G000144683

Current Law

Case Citator

2005

THOMSON

™

SWEET & MAXWELL

AUSTRALIA
LBC Information Services
Sydney

CANADA and USA
Carswell
Toronto

NEW ZEALAND
Brooker's
Auckland

SINGAPORE and MALAYSIA
Sweet & Maxwell Asia
Singapore and Kuala Lumpur

Current Law

Case Citator

2005

THOMSON

SWEET & MAXWELL

Published in 2006 by
Sweet & Maxwell Limited of
100 Avenue Road, Swiss Cottage, London NW3 3PF.
Typeset by Sweet & Maxwell Ltd, Mytholmroyd, Hebden Bridge, West Yorkshire.
Printed in the United Kingdom by Bath Press Ltd.

A CIP catalogue record for this book is available from the British Library.

ISBN-10 0-421-93640-1
ISBN-13 978-0-421-93640-9

No forests were destroyed to make this product; only farmed timber was used and re-planted.

CONTENTS

PREFACE

The Sweet & Maxwell Current Law Service

The Current Law Service began in 1947 and provides a comprehensive guide to developments in case law, primary legislation and secondary legislation in the UK and mainland Europe. The Current Law Service presently consists of the Monthly Digests, the Year Book, Current Law Statutes, the Statute Citator, the Statutory Instrument Citator, the Case Citator, Current Law Week and European Current Law.

Also available is the Current Legal Information CD, which contains an archive of Year Books dating back to 1947, the present year's accumulated Monthly Digests and the English and Scottish Case Citators from 1947 to the current month, as well as a range of other Sweet & Maxwell current awareness products such as the Current Law Legislation Citators, Legal Journals Index and Financial Journals Index.

The Case Citators

The Current Law Case Citators comprise four cumulative volumes covering the years 1947-1976, 1977-1997, 1998-2001, 2002-2004 and a single volume covering 2005. Together they provide a comprehensive reference guide to case law after 1946.

How to use the Citators

When searching for a case, users should consult the most recent citator volume first, since it provides the most comprehensive and authoritative information. The current volume contains a guide to the complete history of cases digested or judicially considered in 2005. For earlier case law not considered since 2004, users should consult either the previous citator volumes (2002-2004, 1998-2001, 1977-1997, and 1947-1976), the Current Legal Information CD.

The material in this volume is arranged in alphabetical order in three sections:

English Citator
Scottish Citator
Ships' Names Index

The details in each entry can be used on a number of different levels, including identifying law report series in which a full report of a case can be found, the judicial history of a case and the location of an abstract of a case within a Current Law Yearbook. The following information is provided:

(a) The full name of any case reported between 1947 and 2005

Cases are listed alphabetically by the first party's name, giving the most recent Current Law Year Book paragraph reference to the appropriate digest. Most references have a year before the paragraph number, e.g. 05/**239** alludes to the 2005 Year Book, paragraph 239. If no year is given, the case is contained in the Current Law Consolidation 1947-1951. (For Scotland see the Scottish Year Books 1948-1951)

(b) An extensive list of references to the law reports and journals reporting each case

Each entry gives details about one case, beginning with the case name and any joined cases or other names by which the case might be known, followed by the reports in descending order of authority and the court in which the case was heard. Where cases go on to an appellate court, the entry states whether the higher court affirmed or reversed the decision of the lower court.

(c) The judicial history of a case

If a case has been applied, considered, approved, distinguished, overruled, etc., since it was decided, Current Law Year Book references to digests of cases in which the judicial consideration took place are provided. These references are in normal type while the paragraph number of the actual digest of each case is given in bold.

(d) Details of Scottish cases

Part II of the Citator contains details of cases decided or judicially considered in the Scottish Courts. References to English cases judicially considered in Scotland are also included in this part, so subscribers wishing to follow the full history of an English case should consult both parts of the Citator. Scottish cases published in English Law Reports are included in both the Scottish and English sections.

(e) Ships' Names Index

This is an alphabetical listing of all ships' names and their law report citations to assist where only the ship's name is known by the user. The official party names for these cases will be located in the main body of the Citator.

Whilst every effort has been made to ensure that details of cases in this citator are correct, there may be occasions when a citation is wrong. The editor would be grateful for notification of any errors to enable them to be rectified on the database from which this volume was derived.

Case Citator Editor
Sweet & Maxwell Ltd
The Hatchery
Hall Bank Lane
Mytholmroyd, Hebden Bridge
West Yorkshire
HX7 5HQ
email: smg.casecitatoreditor@thomson.com
or casecitatoreditor@sweetandmaxwell.co.uk

TABLE OF ABBREVIATIONS

Courts Abbreviations

AAT = Administrative Appeals Tribunal (Australia)
Afr Comm HPR = African Commission on Human and Peoples Rights
AG = Amtsgericht (Germany)
AGO = Advocate Generals Opinion
App (B) = Cour d'Appel (Belgium)
App (I) = Corte di Appello (Italy)
App Person = Trade Marks Registry (Appointed Person)
Ar Pag = Areios Pagos (Greece)
ArbG = Arbeitsgericht (Germany)
ARRS = Afdeling Rechtspraak van de Raad van State (NL)
As Tic Mah = Asliye Ticaret Mahkemesi (Turkey)
Aud = Audiencia Provincial (Spain)
BAG = Bundesarbeitsgericht (Germany)
Bd of Trade = Board of Trade
BezG = Bezirksgericht (Switzerland)
BFH = Bundesfinanzhof (Germany)
BG = Bundesgericht (Switzerland)
BGH = Bundesgerichtshof (Germany)
BKA = Bundeskartellamt (Germany)
BPG = Bundespatentgericht (Germany)
BRB = Burgerlijke Rechtbank (Belgium)
BsozG = Bundessozialgericht (Germany)
BverfG = Bundesverfassungsgericht (Germany)
BverwG = Bundesverwaltungsgericht (Germany)
C Adm A = Cour Administrative d'Appel (Belgium/France)
C Concurrence = Conseil de la Concurrence (Belgium/France)
C Cost = Corte Costituzionale (Italy)
C d'A = Cour d'Appel (France/Luxembourg)
CA = Court of Appeal
CA (Civ Div) = Court of Appeal (Civil Division)
CA (Crim Div) = Court of Appeal (Criminal Division)
CAC = Central Arbitration Committee
CAEW = Central Authority for England and Wales
Care Standards Tr = Care Standards Tribunal
Cass = Cour de Cassation (Belgium/France/Luxembourg)
CAT = Competition Appeal Tribunal
CC = County Court
CCA = Court of Criminal Appeal
CCAT = Competition Commission Appeal Tribunal
CCP = Court of Common Pleas
CE = Conseil d'Etat (Belgium/France)
CEC = Commission of the European Communities
Cent Crim Ct = Central Criminal Court (Ireland)
Central Crim Ct = Central Criminal Court
CFA (HK) = Court of Final Appeal (Hong Kong)
CFI = Court of First Instance
CFI (HK) = Court of First Instance of the High Court (Hong Kong Special Administrative Region)
CFI (Phl) = Court of First Instance (Philippines)
Ch D = Chancery Division
Ch D (Bankruptcy Ct) = Chancery Divison (Bankruptcy Court)
Ch D (Companies Ct) = Chancery Division (Companies Court)
Ch D (Irl) = Chancery Division (Ireland)
Ch D (NI) = Chancery Division (Northern Ireland)
Ch D (Patents Ct) = Chancery Division (Patents Court)

Ch D (RPC) = Chancery Division (Restrictive Practices Court)
CICA = Criminal Injuries Compensation Authority
CICAP = Criminal Injuries Compensation Appeals Panel
CICB = Criminal Injuries Compensation Board
Circ Ct = Circuit Court (Ireland)
CJ = Court of Justice
CJ (Gen Div) (Ont) = Ontario Court of Justice (General Division)
CMAC = Courts Martial Appeal Court
CollvB = College van Beroep voor het Bedrijfsleven (NL)
Comm Cartels = Commission des Cartels (Switzerland)
Comm Conc = Commission de la Concurrence (France)
Comm Ministers = Committee of Ministers
Commr Pat = Commissioner of Patents (Australia)
Comm Sec Cons (F) = Commission de la Securite des Consommateurs
Comm Tributaria PG = Commissione Tributaria di Primo Grado (Italy)
Comm Tributaria SG = Commissione Tributaria di Secondo Grado (Italy)
Comp Auth = Competition Authority (Ireland)
Cons Const = Conseil Constitutionnel (France)
Cons Ct = Consistory Court
Cons Stato = Consiglio di Stato (Italy)
Const Ct = Constitutional Court
Cour d'Arb = Cour d'Arbitrage (Belgium)
CP = Court of Protection
CPD = Common Pleas Division
CRC = Commission Federale de Recours en Matiere de Contributions (Switzerland)
Crim CA = Criminal Court of Appeal (Ireland)
CRvB = Centrale Raad van Beroep (Netherlands)
CS = Court of Session
CSJ = Cour Superieure de Justice (Luxembourg)
Ct Sup = Corte Suprema de Justicia (Argentina)
DC = Divisional Court
DR = District Registry
EAT = Employment Appeal Tribunal
EC Council = European Council
Eccl Ct = Court of Ecclesiastical Causes Reserved
ECHR = European Court of Human Rights
ECHR (Grand Chamber) = European Court of Human Rights (Grand Chamber)
ECJ = European Court of Justice
ECSR = European Committee of Social Rights
ED = Eparhiako Dikastrio (Cyprus)
EFTA = EFTA Court of Justice
Epit Antag = Epitropi Antagonismou (Greece)
EPO = European Patent Office
ERGI (Swi) = Edigenossische Rekurskommission fur Geistiges Eigentum (Switzerland)
ES = Eidgenossisches Steuerrekurskommission (Switzerland)
ET = Employment Tribunal
Eur Comm HR = European Commission on Human Rights
Ex Chamber = Court of Exchequer Chamber
Ex Ct = Court of Exchequer
Ex Div = Extra Division
Fam Ct = Family Court
Fam Div = Family Division

v

TABLE OF ABBREVIATIONS

FAS Mosk Okr (RF) = Federalnyi Arbitrazhnyi Sud Moskovskogo Okruga (Russian Federation)
Fed CA = Federal Court of Appeal
Fed Ct = Federal Court
Fed HC = Federal High Court
FG = Finanzgericht (Germany)
FSMT = Financial Services & Markets Tribunal
GC = Giudice Conciliatore (Italy)
HC = High Court
HCJ = High Court of Justiciary
HD = Hogsta Domstolen (Finland/Sweden)
HerrR = Herredsrett (Norway)
HFD = Hogsta forvaltningsdomstolen (Finland)
HL = House of Lords
HO = Hovioikeus/Hovratt (Finland)
Hof = Gerechtshof (Netherlands)
HR (DK) = Hojesteret (Denmark)
HR (N) = Hoyesterett (Norway)
HR (NL) = Hoge Raad (NL)
HR (Swe) = Hovratt (Sweden)
HR Ch = Human Rights Chamber for Bosnia and Herzegovina
HvB = Hof van Beroep (Belgium)
HvC = Hof van Cassatie (Belgium)
IA Comm HR = Inter American Commission on Human Rights
IACHR = Inter American Court of Human Rights
IAT = Immigration Appeal Tribunal
ICC = International Chamber of Commerce, Arbitration Tribunal
ICJ = International Court of Justice
ICTA Tr = Tribunal constituted under the Income and Corporation Taxes Act 1988 s.706
IH = Inner House
IH = Court of Session (Inner House)
IH (1 Div) = Court of Session (Inner House, First Division)
IH (2 Div) = Court of Session (Inner House, Second Division)
IH (Ex Div) = Court of Session (Inner House, Extra Division)
IT = Industrial Tribunal
ITAT (Ind) = Income Tax Appellate Tribunal (India)
It Cass = Corte di Cassazione (Italy)
J de Paix = Justices de la Paix (Luxembourg)
JP = Juge de Paix (Belgium)
JPI = Juzgado de Primera Instancia (Spain)
KBD = King's Bench Division
KBD (Comm) = King's Bench Division (Commercial Court)
KBD (Irl) = King's Bench Division (Ireland)
KBD (NI) = King's Bench Division (Northern Ireland)
KG (Ger) = Kammergericht (Germany)
KG (Swi) = Kassationsgericht (Switzerland)
KHO = Korkein Hallinto-Oikeus (Finland)
KKO = Korkein Oikeus (Finland)
KO = Kihlakunnanoikeus/Haradsratt (Finland)
Ktg = Kantongerecht (Netherlands)
Lab Ct = Labour Court (Ireland)
Land Ct (IoM) = Land Court (Isle of Man)
LArbG = Landesarbeitsgericht (Germany)
LCD = Lord Chancellors Department
Legf Bir = Legfelsobb Birosag (Hungary)
LG (A) = Landesgericht (Austria)
LG (Ger) = Landgericht (Germany)
LGO = Local Government Ombudsman
LJ in Lunacy = Lords Justices sitting in Lunacy
LR = Lagmannsrett (Norway)
LSozG = Landessozialgericht (Germany)

LVAC = Lands Valuation Appeal Court
LVT = Leasehold Valuation Tribunal
MC = Magistrates Court
MCLC = Mayor's and City of London Court
MD = Marknadsdomstolen (Sweden)
MMC = Monopolies and Mergers Commission
MR = Markedsradet (Norway)
Nat Ct = National Court
NI Comm = National Insurance Commissioner
NIRC = National Industrial Relations Court
NO = Naringsfrihetotombudsman (Swe)
NS CR = Nejvyssi soud Ceske republiky (Czech Republic)
NSA (PL) = Naczelny Sad Administracyjny (Poland)
ObG = Obergericht (Switzerland)
ODEI = Office of the Director of Equality Investigations (Ireland)
OGH = Oberster Gerichtshof (Austria)
OH = Outer House
OHIM = Office for Harmonization in the Internal Market
Okr Sod = Okrozno Sodisce (Slovenia)
OL = Ostre Landsret (Denmark)
OLG = Oberlandesgericht (Austria/Germany)
OPM = Oberster Patent- und Markensenat (Austria)
OR = Official Referee
OVG = Oberverwaltungsgericht (Germany)
Pat App Tr = Patents Appeal Tribunal
Pat Val Apel Pad = Patentu Valdes Apelacijas Padome (Latvia)
PC = Privy Council
PCA = Parliamentary Commissioner for Administration
PCC = Patents County Court
PDAD = Probate, Divorce & Admiralty Division
PO = Patent Office
Prer Ct = Prerogative Court
Pret = Pretura (Italy)
PVO = Plant Variety Office
PVST = Plant Varieties & Seeds Tribunal
QB = Court of Queen's Bench
QBD = Queen's Bench Division
QBD (Admin) = Queen's Bench Division (Administrative Court)
QBD (Admlty) = Queen's Bench Division (Admiralty Court)
QBD (Comm) = Queen's Bench Division (Commercial Court)
QBD (Merc) = Queen's Bench Division (Mercantile Court)
QBD (NI) = Queen's Bench Division (Northern Ireland)
QBD (OR) = Queen's Bench Division (Official Referee)
QBD (TCC) = Queen's Bench Division (Technology & Construction Court)
QBD (UK-Irl) = Queen's Bench Division (UK - Ireland)
RB (B) = Tribunal de Premiere Instance (Belgium)
RB (NL) = Arrondissementsrechtbank (Netherlands)
RDAT = Registered Designs Appeal Tribunal
Refugees Status Apps = Refugees Status Appeals Authority (New Zealand)
Rel = Tribunal de Relacao (Portugal)
RP Comm = Restrictive Practices Commission (Ireland)
RPC = Restrictive Practices Court
RR = Regeringsratten (Sweden)
RvK = Rechtbank van Koophandel (Belgium)
Ry & Canal Comm = Railway and Canal Commission
Ry Rates Tr = Railway Rates Tribunal
SCSL (UN) = Special Court for Sierra Leone (Appeals Chamber)
SENT = Special Educational Needs Tribunal
SH = So- og Handelsret (Denmark)

TABLE OF ABBREVIATIONS

Sh Ct = Sheriff Court
Sh Pr = Sheriff Principal
Solicitors Disc Ctte (SC) = Solicitors Discipline
  (Scotland) Committee
SozG = Sozialgericht (Germany)
Sp Comm = Special Commissioners
Sp Imm App Comm = Special Immigration Appeals
  Commission
Spec Crim Ct = Special Criminal Court (Ireland)
SS Comm = Social Security Commissioner
Sup Ct = Supreme Court
Sup Trib = Supremo Tribunal de Justica (Portugal)
Sup Trib Admin = Supremo Tribunal Administrativo
  (Portugal)
Sym Ep = Symvoulio tis Epikrateias (Greece)
TAR = Tribunale Amministrativo (Italy)
TMR = Trade Marks Registry
Tr = Tribunal
TR = Tingsratt (Sweden)
Transport Arb Tr = Transport Arbitration Tribunal
Trib = Tribunale (Italy)
Trib Ad = Tribunal Administratif (France)
Trib Civil = Tribunal Civil (Belgium)
Trib Comm = Tribunal de Commerce (Belgium/France)
Trib Comp = Tribunal de Defensa de la Competencia
  (Spain)
Trib Const = Tribunal Constitucional (Spain)

Trib Corr = Tribunal Correctionnel (France)
Trib Correct = Tribunal Correctionnel (Belgium)
Trib d'Arr = Tribunal d'Arrondissement (Luxembourg)
Trib Fed = Tribunal Federal (Switzerland)
Trib Gde Inst = Tribunal de Grande Instance (Belgium/
  France)
Trib Police = Tribunal de Police (France)
Trib Prem Inst = Tribunal de Premiere Instance
  (Monaco)
Trib Sup = Tribunal Supremo (Spain)
Trib Travail = Tribunal du Travail (Belgium)
UN CAT = UN Committee Against Torture
UN CERD = UN Committee on the Elimination of Racial
  Discrimination
UN HRC = UN Human Rights Committee
UN ICT = UN International Criminal Tribunal
US Ct = US Court
V&DTr = VAT and Duties Tribunal
VAC = Valuation Appeal Court
VfGH = Verfassungsgerictshof (Austria)
VGH = Verwaltungsgericht (Germany/Switzerland)
Visje Sod = Visje Sodisce (Slovenia)
VL = Vestre Landsret (Denmark)
VrS = Vrchni soud (Prague)
VT = Valuation Tribunal
VwGH = Verwaltungsgerichtshof (Austria)
Yrg = Yargitay (Turkey)

Jurisdiction Abbreviations

A = Austria
Abu = Abu Dhabi (United Arab Emirates)
ACT = Australian Capital Territory
Afg = Afghanistan
Al = Ascension Island (St Helena)
AL = Albania
Ald = Alderney
Alg = Algeria
Alta = Alberta
And = Andorra
Ang = Anguilla
Ango = Angola
Ant = Antigua and Barbuda
Arg = Argentina
Arm = Armenia (CIS)
Aus = Australia
Aze = Azerbaijan (CIS)
B = Belgium
Bah = Bahamas
Bahr = Bahrain
Bang = Bangladesh
Bar = Barbados
BC = British Columbia
BEL = Belarus (CIS)
Ben = Benin
Ber = Bermuda
BF = Burkina Faso
BG = British Guiana
BH = British Honduras
Bhu = Bhutan
BIH = Bosnia Herzegovina
Bol = Bolivia
Bots = Botswana
Bru = Brunei
Bul = Bulgaria
Bur = Burundi
BVI = British Virgin Islands
Bze = Belize

Bzl = Brazil
Camb = Cambodia
Camn = Cameroon
Can = Canada
Canary I = Canary Islands (Spain)
Cape = Cape of Good Hope
CAR = Central African Republic
Cey = Ceylon
CI = Cayman Islands
CIS = Commonwealth of Independent States
Com = Comoros
Con = Congo
Cook I = Cook Islands
CR = Costa Rica
CV = Cape Verde
Cy = Cyprus
CZ = Czech Republic
Dji = Djibouti
DK = Denmark
Dom = Dominica
DomR = Dominican Republic
Dub = Dubai
EA = Eastern Africa
EC = European Communities
ECHR = European Commission on Human Rights
Ecu = Ecuador
Egy = Egypt
EIS = El Salvador
EPO = European Patent Office
EqG = Equatorial Guinea
Eri = Eritrea
Eth = Ethiopia
EU = European Union
EW = Estonia
F = France
FI = Falkland Islands
Fin = Finland
FL = Lichtenstein/Liechtenstein

TABLE OF ABBREVIATIONS

FMS = Federated Malay States
FRY = Yugoslavia
Gab = Gabon
Gam = Gambia, The
GBi = Guinea Bissau
Geo = Georgia (CIS)
Ger = Germany
Gha = Ghana
Gib = Gibraltar
Gld = Greenland (Denmark)
GR = Greece
Gren = Grenada
Gua = Guatemala
Gue = Guernsey
Gui = Guinea
Guy = Guyana
H = Hungary
HK = Hong Kong
Hon = Honduras
HR = Croatia
I = Italy
IACHR = Inter American Court of Human Rights
ICC = International Chamber of Commerce
ICJ = International Court of Justice
Ind = India
Indo = Indonesia
IoM = Isle of Man
Iran = Iran
Iraq = Iraq
Irl = Ireland
IS = Iceland
Isr = Israel
Ivo = Ivory Coast
Jam = Jamaica
Jer = Jersey
Jor = Jordan
Jpn = Japan
Kaz = Kazakhstan (CIS)
Ken = Kenya
Kir = Kiribati
Kuw = Kuwait
Kyr = Kyrgyzstan (CIS)
L = Luxembourg
LA = Latvia
Leb = Lebanon
Les = Lesotho
Libe = Liberia
Libya = Libya
LT = Lithuania
M = Malta
Mace = Macedonia
Mad = Madagascar
Made = Madeira (Portugal)
Mal = Malaysia
Man = Manitoba
Mar = Martinique
Marshall I = Marshall Islands (Micronesia)
Mau = Mauritius
MC = Monaco
Mex = Mexico
Mic = Micronesia
Mnegro = Montenegro (Yugoslavia)
Mnia = Mauritania
Mol = Moldova (CIS)
Mong = Mongolia
Mor = Morocco
Moz = Mozambique
Mrat = Montserrat
Mves = Maldives

Mwi = Malawi
Mya = Myanmar
N = Norway
Nam = Namibia
NAnt = Netherlands Antilles
Nau = Nauru
NB = New Brunswick
Nfld = Newfoundland
NI = Northern Ireland
Nic = Nicaragua
Nig = Nigeria
NK = North Korea
NL = Netherlands
NS = Nova Scotia
NSW = New South Wales
NT = Northern Territory
NWT = North West Territories
NZ = New Zealand
OAS = Organisation of American States
OAU = Organisation of African Unity
OHIM = Office for Harmonisation in the Internal Market
Oman = Oman
Ont = Ontario
P = Portugal
Pak = Pakistan
Pal = Palestine
Pan = Panama
Par = Paraguay
PEI = Prince Edward Island
Phl = Philippines
PI = Pitcairn Islands (New Zealand)
PL = Poland
PNG = Papua New Guinea
Poly = Polynesia
PR = Puerto Rico
PRC = People's Republic of China
Qat = Qatar
Qld = Queensland
Que = Quebec
RF = Russian Federation
Rho = Rhodesia
RI = Rhode Island
RO = Romania
Rwa = Rwanda
SA = South Africa
Sask = Saskatchewan
Saudi = Saudi Arabia
SAus = South Australia
SC = Scotland
Sen = Senegal
Serb = Serbia
Sey = Seychelles
Sing = Singapore
SK = South Korea
SL = Sierra Leone
Slo = Slovakia
Slove = Slovenia
Smld = Somaliland
Sol = Solomon Islands
Som = Somalia
Sp = Spain
SrL = Sri Lanka
StC = Saint Christopher and Nevis
StH = St Helena
StL = Saint Lucia
StV = Saint Vincent and the Grenadines
Sud = Sudan
Sur = Surinam
Swa = Swaziland

TABLE OF ABBREVIATIONS

Swe = Sweden
Swi = Switzerland
Syria = Syria
Tai = Taiwan
Taj = Tajikistan (CIS)
Tan = Tanzania
Tas = Tasmania
TCI = Turks and Caicos Islands
TDC = Tristan Da Cunha (St Helena)
Thai = Thailand
Tka = Tanganyika
Ton = Tonga
TR = Turkey
Trin = Trinidad and Tobago
Tun = Tunisia
Turkn = Turkmenistan (CIS)
Tuv = Tuvalu
UAE = United Arab Emirates
Ug = Uganda
UK = United Kingdom
UK-Irl = UK - Ireland (pre 1922)

UKEW = England and Wales
UKR = Ukraine (CIS)
UN = United Nations
UN ICT = United Nations International Criminal Tribunal
Uru = Uruguay
US = United States
Uzb = Uzbekistan (CIS)
Van = Vanuatu
Ven = Venezuela
VI = Virgin Islands
Vic = Victoria
Viet = Vietnam
WA = Western Australia
WI = West Indies
Wind = Windward Islands
WS = Western Samoa
WSah = Western Sahara
YT = Yukon Territory
Zai = Zaire
Zam = Zambia
Zim = Zimbabwe

Law Report/Journal Abbreviations

A.2d = Atlantic Reporter 2nd
A.B.C. = Australian Bankruptcy Cases
A.C. = Appeal Cases
A.C.D. = Administrative Court Digest
A.C.L.C. = Australian Company Law Cases
A.C.L.R. = Australian Company Law Reports
A.C.S.R. = Australian Companies and Securities
    Reports
A.C.T.R. = Australian Capital Territory Reports
A.D. = Appellate Division Reports (NY)
A.D.2d = Appellate Division Reports 2nd (NY)
A.F.T.R. = American Federal Tax Reports
A.I.R. All. = All India Reporter, Allahabad Series
A.I.R. Bom. = All India Reporter, Bombay Series
A.I.R. Delhi = All India Reporter, Delhi Series
A.I.R. Mad. = All India Reporter, Madras Series
A.I.R. P.C. = All India Reporter, Privy Council Series
A.I.R. S.C. = All India Reporter, Supreme Court Series
A.L.J. = Australian Law Journal
A.L.J.R. = Australian Law Journal Reports
A.L.M.D. = Australian Legal Monthly Digest
A.L.R. = Australian Law Reports
A.L.R. = American Law Reports
A.L.R. (C.N.) = Argus Law Reports, Current Notes
    (Australia)
A.L.R. Fed. = American Law Reports Federal
A.L.R.2d = American Law Reports 2nd
A.L.R.3d = American Law Reports 3rd
A.M.C. = American Maritime Cases
A.R. = Alberta Reports
A.T.C. = Annotated Tax Cases
A.T.R. = Australian Tax Reports
Ad. & El. = Adolphus & Ellis' Reports
Adam = Adam's Justiciary Reports (Scotland)
Add. = Addams' Ecclesiastical Reports
Admin. L.R. = Administrative Law Reports
All E.R. = All England Law Reports
All E.R. (Comm) = All England Law Reports
    (Commercial Cases)
All E.R. (EC) = All England Law Reports (European
    Cases)
All E.R. Rep. = All England Law Reports Reprints
All N.L.R. = All Nigeria Law Reports
Am.Dec. = American Decisions

Am.Rep. = American Reports
Am.St.Rep. = American State Reports
Amb. = Ambler's Chancery Reports
And. = Anderson's Common Pleas Reports
Ark. = Arkley's Justiciary Reports (Scotland)
Asp. = Aspinall's Maritime Cases (1870-1940)
Atk. = Atkyn's Chancery Reports
B. & Ad. = Barnewall and Adolphus King's Bench
    Reports
B. & Ald. = Barnewall and Alderson King's Bench
    Reports
B. & C. = Barnewall and Cresswell King's Bench
    Reports
B. & C.R. = Reports of Bankruptcy and Companies
    (Winding up) Cases (1918-41)
B. & S. = Best and Smith's Queen's Bench Reports
B.C.C. = British Company Law Cases
B.C.L.C. = Butterworths Company Law Cases
B.C.L.R. = British Columbia Law Reports
B.H.R.C. = Butterworths Human Rights Cases
B.L.G.R. = Butterworths Local Government Reports
B.L.R. = Building Law Reports
B.M.L.R. = Butterworths Medico Legal Reports
B.P.I.R. = Bankruptcy and Personal Insolvency Reports
B.R. = Bankruptcy Reporter
B.T.A. = Board of Tax Appeals Reports
B.T.C. = British Tax Cases
B.V.C. = British VAT Cases
B.W.C.C. = Butterworths Workmen's Compensation
    Cases
Bank. L.R. = Banking Law Reports
Bankr.Ct.Dec. = Bankruptcy Court Decisions (CRR)
Barnes = Barnes' Notes of Cases in Common Pleas
Beat. = Beatty's Irish Chancery Reports
Beav. = Beavan's Rolls Court Reports
Bell C.C. = Bell's Crown Cases Reserved
Bing. = Bingham's Common Pleas Reports
Bing. N.C. = Bingham, New Cases, English Common
    Pleas
Binn. = Binney's Reports (U.S.A.)
Bli. = Bligh's House of Lords Reports
Bli. N.S. = Bligh's House of Lords Reports, New Series
Bos. & P. = Bosanquet and Puller's Common Pleas
    Reports

TABLE OF ABBREVIATIONS

os. & P.N.R. = Bosanquet and Puller's New Reports, Common Pleas

ott P.L. = Bott's Poor Law Cases

r. & Col. Pri. Cas. = British and Colonial Prize Cases

ro. C.C. = W. Brown's Chancery Reports

ro. P.C. = J. Brown's Parliamentary Cases

rod. & Bing. = Broderip and Bingham's Common Pleas Reports

roun = Broun's Justiciary Reports (Scotland)

rown. & Lush. = Browning and Lushington's Admiralty Reports

rownl. = Brownlow and Goldesborough's Common Pleas Reports

ulst. = Bulstrode's King's Bench Reports

unb. = Bunbury's Exchequer Reports

urr. = Burrow's King's Bench Reports, tempore Mansfield

. Rob. = Christopher Robinson's Admiralty Reports

.B. = Common Bench Reports (Manning)

.B. N.S. = Common Bench Reports (Manning), New Series

.C.C. = Canadian Criminal Cases

.C.C. (2d) = Canadian Criminal Cases, 2nd Series

.C.C. (3d) = Canadian Criminal Cases, 3rd Series

.C.L. = Canadian Current Law

.C.L. Rep. = Community Care Law Reports

.C.L.R. = Consumer Credit Law Reports

.C.L.T. = Canadian Cases on the Law of Torts

.C.P.A. = Court of Customs & Patent Appeals Reports

.E.C. = European Community Cases

.I.L.L. = Construction Industry Law Letter

.I.L.R. = Cayman Islands Law Reports

.L.C. = Commercial Law Cases

.L.R. = Commonwealth Law Reports

.M.L. Rev. = Common Market Law Review

.M.L.R. = Common Market Law Reports

.M.L.R. D = Common Market Law Reports Restrictive Practices Supplement

.M.L.R. M = Common Market Law Reports Merger Decisions

.O.D. = Crown Office Digest

.P. Rep. = Civil Procedure Reports

.P.C. (2d) = Carswell's Practice Cases, Second Series

.P.C. (3d) = Carswell's Practice Cases, Third Series

.P.L. = Current Property Law (1952-53)

.P.L.R. = Civil Practice Law Reports

.P.R. = Canadian Patent Reporter

.P.R. (2d) = Canadian Patent Reporter, 2nd Series

.P.R. (3d) = Canadian Patent Reporter, 3rd Series

.P.R. (4th) = Canadian Patent Reporter, 4th Series

.R. = Criminal Reports (Canada)

.R. N.S. = Criminal Reports (New Series) (Canada)

.R.R. = Canadian Rights Reporter

.S. = Rapports Judiciaires de Quebec, Cour Superieure

J C.A.R. = Colorado Appellate Report

ab. & Ell. = Cababe and Ellis' Queen's Bench Reports

al. = California Reports

al. Daily Op. Serv. = California Daily Opinion Service

al.3d = California Reports 3rd

al.4th = California Reports, 4th Series

al.Rptr.2d = California Reporter 2d (West's)

amp. = Campbell's Nisi Prius Reports

an. B.R. = Canadian Bar Review

ar. & K. = Carrington and Kirwan's Nisi Prius Reports

ar. & M. = Carrington and Marshman's Nisi Prius Reports

ar. & P. = Carrington and Payne's Nisi Prius Reports

arswellFor = Carswell Foreign

Cart. = Carter's Common Pleas Reports

CAT = Competition Appeal Tribunal

Ch. = Chancery Division

Ch. Cas. = Cases in Chancery

Chit. = Chitty's King's Bench Practice Reports

Civ. = New York District Court transcript

Cl. & F. = Clark and Finnelly's House of Lords Reports

Clark's Rep. = Clark's Reports (Jamaica)

Clay. = Clayton's Reports and Pleas of Assises at Yorke

Clunet = Journal du Droit International (France)

Co. Rep. = Coke's King's Bench Reports

Coll. = Collyer's Chancery Cases, tempore Bruce

Com. = Comyn's Reports, King's Bench

Com. Cas. = Commercial Cases

Com. L.R. = Commercial Law Reports

Comb. = Comberbach's King's Bench Reports

Comp. A.R. = Competition Appeal Reports

Con. L.R. = Construction Law Reports

Const. L.J. = Construction Law Journal

Coop. t. Cott. = Cooper's Chancery Reports, tempore Cottenham

Costs L.R. = Costs Law Reports

Costs L.R. (Core Vol.) = Costs Law Reports, Core Volume

Coup. = Couper's Justiciary Reports (Scotland)

Cowp. = Cowper's King's Bench Reports

Cox = Cox's Chancery Reports

Cox C.C. = Cox's Criminal Cases

Cox Eq. Cas. = Cox's Equity Cases

Cr. & J. = Crompton and Jervis' Exchequer Reports

Cr. & M. = Crompton and Meeson's Exchequer Reports

Cr. & Ph. = Craig and Phillip's Chancery Reports

Cr. App. R. = Criminal Appeal Reports

Cr. App. R. (S.) = Criminal Appeal Reports (Sentencing)

Cr. M & R. = Crompton, Meeson and Roscoe's Exchequer Reports

Cr. S. & P. = Craigie, Stewart and Paton's Scottish Appeal Cases

Cranch = Cranch's United States Supreme Court Reports

Crim. L.R. = Criminal Law Review

Cro. Eliz. = Croke's King's Bench Reports, tempore Elizabeth

Cro. Jac. = Croke's King's Bench Reports, tempore James

Curt. = Curteis' Ecclesiastical Reports

D. = Dunlop, Bell and Murray's Reports, Session Cases, 2nd series (Scotland)

D. & R. = Decisions and Reports of the European Commission of Human Rights

D. (H.L.) = Dunlop's Session Cases, 2nd Series (House of Lords cases, Scotland)

D.L.R. = Dominion Law Reports

D.L.R. (2d) = Dominion Law Reports (2d)

D.L.R. (3d) = Dominion Law Reports (3d)

D.L.R. (4th) = Dominion Law Reports (4th)

D.R.A. = De-rating Appeals

D.T.C. = Dominion Tax Cases

Daily Telegraph = Daily Telegraph

De G. = De Gex's Bankruptcy Reports

De G. & J. = De Gex and Jones' Chancery Reports

De G. & Sm. = De Gex and Smales Chancery Reports

De G.F. & J. = De Gex, Fisher and Jones' Chancery Reports

De G.J. & S. = De Gex, Jones and Smith's Chancery Reports

De G.M. & G. = De Gex, Macnaghten and Gordons' Chancery Reports

TABLE OF ABBREVIATIONS

Dea. & Sw. = Deane and Swabey's Ecclesiastical Reports
Deac. & Ch. = Deacon and Chitty's Bankruptcy Reports
Dears. = Dearsley's Crown Cases Reserved
Dears. & B. = Dearsley and Bell's Crown Cases Reserved
Den. = Denison and Pearce's Crown Cases Reserved
Dick. = Dickens' Chancery Reports
Disc. L.R. = Discrimination Law Reports
Dods. = Dodson's Admiralty Reports
Doug. K.B. = Douglas' King's Bench Reports
Dow = Dow's House of Lords Cases
Dowl. & L. = Dowling and Lowndes' Bail Court Reports
Dowl. & Ry. K.B. = Dowling and Ryland's King's Bench Reports
Dowl. N.S. = Dowling's Bail Court Reports, New Series
Dowl. Pr. Cas. = Dowling's Bail Court Practice Cases
Dr. & War. = Drury and Warren's Irish Chancery Reports
Drew. = Drewry's Chancery Reports, tempore Kindersley
Drew. & Sm. = Drewry and Smales' Chancery Reports
Dyer = Dyer's King's Bench Reports
E.A. = East African Law Reports
E.A.C.A. = Law Reports of the Court of Appeals for Eastern Africa
E.A.T.C. = East African Tax Cases
E.B.L.R. = Electronic Business Law Reports
E.C.C. = European Commercial Cases
E.C.D.R. = European Copyright and Design Reports
E.C.D.R. CN = European Copyright and Design Reports Case Notes
E.C.R. = European Court Reports
E.C.R. IA = European Court Reports
E.G. = Estates Gazette
E.G.C.S. = Estates Gazette Case Summaries
E.G.D. = Estates Gazette Digest of Cases
E.G.L.R. = Estates Gazette Law Reports (Bound Volume)
E.H.L.R. = Environmental Health Law Reports
E.H.L.R. Dig. = Environmental Health Reports Digest Pages
E.H.R.R. = European Human Rights Reports
E.H.R.R. CD = European Human Rights Reports, Commission Decisions
E.H.R.R. SE = European Human Rights Reports, Summaries & Extracts
E.L.R. = Education Law Reports
E.M.L.R. = Entertainment and Media Law Reports
E.N.P.R. = European National Patent Reports
E.P.O.R. = European Patent Office Reports
E.P.O.R. A = European Patent Office Reports
E.P.O.R. B = European Patent Office Reports
E.P.O.R. C = European Patent Office Reports
E.P.T. Leaflet = Excess Profits Tax Leaflet
E.R. = English Reports
E.T.M.R. = European Trade Mark Reports
E.T.M.R. CN = European Trade Mark Reports Case Notes
ERC = Environment Reporter Cases (BNA)
EWCA Civ = Court of Appeal (Civil)
EWCA Crim = Court of Appeal (Criminal)
EWHC = High Court
EWHC Admin = High Court (Administrative Court)
East = East's Term Reports, King's Bench
East P.C. = East's Pleas of the Crown
Ed. C.R. = Education Case Reports
Ed. Law Rep. = Education Law Reporter

Edw. = Edward's Admiralty Reports
El. & Bl. = Ellis and Blackburn's Queen's Bench Reports
El. & El. = Ellis and Ellis' Queen's Bench Reports
El. Bl. & El. = Ellis, Blackburn and Ellis' Queen's Bench Reports
Emp. L.R. = Employment Law Reports
Employee Benefits Cas. = Employee Benefits Cases
Env. L.R. = Environmental Law Reports
Env. L.R. D = Environmental Law Reports Digest Pages
Envtl. L. Rep. = Environmental Law Reporter (ELR) (cases only)
Eq. Cas. Abr. = Abridgment of Cases in Equity
Esp. = Espinasse's Nisi Prius Reports
Eu. L.R. = European Law Reports
Ex. = Exchequer Reports (Welsby, Hurlstone and Gordon)
Ex. C.R. = Canada Law Reports, Exchequer Court
F. = Federal Reporter (U.S.A.)
F. & F. = Foster and Finlason's Nisi Prius Reports
F. (Ct. of Sess.) = Faculty Decisions, Court of Session (Scotland)
F. (H.L.) = Fraser's Session Cases, 5th Series (House of Lords, Scotland)
F. (J.) = Fraser's Session Cases, 5th Series (Justiciary cases, Scotland)
F.2d = Federal Reporter, 2nd Series (U.S.A.)
F.3d = Federal Reporter, 3rd Series (U.S.A.)
F.C. = Canada Law Reports, Federal Court
F.C.R. = Family Court Reporter
F.L.R. = Family Law Reports
F.R.D. = Federal Rules Decisions (U.S.A.)
F.S.R. = Fleet Street Reports
F.Supp. = Federal Supplement (U.S.A.)
F.Supp.2d = Federal Supplement, Second Series
F.T.L.R. = Financial Times Law Reports
F.T.R. = Federal Trial Reports
Fam. = Family Division
Fam. L.R. = Family Law Reports (Scottish)
Fam. Law = Family Law
Fed. L.R. = Federal Law Reports (Australia)
Fed. R. Evid. Serv. = Federal Rules of Evidence Service (Callaghan's)
Fed. Sec. L. Rep. P = Federal Securities Law Reports (CCH)
Fed.R.Serv.2d = Federal Rules Service 2nd (Callaghan's)
Fed.R.Serv.3d = Federal Rules Service 3rd (Callaghan's)
Fed.Sent.R. = Federal Sentencing Reporter
Fin. L.R. = Financial Law Reports
Financial Times = Financial Times
Fla. L. Weekly Fed. S = Florida Law Weekly, United States Supreme Court
Fost. = Foster's Crown Cases
Freem. Ch. = Freeman's Chancery Reports
G.W.D. = Green's Weekly Digest (Scottish)
GRUR = Gewerblicher Rechtsschutz und Urheberrecht
Ga. = Georgia Reports
Giff. = Giffard's Chancery Reports
Gilb. K.B. = Gilbert's Cases in Law and Equity
Gl. & J. = Glyn and Jameson's Bankruptcy Reports
Gould. = Gouldsborough's King's Bench Reports
Guardian = Guardian
H. Bl. = H. Blackstone's Common Pleas Reports
H.B.R. = Hansell's Bankruptcy Reports (1915-17)
H.K. Cases = Hong Kong Cases
H.K.L.R. = Hong Kong Law Reports
H.K.L.R.D. = Hong Kong Law Reports and Digest
H.L. Cas. = Clark's House of Lords Cases

TABLE OF ABBREVIATIONS

H.L.R. = Housing Law Reports
H.R.C.D. = Human Rights Case Digest
H.R.L.R. = Human Rights Law Reports - UK Cases
Hag. Adm. = Haggard's Admiralty Reports
Hag. Con. = Haggard's Consistorial Reports
Hag. Ecc. = Haggard's Ecclesiastical Reports
Hardres = Hardres' Exchequer Reports
Hare = Hare's Chancery Reports
Hem. & M. = Hemming and Miller's Chancery Reports
Het. = Hetley's Reports
Hob. = Hobart's Reports (Common Pleas and King's
    Bench)
Hodg. = Hodges' Common Pleas Reports
Holt K.B. = Holt's King's Bench Reports
Holt N.P. = F Holt's Nisi Prius Reports
Hous. L.R. = Housing Law Reports (Scottish)
How. = Howard's United States Supreme Court
    Reports
Hume = Hume's Session Cases (Scotland)
Hurl. & C. = Hurlstone and Coltman's Exchequer
    Reports
Hurl. & N. = Hurlstone and Norman's Exchequer
    Reports
I.C.L.R. = Irish Common Law Reports, Second Series
    (1850-66)
I.C.R. = Industrial Cases Reports
I.H.R.R. = International Human Rights Reports
I.L.Pr. = International Litigation Procedure
I.L.R. = International Law Reports
I.L.R.M. = Irish Law Reports Monthly
I.L.T. = Irish Law Times
I.L.T.R. = Irish Law Times Reports
I.N.L.R. = Immigration and Nationality Law Reports
I.P.D. = Intellectual Property Decisions
I.P.L.R. = Industrial Property Law Reports (India)
I.P.R. = Intellectual Property Reports (Australia)
I.R. = Irish Reports
I.R. C.L. = Irish Reports, Common Law
I.R.L.R. = Industrial Relations Law Reports
I.T.C. = Srinivasan's Reports of Income Tax Cases (India)
I.T.C.L.R. = IT & Communications Law Reports
I.T.E.L.R. = International Trust and Estate Law Reports
I.T.L. Rep. = International Tax Law Reports
I.T.R. = Industrial Tribunal Reports
ITRD = International Trade Reporter Decisions (BNA)
Ill.2d = Illinois Reports, 2nd Series
Ill.Dec. = Illinois Decisions
Imm. A.R. = Immigration Appeal Reports
Ind. = Indiana Reports
Ind. Cas. = Indian Cases
Ind. L.R. = Indian Law Reports
Ind. L.R. All. = Indian Law Reports, Allahabad Series
Ind. L.R. Cal. = Indian Law Reports, Calcutta Series
Ind. L.R. Mad. = Indian Law Reports, Madras Series
Ind. L.R. Pat. = Indian Law Reports, Patna Series
Independent = Independent
Info. T.L.R. = Information Technology Law Reports
Ir. Ch. R. = Irish Chancery Reports (1850-66)
Ir. Eq. = Irish Reports, Equity (1866-77)
Ir. Eq. R. = Irish Equity Reports, First Series (1838-50)
Ir. Jur. Rep. = Irish Jurist Reports
Ir. L.J. = Irish Law Journal
Ir. L.R. = Irish Law Reports
Irvine = Irvine's High Court and Circuit Courts of
    Justiciary Reports (Scotland)
J. & Lat. = Jones and La Touche's Irish Chancery
    Reports (1844-46)
J. Bridg. = Sir John Bridgman's Reports
J.C. = Justiciary Cases (Scotland)

J.J. = Jersey Judgments
J.L.R. = Jamaica Law Reports
J.P. = Justice of the Peace Reports
J.P. Rep. = Local Government Review Reports
J.P.I. Law = Journal of Personal Injury Law
J.P.I.L. = Journal of Personal Injury Litigation
J.P.L. = Journal of Planning & Environment Law
J.P.N. = Justice of the Peace Notes of Cases
Jac. & W. = Jacob and Walker's Chancery Reports
Jebb. & Sym. = Jebb and Syme's Queen's Bench
    Reports (Ireland, 1838-41)
Jer. L.R. = Jersey Law Reports
John. = Johnson's Chancery Reports
John. & H. = Johnson and Hemmings Chancery
    Reports
Jones = Sir Thomas Jones' King's Bench Reports
Jur. = Jurist
Jur. N.S. = Jurist, New Series
K.B. = Kings Bench
K.I.R. = Knight's Industrial Law Reports
Kay & J. = Kay and Johnson's Vice Chancellors Reports
Keen = Keen's Rolls Court Reports
Kn. = Knapp's Privy Council Appeal Cases
Ky. = Kentucky Reports
L. & T.R. = Landlord and Tenant Reports
L.D.B. = Legal Decisions Affecting Bankers
L.Ed. = Lawyers' Edition, United States Supreme Court
    Reporter
L.Ed.2d = Lawyers' Edition 2nd Series, United States
    Supreme Court Reporter
L.G. Rev. = Local Government Review
L.G.L.R. = Local Government Law Reports
L.G.R. = Local Government Reports
L.G.R.A. = Local Government Reports of Australia
L.J. = Law Journal (Newspaper)
L.J. Bcy. = Law Journal Reports, Bankruptcy (1832-
    80)
L.J. C.P. = Law Journal Reports, Common Pleas (1831-
    75)
L.J. Ch. = Law Journal Reports, Chancery (1831-1946)
L.J. Ex. = Law Journal Reports, Exchequer (1831-75)
L.J. K.B. = Law Journal Reports, King's Bench (1831-
    1946)
L.J. M.C. = Law Journal Reports, Magistrates Cases
    (1831-96)
L.J. N.C. = Law Journal, Notes of Cases
L.J. N.C.C.R. = Law Journal, County Court Reports
    (1934-47)
L.J. N.S. = Law Journal Reports, New Series (1832-
    1946)
L.J. O.S. = Law Journal Reports, Old Series (1822-31)
L.J. P. = Law Journal Reports, Probate, Divorce and
    Admiralty (1875-1946)
L.J. P. & M. = Law Journal Reports, Probate, Divorce
    and Matrimonial (1858-59, 1866-75)
L.J. P.C. = Law Journal Reports, Privy Council (1831-
    1946)
L.J. P.M. & A. = Law Journal Reports, Probate,
    Matrimonial and Admiralty (1860-65)
L.J. Q.B. = Law Journal Reports, Queen's Bench
    (1831-1946)
L.J.R. = Law Journal Reports (1947-49)
L.M.C.L.Q. = Lloyd's Maritime and Commercial Law
    Quarterly
L.R. A. & E. = Admiralty and Ecclesiastical Cases
    (1865-75)
L.R. App. Cas. = Appeal Cases (1875-90)
L.R. C.C.R. = Crown Cases Reserved
L.R. C.P. = Common Pleas (1865-75)

TABLE OF ABBREVIATIONS

L.R. C.P.D. = Common Pleas Division (1875-80)
L.R. Ch. App. = Chancery Appeals (1865-75)
L.R. Ch. D. = Chancery Division (1875-90)
L.R. Eq. = Equity Cases
L.R. Ex. = Exchequer (1865-75)
L.R. Ex. D. = Exchequer Division (1875-80)
L.R. H.L. = English and Irish Appeals (1866-75)
L.R. Ind. App. = Indian Appeals
L.R. Ir. = Ireland
L.R. P. & D. = Probate and Divorce (1865-75)
L.R. P.C. = Privy Council
L.R. P.D. = Probate Division (1875-90)
L.R. Q.B. = Queen's Bench (1865-75)
L.R. Q.B.D. = Queen's Bench Division (1875-90)
L.R. R.P. = Restrictive Practices (1958-72)
L.R. Sc. = Scotch and Divorce Appeals
L.R.B. = Law Reports of the Bahamas
L.R.C. = Law Reports of the Commonwealth
L.R.C. (Const) = Law Reports of the Commonwealth (Constitutional & Administrative Reports)
L.R.L.R. = Lloyd's Reinsurance Law Reports
L.R.R.M. (BNA) = Labor Relations Reference Manual (BNA)
L.S.G. = Law Society Gazette
L.T. = Law Times (1859-1965)
L.T. O.S. = Law Times (Old Series) (1843-59)
L.T.R. = Law Times Reports (1859-1947)
Lab.Cas. P = Labor Cases (CCH)
Lat. = Latch's King's Bench Reports
Ld. Raym. = Lord Raymond's King's Bench Reports
Le. & Ca. = Leigh and Cave's Crown Cases Reserved
Leach = Leach's Cases in Crown Law
Lee = Lee's Ecclesiastical Reports
Lee temp Hard. = Lee's King's Bench Cases tempore Hardwicke
Leo. = Leonard's Reports
Lev. = Levinz's King's Bench and Common Pleas Reports
Lewin = Lewin's Crown Cases Reserved
Ll. L. Pr. Cas. = Lloyd's List Prize Cases (1914-24)
Ll. L. Pr. Cas. (N.S.) = Lloyd's List Prize Cases, Second Series (1939-53)
Ll. L. Rep. = Lloyd's List Law Reports (1919-50)
Lloyd's List = Lloyd's List
Lloyd's Rep. = Lloyd's Law Reports (1951-)
Lloyd's Rep. Bank. = Lloyd's Law Reports Banking
Lloyd's Rep. I.R. = Lloyd's Law Reports, Insurance & Reinsurance
Lloyd's Rep. Med. = Lloyd's Law Reports Medical
Lloyd's Rep. P.N. = Lloyd's Law Reports Professional Negligence
Lofft = Lofft's King's Bench Reports
Lush. = Lushington's Admiralty Reports
Lutw. = Lutwyche's Entries and Reports, Common Pleas
M. = Macpherson's Session Cases, 3rd Series (Scotland)
M. & S. = Maule and Selwyn's King's Bench Reports
M. & W. = Meeson and Welsby's Exchequer Reports
M. (H.L.) = Macpherson's Session Cases, 3rd Series (House of Lords cases, Scotland)
M.C.C. = MacGillivray's Copyright Cases
M.L.J. = Malaysian Law Journal
M.P.L.R. = Municipal and Planning Law Reports (Canada)
M.P.R. = Maritime Provinces Reports (Canada)
M.R. = Mauritius Reports
Mac. & G. = Macnaghten and Gordon's Chancery Reports

Macq. = Macqueen's Scottish Appeal Cases
Madd. = Maddock's Chancery Reports
Man. & G. = Manning and Granger's Common Pleas Reports
Man. Law = Managerial Law
Mans. = Manson's Bankruptcy and Companies Winding up Cases (1894-1913)
Manx L.R. = Manx Law Reports
Masons C.L.R. = Masons Computer Law Reports
Masons C.L.R. Rep. = Masons Computer Law Reports Reprints (Case Digests, 1994-97)
Mass. = Massachusetts Reports
Med. L.R. = Medical Law Reports
Media L. Rep. = Media Law Reporter (BNA)
Mer. = Merivale's Chancery Reports
Misc. = New York Miscellaneous Reports
Misc.2d = Miscellaneous Reports, 2nd Series (New York)
Mod. = Modern Reports
Mol. = Molloy's Chancery Reports (Ireland, 1927-31)
Mont. D. & De G. = Montagu, Deacon and De Gex Bankruptcy Reports
Moo. K.B. = Moore's King's Bench Reports
Moo. P.C. = Moore's Privy Council Cases
Moo. P.C. N.S. = Moore's Privy Council Cases, New Series
Mood. & R. = Moody and Robinson's Nisi Prius Reports
Mood. C.C. = Moody's Crown Cases Reserved
Mor. Dic. = Morison's Dictionary of Decisions (Scotland)
Morr. = Morrell's Bankruptcy Reports
Mos. = Moseley's Chancery Reports
My. & C. = Mylne and Craig's Chancery Reports
My. & K. = Mylne and Keen's Chancery Reports
N.B. Eq. = New Brunswick Equity Reports
N.B.R. = National Bankruptcy Register Reports
N.B.R. 2d = New Brunswick Reports, 2nd Series
N.C. = Notes of Cases, Ecclesiastical and Maritime (ed. Thornton)
N.E. = North Eastern Reporter (U.S.A.)
N.E.2d = North Eastern Reporter 2nd
N.H. = New Hampshire Reports
N.I. = Northern Ireland Law Reports
N.I.J.B. = Northern Ireland Judgment Bulletin
N.I.L.Q. = Northern Ireland Legal Quarterly
N.J. = New Jersey Reports
N.L.J. = New Law Journal
N.L.J. Rep. = New Law Journal Reports
N.L.R. = New Law Reports (Sri Lanka)
N.P.C. = New Property Cases
N.R. = National Reporter (Canada)
N.S.R. 2d = Nova Scotia Reports, 2nd Series
N.S.W.L.R. = New South Wales Law Reports
N.S.W.R. = New South Wales Reports (1960-70)
N.W. = North Western Reporter (U.S.A.)
N.W.2d = North Western Reporter, 2nd Series (U.S.A.)
N.Y. = New York Reports
N.Y.2d = New York Reports, 2nd Series
N.Y.S. = New York Supplement Reporter
N.Y.S.2d = New York Supplement Reporter, 2nd Series
N.Z.L.R. = New Zealand Law Reports
NDLR P = National Disability Law Reporter
Nev. & M.K.B. = Neville and Manning's King's Bench Reports
New Rep. = New Reports
Nfld. & P.E.I.R. = Newfoundland and Prince Edward Island Reports

TABLE OF ABBREVIATIONS

O'M. & H. = O'Malley and Hardcastle's Election Cases (1869-1929)
O.F.L.R. = Offshore Financial Law Reports
O.J. E.P.O. = Official Journal of the European Patent Office
O.L.R. = Ontario Law Reports (1901-30)
O.P.L.R. = Occupational Pensions Law Reports
O.R. = Ontario Reports (1882-1900, 1931-)
O.R. (2d) = Ontario Reports, 2nd Series
O.R. (3d) = Ontario Reports, 3rd Series
Owen = Owen's King's Bench and Common Pleas Reports
P. = Pacific Reporter (U.S.A.)
P. = Probate
P. & C.R. = Property, Planning and Compensation Reports
P. & C.R. DG = Property, Planning and Compensation Reports Digest Pages
P. & C.R. D = Property and Compensation Reports Digest Pages
P.Wms. = Peere Williams Chancery Reports
P.2d = Pacific Reporter, 2nd Series (U.S.A.)
P.A.D. = Planning Appeal Decisions
P.C.C. = Palmer's Company Cases
P.I.Q.R. P = Personal Injury and Quantum Reports
P.I.Q.R. Q = Personal Injury and Quantum Reports
P.L.C.R. = Planning Law Case Reports
P.L.R. = Planning Law Reports
P.N.G.L.R. = Papua New Guinea Law Reports
P.N.L.R. = Professional Negligence and Liability Reports
P.T. Leaflet = Profits Tax Leaflet
Pal. L.R. = Palestine Law Reports
Park on Ins. = Park on Insurance, 8th ed.
Pat. = Paton's Scottish Appeals, House of Lords
Peake = Peake's Nisi Prius Reports
Peake Add. Cas. = Peake's Additional Cases
Pens. App. R. = Pensions Appeal Reports
Pens. L.R. = Pensions Law Reports
Perry & K. = Perry and Knapp's Election Cases
Ph. = Phillip's Chancery Reports
Phil. Ecc. = Phillimore's Ecclesiastical Reports
Plow. = Plowden's Commentaries
Pop. = Sir John Popham's Reports
Prec. Ch. = Precedents in Chancery
Price = Price's Exchequer Reports
Q.B. = Queens Bench
Q.J.P. = Queensland Justice of the Peace Reports
Q.L.J. = Queensland Law Journal Reports (1897-1901)
Q.R. = Quantum Reports (Kemp & Kemp)
Q.S.R. = Queensland State Reports (1902-57)
Q.W.N. = Queensland Law Reporter and Weekly Notes (1908-72)
Qd. R. = Queensland State Reports (1958-)
R. = Retties Session Cases, 4th Series (Scotland)
R. & I.T. = Rating and Income Tax Reports
R. (H.L.) = Retties Session Cases, 4th Series (House of Lords cases, Scotland)
R. (J.) = Retties Session Cases, 4th Series (Justiciary cases, Scotland)
R.A. = Rating Appeals
R.C.N. = Rating Case Notes
R.F.L. = Reports of Family Law (Canada)
R.I.C.S. = Royal Institution of Chartered Surveyors, Scottish Lands Valuation Appeal Reports
R.J.Q. B.R. = Rapports Judiciares de Quebec, Cour du Banc du Roi (1875-91)
R.L.R. = Road Law Reports
R.P.C. = Reports of Patent Cases

R.P.R. = Real Property Reports (Canada)
R.R.C. = Ryde's Rating Cases
R.T.R. = Road Traffic Reports
R.V.R. = Rating and Valuation Reporter
RICO Bus.Disp.Guide = RICO Business Disputes Guide (CCH)
Ram. = Ramanathan's Reports, Sri Lanka
Re. L.R. = Reinsurance Law Reports
Recueil = Recueil de la Jurisprudence de la Cour (ECJ)
Rep. L.R. = Reparation Law Reports (Scottish)
Rep. L.R. (Quantum) = Reparation Law Reports, Quantum Cases (Scottish)
Rob. = Robinson's Scottish Appeal Cases, House of Lords
Rob. Ecc. = Robertson's Ecclesiastical Reports
Roll. Abr. = Rolle's Abridgment des Plusieurs Cases
Russ. = Russell's Chancery Reports
Russ. & M. = Russell and Mylne's Chancery Reports
Russ. & Ry. = Russell and Ryan's Crown Cases Reserved
Russ. Cr. = Russell on Crime
Ry. & M. = Ryan and Moody's Nisi Prius Reports
S. = Shaw's Session Cases, 1st Series (Scotland)
S.A. = South African Law Reports
S.A. (A.D.) = South African Law Reports (Appellate Division)
S.A. (T.P.D.) = South African Law Reports (Transvaal Provincial Division)
S.A.C.R. = South African Criminal Law Reports
S.A.L.J. = South African Law Journal
S.A.S.R. = South Australian State Reports
S.C. = Session Cases (Scotland)
S.C. (H.L.) = Session Cases (House of Lords cases, Scotland)
S.C. (J.) = Session Cases (Justiciary 1907-16, Scotland)
S.C. (P.C.) = Session Cases (Privy Council Cases, Scotland)
S.C. (S.A.) = Supreme Court Reports (South Africa)
S.C.C.R. = Scottish Criminal Case Reports
S.C.C.R. (Supp.) = Scottish Criminal Case Reports Supplement
S.C.L.R. = Scottish Civil Law Reports
S.C.R. = Canada Law Reports, Supreme Court
S.Ct. = Supreme Court Reporter
S.E. = South Eastern Reporter (U.S.A.)
S.E.2d = South Eastern Reporter, 2nd Series (U.S.A.)
S.J. = Solicitors Journal (Old)
S.J.L.B. = Solicitors Journal Law Brief
S.L.C.R. = Scottish Land Court Reports
S.L.C.R. App. = Scottish Land Court Reports (Appendix)
S.L.L.P. = Scottish Licensing Law and Practice
S.L.R. = Scottish Law Reporter (1865-1924)
S.L.T. = Scots Law Times
S.L.T. (Land Ct) = Scots Law Times (Land Court Reports)
S.L.T. (Land Ct.) = Scots Law Times (Land Ct)
S.L.T. (Lands Tr) = Scots Law Times (Lands Tribunal Reports)
S.L.T. (Lands Tr.) = Scots Law Times (Lands Tr)
S.L.T. (Lyon Ct) = Scots Law Times (Lyon Court Reports)
S.L.T. (Lyon Ct.) = Scots Law Times (Lyon Ct)
S.L.T. (Notes) = Scots Law Times (Notes)
S.L.T. (P.L.) = Scots Law Times (Poor Law Reports)
S.L.T. (Sh Ct) = Scots Law Times (Sheriff Court Reports)
S.L.T. (Sh Ct.) = Scots Law Times (Sheriff Court)

TABLE OF ABBREVIATIONS

S.L.T. (Sh. Ct.) = Scots Law Times (Sheriff Court)
S.N. = Session Notes
S.R. (N.S.W.) = New South Wales State Reports (1901-)
S.S.L.R. = Straits Settlements Law Reports (Malaysia)
S.T.C. = Simons Tax Cases
S.T.C. (S.C.D.) = Simons Tax Cases: Special
  Commissioners Decisions
S.T.I. = Simon's Tax Intelligence
S.W.2d = South Western Reporter, 2nd Series (U.S.A.)
Salk. = Salkeld's King's Bench Reports
Sask. R. = Saskatchewan Reports
Saund. = Saunder's King's Bench Reports
Sc. Jur. = Scottish Jurist
Sch. & L. = Schoales and Lefroy's Irish Chancery
  Reports
Scotsman = Scotsman
Scott N.R. = Scott's New Common Pleas Reports
Sel. Cas. Ch. = Select Cases in Chancery, tempore King
Sess. Cas. K.B. = Session Cases touching settlements
  (England, 1710-48)
Sh. App. = Shaw's Scottish Appeal Cases, House of
  Lords
Sh. Ct. Rep. = Scottish Law Review, Sheriff Court
  Reports (1885-1963)
Shaw = Shaw's Justiciary Cases (Scotland)
Ship. Gaz. = Shipping Gazette
Sid. = Siderfin's King's Bench Reports
Sim. = Simon's Vice Chancellors Reports
Sim. & St. = Simon and Stuart's Vice Chancellor's
  Reports
Sim. N.S. = Simon's Vice Chancellors Reports, New
  Series
Skin. = Skinner's King's Bench Reports
Sm. & G. = Smales and Giffard's Chancery Reports
Smith & B. = Smith and Batty's King's Bench Reports
  (Ireland, 1824-25)
Smith L.C. = Smith's Leading Cases on Various
  Branches of the Law
Sneed (TN) = Sneed's Tennessee Reports
So.2d = Southern Reporter, 2nd Series (U.S.A.)
Sol. = The Solicitor
Sp. Ecc. & Ad. = Spink's Ecclesiastical and Admiralty
  Reports
St. Tr. = Cobbett and Howell's State Trials
St. Tr. (N.S.) = MacDonnell's State Trials, New Series
Stark. = Starkie's Nisi Prius Reports
Str. = Strange's King's Bench Reports
Sw. & Tr. = Swabey and Tristram's Reports
Sw. Admr. = Swabey's Admiralty Reports
Swans. = Swanston's Chancery Reports
Syme = Syme's Justiciary Reports (Scotland)
T. Raym. = Sir Thomas Raymond's King's Bench
  Reports
T.C. = Tax Cases
T.C.L.R. = Technology and Construction Law Reports
T.L.R. = Times Law Reports
T.R. = Taxation Reports (1939-81)
T.S. = Transvaal Supreme Court Reports (South Africa)
Tang. L.R. (R.) = Tanganyika Law Reports
Tas. R. = Tasmanian Reports (1979-)
Tas. S.R. = Tasmanian State Reports (1941-98)
Taunt. = Taunton's Common Pleas Reports
Tenn. = Tennessee Reports
Term Rep. = Durnford and East's Term Reports
Times = Times
Tr. Consist. J. = Tristram's Consistory Judgments
Tr. L. = Trading Law
Tr. L.R. = Trading Law Reports

Traff. Cas. = Traffic Cases
Trin. L.R. = Trinidad Law Reports
Turn. & R. = Turner and Russell's Chancery Reports
Tyr. = Tyrwhitt's Exchequer Reports
U.C.R. = Upper Canada Reports
U.K.C.L.R. = UK Competition Law Reports
U.K.H.R.R. = United Kingdom Human Rights Reports
U.K.T. = UK Transcripts
U.S. = United States Supreme Court Reports
U.S.App.D.C. = United States District Court for the
  District of Columbia
U.S.P.Q. = United States Patent Quarterly (BNA)
U.S.P.Q.2d = United States Patent Quarterly 2nd
  (BNA)
UCC Rep.Serv. = Uniform Commercial Code Reporting
  Service (Callaghan's)
UKHL = House of Lords
UKIAT = Immigration Appeal Tribunal
UKPC = Privy Council
UKPC D = Privy Council (Devolution)
USLW = United States Law Week
V. & B. = Vesey and Beames' Chancery Reports
V. & D.R. = Value Added Tax and Duties Reports
V.A.T.T.R. = Value Added Tax Tribunal Reports
V.L.R. = Victorian Law Reports (1875-1956)
V.R. = Victorian Reports (1957 -)
Va. = Virginia Reports
Vaugh. = Vaughan's Common Pleas Reports
Vent. = Ventris' King's Bench Reports
Vern. = Vernon's Chancery Reports
Ves. Jr. = Vesey Junior's Chancery Reports
Ves. Sen. = Vesey Senior's Chancery Reports
W. & S. = Wilson and Shaw's Scottish Appeal Cases,
  House of Lords
W. Jones = Sir William Jones' Reports
W. Rob. = W. Robinson's Admiralty Reports
W.A.C.A. = West African Court of Appeal Reports
W.A.L.R. = Western Australian Law Reports (1875-
  1956)
W.A.R. = Western Australian Reports (1957-)
W.I.R. = West Indian Reports
W.L.R. = Weekly Law Reports
W.N. = Weekly Notes (1866-1952)
W.N. (N.S.W.) = Weekly Notes, New South Wales
W.P.A.R. = War Pensions Appeal Reports
W.P.C. = Webster's Patent Cases
W.R. = Weekly Reporter (1853-1906)
W.T.L.R. = Wills & Trusts Law Reports
W.W.R. = Western Weekly Law Reports (Canada)
Wall. = Wallace's United States Supreme Court Reports
Wheat. = Wheaton's Supreme Court Reports (U.S.A.)
White = White's Justiciary Reports (Scotland)
Will. Woll. & Dav. = Willmore, Wollaston and Davison's
  Queen's Bench Reports
Willes = Willes' Common Pleas Reports
Wilm. = Wilmot's Notes and Opinions, King's Bench
Wils. K.B. = Wilson's King's Bench Reports
Wm. Bl. = W. Blackstone's King's Bench Reports
Wms. Saund. = William's Notes to Saunders' Reports
Y. & C. Ch. = Younge and Collier's Chancery Cases
Y. & C. Ex. = Younge and Collier's Exchequer Reports
Y. & J. = Younge and Jervis' Exchequer Reports
Y.B. = Year Books
Y.B. (R.S.) = Year Books, Rolls Series
Y.B. (S.S.) = Year Books, Selden Society
Yer. = Yerger's Tennessee Reports
Z.L.R. = Zimbabwe Law Reports

CURRENT LAW
PART I
CASE CITATOR 2005 (ENGLAND)

The Current Law Case Citator comprises in a single table:
(i) Full case name of cases reported in 2005
(ii) The judicial history of any case of whatever date which has been considered, applied, overruled, etc., in 2005
Note: Figures appearing in bold type indicate the paragraph in the Current Law Year Book at which the case is digested

1 Pump Court Chambers v. Horton; *sub nom* Higham v. Horton; Horton v. 1 Pump Court
    Chambers; Horton v. Higham [2004] EWCA Civ 941; [2004] 3 All E.R. 852;
    [2005] I.C.R. 292; (2004) 101(33) L.S.G. 34; (2004) 148 S.J.L.B. 911; *Times,*
    July 21, 2004; *Independent,* July 28, 2004, CA (Civ Div); affirming *Times,* April
    14, 2004, EAT . . . .   *Digested,* 04/**1216**

3M United Kingdom Plc v. Linklaters & Paines (A Firm) A3/2005/1496, CA (Civ Div)
    [2005] EWHC 1382; [2005] P.N.L.R. 46; [2005] N.P.C. 87, Ch D . . . .   *Digested,* 05/**433**
3M/Correction (T309/03) [2004] E.P.O.R. 34, EPO (Technical Bd App) . . . .   *Applied,* 05/2455

4Cast Ltd v. Mitchell (Inspector of Taxes) [2005] S.T.C. (S.C.D.) 287; [2005] S.T.I. 162,
    Sp Comm . . . .   *Digested,* 05/**4041**

7 Strathray Gardens Ltd v. Pointstar Shipping & Finance Ltd; *sub nom* Pointstar
    Shipping & Finance Ltd v. 7 Strathray Gardens Ltd [2004] EWCA Civ 1669;
    [2005] H.L.R. 20; [2005] L. & T.R. 16; [2005] 1 E.G.L.R. 53; [2005] 07 E.G.
    144; [2005] 1 E.G.C.S. 95; (2005) 102(6) L.S.G. 32; (2005) 149 S.J.L.B. 58;
    [2005] 1 P. & C.R. DG23; *Times,* January 10, 2005; *Independent,* January 19,
    2005, CA (Civ Div) . . . .   *Digested,* 05/**2652**

9 Cornwall Crescent London Ltd v. Kensington and Chelsea RLBC [2005] EWCA Civ
    324; [2005] 4 All E.R. 1207; [2005] H.L.R. 40; [2005] L. & T.R. 19; [2005] 2
    E.G.L.R. 131; [2005] 14 E.G.C.S. 128; (2005) 149 S.J.L.B. 391; [2005] N.P.C.
    47; *Times,* March 29, 2005; *Independent,* April 14, 2005, CA (Civ Div). . . . .   *Digested,* 05/**3386**

19TV Ltd v. Freemantle Media Ltd [2005] EWHC 1876; (2005) 28(9) I.P.D. 28068,
    Ch D

420093 BC Ltd v. Bank of Montreal (1995) 128 D.L.R. (4th) 488, CA (Alta) . . . .   *Considered,* 05/4310

A v. A (A Child) (Removal from Jurisdiction) (1980) 1 F.L.R. 380, CA (Civ Div) . . . .   *Applied,* 01/2596,
                                        05/1590
A v. B [2005] EWHC 1651; [2005] E.M.L.R. 36; (2005) 28(8) I.P.D. 28060, QBD
A v. B (Ancillary Relief: Separation Agreement) see A v. B (Financial Relief:
    Agreements)
A v. B (Financial Relief: Agreements); *sub nom* A v. B (Ancillary Relief: Separation
    Agreement) [2005] EWHC 314; [2005] 2 F.L.R. 730; *Times,* March 23, 2005,
    Fam Div . . . .   *Digested,* 05/**1688**
A v. Birmingham City Council [2004] EWHC 156; [2004] E.L.R. 563; [2005] A.C.D.
    7, QBD (Admin) . . . .   *Digested,* 05/**1143**
A v. Chief Constable of West Yorkshire see Chief Constable of West Yorkshire v. A
A v. France (A/277-B) (1994) 17 E.H.R.R. 462, ECHR . . . .   *Digested,* 94/**2432**:
                                         Applied, 05/2115
A v. General Medical Council [2004] EWHC 880; [2004] A.C.D. 54, QBD (Admin) . . .   *Considered,* 05/1802
A v. Headteacher and Governors of Lord Grey School see Ali v. Lord Grey School
    Governors

A *v.* Hoare; H *v.* Suffolk CC; X *v.* Wandsworth LBC; B3/2005/2417, B3/2005/0613 &
     B3/2005/0613(A), B3/2005/2820 & B3/2005/2341, CA (Civ Div); affirming
     [2005] EWHC 2161; (2005) 102(44) L.S.G. 30; (2005) 155 N.L.J. 1601; *Times,*
     October 27, 2005, QBD. . . . .   *Digested,* 05/**432**
A *v.* Inner South London Coroner see R. (on the application of A) *v.* HM Coroner for
     Inner South London
A *v.* Leeds Teaching Hospital NHS Trust; *sub nom* AB *v.* Leeds Teaching Hospital NHS
     Trust; Organ Retention Group Litigation, Re [2004] EWHC 644; [2005] Q.B.
     506; [2005] 2 W.L.R. 358; [2004] 2 F.L.R. 365; [2004] 3 F.C.R. 324; [2005]
     Lloyd's Rep. Med. 1; (2004) 77 B.M.L.R. 145; [2004] Fam. Law 501; (2004)
     101(16) L.S.G. 28; (2004) 154 N.L.J. 497; *Times,* April 12, 2004, QBD . . . .   *Digested,* 04/**2705**
A *v.* Minister for Immigration and Ethnic Affairs 2 B.H.R.C. 143; [1998] I.N.L.R. 1;
     (1997) 71 A.L.J.R. 381, HC (Aus). . . . .   *Digested,* 97/**2934**:
                              Approved, 97/2851: *Considered,* 05/2223
A *v.* Secretary of State for the Home Department; *sub nom* X *v.* Secretary of State for
     the Home Department [2004] UKHL 56; [2005] 2 A.C. 68; [2005] 2 W.L.R.
     87; [2005] 3 All E.R. 169; [2005] H.R.L.R. 1; [2005] U.K.H.R.R. 175; 17 B.H.R.C.
     496; [2005] Imm. A.R. 103; (2005) 155 N.L.J. 23; (2005) 149 S.J.L.B. 28;
     Times, December 17, 2004; *Independent,* December 21, 2004, HL; reversing
     [2002] EWCA Civ 1502; [2004] Q.B. 335; [2003] 2 W.L.R. 564; [2003] 1 All
     E.R. 816; [2003] H.R.L.R. 3; [2002] U.K.H.R.R. 1141; 13 B.H.R.C. 394; [2003]
     A.C.D. 10; (2002) 99(46) L.S.G. 33; (2002) 146 S.J.L.B. 246; *Times,* October
     29, 2002, CA (Civ Div); reversing [2002] H.R.L.R. 45; [2002] A.C.D. 98, Sp
     Imm App Comm . . . .   *Digested,* 05/**2105**:
                                    Applied, 04/2004, 05/1139
A *v.* Secretary of State for the Home Department; *sub nom* CA *v.* Secretary of State
     for the Home Department [2004] EWCA Civ 1165; [2004] Imm. A.R. 640;
     [2004] I.N.L.R. 453; [2004] A.C.D. 91; (2004) 101(34) L.S.G. 30; *Times,*
     August 3, 2004, CA (Civ Div) . . . .   *Digested,* 05/**2165**:
                                    Applied, 05/2179, 05/2217
A *v.* Secretary of State for the Home Department; C *v.* Secretary of State for the Home
     Department; D *v.* Secretary of State for the Home Department [2005] UKHL
     71; [2005] 3 W.L.R. 1249; 19 B.H.R.C. 441; (2005) 155 N.L.J. 1924; *Times,*
     December 9, 2005; *Independent,* December 14, 2005, HL; reversing [2004]
     EWCA Civ 1123; [2005] 1 W.L.R. 414; [2004] H.R.L.R. 38; (2004) 154 N.L.J.
     1291; (2004) 148 S.J.L.B. 1029; *Times,* October 5, 2004, CA (Civ Div) . . . .   *Digested,* 04/**2004**
A (A Child) *v.* Ansell [2005] 2 Q.R. 23; [2004] 5 Q.R. 8, CC (Dudley) [*Ex rel.* Stephen
     Garner, Barrister, No.8 Chambers, Fountain Court, Steelhouse Lane,
     Birmingham.]. . . . .   *Digested,* 04/**2975**
A (A Child) *v.* Guru (Unreported, November 1, 2004), CC (Coventry) [*Ex rel.* Stephen
     Garner, Barrister, No.8 Chambers, Fountain Court, Steelhouse Lane,
     Birmingham.]. . . . .   *Digested,* 05/**3228**
A (A Child) *v.* Ministry of Defence [2004] EWCA Civ 641; [2005] Q.B. 183; [2004] 3
     W.L.R. 469; [2004] P.I.Q.R. P35; [2004] Lloyd's Rep. Med. 351; (2005) 82
     B.M.L.R. 149; (2004) 101(22) L.S.G. 32; *Times,* May 17, 2004; *Independent,*
     May 13, 2004, CA (Civ Div); affirming [2003] EWHC 849; [2003] P.I.Q.R. P33;
     [2003] Lloyd's Rep. Med. 339; (2003) 100(26) L.S.G. 39; *Times,* May 16,
     2003, QBD . . . .   *Digested,* 04/**2697**
A (A Child) *v.* Morrish (Unreported, September 23, 2004), CC (Watford) [*Ex rel.*
     Joanna Kerr, Barrister, Lamb Chambers, Lamb Building, Temple, London] . . . . . .   *Digested,* 05/**3217**
A (A Child) (Contact: Risk of Violence), Re [2005] EWHC 851; [2005] Fam. Law 939, Fam
     Div
A (A Child) (Foreign Contact Order: Jurisdiction), Re; *sub nom* J *v.* C [2003] EWHC
     2911; [2004] 1 All E.R. 912; [2004] 1 F.L.R. 641; [2004] 1 F.C.R. 371; [2004]
     Fam. Law 336; (2004) 101(3) L.S.G. 32; *Times,* December 10, 2003, Fam Div. .   *Digested,* 04/**1485**:
                         Considered, 05/1590: *Previous proceedings,* 02/1655
A (A Child) (Temporary Removal from Jurisdiction), Re; *sub nom* W *v.* A [2004] EWCA
     Civ 1587; [2005] 1 F.L.R. 639; [2005] Fam. Law 215; *Times,* November 10,
     2004, CA (Civ Div) . . . .   *Digested,* 05/**1575**
A (A Minor) (Abduction: Non-Convention Country), Re see JA (A Minor) (Child
     Abduction: Non-Convention Country), Re
A (A Minor) (Adoption: Contact Order), Re [1993] 2 F.L.R. 645; *Times,* June 24, 1993;
     Independent, July 2, 1993, CA (Civ Div) . . . .   *Digested,* 94/**3092**:
                                    Considered, 05/1497
A (Adoption: Placement Outside Jurisdiction), Re; *sub nom* B *v.* Birmingham City
     Council; B (Children) (Adoption: Removal from Jurisdiction), Re [2004] EWCA
     Civ 515; [2005] Fam. 105; [2004] 3 W.L.R. 1207; [2004] 2 F.L.R. 337;
     [2004] 2 F.C.R. 129; [2004] Fam. Law 560; *Times,* June 10, 2004; *Independent,*
     May 6, 2004, CA (Civ Div) . . . .   *Digested,* 04/**1444**
A (Afghanistan) *v.* Secretary of State for the Home Department see R (Iran) *v.*
     Secretary of State for the Home Department
A (Iraq) *v.* Secretary of State for the Home Department [2005] EWCA Civ 1438;
     Independent, December 6, 2005, CA (Civ Div)
A (Medical Treatment: Male Sterilisation), Re see A (Mental Patient: Sterilisation), Re

A (Mental Patient: Sterilisation), Re; *sub nom* A (Medical Treatment: Male Sterilisation), Re; R–B (A Patient) *v.* Official Solicitor; RB (Male Patient: Sterilisation), Re [2000] 1 F.L.R. 549; [2000] 1 F.C.R. 193; [2000] Lloyd's Rep. Med. 87; (2000) 53 B.M.L.R. 66; [2000] Fam. Law 242; (2000) 97(2) L.S.G. 30; *Times,* March 15, 2000, CA (Civ Div) . . . . *Digested,* 00/**2780**:
Applied, 04/3648, 05/1794, 05/1848: *Considered,* 04/1690
A (Placement of Child in Contravention of Adoption Act 1976 s.11), Re [2005] 2 F.L.R. 727, Fam Div
A County Council *v.* DP see Oxfordshire CC *v.* DP
A County Council *v.* K see A Local Authority *v.* K
A County Council *v.* M [2005] EWHC 31; [2005] 2 F.L.R. 129; [2005] Fam. Law 350, Fam Div . . . . *Digested,* 05/**1559**
A Fulton Co Ltd *v.* Grant Barnett & Co Ltd [2001] R.P.C. 16; (2001) 24(1) I.P.D. 24003, Ch D . . . . *Digested,* 01/**3861**:
Approved, 04/2265: *Considered,* 05/2589
A Local Authority *v.* B (Emergency Protection Orders); *sub nom* X Council *v.* B (Emergency Protection Orders) [2004] EWHC 2015; [2005] 1 F.L.R. 341; [2005] Fam. Law 13, Fam Div . . . . *Digested,* 05/**1530**
A Local Authority *v.* DW; *sub nom* X CC *v.* DW [2005] EWHC 162; [2005] 2 F.L.R. 508; [2005] Fam. Law 448, Fam Div
A Local Authority *v.* K; *sub nom* A County Council *v.* K [2005] EWHC 144; [2005] 1 F.L.R. 851; [2005] Fam. Law 450, Fam Div . . . . *Digested,* 05/**1529**
A Local Authority *v.* PD [2005] EWHC 1832; [2005] E.M.L.R. 35, Fam Div
A Local Authority *v.* S [2004] EWHC 1270; [2004] 2 F.L.R. 129; [2004] Fam. Law 636, Fam Div . . . . *Digested,* 05/**1560**
A Local Authority *v.* W see W (Children) (Identification: Restrictions on Publication), Re
A Local Authority *v.* Z see Z (Local Authority: Duty), Re
A Oy, Re 7 I.T.L. Rep. 288, KHO (Fin)
A&S Enterprises Ltd *v.* Kema Holdings Ltd [2005] EWHC 3365; [2005] B.L.R. 76, QBD (TCC) . . . . *Digested,* 05/**645**
AA *v.* Secretary of State for the Home Department; *sub nom* AA (Third Party Maintenance: R297(V): Bangladesh), Re; Entry Clearance Officer, Dhaka *v.* AA [2005] UKIAT 105; [2005] Imm. A.R. 328, IAT
AA *v.* Secretary of State for the Home Department; *sub nom* AA (Exclusion Clause: Palestine), Re [2005] UKIAT 104; [2005] Imm. A.R. 593, IAT
AA Mutual International Insurance Co Ltd, Re [2004] EWHC 2430; [2005] 2 B.C.L.C. 8, Ch D (Companies Ct) . . . . *Digested,* 05/**2264**
AA (Exclusion Clause: Palestine), Re see AA *v.* Secretary of State for the Home Department
AA (Third Party Maintenance: R297(V): Bangladesh), Re see AA *v.* Secretary of State for the Home Department
AAA *v.* Financial Directorate 8 I.T.L. Rep. 178, NS CR (CZ)
Aalborg Portland A/S *v.* Commission of the European Communities (C204/00 P) [2004] E.C.R. I-123; [2005] 4 C.M.L.R. 4, ECJ (5th Chamber) . . . . *Digested,* 05/**1435**:
Previous proceedings, 00/710
Aaron *v.* Shelton [2004] EWHC 1162; [2004] 3 All E.R. 561; [2004] 3 Costs L.R. 488; (2004) 154 N.L.J. 853, QBD . . . . *Digested,* 04/**327**:
Applied, 05/379
AB *v.* Leeds Teaching Hospital NHS Trust see A *v.* Leeds Teaching Hospital NHS Trust
AB & Co, Re see Cooke *v.* Charles A Vogeler Co
Abacus Trust Co (Isle of Man) Ltd *v.* Barr; *sub nom* Barr's Settlement Trusts, Re [2003] EWHC 114; [2003] Ch. 409; [2003] 2 W.L.R. 1362; [2003] 1 All E.R. 763; [2003] W.T.L.R. 149; (2002-03) 5 I.T.E.L.R. 602; (2003) 100(13) L.S.G. 27; *Times,* February 28, 2003; *Independent,* March 31, 2003 (C.S), Ch D . . . . *Digested,* 03/**4501**:
Considered, 05/4305
Abacus Trust Co (Isle of Man) Ltd *v.* National Society for the Prevention of Cruelty to Children see Abacus Trust Co (Isle of Man) Ltd *v.* NSPCC
Abacus Trust Co (Isle of Man) Ltd *v.* NSPCC; *sub nom* Abacus Trust Co (Isle of Man) Ltd *v.* National Society for the Prevention of Cruelty to Children [2001] S.T.C. 1344; [2002] B.T.C. 178; [2001] W.T.L.R. 953; (2000-01) 3 I.T.E.L.R. 846; [2001] S.T.I. 1225; (2001) 98(35) L.S.G. 37; *Times,* September 25, 2001, Ch D . . . . . . *Digested,* 01/**5532**:
Applied, 03/4497, 05/4305
ABB Asea Brown Boveri Ltd *v.* Commission of the European Communities (C213/02 P) see Dansk Rorindustri A/S *v.* Commission of the European Communities (C189/02 P)
Abbey National Plc, Re [2004] EWHC 2776; [2005] 2 B.C.L.C. 15, Ch D (Companies Ct)   *Digested,* 05/**535**
Abbey National Plc *v.* Customs and Excise Commissioners [2005] EWHC 1187; [2005] B.T.C. 5317; [2005] BV.C. 348; [2005] S.T.I. 1095, Ch D; affirming [2003] B.V.C. 2626; [2003] S.T.I. 2195, V&DTr . . . . *Digested,* 05/**4341**
Abbey National Plc *v.* Customs and Excise Commissioners [2005] EWHC 831; [2005] 3 E.G.L.R. 73; [2005] 43 E.G. 190; [2005] B.T.C. 5300; [2005] BV.C. 331; [2005] S.T.I. 906; [2005] 19 E.G.C.S. 175; [2005] N.P.C. 61, Ch D; reversing in part [2004] B.V.C. 2367; [2004] V. & D.R. 267; [2004] S.T.I. 2311, V&DTr . . . . . *Digested,* 05/**4403**

Abbey National Plc v. Customs and Excise Commissioners (C408/98) [2001] 1 W.L.R.
769; [2001] All E.R. (EC) 385; [2001] S.T.C. 297; [2001] E.C.R. I-1361; [2001]
2 C.M.L.R. 28; [2001] C.E.C. 80; [2001] B.T.C. 5481; [2001] B.V.C. 581; [2001]
S.T.I. 244; *Times*, March 13, 2001, ECJ (5th Chamber) . . . .   *Digested*, 01/**5586**:
                         Applied, 05/4380: *Considered*, 01/5585, 03/4555: *Followed*, 05/4363
Abbey National Plc v. JSF Financial & Currency Exchange Co Ltd [2005] EWHC 1730;
[2005] B.P.I.R. 1256, Ch D (Companies Ct)
Abbey National Plc v. O'Hara [2005] R.A. 247, Lands Tr
Abbott v. Condici Ltd [2005] 2 Lloyd's Rep. 450, CC (Central London)
Abbott v. Will Gannon & Smith Ltd [2005] EWCA Civ 198; [2005] B.L.R. 195; 103
Con. L.R. 92; [2005] P.N.L.R. 30; [2005] 10 E.G.C.S. 154; [2005] N.P.C. 30;
Times, April 28, 2005, CA (Civ Div) . . . .   *Digested*, 05/**436**
Abbott Laboratories v. Approved Prescriptions Services Ltd see Abbott Laboratories v.
Ranbaxy Europe Ltd
Abbott Laboratories v. Generics (UK) Ltd see Abbott Laboratories v. Ranbaxy Europe
Ltd
Abbott Laboratories v. Ranbaxy Europe Ltd; Abbott Laboratories v. Approved
Prescriptions Services Ltd; Abbott Laboratories v. Generics (UK) Ltd [2004]
EWHC 2723; (2005) 28(1) I.P.D. 27111, Ch D
ABBOTT LABORATORIES/Controlled Release Formulation (T453/01) [2005] E.P.O.R.
30, EPO (Technical Bd App)
ABC Ltd v. M (Inspector of Taxes) see Barclays Mercantile Business Finance Ltd v.
Mawson (Inspector of Taxes)
Abdi v. Secretary of State for the Home Department see R. (on the application of
Nadarajah) v. Secretary of State for the Home Department
Abdoulaye v. Regie Nationale des Usines Renault SA (C218/98) [1999] E.C.R. I-
5723; [2001] 2 C.M.L.R. 18; [2001] I.C.R. 527; [1999] I.R.L.R. 811; *Times*,
October 20, 1999, ECJ (5th Chamber) . . . .   *Digested*, 99/**2114**:
                                        Followed, 05/1282
Abdullah v. Shropshire CC see R. v. Barnet LBC Ex p. Shah (Nilish)
Abdullahi v. Mudashiru [2003] EWHC 2836; [2004] W.T.L.R. 913, Ch D . . . .   *Digested*, 05/**3966**
Abercromby Motor Group Ltd v. Customs and Excise Commissioners [2005] B.V.C.
2549; [2005] S.T.I. 910, V&DTr
Aberdeen Construction Group Ltd v. Inland Revenue Commissioners [1978] A.C. 885;
[1978] 2 W.L.R. 648; [1978] 1 All E.R. 962; [1978] S.T.C. 127; 1978 S.C. (H.L.)
72; 1978 S.L.T. 146; 52 T.C. 281; [1978] T.R. 25; 122 S.J. 249, HL; reversing in
part [1977] S.T.C. 302; 1977 S.C. 265, IH (1 Div) . . . .   *Digested*, 79/**371**:
          Applied, 79/1450: *Cited*, 97/1073: *Considered*, 97/1071:
      Distinguished, 80/1453: *Followed*, 78/359, 05/4003: *Referred to*, 95/527
Aberdeen Journals Ltd v. Director General of Fair Trading [2002] CAT 4; [2002] Comp.
A.R. 167, CCAT . . . .   *Digested*, 03/**5306**:
                                        Followed, 05/565
Aberdeen Journals Ltd v. Director General of Fair Trading (Confidentiality of Judgment)
[2003] CAT 14; [2004] Comp. A.R. 71, CCAT . . . .   *Digested*, 04/**511**:
                                     Considered, 05/580
Abertal Sat Limitada v. Commission of the European Communities (C213/91) [1993]
E.C.R. I-3177, ECJ . . . .   *Digested*, 93/**4196**:
                                        Followed, 05/550
Ablack v. Inner London Education Authority see R. v. Barnet LBC Ex p. Shah (Nilish)
Ableway Ltd v. Customs and Excise Commissioners see Ableway Ltd v. Inland
Revenue Commissioners
Ableway Ltd v. Inland Revenue Commissioners; *sub nom* Ableway Ltd v. Customs and
Excise Commissioners [2002] S.T.C. (S.C.D.) 1; [2001] S.T.I. 1527, Sp Comm. . .   *Digested*, 02/**4229**:
                                     Followed, 05/3895
Abrahamsson v. Fogelqvist (C407/98) [2000] E.C.R. I-5539; [2002] I.C.R. 932;
[2000] I.R.L.R. 732, ECJ (5th Chamber) . . . .   *Digested*, 00/**2170**:
                                     Followed, 05/1269
Absalom v. TCRU Ltd (formerly Monument Insurance Brokers Ltd) [2005] EWCA Civ
1586, CA (Civ Div); affirming [2005] EWHC 1090; [2005] 2 Lloyd's Rep. 735,
QBD (Comm)
Abu-Qulbain v. Secretary of State for the Home Department see Huang v. Secretary of
State for the Home Department
Abu-Romia v. General Medical Council [2003] EWHC 2515; (2004) 80 B.M.L.R. 1,
QBD (Admin) . . . .   *Digested*, 05/**1803**
AC v. Secretary of State for the Home Department; *sub nom* AC (Witness with
Refugee Status: Effect: Somalia), Re [2005] UKIAT 124; [2005] Imm. A.R. 714,
IAT
AC v. Secretary of State for the Home Department; *sub nom* AC (Regularisation
Period: Rights of Appeal: Zimbabwe), Re [2005] UKIAT 128; [2005] Imm. A.R.
719, IAT
AC Hatrick (NZ) v. Nelson Carlton Construction Co (In Liquidation) [1964] N.Z.L.R.
72, Sup Ct (NZ) . . . .   *Digested*, 64/**363**:
                                       Applied, 05/665

AC (Regularisation Period: Rights of Appeal: Zimbabwe), Re see AC *v.* Secretary of State for the Home Department
AC (Witness with Refugee Status: Effect: Somalia), Re see AC *v.* Secretary of State for the Home Department
Access to Higher Education, Re (C147/03) see Commission of the European Communities *v.* Austria (C147/03)
Acciai Speciali Terni SpA *v.* Commission of the European Communities (T47/98) see Krupp Thyssen Stainless GmbH *v.* Commission of the European Communities (T45/98)
Accident Assistance Ltd *v.* Hammond Suddards Edge (A Firm) [2005] EWHC 202; [2005] P.N.L.R. 29, Ch D . . . . *Digested,* 05/**2878**
Acclivus Corp's Community Trade Mark Application [2005] E.T.M.R. 24, OHIM (3rd Bd App) . . . . *Digested,* 05/**2550**
Accountant *v.* Inspector of Taxes [2000] S.T.C. (S.C.D.) 522; [2000] S.T.I. 1518, Sp Comm . . . . *Digested,* 01/**5314**:
Applied, 05/**4088**: *Followed,* 04/**3823**
Ace Telecom Ltd *v.* Revenue and Customs Commissioners [2005] S.T.I. 2039, V&DTr (Manchester)
ACF Chemiefarma NV *v.* Commission of the European Communities (41/69) [1970] E.C.R. 661, ECJ. . . . . *Applied,* 05/**555**
Achour *v.* France (67335/01) (2005) 41 E.H.R.R. 36, ECHR
Acimovic *v.* Croatia (61237/00) (2005) 40 E.H.R.R. 23; (2004) 39 E.H.R.R. 27, ECHR .   *Digested,* 05/**2073**
Ackinclose *v.* Gateshead MBC [2005] I.R.L.R. 79, EAT . . . .   *Digested,* 05/**1339**
Action Navigation Inc *v.* Bottiglieri di Navigatione SpA (The Kitsa); *sub nom* Action Navigation Inc *v.* Bottigliere Navigation SpA [2005] EWHC 177; [2005] 1 Lloyd's Rep. 432; [2005] 1 C.L.C. 153, QBD (Comm) . . . .   *Digested,* 05/**3814**
Actionstrength Ltd (t/a Vital Resources) *v.* International Glass Engineering IN.GL.EN SpA [2003] UKHL 17; [2003] 2 A.C. 541; [2003] 2 W.L.R. 1060; [2003] 2 All E.R. 615; [2003] 2 All E.R. (Comm) 331; [2005] 1 B.C.L.C. 606; [2003] 1 C.L.C. 1003; [2003] B.L.R. 207; 88 Con. L.R. 208; (2003) 153 N.L.J. 563; (2003) 147 S.J.L.B. 418; *Times,* April 4, 2003, HL; affirming [2001] EWCA Civ 1477; [2002] 1 W.L.R. 566; [2002] 4 All E.R. 468; [2002] C.L.C. 153; [2002] B.L.R. 44; [2002] T.C.L.R. 10; *Independent,* December 3, 2001, CA (Civ Div) . . . .   *Digested,* 03/**1422**
Adam *v.* Administration de l'Enregistrement et des Domaines (C267/99); *sub nom* Urbing *v.* Administration de l'Enregistrement et des Domaines (C267/99) [2001] E.C.R. I-7467; [2003] 2 C.M.L.R. 33; [2003] B.T.C. 5240; [2003] B.V.C. 296, ECJ (2nd Chamber) . . . .   *Digested,* 03/**4597**:
Applied, 05/**4348**
Adami *v.* Ethical Standards Officer of the Standards Board for England [2005] EWCA Civ 1754; *Times,* December 2, 2005, CA (Civ Div)
Adams, Re [2004] EWHC 2739; (2005) 102(2) L.S.G. 28; *Times,* December 6, 2004, QBD . . . .   *Digested,* 05/**844**
Adams *v.* Bracknell Forest BC; *sub nom* Bracknell Forest BC *v.* Adams [2004] UKHL 29; [2005] 1 A.C. 76; [2004] 3 W.L.R. 89; [2004] 3 All E.R. 897; [2004] E.L.R. 459; [2005] P.I.Q.R. P2; (2004) 101(26) L.S.G. 28; (2004) 148 S.J.L.B. 761; *Times,* June 24, 2004, HL; reversing [2003] EWCA Civ 706; [2003] E.L.R. 409; (2003) 100(26) L.S.G. 39; (2003) 147 S.J.L.B. 599; *Times,* May 14, 2003; *Independent,* May 15, 2003, CA (Civ Div) . . . .   *Digested,* 04/**372**:
Applied, 05/**438**
Adams *v.* Green [1978] 2 E.G.L.R. 46; (1978) 247 E.G. 49, CA (Civ Div) . . . .   *Digested,* 79/**1576**:
Applied, 90/**3378**: *Considered,* 90/**2771**, 94/**1758**, 05/**2671**
Adams *v.* Mason Bullock (A Firm) [2004] EWHC 2910; [2005] B.P.I.R. 241; (2005) 102(4) L.S.G. 30; *Times,* January 6, 2005, Ch D . . . .   *Digested,* 05/**2279**
Adams *v.* United Kingdom (Admissibility) (28979/95); *sub nom* Benn *v.* United Kingdom (30343/96) (1997) 23 E.H.R.R. CD160, Eur Comm HR . . . .   *Considered,* 05/**2149**
Adan *v.* Securicor Custodial Services Ltd [2004] EWHC 394; [2004] C.P. Rep. 33; [2005] P.I.Q.R. P6, QBD . . . .   *Digested,* 05/**462**
Adan (Hassan Hussein) *v.* Secretary of State for the Home Department; *sub nom* Secretary of State for the Home Department *v.* Adan (Hassan Hussein); R. *v.* Secretary of State for the Home Department Ex p. Adan (Hassan Hussein); Nooh *v.* Secretary of State for the Home Department; Lazarevic *v.* Secretary of State for the Home Department; Radivojevic *v.* Secretary of State for the Home Department [1999] 1 A.C. 293; [1998] 2 W.L.R. 702; [1998] 1 W.L.R. 624; [1998] 2 All E.R. 453; [1998] Imm. A.R. 338; [1998] I.N.L.R. 325; (1998) 95(18) L.S.G. 33; (1998) 148 N.L.J. 552; (1998) 142 S.J.L.B. 139; *Times,* April 6, 1998, HL; reversing [1997] 1 W.L.R. 1107; [1997] 2 All E.R. 723; 2 B.H.R.C. 65; [1997] Imm. A.R. 251; [1997] I.N.L.R. 1; *Times,* March 7, 1997; *Independent,* March 12, 1997, CA (Civ Div) . . . .   *Digested,* 98/**3241**:
Applied, 99/**3183**, 03/**5732**, 05/**2177**: *Considered,* 00/**3319**:
Followed, 00/**6491**, 01/**3639**: *Not followed,* 01/**3694**
Addax BV Geneva Branch *v.* Coral Suki SA [2004] EWHC 2882; [2005] 2 All E.R. (Comm) 137, QBD (Comm)
Addey and Stanhope School *v.* Vakante see Vakante *v.* Addey and Stanhope School Governing Body

Addin Investments Ltd v. Secretary of State for the Environment [1997] 1 E.G.L.R. 99;
  [1997] 14 E.G. 132; [1996] E.G.C.S. 195, Ch D . . . . *Digested,* 97/**3322**:
                                             Distinguished, 05/2667
Addington v. Texas 504 U.S. 71, US Ct . . . . *Considered,* 05/2825
Addison v. Babcock FATA Ltd; *sub nom* Babcock FATA Ltd v. Addison [1988] Q.B.
  280; [1987] 3 W.L.R. 122; [1987] 2 All E.R. 784; [1987] I.C.R. 805; [1987]
  I.R.L.R. 173; [1987] 1 F.T.L.R. 505; (1987) 84 L.S.G. 1409, CA (Civ Div);
  reversing [1987] I.C.R. 45; [1986] I.R.L.R. 388; (1986) 83 L.S.G. 2568; *Times,*
  July 10, 1986, EAT . . . . *Digested,* 87/**1388**:
                   Applied, 05/1331: *Considered,* 88/1336: *Followed,* 93/1816
Addison v. Esso Petroleum Co Ltd see Esso Petroleum Co Ltd v. Addison
Aden Refinery Co Ltd v. Ugland Management Co Ltd (The Ugland Obo One) [1987]
  Q.B. 650; [1986] 3 W.L.R. 949; [1986] 3 All E.R. 737; [1986] 2 Lloyd's Rep.
  336, CA (Civ Div) . . . . *Digested,* 86/**91**:
                                                  Considered, 05/325
ADI (UK) Ltd v. Firm Security Group Ltd [2001] EWCA Civ 971; [2001] 3 C.M.L.R. 8;
  [2001] I.R.L.R. 542; [2001] Emp. L.R. 969, CA (Civ Div); reversing EAT/11/99,
  EAT . . . . *Digested,* 01/**2338**:
                   Applied, 02/1429, 03/1329: *Considered,* 03/1328, 05/1313
Adidas AG v. H&M Hennes & Mauritz Netherlands BV [2005] E.T.M.R. CN8, Hof ('s-
  Hertogenbosch)
Adidas Sarragan France v. Subo [2005] E.T.M.R. 4, C d'A (Paris)
Adidas-Salomon AG v. Dolce & Gabbana Germany GmbH (26 U 5518/03) [2005]
  E.T.M.R. 2, OLG (Munchen)
Adidas-Salomon AG v. Fitnessworld Trading Ltd (C408/01) [2004] Ch. 120; [2004] 2
  W.L.R. 1095; [2003] E.C.R. I-12537; [2004] 1 C.M.L.R. 14; [2004] C.E.C. 3;
  [2004] E.T.M.R. 10; [2004] F.S.R. 21; *Times,* October 31, 2003, ECJ (6th
  Chamber) [2003] E.T.M.R. 91, AGO . . . . *Digested,* 04/**2390**:
                                                  Applied, 05/2562
Adidas-Salomon AG v. Nike International Ltd [2005] E.T.M.R. 91, LG (Koln)
Adidas-Salomon AG v. Shoes Partners SAS di Fabrizi Manuela & Co [2005] E.T.M.R.
  3, Trib (Rome)
Adidas-Salomon AG v. Spanish Patent and Trade Mark Office [2005] E.T.M.R. 113, Trib
  Sup (Sp)
Administration des Douanes et Droits Indirect v. Legros (C163/90) [1992] E.C.R. I-
  4625; *Financial Times,* August 14, 1992, ECJ . . . . *Digested,* 92/**4749**:
                                  Considered, 96/5619: *Followed,* 06/943
Adojutelegan v. Clark [2004] S.T.C. (S.C.D.) 524; [2004] S.T.I. 2241, Sp Comm . . . . . . *Digested,* 05/**3893**
Adolf v. Austria (A/49) (1982) 4 E.H.R.R. 313, ECHR . . . . *Considered,* 03/5307:
                                                  Distinguished, 05/925
Adoption Application (AA 125/1983), Re see Y (Minors) (Adoption: Jurisdiction), Re
Adoui v. Belgium (115/81); Cornuaille v. Belgium (116/81) [1982] E.C.R. 1665; [1982]
  3 C.M.L.R. 631, ECJ . . . . *Digested,* 83/**1400**:
                                                  Followed, 05/1462
Adria Wien Pipeline GmbH v. Finanzlandesdirektion fur Karnten (C143/99) [2002] All
  E.R. (EC) 306; [2001] E.C.R. I-8365; [2002] 1 C.M.L.R. 38, ECJ (5th
  Chamber) . . . . *Digested,* 02/**616**:
                                                  Followed, 05/2380
Adriatica di Navigazione SpA v. Commission of the European Communities (T61/99)
  [2003] E.C.R. II-5349; [2005] 5 C.M.L.R. 30, CFI (5th Chamber)
Advanced Building Solutions Ltd v. Yates (Unreported, May 7, 2004), Ch D [*Ex rel.* Ian
  Strongman, Barrister, No. 8 Chambers, Fountain Court, Steelhouse Lane,
  Birmingham] . . . . *Digested,* 05/**474**
Advanced Totes Ltd v. Bord na gCon [2005] Eu. L.R. 873, HC (Irl)
Advent Capital Plc v. GN Ellinas Imports-Exports Ltd [2005] EWHC 1242; [2005] 2
  Lloyd's Rep. 607; [2005] 1 C.L.C. 1058; [2005] I.L.Pr. 57, QBD (Comm) . . . . . . *Digested,* 05/**420**
Advocate General for Scotland v. MacDonald; *sub nom* Secretary of State for Defence
  v. MacDonald; MacDonald v. Ministry of Defence; MacDonald v. Advocate
  General for Scotland; Pearce v. Mayfield Secondary School Governing Body
  [2003] UKHL 34; [2004] 1 All E.R. 339; 2003 S.C. (H.L.) 35; 2003 S.L.T. 1158;
  2003 S.C.L.R. 814; [2003] I.C.R. 937; [2003] I.R.L.R. 512; [2003] E.L.R. 655;
  (2003) 100(29) L.S.G. 36; (2003) 147 S.J.L.B. 782; 2003 G.W.D. 23-677;
  Times, June 20, 2003, HL; affirming 2002 S.C. 1; 2001 S.L.T. 819; 2001 S.C.L.R.
  795; [2002] I.C.R. 174; [2001] I.R.L.R. 431; [2001] Emp. L.R. 793; 2001
  G.W.D. 19-731, IH (Ex Div); reversing [2001] 1 All E.R. 620; [2001] I.C.R. 1;
  [2000] I.R.L.R. 748; [2001] Emp. L.R. 105; [2001] H.R.L.R. 5; *Independent,*
  November 27, 2000 (C.S), EAT . . . . *Digested,* 03/**1309**:
                Applied, 05/1298: *Considered,* 01/2315: *Previous proceedings,* 01/2315
Aectra Refining & Manufacturing Inc v. Exmar NV (The New Vanguard and The Pacifica)
  [1994] 1 W.L.R. 1634; [1995] 1 All E.R. 641; [1995] 1 Lloyd's Rep. 191; *Times,*
  August 15, 1994; *Independent,* August 22, 1994 (C.S.), CA (Civ Div) . . . . *Digested,* 95/**4213**:
                                                  Considered, 05/206

AEG Telefunken AG v. Commission of the European Communities (107/82 R) [1982]
E.C.R. 1549, ECJ . . . . *Followed,* 01/2451,
05/544
Aegis Group Plc v. Inland Revenue Commissioners [2005] EWHC 1468; [2005] S.T.I.
989, Ch D
AEI Rediffusion Music Ltd v. Phonographic Performance Ltd (Costs); *sub nom*
Phonographic Performance Ltd v. AEI Rediffusion Music Ltd (Costs) [1999] 1
W.L.R. 1507; [1999] 2 All E.R. 299; [1999] C.P.L.R. 551; [1999] E.M.L.R. 335;
[1999] R.P.C. 599; (1999) 22(5) I.P.D. 22046; (1999) 96(12) L.S.G. 33; (1999)
143 S.J.L.B. 97; *Times,* March 3, 1999; *Independent,* February 24, 1999, CA
(Civ Div); affirming [1999] E.M.L.R. 129; (1998) 21(12) I.P.D. 21130, Ch D;
reversing [1998] E.M.L.R. 459, CopyrightTr . . . . *Digested,* 99/**3456**:
Applied, 04/500: *Considered,* 00/396, 00/457, 01/470, 02/371, 02/2837,
03/360, 03/3583, 05/357: *Followed,* 01/460
AEM SpA v. Autorita per l'Energia Elettrica e per il Gas (C128/03) [2005] E.C.R. I-
2861; [2005] 2 C.M.L.R. 60, ECJ (3rd Chamber)
Aerlink Leisure Ltd (In Liquidation) v. First Secretary of State; *sub nom* R. (on the
application of Aerlink Leisure Ltd (In Liquidation)) v. First Secretary of State
[2004] EWHC 3198; [2005] 2 P. & C.R. 15, QBD (Admin) . . . . *Digested,* 05/**3260**
Aeroports de Paris v. Commission of the European Communities (C82/01 P); *sub nom*
Aeroports de Paris v. Commission of the European Communities (T128/98)
[2002] E.C.R. I-9297; [2003] 4 C.M.L.R. 12, ECJ (6th Chamber); affirming
[2000] E.C.R. II-3929; [2001] 4 C.M.L.R. 38, CFI (3rd Chamber) . . . . *Digested,* 03/**550**:
Considered, 05/575
Aeroports de Paris v. Commission of the European Communities (T128/98) see
Aeroports de Paris v. Commission of the European Communities (C82/01 P)
AES Barry Ltd v. TXU Europe Energy Trading (In Administration) [2004] EWHC 1757;
[2005] 2 B.C.L.C. 22, Ch D . . . . *Digested,* 05/**2258**
AES Drax Power Ltd v.Valuation Officer [2005] R.V.R. 299,VT
AF (A Minor) (Abduction), Re see F (A Minor) (Child Abduction), Re
Affymetrix Inc v. Multilyte Ltd [2004] EWHC 291; [2005] I.L.Pr. 34; [2005] F.S.R. 1;
(2004) 27(5) I.P.D. 27053, Ch D (Patents Ct)
AG v. Secretary of State for the Home Department; *sub nom* AG (CA: Fresh
Evidence: Turkey), Re [2005] UKIAT 14; [2005] Imm. A.R. 187, IAT
AG (CA: Fresh Evidence: Turkey), Re see AG v. Secretary of State for the Home
Department
Agapitos v. Agnew (The Aegeon) (No.1) [2002] EWCA Civ 247; [2003] Q.B. 556;
[2002] 3 W.L.R. 616; [2002] 1 All E.R. (Comm) 714; [2002] 2 Lloyd's Rep. 42;
[2002] C.L.C. 886; [2002] Lloyd's Rep. I.R. 573; (2002) 99(16) L.S.G. 38;
(2002) 146 S.J.L.B. 66, CA (Civ Div); affirming [2002] Lloyd's Rep. I.R. 191,
QBD (Comm) . . . . *Digested,* 02/**2732**:
Considered, 05/2359: *Referred to,* 05/2387
Agassi v. Robertson (Inspector of Taxes) see Agassi v. Robinson (Inspector of Taxes)
Agassi v. Robinson (Inspector of Taxes); *sub nom* Set v. Robinson (Inspector of Taxes);
Agassi v. Robertson (Inspector of Taxes) [2004] EWCA Civ 1518; [2005] 1
W.L.R. 1090; [2005] S.T.C. 303; [2004] B.T.C. 467; 7 I.T.L. Rep. 353; [2004]
S.T.I. 2401; (2004) 101(47) L.S.G. 30; (2004) 154 N.L.J. 1789; (2004) 148
S.J.L.B. 1401; *Times,* November 27, 2004; *Independent,* November 24, 2004, CA
(Civ Div); reversing [2004] EWHC 487; [2004] S.T.C. 610; [2004] B.T.C. 170;
6 I.T.L. Rep. 705; [2004] S.T.I. 893; *Times,* April 1, 2004, Ch D; affirming [2003]
S.T.C. (S.C.D.) 382; 6 I.T.L. Rep. 52, Sp Comm . . . . *Digested,* 05/**4104**
Agassi v. Robinson (Inspector of Taxes) (Costs) [2005] EWCA Civ 1507; [2005] S.T.I.
1994; (2005) 155 N.L.J. 1885; [2005] N.P.C. 140; *Times,* December 22, 2005;
Independent, December 7, 2005, CA (Civ Div)
AGCO Ltd v. Massey Ferguson Works Pension Trust Ltd [2003] EWCA Civ 1044;
[2004] I.C.R. 15; [2003] I.R.L.R. 783; [2003] O.P.L.R. 199; [2003] Pens. L.R.
241; (2003) 100(35) L.S.G. 37; (2003) 147 S.J.L.B. 1085; *Times,* July 24, 2003,
CA (Civ Div); affirming in part [2002] EWHC 2878; [2003] O.P.L.R. 119;
[2003] Pens. L.R. 47, Ch D . . . . *Digested,* 03/**3098**:
Considered, 05/1213
Agence France Presse v. D [2005] E.T.M.R. 105,Trib Gde Inst (Paris)
Aggeliki Charis Compania Maritima SA v. Pagnan SpA (The Angelic Grace) [1995] 1
Lloyd's Rep. 87, CA (Civ Div); affirming [1994] 1 Lloyd's Rep. 168, QBD
(Comm) . . . . *Digested,* 94/**4066**:
Applied, 98/239, 05/599, 05/2357: *Considered,* 97/880, 99/733, 99/745,
99/4441, 01/950, 05/625
Agilent Technologies Deutschland GmbH v. Waters Corp [2005] EWCA Civ 987;
(2005) 28(10) I.P.D. 28072, CA (Civ Div); affirming [2004] EWHC 2992, Ch D
(Patents Ct)
Agip SpA v. Navigazione Alta Italia SpA (The Nai Genova and The Nai Superba)
[1984] 1 Lloyd's Rep. 353, CA (Civ Div); affirming [1983] 2 Lloyd's Rep. 333;
[1983] Com. L.R. 170; (1983) 133 N.L.J. 621, QBD (Comm) . . . . *Digested,* 84/**378**:
Applied, 95/3063, 96/3756, 96/3815, 05/2386: *Considered,* 05/717:
Followed, 94/558

Agip (Africa) Ltd *v.* Jackson [1991] Ch. 547; [1991] 3 W.L.R. 116; [1992] 4 All E.R. 451; (1991) 135 S.J. 117; *Times*, January 9, 1991; *Financial Times*, January 18, 1991, CA (Civ Div); affirming [1990] Ch. 265; [1989] 3 W.L.R. 1367; [1992] 4 All E.R. 385; (1989) 86(3) L.S.G. 34; (1990) 134 S.J. 198; *Times*, June 5, 1989, Ch D . . . . *Digested*, 92/**2039**:
                 Applied, 96/421, 00/4316: *Considered*, 90/4259, 91/3379, 95/3601, 00/520,
                                                      05/**621**

Agnew *v.* Inland Revenue Commissioner see Brumark Investments Ltd, Re

Agros Trading Co Ltd *v.* Glencore Grain Ltd see Glencore Grain Ltd *v.* Agros Trading Co Ltd

Agudas Israel Housing Association Ltd *v.* Customs and Excise Commissioners [2005] S.T.I. 116, V&D Tr

Agulian *v.* Cyganik see Cyganik *v.* Agulian

Ahad *v.* Uddin [2005] EWCA Civ 883; (2005) 149 S.J.L.B. 772; *Times*, June 30, 2005, CA (Civ Div) . . . . *Digested*, 05/**481**

Ahajot (Count Artsrunik) *v.* Waller (Inspector of Taxes) [2005] B.P.I.R. 82; [2004] S.T.C. (S.C.D.) 151; [2004] S.T.I. 1086, Sp Comm . . . . *Digested*, 05/**4061**

AHLR, Petitioner see R *v.* Secretary of State for Scotland

Ahmad *v.* Inland Revenue Commissioners [2004] EWHC 2292; [2005] B.P.I.R. 541, Ch D

Ahmad *v.* United Kingdom (8160/78) (1982) 4 E.H.R.R. 126, Eur Comm HR . . . .   *Applied*, 05/**1328**

Ahmed *v.* Austria (1997) 24 E.H.R.R. 278; [1998] I.N.L.R. 65, ECHR . . . .   *Digested*, 97/**2764**:
                                                         Applied, 05/**2167**

Ahmed *v.* Butt [2005] EWCA Civ 1448; (2005) 149 S.J.L.B. 1352, CA (Civ Div)

Ahmed *v.* Secretary of State for Work and Pensions; *sub nom* Secretary of State for Work and Pensions *v.* Ahmed [2005] EWCA Civ 535; *Times*, May 19, 2005, CA (Civ Div) . . . . *Digested*, 05/**2233**

Ahmed (Iftikhar) *v.* Secretary of State for the Home Department; *sub nom* Secretary of State for the Home Department *v.* Ahmed (Iftikhar) [2000] I.N.L.R. 1; *Times*, December 8, 1999, CA (Civ Div) . . . . *Digested*, 00/**3313**:
                       Applied, 05/2164: *Considered*, 05/2140

AIC Ltd *v.* ITS Testing Services (UK) Ltd [2005] EWHC 2122; [2005] 2 C.L.C. 490, QBD (Comm)

Aid to Eni-Lanerossi, Re (C303/88) see Italy *v.* Commission of the European Communities (C303/88)

Aid to Olympic Airways, Re (C415/03) see Commission of the European Communities *v.* Greece (C415/03)

Aid to Pig Farmers (C110/02), Re see Commission of the European Communities *v.* Council of the European Union (C110/02)

Aid to Seleco, Re (C328/99) see Italy *v.* Commission of the European Communities (C328/99)

Aid to Stardust Marine (C482/99), Re see France *v.* Commission of the European Communities (C482/99)

Aid to Tirrenia Group, Re (C400/99) see Italy *v.* Commission of the European Communities (C400/99)

Aid to Tubemeuse (C142/87), Re see Belgium *v.* Commission of the European Communities (C142/87)

Aim Underwriting Agencies (Ireland) Ltd, Re [2004] EWHC 2114; [2005] I.L.Pr. 22, Ch D (Companies Ct) . . . . *Digested*, 05/**2259**

Ainsdale Investments Ltd *v.* First Secretary of State [2004] EWHC 1010; [2004] H.L.R. 50; [2004] 2 E.G.L.R. 9; [2004] 35 E.G. 68; [2005] R.V.R. 135; [2004] 22 E.G.C.S. 141; (2004) 101(22) L.S.G. 31; *Times*, June 2, 2004, QBD (Admin) . . .   *Digested*, 05/**3258**

Ainsworth *v.* Inland Revenue Commissioners see Inland Revenue Commissioners *v.* Ainsworth

Air Canada *v.* M&L Travel Ltd [1993] 3 S.C.R. 787, Sup Ct (Can) . . . .   *Applied*, 03/4474,
                                                          05/**4307**

Airedale NHS Trust *v.* Bland [1993] A.C. 789; [1993] 2 W.L.R. 316; [1993] 1 All E.R. 821; [1993] 1 F.L.R. 1026; [1994] 1 F.C.R. 485; [1993] 4 Med. L.R. 39; (1993) 12 B.M.L.R. 64; [1993] Fam. Law 473; (1993) 143 N.L.J. 199; *Times*, February 5, 1993; *Independent*, February 5, 1993; *Guardian*, February 5, 1993, HL; affirming (1992) 142 N.L.J. 1755; *Times*, December 10, 1992; *Independent*, December 10, 1992, CA (Civ Div); affirming (1992) 142 N.L.J. 1648; *Times*, November 23, 1992; *Independent*, November 20, 1992, Fam Div . . . .   *Digested*, 93/**2712**:
                          Applied, 94/3015, 94/3850, 95/4266, 01/2934, 05/3946:
                   Considered, 94/1004, 95/4104, 96/2978, 97/2593, 97/6070, 98/958,
               00/3246, 01/2662, 01/2935: *Distinguished*, 97/5783: *Followed*, 98/2650,
                                          98/2651, 01/3571, 02/1888

Airey *v.* Ireland (A/32) (1979-80) 2 E.H.R.R. 305, ECHR . . . .   *Applied*, 02/3117,
                          05/2089: *Considered*, 98/3154, 01/3439

Airfreight Express (UK) Ltd (In Liquidation), Re; *sub nom* Wood *v.* AFX Engineering [2005] B.P.I.R. 250, Ch D . . . .   *Digested*, 05/**2345**

Airwave MM02 Ltd *v.* First Secretary of State [2005] EWHC 1701; (2005) 102(28) L.S.G. 33, QBD (Admin)

Airways Pension Scheme, Re see Stevens *v.* Bell

AITC Foundation's Application for Registration as a Charity [2005] W.T.L.R.1265
AJ, Re (Unreported, December 9,1992), CA (Civ Div)...................... *Applied,* 05/926
AK v. Secretary of State for the Home Department; *sub nom* AK (Tribunal Appeal: Out of Time: Bulgaria), Re [2004] UKIAT 201; [2004] Imm. A.R. 486; [2004] I.N.L.R. 549, IAT .... *Digested,* 05/**2221**
AK (Tribunal Appeal: Out of Time: Bulgaria), Re see AK v. Secretary of State for the Home Department
Akaeke v. Secretary of State for the Home Department; *sub nom* Secretary of State for the Home Department v. Akaeke [2005] EWCA Civ 947; [2005] Imm. A.R. 701; [2005] I.N.L.R. 575; *Times,* September 23, 2005, CA (Civ Div) .... *Digested,* 05/**2211**
Akai Pty Ltd v. People's Insurance Co Ltd [1998] 1 Lloyd's Rep. 90; [1997] C.L.C. 1508; [1999] I.L.Pr. 24, QBD (Comm)............................... *Digested,* 98/**771**:
  Approved, 05/627: *Considered,* 00/3516
Akbarali v. Brent LBC see R. v. Barnet LBC Ex p. Shah (Nilish)
Akester v. Kingston Communications (Hull) Plc [2005] Pens. L.R.153, Ch D .... *Digested,* 05/**2991**
Akhtar v. Rafiq [2005] Fam. Law 856, Fam Div
Akici v. LR Butlin Ltd [2005] EWCA Civ 1296; [2005] 45 E.G.C.S. 168; (2005) 149 S.J.L.B.1352; [2005] N.P.C.126, CA (Civ Div)
Akram v. Adam (No.2) [2004] EWCA Civ 1601; [2005] 1 W.L.R. 2762; [2005] 1 All E.R. 741; [2005] C.P. Rep.14; [2005] H.L.R. 14; [2005] L. & T.R. 9; [2004] 50 E.G.C.S. 84; (2005) 102(5) L.S.G. 28; (2004) 148 S.J.L.B. 1433; [2004] N.P.C.182; [2005] 1 P. & C.R. DG13; *Times,* December 29, 2004, CA (Civ Div) . *Digested,* 05/**467**
Aktieselskabet Olivebank v. Danck Svovlsyre Fabrik see Olivebank A/S v. Dansk Svovlsyre Fabrik
Akumah v. Hackney LBC [2005] UKHL 17; [2005] 1 W.L.R. 985; [2005] 2 All E.R. 148; [2005] H.L.R. 26; [2005] B.L.G.R. 399; [2005] 10 E.G.C.S. 155; (2005) 102(17) L.S.G. 31; (2005) 149 S.J.L.B. 299; [2005] N.P.C. 31; *Times,* March 4, 2005, HL; affirming [2002] EWCA Civ 582; [2003] H.L.R. 5, CA (Civ Div).... *Digested,* 05/**2001**
Akyuz v. Secretary of State for the Home Department see R. (on the application of Ozturk) v. Secretary of State for the Home Department
Akzo Nobel Chemicals Ltd v. Commission of the European Communities (T125/03 R) [2003] E.C.R. II-4771; [2004] 4 C.M.L.R. 15, CFI..................... *Digested,* 04/**496**:
  Overruled in part, 05/546
Al Hamwi v. Johnston [2005] EWHC 206; [2005] Lloyd's Rep. Med. 309, QBD
Al-Bassam v. Al-Bassam [2004] EWCA Civ 857; [2004] W.T.L.R. 757; (2004) 148 S.J.L.B. 826; *Times,* July 22, 2004, CA (Civ Div); reversing in part [2003] EWHC 2278; [2004] W.T.L.R.157, Ch D .... *Digested,* 05/**412**:
  Previous proceedings, 03/4129
Al-Bassam v. Al-Bassam (Preliminary Issues) [2002] EWHC 2281; [2003] W.T.L.R.1, Ch D .... *Digested,* 03/**4129**:
  Overruled in part, 05/412
Al-Fayed v. Commissioner of Police of the Metropolis (No.3) [2004] EWCA Civ 1579; (2004) 148 S.J.L.B.1405, CA (Civ Div); affirming [2002] EWHC1734, QBD... *Applied,* 05/**3339**
Al-Kandari v. JR Brown & Co [1988] Q.B. 665; [1988] 2 W.L.R. 671; [1988] 1 All E.R. 833; [1988] Fam. Law 382; (1988) 85(14) L.S.G. 50; (1988) 138 N.L.J. Rep. 62; (1988) 132 S.J. 462, CA (Civ Div); reversing [1987] Q.B. 514; [1987] 2 W.L.R. 469; [1987] 2 All E.R. 302; (1987) 84 L.S.G. 825; (1987) 137 N.L.J. 36; (1987) 131 S.J. 225, QBD .... *Digested,* 88/**3376**:
  Considered, 94/3345, 95/3652: *Doubted,* 05/2845
Al-Khatib v. Masry [2004] EWCA Civ 1353; [2005] 1 F.L.R. 381; [2004] 3 F.C.R. 573; *Times,* October 21, 2004, CA (Civ Div); reversing [2002] EWHC108; [2002] 1 F.L.R.1053; [2002] 2 F.C.R. 539; [2002] Fam. Law 420, Fam Div .... *Digested,* 05/**1676**:
  Followed, 05/1657
Al-Mehdawi v. Secretary of State for the Home Department see R. v. Secretary of State for the Home Department Ex p. Al-Mehdawi
Al-Sabah v. Grupo Torras SA [2005] UKPC 1; [2005] 2 A.C. 333; [2005] 2 W.L.R. 904; [2005] 1 All E.R. 871; [2005] B.P.I.R. 544; (2004-05) 7 I.T.E.L.R. 531; (2005) 102(9) L.S.G. 29; (2005) 149 S.J.L.B. 112; *Times,* January 14, 2005, PC (CI) .... *Digested,* 05/**2282**
Alabaster v. Barclays Bank Plc (formerly Woolwich Plc) see Alabaster v. Woolwich Plc
Alabaster v. Woolwich Plc; *sub nom* Alabaster v. Barclays Bank Plc (formerly Woolwich Plc) [2005] EWCA Civ 508; [2005] 2 C.M.L.R. 19; [2005] Eu. L.R. 824; [2005] I.C.R. 1246; [2005] I.R.L.R. 576; *Times,* May 27, 2005, CA (Civ Div); reversing [2000] I.C.R. 1037; [2000] I.R.L.R. 754; *Times,* April 19, 2000, EAT .... *Digested,* 05/**1262**:
  Subsequent proceedings, 02/1364
Alabaster v. Woolwich Plc (C147/02) [2005] All E.R. (EC) 490; [2004] E.C.R. I-3101; [2004] 2 C.M.L.R. 9; [2004] C.E.C. 261; [2005] I.C.R. 695; [2004] I.R.L.R. 486, ECJ .... *Digested,* 04/**1257**:
  Considered, 05/1262: *Previous proceedings,* 02/1364
Alarakhia v. Bayley (Unreported, January 17, 2005), CC (Willesden) [*Ex rel.* Sadie Crapper, Pupil Barrister, 3, Paper Buildings,Temple, London] .... *Digested,* 05/**3105**
Albacom SpA v. Ministero del Tesoro, del Bilancio e della Programmazione Economica (C292/01) [2003] E.C.R. I-9449; [2003] Info.T.L.R. 446, ECJ (5th Chamber) . *Digested,* 05/**4183**

Albania v. Bleta [2005] EWHC 475; [2005] 1 W.L.R. 3576; [2005] 3 All E.R. 351,
    QBD (Admin) . . . .   *Digested*, 05/**1488**
Albion Water Ltd v. Director General of Water Services (Application to Intervene)
    [2004] CAT 19; [2005] Comp. A.R. 404, CAT . . . .   *Digested*, 05/**597**
Albion Water Ltd v. Director General of Water Services (Application to Stay Appeal)
    [2004] CAT 21; [2005] Comp. A.R. 461, CAT . . . .   *Digested*, 05/**559**
Albion Water Ltd v. Director General of Water Services (Application to Strike Out)
    [2005] CAT 23; [2005] Comp. A.R. 1129, CAT
Albion Water Ltd v. Director General of Water Services (Consent Order: Clarification)
    [2005] CAT 19; [2005] Comp. A.R. 993, CAT
Albion Water Ltd v. Director General of Water Services (Interim Measures: Jurisdiction)
    [2004] CAT 9; [2004] Comp. A.R. 667, CAT . . . .   *Digested*, 05/**556**
Albion Water Ltd v. Director General of Water Services (Submission of Further Witness
    Statement) [2005] CAT 18; [2005] Comp. A.R. 991, CAT
Alcan Aluminium UK Ltd v. Highland and Western Isles Valuation Joint Board Assessor
    [2005] R.A. 161, Lands Tr (Scot) . . . .   *Digested*, 05/**5621**
Alcan Extrusions v. Yates [1996] I.R.L.R. 327, EAT. . . . .   *Digested*, 96/**2657**:
                                                                                          Applied, 05/1204
Alcatel Austria AG v. Bundesministerium fur Wissenschaft und Verkehr (C81/98) [1999]
    E.C.R. I-7671; (2000) 2 T.C.L.R. 894, ECJ (6th Chamber) . . . .   *Digested*, 01/**2518**:
                                                                                          Considered, 05/73
Alcock v. Chief Constable of South Yorkshire; *sub nom* Jones v. Wright; Penk v. Wright;
    Jones v. Chief Constable of South Yorkshire; Copoc v. Chief Constable of South
    Yorkshire [1992] 1 A.C. 310; [1991] 3 W.L.R. 1057; [1991] 4 All E.R. 907;
    [1992] P.I.Q.R. P1; (1992) 89(3) L.S.G. 34; (1991) 141 N.L.J. 166; (1992) 136
    S.J.L.B. 9; *Times*, November 29, 1991; *Independent*, November 29, 1991;
    Guardian, December 11, 1991, HL; affirming [1991] 3 All E.R. 88; *Times*, May 6,
    1991; *Independent*, May 10, 1991; *Guardian*, May 9, 1991, CA (Civ Div); affirming
    [1991] 2 W.L.R. 814; [1991] 1 All E.R. 353; (1990) 140 N.L.J. 1717;
    Independent, December 7, 1990, QBD . . . .   *Digested*, 92/**3250**:
                      Applied, 92/3253, 93/2972, 95/6157, 98/3938, 00/531, 01/5352, 01/6665,
                      02/948, 03/5828: *Considered*, 95/3682, 97/2615, 98/4035, 99/4059,
                                      00/4213, 00/4220, 00/6598, 03/3132, 03/5844, 05/2834:
                                                                                    Distinguished, 03/3028
Alcon Inc v. Office for Harmonisation in the Internal Market (Trade Marks and Designs)
    (OHIM) (C192/03 P) [2004] E.C.R. I-8993; [2005] E.T.M.R. 69, ECJ (6th
    Chamber) . . . .   *Digested*, 05/**2518**:
                                                                          Previous proceedings, 03/2604
Aldi Stores Ltd v. Holmes Buildings Plc [2003] EWCA Civ 1882; [2005] P.N.L.R. 9,
    CA (Civ Div) . . . .   *Digested*, 05/**313**
Alexander v. Arts Council of Wales [2001] EWCA Civ 514; [2001] 1 W.L.R. 1840;
    [2001] 4 All E.R. 205; [2001] E.M.L.R. 27; (2001) 98(22) L.S.G. 35; (2001)
    145 S.J.L.B. 123; *Times*, April 27, 2001; *Independent*, April 27, 2001, CA (Civ
    Div) . . . .   *Digested*, 01/**1827**:
                                             Applied, 02/952, 05/486: *Considered*, 01/1821, 04/928:
                                                                                      Distinguished, 03/959
Alexander v. Home Office see Alexander v. Secretary of State for the Home
    Department
Alexander v. Rayson [1936] 1 K.B. 169; 114 A.L.R. 357, CA . . . .   *Applied*, 47-51/1751,
                      47-51/5327, 47-51/5378, 47-51/5609, 47-51/7929, 53/1004, 59/542, 78/3048,
                      87/432, 88/437, 04/238, 05/493: *Approved*, 01/676: *Considered*, 54/1809,
                      57/998, 61/7207, 70/144, 71/640, 76/384, 87/1826: *Distinguished*, 53/3754,
                                                                            55/1148, 55/1502, 60/956
Alexander v. Secretary of State for the Home Department; *sub nom* Alexander v.
    Home Office [1988] 1 W.L.R. 968; [1988] 2 All E.R. 118; [1988] I.C.R. 685;
    [1988] I.R.L.R. 190; (1988) 85(40) L.S.G. 45, CA (Civ Div) . . . .   *Digested*, 88/**1295**:
                      Applied, 96/2606, 98/2099, 04/1276: *Approved*, 98/5150:
                                                      Considered, 00/2181: *Followed*, 05/1318
Alexander Forbes Trustee Services Ltd v. Jackson; *sub nom* T&N Retirement Benefits
    Scheme (1989), Re [2004] EWHC 2448; [2004] O.P.L.R. 391; [2005] Pens.
    L.R. 33, Ch D . . . .   *Digested*, 05/**2996**
Alford v. Secretary of State for the Environment, Food and Rural Affairs; *sub nom*
    Department for Environment, Food and Rural Affairs v. Alford; Secretary of State
    for the Environment, Food and Rural Affairs v. Alford [2005] EWHC 808;
    [2005] Env. L.R. 43; [2005] 3 E.G.L.R. 11; [2005] 36 E.G. 278; [2005] N.P.C.
    59; *Times*, May 30, 2005, QBD (Admin). . . . .   *Digested*, 05/**1363**
Alford v. West Bromwich Building Society see Investors Compensation Scheme Ltd v.
    West Bromwich Building Society (No.1)
Alfred C Toepfer v. Peter Cremer GmbH & Co; *sub nom* Toepfer v. Cremer [1975] 2
    Lloyd's Rep. 118; (1975) 119 S.J. 506, CA (Civ Div); affirming [1975] 1 Lloyd's
    Rep. 406, QBD (Comm) . . . .   *Digested*, 75/**3059**:
                      Applied, 77/2669, 78/2640, 03/709: *Considered*, 80/2381, 05/454:
                                                                                      Followed, 78/2637

Alfred McAlpine Capital Projects Ltd v. Tilebox Ltd [2005] EWHC 281; [2005] B.L.R.
 271; (2005) 21 Const. L.J. 539, QBD (TCC)
Alfred McAlpine Plc v. BAI (Run-Off) Ltd [2000] 1 All E.R. (Comm) 545; [2000] 1
 Lloyd's Rep. 437; [2000] C.L.C. 812; (2001) 3 T.C.L.R. 5; 69 Con. L.R. 87;
 [2000] Lloyd's Rep. I.R. 352, CA (Civ Div); affirming [1998] 2 Lloyd's Rep. 694;
 [1998] C.L.C. 1145; (1999) 1 T.C.L.R. 92; 66 Con. L.R. 57, QBD (Comm). . . . . .   *Digested,* 00/**3532:**
                                                                                   Applied, 04/2219: *Doubted,* 05/2377
Alhamrani v. Russa Management Ltd; *sub nom* Internine Trust and Intertraders Trust, Re
 (2004-05) 7 I.T.E.L.R. 308, CA (Jer). . . . .   *Digested,* 05/**4303**
Ali v. Hudson (t/a Hudson Freeman Berg) [2003] EWCA Civ 1793; [2004] C.P. Rep.
 15, CA (Civ Div). . . . .   *Digested,* 05/**482**
Ali v. Lord Grey School Governors; *sub nom* A v. Headteacher and Governors of Lord
 Grey School; TNS, HL; reversing [2004] EWCA Civ 382; [2004] Q.B. 1231;
 [2004] 2 W.L.R. 1442; [2004] 4 All E.R. 628; [2005] B.L.G.R. 212; [2004]
 E.L.R. 169; (2004) 101(14) L.S.G. 25; (2004) 148 S.J.L.B. 417; *Times,* April 9,
 2004; *Independent,* April 1, 2004, CA (Civ Div); reversing in part [2003] EWHC
 1533; [2003] 4 All E.R. 1317; [2003] E.L.R. 517; (2003) 100(34) L.S.G. 29;
 Times, August 14, 2003, QBD . . . .   *Digested,* 04/**1022:**
                                                                                   Considered, 04/1023
Ali v. McDonagh see Triesman v. Ali
Ali v. Office of National Statistics; *sub nom* Office of National Statistics v. Ali [2004]
 EWCA Civ 1363; [2005] I.R.L.R. 201; (2004) 148 S.J.L.B. 1250, CA (Civ Div);
 affirming UKEAT/0114/04/RN, EAT . . . .   *Digested,* 05/**1278**
Ali v. Parvez (t/a KK Auto Salvage) [2005] 2 Q.R. 11; [2004] 6 Q.R. 6, CC (Bradford)
 [*Ex rel.* Emsleys Solicitors, 35b Main Street, Garforth, Leeds] . . . .   *Digested,* 04/**2870**
Ali v. Usman (Unreported, December 18, 2003), CC (Manchester) [*Ex rel.* Claire Hill,
 Pupil Barrister, St James's Chambers, 68 Quay Street, Manchester.]. . . . .   *Digested,* 05/**3166**
Allan Water Developments Ltd v. Revenue and Customs Commissioners [2005] S.T.I.
 661, V&DTr (Edinburgh)
Allard v. Institut National d'Assurances Sociales pour Travailleurs Independants
 (INASTI) (C249/04) [2005] 3 C.M.L.R. 8, ECJ (5th Chamber)
Allard v. Sweden (35179/97) (2004) 39 E.H.R.R. 14, ECHR . . . .   *Digested,* 05/**2071**
Allardyce v. Roebuck; *sub nom* Gray (Deceased), Re [2004] EWHC 1538; [2005] 1
 W.L.R. 815; [2004] 3 All E.R. 754; [2004] W.T.L.R. 779; (2004-05) 7 I.T.E.L.R.
 232; [2004] N.P.C. 109, Ch D . . . .   *Digested,* 04/**3675**
Allason v. Random House (UK) Ltd (No.2) [2002] EWHC 1030, Ch D . . . .   *Applied,* 05/414
Allcard v. Skinner (1887) L.R. 36 Ch. D. 145, CA . . . .   *Applied,* 52/1485,
                   70/1145, 70/1706, 73/419, 74/1691, 81/1251, 82/285, 83/1361.b, 85/396,
                          86/426, 87/456, 01/4880, 02/4314, 05/3401: *Approved,* 53/1532:
                    Considered, 60/1802, 88/1733, 89/1829, 05/4291: *Distinguished,* 77/1207:
                                                    Followed, 97/4270: *Referred to,* 75/112.u
Allchin v. R. 7 I.T.L. Rep. 851, Tax Ct (Can)
Allders Department Stores Ltd (In Administration), Re [2005] EWHC 172; [2005] 2 All E.R.
 122; [2005] B.C.C. 289; [2005] I.C.R. 867; (2005) 102(15) L.S.G. 34, Ch D . .   *Digested,* 05/**2260**
Allen v. British Rail Engineering Ltd (BREL) [2001] EWCA Civ 242; [2001] I.C.R. 942;
 [2001] P.I.Q.R. Q10, CA (Civ Div); affirming C970197, QBD . . . .   *Digested,* 01/**4448:**
                                                                                   Considered, 05/965
Allen v. Revenue and Customs Commissioners [2005] S.T.C. (S.C.D.) 614; 8 I.T.L. Rep.
 108; [2005] W.T.L.R. 937, Sp Comm
Allen v. Unigate Dairies Ltd see Ridehalgh v. Horsefield
Allen & Hanburys Ltd's (Salbutamol) Patent [1987] R.P.C. 327, CA (Civ Div) . . . .   *Digested,* 87/**2803:**
                                                                                   Applied, 98/3458, 05/2436
Allen Wilson Shopfitters v. Buckingham [2005] EWHC 1165; 102 Con. L.R. 154, QBD
 (TCC)
Alliance & Leicester International Ltd, Re [2004] W.T.L.R. 927, HC (IoM). . . . .   *Digested,* 05/**261**
Alliance Spring Co Ltd v. First Secretary of State [2005] EWHC 18; [2005] 3 P.L.R. 76;
 [2005] N.P.C. 7, QBD (Admin)
Allianz Marine Aviation (France) v. GE Frankona Reinsurance Ltd (The Treasure Bay)
 [2005] EWHC 101; [2005] Lloyd's Rep. I.R. 437, QBD (Comm) . . . .   *Digested,* 05/**2404**
Allied Dunbar Assurance Plc, Re [2005] EWHC 28; [2005] 2 B.C.L.C. 220, Ch D
 (Companies Ct) . . . .   *Digested,* 05/**2362**
Allied Dunbar Assurance Plc v. Homebase Ltd; *sub nom* Homebase Ltd v. Allied Dunbar
 Assurance Plc [2002] EWCA Civ 666; [2003] 1 P. & C.R. 6; [2002] L. & T.R.
 27; [2002] 2 E.G.L.R. 23; [2002] 27 E.G. 144; [2002] 22 E.G.C.S. 134; (2002)
 99(24) L.S.G. 38, CA (Civ Div); affirming [2002] 1 P. & C.R. 1; [2002] L. &
 T.R. 1; [2001] 16 E.G.C.S. 146; (2001) 98(17) L.S.G. 40; [2001] N.P.C. 76, Ch D
 . . . .   *Digested,* 02/**3048:**
                                                                                   Applied, 05/2693: *Distinguished,* 05/2694

Allied Maples Group Ltd v. Simmons & Simmons [1995] 1 W.L.R. 1602; [1995] 4 All
E.R. 907; [1996] C.L.C. 153; 46 Con. L.R. 134; [1955-95] P.N.L.R. 701; (1995)
145 N.L.J.1646; [1995] N.P.C. 83; (1995) 70 P. & C.R. D14, CA (Civ Div). . . . . *Digested,* 96/**4489**:
Applied, 97/3832, 98/1447, 98/3604, 00/4266, 00/4276, 03/946, 03/3015,
05/2880, 05/3419: *Considered,* 95/1843, 96/4482, 96/4505, 97/3839,
97/3903, 00/4264, 02/1318: *Distinguished,* 03/3121, 04/913:
Followed, 05/2877: *Not applied,* 01/537: *Referred to,* 97/3917
Allinson v. General Council of Medical Education and Registration [1894] 1 Q.B. 750;
[1891-94] All E.R. Rep. 768, CA . . . . *Applied,* 52/3361,
52/3505, 55/2630, 65/2513, 05/13: *Considered,* 60/1958, 60/2603, 67/2468,
79/1750, 80/1760: *Distinguished,* 57/348
Allobrogia Steamship Corp, Re [1978] 3 All E.R. 423; [1979] 1 Lloyd's Rep. 190, Ch D
(Companies Ct) . . . . *Digested,* 78/**262**:
Considered, 05/2366
Allonby v. Accrington and Rossendale College; Allonby v. Education Lecturing
Services; Allonby v. Department for Education and Employment [2001] EWCA
Civ 529; [2001] 2 C.M.L.R. 27; [2001] I.C.R. 1189; [2001] I.R.L.R. 364; [2001]
Emp. L.R. 613; [2001] E.L.R. 679; [2001] Pens. L.R. 185; *Times,* April 3, 2001,
CA (Civ Div); reversing in part EAT/1300/97, EAT/1080/98, EAT/1081/98, EAT. *Digested,* 01/**2319**:
Applied, 05/1294
Allonby v. Accrington and Rossendale College (C256/01) [2005] All E.R. (EC) 289;
[2004] E.C.R. I-873; [2004] 1 C.M.L.R. 35; [2004] I.C.R. 1328; [2004] I.R.L.R.
224; [2004] O.P.L.R. 83; [2004] Pens. L.R. 199, ECJ [2004] E.C.R. I-873;
[2003] Pens. L.R. 97, AGO . . . . *Digested,* 04/**1258**
Allonby v. Department for Education and Employment see Allonby v. Accrington and
Rossendale College
Allonby v. Education Lecturing Services see Allonby v. Accrington and Rossendale
College
Allsports Ltd v. Office of FairTrading see JJB Sports Plc v. Office of FairTrading
Allsports Ltd v. Office of Fair Trading (Application for Summary Judgment) [2004]
CAT 1; [2004] Comp. A.R. 323, CAT . . . . *Digested,* 05/**565**
Allum v. Marsh (Inspector of Taxes) [2005] S.T.C. (S.C.D.) 191; [2005] S.T.I. 97, Sp
Comm . . . . *Digested,* 05/**4016**
Alphapoint Shipping Ltd v. Rotem Amfert Negev Ltd (The Agios Dimitrios) [2004]
EWHC 2232; [2005] 1 Lloyd's Rep. 23, QBD (Comm) . . . . *Digested,* 05/**3795**
Alsop Wilkinson v. Neary [1996] 1 W.L.R. 1220; [1995] 1 All E.R. 431; *Times,* November
4, 1994; *Independent,* November 3, 1994, Ch D . . . . *Digested,* 95/**2213**:
Applied, 05/4290: *Considered,* 97/3952, 97/4939, 03/4470:
Distinguished, 05/4314
ALTHIN MEDICAL/Declaration in lieu of an oath (T474/04) [2005] E.P.O.R. 47, EPO
(Technical Bd App)
Altmark Trans GmbH v. Nahverkehrsgesellschaft Altmark GmbH (C280/00) [2005] All
E.R. (EC) 610; [2003] E.C.R. I-7747; [2003] 3 C.M.L.R. 12, ECJ . . . . *Digested,* 03/**4444**:
Applied, 04/551
Alto de Casablanca SA v. Office for Harmonisation in the Internal Market (Trade Marks
and Designs) (OHIM) (T14/04) [2005] E.T.M.R. 71, CFI (5th Chamber) . . . . *Digested,* 05/**2586**
Alzitrans SL v. Customs and Excise Commissioners see Customs and Excise
Commissioners v. Alzitrans SL
AM v. Secretary of State for the Home Department; *sub nom* AM (Upgrade Appeals:
Art 6: Afghanistan) [2004] UKIAT 186; [2004] Imm. A.R. 530, IAT . . . . *Digested,* 05/**2149**
AM (Upgrade Appeals: Art 6: Afghanistan) see AM v. Secretary of State for the Home
Department
AM&S Europe Ltd v. Commisson of the European Communities (155/79) see
Australian Mining & Smelting Europe Ltd v. Commission of the European
Communities (155/79)
Amalgamated Metal Trading Ltd v. International Tin Council see JH Rayner (Mincing
Lane) Ltd v. Department of Trade and Industry
Amara v. Netherlands (Admissibility) (6914/02) (2005) 40 E.H.R.R. SE5, ECHR
AMB Generali Holding AG v. Manches see SEB Trygg Holding AB v. Manches
AMB Generali Holding AG v. SEB Trygg Liv Holding AB see SEB Trygg Holding AB v.
Manches
Amber v. Stacey [2001] 1 W.L.R. 1225; [2001] 2 All E.R. 88; [2001] C.P. Rep. 26;
[2001] C.P.L.R. 37; (2001) 3 T.C.L.R. 20; [2001] 2 Costs L.R. 325; (2000) 150
N.L.J.1755; *DailyTelegraph,* November 28, 2000, CA (Civ Div) . . . . *Digested,* 01/**503**:
Applied, 01/502: *Considered,* 05/374
Ambulanter Pflegedienst Kugler GmbH v. Finanzamt fur Korperschaften I in Berlin
(C141/00) [2002] E.C.R. I-6833; [2004] 3 C.M.L.R. 54; [2004] B.T.C. 5690;
[2004] B.V.C. 749; [2002] S.T.I. 1277, ECJ (6th Chamber) [2002] E.C.R. I-
6833, AGO . . . . *Digested,* 05/**4349**:
Followed, 04/1206, 04/3975
AMC Trust v. Commissioner of Internal Revenue (2005-06) 8 I.T.E.L.R. 207, US Ct

AMEC Capital Projects Ltd v. Whitefriars City Estates Ltd [2004] EWCA Civ 1418; [2005] 1 All E.R. 723; [2005] B.L.R. 1; 96 Con. L.R. 142; (2005) 21 Const. L.J. 249; (2004) 154 N.L.J. 1690; (2004) 148 S.J.L.B. 1285; *Times*, November 8, 2004, CA (Civ Div); reversing [2004] EWHC 393; (2004) 20 Const. L.J. 338, QBD (TCC) .... *Digested*, 05/**646**

Amec Civil Engineering Ltd v. Secretary of State for Transport [2005] EWCA Civ 291; [2005] 1 W.L.R. 2339; [2005] B.L.R. 227; 101 Con. L.R. 26; (2005) 21 Const. L.J. 640; [2005] 12 E.G.C.S. 219; (2005) 102(20) L.S.G. 30; *Times*, March 22, 2005, CA (Civ Div); affirming [2004] EWHC 2339, QBD (TCC) .... *Digested*, 05/**665**

Amec Developments Ltd v. Jury's Hotel Management (UK) Ltd [2002] T.C.L.R. 13; (2001) 82 P. & C.R. 22; [2001] 1 E.G.L.R. 81; [2001] 07 E.G. 163; [2000] E.G.C.S. 138; [2000] N.P.C. 125, Ch D .... *Digested*, 01/**1549**
Applied, 05/**2693**

Amegnigan v. Netherlands (Unreported, November 24, 2004) .... *Considered*, 05/**2160**

Amendment No.10 to the Consolidated Criminal Practice Direction (Forms for use in Criminal Proceedings) see Practice Direction (Sup Ct: Criminal Proceedings: Forms)

Amendment No.11 to the Consolidated Criminal Practice Direction (Case Management) see Practice Direction (Sup Ct: Criminal Proceedings: Case Management)

Amendment No.9 to the Consolidated Criminal Practice Direction (Jury Service) see Practice Direction (Sup Ct: Jury Service: Excusal)

American Airlines Inc v. Hope; *sub nom* Banque Sabbag SAL v. Hope [1974] 2 Lloyd's Rep. 301, HL; affirming [1973] 1 Lloyd's Rep. 233, CA (Civ Div); affirming [1972] 1 Lloyd's Rep. 253, QBD (Comm) .... *Digested*, 75/**1693**
Applied, 05/**2385**

American International Marine Agency of New York Inc v. Dandridge [2005] EWHC 829; [2005] 2 All E.R. (Comm) 496; [2005] 1 C.L.C. 1102; [2005] Lloyd's Rep. I.R. 643, QBD (Comm) .... *Digested*, 05/**2405**

American International Specialty Lines Insurance Co v. Abbott Laboratories [2002] EWHC 2714; [2003] 1 Lloyd's Rep. 267; [2004] Lloyd's Rep. I.R. 815, QBD (Comm) .... *Digested*, 05/**2371**

Amicus v. Dynamex Friction Ltd [2005] I.R.L.R. 724, QBD

Amicus v. GBS Tooling Ltd (In Administration) [2005] I.R.L.R. 683, EAT .... *Digested*, 05/**1296**

Amihalachioaie v. Moldova (60115/00) (2005) 40 E.H.R.R. 35; 17 B.H.R.C. 689, ECHR .... *Digested*, 05/**2045**

Amihiya v. Official Receiver [2004] EWHC 2617; [2005] B.P.I.R. 264, Ch D .... *Digested*, 05/**2283**

Amin v. Brown [2005] EWHC 1670; [2005] A.C.D. 95; (2005) 155 N.L.J. 1278; [2005] N.P.C. 104; *Times*, August 24, 2005, Ch D .... *Digested*, 05/**444**

Ammann-Yanmar SA v. Zwaans BVA [2005] E.C.C. 16, Cass (F)

Amministrazione delle Finanze dello Stato v. Meridionale Industria Salumi Srl (212/80) [1981] E.C.R. 2735, ECJ .... *Considered*, 05/**1431**

Amoco (UK) Exploration Co v. British American Offshore Ltd (Costs: Indemnity Basis) [2002] B.L.R. 135, QBD (Comm) .... *Considered*, 05/**355**

AMP General Insurance Ltd v. Macalister Todd Phillips Bodkins see Macalister Todd Phillips Bodkins v. AMP General Insurance Ltd

AMP (UK) Plc v. Barker [2001] O.P.L.R. 197; [2001] Pens. L.R. 77; [2001] W.T.L.R. 1237; (2000-01) 3 I.T.E.L.R. 414, Ch D .... *Digested*, 01/**4595**
Applied, 05/3420: *Followed*, 05/**2990**

Ampafrance SA v. Directeur des Services Fiscaux de Maine-et-Loire (C177/99); Sanofi Synthelabo SA v. Directeur des Services Fiscaux du Val-de-Marne (C181/99) [2000] E.C.R. I-7013; [2002] B.T.C. 5520; [2002] B.V.C. 664, ECJ (5th Chamber) [2000] E.C.R. I-7013, AGO .... *Digested*, 03/**4546**
Distinguished, 05/**436**

Ampafrance SA v. Office for Harmonisation in the Internal Market (Trade Marks and Designs) (OHIM) (T164/03) [2005] E.T.M.R. 107, CFI (3rd Chamber)

Amrit Holdings Co Ltd v. Shahbakhti [2005] EWCA Civ 339; [2005] H.L.R. 30; [2005] L. & T.R. 18; (2005) 149 S.J.L.B. 298, CA (Civ Div); affirming (Unreported, July 15, 2004), CC (London) .... *Digested*, 05/**267**

AN v. Secretary of State for the Home Department; *sub nom* AN (Only Loser can Appeal: Afghanistan), Re [2005] UKIAT 97; [2005] Imm. A.R. 390, IAT

AN (Only Loser can Appeal: Afghanistan), Re see AN v. Secretary of State for the Home Department

Anchor International Ltd v. Inland Revenue Commissioners; *sub nom* Inland Revenue Commissioners v. Anchor International Ltd [2005] S.T.C. 411; 2005 S.C. 76; 2005 S.L.T. 710; 2004 S.C.L.R. 1045; 77 T.C. 38; [2005] B.T.C. 97; [2004] S.T.I. 2298; 2004 G.W.D. 35-712, IH (Ex Div); affirming [2003] S.T.C. (S.C.D.) 115; [2003] S.T.I. 246, Sp Comm .... *Digested*, 05/**5691**

Anderson, Re see Anderson v. KAS Bank NV

Anderson v. Customs and Excise Commissioners see Hughes v. Customs and Excise Commissioners

Anderson v. KAS Bank NV; *sub nom* Anderson, Re [2004] EWHC 532; [2004] B.P.I.R. 685, Ch D .... *Digested*, 05/**2286**

Anderson v. Wall (Unreported, January 10, 2005), CC (Birmingham) [*Ex rel.* Matthew Brunning, Barrister, No. 5 Chambers, Steelhouse Lane, Birmingham] .... *Digested*, 05/**3116**

Anderton v. Clwyd CC see Phelps v. Hillingdon LBC
Anderton v. Clwyd CC; *sub nom* Bryant v. Pech; Home Office v. Dorgan; Cummins v.
Shell International Trading & Shipping Ltd; Bryant v. Mike Beer Transport Ltd;
Dorgan v. Home Office; Chambers v. Southern Domestic Electrical Services Ltd;
Cummins v. Shell International Manning Services Ltd [2002] EWCA Civ 933;
[2002] 1 W.L.R. 3174; [2002] 3 All E.R. 813; [2002] C.P. Rep. 71; (2002)
99(35) L.S.G. 38; (2002) 152 N.L.J. 1125; (2002) 146 S.J.L.B. 177; *Times*, July
16, 2002; *Independent*, July 11, 2002, CA (Civ Div); reversing [2001] C.P. Rep.
110, QBD .... *Digested*, 02/**491**:
   Applied, 02/476, 03/455, 03/456, 04/412: *Considered*, 03/2724, 04/383:
   Followed, 05/341
Andrea Merzario Ltd v. Internationale Spedition Leitner Gesellschaft GmbH [2001]
EWCA Civ 61; [2001] 1 All E.R. (Comm) 883; [2001] 1 Lloyd's Rep. 490; [2001]
C.L.C. 643; [2002] I.L.Pr. 26; (2001) 98(9) L.S.G. 41; (2001) 145 S.J.L.B. 54;
Times, February 27, 2001; *Daily Telegraph*, February 13, 2001, CA (Civ Div);
affirming 1999 Folio 1256, QBD (Comm) .... *Digested*, 01/**5419**:
   Considered, 05/618
Andrew Weir Shipping Ltd v. Wartsila UK Ltd [2004] EWHC 1284; [2004] 2 Lloyd's
Rep. 377, QBD (Comm). .... *Digested*, 05/**427**
Andrews v. Hill (Unreported, May 21, 2004), CC (Romford) [*Ex rel.* Joanna Kerr,
Barrister, Lamb Chambers, Lamb Building, London] .... *Digested*, 05/**3235**
Andrews v. Reading BC (No.1) [2004] EWHC 970; [2005] Env. L.R. 2; [2004]
U.K.H.R.R. 599; [2004] R.V.R. 272; [2005] A.C.D. 11, QBD (Admin)......... *Digested*, 04/**1373**
Angel v. New Possibilities NHS Trust see Rhys-Harper v. Relaxion Group Plc
Anglia Home Improvements Ltd v. Kelly see Anglian Home Improvements Ltd v. Kelly
Anglia Regional Cooperative Society Ltd v. Customs and Excise Commissioners [2005]
B.V.C. 2508; [2005] V. & D.R. 100; [2005] S.T.I. 894,V&DTr (London)
Anglian Home Improvements Ltd v. Kelly; *sub nom* Anglia Home Improvements Ltd v.
Kelly [2004] EWCA Civ 901; [2005] I.C.R. 242; [2004] I.R.L.R. 793; (2004)
101(28) L.S.G. 33; (2004) 148 S.J.L.B. 760; *Times*, June 30, 2004, CA (Civ
Div) .... *Digested*, 04/**1309**
Anglo African Merchants Ltd v. Bayley; Exmouth Clothing Co Ltd v. Bayley [1970] 1
Q.B. 311; [1969] 2 W.L.R. 686; [1969] 2 All E.R. 421; [1969] 1 Lloyd's Rep. 268;
113 S.J. 281, QBD (Comm) .... *Digested*, 69/**1810**:
   Applied, 05/2355: *Considered*, 75/1712: *Followed*, 71/111
Anglo-Egyptian Navigation Co v. Rennie (1874-75) L.R. 10 C.P. 271, CCP.......... *Applied*, 05/**2389**
Anglorom Trans (UK) Ltd, Re; *sub nom* Paramount Kitchens Ltd, Re [2004] EWCA Civ
998; [2005] R.T.R. 6, CA (Civ Div) .... *Digested*, 05/**3458**
Angora Trust, Re see Schmidt v. Rosewood Trust Ltd
Anheuser-Busch Inc v. Budejovicky Budvar Narodni Podnik (C245/02) [2004] E.C.R.
I-10989; [2005] E.T.M.R. 27, ECJ .... *Digested*, 05/**2587**
Ani v. Barclays Private Bank & Trust Ltd [2005] W.T.L.R. 469, Royal Ct (Jer)
Anisminic Ltd v. Foreign Compensation Commission [1969] 2 A.C. 147; [1969] 2
W.L.R. 163; [1969] 1 All E.R. 208; (1968) 113 S.J. 55; *Times*, December 18,
1968, HL; reversing [1968] 2 Q.B. 862; [1967] 3 W.L.R. 382; [1967] 3 All E.R.
986; 111 S.J. 374, CA (Civ Div); reversing [1969] 2 A.C. 223, QBD .... *Digested*, 69/**1866**:
   Applied, 70/2778, 74/3742, 78/2324, 79/19, 80/163, 84/447, 92/2435,
   93/2167, 96/4839, 00/5979, 01/81: *Considered*, 68/1909, 70/2436,
   84/364.A, 84/3483, 85/2791, 85/3415, 86/950, 88/2417, 88/3418,
   89/3626, 90/4424, 94/1896, 96/2508, 02/658, 03/66, 05/2163:
   Distinguished, 76/19, 92/2740, 92/3464, 94/5367: *Explained*, 80/273:
   Not applied, 92/163, 93/63: *Referred to*, 92/6511
Anker v. Germany (C47/02) [2003] E.C.R. I-10447; [2004] 2 C.M.L.R. 35, ECJ ..... *Digested*, 05/**1457**
Anns v. Merton LBC; *sub nom* Anns v. Walcroft Property Co Ltd [1978] A.C. 728;
[1977] 2 W.L.R. 1024; [1977] 2 All E.R. 492; 75 L.G.R. 555; (1977) 243 E.G.
523; (1988) 4 Const. L.J. 100; [1977] J.P.L. 514; (1987) 84 L.S.G. 319; (1987)
137 N.L.J. 794; 121 S.J. 377, HL; affirming [1976] Q.B. 882; [1976] 2 W.L.R.
512; 74 L.G.R. 374; (1976) 241 E.G. 311; 120 S.J. 216, CA (Civ Div); reversing
(Unreported, October 24, 1975), HC. .... *Digested*, 77/**2030**:
   Applied, 78/1550, 78/2067, 79/213, 79/1865, 79/2570, 80/198, 81/1837,
   81/1849, 81/1859, 81/1860, 81/3409, 82/339, 82/2134, 82/4055, 83/2531,
   83/2535, 83/2538, 83/2746, 84/2337, 84/3044, 85/952, 85/1603,
   85/2303, 86/210, 87/241, 87/242, 87/2579, 87/2857, 87/3153, 88/2442,
   90/5493, 95/3452, 99/274, 02/3313: *Cited*, 00/4232: *Considered*, 80/1878,
   82/2266, 84/2298, 84/2300, 84/2566, 85/2305, 85/3549, 86/2252,
   86/2259, 86/4338, 87/2580, 87/2586, 87/2591, 87/3466, 88/2418,
   88/2433, 88/2435, 88/2438, 88/2444, 88/2457, 88/2465, 88/3409,
   88/3410, 89/259, 89/469, 89/2564, 89/2566, 90/3270, 94/2278, 94/3749,
   94/4517, 94/5335, 95/3659, 95/3681, 95/4189, 05/2856:
   Distinguished, 78/1547, 83/2523, 87/2709.a, 92/3197: *Followed*, 78/2062,
   80/1879, 82/763, 82/2125, 82/2133: *Not followed*, 86/2274:
   Overruled, 76/1873, 90/3288, 91/2661: *Referred to*, 78/2074, 79/1866,
   79/1884, 83/2521, 87/3582
Anns v. Walcroft Property Co Ltd see Anns v. Merton LBC

Ansell Computer Services Ltd *v.* Richardson (Inspector of Taxes) [2004] S.T.C. (S.C.D.)
472; [2004] S.T.I. 1995, Sp Comm . . . . *Digested,* 05/**4128**
Anson *v.* Anson (2004-05) 7 I.T.E.L.R. 318, Sup Ct (NSW) . . . . *Digested,* 05/**4300**
Ansul BV *v.* Ajax Brandbeveiliging BV (C40/01) [2005] Ch. 97; [2004] 3 W.L.R.
1048; [2003] E.C.R. I-2439; [2005] 2 C.M.L.R. 36; [2003] E.T.M.R. 85;
[2003] R.P.C. 40; (2005) 28(4) I.P.D. 28022, ECJ [2003] E.C.R. I-2439,
AGO. . . . . *Digested,* 04/**2386**:
Applied, 04/2416, 05/2540, 05/2582: *Considered,* 03/2635
Antaios Compania Naviera SA *v.* Salen Rederierna AB (The Antaios) [1985] A.C. 191;
[1984] 3 W.L.R. 592; [1984] 3 All E.R. 229; [1984] 2 Lloyd's Rep. 235; (1984)
81 L.S.G. 2776; (1984) 128 S.J. 564, HL; affirming [1983] 1 W.L.R. 1362;
[1983] 3 All E.R. 777; [1983] 2 Lloyd's Rep. 473; [1983] Com. L.R. 262; (1983)
127 S.J. 730, CA (Civ Div) . . . . *Digested,* 84/**96**:
Applied, 85/113, 86/1909, 90/193, 90/2850, 92/2745, 98/807, 00/874,
01/332: *Considered,* 85/2602, 86/91, 86/92, 86/1907, 86/2711, 87/146,
89/104, 90/180, 91/201, 91/203, 91/2269, 92/2721, 94/2760, 02/208,
03/204, 05/475: *Referred to,* 87/2216
Antillean Rice Mills NV *v.* Commission of the European Communities (C390/95 P); *sub
nom* Antillean Rice Mills NV *v.* Commission of the European Communities
(T480/93); Antillean Rice Mills NV *v.* Commission of the European Communities
(T483/93) [1999] E.C.R. I-769, ECJ (6th Chamber) . . . . *Considered,* 05/1471:
Followed, 02/1536, 02/1543
Antillean Rice Mills NV *v.* Commission of the European Communities (T480/93) see
Antillean Rice Mills NV *v.* Commission of the European Communities (C390/95
P)
Antillean Rice Mills NV *v.* Commission of the European Communities (T483/93) see
Antillean Rice Mills NV *v.* Commission of the European Communities (C390/95
P)
Antillean Rice Mills NV *v.* Council of the European Union (C451/98) [2001] E.C.R. I-
8949, ECJ . . . . *Considered,* 05/1474
Anton Durbeck GmbH *v.* Den Norske Bank ASA [2005] EWHC 2497; [2005] 2 C.L.C.
783, QBD (Comm)
Antonelli *v.* Wade Gery Farr (A Firm) see Ridehalgh *v.* Horsefield
Antonio Jorge Lda *v.* Fazenda Publica (C536/03) [2005] S.T.I. 1017, ECJ
Anufrijeva *v.* Southwark LBC; *sub nom* R. (on the application of Anufrijeva) *v.*
Southwark LBC; R. (on the application of N) *v.* Secretary of State for the Home
Department; R. (on the application of M) *v.* Secretary of State for the Home
Department [2003] EWCA Civ 1406; [2004] Q.B. 1124; [2004] 2 W.L.R. 603;
[2004] 1 All E.R. 833; [2004] 1 F.L.R. 8; [2003] 3 F.C.R. 673; [2004] H.R.L.R.
1; [2004] U.K.H.R.R. 1; 15 B.H.R.C. 526; [2004] H.L.R. 22; [2004] B.L.G.R.
184; (2003) 6 C.C.L. Rep. 415; [2004] Fam. Law 12; (2003) 100(44) L.S.G.
30; *Times,* October 17, 2003; *Independent,* October 23, 2003, CA (Civ Div);
affirming in part [2002] EWHC 3163; (2003) 6 C.C.L. Rep. 25, QBD . . . . *Digested,* 04/**1986**:
Applied, 03/2246, 05/3947: *Previous proceedings,* 03/2246
Aon Training Ltd (formerly Totalamber Plc) *v.* Dore see Dore *v.* Aon Training Ltd (formerly
Totalamber Plc)
Aon Trust Corp Ltd *v.* KPMG [2005] EWCA Civ 1004; [2005] O.P.L.R. 189; [2005]
Pens. L.R. 301; *Times,* September 7, 2005, CA (Civ Div); reversing in part
[2004] EWHC 1844; [2005] 1 W.L.R. 995; [2005] 3 All E.R. 587; [2004]
O.P.L.R. 373; [2004] Pens. L.R. 337; (2004) 101(36) L.S.G. 34; (2004) 154
N.L.J. 1326; *Times,* August 24, 2004, Ch D . . . . *Digested,* 05/**3042**
Apex Asphalt & Paving Co Ltd *v.* Office of Fair Trading [2005] CAT 4; [2005] Comp.
A.R. 507, CAT
Apex Asphalt & Paving Co Ltd *v.* Office of Fair Trading (Costs) [2005] CAT 11; [2005]
Comp. A.R. 825, CAT
Apotex Europe Ltd *v.* SmithKline Beecham Plc; *sub nom* SmithKline Beecham Plc *v.*
Apotex Europe Ltd [2004] EWCA Civ 1568; [2005] F.S.R. 23; (2005) 28(2)
I.P.D. 28003, CA (Civ Div); reversing in part [2003] EWHC 2939; [2004] F.S.R.
26; (2004) 27(2) I.P.D. 27014, Ch D (Patents Ct) . . . . *Digested,* 05/**2478**:
Subsequent proceedings, 04/2275
Appellant S 395/2002 *v.* Minister for Immigration and Multicultural Affairs [2004]
I.N.L.R. 233, HC (Aus) . . . . *Digested,* 05/**2164**
APPLERA/Dibenzorhodamine dye (T1255/04) [2005] E.P.O.R. 38, EPO (Technical Bd
App)
Application by the Landlords Association for Northern Ireland, Re [2005] 15 E.G.C.S. 122,
QBD (NI)
Application to Vary the Undertakings of A, Re [2005] S.T.C. (S.C.D.) 103; [2005] W.T.L.R. 1;
[2004] S.T.I. 2502; (2004) 148 S.J.L.B. 1432, Sp Comm . . . . *Digested,* 05/**4121**
Application under s 83.28 of the Criminal Code, Re 18 B.H.R.C. 361, Sup Ct (Can)
Applications Pursuant to r.7.28 of the Insolvency Rules 1986, Re see Austintel Ltd, Re
Applied Molecular Evolution Inc *v.* Office for Harmonisation in the Internal Market (Trade
Marks and Designs) (OHIM) (T183/03) [2005] E.T.M.R. 60, CFI . . . . *Digested,* 05/**2543**
APPLIED RESEARCH SYS/Endogenous gene expression (T431/04) [2005] E.P.O.R. 14,
EPO (Technical Bd App) . . . . *Digested,* 05/**2465**

Applied Technologies Manufacturing Ltd's Trade Mark Application (No.2149359); *sub nom* MOVIESTAR Trade Mark [2005] R.P.C. 26, App Person. . . . .   *Digested*, 05/**2584**

AR v. Homefirst Community Trust [2005] N.I. 435, CA (NI)

Arab Bank Plc v. Zurich Insurance Co; Banque Bruxelles Lambert SA v. Zurich Insurance Co [1999] 1 Lloyd's Rep. 262; [1998] C.L.C. 1351, QBD (Comm) . . . .   *Digested*, 99/**3382**:
                    Distinguished, 05/2307

Arab National Bank v. El-Abdali [2004] EWHC 2381; [2005] 1 Lloyd's Rep. 541, QBD (Comm) . . . .   *Digested*, 05/**197**

Aragonesa de Publicidad Exterior SA v. Departmento de Sanidad y Seguridad Social de la Generalitat de Cataluna (C1/90); Publivia SAE v. Departmento de Sanidad y Seguridad Social de la Generalitat de Cataluna (C176/90) [1991] E.C.R. I-4151; [1994] 1 C.M.L.R. 887, ECJ. . . . .   *Applied*, 05/1463,
                    05/1464

Aratra Potato Co Ltd v. Egyptian Navigation Co (The El Amria) [1981] 2 Lloyd's Rep. 119; [1981] Com. L.R. 136, CA (Civ Div); affirming [1980] 1 Lloyd's Rep. 390, QBD (Admlty). . . . .   *Digested*, 81/**2198**:
                    Applied, 83/387, 93/454, 00/760, 02/4688, 05/2406: *Considered*, 85/1291,
                    97/872, 97/881: *Followed*, 98/771

Arbed SA v. Commission of the European Communities (C176/99 P) [2005] 4 C.M.L.R. 6, ECJ (5th Chamber) . . . .   *Digested*, 05/**595**

Arbed SA v. Commission of the European Communities (T137/94) [1999] E.C.R. II-303, CFI . . . .   *Overruled*, 05/595

Arbib v. Earl Cadogan; Earl Cadogan v. 55/57 Cadogan Square Freehold Ltd; Earl Cadogan v. Moussaieff; Day v. 32 Rosary Gardens (Freehold) Ltd; Cadogan (9 Astell Street), Re [2005] 3 E.G.L.R. 139; [2005] R.V.R. 401; [2005] 41 E.G.C.S. 204, Lands Tr

Arbuthnot Pensions & Investments Ltd v. Padden see Padden v. Arbuthnot Pensions & Investments Ltd

Archibald v. Fife Council [2004] UKHL 32; [2004] 4 All E.R. 303; 2004 S.C. (H.L.) 117; 2004 S.L.T. 942; 2004 S.C.L.R. 971; [2004] I.C.R. 954; [2004] I.R.L.R. 651; (2005) 82 B.M.L.R. 185; (2004) 101 (31) L.S.G. 25; (2004) 148 S.J.L.B. 826; 2004 G.W.D. 23-505; *Times*, July 5, 2004, HL; reversing 2004 S.C. 495; 2004 S.L.T. 931; [2004] I.R.L.R. 197; 2004 G.W.D. 11-247; *Times*, January 23, 2004, IH (Ex Div); affirming EATS/0025/02, EAT . . . .   *Digested*, 04/**4707**:
                    Applied, 05/1229

ARCO Chemie Nederland Ltd v. Minister van Volkshuisvesting, Ruimtelijke Ordening en Milieubeheer (C418/97); *sub nom* Epon (C419/97), Re; Vereniging Dorpsbelang Hees v. Directeur van de dienst Milieu en Water van de provincie Gelderland (C419/97) [2002] Q.B. 646; [2002] 2 W.L.R. 1240; [2003] All E.R. (EC) 237; [2000] E.C.R. I-4475; [2003] Env. L.R. 2; [2001] Env. L.R. D6, ECJ (5th Chamber) . . . .   *Digested*, 02/**1519**:
                    Applied, 02/1520, 02/1521: *Considered*, 01/2413, 05/1362: *Followed*, 05/1414

Area Cova SA v. Commission of the European Communities (T196/99) [2001] E.C.R. II-3597, CFI. . . . .   *Followed*, 05/1441

Arena Corp Ltd, Re see Customs and Excise Commissioners v. Arena Corp Ltd (In Provisional Liquidation)

Arena Corp Ltd (In Provisional Liquidation) v. Customs and Excise Commissioners see Customs and Excise Commissioners v. Arena Corp Ltd (In Provisional Liquidation)

Arena Corp Ltd (In Provisional Liquidation) v. Schroeder see Customs and Excise Commissioners v. Arena Corp Ltd (In Provisional Liquidation)

Argo Fund Ltd v. Essar Steel Ltd; *sub nom* Essar Steel Ltd v. Argo Fund Ltd; A3/2005/1135, CA (Civ Div); affirming [2005] EWHC 600; [2005] 2 Lloyd's Rep. 203; [2005] 2 C.L.C. 209, QBD (Comm).   *Digested*, 05/**267**

Argos Distributors Ltd v. Customs and Excise Commissioners (C288/94) [1997] Q.B. 499; [1997] 2 W.L.R. 477; [1996] S.T.C. 1359; [1996] E.C.R. I-5311; [1996] 3 C.M.L.R. 569; [1996] C.E.C. 963; [1997] B.V.C. 64; *Times*, November 18, 1996; *Independent*, November 25, 1996 (C.S.), ECJ (6th Chamber) . . . .   *Digested*, 96/**5909**:
                    Applied, 99/6472, 02/4775, 03/4580, 05/4417: *Distinguished*, 00/5364,
                    01/5614: *Followed*, 97/4980: *Referred to*, 00/5317

Argos Ltd v. Office of Fair Trading [2004] CAT 24; [2005] Comp. A.R. 588, CAT

Argos Ltd v. Office of Fair Trading (Case Management: Witness Statements) [2003] CAT 16; [2004] Comp. A.R. 80, CAT . . . .   *Digested*, 04/**510**:
                    Followed, 05/565

Argos Ltd v. Office of Fair Trading (Costs) [2005] CAT 15; [2005] Comp. A.R. 996, CAT

Argos Ltd v. Office of Fair Trading (Disclosure) [2004] CAT 5; [2004] Comp. A.R. 513, CAT . . . .   *Digested*, 05/**580**

Argos Ltd v. Office of Fair Trading (Penalties) [2005] CAT 13; [2005] Comp. A.R. 834, CAT

Argos Ltd v. Office of Fair Trading (Permission to Appeal) [2005] CAT 16; [2005] Comp. A.R. 1000, CAT

Argosam Finance Co Ltd v. Oxby (Inspector of Taxes); *sub nom* FA & AB Ltd v. Lupton (Inspector of Taxes) [1965] Ch. 390; [1964] 3 W.L.R. 774; [1964] 3 All E.R. 561; (1964) 43 A.T.C. 240; [1964] T.R. 255; 108 S.J. 541, CA; affirming [1964] 2 W.L.R. 882; [1964] 1 All E.R. 791; (1964) 43 A.T.C. 26; [1964] T.R. 31; 108 S.J. 335, Ch D . . . . *Digested*, 64/**1813**
Applied, 91/586, 05/4056: *Distinguished*, 70/11, 77/1600, 92/611

Argyle v. Photobition Ltd (Unreported, May 13, 2004), CC (Southampton) [*Ex rel.* James Counsell, Barrister, Outer Temple Chambers, Outer Temple, 222 Strand, London] . . . . *Digested*, 05/**3146**

Arkin v. Borchard Lines Ltd (Costs: Third Party Proceedings) [2003] EWHC 3088; [2004] 1 Lloyd's Rep. 636; [2004] 2 Costs L.R. 267; (2004) 154 N.L.J. 22, QBD (Comm) . . . . *Digested*, 04/**313**
Overruled in part, 05/**385**

Arkin v. Borchard Lines Ltd (Costs Order) [2005] EWCA Civ 655; [2005] 1 W.L.R. 3055; [2005] 3 All E.R. 613; [2005] 2 Lloyd's Rep. 187; [2005] C.P. Rep. 39; [2005] 4 Costs L.R. 643; (2005) 155 N.L.J. 902; *Times*, June 3, 2005; *Independent*, June 7, 2005, CA (Civ Div); reversing in part [2003] EWHC 2844; [2004] 1 Lloyd's Rep. 88; [2004] 2 Costs L.R. 231; (2003) 153 N.L.J. 1903, QBD (Comm) . . . . *Digested*, 05/**385**
Previous proceedings, 04/31?

Arkwright (Williams Personal Representative) v. Inland Revenue Commissioners; *sub nom* Inland Revenue Commissioners v. Arkwright [2004] EWHC 1720; [2005] 1 W.L.R. 1411; [2004] S.T.C. 1323; [2005] R.V.R. 266; 76 T.C. 788; [2004] B.T.C. 8082; [2004] W.T.L.R. 855; [2004] S.T.I. 1724; (2004) 101(31) L.S.G. 26; *Times*, August 4, 2004, Ch D; reversing [2004] S.T.C. (S.C.D.) 89; [2004] W.T.L.R. 181; [2004] S.T.I. 147, Sp Comm . . . . *Digested*, 04/**3794**

Armagas Ltd v. Mundogas SA (The Ocean Frost) [1986] A.C. 717; [1986] 2 W.L.R. 1063; [1986] 2 All E.R. 385; [1986] 2 Lloyd's Rep. 109; (1986) 83 L.S.G. 2002; (1986) 130 S.J. 430, HL; affirming [1985] 3 W.L.R. 640; [1985] 3 All E.R. 795; [1985] 1 Lloyd's Rep. 1; (1984) 81 L.S.G. 2169; (1984) 129 S.J. 362, CA (Civ Div) . . . . *Digested*, 86/**37**
Applied, 89/55, 94/537, 95/763, 99/456, 05/2959: *Considered*, 93/64, 94/106

Armitage v. Staveley Industries Plc [2005] EWCA Civ 792; [2005] O.P.L.R. 177, CA (Civ Div); reversing [2004] EWHC 2320; [2005] O.P.L.R. 165; [2004] Pens. L.R. 385, Ch D . . . . *Digested*, 05/**711**

Armitage v. West Bromwich Building Society see Investors Compensation Scheme Ltd v. West Bromwich Building Society (No.1)

Armory v. Delamirie 93 E.R. 664; (1722) 1 Str. 504 . . . . *Applied*, 05/**957**

Armstrong v. British Coal Corp (Unreported, July 31, 1998), CA (Civ Div) . . . . *Digested*, 98/**2842**
Considered, 05/965: *Followed*, 04/2714

Armstrong v. First York Ltd [2005] EWCA Civ 277; [2005] 1 W.L.R. 2751; [2005] C.P. Rep. 25; [2005] R.T.R. 19; *Times*, January 19, 2005, CA (Civ Div) . . . . *Digested*, 05/**297**

Armstrong v. Times Newspapers Ltd [2005] EWCA Civ 1007; [2005] E.M.L.R. 33, CA (Civ Div); reversing in part [2004] EWHC 2928, Ch D

Armstrong (Deceased), Re see Perpetual Trust Ltd v. Roman Catholic Bishop of the Diocese of Christchurch

Arnold v. Zako (Unreported, May 12, 2004), CC (Birmingham) [*Ex rel.* Stephen Garner, Barrister, No.8 Chambers, Fountain Court, Steelhouse Lane, Birmingham.] . . . . . *Digested*, 05/**3141**

Arnold Andre GmbH & Co KG v. Landrat des Kreises Herford (C434/02) [2004] E.C.R. I-11825; [2005] 1 C.M.L.R. 25, ECJ . . . . *Digested*, 05/**1434**

Arnold (Inspector of Taxes) v. G-Con Ltd [2005] EWHC 2456; [2005] S.T.I. 364; (2005) 102(18) L.S.G. 24; *Times*, March 14, 2005, Ch D

Arrmet SL's Community Design [2004] E.C.D.R. 24, OHIM (Cancellation Div) . . . . *Digested*, 05/**2415**

Arros Invest Ltd v. Nishanov [2004] EWHC 576; [2004] I.L.Pr. 22, Ch D . . . . *Digested*, 05/**472**

Arrow Trading & Investments Est 1920 v. Edwardian Group Ltd (No.2) [2004] EWHC 1319; [2004] B.C.C. 955; [2005] 1 B.C.L.C. 696, Ch D (Companies Ct)

Arrowfield Services Ltd v. BP Collins (A Firm) [2003] EWHC 830; [2005] 2 Costs L.R. 171, Ch D . . . . *Applied*, 05/**361**

Arscott v. Coal Authority [2004] EWCA Civ 892; [2005] Env. L.R. 6; (2004) 148 S.J.L.B. 880; [2004] N.P.C. 114, CA (Civ Div); affirming [2003] EWHC 1690, QBD . . . . *Digested*, 05/**289**

Arthur JS Hall & Co v. Simons; *sub nom* Harris v. Scholfield Roberts & Hall; Barratt v. Ansell (t/a Woolf Seddon); Barratt v. Woolf Seddon; Cockbone v. Atkinson Dacre & Slack; Harris v. Scholfield Roberts & Hill [2002] 1 A.C. 615; [2000] 3 W.L.R. 543; [2000] 3 All E.R. 673; [2000] B.L.R. 407; [2000] E.C.C. 487; [2000] 2 F.L.R. 545; [2000] 2 F.C.R. 673; [2001] P.N.L.R. 6; [2000] Fam. Law 806; [2000] E.G.C.S. 99; (2000) 97(32) L.S.G. 38; (2000) 150 N.L.J. 1147; (2000) 144 S.J.L.B. 238; [2000] N.P.C. 87; *Times*, July 21, 2000; *Independent*, July 25, 2000, HL; affirming [1999] 3 W.L.R. 873; [1999] 1 F.L.R. 536; [1999] 2 F.C.R. 193; [1999] Lloyd's Rep. P.N. 47; [1999] P.N.L.R. 374; [1999] Fam. Law 215; [1998] N.P.C. 162; *Times*, December 18, 1998; *Independent*, December 18, 1998, CA (Civ Div); affirming [1998] 2 F.L.R. 679; [1999] P.N.L.R. 208; [1998] Fam. Law 524, QBD . . . . *Digested*, 00/**4269**:
         Applied, 00/597, 03/509, 05/363, 05/2869: *Cited*, 01/525:
         Considered, 01/4515

Arthurton (Errol) v. Queen, The [2004] UKPC 25; [2005] 1 W.L.R. 949; [2004] 2 Cr. App. R. 33, PC (BVI) . . . . *Digested*, 04/**848**

Arun DC v. First Secretary of State; *sub nom* R. (on the application of Arun DC) v. First Secretary of State [2005] EWHC 2520; *Times*, October 13, 2005, QBD (Admin)

Arun DC v. Searle [2005] P.A.D. 92, Planning Inspector

AS Screenprinting Ltd v. British Reserve Insurance Co Ltd [1996] C.L.C. 1470; [1999] Lloyd's Rep. I.R. 430, CA (Civ Div) . . . . *Digested*, 99/**3397**:
         Applied, 05/2375

Asahi Glass Fluoropolymers UK Ltd v. Stop Huntingdon Animal Cruelty see Daiichi Pharmaceuticals UK Ltd v. Stop Huntingdon Animal Cruelty

Ashan v. Carter see Carter v. Ahsan (No.1)

Ashborder BV v. Green Gas Power Ltd [2004] EWHC 1517; [2005] B.C.C. 634; [2005] 1 B.C.L.C. 623, Ch D

Ashby v. White (1703) 2 Ld. Raym. 938; (1703) 1 Smith L.C. 253 . . . . *Applied*, 05/**4193**:
         Considered, 90/1571, 91/2512

Ashdown v. Telegraph Group Ltd [2001] EWCA Civ 1142; [2002] Ch. 149; [2001] 3 W.L.R. 1368; [2001] 4 All E.R. 666; [2002] E.C.C. 19; [2002] E.C.D.R. 32; [2001] E.M.L.R. 44; [2001] H.R.L.R. 57; [2001] U.K.H.R.R. 1242; [2002] R.P.C. 5; (2001) 24(9) I.P.D. 24058; (2001) 98(33) L.S.G. 29; (2001) 145 S.J.L.B. 201; *Times*, August 1, 2001; *Independent*, July 20, 2001; *Daily Telegraph*, July 24, 2001, CA (Civ Div); affirming [2001] Ch. 685; [2001] 2 W.L.R. 967; [2001] 2 All E.R. 370; [2001] E.C.D.R. 21; [2001] E.M.L.R. 20; [2001] H.R.L.R. 30; [2001] R.P.C. 34; (2001) 98(8) L.S.G. 47; (2001) 151 N.L.J. 58; (2001) 145 S.J.L.B. 31; *Times*, February 6, 2001; *Independent*, February 26, 2001 (C.S), Ch D . . . . *Digested*, 01/**3850**:
         Considered, 05/2420

Ashton, Re; *sub nom* R. v. Manchester Crown Court Ex p. DPP [1994] 1 A.C. 9; [1993] 2 W.L.R. 846; [1993] 2 All E.R. 663; (1993) 97 Cr. App. R. 203; (1994) 6 Admin. L.R. 329; [1993] Crim. L.R. 959; (1993) 157 J.P.N. 362; (1993) 90(24) L.S.G. 40; (1993) 143 N.L.J. 687; (1993) 137 S.J.L.B. 144; *Times*, May 7, 1993; *Independent*, May 10, 1993; *Guardian*, May 7, 1993, HL; reversing [1992] C.O.D. 444, QBD . . . . *Digested*, 93/**15**:
         Applied, 94/19, 00/2420, 05/71: *Followed*, 96/1550

Ashton v. Securum Finance Ltd see Securum Finance Ltd v. Ashton (No.1)

Ashurst v. Pollard; *sub nom* Pollard v. Ashurst [2001] Ch. 595; [2001] 2 W.L.R. 722; [2001] 2 All E.R. 75; [2001] B.P.I.R. 131; (2001) 98(3) L.S.G. 42; (2000) 150 N.L.J. 1787; *Times*, November 29, 2000, CA (Civ Div); affirming [2000] 2 All E.R. 772; [2001] I.L.Pr. 7; [2000] B.P.I.R. 347; [2000] 2 E.G.L.R. 29; [2000] 24 E.G. 171; [2000] E.G.C.S. 18; [2000] N.P.C. 11; *Times*, March 16, 2000, Ch D . . . *Digested*, 01/**3736**:
         Applied, 05/619

Ashville Investments Ltd v. Elmer Contractors Ltd; *sub nom* Elmer Contractors Ltd v. Ashville Investments Ltd [1989] Q.B. 488; [1988] 3 W.L.R. 867; [1988] 2 All E.R. 577; [1988] 2 Lloyd's Rep. 73 (Note); 37 B.L.R. 55; 10 Con. L.R. 72; (1987) 3 Const. L.J. 193; (1988) 132 S.J. 1553, CA (Civ Div) . . . . *Digested*, 88/**136**:
         Considered, 04/186, 05/716: *Followed*, 88/144: *Referred to*, 95/5027

Ashworth Frazer Ltd v. Gloucester City Council [2001] UKHL 59; [2001] 1 W.L.R. 2180; [2002] 1 All E.R. 377; [2002] L. & T.R. 2; [2002] 1 E.G.L.R. 15; [2002] 05 E.G. 133; [2001] 46 E.G.C.S. 180; (2001) 98(45) L.S.G. 27; (2001) 151 N.L.J. 1695; *Times*, November 12, 2001; *Independent*, November 13, 2001, HL; reversing in part (2000) 80 P. & C.R. 11; [2000] 1 E.G.L.R. 44; [2000] 12 E.G. 149; [2000] E.G.C.S. 3; *Times*, February 3, 2000 ; *Independent*, January 20, 2000, CA (Civ Div); reversing *Times*, April 1, 1999, Ch D . . . . *Digested*, 01/**4185**:
         Applied, 05/2643: *Considered*, 05/2639

Ashworth Hospital Authority v. MGN Ltd; *sub nom* Ashworth Security Hospital v.
MGN Ltd [2002] UKHL 29; [2002] 1 W.L.R. 2033; [2002] 4 All E.R. 193;
[2002] C.P.L.R. 712; [2002] E.M.L.R. 36; [2002] H.R.L.R. 41; [2002]
U.K.H.R.R. 1263; 12 B.H.R.C. 443; [2003] F.S.R. 17; (2002) 67 B.M.L.R. 175;
(2002) 99(30) L.S.G. 37; (2002) 146 S.J.L.B. 168; *Times,* July 1, 2002;
Independent, July 3, 2002, HL; affirming [2001] 1 W.L.R. 515; [2001] 1 All E.R.
991; [2001] E.M.L.R. 11; [2001] F.S.R. 33; (2001) 61 B.M.L.R. 48; (2001)
98(6) L.S.G. 46; (2001) 145 S.J.L.B. 20; *Times,* January 10, 2001; *Independent,*
January 18, 2001; *Daily Telegraph,* January 9, 2001, CA (Civ Div); affirming HQ
0000397, QBD . . . . *Digested,* 02/**3221**:
                    Considered, 02/415, 05/2064: *Distinguished,* 03/2922
Ashworth Security Hospital v. MGN Ltd see Ashworth Hospital Authority v. MGN Ltd
Asia Pacific (HK) Ltd v. Hanjin Shipping Co Ltd [2005] EWHC 2443; [2005] 2 C.L.C.
747; (2005) 102(46) L.S.G. 25, QBD (Comm)
Ask v. ABB Offshore Technology AS (E3/96) [1997] 2 C.M.L.R. 954, EFTA . . . . *Followed,* 05/**1314**
Askarov v. Turkey (46951/99) see Mamatkulov v. Turkey (46827/99)
Assanidze v. Georgia (71503/01) (2004) 39 E.H.R.R. 32, ECHR . . . . *Digested,* 05/**2111**:
                                                                Applied, 05/2065
Assicurazioni Generali SpA v. Arab Insurance Group (BSC) [2002] EWCA Civ 1642;
[2003] 1 W.L.R. 577; [2003] 1 All E.R. (Comm) 140; [2003] 2 C.L.C. 242;
[2003] Lloyd's Rep. I.R. 131; (2003) 100(3) L.S.G. 34; *Times,* November 29,
2002, CA (Civ Div); affirming [2002] C.L.C. 164; [2002] Lloyd's Rep. I.R. 633,
QBD (Comm) . . . . *Digested,* 03/**2480**:
                    Applied, 03/257, 05/10: *Considered,* 03/2725
Assimina Maritime Ltd v. Pakistan National Shipping Corp (The Tasman Spirit) [2004]
EWHC 3005; [2005] 1 All E.R. (Comm) 460; [2005] 1 Lloyd's Rep. 525;
[2005] 2 C.L.C. 448, QBD (Comm) . . . . *Digested,* 05/**211**
Associacao Comercial de Aveiro (ACA) v. Commission of the European Communities
(T80/00) [2002] E.C.R. II-2465, CFI . . . . *Followed,* 05/**1436**
ASSOCIATED ENGINEERING ITALY/Decisions by formalities officers (J3/83) [1979-85]
E.P.O.R. A164, EPO (Legal Bd App) . . . . *Applied,* 05/**2457**
Association de Soutien aux Travailleurs Immigres (ASTI) v. Chambre des Employes Prives
(C213/90) [1991] E.C.R. I-3507; [1993] 3 C.M.L.R. 621, ECJ. . . . . *Followed,* 05/**1234**
Astle v. Cheshire CC [2005] I.R.L.R. 12, EAT . . . . *Digested,* 05/**1313**
Astley v. Celtec Ltd (C478/03) see Celtec Ltd v. Astley (C478/03)
Atack v. Lee; Ellerton v. Harris [2004] EWCA Civ 1712; [2005] 1 W.L.R. 2643; [2005]
2 Costs L.R. 308; [2005] P.I.Q.R. Q6; (2005) 155 N.L.J. 24; (2005) 149
S.J.L.B. 60; *Times,* December 28, 2004, CA (Civ Div) . . . . *Digested,* 05/**2704**
Athanasakos v. Hatramo Haven en Transportbedrijf Moerdijk BV [2005] I.L.Pr. 49, Ar
Pag (GR)
Athanasios v. Norway (E3/04) [2005] 1 C.M.L.R. 29, EFTA
Atkins v. Dunn & Baker (A Firm) [2004] EWCA Civ 263; [2004] W.T.L.R. 477;
(2004) 148 S.J.L.B. 263, CA (Civ Div) . . . . *Digested,* 05/**2875**
Atkinson v. DPP [2004] EWHC 1457; [2005] 1 W.L.R. 96; [2004] 3 All E.R. 971;
(2004) 168 J.P. 472; (2004) 168 J.P.N. 700, QBD (Admin) . . . . *Digested,* 05/**887**
Atkinson v. United States; *sub nom* R. v. Brixton Prison Governor Ex p. Atkinson;
United States v. Atkinson [1971] A.C. 197; [1969] 3 W.L.R. 1074; [1969] 3 All
E.R. 1317; 113 S.J. 901, HL; affirming in part [1969] 2 All E.R. 1146; (1969) 133
J.P. 617; 113 S.J. 690, QBD . . . . *Digested,* 69/**2155**:
                    Applied, 69/1452, 71/7105, 91/1750, 92/2084, 93/1871, 05/1362:
                    Considered, 85/2128, 90/2267, 94/1115: *Distinguished,* 02/1593
Atkinson (Inspector of Taxes) v. Camas Plc see Camas Plc v. Atkinson (Inspector of
Taxes)
Atlantic Computer Systems Plc, Re [1992] Ch. 505; [1992] 2 W.L.R. 367; [1992] 1 All E.R.
476; [1990] B.C.C. 859; [1991] B.C.L.C. 606; *Financial Times,* August 1, 1990, CA
(Civ Div); reversing [1990] B.C.C. 454; [1990] B.C.L.C. 729; *Times,* June 20,
1990; *Financial Times,* June 13, 1990, Ch D (Companies Ct) . . . . *Digested,* 91/**2127**:
                    Applied, 93/2325, 93/4812, 03/644, 05/2258: *Considered,* 99/3349,
                    00/3432, 01/507, 01/733: *Distinguished,* 96/400: *Followed,* 93/2314,
                    93/2315, 94/2591, 99/3267, 99/3358: *Referred to,* 90/514
Atlantic Container Line AB v. Commission of the European Communities (T191/98)
[2003] E.C.R. II-3275; [2005] 4 C.M.L.R. 20, CFI (3rd Chamber)
Atos Consulting Ltd v. Avis Europe Plc [2005] EWHC 982; [2005] C.P. Rep. 43;
[2005] T.C.L.R. 7, QBD (TCC)
Atos Origin IT Services UK Ltd v. Haddock [2005] I.C.R. 277; [2005] I.R.L.R. 20, EAT . *Digested,* 05/**1277**
Atos Origin UK Ltd v. Amicus (AMPS) UKEAT/0566/03/DM, EAT . . . . *Considered,* 05/**1313**
Attar v. Attar (No.2) [1985] Fam. Law 252, Fam Div . . . . *Digested,* 85/**1054**:
                                                                Doubted, 05/1656
Attheraces Ltd v. British Horseracing Board Ltd (Preliminary Issues) [2005] EWHC
1553; [2005] U.K.C.L.R. 757, Ch D . . . . *Digested,* 05/**484**
Attorney General v. Barker (Civil Proceedings Order) [2000] 1 F.L.R. 759; [2000] 2
F.C.R. 1; [2000] Fam. Law 400; (2000) 97(10) L.S.G. 37; *Times,* March 7, 2000,
DC . . . . *Digested,* 00/**631**:
                                                                Applied, 01/92, 05/339

Attorney General v. Blake [2001] 1 A.C. 268; [2000] 3 W.L.R. 625; [2000] 4 All E.R. 385; [2000] 2 All E.R. (Comm) 487; [2001] I.R.L.R. 36; [2001] Emp. L.R. 329; [2000] E.M.L.R. 949; (2000) 23(12) I.P.D. 23098; (2000) 97(32) L.S.G. 37; (2000) 150 N.L.J. 1230; (2000) 144 S.J.L.B. 242; *Times*, August 3, 2000; *Independent*, November 6, 2000 (C.S), HL; affirming [1998] Ch. 439; [1998] 2 W.L.R. 805; [1998] 1 All E.R. 833; [1998] E.M.L.R. 309; (1998) 95(4) L.S.G. 33; (1998) 148 N.L.J. 15; (1998) 142 S.J.L.B. 35; *Times*, December 22, 1997; *Independent*, December 19, 1997, CA (Civ Div); reversing [1997] Ch. 84; [1996] 3 W.L.R. 741; [1996] 3 All E.R. 903; [1996] E.M.L.R. 382; [1996] F.S.R. 727; (1996) 19(7) I.P.D. 19066; *Times*, April 23, 1996, Ch D . . . . *Digested*, 00/**797**:
           Applied, 00/2132: *Considered*, 03/717, 04/912, 05/956
Attorney General v. British Museum Trustees [2005] EWHC 1089; [2005] Ch. 397; [2005] 3 W.L.R. 396; [2005] W.T.L.R. 781; (2005) 155 N.L.J. 865; *Times*, June 2, 2005, Ch D . . . . *Digested*, 05/**241**
Attorney General v. Chitolie [2004] EWHC 1943; [2005] B.P.I.R. 267, QBD (Admin) . .   *Digested*, 05/**339**
Attorney General v. D see Attorney General's Reference (No.4 of 2004), Re
Attorney General v. Ebert [2005] EWHC 1254; [2005] B.P.I.R. 1056, QBD (Admin)
Attorney General v. Ebert (Civil Proceedings Order) [2005] B.P.I.R. 1029, QBD
Attorney General v. Express Newspapers [2004] EWHC 2859; [2005] E.M.L.R. 13; [2005] A.C.D. 41, QBD (Admin) . . . . *Digested*, 05/**848**
Attorney General v. Great Eastern Railway Co (1879-80) L.R. 5 App. Cas. 473, HL; affirming (1879) L.R. 11 Ch. D. 449, CA . . . . *Applied*, 53/500,
       54/2747, 61/3959, 62/1428, 62/2440, 71/1531, 72/2835, 94/60, 95/1173,
       95/6406, 01/5642, 05/2001: *Considered*, 03/4960
Attorney General v. Greater Manchester Newspapers Ltd see Venables v. News Group International (Breach of Injunction)
Attorney General v. Heinemann Publishers Australia Pty Ltd [1989] 2 F.S.R. 631; 165 C.L.R. 30; (1988) 78 A.L.R. 449; (1988) 138 N.L.J. Rep. 170; *Independent*, June 8, 1988, HC (Aus); affirming [1989] 2 F.S.R. 349, CA (NSW) . . . . *Digested*, 88/**1982**:
           Applied, 03/621, 05/621
Attorney General v. Pelling [2005] EWHC 414; [2005] A.C.D. 82; [2005] Fam. Law 854, QBD (Admin)
Attorney General v. Scotcher [2005] UKHL 36; [2005] 1 W.L.R. 1867; [2005] 3 All E.R. 1; [2005] 2 Cr. App. R. 35; [2005] U.K.H.R.R. 637; [2005] Crim. L.R. 791; (2005) 155 N.L.J. 828; *Times*, May 20, 2005, HL; affirming [2003] EWHC 1380; [2004] A.C.D. 2, QBD (Admin) . . . . *Digested*, 05/**849**
Attorney General v. Zaoui 19 B.H.R.C. 147, Sup Ct (NZ)
Attorney General Ex rel Bedfordshire CC v. Howard United Reformed Church Trustees, Bedford; *sub nom* Attorney General Ex rel Bedfordshire CC v. Trustees of the Howard United Reformed Church, Bedford [1976] A.C. 363; [1975] 2 W.L.R. 961; [1975] 2 All E.R. 337; 73 L.G.R. 364; (1975) 30 P. & C.R. 47; 119 S.J. 376, HL; reversing [1975] Q.B. 41; [1974] 3 W.L.R. 368; [1974] 3 All E.R. 273; 72 L.G.R. 664; (1974) 28 P. & C.R. 431; [1975] R.A. 1; 118 S.J. 628, CA (Civ Div); reversing [1974] Q.B. 332; [1973] 3 W.L.R. 661; [1973] 3 All E.R. 878; 72 L.G.R. 190; (1974) 27 P. & C.R. 113; [1973] J.P.L. 595; 117 S.J. 814, QBD . . . . *Digested*, 75/**3354**:
           Applied, 05/3367
Attorney General Ex rel Bedfordshire CC v. Trustees of the Howard United Reformed Church, Bedford see Attorney General Ex rel Bedfordshire CC v. Howard United Reformed Church Trustees, Bedford
Attorney General of Gibraltar v. Shimidzu [2005] UKPC 26; [2005] 1 W.L.R. 3335, PC (Gib) . . . . *Digested*, 05/**633**
Attorney General of Hong Kong v. Reid [1994] 1 A.C. 324; [1993] 3 W.L.R. 1143; [1994] 1 All E.R. 1; (1993) 143 N.L.J. 1569; (1993) 137 S.J.L.B. 251; [1993] N.P.C. 144; *Times*, November 12, 1993; *Independent*, November 24, 1993, PC (NZ) . . . . *Digested*, 94/**2083**:
           Applied, 03/4481, 04/1197: *Considered*, 05/3443
Attorney General of Jersey v. Holley [2005] UKPC 23; [2005] 2 A.C. 580; [2005] 3 W.L.R. 29; [2005] 3 All E.R. 371; [2005] 2 Cr. App. R. 36; [2005] Crim. L.R. 966; (2005) 155 N.L.J. 1009; (2005) 149 S.J.L.B. 774; *Times*, June 21, 2005; *Independent*, June 22, 2005, PC (Jer) . . . . *Digested*, 05/**807**
Attorney General of Trinidad and Tobago v. Ramanoop [2005] UKPC 15; [2005] 2 W.L.R. 1324, PC (Trin)
Attorney General's Reference (No.9 of 1989), Re; *sub nom* R. v. Lacey (Steven Lloyd) (1990-91) 12 Cr. App. R. (S.) 7; [1990] Crim. L.R. 437, CA (Crim Div) . . . . *Digested*, 91/**1214**:
       Applied, 92/1399, 93/1101: *Cited*, 93/1274: *Considered*, 92/1155, 92/1392,
       96/2060, 97/1596, 00/1137, 00/1421, 01/1400, 01/1478, 03/3761, 03/3857,
       04/3432: *Followed*, 97/1699, 05/3729: *Referred to*, 99/1331
Attorney General's Reference (Nos.3, 4, 8, 9, 10, 11, 14 and 16 of 1990), Re; *sub nom* R. v. Dickson (Robert Leslie); R. v. Mendy (Alphonse Francis); R. v. Singleton (Edward); R. v. Hodgkins (Barry Kenneth); R. v. Ryan (James Francis); R. v. Walsh (Martin Peter Andrew); R. v. Duffy (Warren Edward) (1991) 92 Cr. App. R. 166; (1990-91) 12 Cr. App. R. (S.) 479; [1991] Crim. L.R. 304, CA (Crim Div) . .   *Digested*, 91/**1213**:
       Cited, 92/1393, 92/1394, 93/1274, 93/1277, 93/1278, 93/1279:
       Considered, 96/2060, 05/3779

Attorney General's Reference (Nos.14 and 24 of 1993), Re; *sub nom* R. *v.* Shepherd (Peter
James); R. *v.* Wernet (Robert Stewart) [1994] 1 W.L.R. 530; [1994] 2 All E.R.
242; (1994) 99 Cr. App. R. 39; (1994) 15 Cr. App. R. (S.) 640; [1994] R.T.R. 49;
(1994) 138 S.J.L.B. 23; *Times,* December 27, 1993, CA (Crim Div) . . . .   *Digested,* 94/**119**3
Applied, 95/1319, 02/4026: *Approved,* 96/1836: *Considered,* 96/175€
96/1757, 96/1762, 96/1763, 96/1767, 96/1822, 96/1824, 96/1826, 96/182`
96/1828, 96/1829, 96/1835, 97/1662, 97/1668, 97/1669, 97/1671, 97/167`
99/1326, 00/1197, 00/1364, 03/3645, 05/3766: *Distinguished,* 96/175€
Followed, 96/1761, 97/1678: *Referred to,* 94/1193.a, 95/1344, 97/166`
97/1665, 97/166

Attorney General's Reference (No.35 of 1994), Re; *sub nom* R. *v.* H (Terence) (1995) 16
Cr. App. R. (S.) 635, CA (Crim Div) . . . .   *Digested,* 96/**178**2
Considered, 99/1195, 00/1280: *Followed,* 05/363

Attorney General's Reference (No.47 of 1994), Re; *sub nom* R. *v.* Smith (Robert John)
(1995) 16 Cr. App. R. (S.) 865, CA (Crim Div) . . . .   *Digested,* 96/**191**C
Applied, 03/3723, 05/3617: *Considered,* 97/1556, 97/1559, 97/1561, 97/156`
98/1236, 02/4085: *Referred to,* 97/157

Attorney General's Reference (No.3 of 1995), Re; *sub nom* R. *v.* H (Cyril Arthur) [1996]
1 Cr. App. R. (S.) 26, CA (Crim Div) . . . .   *Digested,* 96/**177**€
Considered, 97/1453, 00/1395, 05/373

Attorney General's Reference (No.29 of 1995), Re; *sub nom* R. *v.* Mighty (Daniel Ivor)
[1996] 2 Cr. App. R. (S.) 60, CA (Crim Div) . . . .   *Digested,* 96/**207**4
Considered, 99/1339, 00/1424, 05/372

Attorney General's Reference (Nos.32 and 33 of 1995), Re; *sub nom* R. *v.* Pegg (Shane
Robin); R. *v.* Martin (Mark Anthony) [1996] 2 Cr. App. R. (S.) 346, CA (Crim
Div) . . . .   *Digested,* 97/**142**1
Considered, 97/1700, 98/1132, 00/1414, 02/4084, 04/3437, 05/372€
Referred to, 97/141

Attorney General's Reference (No.35 of 1995), Re; *sub nom* R. *v.* Hartley (Russell)
[1996] 1 Cr. App. R. (S.) 413, CA (Crim Div) . . . .   *Digested,* 96/**190**4
Applied, 05/361

Attorney General's Reference (No.38 of 1995), Re; *sub nom* R. *v.* Harvey (Michael)
[1996] 2 Cr. App. R. (S.) 103, CA (Crim Div) . . . .   *Digested,* 96/**206**€
Considered, 98/1328, 98/1372, 99/1239, 05/372·

Attorney General's Reference (Nos.60 and 61 of 1995), Re; *sub nom* R. *v.* Sunderland
(Kevin Thomas); R. *v.* Collier (Michael Anthony) [1996] 2 Cr. App. R. (S.) 243,
CA (Crim Div) . . . .   *Digested,* 97/**169**€
Considered, 05/3732: *Followed,* 97/169

Attorney General's Reference (No.18 of 1997), Re; *sub nom* R. *v.* Cutler (Saul Roland)
[1998] 1 Cr. App. R. (S.) 151, CA (Crim Div) . . . .   *Digested,* 97/**169**4
Considered, 05/3732: *Distinguished,* 03/385'

Attorney General's Reference (Nos.64 and 65 of 1997), Re; *sub nom* R. *v.* O'Gorman
(John); R. *v.* Hibbard (Terence) [1999] 1 Cr. App. R. (S.) 237, CA (Crim Div) . . .   *Digested,* 99/**114**€
Considered, 05/359

Attorney General's Reference (No.4 of 1998), Re; *sub nom* R. *v.* Ward (Mark Richard)
[1998] 2 Cr. App. R. (S.) 388, CA (Crim Div) . . . .   *Digested,* 98/**140**7
Considered, 03/3879, 05/362·

Attorney General's Reference (No.54 of 1998), Re; *sub nom* R. *v.* W (Michael Paul) (A
Juvenile) [2000] 1 Cr. App. R. (S.) 219, CA (Crim Div) . . . .   *Digested,* 99/**131**€
Considered, 05/372

Attorney General's Reference (Nos.59, 60 and 63 of 1998), Re; *sub nom* R. *v.* Goodwin
(Frankie); R. *v.* JO'B (A Juvenile); R. *v.* TH (A Juvenile) [1999] 2 Cr. App. R.
(S.) 128; [1999] Crim. L.R. 341; *Times,* December 28, 1998, CA (Crim Div) . . . .   *Digested,* 99/**137**'
Applied, 03/3767: *Considered,* 00/1322, 00/1323, 03/3879, 05/378

Attorney General's Reference (No.76 of 1998), Re; *sub nom* R. *v.* Kirkham (Gary) [1999]
2 Cr. App. R. (S.) 361, CA (Crim Div) . . . .   *Digested,* 99/**117**€
Applied, 05/361

Attorney General's Reference (Nos.78, 79 and 85 of 1998), Re; *sub nom* R. *v.* Russell
(Robert John); R. *v.* O (Jason Patrick) (A Juvenile); R. *v.* M (Sarah Ruth) (A
Juvenile) [2000] 1 Cr. App. R. (S.) 371, CA (Crim Div) . . . .   *Digested,* 00/**113**2
Considered, 00/1130, 01/1375, 05/365€

Attorney General's Reference (No.3 of 1999), Re; *sub nom* R. *v.* B [2001] 2 A.C. 91;
[2001] 2 W.L.R. 56; [2001] 1 All E.R. 577; [2001] 1 Cr. App. R. 34; [2001]
H.R.L.R. 16; [2001] Crim. L.R. 394; (2001) 98(7) L.S.G. 39; (2000) 150 N.L.J.
1889; (2001) 145 S.J.L.B. 8; *Times,* December 15, 2000; *Independent,*
December 19, 2000, HL; reversing [2000] 3 W.L.R. 1164; [2000] 4 All E.R. 360;
[2000] 2 Cr. App. R. 416; [2000] Crim. L.R. 994; (2000) 144 S.J.L.B. 222;
Times, June 16, 2000; *Independent,* June 9, 2000, CA (Crim Div) . . . .   *Digested,* 01/**973**
Applied, 01/718, 02/858, 05/842: *Considered,* 02/3769: *Followed,* 00/91`

Attorney General's Reference (No.19 of 1999), Re; *sub nom* R. *v.* Kitchener (Marvine
Wayne) [2000] 1 Cr. App. R. (S.) 287, CA (Crim Div) . . . .   *Digested,* 99/**125**€
Considered, 05/366·

Attorney General's Reference (No.43 of 1999), Re; *sub nom* R. *v.* GGM [2000] 1 Cr. App. R. (S.) 398, CA (Crim Div) . . . . *Digested,* 00/**1287**: *Considered,* 01/1358, 05/3641

Attorney General's Reference (No.49 of 1999), Re; *sub nom* R. *v.* Hinchliffe (Allen Patrick) [2000] 1 Cr. App. R. (S.) 436, CA (Crim Div) . . . . *Digested,* 00/**1244**: *Considered,* 01/1312, 03/3716, 04/3411, 05/3759: *Followed,* 02/3942

Attorney General's Reference (No.68 of 1999), Re; *sub nom* R. *v.* Thomas (Nigel Wynn) [2000] 2 Cr. App. R. (S.) 50, CA (Crim Div) . . . . *Digested,* 00/**1423**: *Considered,* 05/3732

Attorney General's Reference (No.3 of 2000), Re; *sub nom* R. *v.* G (Entrapment); R. *v.* Loosley (Grant Spencer) (No.2); R. *v.* Loosely (Grant Spencer); R. *v.* Looseley (Grant Spencer) (No.2) [2001] UKHL 53; [2001] 1 W.L.R. 2060; [2001] 4 All E.R. 897; [2002] 1 Cr. App. R. 29; [2002] H.R.L.R. 8; [2002] U.K.H.R.R. 333; [2002] Crim. L.R. 301; (2001) 98(45) L.S.G. 25; (2001) 145 S.J.L.B. 245; *Times,* October 29, 2001; *Independent,* November 2, 2001; *Daily Telegraph,* November 6, 2001, HL; reversing [2001] EWCA Crim 1214; [2001] 2 Cr. App. R. 26; [2001] H.R.L.R. 47; [2001] Crim. L.R. 645; *Times,* June 27, 2001; *Independent,* May 25, 2001, CA (Crim Div) . . . . *Digested,* 01/**992**: *Applied,* 05/1487

Attorney General's Reference (No.48 of 2000), Re; *sub nom* R. *v.* Johnson (Martin Clive) [2001] 1 Cr. App. R. (S.) 123, CA (Crim Div) . . . . *Digested,* 00/**1413**: *Considered,* 04/3437, 05/3725

Attorney General's Reference (No.78 of 2000), Re; *sub nom* R. *v.* Jones (Jason) [2001] EWCA Crim 2114; [2002] 1 Cr. App. R. (S.) 116, CA (Crim Div) . . . . *Digested,* 01/**1334**: *Considered,* 05/3619

Attorney General's Reference (No.88 of 2000), Re; *sub nom* R. *v.* Heighton (Mark Kristian) [2001] EWCA Crim 68, CA (Crim Div) . . . . *Digested,* 01/**1335**: *Considered,* 05/3530

Attorney General's Reference (No.89 of 2000), Re; *sub nom* R. *v.* Jones (Neil Andrew) [2001] EWCA Crim 137; [2001] 2 Cr. App. R. (S.) 65, CA (Crim Div) . . . . *Digested,* 01/**1202**: *Considered,* 03/3728, 05/3625

Attorney General's Reference (No.2 of 2001), Re; *sub nom* R. *v.* J (Unreasonable Delay) [2003] UKHL 68; [2004] 2 A.C. 72; [2004] 2 W.L.R. 1; [2004] 1 All E.R. 1049; [2004] 1 Cr. App. R. 25; [2004] H.R.L.R. 16; [2004] U.K.H.R.R. 193; 15 B.H.R.C. 472; [2004] Crim. L.R. 574; (2004) 101(4) L.S.G. 30; (2004) 148 S.J.L.B. 25; *Times,* December 12, 2003; *Independent,* December 16, 2003, HL; affirming [2001] EWCA Crim 1568; [2001] 1 W.L.R. 1869; [2002] 1 Cr. App. R. 24; [2001] U.K.H.R.R. 1265; [2002] Crim. L.R. 207; (2001) 98(32) L.S.G. 36; (2001) 145 S.J.L.B. 172; *Times,* July 12, 2001, CA (Crim Div) . . . . *Digested,* 04/**884**: *Applied,* 03/820, 03/3385: *Considered,* 04/3439, 05/925

Attorney General's Reference (No.7 of 2001), Re see Attorney General's Reference (No.71 of 2001), Re

Attorney General's Reference (Nos.19, 20 and 21 of 2001), Re; *sub nom* R. *v.* Byrne (Alan); R. *v.* Field (Jason); R. *v.* C (Craig) (A Juvenile) [2001] EWCA Crim 1432; [2002] 1 Cr. App. R. (S.) 33, CA (Crim Div) . . . . *Digested,* 02/**4032**: *Applied,* 03/3786, 05/3758: *Considered,* 01/1434, 03/3794, 05/3670: *Distinguished,* 03/3797: *Followed,* 03/3790

Attorney General's Reference (No.25 of 2001), Re; *sub nom* R. *v.* Moran (Frank Adam); Moran, Re [2001] EWCA Crim 1770; [2002] 1 W.L.R. 253; [2001] S.T.C. 1309; [2002] 1 Cr. App. R. (S.) 95; [2001] B.T.C. 351; [2001] Crim. L.R. 825; [2001] S.T.I. 1142; (2001) 98(37) L.S.G. 38; (2001) 145 S.J.L.B. 218; *Times,* August 8, 2001, CA (Crim Div) . . . . *Digested,* 01/**1111**: *Considered,* 05/3595: *Distinguished,* 03/3647

Attorney General's Reference (No.35 of 2001), Re; *sub nom* R. *v.* Girt (Stuart Barry) [2001] EWCA Crim 1271; [2002] 1 Cr. App. R. (S.) 44, CA (Crim Div) . . . . *Digested,* 02/**3870**: *Applied,* 04/3282: *Considered,* 04/3281, 05/3525: *Referred to,* 03/3622

Attorney General's Reference (Nos.41 and 42 of 2001), Re; *sub nom* R. *v.* TL (A Juvenile); R. *v.* TH (A Juvenile) [2001] EWCA Crim 1294, CA (Crim Div) . . . . *Considered,* 05/3644

Attorney General's Reference (No.52 of 2001), Re; *sub nom* R. *v.* Lamoon (Johnathon Joe) [2001] EWCA Crim 1906, CA (Crim Div) . . . . *Digested,* 01/**1501**: *Considered,* 05/3623

Attorney General's Reference (No.64 of 2001), Re; *sub nom* R. *v.* Little (David) [2001] EWCA Crim 2028; [2002] 1 Cr. App. R. (S.) 94, CA (Crim Div) . . . . *Digested,* 01/**1426**: *Considered,* 05/3771

Attorney General's Reference (No.71 of 2001), Re; *sub nom* Attorney General's Reference (No.7 of 2001), Re; R. *v.* Nixon (Tyrone Carlos) [2001] EWCA Crim 2838; [2002] 2 Cr. App. R. (S.) 23, CA (Crim Div) . . . . *Digested,* 02/**3942**: *Considered,* 03/3716, 04/3411, 05/3759

Attorney General's Reference (Nos.148, 149, 150, 151, 152, 153, 154 and 155 of 2001), Re; *sub nom* R. *v.* Russell (Graham); R. *v.* Burwood (James); R. *v.* Jary (Stephen); R. *v.* Tapken (Christopher); R. *v.* Batty (Christopher Andrew); R. *v.* Miller (Christopher Richard); R. *v.* Clements (Paul); R. *v.* Wilson (Mark); R. *v.* Leng (Darren Shaun); R. *v.* Sharp (John Wilson) [2002] EWCA Crim 1313, CA (Crim Div) . . . . *Digested*, 02/**4079**
Considered, 05/**3573**

Attorney General's Reference (No.4 of 2002), Re see Sheldrake *v.* DPP
Attorney General's Reference (Nos.4 and 7 of 2002), Re; *sub nom* R. *v.* Lobban (Adrian Michael); R. *v.* Sawyers (Christopher); R. *v.* Q (Steven James) (A Juvenile) [2002] EWCA Crim 127; [2002] 2 Cr. App. R. (S.) 77; [2002] Crim. L.R. 333; *Times*, February 11, 2002, CA (Crim Div) . . . . *Digested*, 02/**4066**
Applied, 02/4008, 03/3762, 03/3764, 04/802: *Considered*, 02/4057
03/3763, 03/3839, 04/874, 04/3432, 04/3433, 04/3435, 05/3726
05/3735, 05/3777, 05/3780: *Followed*, 03/3848, 03/3849, 03/3850
03/3858

Attorney General's Reference (No.5 of 2002), Re; *sub nom* R. *v.* W; Attorney General's Reference (No.5 of 2003), Re [2004] UKHL 40; [2005] 1 A.C. 167; [2004] 3 W.L.R. 957; [2004] 4 All E.R. 901; [2005] 1 Cr. App. R. 20; [2004] H.R.L.R. 37; [2005] Crim. L.R. 220; (2004) 101 (42) L.S.G. 29; (2004) 148 S.J.L.B. 1215; *Times*, October 18, 2004; *Independent*, October 19, 2004, HL; affirming [2003] EWCA Crim 1632; [2003] 1 W.L.R. 2902; [2004] 1 Cr. App. R. 2; [2003] Crim. L.R. 793; (2003) 100(27) L.S.G. 34; (2003) 147 S.J.L.B. 816; *Times*, June 16, 2003; *Independent*, July 21, 2003, CA (Crim Div) . . . . *Digested*, 04/**700**
Attorney General's Reference (Nos.48, 49, 50 and 51 of 2002), Re; *sub nom* R. *v.* Paulssen (Hans Constantin); R. *v.* Newmarch (Jennifer Leslie); R. *v.* Lizziemore (Bryan Roger); R. *v.* Geraghty (Desmond) [2002] EWCA Crim 3165; [2003] 2 Cr. App. R. (S.) 36, CA (Crim Div) . . . . *Considered*, 05/**911**
Attorney General's Reference (No.77 of 2002), Re; *sub nom* R. *v.* Scotney (Stephen Reginald) [2002] EWCA Crim 2312; [2003] 1 Cr. App. R. (S.) 111; [2003] Crim. L.R. 52, CA (Crim Div) . . . . *Digested*, 03/**3645**
Distinguished, 05/**3546**
Attorney General's Reference (Nos.91, 119 and 120 of 2002), Re; *sub nom* R. *v.* CCE; R. *v.* NJK; R. *v.* TAG [2003] EWCA Crim 5; [2003] 2 All E.R. 955; [2003] 2 Cr. App. R. 9; [2003] 2 Cr. App. R. (S.) 55; [2003] 1 F.C.R. 760; *Times*, February 7, 2003, CA (Crim Div) . . . . *Digested*, 03/**3866**
Applied, 04/3373, 04/3445: *Considered*, 04/3368, 05/3740, 05/3741
Attorney General's Reference (No.121 of 2002), Re; *sub nom* R. *v.* AF (A Juvenile) [2003] EWCA Crim 684; (2003) 147 S.J.L.B. 267, CA (Crim Div) . . . . *Digested*, 03/**3768**
Considered, 05/**3781**

Attorney General's Reference (No.146 of 2002), Re; *sub nom* R. *v.* Stewart (Robert) [2003] EWCA Crim 1010; [2003] 2 Cr. App. R. (S.) 107, CA (Crim Div) . . . . *Digested*, 03/**3691**
Considered, 05/**3587**

Attorney General's Reference (Nos.150 and 151 of 2002), Re; *sub nom* R. *v.* Warren (Ashley Leon); R. *v.* Whellams (Kyrt Anthony) [2003] EWCA Crim 1165; [2003] 2 Cr. App. R. (S.) 111, CA (Crim Div) . . . . *Digested*, 03/**3849**
Considered, 05/**3726**

Attorney General's Reference (No.152 of 2002), Re; *sub nom* R. *v.* Crump (Richard James); R. *v.* Cooksley (Robert Charles); R. *v.* Stride (Ian Paul); R. *v.* Cook (Neil Terence) [2003] EWCA Crim 996; [2003] 3 All E.R. 40; [2003] 2 Cr. App. R. 18; [2004] 1 Cr. App. R. (S.) 1; [2003] R.T.R. 32; (2003) 100(23) L.S.G. 36; *Times*, April 8, 2003; *Independent*, June 30, 2003 (C.S), CA (Crim Div) . . . . . . *Digested*, 04/**3333**
Applied, 04/3294, 04/3295, 04/3296, 04/3298, 05/3547, 05/3550
05/3554: *Considered*, 04/3297, 05/3546, 05/3549, 05/3551, 05/3552
05/3553, 05/3581, 05/3766, 05/5657: *Followed*, 04/3467, 04/4371
05/3548

Attorney General's Reference (No.2 of 2003), Re [2004] EWCA Crim 785; [2004] 1 W.L.R. 2062; [2005] 3 All E.R. 149; (2005) 84 B.M.L.R. 1; (2004) 101(17) L.S.G. 30; *Times*, April 21, 2004, CA (Crim Div) . . . . *Digested*, 04/**1637**
Attorney General's Reference (No.3 of 2003), Re see Attorney General's Reference (No.4 of 2003), Re
Attorney General's Reference (No.3 of 2003), Re [2004] EWCA Crim 868; [2005] Q.B.73; [2004] 3 W.L.R. 451; [2005] 4 All E.R. 303; [2004] 2 Cr. App. R. 23; *Times*, April 22, 2004, CA (Crim Div) . . . . *Digested*, 04/**753**
Attorney General's Reference (No.4 of 2003), Re; *sub nom* R. *v.* Suchedina (Hasnain Mohammed); Attorney General's Reference (No.3 of 2003), Re [2004] EWCA Crim 1944; [2005] 1 W.L.R. 1574; [2005] 1 Cr. App. R. 2; [2005] 1 Cr. App. R. (S.) 79; (2004) 148 S.J.L.B. 941; *Times*, September 9, 2004, CA (Crim Div) . . . . *Digested*, 04/**3313**
Attorney General's Reference (No.5 of 2003), Re see Attorney General's Reference (No.5 of 2002), Re

Attorney General's Reference (Nos.31, 42, 43, 45, 50 and 51 of 2003), Re; *sub nom* R. *v.* McInerney (Thomas); R. *v.* McLean (Adele); R. *v.* Burgess (Daniel); R. *v.* AC; R. *v.* Lehal (Surinder); R. *v.* Lehal (Bhupinder); Attorney General's References (Nos.31, 42, 43, 44, 50 and 51 of 2004), Re [2004] EWCA Crim 1934; [2005] 1 Cr. App. R. (S.) 76; *Times*, July 20, 2004, CA (Crim Div) . . . . *Digested*, 04/**3304**: *Considered*, 05/**3725**

Attorney General's Reference (Nos.37, 38, 44, 54, 51, 53, 35, 40, 43, 45, 41 and 42 of 2003), Re; R. *v.* HN; R. *v.* TG; R. *v.* Coles (Dean); R. *v.* RD; R. *v.* Hodgkins (Daniel); R. *v.* EE; R. *v.* EM; R. *v.* AC; R. *v.* TC; R. *v.* JC; R. *v.* GS; R. *v.* DS [2003] EWCA Crim 2973; [2004] 1 Cr. App. R. (S.) 84, CA (Crim Div) . . . . *Digested*, 04/**3373**: *Applied*, 04/**3364**: *Cited*, 04/**3444**: *Considered*, 04/**3363**, 04/**3372**, 05/**3741**

Attorney General's Reference (No.39 of 2003), Re see Attorney General's Reference (No.42 of 2003), Re

Attorney General's Reference (No.42 of 2003), Re; *sub nom* R. *v.* Wheeler (Michael Anthony); Attorney General's Reference (No.39 of 2003), Re [2003] EWCA Crim 3068; [2004] 1 Cr. App. R. (S.) 79; (2003) 147 S.J.L.B. 1208; *Times*, October 23, 2003, CA (Crim Div) . . . . *Digested*, 03/**3864**: *Considered*, 05/**3644**

Attorney General's Reference (No.52 of 2003), Re; *sub nom* R. *v.* Webb (Ian David) [2003] EWCA Crim 3731; [2004] Crim. L.R. 306; *Times*, December 12, 2003, CA (Crim Div) . . . . *Digested*, 04/**3443**: *Considered*, 05/**3743**

Attorney General's Reference (No.59 of 2003), Re [2003] EWCA Crim 3010, CA (Crim Div)   *Considered*, 05/**3762**

Attorney General's Reference (No.64 of 2003), Re see Attorney General's Reference (No.66 of 2003), Re

Attorney General's Reference (No.64 of 2003), Re; *sub nom* R. *v.* Britton (Gary Michael) [2003] EWCA Crim 3948; [2004] 2 Cr. App. R. (S.) 38, CA (Crim Div) . . . . . . *Digested*, 04/**3367**: *Approved*, 05/**3746**: *Considered*, 04/**3454**

Attorney General's Reference (No.66 of 2003), Re; *sub nom* R. *v.* Boujettif (Moussin); Attorney General's Reference (No.64 of 2003), Re; R. *v.* Harrison (John) [2003] EWCA Crim 3514; [2004] 2 Cr. App. R. (S.) 22; [2004] Crim. L.R. 241; *Times*, December 1, 2003, CA (Crim Div) . . . . *Digested*, 04/**3344**: *Applied*, 05/**3700**: *Considered*, 04/**3280**

Attorney General's Reference (No.70 of 2003), Re; *sub nom* R. *v.* Bates (Alan Roy) [2004] EWCA Crim 163; [2004] 2 Cr. App. R. (S.) 49, CA (Crim Div) . . . . . . *Digested*, 05/**3636**

Attorney General's Reference (No.73 of 2003), Re; *sub nom* R. *v.* Ranganathan (Umaharan) [2004] EWCA Crim 183; [2004] 2 Cr. App. R. (S.) 62, CA (Crim Div) . . . . *Digested*, 04/**3320**: *Considered*, 05/**3612**: *Distinguished*, 05/3614

Attorney General's Reference (No.77 of 2003), Re; *sub nom* R. *v.* Grierson (Ernest Roy) [2004] EWCA Crim 3394, CA (Crim Div) . . . . *Digested*, 05/**3695**

Attorney General's Reference (No.80 of 2003), Re; *sub nom* R. *v.* Harris (Adrian) [2004] EWCA Crim 398, CA (Crim Div) . . . . *Digested*, 04/**3414**: *Considered*, 05/**3590**

Attorney General's Reference (No.81 of 2003), Re; *sub nom* R. *v.* Attiq (Mohammed) [2004] EWCA Crim 994; [2005] 1 Cr. App. R. (S.) 3, CA (Crim Div) . . . . *Digested*, 05/**3703**

Attorney General's Reference (No.87 of 2003), Re; *sub nom* R. *v.* Leer (Nicholas) [2004] EWCA Crim 1144; [2005] 1 Cr. App. R. (S.) 17, CA (Crim Div) . . . . *Digested*, 04/**3465**

Attorney General's Reference (No.99 of 2003), Re [2004] EWCA Crim 1622; [2005] 1 Cr. App. R. (S.) 33, CA (Crim Div) . . . . *Digested*, 05/**3617**

Attorney General's Reference (No.1 of 2004), Re; *sub nom* R. *v.* Edwards (Caroline Patricia); R. *v.* Denton (Errol); R. *v.* Jackson (Ruth); R. *v.* Hendley (Ian); R. *v.* Crowley (Helen) [2004] EWCA Crim 1025; [2004] 1 W.L.R. 2111; [2005] 4 All E.R. 457 (Note); [2004] 2 Cr. App. R. 27; [2004] H.R.L.R. 23; [2004] U.K.H.R.R. 608; [2004] B.P.I.R. 1073; (2004) 101(20) L.S.G. 34; (2004) 148 S.J.L.B. 568; *Times*, April 30, 2004, CA (Crim Div) . . . . *Digested*, 04/**800**: *Applied*, 05/**780**, 05/**812**

Attorney General's Reference (No.2 of 2004), Re see R. *v.* Quayle (Barry)

Attorney General's Reference (No.2 of 2004), Re; *sub nom* R. *v.* Neville (Daniel John) [2004] EWCA Crim 1280; [2005] 1 Cr. App. R. (S.) 14, CA (Crim Div) . . . . *Digested*, 05/**3604**

Attorney General's Reference (No.3 of 2004), Re; *sub nom* R. *v.* Akuffo (Andrew Frank) [2004] EWCA Crim 1532; [2005] 1 Cr. App. R. (S.) 52, CA (Crim Div) . . . . *Digested*, 04/**3410**

Attorney General's Reference (No.4 of 2004), Re; *sub nom* R. *v.* Green (Joseph) [2004] EWCA Crim 1197; [2005] 1 Cr. App. R. (S.) 23, CA (Crim Div) . . . . *Digested*, 04/**3282**

Attorney General's Reference (No.4 of 2004), Re; *sub nom* Attorney General *v.* D [2005] EWCA Crim 889; [2005] 1 W.L.R. 2810; [2005] 2 Cr. App. R. 26; [2005] Crim. L.R. 799; *Times*, May 17, 2005, CA (Crim Div) . . . . *Digested*, 05/**814**

Attorney General's Reference (No.6 of 2004), Re; *sub nom* R. *v.* Plakici (Luan) [2004] EWCA Crim 1275; [2005] 1 Cr. App. R. (S.) 19; (2004) 148 S.J.L.B. 541; *Times*, May 6, 2004, CA (Crim Div) . . . . *Digested*, 05/**3536**

Attorney General's Reference (No.9 of 2004), Re; *sub nom* R. *v.* Uddin (Alim); Attorney General's Reference (No.9 of 2005), Re [2005] EWCA Crim 812; [2005] 2 Cr. App. R. (S.) 105, CA (Crim Div) . . . . *Digested*, 05/**3671**

Attorney General's Reference (No.10 of 2004), Re; *sub nom* R. v. Teesdale (Simon Walker) [2004] EWCA Crim 1530; [2005] 1 Cr. App. R. (S.) 20, CA (Crim Div) . *Digested*, 04/**329**
Attorney General's Reference (No.12 of 2004), Re; *sub nom* R. v. Weekes (Alfred Washington) [2004] EWCA Crim 1623; [2005] 1 Cr. App. R. (S.) 32, CA (Crim Div) . . . . *Digested*, 04/**335**
Attorney General's Reference (Nos.13, 14, 15, 16, 17 and 18 of 2004), Re; *sub nom* R. v. McKeown (Sharon Ann); R. v. Baria (Peter); R. v. McKeown (Jason); R. v. Parsons (Adam); R. v. Jones (Leon); R. v. McKeown (Nigel) [2004] EWCA Crim 1885; [2005] 1 Cr. App. R. (S.) 66; *Times*, August 17, 2004, CA (Crim Div) . . . . *Digested*, 04/**3450**
　　　　　　　　　　　　　　　　　　　　　　　　　　　　　　　　　　　Considered, 05/375٠
Attorney General's Reference (No.19 of 2004), Re; *sub nom* R. v. Charlton (Brett) [2004] EWCA Crim 1239; [2005] 1 Cr. App. R. (S.) 18; (2004) 148 S.J.L.B. 539; (2004) 148 S.J.L.B. 568, CA (Crim Div) . . . . *Digested*, 05/**376**
Attorney General's Reference (No.20 of 2004), Re; *sub nom* R. v. Barker (Daniel) [2004] EWCA Crim 2723; [2005] 1 Cr. App. R. (S.) 111, CA (Crim Div) . . . . *Digested*, 05/**376:**
Attorney General's Reference (No.25 of 2004), Re; *sub nom* R. v. Gay (Alan Thomas) [2004] EWCA Crim 1203; [2005] 1 Cr. App. R. (S.) 15, CA (Crim Div) . . . . *Digested*, 05/**356**
Attorney General's Reference (No.26 of 2004), Re; *sub nom* R. v. Khan (Jameel) [2004] EWCA Crim 1384; [2005] 1 Cr. App. R. (S.) 25, CA (Crim Div) . . . . *Digested*, 04/**335**
Attorney General's Reference (No.28 of 2004), Re; *sub nom* R. v. McCluskie (George) [2004] EWCA Crim 1440; [2005] 1 Cr. App. R. (S.) 35, CA (Crim Div) . . . . *Digested*, 05/**378**
Attorney General's Reference (No.30 of 2004), Re; *sub nom* R. v. Taroni (Ross Paul) [2004] EWCA Crim 1754; [2005] 1 Cr. App. R. (S.) 48, CA (Crim Div) . . . . *Digested*, 04/**346**
Attorney General's Reference (No.32 of 2004), Re [2004] EWCA Crim 2644, CA (Crim Div) . . . . *Digested*, 05/**378:**
Attorney General's Reference (No.34 of 2004), Re; *sub nom* R. v. Webb (Michael John) [2004] EWCA Crim 1470; [2005] 1 Cr. App. R. (S.) 37, CA (Crim Div) . . . . *Digested*, 04/**337:**
Attorney General's Reference (No.37 of 2004), Re; *sub nom* R. v. Dawson (James Anthony) [2004] EWCA Crim 1854; [2005] 1 Cr. App. R. (S.) 65, CA (Crim Div) . . . . *Digested*, 04/**343**
Attorney General's Reference (Nos.38 and 39 of 2004), Re; *sub nom* R. v. Randall (Aaron); R. v. Donaghue (Troy) [2004] EWCA Crim 1820; [2005] 1 Cr. App. R. (S.) 60, CA (Crim Div) . . . . *Digested*, 04/**343**
Attorney General's Reference (No.44 of 2004), Re; *sub nom* R. v. E (Keith) [2004] EWCA Crim 2038; [2005] 1 Cr. App. R. (S.) 59, CA (Crim Div) . . . . *Digested*, 04/**342**
Attorney General's Reference (No.49 of 2004), Re; *sub nom* R. v. Quinn (Kieran James) [2004] EWCA Crim 1952; [2005] 1 Cr. App. R. (S.) 72, CA (Crim Div) . . . . *Digested*, 05/**366**
Attorney General's Reference (No.53 of 2004), Re; *sub nom* R. v. Lowe (Allan) [2004] EWCA Crim 1831; [2005] 1 Cr. App. R. (S.) 61, CA (Crim Div) . . . . *Digested*, 04/**336:**
Attorney General's Reference (Nos.54, 55 and 56 of 2004), Re [2004] EWCA Crim 2062; [2005] 1 Cr. App. R. (S.) 78, CA (Crim Div) . . . . *Digested*, 04/**346:**
Attorney General's Reference (No.59 of 2004), Re; *sub nom* R. v. Pound (Guy); R. v. Green (Anthony); R. v. Beard (Peter); Attorney General's Reference (No.60 of 2004), Re; Attorney General's Reference (No.61 of 2004), Re [2004] EWCA Crim 2488, CA (Crim Div) . . . . *Digested*, 05/**361**
Attorney General's Reference (No.60 of 2004), Re see Attorney General's Reference (No.59 of 2004), Re
Attorney General's Reference (No.61 of 2004), Re see Attorney General's Reference (No.59 of 2004), Re
Attorney General's Reference (No.64 of 2004), Re [2004] EWCA Crim 2618; [2005] 1 Cr. App. R. (S.) 107, CA (Crim Div) . . . . *Digested*, 05/**367**
Attorney General's Reference (Nos.74 and 75 of 2004), Re; *sub nom* R. v. Scott (Mark Raymond); R. v. Holmes (Anthony James) [2005] EWCA Crim 262, CA (Crim Div) . . . . *Digested*, 05/**374:**
Attorney General's Reference (No.76 of 2004), Re; *sub nom* R. v. B (Colin) [2004] EWCA Crim 2310, CA (Crim Div) . . . . *Digested*, 05/**374**
Attorney General's Reference (No.77 of 2004), Re [2004] EWCA Crim 2464, CA (Crim Div) *Digested*, 05/**362**
Attorney General's Reference (No.79 of 2004), Re; *sub nom* R. v. Husain (Syed); R. v. Hussain (Syed) [2004] EWCA Crim 2722; [2005] 1 Cr. App. R. (S.) 112, CA (Crim Div) . . . . *Digested*, 05/**364:**
Attorney General's Reference (No.81 of 2004), Re; *sub nom* R. v. Thompson (Jaime Ian) [2004] EWCA Crim 3315; (2005) 149 S.J.L.B. 58, CA (Crim Div)
Attorney General's Reference (Nos.83 and 85 of 2004), Re; *sub nom* R. v. Gardner (Matthew); R. v. Afzal (Mohammed) [2005] EWCA Crim 1537; (2005) 149 S.J.L.B. 770, CA (Crim Div) . . . . *Digested*, 05/**375**
Attorney General's Reference (Nos.86, 87 and 88 of 2004), Re; *sub nom* R. v. Sellars (Dylan Brian); R. v. Broad (Simon Ronald); R. v. Matthews (Jamie Lee) [2005] EWCA Crim 527; [2005] 2 Cr. App. R. (S.) 91, CA (Crim Div) . . . . *Digested*, 05/**362:**
Attorney General's Reference (No.89 of 2004), Re; *sub nom* R. v. Cox (Earl Webster) [2004] EWCA Crim 3222; *Times*, January 10, 2005, CA (Crim Div) . . . . *Digested*, 05/**364**
Attorney General's Reference (No.90 of 2004), Re; *sub nom* R. v. Chambers (Stephen Paul) [2004] EWCA Crim 3285, CA (Crim Div) . . . . *Digested*, 05/**354**
Attorney General's Reference (No.92 of 2004), Re [2004] EWCA Crim 2823, CA (Crim Div) . . . . *Digested*, 05/**352**

Attorney General's Reference (No.96 of 2004), Re; *sub nom* R. *v.* Keenan (Martin Thomas) [2004] EWCA Crim 2853, CA (Crim Div) . . . .   *Digested,* 05/**3726**

Attorney General's Reference (No.97 of 2004), Re; *sub nom* R. *v.* FK [2004] EWCA Crim 2311, CA (Crim Div) . . . .   *Digested,* 05/**3641**

Attorney General's Reference (No.98 of 2004), Re; *sub nom* R. *v.* Meakin (Joel) [2004] EWCA Crim 2769; [2005] 1 Cr. App. R. (S.) 125, CA (Crim Div) . . . .   *Digested,* 05/**3777**

Attorney General's Reference (Nos.99, 100, 101 and 102 of 2004), Re; *sub nom* R. *v.* Whiteway (Jules Devere); R. *v.* Nadarajah (Milroy); R. *v.* Long (James); R. *v.* Connell (Tom) [2005] EWCA Crim 294; [2005] 2 Cr. App. R. (S.) 82, CA (Crim Div) . . . .   *Digested,* 05/**3750**

Attorney General's Reference (No.104 of 2004), Re; *sub nom* R. *v.* Garvey (Wayne) [2004] EWCA Crim 2672; [2005] 1 Cr. App. R. (S.) 117; [2005] Crim. L.R. 150; (2004) 148 S.J.L.B. 1283; *Times,* October 29, 2004; *Independent,* December 16, 2004, CA (Crim Div) . . . .   *Digested,* 04/**3285**: *Followed,* 05/3532

Attorney General's Reference (No.105 of 2004), Re; *sub nom* R. *v.* H [2004] EWCA Crim 3295; [2005] 2 Cr. App. R. (S.) 42, CA (Crim Div) . . . .   *Digested,* 05/**3562**

Attorney General's Reference (No.106 of 2004), Re; *sub nom* R. *v.* Kabir (Shahajan) [2004] EWCA Crim 2751; [2005] 1 Cr. App. R. (S.) 120; [2005] Crim. L.R. 156, CA (Crim Div) . . . .   *Digested,* 05/**3677**

Attorney General's Reference (No. 112 of 2004), Re; *sub nom* R. *v.* Yemm (Andrew Neil) [2005] EWCA Crim 961, CA (Crim Div) . . . .   *Digested,* 05/**3558**

Attorney General's Reference (No.113 of 2004), Re; *sub nom* R. *v.* Follows (Dean John) [2004] EWCA Crim 3209, CA (Crim Div). . . . .   *Digested,* 05/**3731**

Attorney General's Reference (No.114 of 2004), Re; *sub nom* R. *v.* McDowell (Steven) [2004] EWCA Crim 2954; [2005] 2 Cr. App. R. (S.) 6; [2005] Crim. L.R. 142; (2004) 148 S.J.L.B. 1316, CA (Crim Div) . . . .   *Digested,* 05/**3608**

Attorney General's Reference (Nos.115 and 116 of 2004), Re; *sub nom* R. *v.* Hiscock (Christopher); R. *v.* Coombes (Jeffrey Ian) [2004] EWCA Crim 3487, CA (Crim Div) . . . .   *Digested,* 05/**3699**

Attorney General's Reference (No.118 of 2004), Re; *sub nom* R. *v.* Barrett (Michael) [2004] EWCA Crim 3220; [2005] 2 Cr. App. R. (S.) 18; (2005) 169 J.P. 51; (2005) 169 J.P.N. 98; *Times,* November 29, 2004, CA (Crim Div) . . . .   *Digested,* 05/**3583**

Attorney General's Reference (No.119 of 2004), Re; *sub nom* R. *v.* Jackson (Leanna) [2005] EWCA Crim 69; [2005] 2 Cr. App. R. (S.) 52, CA (Crim Div) . . . .   *Digested,* 05/**3620**

Attorney General's Reference (Nos.120 and 121 of 2004), Re; *sub nom* R. *v.* Herbert (Stephen Ronald); R. *v.* Beard (Gary Colin) [2005] EWCA Crim 890, CA (Crim Div) . . . .   *Digested,* 05/**3609**

Attorney General's Reference (No.122 and 123 of 2004), Re; *sub nom* R. *v.* Eyre (Nathan Oliver); R. *v.* Hawthorne (Raymond Colin) [2005] EWCA Crim 1059, CA (Crim Div) . . . .   *Digested,* 05/**3655**   *Digested,* 05/**3715**

Attorney General's Reference (No.125 of 2004), Re [2005] EWCA Crim 259, CA (Crim Div)

Attorney General's Reference (No.126 of 2004), Re; *sub nom* R. *v.* Portillo (Jose) [2004] EWCA Crim 3218; [2005] 2 Cr. App. R. (S.) 20, CA (Crim Div) . . . .   *Digested,* 05/**3728**

Attorney General's Reference (No.127 of 2004), Re; *sub nom* R. *v.* Briggs (David Michael) [2005] EWCA Crim 257; [2005] 2 Cr. App. R. (S.) 74, CA (Crim Div) .   *Digested,* 05/**3644**

Attorney General's Reference (No.128 of 2004), Re; *sub nom* R. *v.* Holness (Peter Phillip) [2004] EWCA Crim 3066; [2005] 2 Cr. App. R. (S.) 17, CA (Crim Div) . . . .   *Digested,* 05/**3532**

Attorney General's Reference (No.129 of 2004), Re; *sub nom* R. *v.* Ssan (Archit) [2005] EWCA Crim 363, CA (Crim Div) . . . .   *Digested,* 05/**3537**

Attorney General's Reference (No.130 of 2004), Re; *sub nom* R. *v.* Thornhill (Leigh James) [2005] EWCA Crim 278; [2005] 2 Cr. App. R. (S.) 75, CA (Crim Div) . .   *Digested,* 05/**3676**

Attorney General's Reference (No.131 of 2004), Re; *sub nom* R. *v.* Goad (William Alexander) [2005] EWCA Crim 16; (2005) 149 S.J.L.B. 112, CA (Crim Div) . . . .   *Digested,* 05/**3542**

Attorney General's Reference (Nos.132 and 133 of 2004), Re; *sub nom* R. *v.* Burden (Sarah); R. *v.* Hill (Debra) [2005] EWCA Crim 354; *Times,* March 21, 2005, CA (Crim Div) . . . .   *Digested,* 05/**3755**

Attorney General's Reference (No.134 of 2004), Re; *sub nom* R. Roberts (Michael John) [2004] EWCA Crim 3286; [2005] 2 Cr. App. R. (S.) 47; [2005] Crim. L.R. 321, CA (Crim Div) . . . .   *Digested,* 05/**3665**

Attorney General's Reference (No.138 of 2004), Re; *sub nom* R. *v.* White (Shane) [2005] EWCA Crim 198, CA (Crim Div) . . . .   *Digested,* 05/**3757**

Attorney General's Reference (No.139 of 2004), Re; *sub nom* R. *v.* Worth (Duncan) [2005] EWCA Crim 749, CA (Crim Div) . . . .   *Digested,* 05/**3705**

Attorney General's Reference (No.141 of 2004), Re; *sub nom* R. *v.* Thomas (Kenneth Kince) [2005] EWCA Crim 653; [2005] 2 Cr. App. R. (S.) 94; (2005) 149 S.J.L.B. 299, CA (Crim Div) . . . .   *Digested,* 05/**3612**

Attorney General's Reference (No.142 of 2004), Re; *sub nom* R. *v.* G (Richard Shane) [2005] EWCA Crim 654, CA (Crim Div). . . . .   *Digested,* 05/**3643**

Attorney General's Reference (No.143 of 2004), Re; *sub nom* R. *v.* Hasan (Miriwan Ali) [2005] EWCA Crim 506, CA (Crim Div) . . . .   *Digested,* 05/**3720**

Attorney General's Reference (Nos.144 and 145 of 2004), Re; *sub nom* R. *v.* Johnston (George); R. *v.* McShefferty (Jason) [2005] EWCA Crim 280; [2005] 2 Cr. App. R. (S.) 77, CA (Crim Div) . . . .   *Digested,* 05/**3724**

Attorney General's Reference (No.146 of 2004), Re [2005] EWCA Crim 246, CA (Crim Div) *Digested*, 05/**3769**
Attorney General's Reference (No.147 of 2004), Re; *sub nom* R. *v.* Chappell (Edwin
    John) [2005] EWCA Crim 845, CA (Crim Div) . . . . *Digested*, 05/**3533**
Attorney General's Reference (No.150 of 2004), Re [2005] EWCA Crim 680, CA (Crim Div) *Digested*, 05/**3739**
Attorney General's Reference (No.152 of 2004), Re; *sub nom* R. *v.* Packer (Peter) [2005]
    EWCA Crim 456; [2005] 2 Cr. App. R. (S.) 90, CA (Crim Div). . . . . *Digested*, 05/**3590**
Attorney General's Reference (No.154 of 2004), Re; *sub nom* R. *v.* Henry (Andrew John)
    [2005] EWCA Crim 455, CA (Crim Div). . . . . *Digested*, 05/**3729**
Attorney General's Reference (No.155 of 2004), Re; *sub nom* R. *v.* Martin (Deborah)
    [2005] EWCA Crim 968, CA (Crim Div) . . . . *Digested*, 05/**3759**
Attorney General's Reference (No.156 of 2004), Re; *sub nom* R. *v.* S (Christopher)
    [2005] EWCA Crim 724, CA (Crim Div). . . . . *Digested*, 05/**3637**
Attorney General's Reference (No.157 of 2004), Re; *sub nom* R. *v.* Green (Ryan Keith)
    [2005] EWCA Crim 537, CA (Crim Div). . . . . *Digested*, 05/**3546**
Attorney General's Reference (No.158 of 2004), Re; *sub nom* R. *v.* Ellis (Russell John)
    [2005] EWCA Crim 1588, CA (Crim Div) . . . . *Digested*, 05/**3554**
Attorney General's Reference (No.311 of 2004), Re; *sub nom* R. *v.* Dad (Arif Mahmood);
    R. *v.* Teale (Joseph Michael) [2005] EWCA Crim 1837, CA (Crim Div) . . . . *Digested*, 05/**3696**
Attorney General's Reference (Nos.3 and 4 of 2005), Re; *sub nom* R. *v.* Crawley
    (Alexander Steven); R. *v.* Llewellyn (David Stephen) [2005] EWCA Crim 574;
    [2005] 2 Cr. App. R. (S.) 98, CA (Crim Div) . . . . *Digested*, 05/**3667**
Attorney General's Reference (No.5 of 2005), Re; *sub nom* R. *v.* Orr (Robert Horatio)
    [2005] EWCA Crim 880, CA (Crim Div) . . . . *Digested*, 05/**3697**
Attorney General's Reference (No.6 of 2005), Re; *sub nom* R. *v.* N (James) [2005]
    EWCA Crim 844, CA (Crim Div) . . . . *Digested*, 05/**3639**
Attorney General's Reference (No.6 of 2005) (Unduly Lenient Sentence), Re; *sub nom* R.
    v. N (James) (Unduly Lenient Sentence) [2005] EWCA Crim 500, CA (Crim
    Div) . . . . *Digested*, 05/**3638**
Attorney General's Reference (No.8 of 2005), Re [2005] EWCA Crim 1002, CA (Crim Div) *Digested*, 05/**3716**
Attorney General's Reference (No.9 of 2005), Re see Attorney General's Reference (No.9 of
    2004), Re
Attorney General's Reference (Nos.11 and 12 of 2005), Re; *sub nom* R. Matthews (David
    George); R. *v.* Lopez (Michael) [2005] EWCA Crim 450, CA (Crim Div) . . . . . . *Digested*, 05/**3551**
Attorney General's Reference (No.16 of 2005), Re; *sub nom* R. *v.* Wilson (Rebecca)
    [2005] EWCA Crim 1285, CA (Crim Div) . . . . *Digested*, 05/**3659**
Attorney General's Reference (No.20 of 2005), Re; *sub nom* R. *v.* May (Michael
    Anthony) [2005] EWCA Crim 1861, CA (Crim Div). . . . . *Digested*, 05/**3747**
Attorney General's Reference (No.21 of 2005), Re; *sub nom* R. *v.* Corriette (Jean-Yves)
    [2005] EWCA Crim 1675, CA (Crim Div) . . . . *Digested*, 05/**3587**
Attorney General's Reference (No.26 of 2005), Re [2005] EWCA Crim 1973, CA (Crim Div) *Digested*, 05/**3779**
Attorney General's Reference (Nos.27, 28, 29 and 30 of 2005), Re; *sub nom* R. *v.* Chellouj
    (Tariq); R. *v.* Kamel (Izem); R. *v.* Rouvier (Delphine); R. *v.* Smaine (Moumen)
    [2005] EWCA Crim 2081, CA (Crim Div) . . . . *Digested*, 05/**3605**
Attorney General's Reference (No.31 of 2005), Re; *sub nom* R. *v.* Keane (Michael)
    [2005] EWCA Crim 1589, CA (Crim Div) . . . . *Digested*, 05/**3762**
Attorney General's Reference (No.34 of 2005), Re; *sub nom* R. *v.* Whyte (Lincoln)
    [2005] EWCA Crim 1750, CA (Crim Div) . . . . *Digested*, 05/**3752**
Attorney General's Reference (No.38 of 2005), Re; *sub nom* R. *v.* Wilson (Daniel) [2005]
    EWCA Crim 1678, CA (Crim Div) . . . . *Digested*, 05/**3725**
Attorney General's Reference (Nos.39, 40 and 41 of 2005); *sub nom* R. *v.* Dale (Adam);
    R. *v.* Shearman (Peter); R. *v.* W [2005] EWCA Crim 1961, CA (Crim Div) . . . . . . *Digested*, 05/**3764**
Attorney General's Reference (No.42 of 2005), Re; *sub nom* R. *v.* Cameron (David)
    [2005] EWCA Crim 1722, CA (Crim Div) . . . . *Digested*, 05/**3700**
Attorney General's Reference (No.44 of 2005), Re; *sub nom* R. *v.* Guirdham (Daniel)
    [2005] EWCA Crim 2211, CA (Crim Div) . . . . *Digested*, 05/**3564**
Attorney General's Reference (No.46 of 2005), Re; *sub nom* R. *v.* Stephenson (Matthew
    John) [2005] EWCA Crim 2146, CA (Crim Div) . . . . *Digested*, 05/**3753**
Attorney General's Reference (No.54 of 2005), Re; *sub nom* R. *v.* Mann (Keith) [2005]
    EWCA Crim 1896, CA (Crim Div) . . . . *Digested*, 05/**3543**
Attorney General's Reference (No.66 of 2005), Re; *sub nom* R. *v.* Gormanly (Fraser)
    [2005] EWCA Crim 2445, CA (Crim Div) . . . . *Digested*, 05/**3732**
Attorney General's Reference (Nos.135, 136 and 137), Re; *sub nom* R. *v.* Dervishi
    (Markel); R. *v.* Sejdial (Gentian); R. *v.* Kalemi (Alban) [2005] EWCA Crim 468,
    CA (Crim Div) . . . . *Digested*, 05/**3727**
Attorney General's References (Nos.31, 42, 43, 44, 50 and 51 of 2004), Re see Attorney
    General's Reference (Nos.31, 42, 43, 45, 50 and 51 of 2003), Re
Audi AG *v.* Office for Harmonisation in the Internal Market (Trade Marks and Designs)
    (OHIM) (T16/02) [2003] E.C.R. II-5167; [2004] E.T.M.R. 59, CFI (2nd
    Chamber) . . . . *Digested*, 05/**2524**
Audit Commission for England and Wales *v.* Ealing LBC see R. (on the application of
    Ealing LBC) *v.* Audit Commission
Aujla *v.* Sanghera [2004] EWCA Civ 121; [2004] C.P. Rep. 31; (2004) 148 S.J.L.B.
    147, CA (Civ Div) . . . . *Digested*, 05/**491**

Austin v. Commissioner of Police of the Metropolis [2005] EWHC 480; [2005] H.R.L.R. 20; [2005] U.K.H.R.R. 1039; (2005) 155 N.L.J. 515; *Times*, April 14, 2005, QBD .... *Digested*, 05/**3339**

Austin v. Price (Inspector of Taxes) [2004] S.T.C. (S.C.D.) 487; [2004] S.T.I. 2071; (2004) 148 S.J.L.B. 1120, Sp Comm .... *Digested*, 05/**4130**

Austin Knight (UK) Ltd v. Hinds [1994] F.S.R. 52, Ch D .... *Digested*, 94/**1925**: *Considered*, 05/1208

Austin Rover Group Ltd v. HM Inspector of Factories; *sub nom* Mailer v. Austin Rover Group [1990] 1 A.C. 619; [1989] 3 W.L.R. 520; [1989] 2 All E.R. 1087; [1990] I.C.R. 133; [1989] I.R.L.R. 404; [1990] C.O.D. 35; (1989) 133 S.J. 1661, HL; affirming [1988] Crim. L.R. 752, DC .... *Digested*, 90/**2446**: *Considered*, 94/2280, 05/1955

Austintel Ltd, Re; Applications Pursuant to r.7.28 of the Insolvency Rules 1986, Re; Creditnet Ltd, Re; Debtor Management Ltd, Re [1997] 1 W.L.R. 616; [1997] B.C.C. 362; [1997] 1 B.C.L.C. 233; [2000] B.P.I.R. 223; (1996) 93(43) L.S.G. 26; (1996) 140 S.J.L.B. 254; *Times*, November 11, 1996; *Independent*, November 25, 1996 (C.S.), CA (Civ Div); affirming [1996] 1 W.L.R. 1291; [1996] B.C.C. 444; [1996] 2 B.C.L.C. 133; (1996) 146 N.L.J. 916; *Times*, May 22, 1996, Ch D .... *Digested*, 96/**3535**: *Considered*, 05/2313

Australian Mining & Smelting Europe Ltd v. Commission of the European Communities (155/79); *sub nom* AM&S Europe Ltd v. Commisson of the European Communities (155/79) [1983] Q.B. 878; [1983] 3 W.L.R. 17; [1983] 1 All E.R. 705; [1982] E.C.R. 1575; [1982] 2 C.M.L.R. 264; [1982] F.S.R. 474; (1983) 127 S.J. 410; *Times*, May 20, 1982, ECJ .... *Digested*, 83/**1593**: *Considered*, 04/496, 05/2586

Australian Mutual Provident Society v. National Mutual Life Association of Australasia Ltd [1995] 1 N.Z.L.R. 581, CA (NZ) .... *Followed*, 05/2667

Auto Lease Holland BV v. Bundesamt fur Finanzen (C185/01) [2005] S.T.C. 598; [2003] E.C.R. I-1317; [2005] B.T.C. 5151; [2005] B.V.C. 182; [2003] S.T.I. 202, ECJ (5th Chamber) [2003] E.C.R. I-1317, AGO .... *Digested*, 05/**4395**: *Considered*, 04/4021: *Distinguished*, 04/3992

Autocity Networks SA v. Het Parool BV (R544/2004-1) [2005] E.T.M.R. 117, OHIM (1st Bd App)

Autologic Holdings Plc v. Inland Revenue Commissioners; *sub nom* Test Claimants in Loss Relief Group Litigation v. Inland Revenue Commissioners; Loss Relief Group Litigation Order Claimants v. Inland Revenue Commissioners [2005] UKHL 54; [2005] 3 W.L.R. 339; [2005] 4 All E.R. 1141; [2005] S.T.C. 1357; [2005] 3 C.M.L.R. 2; [2005] B.T.C. 402; [2005] S.T.I. 1336; (2005) 155 N.L.J. 1277; *Times*, August 1, 2005, HL; reversing [2004] EWCA Civ 680; [2005] 1 W.L.R. 52; [2004] 3 All E.R. 957; [2004] S.T.C. 1054; [2004] 2 C.M.L.R. 60; [2004] Eu. L.R. 865; [2004] B.T.C. 255; 6 I.T.L. Rep. 1043; [2004] S.T.I. 1323; (2004) 148 S.J.L.B. 698, CA (Civ Div); reversing [2004] EWHC 358; [2004] S.T.C. 594; [2004] S.T.I. 557; (2004) 101(12) L.S.G. 37; *Times*, March 10, 2004, Ch D .... *Digested*, 05/**4056**

Automobili Lamborghini Holding SpA's Community Trade Mark Application (R772/2001-1) [2005] E.T.M.R. 43, OHIM (1st Bd App) .... *Digested*, 05/**2548**

AVECIA/Phosphoramidites (T713/02) [2005] E.P.O.R. 46, EPO (Technical Bd App)

Aveda Corp's Community Trade Mark Application [2005] E.T.M.R. 75, OHIM (1st Bd App) .... *Digested*, 05/**2528**

Avex Inc v. Office for Harmonisation in the Internal Market (Trade Marks and Designs) (OHIM) (T115/02) [2005] E.T.M.R. 30, CFI (2nd Chamber) .... *Digested*, 05/**2513**

Avonridge Property Co Ltd v. London Diocesan Fund see Avonridge Property Co Ltd v. Mashru

Avonridge Property Co Ltd v. Mashru; *sub nom* London Diocesan Fund v. Phithwa; Mashru v. Avonridge Property Co Ltd; Avonridge Property Co Ltd v. London Diocesan Fund; London Diocesan Fund v. Avonridge Property Co Ltd [2005] UKHL 70; [2005] 1 W.L.R. 3956; [2005] 49 E.G.C.S. 88; [2005] N.P.C. 138; *Times*, December 5, 2005, HL; reversing [2004] EWCA Civ 1306; [2005] 1 W.L.R. 236; [2005] 1 P. & C.R. 23; [2005] L. & T.R. 5; [2005] 1 E.G.L.R. 15; [2005] 05 E.G. 204; (2004) 148 S.J.L.B. 1217; [2005] 1 P. & C.R. DG9, CA (Civ Div) .... *Digested*, 05/**2665**

Awotona v. South Tyneside Healthcare NHS Trust; *sub nom* South Tyneside Healthcare NHS Trust v. Awotona [2005] EWCA Civ 217; [2005] I.C.R. 958, CA (Civ Div); reversing UKEAT/0599/03/SM, EAT .... *Digested*, 05/**1320**

Axa General Insurance Ltd v. Gottlieb; *sub nom* Gottleib v. Axa General Insurance Ltd [2005] EWCA Civ 112; [2005] 1 All E.R. (Comm) 445; [2005] 1 C.L.C. 62; [2005] Lloyd's Rep. I.R. 369; [2005] N.P.C. 20; *Times*, March 3, 2005, CA (Civ Div) .... *Digested*, 05/**2359**

Axion SA v. Office for Harmonisation in the Internal Market (Trade Marks and Designs) (OHIM) (T324/01) [2003] E.C.R. II-1897; [2005] E.T.M.R. 72; (2003) 26(8) I.P.D. 26050, CFI (4th Chamber) .... *Digested*, 05/**2506**

Ayaz v. Land Baden-Wurttemberg (C275/02) [2004] E.C.R. I-8765; [2005] 1 C.M.L.R. 50, ECJ (2nd Chamber) .... *Digested*, 05/**2204**

Aydinli *v.* Land Baden-Wurttemberg (C373/03) [2005] 3 C.M.L.R. 43, ECJ (5th Chamber)
Ayliffe *v.* DPP see R. *v.* Jones (Margaret)
Ayliffe *v.* DPP; Swain *v.* DPP; Percy *v.* DPP [2005] EWHC 684; [2005] 3 W.L.R. 628; [2005] 3 All E.R. 330; [2005] Crim. L.R. 959; [2005] A.C.D. 86, QBD (Admin) . . . . *Digested*, 05/**754**
AZ (Risk on Return) Ivory Coast CG, Re [2004] UKIAT 170, IAT . . . . *Considered*, 05/2166
Azinas *v.* Cyprus (56679/00) (2005) 40 E.H.R.R. 8, ECHR . . . . *Digested*, 05/**2030**
Aziz *v.* Cyprus (69949/01) (2005) 41 E.H.R.R. 11; 19 B.H.R.C. 510, ECHR . . . . *Digested*, 05/**2127**
Aziz *v.* Norman see Norman *v.* Ali (Limitation Period)
Aziz *v.* Yemen; *sub nom* Yemen *v.* Aziz [2005] EWCA Civ 745; [2005] I.C.R. 1391; *Times*, June 22, 2005; *Independent*, June 23, 2005, CA (Civ Div) . . . . *Digested*, 05/**495**

B, Re see R. (on the application of Hoxha) *v.* Special Adjudicator
B *v.* A [2005] Fam. Law 944, Fam Div
B *v.* B [2005] EWCA Civ 237; [2005] C.P. Rep. 30, CA (Civ Div) . . . . *Digested*, 05/**306**
B *v.* B (Divorce: Stay of Foreign Proceedings) [2002] EWHC 1711; [2003] 1 F.L.R. 1, Fam Div . . . . *Digested*, 03/**1554**: *Applied*, 05/1623
B *v.* B (Post Nuptial Settlements) (Pension Fund), Re see Brooks *v.* Brooks
B *v.* B (Residence: Condition Limiting Geographic Area) [2004] 2 F.L.R. 979; [2004] Fam. Law 651, Fam Div . . . . *Digested*, 05/**1576**
B *v.* BAA Plc [2005] I.C.R. 1530; [2005] I.R.L.R. 927, EAT . . . . *Digested*, 05/**1335**
B *v.* Birmingham City Council see A (Adoption: Placement Outside Jurisdiction), Re
B *v.* Chief Constable of Avon and Somerset [2001] 1 W.L.R. 340; [2001] 1 All E.R. 562, DC . . . . *Digested*, 01/**87**:
          Applied, 01/10, 02/1579: *Considered*, 05/829: *Distinguished*, 04/1458
B *v.* O (Residence Orders: Parental Contact) see H (Agreed Joint Residence: Mediation), Re
B *v.* R see R (A Child) (IVF: Paternity of Child), Re
B *v.* Secretary of State for the Home Department see R. (on the application of Hoxha) *v.* Special Adjudicator
B *v.* Secretary of State for the Home Department [2003] UKIAT 20; [2003] Imm. A.R. 591, IAT . . . . *Considered*, 05/2178
B *v.* Secretary of State for the Home Department [2004] UKIAT 76, IAT . . . . *Not applied*, 05/322
B *v.* Secretary of State for the Home Department [2005] EWCA Civ 61; *Independent*, February 4, 2005, CA (Civ Div) . . . . *Digested*, 05/**2173**
B *v.* Secretary of State for Work and Pensions [2005] EWCA Civ 929; [2005] 1 W.L.R. 3796; *Times*, September 16, 2005, CA (Civ Div)
B *v.* United Kingdom (36536/02) [2005] 3 F.C.R. 353; 19 B.H.R.C. 430; [2005] Fam. Law 943; *Times*, October 5, 2005, ECHR
B (A Child) *v.* B (Unreported, November 9, 2004), CC (Maidstone) [*Ex rel.* Mathew Gullick, Barrister, 3 Paper Buildings, Temple, London] . . . . *Digested*, 05/**3232**
B (A Child) *v.* Barking and Dagenham LBC (Unreported, September 28, 2004), CC (Romford) [*Ex rel.* Joanna Kerr, Barrister, Lamb Chambers, Lamb Building, Temple, London] . . . . *Digested*, 05/**3184**
B (A Child) *v.* Barnickle (Unreported, February 9, 2004), CC (Coventry) [*Ex rel.* Stephen Garner, Barrister, No.8 Chambers, Fountain Court, Steelhouse Lane, Birmingham.] . . . . *Digested*, 05/**3131**
B (A Child) *v.* Botfield (Unreported, October 22, 2004), CC (Scunthorpe) [*Ex rel.* Martin & Haigh, Solicitors, 12-18 Frances Street, Scunthorpe, North Lincolnshire] . . . . *Digested*, 05/**3221**
B (A Child) *v.* Carter (Unreported, July 6, 2004), CC (Romford) [*Ex rel.* Gurion Taussig, Barrister, 199 Strand, London] . . . . *Digested*, 05/**3204**
B (A Child) *v.* DPP [2000] 2 A.C. 428; [2000] 2 W.L.R. 452; [2000] 1 All E.R. 833; [2000] 2 Cr. App. R. 65; [2000] Crim. L.R. 403; (2000) 97(11) L.S.G. 36; (2000) 144 S.J.L.B. 108; *Times*, February 25, 2000; *Independent*, April 10, 2000 (C.S.), HL; reversing [1999] 3 W.L.R. 116; [1998] 4 All E.R. 265; [1999] 1 Cr. App. R. 163; (1998) 148 N.L.J. 1177, DC . . . . *Digested*, 00/**1002**:
          Applied, 00/5063, 01/1070: *Considered*, 04/751: *Followed*, 05/758
B (A Child) *v.* Evans (Unreported, June 28, 2002), CC (Telford) [*Ex rel.* Stephen Garner, Barrister, No.8 Chambers, Fountain Court, Steelhouse Lane, Birmingham.] . . . . *Digested*, 03/**3296**:
          Considered, 05/3116
B (A Child) *v.* Galway (Unreported, July 5, 2004), CC (Croydon) [*Ex rel.* Mathew Gullick, Barrister, 3, Paper Buildings, Temple, London] . . . . *Digested*, 05/**3231**
B (A Child) *v.* Munda (Unreported, September 8, 2004), CC (Birmingham) [*Ex rel.* Stephen Garner, Barrister, No.8 Chambers, Fountain Court, Steelhouse Lane, Birmingham.] . . . . *Digested*, 05/**3117**
B (A Child) *v.* Naik (Unreported, June 23, 2004), CC (Central London) [*Ex rel.* Joanna Kerr, Barrister, Lamb Chambers, Lamb Building, Temple, London] . . . . *Digested*, 05/**3108**
B (A Child) *v.* Ostermeyer (Unreported, July 29, 2004), CC (Basildon) [*Ex rel.* Joanna Kerr, Barrister, Lamb Chambers, Lamb Building, Temple, London] . . . . *Digested*, 05/**3219**

B (A Child) v. Patel [2005] 2 Q.R. 16; [2004] 6 Q.R. 8, CC (Wolverhampton) [*Ex rel.* Stephen Garner, Barrister, No.8 Chambers, Fountain Court, Steelhouse Lane, Birmingham.] . . . . *Digested,* 04/**2901**
B (A Child) (Non-Accidental Injury: Compelling Medical Evidence), Re see O and N (Children) (Non-Accidental Injury: Burden of Proof), Re
B (A Child) (Serious Injury: Standard of Proof), Re see U (A Child) (Serious Injury: Standard of Proof), Re
B (A Minor), Re see V-B (Abduction: Rights of Custody), Re
B (A Minor) (Wardship: Medical Treatment), Re [1981] 1 W.L.R.1421; 80 L.G.R.107; 125 S.J. 608, CA (Civ Div) . . . . *Digested,* 81/**1790**:
                     Applied, 00/3247: *Considered,* 82/3117, 90/3197, 91/2588, 05/1794:
                                                  Referred to, 00/3246
B (A Patient) (Court of Protection: Appeal), Re; *sub nom* MB (A Patient) (Court of Protection: Appeal), Re [2005] EWCA Civ 1293; (2005) 155 N.L.J. 1714; (2005) 149 S.J.L.B. 1351; *Times,* November 10, 2005; *Independent,* November 15, 2005, CA (Civ Div)
B (Appeal: Lack of Reasons), Re [2003] EWCA Civ 881; [2003] 2 F.L.R. 1035; [2003] Fam. Law 716, CA (Civ Div) . . . . *Applied,* 05/1533
B (Children), Re see O and N (Children) (Non-Accidental Injury: Burden of Proof), Re
B (Children), Re [2005] EWCA Civ 779; [2005] 4 Costs L.R. 675; *Times,* June 8, 2005, CA (Civ Div)
B (Children) (Adoption: Removal from Jurisdiction), Re see A (Adoption: Placement Outside Jurisdiction), Re
B (Children) (Leave to Remove: Impact of Refusal), Re; *sub nom* B (Children) (Parental Contact: Relocation), Re; B (Children) (Termination of Contact), Re [2004] EWCA Civ 956; [2005] 2 F.L.R. 239; [2005] 1 F.C.R. 480; [2005] Fam. Law 462, CA (Civ Div) . . . . *Digested,* 05/**1572**:
                                                  Considered, 05/1574
B (Children) (Parental Contact: Relocation), Re see B (Children) (Leave to Remove: Impact of Refusal), Re
B (Children) (Termination of Contact), Re see B (Children) (Leave to Remove: Impact of Refusal), Re
B (Minors) (Care: Contact: Local Authority's Plans), Re see B (Minors) (Termination of Contact: Paramount Consideration), Re
B (Minors) (Care Proceedings: Practice), Re; *sub nom* CB and JB (Minors) (Care Proceedings: Guidelines), Re [1999] 1 W.L.R. 238; [1998] 2 F.L.R. 211; [1998] 2 F.C.R. 313; [1998] Fam. Law 454; *Times,* May 13, 1998, Fam Div . . . . *Digested,* 98/**2401**:
                         Applied, 03/1517: *Considered,* 05/1559: *Followed,* 99/2358
B (Minors) (Contact), Re [1994] 2 F.L.R. 1; [1994] 2 F.C.R. 812; [1994] Fam. Law 491; *Independent,* February 7, 1994 (C.S.), CA (Civ Div) . . . . *Digested,* 95/**3491**:
                                          Considered, 96/497, 05/1679
B (Minors) (Termination of Contact: Paramount Consideration), Re; *sub nom* B (Minors) (Care: Contact: Local Authority's Plans), Re [1993] Fam. 301; [1993] 3 W.L.R. 63; [1993] 3 All E.R. 542; [1993] 1 F.L.R. 543; [1993] 1 F.C.R. 363; 91 L.G.R. 311; [1993] Fam. Law 291; (1993) 137 S.J.L.B. 13; *Times,* December 31, 1992, CA (Civ Div) . . . . *Digested,* 93/**2771**:
              Applied, 94/3094, 94/3120, 95/3363, 95/3391, 95/3394, 95/3398,
                    95/3421, 95/3514, 05/1566: *Considered,* 95/3389, 95/3395, 95/3396,
                                            95/3554, 96/482, 97/364
Baars v. Netherlands (44320/98) (2004) 39 E.H.R.R. 25, ECHR . . . . *Considered,* 05/2090
Babar v. Anis [2005] EWHC 1384; [2005] 3 F.C.R. 216, Ch D . . . . *Digested,* 05/**3423**
Babcock FATA Ltd v. Addison see Addison v. Babcock FATA Ltd
Babcock International Ltd v. National Grid Co Plc see Fairchild v. Glenhaven Funeral Services Ltd (t/a GH Dovener & Son)
Bacardi France SAS (formerly Bacardi-Martini SAS) v. Television Francaise 1 SA (TF1) (C429/02) [2004] E.C.R. I-6613; [2004] 3 C.M.L.R. 2, ECJ . . . . *Digested,* 05/**1463**
Baccini v. Celador Productions Ltd see Celador Productions Ltd v. Melville
Baccus Srl v. Servicio Nacional del Trigo [1957] 1 Q.B. 438; [1956] 3 W.L.R. 948; [1956] 3 All E.R. 715; [1956] 2 Lloyd's Rep. 448; 100 S.J. 872, CA . . . . *Digested,* 56/**6979**:
                            Applied, 98/2233, 05/495: *Considered,* 71/6115, 72/1824
Bachmaier v. Austria (Admissibility) (77413/01) (2005) 40 E.H.R.R. SE17, ECHR
Bachmann v. Belgium (C204/90); *sub nom* Insurance Premiums, Re (C204/90) [1994] S.T.C. 855; [1992] E.C.R. I-249; [1993] 1 C.M.L.R. 785, ECJ [1992] E.C.R. I-249, AGO . . . . *Digested,* 92/**4805**:
                  Applied, 95/2773, 98/4517, 03/1447, 05/4034: *Considered,* 05/4134:
                                            Distinguished, 03/4226
Back v. Finland (37598/97) (2005) 40 E.H.R.R. 48; [2005] B.P.I.R. 1, ECHR
Bactria Industriehygiene-Service Verwaltungs GmbH v. Commission of the European Communities (C258/02 P) [2003] E.C.R. I-15105; [2004] 2 C.M.L.R. 42, ECJ (5th Chamber) . . . . *Digested,* 05/**1444**
Badeck's Application (C158/97), Re [2000] All E.R. (EC) 289; [2000] E.C.R. I-1875; [2001] 2 C.M.L.R. 6; [2000] C.E.C. 218; [2000] I.R.L.R. 432; *Times,* March 31, 2000, ECJ . . . . *Digested,* 00/**2171**:
                            Considered, 00/2170: *Followed,* 05/1269

Baden v. Societe Generale pour Favoriser le Developpement du Commerce et de
l'Industrie en France SA [1993] 1 W.L.R. 509; [1992] 4 All E.R. 161, Ch D . . . . . *Digested*, 92/**214**:
Considered, 90/1993, 99/2217, 00/2315, 05/261: *Followed*, 94/558
Badger v. Ministry of Defence [2005] EWHC 2941; *Times*, December 30, 2005, QBD
BAE YOUN SOO/Postponement of decision (T1184/03) [2005] E.P.O.R. 50, EPO
(Technical Bd App)
Baggott v. Asda Stores Ltd (Unreported, February 6, 2004), CC (Stourbridge) [*Ex rel.*
Alastair Smail, Barrister, St Philips Chambers, 55 Temple Row, Birmingham] . . . . *Digested*, 05/**3192**
Bagley v. Phillips (Unreported, October 29, 2004), CC (Birkenhead) [*Ex rel.* Justin
Valentine, Barrister, Atlantic Chambers, 4-6 Cook Street, Liverpool] . . . . *Digested*, 05/**3135**
Bailey v. Home Office see Home Office v. Bailey
Bailey v. Warren B3/2005/0798/PTA+A, B3/2005/0798(A)FC3, CA (Civ Div);
affirming [2005] P.I.Q.R. P15, QBD . . . . *Digested*, 05/**473**
Baines v. Army Prosecuting Authority [2005] EWHC 1399; (2005) 155 N.L.J. 1207,
QBD (Admin)
Baines & Ernst Ltd v. Customs and Excise Commissioners; *sub nom* Baines & Ernst Ltd
v. Revenue and Customs Commissioners [2005] EWHC 2300; [2005] B.T.C.
5785; [2005] S.T.I. 1775, Ch D; reversing [2004] S.T.I. 2572, V&DTr
(Manchester)
Baines & Ernst Ltd v. Revenue and Customs Commissioners see Baines & Ernst Ltd v.
Customs and Excise Commissioners
Baird v. Thurrock BC [2005] EWCA Civ 1499; *Times*, November 15, 2005, CA (Civ
Div)
Bairstow Eves London Central Ltd v. Smith [2004] EWHC 263; [2004] 2 E.G.L.R. 25;
[2004] 29 E.G. 118, QBD. . . . . *Digested*, 05/**721**
Baker v. Potter [2004] EWHC 1422; [2005] B.C.C. 855, Ch D (Companies Ct)
Baker & Davies Plc v. Leslie Wilks Associates [2005] EWHC 1179; [2005] 3 All E.R.
603; [2005] B.L.R. 425; 101 Con. L.R. 82; *Times*, August 16, 2005, QBD
(TCC)
Baker Refractories Ltd v. Bishop see Barber v. Somerset CC
Bakewell Management Ltd; *sub nom* Brandwood v. Bakewell Management Ltd [2004]
UKHL 14; [2004] 2 A.C. 519; [2004] 2 W.L.R. 955; [2004] 2 All E.R. 305;
[2004] R.T.R. 26; [2005] 1 P. & C.R. 1; [2004] 2 E.G.L.R. 15; [2004] 20 E.G.
168; [2004] 15 E.G.C.S. 104; (2004) 101(18) L.S.G. 34; (2004) 154 N.L.J.
553; (2004) 148 S.J.L.B. 418; [2004] N.P.C. 53; [2004] 2 P. & C.R. DG6;
Times, April 2, 2004; *Independent*, April 6, 2004, HL; reversing [2003] EWCA
Civ 23; [2003] 1 W.L.R. 1429; [2003] R.T.R. 30; [2003] 1 P. & C.R. 27; [2003]
1 E.G.L.R. 17; [2003] 09 E.G. 198; [2003] 6 E.G.C.S. 146; (2003) 100(11)
L.S.G. 33; [2003] N.P.C. 12; [2003] 1 P. & C.R. DG22; *Times*, February 5, 2003;
Independent, February 7, 2003, CA (Civ Div); affirming [2002] EWHC 472;
[2003] J.P.L. 75; [2002] 14 E.G.C.S. 124; (2002) 99(19) L.S.G. 30; (2002) 146
S.J.L.B. 102; *Times*, April 19, 2002, Ch D . . . . *Digested*, 04/**3224**:
Followed, 05/3404
Bakranich v. Robertson (2004-05) 7 I.T.E.L.R. 609, Sup Ct (WA) (Sgl judge). . . . . *Digested*, 05/**3975**
Balabel v. Air India [1988] Ch. 317; [1988] 2 W.L.R. 1036; [1988] 2 All E.R. 246;
[1988] E.G.C.S. 38; (1988) 138 N.L.J. Rep. 85; (1988) 132 S.J. 699, CA (Civ
Div); reversing *Daily Telegraph*, February 8, 1988, Ch D . . . . *Digested*, 88/**1594**:
Applied, 89/1932, 95/4114, 01/399: *Approved*, 05/299:
Considered, 90/3666.a, 94/1027, 99/879, 04/257: *Followed*, 98/355
Baldinger v. Pensionsversicherungsanstalt der Arbeiter (C386/02) [2005] 1 C.M.L.R.
20; [2005] C.E.C. 349, ECJ (2nd Chamber) . . . . *Digested*, 05/**1455**
Baldock v. Webster [2004] EWCA Civ 1869; [2005] 3 All E.R. 655; (2005) 102(7)
L.S.G. 27; *Times*, January 13, 2005, CA (Civ Div) . . . . *Digested*, 05/**36**
Balendran v. Law Society (No.2) [2004] EWHC 495; [2004] B.P.I.R. 859, Ch D . . . . . *Digested*, 05/**2284**
Balfour Beatty Construction Ltd v. Lambeth LBC [2002] EWHC 597; [2002] B.L.R.
288; [2002] T.C.L.R. 25; 84 Con. L.R. 1; (2002) 18 Const. L.J. 405, QBD
(TCC) . . . . *Digested*, 02/**662**:
Applied, 05/644
BALI Trade Mark (No.1) see Berlei (UK) Ltd v. Bali Brassiere Co Inc (No.1)
Ball v. Druces & Attlee (A Firm) (No.2) [2004] EWHC 1402; [2004] P.N.L.R. 39,
QBD . . . . *Digested*, 05/**2877**
Ball v. Street [2005] EWCA Civ 76; [2005] P.I.Q.R. P22, CA (Civ Div) . . . . *Digested*, 05/**1960**
Ballast Plc (In Administration), Re [2004] EWHC 2356; [2005] 1 W.L.R. 1928; [2005] 1 All
E.R. 630; [2005] B.C.C. 96; [2005] 1 B.C.L.C. 446; (2004) 101(44) L.S.G. 33;
Times, October 28, 2004, Ch D (Companies Ct). . . . . *Digested*, 04/**2115**
Balmoral Ltd v. Revenue and Customs Commissioners [2005] S.T.I. 2041, V&DTr
Balogh v. St Albans Crown Court [1975] Q.B. 73; [1974] 3 W.L.R. 314; [1974] 3 All
E.R. 283; 118 S.J. 582, CA (Civ Div) . . . . *Digested*, 74/**2912**:
Applied, 76/2118, 92/3402: *Considered*, 78/432, 79/2119, 94/1003, 95/4660,
96/1564, 03/47, 05/847: *Distinguished*, 78/595.7, 79/406
Baltrusaitis v. Byrne (Officer of the Board) [2005] S.T.C. (S.C.D.) 188; [2005] S.T.I.
24, Sp Comm . . . . *Digested*, 05/**4108**
Balyan v. Pensions Ombudsman [2003] EWHC 1826; [2003] O.P.L.R. 387, Ch D . . . . *Digested*, 05/**3043**

Bamber *v.* Eaton; *sub nom* Osea Road Camp Sites Ltd, Re [2004] EWHC 2437; [2005] 1 W.L.R. 760; [2005] 1 All E.R. 820; (2004) 101(40) L.S.G. 28; *Times,* October 22, 2004, Ch D . . . . *Digested,* 05/**453**

Bambino Holdings Ltd *v.* Speed Investments Ltd see Speed Investments Ltd *v.* Formula One Holdings Ltd (No.2)

Bance Ltd's Licence of Right (Copyright) Application, Re [1996] R.P.C. 667, PO . . . . . *Digested,* 97/**1044**: *Considered,* 01/3854: *Distinguished,* 00/3579: *Followed,* 05/2436

Bangs *v.* Connex South Eastern Ltd; *sub nom* Connex South Eastern Ltd *v.* Bangs [2005] EWCA Civ 14; [2005] 2 All E.R. 316; [2005] I.C.R. 763; [2005] I.R.L.R. 389; (2005) 149 S.J.L.B. 148; *Times,* February 15, 2005, CA (Civ Div) . . . . *Digested,* 05/**1249**: *Previous proceedings,* 04/1241

Banham *v.* Scottish & Newcastle Plc (Unreported, April 23, 2004), CC (Leeds) [*Ex rel.* Tom Nossiter, Barrister, Park Lane Chambers, 19, Westgate, Leeds] . . . . *Digested,* 05/**3190**

Banjo *v.* Brent LBC [2005] EWCA Civ 292; [2005] 1 W.L.R. 2520; [2005] H.L.R. 32; [2005] 13 E.G.C.S. 134; [2005] N.P.C. 42; [2005] 2 P. & C.R. DG12; *Times,* March 29, 2005, CA (Civ Div) . . . . *Digested,* 05/**2690**

Bank Austria Trade Services Gesellschaft mbH *v.* Customs and Excise Commissioners [2001] S.T.I. 528, V&DTr . . . . *Followed,* 05/4376

Bank of Baroda *v.* Vysya Bank Ltd [1994] 2 Lloyd's Rep. 87; [1994] 3 Bank. L.R. 216, QBD (Comm) . . . . *Digested,* 95/**398**: *Applied,* 05/628: *Considered,* 04/554

Bank of Credit & Commerce Hong Kong Ltd *v.* Sonali Bank [1995] 1 Lloyd's Rep. 227; *Independent,* October 20, 1994, QBD (Comm) . . . . *Digested,* 96/**1082**: *Applied,* 05/628

Bank of Credit and Commerce International SA (In Liquidation) *v.* Al-Saud [1997] 6 Bank. L.R. 121; [1997] B.C.C. 63; [1997] 1 B.C.L.C. 457; (1996) 93(36) L.S.G. 35; (1996) 140 S.J.L.B. 209; *Times,* August 12, 1996, CA (Civ Div) . . . . *Digested,* 96/**3505**: *Applied,* 05/258

Bank of Credit and Commerce International SA (In Liquidation) (No.8), Re; *sub nom* Morris *v.* Rayners Enterprises Inc; Morris *v.* Agrichemicals Ltd [1998] A.C. 214; [1997] 3 W.L.R. 909; [1997] 4 All E.R. 568; [1998] Lloyd's Rep. Bank. 48; [1997] B.C.C. 965; [1998] 1 B.C.L.C. 68; [1998] B.P.I.R. 211; (1997) 94(44) L.S.G. 35; (1997) 147 N.L.J. 1653; (1997) 141 S.J.L.B. 229; *Times,* November 13, 1997, HL; affirming [1996] Ch. 245; [1996] 2 W.L.R. 631; [1996] 2 All E.R. 121; [1996] B.C.C. 204; [1996] 2 B.C.L.C. 254; (1996) 140 S.J.L.B. 36; *Times,* January 8, 1996, CA (Civ Div); affirming [1995] Ch. 46; [1994] 3 W.L.R. 911; [1994] 3 All E.R. 565; [1994] 1 B.C.L.C. 758; *Times,* March 22, 1994, Ch D . . . . *Digested,* 97/**3047**: *Applied,* 05/2339: *Considered,* 98/3314

Bank of Credit and Commerce International SA (In Liquidation) (No.9), Re; *sub nom* Morris *v.* Mahfouz; Mahfouz *v.* Morris; Bank of Credit and Commerce International SA (Overseas), Re [1994] 1 W.L.R. 708; [1994] 3 All E.R. 764; [1994] 2 B.C.L.C. 664; [1994] I.L.Pr. 300; *Times,* November 30, 1993, CA (Civ Div); reversing in part *Times,* August 11, 1993; *Independent,* September 20, 1993 (C.S.), Ch D . . . . *Digested,* 95/**2870**: *Approved,* 97/3045: *Considered,* 96/2673, 05/2301

Bank of Credit and Commerce International SA (In Liquidation) (No.15), Re see Morris *v.* Bank of India

Bank of Credit and Commerce International SA (Overseas), Re see Bank of Credit and Commerce International SA (In Liquidation) (No.9), Re

Bank of Credit and Commerce International (Overseas) Ltd *v.* Akindele; *sub nom* BCCI *v.* Chief Labode Onadimaki Akindele [2001] Ch. 437; [2000] 3 W.L.R. 1423; [2000] 4 All E.R. 221; [2000] Lloyd's Rep. Bank. 292; [2000] B.C.C. 968; [2000] W.T.L.R. 1049; (1999-2000) 2 I.T.E.L.R. 788; (2000) 97(26) L.S.G. 36; (2000) 150 N.L.J. 950; *Times,* June 22, 2000; *Independent,* June 29, 2000, CA (Civ Div); affirming [1999] B.C.C. 669, Ch D . . . . *Digested,* 00/**2315**: *Applied,* 03/529, 05/3444

Bank of India *v.* Morris see Morris *v.* Bank of India

Bank of Scotland *v.* A Ltd [2001] EWCA Civ 52; [2001] 1 W.L.R. 751; [2001] 3 All E.R. 58; [2001] 1 All E.R. (Comm) 1023; [2001] Lloyd's Rep. Bank. 73; (2000-01) 3 I.T.E.L.R. 503; (2001) 98(9) L.S.G. 41; (2001) 151 N.L.J. 102; (2001) 145 S.J.L.B. 21; *Times,* February 6, 2001; *Independent,* January 23, 2001, CA (Civ Div); affirming [2000] Lloyd's Rep. Bank. 271; [2001] C.P. Rep. 14; *Times,* July 18, 2000; *Independent,* July 31, 2000 (C.S.), Ch D . . . . *Digested,* 01/**370**: *Considered,* 03/1598, 05/261: *Distinguished,* 03/795

Bank of Scotland *v.* Bennett see Royal Bank of Scotland Plc *v.* Etridge (No.2)

Bank of Tokyo-Mitsubishi Ltd *v.* Baskan Gida Sanayi Ve Pazarlama AS [2004] EWHC 945; [2004] 2 Lloyd's Rep. 395; [2004] I.L.Pr. 26, Ch D . . . . *Digested,* 05/**607**

Bankovic *v.* Belgium (52207/99) 11 B.H.R.C. 435, ECHR . . . . *Digested,* 02/**2535**: *Applied,* 05/2065, 05/2129: *Considered,* 03/2162, 04/2008

Banks *v.* Ablex Ltd [2005] EWCA Civ 173; [2005] I.C.R. 819; [2005] I.R.L.R. 357; (2005) 149 S.J.L.B. 269; *Times,* March 21, 2005, CA (Civ Div)

Banks *v.* Goodfellow (1869-70) L.R. 5 Q.B. 549, QB . . . . *Applied,* 47-51/10956, 47-51/10958, 01/5165, 01/5167, 02/4328, 05/3971: *Considered,* 78/351.u

Banner Homes Holdings Ltd (formerly Banner Homes Group Plc) *v.* Luff Developments
Ltd (No.1) [2000] 2 All E.R. 117; [2000] 2 B.C.L.C. 269; [2000] W.T.L.R. 473;
(1999-2000) 2 I.T.E.L.R. 525; [2000] E.G.C.S. 15; (2000) 97(6) L.S.G. 35;
(2000) 97(6) L.S.G. 37; (2000) 144 S.J.L.B. 83; (2000) 79 P. & C.R. D29;
Times, February 17, 2000; *Independent*, February 11, 2000, CA (Civ Div) . . . . . .   *Digested*, 00/**2327**:
                                                                                              Considered, 05/**695**

Banner Homes Holdings Ltd (formerly Banner Homes Group Plc) *v.* Luff Developments
Ltd (No.2) [2000] Ch. 372; [2000] 2 W.L.R. 772, CA (Civ Div) . . . .   *Digested*, 00/**2317**:
                                                                                              Applied, 05/**3379**

Banque Bruxelles Lambert SA *v.* Zurich Insurance Co see Arab Bank Plc *v.* Zurich
Insurance Co
Banque Bruxelles Lambert SA (BBL) *v.* Belgium (C8/03) [2004] S.T.C. 1643; [2004]
E.C.R. I-10157; [2005] 1 C.M.L.R. 13; [2004] C.E.C. 485; [2004] S.T.I. 2256,
ECJ (1st Chamber) . . . . *Digested*, 05/**4412**
Banque de France *v.* Editions Catherine Audval [2005] E.C.C. 7, Cass (F); affirming
[2001] E.C.C. 20, C d'A (Paris)
Banque Sabbag SAL *v.* Hope see American Airlines Inc *v.* Hope
Barbelivien *v.* Agence Business [2005] E.C.C. 42, Cass (F)
Barber *v.* Crown Prosecution Service [2004] EWHC 2605; [2005] A.C.D. 20, QBD
(Admin)
Barber *v.* Guardian Royal Exchange Assurance Group (C262/88) [1991] 1 Q.B. 344;
[1991] 2 W.L.R. 72; [1990] 2 All E.R. 660; [1990] E.C.R. I-1889; [1990] 2
C.M.L.R. 513; [1990] I.C.R. 616; [1990] I.R.L.R. 240; [1990] 1 P.L.R. 103;
(1990) 140 N.L.J. 925; *Times*, May 18, 1990; *Independent*, May 23, 1990;
Financial Times, May 25, 1990; *Guardian*, July 12, 1990, ECJ . . . . *Digested*, 90/**1915**:
      Applied, 91/1636, 91/1669, 92/1979, 93/1751, 94/4820, 94/4824, 95/1997,
      95/1998, 95/2001, 98/2240, 98/4133, 01/2277, 01/2281, 02/1367, 02/3380,
      04/2799, 05/3000: *Cited*, 92/1940, 92/1968, 94/2013, 95/2095, 00/4382:
      Considered, 93/3060, 94/1982, 94/4814, 94/4821, 94/4822, 94/4826,
      95/2000, 95/2039, 95/2052, 96/2629, 96/4609, 97/5378, 01/4605,
      05/1257: *Followed*, 00/2159: *Referred to*, 97/2214, 97/3947
Barber *v.* Somerset CC; *sub nom* Jones *v.* Sandwell MBC; Hatton *v.* Sutherland;
Bishop *v.* Baker Refractories Ltd; Somerset CC *v.* Barber; Baker Refractories Ltd
v. Bishop; Sutherland *v.* Hatton; Sandwell MBC *v.* Jones [2004] UKHL 13;
[2004] 1 W.L.R. 1089; [2004] 2 All E.R. 385; [2004] I.C.R. 457; [2004]
I.R.L.R. 475; [2004] E.L.R. 199; [2004] P.I.Q.R. P31; (2004) 77 B.M.L.R. 219;
(2004) 101(18) L.S.G. 34; (2004) 148 S.J.L.B. 419; *Times*, April 5, 2004, HL;
reversing [2002] EWCA Civ 76; [2002] 2 All E.R. 1; [2002] I.C.R. 613; [2002]
I.R.L.R. 263; [2002] Emp. L.R. 288; [2002] P.I.Q.R. P21; (2002) 68 B.M.L.R.
115; (2002) 99(12) L.S.G. 34; (2002) 146 S.J.L.B. 43; *Times*, February 12,
2002; *Independent*, February 13, 2002; *Daily Telegraph*, February 14, 2002, CA
(Civ Div) . . . . *Digested*, 04/**2713**:
            Applied, 03/3134, 03/3135, 04/1194, 04/2860, 05/2883, 05/2884:
                                       Considered, 03/5830, 05/2883
Barca *v.* Mears [2004] EWHC 2170; [2005] 2 F.L.R. 1; [2005] B.P.I.R. 15; [2005]
Fam. Law 444; [2004] N.P.C. 141; [2005] 1 P. & C.R. DG7, Ch D . . . .   *Digested*, 05/**2272**
Barclays Bank Ltd *v.* Quistclose Investments Ltd; *sub nom* Quistclose Investments Ltd
v. Rolls Razor Ltd (In Voluntary Liquidation) [1970] A.C. 567; [1968] 3 W.L.R.
1097; [1968] 3 All E.R. 651; 112 S.J. 903, HL; affirming [1968] Ch. 540; [1968]
2 W.L.R. 478; [1968] 1 All E.R. 613; (1967) 118 N.L.J. 13; 112 S.J. 85; *Times*,
December 18, 1967, CA (Civ Div); reversing [1967] Ch. 910; [1967] 2 W.L.R.
1064; [1967] 1 All E.R. 864; 111 S.J. 190, Ch D . . . .   *Digested*, 68/**459**:
            Applied, 84/332, 87/345, 89/178, 94/489, 05/2325: *Considered*, 75/160,
                        79/153, 94/2098, 95/2938, 99/294, 00/437, 01/3835:
            Distinguished, 68/3706, 69/2281, 69/3367, 77/1205, 78/142, 95/4151,
                                                                      03/2427
Barclays Bank Plc *v.* Bean [2005] B.P.I.R. 563; [2004] 3 E.G.L.R. 71; [2004] 41 E.G.
152, Ch D . . . . *Digested*, 05/**3429**
Barclays Bank Plc *v.* Coleman see Royal Bank of Scotland Plc *v.* Etridge (No.2)
Barclays Bank Plc *v.* Harris see Royal Bank of Scotland Plc *v.* Etridge (No.2)
Barclays Bank Plc *v.* Kapur [1991] 2 A.C. 355; [1991] 2 W.L.R. 401; [1991] 1 All E.R.
646; [1991] I.C.R. 208; [1991] I.R.L.R. 136; *Times*, January 25, 1991;
Independent, February 6, 1991; *Financial Times*, January 30, 1991; *Guardian*,
January 31, 1991; *Daily Telegraph*, February 7, 1991, HL; affirming [1989] I.C.R.
753; [1989] I.R.L.R. 387; *Times*, July 5, 1989; *Independent*, July 10, 1989 (C.S.);
Financial Times, July 5, 1989; *Daily Telegraph*, August 24, 1989, CA (Civ Div);
reversing [1989] I.C.R. 142; [1989] I.R.L.R. 57; (1989) 86(5) L.S.G. 41; *Times*,
December 31, 1988; *Daily Telegraph*, January 23, 1989, EAT . . . .   *Digested*, 91/**1652**:
            Applied, 05/1232: *Considered*, 96/2583, 97/3602: *Distinguished*, 92/1962

Barclays Mercantile Business Finance Ltd *v.* Mawson (Inspector of Taxes); *sub nom* ABC Ltd *v.* M (Inspector of Taxes) [2004] UKHL 51; [2005] 1 A.C. 684; [2004] 3 W.L.R. 1383; [2005] 1 All E.R. 97; [2005] S.T.C. 1; 76 T.C. 446; [2004] B.T.C. 414; 7 I.T.L. Rep. 383; [2004] S.T.I. 2435; (2004) 154 N.L.J. 1830; (2004) 148 S.J.L.B. 1403; *Times*, November 27, 2004, HL; affirming [2002] EWCA Civ 1853; [2003] S.T.C. 66; [2003] B.T.C. 81; [2002] S.T.I. 1809; (2003) 100(9) L.S.G. 29; *Times*, December 27, 2002; *Independent*, December 18, 2002, CA (Civ Div); reversing [2002] EWHC 1527; [2002] S.T.C. 1068; [2002] B.T.C. 388; [2002] S.T.I. 1066; (2002) 99(38) L.S.G. 34; *Times*, August 26, 2002, Ch D; affirming [2002] S.T.C. (S.C.D.) 78; [2002] S.T.I. 47, Sp Comm . . . .   *Digested*, 05/**3988**:
         Followed, 05/4022

Barder *v.* Barder see Barder *v.* Caluori
Barder *v.* Caluori; *sub nom* Barder *v.* Barder [1988] A.C. 20; [1987] 2 W.L.R. 1350; [1987] 2 All E.R. 440; [1987] 2 F.L.R. 480; [1988] Fam. Law 18; (1987) 84 L.S.G. 2046; (1987) 137 N.L.J. 497; (1987) 131 S.J. 776, HL; reversing [1987] Fam. 24; [1986] 3 W.L.R. 145; [1986] 2 All E.R. 918; [1987] 1 F.L.R. 18; [1986] Fam. Law 331; (1986) 83 L.S.G. 1996; (1986) 136 N.L.J. 561; (1986) 130 S.J. 524, CA (Civ Div) . . . .   *Digested*, 87/**1746**:
   Applied, 92/2085, 95/2320, 95/2323, 96/2857, 04/1528, 05/1660, 05/1661:
   Considered, 94/2188, 96/2888, 97/2476, 99/370: *Distinguished*, 02/1681:
         Followed, 96/2868: *Referred to*, 95/2321

Baring Securities (Hong Kong) Ltd *v.* Inland Revenue Commissioner 7 I.T.L. Rep. 873, CFI (HK)
Barings Plc (No.6), Re see Secretary of State for Trade and Industry *v.* Baker (No.6)
Bark *v.* Hawley [2004] EWHC 144; [2005] P.N.L.R. 3, QBD
Barke *v.* Seetec Business Technology Centre Ltd [2005] EWCA Civ 578; [2005] I.C.R. 1373; [2005] I.R.L.R. 633; *Times*, May 26, 2005, CA (Civ Div) . . . .   *Digested*, 05/**1256**
Barker *v.* Corus (UK) Plc see Barker *v.* Saint Gobain Pipelines Plc
Barker *v.* Jones (Unreported, January 19, 2005), CC (Luton) [*Ex rel.* Adam Farrer, Barrister, 5, Fountain Court, Steelhouse Lane, Birmingham] . . . .   *Digested*, 05/**3202**
Barker *v.* Saint Gobain Pipelines Plc; *sub nom* Barker *v.* Corus (UK) Plc; Murray (Deceased) *v.* British Shipbuilders (Hydrodynamics) Ltd ; Patterson (Deceased) *v.* Smiths Dock Ltd; TNS, HL; reversing [2004] EWCA Civ 545; [2005] 3 All E.R. 661; [2004] P.I.Q.R. P34; (2004) 148 S.J.L.B. 570; *Independent*, May 12, 2004, CA (Civ Div) . . . .   *Digested*, 04/**2693**
Barkin Construction Ltd *v.* Re-Source America International Ltd see Re-Source America International Ltd *v.* Platt Site Services Ltd (Damages)
Barking and Dagenham LBC *v.* Home Charm Retail see Stoke on Trent City Council *v.* B&Q (Retail) Ltd
Barlow Clowes International Ltd (In Liquidation) *v.* Eurotrust International Ltd [2005] UKPC 37; [2005] W.T.L.R. 1453; (2005-06) 8 I.T.E.L.R. 347; (2005) 102(44) L.S.G. 32, PC (IoM)
Barlow Clowes International Ltd (In Liquidation) *v.* Vaughan; *sub nom* Vaughan *v.* Barlow Clowes International Ltd [1992] 4 All E.R. 22; [1992] B.C.L.C. 910; *Times*, March 6, 1992, CA (Civ Div) . . . .   *Digested*, 92/**2576**:
   Applied, 05/3444: *Considered*, 95/2210: *Distinguished*, 03/253
Barnes *v.* Addy (1873-74) L.R. 9 Ch. App. 244; (1874) 22 W.R. 505; (1874) 43 L.J. Ch. 513; (1874) 30 L.T. 4, CA in Chancery . . . .   *Applied*, 68/3706,
   69/3367, 78/242, 80/279, 92/2039, 05/522: *Considered*, 86/170:
         Distinguished, 66/11052, 98/4871
Barnes *v.* Taylor [2005] 3 Q.R. 10, CC (Birmingham) [*Ex rel.* Stephen Garner, Barrister, No.8 Chambers, Fountain Court, Steelhouse Lane, Birmingham.] . . . .   *Digested*, 05/**3175**
Barnes (Deceased), Re [1939] 1 K.B. 316, CA; affirming [1938] 2 K.B. 684, KBD . . . . .   *Applied*, 05/**4117**
Barnes (Inspector of Taxes) *v.* Hilton Main Construction Ltd [2005] EWCA Civ 1241, CA (Civ Div); affirming [2005] EWHC 1355; [2005] S.T.C. 1532; 77 T.C. 255; [2005] B.T.C. 568; [2005] S.T.I. 834, Ch D . . . .   *Digested*, 05/**4036**
Barnet LBC *v.* Simon Holdings [2005] P.A.D. 81, Planning Inspector
Barnet LBC *v.* Zerdin [2005] P.A.D. 32, Planning Inspector
Barnett *v.* Lambeth LBC see Kay *v.* Lambeth LBC
Barnicoat *v.* Knight; *sub nom* Barnicoat *v.* Knights [2004] EWHC 330; [2004] 2 B.C.L.C. 464, Ch D . . . .   *Digested*, 05/**537**
Barns *v.* Barns [2005] W.T.L.R. 1093, HC (Aus)
Barns (NE) Ltd *v.* Newcastle upon Tyne City Council see Newcastle upon Tyne City Council *v.* Barns (NE) Ltd
Barr's Settlement Trusts, Re see Abacus Trust Co (Isle of Man) Ltd *v.* Barr
Barraclough *v.* Brown [1897] A.C. 615, HL . . . .   *Applied*, 64/1813,
   82/1264, 82/2928, 84/2379, 87/2666, 98/281, 05/4056: *Considered*, 93/3391:
         Distinguished, 58/3343, 59/3260, 69/2896, 70/11
Barratt *v.* Ansell (t/a Woolf Seddon) see Arthur JS Hall & Co *v.* Simons
Barratt *v.* Woolf Seddon see Arthur JS Hall & Co *v.* Simons
Barrett *v.* Duckett [1995] B.C.C. 362; [1995] 1 B.C.L.C. 243; *Independent*, August 15, 1994 (C.S.), CA (Civ Div); reversing [1993] B.C.C. 778; [1995] 1 B.C.L.C. 73, Ch D . . . .   *Digested*, 96/**1033**:
   Considered, 05/392: *Not applied*, 03/5304

Barrett v. Tower Hamlets LBC see Tower Hamlets LBC v. Barrett
Barros Mattos Junior v. General Securities & Finance Co Ltd see Barros Mattos Junior
    v. MacDaniels Ltd
Barros Mattos Junior v. MacDaniels Ltd; *sub nom* Mattos Junior v. MacDaniels Ltd;
    Barros Mattos Junior v. General Securities & Finance Co Ltd [2004] EWHC
    1188; [2005] 1 W.L.R. 247; [2004] 3 All E.R. 299; [2004] 2 All E.R. (Comm)
    501; [2004] 2 Lloyd's Rep. 475, Ch D . . . . *Digested*, 04/**3264**
Barros Mattos Junior v. MacDaniels Ltd (Amendments) [2005] EWHC 1323; [2005]
    I.L.Pr. 45, Ch D . . . . *Digested*, 05/**448**
Barton v. DPP [2001] EWHC Admin 223; (2001) 165 J.P. 779; (2001) 165 J.P.N. 887,
    QBD (Admin) . . . . *Digested*, 02/**866**:
                                 Considered, 05/3742
Barton v. Investec Henderson Crosthwaite Securities Ltd [2003] I.C.R. 1205; [2003]
    I.R.L.R. 332; (2003) 100(22) L.S.G. 29; *Times*, April 16, 2003, EAT . . . . *Digested*, 03/**1271**:
                       Applied, 05/1292: *Approved*, 05/1221
Barton v. Morris [1985] 1 W.L.R. 1257; [1985] 2 All E.R. 1032; (1986) 51 P. & C.R. 84;
    (1986) 83 L.S.G. 118; *Times*, May 1, 1985, Ch D . . . . *Digested*, 85/**2944**:
                                 Distinguished, 05/2900
Barvis v. Secretary of State for the Environment (1971) 22 P. & C.R. 710, QBD . . . . *Digested*, 71/**11383**:
              Applied, 99/4171, 05/3243: *Considered*, 93/3827, 94/4326, 00/4415
Base Metal Trading Ltd v. Shamurin [2004] EWCA Civ 1316; [2005] 1 W.L.R. 1157;
    [2005] 1 All E.R. (Comm) 17; [2005] B.C.C. 325; [2005] 2 B.C.L.C. 171; [2004]
    2 C.L.C. 916; (2004) 148 S.J.L.B. 1281; *Times*, November 1, 2004, CA (Civ
    Div); affirming [2003] EWHC 2419; [2004] 1 All E.R. (Comm) 159; [2004]
    I.L.Pr. 5, QBD (Comm) . . . . *Digested*, 05/**615**
Base Metal Trading Ltd v. Shamurin (Application for Summary Judgment) [2002] C.L.C.
    322, QBD (Comm) . . . . *Digested*, 02/**620**:
                                    Approved, 05/615
Bashir v. Secretary of State for the Home Department [2004] EWCA Civ 696; [2004]
    I.N.L.R. 591; (2004) 101(23) L.S.G. 32, CA (Civ Div) . . . . *Digested*, 05/**2214**
Basic Trademark SA's Trade Mark Application [2005] R.P.C. 25; (2005) 102(36) L.S.G. 31,
    App Person . . . . *Digested*, 05/**2580**
Basildon DC v. Davis [2005] P.A.D. 28, Planning Inspector
Basildon DC v. Secretary of State for the Environment, Transport and the Regions
    [2001] J.P.L. 1184, QBD (Admin) . . . . *Digested*, 01/**4708**:
                              Considered, 03/3391, 05/3264
Basingstoke and Deane BC v. Host Group [1988] 1 W.L.R. 348; [1988] 1 All E.R. 824;
    (1988) 56 P. & C.R. 31; (1987) 284 E.G. 1587; (1988) 85(6) L.S.G. 37; (1988)
    132 S.J. 158; *Independent*, November 16, 1987, CA (Civ Div); reversing [1986] 2
    E.G.L.R. 107; (1986) 279 E.G. 505, Ch D . . . . *Digested*, 88/**2069**:
        Applied, 92/2722, 92/2730, 92/2739: *Approved*, 99/6325:
        Considered, 88/2074, 89/2183, 90/180, 90/2857, 90/2886, 91/203,
        91/2268, 91/2269, 92/2721, 92/2735, 92/2738, 92/2740, 93/2524,
        93/2531, 96/3805, 04/2495: *Explained*, 05/2667: *Referred to*, 90/2791
Basna v. Punjab National Bank see Bhogal v. Punjab National Bank
Bassett v. Bassett [2005] W.T.L.R. 51, Sup Ct (NSW) . . . . *Digested*, 05/**3978**
Batayav v. Secretary of State for the Home Department (No.1) [2003] EWCA Civ
    1489; [2004] I.N.L.R. 126; [2004] A.C.D. 5, CA (Civ Div) . . . . *Digested*, 04/**2047**:
                                   Applied, 05/2166
Bath and North East Somerset DC v. Mowlem Plc [2004] EWCA Civ 115; [2004] B.L.R.
    153; 100 Con. L.R. 1; (2004) 148 S.J.L.B. 265, CA (Civ Div)
Bath and North East Somerset DC v. Nicholson; *sub nom* Bath and North Somerset DC
    v. Nicholson [2002] 10 E.G.C.S. 156, Ch D . . . . *Applied*, 05/**3439**
Bathurst v. Scarborow; *sub nom* Bathurst v. Scarborough [2004] EWCA Civ 411;
    [2005] 1 P. & C.R. 4; (2004) 148 S.J.L.B. 420, CA (Civ Div). . . . . *Digested*, 05/**2900**
Batram v. Chapman [2005] 3 Q.R. 11, CC (Norwich) [*Ex rel.* Jackman Smith & Mulley,
    Solicitors, Oak House, Northgate Street, Ipswich, Suffolk] . . . . *Digested*, 05/**3199**
Batsford Estates (1983) Co Ltd v. Taylor [2005] EWCA Civ 489; [2005] 2 E.G.L.R. 12;
    [2005] 33 E.G. 68; [2005] 19 E.G.C.S. 174, CA (Civ Div)
Batt v. Highgate Private Hospital [2004] EWHC 707; [2005] P.I.Q.R. Q1, Ch D . . . . . . *Digested*, 04/**916**
Baumbast v. Secretary of State for the Home Department (C413/99) [2002] E.C.R. I-
    7091; [2002] 3 C.M.L.R. 23; [2003] I.C.R. 1347; [2003] I.N.L.R. 1; *Times*,
    October 8, 2002, ECJ [2002] E.C.R. I-7091, AGO . . . . *Digested*, 02/**2628**:
                    Distinguished, 05/3856: *Followed*, 05/2204
Baumgartner v. Baumgartner 164 C.L.R. 137, HC (Aus) . . . . *Applied*, 05/**4300**:
                                  Considered, 03/4479
Baumler (UK) Ltd, Re see Gerrard v. Koby
Bayer AG v. Commission of the European Communities (C2/01 P) see Bundesverband
    der Arzneimittel Importeure eV v. Bayer AG (C2/01 P)
Bayer AG v. Commission of the European Communities (T41/96) [2001] All E.R. (EC)
    1; [2000] E.C.R. II-3383; [2001] 4 C.M.L.R. 4; [2001] I.C.R. 735; (2002) 63
    B.M.L.R. 71; *Times*, February 9, 2001, CFI (5th Chamber) . . . . *Digested*, 01/**776**:
        Applied, 03/556, 04/487, 05/555: *Subsequent proceedings*, 04/494

Bayer AG *v.* Commission of the European Communities (T41/96 R) [1996] E.C.R. II-
381; [1996] 5 C.M.L.R. 290, CFI . . . . *Followed,* 05/550
Bayer AG *v.* Paranova A/S (C436/93) see Bristol Myers Squibb Co *v.* Paranova A/S
(C427/93)
Bayerische Hypo- und Vereinsbank AG *v.* Commission of the European Communities
(T56/02) [2004] 5 C.M.L.R. 29, CFI (5th Chamber) . . . . *Digested,* 05/**555**
Bayerische Motorenwerke AG *v.* Deenik (C63/97); *sub nom* BMW AG *v.* Deenik (C63/
97) [1999] All E.R. (EC) 235; [1999] E.C.R. I-905; [1999] 1 C.M.L.R. 1099;
[1999] C.E.C. 159; [1999] E.T.M.R. 339, ECJ [1999] E.C.R. I-905; [1998]
E.T.M.R. 348, AGO . . . . *Digested,* 99/**3554**
Applied, 05/2571: *Considered,* 99/3553: *Followed,* 01/4029, 04/2411
Baynton *v.* South West Trains Ltd [2005] I.C.R. 1730, EAT . . . . *Digested,* 05/**1229**
Bayoil SA, Re; *sub nom* Seawind Tankers Corp *v.* Bayoil SA [1999] 1 W.L.R. 147;
[1999] 1 All E.R. 374; [1999] 1 Lloyd's Rep. 211; [1998] B.C.C. 988; [1999] 1
B.C.L.C. 62; (1998) 142 S.J.L.B. 251; *Times,* October 12, 1998, CA (Civ Div) . . . *Digested,* 98/**3324**
Applied, 99/3351, 00/3486, 02/2723: *Considered,* 99/3254, 99/3350,
04/2180, 05/2346: *Subsequent proceedings,* 02/4101
Bazayeva *v.* Russia (57949/00) see Isayeva *v.* Russia (57947/00)
BCCI *v.* Chief Labode Onadimaki Akindele see Bank of Credit and Commerce
International (Overseas) Ltd *v.* Akindele
BCCI SA, Re see Malik *v.* Bank of Credit and Commerce International SA (In
Liquidation)
BCL Old Co Ltd *v.* Aventis SA (Application to Strike Out) [2005] CAT 1; [2005] Comp.
A.R. 470, CAT . . . . *Digested,* 05/**564**
BCL Old Co Ltd *v.* Aventis SA (Security for Costs) [2005] CAT 2; [2005] Comp. A.R.
485; [2005] E.C.C. 39, CAT . . . . *Digested,* 05/**560**
BD *v.* Secretary of State for the Home Department; *sub nom* BD (Application of SK
and DK) Croatia [2004] UKIAT 32; [2004] Imm. A.R. 226, IAT . . . . *Digested,* 05/**2215**:
Applied, 05/2208
BD (Application of SK and DK) Croatia see BD *v.* Secretary of State for the Home
Department
BE Studios Ltd *v.* Smith & Williamson Ltd [2005] EWHC 1506; [2005] B.T.C. 361;
[2005] S.T.I. 1260, Ch D . . . . *Digested,* 05/**2872**
BE Studios Ltd *v.* Smith & Williamson Ltd (Costs) [2005] EWHC 2730; *Times,*
December 16, 2005, Ch D
Beadle (Deceased), Re; *sub nom* Mayes *v.* Beadle [1974] 1 W.L.R. 417; [1974] 1 All
E.R. 493; (1973) 118 S.J. 170, Ch D . . . . *Digested,* 74/**4011**:
Approved, 05/3980
Beale *v.* United Kingdom (Admissibility) (16743/03) (2005) 40 E.H.R.R. SE6, ECHR
Beaney *v.* Ashford BC [2005] P.A.D. 59, Planning Inspector
Bearman (A Bankrupt), Re see Saunders (A Bankrupt), Re
Beary *v.* Pall Mall Investments [2005] EWCA Civ 415; [2005] P.N.L.R. 35, CA (Civ
Div); affirming [2004] EWHC 1608, Ch D . . . . *Digested,* 05/**2863**
Beaufort Developments (NI) Ltd *v.* Gilbert-Ash (NI) Ltd [1999] 1 A.C. 266; [1998] 2
W.L.R. 860; [1998] 2 All E.R. 778; [1998] N.I. 144; [1998] C.L.C. 830; 88
B.L.R. 1; 59 Con. L.R. 66; (1998) 14 Const. L.J. 280; [1998] E.G.C.S. 85;
(1998) 95(24) L.S.G. 33; (1998) 95(31) L.S.G. 34; (1998) 148 N.L.J. 869;
(1998) 142 S.J.L.B. 172; [1998] N.P.C. 91; [1998] N.P.C. 93; *Times,* June 8,
1998, HL (NI); reversing [1997] N.I. 142; 83 B.L.R. 1; (1997) 13 Const. L.J. 321,
CA (NI). . . . . *Digested,* 98/**5055**:
Applied, 00/815, 00/820: *Considered,* 02/5322, 05/656:
Distinguished, 02/5407: *Followed,* 99/792, 00/237
Beaulane Properties Ltd *v.* Palmer [2005] EWHC 817; [2005] 3 W.L.R. 554; [2005] 4
All E.R. 461; [2005] H.R.L.R. 19; [2005] 3 E.G.L.R. 85; [2005] 14 E.G.C.S.
129; [2005] 2 P. & C.R. DG13; *Times,* April 13, 2005, Ch D . . . . *Digested,* 05/**3376**
Beazley *v.* Horizon Offshore Contractors Inc [2004] EWHC 2555; [2005] I.L.Pr. 11;
[2005] Lloyd's Rep. I.R. 231, QBD (Comm) . . . . *Digested,* 05/**625**
Becheret Thierry *v.* Industrie Guido Malvestio SpA [2005] B.C.C. 974, C d'A
(Versailles)
Beck *v.* Ministry of Defence [2003] EWCA Civ 1043; [2005] 1 W.L.R. 2206; [2003]
C.P. Rep. 62; [2004] P.I.Q.R. P1; (2003) 100(31) L.S.G. 31; *Times,* July 21,
2003, CA (Civ Div) . . . . *Digested,* 03/**400**:
Explained, 05/296
Beck Peppiatt Ltd *v.* Norwest Holst Construction Ltd [2003] EWHC 822; [2003]
B.L.R. 316, QBD (TCC) . . . . *Digested,* 04/**652**:
Applied, 05/642: *Considered,* 04/588
Beckenham MC Ltd *v.* Centralex Ltd [2004] EWHC 1287; [2004] 2 B.C.L.C. 764;
[2004] B.P.I.R. 1112, Ch D . . . . *Digested,* 05/**2340**
Beckles *v.* United Kingdom (44652/98) (2003) 36 E.H.R.R. 13; 13 B.H.R.C. 522;
Times, October 15, 2002, ECHR . . . . *Digested,* 02/**2461**:
Applied, 05/927: *Subsequent proceedings,* 05/901
Bedford Estates, Re see Sieff *v.* Fox
Beecham Group Plc's Community Trade Mark Application (R118/2003-2) [2004] E.T.M.R.
98, OHIM (2nd Bd App) . . . . *Digested,* 05/**2545**

Beeken *v.* Beeken [1948] P. 302; 92 S.J. 498, CA . . . . *Digested,* 47-51/**2947**:
Considered, 05/3883
Beeston Shipping Ltd *v.* Babanaft International SA (The Eastern Venture) [1985] 1 All
E.R. 923; (1983) 80 L.S.G. 2683; (1983) 127 S.J. 682, CA (Civ Div) . . . . *Digested,* 85/**2628**:
Distinguished, 05/345
Beet *v.* United Kingdom (47676/99) (2005) 41 E.H.R.R. 23; *Times,* March 10, 2005,
ECHR
Begum *v.* Klarit (Costs) [2005] EWCA Civ 210; [2005] 3 Costs L.R. 452; (2005)
102(15) L.S.G. 32; *Times,* March 18, 2005, CA (Civ Div)
Begum *v.* Social Security Commissioner [2003] EWHC 3380; (2003) 100(48) L.S.G.
18; *Times,* December 4, 2003, QBD . . . . *Digested,* 04/**3590**:
Considered, 05/2233
Begum (Rikha) *v.* Tower Hamlets LBC; *sub nom* Tower Hamlets LBC *v.* Begum (Rikha)
[2005] EWCA Civ 340; [2005] 1 W.L.R. 2103; [2005] H.L.R. 34; [2005]
B.L.G.R. 503; (2005) 149 S.J.L.B. 393; [2005] N.P.C. 49; *Independent,* April 6,
2005, CA (Civ Div) . . . . *Digested,* 05/**1986**
Beiersdorf AG *v.* Ramlort Ltd [2004] EWHC 117; [2005] E.T.M.R. 15, Ch D . . . . *Digested,* 05/**488**
Belgacom Mobile SA *v.* Commune de Schaerbeek (C545/03) see Mobistar SA *v.*
Commune de Fleron (C544/03)
Belgium *v.* Commission of the European Communities (C142/87); *sub nom* Aid to
Tubemeuse (C142/87), Re [1990] E.C.R. I-959; [1991] 3 C.M.L.R. 213, ECJ . . . *Digested,* 91/**4113**:
Followed, 02/587, 05/590
Belgium *v.* Ghent Coal Terminal NV (C37/95) [1998] All E.R. (EC) 223; [1998] S.T.C.
260; [1998] E.C.R. I-1; [1998] 1 C.M.L.R. 950; [1998] C.E.C. 137; [1998] B.T.C.
5121; [1998] B.V.C. 139; *Times,* February 4, 1998, ECJ (2nd Chamber) [1998]
E.C.R. I-1, AGO . . . . *Digested,* 98/**4918**:
Applied, 01/5577: *Followed,* 05/4363
Belgium *v.* GW 7 I.T.L. Rep. 442, Cass (B)
Belgium *v.* Mesbah (C179/98) [1999] E.C.R. I-7955, ECJ . . . . *Followed,* 05/2204
Belgium *v.* Postlethwaite; *sub nom* R. *v.* Governor of Ashford Remand Centre Ex p.
Postlethwaite; Postlethwaite, Re [1988] A.C. 924; [1987] 3 W.L.R. 365; [1987]
2 All E.R. 985; (1987) 84 L.S.G. 2449; (1987) 137 N.L.J. 666; (1987) 131 S.J.
1038, HL. . . . . *Digested,* 87/**1703**:
Applied, 05/1490: *Considered,* 01/5783: *Followed,* 97/2439
Belgium *v.* Temco Europe SA (C284/03) [2005] S.T.C. 1451; [2004] E.C.R. I-11237;
[2005] 1 C.M.L.R. 23; [2005] C.E.C. 20; [2004] S.T.I. 2399; *Times,* November
25, 2004, ECJ (1st Chamber) . . . . *Digested,* 05/**4351**
Belgocodex SA *v.* Belgium (C381/97) [2000] S.T.C. 351; [1998] E.C.R. I-8153; [2001]
1 C.M.L.R. 11; [2000] B.T.C. 5168; [2000] B.V.C. 211, ECJ (5th Chamber) . . . . . *Digested,* 00/**5305**:
Followed, 05/4384
Bell *v.* Canterbury City Council 86 L.G.R. 635; (1988) 56 P. & C.R. 211; [1988] 2
P.L.R. 69; [1988] 22 E.G. 86; [1988] R.V.R. 96; [1988] J.P.L. 536; (1988) 152
L.G. Rev. 1008; [1988] E.G.C.S. 31; *Times,* March 11, 1988; *Independent,* March
14, 1988, CA (Civ Div); affirming (1986) 52 P. & C.R. 428; [1986] 2 E.G.L.R.
209; (1986) 279 E.G. 767; [1986] R.V.R. 15; [1986] J.P.L. 844, Lands Tr . . . . . . *Digested,* 88/**3533**:
Followed, 05/3317
Bell *v.* Lever Brothers Ltd; *sub nom* Lever Bros Ltd *v.* Bell [1932] A.C. 161, HL;
reversing [1931] 1 K.B. 557, CA . . . . *Applied,* 47-51/1785,
47-51/1786, 47-51/4202, 47-51/9247, 47-51/9254, 53/3290, 57/596, 80/592,
83/430, 88/449, 89/430, 91/408, 91/425, 02/720: *Considered,* 47-51/4201,
47-51/8914, 68/3999, 69/1819, 99/2111: *Distinguished,* 66/1854, 68/2240,
83/1254, 03/518, 05/524
Bell *v.* Patterson (Unreported, February 26, 2004), CC (Southport) [*Ex rel.* Claire Hill,
Pupil Barrister, St James's Chambers, 68 Quay Street, Manchester.] . . . . *Digested,* 05/**3100**
Bell *v.* Peter Browne & Co [1990] 2 Q.B. 495; [1990] 3 W.L.R. 510; [1990] 3 All E.R.
124; (1990) 140 N.L.J. 701; *Independent,* May 9, 1990, CA (Civ Div) . . . . *Digested,* 91/**2343**:
Applied, 02/3304: *Considered,* 93/2997, 94/2912, 00/2621:
Distinguished, 05/443
Bell *v.* South and East Belfast Health and Social Services Trust [2005] R.V.R. 215,
Lands Tr (NI)
Bell Concord Trust Ltd *v.* Customs and Excise Commissioners see Customs and Excise
Commissioners *v.* Bell Concord Educational Trust Ltd
Bell Davies Trading Ltd *v.* Secretary of State for Trade and Industry see Secretary of
State for Trade and Industry *v.* Bell Davies Trading Ltd
Bellarby *v.* Worthing and Southlands Hospitals NHS Trust [2005] EWHC 2089;
(2005) 86 B.M.L.R. 1, QBD
Bellcourt Estates Ltd *v.* Adesina [2005] EWCA Civ 208; [2005] 2 E.G.L.R. 33; [2005]
18 E.G. 150; (2005) 149 S.J.L.B. 265, CA (Civ Div) . . . . *Digested,* 05/**2669**
Bellio Fratelli Srl *v.* Prefettura di Treviso (C286/02) [2004] E.C.R. I-3465; [2004] 3
C.M.L.R. 34, ECJ (3rd Chamber) . . . . *Digested,* 05/**136**
Bellouti *v.* Wandsworth LBC [2005] EWCA Civ 602; [2005] H.L.R. 46; [2005] N.P.C.
68, CA (Civ Div)
Bellway Urban Renewal Southern *v.* Gillespie see Gillespie *v.* First Secretary of State

Beltekian v. Westminster City Council [2004] EWCA Civ 1784; [2005] A.C.D. 76;
 Times, December 15, 2004, CA (Civ Div) . . . . *Digested,* 05/**3875**
Benaim (UK) Ltd v. Davies Middleton & Davies Ltd (No.2) [2005] EWHC 1370; 102
 Con. L.R.1, QBD (TCC)
Benamar v. Netherlands (43786/04) (Admissibility) (2005) 41 E.H.R.R. SE4, ECHR
Benbow v. United States see Jenkins v. United States
Benford Ltd v. Lopecan SL (No.2) [2004] EWHC 1897; [2004] 2 Lloyd's Rep. 618;
 [2005] 2 B.C.L.C. 258, QBD (Comm) . . . . *Digested,* 05/**388**
Benham Ltd v. Kythira Investments Ltd; *sub nom* Benhams Investments Ltd (t/a
 Benham & Reeves) v. Kythira Investments Ltd [2003] EWCA Civ 1794; [2004]
 C.P. Rep. 17; (2004) 154 N.L.J. 21, CA (Civ Div); reversing [2003] EWHC 1210,
 QBD . . . . *Digested,* 05/**493**
Benhams Investments Ltd (t/a Benham & Reeves) v. Kythira Investments Ltd see
 Benham Ltd v. Kythira Investments Ltd
Benhams Ltd v. Kythira Investments Ltd [2004] EWHC 2973, QBD . . . . *Digested,* 05/**91**
Benjamin (Deceased), Re (1934) 150 L.T. 417 . . . . *Disapproved,* 05/**3980**
Benn v. United Kingdom (30343/96) see Adams v. United Kingdom (Admissibility)
 (28979/95)
Bennet v. Bellm (Unreported, April 28, 2004), CC (Winchester) [*Ex rel.* Guy
 Opperman, Barrister, 3 Paper Buildings, Temple, London] . . . . *Digested,* 05/**189**
Bennett v. A see R. (on the application of A) v. HM Coroner for Inner South London
Bennett v. Compass Group UK & Ireland Ltd [2002] EWCA Civ 642; [2002] C.P.
 Rep. 58; [2002] C.P.L.R. 452; [2002] I.C.R.1177, CA (Civ Div) . . . . *Digested,* 03/**402:**
 Cited, 05/3073
Bennett v. FMK Construction Ltd [2005] EWHC 1268; 101 Con. L.R. 92, QBD (TCC)
Bennett v. Horseferry Road Magistrates Court see R. v. Horseferry Road Magistrates
 Court Ex p. Bennett (No.1)
Bennett (Florence Lilian), In the Estate of see Papouis v. Gibson-West
Bensoor v. Devine (Inspector of Taxes) [2005] S.T.C. (S.C.D.) 297; [2005] S.T.I. 164,
 Sp Comm . . . . *Digested,* 05/**4136**
Bentley v. Secretary of State for Trade and Industry see Rutherford v. Secretary of
 State for Trade and Industry
Benyon v. Customs and Excise Commissioners see Beynon v. Customs and Excise
 Commissioners
Beoco Ltd v. Alfa Laval Co Ltd [1995] Q.B. 137; [1994] 3 W.L.R. 1179; [1994] 4 All
 E.R. 464; 66 B.L.R. 1; (1994) 144 N.L.J. 233; *Times,* January 12, 1994, CA (Civ
 Div) . . . . *Digested,* 94/**1442:**
 Considered, 04/4117, 05/816: *Referred to,* 02/328
Berezovsky v. Forbes Inc (No.1); *sub nom* Berezovsky v. Michaels; Glouchkov v.
 Michaels; Glouchkov v. Forbes Inc [2000] 1 W.L.R.1004; [2000] 2 All E.R. 986;
 [2001] I.L.Pr. 21; [2000] E.M.L.R. 643; (2000) 97(22) L.S.G. 44; (2000) 150
 N.L.J. 741; *Times,* May 16, 2000; *Independent,* May 18, 2000, HL; affirming
 [1999] I.L.Pr. 358; [1999] E.M.L.R. 278; *Times,* November 27, 1998, CA (Civ
 Div); reversing *Times,* January 19, 1998, QBD . . . . *Digested,* 00/**769:**
 Applied, 01/1825, 05/974, 05/978: *Distinguished,* 99/750
Berezovsky v. Forbes Inc (No.2) [2001] EWCA Civ 1251; [2001] E.M.L.R. 45, CA (Civ
 Div) . . . . *Digested,* 01/**1824:**
 Applied, 03/953, 05/978
Berezovsky v. Michaels see Berezovsky v. Forbes Inc (No.1)
Berg v. IML London Ltd [2002] 1 W.L.R. 3271; [2002] 4 All E.R. 87, QBD . . . . *Applied,* 05/**647**
Bergandi v. Directeur General des Impots, La Manche (252/86) [1991] S.T.C. 529;
 [1988] E.C.R.1343; [1989] 2 C.M.L.R. 933, ECJ . . . . *Digested,* 91/**4152:**
 Followed, 05/2380
Berkeley v. North & South Trust Co see North & South Trust Co v. Berkeley
Berkeley v. Secretary of State for the Environment, Transport and the Regions (No.1)
 [2001] 2 A.C. 603; [2000] 3 W.L.R. 420; [2000] 3 All E.R. 897; [2001] 2
 C.M.L.R. 38; [2001] Env. L.R. 16; (2001) 81 P. & C.R. 35; [2000] 3 P.L.R. 111;
 [2001] J.P.L. 58; [2000] E.G.C.S. 86; [2000] N.P.C. 77; *Times,* July 7, 2000,
 HL; reversing [1999] 1 C.M.L.R. 945; [1998] Env. L.R. 741; [1998] 3 P.L.R. 39;
 [1998] P.L.C.R. 97; [1998] N.P.C.18; *Times,* March 2, 1998, CA (Civ Div) . . . . . *Digested,* 00/**4460:**
 Applied, 02/3717, 04/3074, 05/1402: *Considered,* 01/4726, 04/3054,
 04/3084, 05/3308: *Distinguished,* 00/4505
Berkholz v. Finanzamt Hamburg Mitte-Altstadt (168/84) [1985] E.C.R. 2251; [1985]
 3 C.M.L.R. 667, ECJ (2nd Chamber) . . . . *Digested,* 86/**1495:**
 Applied, 01/5588, 04/4022: *Considered,* 96/5902, 97/5021:
 Followed, 05/4382, 05/4404
Berlei (UK) Ltd v. Bali Brassiere Co Inc (No.1); *sub nom* BALI Trade Mark (No.1) [1969]
 1 W.L.R. 1306; [1969] 2 All E.R. 812; [1969] F.S.R. 288; [1969] R.P.C. 472;
 113 S.J. 720, HL; reversing [1968] F.S.R. 1; [1968] R.P.C. 426, CA (Civ Div);
 reversing [1966] F.S.R. 8; [1966] R.P.C. 387, Ch D . . . . *Digested,* 69/**3565:**
 Applied, 74/3830, 75/3432, 97/4893, 99/3537, 00/3770, 03/2629,
 04/2399: *Considered,* 72/3435, 93/3990, 96/5723, 98/3534, 98/3539,
 98/3540: *Followed,* 95/4946, 97/4899, 00/3774, 00/3786, 05/2577:
 Referred to, 00/3795

Bernard *v.* Attorney General of Jamaica [2004] UKPC 47; [2005] I.R.L.R. 398; (2004) 148 S.J.L.B. 1281, PC (Jam)................................ *Digested,* 05/**4200**: *Applied,* 05/4199

Bernhard Schulte GmbH & Co KG *v.* Nile Holdings Ltd [2004] EWHC 977; [2004] 2 Lloyd's Rep. 352, QBD (Comm).. *Digested,* 05/**309**

Besix SA *v.* Wasserreinigungsbau Alfred Kretzschmar GmbH & Co KG (WABAG) (C256/00) [2003] 1 W.L.R. 1113; [2004] All E.R. (EC) 229; [2004] 1 All E.R. (Comm) 521; [2002] E.C.R. I-1699; [2003] I.L.Pr. 8, ECJ................ *Digested,* 04/**578**: *Applied,* 05/604

Bessant *v.* South Cone Inc see REEF Trade Mark

Best *v.* Staffordshire University see Hartman *v.* South Essex Mental Health and Community Care NHS Trust

BESTrustees *v.* Stuart [2001] O.P.L.R. 341; [2001] Pens. L.R. 283, Ch D .... *Digested,* 02/**3380**: *Considered,* 05/4305

Betney *v.* Rowlands Mallard (Unreported, May 8, 1992), CC (Liverpool)........... *Digested,* 92/**1786**: *Considered,* 05/406

BetterCare Group Ltd *v.* Director General of Fair Trading (Admissibility of Appeal) [2002] CAT 6; [2002] Comp. A.R. 226; [2003] E.C.C. 39, CCAT........... *Digested,* 03/**568**: *Applied,* 03/569, 04/516: *Followed,* 05/586

Bettray *v.* Staatssecretaris van Justitie (344/87) [1989] E.C.R. 1621; [1991] 1 C.M.L.R. 459; *Times,* June 16, 1989, ECJ .... *Digested,* 91/**4000**: *Distinguished,* 05/2206

Beynon *v.* Customs and Excise Commissioners; *sub nom* Benyon *v.* Customs and Excise Commissioners [2004] UKHL 53; [2005] 1 W.L.R. 86; [2004] 4 All E.R. 1091; [2005] S.T.C. 55; [2004] B.T.C. 5794; [2005] B.V.C. 3; [2004] S.T.I. 2434; (2004) 148 S.J.L.B. 1404; *Times,* November 26, 2004, HL; reversing [2002] EWCA Civ 1870; [2003] S.T.C. 169; [2003] B.T.C. 5071; [2003] B.V.C. 127; [2003] S.T.I. 31; *Times,* January 15, 2003, CA (Civ Div); reversing [2002] EWHC 518; [2002] S.T.C. 699; [2002] B.T.C. 5366; [2002] B.V.C. 494; [2002] S.T.I. 401, Ch D; affirming [2001] B.V.C. 2331; [2001] S.T.I. 1323, V&DTr....... *Digested,* 05/**4397**

Bhandari *v.* Advocates Committee [1956] 1 W.L.R. 1442; [1956] 3 All E.R. 742; 100 S.J. 836, PC (EA) .... *Digested,* 56/**6608**: *Considered,* 92/4089, 05/2727

Bhanderi *v.* Customs and Excise Commissioners; *sub nom* Turnstem Ltd, Re [2004] EWHC 1765; [2005] 1 B.C.L.C. 388; [2005] B.P.I.R. 659, Ch D (Companies Ct) .... *Digested,* 05/**2348**

Bhatia Shipping & Agencies Pvt Ltd *v.* Alcobex Metals Ltd [2004] EWHC 2323; [2005] 2 Lloyd's Rep. 336, QBD (Comm) .... *Digested,* 05/**434**

BHB Enterprises Plc *v.* Victor Chandler (International) Ltd; *sub nom* Victor Chandler (International) Ltd *v.* BHB Enterprises Plc [2005] EWHC 1074; [2005] U.K.C.L.R. 787; [2005] E.C.C. 40; [2005] Eu. L.R. 924, Ch D .... *Digested,* 05/**573**: *Distinguished,* 05/484

Bhe *v.* Magistrate of Khayelitsha; Shibi *v.* Sithole; South African Human Rights Commission *v.* President of South Africa 18 B.H.R.C. 52, Const Ct (SA)

Bhogal *v.* Punjab National Bank; Basna *v.* Punjab National Bank [1988] 2 All E.R. 296; [1988] F.L.R. 97; [1988] 1 F.T.L.R. 161, CA (Civ Div) .... *Digested,* 88/**186**: *Applied,* 89/162: *Followed,* 05/258

BHP Petroleum Great Britain Ltd *v.* Chesterfield Properties Ltd; *sub nom* Chesterfield Properties Ltd *v.* BHP Petroleum Great Britain Ltd; BHP Great Britain Petroleum Ltd *v.* Chesterfield Properties Ltd [2001] EWCA Civ 1797; [2002] Ch. 194; [2002] 2 W.L.R. 672; [2002] 1 All E.R. 821; [2002] 2 P. & C.R. 9; [2002] L. & T.R. 18; [2002] 2 E.G.L.R. 121; [2001] 50 E.G.C.S. 88; (2002) 99(5) L.S.G. 29; (2002) 146 S.J.L.B. 5; [2001] N.P.C. 174; [2002] 1 P. & C.R. DG17; *Times,* February 21, 2002; *Independent,* December 6, 2001, CA (Civ Div); reversing in part [2002] Ch. 12; [2001] 3 W.L.R. 277; [2001] 2 All E.R. 914; [2002] 1 P. & C.R. 2; [2001] L. & T.R. 28; [2001] 2 E.G.L.R. 11; [2001] 22 E.G. 155; [2001] 10 E.G.C.S. 158; (2001) 98(15) L.S.G. 32; (2001) 98(10) L.S.G. 46; (2001) 145 S.J.L.B. 76; [2001] N.P.C. 47; (2001) 82 P. & C.R. DG11; *Times,* March 30, 2001, Ch D .... *Digested,* 02/**3033**: *Applied,* 05/2665

Bibi *v.* Immigration Appeal Tribunal see R. (on the application of Bibi) *v.* Immigration Appeal Tribunal

Bice *v.* Birmingham Motor Tyres (Unreported, May 3, 2005), CC (Birmingham) [*Ex rel.* Stephen Garner, Barrister, No.8 Chambers, Fountain Court, Steelhouse Lane, Birmingham.].. *Digested,* 05/**3206**

Bick *v.* Royal School for the Deaf [1976] I.R.L.R. 326, IT .... *Digested,* 76/**950**: *Not followed,* 05/1304

Biehl *v.* Administration des Contributions du Grand-Duche de Luxembourg (C175/88) [1991] S.T.C. 575; [1990] E.C.R. I-1779; [1990] 3 C.M.L.R. 143, ECJ (5th Chamber) .... *Considered,* 05/3827

Bigott *v.* Phillip Morris Products Inc [2004] UKPC 28; [2005] F.S.R. 4; (2004) 27(8) I.P.D. 27081; (2004) 148 S.J.L.B. 789, PC (Trin) .... *Digested,* 05/**2579**

Bijl *v.* General Medical Council [2001] UKPC 42; [2002] Lloyd's Rep. Med. 60; (2002) 65 B.M.L.R. 10; *Times*, October 24, 2001, PC (UK) . . . . *Digested*, 01/**3287**: *Applied*, 05/1919

Bild-Kunst *v.* Focus (I ZR 117/00) [2005] E.C.D.R. 6, BGH (Ger)

Bim Kemi AB *v.* Blackburn Chemicals Ltd (Application to Strike Out); *sub nom* Blackburn Chemicals Ltd *v.* Bim Kemi AB (Application to Strike Out) [2004] EWCA Civ 1490; [2005] U.K.C.L.R. 1; [2005] Eu. L.R. 176; (2004) 101(46) L.S.G. 34; *Times*, November 22, 2004, CA (Civ Div); affirming [2004] EWHC 166; [2004] U.K.C.L.R. 364; [2004] Eu. L.R. 575, QBD (Comm) . . . .   *Digested*, 05/**329**

Binder *v.* Alachouzos [1972] 2 Q.B. 151; [1972] 2 W.L.R. 947; [1972] 2 All E.R. 189; [1972] 1 Lloyd's Rep. 524; 116 S.J. 139, CA (Civ Div) . . . . *Digested*, 72/**2194**: *Considered*, 05/241

Biogen Inc *v.* SmithKline Beecham Biologicals SA (C181/95) [1997] E.C.R. I-357; [1997] R.P.C. 833; (1997) 38 B.M.L.R. 94, ECJ (6th Chamber) . . . .   *Digested*, 98/**3481**: *Considered*, 05/2473: *Distinguished*, 04/2351

Bioid AG (In Liquidation) *v.* Office for Harmonisation in the Internal Market (Trade Marks and Designs) (OHIM) (C37/03) [2005] E.T.M.R. CN5, AGO

Birmingham City Council *v.* Mtize see Kwamin *v.* Abbey National Plc

Birmingham City Council *v.* Yardley [2004] EWCA Civ 1756; (2005) 102(5) L.S.G. 29; *Times*, December 13, 2004, CA (Civ Div) . . . .   *Digested*, 05/**490**

Birmingham Midshires Mortgage Services Ltd *v.* Sabherwal (Equitable Interest) (2000) 80 P. & C.R. 256, CA (Civ Div) . . . . *Digested*, 00/**4658**: *Applied*, 05/3437

Birse Construction Ltd *v.* McCormick (UK) Ltd (formerly McCormick (UK) Plc) [2005] EWCA Civ 940; [2005] B.L.R. 523, CA (Civ Div); affirming [2004] EWHC 3053; 99 Con. L.R. 181, QBD (TCC). . . . .   *Digested*, 05/**657**

Bishop *v.* Baker Refractories Ltd see Barber *v.* Somerset CC

Bishop *v.* Uxbridge Magistrates Court [2001] EWHC Admin 104, QBD (Admin) . . . . . .   *Considered*, 05/734

Bishopsgate Foundation *v.* Curtis [2004] 3 E.G.L.R. 57; [2004] 46 E.G. 152, CC (Central London) . . . .   *Digested*, 05/**2656**

Bishopsgate Space Management Ltd *v.* London Underground Ltd [2004] 2 E.G.L.R. 175; [2004] R.V.R. 89, Lands Tr . . . .   *Digested*, 04/**3207**: *Considered*, 05/3251

Bjornekulla Fruktindustrier AB *v.* Procordia Food AB (C371/02) [2004] E.C.R. I-5791; [2005] 3 C.M.L.R. 16; [2004] E.T.M.R. 69; [2004] R.P.C. 45, ECJ (6th Chamber) . . . .   *Digested*, 05/**2566**

Black *v.* Pastouna; *sub nom* Pastouna *v.* Black [2005] EWCA Civ 1389; (2005) 155 N.L.J. 1847; *Independent*, December 2, 2005, CA (Civ Div)

Black *v.* Sumitomo Corp [2001] EWCA Civ 1819; [2002] 1 W.L.R. 1562; [2003] 3 All E.R. 643; [2002] 1 Lloyd's Rep. 693; [2002] C.P.L.R. 148; *Times*, January 25, 2002; *Independent*, December 13, 2001, CA (Civ Div); reversing TNS, QBD (Comm) . . . .   *Digested*, 02/**422**: *Applied*, 02/426, 05/456

Black & Decker Corp *v.* Muko Tekstil Kot San ve Tic Ltd Sti [2005] E.T.M.R. 64, Yrg (TR)

Black Clawson International Ltd *v.* Papierwerke Waldhof-Aschaffenburg AG [1975] A.C. 591; [1975] 2 W.L.R. 513; [1975] 1 All E.R. 810; [1975] 2 Lloyd's Rep. 11; 119 S.J. 221, HL; reversing [1974] Q.B. 660; [1974] 2 W.L.R. 789; [1974] 2 All E.R. 611; [1974] 1 Lloyd's Rep. 573; 118 S.J. 365, CA (Civ Div) . . . .   *Digested*, 75/**361**: *Applied*, 79/140, 94/165: *Considered*, 87/405, 05/970: *Followed*, 77/2486.6, 77/3464, 78/839.1, 78/3384

Blackburn Chemicals Ltd *v.* Bim Kemi AB (Application to Strike Out) see Bim Kemi AB *v.* Blackburn Chemicals Ltd (Application to Strike Out)

Blackburn Rovers Football & Athletic Club Plc *v.* Avon Insurance Plc (Preliminary Issues) [2005] EWCA Civ 423; [2005] 1 C.L.C. 554; [2005] Lloyd's Rep. I.R. 447, CA (Civ Div); reversing [2004] EWHC 2625; [2005] Lloyd's Rep. I.R. 239, QBD (Comm) . . . .   *Digested*, 05/**2374**

Blackham *v.* Entrepose UK [2004] EWCA Civ 1109; [2005] C.P. Rep. 7; [2005] 1 Costs L.R. 68; (2004) 101(35) L.S.G. 33; (2004) 148 S.J.L.B. 945; *Times*, September 28, 2004, CA (Civ Div)

Blackpool Pleasure Beach (Holdings) Ltd *v.* Customs and Excise Commissioners [2005] B.V.C. 2536; [2005] S.T.I. 909, V&D Tr

Blackstock *v.* United Kingdom (59512/00), *Times*, June 29, 2005, ECHR

Blagdon Cemetery, Re [2002] Fam. 299; [2002] 3 W.L.R. 603; [2002] 4 All E.R. 482; (2002) 99(20) L.S.G. 31; (2002) 146 S.J.L.B. 108, Arches Ct . . . .   *Applied*, 04/943, 05/993

Blamaud *v.* Les Oliviers (Societe) [2005] I.L.Pr. 50, Cass (F)

Blanc Canet *v.* Europcar France SA [2005] E.C.C. 34, Cass (F)

Blanckaert *v.* Inspecteur van de Belastingdienst/Particulieren/Ondernemingen Buitenland te Heerlen (C512/03) [2005] S.T.C. 1574; [2005] 3 C.M.L.R. 39; 8 I.T.L. Rep. 146; [2005] S.T.I. 1586, ECJ (1st Chamber)

Blasi *v.* Finanzamt Munchen I (C346/95) [1998] All E.R. (EC) 211; [1998] S.T.C. 336; [1998] E.C.R. I-481; [1998] C.E.C. 408; [1998] B.T.C. 5188; [1998] B.V.C. 247, ECJ (5th Chamber) . . . .   *Digested*, 98/**4897**: *Considered*, 04/3976, 05/4351

Blecic v. Croatia (59532/00) (2005) 41 E.H.R.R. 13, ECHR

Blewitt v. Derbyshire Waste Ltd see R. (on the application of Blewett) v. Derbyshire CC

Blom-Cooper v. Customs and Excise Commissioners; *sub nom* Customs and Excise Commissioners v. Blom-Cooper [2003] EWCA Civ 493; [2003] S.T.C. 669; [2003] B.T.C. 5359; [2003] B.V.C. 415; [2003] S.T.I. 587; [2003] 20 E.G.C.S. 148; (2003) 100(23) L.S.G. 39; (2003) 147 S.J.L.B. 416; [2003] N.P.C. 49; *Times*, May 15, 2003, CA (Civ Div); reversing [2002] EWHC 1421; [2002] S.T.C. 1061; [2002] B.T.C. 5458; [2002] B.V.C. 586; [2002] S.T.I. 1010; [2002] N.P.C. 97; *Times*, July 20, 2002, Ch D; affirming [2002] S.T.I. 798, V&DTr . . . . .   *Digested*, 03/**4570**:
Considered, 05/4381

Blower v. Mercadel Plant & Machinery Ltd (Unreported, June 16, 2004), CC (Lincoln) [*Ex rel.* Andrew Maguire, Barrister, St Philips Chambers, 55 Temple Row, Birmingham] . . . .   *Digested*, 05/**3077**

Bluck v. Salton (Inspector of Taxes) (No.2) [2004] S.T.C. (S.C.D.) 177; [2004] S.T.I. 991, Sp Comm . . . .   *Digested*, 05/**4103**

Bluett v. Suffolk CC [2004] EWCA Civ 1707; [2005] 1 F.C.R. 89, CA (Civ Div) . . . .   *Digested*, 05/**2852**

Blumenthal v. Church Commissioners for England [2004] EWCA Civ 1688; [2005] 2 P. & C.R. 20; [2005] 1 E.G.L.R. 78; [2005] 12 E.G. 220; (2005) 149 S.J.L.B. 56, CA (Civ Div) . . . .   *Digested*, 05/**3415**

Blunkett v. Quinn [2004] EWHC 2816; [2005] 1 F.L.R. 648; [2005] 1 F.C.R. 103; [2005] Fam. Law 213; (2005) 102(5) L.S.G. 29; *Times*, December 7, 2004, Fam Div . . . .   *Digested*, 05/**1630**

BMI Bertollo Srl v. Office for Harmonisation in the Internal Market (Trade Marks and Designs) (OHIM) (T186/02) [2005] E.T.M.R. 32, CFI (4th Chamber) . . . .   *Digested*, 05/**2515**

BMW AG v. Deenik (C63/97) see Bayerische Motorenwerke AG v. Deenik (C63/97)

BMW Motorhaube (BMW Engine Hood), Re (28 W (PAT) 174/03) [2005] E.T.M.R. 77, BPG (Ger)

BNP Paribas v. Deloitte & Touche LLP [2003] EWHC 2874; [2004] 1 Lloyd's Rep. 233; [2004] 1 C.L.C. 530; [2004] B.L.R. 90; (2003) 153 N.L.J. 1841, QBD (Comm) . . . .   *Digested*, 05/**209**:
Applied, 05/211

Board of Trustees of the National Provident Fund v. Shortland Securities Ltd [1996] 1 N.Z.L.R. 45, CA (NZ) . . . .   *Followed*, 05/2667

Boardman v. Phipps; *sub nom* Phipps v. Boardman [1967] 2 A.C. 46; [1966] 3 W.L.R. 1009; [1966] 3 All E.R. 721; 110 S.J. 853, HL; affirming [1965] Ch. 992; [1965] 2 W.L.R. 839; [1965] 1 All E.R. 849; 109 S.J. 197, CA; affirming [1964] 1 W.L.R. 993; [1964] 2 All E.R. 187; 108 S.J. 619, Ch D . . . .   *Digested*, 66/**11052**:
Applied, 72/361, 72/487, 81/2624, 93/1834, 94/2083, 01/5525, 03/520, 04/456, 05/2812, 05/4307: *Considered*, 77/2708, 87/3552, 89/459, 90/487, 01/951: *Distinguished*, 04/3940

Boehringer Ingelheim KG v. Dowelhurst Ltd (Form of Reference to ECJ) see Boehringer Ingelheim KG v. Swingward Ltd (Form of Reference to ECJ)

Boehringer Ingelheim KG v. Swingward Ltd (Form of Reference to ECJ); Boehringer Ingelheim KG v. Dowelhurst Ltd (Form of Reference to ECJ); Glaxo Group Ltd v. Swingward Ltd (Form of Reference to ECJ); Glaxo Group Ltd v. Dowelhurst Ltd (Form of Reference to ECJ); Smithkline Beecham Plc v. Dowelhurst Ltd (Form of Reference to ECJ); Eli Lilly & Co v. Dowelhurst Ltd (Form of Reference to ECJ) [2004] EWCA Civ 757; [2004] 3 C.M.L.R. 4; [2004] Eu. L.R. 959; (2004) 27(7) I.P.D. 27075; (2004) 148 S.J.L.B. 789, CA (Civ Div) . . . .   *Digested*, 05/**2444**:
Previous proceedings, 04/2400

Bolam v. Friern Hospital Management Committee [1957] 1 W.L.R. 582; [1957] 2 All E.R. 118; [1955-95] P.N.L.R. 7; 101 S.J. 357, QBD . . . .   *Digested*, 57/**2431**:
Applied, 67/2729, 83/2548, 83/2576, 84/2322, 84/2326, 85/2318, 86/2278, 87/2601, 87/2605, 90/3279, 91/2654, 92/3213, 93/2999, 94/3399, 95/3679, 97/3789, 97/3797, 99/3997, 00/2779, 00/4250, 01/4513, 02/1120, 04/996, 04/2742, 05/2839, 05/2854: *Approved*, 75/245: *Cited*, 00/4248, 00/4283, 03/1161: *Considered*, 88/2453, 89/3044, 93/2712, 94/1535, 94/3359, 95/3714, 96/3580, 02/1637, 03/2958, 04/2705: *Distinguished*, 74/265, 92/233, 92/3242, 93/233, 96/4469: *Followed*, 97/2142, 98/3986, 99/789, 99/4056: *Not applied*, 99/3992, 99/3995

Boland v. Welsh Development Agency [2005] R.V.R. 279, Lands Tr

Boland v. Welsh Development Agency (Permission to Appeal) [2005] EWCA Civ 1096; [2005] R.V.R. 383, CA (Civ Div)

Bold Transmission Parts Ltd v. Taree see Brown v. Kigass Aero Components Ltd

Boldrini v. Boldrini [1932] P. 9, CA . . . .   *Applied*, 05/**1627**:
Followed, 47-51/1586, 47-51/2910, 71/3603

Bolitho (Deceased) v. City and Hackney HA [1998] A.C. 232; [1997] 3 W.L.R. 1151; [1997] 4 All E.R. 771; [1998] P.I.Q.R. P10; [1998] Lloyd's Rep. Med. 26; (1998) 39 B.M.L.R. 1; [1998] P.N.L.R. 1; (1997) 94(47) L.S.G. 30; (1997) 141 S.J.L.B. 238; *Times*, November 27, 1997, HL; affirming [1993] P.I.Q.R. P334; [1993] 4 Med. L.R. 381, CA (Civ Div) . . . . *Digested*, 97/**3789**:
Applied, 98/3977, 99/3994, 01/4263, 01/4542, 02/3294, 03/5826, 04/2698: *Considered*, 98/3986, 03/2989: *Distinguished*, 98/3969, 05/2863: *Followed*, 98/3963, 99/3989
Bolkiah v. KPMG; *sub nom* HRH Prince Jefri Bolkiah v. KPMG [1999] 2 A.C. 222; [1999] 2 W.L.R. 215; [1999] 1 All E.R. 517; [1999] 1 B.C.L.C. 1; [1999] C.L.C. 175; [1999] P.N.L.R. 220; (1999) 149 N.L.J. 16; (1999) 143 S.J.L.B. 35; *Times*, April 20, 1999; *Independent*, January 12, 1999, HL; reversing (1998) 95(42) L.S.G. 33; (1998) 148 N.L.J. 1602; (1998) 142 S.J.L.B. 268; *Times*, October 22, 1998; *Independent*, October 22, 1998, CA (Civ Div); reversing *Times*, September 25, 1998, Ch D . . . . *Digested*, 99/**1**:
Applied, 00/2504, 00/4008, 02/216, 02/3108, 04/2569, 05/2724: *Considered*, 99/2, 99/3796, 00/4007, 03/2821: *Followed*, 00/2469
Bolton v. Law Society [1994] 1 W.L.R. 512; [1994] 2 All E.R. 486; [1994] C.O.D. 295; *Times*, December 8, 1993, CA (Civ Div) . . . . *Digested*, 94/**4220**:
Applied, 98/3724, 03/1724, 05/1807, 05/3349: *Approved*, 03/1733: *Followed*, 97/3375, 05/1805
Bolton MDC v. Manchester Ship Canal Co (Costs) see Bolton MDC v. Secretary of State for the Environment (Costs)
Bolton MDC v. Secretary of State for the Environment (Costs); Bolton MDC v. Manchester Ship Canal Co (Costs); Bolton MDC v. Trafford Park Development Corp (Costs) [1995] 1 W.L.R. 1176; [1996] 1 All E.R. 184; [1995] 3 P.L.R. 37; [1996] J.P.L. 300; [1995] E.G.C.S. 126; [1995] N.P.C. 99A; *Times*, July 17, 1995, HL . . . . *Digested*, 95/**4755**:
Applied, 04/501, 05/348
Bolton MDC v. Trafford Park Development Corp (Costs) see Bolton MDC v. Secretary of State for the Environment (Costs)
Bolton Pharmaceutical Co 100 Ltd v. Doncaster Pharmaceuticals Group Ltd see Bolton Pharmaceutical Co 100 Ltd v. Swinghope Ltd
Bolton Pharmaceutical Co 100 Ltd v. Swinghope Ltd; Bolton Pharmaceutical Co 100 Ltd v. Doncaster Pharmaceuticals Group Ltd [2005] EWHC 1600; (2005) 28(9) I.P.D. 28066, Ch D
Bond v. Hackney Citizens Advice Bureau see Rhys-Harper v. Relaxion Group Plc
Bond House Systems Ltd v. Customs and Excise Commissioners [2004] V. & D.R. 125, Ch D [2003] B.V.C. 2319; [2003] V. & D.R. 210; [2003] S.T.I. 1431, V&DTr (Manchester) . . . . *Digested*, 05/**4368**
Bondi v. Bank of America NA (C341/04 R) see Eurofood IFSC Ltd, Re (C341/04)
Bongrain SA's Trade Mark Application (No.2134604) [2004] EWCA Civ 1690; [2005] E.T.M.R. 47; [2005] R.P.C. 14, CA (Civ Div); affirming [2003] EWHC 531, Ch D *Digested*, 05/**2532**
Bonnard v. Perryman [1891] 2 Ch. 269; [1891-94] All E.R. Rep. 965, CA . . . . *Applied*, 59/3338,
75/1950, 77/1787, 79/1656, 86/1990, 05/970: *Considered*, 86/2598, 91/2885, 98/1773: *Distinguished*, 87/2298: *Followed*, 68/3133
Bonner v. Cox; *sub nom* Bonner v. Cox Dedicated Corporate Member Ltd [2005] EWCA Civ 1512, CA (Civ Div); affirming [2004] EWHC 2963; [2005] Lloyd's Rep. I.R. 569, QBD (Comm) . . . . *Digested*, 05/**2397**
Bonner v. Cox Dedicated Corporate Member Ltd see Bonner v. Cox
Bonner v. DPP; *sub nom* R. (on the application of Bonner) v. DPP [2004] EWHC 2415; [2005] A.C.D. 56, QBD (Admin)
Bonnick v. Morris [2002] UKPC 31; [2003] 1 A.C. 300; [2002] 3 W.L.R. 820; [2002] E.M.L.R. 37; 12 B.H.R.C. 558; (2002) 146 S.J.L.B. 161; *Times*, June 18, 2002, PC (Jam) . . . . *Digested*, 02/**953**:
Considered, 05/977
Bonus Malus System, Re (C346/02) see Commission of the European Communities v. Luxembourg (C346/02)
Bonus Malus System, Re (C347/02) see Commission of the European Communities v. France (C347/02)
Boodhoo v. Attorney General of Trinidad and Tobago [2004] UKPC 17; [2004] 1 W.L.R. 1689; 18 B.H.R.C. 429; (2004) 101 (15) L.S.G. 28; *Times*, April 9, 2004, PC (Trin) . . . . *Digested*, 04/**40**
Bookit Ltd v. Customs and Excise Commissioners see Bookit Ltd v. Revenue and Customs Commissioners
Bookit Ltd v. Revenue and Customs Commissioners; *sub nom* Bookit Ltd v. Customs and Excise Commissioners; C3/2005/1912, CA (Civ Div); affirming [2005] EWHC 1689; [2005] S.T.C. 1481; [2005] B.T.C. 5581; [2005] B.V.C. 612; [2005] S.T.I. 1337, Ch D; reversing [2004] B.V.C. 2229; [2004] V. & D.R. 421; [2004] S.T.I. 1949, V&DTr (London)
Boone v. ITV Network see Celador Productions Ltd v. Melville
Boor (nee Delahaye) v. Ministre de la Fonction Publique et de la Reforme Administrative (C425/02) see Delahaye v. Ministre de la Fonction Publique et de la Reforme Administrative (C425/02)

Borders (UK) Ltd *v.* Commissioner of Police of the Metropolis [2005] EWCA Civ 197; (2005) 149 S.J.L.B. 301; *Times,* April 15, 2005, CA (Civ Div) . . . . *Digested,* 05/**956**

Borgship Tankers Inc *v.* Product Transport Corp Ltd (The Casco) [2005] EWHC 273; [2005] 1 Lloyd's Rep. 565; [2005] 1 C.L.C. 232, QBD (Comm) . . . . *Digested,* 05/**3816**

Borthwick *v.* Elderslie Steamship Co Ltd (No.1) see Elderslie Steamship Co Ltd *v.* Borthwick

Boston Deep Sea Fishing & Ice Co *v.* Ansell (1888) L.R. 39 Ch. D. 339, CA . . . . *Applied,* 47-51/**525,** 47-51/3579, 47-51/5255, 72/2781: *Approved,* 66/4401, 67/1429: *Considered,* 00/313: *Distinguished,* 74/39, 05/524: *Followed,* 81/941: *Not applied,* 70/901

Botham *v.* Khan (Costs); *sub nom* Botham *v.* Niazi (Costs); Lamb *v.* Khan (Costs) [2004] EWHC 2602; [2005] 2 Costs L.R. 259, QBD . . . . *Digested,* 05/**360**

Botham *v.* Ministry of Defence see Lawson *v.* Serco Ltd

Botham *v.* Niazi (Costs) see Botham *v.* Khan (Costs)

Botten *v.* Norway (16206/90) (2001) 32 E.H.R.R. 3, ECHR (1994) 18 E.H.R.R. CD45, Eur Comm HR . . . . *Digested,* 02/**2402:** *Considered,* 04/3471: *Followed,* 05/2095

Bottiglieri di Navigazione SpA *v.* Cosco Qingdao Ocean Shipping Co (The Bunga Saga Lima) [2005] EWHC 244; [2005] 2 Lloyd's Rep. 1, QBD (Comm)

Boughy *v.* Somerset CC (Unreported, February 3, 2005), CC (Yeovil) [*Ex rel.* Veitch Penny Solicitors, 1 Manor Court, Dix's Field, Exeter, Devon] . . . . *Digested,* 05/**2855**

Boultif *v.* Switzerland (54273/00) [2001] 2 F.L.R. 1228; (2001) 33 E.H.R.R. 50; [2001] Fam. Law 875, ECHR . . . . *Digested,* 02/**2516:** *Considered,* 04/2063, 05/2120

Bournemouth Symphony Orchestra *v.* Customs and Excise Commissioners [2005] EWHC 1566; [2005] S.T.C. 1406; [2005] B.T.C. 5516; [2005] B.V.C. 547; [2005] S.T.I. 1311; *Times,* September 6, 2005, Ch D; affirming [2005] S.T.I. 117, V&DTr. . . . . *Digested,* 05/**4356**

Bouygues UK Ltd *v.* Dahl-Jensen UK Ltd [2001] 1 All E.R. (Comm) 1041; [2001] C.L.C. 927; [2000] B.L.R. 522; (2001) 3 T.C.L.R. 2; 73 Con. L.R. 135; (2000) 97(35) L.S.G. 36; *Times,* August 17, 2000, CA (Civ Div); affirming [2000] B.L.R. 49; (2000) 2 T.C.L.R. 308; 70 Con. L.R. 41; *Independent,* February 7, 2000 (C.S.), QBD (TCC) . . . . *Digested,* 00/**3489:** *Applied,* 02/654, 03/667, 05/644: *Considered,* 02/655: *Followed,* 01/6289

Bowles *v.* Bank of England [1913] 1 Ch. 57, Ch D . . . . *Applied,* 05/**4102**

Bowman *v.* Fels [2005] EWCA Civ 226; [2005] 1 W.L.R. 3083; [2005] 4 All E.R. 609; [2005] 2 Cr. App. R. 19; [2005] 2 C.M.L.R. 23; [2005] 2 F.L.R. 247; [2005] W.T.L.R. 481; [2005] Fam. Law 546; (2005) 102(18) L.S.G. 24; (2005) 155 N.L.J. 413; (2005) 149 S.J.L.B. 357; [2005] N.P.C. 36; *Times,* March 14, 2005, CA (Civ Div) . . . . *Digested,* 05/**811**

Bowman *v.* United Kingdom (24839/94) (1998) 26 E.H.R.R. 1; 4 B.H.R.C. 25; [1998] H.R.C.D. 273; *Times,* February 23, 1998, ECHR (1996) 22 E.H.R.R. CD13, Eur Comm HR . . . . *Digested,* 98/**3086:** *Applied,* 02/3226: *Followed,* 05/2089

Boyce *v.* Wyatt Engineering [2001] EWCA Civ 692; [2001] C.P. Rep. 87; [2001] C.P.L.R. 343; *Times,* June 14, 2001, CA (Civ Div) . . . . *Digested,* 01/**676:** *Applied,* 02/414, 05/333: *Considered,* 02/428

Boyce (Lennox Ricardo) *v.* Queen, The; Joseph (Jeffrey) *v.* Queen, The [2004] UKPC 32; [2005] 1 A.C. 400; [2004] 3 W.L.R. 786; 17 B.H.R.C. 118; (2004) 101(32) L.S.G. 35; *Times,* July 14, 2004, PC (Bar) . . . . *Digested,* 04/**3335:** *Referred to,* 04/3336

Boyden *v.* Watson [2004] B.P.I.R. 1131, CC (Manchester) . . . . *Digested,* 05/**2274**

Boyle *v.* Collins [2004] EWHC 271; [2004] 2 B.C.L.C. 471, Ch D . . . . *Digested,* 05/**525**

Boys *v.* Chaplin; *sub nom* Chaplin *v.* Boys [1971] A.C. 356; [1969] 3 W.L.R. 322; [1969] 2 All E.R. 1085; [1969] 2 Lloyd's Rep. 487; 113 S.J. 608, HL; affirming [1968] 2 Q.B. 1; [1968] 2 W.L.R. 328; [1968] 1 All E.R. 283; 111 S.J. 968; *Times,* December 7, 1967, CA (Civ Div); affirming [1967] 3 W.L.R. 266; [1967] 2 All E.R. 665; 111 S.J. 297, QBD . . . . *Digested,* 69/**469:** *Applied,* 76/2174, 92/477, 04/568: *Considered,* 89/3528, 91/514, 92/1916, 94/4282, 95/4724, 95/4736, 02/634, 05/608: *Explained,* 91/2841, 92/3456: *Followed,* 83/360, 00/1463

Bozkurt *v.* Staatssecretaris van Justitie (C434/93) [1995] E.C.R. I-1475, ECJ . . . . *Digested,* 95/**2007:** *Followed,* 05/2204

BP Exploration Operating Co Ltd *v.* Kvaerner Oilfield Products Ltd [2004] EWHC 999; [2004] 2 All E.R. (Comm) 266; [2005] 1 Lloyd's Rep. 307, QBD (Comm) . . . . . *Digested,* 04/**2205**

BP International Ltd *v.* Energy Infrastructure Group Ltd [2003] EWHC 2924; [2004] 1 C.L.C. 539, QBD (Comm) . . . . *Digested,* 05/**613**

BP International Ltd *v.* Newcastle International Airport Ltd [2005] 1 P. & C.R. DG18, CC (Newcastle)

BP Oil Grangemouth Refinery Ltd *v.* Central Scotland Assessor [2005] R.A. 277, Lands Tr (Scot)

BP Oil UK Ltd *v.* LloydsTSB Bank Plc; Mobil Exploration & Production UK Ltd *v.* Lloyds
TSB Bank Ltd [2004] EWCA Civ 1710; [2005] 1 E.G.L.R. 61; [2005] 10 E.G.
156; [2005] 3 E.G.C.S. 116; (2005) 102(9) L.S.G. 29; *Times,* January 12, 2005,
CA (Civ Div); affirming [2004] EWHC 496; [2004] 12 E.G.C.S. 171; (2004)
101(12) L.S.G. 38; [2004] N.P.C. 38, Ch D . . . .   *Digested,* 05/**2672**
BP Properties Ltd *v.* Buckler (1988) 55 P. & C.R. 337; (1987) 284 E.G. 375; (1987)
137 N.L.J. 899, CA (Civ Div) . . . .   *Digested,* 88/**2155**:
                            Applied, 01/578: *Considered,* 05/3439: *Followed,* 01/4842
Brabon, Re; *sub nom* Treharne *v.* Brabon [2000] B.C.C. 1171; [2001] 1 B.C.L.C. 11;
[2000] B.P.I.R. 537; [2000] E.G.C.S. 38; [2000] N.P.C. 21, Ch D . . . .   *Digested,* 00/**3450**:
                                               Distinguished, 05/135
BRAC Rent-A-Car International Inc, Re; *sub nom* BRAC Rent-A-Car Ltd, Re [2003]
EWHC 128; [2003] 1 W.L.R. 1421; [2003] 2 All E.R. 201; [2003] B.C.C. 248;
[2003] 1 B.C.L.C. 470; [2003] B.P.I.R. 531; (2003) 100(14) L.S.G. 28; *Times,*
February 24, 2003, Ch D (Companies Ct) . . . .   *Digested,* 03/**2393**:
                              Applied, 03/2381: *Considered,* 05/2265
Bracknell Forest BC *v.* Adams see Adams *v.* Bracknell Forest BC
Bradford & Bingley Plc *v.* Ross [2005] EWCA Civ 394; (2005) 102(19) L.S.G. 34;
Times, May 3, 2005, CA (Civ Div) . . . .   *Digested,* 05/**3428**
Bradley *v.* Jockey Club [2005] EWCA Civ 1056; *Times,* July 14, 2005, CA (Civ Div);
affirming [2004] EWHC 2164, QBD. . . . .   *Digested,* 05/**3959**
Bradley-Hole (A Bankrupt), Re [1995] 1 W.L.R.1097; [1995] 4 All E.R. 865; [1995] B.C.C.
418; [1995] 2 B.C.L.C.163; [1995] 2 F.L.R. 838; [1996] 2 F.C.R. 259; [1995] Fam.
Law 673, Ch D . . . .   *Digested,* 95/**428**:
               Applied, 03/2443: *Approved,* 99/3242: *Considered,* 05/2276:
                                  Distinguished, 96/3516, 96/3522
Braintree DC *v.* Thompson; *sub nom* Thompson *v.* Braintree DC [2005] EWCA Civ 178;
[2005] H.L.R. 37; [2005] N.P.C. 35; *Times,* April 5, 2005, CA (Civ Div) . . . . . .   *Digested,* 05/**3872**
Braithwaite *v.* First West Yorkshire Ltd (Unreported, July 23, 2004), CC (Leeds) [*Ex
rel.* Tom Nossiter, Barrister, Park Lane Chambers, 19, Westgate, Leeds] . . . .   *Digested,* 05/**3089**
Brand *v.* Compro Computer Services Ltd [2004] EWCA Civ 204; [2005] I.R.L.R. 196,
CA (Civ Div); reversing EAT/1164/02 DA, EAT . . . .   *Digested,* 05/**1218**
Brand *v.* Netherlands (49902/99) 17 B.H.R.C. 398, ECHR . . . .   *Digested,* 05/**2108**
Brandwood *v.* Bakewell Management Ltd see Bakewell Management Ltd
Brasseries Kronenbourg *v.* Cafe Le Victor Hugo [2005] E.C.C. 45, Trib Gde
Inst(Strasbourg)
Brasseries Kronenbourg *v.* JBEG Sarl [2005] E.C.C. 46, Trib Gde Inst(Strasbourg)
Bratko *v.* Beloit Walmsley Ltd [1996] I.C.R. 76; [1995] I.R.L.R. 629, EAT . . . .   *Digested,* 96/**2604**:
                                              Applied, 05/**1241**
Brazil *v.* Rickell [2005] 3 Q.R. 9, CC (Doncaster) [*Ex rel.* Tom Nossiter, Barrister, Park
Lane Chambers, Leeds]. . . . .   *Digested,* 05/**3104**
Breach of an EC Regulation, Re [2005] 2 C.M.L.R. 16, HR (NL)
Breen *v.* Amalgamated Engineering Union [1971] 2 Q.B. 175; [1971] 2 W.L.R. 742;
[1971] 1 All E.R. 1148; 10 K.I.R. 120; 115 S.J. 203, CA (Civ Div) . . . .   *Digested,* 71/**11754**:
                              Applied, 05/3459: *Considered,* 75/3453, 77/3072
Breeze *v.* Ahmad [2005] EWCA Civ 223; [2005] C.P. Rep. 29, CA (Civ Div) . . . .   *Digested,* 05/**2838**
Brennan *v.* Bolt Burdon; *sub nom* Brennan *v.* Bolt Burden; Brennan *v.* Islington LBC
[2004] EWCA Civ 1017; [2005] Q.B. 303; [2004] 3 W.L.R. 1321; [2004] C.P.
Rep. 43; (2004) 101(34) L.S.G. 31; (2004) 148 S.J.L.B. 972; [2004] N.P.C.
133; *Times,* August 27, 2004, CA (Civ Div); reversing [2003] EWHC 2493;
[2004] 1 W.L.R. 1240; *Times,* November 7, 2003, QBD . . . .   *Digested,* 04/**383**
Brennan *v.* Islington LBC see Brennan *v.* Bolt Burdon
Brennan *v.* Lambeth LBC (1998) 30 H.L.R. 481, CA (Civ Div) . . . .   *Digested,* 98/**3028**:
                                              Applied, 05/2660
Brennan *v.* London Regional Transport Pension Fund Trustee Co Ltd; *sub nom* Brennan
v. LRT Pension Fund Trustee Co Ltd [2003] EWHC 3301; [2004] O.P.L.R. 195,
Ch D . . . .   *Digested,* 05/**2970**
Brennan *v.* London Regional Transport Pension Fund Trustee Co Ltd; *sub nom* Brennan
v. LRT Pension Fund Trustee Co Ltd [2005] EWHC 2767; [2005] Pens. L.R.
417, Ch D
Brennan *v.* LRT Pension Fund Trustee Co Ltd see Brennan *v.* London Regional
Transport Pension Fund Trustee Co Ltd
Brennan *v.* LRT Pension Fund Trustee Co Ltd see Brennan *v.* London Regional
Transport Pension Fund Trustee Co Ltd
Brenner *v.* Revenue and Customs Commissioners; *sub nom* Modern Jet Support
Centre Ltd, Re [2005] EWHC 1611; [2005] 1 W.L.R. 3880; [2005] B.P.I.R.
1382; [2005] R.V.R. 379; *Times,* September 19, 2005, Ch D (Companies Ct) . . .   *Digested,* 05/**2343**
Brent LBC *v.* N [2005] EWHC 1676; [2005] Fam. Law 855, Fam Div
Brentwood BC *v.* Gladen [2004] EWHC 2500; [2005] R.T.R. 12; [2005] A.C.D. 21;
Times, November 1, 2004, QBD (Admin) . . . .   *Digested,* 05/**2767**
Brett *v.* Beaven & Sons [2005] 2 Q.R. 21, CC (Bristol) [*Ex rel.* Jonathan Clarke,
Barrister, Old Square Chambers, 3 Orchard Court, St Augustine's Yard, Bristol] . .   *Digested,* 04/**2959**
Bretton *v.* Hancock [2005] EWCA Civ 404; [2005] R.T.R. 22; [2005] Lloyd's Rep.
I.R. 454; *Independent,* April 20, 2005, CA (Civ Div) . . . .   *Digested,* 05/**2843**

Brewer *v.* DPP [2004] EWHC 355; [2005] R.T.R. 5; *Times*, March 5, 2004, QBD
(Admin) . . . . *Digested*, 04/**738**
Brian Cooper & Co *v.* Fairview Estates (Investments) [1987] 1 E.G.L.R. 18; (1987) 282
E.G. 1131, CA (Civ Div); affirming [1986] 1 E.G.L.R. 34; (1986) 278 E.G. 1094,
QBD . . . . *Digested*, 87/**60**:
Applied, 89/54, 05/90
Brian Warwicker Partnership Plc *v.* HOK International Ltd; *sub nom* Burford NW3 Ltd *v.*
Brian Warwicker Partnership Plc [2005] EWCA Civ 962; 103 Con. L.R. 112;
[2005] Lloyd's Rep. Med. 464; *Times*, September 19, 2005, CA (Civ Div);
affirming [2004] EWHC 2642, QBD (TCC) . . . . *Digested*, 05/**2833**
Brick Farm Management Ltd *v.* Richmond Housing Partnership Ltd; *sub nom* Richmond
Housing Partnership Ltd *v.* Brick Farm Management Ltd [2005] EWHC 1650;
[2005] 1 W.L.R. 3934; [2005] 3 E.G.L.R. 57; [2005] 48 E.G. 224; (2005) 155
N.L.J. 1483; [2005] N.P.C. 108; *Times*, August 30, 2005, QBD . . . . *Digested*, 05/**3385**
Bridgestart Properties Ltd *v.* London Underground Ltd [2004] EWCA Civ 793; [2005]
1 P. & C.R. 15; [2004] R.V.R. 196; (2004) 148 S.J.L.B. 793; [2004] N.P.C. 104,
CA (Civ Div); affirming [2004] R.V.R. 18, LandsTr . . . . *Digested*, 04/**3029**
Briggs *v.* Burntwood Sports Ltd [2005] 2 Q.R. 21; [2004] 6 Q.R. 12, CC (Sheffield)
[*Ex rel.* Tom Nossiter, Barrister, Park Lane Chambers, 19, Westgate, Leeds] . . . . . *Digested*, 04/**3013**
Briggs & Forrester Electrical Ltd *v.* Southfield School for Girls Governors [2005] EWHC
1734; [2005] B.L.R. 468, QBD (TCC)
Bright *v.* Barnsley District General Hospital NHS Trust [2005] Lloyd's Rep. Med. 449,
QBD
Brighton *v.* Jones [2004] EWHC 1157; [2004] E.M.L.R. 26; [2005] F.S.R. 16; (2004)
27(7) I.P.D. 27073, Ch D . . . . *Digested*, 04/**2257**
Brighton and Hove City Council *v.* Collinson [2004] EWCA Civ 678; [2004] L. & T.R.
24; [2004] 2 E.G.L.R. 65; [2004] 28 E.G. 178; [2004] 21 E.G.C.S. 150; (2004)
148 S.J.L.B. 630; [2004] 2 P. & C.R. DG11, CA (Civ Div) . . . . *Digested*, 05/**2650**
Briheche *v.* Ministre de l'Interieur (C319/03); *sub nom* Briheche *v.* Ministere de
l'Interieur, de la Securite Interieure et des Libertes Locales (C319/03) [2004]
E.C.R. I-8807; [2005] 1 C.M.L.R. 4; [2005] C.E.C. 106, ECJ (2nd Chamber). . . *Digested*, 05/**1269**
Brinkley's Will Trusts, Re; *sub nom* Westminster Bank Ltd *v.* Brinkley [1968] Ch. 407;
[1968] 2 W.L.R. 217; [1967] 3 All E.R. 805; 111 S.J. 852, Ch D . . . . *Digested*, 67/**4095**:
Applied, 05/3976
Brinks *v.* Netherlands (9940/04) (2005) 41 E.H.R.R. SE5, ECHR
Brioland Ltd *v.* Searson see Searson *v.* Brioland Ltd
Bristol and West Building Society *v.* Evans Bullock & Co QBENI 95/1744/E, CA (Civ
Div) . . . . *Digested*, 96/**695**:
Applied, 05/374
Bristol and West Building Society *v.* Mothew (t/a Stapley & Co); *sub nom* Mothew *v.*
Bristol and West Building Society [1998] Ch. 1; [1997] 2 W.L.R. 436; [1996] 4
All E.R. 698; [1997] P.N.L.R. 11; (1998) 75 P. & C.R. 241; [1996] E.G.C.S. 136;
(1996) 146 N.L.J. 1273; (1996) 140 S.J.L.B. 206; [1996] N.P.C. 126; *Times*,
August 2, 1996, CA (Civ Div) . . . . *Digested*, 96/**4503**:
Applied, 97/3822, 97/3823, 98/859, 99/458, 00/2334, 03/3015, 04/2569:
Considered, 97/3827, 98/2298, 99/3796, 00/649, 00/2323, 00/5270,
05/2873: *Followed*, 99/3814, 99/4037, 03/5827
Bristol and West Building Society *v.* Saunders see Saunders (A Bankrupt), Re
Bristol & West Plc *v.* Bartlett; Paragon Finance Plc *v.* Banks; Halifax Plc *v.* Grant [2002]
EWCA Civ 1181; [2003] 1 W.L.R. 284; [2002] 4 All E.R. 544; [2002] 2 All
E.R. (Comm) 1105; [2003] H.L.R. 22; [2003] 1 E.G.L.R. 85; [2003] 01 E.G. 69;
[2002] 33 E.G.C.S. 97; (2002) 99(38) L.S.G. 34; [2002] N.P.C. 109; *Times*,
September 9, 2002, CA (Civ Div) . . . . *Digested*, 02/**3838**:
Applied, 05/435: *Cited*, 03/3586: *Considered*, 03/260
Bristol City Council *v.* Lovell [1998] 1 W.L.R. 446; [1998] 1 All E.R. 775; (1998) 30
H.L.R. 770; [1999] L. & T.R. 66; [1998] R.V.R. 133; [1998] E.G.C.S. 29; (1998)
95(14) L.S.G. 32; (1998) 95(9) L.S.G. 30; (1998) 148 N.L.J. 329; (1998) 142
S.J.L.B. 116; [1998] N.P.C. 31; *Times*, February 27, 1998, HL; reversing (1997) 29
H.L.R. 528; [1996] E.G.C.S. 140; [1996] N.P.C. 130, CA (Civ Div) . . . . *Digested*, 98/**3055**:
Considered, 05/2674: *Followed*, 98/3056
Bristol Myers Squibb Co *v.* Paranova A/S (C427/93); CH Boehringer Sohn *v.* Paranova
A/S (C429/93); Bayer AG *v.* Paranova A/S (C436/93) [2003] Ch. 75; [2002]
3 W.L.R. 1746; [1996] E.C.R. I-3457; [1997] 1 C.M.L.R. 1151; [1996] C.E.C. 716;
[1996] E.T.M.R. 1; [1997] F.S.R. 102; (1997) 34 B.M.L.R. 59, ECJ [1996]
E.C.R. I-3457; [1996] F.S.R. 225, AGO . . . . *Digested*, 97/**4879**:
Applied, 97/3892, 98/3506, 00/3706, 00/3709, 04/2400: *Cited*, 00/3703:
Considered, 98/3514, 98/3544, 99/3560, 02/2916, 03/2641:
Distinguished, 98/3426: *Followed*, 99/3558, 04/2411: *Referred to*, 05/2444
Bristow Helicopters Ltd *v.* Sikorsky Aircraft Corp [2004] EWHC 401; [2004] 2 Lloyd's
Rep. 150; [2005] 2 C.L.C. 856, QBD (Comm) . . . . *Digested*, 05/**622**:
Considered, 05/434
Britannic Asset Management Ltd *v.* Pensions Ombudsman see R. (on the application of
Britannic Asset Management Ltd) *v.* Pensions Ombudsman

British Airways Board *v.* Parish [1979] 2 Lloyd's Rep. 361; 123 S.J. 319, CA (Civ Div) ..   *Digested*, 80/**261**:
                               Followed, 05/265

British Airways Pension Trustees Ltd *v.* British Airways Plc see Stevens *v.* Bell

British Airways Plc *v.* Commission of the European Communities (T219/99) [2004] All
E.R. (EC) 1115; [2004] 4 C.M.L.R. 19, CFI (1st Chamber) . . . .   *Digested*, 05/**575**

British Airways Plc *v.* Starmer [2005] I.R.L.R. 863, EAT . . . .   *Digested*, 05/**1299**

British American Racing (Holdings) Ltd, Re [2004] EWHC 2947; [2005] B.C.C. 110;
[2005] 2 B.C.L.C. 234, Ch D (Companies Ct) . . . .   *Digested*, 05/**2263**

British American Tobacco International Ltd *v.* Belgium (C435/03); *sub nom* British
American Tobacco International Ltd *v.* Ministerie van Financien (C435/03)
[2005] 3 C.M.L.R. 33; [2005] B.T.C. 5724; [2005] B.V.C. 755; [2005] S.T.I.
1256, ECJ (3rd Chamber)

British American Tobacco International Ltd *v.* Ministerie van Financien (C435/03) see
British American Tobacco International Ltd *v.* Belgium (C435/03)

British & Foreign Marine Insurance Co Ltd *v.* Gaunt; *sub nom* Gaunt *v.* British & Foreign
Marine Insurance Co Ltd (No.3) [1921] 2 A.C. 41; (1921) 7 Ll. L. Rep. 62, HL;
affirming [1920] 1 K.B. 903; (1920) 5 Ll. L. Rep. 202, CA . . . .   *Applied*, 55/2596,
81/2508, 82/2905, 05/2383: *Considered*, 86/1771

British Basic Slag *v.* Registrar of Restrictive Trading Agreements see British Basic Slag
Ltd's Agreements (No.1), Re

British Basic Slag Ltd's Agreements (No.1), Re; *sub nom* British Basic Slag *v.* Registrar of
Restrictive Trading Agreements; Colvilles Application, Re; Colville *v.* Registrar of
Restrictive Trading Agreements [1963] 1 W.L.R. 727; [1963] 2 All E.R. 807; 107
S.J. 457, CA; affirming [1962] 1 W.L.R. 986; [1962] 3 All E.R. 247; 106 S.J.
590, Ch D . . . .   *Digested*, 63/**3475**:
Applied, 65/3895, 66/12053, 86/3401, 05/685: *Considered*, 65/3892,
65/3893

British Beer & Pub Association *v.* Canterbury City Council [2005] EWHC 1318; (2005)
169 J.P. 521; (2005) 169 J.P.N. 859; [2005] N.P.C. 82; *Times*, July 11, 2005,
QBD (Admin) . . . .   *Digested*, 05/**2752**

British Building & Engineering Appliances *v.* Dedman see Dedman *v.* British Building &
Engineering Appliances

British Celanese Ltd *v.* Courtaulds Ltd (1935) 52 R.P.C. 171 . . . .   *Applied*, 05/2480:
Approved, 98/3462

British Coal Corp *v.* Commission of the European Communities (T367/94) see National
Power Plc, Re (C151/97 P (I))

British Coal Corp *v.* Keeble [1997] I.R.L.R. 336, EAT . . . .   *Digested*, 97/**2266**:
Applied, 98/2195: *Considered*, 05/1301

British Compressed Air Society *v.* Wall see Wall *v.* British Compressed Air Society

British Eagle International Airlines Ltd *v.* Compagnie Nationale Air France [1975] 1
W.L.R. 758; [1975] 2 All E.R. 390; [1975] 2 Lloyd's Rep. 43; 119 S.J. 368, HL;
reversing in part [1974] 1 Lloyd's Rep. 429, CA (Civ Div); affirming [1973] 1
Lloyd's Rep. 414, Ch D . . . .   *Digested*, 75/**320**:
Applied, 92/292, 97/5287: *Considered*, 99/3305, 01/3778:
Distinguished, 84/332, 93/289, 93/2319: *Followed*, 05/2407

British Horseracing Board Ltd *v.* William Hill Organisation Ltd [2001] EWCA Civ 1268;
[2002] E.C.C. 24; [2002] E.C.D.R. 4; [2002] Masons C.L.R. 1; (2001) 24(9)
I.P.D. 24059, CA (Civ Div); reversing in part [2001] 2 C.M.L.R. 12; [2002]
E.C.C. 23; [2001] E.C.D.R. 20; [2001] E.B.L.R. 71; [2001] R.P.C. 31; [2001]
Masons C.L.R. 79; (2001) 151 N.L.J. 271; *Times*, February 23, 2001;
Independent, March 26, 2001 (C.S), Ch D (Patents Ct) . . . .   *Digested*, 02/**2775**:
Overruled, 05/2433: *Subsequent proceedings*, 05/2429

British Horseracing Board Ltd *v.* William Hill Organisation Ltd [2005] EWCA Civ 863;
[2005] E.C.D.R. 28; [2005] R.P.C. 35; (2005) 155 N.L.J. 1183, CA (Civ Div) ..   *Digested*, 05/**2433**:
Considered, 05/484: *Previous proceedings*, 05/2429

British Horseracing Board Ltd *v.* William Hill Organisation Ltd (C203/02) [2004] E.C.R.
I-10415; [2005] 1 C.M.L.R. 15; [2005] C.E.C. 68; [2005] E.C.D.R. 1; [2005]
Info. T.L.R. 157; [2005] R.P.C. 13, ECJ [2004] E.C.R. I-10415; [2004] Info. T.L.R.
315, AGO . . . .   *Digested*, 05/**2429**:
Considered, 05/573: *Previous proceedings*, 02/2775:
Subsequent proceedings, 05/2433

British Industrial Plastics Ltd *v.* Ferguson [1940] 1 All E.R. 479, HL. . . . .   *Applied*, 05/4198

British Medical Association *v.* Chaudhary (No.1); Chaudhary *v.* Royal College of
Surgeons of Great Britain and Ireland Senate (Appeal: Multiple Application);
Chaudhary *v.* Secretary of State for Health (Appeal: Multiple Application);
Chaudhary *v.* Medical Royal Colleges Specialist Training Authority (Appeal:
Multiple Application); Platt *v.* Chaudhary (Appeal: Multiple Application) [2003]
EWCA Civ 645; [2003] I.C.R. 1510; [2003] Lloyd's Rep. Med. 409; (2003) 147
S.J.L.B. 629; *Times*, May 21, 2003; *Independent*, May 21, 2003, CA (Civ Div) ..   *Digested*, 03/**1294**:
Applied, 05/1293

British Motor Trade Association *v.* Salvadori [1949] Ch. 556; [1949] 1 All E.R. 208; 65
T.L.R. 44; [1949] L.J.R. 1304, Ch D . . . .   *Digested*, 47-51/**1721**:
Applied, 64/3125, 04/364, 05/2421: *Considered*, 87/516:
Distinguished, 94/4300

British Movietonews v. London and District Cinemas [1952] A.C. 166; [1951] 2 All E.R.
617; [1951] 2 T.L.R. 571; 95 S.J. 499, HL; reversing [1951] 1 K.B. 190; [1950] 2
All E.R. 390; 66 T.L.R. (Pt. 2) 203; 94 S.J. 504, CA . . . . *Digested*, 47-51/**1745**:
Applied, 55/271, 56/874: *Considered*, 52/628, 76/133, 80/350:
Followed, 05/711

British Railways Board v. Glass [1965] Ch. 538; [1964] 3 W.L.R. 913; [1964] 3 All E.R.
418; 108 S.J. 673, CA; affirming [1964] 1 W.L.R. 294; [1964] 1 All E.R. 418;
108 S.J. 198, Ch D . . . . *Digested*, 64/**1204**:
Applied, 71/3752, 80/817, 05/3403

British Sugar Plc v. Commission of the European Communities (C359/01 P) [2004]
E.C.R. I-4933; [2004] 5 C.M.L.R. 8, ECJ (5th Chamber) . . . . *Digested*, 05/**549**:
Previous proceedings, 01/760

British Sugar Plc v. Fratelli Babbini di Lionello Babbini & Co SAS; *sub nom* Fratelli
Babbini di Lionello Babbini & Co SAS v. BF Engineering SpA [2004] EWHC
2560; [2005] 1 All E.R. (Comm) 55; [2005] 1 Lloyd's Rep. 332; 100 Con. L.R.
122; [2005] I.L.Pr. 20, QBD (TCC). . . . . *Digested*, 05/**626**

British Telecommunications Plc v. Office of Communications (formerly Director General
of Telecommunications) [2004] CAT 8; [2004] Comp. A.R. 574, CAT . . . . *Digested*, 05/**4184**

Britnell v. Secretary of State for Social Services see R. v. Secretary of State for Social
Services Ex p. Britnell

Broadbent v. Parole Board see R. (on the application of Broadbent) v. Parole Board

Broadhurst v. United Kingdom (69187/01) [2005] R.V.R. 56, ECHR . . . . *Digested*, 05/**2096**

Broadwick Financial Services Ltd v. Spencer [2002] EWCA Civ 35; [2002] 1 All E.R.
(Comm) 446; (2002) 99(11) L.S.G. 36; (2002) 146 S.J.L.B. 53, CA (Civ Div). . *Digested*, 02/**694**:
Considered, 05/3421

Brocklebank v. General Medical Council [2003] UKPC 57; (2004) 79 B.M.L.R. 122;
(2003) 147 S.J.L.B. 1084, PC (UK) . . . . *Digested*, 05/**1798**

Broere v. Mourant & Co (Trustees) Ltd [2004] W.T.L.R. 1417, CA (Jer) . . . . *Digested*, 05/**4293**

Brogan v. United Kingdom (11209/84) see Brogan v. United Kingdom (A/145-B)

Brogan v. United Kingdom (A/145-B); *sub nom* Brogan v. United Kingdom (11209/
84); Tracey v. United Kingdom; Coyle v. United Kingdom (11266/84); McFadden
v. United Kingdom (11365/85) (1989) 11 E.H.R.R. 117; *Times*, November 30,
1988; *Independent*, November 30, 1988; *Guardian*, December 7, 1988, ECHR
(1987) 9 E.H.R.R. CD378, Eur Comm HR . . . . *Digested*, 88/**1804**:
Applied, 03/2157, 05/2130: *Followed*, 98/3073

Bromley LBC v. Chislehurst Service Station [2005] P.A.D. 35, Planning Inspector

Bromley LBC v. Greater London Council [1983] 1 A.C. 768; [1982] 2 W.L.R. 92;
[1982] 1 All E.R. 153; 126 S.J. 16, HL; affirming [1982] 2 W.L.R. 62; [1982] 1 All
E.R. 129, CA (Civ Div) . . . . *Digested*, 82/**1910**:
Applied, 83/288: *Considered*, 86/2017, 87/3159, 88/3026, 89/3186,
05/1415: *Distinguished*, 82/1911: *Referred to*, 94/549, 95/771

Bromley LBC v. Maughan see South Cambridgeshire DC v. Gammell

Broniowski v. Poland (31443/96) (2005) 40 E.H.R.R. 21; 16 B.H.R.C. 573, ECHR
(Grand Chamber) . . . . *Digested*, 04/**1933**

Brook Leisure Holdings Ltd v. Revenue and Customs Commissioners [2005] S.T.I. 1732,
V&DTr

Brook Street Bureau (UK) Ltd v. Dacas see Dacas v. Brook Street Bureau (UK) Ltd

Brooker v. DPP [2005] EWHC 1132; (2005) 169 J.P. 368; (2005) 169 J.P.N. 497;
Times, May 5, 2005, QBD (Admin) . . . . *Digested*, 05/**797**

Brooklands Selangor Holdings v. Inland Revenue Commissioners; Kuala Pertang
Syndicate v. Inland Revenue Commissioners [1970] 1 W.L.R. 429; [1970] 2 All
E.R. 76; [1969] T.R. 485; (1969) 114 S.J. 170, Ch D . . . . *Digested*, 70/**2715**:
Applied, 91/3390, 02/4358, 05/2335

Brooks v. Brooks; *sub nom* B v. B (Post Nuptial Settlements) (Pension Fund), Re
[1996] A.C. 375; [1995] 3 W.L.R. 141; [1995] 3 All E.R. 257; [1995] 2 F.L.R. 13;
[1995] 3 F.C.R. 214; [1995] Fam. Law 545; (1995) 145 N.L.J. 995; (1995)
139 S.J.L.B. 165; *Times*, July 3, 1995; *Independent*, July 4, 1995, HL; affirming
[1995] Fam. 70; [1994] 3 W.L.R. 1292; [1994] 4 All E.R. 1065; [1994] 2 F.L.R.
10; [1995] 1 F.C.R. 220; [1994] O.P.L.R. 41; [1994] Fam. Law 382; (1994) 144
N.L.J. 830; *Times*, May 27, 1994; *Independent*, May 27, 1994, CA (Civ Div);
affirming [1993] Fam. 322; [1993] 3 W.L.R. 548; [1993] 4 All E.R. 917; [1993]
2 F.L.R. 491; [1993] Fam. Law 576; (1993) 143 N.L.J. 723; *Times*, May 5,
1993; *Independent*, May 14, 1993, Fam Div . . . . *Digested*, 95/**2354**:
Distinguished, 05/1682

Brooks v. Camden LBC (Unreported, February 12, 2004), CC (Clerkenwell) [*Ex rel.*
Colin Mendoza, Barrister, Devereux Chambers, Devereux Court, London] . . . . . *Digested*, 05/**3178**

Brooks v. Commissioner of Police of the Metropolis [2005] UKHL 24; [2005] 1
W.L.R. 1495; [2005] 2 All E.R. 489; (2005) 155 N.L.J. 653; *Times*, April 26,
2005, HL; reversing [2002] EWCA Civ 407; *Daily Telegraph*, April 11, 2002, CA
(Civ Div). . . . . *Digested*, 05/**3342**

Brotherton *v.* Aseguradora Colseguros SA (No.2); *sub nom* Brotherton *v.* La Previsora
SA Compania de Seguros [2003] EWCA Civ 705; [2003] 2 All E.R. (Comm)
298; [2003] 2 C.L.C. 629; [2003] Lloyd's Rep. I.R. 746; (2003) 147 S.J.L.B.
658, CA (Civ Div); affirming [2003] EWHC 335; [2003] 1 All E.R. (Comm) 774,
QBD (Comm) . . . .   *Digested*, 03/**2476**:
Followed, 05/614
Brotherton *v.* La Previsora SA Compania de Seguros see Brotherton *v.* Aseguradora
Colseguros SA (No.2)
Brotherton *v.* Young (Unreported, November 19, 2004), CC (Salford) [*Ex rel.* Chris
Middleton, Oriel Chambers, 14 Water Street, Liverpool] . . . .   *Digested*, 05/**3114**
Brown *v.* FE Thorpe & Sons (Unreported, May 7, 2004), CC (Willesden) [*Ex rel.*
Joanna Kerr, Barrister, Lamb Chambers, Lamb Building, Temple, London] . . . . . .   *Digested*, 05/**964**
Brown *v.* Kigass Aero Components Ltd; *sub nom* Kigass Aero Components Ltd *v.*
Brown; Bold Transmission Parts Ltd *v.* Taree; Taree *v.* Bold Transmission Parts Ltd;
Macredie *v.* Thrapston Garage [2002] I.C.R. 697; [2002] I.R.L.R. 312; [2002]
Emp. L.R. 900, EAT . . . .   *Digested*, 02/**1377**:
Distinguished, 04/1267: *Overruled*, 05/1273
Brown *v.* Mcasso Music Production Ltd [2005] F.S.R. 40; (2005) 28(7) I.P.D.
28053, PCC . . . .   *Digested*, 05/**2417**
Brown *v.* United Kingdom (Admissibility) (44223/98) (2002) 35 E.H.R.R. CD197,
ECHR . . . .   *Applied*, 05/815
Brown (CICA: Quantum: 2003), Re [2005] 2 Q.R. 13; [2004] 4 Q.R. 5, CICB (Plymouth)
[*Ex rel.* Daniel Bennett, Barrister, Old Square Chambers, 3 Orchard Court, St
Augustine's Yard, Bristol] . . . .   *Digested*, 04/**2918**
Brown (Uriah) *v.* Queen, The; *sub nom* R. *v.* Brown (Uriah) [2005] UKPC 18; [2005] 2
W.L.R. 1558, PC (Jam) . . . .   *Digested*, 05/**757**
Browne *v.* Chief Constable of Greater Manchester see Mohindra *v.* DPP
Browne *v.* DPP see Mohindra *v.* DPP
Browne *v.* Dunn (1894) 6 R. 67 . . . .   *Applied*, 80/466,
81/405, 05/2448: *Considered*, 71/728, 77/728: *Referred to*, 90/2246
Browne *v.* Queen, The [2000] 1 A.C. 45; [1999] 3 W.L.R. 1158; (1999) 143 S.J.L.B.
181; *Times*, May 11, 1999, PC (StC) . . . .   *Digested*, 99/**781**:
Applied, 05/773: *Considered*, 03/635, 04/3334
Browning *v.* Brachers (A Firm) (Damages) [2005] EWCA Civ 753; [2005] P.N.L.R.
44, CA (Civ Div); reversing [2004] EWHC 16; [2004] P.N.L.R. 28, QBD . . . . . .   *Digested*, 05/**957**
Bruce *v.* Dignity Funerals Ltd; *sub nom* Dignity Funerals Ltd *v.* Bruce 2005 S.C. 59;
2004 S.L.T. 1223; 2005 S.C.L.R. 951; [2005] I.R.L.R. 189; (2004) 148 S.J.L.B.
1313; 2004 G.W.D. 32-662, IH (2 Div); reversing EATS/0015/02, EAT (SC) . . . .   *Digested*, 05/**5217**
Bruce's Estate, Re (2004-05) 7 I.T.E.L.R. 280, Sup Ct (PEI) . . . .   *Digested*, 05/**3973**
Brugg Rohrsysteme GmbH *v.* Commission of the European Communities (C207/02 P)
see Dansk Rorindustri A/S *v.* Commission of the European Communities (C189/
02 P)
Brugger *v.* Medicaid Ltd (No.2) [1996] R.P.C. 635, Ch D (Patents Ct) . . . .   *Digested*, 97/**3905**:
Applied, 03/2587, 05/2481
Brumark Investments Ltd, Re; *sub nom* Inland Revenue Commissioner *v.* Agnew;
Agnew *v.* Inland Revenue Commissioner [2001] UKPC 28; [2001] 2 A.C. 710;
[2001] 3 W.L.R. 454; [2001] Lloyd's Rep. Bank. 251; [2001] B.C.C. 259; [2001]
2 B.C.L.C. 188; *Independent*, July 16, 2001 (C.S); *Daily Telegraph*, June 12,
2001, PC (NZ); affirming [2000] 1 B.C.L.C. 353, CA (NZ) . . . .   *Digested*, 01/**732**:
Applied, 02/2644, 05/2320
Brumfitt *v.* Ministry of Defence [2005] I.R.L.R. 4; (2004) 148 S.J.L.B. 1028, EAT . . . . .   *Digested*, 05/**1298**
Bruncrona *v.* Finland (41673/98) (2005) 41 E.H.R.R. 28, ECHR
Brunel University *v.* Webster see Wong *v.* Igen Ltd (formerly Leeds Careers Guidance)
Brunnhofer *v.* Bank der Osterreichischen Postsparkasse AG (C381/99) [2001] All E.R.
(EC) 693; [2001] E.C.R. I-4961; [2001] 3 C.M.L.R. 9; [2001] I.R.L.R. 571;
[2001] Emp. L.R. 1176; *Times*, July 9, 2001, ECJ (6th Chamber) . . . .   *Digested*, 01/**2277**:
Applied, 05/1268: *Considered*, 04/1255
Brunt *v.* Southampton International Airport Ltd [2005] EWCA Civ 93; [2005] Env.
L.R. 28; [2005] 2 P. & C.R. 21; [2005] 2 E.G.L.R. 105; [2005] R.V.R. 120;
[2005] J.P.L. 1318; (2005) 102(15) L.S.G. 34; [2005] N.P.C. 17; *Times*,
February 15, 2005, CA (Civ Div); affirming [2004] R.V.R. 81, Lands Tr . . . .   *Digested*, 05/**3390**
Brutus *v.* Cozens [1973] A.C. 854; [1972] 3 W.L.R. 521; [1972] 2 All E.R. 1297; (1972)
56 Cr. App. R. 799; [1973] Crim. L.R. 56; 116 S.J. 647, HL; reversing [1972] 1
W.L.R. 484; [1972] 2 All E.R. 1; 116 S.J. 217, QBD . . . .   *Digested*, 72/**706**:
Applied, 72/746, 73/602, 73/655, 74/2726, 79/2532, 91/974, 92/1129,
93/977, 93/4067, 98/4669, 04/770, 05/796: *Considered*, 82/632, 86/1238,
88/3243, 89/3395, 91/2373, 95/5116, 95/5119, 96/1506, 03/4560:
Distinguished, 90/4372: *Followed*, 97/2863
Bruvik *v.* Emi Norsk AS [2005] E.C.D.R. 23, LR (Eidsivating)
Bryan *v.* Maloney 74 B.L.R. 35; 51 Con. L.R. 29; 182 C.L.R. 609; (1995) 11 Const. L.J.
274, HC (Aus) . . . .   *Digested*, 96/**4436**:
Disapproved, 05/2847: *Followed*, 98/3924
Bryan Haulage Ltd *v.* Vehicle Inspectorate (No.1) (Unreported, June 25, 2002),
Transport Tr . . . .   *Approved*, 05/3458

Bryant v. Mike Beer Transport Ltd see Anderton v. Clwyd CC
Bryant v. Pech see Anderton v. Clwyd CC
Bryen & Langley Ltd v. Boston [2005] EWCA Civ 973; [2005] B.L.R. 508, CA (Civ
 Div); reversing [2004] EWHC 2450; [2005] B.L.R. 28; 98 Con. L.R. 82; [2004]
 N.P.C. 165, QBD (TCC) . . . .   *Digested*, 05/**194**
BT Fleet Ltd v. McKenna [2005] EWHC 387; (2005) 102(21) L.S.G. 33; *Times*, April 5,
 2005, QBD (Admin)
BT Pension Scheme, Re see BT Pension Scheme Trustees v. Revenue and Customs
 Commissioners
BT Pension Scheme Trustees v. Revenue and Customs Commissioners; *sub nom* BT
 Pension Scheme, Re [2005] EWHC 3088; [2005] S.T.I. 1842, Ch D
BTG/Magnetic field screen (T473/98) [2001] E.P.O.R. 64, EPO (Technical Bd App) . . .   *Digested*, 02/**2808**:
                                                                                       Considered, 05/2451
Bubbins v. United Kingdom (50196/99) (2005) 41 E.H.R.R. 24; *Times*, March 30,
 2005, ECHR
Buchanan v. Broadleigh Developments Ltd [2005] 3 Q.R. 7, CC (Sheffield) [*Ex rel.*
 Pankaj Madan, Barrister, Zenith Chambers, 10 Park Square, Leeds] . . . .   *Digested*, 05/**3086**
Buchanan v. Jennings; *sub nom* Jennings v. Buchanan [2004] UKPC 36; [2005] 1
 A.C. 115; [2004] 3 W.L.R. 1163; [2005] 2 All E.R. 273; [2004] E.M.L.R. 22;
 (2004) 101 (33) L.S.G. 34; *Times*, July 19, 2004, PC (NZ). . . . .   *Digested*, 04/**927**
Buck v. Attorney General [1965] Ch. 745; [1965] 2 W.L.R. 1033; [1965] 1 All E.R.
 882; 109 S.J. 291, CA; affirming [1964] 3 W.L.R. 850; [1964] 2 All E.R. 663;
 108 S.J. 601, Ch D . . . .   *Digested*, 65/**325**:
                                                            Considered, 90/3689, 95/2939, 96/3659, 05/634
Buckland v. Palmer [1984] 1 W.L.R. 1109; [1984] 3 All E.R. 554; [1985] R.T.R. 5;
 (1984) 81 L.S.G. 2300; (1984) 128 S.J. 565, CA (Civ Div) . . . .   *Digested*, 84/**2549**:
                                           Considered, 97/688, 05/306: *Distinguished*, 01/585: *Referred to*, 94/3773
Buckler v. JF Finnegan Ltd see Buckler v. Sheffield City Council
Buckler v. Sheffield City Council; *sub nom* Buckler v. JF Finnegan Ltd [2004] EWCA
 Civ 920; [2005] P.I.Q.R. P3; (2004) 148 S.J.L.B. 791, CA (Civ Div) . . . .   *Digested*, 05/**440**
Buckley v. Revenue and Customs Commissioners [2005] S.T.C. (S.C.D.) 860; [2005]
 S.T.I. 1799, Sp Comm
BUCKMAN LABORATORIES INTERNATIONAL/Synergistic combination (T393/01)
 [2005] E.P.O.R. 8, EPO (Technical Bd App) . . . .   *Digested*, 05/**2464**
Bucknell v. Currie [2005] 2 Q.R. 8; [2004] 6 Q.R. 6, CC (Cambridge) [*Ex rel.* Andrew
 Granville Stafford, Barrister, 4 King's Bench Walk, Temple, London] . . . .   *Digested*, 04/**2868**
Budden v. Police Aviation Services Ltd [2005] P.I.Q.R. P23, QBD
Buddington v. Secretary of State for the Home Department see R. (on the application
 of Buddington) v. Secretary of State for the Home Department
Budejovicky Budvar Narodni Podnik v. Rudolf Ammersin GmbH (C216/01) [2003]
 E.C.R. I-13617; [2005] 1 C.M.L.R. 56; [2004] E.T.M.R. 21, ECJ . . . .   *Digested*, 04/**1408**
Bugdaycay v. Secretary of State for the Home Department; *sub nom* R. v. Secretary of
 State for the Home Department Ex p. Bugdaycay; Nelidow Santis v. Secretary of
 State for the Home Department; Norman v. Secretary of State for the Home
 Department; Musisi v. Secretary of State for the Home Department [1987] A.C.
 514; [1987] 2 W.L.R. 606; [1987] 1 All E.R. 940; [1987] Imm. A.R. 250;
 (1987) 84 L.S.G. 902; (1987) 137 N.L.J. 199; (1987) 131 S.J. 297, HL; affirming
 [1986] 1 W.L.R. 155; [1986] 1 All E.R. 458; [1986] Imm. A.R. 8; (1986) 83
 L.S.G. 700; (1986) 130 S.J. 129; *Times*, November 12, 1985, CA (Civ Div);
 affirming *Times*, July 11, 1985, DC . . . .   *Digested*, 87/**1989**:
        Applied, 87/1926, 89/1951, 89/1954, 92/2402, 92/2450, 93/2233, 94/2452,
                           96/3220, 97/4111, 01/3421, 03/3944: *Cited*, 94/2498, 95/2695:
                       Considered, 87/23, 87/1983, 88/14, 90/2572, 91/1965, 94/2455, 96/3236,
                                  96/3278, 05/3882: *Followed*, 96/3300, 97/2929, 98/3196:
                                                                 Referred to, 89/1939, 95/2676
Bugle Press, Re; *sub nom* Houses & Estates Ltd, Re; HC Treby's Application [1961] Ch.
 270; [1960] 3 W.L.R. 956; [1960] 3 All E.R. 791; 104 S.J. 1057, CA; affirming
 [1960] 2 W.L.R. 658; [1960] 1 All E.R. 768; 104 S.J. 289, Ch D . . . .   *Digested*, 60/**435**:
                                           Applied, 75/301, 78/232: *Considered*, 69/137, 69/187, 02/525:
                                                                                 Distinguished, 05/2263
Building Product Design Ltd v. Sandtoft Roof Tiles Ltd (No.1) [2004] F.S.R. 40, PCC . .   *Digested*, 05/**2476**
Building Product Design Ltd v. Sandtoft Roof Tiles Ltd (No.2) [2004] F.S.R. 41, PCC . .   *Digested*, 05/**2477**
Buildlead Ltd (In Creditors Voluntary Liquidation) (No.1), Re see Quicksons (South & West)
 Ltd v. Katz (No.1)
Buildlead Ltd (In Creditors Voluntary Liquidation) (No.2), Re see Quicksons (South & West)
 Ltd v. Katz (No.2)
Bulbul v. Secretary of State for the Home Department see Sepet v. Secretary of State
 for the Home Department
Bulfracht (Cyprus) Ltd v. Boneset Shipping Co Ltd (The Pamphilos) [2002] EWHC
 2292; [2002] 2 Lloyd's Rep. 681, QBD (Comm) . . . .   *Digested*, 03/**3894**:
                                                                                       Applied, 05/205
Bull v. Thomas (Unreported, October 15, 2004), CC (Northampton) [*Ex rel.* Cogent
 Solicitors, 3 Bedford Court, Croydon CR9 2ZL] . . . .   *Digested*, 05/**3163**

Bultitude *v.* Law Society; *sub nom* Law Society *v.* Bultitude [2004] EWCA Civ 1853; (2005) 102(9) L.S.G. 29; *Times*, January 14, 2005, CA (Civ Div); reversing [2004] EWHC 1370, QBD (Admin) . . . .   *Digested*, 05/**2732**

Bunce *v.* Postworth Ltd (t/a Skyblue) [2005] EWCA Civ 490; [2005] I.R.L.R. 557, CA (Civ Div); affirming UKEAT/0052/04/MH, EAT . . . .   *Digested*, 05/**1214**

Bundesverband der Arzneimittel Importeure eV *v.* Bayer AG (C2/01 P); *sub nom* Bayer AG *v.* Commission of the European Communities (C2/01 P) [2004] All E.R. (EC) 500; [2004] E.C.R. I-23; [2004] 4 C.M.L.R. 13; [2004] E.T.M.R. 100; [2005] I.C.R. 834; (2004) 78 B.M.L.R. 91, ECJ . . . .   *Digested*, 04/**494**:
       Previous proceedings, 01/776

Bunting *v.* W [2005] EWHC 1274; (2005) 86 B.M.L.R. 39; [2005] W.T.L.R. 955, CP . .   *Digested*, 05/**2827**

BUPA Purchasing Ltd *v.* Revenue and Customs Commissioners; *sub nom* BUPA Purchasing Ltd *v.* Customs and Excise Commissioners (No.2) [2005] EWHC 2117; [2005] B.T.C. 5637; [2005] B.V.C. 668; [2005] S.T.I. 1675, Ch D

Burchell *v.* Bullard [2005] EWCA Civ 358; [2005] C.P. Rep. 36; [2005] B.L.R. 330; [2005] 3 Costs L.R. 507; (2005) 155 N.L.J. 593; *Independent*, April 21, 2005, CA (Civ Div) . . . .   *Digested*, 05/**356**

Burden *v.* Harrods Ltd [2005] EWHC 410; [2005] P.I.Q.R. P17, QBD . . . .   *Digested*, 05/**311**

Bureau Rik Decan-Business Research & Development NV (BRD) *v.* Belgium (C401/95) see Garage Molenheide BVBA *v.* Belgium (C286/94)

Bureau Veritas *v.* Societe Silja Oyj ABP [2005] I.L.Pr. 42, Cass (F)

Burford *v.* Durkin (Inspector of Taxes) [1991] S.T.C. 7; 63 T.C. 645, CA (Civ Div); affirming [1990] S.T.C. 845; [1990] S.T.I. 825; *Times*, October 26,1989, Ch D . .   *Digested*, 91/**2081**:
       Applied, 05/4340

Burford NW3 Ltd *v.* Brian Warwicker Partnership Plc see Brian Warwicker Partnership Plc *v.* HOK International Ltd

Burgess (t/a JJ Burgess & Sons) *v.* Office of Fair Trading [2005] CAT 25; [2005] Comp. A.R. 1151, CAT

Burghartz *v.* Switzerland (A/280-B) [1994] 2 F.C.R. 235; (1994) 18 E.H.R.R. 101; [1995] Fam. Law 71; *Times*, April 8, 1994, ECHR . . . .   *Digested*, 94/**2427**:
       Applied, 97/2819, 05/2128

Burghill Valley Golf Club *v.* Customs and Excise Commissioners [2005] B.V.C. 2281, V&DTr

Burke *v.* Uvex Sports GmbH [2005] I.L.Pr. 26, HC (Irl)

Burman *v.* Mount Cook Land Ltd [2001] EWCA Civ 1712; [2002] Ch. 256; [2002] 2 W.L.R. 1172; [2002] 1 All E.R. 144; [2002] H.L.R. 45; [2002] L. & T.R. 19; [2002] 1 E.G.L.R. 61; [2002] 06 E.G. 156; [2001] 48 E.G.C.S. 128; (2002) 99(3) L.S.G. 26; (2001) 98(46) L.S.G. 37; (2002) 146 S.J.L.B. 12; [2001] N.P.C. 166; [2002] 1 P. & C.R. DG16; *Independent*, November 30, 2001, CA (Civ Div); reversing [2001] 1 E.G.L.R. 62; [2001] 10 E.G. 164, CC (Central London) .   *Digested*, 01/**4181**:
       Applied, 03/2745, 05/2652

Burnden Group Plc *v.* Northstar Systems Ltd see Burnden Group Plc *v.* Ultraframe (UK) Ltd

Burnden Group Plc *v.* Northstar Systems Ltd (In Liquidation) see Ultraframe (UK) Ltd *v.* Fielding

Burnden Group Plc *v.* Ultraframe (UK) Ltd; Burnden Group Plc *v.* Northstar Systems Ltd [2005] EWCA Civ 867; (2005) 28(9) I.P.D. 28063, CA (Civ Div)

Burns *v.* Burns [2004] EWCA Civ 1258; [2004] 3 F.C.R. 263, CA (Civ Div) . . . .   *Digested*, 05/**1661**

Burns *v.* Consignia Plc (No.2) see Burns *v.* Royal Mail Group Plc (formerly Consignia Plc)

Burns *v.* Royal Mail Group Plc (formerly Consignia Plc); *sub nom* Burns *v.* Consignia Plc (No.2) [2004] I.C.R. 1103; [2004] I.R.L.R. 425; *Times*, June 24, 2004, EAT .   *Digested*, 04/**1248**:
       Applied, 05/1256

Burns International Security Services (UK) *v.* Butt [1983] I.C.R. 547; [1983] I.R.L.R. 438, EAT . . . .   *Digested*, 83/**1241**:
       Applied, 05/1279: *Followed*, 85/1254

Burns-Anderson Independent Network Plc *v.* Wheeler [2005] EWHC 575; [2005] 1 Lloyd's Rep. 580; [2005] I.L.Pr. 38, QBD (Merc) . . . .   *Digested*, 05/**485**

Burrell *v.* Burrell [2005] EWHC 245; [2005] S.T.C. 569; [2005] Pens. L.R. 289; [2005] B.T.C. 8011; [2005] W.T.L.R. 313; (2004-05) 7 I.T.E.L.R. 622, Ch D . . .   *Digested*, 05/**4305**

Burris *v.* Azadani [1995] 1 W.L.R. 1372; [1995] 4 All E.R. 802; [1996] 1 F.L.R. 266; [1996] 1 F.C.R. 618; [1996] Fam. Law 145; (1995) 145 N.L.J. 1330; *Times*, August 9, 1995, CA (Civ Div). . . . .   *Digested*, 96/**5693**:
       Applied, 05/419

Burstein *v.* Times Newspapers Ltd [2001] 1 W.L.R. 579; [2001] E.M.L.R. 14; (2001) 98(8) L.S.G. 44; (2001) 145 S.J.L.B. 30; *Times*, January 31, 2001, CA (Civ Div); affirming 1999 TLQ (J) 1205, QBD. . . . .   *Digested*, 01/**1820**:
       Considered, 01/1818, 03/960, 05/834, 05/969

Burton *v.* Bevan [1908] 2 Ch. 240, Ch D . . . .   *Considered*, 05/1708

Burton *v.* British Railways Board (19/81) [1982] Q.B. 1080; [1982] 3 W.L.R. 387; [1982] 3 All E.R. 537; [1982] E.C.R. 554; [1982] E.C.R. 555; [1982] 2 C.M.L.R. 136; [1982] I.C.R. 329; [1982] I.R.L.R. 116; 126 S.J. 480, ECJ. . . . .   *Digested*, 82/**1220**:
       Considered, 83/1294, 87/1637, 91/1636, 05/1257

Burton v. M&S Thompson Plant Hire Ltd (Unreported, May 13, 2004), CC (York) [*Ex rel.* Tom Nossiter, Barrister, Park Lane Chambers, 19, Westgate, Leeds] . . . .   *Digested*, 05/**3150**
Burton v. New Forest DC [2004] EWCA Civ 1510; (2004) 148 S.J.L.B. 1371; *Independent*, November 18, 2004, CA (Civ Div) . . . .   *Digested*, 05/**3873**
Buscarini v. San Marino (24645/94) (2000) 30 E.H.R.R. 208; 6 B.H.R.C. 638, ECHR. .   *Digested*, 00/**3195**:
    Considered, 05/2101

Bushell v. Secretary of State for the Environment [1981] A.C. 75; [1980] 3 W.L.R. 22; [1980] 2 All E.R. 608; 78 L.G.R. 269; (1980) 40 P. & C.R. 51; [1980] J.P.L. 458; 125 S.J. 168, HL; reversing 78 L.G.R. 10; (1980) 39 P. & C.R. 341; [1980] J.P.L. 27; 123 S.J. 605, CA (Civ Div); reversing 76 L.G.R. 460; (1978) 36 P. & C.R. 363; [1978] J.P.L. 310; 122 S.J. 110, QBD . . . .   *Digested*, 80/**1337**:
    Applied, 80/308, 82/9, 84/1614, 02/6041: *Considered*, 83/38, 86/2017,
    87/35, 87/3162, 88/3604, 96/4751, 05/59: *Distinguished*, 94/1874:
    Followed, 95/4845: *Referred to*, 91/5756
Businessman v. Inspector of Taxes see Weston v. Garnett (Inspector of Taxes)
Butler, Re; *sub nom* Camberwell (Wingfield Mews) No.2 Clearance Order 1936, Re [1939] 1 K.B. 570, CA; affirming [1938] 2 K.B. 210, KBD . . . .   *Applied*, 65/520,
    66/1538: *Distinguished*, 65/522: *Followed*, 05/3258
Butler v. Butler see M v. P (Contempt of Court: Committal Order)
Butler v. Derby City Council [2005] EWHC 2835; (2005) 102(48) L.S.G. 19, QBD (Admin)
Butler Machine Tool Co v. Ex-cell-o Corp (England) [1979] 1 W.L.R. 401; [1979] 1 All E.R. 965; 121 S.J. 406, CA (Civ Div) . . . .   *Digested*, 79/**338**:
    Considered, 05/654
Butterworth v. Soutter [2000] B.P.I.R. 582, Ch D . . . .   *Digested*, 01/**3717**:
    Applied, 05/2270

Buttes Gas & Oil Co v. Hammer (No.3); Occidental Petroleum Corp v. Buttes Gas & Oil Co (No.2) [1982] A.C. 888; [1981] 3 W.L.R. 787; [1981] 3 All E.R. 616; [1981] Com. L.R. 257; 125 S.J. 776; *Times*, October 31, 1981, HL; reversing [1981] Q.B. 223; [1980] 3 W.L.R. 668; [1980] 3 All E.R. 475; 124 S.J. 630, CA (Civ Div) . . . .   *Digested*, 81/**1473**:
    Applied, 87/3060, 95/2939, 96/3659: *Cited*, 93/3224: *Considered*, 84/2700,
    91/2860, 92/3479, 96/681, 96/1086, 98/3552, 99/723, 00/1756, 00/5107,
    03/4204, 05/212: *Distinguished*, 85/2651, 90/3689: *Not followed*, 88/1595,
    89/1699
Button v. Bexley LBC [2005] P.A.D. 63, Planning Inspector
Bwllfa and Merthyr Dare Steam Collieries (1891) Ltd v. Pontypridd Waterworks Co; *sub nom* Bwllfa and Merthyr Dare Steam Collieries (1891) Ltd and Pontypridd Waterworks Co's Arbitration, Re [1903] A.C. 426, HL; reversing [1902] 2 K.B. 135, CA; reversing [1901] 2 K.B. 798, KBD . . . .   *Applied*, 62/2560,
    68/1862, 68/4074, 75/3666, 79/297, 03/3023: *Considered*, 69/433,
    82/20.au, 95/4829, 03/1230, 05/2671: *Distinguished*, 79/2873, 83/3143,
    91/3062

C v. C (Ancillary Relief: Nuptial Settlement); *sub nom* C v. C (Financial Provision: Post Nuptial Settlements); C v. C (Variation of Post Nuptial Settlement) [2004] EWCA Civ 1030; [2005] Fam. 250; [2005] 2 W.L.R. 241; [2004] 2 F.L.R. 1093; [2004] 2 F.C.R. 721; [2004] W.T.L.R. 1061; [2004] Fam. Law 861; *Times*, September 7, 2004, CA (Civ Div); affirming [2004] EWHC 742; [2004] Fam. 141; [2004] 2 W.L.R. 1467; [2004] 2 F.L.R. 1; [2004] Fam. Law 483; (2004) 101(18) L.S.G. 34; *Times*, April 29, 2004, Fam Div . . . .   *Digested*, 05/**1682**
C v. C (Brussels II: French Conciliation and Divorce Proceedings) see C v. C (Divorce: Jurisdiction)
C v. C (Divorce: Jurisdiction); *sub nom* C v. C (Brussels II: French Conciliation and Divorce Proceedings) [2005] EWCA Civ 68; [2005] 1 W.L.R. 469; [2005] 2 F.L.R. 38; [2005] Fam. Law 276; (2005) 102(9) L.S.G. 28; (2005) 149 S.J.L.B. 113; *Times*, January 18, 2005, CA (Civ Div); reversing [2004] EWHC 1959; [2005] 2 F.L.R. 14; [2005] Fam. Law 15, Fam Div . . . .   *Digested*, 05/**1624**
C v. C (Financial Provision: Post Nuptial Settlements) see C v. C (Ancillary Relief: Nuptial Settlement)
C v. C (Variation of Post Nuptial Settlement) see C v. C (Ancillary Relief: Nuptial Settlement)
C v. East Sussex CC [2004] EWHC 3122; [2005] E.L.R. 367, QBD (Admin) . . . .   *Digested*, 05/**1142**
C v. Merseyside Regional Ambulance Service NHS Trust [2003] EWHC 250; [2004] 3 Costs L.R. 363, Fam Div . . . .   *Digested*, 05/**2702**
C v. Middlesbrough BC [2004] EWCA Civ 1746; [2005] 1 F.C.R. 76; [2005] E.L.R. 91, CA (Civ Div); affirming [2004] EWHC 1386, QBD . . . .   *Digested*, 05/**2859**
C v. Secretary of State for the Home Department see A v. Secretary of State for the Home Department
C v. United Kingdom (A/184) see Cossey v. United Kingdom (A/184)
C (A Child) v. Edge [2005] 2 Q.R. 12, CC (Watford) [*Ex rel.* Mr Sharpe, Barrister, 1 Temple Gardens, Temple, London] . . . .   *Digested*, 04/**2873**

C (A Child) v. Forrest (Unreported, February 16, 2004), CC (Worcester) [*Ex rel.* Stephen Garner, Barrister, No.8 Chambers, Fountain Court, Steelhouse Lane, Birmingham.].. *Digested*, 05/**3230**
C (A Child) v. Patel (Unreported, February 17, 2004), CC (Wolverhampton) [*Ex rel.* Stephen Garner, Barrister, No.8 Chambers, Fountain Court, Steelhouse Lane, Birmingham.].. *Digested*, 05/**3218**
C (A Child) v. Powell [2005] 2 Q.R. 17, CC (Cambridge) [*Ex rel.* Joanna Kerr, Barrister, 8 Stone Buildings, Lincoln's Inn, London]............................ *Digested*, 04/**2994**
C (A Child) v. Samuda (Unreported, July 23, 2004), CC (Brentford) [*Ex rel.* David McHugh, Barrister, 1, Essex Court Chambers, 1st Floor, Temple, London]...... *Digested*, 05/**3133**
C (A Child) v. Slater [2005] 2 Q.R. 16; [2004] 5 Q.R. 4, CC (Birmingham) [*Ex rel.* Stephen Garner, Barrister, No.8 Chambers, Fountain Court, Steelhouse Lane, Birmingham.].. *Digested*, 04/**2900**
C (A Child) v. Waltham Forest LBC (Unreported, April 22, 2005), CC (Bow) [*Ex rel.* Adam Walker, Barrister, Lamb Chambers, Lamb Building, Elm Court, Temple, London]... *Digested*, 05/**3094**
C (A Child) (Care Order: Application to Discharge), Re; *sub nom* NP v. South Gloucestershire CC [2005] EWCA Civ 1329; (2005) 102(46) L.S.G. 26; *Independent*, November 16, 2005, CA (Civ Div)
C (A Child) (Care Proceedings: Disclosure of Local Authority's Decision Making Process), Re see L (A Child) (Care: Assessment: Fair Trial), Re
C (A Child) (Contact Order), Re [2005] EWCA Civ 1330; [2005] 3 F.C.R. 571, CA (Civ Div)
C (Abduction: Settlement) (No.1), Re see Cannon v. Cannon
C (Abduction: Settlement) (No.2), Re [2005] 1 F.L.R. 938; [2005] Fam. Law 440, Fam Div　*Digested*, 05/**1546**:
　　　　　　　　　　　　　　　　　　　　　　　　　　　Previous proceedings, 05/1539
C (Children) v. Zanaga (Unreported, June 28, 2004), MCLC [*Ex rel.* Joanna Kerr, Barrister, Lamb Chambers, Lamb Building, Temple, London]............... *Digested*, 05/**3167**
C (Minors) (Adoption by Relative), Re [1989] 1 W.L.R. 61; [1989] 1 All E.R. 395; [1989] 1 F.L.R. 222; [1989] F.C.R. 774; 87 L.G.R. 73; [1989] Fam. Law 107; (1989) 153 J.P.N. 658; (1989) 86(46) L.S.G. 38; (1989) 133 S.J. 20; *Independent*, October 17, 1988 (C.S.), CA (Civ Div)... *Digested*, 89/**2417**:
　　　　　　　　　　　　　　　　　　　　　　　　　　　Followed, 05/1509
C (Permission to Remove from Jurisdiction), Re see IHC v. AC
C&H Engineering v. F Klucznik & Sons Ltd (No.1) [1992] F.S.R. 421, Ch D.......... *Digested*, 93/**3023**:
　　　　　　　　　　Applied, 05/2435: *Considered*, 02/2776: *Followed*, 97/1035
CA v. Secretary of State for the Home Department see A v. Secretary of State for the Home Department
CA v. Secretary of State for the Home Department; *sub nom* CA (Date of Decision: Evidence: Nigeria), Re [2004] UKIAT 243; [2005] Imm. A.R. 26, IAT
CA Sheimer (M) Sdn Bhd's Trade Mark Application [2000] E.T.M.R. 1170 (Note); [2000] R.P.C. 484, App Person... *Digested*, 00/**3768**:
　　　　　　　　　　　　　　　　　　　　　　　　　　　Applied, 05/2561
CA Stewart & Co v. PHS Van Ommeren (London) Ltd [1918] 2 K.B. 560, CA........　*Applied*, 05/3789
CA Webber (Transport) Ltd v. Network Rail Infrastructure Ltd (formerly Railtrack Plc) see CA Webber (Transport) Ltd v. Railtrack Plc
CA Webber (Transport) Ltd v. Railtrack Plc; *sub nom* CA Webber (Transport) Ltd v. Network Rail Infrastructure Ltd (formerly Railtrack Plc) [2003] EWCA Civ 1167; [2004] 1 W.L.R. 320; [2004] 3 All E.R. 202; [2004] 1 P. & C.R. 20; [2004] L. & T.R. 2; [2004] 1 E.G.L.R. 49; [2004] 14 E.G. 142; (2003) 100(36) L.S.G. 40; (2003) 147 S.J.L.B. 902; [2003] 2 P. & C.R. DG21; *Times*, August 5, 2003, CA (Civ Div).. *Digested*, 03/**2757**:
　　　　　　　　　　　　　　　　　　　　　　　　　　　Considered, 05/2584
CA (Date of Decision: Evidence: Nigeria), Re see CA v. Secretary of State for the Home Department
Cable & Wireless Plc v. British Telecommunications Plc [1998] F.S.R. 383; (1998) 21(4) I.P.D. 21042, Ch D.. *Digested*, 98/**3507**:
　　　　　　　　　　　　　　　Applied, 01/4023, 05/2570: *Followed*, 99/3535
Cable & Wireless Plc v. Valentine see Willis Management (Isle of Man) Ltd v. Cable & Wireless Plc
Cable Television Broadcasts, Re (C11/95) see Commission of the European Communities v. Belgium (C11/95)
Cabletel Installations Ltd (In Liquidation), Re [2005] B.P.I.R. 28, Ch D
Cableuropa SA v. Commission of the European Communities (T346/02) [2003] E.C.R. II-4251; [2004] 5 C.M.L.R. 25, CFI (3rd Chamber)................. *Digested*, 05/**583**
Cabvision Ltd v. Feetum see Feetum v. Levy
Cachia v. Faluyi [2001] EWCA Civ 998; [2001] 1 W.L.R. 1966; [2002] 1 All E.R. 192; [2001] C.P. Rep. 102; [2002] P.I.Q.R. P5; (2001) 98(29) L.S.G. 39; (2001) 145 S.J.L.B. 167; *Times*, July 11, 2001; *Daily Telegraph*, July 3, 2001, CA (Civ Div) ... *Digested*, 01/**411**:
　　　　　　　　　　　　　　　　　　　　　　　　　　　Considered, 05/2584
Cadbury Schweppes Plc v. Williams (Inspector of Taxes) [2005] EWHC 1610; [2005] B.T.C. 436; [2005] S.T.I. 1313, Ch D; affirming [2005] S.T.C. (S.C.D.) 151; [2004] S.T.I. 2440, Sp Comm.. *Digested*, 05/**4059**

Cadman *v.* Health and Safety Executive; *sub nom* Health and Safety Executive *v.*
  Cadman [2004] EWCA Civ 1317; [2005] I.C.R. 1546; [2004] I.R.L.R. 971;
  (2004) 148 S.J.L.B. 1246, CA (Civ Div); reversing in part [2004] I.C.R. 378;
  [2004] I.R.L.R. 29; (2003) 147 S.J.L.B. 1273, EAT . . . . *Digested,* 05/**1261**
Cadogan *v.* Search Guarantees Plc see Earl Cadogan *v.* Search Guarantees Plc
Cadogan Estates Ltd *v.* Morris see Viscount Chelsea *v.* Morris
Cadogan Holdings Ltd *v.* Pockney [2005] R.V.R. 197, Lands Tr . . . . *Digested,* 05/**3406**
Cadogan (9 Astell Street), Re see Arbib *v.* Earl Cadogan
Cahill Droge *v.* United Airlines Inc [2005] I.L.Pr. 15, Cass (F)
Caisse Nationale d'Assurance Vieillesse des Travailleurs Salaries (CNAVTS) *v.* Thibault
  (C136/95); *sub nom* Thibault *v.* Caisse Nationale d'Assurance Vieillesse des
  Travailleurs Salaries (C136/95) [1998] All E.R. (EC) 385; [1998] E.C.R. I-2011;
  [1998] 2 C.M.L.R. 516; [1999] I.C.R. 160; [1998] I.R.L.R. 399; *Times,* May 13,
  1998, ECJ (6th Chamber) . . . . *Digested,* 98/**2150**
                                                                                    Considered, 05/**1266**
Caisse Nationale des Prestations Familiales *v.* Schwarz (nee Weide) (C153/03) [2005]
  3 C.M.L.R. 42, ECJ (1st Chamber)
Caixa Bank France *v.* Ministere de l'Economie, des Finances et de l'Industrie (C442/02)
  [2004] E.C.R. I-8961; [2005] 1 C.M.L.R. 2; [2005] C.E.C. 121, ECJ
Calder Gravel Ltd *v.* Kirklees MBC (1990) 60 P. & C.R. 322; [1990] 2 P.L.R. 26;
  [1989] E.G.C.S. 137; *Times,* October 16, 1989; *Independent,* October 30, 1989,
  Ch D . . . . *Digested,* 91/**3516**
                                                                                    Distinguished, 05/**3306**
Calderdale MBC *v.* Gorringe see Gorringe *v.* Calderdale MBC
Calderdale MBC *v.* S [2004] EWHC 2529; [2005] 1 F.L.R. 751; [2005] Fam. Law
  353; (2004) 101 (47) L.S.G. 30; *Times,* November 18, 2004, Fam Div . . . . *Digested,* 05/**1629**
Calfa, Re (C348/96) see Criminal Proceedings against Calfa (C348/96)
Callery *v.* Gray (No.1); *sub nom* Callery *v.* Gray (No.2); Callery *v.* Gray (Nos.1 and 2);
  Russell *v.* Pal Pak Corrugated Ltd (No.1) [2002] UKHL 28; [2002] 1 W.L.R.
  2000; [2002] 3 All E.R. 417; [2002] 2 Costs L.R. 205; [2003] R.T.R. 4; [2003]
  Lloyd's Rep. I.R. 203; [2002] P.I.Q.R. P32; (2002) 152 N.L.J. 1031; *Times,* July
  2, 2002; *Independent,* July 2, 2002; *Daily Telegraph,* July 11, 2002, HL; affirming
  [2001] EWCA Civ 1117; [2001] 1 W.L.R. 2112; [2001] 3 All E.R. 833; [2001] 2
  Costs L.R. 163; [2001] Lloyd's Rep. I.R. 743; [2001] P.I.Q.R. P32; (2001) 151
  N.L.J. 1129; *Times,* July 18, 2001; *Independent,* July 24, 2001; *Daily Telegraph,*
  July 24, 2001, CA (Civ Div); reversing in part [2002] R.T.R. 10, CC (Chester) [*Ex
  rel.* Amelans, Solicitors, Barlow House, 708-710 Wilmslow Road, Manchester] . *Digested,* 02/**360**
                            Applied, 02/322, 03/330, 03/332, 05/2704: *Cited,* 03/331:
                         Considered, 05/2703: *Distinguished,* 04/2552: *Previous proceedings,* 01/492
Callery *v.* Gray (No.2) see Callery *v.* Gray (No.1)
Callery *v.* Gray (Nos.1 and 2) see Callery *v.* Gray (No.1)
Calveley *v.* Chief Constable of Merseyside; Worrall *v.* Chief Constable of Merseyside;
  Park *v.* Chief Constable of Greater Manchester [1989] A.C. 1228; [1989] 2
  W.L.R. 624; [1989] 1 All E.R. 1025; (1989) 153 L.G. Rev. 686; (1989) 86 (15)
  L.S.G. 42; (1989) 139 N.L.J. 469; (1989) 133 S.J. 456, HL; affirming [1989]
  Q.B. 136; [1988] 3 W.L.R. 1020; [1988] 3 All E.R. 385; [1989] C.O.D. 229;
  (1988) 138 N.L.J. Rep. 267; (1988) 132 S.J. 1244, CA (Civ Div) . . . . *Digested,* 89/**2863**
                            Applied, 05/2884: *Considered,* 00/5117: *Distinguished,* 00/4229:
                                                                                    Followed, 97/4150
Calvelli *v.* Italy (32967/96) (Unreported, January 17, 2002), ECHR . . . . *Considered,* 05/34:
                                                                                    Distinguished, 05/2113
Calvin *v.* Carr [1980] A.C. 574; [1979] 2 W.L.R. 755; [1979] 2 All E.R. 440; 123 S.J.
  112, PC (Aus) . . . . *Digested,* 79/**14**
                            Applied, 80/315, 80/2904, 89/1500, 02/704, 05/720: *Considered,* 87/3162,
                                  95/3252, 00/6628: *Distinguished,* 97/63: *Followed,* 91/43, 93/31:
                                                                                    Referred to, 81/108
Camacho *v.* Law Society (No.2); *sub nom* R. (on the application of Camacho) *v.* Law
  Society (No.2) [2004] EWHC 1675; [2004] 1 W.L.R. 3037; [2004] 4 All E.R.
  126; (2004) 101 (33) L.S.G. 37; *Times,* October 5, 2004, QBD (Admin) . . . . *Digested,* 05/**2735**
Camas Plc *v.* Atkinson (Inspector of Taxes); *sub nom* Atkinson (Inspector of Taxes) *v.*
  Camas Plc [2004] EWCA Civ 541; [2004] 1 W.L.R. 2392; [2004] S.T.C. 860; 76
  T.C. 641; [2004] B.T.C. 190; [2004] S.T.I. 1163; (2004) 101 (22) L.S.G. 33;
  (2004) 148 S.J.L.B. 571; *Times,* May 27, 2004, CA (Civ Div); affirming [2003]
  EWHC 1600; [2003] S.T.C. 968; [2003] B.T.C. 296; [2003] S.T.I. 1145; (2003)
  100 (35) L.S.G. 38; *Times,* July 18, 2003, Ch D; reversing [2003] S.T.C. (S.C.D.)
  1; [2002] S.T.I. 1545, Sp Comm . . . . *Digested,* 04/**3713**
Camberwell (Wingfield Mews) No.2 Clearance Order 1936, Re see Butler, Re
Cambridge Antibody Technology Ltd *v.* Abbott Biotechnology Ltd [2004] EWHC 2974;
  [2005] F.S.R. 27, Ch D (Patents Ct)
Cambridge Display Technology Ltd *v.* El Dupont de Nemours & Co [2005] EWCA Civ
  224, CA (Civ Div); affirming [2004] EWHC 1415; [2005] F.S.R. 14, Ch D . . . . . *Digested,* 05/**713**
Cambridgeshire and Isle of Ely CC *v.* Rust [1972] 2 Q.B. 426; [1972] 3 W.L.R. 226;
  [1972] 3 All E.R. 232; 70 L.G.R. 444; [1972] Crim. L.R. 433; 116 S.J. 564, DC . . *Digested,* 72/**1641**
                            Applied, 74/1723, 05/774: *Considered,* 73/504, 74/556

Cambridgeshire CC *v.* Associated Lead Mills Ltd [2005] EWHC 1627; (2005) 169 J.P.
489; (2005) 169 J.P.N. 778, QBD (Admin) . . . . *Digested,* 05/**818**
Camilla Cotton Oil Co *v.* Granadex SA; Shawnee Processors Inc *v.* Granadex SA [1976]
2 Lloyd's Rep. 10, HL; reversing [1975] 1 Lloyd's Rep. 470; (1975) 119 S.J. 115,
CA (Civ Div). . . . . *Digested,* 76/**99**:
Applied, 84/99, 88/136, 98/3528: *Considered,* 85/2743, 05/434:
Followed, 97/890
Camm *v.* Camm (1983) 4 F.L.R. 577; (1983) 13 Fam. Law 112, CA (Civ Div). . . . . *Digested,* 83/**1100**:
Applied, 95/2340: *Cited,* 00/2519: *Followed,* 95/2341, 05/1688
Campbell *v.* Hamlet (Executrix of Simon Alexander) [2005] UKPC 19; [2005] 3 All
E.R. 1116, PC (Trin) . . . . *Digested,* 05/**2727**
Campbell *v.* Inland Revenue Commissioners [2004] S.T.C. (S.C.D.) 396; 7 I.T.L. Rep.
211; [2004] S.T.I. 1831, Sp Comm. . . . . *Digested,* 05/**4084**
Campbell *v.* MGN Ltd see Campbell *v.* Mirror Group Newspapers Ltd
Campbell *v.* MGN Ltd (Costs) see Campbell *v.* Mirror Group Newspapers Ltd (Costs)
Campbell *v.* MGN Ltd (No.2) see Campbell *v.* Mirror Group Newspapers Ltd (Costs)
Campbell *v.* Mirror Group Newspapers Ltd; *sub nom* Campbell *v.* MGN Ltd [2004]
UKHL 22; [2004] 2 A.C. 457; [2004] 2 W.L.R. 1232; [2004] 2 All E.R. 995;
[2004] E.M.L.R. 15; [2004] H.R.L.R. 24; [2004] U.K.H.R.R. 648; 16 B.H.R.C.
500; (2004) 101(21) L.S.G. 36; (2004) 154 N.L.J. 733; (2004) 148 S.J.L.B.
572; *Times,* May 7, 2004; *Independent,* May 11, 2004, HL; reversing [2002]
EWCA Civ 1373; [2003] Q.B. 633; [2003] 2 W.L.R. 80; [2003] 1 All E.R. 224;
[2003] E.M.L.R. 2; [2003] H.R.L.R. 2; (2002) 99(42) L.S.G. 38; (2002) 146
S.J.L.B. 234; *Times,* October 16, 2002; *Independent,* October 18, 2002, CA (Civ
Div); reversing [2002] EWHC 499; [2002] E.M.L.R. 30; [2002] H.R.L.R. 28;
(2002) 99(19) L.S.G. 28; (2002) 146 S.J.L.B. 107; *Times,* March 29, 2002; *Daily
Telegraph,* April 11, 2002, QBD . . . . *Digested,* 04/**2673**:
Applied, 03/1217, 05/2121, 05/2812: *Considered,* 03/2923: *Followed,* 05/979
Campbell *v.* Mirror Group Newspapers Ltd (Costs); *sub nom* Campbell *v.* MGN Ltd
(Costs); Campbell *v.* MGN Ltd (No.2) [2005] UKHL 61; [2005] 1 W.L.R. 3394;
[2005] 4 All E.R. 793; (2005) 102(42) L.S.G. 23; (2005) 155 N.L.J. 1633;
Times, October 21, 2005, HL
Campbell *v.* United Kingdom (A/182) see Fox *v.* United Kingdom (A/182)
Campbell *v.* United Kingdom (A/80); Fell *v.* United Kingdom (A/80) (1985) 7
E.H.R.R. 165, ECHR (1983) 5 E.H.R.R. 207, Eur Comm HR . . . . *Applied,* 03/428,
05/2909: *Considered,* 88/2973: *Distinguished,* 85/2447: *Followed,* 03/2141
Campbell and Cosans *v.* United Kingdom (A/48) (1982) 4 E.H.R.R. 293, ECHR . . . . . . *Applied,* 97/2787:
Considered, 03/1114: *Distinguished,* 05/1019
Campbell-James *v.* Guardian Media Group Plc [2005] EWHC 893; [2005] E.M.L.R.
24, QBD . . . . *Digested,* 05/**972**
Campden Hill Ltd *v.* Chakrani [2005] EWHC 911; [2005] N.P.C. 65, Ch D
Campina Melkunie BV *v.* Benelux-Merkenbureau (C265/00) [2004] E.C.R. I-1699;
[2005] 2 C.M.L.R. 9; [2005] C.E.C. 676; [2004] E.T.M.R. 58, ECJ (6th
Chamber) . . . . *Digested,* 05/**2564**
Campomar SL *v.* Nike International Ltd [2005] E.T.M.R. 1, Sup Trib (P)
Canada Inc *v.* Strother (2004-05) 7 I.T.E.L.R. 748, CA (BC). . . . . *Digested,* 05/**4307**
Canada Life Ltd *v.* Gray [2004] I.C.R. 673, EAT. . . . . *Digested,* 04/**1267**:
Overruled, 05/1273
Canada Trust Co *v.* Stolzenberg (No.2) [2002] 1 A.C. 1; [2000] 3 W.L.R. 1376; [2000]
4 All E.R. 481; [2001] C.L.C. 118; [2001] I.L.Pr. 40; (2000) 97(42) L.S.G. 44;
(2000) 150 N.L.J. 1537; (2000) 144 S.J.L.B. 256; *Times,* October 17, 2000;
Independent, October 17, 2000, HL; affirming [1998] 1 W.L.R. 547; [1998] 1 All
E.R. 318; [1998] C.L.C. 23; [1998] I.L.Pr. 290; *Times,* November 10, 1997, CA
(Civ Div); affirming (Unreported, May 23, 1997), Ch D . . . . *Digested,* 00/**744**:
Applied, 02/714, 03/595, 03/625, 05/2293: *Followed,* 98/584, 99/526
Canada Trustco Mortgage Co *v.* Canada 8 I.T.L. Rep. 276, Sup Ct (Can)
Canadian Foundation for Children, Youth and the Law *v.* Attorney General 19 B.H.R.C. 39,
Sup Ct (Can)
CANADIAN LIQUID AIR/Shielding gases (T4/00) [2005] E.P.O.R. 9, EPO (Technical Bd
App). . . . . *Digested,* 05/**2488**
Canali Ireland Ltd *v.* Office for Harmonisation in the Internal Market (Trade Marks and
Designs) (OHIM) (T301/03) [2005] E.T.M.R. 97, CFI (1st Chamber)
Candlewood Navigation Corp *v.* Mitsui Osk Lines (The Mineral Transporter and The
Ibaraki Maru) [1986] A.C. 1; [1985] 3 W.L.R. 381; [1985] 2 All E.R. 935; [1985]
2 Lloyd's Rep. 303; (1985) 82 L.S.G. 2912; (1985) 135 N.L.J. 677; (1985) 129
S.J. 506, PC (Aus) . . . . *Digested,* 85/**2310**:
Applied, 05/3239: *Considered,* 85/2311, 86/2252, 86/2270:
Distinguished, 90/1535: *Referred to,* 87/3582, 88/3408
Candolin *v.* Vahinkovakuutusosakeyhtio Pohjola (C537/03) [2005] E.C.R. I-5745;
[2005] 3 C.M.L.R. 17, ECJ (1st Chamber)

Canelhas Comercio Importacao e Exportacao Ltd v. Wooldridge; *sub nom* Wooldridge v.
Canelhas Comercio Importacao e Exportacao Ltda [2004] EWCA Civ 984;
[2005] 1 All E.R. (Comm) 43; [2004] 2 C.L.C. 469; [2004] Lloyd's Rep. I.R.
915; (2004) 148 S.J.L.B. 943, CA (Civ Div); affirming [2004] EWHC 643, QBD
(Comm) . . . .   *Digested,* 05/**2367**
Canmer International Inc v. UK Mutual Steamship Assurance Association (Bermuda)
Ltd (The Rays) [2005] EWHC 1694; [2005] 2 Lloyd's Rep. 479, QBD (Comm) .   *Digested,* 05/**3811**
Cannon v. Cannon; *sub nom* C (Abduction: Settlement) (No.1), Re [2004] EWCA Civ
1330; [2005] 1 W.L.R. 32; [2005] 1 F.L.R. 169; [2004] 3 F.C.R. 438; [2005]
Fam. Law 8; (2004) 101(44) L.S.G. 31; *Times,* October 28, 2004, CA (Civ Div);
reversing [2004] EWHC 1245; [2005] 1 F.L.R. 127; [2004] Fam. Law 782,
Fam Div . . . .   *Digested,* 05/**1539**:
                                                                                  Subsequent proceedings, 05/1546
Cannon Screen Entertainment Ltd v. Handmade Films (Distributors) Ltd; *sub nom* Pathe
Screen Entertainments Ltd v. Hand Made Films Ltd (Unreported, July 11, 1989),
QBD (Comm) . . . .   *Applied,* 05/600:
                                                            Considered, 02/5381: *Distinguished,* 04/573
Canon Kabushiki Kaisha v. Metro Goldwyn Mayer Inc (C39/97) [1998] All E.R. (EC)
934; [1998] E.C.R. I-5507; [1999] 1 C.M.L.R. 77; [1998] C.E.C. 920; [1999]
E.T.M.R. 1; [1999] F.S.R. 332; [1999] R.P.C. 117; *Times,* October 10, 1998, ECJ
[1998] E.C.R. I-5507; [1998] E.T.M.R. 366, AGO . . . .   *Digested,* 98/**3526**:
               Applied, 00/3742, 00/3748, 01/3987, 01/4025, 01/4036, 05/2540, 05/2559:
                             Considered, 99/3531, 00/3728, 03/2651: *Followed,* 00/3701, 01/4029:
                                               Not followed, 99/3544: *Referred to,* 01/4024
Canterbury City Council v. Lowe (2001) 33 H.L.R. 53; [2001] L. & T.R. 14, CA (Civ
Div) . . . .   *Digested,* 01/**3440**:
                                                                                           Followed, 05/2642
Canterbury Hockey Club v. Revenue and Customs Commissioners [2005] B.V.C. 2709;
[2005] S.T.I. 1729, V&DTr (London)
Canterbury Pipe Lines Ltd v. Christchurch Drainage Board 16 B.L.R. 76, CA (NZ) . . . . .   *Applied,* 05/665
Cantine Mezzacorona SCARL v. Miguel Torres SA see Miguel Torres SA v. Cantine
Mezzacorona SCARL
Cantor Fitzgerald International v. Horkulak see Horkulak v. Cantor Fitzgerald
International
Caparo Industries Plc v. Dickman [1990] 2 A.C. 605; [1990] 2 W.L.R. 358; [1990] 1
All E.R. 568; [1990] B.C.C. 164; [1990] B.C.L.C. 273; [1990] E.C.C. 313; [1955-
95] P.N.L.R. 523; (1990) 87(12) L.S.G. 42; (1990) 140 N.L.J. 248; (1990) 134
S.J. 494; *Times,* February 12, 1990; *Independent,* February 16, 1990; *Financial
Times,* February 13, 1990; *Guardian,* February 15, 1990; *Daily Telegraph,* February
15, 1990, HL; reversing [1989] Q.B. 653; [1989] 2 W.L.R. 316; [1989] 1 All
E.R. 798; (1989) 5 B.C.C. 105; [1989] B.C.L.C. 154; [1989] P.C.C. 125; (1988)
138 N.L.J. Rep. 289; (1989) 133 S.J. 221; *Times,* August 8, 1988; *Independent,*
August 10, 1988; *Financial Times,* August 5, 1988; *Daily Telegraph,* August 26,
1988, CA (Civ Div); reversing in part (1988) 4 B.C.C. 144; [1988] B.C.L.C. 387,
QBD . . . .   *Digested,* 90/**3266**:
                        Applied, 89/2540, 90/3254, 90/3265, 91/2650, 91/2652, 92/1915,
                 92/2605, 92/3201, 93/2953, 93/2982, 94/3335, 94/3352, 94/3365,
                        95/2906, 95/3668, 95/3686, 95/3701, 95/4519, 95/4730, 96/4440,
                 96/4484, 97/331, 97/3778, 97/3816, 98/3997, 99/3956, 99/3963, 99/3966,
                        99/4025, 99/5435, 00/679, 00/4201, 00/4246, 00/4249, 00/6162,
                 00/6586, 01/1509, 01/1989, 01/4462, 01/4464, 01/4541, 04/658, 04/2119,
                 04/2704, 05/2845, 05/2848, 05/2851, 05/2861, 05/2868: *Cited,* 00/4218:
                        Considered, 90/3315, 91/2657, 93/2044, 93/2958, 93/2983, 93/2997,
                 94/3345, 95/3452, 95/3652, 98/3921, 98/3951, 98/3999, 99/3953,
                        00/4205, 01/550, 03/5821, 04/386, 04/5103, 05/2891:
                 Distinguished, 91/2653: *Followed,* 90/3281, 93/5553, 97/424, 97/4087,
                        98/3930, 98/3987, 99/3959, 99/4015, 00/4219, 00/4224, 01/4470:
                                      Referred to, 92/6078, 94/6386, 95/5841, 99/4023
Capewell v. Customs and Excise Commissioners [2004] EWCA Civ 1628; [2005] 1
All E.R. 900; [2005] B.P.I.R. 1266; *Times,* December 15, 2004, CA (Civ Div) . . .   *Digested,* 05/**2332**
Capewell v. Customs and Excise Commissioners (Costs) [2005] EWCA Civ 964;
[2005] B.P.I.R. 1266; *Times,* September 20, 2005, CA (Civ Div) . . . .   *Digested,* 05/**349**
Capital Bank Plc v. Stickland [2004] EWCA Civ 1677; [2005] 1 W.L.R. 3914; [2005] 2
All E.R. 544; [2005] C.P. Rep. 15, CA (Civ Div) . . . .   *Digested,* 05/**446**
Capital Cranfield Trustees Ltd v. Pinsent Curtis (A Firm) see Pinsent Curtis v. Capital
Cranfield Trustees Ltd
Capital Cranfield Trustees Ltd v. Walsh see Pinsent Curtis v. Capital Cranfield Trustees
Ltd
Capital One Bank (Europe) Plc v. Revenue and Customs Commissioners [2005] S.T.I.
2042, V&DTr (Manchester)
Capital One Developments Ltd v. Customs and Excise Commissioners [2002] EWHC
197; [2002] S.T.C. 479; [2002] B.T.C. 5300; [2002] B.V.C. 428; [2002] S.T.I.
169; (2002) 99(11) L.S.G. 38; *Times,* February 19, 2002, Ch D . . . .   *Digested,* 02/**449**:
                                                         Applied, 05/4373: *Doubted,* 05/4420

Carabott v. Huxley (2005) 102(34) L.S.G. 30, CA (Civ Div)
Carafe Trust, Re (2005-06) 8 I.T.E.L.R. 29, Royal Ct (Jer)
Carbonati Apuani Srl v. Comune di Carrara (C72/03) [2004] E.C.R. I-8027; [2004] 3
    C.M.L.R. 59, ECJ (1st Chamber) . . . .   *Digested*, 05/**943**
Card Protection Plan Ltd v. Customs and Excise Commissioners (C349/96) [1999] 2
    A.C. 601; [1999] 3 W.L.R. 203; [1999] All E.R. (E.C.) 339; [1999] S.T.C. 270;
    [1999] E.C.R. I-973; [1999] 2 C.M.L.R. 743; [1999] C.E.C. 133; [1999] B.T.C.
    5121; [1999] B.V.C. 155; *Times*, March 18, 1999, ECJ (6th Chamber) . . . .   *Digested*, 99/**4972**:
        Applied, 00/5343, 00/5346, 00/5369, 02/4745, 02/4750, 02/4782,
        03/4538, 03/4545, 03/4576, 03/4580, 04/3968, 04/4009, 05/4354,
        05/4355, 05/4397: *Considered*, 01/5599, 03/4537, 03/4558, 04/3977,
        04/4018, 05/4419: *Distinguished*, 00/5294, 01/5564, 05/4394:
        Followed, 99/4983, 00/5344, 04/3981: *Referred to*, 04/4020:
        Subsequent proceedings, 01/5600
Carden v. Pickerings Europe Ltd [2005] I.R.L.R. 721, EAT
Cargill v. Gotts [1981] 1 W.L.R. 441; [1981] 1 All E.R. 682; (1981) 41 P. & C.R. 300;
    [1981] J.P.L. 515; 125 S.J. 99, CA (Civ Div); reversing [1980] 1 W.L.R. 521;
    [1980] 2 All E.R. 49; (1980) 40 P. & C.R. 122; [1980] J.P.L. 602, Ch D . . . . . .   *Digested*, 81/**742**:
        Applied, 05/3403
Carglass Luxembourg Sarl's Community Trade Mark (R 703/2004-1) (2005) 28(4) I.P.D.
    28029, OHIM (1st Bd App)
Cargo of the Alfonsina, Re (68/88) see Commission of the European Communities v.
    Greece (68/88)
Carillion Construction Ltd v. Devonport Royal Dockyard Ltd [2005] EWCA Civ 1358;
    (2005) 102(47) L.S.G. 26; *Times*, November 24, 2005, CA (Civ Div); affirming
    [2005] EWHC 778; [2005] B.L.R. 310; 102 Con. L.R. 167, QBD (TCC) . . . .   *Digested*, 05/**644**
Carisbrooke Shipping CV5 v. Bird Port Ltd [2005] EWHC 1974; [2005] 2 Lloyd's Rep.
    626, QBD (Admlty)
Carman v. Yates see Yates (A Bankrupt), Re
Carmichael v. National Power Plc [1999] 1 W.L.R. 2042; [1999] 4 All E.R. 897;
    [1999] I.C.R. 1226; [2000] I.R.L.R. 43; (1999) 96(46) L.S.G. 38; (1999) 143
    S.J.L.B. 281; *Times*, November 23, 1999 ; *Independent*, November 25, 1999, HL;
    reversing [1998] I.C.R. 1167; [1998] I.R.L.R. 301; (1998) 95(19) L.S.G. 23;
    (1998) 142 S.J.L.B. 140; *Times*, April 2, 1998, CA (Civ Div) . . . .   *Digested*, 99/**2002**:
        Applied, 03/1280, 05/667, 05/1213: *Considered*, 01/2262: *Followed*, 03/1257
Carnegie v. Giessen [2005] EWCA Civ 191; [2005] 1 W.L.R. 2510; [2005] C.P. Rep.
    24; [2005] 1 C.L.C. 259; (2005) 102(18) L.S.G. 23; *Times*, March 14, 2005;
    Independent, March 18, 2005, CA (Civ Div); affirming [2004] EWHC 1782,
    Ch D . . . .   *Digested*, 05/**330**
Carreras Group Ltd v. Stamp Commissioner; *sub nom* Stamp Commissioner v. Carreras
    Group Ltd [2004] UKPC 16; [2004] S.T.C. 1377; [2004] B.T.C. 8077; [2004]
    S.T.I. 990; (2004) 148 S.J.L.B. 473, PC (Jam) . . . .   *Digested*, 05/**4037**
Carrickdale Hotel Ltd v. Controller of Patents, Designs and Trade Marks [2005]
    E.C.D.R. CN1, HC (Irl)
Carruthers v. Whitaker [1975] 2 N.Z.L.R. 667, CA (NZ) . . . .   *Considered*, 05/4318
Carson v. Secretary of State for Work and Pensions see R. (on the application of
    Carson) v. Secretary of State for Work and Pensions
Carter v. Ahsan (No.1); *sub nom* Labour Party v. Ahsan; Ashan v. Carter [2005]
    EWCA Civ 990; [2005] I.C.R. 1817; *Times*, August 23, 2005, CA (Civ Div);
    reversing [2004] I.C.R. 938, EAT. . . . .   *Digested*, 05/**429**
Carter v. Ahsan (No.2) UKEAT/0907/03/(2)/DM, EAT . . . .   *Overruled*, 05/429
Carter v. Wandsworth LBC see Hall v. Wandsworth LBC
Carter Commercial Developments Ltd (In Administration) v. Secretary of State for
    Transport, Local Government and the Regions [2002] EWCA Civ 1994; [2003]
    J.P.L. 1048, CA (Civ Div); affirming [2002] EWHC 1200; [2003] J.P.L. 35,
    QBD (Admin) . . . .   *Digested*, 03/**3411**:
        Considered, 05/3303
Carter (t/a Michael Carter Partnership) v. Harold Simpson Associates (Architects) Ltd
    [2004] UKPC 29; [2005] 1 W.L.R. 919; [2004] 2 Lloyd's Rep. 512; [2004] 2
    C.L.C. 1053; (2004) 101(27) L.S.G. 29; (2004) 148 S.J.L.B. 759; *Times*, June
    25, 2004, PC (Jam) . . . .   *Digested*, 04/**189**
Carter (t/a New Chapel Developments) v. TG Baynes & Sons [1998] E.G.C.S. 109, Ch D
        Doubted, 05/2866
Cartledge v. E Jopling & Sons Ltd [1963] A.C. 758; [1963] 2 W.L.R. 210; [1963] 1 All
    E.R. 341; [1963] 1 Lloyd's Rep. 1; 107 S.J. 73, HL; affirming [1962] 1 Q.B. 189;
    [1961] 3 W.L.R. 838; [1961] 3 All E.R. 482; [1961] 2 Lloyd's Rep. 61; 105 S.J.
    884, CA . . . .   *Digested*, 63/**2023**:
        Applied, 64/3468, 82/1850, 83/2215, 83/2216, 87/229, 88/2158, 05/955:
        Considered, 66/7087, 69/1575, 76/1873, 84/1098, 93/2997, 94/3079
Cartwright v. Superintendent of HM Prison [2004] UKPC 10; [2004] 1 W.L.R. 902;
    (2004) 148 S.J.L.B. 232, PC (Bah) . . . .   *Digested*, 04/**1437**:
        Applied, 05/1488: *Considered*, 05/1486
Cartwright (Valuation Officer) v. Nickerson Zwann Ltd [2005] R.V.R. 319, Lands Tr

Carty v. Croydon LBC [2005] EWCA Civ 19; [2005] 1 W.L.R. 2312; [2005] 2 All E.R. 517; [2005] 1 F.C.R. 554; [2005] B.L.G.R. 319; [2005] E.L.R. 104; (2005) 102(10) L.S.G. 30; *Times*, February 3, 2005, CA (Civ Div); affirming [2004] EWHC 228; [2004] E.L.R. 226, QBD . . . . *Digested*, 05/**2861**

Carver v. Saudi Arabian Airlines [1999] 3 All E.R. 61; [1999] I.C.R. 991; [1999] I.R.L.R. 370; [1999] Disc. L.R. 216; (1999) 149 N.L.J. 521; *Times*, March 24, 1999; *Independent*, March 23, 1999, CA (Civ Div) . . . . *Digested*, 99/**2055**: *Considered*, 05/1252

Carvill v. Frost (Inspector of Taxes) (No.1) [2005] S.T.C. (S.C.D.) 208; [2005] S.T.I. 257, Sp Comm . . . . *Digested*, 05/**4069**

Carvill v. Frost (Inspector of Taxes) (No.2) [2005] S.T.I. 838, Sp Comm

Carvill v. Inland Revenue Commissioners (Transfer Purpose) [2000] S.T.C. (S.C.D.) 143; [2000] S.T.I. 584, Sp Comm. . . . . *Digested*, 00/**5021**: *Considered*, 05/4041

Carvill America Inc v. Camperdown UK Ltd; Carvill America Inc v. XL Speciality Insurance Co Ltd [2005] EWCA Civ 645; [2005] 2 Lloyd's Rep. 457; [2005] 1 C.L.C. 845, CA (Civ Div); affirming [2004] EWHC 2221; [2005] Lloyd's Rep. I.R. 55, QBD (Comm) . . . . *Digested*, 05/**2396**

Carvill America Inc v. XL Speciality Insurance Co Ltd see Carvill America Inc v. Camperdown UK Ltd

Castillo v. Spain see R. (on the application of Castillo) v. Spain

Castorina v. Chief Constable of Surrey (1996) 160 L.G. Rev. 241; (1988) 138 N.L.J. Rep.180; *Times*, June 15, 1988; *Independent*, June 16, 1988; *Guardian*, June 15, 1988, CA (Civ Div) . . . . *Digested*, 88/**578**:
Applied, 97/1359, 05/3339: *Considered*, 95/1039, 04/3146

Casulli v. Patel (Unreported, July 22, 2004), CC (Shoreditch) [*Ex rel.* Nigel Ffitch, Barrister, Phoenix Chambers, Gray's Inn Chambers, Gray's Inn, London] . . . . . . *Digested*, 05/**378**

Catchpole v. Young & Co's Brewery Plc (Unreported, August 16, 2004), CC (St Helens) [*Ex rel.* Chris Middleton, Barrister, Oriel Chambers, 14 Water Street, Liverpool] . . . . *Digested*, 05/**3073**

Catnic Components Ltd v. Hill & Smith Ltd (No.1); *sub nom* Catnic Components Ltd v. Hills & Rutter [1981] F.S.R. 60; [1982] R.P.C. 183, HL; reversing [1979] F.S.R. 619, CA (Civ Div); reversing in part [1978] F.S.R. 405, Ch D . . . . *Digested*, 81/**2042**:
Applied, 91/2699, 91/2700, 91/2708, 92/3291, 92/3302, 93/3028, 93/3041, 95/3758, 95/3777, 00/3624, 04/2337, 04/2339, 04/2346, 05/2479:
Considered, 91/2698, 95/3799, 99/3472: *Followed*, 84/2496, 98/3467, 02/2841, 02/2842: *Not followed*, 83/2772, 84/434, 94/3434, 95/3757:
Referred to, 84/2495, 93/3029, 94/3430, 99/3480, 00/3679

Catnic Components Ltd v. Hills & Rutter see Catnic Components Ltd v. Hill & Smith Ltd (No.1)

Caulfield v. Marshalls Clay Products Ltd see Marshalls Clay Products Ltd v. Caulfield

Causey v. DPP [2004] EWHC 3164; (2005) 169 J.P. 331; (2005) 169 J.P.N. 438, QBD (Admin) . . . . *Digested*, 05/**739**

Causton v. Chambers (Unreported, March 4, 2004), CC (Oxford) [*Ex rel.* Jude Durr, Barrister, East Anglian Chambers, 53 North Hill, Colchester, Essex] . . . . *Digested*, 05/**3176**

Cave v. Robinson Jarvis & Rolf; *sub nom* Robinson Jarvis & Rolf v. Cave; Cave v. Robinson Jarvis & Rolfe [2002] UKHL 18; [2003] 1 A.C. 384; [2002] 2 W.L.R. 1107; [2002] 2 All E.R. 641; [2003] 1 C.L.C. 101; 81 Con. L.R. 25; [2002] P.N.L.R. 25; [2002] 19 E.G.C.S. 146; (2002) 99(20) L.S.G. 32; (2002) 152 N.L.J. 671; (2002) 146 S.J.L.B. 109; *Times*, May 7, 2002; *Independent*, April 30, 2002, HL; reversing [2001] EWCA Civ 245; [2002] 1 W.L.R. 581; [2001] C.P. Rep. 66; 78 Con. L.R. 1; [2001] Lloyd's Rep. P.N. 290; [2001] P.N.L.R. 23; (2001) 17 Const. L.J. 262; [2001] 9 E.G.C.S. 229; [2001] N.P.C. 36; *Independent*, April 9, 2001 (C.S), CA (Civ Div) . . . . *Digested*, 02/**466**:
Applied, 04/380, 04/381, 05/461: *Considered*, 04/377

CB and JB (Minors) (Care Proceedings: Guidelines), Re see B (Minors) (Care Proceedings: Practice), Re

CBC Union SRO v. Czech Republic (Admissibility) (68741/01) 8 I.T.L. Rep. 224, ECHR

CCP SA (t/a Fel2) v. Ginger Sarl [2005] E.C.C. 43; [2004] E.C.D.R. 14, Cass (F)

CD (A Child) v. Isle of Anglesey CC see R. (on the application of CD) v. Isle of Anglesey CC

CD (A Child) v. O see D (A Child) v. O

CDC2020 Plc v. Ferreira [2005] EWCA Civ 611; [2005] 3 E.G.L.R. 15; [2005] 35 E.G. 112; [2005] 2 P. & C.R. DG15, CA (Civ Div) . . . . *Digested*, 05/**3436**

Celador Productions Ltd v. Melville; Boone v. ITV Network; Baccini v. Celador Productions Ltd [2004] EWHC 2362; (2005) 28(1) I.P.D. 27112, Ch D

Celltech R&D v. MedImmune Inc [2004] EWHC 2760; (2005) 28(2) I.P.D. 28007, Ch D

Celltech R&D Ltd v. MedImmune Inc [2004] EWCA Civ 1331; [2005] F.S.R. 21; (2005) 28(1) I.P.D. 27109; (2004) 148 S.J.L.B. 1250; *Independent*, November 12, 2004, CA (Civ Div); affirming [2004] EWHC 1522; (2004) 27(9) I.P.D. 27096, Ch D (Patents Ct) . . . . *Digested*, 04/**2344**

Celtec Ltd v. Astley (C478/03); *sub nom* Astley v. Celtec Ltd (C478/03) [2005] E.C.R. I-4389; [2005] 3 C.M.L.R. 9; [2005] I.C.R. 1409; [2005] I.R.L.R. 647; *Times*, June 9, 2005, ECJ (1st Chamber) . . . . *Previous proceedings,* 02/1430

Celtic Football & Athletic Co Ltd v. Customs and Excise Commissioners [1983] S.T.C. 470; 1983 S.C. 215; 1983 S.L.T. 662, IH (1 Div) . . . . *Digested,* 83/**5078**: *Applied,* 05/4361: *Considered,* 98/4915

Cemm v. Bryant (Quantum) (Unreported, December 2, 2004), CC (Stourbridge) [*Ex rel.* Stephen Garner, Barrister, No.8 Chambers, Fountain Court, Steelhouse Lane, Birmingham.] . . . . *Digested,* 05/**3079**

Cenlon Finance Co Ltd v. Ellwood (Inspector of Taxes); *sub nom* Tableau Holdings v. Williams [1962] A.C. 782; [1962] 2 W.L.R. 871; [1962] 1 All E.R. 854; 40 T.C. 176; (1962) 41 A.T.C. 11; [1962] T.R. 1; 106 S.J. 280, HL; affirming [1961] Ch. 634; [1961] 3 W.L.R. 242; [1961] 2 All E.R. 859; (1961) 40 A.T.C. 99; [1961] T.R. 103; 105 S.J. 422, CA; reversing in part [1961] Ch. 50; [1960] 3 W.L.R. 690; [1960] 3 All E.R. 390; 53 R. & I.T. 578; (1960) 39 A.T.C. 201; [1960] T.R. 239; 104 S.J. 850, Ch D . . . . *Digested,* 62/**1491**: *Applied,* 63/1721, 05/4062: *Considered,* 64/1813, 66/5971, 70/1300, 84/1773: *Disapproved,* 64/1810

Central Arbitration Committee v. Ultraframe (UK) Ltd see R. (on the application of Ultraframe (UK) Ltd) v. Central Arbitration Committee

Central Sunderland Housing Co Ltd v. Wilson see Sheffield City Council v. Smart

Centrale Generale des Services Publics (CGSP) v. Belgium (25/2004) (2005) 41 E.H.R.R. SE20, ECSR

Centre Reinsurance International Co v. Curzon Insurance Ltd; Freakley v. Centre Reinsurance International Co; Centre Reinsurance International Co v. Freakley [2005] EWCA Civ 115; [2005] 2 All E.R. (Comm) 65; [2005] 1 C.L.C. 78; [2005] Lloyd's Rep. I.R. 303; *Times*, February 28, 2005, CA (Civ Div); affirming in part [2004] EWHC 200; [2004] 2 All E.R. (Comm) 28; [2004] 2 C.L.C. 586; [2004] Lloyd's Rep. I.R. 622; (2004) 101(11) L.S.G. 34; *Times*, February 27, 2004, Ch D . . . . *Digested,* 05/**2366**: *Previous proceedings,* 05/2372

Centre Reinsurance International Co v. Freakley see Centre Reinsurance International Co v. Curzon Insurance Ltd

Cetelem SA v. Roust Holdings Ltd [2005] EWCA Civ 618; [2005] 1 W.L.R. 3555; [2005] 4 All E.R. 52; [2005] 2 All E.R. (Comm) 203; [2005] 2 Lloyd's Rep. 494; [2005] 1 C.L.C. 821; *Times*, June 13, 2005, CA (Civ Div); affirming [2004] EWHC 3175, QBD . . . . *Digested,* 05/**325**

CFPH LLC's Patent Applications (Nos.0226884.3 and 0419317.3) [2005] EWHC 1589; (2005) 28(9) I.P.D. 28070, Ch D (Patents Ct)

CH v. Sutton and Merton Primary Care Trust; MH v. Sutton and Merton Primary Care Trust [2004] EWHC 2984; (2005) 8 C.C.L. Rep. 5; [2005] A.C.D. 40, QBD (Admin) . . . . *Digested,* 05/**1837**

CH Boehringer Sohn v. Paranova A/S (C429/93) see Bristol Myers Squibb Co v. Paranova A/S (C427/93)

Chelle Properties (NZ) Ltd v. Inland Revenue Commissioner 7 I.T.L. Rep. 33, HC (NZ) . . *Digested,* 05/**4159**

Chadwick v. Abbotswood Properties Ltd; *sub nom* Chadwick v. Hauser [2004] EWHC 1058; [2005] 1 P. & C.R. 10; [2004] N.P.C. 80, Ch D . . . . *Digested,* 05/**3383**

Chadwick v. Hauser see Chadwick v. Abbotswood Properties Ltd

Chaffeur Bikes Ltd v. Leeds City Council see Chauffeur Bikes Ltd v. Leeds City Council

Chagos Islanders v. Attorney General [2004] EWCA Civ 997; *Times*, September 21, 2004, CA (Civ Div); affirming [2003] EWHC 2222; *Times*, October 10, 2003, QBD . . . . *Digested,* 05/**4197**

Chahal v. Mahal [2005] EWCA Civ 898; [2005] 2 B.C.L.C. 655; *Independent*, July 21, 2005, CA (Civ Div); affirming [2005] EWHC 2859, Ch D . . . . *Digested,* 05/**2898**

Chahal v. United Kingdom (22414/93) (1997) 23 E.H.R.R. 413; 1 B.H.R.C. 405; *Times*, November 28, 1996; *Independent*, November 20, 1996, ECHR (1994) 18 E.H.R.R. CD193; (1995) 20 E.H.R.R. CD19, Eur Comm HR . . . . *Digested,* 96/**3130**: *Applied,* 97/2764, 05/2167: *Considered,* 03/2256: *Followed,* 98/3069, 04/2034

Challinor v. Challinor [2004] EWCA Civ 1674; (2005) 149 S.J.L.B. 56, CA (Civ Div)

Chambelin Solicitors v. Emokpae see Wong v. Igen Ltd (formerly Leeds Careers Guidance)

Chamberlin Solicitors v. Emokpae see Emokpae v. Chamberlin Solicitors

Chambers v. Kingham (1878-79) L.R. 10 Ch. D. 743, Ch D . . . . *Applied,* 05/**3431**

Chambers v. Southern Domestic Electrical Services Ltd see Anderton v. Clwyd CC

Chan U Seek v. Alvis Vehicles Ltd; *sub nom* Guardian Newspapers Ltd (Court Record: Disclosure), Re [2004] EWHC 3092; [2005] 1 W.L.R. 2965; [2005] 3 All E.R. 155; [2005] E.M.L.R. 19; *Times*, December 14, 2004, Ch D . . . . *Digested,* 05/**396**

Chancebutton Ltd v. Compass Services UK & Ireland Ltd; *sub nom* Deletenumber Ltd v. Compass Services UK & Ireland Ltd [2004] EWHC 1293; [2005] 1 P. & C.R. 8; [2004] 2 E.G.L.R. 47; [2004] 31 E.G. 94, Ch D . . . . *Digested,* 04/**2523**

Chandler v. Church (1987) 137 N.L.J. 451; *Independent*, April 30, 1987, Ch D . . . . *Digested,* 87/**3059**: *Applied,* 99/3330: *Approved,* 05/294

Channel Hotels & Properties (UK) Ltd v. Al-Tamimi see First Penthouse Ltd v. Channel Hotels & Properties (UK) Ltd

Channon v. Lindley Johnstone (A Firm) (Measure of Damages) [2002] EWCA Civ 353; [2002] Lloyd's Rep. P.N. 342; [2002] P.N.L.R. 41, CA (Civ Div) . . . . *Digested*, 03/**946**: *Applied*, 05/957

Chantrey Vellacott v. Convergence Group Plc; *sub nom* Convergence Group Plc v. Chantrey Vellacott (A Firm) [2005] EWCA Civ 290; *Times*, April 25, 2005, CA (Civ Div); reversing [2004] EWHC 1597, Ch D . . . . *Digested*, 05/**479**

Chaplin v. Boys see Boys v. Chaplin

Chapman v. Letheby & Christopher Ltd [1981] I.R.L.R. 440, EAT . . . . *Digested*, 82/**1115**: *Applied*, 85/1243, 05/4093

Chapman v. United Kingdom (27238/95) (2001) 33 E.H.R.R. 18; 10 B.H.R.C. 48; *Times*, January 30, 2001, ECHR (1998) 25 E.H.R.R. CD64, Eur Comm HR . . . . . *Digested*, 01/**4744**: *Applied*, 02/3684, 03/3380, 03/3485, 05/3285: *Considered*, 02/3686, 03/3424, 04/1376, 04/3040, 04/3095: *Distinguished*, 02/3069, 04/1992

Chappel v. Hart [1999] Lloyd's Rep. Med. 223; 195 C.L.R. 232, HC (Aus) . . . . *Digested*, 99/**3987**: *Considered*, 02/3279, 05/2841: *Followed*, 02/3254

Chappell v. United Kingdom (10461/83) see Chappell v. United Kingdom (A/152)

Chappell v. United Kingdom (A/152); *sub nom* Chappell v. United Kingdom (10461/ 83) (1990) 12 E.H.R.R. 1; [1989] 1 F.S.R. 617; *Times*, April 6, 1989; *Independent*, April 21, 1989; *Guardian*, April 18, 1989, ECHR (1989) 11 E.H.R.R. CD543; (1985) 7 E.H.R.R. CD589, Eur Comm HR . . . . *Digested*, 89/**1921**: *Considered*, 05/2116

Charles v. Hugh James Jones & Jenkins [2000] 1 W.L.R. 1278; [2000] 1 All E.R. 289; [2001] P.I.Q.R. P1; [2000] Lloyd's Rep. P.N. 207; *Times*, December 22, 1999, CA (Civ Div) . . . . *Digested*, 00/**1468**: *Applied*, 05/957

Charles v. Staatssecretaris van Financien (C434/03) [2005] 3 C.M.L.R. 38; [2005] S.T.I. 1258, ECJ

Charlton v. Charlton Thermosystems (Romsey) Ltd; Charlton v. Ellis [1995] I.C.R. 56; [1995] I.R.L.R. 79, EAT . . . . *Digested*, 95/**2068**: *Applied*, 05/1277

Charlton v. Ellis see Charlton v. Charlton Thermosystems (Romsey) Ltd

Chartered Accountants Firm v. Braisby (Inspector of Taxes) [2005] S.T.C. (S.C.D.) 389; [2005] S.T.I. 725, Sp Comm . . . . *Digested*, 05/**4089**

Charterhall Marketing Ltd v. Customs and Excise Commissioners [2005] B.V.C. 2566; [2005] S.T.I. 1027,V&DTr (Edinburgh)

Chatfield v. Kohler [2005] 2 Q.R. 12; [2004] 4 Q.R. 5, CC (Milton Keynes) [*Ex rel.* Geoffrey Mott, Barrister, Renaissance Chambers, Gray's Inn, London] . . . . *Digested*, 04/**2875**

Chatterley-Whitfield Collieries Ltd, Re see Prudential Assurance Co Ltd v. Chatterley-Whitfield Collieries Ltd

Chaudhary v. Medical Royal Colleges Specialist Training Authority (Appeal: Multiple Application) see British Medical Association v. Chaudhary (No.1)

Chaudhary v. Royal College of Surgeons of Great Britain and Ireland Senate (Appeal: Multiple Application) see British Medical Association v. Chaudhary (No.1)

Chaudhary v. Secretary of State for Health (Appeal: Multiple Application) see British Medical Association v. Chaudhary (No.1)

Chaudhary v. Specialist Training Authority Appeal Panel; Pathak v. Secretary of State for Health [2005] EWCA Civ 282; [2005] I.C.R. 1086, CA (Civ Div); affirming (2004) 80 B.M.L.R. 151, EAT. . . . . *Digested*, 05/**1293**

Chauffeur Bikes Ltd v. Leeds City Council; Chaffeur Bikes Ltd v. Leeds City Council [2005] EWHC 2369; *Times*, October 20, 2005, QBD (Admin)

Chauhan v. Wilson (Inspector of Taxes) [2004] EWHC 3364; [2005] S.T.C. 1786; [2004] S.T.I. 2397, Ch D

Chauvy v. France (64915/01) (2005) 41 E.H.R.R. 29, ECHR

Cheapside Land Development Co Ltd v. Messels Service Co see United Scientific Holdings Ltd v. Burnley BC

Checkpoint Ltd v. Strathclyde Pension Fund [2003] EWCA Civ 84; [2003] L. & T.R. 22; [2003] 1 E.G.L.R. 1; [2003] 14 E.G. 124; [2003] 8 E.G.C.S. 128; (2003) 100(12) L.S.G. 29; (2003) 147 S.J.L.B. 233; [2003] N.P.C. 23; *Times*, February 12, 2003, CA (Civ Div); affirming [2002] EWHC 439; [2002] 2 E.G.L.R. 97; [2002] 13 E.G.C.S. 101, Ch D . . . . *Digested*, 03/**190**: *Applied*, 03/2778: *Considered*, 05/2678

Chelmsford BC v. First Secretary of State see R. (on the application of Chelmsford BC) v. First Secretary of State

Cheltenham Old People's Housing Society Ltd v. Customs and Excise Commissioners [2005] B.V.C. 2200,V&DTr (London)

Chen v. Secretary of State for the Home Department (C200/02); Zhu v. Secretary of State for the Home Department (C200/02) [2005] Q.B. 325; [2004] 3 W.L.R. 1453; [2005] All E.R. (EC) 129; [2004] E.C.R. I-9925; [2004] 3 C.M.L.R. 48; [2004] C.E.C. 503; [2004] Imm. A.R. 754; [2005] I.N.L.R. 1; *Times*, October 21, 2004, ECJ [2004] E.C.R. I-9925; [2004] Imm. A.R. 333, AGO . . . . *Digested*, 05/**2207**

Chernobyl Accident, Re (C62/88) see Greece v. Council of Ministers of the European Communities (C62/88)

Cherry v. Malta Bargain Ltd (Unreported, May 5, 2005), CC (Gravesend) [*Ex rel.* Nicholas Preston, Barrister, 53 Curzon Road, London] . . . .   *Digested*, 05/**1978**

Cherry Tree Machine Co Ltd v. Dawson see Shell Tankers UK Ltd v. Jeromson

Chester v. Afshar [2004] UKHL 41; [2005] 1 A.C. 134; [2004] 3 W.L.R. 927; [2004] 4 All E.R. 587; [2005] P.I.Q.R. P12; [2005] Lloyd's Rep. Med. 109; (2005) 81 B.M.L.R. 1; [2005] P.N.L.R. 14; (2004) 101(43) L.S.G. 34; (2004) 154 N.L.J. 1589; (2004) 148 S.J.L.B. 1215; *Times*, October 19, 2004, HL; affirming [2002] EWCA Civ 724; [2003] Q.B. 356; [2002] 3 W.L.R. 1195; [2002] 3 All E.R. 552; [2002] Lloyd's Rep. Med. 305; (2002) 67 B.M.L.R. 66; (2002) 99(29) L.S.G. 33; (2002) 146 S.J.L.B. 167; *Times*, June 13, 2002; *Daily Telegraph*, June 13, 2002, CA (Civ Div); affirming 1997 C No. 198, HQ 9902422, QBD . . . .   *Digested*, 05/**2841**:
Distinguished, 05/2863

Chester CC v. Evans [2005] P.A.D. 55, Planning Inspector

Chesterfield Properties Ltd v. BHP Petroleum Great Britain Ltd see BHP Petroleum Great Britain Ltd v. Chesterfield Properties Ltd

Chesterton International Group Plc v. Deka Immobilien Inv GmbH [2005] EWHC 656; [2005] B.P.I.R. 1103, Ch D

CHEVRON/Fuel additive (T123/02) [2005] E.P.O.R. 29, EPO (Technical Bd App)

Chichester DC v. First Secretary of State; *sub nom* First Secretary of State v. Chichester DC [2004] EWCA Civ 1248; [2005] 1 W.L.R. 279; [2005] 1 F.C.R. 231; [2005] B.L.G.R. 427; [2005] 3 P.L.R. 39; [2005] J.P.L. 1029; (2004) 154 N.L.J. 1498; (2004) 148 S.J.L.B. 1152; [2004] N.P.C. 142; *Times*, October 14, 2004, CA (Civ Div); reversing [2003] EWHC 1924; [2003] N.P.C. 99, QBD (Admin) . . . .   *Digested*, 05/**3292**

Chichester DC v. Searle see South Buckinghamshire DC v. Porter (No.1)

Chief Constable of Leicestershire v. M [1989] 1 W.L.R. 20; [1988] 3 All E.R. 1015; (1988) 138 N.L.J. Rep. 295, Ch D . . . .   *Digested*, 88/**2877**:
Applied, 05/2804: *Distinguished*, 89/3210

Chief Constable of Leicestershire v. Tatam; *sub nom* Chief Constable of Leicestershire v. Tatem [2005] EWHC 912; (2005) 169 J.P. 485, QBD (Admin)

Chief Constable of Leicestershire v. Tatem see Chief Constable of Leicestershire v. Tatam

Chief Constable of Merseyside v. Husain see Yearwood v. Commissioner of Police of the Metropolis

Chief Constable of Merseyside v. Reynolds [2004] EWHC 2862; [2005] A.C.D. 44; *Times*, November 27, 2004, QBD . . . .   *Digested*, 05/**892**

Chief Constable of Norfolk v. Clayton; *sub nom* Clayton, Re; R. v. Hunstanton Justices Ex p. Clayton [1983] 2 A.C. 473; [1983] 2 W.L.R. 555; [1983] 1 All E.R. 984; (1983) 77 Cr. App. R. 24; [1983] Crim. L.R. 552; *Times*, March 19, 1983, HL; reversing [1982] Crim. L.R. 683, DC . . . .   *Digested*, 83/**2376**:
Applied, 05/905: *Considered*, 84/2109, 86/2085: *Distinguished*, 83/2316

Chief Constable of Surrey v. JHG see R. (on the application of T) v. St Albans Crown Court

Chief Constable of the West Midlands v. Billingham [1979] 1 W.L.R. 747; [1979] 2 All E.R. 182; [1979] R.T.R. 446; [1979] Crim. L.R. 256; 123 S.J. 98, QBD . . . .   *Digested*, 79/**2311**:
Applied, 05/755

Chief Constable of West Mercia v. Boorman [2005] EWHC 2559; (2005) 169 J.P. 669; *Times*, November 17, 2005, QBD (Admin)

Chief Constable of West Yorkshire v. A; *sub nom* A v. Chief Constable of West Yorkshire [2004] UKHL 21; [2005] 1 A.C. 51; [2004] 2 W.L.R. 1209; [2004] 3 All E.R. 145; [2004] 2 C.M.L.R. 37; [2004] Eu. L.R. 841; [2004] I.C.R. 806; [2004] I.R.L.R. 573; [2004] 2 F.C.R. 160; [2004] H.R.L.R. 25; [2004] U.K.H.R.R. 694; 17 B.H.R.C. 585; (2004) 101(20) L.S.G. 34; (2004) 154 N.L.J. 734; (2004) 148 S.J.L.B. 572; *Times*, May 7, 2004, HL; affirming [2002] EWCA Civ 1584; [2003] 1 All E.R. 255; [2003] 1 C.M.L.R. 25; [2003] I.C.R. 161; [2003] I.R.L.R. 32; [2003] 1 F.L.R. 223; [2002] 3 F.C.R. 751; [2003] H.R.L.R. 5; [2003] Fam. Law 98; (2003) 100(1) L.S.G. 24; (2002) 146 S.J.L.B. 254; *Times*, November 14, 2002, CA (Civ Div); reversing [2002] I.C.R. 552; [2002] I.R.L.R. 103; *Daily Telegraph*, October 9, 2001, EAT . . . .   *Digested*, 04/**1261**

Chief Constable of West Yorkshire v. Khan; *sub nom* Khan v. Chief Constable of West Yorkshire [2001] UKHL 48; [2001] 1 W.L.R. 1947; [2001] 4 All E.R. 834; [2001] I.C.R. 1065; [2001] I.R.L.R. 830; [2001] Emp. L.R. 1399; (2001) 98(42) L.S.G. 37; (2001) 145 S.J.L.B. 230; *Times*, October 16, 2001; *Daily Telegraph*, October 16, 2001, HL; reversing [2000] I.C.R. 1169; [2000] I.R.L.R. 324; (2000) 150 N.L.J. 308; *Times*, March 15, 2000; *Independent*, March 3, 2000, CA (Civ Div); affirming (Unreported, July 28, 1998), EAT . . . .   *Digested*, 01/**2302**:
Applied, 05/1232, 05/1235: *Cited*, 00/2186: *Followed*, 03/1354

Chief Constable of West Yorkshire v. Vento (No.2) see Vento v. Chief Constable of West Yorkshire

Chief Inspector Shields v. Devenney [2005] N.I. 375, CA (NI)

Chiltern DC v. Hodgetts see Hodgetts v. Chiltern DC

CHINAWHITE Trade Mark see Harrison v. Teton Valley Trading Co Ltd

Chios Investment Property Co v. Lopez (1988) 20 H.L.R. 120; [1988] 05 E.G. 57;
[1988] Fam. Law 384; (1988) 138 N.L.J. Rep. 20; *Times*, November 3, 1987, CA
(Civ Div) . . . . *Digested*, 88/**2086**:
Considered, 05/2641
Chiron Corp's and Novo Nordisk A/S's SPC Application [2005] R.P.C. 24, PO . . . . *Digested*, 05/**2473**
Chivers v. Metcalfe (Unreported, June 16, 2004), QBD [*Ex rel.* Graham Leigh Pfeffer &
Co, Solicitors, Maple House, Haymarket Street, Bury] . . . . *Digested*, 05/**3237**
Chohan v. Derby Law Centre [2004] I.R.L.R. 685, EAT . . . . *Digested*, 05/**1301**:
Applied, 05/1229
Chorley v. Archcraft Ltd see Forshaw v. Archcraft Ltd
Christ's Hospital v. Revenue and Customs Commissioners [2005] S.T.I. 1660, V&DTr
(London)
Christchurch Sparkbrook, Re, *Times*, December 19, 2005, Cons Ct (Birmingham)
Christiani & Nielsen Ltd v. Lowry Centre Development Co Ltd [2005] T.C.L.R. 2, QBD
(TCC) . . . . *Digested*, 05/**650**
Christie Owen & Davies Plc v. Ryelance [2005] 18 E.G.C.S. 148, CC (Liverpool)
Christmas v. Hampshire CC (Duty of Care) see X (Minors) v. Bedfordshire CC
Christoph-Dornier-Stiftung fur Klinische Psychologie v. Finanzamt Giessen (C45/01)
[2005] S.T.C. 228; [2004] 1 C.M.L.R. 30; [2004] C.E.C. 144; [2005] B.T.C.
5232; [2005] B.V.C. 263; [2003] S.T.I. 1935, ECJ (5th Chamber) . . . . *Digested*, 04/**3975**
Chubb Insurance Co of Europe SA v. Davies [2004] EWHC 2138; [2004] 2 All E.R.
(Comm) 827; [2005] Lloyd's Rep. I.R. 1, QBD (Comm) . . . . *Digested*, 05/**424**
Church of England Children's Society v. Customs and Excise Commissioners; *sub nom*
Church of England Children's Society v. Revenue and Customs Commissioners
[2005] EWHC 1692; [2005] S.T.C. 1644; [2005] B.T.C. 5559; [2005] B.V.C.
590; [2005] S.T.I. 1340; (2005) 102(34) L.S.G. 33; *Times*, September 21, 2005,
Ch D; reversing [2004] B.V.C. 2317; [2004] V. & D.R. 178; [2004] S.T.I. 1953,
V&DTr (London) . . . . *Digested*, 05/**4371**
Church of England Children's Society v. Revenue and Customs Commissioners see
Church of England Children's Society v. Customs and Excise Commissioners
Church of Scientology's Application for Registration as a Charity [2005] W.T.L.R. 1151
Church of the Blessed Virgin Mary, Batcombe, Re (2005) 102(8) L.S.G. 29; *Times*, January
13, 2005, Cons Ct (Bath & Wells) . . . . *Digested*, 05/**990**
Church Schools Foundation Ltd v. Customs and Excise Commissioners; *sub nom*
Customs and Excise Commissioners v. Church Schools Foundation Ltd [2001]
EWCA Civ 1745; [2001] S.T.C. 1661; [2002] B.T.C. 5003; [2002] B.V.C. 114;
[2001] S.T.I. 1519, CA (Civ Div); reversing [2000] S.T.C. 651; [2000] B.T.C.
5326; [2000] B.V.C. 353; [2000] S.T.I. 1000; [2000] E.G.C.S. 93; [2000] N.P.C.
81, Ch D; reversing [2000] B.V.C. 2213; [2000] S.T.I. 759, V&DTr. . . . . *Digested*, 02/**4790**:
Distinguished, 05/4419
Churchill Retirement Living v. Poole BC [2005] P.A.D. 67, Planning Inspector
Ci4Net.com.Inc, Re; DBP Holdings, Re [2004] EWHC 1941; [2005] B.C.C. 277, Ch D
(Companies Ct) . . . . *Digested*, 05/**2265**
Cia de Seguros Imperio v. Heath (REBX) Ltd (formerly CE Heath & Co (America) Ltd);
sub nom Companhia de Seguros Imperio v. Heath (REBX) Ltd [2001] 1 W.L.R.
112; [2000] 2 All E.R. (Comm) 787; [2000] C.L.C. 1543; [2001] Lloyd's Rep.
I.R. 109; [2000] Lloyd's Rep. P.N. 795; (2000-01) 3 I.T.E.L.R. 134; *Times*,
September 26, 2000; *Independent*, October 23, 2000 (C.S), CA (Civ Div);
affirming [1999] 1 All E.R. (Comm) 750; [1999] C.L.C. 997; [1999] Lloyd's Rep.
I.R. 571; [1999] Lloyd's Rep. P.N. 571; *Independent*, May 3, 1999 (C.S.), QBD
(Comm) . . . . *Digested*, 00/**513**:
Applied, 05/314
CIB Properties Ltd v. Birse Construction Ltd [2005] 1 W.L.R. 2252; [2005] B.L.R. 173,
QBD (TCC)
CIBC Mellon Trust Co v. Mora Hotel Corp NV [2002] EWCA Civ 1688; [2003] 1 All E.R.
564; [2003] C.P. Rep. 19; (2003) 100(3) L.S.G. 30; *Times*, November 28,
2002; *Independent*, November 26, 2002, CA (Civ Div) . . . . *Digested*, 03/**363**:
Applied, 05/482
CIBC Mellon Trust Co v. Stolzenberg (Costs) [2005] EWCA Civ 628; [2005] C.P. Rep.
45; [2005] 2 B.C.L.C. 618; [2005] 4 Costs L.R. 617; *Times*, June 8, 2005, CA
(Civ Div); reversing [2004] EWHC 413, Ch D . . . . *Digested*, 05/**386**
Cibo Participations SA v. Directeur Regional des Impots du Nord Pas de Calais (C16/
00) [2002] S.T.C. 460; [2001] E.C.R. I-6663; [2002] 1 C.M.L.R. 23; [2002]
B.T.C. 5500; [2002] B.V.C. 605; [2001] S.T.I. 1377, ECJ (1st Chamber) . . . . *Digested*, 02/**4746**:
Applied, 03/4555: *Followed*, 05/4345, 05/4363
Cie Maritime Belge Transports SA v. Commission of the European Communities (C395/
96 P) see Compagnie Maritime Belge Transports SA v. Commission of the
European Communities (C395/96 P)
Cigna Life Insurance New Zealand Ltd v. Westpac Securities Ltd [1996] 1 N.Z.L.R. 80,
HC (NZ) . . . . *Considered*, 05/621
Cimber Air A/S v. Skatteministeriet (C382/02) [2005] S.T.C. 547; [2004] 3 C.M.L.R.
55; [2004] S.T.I. 2120, ECJ (2nd Chamber) . . . . *Digested*, 05/**4344**

Cimenteries CBR SA v. Commission of the European Communities (T25/95) [2000]
E.C.R. II-491; [2000] 5 C.M.L.R. 204, CFI (4th Chamber) . . . . *Digested*, 00/**710**:
Followed, 05/**553**: *Subsequent proceedings*, 05/**1435**
Cinpres Gas Injection Ltd v. Melea Ltd [2005] EWHC 3180; *Times*, December 21, 2005,
Ch D (Patents Ct)
Circle 33 Housing Trust Ltd v. Ellis [2005] EWCA Civ 1233; (2005) 102(39) L.S.G. 31,
CA (Civ Div); reversing [2005] EWHC 2090, QBD
Circular Facilities (London) Ltd v. Sevenoaks DC [2005] EWHC 865; [2005] Env. L.R.
35; [2005] J.P.L. 1624, QBD (Admin); reversing (Unreported, June 14, 2004),
MC . . . . *Digested*, 05/**1388**
Cirdan Sailing Trust v. Revenue and Customs Commissioners [2005] EWHC 2999;
[2005] S.T.I. 1062, Ch D; affirming [2005] B.V.C. 2245; [2004] V. & D.R. 501,
V&DTr (London)
Citadel General Insurance Co v. Lloyd's Bank Canada; *sub nom* Citadel General
Insurance Co v. Lloyds Bank Canada [1997] 3 S.C.R. 805, Sup Ct (Can) . . . . . . *Applied*, 05/**4307**
Citro (Carmine) (A Bankrupt), Re see Citro (Domenico) (A Bankrupt), Re
Citro (Domenico) (A Bankrupt), Re; Citro (Carmine) (A Bankrupt), Re [1991] Ch. 142;
[1990] 3 W.L.R. 880; [1990] 3 All E.R. 952; [1991] 1 F.L.R. 71; [1990] E.G.C.S.
78; (1990) 154 N.L.J. 1073; (1990) 134 S.J. 806, CA (Civ Div) . . . . *Digested*, 91/**261**:
Applied, 01/3723, 05/2272: *Considered*, 92/2131, 98/3291:
Distinguished, 93/1846, 94/3303, 95/2214: *Followed*, 95/2365
City Branch Group Ltd, Re see Gross v. Rackind
City of London v. Intercede Ltd see Mayor and Commonalty and Citizens of the City of
London v. Intercede 1765 Ltd
City of London v. Wardens and Commonality of the Mystery of Mercers in the City of
London see Mayor and Commonalty and Citizens of the City of London v.
Intercede 1765 Ltd
City of London Corp v. Bovis Construction Ltd [1992] 3 All E.R. 697; 49 B.L.R. 1; 84
L.G.R. 660; (1988) 4 Const. L.J. 203; [1989] J.P.L. 263; (1989) 153 L.G. Rev.
166; [1988] E.G.C.S. 56; *Times*, April 21, 1988, CA (Civ Div); affirming [1988]
E.G.C.S. 23, Ch D . . . . *Digested*, 89/**3133**:
Applied, 89/2990, 90/3704, 90/4131, 91/3303, 93/3852: *Cited*, 01/4706:
Considered, 92/4263: *Distinguished*, 94/4421, 95/4841, 95/4875:
Followed, 05/2804
City of London Corp v. Eurostar (UK) Ltd; *sub nom* London Corp v. Eurostar (UK) Ltd
[2004] EWHC 187; (2005) 169 J.P. 263; [2004] A.C.D. 64, QBD (Admin) . . . . *Digested*, 05/**774**
City of London Corp v. Secretary of State for the Environment, Food and Rural Affairs
see R. (on the application of London Corp) v. Secretary of State for the
Environment, Food and Rural Affairs
City of London Police Authority v. Medical Referee [2004] EWHC 897, QBD (Admin) . *Approved*, 05/**3332**
Citybranch Group Ltd, Re see Gross v. Rackind
Civil Service Pensioners Alliance v. Customs and Excise Commissioners [2005] B.V.C.
2319, V&DTr
Claim 13 Plc v. HMRC [2005] S.T.I. 1657, VAT Tr
Claim by a German Lottery Company, Re (6 U 135/03) [2005] I.L.Pr. 35, OLG (Koln)
Claim for Payment of Prize Money, Re (III ZR 226/03) [2005] I.L.Pr. 19, BGH (Ger)
Claims Direct Test Cases (Case Management), Re [2002] EWCA Civ 428; [2002] P.I.Q.R.
Q11; *Times*, April 4, 2002, CA (Civ Div) . . . . *Digested*, 02/**289**:
Applied, 05/452
Claire & Co Ltd v. Thames Water Utilities Ltd [2005] EWHC 1022; [2005] B.L.R. 366,
QBD (TCC)
Clare v. Perry (t/a Widemouth Manor Hotel) [2005] EWCA Civ 39; (2005) 149
S.J.L.B. 114, CA (Civ Div)
Clare Civil Engineering Ltd v. Mayo CC [2005] Eu. L.R. 335, HC (Irl)
Clariant GmbH v. Air Products & Chemicals Inc (T85/03) (2005) 28(4) I.P.D. 28032,
EPO (Technical Bd App)
Clarins Paris SA v. Supermercados Sabeco SA [2005] E.T.M.R. 110, Aud (Sp)
Clark v. BET Plc [1997] I.R.L.R. 348; [1997] O.P.L.R. 1, QBD . . . . *Digested*, 97/**2207**:
Considered, 05/1212: *Distinguished*, 05/5220
Clark v. Devon CC; *sub nom* Devon CC v. Clarke [2005] EWCA Civ 266; [2005] C.P.
Rep. 42; [2005] 2 F.L.R. 747; [2005] 1 F.C.R. 752; [2005] E.L.R. 375; *Times*,
April 22, 2005, CA (Civ Div) . . . . *Digested*, 05/**2871**
Clark v. Midland Packaging Ltd; *sub nom* Midland Packaging Ltd v. Clark [2005] 2 All
E.R. 266, EAT . . . . *Disapproved*, 05/**1244**
Clark v. Nomura International Plc [2000] I.R.L.R. 766, QBD . . . . *Digested*, 00/**2098**:
Approved, 05/1212: *Considered*, 03/1316
Clark v. Novacold Ltd see Clark v. TDG Ltd (t/a Novacold Ltd)
Clark v. Revenue and Customs Commissioners [2005] S.T.C. (S.C.D.) 823; [2005]
W.T.L.R. 1465; [2005] S.T.I. 1758, Sp Comm

Clark v. TDG Ltd (t/a Novacold Ltd); *sub nom* Clark v. Novacold Ltd [1999] 2 All E.R.
977; [1999] I.C.R. 951; [1999] I.R.L.R. 318; [1999] Disc. L.R. 240; (1999) 48
B.M.L.R. 1; *Times*, April 1, 1999, CA (Civ Div); reversing [1998] I.C.R. 1044;
[1998] I.R.L.R. 420; [1999] Disc. L.R. 22; (1998) 42 B.M.L.R. 101; *Times*, June
11, 1998, EAT . . . . *Digested*, 99/**2022**:
    Applied, 99/2024, 01/2239, 01/2240, 01/6461, 03/5477, 04/1077, 04/1220,
    05/1229: *Followed*, 00/2127
Clark v. Torre Kitchens & Bathrooms [2005] 2 Q.R. 20; [2004] 6 Q.R. 10, CC
(Torquay) [*Ex rel.* Michael Melville-Shreeve, Barrister, Walnut House, 63 St
David's Hill, Exeter, Devon] . . . . *Digested*, 04/**2940**
Clark v. University of Lincolnshire and Humberside [2000] 1 W.L.R. 1988; [2000] 3
All E.R. 752; [2000] Ed. C.R. 553; [2000] E.L.R. 345; [2000] C.O.D. 293;
(2000) 150 N.L.J. 616; (2000) 144 S.J.L.B. 220; *Times*, May 3, 2000;
Independent, May 3, 2000, CA (Civ Div) . . . . *Digested*, 00/**2001**:
    Applied, 05/2497
Clark Boyce v. Mouat [1994] 1 A.C. 428; [1993] 3 W.L.R. 1021; [1993] 4 All E.R. 268;
(1993) 143 N.L.J. 1440; (1993) 137 S.J.L.B. 231; [1993] N.P.C. 128; *Times*,
October 7, 1993; *Independent*, October 12, 1993, PC (NZ) . . . . *Digested*, 93/**3750**:
    Applied, 00/4247, 05/4307: *Considered*, 99/4390: *Distinguished*, 00/4273
Clark (Inspector of Taxes) v. Oceanic Contractors Inc [1983] 2 A.C. 130; [1983] 2
W.L.R. 94; [1983] 1 All E.R. 133; [1983] S.T.C. 35; 56 T.C. 183; (1982) 13 A.T.R.
901; (1983) 133 N.L.J. 62; (1983) 127 S.J. 54, HL; reversing [1982] 1 W.L.R.
222; [1982] S.T.C. 66; [1982] E.C.C. 224; [1981] T.R. 463; 124 S.J. 34; *Times*,
November 11, 1981, CA (Civ Div); reversing [1981] 1 W.L.R. 59; [1980] S.T.C.
656; [1980] E.C.C. 485; [1980] T.R. 341; 124 S.J. 595, Ch D . . . . *Digested*, 85/**1766**:
    Applied, 87/209, 05/685, 05/4104: *Considered*, 88/190, 04/3758:
    Distinguished, 85/318
Clarke v. Frank Staddon Ltd see Marshalls Clay Products Ltd v. Caulfield
Clarke v. Harlowe [2005] EWHC 3062; [2005] W.T.L.R. 1473, Ch D
Clarke v. Hynes (Unreported, November 4, 2004), CC (Doncaster) [*Ex rel.* Tom
Nossiter, Barrister, Park Lane Chambers, 19 Westgate, Leeds] . . . . *Digested*, 05/**3123**
Clarke v. United Kingdom (57419/00) see Whitfield v. United Kingdom (46387/99)
Claussen v. Yeates see Cranfield v. Bridgegrove Ltd
Claygreen Ltd, Re see Romer-Ormiston v. Claygreen Ltd
Claymore Dairies Ltd v. Director General of Fair Trading (Preliminary Issues) [2003]
CAT 3; [2004] Comp. A.R. 1, CAT . . . . *Digested*, 04/**516**:
    Applied, 04/519: *Followed*, 05/586
Claymore Dairies Ltd v. Office of Fair Trading (Disclosure: Further Information) [2004]
CAT 16; [2005] Comp. A.R. 1, CAT . . . . *Digested*, 05/**5061**
Claymore Dairies Ltd v. Office of Fair Trading (Stay of Proceedings) [2003] CAT 18;
[2004] Comp. A.R. 177, CAT . . . . *Digested*, 04/**542**:
    Applied, 05/570
Clayton, Re see Chief Constable of Norfolk v. Clayton
Clayton v. HM Coroner for South Yorkshire (East District) [2005] EWHC 1196; [2005]
A.C.D. 97, QBD (Admin)
Clayton's Case; *sub nom* Devaynes v. Noble [1814-23] All E.R. Rep. 1; (1816) 1 Mer.
572. . . . . *Applied*, 47-51/1409,
    54/1570, 55/2066, 64/476, 64/481, 79/169, 82/3432, 84/1598, 85/1579:
    Considered, 62/385, 91/1719, 92/2050, 92/2576, 94/2935:
    Distinguished, 61/5024: *Not followed*, 05/3444
Clear Channel UK Ltd v. Manchester City Council [2005] EWCA Civ 1304, CA (Civ
Div); affirming [2004] EWHC 2873; [2005] 2 P. & C.R. 2; [2005] L. & T.R. 10;
[2005] 1 E.G.L.R. 128; [2005] 1 P. & C.R. DG19, Ch D . . . . *Digested*, 05/**2670**
Cleveland Trust, Re [1991] B.C.C. 33; [1991] B.C.L.C. 424, Ch D (Companies Ct) . . . . . *Digested*, 91/**425**:
    Approved, 05/516: *Distinguished*, 04/472
Clifford Harris & Co v. Solland International Ltd (No.2) [2005] EWHC 141; [2005] 2 All
E.R. 334; [2005] 3 Costs L.R. 414; (2005) 102(17) L.S.G. 32; *Times*, March
10, 2005, Ch D . . . . *Digested*, 05/**2720**
Clingham v. Kensington and Chelsea RLBC see R. (on the application of McCann) v.
Manchester Crown Court
Cloverbay Ltd (Joint Administrators) v. Bank of Credit and Commerce International SA
[1991] Ch. 90; [1990] 3 W.L.R. 574; [1991] 1 All E.R. 894; [1991] B.C.L.C.
135; *Independent*, May 4, 1990, CA (Civ Div) . . . . *Digested*, 91/**2160**:
    Applied, 92/2580, 05/2294: *Considered*, 91/2856, 93/2317:
    Followed, 02/2687
Clowance Owners Club Ltd v. Customs and Excise Commissioners [2005] B.V.C. 2169;
[2004] S.T.I. 2579, V&DTr
Clowes Developments (UK) Ltd v. Walters [2005] EWHC 669; [2005] 17 E.G.C.S. 123,
Ch D
Clydesdale Bank Plc v. Lanarkshire Valuation Joint Board Assessor see Lanarkshire
Valuation Joint Board Assessor v. Clydesdale Bank Plc
CM v. Secretary of State for the Home Department; *sub nom* CM (Deportation:
Article 8: Jamaica), Re [2005] UKIAT 103; [2005] Imm. A.R. 397, IAT

CM (Deportation: Article 8: Jamaica), Re see CM *v.* Secretary of State for the Home Department

CN *v.* Secretary of State for the Home Department see MM *v.* Secretary of State for the Home Department

CNA Insurance Co Ltd *v.* Office Depot International (UK) Ltd [2005] EWHC 456; [2005] Lloyd's Rep. I.R. 658, QBD (Comm)

Co-Frutta Coop Srl *v.* Commission of the European Communities (T47/01) [2003] E.C.R. II-4441; [2005] 2 C.M.L.R. 22, CFI (5th Chamber) . . . .   *Digested,* 05/**1426**

Co-operative Group (CWS) Ltd *v.* Stansell Ltd (formerly Stansell (Builders) Ltd see Stansell Ltd (formerly Stansell (Builders) Ltd *v.* Co-operative Group (CWS) Ltd

Coates *v.* South Buckinghamshire DC see South Buckinghamshire DC *v.* Coates

Cobbe *v.* Yeomans Row Management Ltd (No.1) [2005] EWHC 266; [2005] W.T.L.R. 625; [2005] N.P.C. 29; [2005] 2 P. & C.R. DG1, Ch D

Cobbold *v.* Greenwich LBC (Unreported, August 9, 1999), CA (Civ Div) . . . .   *Applied,* 05/**454**:
                                                                                            Considered, 04/**270**

Coburn *v.* Colledge [1897] 1 Q.B. 702, CA. . . . .   *Applied,* 56/**5436**,
                                                  62/**1122**, 62/**1770**, 86/**2000**, 05/**657**: *Considered,* 85/**2006**

Coburn *v.* Sonora Foods (Unreported, February 17, 2005), CC (Nuneaton) [*Ex rel.* Stephen Garner, Barrister, No.8 Chambers, Fountain Court, Steelhouse Lane, Birmingham.]. . . . .   *Digested,* 05/**3187**

Cockbone *v.* Atkinson Dacre & Slack see Arthur JS Hall & Co *v.* Simons

Codeviandes SA *v.* Maillard [2005] I.L.Pr. 41, Cass (F)

Codona *v.* Mid-Bedfordshire DC [2004] EWCA Civ 925; [2005] H.L.R. 1; [2005] B.L.G.R. 241; [2005] A.C.D. 10; (2004) 148 S.J.L.B. 910; [2004] N.P.C. 120; *Times,* July 21, 2004, CA (Civ Div). . . . .   *Digested,* 04/**1890**

Coffey *v.* Warner/Chappell Music Ltd [2005] EWHC 449; [2005] E.C.D.R. 21; [2005] F.S.R. 34; (2005) 28(6) I.P.D. 28046, Ch D . . . .   *Digested,* 05/**2423**

Coflexip SA *v.* Stolt Offshore MS Ltd [2004] EWCA Civ 213; [2004] F.S.R. 34; (2004) 27(5) I.P.D. 27047; (2004) 148 S.J.L.B. 297, CA (Civ Div); affirming [2003] EWHC 1892; [2004] F.S.R. 7; (2003) 26(10) I.P.D. 26066, Ch D (Patents Ct) . . . .   *Digested,* 04/**2338**:
                                                  Considered, 05/**2505**: *Followed,* 05/329

Cohen *v.* Kingsley Napley (A Firm) A2/2005/1164, CA (Civ Div); reversing in part [2005] EWHC 899; [2005] P.N.L.R. 37, QBD . . . .   *Digested,* 05/**461**

Cohen *v.* Knowsley MBC [2005] R.V.R. 40, Lands Tr . . . .   *Digested,* 05/**3255**

Cohen *v.* Selby; *sub nom* Simmon Box (Diamonds) Ltd, Re [2002] B.C.C. 82; [2001] 1 B.C.L.C. 176, CA (Civ Div); reversing [2000] B.C.C. 275, Ch D . . . .   *Digested,* 01/**3745**:
                                                                                            Applied, 05/2296

Cole *v.* Lambeth LBC see Kay *v.* Lambeth LBC

Colegio de Oficiales de la Marina Mercante Espanola *v.* Administracion del Estado (C405/01) [2003] E.C.R. I-10391; [2005] 2 C.M.L.R. 13, ECJ . . . .   *Digested,* 05/**1459**

Colin Dawson Windows Ltd *v.* Howard see Colin Dawson Windows Ltd *v.* King's Lynn and West Norfolk BC

Colin Dawson Windows Ltd *v.* King's Lynn and West Norfolk BC; *sub nom* Colin Dawson Windows Ltd *v.* Howard [2005] EWCA Civ 9; [2005] 2 P. & C.R. 19; [2005] N.P.C. 8, CA (Civ Div) . . . .   *Digested,* 05/**3439**

Collector of Stamp Revenue *v.* Arrowtown Assets Ltd 6 I.T.L. Rep. 454, CFA (HK) . . . .   *Considered,* 05/**4084**

Colleg Elidyr (Camphill Communities Wales) Ltd *v.* Koeller see Koeller *v.* Coleg Elidyr (Camphill Communities Wales) Ltd

College Credit Ltd *v.* National Guarantee Corp Ltd [2004] EWHC 978; [2004] 2 All E.R. (Comm) 409; [2005] Lloyd's Rep. I.R. 5, QBD (Comm). . . . .   *Digested,* 04/**2232**

College of Estate Management *v.* Customs and Excise Commissioners; *sub nom* College of Estate Management *v.* Revenue and Customs Commissioners [2005] UKHL 62; [2005] 1 W.L.R. 3351; [2005] 4 All E.R. 933; [2005] S.T.C. 1957; [2005] B.T.C. 5673; [2005] B.V.C. 704; [2005] S.T.I. 1753; (2005) 102(44) L.S.G. 32; [2005] N.P.C. 118; *Times,* October 26, 2005, HL; reversing [2004] EWCA Civ 1086; [2004] S.T.C. 1471; [2004] B.T.C. 5754; [2004] B.V.C. 813; [2004] S.T.I. 1972; (2004) 101(37) L.S.G. 36; (2004) 148 S.J.L.B. 1030; *Times,* October 11, 2004, CA (Civ Div); reversing [2003] EWHC 2712; [2004] S.T.C. 235; [2004] B.T.C. 5335; [2004] B.V.C. 395; [2004] S.T.I. 1867; [2003] S.T.I. 2119, Ch D; affirming [2003] V. & D.R.165; [2003] S.T.I.1087, V&DTr . . . .   *Digested,* 04/**3985**

College of Estate Management *v.* Revenue and Customs Commissioners see College of Estate Management *v.* Customs and Excise Commissioners

Colley *v.* Clements (Inspector of Taxes) [2005] S.T.C. (S.C.D.) 633, Sp Comm

Collins *v.* Addies (Inspector of Taxes); Greenfield *v.* Bains (Inspector of Taxes) [1992] S.T.C. 746; *Times,* August 25, 1992; *Independent,* August 24, 1992, CA (Civ Div); affirming [1991] S.T.C. 445; *Times,* July 16, 1991, Ch D . . . .   *Digested,* 93/**2267**:
                                                                                            Applied, 05/4020

Collins *v.* Equity Trustees Executors & Agency Co Ltd [1997] V.R. 166 . . . .   *Applied,* 05/3978

Collins *v.* Laing (Inspector of Taxes) see Xi Software Ltd *v.* Laing (Inspector of Taxes)

Collins *v.* Laing (Inspector of Taxes) (Costs) see Xi Software Ltd *v.* Laing (Inspector of Taxes) (Costs)

Collins v. Royal National Theatre Board Ltd; *sub nom* Royal National Theatre Board
   Ltd v. Collins [2004] EWCA Civ 144; [2004] 2 All E.R. 851; [2004] I.R.L.R. 395;
   (2004) 78 B.M.L.R. 62; (2004) 148 S.J.L.B. 236, CA (Civ Div); reversing EAT/
   0642/02/MAA, EAT . . . .   *Digested,* 04/**1219:**
                                                                                Applied, 05/1223
Collins v. Secretary of State for Work and Pensions (C138/02) [2005] Q.B. 145;
   [2004] 3 W.L.R. 1236; [2004] All E.R. (EC) 1005; [2004] E.C.R. I-2703;
   [2004] 2 C.M.L.R. 8; [2004] C.E.C. 436; [2005] I.C.R. 37; *Times,* March 30,
   2004, ECJ . . . .   *Digested,* 04/**3597:**
                                      Applied, 05/3856: *Considered,* 04/1419, 05/2004
Collins and Beckett Ltd v. Revenue and Customs Commissioners [2005] S.T.I. 2038,
   V&DTr
Collins Stewart Ltd v. Financial Times Ltd (No.1) [2004] EWHC 2337; [2005] E.M.L.R.
   5; (2004) 101(43) L.S.G. 33; *Times,* October 26, 2004, QBD . . . .   *Digested,* 04/**334**
Collins (Contractors) Ltd v. Baltic Quay Management (1994) Ltd [2004] EWCA Civ
   1757; [2005] B.L.R. 63; [2005] T.C.L.R. 3; 99 Con. L.R. 1; (2005) 102(5)
   L.S.G. 26; *Times,* January 3, 2005, CA (Civ Div) . . . .   *Digested,* 05/**198:**
                                                                                Applied, 05/665
Colls v. Home & Colonial Stores Ltd; *sub nom* Home & Colonial Stores Ltd v. Colls
   [1904] A.C. 179, HL; reversing [1902] 1 Ch. 302, CA . . . .   *Applied,* 64/1200,
                             70/825, 71/3750, 78/2205, 79/797, 84/1150, 85/1085, 05/3434:
                                                                       Considered, 00/4633
Colville v. Registrar of Restrictive Trading Agreements see British Basic Slag Ltd's
   Agreements (No.1), Re
Colvilles Application, Re see British Basic Slag Ltd's Agreements (No.1), Re
Comfort v. Department of Constitutional Affairs (2005) 102(35) L.S.G. 42, EAT . . . . .   *Digested,* 05/**300**
Comite Andaluz de Agricultura Ecologica v. Administracion General del Estado (C107/
   04) [2005] 3 C.M.L.R. 32, ECJ (1st Chamber)
Commercial Land Ltd v. Secretary of State for Transport, Local Government and the
   Regions; *sub nom* Imperial Resources SA v. Secretary of State for Transport,
   Local Government and the Regions [2002] EWHC 1264; [2003] J.P.L. 358,
   QBD (Admin) . . . .   *Digested,* 03/**3430:**
                                                                                Followed, 05/3260
Commerzbank AG v. IMB Morgan Plc [2004] EWHC 2771; [2005] 2 All E.R. (Comm)
   564; [2005] 1 Lloyd's Rep. 298; [2005] W.T.L.R. 1485; [2005] 1 P. & C.R.
   DG17, Ch D . . . .   *Digested,* 05/**3444**
Commission for the New Towns v. Cooper (Great Britain) Ltd (formerly Coopind UK);
   sub nom Milton Keynes Development Corp v. Cooper (Great Britain) [1995] Ch.
   259; [1995] 2 W.L.R. 677; [1995] 2 All E.R. 929; (1996) 72 P. & C.R. 270;
   [1995] 2 E.G.L.R. 113; [1995] E.G.C.S. 30; (1995) 139 S.J.L.B. 87; [1995]
   N.P.C. 34; (1995) 69 P. & C.R. D40; *Times,* March 3, 1995; *Independent,* March
   15, 1995, CA (Civ Div); affirming in part (1995) 69 P. & C.R. 221; [1993]
   E.G.C.S. 142; [1993] N.P.C. 115, Ch D . . . .   *Digested,* 95/**780:**
                                      Applied, 96/3756, 99/3658, 05/717, 05/2386: *Considered,* 04/675
Commission of the European Communities v. Akzo Nobel Chemicals Ltd (C7/04 P (R))
   [2004] E.C.R. I-8739; [2004] 5 C.M.L.R. 24, ECJ . . . .   *Digested,* 05/**546:**
                                                                       Previous proceedings, 04/496
Commission of the European Communities v. Anic Partecipazioni SpA (C49/92) [1999]
   E.C.R. I-4125; [2001] 4 C.M.L.R. 17, ECJ (6th Chamber) . . . .   *Digested,* 01/**758:**
                                      Applied, 03/558: *Distinguished,* 04/494: *Followed,* 05/1435
Commission of the European Communities v. Austria (C147/03); *sub nom* Access to
   Higher Education, Re (C147/03) [2005] 3 C.M.L.R. 23; [2005] C.E.C. 758, ECJ
   (2nd Chamber)
Commission of the European Communities v. Austria (C203/03); *sub nom* Law
   Prohibiting Employment of Women in Specific Posts, Re (C203/03) [2005]
   E.C.R. I-935; [2005] 2 C.M.L.R. 14, ECJ . . . .   *Digested,* 05/**1440**
Commission of the European Communities v. Austria (C465/01) [2004] 3 C.M.L.R. 58,
   ECJ (2nd Chamber) . . . .   *Digested,* 05/**1234**
Commission of the European Communities v. Belgium (C11/95); *sub nom* Cable
   Television Broadcasts, Re (C11/95) [1996] E.C.R. I-4115; [1997] 2 C.M.L.R.
   289; [1998] E.M.L.R. 71, ECJ . . . .   *Digested,* 98/**3856:**
                                                        Applied, 97/3569: *Considered,* 05/1440
Commission of the European Communities v. Belgium (C287/03); *sub nom* Customer
   Loyalty Schemes, Re (C287/03) [2005] 2 C.M.L.R. 47, ECJ (2nd Chamber) . .   *Digested,* 05/**1447**
Commission of the European Communities v. Belgium (No.1) (149/79); *sub nom* Public
   Employees (No.1) (149/79), Re [1980] E.C.R. 3881; [1981] 2 C.M.L.R. 413,
   ECJ . . . .   *Digested,* 81/**1049:**
                                      Applied, 99/5272, 01/5769: *Considered,* 05/1457
Commission of the European Communities v. Ceva Sante Animale SA (C198/03 P)
   [2005] 3 C.M.L.R. 30, ECJ
Commission of the European Communities v. CMA CGM (C236/03 P) [2005] 4
   C.M.L.R. 7, ECJ (2nd Chamber). . . . .   *Digested,* 05/**545:**
                                                                       Previous proceedings, 04/486

Commission of the European Communities v. Council of Ministers of the European
Communities (16/88) [1989] E.C.R. 3457, ECJ . . . .   *Applied*, 05/1446
Commission of the European Communities v. Council of the European Union (C110/02);
   sub nom Aid to Pig Farmers (C110/02), Re [2005] All E.R. (EC) 397; [2004] 2
   C.M.L.R. 58, ECJ . . . .   *Digested*, 05/**1430**
Commission of the European Communities v. Council of the European Union (C176/03)
   [2005] 3 C.M.L.R. 20; *Times*, September 28, 2005, ECJ
Commission of the European Communities v. Council of the European Union (C257/01);
   sub nom Schengen Implementing System, Re (C257/01) [2005] E.C.R. I-345;
   [2005] 1 C.M.L.R. 33, ECJ . . . .   *Digested*, 05/**1446**
Commission of the European Communities v. Denmark (106/84); *sub nom* Taxation of
   Wine, Re (106/84) [1986] E.C.R. 833; [1987] 2 C.M.L.R. 278, ECJ . . . .   *Digested*, 87/**1659**:
                                       Followed, 05/4009
Commission of the European Communities v. Denmark (C192/01); *sub nom* Prohibition
   of Marketing of Enriched Foods (C192/01), Re [2003] E.C.R. I-9693; [2003]
   3 C.M.L.R. 29, ECJ . . . .   *Digested*, 04/**1600**:
                           Applied, 05/1450: *Followed*, 05/1732
Commission of the European Communities v. First NV (C275/00) [2002] E.C.R. I-
   10943; [2005] 2 C.M.L.R. 12, ECJ
Commission of the European Communities v. France (C233/00) [2003] E.C.R. I-6625,
   ECJ . . . .   *Distinguished*, 05/57
Commission of the European Communities v. France (C24/00) [2004] E.C.R. I-1277;
   [2004] 3 C.M.L.R. 25, ECJ (6th Chamber) . . . .   *Digested*, 05/**1450**
Commission of the European Communities v. France (C262/02) [2005] All E.R. (EC)
   157; [2004] E.C.R. I-6569; [2004] 3 C.M.L.R. 1, ECJ. . . . .   *Digested*, 05/**1464**
Commission of the European Communities v. France (C280/02) [2005] Env. L.R. D1,
   ECJ
Commission of the European Communities v. France (C304/02); *sub nom* Control
   Measures for Fishing Activities, Re (C304/02) [2005] 3 C.M.L.R. 13, ECJ
Commission of the European Communities v. France (C334/02); *sub nom* Levy to
   Income on Investments, Re (C334/02) [2004] E.C.R. I-2229; [2005] 2
   C.M.L.R. 24; 6 I.T.L. Rep. 642; [2004] S.T.I. 558, ECJ (5th Chamber) . . . .   *Digested*, 04/**3772**
Commission of the European Communities v. France (C344/90) [1992] E.C.R. I-4719,
   ECJ . . . .   *Followed*, 05/1732
Commission of the European Communities v. France (C347/02); *sub nom* Bonus Malus
   System, Re (C347/02) [2004] E.C.R. I-7557; [2004] 3 C.M.L.R. 51; [2005]
   Lloyd's Rep. I.R. 247, ECJ . . . .   *Digested*, 05/**2381**
Commission of the European Communities v. France (C35/97) [1998] E.C.R. I-5325,
   ECJ (5th Chamber). . . . .   *Followed*, 05/3860
Commission of the European Communities v. France (C384/01) [2003] E.C.R. I-4395;
   [2005] B.T.C. 5429; [2005] B.V.C. 460, ECJ (5th Chamber)
Commission of the European Communities v. France (C404/99) [2001] E.C.R. I-2667,
   ECJ . . . .   *Considered*, 04/4021,
                                            05/4419
Commission of the European Communities v. France (C62/89); *sub nom* Redfish
   Quotas, Re (C62/89) [1990] E.C.R. I-925; [1991] 2 C.M.L.R. 600, ECJ . . . . . .   *Digested*, 91/**3957**:
                                       Followed, 05/1447
Commission of the European Communities v. France (C76/99) [2001] E.C.R. I-249;
   [2001] 1 C.M.L.R. 48, ECJ (6th Chamber) . . . .   *Digested*, 01/**5560**:
                                       Considered, 05/4355
Commission of the European Communities v. Germany (205/84); *sub nom* Insurance
   Services (205/84), Re [1986] E.C.R. 3755; [1987] 2 C.M.L.R. 69; *Times*,
   January 13, 1987, ECJ . . . .   *Digested*, 87/**1631**:
                         Applied, 04/3685: *Followed*, 05/2330
Commission of the European Communities v. Germany (C103/01); *sub nom* Personal
   Protective Equipment for Firefighters, Re (C103/01) [2003] E.C.R. I-5369;
   [2005] 2 C.M.L.R. 4, ECJ (5th Chamber) . . . .   *Digested*, 05/**1451**
Commission of the European Communities v. Germany (C109/02) [2003] E.C.R. I-
   12691; [2005] B.T.C. 5511; [2005] B.V.C. 542; [2003] S.T.I. 1850, ECJ (5th
   Chamber) . . . .   *Applied*, 05/4348
Commission of the European Communities v. Germany (C217/97) [1999] E.C.R. I-5087;
   [1999] 3 C.M.L.R. 277; [2000] Env. L.R. 141, ECJ (6th Chamber) . . . .   *Digested*, 00/**2394**:
                                       Followed, 05/1447
Commission of the European Communities v. Germany (C228/00) [2003] E.C.R. I-
   1439; [2003] Env. L.R. D13, ECJ. . . . .   *Applied*, 05/1417
Commission of the European Communities v. Germany (C341/02); *sub nom* Law on the
   Posting of Workers, Re (C341/02) [2005] 3 C.M.L.R. 4, ECJ (1st Chamber)
Commission of the European Communities v. Germany (C387/99) [2004] E.C.R. I-
   3751, ECJ. . . . .   *Followed*, 05/1447
Commission of the European Communities v. Germany (C427/98); *sub nom* Coupon
   Scheme (C427/98), Re [2003] S.T.C. 301; [2002] E.C.R. I-8315; [2003] 1
   C.M.L.R. 4; [2003] B.T.C. 5149; [2003] B.V.C. 205; [2003] S.T.I. 101, ECJ
   [2002] E.C.R. I-8315, AGO . . . .   *Applied*, 03/4579:
                                       Considered, 05/4341

Commission of the European Communities *v.* Germany (C463/01); *sub nom* Verpack V, Re (C463/01) [2004] E.C.R. I-11705; [2005] 1 C.M.L.R. 34, ECJ . . . .   *Digested*, 05/**1476**

Commission of the European Communities *v.* Germany (C5/89); *sub nom* State Aid to Bug-Alutechnik GmbH (C5/89), Re [1990] E.C.R. I-3437; [1992] 1 C.M.L.R. 117; *Times*, November 8, 1990, ECJ. . . . .   *Digested*, 90/**2217**: *Applied*, 04/1404, 05/594

Commission of the European Communities *v.* Greece (68/88); *sub nom* Cargo of the Alfonsina, Re (68/88) [1989] E.C.R. 2965; [1991] 1 C.M.L.R. 31; *Times*, October 28, 1989, ECJ . . . .   *Digested*, 91/**3915**: *Applied*, 05/1437: *Considered*, 99/2232

Commission of the European Communities *v.* Greece (C119/02) [2005] Env. L.R. 5, ECJ

Commission of the European Communities *v.* Greece (C140/03); *sub nom* Establishment of Opticians Shops, Re (C140/03) [2005] 3 C.M.L.R. 5, ECJ (2nd Chamber)

Commission of the European Communities *v.* Greece (C365/93) [1995] E.C.R. I-499, ECJ . . . .   *Digested*, 95/**1897**: *Considered*, 05/4185

Commission of the European Communities *v.* Greece (C415/03); *sub nom* Aid to Olympic Airways, Re (C415/03) [2005] E.C.R. I-3875; [2005] 3 C.M.L.R. 10, ECJ (2nd Chamber)

Commission of the European Communities *v.* Greencore Group Plc (C123/03 P) [2004] E.C.R. I-11647; [2005] 4 C.M.L.R. 1, ECJ (2nd Chamber)

Commission of the European Communities *v.* Ireland (C494/01) [2005] E.C.R. I-3331; [2005] 3 C.M.L.R. 14; [2005] Env. L.R. 36, ECJ

Commission of the European Communities *v.* Italy (C103/02) [2004] E.C.R. I-9127; [2005] Env. L.R. 21, ECJ [2004] E.C.R. I-9127, AGO . . . .   *Digested*, 05/**1416**

Commission of the European Communities *v.* Italy (C14/00); *sub nom* Marketing of Chocolate, Re (C14/00) [2003] E.C.R. I-513; [2005] 2 C.M.L.R. 34; [2003] E.T.M.R. CN9; *Times*, January 21, 2003, ECJ (6th Chamber) . . . .   *Digested*, 03/**1441**

Commission of the European Communities *v.* Italy (C270/02) [2004] 3 C.M.L.R. 26, ECJ (3rd Chamber) . . . .   *Digested*, 05/**687**

Commission of the European Communities *v.* Italy (C278/03); *sub nom* Recruitment of Teaching Staff, Re (C278/03) [2005] E.C.R. I-3747; [2005] 2 C.M.L.R. 39, ECJ (2nd Chamber)

Commission of the European Communities *v.* Italy (C385/02); *sub nom* Flood Safety Works in the River Po, Re (C385/02) [2005] 1 C.M.L.R. 52, ECJ (2nd Chamber) . . . .   *Digested*, 05/**3355**

Commission of the European Communities *v.* Italy (C439/99) [2002] E.C.R. I-305, ECJ AGO . . . .   *Followed*, 04/978, 05/1468

Commission of the European Communities *v.* Italy (C59/01) [2003] E.C.R. I-1759, ECJ   *Distinguished*, 05/2381, 05/2382

Commission of the European Communities *v.* Italy (C87/02) [2004] E.C.R. I-5975; [2005] Env. L.R. 3, ECJ

Commission of the European Communities *v.* Jego-Quere et Cie SA (C263/02 P); *sub nom* Jego-Quere & Cie SA *v.* Commission of the European Communities (T177/01) [2005] Q.B. 237; [2005] 2 W.L.R. 179; [2004] All E.R. (EC) 983; [2004] E.C.R. I-3425; [2004] 2 C.M.L.R. 12; [2004] C.E.C. 284, ECJ (6th Chamber); reversing [2003] Q.B. 854; [2003] 2 W.L.R. 783; [2002] All E.R. (EC) 932; [2002] E.C.R. II-2365; [2002] 2 C.M.L.R. 44; *Times*, May 31, 2002, CFI (1st Chamber) . . . .   *Digested*, 05/**1470**: *Followed*, 05/942

Commission of the European Communities *v.* Kvaerner Warnow Werft GmbH (C181/02 P); *sub nom* Kvaerner Warnow Werft GmbH *v.* Commission of the European Communities (T227/99) [2004] E.C.R. I-5703; [2004] 2 C.M.L.R. 19, ECJ (5th Chamber); affirming [2002] E.C.R. II-1205; [2003] 2 C.M.L.R. 17, CFI (4th Chamber) . . . .   *Digested*, 05/**589**

Commission of the European Communities *v.* Luxembourg (C118/92) [1994] E.C.R. I-1891, ECJ . . . .   *Digested*, 94/**4891**: *Followed*, 05/1234

Commission of the European Communities *v.* Luxembourg (C346/02); *sub nom* Bonus Malus System, Re (C346/02) [2004] 3 C.M.L.R. 50, ECJ . . . .   *Digested*, 05/**2382**

Commission of the European Communities *v.* Luxembourg (C445/03); *sub nom* Law on Work Permits for Foreign Workers Employed by Cross Border Service Providers, Re (C445/03) [2004] E.C.R. I-10191; [2005] 1 C.M.L.R. 22; [2005] C.E.C. 529, ECJ (1st Chamber) . . . .   *Digested*, 05/**1466**

Commission of the European Communities *v.* Luxembourg (C519/03); *sub nom* Parental Leave, Re (C519/03) [2005] 3 C.M.L.R. 1, ECJ

Commission of the European Communities *v.* Luxembourg (C97/01) [2003] E.C.R. I-5797; [2003] Info. T.L.R. 420, ECJ. . . . .   *Digested*, 05/**4185**

Commission of the European Communities *v.* Netherlands (C113/02) [2004] E.C.R. I-9707; [2005] Env. L.R. 22, ECJ. . . . .   *Digested*, 05/**1417**

Commission of the European Communities v. Netherlands (C146/04) [2005] Env. L.R. 39, ECJ

Commission of the European Communities v. Netherlands (C246/00) [2003] E.C.R. I-7485, ECJ [2003] E.C.R. I-7485, AGO . . . . *Followed*, 05/**1438**

Commission of the European Communities v. Netherlands (C350/02) [2004] E.C.R. I-6213; [2004] Info. T.L.R. 229, ECJ (1st Chamber) . . . . *Digested*, 05/**4186**

Commission of the European Communities v. Netherlands Antilles (C142/00 P) [2003] E.C.R. I-3483; [2004] 2 C.M.L.R. 41, ECJ (6th Chamber) [2003] E.C.R. I-3483, AGO . . . . *Digested*, 05/**1474**: *Followed*, 05/**1444**: *Previous proceedings*, 02/1543

Commission of the European Communities v. Portugal (C171/02) [2004] E.C.R. I-5645; [2004] Env. L.R. 47, ECJ. . . . . *Digested*, 05/**1366**

Commission of the European Communities v. Portugal (C62/98) [2000] E.C.R. I-5171, ECJ . . . . *Considered*, 05/**1440**

Commission of the European Communities v. Spain (C12/00); *sub nom* Marketing of Chocolate, Re (C12/00) [2003] E.C.R. I-459; [2005] 2 C.M.L.R. 33, ECJ (6th Chamber) . . . . *Digested*, 05/**1449**

Commission of the European Communities v. Spain (C135/03); *sub nom* Organic Labelling, Re (C135/03) [2005] 3 C.M.L.R. 31, ECJ (1st Chamber)

Commission of the European Communities v. Spain (C157/03); *sub nom* Residence Visas, Re (C157/03) [2005] E.C.R. I-2911; [2005] 2 C.M.L.R. 27, ECJ (2nd Chamber) . . . . *Digested*, 05/**1480**

Commission of the European Communities v. Spain (C195/02) [2004] E.C.R. I-7857; [2005] R.T.R. 23; *Times*, October 11, 2004, ECJ

Commission of the European Communities v. Spain (C204/03) [2005] S.T.I. 1676, ECJ (3rd Chamber)

Commission of the European Communities v. Spain (C227/01) [2005] Env. L.R. 20, ECJ . . . . *Digested*, 05/**1365**

Commission of the European Communities v. Spain (C500/01) [2004] E.C.R. I-583; [2004] Info. T.L.R. 99, ECJ (5th Chamber). . . . . *Digested*, 05/**596**

Commission of the European Communities v. Spain (C79/03) [2004] E.C.R. I-11619; [2005] Env. L.R. D4, ECJ

Commission of the European Communities v. Spain (C83/99) [2001] E.C.R. I-445, ECJ   *Applied*, 05/3355

Commission of the European Communities v. T-Mobile Austria GmbH (formerly Max.Mobil Telekommunikation Service GmbH) (C141/02 P) [2005] E.C.R. I-1283; [2005] 4 C.M.L.R. 12; *Times*, March 31, 2005, ECJ . . . . *Digested*, 05/**1473**: *Previous proceedings*, 02/1540

Commission of the European Communities v. Tetra Laval BV (C12/03 P) [2005] All E.R. (EC) 1059; [2005] E.C.R. I-987; [2005] 4 C.M.L.R. 8, ECJ . . . . *Digested*, 05/**542**: *Previous proceedings*, 03/579

Commission of the European Communities v. Tetra Laval BV (C13/03 P) [2005] E.C.R. I-1113; [2005] 4 C.M.L.R. 9, ECJ . . . . *Digested*, 05/**543**: *Previous proceedings*, 03/577

Commission of the European Communities v. United Kingdom (C300/95); *sub nom* Product Liability Directive, Re (C300/95) [1997] All E.R. (EC) 481; [1997] E.C.R. I-2649; [1997] 3 C.M.L.R. 923; *Times*, June 23, 1997, ECJ (5th Chamber) . . . . *Digested*, 97/**975**: *Followed*, 05/1447

Commission of the European Communities v. United Kingdom (C33/03) [2005] S.T.C. 582; [2005] E.C.R. I-1865; [2005] 2 C.M.L.R. 26; [2005] C.E.C. 661; [2005] S.T.I. 366; *Times*, March 15, 2005, ECJ (1st Chamber)

Commission of the European Communities v. United Kingdom (C349/03); *sub nom* Gibraltar Exemption from VAT and Excise Duties, Re (C349/03) [2005] S.T.I. 1314, ECJ

Commission of the European Communities v. United Kingdom (C6/04), *Times*, October 27, 2005, ECJ (2nd Chamber)

Commission of the European Communities v. United Kingdom (C61/03); *sub nom* Disposal of Nuclear Military Reactor, Re (C61/03) [2005] 2 C.M.L.R. 49; [2005] Env. L.R. 34, ECJ . . . . *Digested*, 05/**1406**

Commission of the European Communities v. United Kingdom (C62/03), *Times*, January 6, 2005, ECJ (3rd Chamber)

Commission of the European Communities v. United Kingdom (C88/04) [2005] E.C.D.R. 9, ECJ (6th Chamber) . . . . *Digested*, 05/**1433**

Commissioner of Police of the Metropolis v. Hendricks; *sub nom* Hendricks v. Commissioner of Police of the Metropolis [2002] EWCA Civ 1686; [2003] 1 All E.R. 654; [2003] I.C.R. 530; [2003] I.R.L.R. 96; (2003) 100(5) L.S.G. 30; (2002) 146 S.J.L.B. 274; *Times*, December 6, 2002, CA (Civ Div); reversing [2002] Emp. L.R. 32, EAT . . . . *Digested*, 03/**1298**: *Considered*, 05/1229

Commissioner of Police of the Metropolis v. Hooper [2005] EWHC 340; [2005] 1 W.L.R. 1995; [2005] 4 All E.R. 1095; (2005) 169 J.P. 409; (2005) 169 J.P.N. 596; (2005) 102(16) L.S.G. 28; *Times*, March 3, 2005, QBD (Admin) . . . . *Digested*, 05/**342**

Commissioner of Police of the Metropolis v. Hurst see R. (on the application of Hurst) v. HM Coroner for Northern District London

Commissioner of Police of the Metropolis v. Miller see Yearwood v. Commissioner of
Police of the Metropolis
Commissioners of Crown Lands v. Page see Crown Lands Commissioners v. Page
Commune de Braine le Chateau v. Region Wallonne (C53/02) [2004] E.C.R. I-3251,
ECJ . . . .   *Considered*, 05/1402
Compagnie Maritime Belge Transports SA v. Commission of the European Communities
(C395/96 P); *sub nom* Cie Maritime Belge Transports SA v. Commission of the
European Communities (C395/96 P); Dafra-Lines A/S v. Commission of the
European Communities (C396/96 P) [2000] All E.R. (EC) 385; [2000] E.C.R.
I-1365; [2000] 4 C.M.L.R. 1076, ECJ (5th Chamber) . . . .   *Digested*, 00/**709**:
                                                                                         Followed, 05/595
Compagnie Maritime Belge Transports SA v. Commission of the European Communities
(T24/93) [1996] E.C.R. II-1201; [1997] 4 C.M.L.R. 273, CFI (3rd Chamber) . . .   *Followed*, 05/576
Companhia de Seguros Imperio v. Heath (REBX) Ltd see Cia de Seguros Imperio v.
Heath (REBX) Ltd (formerly CE Heath & Co (America) Ltd)
Compania Espanola para la Fabricacion de Aceros Inoxidables SA (ACERINOX) v.
Commission of the European Communities (C57/02 P) [2005] 5 C.M.L.R. 15,
ECJ (1st Chamber)
Company (No.1573 of 1983), Re [1983] Com. L.R. 202, Ch D (Companies Ct) . . . . . .   *Digested*, 83/**341**:
                                                                                         Distinguished, 05/2263
Company (No.005134 of 1986) Ex p. Harries, Re [1989] B.C.L.C. 383. . . . .   *Digested*, 89/**323**:
                                                                                         Followed, 05/528
Company (No.000709 of 1992), Re see O'Neill v. Phillips
Company (No.2272 of 2004), Re [2005] EWHC 422; [2005] B.P.I.R. 1251, Ch D
Compass Contract Services UK Ltd v. Revenue and Customs Commissioners [2005]
B.V.C. 2590, V&DTr (Manchester)
Compass Publishing BV v. Compass Logistics Ltd [2004] EWHC 520; [2004] R.P.C.
41; (2004) 101(17) L.S.G. 32; *Times*, April 29, 2004, Ch D . . . .   *Digested*, 04/**2394**:
                                                                                         Considered, 05/2568
Compassion in World Farming Ltd v. Secretary of State for the Environment, Food and
Rural Affairs see R. (on the application of Compassion in World Farming Ltd) v.
Secretary of State for the Environment, Food and Rural Affairs
Compton (Marquis of Northampton) v. Compton (Marchioness of Northampton)
[1960] P. 201; [1960] 3 W.L.R. 476; [1960] 2 All E.R. 70; 104 S.J. 705, PDAD. .   *Digested*, 60/**1069**:
                                                                                         Followed, 05/1682
Computer 2000 Distribution Ltd v. ICM Computer Solutions Plc; *sub nom* ICM
Computer Solutions Plc v. Computer 2000 Distribution Ltd [2004] EWCA Civ
1634; [2005] Info. T.L.R. 147; *Times*, December 29, 2004, CA (Civ Div) . . . . . .   *Digested*, 05/**3517**:
COMVIK/Two identities (T641/00) [2004] E.P.O.R. 10, EPO (Technical Bd App) . . . . .   *Digested*, 04/**2329**:
                                                                                         Applied, 05/2484
Concord Trust v. Law Debenture Trust Corp Plc [2005] UKHL 27; [2005] 1 W.L.R.
1591; [2005] 1 All E.R. (Comm) 699; [2005] 2 Lloyd's Rep. 221; [2005] 1
C.L.C. 631; (2005) 155 N.L.J. 692; *Times*, May 3, 2005; *Independent*, May 6,
2005, HL; reversing [2004] EWCA Civ 1001; [2004] 2 All E.R. (Comm) 737;
[2005] 1 Lloyd's Rep. 113; (2004) 148 S.J.L.B. 1062, CA (Civ Div); reversing in
part [2004] EWHC 1216, Ch D . . . .   *Digested*, 05/**263**:
Concorde Enterprises v. Anthony Motors (Hutt) Ltd [1981] 2 N.Z.L.R. 385, CA (NZ) . .   *Digested*, 83/**428**:
                                                                                         Considered, 05/4318
Concordia Bus Finland Oy AB (formerly Stagecoach Finland Oy AB) v. Helsingin Kaupunki
(C513/99) [2004] All E.R. (EC) 87; [2002] E.C.R. I-7213; [2003] 3 C.M.L.R.
20, ECJ [2002] E.C.R. I-7213, AGO . . . .   *Digested*, 04/**3162**:
                                                                                         Followed, 05/3354
Concurrence SA v. Sony SA [2005] E.C.C. 4, Cass (F)
Conde Nast Publications Ltd v. Customs and Excise Commissioners [2005] EWHC
1167; [2005] S.T.C. 1327; [2005] Eu. L.R. 1014; [2005] B.T.C. 5447; [2005]
B.V.C. 478; [2005] S.T.I. 1093, Ch D; affirming [2005] B.V.C. 2259, V&DTr . . . . .   *Digested*, 05/**4367**
Condon Ex p. James, Re (1873-74) L.R. 9 Ch. App. 609; [1874-80] All E.R. Rep. 388, CA in
Chancery . . . .   *Applied*, 69/421,
                      70/310, 72/189, 74/171, 74/357, 75/170: *Considered*, 99/3258, 05/2261:
                                        Distinguished, 72/197, 82/195, 87/3806, 88/3612, 02/2655:
                                                                              Not applied, 99/3230
Condron v. United Kingdom (35718/97) (2001) 31 E.H.R.R. 1; 8 B.H.R.C. 290; [2000]
Crim. L.R. 679; *Times*, May 9, 2000, ECHR . . . .   *Digested*, 00/**1075**:
                          Applied, 00/1076, 01/997, 02/2461, 05/927: *Considered*, 00/1073, 02/2447
Confederation Francaise de l'Encadrement CFE-CGC v. France (2005) 41 E.H.R.R. SE17,
ECHR
Confederation Generale du Travail (CGT) v. France (2005) 41 E.H.R.R. SE8, ECHR
Confiance Ltd v. Timespan Images Ltd [2005] EWHC 1557; [2005] 2 B.C.L.C. 693,
Ch D
Conlon v. Hewitt (Inspector of Taxes) [2005] S.T.C. (S.C.D.) 46; [2004] S.T.I. 2380,
Sp Comm . . . .   *Digested*, 05/**4083**
Conlon's Application for Judicial Review, Re [2005] N.I. 97, QBD (NI)

Connect Austria Gesellschaft fur Telekommunikation GmbH v. Telekom-Control-Kommission (C462/99) [2003] E.C.R. I-5197; [2005] 5 C.M.L.R. 6; [2003] Info. T.L.R. 389, ECJ . . . . *Digested*, 05/**4180**
Connell v. Wycombe DC [2005] P.A.D. 87, Planning Inspector
Connex South Eastern Ltd v. Bangs see Bangs v. Connex South Eastern Ltd
Connex South Eastern Ltd v. Bangs see Kwamin v. Abbey National Plc
Connex South Eastern Ltd v. MJ Building Services Group Plc [2005] EWCA Civ 193; [2005] 1 W.L.R. 3323; [2005] 2 All E.R. 871; [2005] B.L.R. 201; 100 Con. L.R. 16; (2005) 102(18) L.S.G. 23; (2005) 149 S.J.L.B. 296; *Times*, May 13, 2005, CA (Civ Div); reversing [2004] EWHC 1518; [2004] B.L.R. 333; 95 Con. L.R. 43, QBD (TCC) . . . . *Digested*, 05/**649**
Connor's Application for Judicial Review, Re [2005] N.I. 322; (2005) 8 C.C.L. Rep. 328, CA (NI)
Connors v. United Kingdom (40086/98) see Ezeh v. United Kingdom (39665/98)
Connors v. United Kingdom (66746/01) (2005) 40 E.H.R.R. 9; 16 B.H.R.C. 639; [2004] H.L.R. 52; [2004] 4 P.L.R. 16; [2004] N.P.C. 86; *Times*, June 10, 2004, ECHR . . . . *Digested*, 04/**1992**: *Distinguished*, 05/190: *Explained*, 05/3424
Conservators of Ashdown Forest v. Customs and Excise Commissioners [2005] S.T.I. 115, V&DTr
Consignia Plc v. Sealy; *sub nom* Sealy v. Consignia Plc [2002] EWCA Civ 878; [2002] 3 All E.R. 801; [2002] I.C.R. 1193; [2002] I.R.L.R. 624; [2002] Emp. L.R. 983; (2002) 99(30) L.S.G. 39; (2002) 146 S.J.L.B. 162; *Times*, July 3, 2002; *Independent*, June 27, 2002, CA (Civ Div) . . . . *Digested*, 02/**1360**: *Considered*, 03/1250: *Distinguished*, 05/1248
Consolidated Criminal Practice Direction (Amendment No.12) (Classification and Allocation of Business) see Practice Direction (Crown Ct: Classification and Allocation of Business)
Consolidated Criminal Practice Direction (Amendment No.4) (Guidance to Jurors) see Practice Direction (Crown Ct: Guidance to Jurors)
Consolidated Criminal Practice Direction (Amendment No.6) (Mandatory Life Sentences) see Practice Direction (Sup Ct: Crime: Mandatory Life Sentences) (No.1)
Consolidated Criminal Practice Direction (Amendment No.7) (Explanations for the Imposition of Custodial Sentences) see Practice Direction (Sup Ct: Custodial Sentences: Explanations)
Consorzio fra i Caseifici dell'Altopiano di Asiago v. Regione Veneto (C288/97) [1999] E.C.R. I-2575, ECJ . . . . *Followed*, 05/142
Constable v. Executive Connections Ltd [2005] EWHC 3; [2005] 2 B.C.L.C. 638, Ch D
Constantine v. Lambeth LBC see Kay v. Lambeth LBC
Constructive Solutions (Contractors) Ltd (In Liquidation) v. Customs and Excise Commissioners [2005] S.T.I. 815, V&DTr
Consul Development Pty Ltd v. DPC Estates Pty Ltd 132 C.L.R. 373, HC (Aus) . . . . *Applied*, 05/522, 05/4294
Contigroup Companies Inc (formerly Continental Grain Co) v. China Petroleum Technology & Development Corp see LG Caltex Gas Co Ltd v. China National Petroleum Corp
Contigroup Cos Inc v. Glencore AG [2004] EWHC 2750; [2005] 1 Lloyd's Rep. 241, QBD (Comm) . . . . *Digested*, 05/**719**
Continental Illinois National Bank & Trust Co of Chicago v. Bathurst (The Captain Panagos DP) [1985] 1 Lloyd's Rep. 625; [1985] Fin. L.R. 224, QBD (Comm) . . . . *Digested*, 85/**3205**: *Applied*, 05/2386
Control Measures for Fishing Activities, Re (C304/02) see Commission of the European Communities v. France (C304/02)
Convergence Group Plc v. Chantrey Vellacott (A Firm) see Chantrey Vellacott v. Convergence Group Plc
Conway v. Ratiu see Ratiu v. Conway
Coogi Australia Pty Ltd v. Hysport International Pty Ltd (1998) 42 I.P.R. 593, Fed Ct (Aus) (Full Ct) . . . . *Applied*, 05/2423
Cook v. Wood (Inspector of Taxes) [2005] S.T.C. (S.C.D.) 267; [2005] S.T.I. 110, Sp Comm . . . . *Digested*, 05/**4106**
Cooke v. Adatia (1989) 153 J.P. 129; [1989] C.O.D. 327; (1989) 153 L.G. Rev. 189, DC . . . . *Digested*, 89/**2784**: *Applied*, 05/2894
Cooke v. Charles A Vogeler Co; *sub nom* AB & Co, Re [1901] A.C. 102, HL; affirming [1900] 1 Q.B. 541, CA . . . . *Applied*, 47-51/3066, 47-51/3084, 05/685: *Distinguished*, 47-51/640, 47-51/641, 47-51/643, 47-51/9858
Cooke v. Secretary of State for Social Security; *sub nom* Cooke v. Social Security Commissioner [2001] EWCA Civ 734; [2002] 3 All E.R. 279; *Daily Telegraph*, May 1, 2001, CA (Civ Div) . . . . *Digested*, 02/**4236**: *Applied*, 05/2211: *Considered*, 02/483
Cooke v. Social Security Commissioner see Cooke v. Secretary of State for Social Security

Cookies World Vertriebsgesellschaft mbh i L v. Finanzlandesdirektion fur Tirol (C155/01) [2004] S.T.C. 1386; [2003] E.C.R. I-8785; [2004] 2 C.M.L.R. 10; [2005] B.T.C. 5177; [2005] B.V.C. 208; [2003] S.T.I. 1637, ECJ (1st Chamber) [2003] E.C.R. I-8785, AGO.. *Digested,* 05/**4382**
Cookson & Clegg Ltd v. Ministry of Defence [2005] EWCA Civ 811; (2005) 149 S.J.L.B. 771, CA (Civ Div); affirming [2005] EWHC 38; [2005] Eu. L.R. 517; [2005] A.C.D. 48, QBD (Admin)... *Digested,* 05/**73**
Cooley Group Holding Inc's Community Trade Mark Application (R817/2004-1) [2005] E.T.M.R. CN9, OHIM (1st Bd App)
Cooper v. Bucknall [2005] 2 Q.R. 5; [2004] 6 Q.R. 5, QBD [*Ex rel.* Stephen Garner, Barrister, No.8 Chambers, Fountain Court, Steelhouse Lane, Birmingham.]..... *Digested,* 04/**2861**
Cooper v. Floor Cleaning Machines Ltd [2003] EWCA Civ 1649; [2004] R.T.R. 17; (2003) 100(43) L.S.G. 32; *Times,* October 24, 2003, CA (Civ Div) .... *Digested,* 04/**2745**: *Applied,* 05/292
Cooper v. Pure Fishing (UK) Ltd (formerly Outdoor Technology Group (UK) Ltd) [2004] EWCA Civ 375; [2004] 2 Lloyd's Rep. 518; [2004] 2 C.L.C. 412; [2005] E.C.C. 6; [2004] Eu. L.R. 664, CA (Civ Div).................... *Digested,* 04/**90**
Cooper v. Slade (1858) 6 H.L. Cas. 746, HL .... *Applied,* 56/3686, 59/646, 60/641, 80/447, 05/802: *Considered,* 69/251, 70/204, 85/536, 86/524
Cooper v. United Kingdom (48843/99) (2004) 39 E.H.R.R. 8; [2004] Crim. L.R. 577; *Times,* January 12, 2004, ECHR .... *Digested,* 04/**1945**: *Applied,* 05/234
Cooperatieve Vereniging Suiker Unie UA v. Commission of the European Communities (40/73); *sub nom* European Sugar Cartel (40/73), Re; Suiker Unie v. Commission of the European Communities (40/73) [1975] E.C.R. 1663; [1976] 1 C.M.L.R. 295; [1976] F.S.R. 443; *Times,* December 23, 1975, ECJ.......... *Digested,* 76/**1055**: *Considered,* 78/1257, 05/570: *Distinguished,* 05/549
Cooperativa Co-frutta Srl v. Amministrazione delle Finanze dello Stato (193/85) [1987] E.C.R. 2085; *Times,* May 13, 1987, ECJ............................. *Digested,* 87/**1583**: *Followed,* 05/4009
Cooperative Group (CWS) Ltd v. International Computers Ltd [2003] EWCA Civ 1955; [2004] Info. T.L.R. 25; (2004) 27(3) I.P.D. 27023; (2004) 148 S.J.L.B. 112; *Times,* January 19, 2004, CA (Civ Div); reversing [2003] EWHC 1; [2003] Masons C.L.R. 4, QBD (TCC) .... *Digested,* 05/**425**
Cootes v. John Lewis Plc EAT/1414/00, EAT............................... *Disapproved,* 05/1243
Copoc v. Chief Constable of South Yorkshire see Alcock v. Chief Constable of South Yorkshire
Copp v. D'Jan see D'Jan of London, Re
Coppard v. Customs and Excise Commissioners [2003] EWCA Civ 511; [2003] Q.B. 1428; [2003] 2 W.L.R. 1618; [2003] 3 All E.R. 351; (2003) 100(24) L.S.G. 36; (2003) 147 S.J.L.B. 475; *Times,* April 11, 2003, CA (Civ Div); affirming 1998 C No.546, QBD .... *Digested,* 03/**6**: *Applied,* 05/36
Copping v. Surrey CC [2005] EWCA Civ 1604; [2005] N.P.C. 147, CA (Civ Div); affirming [2005] EWHC 754; [2005] H.L.R. 43; [2005] 2 E.G.L.R. 56; [2005] 34 E.G. 110; [2005] 18 E.G.C.S. 149, QBD .... *Digested,* 05/**2014**
Copsey v. WWB Devon Clays Ltd [2005] EWCA Civ 932; [2005] I.C.R. 1789; [2005] I.R.L.R. 811; [2005] H.R.L.R. 32; (2005) 155 N.L.J. 1484; *Times,* August 25, 2005, CA (Civ Div); affirming UKEAT/0438/03/SM, EAT................. *Digested,* 05/**1328**
Copyright and Communication Advisory Agency/Latvian Copyright Agency v. Latvian Radio [2005] E.C.D.R. 11
Copyright in Road Construction Materials Handbooks, Re (I ZR 231/99) [2005] E.C.C. 13, BGH (Ger)
Cordoba Shipping Co v. National State Bank, Elizabeth, New Jersey (The Albaforth) [1984] 2 Lloyd's Rep. 91; (1984) 81 L.S.G. 1360, CA (Civ Div) .... *Digested,* 84/**2671**: *Applied,* 05/978: *Considered,* 00/769
Cordova v. Italy (No.1) (40877/98) (2005) 40 E.H.R.R. 43, ECHR .... *Digested,* 05/**2074**
Cork v. Gill [2004] EWHC 2536; [2005] B.P.I.R. 272, Ch D .... *Digested,* 05/**2329**
Cormack (Inspector of Taxes) v. CBL Cable Contractors Ltd [2005] EWHC 1294; 77 T.C. 239; [2005] S.T.I. 1170; [2005] 26 E.G.C.S. 131, Ch D
Cornelius v. University College of Swansea [1987] I.R.L.R. 141; (1987) 84 L.S.G. 1141; (1987) 131 S.J. 359, CA (Civ Div) .... *Digested,* 87/**1372**: *Applied,* 01/2302, 05/1235
Cornish v. Cunningham (Unreported, April 21, 2004), CC (Guildford) [*Ex rel.* David McHugh, Barrister, 8, Bell Yard Chambers, DX: 416 London/Chancery Lane] ... *Digested,* 05/**3159**
Cornuaille v. Belgium (116/81) see Adoui v. Belgium (115/81)
Cornwell v. Newhaven Port & Properties Ltd [2005] EWHC 1469; [2005] O.P.L.R. 277; [2005] Pens. L.R. 329, Ch D .... *Digested,* 05/**2950**
Corus UK Ltd v. Commission of the European Communities (T171/99) [2002] 1 W.L.R. 970; [2001] E.C.R. II-2967; [2001] 5 C.M.L.R. 34; *Times,* November 15, 2001, CFI (1st Chamber) .... *Digested,* 01/**2483**: *Considered,* 04/3681, 05/3984

Corus UK Ltd v. Commission of the European Communities (T48/00) [2005] 4
C.M.L.R. 3, CFI (2nd Chamber) . . . . *Digested*, 05/**554**:
                                                     Considered, 05/553
Corus UK Ltd v. Erewash BC [2005] EWHC 2821; [2005] N.P.C. 145, QBD (Admin)
Cosmetic Products Directive, Re (C244/03) see France v. European Parliament (C244/
03)
Cossey v. United Kingdom (10843/84) see Cossey v. United Kingdom (A/184)
Cossey v. United Kingdom (A/184); *sub nom* C v. United Kingdom (A/184); Cossey v.
United Kingdom (10843/84) [1991] 2 F.L.R. 492; [1993] 2 F.C.R. 97; (1991) 13
E.H.R.R. 622; [1991] Fam. Law 362; *Times*, October 17, 1990, ECHR (1986) 8
E.H.R.R. CD89, Eur Comm HR . . . . *Digested*, 92/**2371**:
                         Applied, 05/2272: *Referred to*, 93/2156, 98/3163
Costain Ltd v. Bechtel Ltd [2005] EWHC 1018; [2005] T.C.L.R. 6, QBD (TCC)
Costain Ltd v. Strathclyde Builders Ltd 2004 S.L.T. 102; 2004 S.C.L.R. 707; 100 Con.
L.R. 41; 2004 G.W.D. 1-9, OH . . . . *Digested*, 04/**4600**
Costs of a Foreign Correspondence Lawyer, Re (VIII ZB 55/04) [2005] I.L.Pr. 54, BGH
(Ger)
Cotswold DC v. Whayman [2005] P.A.D. 25, Planning Inspector
Cottrell v. King; *sub nom* TA King (Services) Ltd, Re [2004] EWHC 397; [2004]
B.C.C. 307; [2004] 2 B.C.L.C. 413; [2005] W.T.L.R. 63, Ch D . . . . *Digested*, 04/**473**
Coudrat v. Revenue and Customs Commissioners [2005] EWCA Civ 616; [2005]
S.T.C. 1006; [2005] S.T.I. 1018, CA (Civ Div) . . . . *Digested*, 05/**4192**
Coulter v. Chief Constable of Dorset [2004] EWCA Civ 1259; [2005] 1 W.L.R. 130;
[2005] B.P.I.R. 62; (2004) 101(40) L.S.G. 28; (2004) 148 S.J.L.R. 1213; *Times*,
October 22, 2004, CA (Civ Div); affirming [2003] EWHC 3391; [2004] 1
W.L.R. 1425; [2004] B.P.I.R. 462; *Times*, December 24, 2003, Ch D . . . . *Digested*, 05/**2338**
Coulter v. Chief Constable of Dorset [2005] EWCA Civ 1113, CA (Civ Div); reversing
in part [2004] EWHC 2545; [2005] B.P.I.R. 76, Ch D . . . . *Digested*, 05/**2336**
Council for Health Care Regulatory Excellence v. General Medical Council; *sub nom*
Council for the Regulation of Health Care Professionals v. Basiouny; Council for
the Regulation of Health Care Professionals v. General Medical Council [2005]
EWHC 68; (2005) 102(13) L.S.G. 28; *Times*, February 7, 2005, QBD (Admin) . . *Digested*, 05/**1801**
Council for National Parks Ltd v. Pembrokeshire Coast National Park Authority; *sub nom*
R. (on the application of Council for National Parks Ltd) v. Pembrokeshire
Coast National Park Authority [2005] EWCA Civ 888; [2005] N.P.C. 97, CA
(Civ Div); affirming [2004] EWHC 2907; [2005] J.P.L. 1362, QBD (Admin)
Council for the Regulation of Health Care Professionals v. Basiouny see Council for
Health Care Regulatory Excellence v. General Medical Council
Council for the Regulation of Health Care Professionals v. General Dental Council [2005]
EWHC 87; *Times*, February 8, 2005, QBD . . . . *Digested*, 05/**3349**
Council for the Regulation of Health Care Professionals v. General Medical Council see
Council for Health Care Regulatory Excellence v. General Medical Council
Council for the Regulation of Health Care Professionals v. General Medical Council; *sub
nom* Ruscillo v. Council for the Regulation of Health Care Professionals;
Council for the Regulation of Health Care Professionals v. Truscott; Council for
the Regulation of Health Care Professionals v. Nursing and Midwifery Council
[2004] EWCA Civ 1356; [2005] 1 W.L.R. 717; [2005] Lloyd's Rep. Med. 65;
[2005] A.C.D. 69; [2005] A.C.D. 99; (2004) 148 S.J.L.B. 1248; *Times*, October
27, 2004; *Independent*, October 28, 2004, CA (Civ Div); affirming [2004]
EWHC 527; [2004] 1 W.L.R. 2068; [2004] Lloyd's Rep. Med. 365; [2005]
A.C.D. 46; (2004) 101(16) L.S.G. 28; *Times*, April 8, 2004, QBD (Admin) . . . . . *Digested*, 05/**1796**:
                   Applied, 05/1801, 05/1919: *Previous proceedings*, 04/1621
Council for the Regulation of Health Care Professionals v. General Medical Council; *sub
nom* Council for the Regulation of Healthcare Professionals v. General Medical
Council [2004] EWHC 1850; *Times*, September 1, 2004, QBD (Admin) . . . . *Considered*, 05/1807
Council for the Regulation of Health Care Professionals v. Nursing and Midwifery Council
see Council for the Regulation of Health Care Professionals v. General Medical
Council
Council for the Regulation of Health Care Professionals v. Truscott see Council for the
Regulation of Health Care Professionals v. General Medical Council
Council for the Regulation of Healthcare Professionals v. General Medical Council see
Council for the Regulation of Health Care Professionals v. General Medical
Council
Council for the Regulation of Healthcare Professionals v. General Medical Council; *sub
nom* Council for the Regulation of Healthcare Professionals v. Southall [2005]
EWHC 579; [2005] Lloyd's Rep. Med. 365; (2005) 84 B.M.L.R. 7; [2005]
A.C.D. 87, QBD (Admin) . . . . *Digested*, 05/**1919**
Council for the Regulation of Healthcare Professionals v. Southall see Council for the
Regulation of Healthcare Professionals v. General Medical Council
Council of European Municipalities and Regions (CEMR) v. Commission of the European
Communities (T46/98) [2000] E.C.R. II-167, CFI (4th Chamber) . . . . *Followed*, 05/1436

County Personnel (Employment Agency) Ltd *v.* Alan R Pulver & Co [1987] 1 W.L.R. 916; [1987] 1 All E.R. 289; [1986] 2 E.G.L.R. 246; (1987) 84 L.S.G. 1409; (1986) 136 N.L.J. 1138; (1987) 131 S.J. 474; *Times*, October 29, 1986, CA (Civ Div) . . . . *Digested*, 87/**3551**:
Applied, 91/1315, 91/1319, 93/2989, 00/1483: *Considered*, 88/1051, 89/1199, 90/1567, 92/1533, 94/1758, 96/4502, 99/4031: *Distinguished*, 98/4018, 05/2866: *Followed*, 98/3959, 98/4025

County Pharmacy Ltd *v.* Revenue and Customs Commissioners; Morris *v.* Revenue and Customs Commissioners [2005] S.T.C. (S.C.D.) 729; [2005] S.T.I. 1604, Sp Comm

Coupland *v.* Arabian Gulf Oil Co [1983] 1 W.L.R. 1136; [1983] 3 All E.R. 226; (1983) 133 N.L.J. 893; (1983) 127 S.J. 597, CA (Civ Div); affirming [1983] 1 W.L.R. 1136; [1983] 2 All E.R. 434; (1983) 127 S.J. 393, QBD . . . . *Digested*, 83/**360**:
Applied, 05/**615**

Coupon Scheme (C427/98), Re see Commission of the European Communities *v.* Germany (C427/98)

Courage Group's Pension Schemes, Re; Ryan *v.* Imperial Brewing & Leisure [1987] 1 W.L.R. 495; [1987] 1 All E.R. 528; [1987] 1 F.T.L.R. 210; (1987) 84 L.S.G. 1573; (1987) 131 S.J. 507; *Times*, December 22, 1986; *Financial Times*, December 16, 1986, Ch D . . . . *Digested*, 87/**2822**:
Applied, 00/6616, 02/3384, 05/2335: *Considered*, 91/2726:
Distinguished, 01/4628

Courtney Lodge Management Ltd *v.* Blake [2004] EWCA Civ 975; [2005] 1 P. & C.R. 17; [2005] L. & T.R. 2; (2004) 101(31) L.S.G. 26; (2004) 148 S.J.L.B. 908; *Times*, July 15, 2004, CA (Civ Div) . . . . *Digested*, 04/**2512**

Courts Plc *v.* Customs and Excise Commissioners [2004] EWCA Civ 1527; [2005] S.T.C. 27; [2005] B.T.C. 5037; [2005] B.V.C. 68; [2004] S.T.I. 2398; (2004) 148 S.J.L.B. 1373; *Independent*, November 25, 2004, CA (Civ Div); affirming [2003] EWHC 2541; [2004] S.T.C. 690; [2004] B.T.C. 5457; [2004] B.V.C. 517; [2003] S.T.I. 1933, Ch D; affirming [2002] V. & D.R. 482, V&DTr (London) . . . . *Digested*, 05/**4340**

Courts Plc *v.* Customs and Excise Commissioners [2005] B.V.C. 2003; [2004] V. & D.R. 316; [2004] S.T.I. 2566, V&DTr . . . . *Digested*, 05/**4394**

Coutts & Co Plc *v.* Cure see Cure *v.* Coutts & Co Plc

Coventry *v.* Cliff Evans Holdings Ltd [2005] 2 Q.R. 13; [2004] 6 Q.R. 7, CC (Worcester) [*Ex rel.* Stephen Garner, Barrister, No.8 Chambers, Fountain Court, Steelhouse Lane, Birmingham.] . . . . *Digested*, 04/**2876**

Cowen *v.* Whitehead (Unreported, April 29, 2005), CC (St Helens) [*Ex rel.* Stephen Garner, Barrister, No.8 Chambers, Fountain Court, Steelhouse Lane, Birmingham.] . . . . *Digested*, 05/**3172**

Cox *v.* Bankside Members Agency Ltd [1995] 2 Lloyd's Rep. 437; [1995] C.L.C. 671; *Times*, May 16, 1995; *Independent*, June 9, 1995; *Lloyd's List*, August 29, 1995 (I.D.), CA (Civ Div); affirming *Times*, January 27, 1995, QBD . . . . *Applied*, 04/2216, 05/2366: *Considered*, 95/2907, 96/3581, 96/3599

Cox *v.* Jones [2004] EWHC 1486; [2004] 2 F.L.R. 1010; [2004] 3 F.C.R. 693; [2004] Fam. Law 717, Ch D . . . . *Digested*, 05/**3379**

Coyle *v.* United Kingdom (11266/84) see Brogan *v.* United Kingdom (A/145-B)

Coyne *v.* Home Office see Home Office *v.* Coyne

CPL Contracting Ltd *v.* Cadenza Residential Ltd [2005] T.C.L.R. 1, QBD (TCC) . . . . *Digested*, 05/**642**

CPL Industrial Services Holding Ltd *v.* R&L Freeman & Sons [2005] EWCA Civ 539; (2005) 149 S.J.L.B. 115, CA (Civ Div)

Craft Enterprises (International) Ltd *v.* AXA Insurance Co [2004] EWCA Civ 171; [2004] 2 All E.R. (Comm) 123; [2004] 2 C.L.C. 427; [2005] Lloyd's Rep. I.R. 14, CA (Civ Div); affirming [2004] EWHC 106, QBD (Comm) . . . . *Digested*, 04/**572**

Cramp *v.* Hastings BC; Phillips *v.* Camden LBC [2005] EWCA Civ 1005; [2005] 4 All E.R. 1014; [2005] H.L.R. 48; [2005] N.P.C. 109, CA (Civ Div)

Cranage Parish Council *v.* First Secretary of State [2004] EWHC 2949; [2005] 2 P. & C.R. 23; [2005] J.P.L. 1176; [2005] A.C.D. 79, QBD (Admin) . . . . *Digested*, 05/**3295**

Cranfield *v.* Bridgegrove Ltd; Claussen *v.* Yeates; McManus *v.* Sharif; Murphy *v.* Staples UK Ltd; Smith *v.* Hughes [2003] EWCA Civ 656; [2003] 1 W.L.R. 2441; [2003] 3 All E.R. 129; [2003] C.P. Rep. 54; [2003] 21 E.G.C.S. 191; (2003) 147 S.J.L.B. 599; [2003] N.P.C. 66; *Times*, May 16, 2003, CA (Civ Div) . . . . *Digested*, 03/**455**:
Applied, 05/467, 05/485

Craven DC *v.* Skipton Properties [2005] P.A.D. 21, Planning Inspector

Crawford Settlement Trustees *v.* Revenue and Customs Commissioners; *sub nom* Trustees of the Crawford Settlement *v.* Revenue and Customs Commissioners [2005] S.T.C. (S.C.D.) 457; [2005] W.T.L.R. 797, Sp Comm

Cream Holdings Ltd *v.* Banerjee [2004] UKHL 44; [2005] 1 A.C. 253; [2004] 3 W.L.R. 918; [2004] 4 All E.R. 617; [2005] E.M.L.R. 1; [2004] H.R.L.R. 39; [2004] U.K.H.R.R. 1071; 17 B.H.R.C. 464; (2005) 28(2) I.P.D. 28001; (2004) 101(42) L.S.G. 29; (2004) 154 N.L.J. 1589; (2004) 148 S.J.L.B. 1215; *Times,* October 15, 2004, HL; reversing [2003] EWCA Civ 103; [2003] Ch. 650; [2003] 3 W.L.R. 999; [2003] 2 All E.R. 318; [2003] E.M.L.R. 16; [2003] H.R.L.R. 18; (2003) 100(15) L.S.G. 25; *Times,* February 28, 2003; *Independent,* April 7, 2003 (C.S), CA (Civ Div) . . . . *Digested,* 05/**2041**: *Applied,* 04/1924, 05/4191: *Considered,* 05/970: *Not applied,* 04/928

Creation Records Ltd *v.* News Group Newspapers Ltd [1997] E.M.L.R. 444; (1997) 16 Tr. L.R. 544; (1997) 20(7) I.P.D. 20070; (1997) 94(21) L.S.G. 32; (1997) 141 S.J.L.B. 107; *Times,* April 29, 1997, Ch D . . . . *Digested,* 97/**1041**: *Considered,* 05/2812

Creaven *v.* Director of the Assets Recovery Agency see Director of the Assets Recovery Agency *v.* Creaven

Credinfor SA *v.* Artprice.com [2005] E.C.C. 22, C d'A (Paris)

Credit & Industrial Bank *v.* Czech Republic (29010/95) (2004) 39 E.H.R.R. 39, ECHR . *Digested,* 05/**2081**

Credit & Mercantile Plc *v.* Marks [2004] EWCA Civ 568; [2005] Ch. 81; [2004] 3 W.L.R. 489; (2004) 101(22) L.S.G. 32; (2004) 148 S.J.L.B. 632; [2004] N.P.C. 74; [2004] 2 P. & C.R. DG12; *Times,* May 27, 2004, CA (Civ Div) . . . . *Digested,* 04/**3245**

Credit Lyonnais SA *v.* Moon Sarl [2005] E.C.C.18, C d'A (Paris)

CREDITMASTER Trade Mark see Mastercard International Inc *v.* Hitachi Credit (UK) Plc

Creditnet Ltd, Re see Austintel Ltd, Re

Cressey *v.* E Timm & Son Ltd [2005] EWCA Civ 763; [2005] 1 W.L.R. 3926; (2005) 102(28) L.S.G. 33; *Times,* July 25, 2005, CA (Civ Div) . . . . *Digested,* 05/**439**

Crest Nicholson Residential (South) Ltd *v.* McAllister [2004] EWCA Civ 410; [2004] 1 W.L.R. 2409; [2004] 2 All E.R. 991; [2004] 2 P. & C.R. 26; [2004] 2 E.G.L.R. 79; [2004] 24 E.G. 150; [2004] 15 E.G.C.S. 105; (2004) 148 S.J.L.B. 420; [2004] N.P.C. 54; *Times,* May 6, 2004, CA (Civ Div); reversing [2002] EWHC 2443; [2003] 1 All E.R. 46; [2003] 1 E.G.L.R. 165; [2002] 48 E.G.C.S. 140; (2002) 146 S.J.L.B. 265; [2002] N.P.C.148; *Times,* December 10, 2002, Ch D . *Digested,* 04/**3250**: *Applied,* 05/3431: *Considered,* 05/3430

Crestfort Ltd *v.* Tesco Stores Ltd [2005] EWHC 805; [2005] L. & T.R. 20; [2005] 3 E.G.L.R. 25; [2005] 37 E.G. 148; [2005] N.P.C. 74, Ch D . . . . *Digested,* 05/**2693**

Crestfort Ltd *v.* Tesco Stores Ltd [2005] EWHC 2480; [2005] N.P.C.130, Ch D

Crickmore *v.* Bennet Baggs (Unreported, June 27, 1995), CC (Colchester) [*Ex rel.* Marie Kelly, Barrister] . . . . *Digested,* 95/**1633**: *Considered,* 05/2855

Criminal Proceedings against Berlusconi (C387/02) [2005] E.C.R. I-3565; [2005] 2 C.M.L.R. 32, ECJ . . . . *Digested,* 05/**1437**

Criminal Proceedings against Calfa (C348/96); *sub nom* Calfa, Re (C348/96) [1999] All E.R. (EC) 850; [1999] E.C.R. I-11; [1999] 2 C.M.L.R. 1138; [1999] C.E.C. 477; [1999] I.N.L.R. 333; (1999) 96(19) L.S.G. 30; *Times,* January 21, 1999, ECJ . . . . *Digested,* 99/**1132**: *Followed,* 05/1462

Criminal Proceedings against Fornasar (C318/98), Re; *sub nom* Fornasar (C318/98), Re [2000] E.C.R. I-4785; [2001] Env. L.R. D1, ECJ (6th Chamber) . . . . *Followed,* 05/1401

Criminal Proceedings against Georgescu (C51/03) [2004] E.C.R. I-3203; [2005] 1 C.M.L.R. 47, ECJ. . . . . *Digested,* 05/**1479**

Criminal Proceedings against Greenham (C95/01); *sub nom* Ministere Public *v.* Greenham (C95/01) [2005] All E.R. (EC) 903; [2004] 3 C.M.L.R. 33, ECJ (6th Chamber) . . . . *Digested,* 05/**1732**

Criminal Proceedings against Hoffmann (C144/00); *sub nom* Hoffmann (C144/00), Re [2004] S.T.C. 740; [2003] E.C.R. I-2921; [2004] 1 C.M.L.R. 37; [2005] B.T.C. 5010; [2005] B.V.C. 41; [2003] S.T.I. 587; *Times,* April 17, 2003, ECJ (6th Chamber) . . . . *Digested,* 03/**4527**

Criminal Proceedings against Kapper (C476/01); *sub nom* Staatsanwaltschaft Frankenthal (Pfalz) *v.* Kapper (C476/01) [2005] All E.R. (EC) 257; [2004] E.C.R. I-5205, ECJ (5th Chamber). . . . . *Digested,* 05/**1438**

Criminal Proceedings against Keck (C267/91); Criminal Proceedings against Mithouard (C268/91) [1993] E.C.R. I-6097; [1995] 1 C.M.L.R. 101; *Times,* November 25, 1993; *Financial Times,* November 30, 1993, ECJ [1993] E.C.R. I-6097, AGO . . . *Digested,* 94/**4885**: *Applied,* 05/500: *Considered,* 94/4874, 96/2801, 01/2486, 03/1455: *Distinguished,* 05/1449: *Followed,* 98/3855, 00/4165, 04/636

Criminal Proceedings against MacQuen (C108/96); *sub nom* Criminal Proceedings against MacQueen (C108/96) [2001] E.C.R. I-837; [2002] 1 C.M.L.R. 29, ECJ (5th Chamber) . . . . *Digested,* 02/**1581**: *Followed,* 05/1468

Criminal Proceedings against Miraglia (C469/03), Re [2005] E.C.R. I-2009; [2005] 2 C.M.L.R. 6, ECJ (5th Chamber) . . . . *Digested,* 05/**870**

Criminal Proceedings against Mithouard (C268/91) see Criminal Proceedings against Keck (C267/91)

Criminal Proceedings against Pupino (C105/03) [2005] 3 W.L.R.1102; [2005] E.C.R. I-5285; [2005] 2 C.M.L.R. 63; *Times,* July 14, 2005, ECJ

Criminal Proceedings against Raemdonck (C128/04) [2005] E.C.R. I-2445; [2005] R.T.R. 25, ECJ

Criminal Proceedings against Texaco Belgium SA (C1/03) see Criminal Proceedings against Van de Walle (C1/03)

Criminal Proceedings against Van de Walle (C1/03); *sub nom* Ministere Public v. Van de Walle (C1/03); Criminal Proceedings against Texaco Belgium SA (C1/03); Van De Walle v. Texaco Belgium SA (C1/03) [2005] All E.R. (EC) 1139; [2004] E.C.R. I-7613; [2005] 1 C.M.L.R. 8; [2005] Env. L.R. 24; [2004] N.P.C. 137, ECJ (2nd Chamber) . . . . *Digested*, 05/**1414**

Criminal Proceedings against Van Lent (C232/01); *sub nom* Openbaar Ministerie v. Van Lent (C232/01) [2004] 3 C.M.L.R. 23, ECJ (5th Chamber) . . . . *Digested*, 05/**1458**

Criminal Proceedings against Webb (279/80) [1981] E.C.R. 3305; [1982] 1 C.M.L.R. 719, ECJ . . . . *Digested*, 82/**1215**:
Applied, 98/4517: *Followed*, 05/**1468**

Crisp from the Fens Ltd v. Rutland CC (1950) 114 J.P. 105; 48 L.G.R. 210; (1949-51) 1 P. & C.R. 48; [1950] W.N. 72; 94 S.J. 177, CA; affirming (1949) 113 J.P. 426; 47 L.G.R. 647; 93 S.J. 632, DC . . . . *Digested*, 47-51/**10136**:
Cited, 05/3303

Crofts v. Cathay Pacific Airways Ltd see Dickie v. Cathay Pacific Airways Ltd

Crofts v. Veta Ltd see Lawson v. Serco Ltd

Crompton (t/a David Crompton Haulage) v. Department of Transport North Western Area [2003] EWCA Civ 64; [2003] R.T.R. 34; *Times*, February 7, 2003, CA (Civ Div) . . . . *Digested*, 03/**4413**:
Considered, 05/3458

Crookdake v. Drury see Sowden v. Lodge

Croom's Trade Mark Application; *sub nom* McQUEEN CLOTHING CO Trade Mark [2005] R.P.C. 2, App Person . . . . *Digested*, 05/**2560**:
Considered, 05/2565

Cross v. British Airways Plc [2005] I.R.L.R. 423, EAT . . . . *Digested*, 05/**1303**

Cross Levels Developments Ltd v. Customs and Excise Commissioners [2004] V. & D.R. 248; [2004] S.T.I. 2354, V&DTr (London) . . . . *Digested*, 05/**4400**

Cross (Inspector of Taxes) v. London and Provincial Trust Ltd [1938] 1 K.B. 792, CA; affirming [1937] 2 K.B. 718, KBD . . . . *Considered*, 05/4021

Crossland (Inspector of Taxes) v. Hawkins [1961] Ch. 537; [1961] 3 W.L.R. 202; [1961] 2 All E.R. 812; 39 T.C. 493; (1961) 40 A.T.C. 126; [1961] T.R. 113; 105 S.J. 424, CA; reversing 53 R. & I.T. 758; (1960) 39 A.T.C. 461; [1960] T.R. 297 . . . . *Digested*, 61/**4252**:
Applied, 05/4101: *Considered*, 74/1870

Crouch v. King's Healthcare NHS Trust; Murry v. Blackburn, Hyndburn and Ribble Valley Healthcare NHS Trust [2004] EWCA Civ 1332; [2005] 1 W.L.R. 2015; [2005] 1 All E.R. 207; [2005] C.P. Rep. 10; [2005] 2 Costs L.R. 200; [2005] P.I.Q.R. Q4; [2005] Lloyd's Rep. Med. 50; (2004) 83 B.M.L.R. 47; (2004) 101(44) L.S.G. 29; (2004) 154 N.L.J. 1616; (2004) 148 S.J.L.B. 1245; *Times*, November 9, 2004, CA (Civ Div) . . . . *Digested*, 05/**447**:
Considered, 05/374

Crowe v. Stevedoring Employees Retirement Fund Pty Ltd [2003] Pens. L.R. 343; [2005] W.T.L.R. 1271, Sup Ct (Vic) . . . . *Digested*, 04/**2815**

Crown Lands Commissioners v. Page; *sub nom* Commissioners of Crown Lands v. Page [1960] 2 Q.B. 274; [1960] 3 W.L.R. 446; [1960] 2 All E.R. 726; 104 S.J. 642, CA; affirming (1959) 174 E.G. 7 . . . . *Digested*, 60/**1719**:
Considered, 77/376, 78/315, 05/2644: *Followed*, 84/1896, 85/1809, 85/1869

Crown Prosecution Service v. K (Age of Consent: Reasonable Belief) see R. v. K (Age of Consent: Reasonable Belief)

Crowther v. Pleavin [2005] 2 Q.R. 14, CC (Birkenhead) [*Ex rel.* E Rylance, Solicitor, Michael W Halsall Solicitors, 2 The Parks, Newton-le-Willows] . . . . *Digested*, 04/**2913**

Crowther v. United Kingdom (53741/00), *Times*, February 11, 2005, ECHR

CRT France International SA v. Directeur Regional des Impots de Bourgogne (C109/98) [1999] E.C.R. I-2237; (1999) 96(31) L.S.G. 43, ECJ (1st Chamber) . . . . *Followed*, 05/943

Cruh v. Cruh [1945] 2 All E.R. 545, PDAD . . . . *Applied*, 05/1627:
Followed, 71/3603

Cruz Varas v. Sweden; *sub nom* Varas Cruz v. Sweden (1992) 14 E.H.R.R. 1; *Times*, May 8, 1991, ECHR . . . . *Digested*, 92/**2339**:
Applied, 97/2764, 02/2511, 05/2167: *Not followed*, 03/2089

CSSC Properties Ltd v. York CC [2005] P.A.D. 4, Planning Inspector

Culnane v. Morris [2005] EWHC 2438; (2005) 155 N.L.J. 1810, QBD

Cummins v. Shell International Manning Services Ltd see Anderton v. Clwyd CC

Cummins v. Shell International Trading & Shipping Ltd see Anderton v. Clwyd CC

Cumpana v. Romania (33348/96) (2005) 41 E.H.R.R. 14, ECHR (Grand Chamber)

Cumper v. Pothecary [1941] 2 K.B. 58; [1941] 2 All E.R. 516, CA . . . . *Applied*, 53/**2874**,
75/2670, 76/2182, 77/2382, 04/392, 05/446: *Considered*, 97/680:
Not applied, 01/621

Cunliffe v. Fielden; *sub nom* Fielden v. Cunliffe [2005] EWCA Civ 1508; [2005] 3 F.C.R. 593; *Independent*, December 8, 2005, CA (Civ Div)

Cunliffe Owen v. LA Seligmann & Co see Cunliffe-Owen v. Teather & Greenwood

Cunliffe Owen v. Schaverien Habermann, Simon & Co see Cunliffe-Owen v. Teather & Greenwood

Cunliffe-Owen v. Teather & Greenwood; Cunliffe Owen v. Schaverien Habermann, Simon & Co; Cunliffe Owen v. LA Seligmann & Co [1967] 1 W.L.R. 1421; [1967] 3 All E.R. 561; 111 S.J. 866, Ch D . . . . *Digested,* 67/**3740**:
Applied, 05/2355: *Followed,* 96/1282

Cure v. Coutts & Co Plc; *sub nom* Coutts & Co Plc v. Cure [2005] I.C.R. 1098; *Times,* October 25, 2004, EAT . . . . *Digested,* 05/**1232**

Curley v. Parkes [2004] EWCA Civ 1515; [2005] 1 P. & C.R. DG15, CA (Civ Div)

Currey v. Currey [2004] EWCA Civ 1799; [2005] 1 F.L.R. 952; [2005] 1 F.C.R. 25; [2005] Fam. Law 277; *Times,* November 26, 2004, CA (Civ Div) . . . . *Digested,* 05/**1659**

Custodial Ltd v. Cardinal Financial Services Ltd (2004-05) 7 I.T.E.L.R. 512, Sup Ct (Qld) . . . . *Digested,* 05/**4319**

Customer Loyalty Schemes, Re (C287/03) see Commission of the European Communities v. Belgium (C287/03)

Customs and Excise Commissioners v. Alzitrans SL; *sub nom* Alzitrans SL v. Customs and Excise Commissioners [2003] EWHC 75; [2003] V. & D.R. 369; *Times,* February 10, 2003, Ch D . . . . *Digested,* 03/**927**:
Distinguished, 05/944

Customs and Excise Commissioners v. Anglo Overseas Ltd [2004] EWHC 2198; [2005] B.P.I.R. 137, Ch D . . . . *Digested,* 05/**948**

Customs and Excise Commissioners v. Arena Corp Ltd (In Provisional Liquidation); *sub nom* Arena Corp Ltd, Re; Arena Corp Ltd (In Provisional Liquidation) v. Customs and Excise Commissioners; Arena Corp Ltd (In Provisional Liquidation) v. Schroeder [2004] EWCA Civ 371; [2005] Eu. L.R. 15; [2004] B.P.I.R. 415, CA (Civ Div); affirming [2003] EWHC 3032; [2004] B.P.I.R. 375, Ch D . . . . *Digested,* 04/**902**:
Considered, 05/2348

Customs and Excise Commissioners v. Barclays Bank Plc [2004] EWCA Civ 1555; [2005] 1 W.L.R. 2082; [2005] 3 All E.R. 852; [2005] 1 Lloyd's Rep. 165; (2004) 154 N.L.J. 1831; (2004) 148 S.J.L.B. 1402; [2004] N.P.C. 175; *Independent,* December 2, 2004, CA (Civ Div); reversing [2004] EWHC 122; [2004] 1 W.L.R. 2027; [2004] 2 All E.R. 789; [2004] 1 All E.R. (Comm) 960; [2004] 1 Lloyd's Rep. 572; [2004] 2 C.L.C. 1; (2004) 101 (7) L.S.G. 35; (2004) 154 N.L.J. 224; *Times,* February 11, 2004, QBD (Comm) . . . . *Digested,* 05/**2845**

Customs and Excise Commissioners v. Bell Concord Educational Trust Ltd; *sub nom* Bell Concord Trust Ltd v. Customs and Excise Commissioners [1990] 1 Q.B. 1040; [1989] 2 W.L.R. 679; [1989] 2 All E.R. 217; [1989] S.T.C. 264; [1989] 1 C.M.L.R. 845; (1989) 133 S.J. 265; *Times,* February 9, 1989, CA (Civ Div); reversing [1988] S.T.C. 143; [1988] 2 C.M.L.R. 934, QBD; reversing [1987] 3 C.M.L.R. 424; [1986] V.A.T.T.R. 165, VAT Tr (Manchester) . . . . *Digested,* 90/**4616**:
Applied, 05/4346: *Followed,* 97/4984

Customs and Excise Commissioners v. Blom-Cooper see Blom-Cooper v. Customs and Excise Commissioners

Customs and Excise Commissioners v. Church Schools Foundation Ltd see Church Schools Foundation Ltd v. Customs and Excise Commissioners

Customs and Excise Commissioners v. East Midlands Aggregates Ltd see East Midlands Aggregates Ltd v. Customs and Excise Commissioners

Customs and Excise Commissioners v. Ebbcliff Ltd; *sub nom* Ebbcliffe Ltd v. Customs and Excise Commissioners [2004] EWCA Civ 1071; [2004] S.T.C. 1496; [2005] Env. L.R. 8; [2004] B.T.C. 8094; [2004] S.T.I. 1762; (2004) 101 (34) L.S.G. 33; (2004) 148 S.J.L.B. 976, CA (Civ Div); affirming [2003] EWHC 3181; [2004] S.T.C. 391; [2004] Env. L.R. 35; [2004] B.T.C. 8056; [2003] V. & D.R. 415; [2004] S.T.I. 53; *Times,* January 15, 2004, Ch D; reversing [2003] V. & D.R. 291, V&DTr. . . . . *Digested,* 04/**1372**

Customs and Excise Commissioners v. Elm Milk Ltd see Elm Milk Ltd v. Customs and Excise Commissioners

Customs and Excise Commissioners v. Federation of Technological Industries see R. (on the application of Federation of Technological Industries) v. Customs and Excise Commissioners

Customs and Excise Commissioners v. Ferrero UK Ltd [1997] S.T.C. 881; [1997] B.T.C. 5294; [1997] B.V.C. 408; *Times,* May 19, 1997; *Independent,* May 19, 1997 (C.S.), CA (Civ Div); reversing [1996] S.T.C. 866, QBD . . . . *Digested,* 97/**5047**:
Followed, 05/4418

Customs and Excise Commissioners v. First Choice Holidays Plc (C149/01); *sub nom* First Choice Holidays Plc v. Customs and Excise Commissioners (C149/01) [2003] All E.R. (EC) 705; [2003] S.T.C. 934; [2003] E.C.R. I-6289; [2003] 3 C.M.L.R. 1; [2003] C.E.C. 436; [2003] B.T.C. 5500; [2003] B.V.C. 556; [2003] S.T.I. 1126; *Times,* July 11, 2003, ECJ (6th Chamber) [2003] E.C.R. I-6289, AGO . . . . *Digested,* 03/**4588**:
Followed, 05/4406: *Previous proceedings,* 00/5316:
Subsequent proceedings, 04/4024

Customs and Excise Commissioners *v.* General Motors Acceptance Corp (UK) Plc see General Motors Acceptance Corp (UK) Plc *v.* Customs and Excise Commissioners

Customs and Excise Commissioners *v.* Isle of Wight Council see Isle of Wight Council *v.* Customs and Excise Commissioners

Customs and Excise Commissioners *v.* Jacobs see Jacobs *v.* Customs and Excise Commissioners

Customs and Excise Commissioners *v.* Kilroy Television Co Ltd; *sub nom* R. *v.* Customs and Excise Commissioners Ex p. Kilroy Television Co Ltd [1997] S.T.C. 901; [1997] B.T.C. 5308; [1998] C.O.D. 78; *Times*, June 30, 1997; *Independent*, June 9, 1997 (C.S.), QBD . . . . *Digested*, 97/**5004**:
Considered, 05/4361

Customs and Excise Commissioners *v.* Latchmere Properties Ltd see Latchmere Properties Ltd *v.* Customs and Excise Commissioners

Customs and Excise Commissioners *v.* Lord Fisher; *sub nom* Lord Fisher DSC *v.* Customs and Excise Commissioners [1981] 2 All E.R. 147; [1981] S.T.C. 238, QBD; affirming [1979] V.A.T.T.R. 227, VAT Tr . . . . *Digested*, 81/**2849**:
Applied, 84/3038, 03/4606, 05/4383: *Considered*, 88/3454

Customs and Excise Commissioners *v.* Madgett (t/a Howden Court Hotel) (C308/96) see Madgett (t/a Howden Court Hotel) *v.* Customs and Excise Commissioners (C308/96)

Customs and Excise Commissioners *v.* Midland Bank Plc (C98/98) see Midland Bank Plc *v.* Customs and Excise Commissioners (C98/98)

Customs and Excise Commissioners *v.* Musahi Autoparts Europe Ltd see Musashi Autoparts Europe Ltd (formerly TAP Manufacturing Ltd) *v.* Customs and Excise Commissioners

Customs and Excise Commissioners *v.* Plantiflor Ltd; *sub nom* Plantiflor Ltd *v.* Customs and Excise Commissioners [2002] UKHL 33; [2002] 1 W.L.R. 2287; [2002] S.T.C. 1132; [2002] 3 C.M.L.R. 5; [2002] B.T.C. 5413; [2002] B.V.C. 572; [2002] S.T.I. 1093; (2002) 99(36) L.S.G. 39; (2002) 152 N.L.J. 1385; *Times*, July 31, 2002; *Independent*, November 11, 2002 (C.S), HL; reversing [2000] S.T.C. 137; [2000] B.T.C. 5050; [2000] B.V.C. 103; [2000] S.T.I. 128; *Times*, February 10, 2000, CA (Civ Div); reversing [1999] S.T.C. 51; [1999] B.T.C. 5038; [1999] B.V.C. 37; *Times*, November 25, 1998; *Independent*, November 23, 1998 (C.S.), QBD; reversing [1997] B.V.C. 2380; [1997] V. & D.R. 301; [1997] S.T.I. 998, V&D Tr. . . . . *Digested*, 02/**4785**:
Applied, 04/3992, 05/4346: *Approved*, 98/4916

Customs and Excise Commissioners *v.* Primback Ltd (C34/99); *sub nom* Primback Ltd *v.* Customs and Excise Commissioners (C34/99) [2001] 1 W.L.R. 1693; [2001] All E.R. (EC) 714; [2001] S.T.C. 803; [2001] E.C.R. I-3833; [2001] 2 C.M.L.R. 42; [2001] C.E.C. 132; [2001] B.T.C. 5240; [2001] B.V.C. 315; [2001] S.T.I. 835; *Times*, June 8, 2001, ECJ . . . . *Digested*, 01/**5555**:
Applied, 03/4521: *Considered*, 04/3969: *Distinguished*, 04/4006:
Followed, 04/3981: *Previous proceedings*, 96/5891: *Referred to*, 05/4340

Customs and Excise Commissioners *v.* Redrow Group Plc [1999] 1 W.L.R. 408; [1999] 2 All E.R. 1; [1999] S.T.C. 161; [1999] B.T.C. 5062; [1999] B.V.C. 96; [1999] E.G.C.S. 20; (1999) 96(9) L.S.G. 32; (1999) 143 S.J.L.B. 58; [1999] N.P.C. 18; *Times*, February 18, 1999; *Independent*, February 18, 1999, HL; reversing [1997] S.T.C. 1053; [1997] B.T.C. 5347; [1997] B.V.C. 461; [1997] E.G.C.S. 92; *Times*, July 3, 1997; *Independent*, July 14, 1997 (C.S.), CA (Civ Div); reversing [1996] S.T.C. 365; [1995] E.G.C.S. 202, QBD; affirming [1995] V. & D.R. 115, VAT Tr (Manchester) . . . . *Digested*, 99/**4994**:
Applied, 02/4774, 04/3992, 05/4346, 05/4375: *Considered*, 03/4529:
Distinguished, 05/4379

Customs and Excise Commissioners *v.* Robbins see Robbins *v.* Customs and Excise Commissioners

Customs and Excise Commissioners *v.* Schindler (C275/92) [1994] Q.B. 610; [1994] 3 W.L.R. 103; [1994] 2 All E.R. 193; [1994] E.C.R. I-1039; [1995] 1 C.M.L.R. 4; *Times*, March 30, 1994; *Financial Times*, March 29, 1994, ECJ . . . . *Digested*, 94/**4907**:
Considered, 05/1467: *Followed*, 99/588, 99/2250, 00/2384, 00/2397

Customs and Excise Commissioners *v.* St Paul's Community Project Ltd; *sub nom* St Paul's Community Project Ltd *v.* Customs and Excise Commissioners [2004] EWHC 2490; [2005] S.T.C. 95; [2004] B.T.C. 5803; [2005] B.V.C. 12; [2004] S.T.I. 2338, Ch D; affirming [2004] S.T.I. 1007, V&D Tr . . . . *Digested*, 05/**4383**

Customs and Excise Commissioners *v.* Tinsley see Tinsley *v.* Customs and Excise Commissioners

Customs and Excise Commissioners *v.* Total Network SL [2005] EWHC 1; [2005] S.T.C. 637; [2005] B.T.C. 5273; [2005] B.V.C. 304; [2005] S.T.I. 105, QBD . . . . *Digested*, 05/**4190**

Customs and Excise Commissioners *v.* Upton (t/a Fagomatic) [2002] EWCA Civ 520; [2002] S.T.C. 640; [2002] B.T.C. 5323; [2001] B.V.C. 451; [2002] S.T.I. 681; (2002) 99(22) L.S.G. 36; *Times,* May 27, 2002; *Independent,* April 25, 2002, CA (Civ Div); affirming [2001] S.T.C. 912; [2002] B.T.C. 5162; [2002] B.V.C. 285; [2001] S.T.I. 756, Ch D; reversing [2001] B.V.C. 2099; [2000] S.T.I. 1771, V&DTr. . . . . *Digested,* 02/**4766**:
Applied, 04/5161, 05/4362: *Distinguished,* 03/4554, 05/4372:
Followed, 04/3991

Customs and Excise Commissioners *v.* West Herts College; *sub nom* West Herts College *v.* Customs and Excise Commissioners [2001] S.T.C. 1245; [2005] B.T.C. 5551; [2005] B.V.C. 582; [2001] S.T.I. 1057, Ch D; affirming [2001] B.V.C. 2068; [2000] S.T.I. 1555, V&DTr. . . . . *Digested,* 01/**5576**:
Followed, 05/4371

Customs and Excise Commissioners *v.* Yarburgh Children's Trust see Yarburgh Childrens Trust *v.* Customs and Excise Commissioners

Customs and Excise Commissioners *v.* Zoological Society of London (C267/00) see Zoological Society of London *v.* Customs and Excise Commissioners (C267/00)

Cutts *v.* Sharman (Unreported, February 16, 2005), CC (Lincoln) [*Ex rel.* James Earle, Barrister, Regency Chambers, Cathedral Square, Peterborough] . . . . *Digested,* 05/**3201**

CV Scheepvaartonderneming Flintermar *v.* Sea Malta Co Ltd (The Flintermar) [2005] EWCA Civ 17; [2005] 1 All E.R. (Comm) 497; [2005] 1 Lloyd's Rep. 409; [2005] 1 C.L.C. 40, CA (Civ Div) . . . . *Digested,* 05/**3813**

CW *v.* Secretary of State for the Home Department; *sub nom* CW (Deportation: Huang: Proportionality: Jamaica), Re [2005] UKIAT 110; [2005] Imm. A.R. 441, IAT

CW (Deportation: Huang: Proportionality: Jamaica), Re see CW *v.* Secretary of State for the Home Department

Cyganik *v.* Agulian; *sub nom* Agulian *v.* Cyganik; A3/2005/0927, CA (Civ Div); reversing [2005] EWHC 444; [2005] W.T.L.R. 1049; (2004-05) 7 I.T.E.L.R. 831, Ch D . . . . *Digested,* 05/**3965**

Cyprus *v.* Turkey (25781/94) (2002) 35 E.H.R.R. 30; 11 B.H.R.C. 45, ECHR . . . . *Digested,* 02/**2386**:
Applied, 05/2038

D *v.* DPP [2005] EWHC 967; [2005] Crim. L.R. 962, QBD (Admin)

D *v.* East Berkshire Community NHS Trust see JD *v.* East Berkshire Community Health NHS Trust

D *v.* East Sussex County LEA [2005] EWCA Civ 323; [2005] E.L.R. 388; (2005) 102(23) L.S.G. 27; (2005) 149 S.J.L.B. 391; *Times,* April 29, 2005, CA (Civ Div); affirming [2004] EWHC 1834, QBD (Admin) . . . . *Digested,* 05/**1145**

D *v.* Home Office; *sub nom* D *v.* Secretary of State for the Home Department; ID *v.* Home Office [2005] EWCA Civ 38; [2005] I.N.L.R. 278; *Times,* February 10, 2005, CA (Civ Div) . . . . *Digested,* 05/**2163**

D *v.* Inspecteur van de Belastingdienst/Particulieren/Ondernemingen Buitenland te Heerlen (C376/03) [2005] S.T.C. 1211; [2005] 3 C.M.L.R. 19; 7 I.T.L. Rep. 927; [2005] S.T.I. 1233, ECJ

D *v.* Secretary of State for the Home Department see A *v.* Secretary of State for the Home Department

D *v.* Secretary of State for the Home Department see D *v.* Home Office

D *v.* Secretary of State for the Home Department; *sub nom* R. (on the application of D) *v.* Secretary of State for the Home Department [2004] EWHC 2857; *Times,* December 27, 2004, QBD (Admin) . . . . *Digested,* 05/**2915**

D *v.* United Kingdom (30240/96) (1997) 24 E.H.R.R. 423; 2 B.H.R.C. 273; (1998) 42 B.M.L.R. 149; *Times,* May 12, 1997, ECHR (1996) 22 E.H.R.R. CD45, Eur Comm HR . . . . *Digested,* 97/**2763**:
Applied, 04/1692, 04/2029: *Considered,* 01/3611, 05/2160:
Distinguished, 04/2038

D *v.* W (C384/98) [2002] S.T.C. 1200; [2000] E.C.R. I-6795; [2002] B.T.C. 5427; [2002] B.V.C. 541; [2000] S.T.I. 1398; *Times,* October 24, 2000, ECJ (5th Chamber) [2000] E.C.R. I-6795, AGO . . . . *Digested,* 00/**5295**:
Applied, 05/4349: *Considered,* 04/3980

D (A Child), Re (2005) 149 S.J.L.B. 770, CA (Civ Div)

D (A Child) *v.* Burnley Healthcare NHS Trust [2005] 2 Q.R. 17; [2004] 6 Q.R. 9, CC (Manchester) [*Ex rel.* JMW, Solicitors, 5-7 Byrom Street, Manchester] . . . . *Digested,* 04/**2937**

D (A Child) *v.* Noor (Unreported, June 3, 2004), CC (Kingston on Thames) [*Ex rel.* Joanna Kerr, Barrister, Lamb Chambers, Lamb Building, Temple, London] . . . . . . *Digested,* 05/**3115**

D (A Child) *v.* O; *sub nom* CD (A Child) *v.* O [2004] EWHC 1036; [2004] 3 All E.R. 780; [2004] 3 F.C.R. 195; [2004] W.T.L.R. 751; (2004-05) 7 I.T.E.L.R. 63; [2004] 2 P. & C.R. DG13, Ch D . . . . *Digested,* 04/**3956**

D (A Child) *v.* S (Education: Discrimination) see R. (on the application of D (A Child)) *v.* Plymouth High School for Girls Governing Body

D (A Child) v. Walker; sub nom Walker v. D (A Child) [2000] 1 W.L.R. 1382; [2000]
C.P.L.R. 462; [2001] H.R.L.R. 1; [2000] U.K.H.R.R. 648; [2000] P.I.Q.R. P193;
(2000) 97(22) L.S.G. 44; Times, May 17, 2000; Independent, June 12, 2000
(C.S), CA (Civ Div) . . . . Digested, 00/**321**:
Applied, 05/3073: Considered, 01/402: Followed, 01/690
D (A Child) (IVF: Paternity of Child), Re see R (A Child) (IVF: Paternity of Child), Re
D (Abduction: Habitual Residence), Re [2005] EWHC 518; [2005] 2 F.L.R. 403; [2005]
Fam. Law 604, Fam Div
D (Children), Re [2005] EWCA Civ 825; (2005) 102(29) L.S.G. 31; (2005) 155 N.L.J.
1209; Independent, July 8, 2005, CA (Civ Div) . . . . Digested, 05/**1535**
D (CICB: Quantum: 2004: Brain injury), Re (Unreported, May 6, 2004), CICA (London) [Ex
rel. Russell-Cooke, Solicitors, 2 Putney Hill, Putney, London] . . . . Digested, 05/**3080**
D&F Estates Ltd v. Church Commissioners for England [1989] A.C. 177; [1988] 3
W.L.R. 368; [1988] 2 All E.R. 992; 41 B.L.R. 1; 15 Con. L.R. 35; [1988] 2
E.G.L.R. 213; (1988) 4 Const. L.J. 100; [1988] E.G.C.S. 113; (1988) 85(33)
L.S.G. 46; (1988) 138 N.L.J. Rep. 210; (1988) 132 S.J. 1092, HL; affirming 36
B.L.R. 72; 11 Con. L.R. 12; [1987] 1 F.T.L.R. 405; (1987) 3 Const. L.J. 110, CA
(Civ Div); affirming in part 7 Con. L.R. 40, OR . . . . Digested, 88/**3410**:
Applied, 89/3516, 90/3289, 92/3197, 94/321, 05/655: Considered, 89/2537,
90/3288, 90/3884, 90/5485, 90/5487, 91/2661, 92/3219, 93/2997:
Distinguished, 96/4437: Not followed, 98/3924
D'Ambrumenil v. Customs and Excise Commissioners [2004] V. & D.R. 134; [2004]
S.T.I. 1554, V&DTr (London) . . . . Digested, 05/**4353**
D'Ambrumenil v. Customs and Excise Commissioners (C307/01) [2004] Q.B. 1179;
[2004] 3 W.L.R. 174; [2005] S.T.C. 650; [2004] 2 C.M.L.R. 18; [2004] C.E.C.
47; [2005] B.T.C. 5710; [2005] B.V.C. 741; [2003] S.T.I. 2181, ECJ (5th
Chamber) . . . . Digested, 04/**3984**:
Applied, 05/4353, 05/4355
D'Hoop v. Office National de l'Emploi (C224/98); sub nom D'Hoop v. Rijksdienst voor
Arbeidsvoorziening (C224/98); D'Hoop v. Office National d'Emploi (C224/98)
[2003] All E.R. (EC) 527; [2002] E.C.R. I-6191; [2002] 3 C.M.L.R. 12; [2002]
C.E.C. 642; [2004] I.C.R. 137, ECJ . . . . Digested, 03/**1445**:
Applied, 05/3922: Followed, 05/4008
D'Hoop v. Rijksdienst voor Arbeidsvoorziening (C224/98) see D'Hoop v. Office
National de l'Emploi (C224/98)
D'Jan of London, Re; sub nom Copp v. D'Jan [1993] B.C.C. 646; [1994] 1 B.C.L.C.
561, Ch D (Companies Ct) . . . . Digested, 95/**595**:
Applied, 05/521
D'Souza v. Lambeth LBC (No.2) see Rhys-Harper v. Relaxion Group Plc
Da Costa v. Queen, The [1990] 2 A.C. 389; [1990] 2 W.L.R. 1182; (1990) 87(17)
L.S.G. 31; (1990) 134 S.J. 885, PC (Jam) . . . . Digested, 90/**961**:
Applied, 05/2295
Dacas v. Brook Street Bureau (UK) Ltd; sub nom Brook Street Bureau (UK) Ltd v.
Dacas [2004] EWCA Civ 217; [2004] I.C.R. 1437; [2004] I.R.L.R. 358; Times,
March 19, 2004, CA (Civ Div); reversing [2003] I.R.L.R. 190, EAT . . . . Digested, 04/**1204**:
Applied, 05/1214
Dacre Son & Hartley Ltd v. North Yorkshire CC see Dacre Son & Hartley Ltd v. North
Yorkshire Trading Standards
Dacre Son & Hartley Ltd v. North Yorkshire Trading Standards; sub nom Dacre Son &
Hartley Ltd v. North Yorkshire CC [2004] EWHC 2783; (2005) 169 J.P. 59;
[2005] 1 E.G.L.R. 11; [2005] 03 E.G. 118; (2005) 169 J.P.N. 179; [2004] 45
E.G.C.S. 124, QBD (Admin) . . . . Digested, 05/**886**
Dadourian Group International Inc v. Simms A3/2005/0430, CA (Civ Div); affirming
[2005] EWHC 268; [2005] 2 All E.R. 651; [2005] 2 All E.R. (Comm) 224,
Ch D . . . . Digested, 05/**415**
Daewoo Electronics Manufacturing Espana SA (DEMESA) v. Commission of the
European Communities (C183/02 P) [2004] E.C.R. I-10609; [2005] 1 C.M.L.R.
31, ECJ (2nd Chamber) . . . . Digested, 05/**594**
Dafeki v. Landesversicherungsanstalt Wurttemberg (C336/94) [1998] All E.R. (E.C.)
452; [1997] E.C.R. I-6761; [1998] 2 C.M.L.R. 1; Times, December 13, 1997, ECJ . Digested, 98/**4520**:
Distinguished, 05/3889
Dafra-Lines A/S v. Commission of the European Communities (C396/96 P) see
Compagnie Maritime Belge Transports SA v. Commission of the European
Communities (C395/96 P)
Daiichi Pharmaceuticals UK Ltd v. Stop Huntingdon Animal Cruelty; Asahi Glass
Fluoropolymers UK Ltd v. Stop Huntingdon Animal Cruelty; Eisai Ltd v. Stop
Huntingdon Animal Cruelty; Yamanouchi Pharma UK Ltd v. Stop Huntingdon
Animal Cruelty; Sankyo Pharma UK Ltd v. Stop Huntingdon Animal Cruelty
[2003] EWHC 2337; [2004] 1 W.L.R. 1503; [2005] 1 B.C.L.C. 27; (2003)
100(41) L.S.G. 33; Times, October 22, 2003, QBD
Daimler Chrysler AG v. Alavi (t/a Merc); sub nom DaimlerChrysler AG v. Alavi [2001]
E.T.M.R. 98; [2001] R.P.C. 42; (2001) 24(5) I.P.D. 24028; (2001) 98(13) L.S.G.
41; Times, February 16, 2001, Ch D . . . . Digested, 01/**4035**:
Applied, 03/2636: Considered, 05/2562

Daimler Chrysler AG v. Office for Harmonisation in the Internal Market (Trade Marks and Designs) (OHIM) (Tele Aid) (T355/00); *sub nom* DaimlerChrysler AG v. Office for Harmonisation in the Internal Market (Trade Marks and Designs) (OHIM) (Tele Aid) (T355/00) [2002] E.C.R. II-1939, CFI. . . . . *Followed*, 05/2506
Daimler Chrysler's Swedish Design Application [2005] E.C.D.R. 15 . . . . *Digested*, 05/**2500**
DaimlerChrysler AG v. Alavi see Daimler Chrysler AG v. Alavi (t/a Merc)
DaimlerChrysler AG v. Office for Harmonisation in the Internal Market (Trade Marks and Designs) (OHIM) (Tele Aid) (T355/00) see Daimler Chrysler AG v. Office for Harmonisation in the Internal Market (Trade Marks and Designs) (OHIM) (Tele Aid) (T355/00)
Dairy Containers Ltd v. Tasman Orient Line CV (The Tasman Discoverer) [2004] UKPC 22; [2005] 1 W.L.R. 215; [2004] 2 All E.R. (Comm) 667; [2004] 2 Lloyd's Rep. 647; [2004] 2 C.L.C. 794, PC (NZ); affirming [2002] 2 Lloyd's Rep. 528; [2002] 3 N.Z.L.R. 353, CA (NZ); reversing [2001] 2 Lloyd's Rep. 665; [2002] 1 N.Z.L.R. 265, HC (NZ) . . . . *Digested*, 04/**3480**
Daisytek-ISA Ltd, Re [2003] B.C.C. 562; [2004] B.P.I.R. 30, Ch D . . . . *Digested*, 03/**2394**:
Applied, 05/2259: *Considered*, 05/2265
Dalby v. Bodilly; Dalby v. Coloursource Ltd [2004] EWHC 3078; [2005] B.C.C. 627, Ch D (Companies Ct) . . . . *Digested*, 05/**528**
Dalby v. Coloursource Ltd see Dalby v. Bodilly
Daltel Europe Ltd (In Liquidation) v. Makki (No.1) [2004] EWHC 726; [2005] 1 B.C.L.C. 594, Ch D . . . . *Digested*, 05/**2302**
Dame Margaret Hungerford Charity Trustees v. Beazeley (1994) 26 H.L.R. 269; [1993] 29 E.G. 100; [1993] E.G.C.S. 90; [1993] N.P.C. 71; *Times*, May 17, 1993, CA (Civ Div) . . . . *Digested*, 93/**2544**:
Considered, 05/2684
Dangeville SA v. France (36677/97) [2003] S.T.C. 771; (2004) 38 E.H.R.R. 32; [2005] B.T.C. 5599; [2005] B.V.C. 630; 5 I.T.L. Rep. 604; [2003] S.T.I. 964, ECHR . . . . *Digested*, 03/**4562**
Daniel v. Drew see Drew v. Daniel
Daniels v. Commissioner of Police of the Metropolis [2005] EWCA Civ 1312; (2005) 102(44) L.S.G. 30; *Times*, October 28, 2005, CA (Civ Div)
Daniels v. Revenue and Customs Commissioners [2005] S.T.C. (S.C.D.) 684, Sp Comm
Dannatt v. Customs and Excise Commissioners (Appeal) see Gora v. Customs and Excise Commissioners
Dansk Rorindustri A/S v. Commission of the European Communities (C189/02 P); Isoplus Fernwarmetechnik Vertriebsgesellschaft mbH v. Commission of the European Communities (C202/02 P); KE KELIT Kunststoffwerk GmbH v. Commission of the European Communities (C205/02 P); LR af 1998 A/S v. Commission of the European Communities (C206/02 P); Brugg Rohrsysteme GmbH v. Commission of the European Communities (C207/02 P); LR af 1998 (Deutschland) GmbH v. Commission of the European Communities (C208/02 P); ABB Asea Brown Boveri Ltd v. Commission of the European Communities (C213/02 P) [2005] E.C.R. I-5425; [2005] 5 C.M.L.R. 17, ECJ
Danske Bilimportorer v. Skatteministeriet, Told- og Skattestyrelsen (C383/01) [2005] All E.R. (EC) 553; [2003] E.C.R. I-6065; [2003] 2 C.M.L.R. 41; [2003] C.E.C. 543, ECJ . . . . *Digested*, 04/**905**
Danske Busvognmaend v. Commission of the European Communities (T157/01) [2004] E.C.R. II-917; [2004] 2 C.M.L.R. 29, CFI (2nd Chamber) . . . . *Digested*, 05/**592**
Daraydan Holdings Ltd v. Solland International Ltd [2004] EWHC 622; [2005] Ch. 119; [2004] 3 W.L.R. 1106; [2005] 4 All E.R. 73; [2004] W.T.L.R. 815; [2004] N.P.C. 49, Ch D . . . . *Digested*, 05/**3443**
Darby v. National Trust for Places of Historic Interest or Natural Beauty [2001] EWCA Civ 189; (2001) 3 L.G.L.R. 29; [2001] P.I.Q.R. P27; *Times*, February 23, 2001, CA (Civ Div) . . . . *Digested*, 01/**4504**:
Considered, 05/4196
Dardana Ltd v. Yukos Oil Co (No.1); *sub nom* Petroalliance Services Co Ltd v. Yukos Oil Co; Yukos Oil Co v. Dardana Ltd [2002] EWCA Civ 543; [2002] 1 All E.R. (Comm) 819; [2002] 2 Lloyd's Rep. 326; [2002] C.L.C. 1120, CA (Civ Div); reversing in part [2002] 1 Lloyd's Rep. 225, QBD (Comm) . . . . *Digested*, 03/**196**:
Considered, 05/463
Dari v. Secretary of State for the Home Department see R. (on the application of Tum) v. Secretary of State for the Home Department
Darling Island Stevedoring Co v. Long (1957) 31 A.L.J. 208, HC (Aus) . . . . *Digested*, 58/**2280**:
Considered, 05/4199
Darlington BC v. Kaye [2004] EWHC 2836; [2005] R.T.R. 14; [2005] A.C.D. 77, QBD (Admin) . . . . *Digested*, 05/**2754**
Dart Industries Inc v. Office for Harmonisation in the Internal Market (Trade Marks and Designs) (OHIM) (T360/00) [2002] E.C.R. II-3867; [2003] E.T.M.R. 32, CFI (2nd Chamber) . . . . *Digested*, 03/**2603**:
Applied, 05/2519
Dart Major Works Ltd v. Customs and Excise Commissioners [2005] B.V.C. 2105; [2004] S.T.I. 2575; (2004) 148 S.J.L.B. 1280, V&DTr (London)
Dartmoor National Park Authority v. Bovey Castle [2005] P.A.D. 86, Planning Inspector

Dartmoor National Park Authority *v.* Executors of VL Spear (Deceased) [2005] P.A.D.
20, Planning Inspector

Dassonville *v.* Commission of the European Communities (8/74) see Procureur du Roi
v. Dassonville (8/74)

Datec Electronic Holdings Ltd *v.* United Parcels Service Ltd [2005] EWCA Civ 1418;
[2005] 2 C.L.C. 1025, CA (Civ Div); reversing [2005] EWHC 221; [2005] 1
Lloyd's Rep. 470, QBD (Comm) . . . . *Digested*, 05/**3455**

Dattani *v.* Chief Constable of West Mercia [2005] I.R.L.R. 327, EAT . . . . *Digested*, 05/**1292**

David *v.* General Medical Council [2004] EWHC 2977; (2005) 84 B.M.L.R. 30; *Times*,
January 12, 2005, QBD (Admin) . . . . *Digested*, 05/**1799**

David Hendry Cars *v.* Customs and Excise Commissioners [2005] V. & D.R. 169,
V&DTr (London)

Davidson *v.* Scottish Ministers (No.1); *sub nom* Scott *v.* Scottish Ministers; Scott,
Petitioner; Davidson, Petitioner (No.1) [2005] UKHL 74; *Times*, December 19,
2005, HL; reversing 2002 S.C. 205; 2002 S.L.T. 420; 2002 G.W.D. 1-9, IH (Ex
Div); affirming 2002 S.C.L.R. 166; 2001 G.W.D. 35-1341, OH . . . . *Digested*, 02/**5239**

Davidson *v.* Scottish Ministers (No.2); *sub nom* Davidson, Petitioner (No.2) [2004]
UKHL 34; 2005 S.C. (H.L.) 7; 2004 S.L.T. 895; 2004 S.C.L.R. 991; [2004]
H.R.L.R. 34; [2004] U.K.H.R.R. 1079; [2005] A.C.D. 19; 2004 G.W.D. 27-572;
Times, July 16, 2004, HL; affirming in part 2003 S.C. 103; 2002 S.L.T. 1231;
2002 G.W.D. 28-959, IH (2 Div) . . . . *Digested*, 04/**4467**:
Considered, 05/2908: *Followed*, 03/5168

Davidson *v.* Stanley [2004] EWHC 2595; [2005] B.P.I.R. 279, Ch D . . . . *Digested*, 05/**2309**

Davies *v.* Elsby Bros [1961] 1 W.L.R. 519, HL; affirming [1961] 1 W.L.R. 170; [1960] 3
All E.R. 672; 105 S.J. 107, CA . . . . *Digested*, 61/**7111**:
Applied, 66/10122, 80/352, 81/300: *Considered*, 05/710:
Distinguished, 61/7112, 66/9833, 73/2512, 89/2885

Davies *v.* United Kingdom (42007/98) [2005] B.C.C. 401; (2002) 35 E.H.R.R. 29;
Times, August 1, 2002, ECHR . . . . *Digested*, 02/**2421**:
Applied, 05/2093: *Considered*, 03/474

Davies Attbrook (Chemists) Ltd *v.* Benchmark Group Plc, *Times*, November 24, 2005,
Ch D

Davies (Inspector of Taxes) *v.* Hicks see Hicks *v.* Davies (Inspector of Taxes)

Davis *v.* Stena Line Ltd [2005] EWHC 420; [2005] 2 Lloyd's Rep. 13, QBD . . . . *Digested*, 05/**2860**

Davis *v.* Tonbridge and Malling BC see Tonbridge and Malling BC *v.* Davis

Davy's of London (Wine Merchants) Ltd *v.* City of London Corp; Davy's of London
(Wine Merchants) Ltd *v.* Saxon Land BV [2004] EWHC 2224; [2004] 3
E.G.L.R. 39; [2004] 49 E.G. 136; [2004] 42 E.G.C.S. 161; [2004] N.P.C. 144;
[2005] 1 P. & C.R. DG8, Ch D . . . . *Digested*, 05/**2671**

Davy's of London (Wine Merchants) Ltd *v.* Saxon Land BV see Davy's of London (Wine
Merchants) Ltd *v.* City of London Corp

Dawes & Henderson (Agencies) Ltd (In Liquidation) (No.2), Re; *sub nom* Shuttleworth *v.*
Secretary of State for Trade and Industry [2000] B.C.C. 204; [1999] 2 B.C.L.C.
317; (1999) 96(8) L.S.G. 29; *Times*, February 9, 1999, Ch D . . . . *Digested*, 99/**617**:
Applied, 05/519: *Considered*, 01/716

Dawson *v.* Cherry Tree Machine Co Ltd see Shell Tankers UK Ltd *v.* Jeromson

Dawson *v.* Stonham Housing Association see Dunnachie *v.* Kingston upon Hull City
Council

Day *v.* 32 Rosary Gardens (Freehold) Ltd see Arbib *v.* Earl Cadogan

Day *v.* Cook [2001] EWCA Civ 592; [2003] B.C.C. 256; [2002] 1 B.C.L.C. 1; [2001]
Lloyd's Rep. P.N. 551; [2001] P.N.L.R. 32, CA (Civ Div); reversing in part [2000]
P.N.L.R. 178, QBD (Merc) . . . . *Digested*, 01/**749**:
Considered, 05/533

Dbeis *v.* Secretary of State for the Home Department [2005] EWCA Civ 584; *Times*,
May 30, 2005, CA (Civ Div) . . . . *Digested*, 05/**2179**

DBP Holdings, Re see Ci4Net.com.Inc, Re

DC Thomson & Co Ltd *v.* Deakin [1952] Ch. 646; [1952] 2 All E.R. 361; [1952] 2
T.L.R. 105, CA; affirming [1952] 1 T.L.R. 1397, Ch D . . . . *Digested*, 52/**3507**:
Applied, 57/3584, 61/8932, 76/2810, 83/3704, 92/2541, 93/4000, 05/4198:
Considered, 65/3964, 68/3888, 68/3955, 69/3574, 81/30.u, 82/3276

De Baeck *v.* Belgium (C268/03) [2004] 2 C.M.L.R. 57, ECJ (2nd Chamber) . . . . *Digested*, 05/**3993**

De Bergolis *v.* Norinchukin International Plc see Hanly *v.* Norinchukin International Plc

De Campomar *v.* Pettiward's Estate Trustees [2005] 1 E.G.L.R. 83; [2005] 15 E.G. 124,
Lands Tr . . . . *Digested*, 05/**2655**

De Cavel *v.* De Cavel (143/78) [1979] E.C.R. 1055; [1979] 2 C.M.L.R. 547, ECJ. . . . . . *Digested*, 79/**1130**:
Considered, 03/1585, 04/1535, 05/1682

De Cubber *v.* Belgium (9186/80) see De Cubber *v.* Belgium (A/86)

De Cubber *v.* Belgium (A/86); *sub nom* De Cubber *v.* Belgium (9186/80) (1985) 7
E.H.R.R. 236, ECHR (1984) 6 E.H.R.R. CD104, Eur Comm HR . . . . *Considered*, 03/5307,
04/4655: *Followed*, 05/3657

De Dampierre v. De Dampierre [1988] A.C. 92; [1987] 2 W.L.R. 1006; [1987] 2 All
E.R. 1; [1987] 2 F.L.R. 300; [1987] Fam. Law 418; (1987) 84 L.S.G. 1493;
(1987) 131 S.J. 471, HL; reversing [1987] 1 F.L.R. 511; [1986] Fam.
Law 361, CA
(Civ Div) .... *Digested*, 87/**399**:
Applied, 92/475, 95/2334, 99/2403, 02/628, 03/1554, 05/1623:
Considered, 92/3072, 94/3256, 97/2453: *Followed*, 92/5695:
Referred to, 95/2303
De Haes v. Belgium (19983/92) (1998) 25 E.H.R.R. 1, ECHR .... *Digested*, 98/**3089**:
Applied, 98/3088: *Considered*, 98/3092, 05/633
De Haney v. Brent MIND; *sub nom* Haney v. Brent Mind; Dehaney v. Brent Mind
[2003] EWCA Civ 1637; [2004] I.C.R. 348; (2003) 100(45) L.S.G. 29; (2003)
147 S.J.L.B. 1275; *Times*, November 11, 2003, CA (Civ Div); reversing EAT/
0054/03/DA, EAT .... *Digested*, 04/**1232**:
Followed, 05/1253
De Jorio v. Italy (73936/01) (2005) 40 E.H.R.R. 42, ECHR .... *Digested*, 05/**2075**
De Landtsheer v. Veuve Clicquot Ponsardin [2005] E.T.M.R. 12, App (Brussels)
De Lasteyrie du Saillant v. Ministere de l'Economie, des Finances et de l'Industrie (C9/
02) [2005] S.T.C. 1722; [2004] E.C.R. I-2409; [2004] 3 C.M.L.R. 39; 6 I.T.L.
Rep. 666; [2004] S.T.I. 890, ECJ (5th Chamber) .... *Digested*, 04/**3697**
De Maroussem v. Commissioner of Income Tax; *sub nom* Maroussem v. Income Tax
Commissioner [2004] UKPC 43; [2004] 1 W.L.R. 2865; [2005] S.T.C. 125;
[2004] B.T.C. 402; [2004] S.T.I. 2118; *Times*, September 13, 2004, PC (Mau) .. *Digested*, 04/**3768**
De Meyere v. Belgium (A/43) see Le Compte v. Belgium (A/43)
De Mulder v. First Secretary of State [2005] EWHC 2640; [2005] N.P.C. 138, QBD
(Admin)
De Reuck v. Director of Public Prosecutions (Witwaterstrand Local Division) 17
B.H.R.C. 710, Const Ct (SA)
De Weerd v. Bestuur van de Bedrijfsvereniging voor de Gezondheit, Geestelijke en
Maatschappelijke Belangen (C343/92) [1994] E.C.R. I-571; [1994] 2 C.M.L.R.
325, ECJ (6th Chamber) .... *Digested*, 94/**4942**:
Applied, 05/1268
Deakin v. Faulding; Specialist Group International Ltd v. Deakin (2001) 98(35) L.S.G.
32; *Times*, August 29, 2001, Ch D .... *Digested*, 01/**748**:
Considered, 05/470
Dean v. Stout [2004] EWHC 3315; [2005] B.P.I.R. 1113, Ch D
Dean & Dyball Construction Ltd v. Kenneth Grubb Associates Ltd [2003] EWHC 2465;
100 Con. L.R. 92, QBD (TCC)
Debenhams Retail Plc v. Customs and Excise Commissioners; *sub nom* Revenue and
Customs Commissioners v. Debenhams Retail Plc [2005] EWCA Civ 892;
[2005] S.T.C. 1155; [2005] B.T.C. 5394; [2005] B.V.C. 425; [2005] S.T.I. 1262;
(2005) 149 S.J.L.B. 921; *Times*, July 26, 2005, CA (Civ Div); reversing [2004]
EWHC 1540; [2004] S.T.C. 1132; [2004] B.T.C. 5494; [2004] B.V.C. 554;
[2004] S.T.I. 1585; (2004) 154 N.L.J. 1106, Ch D; reversing [2003] B.V.C. 2543;
[2003] S.T.I. 1520, V&DTr. .... *Digested*, 05/**4398**
Debenhams Retail Plc v. Sun Alliance & London Assurance Co Ltd; *sub nom*
Debenhams Retail Plc v. Sun Alliance & London Insurance Co Ltd; Sun Alliance
& London Insurance Co Ltd v. Debenhams Retail Plc [2005] EWCA Civ 868;
[2005] S.T.C. 1443; [2005] 3 E.G.L.R. 34; [2005] 38 E.G. 142; [2005] B.T.C.
5464; [2005] B.V.C. 495; [2005] S.T.I. 1310; [2005] 30 E.G.C.S. 89; (2005)
102(32) L.S.G. 32; (2005) 149 S.J.L.B. 923; [2005] N.P.C. 98; *Times*,
September 29, 2005, CA (Civ Div); reversing [2004] EWHC 2940; [2005]
S.T.C. 171; [2005] 2 P. & C.R. 1; [2005] 1 E.G.L.R. 26; [2005] 11 E.G. 182;
[2004] S.T.I. 2375; [2004] N.P.C. 168; *Times*, November 15, 2004, Ch D ..... *Digested*, 05/**2692**
Debenhams Retail Plc v. Sun Alliance & London Insurance Co Ltd see Debenhams
Retail Plc v. Sun Alliance & London Assurance Co Ltd
Debs, Re CO/1503/97, QBD. .... *Considered*, 04/**1438**:
Followed, 05/1491
Debtor Management Ltd, Re see Austintel Ltd, Re
Debtor (No.1 of 1987), Re [1989] 1 W.L.R. 271; [1989] 2 All E.R. 46; (1989) 86(16) L.S.G.
35; (1989) 133 S.J. 290, CA (Civ Div); affirming [1988] 1 W.L.R. 419; [1988] 1 All
E.R. 959; (1988) 132 S.J. 375; *Independent*, October 19, 1987, Ch D .... *Digested*, 89/**176**:
Applied, 92/231, 05/2338: *Considered*, 88/199, 93/71, 93/230, 94/283,
94/287
Debtor (No.784 of 1991), Re [1992] Ch. 554; [1992] 3 W.L.R. 119; [1992] 3 All E.R. 376;
[1992] S.T.C. 549; 64 T.C. 612, Ch D .... *Digested*, 92/**230**:
Applied, 05/2343
Debtor (No.37 of 1976, Liverpool) Ex p. Taylor [1980] Ch. 565; [1980] 3 W.L.R. 345;
[1980] 1 All E.R. 129; 124 S.J. 645, Ch D .... *Digested*, 80/**145**:
Considered, 05/2285
Debtor (No.32/SD/1991) (No.1), Re [1993] 1 W.L.R. 314; [1993] 2 All E.R. 991, Ch D . *Digested*, 93/**237**:
Considered, 94/2624, 95/424, 05/2277
Debtor (No.97/SD/2003), Re; *sub nom* Di Palmer v. Daejan Properties Ltd; Di Palmer v.
Kensington Hall Gardens Ltd [2003] EWHC 2829; [2005] B.P.I.R. 288, Ch D . *Digested*, 05/**2337**
Decca Music Group Ltd v. Jagger HC 04 C00863, Ch D .... *Overruled*, 05/716

Dedman *v.* British Building & Engineering Appliances; *sub nom* British Building & Engineering Appliances *v.* Dedman [1974] 1 W.L.R. 171; [1974] 1 All E.R. 520; [1974] I.C.R. 53; [1973] I.R.L.R. 379; (1973) 16 K.I.R. 1; (1974) 9 I.T.R. 100; (1973) 117 S.J. 938, CA (Civ Div); affirming [1973] I.C.R. 82; (1973) 8 I.T.R. 130, NIRC. . . . . *Digested,* 74/**1316**:
Applied, 74/1318, 74/1320, 75/1182, 76/969, 77/1105, 77/1187, 78/1084, 78/1085, 79/868, 79/979, 79/982, 80/997, 82/1099: *Considered,* 78/997, 80/1022, 84/1238, 05/1336: *Distinguished,* 78/1082: *Followed,* 80/999

DeepVeinThrombosis and AirTravel Group Litigation, Re [2005] UKHL 72; [2005] 3 W.L.R. 1320; [2005] 2 C.L.C. 1083; (2005) 155 N.L.J. 1925; *Times,* December 12, 2005; *Independent,* December 13, 2005, HL; affirming [2003] EWCA Civ 1005; [2004] Q.B. 234; [2003] 3 W.L.R. 956; [2004] 1 All E.R. 445; [2004] 1 All E.R. (Comm) 459; [2004] 1 Lloyd's Rep. 316; [2003] 2 C.L.C. 884; [2003] P.I.Q.R. P35; (2004) 76 B.M.L.R. 38; (2003) 100(35) L.S.G. 34; (2003) 147 S.J.L.B. 869; *Times,* July 14, 2003; *Independent,* July 8, 2003, CA (Civ Div); affirming [2002] EWHC 2825; [2003] 1 All E.R. 935; [2003] 1 All E.R. (Comm) 418; (2003) 71 B.M.L.R. 82; *Times,* January 17, 2003, QBD . . . . *Digested,* 03/**231**

DEG-Deutsche Investitions- und Entwicklungsgesellschaft mbH *v.* Koshy (Preliminary Issues) [2004] EWHC 2896; [2005] 1 W.L.R. 2434; (2005) 102(4) L.S.G. 31; *Times,* January 7, 2005, Ch D . . . . *Digested,* 05/**380**

Degirmenci *v.* Secretary of State for the Home Department [2004] EWCA Civ 1553; [2005] Imm. A.R. 66, CA (Civ Div) . . . . *Digested,* 05/**2182**

Degnan *v.* Redcar and Cleveland BC see Newcastle uponTyne City Council *v.* Allan

Degnan *v.* Redcar and Cleveland BC see Redcar and Cleveland BC *v.* Degnan

Degussa-Huls AG *v.* Comptroller-General of Patents [2004] EWHC 3213; [2005] R.P.C. 29; (2005) 28(3) I.P.D. 28018, Ch D (Patents Ct) . . . . *Digested,* 05/**2481**

Dehal *v.* Crown Prosecution Service [2005] EWHC 2154; (2005) 169 J.P. 581, QBD (Admin)

Dehaney *v.* Brent Mind see De Haney *v.* Brent MIND

Del Latte *v.* Netherlands (44760/98) (2005) 41 E.H.R.R. 12, ECHR . . . . *Digested,* 05/**2090**

Del Monte Foods Ltd *v.* Mundon [1980] I.C.R. 694; [1980] I.R.L.R. 224, EAT . . . . *Digested,* 81/**962**:
Applied, 05/1193

Delahaye *v.* Ministre de la Fonction Publique et de la Reforme Administrative (C425/02); *sub nom* Boor (nee Delahaye) *v.* Ministre de la Fonction Publique et de la Reforme Administrative (C425/02) [2005] All E.R. (EC) 575; [2004] E.C.R. I-10823; [2005] C.E.C. 592; [2005] I.R.L.R. 61, ECJ (2nd Chamber) . . . . *Digested,* 05/**1315**

Delaney *v.* Staples (t/a De Montfort Recruitment) [1992] 1 A.C. 687; [1992] 2 W.L.R. 451; [1992] 1 All E.R. 944; [1992] I.C.R. 483; [1992] I.R.L.R. 191; (1992) 142 N.L.J. 384; *Times,* March 16, 1992; *Independent,* March 13, 1992, HL; affirming [1991] 2 Q.B. 47; [1991] 2 W.L.R. 627; [1991] 1 All E.R. 609; [1991] I.C.R. 331; [1991] I.R.L.R. 112; (1991) 141 N.L.J. 581, CA (Civ Div); reversing in part [1990] I.C.R. 364; [1990] I.R.L.R. 86; (1990) 87(10) L.S.G. 35, EAT. . . . . *Digested,* 92/**2028**:
Applied, 95/1981, 95/2040, 97/2294, 98/2208, 98/2245, 04/1267, 05/2262, 05/4093: *Considered,* 00/2247, 01/5274: *Distinguished,* 96/2675, 98/5827:
Followed, 99/2017: *Not followed,* 90/1985, 91/1709

Deletenumber Ltd *v.* Compass Services UK & Ireland Ltd see Chancebutton Ltd *v.* Compass Services UK & Ireland Ltd

Deloitte & Touche LLP *v.* Dickinson see Deloitte & Touche LLP *v.* Dickson

Deloitte & Touche LLP *v.* Dickson; *sub nom* Deloitte & Touche LLP *v.* Dickinson [2005] EWHC 721; [2005] A.C.D. 103, Ch D

Deluni Mobile Ltd *v.* Revenue and Customs Commissioners [2005] S.T.I. 2036, V&DTr (Manchester)

Deman *v.* Association of University Teachers (AUT) [2003] EWCA Civ 329; (2003) 100(20) L.S.G. 27, CA (Civ Div); reversing EAT/746/99, EAT . . . . *Followed,* 05/**1291**

Deman *v.* Lord Chancellor's Department see R. (on the application of Deman) *v.* Lord Chancellor's Department

Demarco *v.* Bulley Davey (A Firm); *sub nom* DeMarco *v.* Perkins; A2 2005 1297, CA (Civ Div); reversing in part [2005] EWHC 1461; [2005] B.P.I.R. 1118, QBD. . . . . . *Digested,* 05/**960**

DeMarco *v.* Perkins see Demarco *v.* Bulley Davey (A Firm)

Demco Investments & Commercial SA *v.* SE Banken Forsakring Holding AB [2005] EWHC 1398; [2005] 2 Lloyd's Rep. 650, QBD (Comm)

Demibourne Ltd *v.* Revenue and Customs Commissioners [2005] S.T.C. (S.C.D.) 667, Sp Comm

Demirel *v.* Stadt Schwabisch Gmund (12/86) [1987] E.C.R. 3719; [1989] 1 C.M.L.R. 421, ECJ. . . . . *Digested,* 90/**2040**:
Applied, 96/3277: *Considered,* 96/3292, 05/1377: *Followed,* 90/2151, 91/1996, 00/2380, 02/1554

DEMON ALE Trade Mark [2000] R.P.C. 345, App Person . . . . *Digested,* 00/**3713**:
Applied, 01/4062: *Followed,* 05/2575

Demon Internet Ltd *v.* Young (Inspector of Taxes) [2005] S.T.C. (S.C.D.) 233; [2005] S.T.I. 108, Sp Comm. . . . . *Digested,* 05/**4102**

Den Norske Bank ASA *v.* Acemex Management Co Ltd (The Tropical Reefer) [2003] EWCA Civ 1559; [2004] 1 All E.R. (Comm) 904; [2004] 1 Lloyd's Rep. 1; [2005] 1 B.C.L.C. 274; [2003] 2 C.L.C. 910; *Independent*, November 11, 2003, CA (Civ Div); affirming [2003] EWHC 326; [2003] 2 All E.R. (Comm) 318, QBD (Comm) . . . . *Digested*, 04/**3526**

Dendron GmbH *v.* University of California (Parallel Proceedings: Use of Evidence) [2004] EWHC 589; [2005] 1 W.L.R. 200; [2004] I.L.Pr. 35; [2004] F.S.R. 42; (2004) 27(6) I.P.D. 27063; *Times*, May 24, 2004, Ch D (Patents Ct) . . . . *Digested*, 04/**258**

Denfleet International Ltd *v.* NHS Purchasing and Supply Agency [2005] EWHC 55; [2005] Eu. L.R. 526, QBD (Admin) . . . . *Digested*, 05/**3353**

Denham *v.* Midland Employers Mutual Assurance [1955] 2 Q.B. 437; [1955] 3 W.L.R. 84; [1955] 2 All E.R. 561; [1955] 1 Lloyd's Rep. 467; 99 S.J. 417, CA; affirming [1955] 1 Lloyd's Rep. 245, QBD. . . . . *Digested*, 55/**986**:
Considered, 05/2890: *Distinguished*, 57/2429

Denkavit Nederland BV *v.* Commission of the European Communities (T20/99) [2000] E.C.R. II-3011; [2000] 3 C.M.L.R. 1014, CFI (1st Chamber) . . . . *Digested*, 01/**2502**:
Applied, 05/1425

Denley's Trust Deed, Re; *sub nom* Holman *v.* HH Martyn & Co [1969] 1 Ch. 373; [1968] 3 W.L.R. 457; [1968] 3 All E.R. 65; 112 S.J. 673, Ch D . . . . *Digested*, 68/**3586**:
Applied, 76/2499, 01/5501: *Considered*, 85/2024, 86/2804:
Distinguished, 05/4310

Dennison *v.* Krasner see Krasner *v.* Dennison

Denton *v.* Denton [2004] EWHC 1308; [2004] 2 F.L.R. 594; [2005] Fam. Law 353; *Times*, April 14, 2004, Fam Div . . . . *Digested*, 04/**296**

Denuit *v.* Transorient - Mosaique Voyages & Culture SA (C125/04) [2005] E.C.R. I-923; [2005] 1 C.M.L.R. 48, ECJ (4th Chamber) . . . . *Digested*, 05/**1478**

Department for Environment, Food and Rural Affairs *v.* Alford see Alford *v.* Secretary of State for the Environment, Food and Rural Affairs

Department for Environment, Food and Rural Affairs *v.* Feakins see Secretary of State for Environment, Food and Rural Affairs *v.* Feakins

Department for the Environment, Food and Rural Affairs *v.* Robertson see Robertson *v.* Department for the Environment, Food and Rural Affairs

Department for Work and Pensions *v.* Richards see R. *v.* Richards (Michael)

Department for Work and Pensions *v.* Webley see Webley *v.* Department for Work and Pensions

Department of Economic Policy and Development of the City of Moscow *v.* Bankers Trust Co; *sub nom* Moscow City Council *v.* Bankers Trust Co; Department of Economics, Policy and Development of the City of Moscow *v.* Bankers Trust Co [2004] EWCA Civ 314; [2005] Q.B. 207; [2004] 3 W.L.R. 533; [2004] 4 All E.R. 746; [2004] 2 All E.R. (Comm) 193; [2004] 2 Lloyd's Rep. 179; [2004] 1 C.L.C. 1099; [2004] B.L.R. 229; (2004) 148 S.J.L.B. 389, CA (Civ Div); reversing in part [2003] EWHC 1377; [2003] 1 W.L.R. 2885; *Times*, September 1, 2003, QBD (Comm) . . . . *Digested*, 04/**185**

Department of the Environment for Northern Ireland's Application for Judicial Review, Re [2005] N.I. 119, QBD (NI)

Deponiezweckverband Eiterkopfe *v.* Land Rheinland-Pfalz (C6/03) [2005] E.C.R. I-2753; [2005] 2 C.M.L.R. 52; [2005] Env. L.R. 37, ECJ (1st Chamber) . . . . *Digested*, 05/**1401**

DEPRENYL ANIMAL HEALTH/Use of deprenyl in dogs (T210/02) [2005] E.P.O.R.18, EPO (Technical Bd App) . . . . *Digested*, 05/**2454**

Derbyshire *v.* First Choice Holidays & Flights Ltd (Unreported, October 5, 2004), CC (Central London) [*Ex rel.* Matthew Chapman, Barrister, No.1 Serjeant's Inn, Fleet Street, London] . . . . *Digested*, 05/**1980**

Derbyshire *v.* St Helens MBC see St Helens MBC *v.* Derbyshire

Derbyshire CC *v.* Akrill [2005] EWCA Civ 308; (2005) 8 C.C.L. Rep. 173, CA (Civ Div) . . . . *Digested*, 05/**3951**

Derbyshire Waste Ltd *v.* Blewett see R. (on the application of Blewett) *v.* Derbyshire CC

Design Progression Ltd *v.* Thurloe Properties Ltd [2004] EWHC 324; [2005] 1 W.L.R. 1; [2004] 2 P. & C.R. 31; [2004] L. & T.R. 25; [2004] 1 E.G.L.R. 121; [2004] 10 E.G.C.S. 184; (2004) 101 (12) L.S.G. 36; *Times*, March 2, 2004, Ch D . . . . *Digested*, 04/**2510**

Designer Room Ltd, Re [2004] EWHC 720; [2005] 1 W.L.R. 1581; [2004] 3 All E.R. 679; [2004] B.C.C. 904, Ch D . . . . *Digested*, 04/**2112**

Designers Guild Ltd *v.* Russell Williams (Textiles) Ltd (t/a Washington DC) [2000] 1 W.L.R. 2416; [2001] 1 All E.R. 700; [2001] E.C.D.R. 10; [2001] F.S.R. 11; (2001) 98(3) L.S.G. 42; (2000) 144 S.J.L.B. 290; *Times*, November 28, 2000, HL; reversing [2000] F.S.R. 121; (1999) 22(7) I.P.D. 22067, CA (Civ Div); reversing [1998] F.S.R. 803; (1998) 21 (6) I.P.D. 21064, Ch D . . . . *Digested*, 01/**3859**:
Applied, 03/2508, 05/2427: *Considered*, 02/2776

Deutsche Krankenversicherung AG (DKV) *v.* Office for Harmonisation in the Internal Market (Trade Marks and Designs) (OHIM) (T359/99) [2001] E.C.R. II-1645; [2001] E.T.M.R. 81, CFI (2nd Chamber) . . . . *Digested*, 01/**4006**:
Applied, 05/2519

Deutsche Morgan Grenfell Group Plc v. Inland Revenue Commissioners; *sub nom* Inland Revenue Commissioners v. Deutsche Morgan Grenfell Group Plc [2005] EWCA Civ 78; [2005] 3 All E.R. 1025; [2005] S.T.C. 329; [2005] Eu. L.R. 553; [2005] B.T.C. 126; 7 I.T.L. Rep. 476; [2005] S.T.I. 194; (2005) 102(10) L.S.G. 30; [2005] N.P.C. 18; *Times*, February 15, 2005, CA (Civ Div); reversing in part [2003] EWHC 1779; [2003] 4 All E.R. 645; [2003] S.T.C. 1017; [2003] Eu. L.R. 838; [2003] B.T.C. 497; 5 I.T.L. Rep. 1067; [2003] S.T.I. 1269; (2003) 100(36) L.S.G. 41; (2003) 153 N.L.J. 1171; *Times*, July 30, 2003, Ch D . . . . *Digested*, 05/**4129**
　　　　　　　　　　　　　　　　　　　　　　　　　　　　　　Applied, 04/3173

Deutsche Post Euro Express GmbH v. Office for Harmonisation in the Internal Market (Trade Marks and Designs) (OHIM) (T334/03) [2005] C.E.C. 206, CFI (3rd Chamber) . . . . *Digested*, 05/2519

Deutsche SiSi-Werke GmbH & Co Betriebs KG v. Office for Harmonisation in the Internal Market (Trade Marks and Designs) (OHIM) (T146/02) [2004] E.C.R. II-447; [2004] E.T.M.R. 72, CFI (2nd Chamber) . . . . *Digested*, 05/2547

Deutsche Telekom AG v. E! Entertainment Television Inc (2005) 28(4) I.P.D. 28024, OHIM (2nd Bd App)

Deutscher Apothekerverband eV v. 0800 DocMorris NV (C322/01) [2003] E.C.R. I-14887; [2005] 1 C.M.L.R. 46; (2005) 81 B.M.L.R. 33, ECJ . . . . *Digested*, 05/50C

Deutscher Handballbund eV v. Kolpak (C438/00) [2003] E.C.R. I-4135; [2004] 2 C.M.L.R. 38, ECJ (5th Chamber) . . . . *Digested*, 05/146C

Devaseelan v. Secretary of State for the Home Department [2002] UKIAT 702; [2003] Imm. A.R. 1, IAT . . . . *Digested*, 04/**2013**
　　　　　　　　Applied, 02/2577, 04/2009: *Considered*, 04/2015, 05/2152

Devaynes v. Noble see Clayton's Case

Devon CC v. Clarke see Clark v. Devon CC

Dextra Accessories Ltd v. MacDonald (Inspector of Taxes); *sub nom* MacDonald (Inspector of Taxes) v. Dextra Accessories Ltd [2005] UKHL 47; [2005] 4 All E.R. 107; [2005] S.T.C. 1111; [2005] Pens. L.R. 395; 77 T.C. 146; [2005] B.T.C. 355; [2005] S.T.I. 1235; (2005) 102(29) L.S.G. 33; *Times*, July 11, 2005, HL; affirming [2004] EWCA Civ 22; [2004] S.T.C. 339; [2004] B.T.C. 88; [2004] S.T.I. 234; (2004) 101(9) L.S.G. 32; (2004) 148 S.J.L.B. 150; *Times*, February 3, 2004, CA (Civ Div); reversing [2003] EWHC 872; [2003] S.T.C. 749; [2003] B.T.C. 472; [2003] W.T.L.R. 675; (2003) 100(25) L.S.G. 47; *Times*, April 25, 2003, Ch D; affirming [2002] S.T.C. (S.C.D.) 413; [2003] W.T.L.R. 349; [2002] S.T.I. 1335, Sp Comm. . . . . *Digested*, 05/402C

DG/General authorisation (J9/99) [2004] E.P.O.R. 52, EPO (Legal Bd App) . . . . *Digested*, 05/2453

Dhaliwal (A Child), Re see Kaur v. Dhaliwal

Di Palmer v. Daejan Properties Ltd see Debtor (No.97/SD/2003), Re

Di Palmer v. Kensington Hall Gardens Ltd see Debtor (No.97/SD/2003), Re

Diaby v. Secretary of State for the Home Department [2005] EWCA Civ 651; (2005) 149 S.J.L.B. 769, CA (Civ Div)

Diagnostiko & Therapeftiko Kentro Athinon (Ygeia AE) v. Ypourgos Oikonomikon (C394/04) [2005] S.T.I. 1904, ECJ

Dial v. Trinidad and Tobago; Dottin v. Trinidad and Tobago [2005] UKPC 4; [2005] 1 W.L.R. 1660; (2005) 102(15) L.S.G. 32; *Times*, February 28, 2005, PC (Trin)

Dian AO v. Davis Frankel & Mead (A Firm) [2004] EWHC 2662; [2005] 1 W.L.R. 2951; [2005] 1 All E.R. 1074; [2005] 1 All E.R. (Comm) 482; [2005] C.P. Rep. 18, QBD (Comm) . . . . *Digested*, 05/**397**
　　　　　　　　　　　　　　　　　　　　　　　　　　　　　　Applied, 05/396

Dick v. Kendall Freeman; *sub nom* Vos (Deceased), Re [2005] W.T.L.R. 1619, Ch D (Bankruptcy Ct)

Dick Lexic Ltd's Community Trade Mark Application [2005] E.T.M.R. 99, OHIM (4th Bd App)

Dicker v. Scammell; *sub nom* Scammell v. Dicker [2005] EWCA Civ 405; [2005] 3 All E.R. 838; [2005] 3 E.G.L.R. 61; [2005] 42 E.G. 236; *Times*, April 27, 2005; *Independent*, April 19, 2005, CA (Civ Div); reversing [2003] EWHC 1601; [2003] N.P.C. 90, QBD . . . . *Digested*, 05/**338**

Dickie v. Cathay Pacific Airways Ltd; Crofts v. Cathay Pacific Airways Ltd; Veta Ltd v. Crofts; Sysdeco Ireland Ltd v. Sysdeco Northern Ireland Ltd; Expro Gulf Ltd v. Birnie; SSAFA Forces Help v. McClymont [2005] EWCA Civ 599; [2005] I.C.R. 1436; [2005] I.R.L.R. 624; *Times*, May 31, 2005, CA (Civ Div); reversing in part [2004] I.C.R. 1733, EAT . . . . *Digested*, 05/**132**

Dickins v. Inland Revenue [2004] EWHC 852; [2004] B.P.I.R. 718, Ch D . . . . *Digested*, 05/229C

Diennet v. France (18160/91) see Diennet v. France (A/315-B)

Diennet v. France (A/315-B); *sub nom* Diennet v. France (18160/91) (1996) 21 E.H.R.R. 554, ECHR (1993) 15 E.H.R.R. CD94, Eur Comm HR . . . . *Digested*, 96/**3151**
　　　　　　Applied, 98/3131, 98/3149: *Considered*, 05/2121: *Distinguished*, 98/3127

Dignity Funerals Ltd v. Bruce see Bruce v. Dignity Funerals Ltd

Dike v. Rickman [2005] EWHC 3071; *Times*, December 7, 2005, QBD

Dilexport Srl v. Amministrazione delle Finanze dello Stato (C343/96) [2000] All E.R. (EC) 600; [1999] E.C.R. I-579; [2000] 3 C.M.L.R. 791, ECJ (5th Chamber) . . . *Digested*, 00/**2406**
　　　　　　　　　　　　　　　　　　　　　　　　　　　　　Considered, 05/4387

Diplock v. Wintle see Ministry of Health v. Simpson

Diplock's Estate, Re see Ministry of Health *v.* Simpson

Direct Line Insurance Plc *v.* Khan [2001] EWCA Civ 1794; [2002] Lloyd's Rep. I.R. 364, CA (Civ Div); affirming HQ0005988, QBD . . . .   *Digested,* 02/**2739**:
Considered, 05/2359

Director General of Fair Trading *v.* First National Bank Plc [2001] UKHL 52; [2002] 1 A.C. 481; [2001] 3 W.L.R. 1297; [2002] 1 All E.R. 97; [2001] 2 All E.R. (Comm) 1000; [2002] 1 Lloyd's Rep. 489; [2002] E.C.C. 22; (2001) 151 N.L.J. 1610; *Times,* November 1, 2001; *Daily Telegraph,* October 30, 2001, HL; reversing [2000] Q.B. 672; [2000] 2 W.L.R. 1353; [2000] 2 All E.R. 759; [2000] 1 All E.R. (Comm) 371; [2000] Lloyd's Rep. Bank. 130; [2000] C.C.L.R. 31; (2000) 97(7) L.S.G. 39; *Times,* March 14, 2000, CA (Civ Div); reversing [2000] 1 W.L.R. 98; [2000] 1 All E.R. 240; [1999] Lloyd's Rep. Bank. 427; [2000] E.C.C. 169; (1999) 18 Tr. L.R. 245; *Times,* September 21, 1999 ; *Independent,* November 8, 1999 (C.S.), Ch D . . . .   *Digested,* 01/**910**:
Applied, 01/3832, 03/664, 04/618: *Considered,* 03/2456, 05/194:
Followed, 05/721

Director General of Fair Trading *v.* Proprietary Association of Great Britain; *sub nom* Medicaments and Related Classes of Goods (No.2), Re [2001] 1 W.L.R. 700; [2001] U.K.C.L.R. 550; [2001] I.C.R. 564; [2001] H.R.L.R. 17; [2001] U.K.H.R.R. 429; (2001) 3 L.G.L.R. 32; (2001) 98(7) L.S.G. 40; (2001) 151 N.L.J. 17; (2001) 145 S.J.L.B. 29; *Times,* February 2, 2001; *Independent,* January 12, 2001, CA (Civ Div); reversing (2001) 98(2) L.S.G. 41; (2000) 144 S.J.L.B. 289, Ch D (RPC) . . . .   *Digested,* 01/**14**:
Applied, 01/692, 01/856, 01/857, 02/1618, 02/1838, 03/642, 03/2217,
03/4604, 04/30, 04/2754, 05/647: *Considered,* 02/452:
Distinguished, 02/3100: *Followed,* 02/1105

Director of Buildings and Lands *v.* Shun Fung Ironworks Ltd [1995] 2 A.C. 111; [1995] 2 W.L.R. 404; [1995] 1 All E.R. 846; [1995] 1 E.G.L.R. 19; [1995] 19 E.G. 147; [1995] R.V.R. 124; [1995] E.G.C.S. 36; (1995) 145 N.L.J. 379; (1995) 139 S.J.L.B. 85; *Times,* February 27, 1995, PC (HK) . . . .   *Digested,* 95/**664**:
Applied, 05/3251: *Disapproved,* 01/4662: *Followed,* 98/231

Director of the Assets Recovery Agency *v.* Creaven; *sub nom* R. (on the application of the Director of the Assets Recovery Agency) *v.* Creaven; Creaven *v.* Director of the Assets Recovery Agency [2005] EWHC 2726; *Times,* November 16, 2005, QBD (Admin)

Director of the Assets Recovery Agency *v.* Singh [2005] EWCA Civ 580; [2005] 1 W.L.R. 3747; [2005] Crim. L.R. 665; *Times,* May 31, 2005; *Independent,* May 27, 2005, CA (Civ Div); affirming [2004] EWHC 2335; [2005] A.C.D. 36, QBD (Admin) . . . .   *Digested,* 05/**326**

Director of the Assets Recovery Agency *v.* Walsh see Walsh *v.* Director of the Assets Recovery Agency

DISCOVISION/Appealable decision (G5/91) [1993] E.P.O.R. 120, EPO (Enlarged Bd App)   *Considered,* 05/2453

Disposal of Nuclear Military Reactor, Re (C61/03) see Commission of the European Communities *v.* United Kingdom (C61/03)

Distribution of Shopping Vouchers, Re (I ZR 8/01) [2005] E.C.C. 29, BGH (Ger)

Dixon *v.* Clement Jones Solicitors [2004] EWCA Civ 1005; [2005] P.N.L.R. 6; (2004) 148 S.J.L.B. 878; *Times,* August 2, 2004, CA (Civ Div); affirming [2004] EWHC 379, QBD . . . .   *Digested,* 04/**913**

Dixon *v.* Revenue and Customs Commissioners [2005] S.T.I. 2001, Sp Comm

DJ&C Withers (Farms) Ltd *v.* Ambic Equipment Ltd see English *v.* Emery Reimbold & Strick Ltd

Djavit An *v.* Turkey (20652/92) (2005) 40 E.H.R.R. 45, ECHR . . . .   *Digested,* 05/**2038**
Followed, 05/2215

DK *v.* Secretary of State for the Home Department [2003] UKIAT 153, IAT . . . .   *Followed,* 05/2215

DKV Deutsche Krankenversicherung AG *v.* Office for Harmonisation in the Internal Market (Trade Marks and Designs) (OHIM) (C104/00 P); *sub nom* DKV Deutsche Krankenversicherung AG *v.* Office for Harmonisation in the Internal Market (Trade Marks and Designs) (OHIM) (T19/99) [2002] E.C.R. I-7561; [2003] E.T.M.R. 20, ECJ (5th Chamber); affirming [2000] All E.R. (EC) 193; [2000] E.C.R. II-1; [2000] 1 C.M.L.R. 508; [2000] C.E.C. 102; [2000] E.T.M.R. 271, CFI (4th Chamber) . . . .   *Digested,* 03/**2610**:
Followed, 05/2518

DM (Proportionality: Article 8: Croatia CG), Re see M *v.* Secretary of State for the Home Department

DN *v.* Greenwich LBC [2004] EWCA Civ 1659; [2005] 1 F.C.R. 112; [2005] B.L.G.R. 597; [2005] E.L.R. 133; (2005) 149 S.J.L.B. 25; *Times,* December 23, 2004, CA (Civ Div); affirming [2004] EWHC 3322, QBD . . . .   *Digested,* 05/**1042**:
Considered, 05/2854

Do *v.* Immigration Appeal Tribunal see R. (on the application of Ullah) *v.* Special Adjudicator

Do *v.* Secretary of State for the Home Department see R. (on the application of Ullah) *v.* Special Adjudicator

Dobryden *v.* Wagner; *sub nom* Tkaczuk (Deceased), Re (2004-05) 7 I.T.E.L.R. 496, Sup Ct (SAus) (Sgl judge) . . . .   *Digested,* 05/**3977**

Dobson v. Hastings [1992] Ch. 394; [1992] 2 W.L.R. 414; [1992] 2 All E.R. 94; (1992) 89(8) L.S.G. 27; (1991) 141 N.L.J. 1625; *Times,* November 18, 1991; *Independent,* November 12, 1991; *Guardian,* November 13, 1991, Ch D . . . . *Digested,* 92/**3410**: *Considered,* 05/397

Dodds v. Walker [1981] 1 W.L.R. 1027; [1981] 2 All E.R. 609; (1981) 42 P. & C.R. 131; 125 S.J. 463, HL; affirming [1980] 1 W.L.R. 1061; [1980] 2 All E.R. 507; (1980) 40 P. & C.R. 487; (1980) 255 E.G. 53; 124 S.J. 575, CA (Civ Div) . . . . *Digested,* 81/**1518**: *Applied,* 85/1847, 05/892: *Considered,* 04/4594: *Distinguished,* 05/5214: *Followed,* 04/440

Dodl v. Tiroler Gebietskrankenkasse (C543/03) [2005] 3 C.M.L.R. 41, ECJ

Doerga v. Netherlands (50210/99) (2005) 41 E.H.R.R. 4, ECHR . . . . *Digested,* 05/**2125**

Dogan v. Semali Investments Ltd [2005] EWCA Civ 1036; [2005] 3 E.G.L.R. 51; [2005] 50 E.G. 92, CA (Civ Div)

Dogan v. Sicherheitsdirektion fur das Bundesland Vorarlberg (C383/03) [2005] 3 C.M.L.R. 45, ECJ (5th Chamber)

Dogan v. Turkey (8803/02) (2005) 41 E.H.R.R. 15, ECHR

Doheny v. New India Assurance Co Ltd [2004] EWCA Civ 1705; [2005] 1 All E.R. (Comm) 382; [2005] Lloyd's Rep. I.R. 251, CA (Civ Div); affirming (Unreported, May 21, 2004), QBD . . . . *Digested,* 05/**2365**

Dole Dried Fruit & Nut Co v. Trustin Kerwood Ltd [1990] 2 Lloyd's Rep. 309; *Times,* June 1, 1990; *Independent,* May 22, 1990; *Lloyd's List,* July 13, 1990, CA (Civ Div) . . . . *Digested,* 91/**2965**: *Applied,* 01/941: *Considered,* 99/410, 05/388

Don Pasquale v. Customs and Excise Commissioners [1990] 1 W.L.R. 1108; [1990] S.T.C. 556; [1990] C.O.D. 481; [1990] S.T.I. 471, CA (Civ Div); affirming [1990] S.T.C. 206; *Times,* December 8, 1989; *Independent,* January 15, 1990 (C.S.), QBD . . . . *Digested,* 91/**3632**: *Applied,* 94/4558, 94/4563: *Cited,* 95/5027: *Considered,* 05/4340: *Distinguished,* 95/5024: *Referred to,* 95/5077

Doncaster BC v. Secretary of State for the Environment, Transport and the Regions see Doncaster MBC v. Secretary of State for the Environment, Transport and the Regions

Doncaster MBC v. Secretary of State for the Environment, Transport and the Regions; *sub nom* Doncaster BC v. Secretary of State for the Environment, Transport and the Regions [2002] EWHC 808; [2002] J.P.L. 1509; [2002] 16 E.G.C.S. 181, QBD (Admin) . . . . *Digested,* 03/**3391**: *Considered,* 03/3424, 05/3264

Donohue v. Armco Inc [2001] UKHL 64; [2002] 1 All E.R. 749; [2002] 1 All E.R. (Comm) 97; [2002] 1 Lloyd's Rep. 425; [2002] C.L.C. 440, HL; reversing [2000] 1 All E.R. (Comm) 641; [2000] 1 Lloyd's Rep. 579; [2000] C.L.C. 1090; [2001] I.L.Pr. 48, CA (Civ Div); reversing [2000] 1 All E.R. (Comm) 425; [1999] 2 Lloyd's Rep. 649; [1999] C.L.C. 1748; [2000] I.L.Pr. 321, QBD (Comm) . . . . *Digested,* 02/**643**: *Applied,* 04/193, 05/2406: *Considered,* 03/593, 05/625, 05/2371: *Distinguished,* 04/2344

Donovan v. Laing Wharton and Down Construction Syndicate Ltd [1893] 1 Q.B. 629, CA . . . . *Considered,* 05/2890

Doodes v. Gotham see Gotham v. Doodes

Doolan v. United Kingdom (30678/96) see Wilson v. United Kingdom (30668/96)

Dore v. Aon Training Ltd (formerly Totalamber Plc); *sub nom* Aon Training Ltd (formerly Totalamber Plc) v. Dore [2005] EWCA Civ 411; [2005] I.R.L.R. 891, CA (Civ Div); reversing UKEAT/0974/03/DM, EAT . . . . *Digested,* 05/**1321**: *Considered,* 05/1231

Doree v. First Choice Holidays & Flights Ltd (Unreported, January 12, 2005), CC (Redditch) [*Ex rel.* Ian Miller, Barrister, No.1 Serjeants' Inn, Fleet Street, London]. *Digested,* 05/**3216**

Dorfman v. Customs and Excise Commissioners [2005] S.T.I. 120, V&DTr

Dorgan v. Home Office see Anderton v. Clwyd CC

Dornoch Ltd v. Mauritius Union Assurance Co Ltd A3/2005/2499, CA (Civ Div); affirming [2005] EWHC 1887; (2005) 102(35) L.S.G. 42, QBD (Comm)

Dornoch Ltd v. Royal & Sun Alliance Insurance Plc see Royal & Sun Alliance Insurance Plc v. Dornoch Ltd

Dorr v. Sicherheitsdirektion fur das Bundesland Karnten (C136/03); Unal v. Sicherheitsdirektion fur das Bundesland Vorarlberg (C136/03) [2005] 3 C.M.L.R. 11, ECJ (3rd Chamber)

Doshi v. Andrew (Inspector of Taxes) [2005] S.T.C. (S.C.D.) 427; [2005] S.T.I. 868, Sp Comm . . . . *Digested,* 05/**4098**

Doshi v. Andrew (Inspector of Taxes) (Addendum: Determination of Figures) [2005] S.T.C. (S.C.D.) 680, SS Comm

Dosoruth v. Mauritius [2004] UKPC 51; [2005] Crim. L.R. 474, PC (Mau)

Dottin v. Trinidad and Tobago see Dial v. Trinidad and Tobago

Double Quick Supplyline Ltd v. Office of Fair Trading (Application for Remittal: Defence Material) [2005] CAT 10; [2005] Comp. A.R. 892, CAT

Double Quick Supplyline Ltd v. Office of Fair Trading (Provisional Defence: New Evidence) [2005] CAT 6; [2005] Comp. A.R. 890, CAT

Douglas *v.* Hello! Ltd (No.6); *sub nom* Douglas *v.* Hello! Ltd (Trial Action: Breach of Confidence) (No.3) [2005] EWCA Civ 595; [2005] 3 W.L.R. 881; [2005] 4 All E.R. 128; [2005] E.M.L.R. 28; [2005] 2 F.C.R. 487; [2005] H.R.L.R. 27; (2005) 28(8) I.P.D. 28057; (2005) 155 N.L.J. 828; *Times,* May 24, 2005; *Independent,* May 26, 2005, CA (Civ Div); reversing in part [2003] EWHC 786; [2003] 3 All E.R. 996; [2003] E.M.L.R. 31; (2003) 153 N.L.J. 595; *Independent,* June 16, 2003 (C.S), Ch D .... *Digested,* 05/**2812**:
Applied, 03/1217, 05/4188: *Approved,* 04/1391

Douglas *v.* Hello! Ltd (No.8) [2003] EWHC 2629; [2004] E.M.L.R. 2, Ch D .... *Overruled in part,* 05/2812

Douglas *v.* Hello! Ltd (Trial Action: Breach of Confidence) (No.3) see Douglas *v.* Hello! Ltd (No.6)

Douwe Egberts NV *v.* Westrom Pharma NV (C239/02) [2004] E.C.R. I-7007; [2005] 2 C.M.L.R. 55, ECJ (2nd Chamber)

Dow Jones & Co Inc *v.* Jameel see Jameel *v.* Dow Jones & Co Inc

Dowden *v.* Stack see Stack *v.* Dowden

Dowmunt-Iwaszkiewicz *v.* First Secretary of State [2004] EWHC 2537; [2005] Env. L.R. 19; [2004] N.P.C. 169, QBD (Admin)................. *Digested,* 05/**3296**

Downey *v.* Charles Evans Shopfitters Ltd see Grieves *v.* FT Everard & Sons Ltd

Dowson *v.* Solomon (1859) 1 Drew. & Sm. 1 .... *Considered,* 05/**3418**

Doyle *v.* Revenue and Customs Commissioners [2005] S.T.C. (S.C.D.) 775; [2005] S.T.I. 1650, Sp Comm

DP Anderson & Co Ltd *v.* Lieber Code Co [1917] 2 K.B. 469, KBD .... *Considered,* 05/**2427**:
Distinguished, 81/323, 81/326

DPP *v.* Allen see DPP *v.* O'Connor

DPP *v.* Allett see DPP *v.* O'Connor

DPP *v.* Baker [2004] EWHC 2782; (2005) 169 J.P. 140; (2005) 169 J.P.N. 78, QBD (Admin) .... *Digested,* 05/**734**

DPP *v.* Barker [2004] EWHC 2502; (2004) 168 J.P. 617; (2004) 168 J.P.N. 937, QBD (Admin) .... *Digested,* 05/**780**

DPP *v.* Brown (Andrew Earle); DPP *v.* Teixeira (Jose) [2001] EWHC Admin 931; (2002) 166 J.P. 1; [2002] R.T.R. 23; *Times,* December 3, 2001, QBD (Admin) .. *Digested,* 02/**733**:
Applied, 03/777: *Followed,* 02/873, 05/729

DPP *v.* Camplin see R. *v.* Camplin (Paul)

DPP *v.* Chapman see DPP *v.* O'Connor

DPP *v.* Collins [2005] EWHC 1308; [2005] 3 All E.R. 326; [2005] 2 Cr. App. R. 39; [2005] Crim. L.R. 794; (2005) 155 N.L.J. 1010, QBD (Admin) .... *Digested,* 05/**764**

DPP *v.* Connor see DPP *v.* O'Connor

DPP *v.* Dziurzynski [2002] EWHC 1380; (2002) 166 J.P. 545; [2002] A.C.D. 88; (2002) 166 J.P.N. 689; (2002) 99(35) L.S.G. 36; *Times,* July 8, 2002, QBD (Admin) .... *Digested,* 02/**798**:
Considered, 05/4199

DPP *v.* Evans [2004] EWHC 2785; (2005) 169 J.P. 237; (2005) 169 J.P.N. 319, QBD (Admin) .... *Digested,* 05/**3483**

DPP *v.* Everest; *sub nom* R. (on the application of DPP) *v.* Everest [2005] EWHC 1124; (2005) 169 J.P. 345; (2005) 169 J.P.N. 537, QBD (Admin) .... *Digested,* 05/**828**

DPP *v.* Gane (1991) 155 J.P. 846; [1991] Crim. L.R. 711; (1991) 155 J.P.N. 620, DC.... *Digested,* 92/**926**:
Applied, 05/905

DPP *v.* Glendinning; *sub nom* R. (on the application of DPP) *v.* Glendinning [2005] EWHC 2333; (2005) 169 J.P. 649; (2005) 169 J.P.N. 959, QBD (Admin)

DPP *v.* Hay [2005] EWHC 1395; (2005) 169 J.P. 429; (2005) 169 J.P.N. 699; *Times,* July 13, 2005, QBD (Admin) .... *Digested,* 05/**782**

DPP *v.* Humphrys (Bruce Edward); *sub nom* R. *v.* Humphrys (Bruce Edward) [1977] A.C. 1; [1976] 2 W.L.R. 857; [1976] 2 All E.R. 497; (1976) 63 Cr. App. R. 95; [1976] R.T.R. 339; [1977] Crim. L.R. 421; 120 S.J. 420, HL; reversing [1976] Q.B. 191; [1975] 3 W.L.R. 81; [1975] 2 All E.R. 1023; (1976) 62 Cr. App. R. 1; [1975] Crim. L.R. 708; 119 S.J. 473, CA (Crim Div) .... *Digested,* 76/**488**:
Applied, 82/511, 83/3098, 84/971, 85/485, 85/2126, 00/5485, 05/733:
Considered, 78/464, 81/1682, 83/2309, 94/655: *Distinguished,* 77/633:
Followed, 97/1107, 00/1106

DPP *v.* Hutchinson; *sub nom* R. *v.* Secretary of State for Defence Ex p. Parker; R. *v.* Secretary of State for Defence Ex p. Hayman; DPP *v.* Smith (Georgina) [1990] 2 A.C. 783; [1990] 3 W.L.R. 196; (1991) 155 J.P. 71; 89 L.G.R. 1; (1990) 2 Admin. L.R. 741; [1991] C.O.D. 4; (1990) 154 J.P.N. 674; (1990) 154 L.G. Rev. 872; (1990) 140 N.L.J. 1035; (1990) 134 S.J. 1041, HL; reversing [1989] Q.B. 583; [1989] 3 W.L.R. 281; [1989] 1 All E.R. 1060; (1989) 153 J.P. 453; 87 L.G.R. 347; [1989] Crim. L.R. 208; [1989] C.O.D. 251; (1989) 153 J.P.N. 631; (1989) 153 L.G. Rev. 609; (1989) 133 S.J. 946; *Times,* October 25, 1988; *Independent,* October 21, 1988, QBD .... *Digested,* 91/**87**:
Applied, 90/2645, 91/2084, 97/1, 97/4101, 99/4359, 05/2502:
Considered, 05/59: *Referred to,* 95/870

DPP *v.* Jackson see Hinds *v.* Queen, The

DPP v. M [2004] EWHC 1453; [2004] 1 W.L.R. 2758; [2005] Crim. L.R. 392; (2004)
148 S.J.L.B. 660; *Times*, July 23, 2004, QBD (Admin) . . . . *Digested*, 04/**771**:
Applied, 05/814
DPP v. Mukandiwa [2005] EWHC 2977; *Times*, October 31, 2005, QBD (Admin)
DPP v. O'Connor; DPP v. Allett; DPP v. Connor; DPP v. Chapman; R. v. Chichester
Crown Court Ex p. Moss; DPP v. Allen (1992) 95 Cr. App. R. 135; (1992) 13 Cr.
App. R. (S.) 188; [1992] R.T.R. 66; [1992] C.O.D. 81; *Times*, July 11, 1991;
Independent, August 19, 1991 (C.S.), QBD . . . . *Digested*, 92/**1263**:
Considered, 05/3586
DPP v. P; *sub nom* R. v. P (A Father) [1991] 2 A.C. 447; [1991] 3 W.L.R. 161; [1991] 3
All E.R. 337; (1991) 93 Cr. App. R. 267; (1992) 156 J.P. 125; [1992] Crim. L.R.
41; (1991) 155 J.P.N. 572; (1991) 141 N.L.J. 928; (1991) 135 S.J.L.B. 69; *Times*,
July 1, 1991; *Independent*, June 28, 1991; *Guardian*, July 3, 1991, HL; reversing
(1991) 155 J.P. 65; [1991] Crim. L.R. 291; (1990) 154 J.P.N. 708; *Times*, August
28, 1990; *Independent*, September 20, 1990, CA (Civ Div) . . . . *Digested*, 91/**676**:
Applied, 92/780, 95/938, 95/939, 95/940, 03/278: *Considered*, 94/702,
95/1014, 96/1389, 96/1613, 97/1128, 98/908, 05/302: *Followed*, 92/664,
92/875
DPP v. Parker [2004] EWHC 1248; [2005] R.T.R. 16; *Times*, June 29, 2004, QBD . . . . . *Digested*, 04/**776**
DPP v. Sharma; *sub nom* R. (on the application of DPP) v. Sharma [2005] EWHC
879; [2005] R.T.R. 27, QBD (Admin) . . . . *Digested*, 05/**3586**
DPP v. Smith (Georgina) see DPP v. Hutchinson
DPP v. Stonehouse [1978] A.C. 55; [1977] 3 W.L.R. 143; [1977] 2 All E.R. 909;
(1977) 65 Cr. App. R. 192; [1977] Crim. L.R. 544; 121 S.J. 491, HL. . . . . *Digested*, 77/**1450**:
Applied, 84/511, 85/896, 87/761, 89/804, 05/902: *Considered*, 80/599,
83/731, 84/679, 86/506, 87/808, 89/686, 90/947, 90/1068, 91/774,
91/1743, 92/770, 92/1041, 93/923, 95/1332, 97/1336:
Distinguished, 88/775, 89/817, 90/1086: *Followed*, 89/775, 90/917:
Not followed, 86/930, 87/759, 90/1069
DPP v. Taylor [2004] EWHC 1554; [2005] A.C.D. 23, QBD (Admin)
DPP v. Teixeira (Jose) see DPP v. Brown (Andrew Earle)
DR v. Secretary of State for the Home Department; *sub nom* DR (ECO: Post Decision
Evidence: Morocco), Re [2005] UKIAT 38; [2005] Imm. A.R. 205; [2005]
I.N.L.R. 117, IAT . . . . *Digested*, 05/**2212**
DR (ECO: Post Decision Evidence: Morocco), Re see DR v. Secretary of State for the
Home Department
Dragon Futures Ltd v. Revenue and Customs Commissioners (Stay of Appeal) [2005]
EWHC 2534; [2005] S.T.I. 1718, Ch D
Drake v. Whipp [1996] 1 F.L.R. 826; [1996] 2 F.C.R. 296; (1996) 28 H.L.R. 531;
[1995] N.P.C. 188; (1996) 71 P. & C.R. D32; *Times*, December 19, 1995, CA (Civ
Div) . . . . *Digested*, 96/**5780**:
Applied, 05/987
Drake Insurance Plc v. MacDonald; *sub nom* Drake Insurance Plc v. McDonald [2005]
EWHC 3287; [2005] Pens. L.R. 401, Ch D
Drake Insurance Plc v. McDonald see Drake Insurance Plc v. MacDonald
Draon v. France (1513/03) [2005] 3 F.C.R. 409, ECHR (Grand Chamber)
Dresdner Kleinwort Wasserstein Ltd v. Adebayo [2005] EWCA Civ 991, CA (Civ Div);
affirming [2005] I.R.L.R. 514, EAT
Dresser UK Ltd v. Falcongate Freight Management Ltd (The Duke of Yare) [1992] Q.B.
502; [1992] 2 W.L.R. 319; [1992] 2 All E.R. 450; [1991] 2 Lloyd's Rep. 557;
[1992] I.L.Pr. 164; (1991) 135 S.J.L.B. 126; *Times*, August 8, 1991; *Financial
Times*, August 2, 1991, CA (Civ Div) . . . . *Digested*, 92/**3534**:
Applied, 94/482, 94/487, 01/830: *Considered*, 96/920, 03/595, 05/468:
Distinguished, 92/3401, 93/3127
Drew v. Daniel; *sub nom* Daniel v. Drew [2005] EWCA Civ 507; [2005] 2 F.C.R. 365;
[2005] W.T.L.R. 807; [2005] 2 P. & C.R. DG14; *Times*, May 18, 2005, CA (Civ
Div) . . . . *Digested*, 05/**4291**
Drew v. McHale (Unreported, January 4, 2005), CC (Bristol) [*Ex rel.* Stephen Garner,
Barrister, No.8 Chambers, Fountain Court, Steelhouse Lane, Birmingham.] . . . . . *Digested*, 05/**3139**
Driskel v. Peninsula Business Services Ltd [2000] I.R.L.R. 151, EAT . . . . *Digested*, 00/**2208**:
Considered, 05/1305
Drivertime Recruitment Ltd, Re; DST Ltd, Re [2004] EWHC 1637; [2005] 1 B.C.L.C. 411,
Ch D (Companies Ct) . . . . *Digested*, 05/**2305**
DS v. Gloucestershire CC see S v. Gloucestershire CC
DSM IP/Yeast formulation (T137/00) [2005] E.P.O.R. 41, EPO (Technical Bd App)
DSM Kunststoffen BV v. Commission of the European Communities (C244/99 P) see
Limburgse Vinyl Maatschappij NV (LVM) v. Commission of the European
Communities (C238/99 P)
DST Ltd, Re see Drivertime Recruitment Ltd, Re
DU PONT Trade Mark see ST Dupont v. El Du Pont de Nemours & Co
Dubai Aluminium Co Ltd v. Al-Alawi [1999] 1 W.L.R. 1964; [1999] 1 All E.R. 703;
[1999] 1 All E.R. (Comm.) 1; [1999] 1 Lloyd's Rep. 478; *Times*, January 6, 1999;
Independent, December 21, 1998 (C.S.), QBD (Comm) . . . . *Digested*, 99/**338**:
Applied, 01/398: *Approved*, 05/294

Dubai Aluminium Co Ltd v. Amhurst see Dubai Aluminium Co Ltd v. Salaam
Dubai Aluminium Co Ltd v. Amhurst Brown Martin & Nicholson see Dubai Aluminium
   Co Ltd v. Salaam
Dubai Aluminium Co Ltd v. Salaam; Dubai Aluminium Co Ltd v. Amhurst; Dubai
   Aluminium Co Ltd v. Amhurst Brown Martin & Nicholson [2002] UKHL 48;
   [2003] 2 A.C. 366; [2002] 3 W.L.R. 1913; [2003] 1 All E.R. 97; [2003] 2 All
   E.R. (Comm) 451; [2003] 1 Lloyd's Rep. 65; [2003] 1 B.C.L.C. 32; [2003] 1
   C.L.C. 1020; [2003] I.R.L.R. 608; [2003] W.T.L.R. 163; (2003) 100(7) L.S.G.
   36; (2002) 146 S.J.L.B. 280; *Times*, December 6, 2002; *Independent*,
   December 10, 2002, HL; reversing [2001] Q.B. 113; [2000] 3 W.L.R. 910;
   [2000] 2 Lloyd's Rep. 168; [2000] Lloyd's Rep. P.N. 497; [2000] P.N.L.R. 578;
   Times, April 21, 2000, CA (Civ Div); reversing [1999] 1 Lloyd's Rep. 415;
   (1998) 148 N.L.J. 1301; *Times*, September 4, 1998, QBD (Comm) . . . .   *Digested*, 03/**3046**:
                       Applied, 01/4267, 03/3033, 03/3045, 05/4199, 05/4200:
                                       Distinguished, 03/3613
Dudda v. Finanzamt Bergisch Gladbach (C327/94) [1996] S.T.C. 1290; [1996] E.C.R.
   I-4595; [1996] 3 C.M.L.R. 1063; [1996] C.E.C. 878; [1997] B.V.C. 3, ECJ (6th
   Chamber) . . . .   *Applied*, 05/**4402**:
                                         Followed, 05/**4405**
Dudgeon v. United Kingdom (1982) 4 E.H.R.R. 153, ECHR . . . .   *Considered*, 05/**2102**
Dudson v. Secretary of State see R. (on the application of Smith) v. Secretary of State
   for the Home Department
Duff v. Minister for Agriculture and Food (C63/93) [1996] E.C.R. I-569, ECJ . . . .   *Digested*, 96/**188**:
                                         Applied, 05/**152**
Duffield v. Duffield 4 E.R. 1334; (1829) 3 Bli. N.S. 260, HL . . . .   *Considered*, 05/**3972**
Duggins v. Tipper see Ferrotech Ltd, Re
Duhur-Johnson v. Duhur-Johnson [2005] 2 F.L.R. 1042; *Times*, May 18, 2005, Fam
   Div
Duke of Brunswick v. Harmer Unreported . . . .   *Considered*, 05/**974**
Dumford Trading AG v. OAO Atlantrybflot [2005] EWCA Civ 24; [2005] 1 Lloyd's Rep.
   289, CA (Civ Div); reversing [2004] EWHC 1099; [2004] 2 Lloyd's Rep. 157,
   QBD (Comm) . . . .   *Digested*, 05/**710**
Duncan v. British Coal Corp see White v. Chief Constable of South Yorkshire
Duncan v. Epping Forest DC [2004] R.V.R. 275, Lands Tr . . . .   *Digested*, 05/**3318**
Duncan v. Epping Forest DC (Preliminary Issues) [2004] R.V.R. 213, Lands Tr . . . .   *Digested*, 05/**3317**
Dunham v. Ashford Windows [2005] I.C.R. 1584; [2005] I.R.L.R. 608, EAT . . . .   *Digested*, 05/**1224**
Dunk v. George Waller & Son [1970] 2 Q.B. 163; [1970] 2 W.L.R. 1241; [1970] 2 All
   E.R. 630; 114 S.J. 356, CA (Civ Div) . . . .   *Digested*, 70/**894**:
                         Applied, 05/1219: *Distinguished*, 04/1180
Dunkley v. Queen, The; Robinson v. Queen, The [1995] 1 A.C. 419; [1994] 3 W.L.R.
   1124; [1995] 1 All E.R. 279; (1994) 91(41) L.S.G. 41; (1994) 138 S.J.L.B. 203;
   Independent, November 1, 1994, PC (Jam) . . . .   *Digested*, 95/**2634**:
                               Applied, 05/903: *Followed*, 99/3136
Dunn v. Ward see Hollins v. Russell
Dunnachie v. Kingston upon Hull City Council; *sub nom* Kingston Upon Hull City
   Council v. Dunnachie (No.1); Williams v. Southampton Institute; Dawson v.
   Stonham Housing Association [2004] UKHL 36; [2005] 1 A.C. 226; [2004] 3
   W.L.R. 310; [2004] 3 All E.R. 1011; [2004] I.C.R. 1052; [2004] I.R.L.R. 727;
   (2004) 101(33) L.S.G. 34; (2004) 154 N.L.J. 1156; (2004) 148 S.J.L.B. 909;
   Times, July 16, 2004; *Independent*, July 21, 2004, HL; reversing [2004] EWCA
   Civ 84; [2004] 2 All E.R. 501; [2004] I.C.R. 481; [2004] I.R.L.R. 287; (2004)
   101(10) L.S.G. 27; (2004) 154 N.L.J. 248; (2004) 148 S.J.L.B. 233; *Times*,
   February 26, 2004; *Independent*, February 18, 2004, CA (Civ Div); reversing
   [2003] I.C.R. 1294; [2003] I.R.L.R. 384; *Times*, June 9, 2003, EAT . . . .   *Digested*, 04/**1303**:
               Applied, 03/1337: *Considered*, 05/1322, 05/1331: *Followed*, 04/1307
Duomatic Ltd, Re [1969] 2 Ch. 365; [1969] 2 W.L.R. 114; [1969] 1 All E.R. 161; 112 S.J. 922,
   Ch D . . . .   *Digested*, 69/**412**:
            Applied, 73/324, 74/321, 80/268, 80/269, 99/607, 00/654, 01/748, 03/540,
                        04/472: *Considered*, 98/704, 02/556, 04/458, 05/470:
                                         Distinguished, 90/487
DUPLO/DUPLO (R 802/1999-1) (Unreported, June 5, 2000), OHIM (1st Bd App) . . . .   *Applied*, 04/**2387**:
                                         Followed, 05/**2520**
Dutton v. Bognor Regis Urban DC [1972] 1 Q.B. 373; [1972] 2 W.L.R. 299; [1972] 1
   All E.R. 462; [1972] 1 Lloyd's Rep. 227; 3 B.L.R. 11; 70 L.G.R. 57; (1971) 116 S.J.
   16; *Times*, December 18, 1971, CA (Civ Div); affirming [1971] 2 All E.R. 1003,
   QBD . . . .   *Digested*, 72/**2352**:
           Applied, 75/1961, 76/1862, 79/2570: *Considered*, 76/1874, 78/2067,
                    79/1866, 79/1887, 80/1878, 81/197, 88/2418, 88/3410, 05/2856:
          Doubted, 84/2300: *Explained*, 76/1873, 77/2030: *Followed*, 82/2133:
                       Not followed, 79/1862: *Overruled*, 90/3288, 91/2661
Dutton v. Law Society [2005] EWHC 125; *Times*, January 31, 2005, QBD (Admin) . . .   *Digested*, 05/**2731**
Dyer v. Customs and Excise Commissioners [2005] S.T.C. 715; 2005 S.L.T. 255;
   [2005] B.T.C. 5356; [2005] B.V.C. 387; [2005] S.T.I. 191; 2005 G.W.D. 3-32, IH
   (Ex Div) . . . .   *Digested*, 05/**5720**

Dyment *v.* Boyden [2004] EWCA Civ 1586; [2005] 1 W.L.R. 792; [2005] B.C.C. 79; [2005] 1 B.C.L.C. 163; [2005] 1 E.G.L.R. 19; [2005] 06 E.G. 142; (2004) 101(48) L.S.G. 25; (2004) 148 S.J.L.B. 1406; [2004] N.P.C. 176; *Times*, December 2, 2004, CA (Civ Div); affirming [2004] EWHC 350; [2004] B.C.C. 946; [2004] 2 B.C.L.C. 423, Ch D . . . . *Digested*, 05/**526**

Dymny *v.* Lambeth LBC see Kay *v.* Lambeth LBC

Dymocks Franchise Systems (NSW) Pty Ltd *v.* Todd (Costs) [2004] UKPC 39; [2004] 1 W.L.R. 2807; [2005] 4 All E.R. 195; [2005] 1 Costs L.R. 52; (2004) 154 N.L.J. 1325; (2004) 148 S.J.L.B. 971, PC (NZ) . . . . *Digested*, 04/**328**

Dyson *v.* Leeds City Council (No.2) see Fairchild *v.* Glenhaven Funeral Services Ltd (t/a GH Dovener & Son)

Dyson Appliances Ltd *v.* Hoover Ltd (Costs: Interim Payment); *sub nom* Dyson Ltd *v.* Hoover Ltd (Costs: Interim Payment) [2003] EWHC 624; [2004] 1 W.L.R. 1264; [2003] 2 All E.R. 1042; [2003] C.P. Rep. 45; (2003) 100(15) L.S.G. 25; *Times*, March 18, 2003, Ch D (Patents Ct) . . . . *Digested*, 03/**346**: *Distinguished*, 05/355

Dyson Ltd *v.* Hoover Ltd (Costs: Interim Payment) see Dyson Appliances Ltd *v.* Hoover Ltd (Costs: Interim Payment)

Dyson Ltd *v.* Qualtex (UK) Ltd A3/2005/0406, CA (Civ Div); affirming [2004] EWHC 2981; [2005] R.P.C. 19; (2005) 28(3) I.P.D. 28013, Ch D . . . . *Digested*, 05/**2589**

E *v.* Castro [2003] EWHC 2066; (2004) 80 B.M.L.R. 14, QBD. . . . . *Digested*, 05/**2839**

E *v.* Channel Four Television Corp [2005] EWHC 1144; [2005] E.M.L.R. 30; [2005] 2 F.L.R. 913; [2005] U.K.H.R.R. 789; [2005] Fam. Law 866, Fam Div

E *v.* DPP [2005] EWHC 147; (2005) 102(14) L.S.G. 26; *Times*, February 9, 2005, QBD (Admin) . . . . *Digested*, 05/**2102**

E *v.* Newham LBC; *sub nom* R. (on the application of E) *v.* Newham LBC [2003] EWCA Civ 9; [2003] B.L.G.R. 547; [2003] E.L.R. 286; (2003) 147 S.J.L.B. 113; *Independent*, January 29, 2003, CA (Civ Div) . . . . *Digested*, 03/**1123**: *Applied*, 05/1143

E *v.* Norway (A/181-A) (1994) 17 E.H.R.R. 30, ECHR . . . . *Digested*, 94/**2381**: *Considered*, 95/64, 96/1990, 05/2921

E *v.* Secretary of State for the Home Department; R *v.* Secretary of State for the Home Department [2004] EWCA Civ 49; [2004] Q.B. 1044; [2004] 2 W.L.R. 1351; [2004] I.N.L.R. 268; [2004] B.L.G.R. 463; (2004) 101(7) L.S.G. 35; (2004) 148 S.J.L.B. 180; *Times*, February 9, 2004; *Independent*, February 4, 2004, CA (Civ Div) . . . . *Digested*, 04/**2030**: *Applied*, 05/2208, 05/2213: *Followed*, 05/2215, 05/2224

E (A Child) *v.* Scunthorpe United FC Ltd (Unreported, October 4, 2004), CC (Scunthorpe) [*Ex rel.* Martin & Haigh, Solicitors, 12-18-Frances Street, Scunthorpe, North Lincolnshire] . . . . *Digested*, 05/**3214**

E (A Child) *v.* Walton (Unreported, February 10, 2004), CC (Wolverhampton) [*Ex rel.* Stephen Garner, Barrister, No.8 Chambers, Fountain Court, Steelhouse Lane, Birmingham.]. . . . . *Digested*, 05/**3116**

E (A Child) (Abduction: Rights of Custody), Re; *sub nom* E (A Child) (Custody: Foreign Judgments), Re [2005] EWHC 848; [2005] 2 F.L.R. 759; [2005] Fam. Law 688, Fam Div . . . . *Digested*, 05/**1542**

E (A Child) (Custody: Foreign Judgments), Re see E (A Child) (Abduction: Rights of Custody), Re

E (A Minor) *v.* Dorset CC (Appeal) see X (Minors) *v.* Bedfordshire CC

E (Abduction: Non Convention Country), Re see Osman *v.* Elasha

E (Alleged Patient), Re see Sheffield City Council *v.* E

E-Data Corp *v.* Corbis Corp see E-Data Corp *v.* Getty Images Inc

E-Data Corp *v.* Getty Images Inc; E-Data Corp *v.* Corbis Corp [2005] EWHC 1527; (2005) 28(7) I.P.D. 28054, PCC

E-Data Corp *v.* Getty Images Inc (Costs) (2005) 28(7) I.P.D. 28055, PCC

E-Data Corp *v.* Getty Images Inc (Interim Costs) (2005) 28(7) I.P.D. 28056, PCC

E-UK Controls Ltd's Licence of Right (Copyright) Application [1998] R.P.C. 833, PO . . *Digested*, 99/**3448**: *Applied*, 05/2436: *Considered*, 01/3854: *Referred to*, 00/3579

Eagerpath Ltd *v.* Edwards (Inspector of Taxes) [2001] S.T.C. 26; 73 T.C. 427; [2001] B.T.C. 12; [2000] S.T.I. 1737; (2001) 98(5) L.S.G. 37; *Times*, January 23, 2001, CA (Civ Div); affirming [1999] S.T.C. 771; [1999] B.T.C. 253; *Times*, May 21, 1999, Ch D . . . . *Digested*, 01/**5200**: *Considered*, 05/4062

Eagil Trust Co *v.* Pigott-Brown [1985] 3 All E.R. 119, CA (Civ Div) . . . . *Digested*, 85/**2728**: *Applied*, 88/183, 88/2288, 90/1992, 90/3802: *Considered*, 87/2898, 88/3442, 05/2213: *Followed*, 89/105

Eagle *v.* Chambers (No.2) [2004] EWCA Civ 1033; [2004] 1 W.L.R. 3081; [2005] 1 All E.R. 136; [2005] P.I.Q.R. Q2; [2004] Lloyd's Rep. Med. 413; (2005) 82 B.M.L.R. 22; (2004) 154 N.L.J. 1451; (2004) 148 S.J.L.B. 972; *Times*, August 30, 2004, CA (Civ Div); reversing in part [2003] EWHC 3135, QBD . . . . *Digested*, 04/**2848**

Eagle Star Insurance Co Ltd *v.* Games Video Co (GVC) SA (The Game Boy) [2004] EWHC 15; [2004] 1 All E.R. (Comm) 560; [2004] 1 Lloyd's Rep. 238; [2004] Lloyd's Rep. I.R. 867, QBD (Comm) .... *Digested,* 04/**2211**:
                             Referred to, 05/2387
Eagle Star Insurance Co Ltd *v.* Kausar see Kausar *v.* Eagle Star Insurance Co Ltd
Eagle Star Insurance Co Ltd *v.* Provincial Insurance [1994] 1 A.C. 130; [1993] 3 W.L.R. 257; [1993] 3 All E.R. 1; [1993] 2 Lloyd's Rep. 143; [1993] R.T.R. 328; (1993) 143 N.L.J. 920; (1993) 137 S.J.L.B. 143; *Times,* June 9, 1993, PC (Bah)........ *Digested,* 93/**2399**:
                       Applied, 04/2228: *Distinguished,* 05/2384
Ealing Community Transport Ltd *v.* Ealing LBC [1999] C.O.D. 492, CA (Civ Div) ...... *Applied,* 05/73
Ealing LBC *v.* Audit Commission see R. (on the application of Ealing LBC) *v.* Audit Commission
Ealing LBC *v.* Joymar International Ltd [2005] P.A.D. 49, Planning Inspector
Ealing LBC *v.* Richardson; *sub nom* Richardson *v.* Ealing LBC [2005] EWCA Civ 1798; *Times,* December 14, 2005, CA (Civ Div)
Ealing LBC *v.* Rihal see Rihal *v.* Ealing LBC
Ealing LBC *v.* Surdonja see Mohamed *v.* Hammersmith and Fulham LBC
Earl Cadogan *v.* 55/57 Cadogan Square Freehold Ltd see Arbib *v.* Earl Cadogan
Earl Cadogan *v.* Morris see Viscount Chelsea *v.* Morris
Earl Cadogan *v.* Moussaieff see Arbib *v.* Earl Cadogan
Earl Cadogan *v.* Search Guarantees Plc; *sub nom* Cadogan *v.* Search Guarantees Plc; Search Guarantees Ltd *v.* Earl Cadogan [2004] EWCA Civ 969; [2004] 1 W.L.R. 2768; [2005] 1 All E.R. 280; [2005] H.L.R. 4; [2005] L. & T.R. 1; [2004] 3 E.G.L.R. 55; [2004] 42 E.G. 162; [2004] 33 E.G.C.S. 71; (2004) 101 (35) L.S.G. 34; (2004) 148 S.J.L.B. 945; [2004] N.P.C. 129; *Times,* August 3, 2004; *Independent,* October 21, 2004, CA (Civ Div)........................ *Digested,* 04/**2490**
East Devon DC *v.* M Baker (Property Services) Ltd [2005] P.A.D. 68, Planning Inspector
East Midlands Aggregates Ltd *v.* Customs and Excise Commissioners; *sub nom* Customs and Excise Commissioners *v.* East Midlands Aggregates Ltd [2004] EWHC 856; [2004] S.T.C. 1582; [2005] 1 P. & C.R. 11; [2004] B.T.C. 8107; [2004] S.T.I. 1085; [2004] N.P.C. 66; *Times,* May 24, 2004, Ch D; affirming [2004] 2 P. & C.R. 1; [2003] V. & D.R. 460, V&DTr (Manchester) .... *Digested,* 04/**3684**
Eastaway *v.* United Kingdom (74976/01) (2005) 40 E.H.R.R. 17; *Times,* August 9, 2004, ECHR .... *Digested,* 05/**2093**
Eastern Bazaar *v.* Central London Commercial Estates see JH Edwards & Sons *v.* Central London Commercial Estates
Eastgate *v.* Oxfordshire CC (Unreported, May 5, 2004), CC (Reading) [*Ex rel.* Dr Peter Ellis, Barrister, Lamb Chambers, Lamb Building, Temple, London]............ *Digested,* 05/**1957**
Eastwood *v.* Magnox Electric Plc; McCabe *v.* Cornwall CC [2004] UKHL 35; [2005] 1 A.C. 503; [2004] 3 W.L.R. 322; [2004] 3 All E.R. 991; [2004] I.C.R. 1064; [2004] I.R.L.R. 733; (2004) 101 (32) L.S.G. 36; (2004) 154 N.L.J. 1155; (2004) 148 S.J.L.B. 909; *Times,* July 16, 2004; *Independent,* October 11, 2004 (C.S.), HL; reversing [2002] EWCA Civ 463; [2003] I.C.R. 520; [2002] I.R.L.R. 447; [2002] Emp. L.R. 795, CA (Civ Div) .... *Digested,* 04/**1183**:
            Considered, 03/1246: *Previous proceedings,* 03/1246
Eastwood *v.* Wright [2005] EWCA Civ 564; (2005) 84 B.M.L.R. 51, CA (Civ Div) .... *Digested,* 05/**2835**
Easy Travel Individual Enterprise *v.* Easy Travel [2005] E.T.M.R. 52, Protodikeio (Athens)
Easycar (UK) Ltd *v.* Office of Fair Trading (C336/03) [2005] All E.R. (EC) 834; [2005] E.C.R. I-1947; [2005] 2 C.M.L.R. 2; [2005] C.E.C. 577; *Times,* March 15, 2005, ECJ (1st Chamber) .... *Digested,* 05/**684**
Eaton Ltd *v.* King see King *v.* Eaton Ltd (No.2)
Ebbcliffe Ltd *v.* Customs and Excise Commissioners see Customs and Excise Commissioners *v.* Ebbcliff Ltd
EC-L *v.* DM (Child Abduction: Costs) [2005] EWHC 588; [2005] 4 Costs L.R. 576; [2005] 2 F.L.R. 772; [2005] Fam. Law 606; *Times,* May 10, 2005, Fam Div. .... *Digested,* 05/**1540**
Eclipse Blinds Ltd *v.* Wright 1993 S.L.T. 664, IH (Ex Div)...................... *Digested,* 93/**5272**:
                                Applied, 05/1232
ECM (Vehicle Delivery Services) Ltd *v.* Cox [1999] 4 All E.R. 669; [2000] 1 C.M.L.R. 224; [1999] I.C.R. 1162; [1999] I.R.L.R. 559, CA (Civ Div); affirming [1998] I.C.R. 631; [1998] I.R.L.R. 416; *Times,* June 10, 1998, EAT .... *Digested,* 99/**2133**:
    Applied, 01/2333, 02/1429: *Cited,* 01/2338: *Considered,* 05/1313:
           Distinguished, 03/1328: *Followed,* 00/2226
Eco Jet Ltd *v.* Selafa MJA [2005] B.C.C. 979, C d'A (Paris)
Eco Swiss China Time Ltd *v.* Benetton International NV (C126/97) [1999] 2 All E.R. (Comm) 44; [1999] E.C.R. I-3055; [1999] U.K.C.L.R. 183; [2000] 5 C.M.L.R. 816, ECJ... *Digested,* 99/**238**:
                                Applied, 05/1478
Eco-Energy (GB) Ltd *v.* First Secretary of State [2004] EWCA Civ 1566; [2005] 2 P. & C.R. 5; [2005] 2 P.L.R. 33; [2005] J.P.L. 1079; (2004) 148 S.J.L.B. 1368, CA (Civ Div)

Economides *v.* Commercial Union Assurance Co Plc [1998] Q.B. 587; [1997] 3
W.L.R. 1066; [1997] 3 All E.R. 636; [1997] C.L.C. 1169; [1998] Lloyd's Rep. I.R.
9; *Times*, June 27, 1997, CA (Civ Div) . . . . *Digested*, 97/**3137**:
Applied, 05/2400: *Considered*, 04/3257
Ecuador *v.* Occidental Exploration & Production Co; *sub nom* Occidental Exploration
& Production Co *v.* Ecuador [2005] EWCA Civ 1116; [2005] 2 All E.R. (Comm)
689; [2005] 2 Lloyd's Rep. 707; [2005] 2 C.L.C. 457; (2005) 102(37) L.S.G.
31; *Times*, September 23, 2005, CA (Civ Div); affirming [2005] EWHC 774;
[2005] 2 Lloyd's Rep. 240, QBD (Comm) . . . . *Digested*, 05/**212**
Edgar *v.* Edgar [1980] 1 W.L.R. 1410; [1980] 3 All E.R. 887; (1981) 2 F.L.R. 19; (1980)
11 Fam. Law 20; 124 S.J. 809; *Times*, July 24, 1980, CA (Civ Div) . . . . *Digested*, 80/**791**:
Applied, 91/1794, 95/2323, 95/2340, 95/2344, 96/2857: *Cited*, 04/1514:
Considered, 83/2622, 93/2824, 94/2166, 95/2336, 03/1580:
Distinguished, 83/1100, 96/2875, 97/2477, 99/4635: *Followed*, 83/1104,
84/1118, 05/1688: *Referred to*, 86/1098, 87/1750, 93/5228
Edgewater Motel Ltd *v.* Inland Revenue Commissioner [2004] UKPC 44; [2004] S.T.C.
1382; [2004] S.T.I. 2067; [2004] 33 E.G.C.S. 70, PC (NZ) . . . . *Digested*, 05/**4110**
Edinburgh City Council *v.* Secretary of State for Scotland; Revival Properties Ltd *v.*
Edinburgh City Council; Secretary of State for Scotland *v.* Revival Properties Ltd
[1997] 1 W.L.R. 1447; [1998] 1 All E.R. 174; 1998 S.C. (H.L.) 33; 1998 S.L.T.
120; 1997 S.C.L.R. 1112; [1997] 3 P.L.R. 71; [1998] J.P.L. 224; [1997] E.G.C.S.
140; (1997) 94(42) L.S.G. 31; (1997) 141 S.J.L.B. 228; [1997] N.P.C. 146; 1997
G.W.D. 33-1693; *Times*, October 31, 1997, HL; affirming in part 1996 S.C.L.R.
600, IH (2 Div) . . . . *Digested*, 97/**6350**:
Applied, 99/4178: *Considered*, 99/4218, 01/4743, 05/3295:
Followed, 97/4116, 99/6411
Edinburgh Leisure *v.* Customs and Excise Commissioners [2005] B.V.C. 2146; [2004]
V. & D.R. 394; [2004] S.T.I. 2577, V&DTr (Edinburgh)
Edinburgh Telford College *v.* Customs and Excise Commissioners; *sub nom* Edinburgh's
Telford College *v.* Revenue and Customs Commissioners; TNS, IH (1 Div);
reversing [2005] B.V.C. 2328; [2005] V. & D.R. 71, V&DTr (Edinburgh)
Edinburgh's Telford College *v.* Revenue and Customs Commissioners see Edinburgh
Telford College *v.* Customs and Excise Commissioners
Editions Albert Rene *v.* Office for Harmonisation in the Internal Market (Trade Marks
and Designs) (OHIM) (T311/01) [2003] E.C.R. II-4625; [2004] E.T.M.R. 62, CFI
(4th Chamber) . . . . *Digested*, 05/**2531**
Edlington Properties Ltd *v.* JH Fenner & Co Ltd B2/2005/2477, CA (Civ Div);
affirming [2005] EWHC 2158; [2005] 43 E.G.C.S. 189; [2005] N.P.C. 119;
Times, November 4, 2005, QBD
Edmund Nuttall Ltd *v.* Butterfield [2005] I.R.L.R. 751, EAT
Edwards *v.* Flightline Ltd see Flightline Ltd *v.* Edwards
Edwards *v.* Lloyds TSB Bank Plc [2004] EWHC 1745; [2005] 1 F.C.R. 139; [2004]
B.P.I.R. 1190, Ch D . . . . *Digested*, 05/**278**
Edwards *v.* United Kingdom (38260/97) [2005] R.V.R. 57; *Times*, November 19, 2004,
ECHR . . . . *Digested*, 05/**2097**
Edwards *v.* United Kingdom (39647/98); Lewis *v.* United Kingdom (40461/98) 15
B.H.R.C. 189; [2003] Crim. L.R. 891; (2005) 40 E.H.R.R. 24; *Times*, July 29,
2003; *Times*, November 3, 2004, ECHR (Grand Chamber); affirming . . . . *Digested*, 05/**2088**:
Considered, 05/875: *Distinguished*, 05/840
Effing, Re (C302/02) [2005] E.C.R. I-553; [2005] 1 C.M.L.R. 43; [2005] C.E.C. 457;
[2005] 1 F.C.R. 441, ECJ (1st Chamber) . . . . *Digested*, 05/**3900**
EFTA Surveillance Authority *v.* Liechtenstein (E8/04) [2005] 2 C.M.L.R. 58, EFTA
Egerton *v.* Rutter [1951] 1 K.B. 472; [1951] 1 T.L.R. 58, KBD . . . . *Digested*, 47-51/**143**:
Applied, 52/52: *Distinguished*, 05/2638: *Not followed*, 66/10432
El Du Pont de Nemours & Co *v.* Agnew (No.1) [1987] 2 Lloyd's Rep. 585; [1987] F.L.R.
376; [1987] 2 F.T.L.R. 487, CA (Civ Div). . . . . *Digested*, 88/**407**:
Applied, 02/2736, 04/2236: *Distinguished*, 05/2408
El Du Pont de Nemours & Co *v.* ST Dupont see ST Dupont *v.* El Du Pont de Nemours &
Co
EIC Services Ltd *v.* Phipps [2004] EWCA Civ 1069; [2005] 1 W.L.R. 1377; [2005] 1
All E.R. 338; [2004] B.C.C. 814; [2004] 2 B.C.L.C. 589; (2004) 148 S.J.L.B.
1118, CA (Civ Div); reversing [2003] EWHC 1507; [2003] 1 W.L.R. 2360;
[2003] 3 All E.R. 804; [2003] B.C.C. 957, Ch D . . . . *Digested*, 05/**516**
Eichholz (No.1), Re; *sub nom* Eichholz's Trustee *v.* Eichholz [1959] Ch. 708; [1959] 2
W.L.R. 200; [1959] 1 All E.R. 166, Ch D . . . . *Digested*, 59/**2782**:
Followed, 05/2341
Eichholz's Trustee *v.* Eichholz see Eichholz (No.1), Re
Eidesund *v.* Stavanger Catering AS (E2/95) [1997] 2 C.M.L.R. 672; [1996] I.R.L.R.
684, EFTA. . . . . *Digested*, 97/**2274**:
Followed, 05/1314
Eilbeck (Inspector of Taxes) *v.* Rawling see WT Ramsay Ltd *v.* Inland Revenue
Commissioners
Eisai Ltd *v.* Stop Huntingdon Animal Cruelty see Daiichi Pharmaceuticals UK Ltd *v.*
Stop Huntingdon Animal Cruelty

El Corte Ingles SA v. Office for Harmonisation in the Internal Market (Trade Marks and
Designs) (OHIM) (T183/02) [2004] E.C.R. II-965; [2004] E.T.M.R. 103, CFI
(4th Chamber) .... *Digested*, 05/**2508**
El Greco (Australia) Pty Ltd v. Mediterranean Shipping Co SA [2004] 2 Lloyd's Rep.
537, Fed Ct (Aus) (Full Ct) .... *Digested*, 05/**3786**
El-Rifai v. Secretary of State for the Home Department [2005] EWCA Civ 385; *Times*,
March 1, 2005, CA (Civ Div) .... *Digested*, 05/**2188**
Elderslie Steamship Co Ltd v. Borthwick; *sub nom* Borthwick v. Elderslie Steamship Co
Ltd (No.1) [1905] A.C. 93, HL; affirming [1904] 1 K.B. 319, CA. .... *Applied*, 05/2356:
Considered, 98/4874
Electrocoin Automatics Ltd v. Coinworld Ltd [2004] EWHC 1498; [2005] E.T.M.R. 31;
[2005] F.S.R. 7; (2004) 27(8) I.P.D. 27084, Ch D .... *Digested*, 05/**2574**
Electronics Ltd v. Inspector of Taxes [2005] S.T.C. (S.C.D.) 512, Sp Comm
Electrotechnical Fittings Cartel (C7/01 P (R)), Re see Nederlandse Federatieve Vereniging
voor de Groothandel op Elektrotechnisch Gebied v. Commission of the European
Communities (C7/01 P (R))
Eli Lilly & Co v. Dowelhurst Ltd (Form of Reference to ECJ) see Boehringer Ingelheim
KG v. Swingward Ltd (Form of Reference to ECJ)
Elim Church, Tamworth v. Revenue and Customs Commissioners [2005] S.T.I. 2036,
V&DTr
Elite Business Systems UK Ltd v. Price [2005] EWCA Civ 920; (2005) 102(36) L.S.G.
32, CA (Civ Div)
Elizabeth Claire Care Management Ltd v. Francis [2005] I.R.L.R. 858, EAT
Elleni Holding BV v. Sigla SA [2005] E.T.M.R. 7, OHIM (3rd Bd App) .... *Digested*, 05/**2521**
Ellerton v. Harris see Atack v. Lee
Ellis v. Harris see Ferrotech Ltd, Re
Ellis (t/a Autospray) v. King (Unreported, June 29, 2004), CC (Croydon) [*Ex rel*. Simon
Hill, Barrister, 33 Bedford Row, London] .... *Digested*, 05/**399**
Elm Milk Ltd v. Customs and Excise Commissioners; *sub nom* Customs and Excise
Commissioners v. Elm Milk Ltd; C3/2005/0768, CA (Civ Div); affirming [2005]
EWHC 366; [2005] S.T.C. 776; [2005] B.T.C. 5260; [2005] B.V.C. 291; [2005]
S.T.I. 193, Ch D; affirming [2004] V. & D.R. 166; [2004] S.T.I. 1943, V&DTr
(London) .... *Digested*, 05/**4372**
Elmer Contractors Ltd v. Ashville Investments Ltd see Ashville Investments Ltd v. Elmer
Contractors Ltd
ELMONTAZ Trade Mark [2005] E.T.M.R. 66, NSA (PL)
Elmsbourne Security Ltd v. Manticore Holdings Ltd [2005] EWHC 1315; [2005]
B.P.I.R. 1295, Ch D
Elsner-Lakeberg v. Land Nordrhein-Westfalen (C285/02) [2004] 2 C.M.L.R. 36;
[2005] I.R.L.R. 209, ECJ (1st Chamber) .... *Digested*, 05/**1264**
Elvidge v. Coventry City Council [1994] Q.B. 241; [1993] 3 W.L.R. 976; [1993] 4 All
E.R. 903; [1994] I.C.R. 68; (1994) 26 H.L.R. 281; 92 L.G.R. 237; [1993]
E.G.C.S. 140; [1993] N.P.C. 110, CA (Civ Div) .... *Digested*, 93/**2107**:
Considered, 96/3833, 05/2688
Emcor Drake & Scull Ltd v. Sir Robert McAlpine Ltd [2004] EWCA Civ 1733; 98 Con.
L.R. 1, CA (Civ Div); affirming [2004] EWHC 1017, QBD (TCC) .... *Digested*, 05/**708**
Emcor Drake & Scull Ltd (formerly Drake & Scull Engineering Ltd) v. Costain Construction
Ltd (t/a Costain Skanska Joint Venture) [2004] EWHC 2439; 97 Con. L.R. 142;
(2004) 148 S.J.L.B. 1314, QBD (TCC) .... *Digested*, 05/**643**
Emerald Construction Co v. Lowthian [1966] 1 W.L.R. 691; [1966] 1 All E.R. 1013; 1
K.I.R. 200; 110 S.J. 226, CA. .... *Digested*, 66/**12214**:
Applied, 66/1488, 68/3888: *Distinguished*, 05/4198: *Followed*, 71/3945
Emezie v. Emokpae see Emokpae v. Chamberlin Solicitors
Emin v. Secretary of State for the Environment (1989) 58 P. & C.R. 416; [1989] J.P.L.
909; [1989] E.G.C.S. 16, QBD .... *Digested*, 90/**4357**:
Applied, 05/3262: *Considered*, 89/3536, 91/3433
Emmanuel Church, Bentley, Re, *Times*, December 26, 2005, Arches Ct
Emokpae v. Chamberlin Solicitors see Wong v. Igen Ltd (formerly Leeds Careers
Guidance)
Emokpae v. Chamberlin Solicitors; *sub nom* Chamberlin Solicitors v. Emokpae; Emezie
v. Emokpae [2004] I.C.R. 1476; [2004] I.R.L.R. 592, EAT. .... *Overruled*, 05/1221
Empowerment Enterprises Ltd v. Customs and Excise Commissioners [2005] B.V.C.
2445; [2005] S.T.I. 876, V&DTr (Edinburgh)
Empresa de Desenvolvimento Mineiro SGPS SA (EDM) v. Fazenda Publica (C77/01)
[2005] S.T.C. 65; [2004] E.C.R. I-4295; [2005] 2 C.M.L.R. 1; [2004] S.T.I.
1164, ECJ (5th Chamber) [2004] E.C.R. I-4295, AGO .... *Digested*, 05/**4345**
Emunefe v. Secretary of State for the Home Department [2005] EWCA Civ 1002;
[2005] I.N.L.R. 587, CA (Civ Div)
Enderby v. Frenchay HA (C127/92) [1994] 1 All E.R. 495; [1993] E.C.R. I-5535;
[1994] 1 C.M.L.R. 8; [1994] I.C.R. 112; [1993] I.R.L.R. 591; *Times*, November 12,
1993; *Financial Times*, November 2, 1993, ECJ (1st Chamber) .... *Digested*, 94/**4813**:
Applied, 05/1268: *Considered*, 97/5226: *Distinguished*, 94/1979, 04/1254:
Followed, 96/5713, 03/1275

Enderby v. Frenchay HA (No.2); Evesham v. North Hertfordshire HA; Hughes v. West
Berkshire HA [2000] I.C.R. 612; [2000] I.R.L.R. 257; *Times*, February 29, 2000,
CA (Civ Div); affirming [1999] I.R.L.R. 155, EAT . . . . *Digested*, 00/**2156**:
Explained, 05/1265

Energias de Portugal (EDP) SA v. Commission of the European Communities (T87/05)
[2005] 5 C.M.L.R. 23, CFI (2nd Chamber)
Energy Financing Team Ltd v. Director of the Serious Fraud Office; *sub nom* R. (on the
application of Energy Financing Team Ltd) v. Bow Street Magistrates' Court
[2005] EWHC 1626; [2005] 4 All E.R. 285, QBD (Admin) . . . . *Digested*, 05/**930**
Enertrag (UK) Ltd v. Sea & Land Power & Energy Ltd [2003] EWHC 2196; 100 Con.
L.R. 146, QBD (TCC)
Enfield LBC v. Kruja see Kruja v. Enfield LBC
Enfield LBC v. Lamotey see Lomotey v. Enfield LBC
Enfield LBC v. McCarthy & Stone [2005] P.A.D. 9, Planning Inspector
Enfield LBC v. Sivanandan see Sivanandan v. Enfield LBC
Enforcement of Austrian Judgment, Re (3 W 91/03) [2005] I.L.Pr. 29, OLG (Dusseldorf)
Enforcement of Portuguese Judgment, Re (IX ZB 2/03) [2005] I.L.Pr. 28, BGH (Ger)
Engel v. Netherlands (A/22) (1979-80) 1 E.H.R.R. 647, ECHR . . . . *Applied*, 88/**2973**,
98/3119, 00/3235, 02/3349, 03/866, 03/925, 03/2141, 03/4604, 05/2909,
05/4164: *Considered*, 01/98, 02/2470, 02/2619, 04/2777, 04/3144
Engel v. Peri; *sub nom* Peri v. Engel [2002] EWHC 799; [2002] B.P.I.R. 961; (2002)
99(23) L.S.G. 27; (2002) 146 S.J.L.B. 135, Ch D . . . . *Digested*, 03/**2376**:
Applied, 05/2270

Engil Sociedade de Construcao Civil SA v. Urlaubs- und Lohnausgleichskasse der
Bauwirtschaft (C71/98) see Finalarte Sociedade de Construcao Civil Lda v.
Urlaubs- und Lohnausgleichskasse der Bauwirtschaft (C49/98)
England v. Magill see Porter v. Magill
Engler v. Janus Versand GmbH (C27/02) [2005] E.C.R. I-481; [2005] C.E.C. 187;
[2005] I.L.Pr. 8, ECJ (2nd Chamber) . . . . *Digested*, 05/**623**
Englewood Properties Ltd v. Patel [2005] EWHC 188; [2005] 1 W.L.R. 1961; [2005] 3
All E.R. 307; [2005] 2 E.G.L.R. 77; [2005] 25 E.G. 194; (2005) 102(15)
L.S.G. 34; [2005] N.P.C. 25; *Times*, March 9, 2005, Ch D . . . . *Digested*, 05/**3418**
English v. Emery Reimbold & Strick Ltd; DJ&C Withers (Farms) Ltd v. Ambic
Equipment Ltd; Verrechia (t/a Freightmaster Commercials) v. Commissioner of
Police of the Metropolis [2002] EWCA Civ 605; [2002] 1 W.L.R. 2409; [2002]
3 All E.R. 385; [2002] C.P.L.R. 520; [2003] I.R.L.R. 710; [2002] U.K.H.R.R.
957; (2002) 99(22) L.S.G. 34; (2002) 152 N.L.J. 758; (2002) 146 S.J.L.B. 123;
Times, May 10, 2002; *Independent*, May 7, 2002, CA (Civ Div) . . . . *Digested*, 02/**301**:
Applied, 02/371, 04/2698, 05/950, 05/1212, 05/1256: *Considered*, 03/847,
03/1544, 05/2213: *Distinguished*, 05/1138
English Churches Housing Group v. Shine; *sub nom* English Churches Housing Group v.
Shrine; Shine v. English Churches Housing Group [2004] EWCA Civ 434;
[2004] H.L.R. 42; [2005] L. & T.R. 7; (2004) 101(20) L.S.G. 35; (2004) 148
S.J.L.B. 476; [2004] N.P.C. 61; *Times*, June 2, 2004, CA (Civ Div) . . . . *Digested*, 05/**2683**
English Churches Housing Group v. Shrine see English Churches Housing Group v.
Shine
Enhorn v. Sweden (56529/00) (2005) 41 E.H.R.R. 30; 19 B.H.R.C. 222, ECHR
Ennion v. Hampstead Old People's Housing Trust see Fleming's Will Trusts, Re
Eno v. Dunn (1890) L.R. 15 App. Cas. 252; (1890) 7 R.P.C. 311, HL; reversing (1889)
L.R. 41 Ch. D. 439, CA. . . . . *Considered*, 77/3058:
Followed, 05/2577: *Referred to*, 99/3587
Enron Europe Ltd (In Administration) v. Revenue and Customs Commissioners CH/
2005/APP/0648, Ch D; affirming [2005] S.T.I. 2032, V&DTr (London)
ENRON Metals & Commodity Ltd (In Administration) v. HIH Casualty & General
Insurance Ltd (In Provisional Liquidation) see HIH Casualty & General Insurance
Ltd, Re
Ensco Maritime Ltd v. Deputy Commissioner of Income Tax (Special Range) 7 I.T.L.
Rep. 822, ITAT (Ind)
Enso-Gutzeit Oy v. Commission of the European Communities (T337/94) [1998]
E.C.R. II-1571, CFI . . . . *Followed*, 05/553
Ensor v. Archer [2004] EWHC 1541; [2005] P.N.L.R. 5, QBD. . . . . *Digested*, 05/**2865**
Enterprise Rent-a-Car Co v. Eurodrive Car Rental Ltd [2005] EWHC 1429; [2005]
E.T.M.R. CN14, Ch D
Entry Clearance Officer, Dhaka v. AA see AA v. Secretary of State for the Home
Department
Environment Agency v. Armstrong Environmental Services Ltd [2005] EWHC 633;
[2005] Env. L.R. 40, QBD (Admin) . . . . *Digested*, 05/**1393**
EOS/Intervention (T1007/01) [2005] E.P.O.R. 40, EPO (Technical Bd App)
EPI Environmental Technologies Inc v. Symphony Plastic Technologies Plc A3/2005/
0185, CA (Civ Div); affirming [2004] EWHC 2945; [2005] 1 W.L.R. 3456;
[2005] F.S.R. 22; (2005) 28(3) I.P.D. 28016; (2005) 102(7) L.S.G. 26; *Times*,
January 14, 2005, Ch D . . . . *Digested*, 05/**2416**

Epikouriko Kefalaio *v.* Anaptyxis (C28/03); *sub nom* Epikouriko Kefalaio *v.* Anaptixis (C28/03) [2004] 3 C.M.L.R. 57; [2005] Lloyd's Rep. I.R. 259, ECJ (1st Chamber) . . . . *Digested,* 05/**2330**

EPO Decision (T854/02) Unreported, EPO (Technical Bd App) . . . . *Considered,* 05/2451

Epoch Properties Ltd *v.* British Home Stores (Jersey) Ltd [2004] 3 E.G.L.R. 34; [2004] 48 E.G. 134, CA (Jer) . . . . *Digested,* 05/**2680**

Epon (C419/97), Re see ARCO Chemie Nederland Ltd *v.* Minister van Volkshuisvesting, Ruimtelijke Ordening en Milieubeheer (C418/97)

Epping Forest DC *v.* Keebee Properties Ltd [2005] P.A.D. 14, Planning Inspector

Equitable Life Assurance Society *v.* Hyman [2002] 1 A.C. 408; [2000] 3 W.L.R. 529; [2000] 3 All E.R. 961; [2001] Lloyd's Rep. I.R. 99; [2000] O.P.L.R. 101; [2000] Pens. L.R. 249; (2000) 144 S.J.L.B. 239; *Times,* July 21, 2000; *Independent,* October 30, 2000 (C.S), HL; affirming [2000] 2 W.L.R. 798; [2000] 2 All E.R. 331; [2000] O.P.L.R. 71; [2000] Pens. L.R. 129; (2000) 97(5) L.S.G. 34; (2000) 144 S.J.L.B. 57; *Times,* January 26, 2000 ; *Independent,* January 28, 2000, CA (Civ Div); reversing [1999] O.P.L.R. 213; [1999] Pens. L.R. 297; *Times,* October 12, 1999, Ch D . . . . *Digested,* 00/**4395**:
Cited, 03/2440, 04/455: *Considered,* 05/538

Equitas Ltd *v.* Jacob see Jacob *v.* Equitas Ltd

Equitas Ltd *v.* Wave City Shipping Co Ltd [2005] EWHC 923; [2005] 2 All E.R. (Comm) 301, QBD (Comm)

ER Ives Investment Ltd *v.* High [1967] 2 Q.B. 379; [1967] 2 W.L.R. 789; [1967] 1 All E.R. 504; 110 S.J. 963, CA . . . . *Digested,* 67/**2196**:
Applied, 75/1191, 05/3437: *Considered,* 68/2185, 84/1154, 85/1083:
Distinguished, 68/1313, 00/4658

Erich Gasser GmbH *v.* MISAT Srl (C116/02) [2005] Q.B. 1; [2004] 3 W.L.R. 1070; [2005] All E.R. (EC) 517; [2005] 1 All E.R. (Comm) 538; [2004] 1 Lloyd's Rep. 222; [2003] E.C.R. I-14693; [2004] I.L.Pr. 7; *Times,* December 12, 2003, ECJ . . *Digested,* 04/**564**:
Considered, 05/599

ERICSSON INC/Divisional application (J28/03) [2005] E.P.O.R. 36, EPO (Legal Bd App)

Erikson *v.* Italy (37900/97) (2000) 29 E.H.R.R. CD152, ECHR . . . . *Considered,* 05/34

Ernst *v.* Belgium (33400/96) (2004) 39 E.H.R.R. 35, ECHR . . . . *Digested,* 05/**2048**

Ernst & Young *v.* Central Guaranty Trust Co (No.2) (2004-05) 7 I.T.E.L.R. 69, QB (Alta) . . . . *Digested,* 05/**4310**

Erris Promotions Ltd *v.* Inland Revenue Commissioner 6 I.T.L. Rep. 364, HC (NZ) . . . . . *Considered,* 05/4157

Ertanir *v.* Land Hessen (C98/96) [1997] E.C.R. I-5179, ECJ [1997] E.C.R. I-5179, AGO . . . . *Considered,* 05/2206

ES *v.* Chesterfield and North Derbyshire Royal Hospital NHS Trust; *sub nom* S *v.* A Health Authority [2003] EWCA Civ 1284; [2004] C.P. Rep. 9; [2004] Lloyd's Rep. Med. 90; (2003) 100(38) L.S.G. 34, CA (Civ Div) . . . . *Digested,* 04/**254**:
Applied, 05/1042

Escalus Properties Ltd *v.* Cooper-Smith see Escalus Properties Ltd *v.* Robinson

Escalus Properties Ltd *v.* Dennis see Escalus Properties Ltd *v.* Robinson

Escalus Properties Ltd *v.* Robinson; Escalus Properties Ltd *v.* Dennis; Escalus Properties Ltd *v.* Cooper-Smith; Sinclair Gardens Investments (Kensington) Ltd *v.* Walsh [1996] Q.B. 231; [1995] 3 W.L.R. 524; [1995] 4 All E.R. 852; (1996) 28 H.L.R. 338; (1996) 71 P. & C.R. 47; [1995] 2 E.G.L.R. 23; [1995] 31 E.G. 71; [1995] E.G.C.S. 65; (1995) 92(18) L.S.G. 36; (1995) 139 S.J.L.B. 111; [1995] N.P.C. 62; (1995) 70 P. & C.R. D7; *Times,* April 21, 1995, CA (Civ Div) . . . . *Digested,* 96/**3758**:
Applied, 04/2500, 05/3429: *Considered,* 97/3293: *Followed,* 96/3748

Ess Production Ltd (In Administration) *v.* Sully [2005] EWCA Civ 554; [2005] B.C.C. 435; [2005] 2 B.C.L.C. 547; [2005] B.P.I.R. 691; *Independent,* May 18, 2005, CA (Civ Div) . . . . *Digested,* 05/**2319**

Essar Steel Ltd *v.* Argo Fund Ltd see Argo Fund Ltd *v.* Essar Steel Ltd

Esso Petroleum Co Ltd *v.* Addison; *sub nom* Addison *v.* Esso Petroleum Co Ltd [2004] EWCA Civ 1470; (2004) 101(46) L.S.G. 33; (2004) 148 S.J.L.B. 1400; *Times,* November 16, 2004, CA (Civ Div); affirming [2003] EWHC 1730, QBD (Comm) . . . . *Digested,* 05/**701**

Esso Petroleum Co Ltd *v.* Hall Russell & Co Ltd (The Esso Bernicia) [1989] A.C. 643; [1988] 3 W.L.R. 730; [1989] 1 All E.R. 37; [1989] 1 Lloyd's Rep. 8; 1988 S.L.T. 874; (1988) 85(42) L.S.G. 48; (1988) 132 S.J. 1459; *Times,* October 7, 1988, HL; affirming in part 1988 S.L.T. 33, IH (1 Div) . . . . *Digested,* 89/**3392**:
Considered, 05/2890: *Distinguished,* 03/3613

Esso SA *v.* Total France SA [2005] E.C.C. 3, C d'A (Paris)

Establishment of Opticians Shops, Re (C140/03) see Commission of the European Communities *v.* Greece (C140/03)

Estevez *v.* Spain (56501/00) (Unreported, May 10, 2001), ECHR . . . . *Considered,* 05/2118

ETA/Request with a view to revision (G01/97) [2001] E.P.O.R. 1, EPO (Enlarged Bd App)   *Digested,* 01/**3890**:
Applied, 05/2465: *Followed,* 05/2472: *Referred to,* 04/2303

EU Constitutional Treaty and French Constitution, Re (2004-504 DC) [2005] 1 C.M.L.R. 30, Cons Const (F)

EU Constitutional Treaty and Spanish Constitution (Declaration 1/2004), Re [2005] 1 C.M.L.R. 39, Trib Const (Sp)

EU Wood Trading GmbH v. Sonderabfall Management Gesellschaft Rheinland-Pfalz
 mbH (C277/02) [2005] All E.R. (EC) 967; [2004] E.C.R. I-11957, ECJ
Eugen Schmidberger Internationale Transporte Planzuge v. Austria (C112/00) [2003]
 E.C.R. I-5659; [2003] 2 C.M.L.R. 34; *Times*, June 27, 2003, ECJ . . . . *Applied*, 05/1437
Eugenia Michaelidou Developments Ltd v. Turkey (16163/90) (2004) 39 E.H.R.R. 36,
 ECHR . . . . *Digested*, 05/**2069**
Eurico SpA v. Philipp Bros (The Epaphus) [1987] 2 Lloyd's Rep. 215; [1987] 2 F.T.L.R.
 213; *Times*, May 18, 1987, CA (Civ Div); affirming [1986] 2 Lloyd's Rep. 387,
 QBD (Comm) . . . . *Digested*, 88/**3165**:
 Considered, 05/267
Eurocell Profiles Ltd v. Ultraframe (UK) Ltd [2004] EWHC 2800; (2005) 28(2) I.P.D.
 28008, Ch D (Patents Ct)
Eurocermex SA v. Office for Harmonisation in the Internal Market (Trade Marks and
 Designs) (OHIM) (C286/04 P) [2005] E.T.M.R. 95, ECJ (1st Chamber)
Eurofinacom v. France (Admissibility) (58753/00) [2005] Crim. L.R. 134, ECHR
Eurofood IFSC Ltd, Re (C341/04); *sub nom* Bondi v. Bank of America NA (C341/04 R)
 [2005] B.C.C. 1021, AGO
Eurofood IFSC Ltd (No.1), Re; *sub nom* Eurofoods IFSC Ltd (No.1), Re [2005] B.C.C.
 999; [2005] Eu. L.R. 148; [2005] I.L.Pr. 2, Sup Ct (Irl) [2004] B.C.C. 383, HC
 (Irl)
Eurofood IFSC Ltd (No.2), Re; *sub nom* Eurofoods IFSC Ltd (No.2), Re [2005] I.L.Pr. 3,
 Sup Ct (Irl)
European Capital Trade Finance Ltd v. Antenna Hungaria RT (Unreported, March 27,
 1995), QBD (Comm) . . . . *Applied*, 05/487
European Roma Rights Center v. Greece (Complaint No.15/2003) (2005) 41 E.H.R.R.
 SE14, ECHR
European Roma Rights Centre v. Immigration Officer, Prague Airport see R. (on the
 application of European Roma Rights Centre) v. Immigration Officer, Prague
 Airport
European Sugar Cartel (40/73), Re see Cooperatieve Vereniging Suiker Unie UA v.
 Commission of the European Communities (40/73)
Eurosteel Ltd v. Stinnes AG [2000] 1 All E.R. (Comm) 964; [2000] C.L.C. 470, QBD
 (Comm) . . . . *Digested*, 00/**736**:
 Applied, 05/89
Evangelical Movement of Wales v. Customs and Excise Commissioners [2004] B.V.C.
 2165; [2004] V. & D.R. 138; [2004] S.T.I. 1555, V&DTr (London) . . . . *Digested*, 05/**4346**
Evans, Re; *sub nom* R. v. Governor of Brixton Prison Ex p. Evans [1994] 1 W.L.R.
 1006; [1994] 3 All E.R. 449; [1994] C.O.D. 477; (1994) 91(36) L.S.G. 38;
 (1994) 144 N.L.J. 1095; (1994) 138 S.J.L.B. 184; *Times*, July 22, 1994;
 Independent, August 16, 1994, HL; affirming [1994] Crim. L.R. 593; [1994]
 C.O.D. 208; *Times*, December 10, 1993, QBD . . . . *Digested*, 94/**2132**:
 Applied, 97/2441, 05/1489: *Considered*, 97/2431, 05/1491
Evans v. Amicus Healthcare Ltd; Hadley v. Midland Fertility Services Ltd [2004]
 EWCA Civ 727; [2005] Fam. 1; [2004] 3 W.L.R. 681; [2004] 3 All E.R. 1025;
 [2004] 2 F.L.R. 766; [2004] 2 F.C.R. 530; (2004) 78 B.M.L.R. 181; [2004]
 Fam. Law 647; (2004) 148 S.J.L.B. 823; *Times*, June 30, 2004; *Independent*,
 June 29, 2004, CA (Civ Div); affirming [2003] EWHC 2161; [2004] 2 W.L.R.
 713; [2003] 4 All E.R. 903; [2004] 1 F.L.R. 67; [2003] 3 F.C.R. 577; (2004) 75
 B.M.L.R. 115; [2003] Fam. Law 879; (2003) 100(39) L.S.G. 38; (2003) 153
 N.L.J. 1519; (2003) 147 S.J.L.B. 1150; *Times*, October 2, 2003; *Independent*,
 October 14, 2003, Fam Div . . . . *Digested*, 04/**1673**
Evans v. European Bank Ltd (2004-05) 7 I.T.E.L.R. 19, CA (NSW) . . . . *Digested*, 05/**621**
Evans v. Governor of Brockhill Prison see R. v. Governor of Brockhill Prison Ex p.
 Evans (No.2)
Evans v. HSBC Trust Co (UK) Ltd [2005] W.T.L.R. 1289, Ch D
Evans v. Secretary of State for the Environment, Transport and the Regions (C63/01)
 [2005] All E.R. (EC) 763; [2003] E.C.R. I-14447; [2004] R.T.R. 32; [2004] 1
 C.M.L.R. 47; [2004] Lloyd's Rep. I.R. 391; *Times*, December 9, 2003, ECJ (5th
 Chamber) . . . . *Digested*, 04/**2230**
Everest Trust, Re see Schmidt v. Rosewood Trust Ltd
Evesham v. North Hertfordshire HA see Enderby v. Frenchay HA (No.2)
Evialis SA v. SIAT [2003] EWHC 863; [2003] 2 Lloyd's Rep. 377; [2003] 2 C.L.C.
 802; [2003] I.L.Pr. 43; [2004] Lloyd's Rep. I.R. 187, QBD (Comm) . . . . *Digested*, 03/**609**:
 Considered, 05/614
Ewing v. Office of the Deputy Prime Minister [2005] EWCA Civ 1583; [2005] N.P.C.
 146, CA (Civ Div); affirming [2005] EWHC 825, QBD (Admin)
Exbanor SA v. Patrigeon [2005] E.C.C. 35, C d'A (Paris)
Excess Insurance Co Ltd v. Gibbs Hartley Cooper Ltd see Pryke v. Gibbs Hartley
 Cooper Ltd
Excess Insurance Co Ltd v. Mander [1997] 2 Lloyd's Rep. 119; [1995] L.R.L.R. 358;
 [1995] C.L.C. 838; *Lloyd's List*, May 18, 1995 (I.D.), QBD (Comm) . . . . *Digested*, 95/**2921**:
 Considered, 05/2371: *Followed*, 98/242

Exeter City AFC Ltd *v.* Football Conference Ltd [2004] EWHC 831; [2004] 1 W.L.R.
2910; [2004] 4 All E.R. 1179; [2004] B.C.C. 498; [2005] 1 B.C.L.C. 238;
(2004) 101(9) L.S.G. 31; *Times,* February 12, 2004, Ch D . . . .   *Digested,* 04/**195**
Exmouth Clothing Co Ltd *v.* Bayley see Anglo African Merchants Ltd *v.* Bayley
Exmouth Marina Ltd *v.* First Secretary of State; *sub nom* R. (on the application of
Exmouth Marina Ltd) *v.* First Secretary of State [2004] EWHC 3166; [2005] 3
P.L.R. 1, QBD (Admin)
Experience Hendrix LLC *v.* Purple Haze Records Ltd [2005] EWHC 249; [2005]
E.M.L.R. 18; (2005) 28(3) I.P.D. 28015; *Times,* May 5, 2005, Ch D . . . .   *Digested,* 05/**2496**
Explora Group Ltd *v.* Trading Force Ltd see Explora Group Plc *v.* Hesco Bastion Ltd
Explora Group Plc *v.* Hesco Bastion Ltd; Explora Group Ltd *v.* Trading Force Ltd [2005]
EWCA Civ 646; (2005) 149 S.J.L.B. 924, CA (Civ Div); reversing [2004]
EWHC 1863, QBD
Express & Echo Publications Ltd *v.* Tanton [1999] I.C.R. 693; [1999] I.R.L.R. 367;
(1999) 96(14) L.S.G. 31; *Times,* April 7, 1999; *Independent* April 19, 1999 (C.S.),
CA (Civ Div) . . . .   *Digested,* 99/**2045**:
                                                  Applied, 05/1325: *Distinguished,* 01/6468
Express Ltd (t/a Express Dairies Distribution) *v.* Environment Agency [2004] EWHC
1710; [2005] 1 W.L.R. 223; [2005] Env. L.R. 7; [2005] J.P.L. 242; [2005]
A.C.D. 26; *Times,* August 10, 2004, QBD (Admin) . . . .   *Digested,* 04/**1354**
Expro Gulf Ltd *v.* Birnie see Dickie *v.* Cathay Pacific Airways Ltd
Exxon Corp's Trade Mark Application [2005] E.T.M.R. 89, TMR
EXXON MOBIL/Transitioning between catalysts (T357/02) [2005] E.P.O.R. 27, EPO
(Technical Bd App)
Eyeson *v.* Milton Keynes Council [2005] EWHC 1160; [2005] H.L.R. 38, QBD
(Admin) . . . .   *Digested,* 05/**3917**
Ezeh *v.* United Kingdom (39665/98); Connors *v.* United Kingdom (40086/98)
(2004) 39 E.H.R.R. 1; 15 B.H.R.C. 145; [2004] Crim. L.R. 472; *Times,* October
30, 2003, ECHR (Grand Chamber) . . . .   *Digested,* 03/**2141**:
                                                  Applied, 05/2909: *Previous proceedings,* 02/3342

F *v.* G (Child: Financial Provision) [2004] EWHC 1848; [2005] 1 F.L.R. 261, Fam Div . .   *Digested,* 05/**1652**
F *v.* Newsquest Ltd; *sub nom* X and Y (Children), Re [2004] EWHC 762; [2004]
E.M.L.R. 29, Fam Div . . . .   *Digested,* 05/**2049**:
                                                                              Considered, 05/1686
F *v.* West Berkshire HA; *sub nom* F (Mental Patient: Sterilisation), Re [1990] 2 A.C. 1;
[1989] 2 W.L.R. 1025; [1989] 2 All E.R. 545; [1989] 2 F.L.R. 376; (1989) 139
N.L.J. 789; (1989) 133 S.J. 785, HL; affirming (1989) 86(10) L.S.G. 42; *Times,*
December 8, 1988; *Independent,* December 6, 1988; *Guardian,* December 3,
1988, CA (Civ Div) . . . .   *Digested,* 89/**3044**:
                              Applied, 94/3850, 95/4266: *Considered,* 90/3139, 90/3679.a, 91/2462,
                                    91/2463, 91/2548, 92/2981, 93/2712, 95/3578, 95/4102, 95/4104,
                                    96/2846, 96/7002, 97/2597, 97/6266, 99/2380, 00/2780, 00/4247,
                                                  01/2662: *Followed,* 05/1850: *Referred to,* 91/5262
F (A Minor) (Child Abduction), Re; *sub nom* AF (A Minor) (Abduction), Re [1992] 1
F.L.R. 548; [1992] F.C.R. 269; [1992] Fam. Law 195; *Independent,* October 7,
1991 (C.S.), CA (Civ Div) . . . .   *Digested,* 93/**2797**:
                                                  Applied, 05/1547: *Considered,* 95/3436, 95/3448, 96/534
F (Children) (Contact Orders: Domestic Violence), Re; *sub nom* F (Children)
(Restrictions on Applications), Re [2005] EWCA Civ 499; [2005] 2 F.L.R. 950;
[2005] 2 F.C.R. 176; [2005] Fam. Law 694, CA (Civ Div) . . . .   *Digested,* 05/**1587**
F (Children) (Restrictions on Applications), Re see F (Children) (Contact Orders: Domestic
Violence), Re
F (Mental Patient: Sterilisation), Re see F *v.* West Berkshire HA
F's Applications for Judicial Review, Re [2005] N.I. 280, QBD (NI)
F Hoffmann La Roche & Co AG *v.* Commission of the European Communities (85/76)
[1979] E.C.R. 461; [1979] 3 C.M.L.R. 211; [1980] F.S.R. 13, ECJ . . . .   *Digested,* 79/**1204**:
                                                  Applied, 03/5306: *Considered,* 05/575
F&G Sykes (Wessex) Ltd *v.* Fine Fare Ltd [1967] 1 Lloyd's Rep. 53, CA; reversing in
part [1966] 2 Lloyd's Rep. 205, QBD (Comm) . . . .   *Digested,* 66/**1783**:
                                                  Applied, 76/2586: *Considered,* 05/665
F-K (A Child) (Contact: Departure from Evidence), Re [2005] EWCA Civ 155; [2005] 1
F.C.R. 388; (2005) 149 S.J.L.B. 268, CA (Civ Div)
FA & AB Ltd *v.* Lupton (Inspector of Taxes) see Argosam Finance Co Ltd *v.* Oxby
(Inspector of Taxes)
Fabricom SA *v.* Belgium (C21/03) [2005] E.C.R. I-1559; [2005] 2 C.M.L.R. 25, ECJ
(2nd Chamber) . . . .   *Digested,* 05/**3354**
Fabris *v.* Societe Nationale de Television France 2 SA; *sub nom* France 2 SA *v.* Fabris
[2005] E.C.C. 31, Cass (F); affirming [2002] E.C.C. 30; [2003] E.C.D.R. 13, C
d'A (Paris); reversing [2000] E.C.C. 258; [2002] E.C.D.R. 11, Trib Gde Inst
(Paris)
Fadipe *v.* Reed Nursing Personnel [2001] EWCA Civ 1885; [2005] I.C.R. 1760, CA
(Civ Div)

Fairbank *v.* Lambeth Magistrates Court [2002] EWHC 785; [2003] H.L.R. 7; [2003] R.V.R. 167, QBD (Admin) . . . . *Approved,* 05/**3873**
Fairchild *v.* Glenhaven Funeral Services Ltd (t/a GH Dovener & Son); Babcock International Ltd *v.* National Grid Co Plc; Fox *v.* Spousal (Midlands) Ltd; Matthews *v.* Associated Portland Cement Manufacturers (1978) Ltd; Dyson *v.* Leeds City Council (No.2); Pendleton *v.* Stone & Webster Engineering Ltd; Matthews *v.* British Uralite Plc [2002] UKHL 22; [2003] 1 A.C. 32; [2002] 3 W.L.R. 89; [2002] 3 All E.R. 305; [2002] I.C.R. 798; [2002] I.R.L.R. 533; [2002] P.I.Q.R. P28; [2002] Lloyd's Rep. Med. 361; (2002) 67 B.M.L.R. 90; (2002) 152 N.L.J. 998; *Times,* June 21, 2002; *Independent,* June 25, 2002; *Daily Telegraph,* June 27, 2002, HL; reversing [2001] EWCA Civ 1881; [2002] 1 W.L.R. 1052; [2002] I.C.R. 412; [2002] I.R.L.R. 129; [2002] P.I.Q.R. P27; *Times,* December 13, 2001; *Independent,* December 21, 2001; *Daily Telegraph,* December 20, 2001, CA (Civ Div); affirming 00/TLQ/1284, QBD . . . . *Digested,* 02/**2225**:
Applied, 04/2693, 04/2755: *Considered,* 02/3245, 02/3247, 03/2990, 05/2841
Fairgate International Ltd *v.* Citibank International Plc [2005] EWCA Civ 569; [2005] 2 E.G.L.R. 48; [2005] 27 E.G. 222; [2005] N.P.C. 63, CA (Civ Div); affirming [2004] N.P.C. 78, QBD (TCC) . . . . *Digested,* 05/**2647**
Fairstate Ltd *v.* First Secretary of State; *sub nom* R. (on the application of Fairstate Ltd) *v.* First Secretary of State [2005] EWCA Civ 283; [2005] 2 P.L.R. 127; [2005] J.P.L. 1333; (2005) 102(23) L.S.G. 28; [2005] N.P.C. 48; *Times,* April 13, 2005; *Independent,* April 13, 2005, CA (Civ Div); affirming [2004] EWHC 1807; [2005] J.P.L. 369; (2004) 101(30) L.S.G. 30; [2004] N.P.C. 111, QBD (Admin) . . . . *Digested,* 05/**3263**
Falk *v.* Netherlands (Admissibility) (66273/01) (2005) 40 E.H.R.R. SE7, ECHR
Fallon (Morgan's Executors) *v.* Fellows (Inspector of Taxes); *sub nom* Morgan's Executors *v.* Fellows (Inspector of Taxes) [2001] S.T.C. 1409; 74 T.C. 232; [2001] B.T.C. 438; [2001] S.T.I. 1104, Ch D; reversing [2001] S.T.C. (S.C.D.) 45; [2001] S.T.I. 632, Sp Comm. . . . . *Digested,* 02/**4358**:
Applied, 05/2335
Falshaw *v.* Senjack (Unreported, January 6, 2005), CC (Romford) [*Ex rel.* Justyn Turner, Barrister, 4 King's Bench Walk, Temple, London] . . . . *Digested,* 05/**3111**
Families for Children *v.* Customs and Excise Commissioners [2005] B.V.C. 2357; [2005] V. & D.R. 51; [2005] S.T.I. 817, V&DTr (London)
Family Housing Association *v.* Donnellan; *sub nom* Family Housing Association *v.* Donellan [2002] 1 P. & C.R. 34; [2001] 30 E.G.C.S. 114; [2001] N.P.C. 125, Ch D . . . . *Digested,* 02/**3803**:
Doubted, 05/3376
Family Planning Association of Northern Ireland *v.* Minister for Health, Social Services and Public Safety [2005] N.I. 188, CA (NI)
Faraday *v.* Carmarthenshire CC [2004] EWCA Civ 649; [2004] 2 E.G.L.R. 5; [2004] 33 E.G. 72; [2004] R.V.R. 236; (2004) 101(20) L.S.G. 36; (2004) 148 S.J.L.B. 629, CA (Civ Div) . . . . *Digested,* 05/**3249**
Fareham BC *v.* Crofton Manor Equestrian Centre [2005] P.A.D. 40, Planning Inspector
Fareham BC *v.* Foreman Homes Ltd [2005] P.A.D. 69, Planning Inspector
Farimani *v.* Gates (1984) 271 E.G. 887; (1984) 81 L.S.G. 1999; (1984) 128 S.J. 615, CA (Civ Div) . . . . *Digested,* 84/**1900**:
Considered, 90/2796, 91/2227, 05/2639
Farley *v.* Child Support Agency; *sub nom* Farley *v.* Secretary of State for Work and Pensions (No.2) [2005] EWCA Civ 869; [2005] 2 F.L.R. 1075; [2005] 3 F.C.R. 343; [2005] A.C.D. 94; [2005] Fam. Law 772; (2005) 102(40) L.S.G. 26; *Times,* June 30, 2005; *Independent,* June 28, 2005, CA (Civ Div)
Farley *v.* Secretary of State for Work and Pensions (No.1) [2005] EWCA Civ 778; [2005] 2 F.L.R. 1059; [2005] 3 F.C.R. 327; [2005] Fam. Law 771; (2005) 102(9) L.S.G. 28; *Times,* January 27, 2005, CA (Civ Div); reversing [2004] EWHC 1655; [2005] 1 F.L.R. 1; [2004] Fam. Law 787; (2004) 101(32) L.S.G. 35; *Times,* July 23, 2004, QBD (Admin) . . . . *Digested,* 05/**1554**
Farley *v.* Secretary of State for Work and Pensions (No.2) see Farley *v.* Child Support Agency
Farmacia Chemists Ltd *v.* Pharmacia AB [2005] E.T.M.R. 41, App Person . . . . *Digested,* 05/**2576**
Farmer *v.* Sloan [2004] EWHC 606; [2005] W.T.L.R. 521; [2004] N.P.C. 41, Ch D
Farrell Matthews & Weir *v.* Hansen [2005] I.C.R. 509; [2005] I.R.L.R. 160, EAT. . . . . . . *Digested,* 05/**1196**
Fassihi *v.* Item Software (UK) Ltd see Item Software (UK) Ltd *v.* Fassihi
Fattal *v.* John Lyon Free Grammar School Governors; *sub nom* Fattal *v.* Keepers and Governors of the Possessions Revenues and Goods of the Free Grammar School of John Lyon [2004] EWCA Civ 1530; [2005] 1 W.L.R. 803; [2005] 1 All E.R. 466; [2005] 1 P. & C.R. 29; [2005] L. & T.R. 11; [2005] 1 E.G.L.R. 51; [2005] 04 E.G. 168; [2005] R.V.R. 339; [2004] 50 E.G.C.S. 85; (2004) 148 S.J.L.B. 1433; [2004] N.P.C. 177; *Times,* December 2, 2004; *Independent,* December 10, 2004, CA (Civ Div) LandsTr . . . . *Digested,* 05/**3405**
Fattal *v.* Keepers and Governors of the Possessions Revenues and Goods of the Free Grammar School of John Lyon see Fattal *v.* John Lyon Free Grammar School Governors

Favermead Ltd v. FPD Savills Ltd [2005] EWHC 626; [2005] B.P.I.R. 715, Ch D ..... *Digested*, 05/**90**
Fawdry & Co v. Murfitt [2002] EWCA Civ 643; [2003] Q.B. 104; [2002] 3 W.L.R.
1354; [2003] 4 All E.R. 60; [2002] C.P. Rep. 62; [2002] C.P.L.R. 593;
Independent, May 23, 2002, CA (Civ Div) .... *Digested*, 02/**316**:
Considered, 03/6, 05/36
FC Shepherd & Co v. Jerrom [1987] Q.B. 301; [1986] 3 W.L.R. 801; [1986] 3 All E.R.
589; [1986] I.C.R. 802; [1986] I.R.L.R. 358; (1986) 130 S.J. 665, CA (Civ Div);
reversing [1985] I.C.R. 552; [1985] I.R.L.R. 275; (1985) 82 L.S.G. 2162, EAT.. *Digested*, 86/**1259**:
Considered, 91/1695, 05/1215
Fea v. Roberts [2005] EWHC 2186; (2005-06) 8 I.T.E.L.R. 231, Ch D
Fearnley v. DPP; *sub nom* Fernley v. DPP [2005] EWHC 1393; (2005) 169 J.P. 450;
(2005) 169 J.P.N. 735; *Times*, July 6, 2005, QBD (Admin) .... *Digested*, 05/**729**
Feay v. Barnwell [1938] 1 All E.R. 31.................................. *Considered*, 05/**406**
Federal Trade Commission v. AmeriDebt Inc (2005-06) 8 I.T.E.L.R. 4, US Ct
Federation des Employes et Cadres (CGT-FO)'s Application [2005] E.C.C. 11, CE (F)
Federation Nationale de l'Industrie et des Commerces en Gros des Viandes (FNICGV) v.
Commission of the European Communities (Interim Measures) (T252/03)
[2005] 4 C.M.L.R. 13, CFI (5th Chamber) .... *Digested*, 05/**1432**
Federation Nationale de l'Industrie et des Commerces en Gros des Viandes (FNICGV) v.
Commission of the European Communities (T252/03 R) [2005] 5 C.M.L.R.
10, CFI
Federation Nationale de la Cooperation Betail et Viande (FNCBV) v. Commission of the
European Communities (T217/03) [2004] E.C.R. II-239; [2005] 5 C.M.L.R. 12,
CFI
Federation Nationale des Syndicats d'Exploitants Agricoles (FNSEA) v. Commission of
the European Communities (T245/03) [2004] E.C.R. II-271; [2005] 5 C.M.L.R.
11, CFI
Federation of Wholesale Distributors v. Office of Fair Trading (Leave to Withdraw Appeal:
Costs) [2004] CAT 11; [2004] Comp. A.R. 764, CAT .... *Digested*, 05/**569**
Feetum v. Levy; *sub nom* Cabvision Ltd v. Feetum [2005] EWCA Civ 1601, CA (Civ
Div); affirming [2005] EWHC 349; [2005] 1 W.L.R. 2576; [2005] B.C.C. 484;
(2005) 102(10) L.S.G. 30; *Times*, February 24, 2005, Ch D .... *Digested*, 05/**2266**
Fejde v. Sweden (A/212-C) (1994) 17 E.H.R.R. 14, ECHR...................... *Digested*, 94/**2411**:
Applied, 05/3775
Feld v. Barnet LBC; Pour v. Westminster City Council [2004] EWCA Civ 1307; [2005]
H.L.R. 9; [2005] B.L.G.R. 411; [2005] A.C.D. 49; (2004) 101(42) L.S.G. 30;
(2004) 148 S.J.L.B. 1247; *Times*, October 26, 2004, CA (Civ Div) .... *Digested*, 04/**1904**
Fell v. United Kingdom (A/80) see Campbell v. United Kingdom (A/80)
Fence Gate Ltd v. NEL Construction Ltd 82 Con. L.R. 41, QBD (TCC) .... *Digested*, 03/**194**:
Applied, 05/205
Fengate Developments v. Customs and Excise Commissioners [2004] EWCA Civ 1591;
[2005] S.T.C. 191; [2005] B.T.C. 5003; [2005] B.V.C. 34; [2004] S.T.I. 2500;
(2005) 102(2) L.S.G. 30; (2004) 148 S.J.L.B. 1434; [2004] N.P.C. 179; *Times*,
December 6, 2004, CA (Civ Div); affirming [2004] EWHC 152; [2004] S.T.C.
772; [2004] B.T.C. 5601; [2004] B.V.C. 660; [2004] S.T.I. 313; [2004] N.P.C. 15,
Ch D; affirming in part [2003] S.T.I. 2208, V&DTr .... *Digested*, 05/**4388**
Fenwood Developments Ltd v. Customs and Excise Commissioners; *sub nom* Revenue
and Customs Commissioners v. Fenwood Developments Ltd [2005] EWHC
2954; [2005] N.P.C. 148; *Times*, December 26, 2005, Ch D; affirming [2005]
B.V.C. 2493; [2005] S.T.I. 879, V&DTr (Manchester)
Fernley v. DPP see Fearnley v. DPP
Ferrari SpA v. Turkish Patent Institute [2005] E.T.M.R. 80
Ferrazzini v. Italy (44759/98) [2001] S.T.C. 1314; (2002) 34 E.H.R.R. 45; [2003]
B.T.C. 157; 3 I.T.L. Rep. 918; [2001] S.T.I. 1224, ECHR.................. *Digested*, 01/**5298**:
Applied, 03/2122, 03/4260, 05/2084: *Considered*, 03/4267, 03/4325,
03/4604
Ferrero SpA v. Kindercare Learning Centers Inc [2005] E.T.M.R. 6, OHIM (1st Bd App) . *Digested*, 05/**2511**:
Considered, 05/2523
Ferrero SpA's Trade Marks; *sub nom* KINDER Trade Marks [2004] R.P.C. 29, App
Person .... *Digested*, 05/**2575**:
Applied, 05/2581
Ferriere di Roe Volciano SpA v. Commission of the European Communities (234/82 R)
[1983] E.C.R. 725, ECJ... *Digested*, 84/**1436**:
Followed, 05/544
Ferriere Nord SpA v. Commission of the European Communities (T176/01) [2005] All
E.R. (EC) 851; [2005] Env. L.R. D3, CFI
Ferrotech Ltd, Re see Huddersfield Fine Worsteds Ltd, Re
Ferrotech Ltd, Re; *sub nom* Duggins v. Tipper; Ellis v. Harris; Granville Technology
Group Ltd, Re [2005] EWHC 1848; [2005] B.C.C. 905, Ch D (Companies Ct) . *Subsequent proceed-*
ings, 05/2262
Ferson Contractors Ltd v. Levolux AT Ltd see Levolux AT Ltd v. Ferson Contractors Ltd
Fesil v. EFTA Surveillance Authority (E5/04) [2005] 3 C.M.L.R. 18, EFTA
Fidelity Management SA v. Myriad International Holdings BV [2005] EWHC 1193;
[2005] 2 All E.R. (Comm) 312; [2005] 2 Lloyd's Rep. 508, QBD (Comm) .... *Digested*, 05/**195**

Fidler *v.* First Secretary of State; Fidler *v.* Reigate and Banstead BC [2004] EWCA Civ 1295; [2005] 1 P. & C.R. 12; [2005] J.P.L. 510; (2004) 148 S.J.L.B. 1214; *Independent*, October 22, 2004, CA (Civ Div); affirming [2003] EWHC 2003; [2004] 1 P.L.R. 1; [2004] J.P.L. 630; [2003] N.P.C. 111, QBD (Admin) . . . .   *Digested*, 04/**3048**

Fidler *v.* Reigate and Banstead BC see Fidler *v.* First Secretary of State

Fiduciary Ltd *v.* Morningstar Research Pty Ltd 7 I.T.L. Rep. 159, Sup Ct (NSW) . . . .   *Digested*, 05/**4352**

Fielden *v.* Cunliffe see Cunliffe *v.* Fielden

Figgis, Re; *sub nom* Roberts *v.* MacLaren [1969] 1 Ch. 123; [1968] 2 W.L.R. 1173; [1968] 1 All E.R. 999; 112 S.J. 156, Ch D . . . .   *Digested*, 68/**4065**: *Applied*, 05/4118

Finalarte Sociedade de Construcao Civil Lda *v.* Urlaubs- und Lohnausgleichskasse der Bauwirtschaft (C49/98); Portugaia Construcoes Lda *v.* Urlaubs- und Lohnausgleichskasse der Bauwirtschaft (C70/98); Engil Sociedade de Construcao Civil SA *v.* Urlaubs- und Lohnausgleichskasse der Bauwirtschaft (C71/98); Urlaubs- und Lohnausgleichskasse der Bauwirtschaft *v.* Amilcar Oliveira Rocha (C50/98); Urlaubs- und Lohnausgleichskasse der Bauwirtschaft *v.* Tudor Stone Ltd (C52/98); Urlaubs- und Lohnausgleichskasse der Bauwirtschaft *v.* Tecnamb-Tecnologia do Ambiante Lda (C53/98); Urlaubs- und Lohnausgleichskasse der Bauwirtschaft *v.* Turiprata Construcoes Civil SA (C54/98); Urlaubs- und Lohnausgleichskasse der Bauwirtschaft *v.* Duarte dos Santos Sousa (C68/98); Urlaubs- und Lohnausgleichskasse der Bauwirtschaft *v.* Santos & Kewitz Construcoes Lda (C69/98) [2001] E.C.R. I-7831; [2003] 2 C.M.L.R. 11, ECJ (5th Chamber) [2001] E.C.R. I-7831, AGO . . . .   *Digested*, 03/**1283**: *Considered*, 05/1466

Finance Ltd *v.* Inspector of Taxes [2005] S.T.C. (S.C.D.) 407; [2005] S.T.I. 867, Sp Comm . . . .   *Digested*, 05/**4021**

Financial Services Authority *v.* Fradley (t/a Top Bet Placement Services); *sub nom* Financial Services Authority *v.* Woodward [2005] EWCA Civ 1183; *Times*, December 1, 2005, CA (Civ Div); reversing in part [2004] EWHC 3008; [2005] 1 B.C.L.C. 479; (2004) 101 (45) L.S.G. 31; *Times*, November 8, 2004, Ch D . . . .   *Digested*, 05/**1708**

Financial Services Authority *v.* Martin [2004] EWHC 3255; [2005] 1 B.C.L.C. 495, Ch D . . . .   *Digested*, 05/**273**

Financial Services Authority *v.* Martin [2005] EWCA Civ 1422; *Times*, December 7, 2005, CA (Civ Div)

Financial Services Authority *v.* Matthews [2004] EWHC 2966; [2005] Pens. L.R. 241, Ch D . . . .   *Digested*, 05/**1694**

Financial Services Authority *v.* Woodward see Financial Services Authority *v.* Fradley (t/a Top Bet Placement Services)

Finanzamt Bergisch Gladbach *v.* HE (C25/03) [2005] E.C.R. I-3123; [2005] 2 C.M.L.R. 38; [2005] S.T.I. 864, ECJ

Finanzamt Gladbeck *v.* Linneweber (C453/02); Finanzamt Herne-West *v.* Akritidis (C462/02) [2005] E.C.R. I-1131; [2005] 1 C.M.L.R. 53; [2005] C.E.C. 548; [2005] S.T.I. 255, ECJ (2nd Chamber) . . . .   *Digested*, 05/**4348**

Finanzamt Gummersbach *v.* Bockemuhl (C90/02) [2005] S.T.C. 934; [2004] E.C.R. I-3303; [2004] 3 C.M.L.R. 5; [2004] C.E.C. 303; [2004] S.T.I. 988, ECJ (5th Chamber) . . . .   *Digested*, 05/**4401**

Finanzamt Heidelberg *v.* iSt Internationale Sprach- und Studienreisen GmbH (C200/04) [2005] S.T.I. 1719, ECJ (2nd Chamber)

Finanzamt Herne-West *v.* Akritidis (C462/02) see Finanzamt Gladbeck *v.* Linneweber (C453/02)

Finanzamt Koln-Altstadt *v.* Schumacker (C279/93) [1996] Q.B. 28; [1995] 3 W.L.R. 498; [1995] All E.R. (E.C.) 319; [1995] S.T.C. 306; [1995] E.C.R. I-225; [1996] 2 C.M.L.R. 450; *Times*, February 24, 1995, ECJ . . . .   *Digested*, 95/**2773**: *Applied*, 02/4433, 05/1469: *Considered*, 96/3341: *Followed*, 95/2786, 01/5245, 02/1577

Finanzamt Offenbach am Main-Land *v.* Faxworld Vorgrundungsgesellschaft Peter Hunninghausen & Wolfgang Klein GbR (C137/02) [2005] S.T.C. 1192; [2004] E.C.R. I-5547; [2004] 2 C.M.L.R. 28; [2004] S.T.I. 1166, ECJ (5th Chamber) . .   *Digested*, 05/**4364**

Finanzamt Sulingen *v.* Sudholz (C17/01) [2005] S.T.C. 747; [2004] E.C.R. I-4243; [2004] 2 C.M.L.R. 31; [2004] C.E.C. 377; [2004] S.T.I. 1197, ECJ (5th Chamber) . . . .   *Digested*, 05/**4366**

Finch *v.* Scriven (Unreported, May 13, 2004), CC (Dartford) [*Ex rel.* Nigel Ffitch, Barrister, Phoenix Chambers, Gray's Inn, London] . . . .   *Digested*, 05/**382**

Findlay *v.* United Kingdom (22107/93) (1997) 24 E.H.R.R. 221; *Times*, February 27, 1997; *Independent*, March 4, 1997, ECHR (1996) 21 E.H.R.R. CD7, Eur Comm HR . . . .   *Digested*, 97/**2807**: *Applied*, 97/2808, 05/2104: *Considered*, 97/288, 00/3227, 01/366, 03/5307, 04/1945, 05/234: *Distinguished*, 01/358: *Explained*, 98/256: *Followed*, 99/3090, 99/3091, 00/3215

Finlan *v.* Vale Royal BC [2005] P.A.D. 6, Planning Inspector

Fiorentino Comm Giuseppe Srl *v.* Farnesi [2005] EWHC 160; [2005] 1 W.L.R. 3718; [2005] 2 All E.R. 737; [2005] 1 All E.R. (Comm) 575; [2005] B.C.C. 771; *Times*, March 3, 2005, Ch D . . . .   *Digested*, 05/**265**

FIRETRACE Trade Mark [2002] R.P.C. 15, TMR . . . . *Digested*, 02/**2857**:
Distinguished, 05/2583

Firma C-Trade SA v. Newcastle Protection and Indemnity Association (The Fanti);
Socony Mobil Oil Co Inc v. West of England Shipowners Mutual Insurance
Association (London) Ltd (The Padre Island) (No.2) [1991] 2 A.C. 1; [1990] 3
W.L.R. 78; [1990] 2 All E.R. 705; [1990] 2 Lloyd's Rep. 191; [1990] B.C.L.C.
625; (1990) 134 S.J. 833, HL; reversing [1989] 1 Lloyd's Rep. 239; *Times*,
December 27, 1988, CA (Civ Div); reversing in part [1987] 2 Lloyd's Rep. 299,
QBD (Comm) . . . . *Digested*, 90/**4098**:
Applied, 92/3972, 93/3619, 97/4597, 00/3514, 03/2468:
Considered, 95/2926, 96/1136, 05/2366: *Distinguished*, 98/3354:
Followed, 97/3139, 99/3227, 00/4693: *Previous proceedings*, 88/3239

First Choice Holidays Plc v. Customs and Excise Commissioners (C149/01) see
Customs and Excise Commissioners v. First Choice Holidays Plc (C149/01)

First Global Locums Ltd v. Cosias (Continuation of Restraining Order) [2005] EWHC
1147; [2005] I.R.L.R. 873, QBD . . . . *Digested*, 05/**421**

First Penthouse Ltd v. Channel Hotels & Properties (UK) Ltd; Channel Hotels &
Properties (UK) Ltd v. Al-Tamimi [2004] EWCA Civ 1072; [2004] L. & T.R. 27;
(2004) 148 S.J.L.B. 974, CA (Civ Div); affirming [2003] EWHC 2713; [2004] L.
& T.R. 16; [2004] 1 E.G.L.R. 16; [2004] 05 E.G. 148, Ch D . . . . *Digested*, 05/**2639**

First Secretary of State v. Chichester DC see Chichester DC v. First Secretary of State

First Secretary of State v. Hammersmatch Properties Ltd see Hammersmatch Properties
Ltd v. First Secretary of State

First Secretary of State v. Redrow Homes Ltd see Redrow Homes Ltd v. First Secretary
of State

First Secretary of State v. Sainsbury's Supermarkets Ltd see R. (on the application of
Sainsbury's Supermarkets Ltd) v. First Secretary of State

First Secretary of State v. Simmons see Simmons v. First Secretary of State

Firstdale Ltd v. Quinton [2004] EWHC 1926; [2005] 1 All E.R. 639; (2004) 101 (40)
L.S.G. 29; (2004) 154 N.L.J. 1256; *Times*, October 27, 2004, QBD (Comm) . . . *Digested*, 04/**283**

Fischer v. Finanzamt Donaueschingen (C283/95) [1998] All E.R. (EC) 567; [1998]
S.T.C. 708; [1998] E.C.R. I-3369; [1998] 3 C.M.L.R. 1055; [1998] C.E.C. 879;
[1998] B.T.C. 5423; [1998] B.V.C. 431; *Times*, July 2, 1998, ECJ (6th Chamber) . *Digested*, 98/**4911**:
Applied, 05/4348: *Considered*, 98/4891, 02/4791:
Joined proceedings, 98/4966

Fisher v. Cadman (Application to Reopen Hearing) [2005] EWHC 2424; *Times*, June
23, 2005, Ch D (Companies Ct)

Fisher v. English Nature see R. (on the application of Fisher) v. English Nature

Fitch v. Official Receiver [1996] 1 W.L.R. 242; [1996] B.C.C. 328; [1996] B.P.I.R. 152;
(1996) 93(3) L.S.G. 29; (1996) 140 S.J.L.B. 22; *Times*, November 21, 1995;
Independent, December 13, 1995, CA (Civ Div) . . . . *Digested*, 95/**414**:
Applied, 04/2138: *Considered*, 05/2277

Fitzgibbon v. Attorney General [2005] EWCA Civ 593, CA (Civ Div); affirming [2005]
EWHC 114; (2005) 28(5) I.P.D. 28035; *Times*, March 15, 2005, Ch D . . . . *Digested*, 05/**634**

Fitzpatrick v. Sterling Housing Association Ltd [2001] 1 A.C. 27; [1999] 3 W.L.R. 1113;
[1999] 4 All E.R. 705; [2000] 1 F.L.R. 271; [1999] 2 F.L.R. 1027; [2000] 1
F.C.R. 21; [2000] U.K.H.R.R. 25; 7 B.H.R.C. 200; (2000) 32 H.L.R. 178; [2000]
L. & T.R. 44; [2000] Fam. Law 14; [1999] E.G.C.S. 125; (1999) 96(43) L.S.G.
3; [1999] N.P.C. 127; (2000) 79 P. & C.R. D4; *Times*, November 2, 1999 ;
Independent, November 2, 1999, HL; reversing [1998] Ch. 304; [1998] 2
W.L.R. 225; [1997] 4 All E.R. 991; [1998] 1 F.L.R. 6; [1998] 1 F.C.R. 417; (1998)
30 H.L.R. 576; [1997] Fam. Law 784; [1997] E.G.C.S. 122; (1997) 147 N.L.J.
1275; [1997] N.P.C. 118; *Times*, July 31, 1997; *Independent*, July 29, 1997, CA
(Civ Div) . . . . *Digested*, 99/**3715**:
Applied, 00/4147, 02/1824, 05/2118: *Considered*, 99/24, 02/914, 04/2538

Fitzroy House Epworth Street (No.1) Ltd v. Financial Times Ltd A1/2005/2588, CA (Civ
Div); affirming [2005] EWHC 2391; [2005] 46 E.G.C.S. 176, QBD (TCC)

Fixtures Marketing Ltd v. Organismos Prognostikon Agonon Podosfairou (OPAP)
(C444/02) [2004] E.C.R. I-10549; [2005] 1 C.M.L.R. 16; [2005] C.E.C. 38;
[2005] E.C.D.R. 3, ECJ . . . . *Digested*, 05/**2431**

Fixtures Marketing Ltd v. Oy Veikkaus AB (C46/02) [2004] E.C.R. I-10365; [2005]
E.C.D.R. 2, ECJ . . . . *Digested*, 05/**2432**

Fixtures Marketing Ltd v. Svenska Spel AB (C338/02) [2004] E.C.R. I-10497; [2005]
E.C.D.R. 4, ECJ . . . . *Digested*, 05/**2430**

Flaherty v. National Greyhound Racing Club Ltd; *sub nom* National Greyhound Racing
Club Ltd v. Flaherty [2005] EWCA Civ 1117; (2005) 102(37) L.S.G. 31; *Times*,
October 5, 2005, CA (Civ Div); reversing [2004] EWHC 2838, Ch D . . . . *Digested*, 05/**720**

Flannery v. Halifax Estate Agencies Ltd (t/a Colleys Professional Services) [2000] 1
W.L.R. 377; [2000] 1 All E.R. 373; [2000] C.P. Rep. 18; [1999] B.L.R. 107;
(1999) 11 Admin. L.R. 465; (1999) 15 Const. L.J. 313; (1999) 96(13) L.S.G. 32;
(1999) 149 N.L.J. 284; [1999] N.P.C. 22; *Times*, March 4, 1999; *Independent*,
February 26, 1999, CA (Civ Div) . . . . *Digested*, 99/**37**:
Applied, 00/1476, 01/559, 05/950: *Considered*, 01/50: *Referred to*, 00/3457

Fleming v. Chief Constable of Sussex [2004] EWCA Civ 643; [2005] 1 Costs L.R. 1, CA (Civ Div) . . . . *Digested*, 05/**383**

Fleming (Inspector of Taxes) v. London Produce Co; *sub nom* Inland Revenue Commissioners v. London Produce Co [1968] 1 W.L.R. 1013; [1968] 2 All E.R. 975; 44 T.C. 582; [1968] T.R. 97; (1968) 112 S.J. 356, Ch D . . . . *Digested*, 68/**1857**:
Applied, 05/4130

Fleming (t/a Bodycraft) v. Customs and Excise Commissioners; *sub nom* Fleming (t/a Bodycraft) v. Revenue and Customs Commissioners; C3/2005/0518, CA (Civ Div); reversing [2005] EWHC 232; [2005] S.T.C. 707; [2005] Eu. L.R. 735; [2005] B.T.C. 5215; [2005] B.V.C. 246, Ch D; affirming in part [2004] V. & D.R. 172; [2004] S.T.I. 1560, V&DTr (London) . . . . *Digested*, 05/**4377**:
Followed, 05/4367

Fleming (t/a Bodycraft) v. Revenue and Customs Commissioners see Fleming (t/a Bodycraft) v. Customs and Excise Commissioners

Fleming's Will Trusts, Re; *sub nom* Ennion v. Hampstead Old People's Housing Trust [1974] 1 W.L.R. 1552; [1974] 3 All E.R. 323; 118 S.J. 850, Ch D . . . . *Digested*, 74/**4005**:
Applied, 05/3969

Fletcher v. Blackpool Fylde and Wyre Hospitals NHS Trust; *sub nom* Fletcher v. NHS Pensions Agency [2005] I.C.R. 1458; [2005] I.R.L.R. 689, EAT . . . . *Digested*, 05/**1337**

Fletcher v. Midland Bank Plc (No.2) see Preston v. Wolverhampton Healthcare NHS Trust (No.2)

Fletcher v. Midland Bank Plc (No.3) see Powerhouse Retail Ltd v. Burroughs

Fletcher v. Midland Bank Plc (No.3) see Preston v. Wolverhampton Healthcare NHS Trust (No.3)

Fletcher v. NHS Pensions Agency see Fletcher v. Blackpool Fylde and Wyre Hospitals NHS Trust

Fletcher v. Vooght [2000] B.P.I.R. 435; (2000) 97(12) L.S.G. 39; (2000) 144 S.J.L.B. 135, Ch D . . . . *Considered*, 05/2309

Flett v. Matheson A2/2005/0697, CA (Civ Div); reversing [2005] I.C.R. 1134; [2005] I.R.L.R. 412, EAT . . . . *Digested*, 05/**1219**

Flightline Ltd v. Edwards; *sub nom* Swissair Schweizerische Luftverkehr AG, Re; Edwards v. Flightline Ltd [2003] EWCA Civ 63; [2003] 1 W.L.R. 1200; [2003] 3 All E.R. 1200; [2003] B.C.C. 361; [2003] 1 B.C.L.C. 427; [2003] B.P.I.R. 549; (2003) 100(13) L.S.G. 28; (2003) 147 S.J.L.B. 178; *Times*, February 13, 2003; *Independent*, February 21, 2003, CA (Civ Div); reversing [2002] EWHC 1648; [2002] 1 W.L.R. 2535; [2003] B.P.I.R. 60; (2002) 99(39) L.S.G. 39; *Times*, August 23, 2002, Ch D (Companies Ct) . . . . *Digested*, 03/**2426**:
Applied, 05/709

Fliptex Ltd v. Hogg [2004] EWHC 1280; [2004] B.C.C. 870, Ch D . . . . *Digested*, 05/**2268**

Flitney v. Columbia Marketing Ltd (Unreported, August 31, 2004), CC (Barnet) [*Ex rel.* Gurion Taussig, Barrister, 199 Strand, London] . . . . *Digested*, 05/**3143**

Floe Telecom Ltd v. Office of Communications [2004] CAT 18; [2005] Comp. A.R. 290, CAT . . . . *Digested*, 05/**547**

Floe Telecom Ltd v. Office of Communications (Application to Set Aside Order) [2005] CAT 14; [2005] Comp. A.R. 1004, CAT

Floe Telecom Ltd v. Office of Communications (Extension of Time) [2005] CAT 17; [2005] Comp. A.R. 1058, CAT

Floe Telecom Ltd v. Office of Communications (Remitted Decision: Procedure: Costs) [2004] CAT 22; [2005] Comp. A.R. 463, CAT. . . . . *Digested*, 05/**567**

Floe Telecom Ltd (In Administration) v. Office of Communications (Permission to Amend Notice of Appeal) [2004] CAT 7; [2004] Comp. A.R. 559, CAT . . . . *Digested*, 05/**558**

Floe Telecom Ltd (In Administration) v. Office of Communications (Permission to Appeal) [2005] CAT 28; [2005] Comp. A.R. 1132, CAT

Floe Telecom Ltd (In Administration) v. Office of Communications (Permission to Intervene) [2004] CAT 2; [2004] Comp. A.R. 356, CAT. . . . . *Digested*, 05/**557**

Flood Safety Works in the River Po, Re (C385/02) see Commission of the European Communities v. Italy (C385/02)

Flower v. Inland Revenue Commissioners see Flower's Settlement Trusts, Re

Flower's Settlement Trusts, Re; *sub nom* Flower v. Inland Revenue Commissioners [1957] 1 W.L.R. 401; [1957] 1 All E.R. 462; 50 R. & I.T. 150; (1957) 36 A.T.C. 22; [1957] T.R. 29; 101 S.J. 189, CA; affirming [1956] T.R. 175 . . . . *Digested*, 57/**3277**:
Applied, 59/2990, 69/3664: *Distinguished*, 57/3688, 57/3690, 66/10940, 05/3978

Flynn v. Scougall [2004] EWCA Civ 873; [2004] 1 W.L.R. 3069; [2004] 3 All E.R. 609; [2004] C.P. Rep. 37; [2005] 1 Costs L.R. 38; (2004) 148 S.J.L.B. 880; *Times*, July 21, 2004; *Independent*, July 16, 2004, CA (Civ Div) . . . . *Digested*, 04/**392**

Focsa Services (UK) Ltd v. Birkett [1996] I.R.L.R. 325, EAT. . . . . *Digested*, 96/**2522**:
Applied, 98/2098, 05/1340: *Distinguished*, 00/2131

Fokus Bank ASA v. Norway (E1/04) [2005] 1 C.M.L.R. 10; 7 I.T.L. Rep. 367, EFTA

Fonden Marselisborg Lystbadehavn v. Skatteministeriet (C428/02) [2005] E.C.R. I-1527; [2005] S.T.I. 360, ECJ

Football Association Premier League Ltd *v.* Panini UK Ltd [2003] EWCA Civ 995; [2004] 1 W.L.R. 1147; [2003] 4 All E.R. 1290; [2004] E.C.C. 17; [2003] E.C.D.R. 36; [2004] F.S.R. 1; (2003) 100(35) L.S.G. 35; (2003) 147 S.J.L.B. 874; *Times*, July 17, 2003, CA (Civ Div); affirming [2002] EWHC 2779; [2003] E.C.D.R. 21; [2003] F.S.R. 38; (2003) 26(4) I.P.D. 26022, Ch D . . . .   *Digested*, 03/**2503**:
                                                            Applied, 05/2420

Forbes *v.* Wandsworth HA [1997] Q.B. 402; [1996] 3 W.L.R. 1108; [1996] 4 All E.R. 881; [1996] 7 Med. L.R. 175; (1997) 36 B.M.L.R. 1; (1996) 93(15) L.S.G. 32; (1996) 146 N.L.J. 477; (1996) 140 S.J.L.B. 85; *Times*, March 21, 1996, CA (Civ Div) . . . .   *Digested*, 96/**4466**:
     Applied, 00/517, 03/2981, 03/2982, 05/440: *Considered*, 97/664:
              Distinguished, 97/650, 98/555: *Followed*, 97/666

Ford Motor Co Ltd *v.* Singh see Gill *v.* Ford Motor Co Ltd

Ford Motor Co Ltd's Design Application, Re see R. *v.* Registered Designs Appeal Tribunal Ex p. Ford Motor Co Ltd

Foreman *v.* Kingstone [2005] W.T.L.R. 823; (2003-04) 6 I.T.E.L.R. 841, HC (NZ) . . . . .   *Digested*, 04/**3950**

Forest of Dean DC *v.* Prictor [2005] P.A.D. 48, Planning Inspector

Fornah *v.* Secretary of State for the Home Department [2005] EWCA Civ 680; [2005] 1 W.L.R. 3773; [2005] 2 F.L.R. 1085; [2005] 3 F.C.R. 449; [2005] Imm. A.R. 479; [2005] I.N.L.R. 483; [2005] Fam. Law 849; *Times*, June 16, 2005, CA (Civ Div) . . . .   *Digested*, 05/**2226**

Fornasar (C318/98), Re see Criminal Proceedings against Fornasar (C318/98), Re

Forshaw *v.* Archcraft Ltd; Chorley *v.* Archcraft Ltd [2005] I.R.L.R. 600, EAT

Forster *v.* Outred & Co [1982] 1 W.L.R. 86; [1982] 2 All E.R. 753; 125 S.J. 309, CA (Civ Div) . . . .   *Digested*, 82/**1849**:
   Applied, 81/1621, 83/1765, 84/3170, 85/2012, 89/2585, 90/2941.a, 91/2343,
     01/4526, 01/4527, 04/2740, 05/437: *Considered*, 82/1845, 84/1579,
       93/2997, 94/2912, 00/2621, 01/946: *Distinguished*, 85/2291, 87/229,
         88/2158, 02/3276: *Doubted*, 83/2215: *Followed*, 88/2154, 05/2865

Forsyth *v.* Forsyth [1891] P. 363, PDAD . . . .   *Applied*, 63/3174:
                                                          Followed, 05/1682

Fortis Banque *v.* Mancini [2005] I.L.Pr. 53, Cass (F)

Fortisbank SA *v.* Trenwick International Ltd [2005] EWHC 399; [2005] Lloyd's Rep. I.R. 464, QBD (Comm) . . . .   *Digested*, 05/**705**

Forvaltnings AB Stenholmen *v.* Riksskatteverket (C320/02) [2004] All E.R. (EC) 870; [2004] S.T.C. 1041; [2004] E.C.R. I-3509; [2004] 2 C.M.L.R. 56; [2004] C.E.C. 248; [2004] S.T.I. 989, ECJ (5th Chamber) . . . .   *Digested*, 05/**4396**

Fosberry *v.* Revenue and Customs Commissioners [2005] S.T.I. 2035, V&DTr

Foskett *v.* McKeown [2001] 1 A.C. 102; [2000] 2 W.L.R. 1299; [2000] 3 All E.R. 97; [2000] Lloyd's Rep. I.R. 627; [2000] W.T.L.R. 667; (1999-2000) 2 I.T.E.L.R. 711; (2000) 97(23) L.S.G. 44; *Times*, May 24, 2000; *Independent*, July 3, 2000 (C.S), HL; reversing [1998] Ch. 265; [1998] 2 W.L.R. 298; [1997] 3 All E.R. 392; [1997] N.P.C. 83; *Times*, June 27, 1997, CA (Civ Div) . . . .   *Digested*, 00/**2328**:
                                                          Considered, 05/621

Foster *v.* DPP; Rutherford *v.* DPP [2004] EWHC 2955; [2005] 1 W.L.R. 1400; [2005] 1 F.C.R. 153; [2005] Crim. L.R. 639; [2005] A.C.D. 63; *Times*, January 5, 2005, QBD (Admin) . . . .   *Digested*, 05/**760**

Foster *v.* Foster [2003] EWCA Civ 565; [2003] 2 F.L.R. 299; [2005] 3 F.C.R. 26; [2003] Fam. Law 562; (2003) 100(26) L.S.G. 37; *Times*, May 2, 2003; *Independent*, May 1, 2003, CA (Civ Div) . . . .   *Considered*, 05/1656

Foster Yeoman Ltd *v.* Highland and Western Isles Valuation Joint Board Assessor [2005] R.A. 189, Lands Tr (Scot) . . . .   *Digested*, 05/**5624**

Foughali *v.* Secretary of State for the Home Department (Unreported, June 2, 2000), IAT . . . .   *Approved*, 05/2178

Foulser *v.* MacDougall (Inspector of Taxes) [2005] EWHC 2958, Ch D; affirming [2005] S.T.C. (S.C.D.) 374; [2005] S.T.I. 835, Sp Comm . . . .   *Digested*, 05/**3995**

Four Seasons Healthcare Ltd (formerly Cotswold Spa Retirement Hotels Ltd) *v.* Maughan [2005] I.R.L.R. 324, EAT . . . .   *Digested*, 05/**1215**

Fourie *v.* Le Roux (Application to Continue Freezing Order) [2004] EWHC 2557; [2005] B.P.I.R. 723, Ch D . . . .   *Digested*, 05/**416**:
                                            Subsequent proceedings, 05/423

Fourie *v.* Le Roux (No.1); *sub nom* Herlan Edmunds Engineering (Pty) Ltd, Re [2005] EWCA Civ 204; *Times*, April 25, 2005, CA (Civ Div); affirming in part [2004] EWHC 2260; *Times*, October 8, 2004, Ch D . . . .   *Digested*, 05/**423**:
                                            Previous proceedings, 05/416

Fourie *v.* Le Roux (No.2) [2005] EWHC 922; [2005] B.P.I.R. 779, Ch D . . . .   *Digested*, 05/**2301**

Fox *v.* Spousal (Midlands) Ltd see Fairchild *v.* Glenhaven Funeral Services Ltd (t/a GH Dovener & Son)

Fox *v.* United Kingdom (A/182); Campbell *v.* United Kingdom (A/182); Hartley *v.* United Kingdom (A/182) (1991) 13 E.H.R.R. 157; *Times*, October 16, 1990; *Guardian*, October 4, 1990, ECHR . . . .   *Digested*, 90/**2526**:
   Applied, 98/3110, 04/891: *Considered*, 98/3071: *Distinguished*, 05/2921:
                                            Subsequent proceedings, 92/2334

Foxton *v.* Revenue and Customs Commissioners [2005] S.T.C. (S.C.D.) 661, Sp
Comm

Foxtons Ltd *v.* Thesleff [2005] EWCA Civ 514; [2005] 2 E.G.L.R. 29; [2005] 21 E.G.
140; [2005] 17 E.G.C.S. 122; *Times,* May 17, 2005, CA (Civ Div) . . . .   *Digested,* 05/**704**

Foyle *v.* Bracknell Forest BC (Unreported, January 21, 2005), CC (Slough) [*Ex rel.*
David White, Barrister, 12 King's Bench Walk, Temple, London] . . . .   *Digested,* 05/**2850**

Foyster *v.* Tetsall see Tetsall, Re

France 2 SA *v.* Fabris see Fabris *v.* Societe Nationale de Television France 2 SA

France *v.* Commission of the European Communities (C277/98) [2001] E.C.R. I-
8453, ECJ (6th Chamber) [2001] E.C.R. I-8453, AGO. . . . .   *Followed,* 05/142

France *v.* Commission of the European Communities (C482/99); *sub nom* Aid to
Stardust Marine (C482/99), Re [2003] All E.R. (EC) 330; [2002] E.C.R. I-
4397; [2002] 2 C.M.L.R. 41; [2002] C.E.C. 463, ECJ . . . .   *Followed,* 05/590

France *v.* Commission of the European Communities (C68/94); Societe Commerciale
des Potasses et de l'Azote (SCPA) *v.* Commission of the European Communities
(C30/95) [1998] E.C.R. I-1375; [1998] 4 C.M.L.R. 829, ECJ . . . .   *Applied,* 99/692:
                                                Followed, 01/3886, 05/**542**

France *v.* European Parliament (C244/03); *sub nom* Cosmetic Products Directive, Re
(C244/03) [2005] 3 C.M.L.R. 6, ECJ

Francis *v.* Barclays Bank Plc [2004] EWHC 2787; [2005] P.N.L.R. 18; [2004] 51
E.G.C.S. 88, Ch D . . . .   *Digested,* 05/**3419**

Francis *v.* Revenue and Customs Commissioners [2005] S.T.C. (S.C.D.) 692; [2005]
S.T.I. 1560, Sp Comm

Francis *v.* Secretary of State for Work and Pensions [2005] EWCA Civ 1303; [2005] 3
F.C.R. 526; *Times,* November 17, 2005; *Independent,* November 17, 2005, CA
(Civ Div)

Francis *v.* South Gloucestershire Council [2005] P.A.D. 89, Planning Inspector

Francis (CICA: Quantum: 2003), Re [2005] 2 Q.R. 7, CICAP [*Ex rel.* Karen Johnson,
Barrister, Guildford Chambers, Stoke House, Leapale Lane, Guildford] . . . .   *Digested,* 04/**2865**

Franco *v.* Queen, The [2001] UKPC 38; (2001) 145 S.J.L.B. 216; *Times,* October 11,
2001, PC (Ant) . . . .   *Digested,* 01/**1151**:
                                                Applied, 05/900

Frans Maas Rotterdam BV *v.* Hans Ulrich Peterman Beratungs- und Vertrub GmbH
[2005] I.L.Pr. 56, HR (NL)

Frans Maas (UK) Ltd *v.* Samsung Electronics (UK) Ltd [2004] EWHC 1502; [2005] 2
All E.R. (Comm) 783; [2004] 2 Lloyd's Rep. 251; [2005] 1 C.L.C. 647, QBD
(Comm) . . . .   *Digested,* 04/**655**

Franses *v.* Oomerjee [2005] B.P.I.R. 1320, Ch D

Fraser *v.* Canterbury Diocesan Board of Finance (No.2) [2005] UKHL 65; [2005] 3
W.L.R. 964; [2005] W.T.L.R. 1499; [2005] 44 E.G.C.S. 135; (2005) 102(43)
L.S.G. 30; [2005] N.P.C. 121; *Times,* October 31, 2005; *Independent,* November
2, 2005, HL; reversing [2004] EWCA Civ 15; (2004) 148 S.J.L.B. 149;
Independent, February 6, 2004, CA (Civ Div); reversing [2003] EWHC 1075;
[2003] W.T.L.R. 1125; (2002-03) 5 I.T.E.L.R. 871; [2003] N.P.C. 62, Ch D

Fraser *v.* Gaskell [2004] EWHC 894; [2004] P.N.L.R. 32, QBD . . . .   *Digested,* 04/**2739**:
                                                Applied, 05/960

Fraser *v.* Oystertec Plc (Proposed Amendments) [2004] EWHC 2225; [2005] B.P.I.R.
389, Ch D . . . .   *Digested,* 05/**392**

Fraser *v.* Oystertec Plc (Third Party Debt Order) [2004] EWHC 1582; [2005] B.P.I.R.
381, Ch D . . . .   *Digested,* 05/**2339**

Fraser-Woodward Ltd *v.* BBC [2005] EWHC 472; [2005] E.M.L.R. 22; [2005] F.S.R.
36; (2005) 28(6) I.P.D. 28047; (2005) 102(23) L.S.G. 28; *Times,* April 15,
2005, Ch D . . . .   *Digested,* 05/**2420**

Fratelli Babbini di Lionello Babbini & Co SAS *v.* BF Engineering SpA see British Sugar Plc
v. Fratelli Babbini di Lionello Babbini & Co SAS

Fratrik *v.* Slovakia (Admissibility) (51224/99) 7 I.T.L. Rep. 173, ECHR . . . .   *Digested,* 05/**2068**

Frawley *v.* Neill [2000] C.P. Rep. 20; (1999) 96(12) L.S.G. 33; (1999) 143 S.J.L.B.
98; *Times,* April 5, 1999, CA (Civ Div) . . . .   *Digested,* 99/**4369**:
                                                Applied, 05/3381

Freakley *v.* Centre Reinsurance International Co see Centre Reinsurance International
Co *v.* Curzon Insurance Ltd

Freakley *v.* Centre Reinsurance International Co [2004] EWHC 2740; [2005] 2
B.C.L.C. 530; [2005] Lloyd's Rep. I.R. 264, Ch D . . . .   *Digested,* 05/**2372**:
                                   Subsequent proceedings, 05/2366

Freeman *v.* Customs and Excise Commissioners; *sub nom* Margaretta Ltd (In
Liquidation), Re [2005] EWHC 582; [2005] S.T.C. 610; [2005] B.C.C. 506;
[2005] B.P.I.R. 834; [2005] S.T.I. 256; [2005] 2 P. & C.R. DG7, Ch D
(Companies Ct) . . . .   *Digested,* 05/**2325**

Freeman & Lockyer *v.* Buckhurst Park Properties (Mangal) Ltd [1964] 2 Q.B. 480;
[1964] 2 W.L.R. 618; [1964] 1 All E.R. 630; 108 S.J. 96, CA . . . .   *Digested,* 64/**444**:
                  Applied, 72/525, 73/420, 74/30, 77/2890, 84/27, 85/21, 94/554, 95/775,
                  05/517: *Considered,* 67/33, 72/1649, 80/14, 81/43.u, 83/202, 00/4024:
                  Distinguished, 94/362: *Followed,* 94/5374, 01/6105

Freers v. Deutsche Bundespost (C278/93) [1996] E.C.R. I-1165, ECJ (6th Chamber). .   *Digested*, 96/**2571**:
                                                                                          Considered, 05/1264
Freeserve.com Plc v. Director General of Telecommunications [2003] CAT 5; [2003]
    Comp. A.R. 202, CAT . . . .   *Digested*, 04/**493**:
                                                                                          Considered, 05/558
Freeserve.com Plc v. Director General of Telecommunications (Reconsideration of
    Decision: Time Extension) [2003] CAT 15; [2004] Comp. A.R. 75, CAT. . . . . . .   *Digested*, 04/**537**:
                                                                                          Applied, 05/567
French v. Chief Constable of Sussex see French v. Sussex CC
French v. Sussex CC; *sub nom* French v. Chief Constable of Sussex; B3/2005/0059,
    0167, 0169 & 0170, CA (Civ Div); affirming [2004] EWHC 3217; [2005] P.I.Q.R.
    P18, QBD . . . .   *Digested*, 05/**2884**
Fressoz v. France (29183/95) (2001) 31 E.H.R.R. 2; 5 B.H.R.C. 654, ECHR . . . .   *Digested*, 99/**3105**:
                                                                                          Considered, 05/2030
Friends of the Irish Environment Ltd v. Minister for the Environment, Heritage and Local
    Government [2005] Eu. L.R. 903, HC (Irl)
Friends Provident Life & Pensions Ltd v. Sirius International Insurance Corp [2005]
    EWCA Civ 601; [2005] 2 All E.R. (Comm) 145; [2005] 2 Lloyd's Rep. 517;
    [2005] 1 C.L.C. 794; *Times*, June 8, 2005, CA (Civ Div); reversing in part
    [2004] EWHC 1799; [2004] 2 All E.R. (Comm) 707; [2005] Lloyd's Rep. I.R.
    135, QBD (Comm) . . . .   *Digested*, 05/**2377**
Frischpack GmbH & Co KG v. Office for Harmonisation in the Internal Market (Trade
    Marks and Designs) (OHIM) (T360/03) [2005] E.T.M.R. 48, CFI (5th
    Chamber) . . . .   *Digested*, 05/**2555**
Front National v. European Parliament (C486/01 P) [2004] 2 C.M.L.R. 51, ECJ . . . . . .   *Digested*, 05/**1445**
Front National v. European Parliament (C486/01 P(R)) [2002] E.C.R. I-1843; [2004]
    2 C.M.L.R. 50, ECJ . . . .   *Digested*, 05/**1443**
Frontier International Shipping Corp v. Swissmarine Corp Inc (The Cape Equinox)
    [2005] EWHC 8; [2005] 1 All E.R. (Comm) 528; [2005] 1 Lloyd's Rep. 390;
    [2005] 1 C.L.C. 1, QBD (Comm) . . . .   *Digested*, 05/**3817**
Froom v. Butcher [1976] Q.B. 286; [1975] 3 W.L.R. 379; [1975] 3 All E.R. 520;
    [1975] 2 Lloyd's Rep. 478; [1975] R.T.R. 518; 119 S.J. 613, CA (Civ Div);
    reversing [1974] 1 W.L.R. 1297; [1974] 3 All E.R. 517; [1974] 2 Lloyd's Rep. 541;
    [1974] R.T.R. 528; 118 S.J. 758, QBD . . . .   *Digested*, 75/**2295**:
                    Applied, 80/1875, 84/2292, 01/4447, 02/3258: *Cited*, 05/2842:
                    Considered, 77/2013, 77/2643, 77/3350, 78/738, 78/2611, 79/2965, 82/2157,
                    82/3700, 82/4059, 83/1055, 89/2536, 89/2555, 93/2954, 94/3344:
                    Distinguished, 79/2367: *Followed*, 74/2565, 75/2299: *Referred to*, 99/1378
Frost v. Chief Constable of South Yorkshire see White v. Chief Constable of South
    Yorkshire
Frost Skip Hire (Newcastle) Ltd v. Wood (Inspector of Taxes) [2004] S.T.C. (S.C.D.)
    387; [2004] S.T.I. 1829, Sp Comm . . . .   *Digested*, 05/**3895**
Fryers v. Hirst (Unreported, August 4, 2000), CC (Bradford) [*Ex rel.* David S Dixon,
    Barrister, Sovereign Chambers, 25 Park Square, Leeds] . . . .   *Digested*, 00/**1568**:
                                                                                          Considered, 05/3101
FUJI ELECTRIC/Photoconductor for electrography (T131/03) [2005] E.P.O.R. 34, EPO
    (Technical Bd App) . . . .   *Digested*, 05/**2495**
Fuji Seal Europe Ltd v. Catalytic Combustion Corp [2005] EWHC 1659; 102 Con. L.R.
    47, QBD (TCC)
Fujitsu Computer Products Corp v. Bax Global Inc [2005] EWHC 2289; [2005] 2
    C.L.C. 760; (2005) 102(48) L.S.G. 18; *Independent*, November 18, 2005, QBD
    (Comm)
Fujitsu Ltd's Application (0/121/04) [2004] Info. T.L.R. 200, PO . . . .   *Digested*, 05/**2491**
Fujitsu Ltd's Application (0/125/04) [2004] Info. T.L.R. 213, PO . . . .   *Digested*, 05/**2492**
Fujitsu Ltd's Patent Application (No.9204959.2) [1997-98] Info.T.L.R.103; [1997] R.P.C.
    608; (1997) 16 Tr. L.R. 352; [1998] Masons C.L.R. Rep. 99; (1997) 20(7) I.P.D.
    20060; *Times*, March 14, 1997, CA (Civ Div); affirming [1997-98] Info. T.L.R.
    101; [1996] R.P.C. 511; [1998] Masons C.L.R. Rep. 112; (1996) 19(9) I.P.D.
    19078; *Times*, June 18, 1996, Ch D (Patents Ct) . . . .   *Digested*, 97/**3915**:
                    Applied, 05/2490: *Cited*, 03/2519: *Considered*, 05/2492: *Followed*, 05/2446:
                                                                                          Referred to, 02/2846
Fullarton v. Inland Revenue Commissioners [2004] S.T.C. (S.C.D.) 207; [2004] S.T.I.
    992, Sp Comm . . . .   *Digested*, 05/**4003**
Fuller v. Strum [2001] EWCA Civ 1879; [2002] 1 W.L.R. 1097; [2002] 2 All E.R. 87;
    [2002] 1 F.C.R. 608; [2002] W.T.L.R. 199; (2001-02) 4 I.T.E.L.R. 454; (2002)
    99(7) L.S.G. 35; (2002) 146 S.J.L.B. 21; *Times*, January 22, 2002; *Independent*,
    January 28, 2002 (C.S), CA (Civ Div); reversing [2001] W.T.L.R. 677; (2001)
    98(6) L.S.G. 45; *Times*, February 14, 2001, Ch D . . . .   *Digested*, 02/**4338**:
                                                                                          Applied, 02/4334, 05/3980
Fulton Motors Ltd v. Toyota (GB) Ltd (Costs) [2000] C.P. Rep. 24, CA (Civ Div) . . . . .   *Digested*, 00/**427**:
                                                                                          Applied, 05/386
Funke v. France (A/256-A) [1993] 1 C.M.L.R. 897; (1993) 16 E.H.R.R. 297, ECHR . . . .   *Digested*, 94/**2431**:
                    Applied, 00/5031, 05/4164: *Considered*, 98/3150, 00/6043, 01/974,
                                                                          02/2463: *Distinguished*, 03/3457

Fusion v. Pertemps see Fusion Interactive Communication Solutions Ltd v. Venture
    Investment Placement Ltd (No.1)
Fusion Interactive Communication Solutions Ltd v. Venture Investment Placement Ltd
    (No.1); *sub nom* Fusion v. Pertemps [2005] EWHC 224; [2005] 2 B.C.L.C. 250,
    Ch D
Fusion Interactive Communication Solutions Ltd v. Venture Investment Placement Ltd
    (No.2) [2005] EWHC 736; [2005] 2 B.C.L.C. 571, Ch D
Future Online Ltd v. Faulds (Inspector of Taxes) see Future Online Ltd v. Foulds
    (Inspector of Taxes)
Future Online Ltd v. Foulds (Inspector of Taxes); *sub nom* Future Online Ltd v. Faulds
    (Inspector of Taxes) [2004] EWHC 2597; [2005] S.T.C. 198; 76 T.C. 590;
    [2005] B.T.C. 226; [2005] S.T.I. 190; (2004) 148 S.J.L.B. 1283, Ch D; affirming
    [2004] S.T.C. (S.C.D.) 237; [2004] S.T.I. 1050, Sp Comm . . . .   *Digested*, 05/**4086**
Fytche v. Wincanton Logistics Plc [2004] UKHL 31; [2004] 4 All E.R. 221; [2004]
    I.C.R. 975; [2004] I.R.L.R. 817; [2005] P.I.Q.R. P5; (2004) 101(31) L.S.G. 25;
    (2004) 148 S.J.L.B. 825; *Times*, July 2, 2004; *Independent*, July 8, 2004, HL;
    affirming [2003] EWCA Civ 874; [2003] I.C.R. 1582; [2004] P.I.Q.R. P2;
    (2003) 147 S.J.L.B. 785, CA (Civ Div) . . . .   *Digested*, 04/**1810**:
                                            Distinguished, 05/**1960**

G v. G see G (Removal from Jurisdiction), Re
G v. G (Financial Provision: Separation Agreement); *sub nom* Wyatt-Jones v.
    Goldsmith [2004] 1 F.L.R. 1011, CA (Civ Div); affirming [2000] 2 F.L.R. 18;
    [2000] Fam. Law 472, Fam Div . . . .   *Digested*, 04/**1514**:
                                            Applied, 05/**1656**
G v. G (Matrimonial Property: Rights of Extended Family) [2005] EWHC 1560;
    [2005] Fam. Law 764, Fam Div
G v. Secretary of State for the Home Department [2004] EWCA Civ 265; [2004] 1
    W.L.R. 1349; [2005] 2 All E.R. 882; (2004) 101(13) L.S.G. 35; *Times*, March 15,
    2004; *Independent*, March 17, 2004, CA (Civ Div) . . . .   *Digested*, 04/**782**
G (A Child), Re see Phelps v. Hillingdon LBC
G (A Child) v. Bromley LBC see Phelps v. Hillingdon LBC
G (A Child) v. Dhillon (Unreported, June 23, 2004), CC (Birmingham) [*Ex rel.* Stephen
    Garner, Barrister, No.8 Chambers, Fountain Court, Steelhouse Lane,
    Birmingham.]. . . . .   *Digested*, 05/**3213**
G (A Child) v. Essex CC [2005] 3 Q.R. 7 [*Ex rel.* Hodgkinsons, Solicitors, The Old
    Manse, 14 Lumley Avenue, Skegness, Lincs] . . . .   *Digested*, 05/**3083**
G (A Child) v. Hynes (Unreported, November 4, 2004), CC (Doncaster) [*Ex rel.* Tom
    Nossiter, Barrister, Park Lane Chambers, Leeds] . . . .   *Digested*, 05/**3233**
G (A Child) v. Kingsmill (No.2) [2001] EWCA Civ 934, CA (Civ Div) . . . .   *Applied*, 05/**2870**
G (A Child) v. Makowski (Unreported, June 15, 2004), CC (Hertford) [*Ex rel.* Gurion
    Taussig, Barrister, 199 Strand, London] . . . .   *Digested*, 05/**3153**
G (A Child) v. Russell (Unreported, June 24, 2004), CC (Bedford) [*Ex rel.* Joanna Kerr,
    Barrister, Lamb Chambers, Lamb Building, Temple, London] . . . .   *Digested*, 05/**3125**
G (A Child) (Care Proceedings: Placement for Adoption), Re [2005] EWCA Civ 896;
    [2005] Fam. Law 770; *Times*, August 1, 2005, CA (Civ Div) . . . .   *Digested*, 05/**1533**
G (A Child) (Disclosure: Prohibition), Re see G (A Child) (Litigants In Person), Re
G (A Child) (Interim Care Order: Residential Assessment), Re; *sub nom* G (A Child)
    (Interim Care Orders: Inpatient Assessment), Re; Kent CC v. G [2005] UKHL 68;
    [2005] 3 W.L.R. 1166; [2005] 3 F.C.R. 621; (2005) 102(47) L.S.G. 28; *Times*,
    November 25, *Independent*, November 29, 2005, HL; reversing [2004]
    EWCA Civ 24; [2004] 1 F.L.R. 876; [2004] 1 F.C.R. 317; [2004] Fam. Law 325;
    (2004) 101(9) L.S.G. 31; *Times*, January 29, 2004, CA (Civ Div). . . . .   *Digested*, 04/**1477**
G (A Child) (Interim Care Orders: Inpatient Assessment), Re see G (A Child) (Interim Care
    Order: Residential Assessment), Re
G (A Child) (Litigants In Person), Re; *sub nom* G (A Child) (Disclosure: Prohibition), Re
    [2003] EWCA Civ 1055; [2003] 2 F.L.R. 963; [2003] Fam. Law 808; *Times*,
    July 31, 2003; *Independent*, October 8, 2003, CA (Civ Div) . . . .   *Digested*, 04/**1508**:
                                            Considered, 05/**1646**
G (Care: Challenge to Local Authority's Decision), Re [2003] EWHC 551; [2003] 2 F.L.R.
    42; [2003] Fam. Law 389, Fam Div . . . .   *Digested*, 03/**1521**:
                         Considered, 05/1530: *Distinguished*, 05/318
G (Children) (Foreign Contact Order: Enforcement), Re; *sub nom* G (Children)
    (Restoration of Custody Rights), Re [2003] EWCA Civ 1607; [2004] 1 W.L.R.
    521; [2004] 1 F.L.R. 378; [2004] 1 F.C.R. 266; [2004] Fam. Law 98; (2004)
    101(2) L.S.G. 27; (2003) 147 S.J.L.B. 1364; *Times*, November 19, 2003, CA (Civ
    Div) . . . .   *Digested*, 04/**1532**:
                                  Considered, 04/1485, 05/**1590**
G (Children) (Removal from Jurisdiction), Re, *Times*, February 28, 2005, CA (Civ Div)
G (Children) (Residence: Making of Order), Re [2005] EWCA Civ 1237; *Times*, September
    14, 2005, CA (Civ Div)
G (Children) (Residence: Same Sex Partner), Re [2005] EWCA Civ 462; [2005] 2 F.L.R.
    957; *Times*, April 29, 2005, CA (Civ Div) . . . .   *Digested*, 05/**1579**

G (Children) (Restoration of Custody Rights), Re see G (Children) (Foreign Contact Order: Enforcement), Re
G (Liberia) v. Secretary of State for the Home Department see Yacoubou v. Secretary of State for the Home Department
G (Removal from Jurisdiction), Re; *sub nom* G v. G [2005] EWCA Civ 170; [2005] 2 F.L.R. 166; [2005] Fam. Law 463, CA (Civ Div) . . . . *Digested*, 05/**1574**
Gabalfrisa SL v. Agencia Estatal de Administracion Tributaria (AEAT) (C147/98) [2002] S.T.C. 535; [2000] E.C.R. I-1577; [2002] 1 C.M.L.R. 13; [2002] B.T.C. 5254; [2002] B.V.C. 333; [2000] S.T.I. 502, ECJ . . . . *Digested*, 02/**4737**:
Applied, 01/5577: *Followed*, 05/4363
Gabarri Moreno v. Spain (68066/01) (2004) 39 E.H.R.R. 40, ECHR . . . . *Digested*, 05/**2067**
Gabriel v. Hayward [2004] EWHC 2363; 97 Con. L.R. 136, QBD (TCC) . . . . *Digested*, 05/**449**
Gaca v. Pirelli General Plc; *sub nom* Pirelli General Plc v. Gaca [2004] EWCA Civ 373; [2004] 1 W.L.R. 2683; [2004] 3 All E.R. 348; [2004] P.I.Q.R. Q5; (2004) 101(17) L.S.G. 30; (2004) 148 S.J.L.B. 416; *Times*, April 2, 2004; *Independent*, March 30, 2004, CA (Civ Div) . . . . *Digested*, 04/**2843**:
Applied, 05/1277
Gadget Shop Ltd, Re see Wilkinson v. West Coast Capital (Pre-Trial Review)
Gafford v. Graham (1999) 77 P. & C.R. 73; [1999] 3 E.G.L.R. 75; [1999] 41 E.G. 159; (1999) 96(40) L.S.G. 44; (1998) 95(21) L.S.G. 36; (1998) 142 S.J.L.B. 155; [1998] N.P.C. 66; (1998) 76 P. & C.R. D18; *Times*, May 1, 1998, CA (Civ Div) . . . *Digested*, 98/**4341**:
Distinguished, 05/3410
Galashiels Gas Co Ltd v. Millar; *sub nom* Millar v. Galashiels Gas Co Ltd [1949] A.C. 275; [1949] 1 All E.R. 319; 1949 S.C. (H.L.) 31; 1949 S.L.T. 223; 65 T.L.R. 76; 47 L.G.R. 213; [1949] L.J.R. 540; 93 S.J. 71, HL; affirming 1948 S.C. 191; 1948 S.L.T. 282; 1948 S.L.T. (Notes) 15, IH (2 Div); affirming 1947 S.L.T. (Notes) 46, OH . . . . *Digested*, 49/**1552**:
Applied, 74/3240, 05/1960: *Considered*, 99/2880, 00/4228: *Distinguished*, 53/1441, 53/2513, 55/1078, 59/2062, 60/1994, 02/5767: *Followed*, 52/1386
Galbraith & Grant Ltd v. Block [1922] 2 K.B. 155, KBD . . . . *Applied*, 05/**3517**
Gale v. Superdrug Stores Plc [1996] 1 W.L.R. 1089; [1996] 3 All E.R. 468; [1996] P.I.Q.R. P330; (1996) 93(19) L.S.G. 29; (1996) 140 S.J.L.B. 124; *Times*, May 2, 1996, CA (Civ Div) . . . . *Digested*, 96/**759**:
Applied, 03/295: *Cited*, 99/499, 01/412: *Considered*, 97/1047, 00/353, 00/355, 01/548, 05/312: *Distinguished*, 00/354, 04/337
Galileo Brand Architecture Ltd's Trade Mark Application (No.2280603); *sub nom* GALILEO Trade Mark [2005] R.P.C. 22, App Person . . . . *Digested*, 05/**2568**
GALILEO Trade Mark see Galileo Brand Architecture Ltd's Trade Mark Application (No.2280603)
Gallagher v. Airtours Holidays Ltd (Unreported, October 23, 2000), CC (Preston) [*Ex rel.* Alan Saggerson, Barrister, No. 1 Serjeants' Inn, London] . . . . *Digested*, 01/**4280**:
Applied, 05/1980
Gallagher v. Alpha Catering Services Ltd (t/a Alpha Flight Services) [2004] EWCA Civ 1559; [2005] I.C.R. 673; [2005] I.R.L.R. 102; (2004) 148 S.J.L.B. 1400, CA (Civ Div); affirming [2004] I.C.R. 1489, EAT . . . . *Digested*, 05/**1240**
Gallaher Ltd v. Gallaher Pensions Ltd [2005] EWHC 42; [2005] O.P.L.R. 57; [2005] Pens. L.R. 103, Ch D . . . . *Digested*, 05/**2990**
Galliford Try Construction Ltd v. Michael Heal Associates Ltd [2003] EWHC 2886; 99 Con. L.R. 9, QBD (TCC) . . . . *Digested*, 05/**641**
Galloway v. Telegraph Group Ltd A2/2005/0308, CA (Civ Div); affirming [2004] EWHC 2786; [2005] E.M.L.R. 7; (2004) 148 S.J.L.B. 1436; *Times*, January 13, 2005, QBD
Gambro Hospal Ltd v. Customs and Excise Commissioners; *sub nom* Gambro Hospital Ltd v. Customs and Excise Commissioners [2004] B.V.C. 2191; [2004] V. & D.R. 21; [2004] S.T.I. 1561, V&DTr (London) . . . . *Digested*, 05/**4354**
Gambro Hospital Ltd v. Customs and Excise Commissioners see Gambro Hospal Ltd v. Customs and Excise Commissioners
Ganci v. Italy (41576/98) (2005) 41 E.H.R.R. 16, ECHR
Garage Molenheide BVBA v. Belgium (C286/94); Schepens v. Belgium (C340/95); Bureau Rik Decan-Business Research & Development NV (BRD) v. Belgium (C401/95); Sanders BVBA v. Belgium (C47/96) [1998] All E.R. (E.C.) 61; [1998] S.T.C. 126; [1997] E.C.R. I-7281; [1998] 1 C.M.L.R. 1186; [1998] C.E.C. 208; [1998] B.T.C. 5088; [1998] B.V.C. 106, ECJ (5th Chamber) . . . . *Digested*, 98/**4931**:
Applied, 00/5356, 04/4001, 05/4373, 05/4420: *Considered*, 03/4566: *Followed*, 02/4737
Garbutt v. Edwards [2005] EWCA Civ 1206; (2005) 102(43) L.S.G. 30; [2005] N.P.C. 122; *Times*, November 3, 2005, CA (Civ Div)
Gardiner-Hill v. Roland Berger Technics [1982] I.R.L.R. 498, EAT . . . . *Digested*, 83/**1305**:
Applied, 05/1321
Gardner v. Parker [2004] EWCA Civ 781; [2005] B.C.C. 46; [2004] 2 B.C.L.C. 554; (2004) 148 S.J.L.B. 792, CA (Civ Div); affirming [2003] EWHC 1463; [2004] 1 B.C.L.C. 417, Ch D . . . . *Digested*, 05/**520**

Garrett v. British Airways Plc (Unreported, March 12, 1997), CC (Wandsworth) [Ex rel.
  Rowley Ashworth, Solicitors, 247 The Broadway, Wimbledon, London] . . . .   Digested, 97/**1927**:
                                                                                          Considered, 05/3160
Garston v. Scottish Widows Fund & Life Assurance Society [1998] 1 W.L.R. 1583;
  [1998] 3 All E.R. 596; [1998] L. & T.R. 230; [1998] 2 E.G.L.R. 73; [1998] 32
  E.G. 88; [1998] E.G.C.S. 101; (1998) 95(26) L.S.G. 32; (1998) 142 S.J.L.B. 199;
  [1998] N.P.C. 109; Times, July 14, 1998; Independent, July 7, 1998, CA (Civ
  Div); reversing [1996] 1 W.L.R. 834; [1996] 4 All E.R. 282; [1996] 1 E.G.L.R.
  113; [1996] 23 E.G. 131; [1996] N.P.C. 49, Ch D . . . .   Digested, 98/**3614**:
                                                                                          Applied, 05/2646: Considered, 03/2723
Garton v. Hunter (Valuation Officer) (No.1) [1969] 2 Q.B. 37; [1968] 2 W.L.R. 86;
  [1969] 1 All E.R. 451; 133 J.P. 162; 67 L.G.R. 229; [1969] R.A. 11; 15 R.R.C. 145;
  (1968) S.J. 924; Times, November 15, 1962, CA (Civ Div); reversing 204 E.G.
  1285; [1967] R.A. 448; 13 R.R.C. 375; [1968] J.P.L. 97, Lands Tr . . . .   Digested, 69/**3017**:
                                                                                          Considered, 05/3369: Followed, 76/2260.4
Gascoines Group Ltd v. Inspector of Taxes [2004] EWHC 640; [2004] S.T.C. 844; 76
  T.C. 623; [2004] B.T.C. 279; [2004] S.T.I. 986, Ch D; affirming [2004] S.T.C.
  (S.C.D.) 11; [2004] S.T.I. 144, Sp Comm . . . .   Digested, 04/**3727**
Gascoyne v. Customs and Excise Commissioners [2004] EWCA Civ 1162; [2005] Ch.
  215; [2005] 2 W.L.R. 222, CA (Civ Div); affirming [2003] EWHC 257; [2003]
  Ch. 292; [2003] 2 W.L.R. 1311; (2003) 100(16) L.S.G. 27; Times, March 28,
  2003, Ch D . . . .   Digested, 05/**953**:
                                                                                          Applied, 04/904
Gaskin v. United Kingdom (57410/00) see Whitfield v. United Kingdom (46387/99)
Gate Gourmet London Ltd v. Transport and General Workers Union [2005] EWHC 1889;
  [2005] I.R.L.R. 881; (2005) 102(35) L.S.G. 41, QBD . . . .   Digested, 05/**1283**
Gaudreau v. Canada 7 I.T.L. Rep. 640, Tax Ct (Can)
Gaughan v. Tony McDonagh & Co Ltd [2005] EWHC 739; [2005] P.N.L.R. 36, QBD
  (Comm) . . . .   Digested, 05/**443**
Gaumain-Cerri v. Kaufmannische Krankenkasse-Pflegekasse (C502/01) [2004] E.C.R.
  I-6483; [2004] 3 C.M.L.R. 27, ECJ (2nd Chamber) . . . .   Digested, 05/**3859**
Gaunt v. British & Foreign Marine Insurance Co Ltd (No.3) see British & Foreign
  Marine Insurance Co Ltd v. Gaunt
Gaygusuz v. Austria (17371/90) (1997) 23 E.H.R.R. 364, ECHR . . . .   Digested, 97/**2823**:
                                                                                          Applied, 04/1889: Considered, 05/2035: Explained, 03/2171
Gaymark Investments Pty Ltd v. Walter Construction Group Ltd (formerly Concrete
  Constructions Group Ltd) (2005) 21 Const. L.J. 71, Sup Ct (NT) (Sgl judge) . . .   Digested, 05/**653**
Gazette Media Co Ltd, Re see R. (on the application of Gazette Media Co Ltd) v. Teesside
  Crown Court
Gazley v. Wade [2004] EWHC 2675; [2005] 1 Costs L.R. 129, QBD . . . .   Digested, 05/**367**
GE Capital Bank Ltd v. Rushton [2005] EWCA Civ 1556; Times, December 21, 2005,
  CA (Civ Div)
GE Ion Track Ltd v. Revenue and Customs Commissioners [2005] V. & D.R. 159, V&D Tr
  (London)
Gebhard v. Consiglio dell'Ordine degli Avvocati e Procuratori di Milano (C55/94)
  [1996] All E.R. (EC) 189; [1995] E.C.R. I-4165; [1996] 1 C.M.L.R. 603; [1996]
  C.E.C. 175; Times, December 13, 1995, ECJ . . . .   Digested, 96/**3902**:
                                                                                          Followed, 02/1571, 05/1462, 05/1468
Gee v. Shell UK Ltd [2002] EWCA Civ 1479; [2003] I.R.L.R. 82; (2002) 99(49)
  L.S.G. 19; (2002) 146 S.J.L.B. 245; Times, November 4, 2002, CA (Civ Div) . . .   Digested, 02/**1353**:
                                                                                          Considered, 05/1220, 05/1318
Gemma Ltd v. Gimson [2004] EWHC 1982; 97 Con. L.R. 165, QBD (TCC)
Gemma Ltd v. Gimson (Costs) [2005] EWHC 69; [2005] B.L.R. 163; 102 Con. L.R.
  87, QBD (TCC)
Genc v. Eidarus (Unreported, January 4, 2005), CC (Shoreditch) [Ex rel. Joanna Kerr,
  Barrister, Lamb Chambers, Lamb Building, Temple, London] . . . .   Digested, 05/**3181**
Gencor Ltd v. Commission of the European Communities (T102/96) [1999] All E.R.
  (EC) 289; [1999] E.C.R. II-753; [1999] B.C.C. 877; [1999] 4 C.M.L.R. 971;
  [1999] C.E.C. 395, CFI (5th Chamber) . . . .   Digested, 99/**692**:
                                                                                          Applied, 05/582: Distinguished, 05/542
GENENTECH/Hepatitis B antigen (T796/02) [2004] E.P.O.R. 56, EPO (Technical Bd App)   Digested, 05/**2449**
General Cigar Co Ltd v. Partagas y Cia SA [2005] EWHC 1729; [2005] F.S.R. 45;
  (2005) 28(9) I.P.D. 28067, Ch D . . . .   Digested, 05/**2563**
GENERAL ELECTRIC CO/Variable speed wind turbine (T1110/03) [2005] E.P.O.R. 17, EPO
  (Technical Bd App) . . . .   Digested, 05/**2470**
GENERAL HOSPITAL CORP/Hair removal method (T383/03) [2005] E.P.O.R. 33, EPO
  (Technical Bd App) . . . .   Digested, 05/**2445**
General Motors Acceptance Corp (UK) Plc v. Customs and Excise Commissioners; sub
  nom Customs and Excise Commissioners v. General Motors Acceptance Corp
  (UK) Plc [2004] EWHC 192; [2004] S.T.C. 577; [2004] B.T.C. 5552; [2004]
  B.V.C. 611; [2004] S.T.I. 373, Ch D; affirming [2003] B.V.C. 2358; [2003] S.T.I.
  983, V&D Tr . . . .   Digested, 04/**3983**:
                                                                                          Considered, 05/4341

General Motors Corp v. Yplon SA (C375/97) [1999] All E.R. (EC) 865; [1999] E.C.R.
I-5421; [1999] 3 C.M.L.R. 427; [1999] C.E.C. 528; [1999] E.T.M.R. 950;
[2000] R.P.C. 572; (1999) 22(11) I.P.D. 22112, ECJ [1999] E.C.R. I-5421;
[1999] E.T.M.R. 122, AGO . . . . *Digested,* 00/**3790**:
Considered, 04/2390, 05/2523, 05/2562
General Reinsurance Corp v. Forsakringsaktiebolaget Fennia Patria [1983] Q.B. 856;
[1983] 3 W.L.R. 318; [1983] 2 Lloyd's Rep. 287; (1983) 127 S.J. 389, CA (Civ
Div); reversing [1982] Q.B. 1022; [1982] 2 W.L.R. 518; [1982] 1 Lloyd's Rep.
87; [1981] Com. L.R. 280; 126 S.J. 32; *Times,* November 4, 1981, QBD
(Comm) . . . . *Digested,* 83/**1988**:
Applied, 05/2355

General Star International Indemnity Ltd v. Stirling Cooke Brown Reinsurance Brokers
Ltd [2003] EWHC 3; [2003] I.L.Pr. 19; [2003] Lloyd's Rep. I.R. 719, QBD
(Comm) . . . . *Digested,* 03/**606**:
Applied, 05/600

Generay Ltd v. Containerised Storage Co Ltd [2005] EWCA Civ 478; [2005] 2
E.G.L.R. 7; [2005] 32 E.G. 68, CA (Civ Div) . . . . *Digested,* 05/**3375**
Genetic Systems v. Roche Diagnostics GmbH (G2/03) see PPG/Disclaimer (G1/03)
Genetic Systems/Disclaimer (G2/03) see PPG/Disclaimer (G1/03)
Gennard v. Bridgnorth DC [2005] R.V.R. 275, LandsTr
Gentilhomme v. France (48205/99) (Unreported, May 14, 2002), ECHR . . . . *Applied,* 05/2065
Genzyme Ltd v. Office of FairTrading [2004] CAT 4; [2004] Comp. A.R. 358, CAT. . . . *Digested,* 05/**572**
Geoffrey Inc v. Nails R Us - Instituto de Beleza e Saude Lda [2005] E.T.M.R. 13, Rel
(Lisboa)
George Wimpey International Ltd v. Rolfe (Inspector of Taxes) [1989] S.T.C. 609; 62
T.C. 597, Ch D . . . . *Digested,* 89/**528**:
Considered, 05/4027

George Wimpey UK Ltd v. First Secretary of State [2004] EWHC 2419; [2005] 2 P. &
C.R. 30, QBD (Admin)
George Wimpey UK Ltd (formerly Wimpey Homes Holdings Ltd) v. VI Construction Ltd
(formerly VI Components Ltd); *sub nom* George Wimpey UK Ltd (formerly
Wimpey Homes Holdings Ltd) v. VIC Construction Ltd (formerly Vic Components
Ltd) [2005] EWCA Civ 77; [2005] B.L.R. 135; 103 Con. L.R. 67; (2005)
102(9) L.S.G. 28; (2005) 149 S.J.L.B. 182; [2005] 2 P. & C.R. DG5; *Times,*
February 16, 2005, CA (Civ Div); reversing [2004] EWHC 1374, Ch D . . . . *Digested,* 05/**717**:
Applied, 05/696

George Wimpey UK Ltd (formerly Wimpey Homes Holdings Ltd) v. VIC Construction Ltd
(formerly Vic Components Ltd) see George Wimpey UK Ltd (formerly Wimpey
Homes Holdings Ltd) v. VI Construction Ltd (formerly VI Components Ltd)
Georgiou v. Enfield LBC; *sub nom* R. (on the application of Georgiou) v. Enfield LBC
[2004] EWHC 779; [2004] B.L.G.R. 497; [2004] 2 P. & C.R. 21; [2005] J.P.L.
62; (2004) 101(17) L.S.G. 33, QBD (Admin) . . . . *Digested,* 05/**3279**:
Applied, 05/3278

Geraets-Smits v. Stichting Ziekenfonds VGZ (C157/99); Peerbooms v. Stichting CZ
Groep Zorgverzekeringen (C157/99) [2002] Q.B. 409; [2002] 2 W.L.R. 154;
[2003] All E.R. (EC) 481; [2001] E.C.R. I-5473; [2002] 2 C.M.L.R. 21; (2001)
62 B.M.L.R. 101; *Times,* September 4, 2001, ECJ. . . . . *Digested,* 01/**5133**:
Considered, 03/1799, 04/1688: *Followed,* 05/1849
Gerber Garment Technology Inc v. Lectra Systems Ltd [1997] R.P.C. 443; [1998]
Masons C.L.R. Rep. 135; (1997) 20(5) I.P.D. 20046; *Times,* January 17, 1997, CA
(Civ Div); reversing in part [1995] R.P.C. 383; [1998] Masons C.L.R. Rep. 64,
Ch D (Patents Ct) . . . . *Digested,* 97/**3903**:
Considered, 96/4555, 99/3448, 02/1318: *Distinguished,* 96/1272, 97/1032,
05/2436: *Followed,* 98/3496
Gerling Konzern Speziale Kreditversicherung AG v. Amministrazione del Tesoro dello
Stato (201/82) [1983] E.C.R. 2503; [1984] 3 C.M.L.R. 638, ECJ (3rd
Chamber) . . . . *Digested,* 85/**1453**:
Applied, 85/1452: *Followed,* 05/2368, 05/2369
Germany v. Commission of the European Communities (8/88); *sub nom* Suckler Cows
(8/88), Re [1990] E.C.R. I-2321; [1992] 1 C.M.L.R. 409, ECJ . . . . *Applied,* 05/1427:
Followed, 00/170
Germany v. Kleinschmidt [2005] EWHC 1373; [2005] 3 All E.R. 759, QBD (Admin) . . . *Digested,* 05/**1486**
Gerrard v. Koby; *sub nom* Baumler (UK) Ltd, Re [2004] EWHC 1763; [2005] B.C.C.
181; [2005] 1 B.C.L.C. 92, Ch D (Companies Ct) . . . . *Digested,* 05/**39**
Gerritse v. Finanzamt Neukolln-Nord (C234/01) [2004] S.T.C. 1307; [2003] E.C.R. I-
5933; [2004] 3 C.M.L.R. 22; 5 I.T.L. Rep. 978; [2003] S.T.I. 1145, ECJ (5th
Chamber) . . . . *Digested,* 04/**3760**:
Applied, 05/1469

Gerster v. Freistaat Bayern (C1/95) [1997] E.C.R. I-5253; [1998] 1 C.M.L.R. 303;
[1998] I.C.R. 327; [1997] I.R.L.R. 699; *Times,* November 24, 1997, ECJ (6th
Chamber) . . . . *Digested,* 97/**2217**:
Considered, 05/1261

CASE CITATOR 2005　　　　　　　　　　　　　　GIL

Getmapping Plc v. Ordnance Survey [2002] EWHC 1089; [2002] U.K.C.L.R. 410;
[2002] Eu. L.R. 464; [2003] I.C.R. 1; (2002) 25(9) I.P.D. 25066; (2002)
99(28) L.S.G. 32; (2002) 146 S.J.L.B. 161; *Times*, June 25, 2002, Ch D (Patents
Ct) . . . . *Digested*, 02/**601**:
　　　　　　　　　　　　　　　　　　　　　　　　　　Applied, 03/570, 05/578
Gezer v. Secretary of State for the Home Department see R. (on the application of
Gezer) v. Secretary of State for the Home Department
GH v. Secretary of State for the Home Department; *sub nom* GH (formerly KAZ:
Country Conditions: Effect: Iraq CG), Re [2005] EWCA Civ 1182; (2005)
102(42) L.S.G. 25, CA (Civ Div); affirming [2004] UKIAT 248; [2004] Imm.
A.R. 707, IAT
GH Renton & Co Ltd v. Palmyra Trading Corp of Panama (The Caspiana) [1957] A.C.
149; [1957] 2 W.L.R. 45; [1956] 3 All E.R. 957; [1956] 2 Lloyd's Rep. 379, HL;
affirming [1956] 1 Q.B. 462; [1956] 2 W.L.R. 238; [1956] 1 All E.R. 209;
[1955] 2 Lloyd's Rep. 722; 101 S.J. 43, CA; reversing [1955] 3 W.L.R. 535;
[1955] 3 All E.R. 251; [1955] 2 Lloyd's Rep. 301; 99 S.J. 762, QBD . . . . *Digested*, 57/**3300**:
　　　　　　　　　Considered, 57/3297, 57/3299, 57/3306, 58/565, 58/3141, 69/3293:
　　　　　　　　　　　　　　　　　　Followed, 59/3033, 03/3887, 05/3787
GH (formerly KAZ: Country Conditions: Effect: Iraq CG), Re see GH v. Secretary of State
for the Home Department
Ghadami v. Harlow DC [2004] EWHC 1883; [2005] B.L.G.R. 24; [2005] 1 P. & C.R.
19, QBD (Admin) . . . . *Digested*, 05/**3278**
Ghaidan v. Godin-Mendoza; *sub nom* Ghaidan v. Mendoza; Godin-Mendoza v.
Ghaidan; Mendoza v. Ghaidan [2004] UKHL 30; [2004] 2 A.C. 557; [2004] 3
W.L.R. 113; [2004] 3 All E.R. 411; [2004] 2 F.L.R. 600; [2004] 2 F.C.R. 481;
[2004] H.R.L.R. 31; [2004] U.K.H.R.R. 827; 16 B.H.R.C. 671; [2004] H.L.R. 46;
[2005] 1 P. & C.R. 18; [2005] L. & T.R. 3; [2004] 2 E.G.L.R. 132; [2004] Fam.
Law 641; [2004] 27 E.G.C.S. 128; (2004) 101(27) L.S.G. 30; (2004) 154
N.L.J. 1013; (2004) 148 S.J.L.B. 792; [2004] N.P.C. 100; [2004] 2 P. & C.R.
DG17; *Times*, June 24, 2004, HL; affirming [2002] EWCA Civ 1533; [2003] Ch.
380; [2003] 2 W.L.R. 478; [2002] 4 All E.R. 1162; [2002] 3 F.C.R. 591;
[2003] U.K.H.R.R. 254; 13 B.H.R.C. 608; [2003] H.L.R. 35; [2003] L. & T.R.
14; [2003] A.C.D. 12; [2003] Fam. Law 87; [2002] 46 E.G.C.S. 197; (2003)
100(1) L.S.G. 24; (2002) 152 N.L.J. 1718; (2002) 146 S.J.L.B. 253; [2002]
N.P.C. 138; [2003] 1 P. & C.R. DG14; *Times*, November 14, 2002; *Independent*,
November 22, 2002, CA (Civ Div) . . . . *Digested*, 04/**2538**:
　　　　　　　Applied, 04/1889, 05/2118, 05/2641: *Considered*, 04/707, 04/1312, 05/2129
Ghaidan v. Mendoza see Ghaidan v. Godin-Mendoza
GHE Realisations Ltd (formerly Gatehouse Estates Ltd), Re [2005] EWHC 2400; *Times*,
November 11, 2005, Ch D (Companies Ct)
Gibbon v. Mitchell [1990] 1 W.L.R. 1304; [1990] 3 All E.R. 338, Ch D . . . . *Digested*, 91/**1724**:
　　　　　　　　　　　Applied, 05/3420: *Considered*, 02/4713, 05/4304
Gibbs v. DE McDowell Ltd (Unreported, July 23, 2004), CC (Barnstaple) [*Ex rel.*
Michael Rapp, Barrister, 1 Temple Gardens, Temple, London] . . . . *Digested*, 05/**406**
Gibraltar Exemption from VAT and Excise Duties, Re (C349/03) see Commission of the
European Communities v. United Kingdom (C349/03)
Gibson v. Skibs A/S Marina [1966] 2 All E.R. 476; [1966] 2 Lloyd's Rep. 39; (1966)
112 S.J. 273, Assizes (Liverpool) . . . . *Digested*, 66/**8343**:
　　　　　　　　　　　　　　　　　　　　　　　Considered, 05/3600
GIE Groupe Concorde v. Master of the Vessel Suhadiwarno Panjan (C440/97); *sub
nom* GIE Group Concorde v. Master of the Vessel Suhadiwarno Panjan (C440/
97) [2000] All E.R. (EC) 865; [1999] 2 All E.R. (Comm) 700; [1999] E.C.R. I-
6307; [1999] C.L.C. 1976; [2000] I.L.Pr. 626, ECJ . . . . *Digested*, 00/**764**:
　　　　　　　　　　　　　　　Applied, 05/604: *Considered*, 04/578
Giele v. General Medical Council [2005] EWHC 2143; [2005] 4 All E.R. 1242, QBD
(Admin)
Gifford, Re; *sub nom* Gifford v. Seaman [1944] Ch. 186, Ch D . . . . *Applied*, 05/3975:
　　　　　　　　　　　　　　　　　　　　　　Considered, 84/3661, 85/3640
Gifford v. Seaman see Gifford, Re
Gil v. Baygreen Properties Ltd [2004] EWHC 1732; [2005] B.P.I.R. 95, Ch D
Gil v. Baygreen Properties Ltd (In Liquidation) (Costs) [2004] EWHC 2029; [2005] 1
Costs L.R. 75, Ch D (Companies Ct) . . . . *Digested*, 05/**371**
Gil v. Spain (56673/00) see Iglesias Gil v. Spain (56673/00)
GIL Insurance Ltd v. Customs and Excise Commissioners (C308/01) [2004] All E.R.
(EC) 954; [2004] S.T.C. 961; [2004] E.C.R. I-4777; [2004] 2 C.M.L.R. 22;
[2004] C.E.C. 352; [2005] B.T.C. 5760; [2004] S.T.I. 1119, ECJ (5th Chamber) . *Digested*, 05/**2380**
Gilbert v. Star Newspaper Co Ltd (1894) 51 T.L.R. 4 . . . . *Considered*, 05/2812
Giles v. Law Society (1996) 8 Admin. L.R. 105; (1995) 92(38) L.S.G. 25; *Times*,
October 20, 1995, CA (Civ Div) . . . . *Digested*, 96/**3917**:
　　　　　　　　　　　　　　Applied, 05/2730: *Considered*, 03/2824

Giles v. Rhind [2002] EWCA Civ 1428; [2003] Ch. 618; [2003] 2 W.L.R. 237; [2002] 4 All E.R. 977; [2003] B.C.C. 79; [2003] 1 B.C.L.C. 1; (2002) 99(44) L.S.G. 32; Times, October 23, 2002; Independent, October 24, 2002, CA (Civ Div); reversing [2001] 2 B.C.L.C. 582; (2001) 98(34) L.S.G. 37; (2001) 145 S.J.L.B. 209; Times, August 6, 2001, Ch D . . . . *Digested*, 02/**565**:
Applied, 05/**520**: *Distinguished*, 04/459

Gill v. Ford Motor Co Ltd; *sub nom* Ford Motor Co Ltd v. Singh; Wong v. BAE Systems Operations Ltd [2004] I.R.L.R. 840; (2004) 101(33) L.S.G. 34; Times, August 30, 2004, EAT. . . . . *Digested*, 05/**1338**

Gill v. Quinn [2004] EWHC 883; [2005] B.P.I.R. 129, Ch D

Gill v. Sandhu see Sandhu v. Gill

Gillespie v. First Secretary of State; *sub nom* Bellway Urban Renewal Southern v. Gillespie; R. (on the application of Gillespie) v. First Secretary of State [2003] EWCA Civ 400; [2003] Env. L.R. 30; [2003] 2 P. & C.R. 16; [2003] 3 P.L.R. 20; [2003] J.P.L. 1287; [2003] 14 E.G.C.S. 123; (2003) 100(14) L.S.G. 30; (2003) 147 S.J.L.B. 384; [2003] N.P.C. 43; Times, April 7, 2003; Independent, April 2, 2003, CA (Civ Div); affirming [2003] EWHC 8; [2003] 1 P. & C.R. 30; [2003] N.P.C. 6, QBD (Admin) . . . . *Digested*, 03/**3416**:
Applied, 04/3085, 05/3281: *Approved*, 04/3089: *Distinguished*, 03/3421, 04/3088

Gillespie v. Northern Health and Social Services Board (C342/93) [1996] All E.R. (EC) 284; [1996] E.C.R. I-475; [1996] 2 C.M.L.R. 969; [1996] I.C.R. 498; [1996] I.R.L.R. 214; (1996) 31 B.M.L.R. 65; Times, February 22, 1996, ECJ . . . . *Digested*, 96/**2570**:
Applied, 97/2239, 97/2241, 00/2161, 00/2164, 05/1262: *Considered*, 99/2079, 00/2204, 02/1364: *Followed*, 00/2165, 04/1257

Gillett v. Holt [2001] Ch. 210; [2000] 3 W.L.R. 815; [2000] 2 All E.R. 289; [2000] 2 F.L.R. 266; [2000] 1 F.C.R. 705; [2000] W.T.L.R. 195; [2000] Fam. Law 714; (2000) 97(12) L.S.G. 40; (2000) 144 S.J.L.B. 141; [2000] N.P.C. 25; (2000) 80 P. & C.R. D3; Times, March 17, 2000, CA (Civ Div); reversing [1998] 3 All E.R. 917; [1998] 2 F.L.R. 470; [1998] Fam. Law 596; (1998) 95(26) L.S.G. 31; Times, June 18, 1998, Ch D . . . . *Digested*, 00/**2321**:
Applied, 03/3592, 04/1520, 04/3676: *Considered*, 01/4859, 02/4319: *Distinguished*, 05/3384: *Followed*, 01/5158, 02/3843

Gillette Co v. LA-Laboratories Ltd Oy (C228/03) [2005] All E.R. (EC) 940; [2005] E.C.R. I-2337; [2005] 2 C.M.L.R. 62; [2005] C.E.C. 734; [2005] E.T.M.R. 67; [2005] F.S.R. 37, ECJ (3rd Chamber) . . . . *Digested*, 05/**2571**

Gillick v. BBC [1996] E.M.L.R. 267; Times, October 20, 1995; Independent, October 31, 1995, CA (Civ Div). . . . . *Digested*, 95/**3131**:
Applied, 05/982

Gillmartin (A Bankrupt), Re [1989] 1 W.L.R. 513; [1989] 2 All E.R. 835; (1989) 86(23) L.S.G. 36; (1989) 133 S.J. 877; Independent, November 21, 1988 (C.S.), Ch D . *Digested*, 89/**167**:
Cited, 00/3488: *Considered*, 00/4562, 05/2292

Gimenez-Exposito v. Germany [2005] I.L.Pr. 7, Cass (F)

Glass v. United Kingdom (61827/00) [2004] 1 F.L.R. 1019; [2004] 1 F.C.R. 553; (2004) 39 E.H.R.R. 15; (2005) 8 C.C.L. Rep. 16; (2004) 77 B.M.L.R. 120; [2004] Fam. Law 410; Times, March 11, 2004, ECHR . . . . *Digested*, 04/**1994**:
Considered, 04/1692, 05/1812

Glaverbel SA v. Office for Harmonisation in the Internal Market (Trade Marks and Designs) (OHIM) (C445/02 P) [2005] E.T.M.R. 70, ECJ (5th Chamber) . . . . . . *Digested*, 05/**2527**:
Previous proceedings, 03/2596

Glaxo Group Ltd v. Dowelhurst Ltd [2004] EWCA Civ 290; [2005] E.T.M.R. 104; (2004) 27(6) I.P.D. 27059, CA (Civ Div); reversing in part [2004] E.T.M.R. 39; (2004) 27(1) I.P.D. 27004, Ch D . . . . *Digested*, 04/**2410**

Glaxo Group Ltd v. Dowelhurst Ltd (Form of Reference to ECJ) see Boehringer Ingelheim KG v. Swingward Ltd (Form of Reference to ECJ)

Glaxo Group Ltd v. Inland Revenue Commissioners [1996] S.T.C. 191; 68 T.C. 166; (1996) 140 S.J.L.B. 35; Times, December 26, 1995; Independent, January 8, 1996 (C.S.), CA (Civ Div); affirming [1995] S.T.C. 1075; Times, November 21, 1995; Independent, December 11, 1995 (C.S.), Ch D . . . . *Digested*, 96/**1313**:
Applied, 03/4172: *Approved*, 05/4056: *Considered*, 99/4682

Glaxo Group Ltd v. Swingward Ltd (Form of Reference to ECJ) see Boehringer Ingelheim KG v. Swingward Ltd (Form of Reference to ECJ)

Glaze & Frame Ltd v. Revenue and Customs Commissioners [2005] S.T.C. (S.C.D.) 757; [2005] S.T.I. 1633, Sp Comm

Glencore Grain Ltd v. Agros Trading Co Ltd; *sub nom* Agros Trading Co Ltd v. Glencore Grain Ltd [1999] 2 All E.R. (Comm) 288; [1999] 2 Lloyd's Rep. 410; [1999] C.L.C. 1696; (1999) 96(31) L.S.G. 42; Times, July 12, 1999, CA (Civ Div) . . . . . *Digested*, 99/**2509**:
Considered, 05/388

Glencore Grain Rotterdam BV v. Lebanese Organisation for International Commerce (The Lorico) [1997] 4 All E.R. 514; [1997] 2 Lloyd's Rep. 386; [1997] C.L.C. 1274, CA (Civ Div); reversing [1997] 1 Lloyd's Rep. 578, QBD (Comm) . . . . *Digested*, 97/**4534**:
Applied, 05/697

Glencot Development & Design Co Ltd *v.* Ben Barrett & Son (Contractors) Ltd [2001] B.L.R. 207; (2001) 3 T.C.L.R. 11; 80 Con. L.R. 14; (2001) 17 Const. L.J. 336, QBD (TCC) . . . . *Digested,* 01/**856**:
Considered, 05/647: *Followed,* 01/857
Glenister *v.* Moody [2003] EWHC 3155; [2005] W.T.L.R. 1205, Ch D
Glenwright (Valuation Officer) *v.* St Nicholas Parochial Church Council [1988] R.A. 1, LandsTr . . . . *Digested,* 88/**3007**:
Considered, 05/3367
Glidepath BV *v.* Thompson [2005] EWHC 818; [2005] 2 All E.R. (Comm) 833; [2005] 2 Lloyd's Rep. 549; [2005] 1 C.L.C. 1090, QBD (Comm)
Glidepath Holding BV *v.* Thompson [2004] EWHC 2234; [2005] 1 All E.R. (Comm) 434, QBD
GLN (Copenhagen) Southern Ltd *v.* Tunbridge Wells BC [2005] P.A.D. 38, Planning Inspector
Global Games International Ltd *v.* Customs and Excise Commissioners [2005] V. & D.R. 246,V&DTr (Manchester)
Global Self Drive Ltd *v.* Revenue and Customs Commissioners [2005] S.T.I. 1734, V&DTr (London)
GlobeWorsted Co Ltd, Re see Huddersfield FineWorsteds Ltd, Re
Glossop *v.* Lord High Chancellor [2005] 3 Costs L.R. 359, QBD
Glouchkov *v.* Forbes Inc see Berezovsky *v.* Forbes Inc (No.1)
Glouchkov *v.* Michaels see Berezovsky *v.* Forbes Inc (No.1)
Glover *v.* United Kingdom (Admissibility) (39835/03) (2005) 40 E.H.R.R. SE18, ECHR
Glyn (t/a Priors Farm EquineVeterinary Surgery) *v.* McGarel-Groves [2005] EWHC 1629; (2005) 102(33) L.S.G. 24, QBD
GMB *v.* MAN Truck & Bus UK Ltd [2000] I.C.R. 1101; [2000] I.R.L.R. 636, EAT . . . . . . *Digested,* 00/**2188**:
Applied, 05/1204
Goc *v.* Turkey (36590/97) (Unreported, July 11, 2002), ECHR (Grand Chamber) . . . . . . *Considered,* 05/**3657**,
05/3775
Godbold *v.* Mahmood [2005] EWHC 1002; [2005] Lloyd's Rep. Med. 379, QBD . . . . . *Digested,* 05/**3071**
Godden *v.* Kent and Medway Strategic HA [2004] EWHC 1629; [2004] Lloyd's Rep. Med. 521, QBD . . . . *Digested,* 05/**2891**
Godfrey *v.* Conwy CBC [2001] Env. L.R. 38; [2001] E.H.L.R. 10; [2001] J.P.L. 1162; [2000] E.G.C.S. 131, DC . . . . *Digested,* 01/**4550**:
Considered, 05/2894
Godin-Mendoza *v.* Ghaidan see Ghaidan *v.* Godin-Mendoza
Godsmark *v.* Greenwich LBC [2004] EWHC 1286; [2004] H.L.R. 53; [2004] N.P.C. 91, Ch D . . . . *Digested,* 05/**2688**
Godwin, Re see R. *v.* Southwark Crown Court Ex p. Godwin
Gojkovic *v.* Gojkovic (No.2) [1992] Fam. 40; [1991] 3 W.L.R. 621; [1992] 1 All E.R. 267; [1991] 2 F.L.R. 233; [1991] F.C.R. 913; [1991] Fam. Law 378; *Times,* May 1, 1991, CA (Civ Div) . . . . *Digested,* 92/**2090**:
Applied, 95/3381: *Considered,* 94/3210, 94/3597, 95/2339, 95/2344, 95/3971, 95/4005, 96/2855, 03/1571: *Distinguished,* 92/3418, 93/3138:
Doubted, 05/1656
Gold *v.* Curtis [2005] W.T.L.R. 673, Ch D
Gold *v.* Mincoff Science & Gold (Costs) [2004] EWHC 2036; [2005] 1 Costs L.R. 30, Ch D . . . . *Digested,* 05/**350**
Goldcrest Homes (Central) Ltd *v.* Newham LBC [2005] P.A.D. 73, Planning Inspector
Golden Portfolio Holidays *v.* Cordingley (Unreported, March 20, 1992), CA (Civ Div) . . *Considered,* 05/414
Golden Strait Corp *v.* Nippon Yusen Kubishika Kaisha (The Golden Victory) [2005] EWCA Civ 1190; [2005] 2 Lloyd's Rep. 747; [2005] 2 C.L.C. 576; (2005) 102(43) L.S.G. 31; *Times,* October 21, 2005, CA (Civ Div); affirming [2005] EWHC 161; [2005] 1 All E.R. (Comm) 467; [2005] 1 Lloyd's Rep. 443; [2005] 1 C.L.C. 138; *Times,* March 4, 2005, QBD (Comm)
GOLDEN YELLOW Trade Mark Application [2005] E.T.M.R. CN1, ERGI (Swi)
Golder *v.* United Kingdom (A/18) (1979-80) 1 E.H.R.R. 524, ECHR . . . . *Applied,* 97/**2934**,
04/1615: *Considered,* 01/1099: *Distinguished,* 05/1553
Golf Operations Ltd *v.* Northamptonshire CC [2005] P.A.D. 41, Planning Inspector
Golobiewska *v.* Customs and Excise Commissioners [2005] EWCA Civ 607; *Times,* May 25, 2005, CA (Civ Div); reversing [2004] EWHC 215, Ch D; affirmingV&DTr . . . . *Digested,* 05/**950**
Goodson *v.* Bedfordshire and Luton Coroner see R. (on the application of Goodson) *v.* HM Coroner for Bedfordshire and Luton
Goodson *v.* HM Coroner for Bedfordshire and Luton (Protective Costs); *sub nom* R. (on the application of Goodson) *v.* HM Coroner for Bedfordshire and Luton (Protective Costs) [2005] EWCA Civ 1172; *Times,* November 1, 2005, CA (Civ Div) . . . . *Digested,* 05/**373**
Goodway *v.* Zurich Insurance Co [2004] EWHC 137; 96 Con. L.R. 49, QBD (TCC) . . . . *Digested,* 05/**662**
Goodwin *v.* Patent Office [1999] I.C.R. 302; [1999] I.R.L.R. 4; [1999] Disc. L.R. 104; *Times,* November 11, 1998, EAT . . . . *Digested,* 98/**2114**:
Applied, 00/2125, 01/2242, 04/1209, 05/1147
GoogleTechnology Inc *v.* TS Single Person Ltd [2005] E.T.M.R. 92, Protodikeio (GR)

Goose v. Wilson Sandford & Co (No.1) (1998) 95(12) L.S.G. 27; (1998) 142 S.J.L.B. 92; *Times*, February 19, 1998, CA (Civ Div); reversing(Unreported, April 1, 1996), Ch D . . . . *Digested*, 98/**50**:
Applied, 98/51, 01/49: *Considered*, 05/2727

Gora v. Customs and Excise Commissioners; Dannatt v. Customs and Excise Commissioners (Appeal) [2003] EWCA Civ 525; [2004] Q.B. 93; [2003] 3 W.L.R. 160; (2003) 147 S.J.L.B. 507; *Times*, April 23, 2003; *Independent*, May 8, 2003, CA (Civ Div); affirming [2002] V. & D.R. 49, V&DTr (London) . . . . *Digested*, 03/**923**:
Considered, 05/953: *Followed*, 04/904

Gordon v. JB Wheatley & Co; *sub nom* Gordon v. Wheatley & Co [2000] Lloyd's Rep. P.N. 605; [2000] P.N.L.R. 755; (2000) 97(24) L.S.G. 40; *Times*, June 6, 2000, CA (Civ Div); reversing 1998-G-No.513, QBD. . . . . *Digested*, 00/**4256**:
Distinguished, 05/313, 05/437

Gordon Alison & Co Ltd v. Wallsend Slipway Co Ltd; *sub nom* Gordon Alison & Co v. Wallsend Slipway & Engineering Co Ltd (1927) 27 Ll. L. Rep. 285, CA; affirming (1926) 26 Ll. L. Rep. 159, KBD. . . . . *Applied*, 05/**2356**

Gorman v. Lambeth LBC see Kay v. Lambeth LBC

Gorringe v. Calderdale MBC; *sub nom* Calderdale MBC v. Gorringe [2004] UKHL 15; [2004] 1 W.L.R. 1057; [2004] 2 All E.R. 326; [2004] R.T.R. 27; [2004] P.I.Q.R. P32; (2004) 101(18) L.S.G. 35; (2004) 148 S.J.L.B. 419; *Times*, April 2, 2004, HL; affirming [2002] EWCA Civ 595; [2002] R.T.R. 27; (2002) 99(22) L.S.G. 36; (2002) 146 S.J.L.B. 124; *Times*, May 16, 2002, CA (Civ Div) . . . . *Digested*, 04/**2752**:
Applied, 04/1818, 05/2850, 05/2891

Gorzelik v. Poland (44158/98) (2005) 40 E.H.R.R. 4, ECHR (Grand Chamber) . . . . *Digested*, 05/**2040**

Goshawk Dedicated Ltd v. Tyser & Co Ltd A3/2005/0850, CA (Civ Div); reversing [2005] EWHC 461; [2005] 2 All E.R. (Comm) 115; [2005] Lloyd's Rep. I.R. 379, QBD (Comm) . . . . *Digested*, 05/**2355**

Gotham v. Doodes; *sub nom* Doodes v. Gotham [2005] EWHC 2576; [2005] N.P.C. 134; *Times*, November 25, 2005, Ch D

Gotobed v. Pridmore (1970) 115 S.J. 78, CA (Civ Div) . . . . *Digested*, 71/**3714**:
Considered, 05/3436: *Distinguished*, 84/1152: *Followed*, 92/1803, 93/1619:
Referred to, 95/1857

Gottlieb v. Axa General Insurance Ltd see Axa General Insurance Ltd v. Gottlieb

Grace v. Biagioli [2005] EWCA Civ 1222; (2005) 102(48) L.S.G. 18, CA (Civ Div)

Graham v. Philcox [1984] Q.B. 747; [1984] 3 W.L.R. 150; [1984] 2 All E.R. 643; (1984) 48 P. & C.R. 354; (1984) 81 L.S.G. 1764; (1984) 128 S.J. 470, CA (Civ Div) . . . . *Digested*, 84/**1153**:
Considered, 03/3600, 05/3436

Grange Builders (Quainton) Ltd v. Customs and Excise Commissioners [2005] V. & D.R. 147, V&DTr (London)

Grant v. Lambeth LBC see R. (on the application of Grant) v. Lambeth LBC

Granville Technology Group Ltd, Re see Ferrotech Ltd, Re

Granville Technology Group Ltd, Re see Huddersfield Fine Worsteds Ltd, Re

Gravgaard v. Aldridge & Brownlee (A Firm) [2004] EWCA Civ 1529; [2005] P.N.L.R. 19; (2005) 149 S.J.L.B. 27; [2004] N.P.C. 187, CA (Civ Div) . . . . *Digested*, 05/**438**

Gray v. Going Places Leisure Travel Ltd [2005] EWCA Civ 189; [2005] C.P. Rep. 21; [2005] 3 Costs L.R. 405; [2005] P.N.L.R. 26, CA (Civ Div) . . . . *Digested*, 05/**379**

Gray (Deceased), Re see Allardyce v. Roebuck

Graysim Holdings Ltd v. P&O Property Holdings Ltd [1996] A.C. 329; [1995] 3 W.L.R. 854; [1995] 4 All E.R. 831; 94 L.G.R. 553; [1996] 1 E.G.L.R. 109; [1996] 03 E.G. 124; [1995] E.G.C.S. 182; (1996) 93(2) L.S.G. 28; (1995) 145 N.L.J. 1813; (1996) 140 S.J.L.B. 23; [1995] N.P.C. 183; (1996) 71 P. & C.R. D22; *Times*, November 24, 1995, HL; reversing [1994] 1 W.L.R. 992; [1994] 3 All E.R. 897; 92 L.G.R. 598; (1995) 70 P. & C.R. 605; [1994] 45 E.G. 150; [1994] E.G.C.S. 29; (1994) 91(14) L.S.G. 47; (1994) 138 S.J.L.B. 71; [1994] N.P.C. 23; *Times*, March 2, 1994, CA (Civ Div); reversing [1993] 1 E.G.L.R. 96; [1993] 05 E.G. 141; [1992] E.G.C.S. 108; [1992] N.P.C. 120, Ch D . . . . *Digested*, 95/**2969**:
Applied, 96/3428, 05/2648, 05/2670

Great Eastern Hotel Co Ltd v. John Laing Construction Ltd [2005] EWHC 181; 99 Con. L.R. 45, QBD (TCC) . . . . *Digested*, 05/**652**

Great Future International Ltd v. Sealand Housing Corp (No.7) [2004] EWHC 124; *Times*, March 1, 2004, Ch D . . . . *Digested*, 04/**252**:
Considered, 05/414

Great Peace Shipping Ltd v. Tsavliris Salvage (International) Ltd [2002] EWCA Civ 1407; [2003] Q.B. 679; [2002] 3 W.L.R. 1617; [2002] 4 All E.R. 689; [2002] 2 All E.R. (Comm) 999; [2002] 2 Lloyd's Rep. 653; [2003] 2 C.L.C. 16; (2002) 99(43) L.S.G. 34; (2002) 152 N.L.J. 1616; [2002] N.P.C. 127; *Times*, October 17, 2002; *Independent*, October 22, 2002, CA (Civ Div); affirming (2001) 151 N.L.J. 1696, QBD (Comm). . . . . *Digested*, 02/**720**:
Applied, 04/383, 04/472: *Considered*, 05/516

Grecoair Inc v. Tilling [2004] EWHC 2851; [2005] Lloyd's Rep. I.R. 151, QBD (Comm) . *Digested*, 05/**2350**

Greece *v.* Council of Ministers of the European Communities (C62/88); *sub nom*
    Chernobyl Accident, Re (C62/88) [1990] E.C.R. I-1527; [1991] 2 C.M.L.R. 649,
    ECJ .... *Digested,* 91/**3772**:
                                                               Followed, 05/1406
Greece *v.* Diamantakis (C362/02) see Greece *v.* Tsapalos (C361/02)
Greece *v.* Tsapalos (C361/02); Greece *v.* Diamantakis (C362/02) [2004] S.T.C. 1220;
    6 I.T.L. Rep.1087, ECJ (3rd Chamber) .... *Digested,* 05/**1431**
Greek Telecommunications Organisation (OTE) *v.* National Commission of
    Telecommunications [2005] E.C.C. 2, Efeteio (Athens)
Green *v.* Alexander Johnson (A Firm); *sub nom* Green *v.* Holmes [2005] EWCA Civ
    775; [2005] P.N.L.R. 45; [2005] N.P.C. 85, CA (Civ Div); affirming [2004]
    EWHC 1205; [2004] P.N.L.R. 40; (2004) 101(23) L.S.G. 34, Ch D .... *Digested,* 05/**961**
Green *v.* Associated Newspapers Ltd see Greene *v.* Associated Newspapers Ltd
Green *v.* BDO Stoy Hayward LLP see XL Communications Group Plc (In Liquidation),
    Re
Green *v.* Gaul; *sub nom* Loftus (Deceased), Re [2005] EWHC 406; [2005] 1 W.L.R.
    1890; [2005] 2 All E.R. 700; [2005] W.T.L.R. 1325; (2004-05) 7 I.T.E.L.R. 640;
    (2005) 102(22) L.S.G. 26; *Times,* March 28, 2005, Ch D .... *Digested,* 05/**3967**
Green *v.* Grimsby and Scunthorpe Newspapers Ltd see Hartman *v.* South Essex
    Mental Health and Community Care NHS Trust
Green *v.* Holmes see Green *v.* Alexander Johnson (A Firm)
Green *v.* Inland Revenue Commissioners see St Barbe Green *v.* Inland Revenue
    Commissioners
Green *v.* Victoria Road Primary School Governing Body; *sub nom* Kent CC *v.* Green
    [2004] EWCA Civ 11; [2004] 2 All E.R. 763; [2004] I.C.R. 684; [2004]
    B.L.G.R. 337; [2004] E.L.R. 75; (2004) 148 S.J.L.B. 118, CA (Civ Div); reversing
    [2003] I.C.R. 713; [2003] E.L.R. 455, EAT.......................... *Digested,* 04/**1195**:
                                               Applied, 04/1220: *Considered,* 05/1223
Green Corns Ltd *v.* Claverley Group Ltd [2005] EWHC 958; [2005] E.M.L.R. 31;
    [2005] 2 F.C.R. 309, QBD... *Digested,* 05/**2064**
Green (Valuation Officer) *v.* Barnet LBC [1994] R.A. 235, Lands Tr .... *Digested,* 95/**4297**:
                                                               Considered, 05/3367
Greenalls Management Ltd *v.* Customs and Excise Commissioners [2005] UKHL 34;
    [2005] 1 W.L.R.1754; [2005] 4 All E.R. 274; [2005] 2 C.M.L.R. 40; [2005] Eu.
    L.R. 839; (2005) 102(23) L.S.G. 28; *Times,* May 16, 2005; *Independent,* May
    19, 2005, HL; reversing [2003] EWCA Civ 896; [2003] 1 W.L.R. 2609; (2003)
    100(32) L.S.G. 34; (2003) 147 S.J.L.B. 814; *Times,* July 2, 2003, CA (Civ
    Div); reversing in part [2002] EWHC 1691; [2002] 1 W.L.R. 3333; [2002] V. &
    D.R. 33, Ch D .... *Digested,* 05/**947**:
                                                               Applied, 04/902
Greene *v.* Associated Newspapers Ltd; *sub nom* Green *v.* Associated Newspapers Ltd
    [2004] EWCA Civ 1462; [2005] Q.B. 972; [2005] 3 W.L.R. 281; [2005] 1 All
    E.R. 30; [2005] E.M.L.R. 10; (2004) 101(45) L.S.G. 31; (2004) 148 S.J.L.B.
    1318; *Times,* November 10, 2004; *Independent,* November 9, 2004, CA (Civ
    Div); affirming [2004] EWHC 2322, QBD .... *Digested,* 05/**970**
Greene King No.1 Ltd *v.* Adie (Inspector of Taxes) [2005] S.T.C. (S.C.D.) 398; [2005]
    S.T.I. 726, Sp Comm .... *Digested,* 05/**4020**
Greenfield *v.* Bains (Inspector of Taxes) see Collins *v.* Addies (Inspector of Taxes)
Greenpeace Ltd *v.* Secretary of State for the Environment, Food and Rural Affairs; *sub
    nom* R. (on the application of Greenpeace Ltd) *v.* Secretary of State for the
    Environment, Food and Rural Affairs [2005] EWCA Civ 1656, CA (Civ Div);
    affirming [2005] EWHC 2144; [2005] N.P.C.115, QBD (Admin)
Greenstein (t/a TechMark) *v.* London Stock Exchange Plc (2005) 28(4) I.P.D. 28025,
    OHIM (1st Bd App)
Greenwood *v.* Newman [2004] EWHC 484; [2004] O.P.L.R. 283, Ch D .... *Digested,* 05/**2959**
Greenwoods Tyre Services Ltd *v.* Manchester Corp (1972) 23 P. & C.R. 246; [1972]
    R.V.R. 91, Lands Tr .... *Digested,* 72/**410**:
                                                               Considered, 05/3251
Gregg *v.* Scott [2005] UKHL 2; [2005] 2 A.C. 176; [2005] 2 W.L.R. 268; [2005] 4
    All E.R. 812; [2005] P.I.Q.R. P24; [2005] Lloyd's Rep. Med. 130; (2005) 82
    B.M.L.R. 52; (2005) 149 S.J.L.B. 145; *Times,* January 28, 2005; *Independent,*
    February 3, 2005, HL; affirming [2002] EWCA Civ 1471; [2003] Lloyd's Rep.
    Med. 105; (2003) 71 B.M.L.R. 16; (2002) 99(49) L.S.G. 19; (2002) 99(48)
    L.S.G. 27; (2002) 146 S.J.L.B. 247; *Times,* November 4, 2002, CA (Civ Div) ... *Digested,* 05/**2837**
Gregory *v.* Buncher & Haseler Ltd (Unreported, April 7, 2004), CC (Norwich) [*Ex rel.*
    Cameron Brown, Barrister, 4 King's Bench Walk, Temple, London] .... *Digested,* 05/**3101**
Gregson *v.* Channel Four Television Corp (Amendment of Party Name); *sub nom*
    Gregson *v.* Channel Four Television Co Ltd [2000] C.P. Rep. 60; *Times,* August
    11, 2000; *Independent,* October 2, 2000 (C.S), CA (Civ Div); affirming
    HQ990963, QBD .... *Digested,* 00/**587**:
                                                               Applied, 05/315
Greymalkin Ltd *v.* Copleys (A Firm) [2004] EWCA Civ 1754; [2005] P.N.L.R. 20, CA
    (Civ Div); affirming [2004] EWCA Civ 1155; [2004] P.N.L.R. 44, Ch D .... *Digested,* 05/**2866**

Griesmar v. Ministre de l'Economie, des Finances et de l'Industrie (C366/99) [2001]
E.C.R. I-9383; [2003] 3 C.M.L.R. 5, ECJ . . . . *Digested,* 04/**2800**:
Followed, 05/1282

Grieves v. FT Everard & Sons Ltd; Quinn v. George Clark & Nem Ltd; Mears v. RG
Carter Ltd; Jackson v. Brock Plc; Rothwell v. Chemical & Insulating Co Ltd;
Downey v. Charles Evans Shopfitters Ltd; Storey v. Clellands Shipbuilders Ltd;
Topping v. Benchtown Ltd (formerly Jones Bros (Preston) Ltd); Johnston v. NEI
International Combustion Ltd; Hindson v. Pipe House Wharf (Swansea) Ltd;
B3/2005/0528, B3/2005/0529, B3/2005/0530, B3/2005/0534, B3/2005/
0535, B3/2005/0497, CA (Civ Div); reversing [2005] EWHC 88; [2005]
P.I.Q.R. P25; *Times,* March 22, 2005, QBD . . . . *Digested,* 05/**955**

Grieves v. United Kingdom (57067/00) (2004) 39 E.H.R.R. 2; [2004] Crim. L.R. 578,
ECHR . . . . *Digested,* 04/**1944**:
Applied, 04/202, 05/234: *Considered,* 05/859

Griffith v. Queen, The; *sub nom* R. v. Griffith (Tennyson Winston) [2004] UKPC 58;
[2005] 2 A.C. 235; [2005] 2 W.L.R. 581, PC (Bar) . . . . *Digested,* 05/**773**

Griffiths v. Griffin (Unreported, December 9, 2004), CC (Oxford) [*Ex rel.* Alicia
Collinson, Barrister, Harcourt Chambers, 2, Harcourt Buildings, Temple, London]   *Digested,* 05/**3210**

Griffiths v. Salisbury DC [2004] EWCA Civ 162; [2004] B.L.G.R. 454, CA (Civ Div) . . . *Digested,* 05/**1200**

Griffiths v. Solutia UK Ltd; *sub nom* Solutia UK Ltd (formerly Monsanto Chemicals UK
Ltd) v. Griffiths [2001] EWCA Civ 736; [2001] C.P. Rep. 92; [2001] C.P.L.R.
419; [2001] 2 Costs L.R. 247; [2002] P.I.Q.R. P16, CA (Civ Div); affirming
[2001] 1 Costs L.R. 99, QBD . . . . *Digested,* 01/**523**:
Considered, 05/367

Griggs Group Ltd v. Evans see R Griggs Group Ltd v. Evans (No.1)

Grimmer v. KLM Cityhopper UK [2005] I.R.L.R. 596, EAT . . . . *Digested,* 05/**1279**

Gromax Plasticulture Ltd v. Don & Low Nonwovens Ltd [1999] R.P.C. 367; (1998)
21 (9) I.P.D. 21098, Ch D . . . . *Digested,* 99/**3592**:
Applied, 01/4062, 03/2649, 03/2650, 05/2575: *Followed,* 01/4047:
Referred to, 01/4024

Gross v. Rackind; *sub nom* City Branch Group Ltd, Re; Citybranch Group Ltd, Re;
Rackind v. Gross [2004] EWCA Civ 815; [2005] 1 W.L.R. 3505; [2004] 4 All
E.R. 735; [2005] B.C.C. 11; (2004) 148 S.J.L.B. 661, CA (Civ Div); affirming
[2003] EWHC 3298, Ch D (Companies Ct) . . . . *Digested,* 05/**530**

Grossmann Air Service Bedarfsluftfahrunternehmen GmbH & Co KG v. Austria (C230/
02) [2005] All E.R. (EC) 593; [2004] E.C.R. I-1829; [2004] 2 C.M.L.R. 2,
ECJ (6th Chamber) . . . . *Digested,* 04/**82**

Group Josi Reinsurance Co SA v. Compagnie d'Assurances Universal General Insurance
Co (UGIC) (C412/98) see Universal General Insurance Co (UGIC) v. Group
Josi Reinsurance Co SA (C412/98)

Groupement d'Interet Economique (GIE) Reunion Europeenne v. Zurich Espana (C77/04)
[2005] I.L.Pr. 33, ECJ (1st Chamber) . . . . *Digested,* 05/**2369**

Grove Leisure Ltd. v. Broxbourne BC [2005] P.A.D. 43, Planning Inspector

Groveholt Ltd v. Hughes; *sub nom* Hughes v. Groveholt Ltd [2005] EWCA Civ 897;
[2005] 2 B.C.L.C. 421; [2005] B.P.I.R. 1345, CA (Civ Div); affirming (2005)
149 S.J.L.B. 176, Ch D

Grovit v. Doctor [1997] 1 W.L.R. 640; [1997] 2 All E.R. 417; [1997] C.L.C. 1038;
(1997) 94(20) L.S.G. 37; (1997) 147 N.L.J. 633; (1997) 141 S.J.L.B. 107; *Times,*
April 25, 1997; *Independent,* May 1, 1997, HL; affirming *Independent,*
December 13, 1993 (C.S.), CA (Civ Div) . . . . *Digested,* 97/**489**:
Applied, 98/614, 03/473: *Considered,* 98/611, 98/619, 00/348, 05/461

Gruber v. Bay Wa AG (C464/01) [2005] E.C.R. I-439; [2005] I.L.Pr. 12, ECJ (2nd
Chamber)

Gruber v. Silhouette International Schmied GmbH & Co KG (C249/97) [1999] E.C.R.
I-5295, ECJ . . . . *Followed,* 05/1282

Grundig Italiana SpA v. Ministero delle Finanze (C255/00) [2003] All E.R. (EC) 176;
[2002] E.C.R. I-8003; [2003] 1 C.M.L.R. 36; [2003] C.E.C. 178, ECJ (6th
Chamber) [2002] E.C.R. I-8003, AGO . . . . *Digested,* 03/**1454**:
Applied, 05/4377: *Considered,* 05/4367

Grupo Sada PA SA v. Office for Harmonisation in the Internal Market (Trade Marks and
Designs) (OHIM) (T31/03) [2005] E.C.R. I-10001; [2005] E.T.M.R. CN7, CFI

Grupo Torras SA v. Al-Sabah (No.1) [1996] 1 Lloyd's Rep. 7; [1995] C.L.C. 1025;
[1995] I.L.Pr. 667; *Independent,* July 5, 1995, CA (Civ Div); affirming [1995] 1
Lloyd's Rep. 374, QBD (Comm) . . . . *Digested,* 96/**1112**:
Applied, 05/619: *Followed,* 98/583, 98/588

Grzelczyk v. Centre Public d'Aide Sociale d'Ottignies Louvain la Neuve (C184/99)
[2003] All E.R. (EC) 385; [2001] E.C.R. I-6193; [2002] 1 C.M.L.R. 19; [2002]
I.C.R. 566; *Times,* November 16, 2001, ECJ . . . . *Digested,* 01/**2496**:
Applied, 05/3856, 05/3922

Gschwind v. Finanzamt Aachen-Aussenstadt (C391/97) [2001] S.T.C. 331; [1999]
E.C.R. I-5451; [2001] 1 C.M.L.R. 3; [2000] B.T.C. 294; 2 I.T.L. Rep. 113, ECJ . . . *Digested,* 01/**5245**:
Applied, 05/1469

Guardian Industries Corp v. United States 7 I.T.L. Rep. 842, US Ct

Guardian Newspapers Ltd (Court Record: Disclosure), Re see Chan U Seek *v.* Alvis
    Vehicles Ltd
Guenat *v.* Switzerland (24722/94) Unreported, ECHR . . . .   *Applied,* 05/3339
Guernsey *v.* Jersey Fishermen's Association Ltd [2005] Eu. L.R. 946, CA (Gue)
Guerra *v.* Italy (1998) 26 E.H.R.R. 357; 4 B.H.R.C. 63; [1998] H.R.C.D. 277, ECHR . . . .   *Digested,* 98/**3096**:
            Applied, 01/1544: *Considered,* 98/3154, 02/1500, 02/3714:
            Followed, 05/2113
Guest House Proprietor *v.* Kendall (Inspector of Taxes) [2005] S.T.C. (S.C.D.) 280;
    [2005] S.T.I. 160, Sp Comm. . . . .   *Digested,* 05/**4088**
Guildford BC *v.* Hein [2005] EWCA Civ 979; [2005] B.L.G.R. 797; *Times,* September
    21, 2005, CA (Civ Div) . . . .   *Digested,* 05/**2804**
Gunaydin *v.* Freistaat Bayern (C36/96) [1997] E.C.R. I-5143; [1998] 1 C.M.L.R. 871,
    ECJ (6th Chamber) . . . .   *Considered,* 05/2229
Gunduz *v.* Turkey (35071/97) (2005) 41 E.H.R.R. 5, ECHR . . . .   *Digested,* 05/**2042**
Gunn *v.* Wallsend Slipway and Engineering Co, *Times,* January 23, 1989, QBD . . . .   *Digested,* 89/**2548**:
            Considered, 99/448, 05/2864
Gunter *v.* South Western Staffordshire Primary Care Trust see R. (on the application of
    Gunter) *v.* South Western Staffordshire Primary Care Trust
Gurney (Inspector of Taxes) *v.* Petch see Petch *v.* Gurney (Inspector of Taxes)
Gurol *v.* Bezirksregierung Koln (C374/03); *sub nom* Gurol *v.* Landesamt fur
    Ausbildungsforderung Nordrhein-Westfalen (C374/03) [2005] 3 C.M.L.R. 44,
    ECJ (1st Chamber)
Gurol *v.* Landesamt fur Ausbildungsforderung Nordrhein-Westfalen (C374/03) see
    Gurol *v.* Bezirksregierung Koln (C374/03)
Gurtner *v.* Circuit [1968] 2 Q.B. 587; [1968] 2 W.L.R. 668; [1968] 1 All E.R. 328;
    [1968] 1 Lloyd's Rep. 171; 112 S.J. 63; 112 S.J. 73, CA (Civ Div) . . . .   *Digested,* 68/**3160**:
            Applied, 69/2895: *Considered,* 69/2846, 71/9385, 79/2346, 94/425,
            98/506, 98/528, 98/591, 05/310: *Distinguished,* 00/547
Gurung *v.* Secretary of State for the Home Department [2004] EWCA Civ 1863;
    (2005) 102(6) L.S.G. 32; *Times,* January 4, 2005, CA (Civ Div) . . . .   *Digested,* 05/**2172**
Gurung (Indra) *v.* Secretary of State for the Home Department [2002] UKIAT 4870;
    [2003] Imm. A.R. 115; [2003] I.N.L.R. 133, IAT . . . .   *Digested,* 03/**2259**:
            Considered, 04/277, 05/2228
Gusinskiy *v.* Russia (70276/01) (2005) 41 E.H.R.R. 17; 16 B.H.R.C. 427, ECHR
Gutnick *v.* Dow Jones Unreported, HC (Aus) . . . .   *Considered,* 05/611
Guzzardi *v.* Italy (A/39) (1981) 3 E.H.R.R. 333, ECHR . . . .   *Considered,* 97/2766,
            04/3152, 05/2030: *Distinguished,* 98/3078
GW *v.* Oldham MBC see W *v.* Oldham MBC

H *v.* Entry Clearance Officer, Addis Ababa Unreported . . . .   *Considered,* 05/2195
H *v.* H (Lump Sum: Interest Payable) [2005] EWHC 1513; [2005] Fam. Law 848,
    Fam Div
H *v.* L [1998] 1 W.L.R. 854; *Times,* February 3, 1998; *Independent,* February 4, 1998,
    QBD . . . .   *Digested,* 98/**1078**:
            Applied, 05/918
H *v.* M (Abduction: Rights of Custody) see Hunter *v.* Murrow
H *v.* Northampton CC [2004] EWCA Civ 526; [2005] P.I.Q.R. P7; (2004) 101(21)
    L.S.G. 36; (2004) 148 S.J.L.B. 540, CA (Civ Div)
H *v.* O (Contempt of Court: Sentencing) [2004] EWCA Civ 1691; [2005] 2 F.L.R.
    329; [2005] Fam. Law 532; (2005) 149 S.J.L.B. 59, CA (Civ Div) . . . .   *Digested,* 05/**1621**:
            Considered, 05/343
H *v.* R School see R. (on the application of H) *v.* Special Educational Needs Tribunal
H *v.* Secretary of State for Health see R. (on the application of H) *v.* Secretary of State
    for Health
H *v.* Special Educational Needs and Disability Tribunal see R. (on the application of
    MH) *v.* Special Educational Needs and Disability Tribunal
H *v.* Suffolk CC see A *v.* Hoare
H (A Child) *v.* Ikea Ltd (Unreported, September 15, 2004), CC (Crewe) [*Ex rel.* Richard
    Mullan, Barrister, Sedan House, Stanley Place, Chester] . . . .   *Digested,* 05/**3096**
H (A Child) *v.* Merck & Co Inc see Horne-Roberts *v.* SmithKline Beecham Plc
H (A Child) *v.* Oldroyd (Unreported, April 18, 2005), CC (Wakefield) [*Ex rel.*
    Hodgkinsons, Solicitors, The Old Manse, 14 Lumley Avenue, Skegness,
    Lincolnshire] . . . .   *Digested,* 05/**3200**
H (A Child) *v.* Pulisciano (Unreported, September 22, 2004), CC (Birmingham) [*Ex rel.*
    Stephen Garner, Barrister, No.8 Chambers, Fountain Court, Steelhouse Lane,
    Birmingham.]. . . . .   *Digested,* 05/**3084**
H (A Child) *v.* Redbridge LBC [2005] 3 Q.R. 11, CC (Romford) [*Ex rel.* Nikolas Clarke,
    Barrister, The Chambers of Ami Feder, Lamb Building, Temple, London] . . . .   *Digested,* 05/**3183**
H (A Child) *v.* Shadrack (Unreported, June 2, 2004), CC (Chelmsford) [*Ex rel.* Joanna
    Kerr, Barrister, Lamb Chambers, Lamb Building, Temple, London]. . . . .   *Digested,* 05/**3134**
H (A Child) *v.* SmithKline Beecham Plc see Horne-Roberts *v.* SmithKline Beecham Plc
H (A Child) *v.* Toys R Us Ltd [2005] 2 Q.R. 11; [2004] 6 Q.R. 7, CC (Cambridge) [*Ex*
    rel. LJ Deegan, Barrister, Fenners Chambers, 3 Madingley Road, Cambridge] . . .   *Digested,* 04/**2872**

H (A Child) *v.* West Midlands Ambulance NHS Trust (Unreported, September 22, 2004), CC (Birmingham) [*Ex rel.* Stephen Garner, Barrister, No.8 Chambers, Fountain Court, Steelhouse Lane, Birmingham.] . . . . *Digested,* 05/**3168**

H (Agreed Joint Residence: Mediation), Re; *sub nom* B *v.* O (Residence Orders: Parental Contact) [2004] EWHC 2064; [2005] 1 F.L.R. 8; [2004] Fam. Law 792, Fam Div . . . . *Digested,* 05/**1578**

H (Children) (Abduction), Re see H (Children) (Child Abduction: Grave Risk), Re

H (Children) (Child Abduction: Grave Risk), Re; *sub nom* H (Children) (Abduction), Re [2003] EWCA Civ 355; [2003] 2 F.L.R. 141; [2003] 2 F.C.R. 151; [2003] Fam. Law 468, CA (Civ Div) . . . . *Digested,* 03/**1503**:
Considered, 05/1543, 05/1547

H (Children) (Child Abduction: Objection to Return), Re [2005] EWCA Civ 319; (2005) 149 S.J.L.B. 178, CA (Civ Div)

H (Children) (Contact: Domestic Violence), Re see L (A Child) (Contact: Domestic Violence), Re

H (Children) (Terminating Contact Orders: Local Authorities Powers), Re see H (Children) (Termination of Contact), Re

H (Children) (Termination of Contact), Re; *sub nom* H (Children) (Terminating Contact Orders: Local Authorities Powers), Re [2005] EWCA Civ 318; [2005] 2 F.L.R. 408; [2005] 1 F.C.R. 658; [2005] Fam. Law 526; (2005) 149 S.J.L.B. 179, CA (Civ Div) . . . . *Digested,* 05/**1566**

H (Minors) (Sexual Abuse: Standard of Proof), Re; *sub nom* H (Minors) (Child Abuse: Threshold Conditions), Re; H and R (Child Sexual Abuse: Standard of Proof), Re [1996] A.C. 563; [1996] 2 W.L.R. 8; [1996] 1 All E.R. 1; [1996] 1 F.L.R. 80; [1996] 1 F.C.R. 509; [1996] Fam. Law 74; (1995) 145 N.L.J. 1887; (1996) 140 S.J.L.B. 24; *Times,* December 15, 1995; *Independent,* January 17, 1996, HL; affirming [1995] 1 F.L.R. 643; [1995] 2 F.C.R. 384; [1995] Fam. Law 401; (1995) 159 J.P.N. 338, CA (Civ Div) . . . . *Digested,* 96/**632**:
Applied, 96/490, 96/496, 98/2401, 00/949, 01/1975, 01/2566, 02/1636, 04/1463, 04/1481, 05/570, 05/1529, 05/1559, 05/1560, 05/4191:
Considered, 95/3509, 96/482, 96/610, 01/721, 01/2549:
Distinguished, 01/2550: *Followed,* 02/1105, 04/1458, 05/2825

H and R (Child Sexual Abuse: Standard of Proof), Re see H (Minors) (Sexual Abuse: Standard of Proof), Re

H Lavender & Son Ltd *v.* Minister of Housing and Local Government [1970] 1 W.L.R. 1231; [1970] 3 All E.R. 871; 68 L.G.R. 408; 114 S.J. 636, QBD . . . . *Digested,* 70/**2757**:
Distinguished, 73/12.1, 05/2796

H&M Hennes Ltd *v.* Customs and Excise Commissioners; *sub nom* H&M Hennes Ltd *v.* Revenue and Customs Commissioners [2005] EWHC 1383; [2005] S.T.C. 1749; [2005] B.T.C. 5387; [2005] B.V.C. 418; [2005] S.T.I. 866; *Times,* May 10, 2005, Ch D; affirming [2004] S.T.I. 2356, V&DTr . . . . *Digested,* 05/**4415**

H&M Hennes Ltd *v.* Revenue and Customs Commissioners see H&M Hennes Ltd *v.* Customs and Excise Commissioners

Haase *v.* Germany (11057/02) [2004] 2 F.L.R. 39; [2004] 2 F.C.R. 1; (2005) 40 E.H.R.R. 19; [2004] Fam. Law 500, ECHR . . . . *Digested,* 04/**1988**

Habib Bank Ltd *v.* Ahmed (Permission to Appeal) [2004] EWCA Civ 805; [2004] B.P.I.R. 864; (2004) 154 N.L.J. 1051; (2004) 148 S.J.L.B. 794; *Independent,* June 30, 2004, CA (Civ Div) . . . . *Digested,* 05/**331**

Habib Bank Ltd *v.* Dawood [2004] EWCA Civ 1346; [2004] 2 Lloyd's Rep. 665; (2004) 148 S.J.L.B. 1213, CA (Civ Div) . . . . *Digested,* 05/**454**

Haddonstone Ltd *v.* Sharp [1996] F.S.R. 767; (1996) 19(6) I.P.D. 19046; *Independent,* January 26, 1996, CA (Civ Div) . . . . *Digested,* 96/**3634**:
Followed, 05/346

Hadkinson *v.* Hadkinson [1952] P. 285; [1952] 2 All E.R. 567; [1952] 2 T.L.R. 416, CA . . . . *Digested,* 52/**2648**:
Applied, 65/3225, 84/2660, 85/3504, 85/3513, 97/2484, 05/1645, 05/1664: *Considered,* 84/1671, 84/2593, 86/2835: *Distinguished,* 79/1399

Hadley *v.* Baxendale 156 E.R. 145; (1854) 9 Ex. 341, Ex Ct . . . . *Applied,* 47-51/5368, 47-51/5562, 53/3775, 55/2559, 56/50, 62/829, 66/3146, 66/11174, 66/12340, 67/3623, 77/2881, 79/2391, 80/640, 81/138, 86/980, 90/2764, 91/1316, 93/517, 93/4846, 98/4384, 99/1379, 01/1507, 03/5438, 05/959:
Considered, 47-51/1604, 47-51/2562, 47-51/5222, 47-51/9482, 47-51/9490, 49/3656, 61/2343, 67/3605, 67/3615, 68/1013, 69/881, 73/3466, 86/780, 87/2429, 90/670, 94/5413, 96/401, 96/1196, 97/989, 97/3839, 00/5981:
Distinguished, 47-51/2561, 47-51/2565, 47-51/2566, 47/2561, 85/1282, 99/3946: *Followed,* 67/3527, 69/3379, 88/1065, 98/1472:
Referred to, 76/155.u, 83/1216, 83/4027

Hadley *v.* Midland Fertility Services Ltd see Evans *v.* Amicus Healthcare Ltd

Hague *v.* Deputy Governor of Parkhurst Prison see R. *v.* Deputy Governor of Parkhurst Prison Ex p. Hague

Haines Watts (A Firm), Re [2004] EWHC 1970; [2005] B.P.I.R. 798, Ch D . . . . *Digested,* 05/**2313**

Hair *v.* Prudential Assurance Co [1983] 2 Lloyd's Rep. 667; (1983) 133 N.L.J. 282, QBD . . . . *Digested,* 84/**1826**:
Considered, 05/2365

Hajigeorgiou v. Vasiliou see Vasiliou v. Hajigeorgiou
Halcrow Gilbert & Co Ltd v. Jones see London Fire and Emergency Planning Authority
    (LFEPA) v. Halcrow Gilbert & Co Ltd
Halifax Plc v. Grant see Bristol & West Plc v. Bartlett
Halki Shipping Corp v. Sopex Oils Ltd (The Halki) [1998] 1 W.L.R. 726; [1998] 2 All
    E.R. 23; [1998] 1 Lloyd's Rep. 465; [1998] C.L.C. 583; (1998) 142 S.J.L.B. 44;
    [1998] N.P.C. 4; *Times,* January 19, 1998; *Independent,* January 12, 1998 (C.S.),
    CA (Civ Div); affirming [1997] 1 W.L.R. 1268; [1997] 3 All E.R. 833; [1998] 1
    Lloyd's Rep. 49; (1997) 94(28) L.S.G. 26; (1997) 141 S.J.L.B. 172; *Times,*
    October 13, 1997, QBD (Admlty) . . . .   *Digested,* 98/**246**:
                                      Applied, 03/648, 04/588, 04/593, 05/642: *Considered,* 04/652, 05/198:
                                                                                Followed, 00/227
Hall v. Pertemps Group Ltd, *Times,* December 23, 2005, Ch D
Hall v. Save Newchurch Guinea Pigs (Campaign) [2005] EWHC 372; (2005) 102(21)
    L.S.G. 33; *Times,* April 7, 2005, QBD . . . .   *Digested,* 05/**419**
Hall v. Wandsworth LBC; Carter v. Wandsworth LBC [2004] EWCA Civ 1740; [2005]
    2 All E.R. 192; [2005] H.L.R. 23; [2005] B.L.G.R. 350; (2005) 102(4) L.S.G.
    30; *Times,* January 7, 2005, CA (Civ Div) . . . .   *Digested,* 05/**1991**
Hallett v. Stoddart (Valuation Officer) [2005] R.A. 255, LandsTr
Halliburton Energy Services Inc v. Smith International (North Sea) Inc (Application for
    Disclosure) [2004] EWHC 2286; (2005) 28(1) I.P.D. 27115, Ch D (Patents Ct)
Halliburton Energy Services Inc v. Smith International (North Sea) Ltd [2005] EWHC
    1623, Ch D (Patents Ct) . . . .   *Digested,* 05/**2441**
Hallmark Cards Inc v. Rolex Promotions SA (R 96/2004-2) [2005] E.T.M.R. 29, OHIM
    (2nd Bd App) . . . .   *Digested,* 05/**2526**
Halloran v. Delaney [2002] EWCA Civ 1258; [2003] 1 W.L.R. 28; [2003] 1 All E.R.
    775; [2002] 3 Costs L.R. 503; [2003] R.T.R. 9; [2003] P.I.Q.R. P5; (2002) 152
    N.L.J. 1386; (2002) 146 S.J.L.B. 205, CA (Civ Div) . . . .   *Digested,* 03/**330**:
                                                                        Applied, 03/336, 04/369, 05/2704
Halsey v. Milton Keynes General NHS Trust; Steel v. Joy [2004] EWCA Civ 576;
    [2004] 1 W.L.R. 3002; [2004] 4 All E.R. 920; [2004] C.P. Rep. 34; [2004] 3
    Costs L.R. 393; (2005) 81 B.M.L.R. 108; (2004) 101(22) L.S.G. 31; (2004) 154
    N.L.J. 769; (2004) 148 S.J.L.B. 629; *Times,* May 27, 2004; *Independent,* May
    21, 2004, CA (Civ Div) . . . .   *Digested,* 04/**291**:
                                                          Considered, 04/255, 04/266, 05/356
Hamann v. Finanzamt Hamburg-Eimsbuttel (51/88) [1991] S.T.C. 193; [1989] E.C.R.
    767; [1990] 2 C.M.L.R. 383, ECJ (2nd Chamber). . . . .   *Digested,* 91/**3660**:
                                                                        Followed, 97/5012, 05/4382
Hamblet v. Walkers Snack Foods Ltd see Ramsey v. Walkers Snack Foods Ltd
Hambleton DC v. Done Brothers (Cash Betting) Ltd [2005] P.A.D. 7, Planning
    Inspector
Hamersley v. Newton; *sub nom* Hamersley (Deceased), Re (2005-06) 8 I.T.E.L.R.
    256, Sup Ct (WA) (Sgl judge)
Hamersley (Deceased), Re see Hamersley v. Newton
Hammersmatch Properties Ltd v. First Secretary of State; *sub nom* First Secretary of
    State v. Hammersmatch Properties Ltd [2005] EWCA Civ 1360; [2005] N.P.C.
    131, CA (Civ Div); reversing [2005] EWHC 187, QBD (Admin)
Hammond v. Commissioner of Police of the Metropolis [2004] EWCA Civ 830;
    [2004] I.C.R. 1467; [2005] P.I.Q.R. P1; (2004) 101(27) L.S.G. 30; (2004) 148
    S.J.L.B. 758; *Times,* June 24, 2004, CA (Civ Div) . . . .   *Digested,* 04/**1814**
Hampstead Heath Winter Swimming Club v. London Corp see R. (on the application of
    Hampstead Heath Winter Swimming Club) v. London Corp
Hamsher v. First Secretary of State; *sub nom* R. (on the application of Hamsher) v.
    First Secretary of State [2004] EWHC 2299; [2005] J.P.L. 491, QBD (Admin) .   *Digested,* 05/**3277**
Hancock v. Holliday (Unreported, September 22, 2004), CC (Southampton) [*Ex rel.*
    James Counsell, Barrister, Outer Temple Chambers, Outer Temple, 222 Strand,
    London] . . . .   *Digested,* 05/**3177**
Handa v. High Instance Court of Paris; R. (on the application of Handa) v. Bow Street
    Magistrates Court [2004] EWHC 3116; *Times,* January 6, 2005, DC . . . .   *Digested,* 05/**1484**
Handels- og Kontorfunktionaerernes Forbund i Danmark v. Dansk Arbejdsgiverforening
    Ex p. Danfoss A/S (109/88); *sub nom* Union of Clerical and Commercial
    Employees v. Danish Employers Association Ex p. Danfoss A/S (109/88) [1989]
    E.C.R. 3199; [1991] 1 C.M.L.R. 8; [1991] I.C.R. 74; [1989] I.R.L.R. 532; *Times,*
    October 28, 1989, ECJ . . . .   *Digested,* 91/**4078**:
                                      Applied, 96/6958: *Considered,* 90/1915, 98/5825, 05/1261:
                                                                                Followed, 04/1254
Handelsbanken ASA v. Dandridge (The Aliza Glacial); *sub nom* Svenska
    Handelsbanken AB v. Dandridge [2002] EWCA Civ 577; [2002] 2 All E.R.
    (Comm) 39; [2002] 2 Lloyd's Rep. 421; [2002] C.L.C. 1227; [2003] Lloyd's
    Rep. I.R. 10, CA (Civ Div) . . . .   *Digested,* 02/**4107**:
                                                                                Applied, 05/2352
Handyside v. United Kingdom (A/24) (1979-80) 1 E.H.R.R. 737, ECHR . . . .   *Considered,* 05/692
Haney v. Brent Mind see De Haney v. Brent MIND

119

Hanly v. Norinchukin International Plc; De Bergolis v. Norinchukin International Plc
[2003] I.C.R. 1416, EAT . . . . *Digested*, 04/**1275**:
Distinguished, 05/1294

Hanner, Re (C438/02) [2005] 2 C.M.L.R. 42, ECJ

Hanning v. Top Deck Travel Group Ltd; Top Deck Maintenance v. Repair Centre (1994)
68 P. & C.R. 14; [1993] E.G.C.S. 84; (1993) 90(22) L.S.G. 37; (1993) 137
S.J.L.B. 172; [1993] N.P.C. 73; *Times*, May 6, 1993; *Independent*, June 7, 1993
(C.S.), CA (Civ Div) . . . . *Digested*, 95/**1858**:
Applied, 04/3254: *Considered*, 05/3404: *Followed*, 02/3096, 03/3544:
Overruled, 04/3224

Hanoman v. Southwark LBC [2004] EWHC 2039; [2005] 1 All E.R. 795; [2004] 27
E.G.C.S. 129; [2004] N.P.C. 102, Ch D . . . . *Applied*, 05/2014

Hansen-Tangen v. Sanko Steamship Co Ltd see Reardon Smith Line Ltd v. Hansen-
Tangen (The Diana Prosperity)

Harb v. Aziz (No.1); *sub nom* Harb v. King Fahd Bin Abdul Aziz (No.1) [2005] EWCA
Civ 632; [2005] 2 F.L.R. 1108; [2005] 2 F.C.R. 342; [2005] Fam. Law 778;
Times, June 6, 2005, CA (Civ Div) . . . . *Digested*, 05/**1665**

Harb v. Aziz (No.2); *sub nom* Harb v. King Fahd Bin Abdul Aziz (No.2) [2005] EWCA
Civ 1324; (2005) 102(45) L.S.G. 28; *Times*, November 21, 2005, CA (Civ Div)

Harb v. King Fahd Bin Abdul Aziz (No.1) see Harb v. Aziz (No.1)

Harb v. King Fahd Bin Abdul Aziz (No.2) see Harb v. Aziz (No.2)

Harbour Estates Ltd v. HSBC Bank Plc; *sub nom* HSBC Bank Plc v. Harbour Estates Ltd
[2004] EWHC 1714; [2005] Ch. 194; [2005] 2 W.L.R. 67; [2004] 3 All E.R.
1057; [2005] 1 E.G.L.R. 107; [2004] 32 E.G.C.S. 62, Ch D . . . . *Digested*, 04/**2489**

Hardie v. Devon CC (Unreported, January 14, 2005), CC (Plymouth) [*Ex rel.* Veitch
Penny Solicitors, 1 Manor Court, Dix's Field, Exeter] . . . . *Digested*, 05/**2854**

Harding v. London Underground Ltd see London Underground Ltd v. Ferenc-Batchelor

Harding v. Pub Estate Co Ltd; *sub nom* Pub Estate Co Ltd v. Harding [2005] EWCA
Civ 553; [2005] N.P.C. 62, CA (Civ Div)

Harding v. Wealands [2004] EWCA Civ 1735; [2005] 1 W.L.R. 1539; [2005] 1 All E.R.
415; [2005] 2 C.L.C. 411; [2005] R.T.R. 20; (2005) 155 N.L.J. 59; *Times*,
January 5, 2005, CA (Civ Div); reversing [2004] EWHC 1957, QBD . . . . *Digested*, 05/**608**

Hardy v. Polk Ltd [2005] I.C.R. 557; [2004] I.R.L.R. 420, EAT . . . . *Digested*, 04/**1307**:
Considered, 05/1322: *Distinguished*, 05/1309: *Not followed*, 05/1331

Hardy v. Tourism South East [2005] I.R.L.R. 242, EAT . . . . *Digested*, 05/**1204**

Hardys & Hansons Plc v. Lax; *sub nom* Hardy & Hansons Plc v. Lax [2005] EWCA Civ
846; [2005] I.C.R. 1565; [2005] I.R.L.R. 726; (2005) 102(29) L.S.G. 31;
Times, July 26, 2005, CA (Civ Div) . . . . *Digested*, 05/**1300**:
Applied, 05/1290

Hareford Ltd v. Barnet LBC [2005] 2 E.G.L.R. 72; [2005] 28 E.G. 122; [2005] 23
E.G.C.S. 140, CC (Central London)

Haringey LBC v. C (A Child) [2004] EWHC 2580; [2005] 2 F.L.R. 47; [2005] Fam.
Law 351; *Times*, November 22, 2004, Fam Div . . . . *Digested*, 05/**1531**

Haringey LBC v. Marks & Spencer Plc; Liverpool City Council Trading Standards Office
v. Somerfield Stores Ltd [2004] EWHC 1141; [2005] 1 W.L.R. 1742; [2004] 3
All E.R. 868; (2004) 168 J.P. 381; [2005] A.C.D. 1; (2004) 168 J.P.N. 556;
(2004) 154 N.L.J. 925; [2004] N.P.C. 69, QBD (Admin) . . . . *Digested*, 04/**2583**

Haringey LBC v. Michniewicz [2004] EWHC 1728; (2004) 101(27) L.S.G. 31; *Times*,
July 8, 2004, QBD (Admin) . . . . *Digested*, 05/**824**

Haringey LBC v. Mosner see Harrison v. Hammersmith and Fulham LBC

Hariri v. Secretary of State for the Home Department [2003] EWCA Civ 807; [2003]
A.C.D. 97; (2003) 147 S.J.L.B. 659, CA (Civ Div) . . . . *Considered*, 05/2166

Harker's Will Trusts, Re; *sub nom* Kean v. Harker [1969] 1 W.L.R. 1124; [1969] 3 All E.R.
1; 113 S.J. 588, Ch D . . . . *Digested*, 69/**3664**:
Applied, 05/3978

Harlow v. Loveday; *sub nom* Hill & Tyler Ltd (In Administration), Re [2004] EWHC
1261; [2004] B.C.C. 732; [2005] 1 B.C.L.C. 41; (2004) 101(26) L.S.G. 27;
Times, June 11, 2004, Ch D (Companies Ct) . . . . *Digested*, 04/**464**

Harper v. Buchler (No.1) [2004] B.P.I.R. 724, Ch D . . . . *Digested*, 05/**2285**

Harper v. Buchler (No.2) [2005] B.P.I.R. 577, Ch D

Harper v. Director of the Assets Recovery Agency [2005] S.T.C. (S.C.D.) 874; [2005]
S.T.I. 1906, Sp Comm

Harper v. Virgin Net Ltd [2004] EWCA Civ 271; [2005] I.C.R. 921; [2004] I.R.L.R.
390; (2004) 101(14) L.S.G. 25; (2004) 148 S.J.L.B. 353; *Times*, March 16,
2004, CA (Civ Div); affirming [2003] I.R.L.R. 831, EAT . . . . *Digested*, 05/**1326**:
Followed, 05/1340

Harris v. BRB (Residuary) Ltd [2005] EWCA Civ 900; [2005] I.C.R. 1680; (2005)
149 S.J.L.B. 922, CA (Civ Div) . . . . *Digested*, 05/**2849**

Harris v. Customs and Excise Commissioners [2005] S.T.I. 121, V&DTr

Harris v. Ellis see Huddersfield Fine Worsteds Ltd, Re

Harris v. Globe Travel Ltd (Unreported, September 27, 2004), CC (Edmonton) [*Ex rel.*
Turner & Debenhams Solicitors, Ivy House, 107 St Peter's Street, St Albans,
Herts] . . . . *Digested*, 05/**3191**

Harris v. Lord Shuttleworth (Trustees of the National & Provincial Building Society Pension Fund) [1994] I.C.R. 991; [1994] I.R.L.R. 547; [1994] Pens. L.R. 47; *Independent*, November 26, 1993, CA (Civ Div) . . . . *Digested*, 95/**3837**:
Considered, 05/3033
Harris v. Saunders (Unreported, May 13, 2004), CC (Liverpool) [*Ex rel.* Heather Belbin, Barrister, Oriel Chambers, 14, Water Street, Liverpool] . . . . *Digested*, 05/**3140**
Harris v. Scholfield Roberts & Hall see Arthur JS Hall & Co v. Simons
Harris v. Scholfield Roberts & Hill see Arthur JS Hall & Co v. Simons
Harrison v. Department of Social Security [1997] C.O.D. 220, QBD . . . . *Digested*, 97/**4659**:
Considered, 05/3869: *Followed*, 02/891
Harrison v. Hammersmith and Fulham LBC; Haringey LBC v. Mosner; Watson v. Hackney LBC [1981] 1 W.L.R. 650; [1981] 2 All E.R. 588; 79 L.G.R. 634; (1982) 44 P. & C.R. 131, CA (Civ Div) . . . . *Digested*, 82/**1479**:
Applied, 83/1786, 83/2120: *Considered*, 05/2690
Harrison v. National Coal Board [1951] A.C. 639; [1951] 1 All E.R. 1102; [1951] 1 T.L.R. 1079; 50 L.G.R. 1; 95 S.J. 413, HL; affirming [1950] 1 K.B. 466; [1950] 1 All E.R. 171; 66 T.L.R. (Pt. 1) 300; 114 J.P. 87; 48 L.G.R. 203; 94 S.J. 145, CA; affirming [1949] 2 All E.R. 58, Assizes (Leeds) . . . . *Digested*, 47-51/**6275**:
Considered, 54/2076, 05/4199: *Distinguished*, 53/2283
Harrison v. Seggar [2005] EWHC 411; [2005] B.P.I.R. 583, Ch D *Digested*, 05/**2292**
Harrison v. Teton Valley Trading Co Ltd; *sub nom* CHINAWHITE Trade Mark; Harrison's Trade Mark Application [2004] EWCA Civ 1028; [2004] 1 W.L.R. 2577; [2005] F.S.R. 10; (2004) 27(8) I.P.D. 27083; (2004) 148 S.J.L.B. 1061; *Times*, August 19, 2004, CA (Civ Div); affirming [2002] EWHC 3009; [2004] F.S.R. 13, Ch D (Patents Ct) . . . . *Digested*, 04/**2408**:
Applied, 05/2504

Harrison's Trade Mark Application see Harrison v. Teton Valley Trading Co Ltd
Harrods Ltd v. Secretary of State for the Environment, Transport and the Regions [2002] EWCA Civ 412; [2003] 1 P.L.R. 108; [2002] J.P.L. 1258; [2002] 11 E.G.C.S. 154; (2002) 99(12) L.S.G. 36; *Times*, April 3, 2002, CA (Civ Div); affirming [2001] EWHC Admin 600; [2002] J.P.L. 437; [2001] 31 E.G.C.S. 101; *Times*, November 15, 2001, QBD (Admin) . . . . *Digested*, 02/**3643**:
Considered, 05/3246
Harrods (Buenos Aires) Ltd (No.2), Re [1992] Ch. 72; [1991] 3 W.L.R. 397; [1991] 4 All E.R. 348; [1992] I.L.Pr. 453; *Times*, March 25, 1991; *Financial Times*, March 26, 1991, CA (Civ Div) . . . . *Digested*, 92/**475**:
Applied, 01/814, 03/607, 05/606: *Followed*, 00/763, 01/376
Harrow LBC v. Knight see Knight v. Harrow LBC
Harrow LBC v. Qazi see Qazi v. Harrow LBC
Harrow LBC v. Quazi see Qazi v. Harrow LBC
Hartigan, Re [1989] 2 Qd. R. 401 . . . . *Applied*, 05/**3978**
Hartley v. Magill see Porter v. Magill
Hartley v. Pleasureland Ltd (Unreported, April 15, 2005), CC (Blackpool) [*Ex rel.* Adam Walker, Barrister, Lamb Chambers, Lamb Building, Elm Court, Temple, London] . . . . *Digested*, 05/**3162**
Hartley v. United Kingdom (A/182) see Fox v. United Kingdom (A/182)
Hartman v. South Essex Mental Health and Community Care NHS Trust; Best v. Staffordshire University; Wheeldon v. HSBC Bank Ltd; Green v. Grimsby and Scunthorpe Newspapers Ltd; Moore v. Welwyn Components Ltd; Melville v. Home Office [2005] EWCA Civ 6; [2005] I.C.R. 782; [2005] I.R.L.R. 293; [2005] E.L.R. 237; [2005] P.I.Q.R. P19; (2005) 85 B.M.L.R. 136; (2005) 149 S.J.L.B. 115; *Times*, January 21, 2005; *Independent*, January 25, 2005, CA (Civ Div) . . . . *Digested*, 05/**2883**
HARVARD/Onco-mouse (T19/90) [1990] E.P.O.R. 501, EPO (Technical Bd App) . . . . . *Applied*, 05/2410
HARVARD/Transgenic animal (T315/03) [2005] E.P.O.R. 31, EPO (Technical Bd App) . *Digested*, 05/**2410**
Harvey v. Walters (1872-73) L.R. 8 C.P. 162, CCP . . . . *Considered*, 05/3403
Hasbro UK Ltd v. Director General of Fair Trading (Withdrawal of Appeal: Costs) [2003] CAT 2; [2003] Comp. A.R. 59, CCAT . . . . *Digested*, 03/**565**:
Applied, 05/569
Hashmi v. Inland Revenue Commissioners see Inland Revenue Commissioners v. Hashmi
Hashtroodi v. Hancock [2004] EWCA Civ 652; [2004] 1 W.L.R. 3206; [2004] 3 All E.R. 530; [2005] C.P. Rep. 17; *Times*, June 4, 2004; *Independent*, June 16, 2004, CA (Civ Div) . . . . *Digested*, 04/**284**:
Applied, 05/466: *Considered*, 05/403
Haskins v. Haskins see Norris v. Norris
Hassan (t/a Parade Dry Cleaners) v. Customs and Excise Commissioners [2005] S.T.I. 117, V&DTr
Hasselblad (GB) Ltd v. Commission of the European Communities (86/82 R) [1982] E.C.R. 1555, ECJ . . . . *Followed*, 05/544
Hastings BC v. Jones; *sub nom* R. (on the application of Hastings BC) v. Jones [2004] EWHC 2414; [2004] R.V.R. 270, QBD (Admin) . . . . *Digested*, 05/**3869**
Hastings-Bass Trustees v. Inland Revenue Commissioners see Hastings-Bass (Deceased), Re

Hastings-Bass (Deceased), Re; *sub nom* Hastings-Bass Trustees *v.* Inland Revenue Commissioners [1975] Ch. 25; [1974] 2 W.L.R. 904; [1974] 2 All E.R. 193; [1974] S.T.C. 211; [1974] T.R. 87; 118 S.J. 422, CA (Civ Div) .... *Digested,* 74/**993**:

Applied, 83/3364, 01/5515, 03/4497, 04/2802, 05/4304, 05/4305:

Considered, 01/5508, 03/4501, 05/2997

Hatton *v.* Sutherland see Barber *v.* Somerset CC

Haugland Tankers AS *v.* RMK Marine Gemi Yapim Sanayii ve Deniz Tasimaciligi Isletmesi AS [2005] EWHC 321; [2005] 1 All E.R. (Comm) 679; [2005] 1 Lloyd's Rep. 573; [2005] 1 C.L.C. 271, QBD (Comm) .... *Digested,* 05/**698**

Haven Healthcare (Southern) Ltd *v.* York (Inspector of Taxes) [2005] EWHC 2212; [2005] S.T.C. 1662; [2005] S.T.I. 1754; *Times,* November 1, 2005, Ch D

Havering LBC *v.* Tibbs [2005] P.A.D. 84, Planning Inspector

Hawk Insurance Co Ltd, Re [2001] EWCA Civ 241; [2002] B.C.C. 300; [2001] 2 B.C.L.C. 480, CA (Civ Div); reversing [2001] B.C.C. 57, Ch D (Companies Ct) .... *Digested,* 02/**2714**:

Applied, 02/2715, 03/2440: *Followed,* 05/2333

Hawkes *v.* DPP see R. (on the application of Hawkes) *v.* DPP

Hawkins *v.* Newham LBC; *sub nom* Newham LBC *v.* Hawkins [2005] EWCA Civ 451; [2005] H.L.R. 42; [2005] B.L.G.R. 750; [2005] 2 E.G.L.R. 51; [2005] 29 E.G. 100; [2005] N.P.C. 55; [2005] 2 P. & C.R. DG16; *Times,* May 3, 2005; *Independent,* April 29, 2005, CA (Civ Div)

Hawley *v.* Luminar Leisure Ltd; *sub nom* Hawley *v.* Luminar Leisure Plc; B3/2005/ 0237, B3/2005/0222, CA (Civ Div); affirming [2005] EWHC 5; [2005] Lloyd's Rep. I.R. 275, QBD .... *Digested,* 05/**2889**

Hay & Robertson Plc *v.* Kangol Ltd; *sub nom* Kangol Ltd *v.* Hay & Robertson Plc [2004] EWCA Civ 63; [2004] 2 All E.R. (Comm) 185; [2005] F.S.R. 13; (2004) 27(4) I.P.D. 27043, CA (Civ Div) .... *Digested,* 04/**2407**

Hayes *v.* James & Charles Dodd (A Firm) [1990] 2 All E.R. 815; [1988] E.G.C.S. 107; (1988) 138 N.L.J. Rep. 259, CA (Civ Div) .... *Digested,* 90/**1524**:

Applied, 92/3972, 93/3619, 95/3645, 96/4485: *Considered,* 91/1315:

Distinguished, 05/2866: *Followed,* 94/1444

Hayward *v.* Cammell Laird Shipbuilders Ltd (No.2) [1988] A.C. 894; [1988] 2 W.L.R. 1134; [1988] 2 All E.R. 257; [1988] 2 C.M.L.R. 528; [1988] I.C.R. 464; [1988] I.R.L.R. 257; (1988) 152 L.G. Rev. 501; (1988) 138 N.L.J. Rep. 133, HL; reversing [1988] Q.B. 12; [1987] 3 W.L.R. 20; [1987] 2 All E.R. 344; [1987] 2 C.M.L.R. 489; [1987] I.C.R. 682; [1987] I.R.L.R. 186; (1987) 151 L.G. Rev. 566; (1987) 84 L.S.G. 1491; (1987) 131 S.J. 657, CA (Civ Div); affirming [1986] I.C.R. 862, EAT .... *Digested,* 88/**1271**:

Applied, 03/1234: *Considered,* 05/1259

Hazel (for Lloyd's Syndicate 260) *v.* Whitlam; *sub nom* Whitlam *v.* Lloyds Syndicate 260 (t/a KGM Motor Policies at Lloyds) [2004] EWCA Civ 1600; [2005] Lloyd's Rep. I.R. 168, CA (Civ Div). .... *Digested,* 05/**2373**

HC *v.* Secretary of State for the Home Department [2005] EWCA Civ 893; (2005) 149 S.J.L.B. 923, CA (Civ Div)

HC Treby's Application see Bugle Press, Re

HCL Equipment Ltd *v.* Revenue and Customs Commissioners [2005] S.T.I. 2040, V&DTr

HE *v.* Secretary of State for the Home Department; *sub nom* HE (DRC: Credibility and Psychiatric Reports), Re [2004] UKIAT 321; [2005] Imm. A.R. 119, IAT

HE (DRC: Credibility and Psychiatric Reports), Re see HE *v.* Secretary of State for the Home Department

Head (Valuation Officer) *v.* Tower Hamlets LBC [2005] R.A. 177, Lands Tr .... *Digested,* 05/**3361**

Headley *v.* Trinidad and Tobago see Sealey *v.* Trinidad and Tobago

Health and Safety Executive *v.* Cadman see Cadman *v.* Health and Safety Executive

Hearn *v.* Younger [2002] EWHC 963; [2003] O.P.L.R. 45; [2005] Pens. L.R. 49; [2002] W.T.L.R. 1317, Ch D .... *Digested,* 04/**2802**

Heath *v.* Commissioner of Police of the Metropolis [2004] EWCA Civ 943; [2005] I.C.R. 329; [2005] I.R.L.R. 270; (2004) 148 S.J.L.B. 913; *Times,* July 22, 2004, CA (Civ Div); affirming EAT/454/02/TM, EAT .... *Digested,* 04/**1221**

Heath *v.* Tang; Stevens *v.* Peacock [1993] 1 W.L.R. 1421; [1993] 4 All E.R. 694; *Times,* August 11, 1993; *Independent,* October 14, 1993, CA (Civ Div) .... *Digested,* 93/**222**:

Applied, 98/3293, 00/3442, 03/465, 03/1331, 04/4061:

Considered, 99/3261, 01/3732: *Followed,* 95/419, 01/3718:

Referred to, 94/3445, 95/861

Heath Lambert Ltd *v.* Sociedad de Corretaje de Seguros [2004] EWCA Civ 792; [2004] 1 W.L.R. 2820; [2005] 1 All E.R. 225; [2004] 2 All E.R. (Comm) 656; [2005] 1 Lloyd's Rep. 597; [2005] 2 C.L.C. 366; [2004] Lloyd's Rep. I.R. 905; (2004) 101(28) L.S.G. 34; (2004) 148 S.J.L.B. 793; *Times,* July 2, 2004, CA (Civ Div); affirming [2003] EWHC 2269; [2004] 1 Lloyd's Rep. 495, QBD (Comm) .... *Digested,* 05/**2351**

Heavy Duty Parts Ltd *v.* Anelay [2004] EWHC 960; [2004] B.P.I.R. 729, Ch D ...... *Digested,* 05/**290**

Hedley Byrne & Co Ltd v. Heller & Partners Ltd [1964] A.C. 465; [1963] 3 W.L.R. 101; [1963] 2 All E.R. 575; [1963] 1 Lloyd's Rep. 485; 107 S.J. 454, HL; affirming [1962] 1 Q.B. 396; [1961] 3 W.L.R. 1225; [1961] 3 All E.R. 891; 105 S.J. 910, CA; affirming *Times*, December 21, 1960, QBD .... *Digested*, 63/**2416**:
Applied, 63/330, 67/2677, 69/1998, 70/1493, 70/1880, 70/1881, 71/8000, 71/9949, 72/38, 72/2364, 73/325, 73/2307, 73/2309, 74/2597, 76/341, 76/1868, 77/1804, 77/2886, 78/1512, 78/1695, 78/2822, 79/213, 79/1859, 80/363, 81/1837, 81/1849, 81/1860, 81/2752, 83/2574, 85/2304, 85/2324, 88/2430, 89/56, 90/3266, 94/3362, 95/3701, 97/3787, 97/3818, 01/1508, 02/3277, 02/4542, 02/6000, 04/2706, 05/2868: *Considered*, 65/2671, 65/3076, 66/9394, 67/3099, 68/3054, 69/882, 69/2463, 70/1849, 72/2363, 74/3638, 75/2326, 76/1343, 77/157, 77/370.u, 77/1452, 77/2009, 77/2032, 79/1864, 79/1884, 80/362, 80/1898, 82/1404, 83/1734, 83/2534, 86/215, 87/2579, 87/2580, 87/2591, 87/2619, 88/1710, 88/2433, 88/2444, 88/2456, 88/3409, 89/304, 89/469, 89/2543, 89/2566, 89/2585, 90/3288, 90/4312, 91/2661, 92/3192, 92/3213, 93/2983, 93/2997, 93/2999, 94/3383, 94/4234, 95/770, 95/3667, 95/3689, 95/4838, 96/4531, 98/3920, 00/4200, 00/4205, 02/5421: *Distinguished*, 64/3468, 67/2731, 71/7804, 71/7843, 71/10472, 71/11921, 72/2349, 72/2352, 73/2312, 86/2258, 87/2576, 98/3922: *Explained*, 72/107, 94/1918:
Followed, 64/2565, 65/2727, 74/453, 74/2576, 75/419, 92/6091, 96/1012, 96/4439, 96/4488, 98/3951, 98/3987, 02/6008: *Referred to*, 81/1852, 88/4958, 95/5841

Heidelberger Bauchemie GmbH's Trade Mark Application (C49/02) [2004] E.T.M.R. 99, ECJ (2nd Chamber) .... *Digested*, 05/**2529**
Heintz van Landewyck Sarl v. Commission of the European Communities (209/78) [1980] E.C.R. 3125; [1981] 3 C.M.L.R. 134, ECJ........................ *Digested*, 82/**1301**:
Applied, 84/1373, 85/1326, 05/555: *Followed*, 02/587
Heiser v. Finanzamt Innsbruck (C172/03); *sub nom* Heiser v. Finanzlandesdirektion fur Tirol (C172/03) [2005] E.C.R. I-1627; [2005] 2 C.M.L.R. 18; [2005] C.E.C. 687, ECJ (2nd Chamber)
Heiser v. Finanzlandesdirektion fur Tirol (C172/03) see Heiser v. Finanzamt Innsbruck (C172/03)
Helby v. Rafferty [1979] 1 W.L.R. 13; [1978] 3 All E.R. 1016; (1979) 37 P. & C.R. 376; (1978) 247 E.G. 729; (1978) 8 Fam. Law 207; 122 S.J. 418, CA (Civ Div) ..... *Digested*, 79/**1630**:
Considered, 87/2242, 88/2086, 05/2641
Helena Housing Ltd v. Pinder see Lambeth LBC v. O'Kane
Hellenic Steel Co v. Svolamar Shipping Co Ltd (The Komninos S) [1991] 1 Lloyd's Rep. 370; *Financial Times*, January 16, 1991, CA (Civ Div); reversing [1990] 1 Lloyd's Rep. 541; *Financial Times*, January 16, 1990, QBD (Comm) .... *Digested*, 92/**3925**:
Applied, 05/616
Hemain v. Hemain [1988] 2 F.L.R. 388; [1988] Fam. Law 432; *Independent*, March 7, 1988, CA (Civ Div) .... *Digested*, 89/**1729**:
Applied, 05/1623: *Distinguished*, 03/1554
Hemingway Realty Ltd v. Clothworkers Co; *sub nom* Hemingway Realty Ltd v. Master Wardens and Commonalty of Freeman of the Art or Mystery of Clothworkers of the City of London [2005] EWHC 299; [2005] L. & T.R. 21; [2005] 2 E.G.L.R. 36; [2005] 19 E.G. 176; [2005] 11 E.G.C.S. 181; [2005] N.P.C. 37; [2005] 2 P. & C.R. DG8; *Times*, March 15, 2005, Ch D .... *Digested*, 05/**2667**
Hemingway Realty Ltd v. Master Wardens and Commonalty of Freeman of the Art or Mystery of Clothworkers of the City of London see Hemingway Realty Ltd v. Clothworkers Co
Henaf v. France (65436/01) (2005) 40 E.H.R.R. 44, ECHR .... *Digested*, 05/**2061**
Henao v. Netherlands (13669/03) (Unreported, June 24, 2003), ECHR .... *Considered*, 05/2160
Henderson, Re see Snowden, Re
Henderson v. Attorney General see Snowden, Re
Henderson v. Henderson [1843-60] All E.R. Rep. 378; (1843) 67 E.R. 313; (1843) 3 Hare 100, Ct of Chancery.. *Applied*, 65/100,
67/1498, 91/1736, 97/461, 97/997, 98/80, 98/2162, 98/2163, 98/3454, 99/3313, 99/4025, 00/5111, 01/4678, 02/419, 03/470, 04/264, 05/2505: *Considered*, 75/2463, 84/2704, 88/2920, 89/1534, 93/3308, 94/3285, 94/3746, 95/3894, 96/1105, 98/244, 98/518, 98/618, 98/4067, 99/620, 00/604, 00/785, 01/410, 01/6474, 03/466, 04/425: *Distinguished*, 47-51/3681, 99/549, 99/4384, 00/349, 00/2605: *Followed*, 99/3952, 00/2322, 05/329: *Not applied*, 99/1376, 99/3732: *Referred to*, 99/4014
Henderson v. Stephenson Harwood [2005] EWHC 24; [2005] O.P.L.R. 21; [2005] Pens. L.R. 209; (2005) 102(11) L.S.G. 29; *Times*, January 27, 2005, Ch D .... *Digested*, 05/**2976**
Hendricks v. Commissioner of Police of the Metropolis see Commissioner of Police of the Metropolis v. Hendricks
Henkel KGaA v. Deutsches Patent- und Markenamt (C218/01) [2005] E.T.M.R. 45, ECJ (6th Chamber) .... *Digested*, 05/**2585**:
Applied, 05/2527

Henkel KGaA v. Office for Harmonisation in the Internal Market (Trade Marks and
  Designs) (OHIM) (C456/01 P) [2004] E.C.R. I-5089; [2005] E.T.M.R. 44, ECJ
  (6th Chamber) [2004] E.C.R. I-5089; [2004] E.T.M.R. 87, AGO . . . . *Digested*, 05/**2553**:
  Considered, 05/2532
Henkel KGaA v. Office for Harmonisation in the Internal Market (Trade Marks and
  Designs) (OHIM) (T393/02) [2005] E.T.M.R. 56, CFI . . . . *Digested*, 05/**2552**
Hennelly v. Official Receiver see Hennelly's Utilities Ltd, Re
Hennelly v. Secretary of State for Trade and Industry see Hennelly's Utilities Ltd, Re
Hennelly's Utilities Ltd, Re; *sub nom* Hennelly v. Official Receiver; Hennelly v. Secretary
  of State for Trade and Industry [2004] EWHC 34; [2005] B.C.C. 542, Ch D
  (Companies Ct) . . . . *Digested*, 05/**519**
Henry v. BBC (Costs Capping) [2005] EWHC 2503; (2005) 155 N.L.J. 1780, QBD
Henry Boot Construction Ltd v. Alstom Combined Cycles Ltd [2005] EWCA Civ 814;
  [2005] 1 W.L.R. 3850; [2005] 3 All E.R. 832; [2005] 2 C.L.C. 63; [2005]
  B.L.R. 437; 101 Con. L.R. 52; (2005) 102(30) L.S.G. 28, CA (Civ Div) . . . . *Digested*, 05/**656**
Henry Bros (Magherafelt) Ltd v. Ministry of Defence (Revocation of Patent) [1999]
  R.P.C. 442; (1999) 22(3) I.P.D. 22023, CA (Civ Div); affirming [1997] R.P.C.
  693; (1997) 20(10) I.P.D. 20096, Ch D (Patents Ct) . . . . *Digested*, 99/**3505**:
  Applied, 05/2486: *Considered*, 05/2485
Henry Butcher International Ltd v. KG Engineering [2004] EWCA Civ 1597; [2005] C.P.
  Rep. 13; (2004) 148 S.J.L.B. 1282, CA (Civ Div) . . . . *Digested*, 05/**308**
Henworth v. United Kingdom (505/02) see Henworth v. United Kingdom (515/02)
Henworth v. United Kingdom (515/02); *sub nom* Henworth v. United Kingdom (505/
  02) (2005) 40 E.H.R.R. 33; *Times*, November 22, 2004, ECHR
Herbert Berry Associates Ltd v. Inland Revenue Commissioners; *sub nom* Herbert Berry
  Associates Ltd (In Liquidation), Re [1977] 1 W.L.R. 1437; [1978] 1 All E.R. 161;
  52 T.C. 113; [1977] T.R. 247; 121 S.J. 829, HL; affirming [1977] 1 W.L.R. 617;
  [1977] 3 All E.R. 729; [1977] T.R. 137; 121 S.J. 252, CA (Civ Div); affirming
  [1976] 1 W.L.R. 783; [1976] 3 All E.R. 207; 120 S.J. 538, Ch D . . . . *Digested*, 78/**253**:
  Applied, 85/326: *Followed*, 05/2343
Herbert Berry Associates Ltd (In Liquidation), Re see Herbert Berry Associates Ltd v. Inland
  Revenue Commissioners
Herbert Karner Industrie Auktionen GmbH v. Troostwijk GmbH (C71/02) [2004] E.C.R.
  I-3025; [2004] 2 C.M.L.R. 5; [2004] C.E.C. 327; [2005] E.T.M.R. 59, ECJ
  (5th Chamber) . . . . *Digested*, 04/**636**
Hercules Chemicals NV v. Commission of the European Communities (C51/92 P); *sub
  nom* Polypropylene Cartel (T7/89), Re; Hercules Chemicals NV v. Commission
  of the European Communities (T7/89) [1999] E.C.R. I-4235; [1999] 5 C.M.L.R.
  976, ECJ (6th Chamber); affirming [1991] E.C.R. II-1711; [1992] 4 C.M.L.R. 84,
  CFI (1st Chamber) . . . . *Digested*, 00/**2377**:
  Applied, 05/555: *Followed*, 05/554
Hercules Chemicals NV v. Commission of the European Communities (T7/89) see
  Hercules Chemicals NV v. Commission of the European Communities (C51/92
  P)
Herczegfalvy v. Austria (A/242-B) (1993) 15 E.H.R.R. 437, ECHR . . . . *Digested*, 93/**2154**:
  Applied, 03/2958: *Considered*, 01/4431, 03/2158, 05/2823:
  Referred to, 00/4322
Herd v. Inland Revenue Commissioners see Inland Revenue Commissioners v. Herd
Hereford Waste Watchers Ltd v. Hereford Council see R. (on the application of Hereford
  Waste Watchers Ltd) v. Herefordshire CC
Herefordshire CC v. Duncan Cameron & Sons Ltd [2005] P.A.D. 78, Planning
  Inspector
Herlan Edmunds Engineering (Pty) Ltd, Re see Fourie v. Le Roux (No.1)
Heronsgate Enterprises Ltd v. Harman (Chesham) Ltd (Unreported, January 21, 1993),
  CA (Civ Div) . . . . *Applied*, 05/3418
Hertel v. Switzerland (25181/94) (1999) 28 E.H.R.R. 534; 5 B.H.R.C. 260; [1998]
  H.R.C.D. 817, ECHR . . . . *Digested*, 99/**3111**:
  Followed, 05/2089: *Referred to*, 01/3533
Hertfordshire Investments Ltd v. Bubb [2000] 1 W.L.R. 2318; [2001] C.P. Rep. 38;
  [2000] C.P.L.R. 588; *Times*, August 31, 2000, CA (Civ Div) . . . . *Digested*, 00/**562**:
  Applied, 03/274, 03/2597: *Considered*, 02/506, 05/2671
Hertsmere BC v. Harty see South Buckinghamshire DC v. Porter (No.1)
Hertsmere Primary Care Trust v. Rabindra-Anandh [2005] EWHC 320; [2005] 3 All
  E.R. 274; [2005] C.P. Rep. 41; *Times*, April 25, 2005, Ch D
Hess v. United Kingdom (1975) 2 D. & R. 72, Eur Comm HR . . . . *Considered*, 05/2129
Hester v. Inland Revenue Commissioner (2004-05) 7 I.T.E.L.R. 420, CA (NZ) . . . . *Digested*, 05/**282**
Hester v. Personal Representatives of Slater's Estate [2005] 2 Q.R. 10, CC (Leeds)
  [*Ex rel.* Langleys Solicitors, Insurance Claims Department, Queens House,
  Micklegate, York] . . . . *Digested*, 04/**2871**
Hetton Victory Club Ltd v. Swainston see Swainston v. Hetton Victory Club Ltd
Hewlett-Packard Development Co LP v. Expansys UK Ltd [2005] EWHC 1495; [2005]
  E.T.M.R. 111; (2005) 28(8) I.P.D. 28062, Ch D . . . . *Digested*, 05/**2573**
Heyward v. Plymouth Hospital NHS Trust [2005] EWCA Civ 939; *Times*, August 1,
  2005; *Independent*, June 29, 2005, CA (Civ Div)

HF Pension Trustees Ltd *v.* Ellison [1999] Lloyd's Rep. P.N. 489; [1999] P.N.L.R. 894; [1999] O.P.L.R. 67; (1999) 96(8) L.S.G. 30; *Times*, March 5, 1999, Ch D . . . . . *Digested*, 99/**472**: *Considered*, 04/379: *Distinguished*, 05/433

Hickman *v.* Potts see Potts *v.* Hickman

Hicks *v.* Davies (Inspector of Taxes); *sub nom* Davies (Inspector of Taxes) *v.* Hicks [2005] EWHC 847; [2005] S.T.C. 850; [2005] B.T.C. 331; [2005] S.T.I. 918; *Times*, May 27, 2005, Ch D; affirming [2005] S.T.C. (S.C.D.) 165; [2005] W.T.L.R. 329; [2004] S.T.I. 2544, Sp Comm . . . . *Digested*, 05/**4005**

Higham *v.* Horton see 1 Pump Court Chambers *v.* Horton

Higham *v.* University of Plymouth [2005] EWHC 1492; [2005] E.L.R. 547, QBD (Admin)

Highfield Commodities Ltd, Re [1985] 1 W.L.R. 149; [1984] 3 All E.R. 884; [1985] P.C.C. 191; (1984) 81 L.S.G. 3589; (1984) 128 S.J. 870, Ch D . . . . *Digested*, 85/**324**: *Considered*, 94/3740, 05/2344

Highgrade Traders, Re [1984] B.C.L.C. 151; *Times*, December 20, 1983, CA (Civ Div); reversing *Times*, December 9, 1982 . . . . *Digested*, 84/**1527**: *Applied*, 97/3367: *Considered*, 87/3060, 05/293: *Distinguished*, 03/403

HIGHLAND INDUSTRIES/Request for reimbursement of appeal fee (G3/03) see HIGHLAND INDUSTRIES/Request for reimbursement of appeal fee (J12/01)

HIGHLAND INDUSTRIES/Request for reimbursement of appeal fee (J12/01); *sub nom* HIGHLAND INDUSTRIES/Request for reimbursement of appeal fee (G3/03) [2005] E.P.O.R. 25, EPO (Enlarged Bd App) [2004] E.P.O.R. 17, EPO (Legal Bd App) . . . . *Digested*, 04/**2248**

HIH Casualty & General Insurance Ltd, Re; *sub nom* ENRON Metals & Commodity Ltd (In Administration) *v.* HIH Casualty & General Insurance Ltd (In Provisional Liquidation) (2005) 102(19) L.S.G. 33; *Times*, April 6, 2005, Ch D

HIH Casualty & General Insurance Ltd *v.* Axa Corporate Solutions (formerly Axa Reassurance SA); HIH Casualty & General Insurance Ltd *v.* New Hampshire Insurance Co [2002] EWCA Civ 1253; [2002] 2 All E.R. (Comm) 1053; [2003] Lloyd's Rep. I.R. 1, CA (Civ Div); affirming [2002] Lloyd's Rep. I.R. 325, QBD . . *Digested*, 03/**2483**: *Applied*, 05/705

HIH Casualty & General Insurance Ltd *v.* New Hampshire Insurance Co see HIH Casualty & General Insurance Ltd *v.* Axa Corporate Solutions (formerly Axa Reassurance SA)

HIH Casualty & General Insurance Ltd *v.* New Hampshire Insurance Co [2001] EWCA Civ 735; [2001] 2 All E.R. (Comm) 39; [2001] 2 Lloyd's Rep. 161; [2001] C.L.C. 1480; [2001] Lloyd's Rep. I.R. 596, CA (Civ Div); affirming [2001] 1 Lloyd's Rep. 378; [2001] C.L.C. 481, QBD (Comm) . . . . *Digested*, 01/**3840**: *Applied*, 03/3908, 04/2245: *Distinguished*, 05/2405

Hill *v.* Chief Constable of West Yorkshire [1989] A.C. 53; [1988] 2 W.L.R. 1049; [1988] 2 All E.R. 238; (1988) 152 L.G. Rev. 709; (1988) 85(20) L.S.G. 34; (1988) 138 N.L.J. Rep. 126; (1988) 132 S.J. 700, HL; affirming [1988] Q.B. 60; [1987] 2 W.L.R. 1126; [1987] 1 All E.R. 1173; (1987) 151 L.G. Rev. 729; (1987) 84 L.S.G. 982; (1987) 137 N.L.J. 222; (1987) 131 S.J. 626, CA (Civ Div); affirming (1986) 136 N.L.J. 238, QBD . . . . *Digested*, 88/**2435**: *Applied*, 90/3278, 92/3354, 93/2958, 94/3345, 94/3384, 95/3452, 95/3652, 99/3963, 05/3342: *Considered*, 87/2580, 90/5493, 94/3345, 94/4296, 95/3652, 96/4441, 99/3970, 99/4009: *Disapproved*, 98/3102: *Distinguished*, 95/3686, 99/3972, 99/5434, 00/4229: *Followed*, 01/4479

Hill *v.* Secretary of State for the Environment, Food and Rural Affairs [2005] EWHC 696; [2005] B.P.I.R. 1330, Ch D

Hill *v.* Slade [2005] 2 Q.R. 9; [2004] 6 Q.R. 11, CC (Tunbridge Wells) [*Ex rel.* Andrew Granville Stafford, Barrister, 4, King's Bench Walk, Temple, London] . . . . *Digested*, 04/**2867**

Hill *v.* Spread Trustee Co Ltd; *sub nom* Nurkowski, Re [2005] EWHC 336; [2005] B.P.I.R. 842, Ch D . . . . *Digested*, 05/**4313**

Hill *v.* Transport for London [2005] EWHC 856; [2005] Ch. 379; [2005] 3 W.L.R. 471; [2005] 3 All E.R. 677; [2005] 2 E.G.L.R. 1; [2005] 30 E.G. 90; [2005] 21 E.G.C.S. 138; *Times*, May 30, 2005, Ch D . . . . *Digested*, 05/**3377**

Hill & Tyler Ltd (In Administration), Re see Harlow *v.* Loveday

Hill Samuel Life Assurance, Re (Unreported, July 10, 1995) . . . . *Followed*, 05/2361

Hillingdon LBC *v.* Secretary of State for the Environment, Transport and the Regions [2000] Env. L.R. D11, QBD . . . . *Approved*, 05/3261

Hilti AG *v.* Commission of the European Communities (C53/92 P); *sub nom* Hilti AG *v.* Commission of the European Communities (T30/89) [1994] E.C.R. I-667; [1994] 4 C.M.L.R. 614; [1994] F.S.R. 760; *Financial Times*, March 8, 1994, ECJ; affirming [1991] E.C.R. II-1439; [1992] 4 C.M.L.R. 16; [1992] F.S.R. 210, CFI (2nd Chamber) . . . . *Digested*, 94/**4774**: *Followed*, 01/761, 05/547

Hilti AG *v.* Commission of the European Communities (T30/89) see Hilti AG *v.* Commission of the European Communities (C53/92 P)

Hilton *v.* Baker Booth & Eastwood see Hilton *v.* Barker Booth & Eastwood

Hilton *v.* Bariker Booth & Eastwood see Hilton *v.* Barker Booth & Eastwood

Hilton v. Barker Booth & Eastwood; *sub nom* Hilton v. Baker Booth & Eastwood; Hilton v. Bariker Booth & Eastwood [2005] UKHL 8; [2005] 1 W.L.R. 567; [2005] 1 All E.R. 651; [2005] P.N.L.R. 23; [2005] 6 E.G.C.S. 141; (2005) 102(14) L.S.G. 27; (2005) 155 N.L.J. 219; (2005) 149 S.J.L.B. 179; [2005] N.P.C. 14; *Times,* February 4, 2005, HL; reversing [2002] EWCA Civ 723; [2002] Lloyd's Rep. P.N. 500; [2003] P.N.L.R. 32; (2002) 146 S.J.L.B. 152; [2002] N.P.C. 74; *Times,* June 6, 2002; *Independent,* May 29, 2002, CA (Civ Div) . . . . *Digested,* 05/**2881**

Hinchy v. Secretary of State for Work and Pensions [2005] UKHL 16; [2005] 1 W.L.R. 967; [2005] 2 All E.R.129; (2005) 102(17) L.S.G. 32; (2005) 149 S.J.L.B. 299; *Times,* March 4, 2005; *Independent,* March 9, 2005, HL; reversing [2003] EWCA Civ 138; [2003] 1 W.L.R. 2018; [2003] 2 All E.R. 289; (2003) 100(17) L.S.G. 29; *Times,* February 24, 2003; *Independent,* February 26, 2003, CA (Civ Div) . . . . *Digested,* 05/**3834**:
Applied, 05/2211

Hindalco Industries Ltd v. Assistant Commissioner of Income Tax 8 I.T.L. Rep. 1, ITAT (Ind)

Hindawi v. Secretary of State for the Home Department see R. (on the application of Hindawi) v. Secretary of State for the Home Department

Hinds v. Queen, The; DPP v. Jackson [1977] A.C. 195; [1976] 2 W.L.R. 366; [1976] 1 All E.R. 353; [1976] Crim. L.R.124; (1975) 119 S.J. 864, PC (Jam) . . . . *Digested,* 76/**183**:
Applied, 85/174, 92/1223, 94/496, 03/635, 05/630, 05/773:
Considered, 99/781

Hindson v. Pipe House Wharf (Swansea) Ltd see Grieves v. FT Everard & Sons Ltd

Hing Lo (Deceased), Re (Unreported, June 26, 2002), Cons Ct . . . . *Approved,* 05/993

Hinton v. University of East London; *sub nom* University of East London v. Hinton [2005] EWCA Civ 532; [2005] I.C.R. 1260; [2005] I.R.L.R. 552, CA (Civ Div); reversing UKEAT/0495/04/LA, EAT . . . . *Digested,* 05/**1207**

Hipgrave v. Jones; *sub nom* Jones v. Hipgrave [2004] EWHC 2901; [2005] 2 F.L.R. 174; [2005] A.C.D. 67; [2005] Fam. Law 453; (2005) 102(6) L.S.G. 33; *Times,* January 11, 2005, QBD . . . . *Digested,* 05/**4191**

Hiranand v. Harilela (2004-05) 7 I.T.E.L.R. 450, CA (HK)

Hirst v. United Kingdom (74025/01) 19 B.H.R.C. 546; (2005) 155 N.L.J. 1551; *Times,* October 10, 2005, ECHR (Grand Chamber)

Hiscock v. Oxley see Oxley v. Hiscock

Hiscox Underwriting Ltd v. Dickson Manchester & Co Ltd [2004] EWHC 479; [2004] 1 All E.R. (Comm) 753; [2004] 2 Lloyd's Rep. 438, QBD (Comm) . . . . *Digested,* 04/**182**:
Considered, 05/325

Historic Motorsport Ltd v. Customs and Excise Commissioners [2005] S.T.I. 1025, V&DTr

HITACHI/Auction method (T258/03) [2004] E.P.O.R. 55, EPO (Technical Bd App) . . . *Digested,* 05/**2460**

Hitch v. Stone (Inspector of Taxes); *sub nom* Stone (Inspector of Taxes) v. Hitch [2001] EWCA Civ 63; [2001] S.T.C. 214; 73 T.C. 600; [2001] B.T.C. 78; [2001] S.T.I. 104; [2001] N.P.C. 19; *Times,* February 21, 2001, CA (Civ Div); reversing [1999] S.T.C. 431; [1999] B.T.C. 103; [1999] E.G.C.S. 44; [1999] N.P.C. 40; *Times,* April 7, 1999, Ch D . . . . *Digested,* 01/**5319**:
Applied, 04/3954, 05/1657

HJ Banks & Co Ltd v. Snowball (Valuation Officer) see HJ Banks & Co Ltd v. Speight (Valuation Officer)

HJ Banks & Co Ltd v. Speight (Valuation Officer); HJ Banks & Co Ltd v. Snowball (Valuation Officer) [2005] R.A. 61, LandsTr . . . . *Digested,* 05/**3369**

HJ Heinz Co Ltd v. Kenrick [2000] I.C.R. 491; [2000] I.R.L.R.144, EAT . . . . *Digested,* 00/**2129**:
Considered, 05/1193: *Followed,* 00/2127

HL v. United Kingdom (45508/99); *sub nom* L v. United Kingdom (45508/99) (2005) 40 E.H.R.R. 32; 17 B.H.R.C. 418; (2004) 7 C.C.L. Rep. 498; [2005] Lloyd's Rep. Med.169; (2005) 81 B.M.L.R.131; *Times,* October 19, 2004, ECHR . *Digested,* 05/**2109**

Hlozek v. Roche Austria GmbH (C19/02) [2004] E.C.R. I-11491; [2005] 1 C.M.L.R. 28; [2005] C.E.C. 362; [2005] O.P.L.R. 233, ECJ (1st Chamber) . . . . *Digested,* 05/**1257**

HLR v. France (1998) 26 E.H.R.R. 29, ECHR . . . . *Digested,* 98/**3069**:
Applied, 05/2167

HM v. Germany (Admissibility) (62512/00) 8 I.T.L. Rep. 206; (2005) 41 E.H.R.R. SE15, ECHR

HN v. Poland (77710/01) [2005] 3 F.C.R. 85, ECHR

Hobbs v. Sutton LBC (1994) 26 H.L.R.132, CA (Civ Div) . . . . *Digested,* 94/**2325**:
Applied, 05/2002

Hochstrasser (Inspector of Taxes) v. Mayes; Jennings v. Kinder (Inspector of Taxes) [1960] A.C. 376; [1960] 2 W.L.R. 63; [1959] 3 All E.R. 817; 53 R. & I.T. 12; 38 T.C. 673; (1959) 38 A.T.C. 360; [1959] T.R. 355, HL; affirming [1959] Ch. 22; [1958] 3 W.L.R. 215; [1958] 3 All E.R. 285; 51 R. & I.T. 767; (1958) 37 A.T.C. 205; [1958] T.R. 237; 102 S.J. 546, CA; affirming [1958] 2 W.L.R. 982; [1958] 1 All E.R. 369; 51 R. & I.T. 321; (1957) 36 A.T.C. 356; [1957] T.R. 365; 102 S.J. 419, Ch D . . . . *Digested*, 59/**1543**:
Applied, 64/1836, 76/1441, 77/1614, 78/1675, 82/1636, 89/2028, 90/2646, 91/2092, 99/4729, 05/4071: *Considered*, 65/1946, 87/2034:
Distinguished, 76/1438, 86/1762
Hockenjos v. Secretary of State for Social Security [2004] EWCA Civ 1749; [2005] Eu. L.R. 385; [2005] I.R.L.R. 471; [2005] 1 F.L.R. 1009; [2005] 1 F.C.R. 286; [2005] Fam. Law 464; (2005) 102(7) L.S.G. 27; *Times*, January 4, 2005; *Independent*, January 20, 2005, CA (Civ Div) . . . . *Digested*, 05/**3886**
Hocking v. Canyon Holdings Ltd [2004] EWHC 1966; [2005] B.P.I.R. 160, Ch D
Hodgetts v. Chiltern DC; *sub nom* Chiltern DC v. Hodgetts [1983] 2 A.C. 120; [1983] 2 W.L.R. 577; [1983] 1 All E.R. 1057; (1983) 147 J.P. 372; (1983) 45 P. & C.R. 402; [1983] J.P.L. 377, HL. . . . . *Digested*, 83/**3655**:
Applied, 84/2281, 85/908, 85/2084, 86/199, 86/952, 05/821:
Considered, 93/3859, 00/5467: *Distinguished*, 93/3808, 94/4305
Hodgkinson v. Simms [1994] 3 S.C.R. 377, Sup Ct (Can) . . . . *Applied*, 05/**4299**
Hodgson, Re; *sub nom* Nowell v. Flannery [1936] Ch. 203, Ch D . . . . *Applied*, 05/**3975**
Hoechst AG v. Inland Revenue Commissioners (C410/98) see Metallgesellschaft Ltd v. Inland Revenue Commissioners (C397/98)
Hoff v. Atherton [2004] EWCA Civ 1554; [2005] W.T.L.R. 99, CA (Civ Div); affirming [2004] EWHC 177, Ch D . . . . *Digested*, 05/**3971**
HOFFMAN-LA ROCHE/Methods for detection (T1091/02) [2005] E.P.O.R. 1, EPO (Technical Bd App) . . . . *Digested*, 05/**2452**
HOFFMAN-LA ROCHE/Transfer of opposition (G2/04) [2005] E.P.O.R. 35, EPO (Enlarged Bd App)
Hoffmann (C144/00), Re see Criminal Proceedings against Hoffmann (C144/00)
Hofmann v. Barmer Ersatzkasse (184/83) [1984] E.C.R. 3047; [1986] 1 C.M.L.R. 242; [1985] I.C.R. 731, ECJ . . . . *Digested*, 86/**1463**:
Considered, 05/1266: *Followed*, 04/1290
Hogg v. Dover College [1990] I.C.R. 39, EAT . . . . *Digested*, 90/**1963**:
Applied, 05/1204: *Followed*, 96/2657
Holcim (Deutschland) AG (formerly Alsen AG) v. Commission of the European Communities (T28/03) [2005] All E.R. (EC) 1037; [2005] 5 C.M.L.R. 3, CFI (3rd Chamber)
Holder v. Law Society [2003] EWCA Civ 39; [2003] 1 W.L.R. 1059; [2003] 3 All E.R. 62; (2003) 100(11) L.S.G. 34; (2003) 147 S.J.L.B. 117; *Times*, January 29, 2003, CA (Civ Div); reversing [2002] EWHC 1559; *Times*, September 9, 2002, Ch D . . . . *Digested*, 03/**2824**:
Applied, 05/2725
Holding v. First Secretary of State [2003] EWHC 3138; [2004] J.P.L. 1405, QBD (Admin) . . . . *Digested*, 05/**3262**
Holding & Management (Solitaire) Ltd v. Ideal Homes North West Ltd (formerly Broseley Estates Ltd) [2005] EWCA Civ 59, CA (Civ Div); affirming [2004] EWHC 2408; 96 Con. L.R. 114; [2005] P.N.L.R. 16, QBD (TCC) . . . . *Digested*, 05/**655**
Holland (James) v. HM Advocate [2005] UKPC D1; 2005 S.C. (P.C.) 3; 2005 S.L.T. 563; 2005 S.C.C.R. 417; [2005] H.R.L.R. 25; 18 B.H.R.C. 500; 2005 G.W.D. 17-305; *Times*, June 1, 2005, PC (Sc) . . . . *Digested*, 05/**5134**:
Previous proceedings, 03/5338, 04/4672
Holliday (A Bankrupt), Re [1981] Ch. 405; [1981] 2 W.L.R. 996; [1980] 3 All E.R. 385; (1980) 77 L.S.G. 340; 125 S.J. 411, CA (Civ Div) . . . . *Digested*, 80/**1406**:
Considered, 93/1846, 94/3303, 95/2214: *Distinguished*, 91/261, 98/3291, 05/2272: *Followed*, 84/1696
Hollins v. Russell; Tichband v. Hurdman; Dunn v. Ward; Pratt v. Bull; Worth v. McKenna; Sharratt v. London Central Bus Co Ltd (No.3) [2003] EWCA Civ 718; [2003] 1 W.L.R. 2487; [2003] 4 All E.R. 590; [2003] 3 Costs L.R. 423; (2003) 100(28) L.S.G. 30; (2003) 153 N.L.J. 920; (2003) 147 S.J.L.B. 662; *Times*, June 10, 2003; *Independent*, June 3, 2003, CA (Civ Div) . . . . *Digested*, 03/**334**:
Applied, 04/2548, 04/2550, 05/377, 05/2705
Hollis v. Dudley MBC see R. v. Dudley Magistrates Court Ex p. Hollis
Holloway v. DPP [2004] EWHC 2621; (2005) 169 J.P. 14; (2004) 168 J.P.N. 956, QBD (Admin) . . . . *Digested*, 05/**813**
Hollywood SAS v. Souza Cruz SA [2002] E.T.M.R. 64, OHIM (3rd Bd App) . . . . *Digested*, 02/**2872**:
Considered, 05/2523: *Followed*, 05/2521
Holman v. HH Martyn & Co see Denley's Trust Deed, Re
Holman v. Howes [2005] EWHC 2824; [2005] 3 F.C.R. 474, Ch D
Holme v. Brunskill (1877-78) L.R. 3 Q.B.D. 495, CA. . . . . *Applied*, 64/1640,
95/3013: *Considered*, 86/1595, 05/703: *Referred to*, 95/3014
Holme v. Liverpool City Justices see R. (on the application of Holme) v. Liverpool Magistrates Court

Holmes, Re see Holmes v. Governor of Brixton Prison
Holmes v. Governor of Brixton Prison; *sub nom* Holmes, Re [2004] EWHC 2020;
  [2005] 1 W.L.R. 1857; [2005] 1 All E.R. 490; [2005] 1 Cr. App. R. 16; [2005]
  Crim. L.R. 229; (2004) 101(41) L.S.G. 35; *Times*, October 28, 2004, QBD
  (Admin)
Holst Italia SpA v. Comune di Cagliari (C176/98) [1999] E.C.R. I-8607, ECJ (5th
  Chamber) [1999] E.C.R. I-8607, AGO . . . .   *Followed*, 05/3352
Holy Trinity, Bosham, Re [2004] Fam. 125; [2004] 2 W.L.R. 833; [2004] 2 All E.R. 820;
  Times, December 12, 2003, Cons Ct (Chichester) . . . .   *Digested*, 04/**943**:
                                                                                                        Considered, 05/993
Home & Colonial Stores Ltd v. Colls see Colls v. Home & Colonial Stores Ltd
Home Depot Inc, Re [2005] E.T.M.R. 100, OLG (Hamburg)
Home Depot Inc v. Bauhaus [2005] E.T.M.R. 63, LG (Hamburg)
Home Office v. Bailey; *sub nom* Bailey v. Home Office [2005] EWCA Civ 327; [2005]
  I.C.R. 1057; [2005] I.R.L.R. 369; (2005) 102(22) L.S.G. 26; (2005) 149
  S.J.L.B. 390; *Times*, April 8, 2005; *Independent*, April 15, 2005, CA (Civ Div);
  reversing [2004] I.R.L.R. 921; (2004) 148 S.J.L.B. 1028, EAT . . . .   *Digested*, 05/**1265**
Home Office v. Bailey [2005] I.R.L.R. 757, EAT
Home Office v. Coyne; *sub nom* Coyne v. Home Office [2000] I.C.R. 1443; [2000]
  I.R.L.R. 838, CA (Civ Div); reversing EAT/244/97, EAT . . . .   *Digested*, 01/**2316**:
                                                                                                        Applied, 05/1298
Home Office v. Dorgan see Anderton v. Clwyd CC
Home Office v. Lownds see Lownds v. Home Office
Home Office v. Saunders, *Times*, December 2, 2005, EAT
Homebase Ltd v. Allied Dunbar Assurance Plc see Allied Dunbar Assurance Plc v.
  Homebase Ltd
Hong Kong Arbitration Award, Re (2005) 21 Const. L.J. 321
Hong Kong Chop Suey v. Inland Revenue Commissioners see Lee (t/a Hong Kong
  Chop Suey) v. Inland Revenue Commissioners
Hood v. United Kingdom (27267/95) (2000) 29 E.H.R.R. 365; *Times*, March 11, 1999,
  ECHR . . . .   *Digested*, 99/**3090**:
                                                                                                        Applied, 00/3214, 05/2104
Hoogendijk v. Netherlands (Admissibility) (58641/00) (2005) 40 E.H.R.R. SE22,
  ECHR
Hook v. Jewson Ltd [1997] B.C.C. 752; [1997] 1 B.C.L.C. 664; [1997] B.P.I.R. 100,
  Ch D . . . .   *Digested*, 97/**3083**:
                                                                                                        Applied, 00/3473, 02/2713, 03/2361, 05/2309
Hooper v. Prescot Ltd (No.1) [2005] 2 Q.R. 22; [2004] 5 Q.R. 7, CC (Central
  London) [*Ex rel*. David Platt, Barrister, Crown Office Chambers, 2 Crown Office
  Row, Temple, London] . . . .   *Digested*, 04/**2961**
Hooper v. Secretary of State for Work and Pensions see R. (on the application of
  Hooper) v. Secretary of State for Work and Pensions
Hooper v. United Kingdom (42317/98) (2005) 41 E.H.R.R. 1; *Times*, November 19,
  2004, ECHR . . . .   *Digested*, 05/**2100**
Hopcraft v. Customs and Excise Commissioners [2005] S.T.I. 2039, V&DTr (London)
Hopkins v. TL Dallas Group Ltd; Hopkins v. TL Dallas & Co Ltd [2004] EWHC 1379;
  [2005] 1 B.C.L.C. 543, Ch D . . . .   *Digested*, 05/**517**
Horbury Building Systems Ltd v. Hampden Insurance NV [2004] EWCA Civ 418;
  [2004] 2 C.L.C. 453; [2004] B.L.R. 431; (2004) 148 S.J.L.B. 477, CA (Civ
  Div); affirming [2003] EWHC 2110, QBD (Comm) . . . .   *Digested*, 05/**2375**
Horkulak v. Cantor Fitzgerald International; *sub nom* Cantor Fitzgerald International v.
  Horkulak [2004] EWCA Civ 1287; [2005] I.C.R. 402; [2004] I.R.L.R. 942;
  (2004) 148 S.J.L.B. 1218, CA (Civ Div); reversing [2003] EWHC 1918; [2004]
  I.C.R. 697; [2003] I.R.L.R. 756, QBD . . . .   *Digested*, 05/**1212**
Hormel Foods Corp v. Antilles Landscape Investments NV [2005] EWHC 13; [2005]
  E.T.M.R. 54; [2005] R.P.C. 28; (2005) 28(5) I.P.D. 28037; (2005) 102(12)
  L.S.G. 26; *Times*, February 28, 2005, Ch D . . . .   *Digested*, 05/**2505**
Horne-Roberts v. SmithKline Beecham Plc; *sub nom* MMR/MR Vaccine Litigation; H
  (A Child) v. Merk & Co Inc; SmithKline Beecham Plc v. H (A Child); H (A Child)
  v. Merck & Co Inc; H (A Child) v. SmithKline Beecham Plc; Smithkline
  Beecham Plc v. Horne-Roberts [2001] EWCA Civ 2006; [2002] 1 W.L.R. 1662;
  [2002] C.P. Rep. 20; (2002) 65 B.M.L.R. 79; (2002) 99(8) L.S.G. 35; (2002)
  146 S.J.L.B. 19; *Times*, January 10, 2002, CA (Civ Div); affirming [2001] C.P.
  Rep. 80; [2002] P.I.Q.R. P3, QBD . . . .   *Digested*, 02/**507**:
                                                                                                        Applied, 04/286, 05/480: *Considered*, 05/315
Hornsey Local Board v. Monarch Investment Building Society (1890) L.R. 24 Q.B.D. 1,
  CA; affirming (1889) L.R. 23 Q.B.D. 149, QBD . . . .   *Distinguished*, 05/3967
Horrocks v. Lowe [1975] A.C. 135; [1974] 2 W.L.R. 282; [1974] 1 All E.R. 662; 72
  L.G.R. 251; 118 S.J. 149, HL; affirming [1972] 1 W.L.R. 1625; [1972] 3 All E.R.
  1098; 71 L.G.R. 96; 116 S.J. 946; *Times*, October 7, 1972, CA (Civ Div) . . . .   *Digested*, 74/**2144**:
                                                                                                        Applied, 04/937, 04/1308: *Distinguished*, 05/976: *Followed*, 96/5658,
                                                                                                        03/956
Horton v. 1 Pump Court Chambers see 1 Pump Court Chambers v. Horton
Horton v. Higham see 1 Pump Court Chambers v. Horton

Hospital of St John and St Elizabeth v. Revenue and Customs Commissioners [2005]
　　B.V.C. 2693, V&DTr (London)
Hospital Products Ltd v. United States Surgical Corp 156 C.L.R. 41, HC (Aus) . . . .　　　*Applied*, 93/72,
　　　　　　　　　　　　　　　　　　　　　　　　　　　　　　　　　　　　05/4294
Hotchkin v. McDonald [2004] EWCA Civ 519; [2005] 1 P. & C.R. 7; [2004] 18
　　E.G.C.S. 100; [2004] N.P.C. 64, CA (Civ Div) . . . .　　*Digested*, 05/**3433**
Hotel de Girancourt v. SCIR Normandie [2005] E.C.C. 32, Cass (F)
Hotel Scandic Gasaback AB v. Riksskatteverket (C412/03) [2005] S.T.C. 1311; [2005]
　　E.C.R. I-743; [2005] 1 C.M.L.R. 38; [2005] C.E.C. 335; [2005] S.T.I. 138, ECJ
　　(1st Chamber) . . . .　　*Digested*, 05/**4392**
Hotung v. Ho Yuen Ki (2004-05) 7 I.T.E.L.R. 795, CFI (HK)
Hough v. East (Unreported, May 26, 2004), CC (Portsmouth) [*Ex rel.* Andrew
　　Stafford, Barrister, 4 King's Bench Walk, Temple, London] . . . .　　*Digested*, 05/**3106**
Houses & Estates Ltd, Re see Bugle Press, Re
Housieaux v. Delegues du Conseil de la Region de Bruxelles-Capitale (C186/04)
　　[2005] E.C.R. I-3299; [2005] 2 C.M.L.R. 53, ECJ (2nd Chamber) . . . .　　*Digested*, 05/**57**
Howard v. Millrise Ltd (t/a Colourflow) (In Liquidation) [2005] I.C.R. 435; [2005]
　　I.R.L.R. 84, EAT. . . . .　　*Digested*, 05/**1312**
Howard de Walden Estates Ltd v. Malekshad see Malekshad v. Howard de Walden
　　Estates Ltd (No.2)
Howard Smith Ltd v. Ampol Petroleum Ltd [1974] A.C. 821; [1974] 2 W.L.R. 689;
　　[1974] 1 All E.R. 1126; 118 S.J.L.B. 330; 118 S.J. 330, PC (Aus) . . . .　　*Digested*, 74/**332**:
　　　　　　　　　　　　　Applied, 05/528: *Considered*, 92/395: *Distinguished*, 02/570
Howell v. Trippier (Inspector of Taxes); *sub nom* Red Discretionary Trustees v. Inspector
　　of Taxes [2004] EWCA Civ 885; [2004] S.T.C. 1245; 76 T.C. 415; [2004] B.T.C.
　　305; [2004] W.T.L.R. 839; [2004] S.T.I. 1654; (2004) 148 S.J.L.B. 881; *Times*,
　　August 17, 2004, CA (Civ Div); affirming [2004] S.T.C. (S.C.D.) 132; [2004]
　　W.T.L.R. 437; [2004] S.T.I. 314, Sp Comm . . . .　　*Digested*, 04/**3825**
Hoxha v. Secretary of State for the Home Department see R. (on the application of
　　Hoxha) v. Special Adjudicator
Hoy v. Hanlin Construction Ltd see Marshalls Clay Products Ltd v. Caulfield
Hoyland v. Asda Stores Ltd [2005] I.C.R. 1235; [2005] I.R.L.R. 438, EAT
HRH Prince Jefri Bolkiah v. KPMG see Bolkiah v. KPMG
Hrico v. Slovakia (49418/99) (2005) 41 E.H.R.R. 18, ECHR
HSBC Bank Plc v. Harbour Estates Ltd see Harbour Estates Ltd v. HSBC Bank Plc
HSBC International Trustee Ltd v. Tam Mei Kam (2004-05) 7 I.T.E.L.R. 382, CFI (HK) . .　　*Digested*, 05/**4290**
HSBC Rail (UK) Ltd v. Network Rail Infrastructure Ltd (formerly Railtrack Plc) [2005]
　　EWCA Civ 1437; *Times*, December 23, 2005, CA (Civ Div); affirming [2005]
　　EWHC 403; [2005] 1 All E.R. (Comm) 689; [2005] 2 Lloyd's Rep. 343, QBD
　　(Comm) . . . .　　*Digested*, 05/**3239**
HSS Hire Services Group Plc v. BMB Builders Merchants Ltd; HSS Hire Services Group
　　Plc v. Grafton Group (UK) Plc [2004] EWHC 2013, QBD . . . .　　*Overruled in part*,
　　　　　　　　　　　　　　　　　　　　　　　　　　　　　　　　　　　　05/816
HSS Hire Services Group Plc v. BMB Builders Merchants Ltd (Application for Permission
　　to Appeal) [2005] EWCA Civ 626; [2005] 1 W.L.R. 3158; [2005] 3 All E.R.
　　486; *Times*, May 31, 2005, CA (Civ Div) . . . .　　*Digested*, 05/**816**
HSS Hire Services Group Plc v. Grafton Group (UK) Plc see HSS Hire Services Group
　　Plc v. BMB Builders Merchants Ltd
Hsu v. Commissioner of Police of the Metropolis see Thompson v. Commissioner of
　　Police of the Metropolis
Huang v. Secretary of State for the Home Department; Abu-Qulbain v. Secretary of
　　State for the Home Department; Kashmiri v. Secretary of State for the Home
　　Department [2005] EWCA Civ 105; [2005] 3 W.L.R. 488; [2005] 3 All E.R.
　　435; [2005] H.R.L.R. 15; [2005] U.K.H.R.R. 651; [2005] Imm. A.R. 240;
　　[2005] I.N.L.R. 247; (2005) 102(20) L.S.G. 30; (2005) 149 S.J.L.B. 297;
　　Times, March 16, 2005, CA (Civ Div) . . . .　　*Digested*, 05/**2192**:
　　　　　　　　　　　　Applied, 05/2179, 05/2193, 05/2211: *Considered*, 05/2213
Huckfield, Re see R. v. Manchester Crown Court Ex p. DPP
Huddersfield Fine Worsteds Ltd, Re; *sub nom* Globe Worsted Co Ltd, Re; Granville
　　Technology Group Ltd, Re; Tipper v. Duggins; Harris v. Ellis; Krasner v. McMath;
　　Ferrotech Ltd, Re [2005] EWCA Civ 1072; [2005] 4 All E.R. 886; [2005]
　　B.C.C. 915; [2005] I.R.L.R. 995; (2005) 155 N.L.J. 1355, CA (Civ Div);
　　reversing [2005] EWHC 1682; [2005] B.C.C. 896, Ch D . . . .　　*Digested*, 05/**2262**
Hudson v. Trustees of Weaver Holdings Ltd Staff Retirement and Death Benefit
　　Scheme [2005] Pens. L.R. 365, Pensions Ombudsman
Hudson Contract Services Ltd v. Revenue and Customs Commissioners [2005] S.T.C.
　　(S.C.D.) 740; [2005] S.T.I. 1630, Sp Comm
Hudson (Inspector of Taxes) v. JDC Services Ltd [2004] EWHC 602; [2004] S.T.C.
　　834; 77 T.C. 134; [2005] B.T.C. 3; [2004] S.T.I. 896; *Times*, April 16, 2004, Ch D
　　. . . . .　　*Digested*, 04/**3710**:
　　　　　　　　　　　　　　　　　　　　　　　　Applied, 05/4017: *Followed*, 05/4036

Hughes v. Customs and Excise Commissioners; *sub nom* R. (on the application of Hughes) v. Customs and Excise Commissioners; R. (on the application of Anderson) v. Customs and Excise Commissioners; R v. DPP; R v. Crown Prosecution Service; Anderson v. Customs and Excise Commissioners [2002] EWCA Civ 734; [2003] 1 W.L.R. 177; [2002] 4 All E.R. 633; (2002) 99(26) L.S.G. 36; (2002) 152 N.L.J. 848; (2002) 146 S.J.L.B. 143; *Times*, May 31, 2002; *Independent*, July 8, 2002, CA (Civ Div) . . . . *Digested*, 02/**907**:
Considered, 04/883, 05/2332

Hughes v. Doncaster MBC [1991] 1 A.C. 382; [1991] 2 W.L.R. 16; [1991] 1 All E.R. 295; 89 L.G.R. 257; (1991) 61 P. & C.R. 355; [1991] 05 E.G. 133; [1991] R.V.R. 10; [1990] E.G.C.S. 153; (1991) 135 S.J. 18, HL; affirming [1990] 1 W.L.R. 845; [1990] 2 All E.R. 53; (1990) 59 P. & C.R. 365; [1990] 26 E.G. 168; [1990] R.V.R. 15; [1990] J.P.L. 665; (1990) 154 L.G. Rev. 154; [1989] E.G.C.S. 152, CA (Civ Div); reversing in part (1988) 55 P. & C.R. 383; [1988] R.V.R. 179, Lands Tr . . . . *Digested*, 91/**453**:
Considered, 93/426: *Followed*, 05/3251

Hughes v. Groveholt Ltd see Groveholt Ltd v. Hughes
Hughes v. Hannover Ruckversicherungs AG [1997] B.C.C. 921; [1997] 1 B.C.L.C. 497; [1999] B.P.I.R. 224; [1997] 6 Re. L.R. 96; *Times*, March 6, 1997, CA (Civ Div) . . *Digested*, 97/**3045**:
Approved, 05/2282: *Considered*, 05/416, 05/2301

Hughes v. Hughes [2005] EWHC 469; [2005] 1 F.C.R. 679, Ch D . . . . *Digested*, 05/**4312**
Hughes v. Newham LBC; Opuku-Donker v. Newham LBC; Thornton v. Newham LBC (2005) 102(34) L.S.G. 30, Sup Ct Costs Office
Hughes v. Prospect Coaches Ltd (Unreported, April 29, 2004), CC (Walsall) [*Ex rel.* Higgs & Sons, Solicitors, Remlane House, 25/27 Hagley Road, Stourbridge] . . . *Digested*, 05/**312**
Hughes v. West Berkshire HA see Enderby v. Frenchay HA (No.2)
Hughes (Inspector of Taxes) v. Viner [1985] 3 All E.R. 40; [1985] S.T.C. 235; 58 T.C. 437; (1985) 82 L.S.G. 1416; (1985) 129 S.J. 225, Ch D . . . . *Digested*, 85/**1760**:
Considered, 05/1486

Hugo v. Plon SA [2005] E.C.D.R. 27, C d'A (Paris)
Hui Chi-Ming v. Queen, The [1992] 1 A.C. 34; [1991] 3 W.L.R. 495; [1991] 3 All E.R. 897; (1992) 94 Cr. App. R. 236; [1992] Crim. L.R. 446; *Times*, September 26, 1991; *Independent*, September 19, 1991; *Guardian*, October 9, 1991, PC (HK) . . . *Digested*, 92/**639**:
Applied, 05/909: *Considered*, 93/917, 93/2525, 95/1272, 05/733:
Followed, 95/1238

Humber Sea Terminal Ltd v. Secretary of State for Transport; *sub nom* Humber Sea Terminals v. Secretary of State for Transport [2005] EWHC 1289; [2005] 20 E.G.C.S. 260, QBD (Admin)
Humber Sea Terminals v. Secretary of State for Transport see Humber Sea Terminal Ltd v. Secretary of State for Transport
Humber Work Boats Ltd v. Owners of the Selby Paradigm [2004] EWHC 1804; [2004] 2 Lloyd's Rep. 714; (2004) 154 N.L.J. 1362, QBD (Admlty) . . . . *Digested*, 05/**310**
Humpherson v. Nevill (Unreported, April 22, 2004), CC (Macclesfield) [*Ex rel.* Matthew Snarr, Barrister, 9 St John Street, Manchester] . . . . *Digested*, 05/**375**
Humphreys v. Humphreys [2004] EWHC 2201; [2005] 1 F.C.R. 712; [2004] W.T.L.R. 1425, Ch D . . . . *Digested*, 05/**4301**
Hundertwasser Haus (I ZR 192/00) [2005] E.C.D.R. 8, BGH (Ger)
Hunkins v. Coventry Magistrates Court [2004] EWHC 3089; [2005] R.V.R. 263, QBD (Admin)
Hunt v. Poole (Unreported, April 7, 2005), CC (Bromley) [*Ex rel.* Nicholas Preston, Barrister, 53, Curzon Road, London] . . . . *Digested*, 05/**3090**
Hunt Technology Ltd v. Don & Low Ltd [2005] EWHC 376; (2005) 28(5) I.P.D. 28036, Ch D
Hunter v. Lex Vehicle Finance Ltd [2005] EWHC 223; [2005] B.P.I.R. 586, Ch D . . . . . *Digested*, 05/**671**
Hunter v. Murrow; *sub nom* H v. M (Abduction: Rights of Custody) [2005] EWCA Civ 976; [2005] 2 F.L.R. 1119; [2005] 3 F.C.R. 1; [2005] Fam. Law 762, CA (Civ Div) . . . . *Digested*, 05/**1541**
Hunter v. Senate Support Services Ltd [2004] EWHC 1085; [2005] 1 B.C.L.C. 175, Ch D . . . . *Digested*, 05/**538**
Hunting Plc, Re [2004] EWHC 2591; [2005] 2 B.C.L.C. 211, Ch D . . . . *Digested*, 05/**532**
Huntingdon v. Attrill see Huntington v. Attrill
Huntingdon Life Sciences Group Plc v. Stop Huntingdon Animal Cruelty [2005] EWHC 2233; *Times*, November 2, 2005, QBD
Huntington v. Attrill; *sub nom* Huntingdon v. Attrill [1893] A.C. 150, PC (Can) . . . . *Applied*, 88/**408**:
Considered, 82/1680, 05/621

Hurren (A Bankrupt), Re; *sub nom* Trustee v. Inland Revenue Commissioners [1983] 1 W.L.R. 183; [1982] 3 All E.R. 982; [1982] S.T.C. 850; 56 T.C. 494; (1983) 80 L.S.G. 93; (1983) 127 S.J. 84, Ch D . . . . *Digested*, 82/**1613**:
Applied, 05/4061

Hurst v. Supperstone; *sub nom* Supperstone v. Hurst [2005] EWHC 1309; [2005] B.P.I.R. 1231; [2005] 25 E.G.C.S. 192; [2005] 2 P. & C.R. DG21, Ch D . . . . *Digested*, 05/**3380**

Hussain v. New Taplow Paper Mills Ltd [1988] A.C. 514; [1988] 2 W.L.R. 266; [1988] 1 All E.R. 541; [1988] I.C.R. 259; [1988] I.R.L.R. 167; (1988) 138 N.L.J. Rep. 45; (1988) 132 S.J. 226, HL; affirming [1987] 1 W.L.R. 336; [1987] 1 All E.R. 417; [1987] I.C.R. 28; (1987) 84 L.S.G. 1242; (1987) 131 S.J. 358, CA (Civ Div) . . . . *Digested*, 88/**1070**: *Applied*, 05/1277: *Considered*, 90/1716, 96/2133, 97/1024, 99/810: *Distinguished*, 90/1718, 99/793

Hutchings v. Dartmoor National Park Authority [2005] P.A.D. 17, Planning Inspector

Hutchinson 3G UK Ltd v. First Secretary of State see T Mobile (UK) Ltd v. First Secretary of State

Hutchison 3G UK Ltd v. Customs and Excise Commissioners [2005] B.V.C. 2114; [2004] S.T.I. 2576, V&DTr

HVC Mildenhall v. Forest Heath DC [2005] P.A.D. 88, Planning Inspector

HW v. Bedfordshire CC [2004] EWHC 560; [2004] E.L.R. 586, QBD (Admin) . . . . . . *Digested*, 05/**1136**

Hyde Park Residence Ltd v. Yelland [2001] Ch. 143; [2000] 3 W.L.R. 215; [2000] E.C.D.R. 275; [2000] E.M.L.R. 363; [2000] R.P.C. 604; (2000) 23(5) I.P.D. 23040; (2000) 97(8) L.S.G. 35; *Times*, February 16, 2000; *Independent*, February 18, 2000, CA (Civ Div); reversing [1999] E.M.L.R. 654; [1999] R.P.C. 655; (1999) 18 Tr. L.R. 217; (1999) 22(7) I.P.D. 22065; *Times*, March 24, 1999, Ch D . . . . *Digested*, 00/**3573**: *Considered*, 01/3850, 05/2420: *Followed*, 99/3437, 01/570

Hydra Plc v. Anatasi [2005] EWHC 1559; (2005) 102(33) L.S.G. 23, QBD . . . . *Digested*, 05/**1208**

Hyperion Records Ltd v. Sawkins see Sawkins v. Hyperion Records Ltd

Hysi v. Secretary of State for the Home Department [2005] EWCA Civ 711; [2005] I.N.L.R. 602; *Times*, June 23, 2005; *Independent*, June 17, 2005, CA (Civ Div) . *Digested*, 05/**2176**

Hyundai Engineering & Construction Co Ltd v. Vigour Ltd [2005] B.L.R. 416, CA (HK)

Hyundai Merchant Marine Co Ltd v. Furness Withy (Australia) Pty (The Doric Pride), CA (Civ Div); affirming [2005] EWHC 945; [2005] 2 Lloyd's Rep. 470; [2005] 1 C.L.C. 780, QBD (Comm) . . . . *Digested*, 05/**3812**

I v. Secretary of State for the Home Department [2005] EWCA Civ 886; *Times*, August 18, 2005, CA (Civ Div) . . . . *Digested*, 05/**2174**

I/S Fini H v. Skatteministeriet (C32/03) [2005] S.T.C. 903; [2005] E.C.R. I-1599; [2005] 2 C.M.L.R. 20; [2005] C.E.C. 638; [2005] S.T.I. 361, ECJ (3rd Chamber) . . . . *Digested*, 05/**4380**

IBA Health Ltd v. Office of Fair Trading; *sub nom* Office of Fair Trading v. IBA Healthcare Ltd [2004] EWCA Civ 142; [2004] 4 All E.R. 1103; [2005] 1 All E.R. (Comm) 147; [2004] U.K.C.L.R. 683; [2005] E.C.C. 1; [2004] I.C.R. 1364; (2004) 101(11) L.S.G. 33; (2004) 154 N.L.J. 352; *Times*, February 25, 2004; *Independent*, March 29, 2004 (C.S), CA (Civ Div); affirming [2003] CAT 27; [2004] Comp. A.R. 235, CAT . . . . *Digested*, 04/**531**

IBA Health Ltd v. Office of Fair Trading (Costs) [2004] CAT 6; [2004] Comp. A.R. 529, CAT . . . . *Digested*, 05/**563**

Ibbotson v. United Kingdom [1999] Crim. L.R. 153; (1999) 27 E.H.R.R. CD332, Eur Comm HR . . . . *Applied*, 05/925: *Considered*, 03/866

Ibe v. McNally (Inspector of Taxes); *sub nom* Redundant Employee v. McNally (Inspector of Taxes) [2005] EWHC 1551; [2005] S.T.C. 1426; [2005] B.T.C. 548, Ch D; affirming [2005] S.T.C. (S.C.D.) 143; [2004] S.T.I. 2439, Sp Comm . . . . . *Digested*, 05/**4093**

IBM Corp v. Commission of the European Communities (60/81); *sub nom* International Business Machines Corp v. Commission of the European Communities (60/81) [1981] E.C.R. 2639; [1981] 3 C.M.L.R. 635, ECJ . . . . *Digested*, 81/**1266**: *Applied*, 03/576, 05/1426: *Considered*, 03/1431: *Followed*, 00/2365, 03/1452, 05/1441

IBM/Electromigration (T963/02) [2005] E.P.O.R. 22, EPO (Technical Bd App) . . . . . . *Digested*, 05/**2461**

ICI Plc v. Colmer (Inspector of Taxes) [1999] 1 W.L.R. 2035; [2000] 1 All E.R. 129; [1999] S.T.C. 1089; [2000] 1 C.M.L.R. 142; 72 T.C. 1; [1999] B.T.C. 440; (1999) 96(46) L.S.G. 40; (2000) 144 S.J.L.B. 7; *Times*, November 24, 1999, HL; reversing [1993] 4 All E.R. 705; [1993] S.T.C. 710; [1993] S.T.I. 1077; (1993) 90(38) L.S.G. 44; *Times*, August 11, 1993; *Independent*, August 9, 1993 (C.S.), CA (Civ Div); affirming [1992] S.T.C. 51; *Times*, December 20, 1991, Ch D . . . . . *Digested*, 99/**4667**: *Considered*, 05/4056: *Previous proceedings*, 98/4620

ICI Plc v. Commission of the European Communities (T36/91) see Solvay et Cie SA v. Commission of the European Communities (C287/95)

ICM Computer Solutions Plc v. Computer 2000 Distribution Ltd see Computer 2000 Distribution Ltd v. ICM Computer Solutions Plc

ICS Incorporation Ltd v. Michael Wilson & Partners Ltd [2005] EWHC 404; [2005] B.P.I.R. 805, Ch D (Companies Ct) . . . . *Digested*, 05/**2347**

ID v. Home Office see D v. Home Office

IDA Ltd v. University of Southampton; *sub nom* University of Southampton's Patent Applications; A3/2005/1249, CA (Civ Div); reversing [2004] EWHC 2107; [2005] R.P.C. 11, Ch D (Patents Ct) . . . . *Digested*, 05/**2485**: *Approved*, 05/2448

Ide Contracting Ltd *v.* RG Carter Cambridge Ltd [2004] EWHC 36; [2004] B.L.R. 172;
102 Con. L.R. 102, QBD (TCC) .... *Digested*, 04/**590**

Idowu *v.* Enfield LBC (Unreported, April 29, 2004), CC (Romford) [*Ex rel.* Richard
Nall-Cain, Barrister, 2-4 St Peters Street, St Albans] .... *Digested*, 05/**2888**

IE Contractors Ltd *v.* Lloyds Bank Plc; IE Contractors Ltd *v.* Rafidain Bank [1990] 2
Lloyd's Rep. 496; (1990) 51 B.L.R. 5; *Financial Times*, July 17, 1990, CA (Civ
Div); reversing in part [1989] 2 Lloyd's Rep. 205, QBD (Comm) .... *Digested*, 91/**256**:
Distinguished, 05/703

IE Contractors Ltd *v.* Rafidain Bank see IE Contractors Ltd *v.* Lloyds Bank Plc

IEP In Extenso Production Sarl *v.* Carrega [2005] E.C.C. 25; [2005] E.C.D.R. 31, C d'A
(Paris)

IFAW Internationaler Tierschutz-Fonds GmbH *v.* Commission of the European
Communities (T168/02) [2005] 1 W.L.R. 1252; [2005] 2 C.M.L.R. 28; *Times*,
December 20, 2004, CFI (5th Chamber) .... *Digested*, 05/**1428**

Igen Ltd (formerly Leeds Careers Guidance) *v.* Wong see Wong *v.* Igen Ltd (formerly
Leeds Careers Guidance)

Iglesias Gil *v.* Spain (56673/00); *sub nom* Gil *v.* Spain (56673/00) [2005] 1 F.L.R.
190; [2005] 1 F.C.R. 210; (2005) 40 E.H.R.R. 3; [2005] Fam. Law 20, ECHR .. *Digested*, 05/**2117**

Ignaccolo-Zenide *v.* Romania (31679/96) (2001) 31 E.H.R.R. 7, ECHR .... *Digested*, 01/**3550**:
Applied, 04/1472: *Considered*, 03/1506, 05/2117

IHC *v.* AC; *sub nom* C (Permission to Remove from Jurisdiction), Re [2003] EWHC
596; [2003] 1 F.L.R. 1066; [2003] Fam. Law 484, Fam Div .... *Applied*, 05/**1590**

Ikea Wholesale Ltd *v.* Customs and Excise Commissioners [2004] EWHC 1758; [2004]
3 C.M.L.R. 28; [2005] Eu. L.R. 87, Ch D; reversing (Unreported, September 8,
2003), V&DTr .... *Digested*, 05/**942**

Ilascu *v.* Moldova (48787/99) (2005) 40 E.H.R.R. 46; 17 B.H.R.C. 141, ECHR (Grand
Chamber) .... *Digested*, 05/**2063**

Immigration Officer (Heathrow) *v.* Obeid [1986] Imm. A.R. 341, IAT............... *Applied*, 96/3281:
Followed, 05/2198

Imperial Chemical Industries (ICI) Ltd *v.* Commission of the European Communities (48/
69) [1972] E.C.R. 619; [1972] C.M.L.R. 557, ECJ...................... *Digested*, 72/**1312**:
Considered, 00/3704, 05/570

Imperial Resources SA *v.* Secretary of State for Transport, Local Government and the
Regions see Commercial Land Ltd *v.* Secretary of State for Transport, Local
Government and the Regions

Improver Corp *v.* Remington Consumer Products Ltd [1990] F.S.R. 181, Ch D (Patents
Ct) .... *Digested*, 91/**2698**:
Applied, 95/3758, 96/4568, 99/3472, 02/2795, 02/2820, 04/2342:
Cited, 04/2339: *Considered*, 00/3639, 05/2479: *Followed*, 95/3799,
97/3901, 98/3467: *Referred to*, 99/3480

IMS Health GmbH & Co OHG *v.* NDC Health GmbH & Co KG (C418/01) [2004] All
E.R. (EC) 813; [2004] E.C.R. I-5039; [2004] 4 C.M.L.R. 28; [2004] E.C.D.R.
23, ECJ (5th Chamber) [2004] E.C.R. I-5039; [2004] E.C.D.R. 9, AGO ...... *Digested*, 05/**574**:
Followed, 05/550

IN Newman Ltd *v.* Adlem [2005] EWCA Civ 741; (2005) 28(8) I.P.D. 28059, CA (Civ
Div)

In the Pink Ltd *v.* North East Lincolnshire Council; PMS International Group Plc *v.* North
East Lincolnshire Council [2005] EWHC 1111; (2005) 169 J.P. 385; (2005)
169 J.P.N. 537, QBD (Admin) .... *Digested*, 05/**686**

Inche Noriah *v.* Shaik Allie bin Omar [1929] A.C. 127; [1928] All E.R. Rep. 189; (1929)
45 T.L.R. 1; (1928) 98 L.J. P.C. 1, PC (Sing) .... *Applied*, 70/1145,
85/396: *Considered*, 77/1458, 05/3401

Inco Europe Ltd *v.* First Choice Distribution [2000] 1 W.L.R. 586; [2000] 2 All E.R.
109; [2000] 1 All E.R. (Comm) 674; [2000] 1 Lloyd's Rep. 467; [2000] C.L.C.
1015; [2000] B.L.R. 259; (2000) 2 T.C.L.R. 487; 74 Con. L.R. 55; (2000)
97(12) L.S.G. 39; (2000) 144 S.J.L.B. 134; [2000] N.P.C. 22; *Times*, March 10,
2000; *Independent*, March 15, 2000, HL; affirming [1999] 1 W.L.R. 270; [1999]
1 All E.R. 820; [1999] C.L.C. 165; (1999) 1 T.C.L.R. 169; (1998) 95(41) L.S.G.
45; (1998) 142 S.J.L.B. 269; *Times*, October 22, 1998; *Independent*, October 12,
1998 (C.S.), CA (Civ Div) .... *Digested*, 00/**220**:
Applied, 02/3792, 02/5549, 03/1962: *Considered*, 05/2742:
Followed, 03/5952

Independent Assessor *v.* O'Brien see R. (on the application of O'Brien) *v.* Independent
Assessor

Independent Jamaica Council for Human Rights (1998) Ltd *v.* Marshall-Burnett [2005]
UKPC 3; [2005] 2 A.C. 356; [2005] 2 W.L.R. 923; (2005) 102(10) L.S.G. 29;
Times, February 8, 2005, PC (Jam) .... *Digested*, 05/**630**

Independent Publishing Co Ltd *v.* Attorney General of Trinidad and Tobago; Trinidad and
Tobago News Centre Ltd *v.* Attorney General of Trinidad and Tobago [2004]
UKPC 26; [2005] 1 A.C. 190; [2004] 3 W.L.R. 611; [2005] 1 All E.R. 499;
[2004] E.M.L.R. 28; 17 B.H.R.C. 661; (2004) 101(26) L.S.G. 27; (2004) 148
S.J.L.B. 757; *Times*, June 24, 2004, PC (Trin) .... *Digested*, 04/**809**

Independent Television Publications Ltd *v.* Commission of the European Communities (C242/91 P) see Radio Telefis Eireann *v.* Commission of the European Communities (C241/91 P)

Indescon Ltd *v.* Ogden [2004] EWHC 2326; [2005] 1 Lloyd's Rep. 31; [2005] B.L.R. 152, QBD

Indiana Investments Ltd *v.* Taylor [2004] 3 E.G.L.R. 63; [2004] 50 E.G. 86, CC (Central London) . . . . *Digested,* 05/**3388**

Indofood International Finance Ltd *v.* JP Morgan Chase Bank NA London Branch 8 I.T.L. Rep. 653, CA (Civ Div); reversing [2005] EWHC 2103; [2005] B.T.C. 8023; 8 I.T.L. Rep. 236; [2005] S.T.I. 1678, Ch D

Industrias Pesqueras Campos SA *v.* Commission of the European Communities (T551/93) [1996] E.C.R. II-247; [1996] 3 C.M.L.R. 142, CFI (4th Chamber) . . . . *Followed,* 05/**1436**

Ingram *v.* Foxon [1984] I.C.R. 685; [1985] I.R.L.R. 5; (1984) 81 L.S.G. 1678; (1984) 134 N.L.J. 473, EAT . . . . *Digested,* 84/**1197**:
Applied, 05/1324: *Not followed,* 98/2231

Ingram *v.* Ingram [1956] P. 390; [1956] 2 W.L.R. 782; [1956] 1 All E.R. 785; 100 S.J. 227, PDAD . . . . *Digested,* 56/**2546**:
Considered, 05/3883: *Distinguished,* 58/957

Initial Electronic Security Systems Ltd *v.* Avdic [2005] I.C.R. 1598; [2005] I.R.L.R. 671, EAT

Inland Revenue Commissioner *v.* Agnew see Brumark Investments Ltd, Re

Inland Revenue Commissioner *v.* Auckland Harbour Board [2001] UKPC 1; [2001] S.T.C. 130; [2001] B.T.C. 360; [2001] S.T.I. 150, PC (NZ) . . . . *Digested,* 01/**5275**:
Considered, 05/4159

Inland Revenue Commissioner *v.* BNZ Investments Ltd [2002] 1 N.Z.L.R. 450, CA (NZ) *Considered,* 05/4105, 05/4159

Inland Revenue Commissioner *v.* Challenge Corp [1987] A.C. 155; [1987] 2 W.L.R. 24; [1986] S.T.C. 548; (1986) 83 L.S.G. 3598; (1987) 131 S.J. 46, PC (NZ) . . . . . . *Digested,* 87/**2036**:
Applied, 03/4228: *Considered,* 87/274, 01/5275, 05/4105

Inland Revenue Commissioner *v.* Cosmotron Manufacturing Co Ltd [1997] 1 W.L.R. 1288; [1997] S.T.C. 1134; 70 T.C. 292; [1997] B.T.C. 465; (1997) 141 S.J.L.B. 215, PC (HK) . . . . *Digested,* 97/**1064**:
Applied, 05/4033

Inland Revenue Commissioner *v.* Ranon Ltd see Inland Revenue Commissioner *v.* Secan Ltd

Inland Revenue Commissioner *v.* Secan Ltd; Inland Revenue Commissioner *v.* Ranon Ltd 74 T.C. 1; 3 I.T.L. Rep. 496, CFA (HK) . . . . *Applied,* 04/**3712**:
Disapproved, 05/4022

Inland Revenue Commissioners *v.* Ainsworth; *sub nom* Ainsworth *v.* Inland Revenue Commissioners; Inland Revenue Commissioners *v.* Kilic; Inland Revenue Commissioners *v.* Stringer; Inland Revenue Commissioners *v.* Thwaites [2005] EWCA Civ 441; [2005] I.C.R. 1149; [2005] I.R.L.R. 465; *Times,* May 16, 2005, CA (Civ Div); reversing UKEAT/0650/03/Tm, UKEAT/0745/03/TM, UKEAT/0798/03/TM, UKEAT/0901/03/TM, EAT. . . . . *Digested,* 05/**1273**

Inland Revenue Commissioners *v.* Anchor International Ltd see Anchor International Ltd *v.* Inland Revenue Commissioners

Inland Revenue Commissioners *v.* Arkwright see Arkwright (Williams Personal Representative) *v.* Inland Revenue Commissioners

Inland Revenue Commissioners *v.* Bullock [1976] 1 W.L.R. 1178; [1976] 3 All E.R. 353; [1976] S.T.C. 409; 51 T.C. 522; [1975] T.R. 179; 120 S.J. 591, CA (Civ Div); reversing [1975] 1 W.L.R. 1436; [1975] 3 All E.R. 541; [1975] S.T.C. 512; [1975] T.R. 179; 119 S.J. 530, Ch D . . . . *Digested,* 76/**1414**:
Applied, 81/2301, 02/5386, 03/4263, 03/4264, 05/3965:
Considered, 99/4638

Inland Revenue Commissioners *v.* Deutsche Morgan Grenfell Group Plc see Deutsche Morgan Grenfell Group Plc *v.* Inland Revenue Commissioners

Inland Revenue Commissioners *v.* Exeter City AFC Ltd [2004] B.C.C. 519, Ch D . . . . . . *Digested,* 05/**477**

Inland Revenue Commissioners *v.* Hashmi; *sub nom* Hashmi *v.* Inland Revenue Commissioners [2002] EWCA Civ 981; [2002] B.C.C. 943; [2002] 2 B.C.L.C. 489; [2002] B.P.I.R. 974; [2002] W.T.L.R. 1027, CA (Civ Div); affirming [2002] B.P.I.R. 271; [2002] W.T.L.R. 19; (2001) 98(41) L.S.G. 34; *Times,* November 2, 2001, Ch D . . . . *Digested,* 03/**4484**:
Applied, 05/2340: *Considered,* 05/4313

Inland Revenue Commissioners *v.* Herd; *sub nom* Herd *v.* Inland Revenue Commissioners [1993] 1 W.L.R. 1090; [1993] 3 All E.R. 56; [1993] S.T.C. 436; 1993 S.C. (H.L.) 35; 1993 S.L.T. 916; 66 T.C. 29; [1993] S.T.I. 1007; (1993) 90(31) L.S.G. 40; (1993) 143 N.L.J. 957; (1993) 137 S.J.L.B. 173; *Times,* June 22, 1993, HL; reversing 1992 S.C. 253; 1992 S.L.T. 766, IH (Ex Div) . . . . *Digested,* 93/**2294**:
Applied, 05/4102

Inland Revenue Commissioners *v.* James Bibby & Sons Ltd [1945] 1 All E.R. 667; (1945) 61 T.L.R. 430; [1945] W.N. 117, HL . . . . *Applied,* 47-51/8034, 47-51/8035, 50/4799, 57/2895, 60/902, 66/6171, 96/1291: *Considered,* 60/1514, 66/6170, 05/2299: *Followed,* 59/909

Inland Revenue Commissioners *v.* John Lewis Properties Plc see John Lewis Properties
    Plc *v.* Inland Revenue Commissioners

Inland Revenue Commissioners *v.* Kahn see Toshoku Finance UK Plc (In Liquidation), Re

Inland Revenue Commissioners *v.* Khan [2005] B.P.I.R. 409, Ch D (Bankruptcy Ct) . . .   *Digested*, 05/**2326**

Inland Revenue Commissioners *v.* Kilic see Inland Revenue Commissioners *v.* Ainsworth

Inland Revenue Commissioners *v.* London Produce Co see Fleming (Inspector of Taxes)
    v. London Produce Co

Inland Revenue Commissioners *v.* Scottish Provident Institution see Scottish Provident
    Institution *v.* Inland Revenue Commissioners

Inland Revenue Commissioners *v.* Soul 51 T.C. 86, CA (Civ Div) . . . .   *Digested*, 79/**1493**:
                                                       Applied, 05/**4060**

Inland Revenue Commissioners *v.* Stringer see Inland Revenue Commissioners *v.*
    Ainsworth

Inland Revenue Commissioners *v.* Thwaites see Inland Revenue Commissioners *v.*
    Ainsworth

Inland Revenue Commissioners *v.* TW Law Ltd [1950] 2 All E.R. 196; 29 T.C. 467;
    [1950] T.R. 137; [1950] W.N. 344; 94 S.J. 436, Ch D . . . .   *Digested*, 47-51/**8083**:
                                                       Considered, 05/**3986**

Inland Revenue Commissioners *v.* William Grant & Sons Distillers Ltd see Revenue and
    Customs Commissioners *v.* William Grant & Sons Distillers Ltd

Inland Revenue Commissioners *v.* Wimbledon Football Club Ltd [2004] EWCA Civ
    655; [2004] B.C.C. 638; [2005] 1 B.C.L.C. 66; [2004] B.P.I.R. 700; (2004) 148
    S.J.L.B. 697; *Independent*, June 10, 2004, CA (Civ Div); affirming [2004]
    EWHC 1020, Ch D (Companies Ct) . . . .   *Digested*, 05/**2295**

INN *v.* Netherlands (Admissibility) (2035/04) (2005) 40 E.H.R.R. SE19, ECHR

Inn Crystal Vertriebs GmbH's Trade Mark Application [2005] E.T.M.R. 102, PO (Irl)

Innova Inc (UK) Ltd *v.* Customs and Excise Commissioners [2005] S.T.I. 893, V&DTr

Institut National d'Assurances Sociales pour Travailleurs Independants (INASTI) *v.* Hervein
    (C393/99); Institut National d'Assurances Sociales pour Travailleurs
    Independants (INASTI) *v.* Lorthiois (C394/99) [2002] E.C.R. I-2829; [2002] 2
    C.M.L.R. 16, ECJ [2002] E.C.R. I-2829, AGO . . . .   *Digested*, 02/**4225**:
                                                       Followed, 05/**4009**

Institut National d'Assurances Sociales pour Travailleurs Independants (INASTI) *v.*
    Lorthiois (C394/99) see Institut National d'Assurances Sociales pour Travailleurs
    Independants (INASTI) *v.* Hervein (C393/99)

Institut pour la Protection des Fragrances (IPF)'s Community Trade Mark Application
    (R186/2000-4) [2005] E.T.M.R. 42, OHIM (4th Bd App) . . . .   *Digested*, 05/**2536**

Institute of Chartered Accountants in England and Wales *v.* Customs and Excise
    Commissioners [1999] 1 W.L.R. 701; [1999] 2 All E.R. 449; [1999] S.T.C. 398;
    [1999] 2 C.M.L.R. 1333; [1999] B.T.C. 5165; [1999] B.V.C. 215; (1999) 96(20)
    L.S.G. 40; (1999) 149 N.L.J. 559; (1999) 143 S.J.L.B. 131; *Times*, March 29,
    1999; *Independent*, April 14, 1999, HL; affirming [1998] 1 W.L.R. 315; [1998] 4
    All E.R. 115; [1997] S.T.C. 1155; [1997] B.T.C. 5355; [1997] B.V.C. 469; (1997)
    94(25) L.S.G. 34; (1997) 141 S.J.L.B. 128; *Times*, May 19, 1997; *Independent*,
    May 22, 1997, CA (Civ Div); affirming [1996] S.T.C. 799; *Times*, February 19,
    1996, QBD; affirming [1995] V. & D.R. 87, VAT Tr (London) . . . .   *Digested*, 99/**4990**:
                                         Applied, 03/**4606**, 05/**4383**

Insurance Premiums, Re (C204/90) see Bachmann *v.* Belgium (C204/90)

Insurance Services (205/84), Re see Commission of the European Communities *v.*
    Germany (205/84)

Intel Corp *v.* Sihra; *sub nom* Sihra's Trade Mark Application (No.2028015) [2003]
    EWHC 17; [2004] E.T.M.R. 44; [2003] R.P.C. 44; (2003) 153 N.L.J. 144, Ch D
    . . . .   *Digested*, 03/**2636**:
                                         Considered, 05/2562

Intense Investments Ltd *v.* Development Ventures Ltd [2005] EWHC 1726; [2005]
    B.L.R. 478, QBD (TCC)

Interface Ltd *v.* Liverpool City Council; Pabo Ltd *v.* Liverpool City Council [2005]
    EWHC 995; [2005] 1 W.L.R. 3118; (2005) 169 J.P. 353; (2005) 169 J.P.N.
    520; (2005) 155 N.L.J. 864; [2005] N.P.C. 72; *Times*, May 31, 2005, QBD
    (Admin) . . . .   *Digested*, 05/**692**

Interlego AG *v.* Tyco Industries Inc [1989] A.C. 217; [1988] 3 W.L.R. 678; [1988] 3 All
    E.R. 949; 1 B.L.R. 271; [1988] 2 F.T.L.R. 133; [1988] R.P.C. 343; (1988) 132 S.J.
    698; *Times*, May 6, 1988; *Financial Times*, May 11, 1988, PC (HK); affirming
    [1987] F.S.R. 409, CA (HK) . . . .   *Digested*, 88/**502**:
          Applied, 95/852: *Considered*, 94/622, 96/1277, 98/3416, 00/3586:
          Distinguished, 97/1036, 00/3572: *Doubted*, 05/2424: *Explained*, 92/577:
                                   Followed, 96/1283, 99/3496

Internation Federation of Human Right Leagues (FIDH) *v.* France (14/2003) (2005) 40
    E.H.R.R. SE25, ECHR

International Brands USA Inc *v.* Goldstein; *sub nom* Shruth Ltd (In Liquidation), Re;
    International Brands USA Inc *v.* Haswell [2005] EWHC 1293; [2005] B.P.I.R.
    1455, Ch D (Companies Ct)

International Brands USA Inc *v.* Haswell see International Brands USA Inc *v.* Goldstein

International Business Machines Corp *v.* Commission of the European Communities
(60/81) see IBM Corp *v.* Commission of the European Communities (60/81)
INTERNATIONAL COMPUTERS/Information modelling (T49/99) [2005] E.P.O.R. 10, EPO
(Technical Bd App) . . . .   *Digested,* 05/**2483**
International Paper SA *v.* Labro Guidetti Inc [2005] E.C.C. 36, Cass (F)
International Power Plc *v.* National Association of Licensed Opencast Operators
(NALOO) (C172/01 P) [2003] E.C.R. I-11421; [2005] 5 C.M.L.R. 19, ECJ (5th
Chamber) . . . .   *Previous proceedings,*
01/2472
International Transport Roth GmbH *v.* Secretary of State for the Home Department; *sub
nom* R. (on the application of International Transport Roth GmbH) *v.* Secretary
of State for the Home Department; Secretary of State for the Home Department
v. International Transport Roth GmbH [2002] EWCA Civ 158; [2003] Q.B. 728;
[2002] 3 W.L.R. 344; [2002] 1 C.M.L.R. 52; [2002] Eu. L.R. 74; [2002]
H.R.L.R. 31; [2002] U.K.H.R.R. 479; [2002] A.C.D. 57; *Times,* February 26,
2002; *Daily Telegraph,* March 7, 2002, CA (Civ Div); reversing in part (2002)
99(2) L.S.G. 27; (2002) 146 S.J.L.B. 5; *Times,* December 11, 2001; *Independent,*
January 28, 2002 (C.S); *Daily Telegraph,* December 13, 2001, QBD (Admin) . . .   *Digested,* 02/**2619**:
Applied, 03/2270, 04/4001: *Considered,* 03/2824, 05/945:
Distinguished, 03/924
International Transport Workers Federation *v.* Viking Line Abp see Viking Line Abp *v.*
International Transport Workers Federation
Internet Auctions of Counterfeit Watches, Re (I ZR 304/01); *sub nom* Rolex Internet
Auction (1 ZR 304/01), Re [2005] E.T.M.R. 25, BGH (Ger)
Internine Trust and Intertraders Trust, Re see Alhamrani *v.* Russa Management Ltd
Interpart Comerciao e Gestao SA *v.* Lexington Insurance Co [2004] Lloyd's Rep. I.R.
690, QBD (Comm) . . . .   *Digested,* 05/**2387**
Interporc Im- und Export GmbH *v.* Commission of the European Communities (C41/00
P); *sub nom* Interporc Im- und Export GmbH *v.* Commission of the European
Communities (T92/98) [2003] E.C.R. I-2125; [2005] 2 C.M.L.R. 17, ECJ;
affirming [1999] E.C.R. II-3521; [2000] 1 C.M.L.R. 181; [2000] C.E.C. 337;
Times, February 2, 2000, CFI (1st Chamber) . . . .   *Digested,* 00/**2371**:
Applied, 05/1425
Interporc Im- und Export GmbH *v.* Commission of the European Communities (T92/98)
see Interporc Im- und Export GmbH *v.* Commission of the European
Communities (C41/00 P)
Intervention Board for Agricultural Produce *v.* Penycoed Farming Partnership (C230/01)
[2004] 3 C.M.L.R. 32, ECJ (6th Chamber) . . . .   *Digested,* 05/**142**
Intuit Inc *v.* Canal+ Technologies SA (2005) 28(4) I.P.D. 28027, OHIM (1st Bd App)
Invercargill City Council *v.* Hamlin [1996] A.C. 624; [1996] 2 W.L.R. 367; [1996] 1 All
E.R. 756; 78 B.L.R. 78; 50 Con. L.R. 105; (1996) 146 N.L.J. 246; (1996) 140
S.J.L.B. 86; *Times,* February 15, 1996, PC (NZ); affirming 72 B.L.R. 39; (1995) 11
Const. L.J. 285, CA (NZ) . . . .   *Digested,* 96/**4438**:
Considered, 05/436: *Distinguished,* 97/1752, 04/600
Inverclyde DC *v.* Lord Advocate see Inverclyde DC *v.* Secretary of State for Scotland
Inverclyde DC *v.* Secretary of State for Scotland; *sub nom* Inverclyde DC *v.* Lord
Advocate 1982 S.C. (H.L.) 64; 1982 S.L.T. 200; (1982) 43 P. & C.R. 375; [1982]
J.P.L. 313, HL; affirming 1980 S.C. 363; 1981 S.L.T. 26, IH (2 Div) . . . .   *Digested,* 82/**4412**:
Applied, 02/3696, 05/3440
Investors Compensation Scheme Ltd *v.* Hopkin & Sons see Investors Compensation
Scheme Ltd *v.* West Bromwich Building Society (No.1)
Investors Compensation Scheme Ltd *v.* West Bromwich Building Society (No.1);
Investors Compensation Scheme Ltd *v.* Hopkin & Sons; Alford *v.* West
Bromwich Building Society; Armitage *v.* West Bromwich Building Society [1998]
1 W.L.R. 896; [1998] 1 All E.R. 98; [1998] 1 B.C.L.C. 531; [1997] C.L.C. 1243;
[1997] P.N.L.R. 541; (1997) 147 N.L.J. 989; *Times,* June 24, 1997, HL; reversing
[1998] 1 B.C.L.C. 521; [1997] C.L.C. 363; [1997] P.N.L.R. 166; [1997] N.P.C.
104; *Times,* November 8, 1996, CA (Civ Div); affirming [1998] 1 B.C.L.C. 493;
[1997] C.L.C. 348; *Times,* October 10, 1996, Ch D . . . .   *Digested,* 97/**2537**:
Applied, 99/852, 99/3420, 99/5795, 00/900, 01/375, 01/959, 01/4272,
01/4950, 01/5508, 02/207, 02/3028, 02/3821, 03/500, 03/530, 03/671,
03/2460, 03/2723, 04/273, 04/653, 04/670, 04/2215, 04/2223, 04/3255,
04/4614, 05/288, 05/469, 05/718, 05/2402: *Cited,* 99/2489:
Considered, 99/2480, 00/878, 00/3686, 00/5932, 01/2430, 02/4683,
04/2205, 04/2407, 04/4988: *Followed,* 98/807, 00/2173
Iorgov *v.* Bulgaria (40653/98) (2005) 40 E.H.R.R. 7, ECHR . . . .   *Digested,* 05/**2058**
IP Metal Ltd *v.* Ruote Oz SpA (No.1) [1993] 2 Lloyd's Rep. 60, QBD (Comm) . . . . . .   *Digested,* 93/**449**:
Applied, 00/754, 03/480: *Considered,* 05/614
IPC Media Ltd *v.* Highbury Leisure Publishing Ltd (Indemnity Costs) [2005] EWHC
283; (2005) 28(3) I.P.D. 28017, Ch D
IPC Media Ltd *v.* Highbury Leisure Publishing Ltd (No.2) [2004] EWHC 2985; [2005]
F.S.R. 20; (2005) 28(2) I.P.D. 28006, Ch D . . . .   *Digested,* 05/**2422**:
Applied, 05/2423

IPC Media Ltd v. News Group Newspapers Ltd [2005] EWHC 317; [2005] E.M.L.R.
23; [2005] F.S.R. 35; (2005) 28(5) I.P.D. 28038, Ch D . . . .   *Digested*, 05/**2418**
IPCO (Nigeria) Ltd v. Nigerian National Petroleum Corp [2005] EWHC 726; [2005] 2
Lloyd's Rep. 326; [2005] 1 C.L.C. 613, QBD (Comm) . . . .   *Digested*, 05/**213**
Iran Continental Shelf Oil Co v. IRI International Corp [2002] EWCA Civ 1024; [2004] 2
C.L.C. 696, CA (Civ Div); reversing [2002] C.L.C. 372, QBD . . . .   *Digested*, 05/**617**
Irish Creamery Milk Suppliers Association v. Ireland (36/80) [1981] E.C.R. 735; [1981]
2 C.M.L.R. 455, ECJ . . . .   *Digested*, 81/**1007**:
                 Considered, 05/**2569**: *Followed*, 04/**503**
Irish Pensions Trust Ltd v. Central Remedial Clinic [2005] O.P.L.R. 137, HC (Irl)
Iron & Steel Trades Confederation v. ASW Ltd (In Liquidation) [2004] I.R.L.R. 926, EAT   *Digested*, 05/**1243**
Irvine v. Commissioner of Police of the Metropolis [2004] EWHC 1536; [2005]
P.I.Q.R. P11, QBD . . . .   *Digested*, 05/**1951**
Irvine v. Commissioner of Police of the Metropolis (Costs) [2005] EWCA Civ 129;
[2005] C.P. Rep. 19; [2005] 3 Costs L.R. 380; (2005) 149 S.J.L.B. 182, CA
(Civ Div) . . . .   *Digested*, 05/**359**
Irwin v. Shipman [2005] 2 Q.R. 15; [2004] 6 Q.R. 9, CC (Watford) [*Ex rel.* Joanna
Kerr, Barrister, 8 Stone Buildings, Lincoln's Inn, London] . . . .   *Digested*, 04/**2884**
Isayeva v. Russia (57947/00); Yusupova v. Russia (57948/00); Bazayeva v. Russia
(57949/00) (2005) 41 E.H.R.R. 39, ECHR
Isayeva v. Russia (57950/00) (2005) 41 E.H.R.R. 38, ECHR
Islam v. Ali [2003] EWCA Civ 612, CA (Civ Div) . . . .   *Applied*, 05/**347**
Islam v. Immigration Appeal Tribunal Ex p. Shah see Islam v. Secretary of State for the
Home Department
Islam v. Secretary of State for the Home Department; *sub nom* R. v. Secretary of State
for the Home Department Ex p. Shah; Islam v. Immigration Appeal Tribunal Ex p.
Shah [1999] 2 A.C. 629; [1999] 2 W.L.R. 1015; [1999] 2 All E.R. 545; 6
B.H.R.C. 356; [1999] Imm. A.R. 283; [1999] I.N.L.R. 144; (1999) 96(17) L.S.G.
24; (1999) 143 S.J.L.B. 115; *Times*, March 26, 1999, HL; reversing [1998] 1
W.L.R. 74; [1998] 4 All E.R. 30; 2 B.H.R.C. 590; [1997] Imm. A.R. 584; [1998]
I.N.L.R. 97; (1997) 94(36) L.S.G. 43; *Times*, October 13, 1997, CA (Civ Div);
reversing [1997] Imm. A.R. 145; *Times*, November 12, 1996; *Independent*,
December 2, 1996 (C.S.), QBD. . . . .   *Digested*, 99/**3172**:
        Applied, 03/**2275**, 05/**2226**, 05/**2227**: *Cited*, 97/**2856**: *Considered*, 00/**3311**,
           01/**3642**, 01/**3651**: *Distinguished*, 00/**3293**, 00/**3315**: *Followed*, 01/**3638**
Isle of Wight Council v. Customs and Excise Commissioners; *sub nom* Customs and
Excise Commissioners v. Isle of Wight Council [2004] EWHC 2541; [2005]
S.T.C. 257; [2005] 1 C.M.L.R. 6; [2005] Eu. L.R. 199; [2005] B.T.C. 5197;
[2005] B.V.C. 228; [2004] S.T.I. 2379; [2004] 48 E.G.C.S. 132, Ch D; reversing
[2004] B.V.C. 2181; [2004] V. & D.R. 68; [2004] S.T.I. 1556, V&DTr (London) . .   *Digested*, 05/**4411**
Islington LBC v. Dornan, *Times*, November 8, 2005, CA (Civ Div)
Islington LBC v. Green; Islington LBC v. O'Shea [2005] EWCA Civ 56; [2005] H.L.R.
35; [2005] L. & T.R. 24; [2005] N.P.C. 11, CA (Civ Div) . . . .   *Digested*, 05/**2691**
Islington LBC v. O'Shea see Islington LBC v. Green
Islington LBC v. Osuala see Islington LBC v. SENDIST
Islington LBC v. SENDIST; *sub nom* Islington LBC v. Osuala [2005] EWHC 1519;
[2005] E.L.R. 581, QBD (Admin)
Islington LBC v. University College London Hospital NHS Trust [2005] EWCA Civ
596; (2005) 8 C.C.L. Rep. 337; [2005] Lloyd's Rep. Med. 387; (2005) 85
B.M.L.R. 171; [2005] N.P.C. 77; *Times*, June 28, 2005, CA (Civ Div); affirming
[2004] EWHC 1754, QBD . . . .   *Digested*, 05/**2857**
Ismail, Re [1999] 1 A.C. 320; [1998] 3 W.L.R. 495; [1998] 3 All E.R. 1007; (1999) 163 J.P.
154; (1999) 11 Admin. L.R. 37; (1998) 95(35) L.S.G. 35; (1998) 148 N.L.J. 1302;
(1998) 142 S.J.L.B. 246; *Times*, August 20, 1998, HL; affirming CO/2905/96,
DC . . . .   *Digested*, 98/**2357**:
            Applied, 01/**5783**, 05/**1488**, 05/**1490**: *Considered*, 05/**1486**
Isoplus Fernwarmetechnik Vertriebsgesellschaft mbH v. Commission of the European
Communities (C202/02 P) see Dansk Rorindustri A/S v. Commission of the
European Communities (C189/02 P)
Issa v. Turkey (31821/96) (2005) 41 E.H.R.R. 27; 17 B.H.R.C. 473, ECHR . . . .   *Digested*, 05/**2065**
It's a Wrap (UK) Ltd (In Liquidation) v. Gula (nee Rogers) A3/2005/2186, CA (Civ Div);
reversing [2005] EWHC 2015; *Times*, October 12, 2005, Ch D
Italy v. Commission of the European Communities (C285/94) [1997] E.C.R. I-3519,
ECJ . . . .   *Applied*, 05/**1426**
Italy v. Commission of the European Communities (C303/88); *sub nom* Aid to Eni-
Lanerossi, Re (C303/88) [1991] E.C.R. I-1433; [1993] 2 C.M.L.R. 1, ECJ . . . . .   *Followed*, 05/**590**
Italy v. Commission of the European Communities (C328/99); *sub nom* Aid to Seleco,
Re (C328/99) [2003] E.C.R. I-4035; [2005] 2 C.M.L.R. 48, ECJ (6th
Chamber) . . . .   *Digested*, 05/**590**
Italy v. Commission of the European Communities (C400/99); *sub nom* Aid to Tirrenia
Group, Re (C400/99) [2005] E.C.R. I-3657; [2005] 3 C.M.L.R. 22, ECJ

Item Software (UK) Ltd v. Fassihi; *sub nom* Fassihi v. Item Software (UK) Ltd [2004]
    EWCA Civ 1244; [2004] B.C.C. 994; [2005] 2 B.C.L.C. 91; [2005] I.C.R. 450;
    [2004] I.R.L.R. 928; (2004) 101 (39) L.S.G. 34; (2004) 148 S.J.L.B. 1153;
    Times, October 21, 2004, CA (Civ Div); reversing in part [2003] EWHC 3116;
    [2003] B.C.C. 858; [2003] 2 B.C.L.C. 1; [2003] I.R.L.R. 769, Ch D . . . .   *Digested*, 05/**524**
ITP SA v. Coflexip Stena Offshore Ltd 2005 S.C. 116; 2004 S.L.T. 1285; 2005 S.C.L.R.
    254; (2005) 28(2) I.P.D. 28002; *Times*, November 29, 2004, IH (1 Div);
    reversing 2003 S.L.T. 1197; 2003 G.W.D. 31-879, OH . . . .   *Digested*, 05/**5452**

J v. C see A (A Child) (Foreign Contact Order: Jurisdiction), Re
J v. C (Child: Financial Provision) [1999] 1 F.L.R. 152; [1998] 3 F.C.R. 79; [1999]
    Fam. Law 78, Fam Div. . . . .   *Digested*, 98/**2474**:
                              Applied, 05/**1666**: *Followed*, 05/1652
J v. CPS see Jennings v. Crown Prosecution Service
J v. Secretary of State for the Home Department [2005] EWCA Civ 629; [2005]
    Imm. A.R. 409, CA (Civ Div)
J (A Child) v. Rossiter (Unreported, September 7, 2004), CC (Ashford) [*Ex rel.*
    Mathew Gullick, Barrister, 3 Paper Buildings, Temple, London] . . . .   *Digested*, 05/**3127**
J (A Child) (Child Returned Abroad: Convention Rights) see J (A Child) (Custody Rights:
    Jurisdiction), Re
J (A Child) (Custody Rights: Jurisdiction), Re; *sub nom* Jomah v. Attar; J (Child
    Returned Abroad: Human Rights), Re; J (A Child) (Return to Foreign
    Jurisdiction: Convention Rights), Re; J (A Child) (Child Returned Abroad:
    Convention Rights) [2005] UKHL 40; [2005] 3 W.L.R. 14; [2005] 3 All E.R.
    291; [2005] 2 F.L.R. 802; [2005] 2 F.C.R. 381; [2005] Fam. Law 689; (2005)
    155 N.L.J. 972; (2005) 149 S.J.L.B. 773; *Times*, June 17, 2005, HL; reversing
    [2004] EWCA Civ 417; [2004] 2 F.L.R. 85; [2004] 2 F.C.R. 337; [2004] Fam.
    Law 489; *Times*, April 14, 2004, CA (Civ Div) . . . .   *Digested*, 05/**1569**
J (A Child) (Return to Foreign Jurisdiction: Convention Rights), Re see J (A Child) (Custody
    Rights: Jurisdiction), Re
J (A Minor) (Consent to Medical Treatment), Re see W (A Minor) (Medical Treatment:
    Court's Jurisdiction), Re
J (A Minor) (Prohibited Steps Order: Circumcision), Re; *sub nom* J (A Minor) (Specific
    Issue Orders: Muslim Upbringing and Circumcision), Re; J (Specific Issue
    Orders: Child's Religious Upbringing and Circumcision), Re [2000] 1 F.L.R. 571;
    [2000] 1 F.C.R. 307; (2000) 52 B.M.L.R. 82; [2000] Fam. Law 246; (1999)
    96(47) L.S.G. 30; *Times*, December 22, 1999, CA (Civ Div); affirming [1999] 2
    F.L.R. 678; [1999] 2 F.C.R. 345; [1999] Fam. Law 543; *Times*, June 1, 1999;
    Independent, June 28, 1999 (C.S.), Fam Div. . . . .   *Digested*, 00/**2484**:
                              Applied, 05/**1580**: *Followed*, 03/1777
J (A Minor) (Specific Issue Orders: Muslim Upbringing and Circumcision), Re see J (A
    Minor) (Prohibited Steps Order: Circumcision), Re
J (A Minor) (Wardship: Medical Treatment), Re [1991] Fam. 33; [1991] 2 W.L.R. 140; [1990]
    3 All E.R. 930; [1991] 1 F.L.R. 366; [1991] F.C.R. 370; [1990] 2 Med. L.R. 67; (1990)
    140 N.L.J. 1533; *Times*, October 23, 1990; *Independent*, October 23, 1990;
    Guardian, October 23, 1990; *Daily Telegraph*, October 23, 1990, CA (Civ Div). . .   *Digested*, 91/**2588**:
            Applied, 00/3247, 05/**1677**: *Considered*, 95/3578, 95/4104, 05/1794,
                                                          05/1848
J (Abduction: Acquiring Custody Rights by Caring for Child), Re [2005] 2 F.L.R. 791;
    [2005] Fam. Law 605, Fam Div
J (Abduction: Objections of Child), Re [2004] EWHC 1985; [2005] 1 F.L.R. 273, Fam Div   *Digested*, 05/**1538**
J (Child Returned Abroad: Human Rights), Re see J (A Child) (Custody Rights:
    Jurisdiction), Re
J (Specific Issue Orders: Child's Religious Upbringing and Circumcision), Re see J (A Minor)
    (Prohibited Steps Order: Circumcision), Re
J Floris Ltd v. Istrad Ltd [2005] E.T.M.R. 8, OHIM (2nd Bd App) . . . .   *Digested*, 05/**2522**
J Sainsbury Plc v. Enfield LBC [1989] 1 W.L.R. 590; [1989] 2 All E.R. 817; (1989) 58
    P. & C.R. 441; [1989] 28 E.G. 134; [1989] E.G.C.S. 4, Ch D . . . .   *Digested*, 89/**473**:
                              Considered, 03/3596: *Distinguished*, 05/357
J Walter Thompson Group Ltd v. Williams see Williams v. J Walter Thompson Group Ltd
JA Chapman & Co Ltd (In Liquidation) v. Kadirga Denizcilik ve Ticaret AS [1998] C.L.C.
    860; [1998] Lloyd's Rep. I.R. 377; *Times*, March 19, 1998, CA (Civ Div) . . . .   *Digested*, 98/**3393**:
                             Considered, 04/2240: *Distinguished*, 05/2351

JA Pye (Oxford) Ltd v. Graham [2002] UKHL 30; [2003] 1 A.C. 419; [2002] 3 W.L.R.
221; [2002] 3 All E.R. 865; [2002] H.R.L.R. 34; [2003] 1 P. & C.R. 10; [2002]
28 E.G.C.S. 129; [2002] N.P.C. 92; [2002] 2 P. & C.R. DG22; *Times*, July 5,
2002; *Independent*, July 9, 2002, HL; reversing [2001] EWCA Civ 117; [2001]
Ch. 804; [2001] 2 W.L.R. 1293; [2001] H.R.L.R. 27; (2001) 82 P. & C.R. 23;
[2001] 2 E.G.L.R. 69; [2001] 18 E.G. 176; [2001] 7 E.G.C.S. 161; (2001) 98(8)
L.S.G. 44; (2001) 145 S.J.L.B. 38; [2001] N.P.C. 29; (2001) 82 P. & C.R. DG1;
Times, February 13, 2001; *Independent*, February 13, 2001, CA (Civ Div);
reversing [2000] Ch. 676; [2000] 3 W.L.R. 242; (2001) 81 P. & C.R. 15; [2000]
2 E.G.L.R. 137; [2000] E.G.C.S. 21; (2000) 97(8) L.S.G. 36; (2000) 97(7)
L.S.G. 42; (2000) 144 S.J.L.B. 107; [2000] N.P.C. 10; *Times*, March 14, 2000;
Independent, March 27, 2000 (C.S.), Ch D . . . . *Digested*, 02/**3805**:
Applied, 03/3536, 03/3537, 03/3538, 04/3192, 05/3376, 05/3422:
Considered, 02/3803: *Distinguished*, 05/3439: *Explained*, 04/3191
JA Pye (Oxford) Ltd v. United Kingdom (44302/02) 19 B.H.R.C. 705; [2005] 3
E.G.L.R. 1; [2005] 49 E.G. 90; [2005] 47 E.G.C.S. 145; [2005] N.P.C. 135;
Times, November 23, 2005, ECHR
JA (A Minor) (Child Abduction: Non-Convention Country), Re; *sub nom* A (A Minor)
(Abduction: Non-Convention Country), Re [1998] 1 F.L.R. 231; [1998] 2 F.C.R.
159; [1997] Fam. Law 718; *Times*, July 3, 1997, CA (Civ Div). . . . . *Digested*, 98/**2381**:
Approved, 05/1569: *Considered*, 03/1548
Jackson v. Attorney General see R. (on the application of Jackson) v. Attorney General
Jackson v. Bishop (1984) 48 P. & C.R. 57, CA (Civ Div). . . . . *Digested*, 84/**3625**:
Distinguished, 05/3383
Jackson v. Brock Plc see Grieves v. FT Everard & Sons Ltd
Jackson v. Farmer (Unreported, March 15, 2005), CC (Guildford) [*Ex rel*. Chris
Middleton, Barrister, Oriel Chambers, 14 Water Street, Liverpool]. . . . . *Digested*, 05/**3142**
Jackson v. Marley Davenport Ltd [2004] EWCA Civ 1225; [2004] 1 W.L.R. 2926;
[2005] C.P. Rep. 8; [2005] B.L.R. 13; [2005] P.I.Q.R. P10; [2005] 1 E.G.L.R.
103; (2004) 101(38) L.S.G. 29; (2004) 148 S.J.L.B. 1121; *Times*, October 7,
2004, CA (Civ Div). . . . . *Digested*, 04/**253**
Jackson v. Royal Bank of Scotland [2005] UKHL 3; [2005] 1 W.L.R. 377; [2005] 2
All E.R. 71; [2005] 1 All E.R. (Comm) 337; [2005] 1 Lloyd's Rep. 366; (2005)
102(11) L.S.G. 29; (2005) 149 S.J.L.B. 146; *Times*, February 2, 2005, HL;
reversing [2000] C.L.C. 1457, CA (Civ Div) . . . . *Digested*, 05/**959**
Jacob v. Equitas Ltd; *sub nom* UIC Insurance Co Ltd (In Provisional Liquidation), Re;
Equitas Ltd v. Jacob [2005] EWHC 1440; [2005] B.P.I.R. 1312, Ch D
Jacobs v. Customs and Excise Commissioners; *sub nom* Customs and Excise
Commissioners v. Jacobs; Revenue and Customs Commissioners v. Jacobs
[2005] EWCA Civ 930; [2005] S.T.C. 1518; [2005] B.T.C. 5659; [2005] B.V.C.
690; [2005] S.T.I. 1316; [2005] 31 E.G.C.S. 80; [2005] N.P.C. 100; *Times*,
September 9, 2005, CA (Civ Div); affirming [2004] EWHC 2358; [2004] S.T.C.
1662; [2004] B.T.C. 5776; [2004] B.V.C. 835; [2004] S.T.I. 2255; [2004] 44
E.G.C.S. 153, Ch D; affirming [2004] V. & D.R. 80; [2004] S.T.I. 1303, V&DTr
(Manchester) . . . . *Digested*, 05/**4381**
Jacobsson v. Sweden (10842/84) see Jacobsson v. Sweden (A/163)
Jacobsson v. Sweden (A/163); *sub nom* Jacobsson v. Sweden (10842/84) (1990) 12
E.H.R.R. 56, ECHR (1989) 11 E.H.R.R. CD562; (1987) 9 E.H.R.R. CD350, Eur
Comm HR . . . . *Applied*, 05/1410
Jacues v. Sevenoaks DC [2005] P.A.D. 91, Planning Inspector
Jafari-Fini v. Skillglass Ltd [2005] EWCA Civ 356; [2005] B.C.C. 842, CA (Civ Div) . . *Digested*, 05/**391**
Jaggard v. Sawyer [1995] 1 W.L.R. 269; [1995] 2 All E.R. 189; [1995] 1 E.G.L.R. 146;
[1995] 13 E.G. 132; [1994] E.G.C.S. 139; [1994] N.P.C. 116; *Independent*,
August 22, 1994 (C.S.), CA (Civ Div); affirming [1993] 1 E.G.L.R. 197, CC
(Weymouth) . . . . *Digested*, 95/**4142**:
Applied, 05/3434: *Cited*, 01/1549: *Considered*, 98/4341, 00/5127, 04/912
Jagger v. Decca Music Group Ltd [2004] EWHC 2542; [2005] F.S.R. 26, Ch D . . . . . *Digested*, 05/**716**
Jahree v. Mauritius [2005] UKPC 7; [2005] 1 W.L.R. 1952; (2005) 102(16) L.S.G. 27;
Times, March 3, 2005, PC (Mau) . . . . *Digested*, 05/**903**
Jakto Transport Ltd v. Hall [2005] EWCA Civ 1327; *Times*, November 28, 2005, CA
(Civ Div)
Jameel v. Dow Jones & Co Inc; *sub nom* Dow Jones & Co Inc v. Jameel [2005]
EWCA Civ 75; [2005] Q.B. 946; [2005] 2 W.L.R. 1614; [2005] E.M.L.R. 16;
(2005) 149 S.J.L.B. 181; *Times*, February 14, 2005; *Independent*, February 10,
2005, CA (Civ Div) . . . . *Digested*, 05/**974**
Jameel v. Wall Street Journal Europe SPRL (No.1) [2003] EWCA Civ 1694; [2004]
E.M.L.R. 6; (2003) 147 S.J.L.B. 1399, CA (Civ Div); reversing in part [2003]
EWHC 2322, QBD . . . . *Digested*, 04/**931**:
Applied, 05/978: *Considered*, 04/932

Jameel *v.* Wall Street Journal Europe SPRL (No.3) [2005] EWCA Civ 74; [2005] Q.B.
    904; [2005] 2 W.L.R. 1577; [2005] 4 All E.R. 356; [2005] E.M.L.R. 17; [2005]
    H.R.L.R. 10; (2005) 102(15) L.S.G. 33; *Times*, February 14, 2005; *Independent*,
    February 9, 2005, CA (Civ Div); affirming [2004] EWHC 37; [2004] E.M.L.R.
    11, QBD . . . . *Digested*, 05/**977**:
                                                    Previous proceedings, 04/933
James *v.* Eastleigh BC [1990] 2 A.C. 751; [1990] 3 W.L.R. 55; [1990] 2 All E.R. 607;
    [1990] I.C.R. 554; [1990] I.R.L.R. 288; (1991) 155 L.G. Rev. 205; (1990) 140
    N.L.J. 926, HL; reversing [1990] 1 Q.B. 61; [1989] 3 W.L.R. 123; [1989] 2 All
    E.R. 914; [1989] I.C.R. 423; [1989] I.R.L.R. 318; 87 L.G.R. 651; (1989) 153 L.G.
    Rev. 848; (1989) 133 S.J. 850, CA (Civ Div) . . . . *Digested*, 90/**2565**:
          Applied, 90/1937, 99/2098, 01/2316: *Considered*, 90/107, 92/1978, 93/1793,
                                94/1999, 95/1989, 95/2028, 95/2047, 00/2187, 03/1295:
          Distinguished, 92/1955, 92/1972, 00/5401, 05/85: *Followed*, 99/2093,
                                              99/2095
James *v.* Hunter (Unreported, March 23, 2005), CC (Birkenhead) [*Ex rel.* Michael W
    Halsall, Solicitors, 2 The Parks, Newton le Willows] . . . . *Digested*, 05/**3158**
James *v.* United Kingdom (8793/79) see James *v.* United Kingdom (A/98)
James *v.* United Kingdom (A/44) see Young *v.* United Kingdom (A/44)
James *v.* United Kingdom (A/98); *sub nom* James *v.* United Kingdom (8793/79);
    Trustees of the Duke of Westminster's Estate *v.* United Kingdom (8793/79)
    (1986) 8 E.H.R.R. 123; [1986] R.V.R. 139, ECHR (1983) 5 E.H.R.R. 440; (1983)
    5 E.H.R.R. CD491; (1984) 6 E.H.R.R. CD475, Eur Comm HR . . . . *Digested*, 86/**1650**:
          Applied, 03/2171, 05/2027: *Considered*, 96/1118, 97/2796, 01/1844,
                  03/2095, 03/2838, 03/3485, 03/5819, 04/1376, 05/3376:
                           Followed, 98/4201, 02/3803
James Hay Pension Trustees Ltd *v.* First Secretary of State [2005] EWHC 2713; [2005]
    N.P.C. 139, QBD (Admin)
James' Trade Mark Application [2005] E.T.M.R. 93, App Person
Janov *v.* Morris [1981] 1 W.L.R. 1389; [1981] 3 All E.R. 780, CA (Civ Div) . . . . *Digested*, 81/**2201**:
        Applied, 05/461: *Considered*, 94/3644: *Distinguished*, 83/2939, 83/3068
Jansen Nielsen Pilkes Ltd *v.* Tomlinson (Inspector of Taxes) [2005] Eu. L.R. 1; [2004]
    S.T.C. (S.C.D.) 226; 6 I.T.L. Rep. 715; [2004] S.T.I. 1048, Sp Comm . . . . *Digested*, 04/**3728**
Jarrold *v.* Houlston (1857) 3 Kay & J. 708 . . . . *Applied*, 67/3169:
                                              Considered, 05/2427
Jarvis *v.* Hampshire CC see Phelps *v.* Hillingdon LBC
Jarvis Homes Ltd *v.* Marshall; *sub nom* Marshall *v.* Jarvis Homes Ltd [2004] EWCA
    Civ 839; [2004] 3 E.G.L.R. 81; [2004] 44 E.G. 154; [2004] 29 E.G.C.S. 116;
    [2004] N.P.C. 110, CA (Civ Div); reversing [2003] EWHC 2949, Ch D . . . . *Digested*, 05/**3432**
Jauzon *v.* American Express Carte France [2005] E.C.C. 38, Cass (F)
JB (Child Abduction: Rights of Custody: Spain), Re [2003] EWHC 2130; [2004] 1 F.L.R.
    796; [2004] Fam. Law 241, Fam Div . . . . *Digested*, 04/**1469**:
                                              Explained, 05/1542
JC Decaux UK Ltd *v.* Brent LBC [2005] P.A.D. 34, Planning Inspector
JD *v.* East Berkshire Community Health NHS Trust; *sub nom* MAK *v.* Dewsbury
    Healthcare NHS Trust; D *v.* East Berkshire Community NHS Trust; K *v.* Dewsbury
    Healthcare NHS Trust; RK *v.* Oldham NHS Trust [2005] UKHL 23; [2005] 2
    A.C. 373; [2005] 2 W.L.R. 993; [2005] 2 All E.R. 443; [2005] 2 F.L.R. 284;
    [2005] 2 F.C.R. 81; (2005) 8 C.C.L. Rep. 185; [2005] Lloyd's Rep. Med. 263;
    (2005) 83 B.M.L.R. 66; [2005] Fam. Law 615; (2005) 155 N.L.J. 654; *Times*,
    April 22, 2005; *Independent*, April 27, 2005, HL; affirming [2003] EWCA Civ
    1151; [2004] Q.B. 558; [2004] 2 W.L.R. 58; [2003] 4 All E.R. 796; [2003] 2
    F.L.R. 1166; [2003] 3 F.C.R. 1; [2003] H.R.L.R. 35; [2003] U.K.H.R.R. 1200;
    (2004) 7 C.C.L. Rep. 63; [2003] Lloyd's Rep. Med. 552; (2004) 76 B.M.L.R.
    61; [2003] Fam. Law 816; (2003) 100(36) L.S.G. 37; *Times*, August 22, 2003;
    Independent, October 1, 2003, CA (Civ Div); affirming [2003] Lloyd's Rep.
    Med. 9, CC (Chester) . . . . *Digested*, 05/**2848**:
                                          Distinguished, 05/3424
Jeancharm Ltd (t/a Beaver International) *v.* Customs and Excise Commissioners; *sub
    nom* Jeancharm Ltd (t/a Beaver International) *v.* Revenue and Customs
    Commissioners; Revenue and Customs Commissioners *v.* Jeancharm Ltd (t/a
    Beaver International) [2005] EWHC 839; [2005] S.T.C. 918; [2005] B.T.C.
    5285; [2005] B.V.C. 316; [2005] S.T.I. 907, Ch D; reversing [2005] S.T.I. 122,
    V&DTr. . . . . *Digested*, 05/**4379**
Jeancharm Ltd (t/a Beaver International) *v.* Revenue and Customs Commissioners see
    Jeancharm Ltd (t/a Beaver International) *v.* Customs and Excise
    Commissioners
Jeans *v.* Nelson (Unreported, July 20, 2004), CC (Uxbridge) [*Ex rel.* Gurion Taussig,
    Barrister, 199 Strand, London] . . . . *Digested*, 05/**3188**
Jeffkins Indentures, Re (Practice Note) [1965] 1 W.L.R. 375; [1965] 1 All E.R. 608 (Note);
    109 S.J. 110, Ch D . . . . *Digested*, 65/**3347**:
            Distinguished, 65/3348, 66/10316: *Followed*, 68/3334, 05/357
Jeffrey *v.* Commissioner of Police of the Metropolis see Yearwood *v.* Commissioner of
    Police of the Metropolis

Jeffrey v. Secretary of State for Transport; *sub nom* Weir v. Secretary of State for Transport [2004] EWHC 2772; [2005] U.K.H.R.R.154, Ch D . . . .   *Digested,* 05/**402**

Jego-Quere & Cie SA v. Commission of the European Communities (T177/01) see Commission of the European Communities v. Jego-Quere et Cie SA (C263/02 P)

Jemma Trust Co Ltd v. Kippax Beaumont Lewis [2005] EWCA Civ 248; [2005] W.T.L.R. 683, CA (Civ Div); reversing in part [2004] EWHC 703; [2004] W.T.L.R. 533; (2004) 101 (15) L.S.G. 29, Ch D . . . .   *Digested,* 05/**2874**

Jemma Trust Co Ltd v. Liptrott (No.2) [2004] EWHC 1404; [2004] 4 Costs L.R. 610; [2005] W.T.L.R.157, Ch D . . . .   *Digested,* 05/**352**

Jenkins v. United States; Benbow v. United States [2005] EWHC 1051, QBD (Admin) .   *Digested,* 05/**1487**

Jennings v. Buchanan see Buchanan v. Jennings

Jennings v. Crown Prosecution Service; *sub nom* J v. CPS [2005] EWCA Civ 746; [2005] 4 All E.R. 391; *Times,* July 12, 2005; *Independent,* June 30, 2005, CA (Civ Div) . . . .   *Digested,* 05/**926**

Jennings v. Kinder (Inspector of Taxes) see Hochstrasser (Inspector of Taxes) v. Mayes

Jennings Motors Ltd v. Secretary of State for the Environment [1982] Q.B. 541; [1982] 2 W.L.R. 131; [1982] 1 All E.R. 471; 80 L.G.R. 226; (1982) 43 P. & C.R. 316; (1982) 261 E.G. 994; [1982] J.P.L. 181, CA (Civ Div); reversing (1981) 41 P. & C.R. 221; [1980] J.P.L. 521, DC . . . .   *Digested,* 82/**3130**:
                                                   Followed, 05/**3304**

Jeromson v. Shell Tankers UK Ltd see Shell Tankers UK Ltd v. Jeromson

Jerzynek v. Customs and Excise Commissioners [2005] B.V.C. 2078; [2004] S.T.I. 2571; (2004) 148 S.J.L.B. 1151, V&DTr (Manchester)

Jewish Community of Oslo v. Norway (30/2003) (2005) 41 E.H.R.R. SE19, UN CERD

Jeyachandran, Re [2002] UKIAT 1869, IAT . . . .   *Considered,* 04/**2021**,
                                   04/**2079**: *Followed,* 05/**2152**

Jeyapragash v. Secretary of State for the Home Department; *sub nom* R. (on the application of Jeyapragash) v. Immigration Appeal Tribunal [2004] EWCA Civ 1260; [2005] 1 All E.R. 412; *Times,* October 12, 2004; *Independent,* October 27, 2004, CA (Civ Div) . . . .   *Digested,* 05/**332**

JFE Engineering Corp v. Commission of the European Communities (T67/00) [2005] 4 C.M.L.R. 2, CFI (2nd Chamber) . . . .   *Digested,* 05/**553**

JH Edwards & Sons v. Central London Commercial Estates; Eastern Bazaar v. Central London Commercial Estates [1984] 2 E.G.L.R. 103; (1984) 271 E.G. 697, CA (Civ Div) . . . .   *Digested,* 84/**1878**:
               Applied, 90/**2784**: *Considered,* 90/**2771**, 05/**2671**

JH Rayner (Mincing Lane) Ltd v. Department of Trade and Industry; Maclaine Watson & Co Ltd v. Department of Trade and Industry; Maclaine Watson & Co Ltd v. International Tin Council; TSB England and Wales v. Department of Trade and Industry; Amalgamated Metal Trading Ltd v. International Tin Council [1990] 2 A.C. 418; [1989] 3 W.L.R. 969; [1989] 3 All E.R. 523; (1989) 5 B.C.C. 872; [1990] B.C.L.C. 102; (1990) 87(4) L.S.G. 68; (1989) 139 N.L.J. 1559; (1989) 133 S.J. 1485, HL; affirming [1989] Ch. 72; [1988] 3 W.L.R. 1033; [1988] 3 All E.R. 257; (1988) 4 BCC. 563; [1988] B.C.L.C. 404; [1989] P.C.C. 1; [1989] P.C.C. 68; (1988) 132 S.J. 1494; *Times,* April 28, 1988; *Independent,* May 9, 1988 (C.S.); *Financial Times,* May 3, 1988, CA (Civ Div); affirming (1987) 3 B.C.C. 413; [1987] B.C.L.C. 667; [1988] P.C.C. 150; [1987] 2 F.T.L.R. 328, Ch D

. . . .   *Digested,* 90/**538**:
     Applied, 90/**614**, 91/**235**, 92/**204**: *Considered,* 93/**3805**, 95/**2939**, 96/**3659**,
        04/**2088**, 05/**212**: *Distinguished,* 91/**2200**: *Followed,* 89/**149**:
                               Referred to, 94/**2098**, 95/**2938**

JI MacWilliam Co Inc v. Mediterranean Shipping Co SA (The Rafaela S) [2005] UKHL 11; [2005] 2 A.C. 423; [2005] 2 W.L.R. 554; [2005] 2 All E.R. 86; [2005] 1 All E.R. (Comm) 393; [2005] 1 Lloyd's Rep. 347; [2005] 1 C.L.C. 172; 2005 A.M.C. 913; *Times,* February 21, 2005, HL; affirming [2003] EWCA Civ 556; [2004] Q.B. 702; [2004] 2 W.L.R. 283; [2003] 3 All E.R. 369; [2003] 2 All E.R. (Comm) 219; [2003] 2 Lloyd's Rep. 113; [2003] 2 C.L.C. 94; 2003 A.M.C. 2035; (2003) 100(26) L.S.G. 38; *Times,* May 5, 2003, CA (Civ Div); reversing [2002] EWHC 593; [2002] 2 Lloyd's Rep. 403; [2002] C.L.C. 1043, QBD (Comm) . . . .   *Digested,* 05/**3785**

Jimenez v. Inland Revenue Commissioners [2004] S.T.C. (S.C.D.) 371; [2004] S.T.I. 1939, Sp Comm . . . .   *Digested,* 05/**4072**

Jindal Iron & Steel Co Ltd v. Islamic Solidarity Shipping Co Jordan Inc; TCI Trans Commodities AG v. Islamic Solidarity Shipping Co Jordan Inc [2004] UKHL 49; [2005] 1 W.L.R. 1363; [2005] 1 All E.R. 175; [2005] 1 All E.R. (Comm) 1; [2005] 1 Lloyd's Rep. 57; [2004] 2 C.L.C. 1172; 2005 A.M.C. 1; (2004) 148 S.J.L.B. 1405; *Times,* November 26, 2004, HL; affirming [2003] EWCA Civ 144; [2003] 1 All E.R. (Comm) 747; [2003] 2 Lloyd's Rep. 87; [2003] 1 C.L.C. 885, CA (Civ Div); reversing in part [2002] EWHC 1268; [2002] 2 All E.R. (Comm) 364, QBD (Comm) . . . .   *Digested,* 05/**3787**

JJ Cafferkey & Co Ltd v. Byrne see Smith v. AJ Morrisroes & Sons Ltd

JJB Sports Plc *v.* Office of Fair Trading; Allsports Ltd *v.* Office of Fair Trading [2004] CAT 17; [2005] Comp. A.R. 29, CAT . . . .　*Digested,* 05/**570**: *Followed,* 05/2825

JJB Sports Plc *v.* Office of Fair Trading (Disclosure of Agreement) [2004] CAT 13; [2005] Comp. A.R. 283, CAT . . . .　*Digested,* 05/**588**

JJB Sports Plc *v.* Office of Fair Trading (Permission to Appeal) [2005] CAT 27; [2005] Comp. A.R. 1145, CAT

JMA Accounting Pty Ltd *v.* Carmody (Commissioner of Taxation) 7 I.T.L. Rep. 274, Fed Ct (Aus) (Full Ct) . . . .　*Digested,* 05/**4165**

Jobsearch Ltd *v.* Relational Designers Ltd; *sub nom* Jobserve Ltd *v.* Skillsite Ltd [2004] EWHC 661; [2004] F.S.R. 36, Ch D . . . .　*Digested,* 05/**346**

Jobserve Ltd *v.* Skillsite Ltd see Jobsearch Ltd *v.* Relational Designers Ltd

Jodrell *v.* Jodrell . . . .　*Applied,* 05/2827

John *v.* MGN Ltd [1997] Q.B. 586; [1996] 3 W.L.R. 593; [1996] 2 All E.R. 35; [1996] E.M.L.R. 229; (1996) 146 N.L.J. 13; *Times,* December 14, 1995, CA (Civ Div) . . .　*Digested,* 96/**5673**: *Applied,* 97/1768: *Considered,* 96/2122, 96/5674, 00/1756, 05/972

John *v.* Trinidad and Tobago see Teeluck *v.* Trinidad and Tobago

John Laing & Son *v.* Kingswood Assessment Committee [1949] 1 K.B. 344; [1949] 1 All E.R. 224; 65 T.L.R. 80; 113 J.P. 111; 47 L.G.R. 64; 42 R. & I.T. 15; 93 S.J. 26, CA; affirming [1948] 2 K.B. 116; [1948] 1 All E.R. 943; 64 T.L.R. 407, KBD . . . .　*Digested,* 47-51/**8292**: *Applied,* 55/2275, 56/6585, 56/7264, 60/2685, 70/2414, 98/4319, 05/3370: *Considered,* 77/2453, 85/2924, 85/2926, 87/3181, 90/3917: *Distinguished,* 75/2776, 99/4333: *Followed,* 99/4335, 01/4821

John Laing Construction Ltd *v.* Amber Pass Ltd [2005] L. & T.R. 12; [2004] 2 E.G.L.R. 128; [2004] 17 E.G.C.S. 128; (2004) 101 (16) L.S.G. 29, Ch D . . . .　*Digested,* 05/**2645**

John Lewis Properties Plc *v.* Inland Revenue Commissioners; *sub nom* Inland Revenue Commissioners *v.* John Lewis Properties Plc [2002] EWCA Civ 1869; [2003] Ch. 513; [2003] 2 W.L.R. 1196; [2003] S.T.C. 117; 75 T.C. 131; [2003] B.T.C. 127; [2003] S.T.I. 29; (2003) 147 S.J.L.B. 180; [2003] N.P.C. 1; *Times,* January 16, 2003, CA (Civ Div); affirming [2002] 1 W.L.R. 35; [2001] S.T.C. 1118; [2001] B.T.C. 213; [2001] S.T.I. 937; (2001) 98(27) L.S.G. 40; (2001) 145 S.J.L.B. 164; *Times,* June 22, 2001; *Independent,* July 30, 2001 (C.S), Ch D; affirming [2000] S.T.C. (S.C.D.) 494; [2000] S.T.I. 1467, Sp Comm . . . .　*Digested,* 03/**4173**: *Considered,* 05/2657, 05/3982

John Lyon's Charity *v.* Shalson see Shalson *v.* John Lyon's Free Grammar School

John Mann International Ltd *v.* Vehicle Inspectorate [2004] EWHC 1236; [2004] 1 W.L.R. 2731; (2005) 169 J.P. 171; [2005] R.T.R. 8; (2005) 169 J.P.N. 299, QBD (Admin) . . . .　*Digested,* 05/**821**

John Mowlem Construction Plc *v.* Neil F Jones & Co Solicitors [2004] EWCA Civ 768; [2004] B.L.R. 387; [2004] T.C.L.R. 7; 96 Con. L.R. 1; [2004] P.N.L.R. 45; (2004) 148 S.J.L.B. 825; *Times,* August 27, 2004, CA (Civ Div); affirming [2003] EWHC 2894, QBD (TCC) . . . .　*Digested,* 05/**2876**

John Pfeiffer Pty Ltd *v.* Rogerson 203 C.L.R. 503, HC (Aus) . . . .　*Considered,* 05/608

John Roberts Architects Ltd *v.* Parkcare Homes (No.2) Ltd A1/2005/1732, CA (Civ Div); reversing [2005] EWHC 1637; [2005] B.L.R. 484, QBD (TCC)

John Taylors (A Firm) *v.* Masons [2001] EWCA Civ 2106; [2005] W.T.L.R. 1519, CA (Civ Div)

Johns *v.* Johns [2005] W.T.L.R. 529; (2005-06) 8 I.T.E.L.R. 287, CA (NZ)

Johnson, Re (LCA/144/2003) [2005] R.V.R. 179, Lands Tr . . . .　*Digested,* 05/**2000**

Johnson *v.* Gore Wood & Co (No.1); *sub nom* Johnson *v.* Gore Woods & Co [2002] 2 A.C. 1; [2001] 2 W.L.R. 72; [2001] 1 All E.R. 481; [2001] C.P.L.R. 49; [2001] B.C.C. 820; [2001] 1 B.C.L.C. 313; [2001] P.N.L.R. 18; (2001) 98(1) L.S.G. 24; (2001) 98(8) L.S.G. 46; (2000) 150 N.L.J. 1889; (2001) 145 S.J.L.B. 29; *Times,* December 22, 2000; *Independent,* February 7, 2001 (C.S), HL; reversing in part [1999] C.P.L.R. 155; [1999] B.C.C. 474; [1999] Lloyd's Rep. P.N. 91; [1999] P.N.L.R. 426; [1998] N.P.C. 151, CA (Civ Div) . . . .　*Digested,* 01/**410**: *Applied,* 99/3313, 01/746, 02/280, 02/281, 02/3286, 02/3310, 03/291, 03/470, 03/4600, 04/265, 04/459, 05/520, 05/533, 05/2448, 05/2505: *Considered,* 01/675, 01/708, 01/5710: *Distinguished,* 02/565, 04/2338: *Followed,* 01/749, 04/425, 04/2733, 05/483

Johnson *v.* Medical Defence Union Ltd [2004] EWHC 2509; [2005] 1 W.L.R. 750; [2005] 1 All E.R. 87; [2005] Info. T.L.R. 119; [2005] F.S.R. 28; (2004) 101(46) L.S.G. 34; *Times,* November 25, 2004, Ch D . . . .　*Digested,* 05/**478**

Johnson *v.* Steelite International Plc (Unreported, April 15, 2004), CC (Stoke on Trent) [*Ex rel.* Adam Farrer, Barrister, 5, Fountain Court, Steelhouse Lane, Birmingham] . . . .　*Digested,* 05/**3224**

Johnson *v.* Unisys Ltd [2001] UKHL 13; [2003] 1 A.C. 518; [2001] 2 W.L.R. 1076; [2001] 2 All E.R. 801; [2001] I.C.R. 480; [2001] I.R.L.R. 279; [2001] Emp. L.R. 469; *Times,* March 23, 2001; *Independent,* March 29, 2001, HL; affirming [1999] 1 All E.R. 854; [1999] I.C.R. 809; [1999] I.R.L.R. 90, CA (Civ Div) . . . . .　*Digested,* 01/**2253**: *Applied,* 03/1216, 03/1332, 03/1337, 04/1183, 05/1340: *Considered,* 03/1246, 03/1333, 04/1303, 04/1307: *Distinguished,* 02/5565: *Followed,* 02/1313, 05/1326

Johnson & Johnson Corp'sWord Mark (R 654/2004-1) (2005) 28(4) I.P.D. 28023, OHIM (1st Bd App)

Johnson Underwood Ltd v. Montgomery see Montgomery v. Johnson Underwood Ltd

Johnston v. NEI International Combustion Ltd see Grieves v. FT Everard & Sons Ltd

Joint London Holdings Ltd v. Mount Cook Land Ltd; *sub nom* Mount Cook Land Ltd v. Joint London Holdings Ltd [2005] EWCA Civ 1171; [2005] 3 E.G.L.R. 119; [2005] 42 E.G.C.S. 234; (2005) 155 N.L.J. 1552; [2005] N.P.C. 113; *Times*, October 11, 2005; *Independent*, October 11, 2005, CA (Civ Div); reversing in part [2005] EWHC 507; *Times*, May 12, 2005, Ch D . . . .   *Digested*, 05/**2668**

Jolley v. Sutton LBC [2000] 1 W.L.R. 1082; [2000] 3 All E.R. 409; [2000] 2 Lloyd's Rep. 65; [2000] 2 F.C.R. 392; (2001) 3 L.G.L.R. 2; [2000] B.L.G.R. 399; [2000] P.I.Q.R. P136; (2000) 97(23) L.S.G. 42; *Times*, May 24, 2000, HL; reversing [1998] 1 W.L.R. 1546; [1998] 3 All E.R. 559; [1998] 2 Lloyd's Rep. 240; [1998] 3 F.C.R. 443; [1998] P.I.Q.R. P377; (1998) 95(28) L.S.G. 31; (1998) 148 N.L.J. 1014; (1998) 142 S.J.L.B. 188; *Times*, June 23, 1998; *Independent*, June 25, 1998, CA (Civ Div); reversing [1998] 1 Lloyd's Rep. 433, QBD . . . .   *Digested*, 00/**4239**:
                   Applied, 00/4214: *Considered*, 05/4196: *Distinguished*, 04/2716

Jomah v. Attar see J (A Child) (Custody Rights: Jurisdiction), Re

Jonas v. Bamford (Inspector of Taxes) [1973] S.T.C. 519; 51 T.C. 1; [1973] T.R. 225 . . . .   *Digested*, 74/**1866**:
                                         Applied, 05/4090, 05/4098

Jones v. 3M Healthcare Ltd (No.1) see Rhys-Harper v. Relaxion Group Plc

Jones v. Associated Tunnelling Co [1981] I.R.L.R. 477, EAT . . . .   *Digested*, 81/**828**:
                                               Applied, 05/1241

Jones v. Callagher (t/a Gallery Kitchens & Bathrooms); *sub nom* Jones v. Gallagher (t/a Gallery Kitchens & Bathrooms) [2004] EWCA Civ 10; [2005] 1 Lloyd's Rep. 377, CA (Civ Div) . . . .   *Digested*, 05/**670**

Jones v. Chief Constable of South Yorkshire see Alcock v. Chief Constable of South Yorkshire

Jones v. Commission for Social Care Inspection; *sub nom* R. (on the application of National Care Standards Commission) v. Jones [2004] EWCA Civ 1713; [2005] 1 W.L.R. 2461; (2005) 149 S.J.L.B. 59; *Times*, January 4, 2005, CA (Civ Div); affirming [2004] EWHC 918; [2004] A.C.D. 77, QBD (Admin) . . . .   *Digested*, 05/**3929**

Jones v. DPP [2001] R.T.R. 80, DC . . . .   *Considered*, 05/818

Jones v. Gallagher (t/a Gallery Kitchens & Bathrooms) see Jones v. Callagher (t/a Gallery Kitchens & Bathrooms)

Jones v. Garnett (Inspector of Taxes) [2005] EWCA Civ 1553, CA (Civ Div); reversing [2005] EWHC 849; [2005] S.T.C. 1667; [2005] B.T.C. 306; [2005] W.T.L.R. 729; [2005] S.T.I. 892; [2005] S.T.I. 903; *Times*, May 17, 2005, Ch D; affirming [2005] S.T.C. (S.C.D.) 9; [2004] W.T.L.R. 1209; [2004] S.T.I. 2263, Sp Comm .   *Digested*, 05/**4101**

Jones v. Hipgrave see Hipgrave v. Jones

Jones v. Llanrwst Urban DC [1911] 1 Ch. 393, Ch D . . . .   *Considered*, 05/3239

Jones v. Maidstone BC [2005] P.A.D. 56, Planning Inspector

Jones v. Minister of the Interior Al-Mamlaka Al-Arabiya AS Saudiya see Jones v. Saudi Arabia

Jones v. National Westminster Bank Plc see National Westminster Bank Plc v. Jones

Jones v. Patel see Patel v. Jones

Jones v. Patnell (Unreported, September 20, 2004), CC (Edmonton) [*Ex rel.* Gurion Taussig, Barrister, 199 Strand, London] . . . .   *Digested*, 05/**3226**

Jones v. Post Office; *sub nom* Post Office v. Jones [2001] EWCA Civ 558; [2001] I.C.R. 805; [2001] I.R.L.R. 384; [2001] Emp. L.R. 527; *Times*, June 5, 2001; *Independent*, April 26, 2001, CA (Civ Div); affirming [2000] I.C.R. 388, EAT . . .   *Digested*, 01/**2236**:
                        Applied, 01/6463, 02/1329, 04/1220: *Considered*, 04/1215, 05/1227:
                                               Distinguished, 04/1219

Jones v. Sandwell MBC see Barber v. Somerset CC

Jones v. Saudi Arabia; *sub nom* Jones v. Minister of the Interior Al-Mamlaka Al-Arabiya AS Saudiya; Mitchell v. Al-Dali [2004] EWCA Civ 1394; [2005] Q.B. 699; [2005] 2 W.L.R. 808; [2005] U.K.H.R.R. 57; [2005] A.C.D. 50; (2004) 101(44) L.S.G. 31; (2004) 154 N.L.J. 1655; (2004) 148 S.J.L.B. 1286; *Times*, November 1, 2004; *Independent*, November 3, 2004, CA (Civ Div); reversing in part TNS, QBD. . . . .   *Digested*, 04/**3849**

Jones v. Whalley [2005] EWHC 931; (2005) 169 J.P. 466; (2005) 169 J.P.N. 679, QBD (Admin) . . . .   *Digested*, 05/**918**

Jones v. Wright see Alcock v. Chief Constable of South Yorkshire

Jones (t/a Shamrock Coaches) v. Department of Transport Welsh Traffic Office; *sub nom* Jones (t/a Shamrock Coaches) v. Department of Transport Welsh Traffic Area [2005] EWCA Civ 58; (2005) 102(11) L.S.G. 31; (2005) 149 S.J.L.B. 114; *Times*, January 24, 2005, CA (Civ Div) . . . .   *Digested*, 05/**86**

Jones (Vivian) v. DPP [2004] EWHC 3165; [2005] R.T.R. 15, QBD (Admin) . . . .   *Digested*, 05/**781**

Jordan v. United Kingdom (Admissibility) (22567/02) (2005) 40 E.H.R.R. SE10, ECHR

Jordan's Application for Judicial Review, Re [2005] N.I. 144, CA (NI)

Joseph v. City of London Real Property Co Ltd see Midtown Ltd v. City of London Real Property Co Ltd

Joseph (Jeffrey) *v.* Queen, The see Boyce (Lennox Ricardo) *v.* Queen, The
Joyce *v.* Revenue and Customs Commissioners [2005] S.T.C. (S.C.D.) 696; [2005]
　　S.T.I. 1561, Sp Comm
JP Garrett Electrical Ltd *v.* Cotton see Woodward *v.* Abbey National Plc (No.2)
JP Morgan Europe Ltd *v.* Primacom AG [2005] EWHC 508; [2005] 2 All E.R. (Comm)
　　764; [2005] 2 Lloyd's Rep. 665; [2005] 1 C.L.C. 493, QBD (Comm)
JSC Zestafoni G Nikoladze Ferroalloy Plant *v.* Ronly Holdings Ltd [2004] EWHC 245;
　　[2004] 2 Lloyd's Rep. 335; [2004] 1 C.L.C. 1146, QBD (Comm) . . . . 　*Digested,* 05/**196**
Judge *v.* Canada (829/1998) (2004) 11 I.H.R.R. 125; (2005) 40 E.H.R.R. SE4, UN
　　HRC
Judge *v.* Crown Leisure Ltd [2005] EWCA Civ 571; [2005] I.R.L.R. 823, CA (Civ
　　Div); affirming UKEAT/0443/04/DA, EAT
Judge (Walden's Personal Representative) *v.* Revenue and Customs Commissioners
　　[2005] S.T.C. (S.C.D.) 863; [2005] W.T.L.R. 1311; [2005] S.T.I. 1800, Sp
　　Comm
Junk *v.* Kuhnel (C188/03) [2005] E.C.R. I-885; [2005] 1 C.M.L.R. 42; [2005] C.E.C.
　　418; [2005] I.R.L.R. 310, ECJ (2nd Chamber) . . . . 　*Digested,* 05/**1203**

K *v.* Croydon Crown Court see R. (on the application of K) *v.* Croydon Crown Court
K *v.* Dewsbury Healthcare NHS Trust see JD *v.* East Berkshire Community Health NHS
　　Trust
K *v.* K (Financial Relief: Management of Difficult Cases) [2005] EWHC 1070; [2005]
　　2 F.L.R. 1137; [2005] Fam. Law 607, Fam Div
K *v.* Knowsley MBC; *sub nom* R. (on the application of K) *v.* Knowsley MBC [2004]
　　EWHC 1933; (2004) 168 J.P. 461; [2005] H.L.R. 3; (2004) 168 J.P.N. 680,
　　QBD (Admin) . . . . 　*Digested,* 05/**831**
K (A Child) *v.* Boye-Doe [2005] 3 Q.R. 13, CC (Edmonton) [*Ex rel.* Joanna Kerr,
　　Barrister, Lamb Chambers, Lamb Building, Temple, London] . . . . 　*Digested,* 05/**3223**
K (A Child) *v.* Harris (Unreported, January 17, 2005), CC (Bolton) [*Ex rel.* Tony
　　Thorndike, Barrister, Central Chambers, 89 Princess Street, Manchester] . . . . . . 　*Digested,* 05/**3132**
K (A Child) *v.* McCallum [2005] 2 Q.R. 15; [2004] 6 Q.R. 11, CC (Southampton) [*Ex*
　　rel. Joanna Kerr, Barrister, Lamb Chambers, Lamb Building, Temple, London] . . . 　*Digested,* 04/**2920**
K (A Child) *v.* Nugent (Unreported, February 10, 2005), CC (Edmonton) [*Ex rel.*
　　Joanna Kerr, Barrister, Lamb Chambers, Lamb Building, Temple, London] . . . . . . 　*Digested,* 05/**3169**
K (Children), Re [2004] EWCA Civ 1821; (2005) 149 S.J.L.B. 28, CA (Civ Div)
K (Children) *v.* Frost (Unreported, July 21, 2004), CC (Romford) [*Ex rel.* David
　　McHugh, Barrister, 1st Floor, 1 Essex Court Chambers, Temple, London] . . . . . . 　*Digested,* 05/**3236**
K (Children) (Adoption: Freeing Order), Re see K (Children) (Non Accidental Injuries:
　　Perpetrator: New Evidence), Re
K (Children) (Adoption Orders: Fresh Evidence), Re see K (Children) (Non Accidental
　　Injuries: Perpetrator: New Evidence), Re
K (Children) (Non Accidental Injuries: Perpetrator: New Evidence), Re; *sub nom* K
　　(Children) (Adoption Orders: Fresh Evidence), Re; K (Children) (Adoption:
　　Freeing Order), Re [2004] EWCA Civ 1181; [2005] 1 F.L.R. 285; [2004] 3 F.C.R.
　　123; [2005] Fam. Law 12, CA (Civ Div) . . . . 　*Digested,* 04/**1462**
K (Children) (Procedure: Family Proceedings Rules), Re [2004] EWCA Civ 1827; [2005] 1
　　F.L.R. 764; [2005] Fam. Law 275; (2005) 149 S.J.L.B. 29, CA (Civ Div) . . . . . 　*Digested,* 05/**1669**
K (CICA: Quantum: 2004: Post Traumatic Stress Disorder), Re (Unreported, July 5, 2004),
　　CICAP [*Ex rel.* Karen Johnson, Barrister, Guildford Chambers, Stoke House,
　　Leapale Lane, Guildford] . . . . 　*Digested,* 05/**3085**
K&J Holdings Ltd, Re see Pinsent Curtis *v.* Capital Cranfield Trustees Ltd
K&L Childcare Services Ltd *v.* Customs and Excise Commissioners [2005] B.V.C. 2559;
　　[2005] V. & D.R. 207; [2005] S.T.I. 1025, V&DTr (Manchester)
Kabushi Kaisha Sony Computer Entertainment Inc *v.* Owen (t/a Neo Technologies); *sub*
　　nom Sony Computer Entertainment *v.* Owen [2002] EWHC 45; [2002]
　　E.C.D.R. 27; [2002] E.M.L.R. 34; [2002] Masons C.L.R. 24; (2002) 25(5)
　　I.P.D. 25030; (2002) 25(5) I.P.D. 25031, Ch D . . . . 　*Digested,* 03/**2489**:
　　　　　　　　　　　　　　　　　　　　　　　　　　　　　　　　　　　　　　　Applied, 05/2421
Kabushiki Kaisha Fernandes *v.* Office for Harmonisation in the Internal Market (Trade
　　Marks and Designs) (OHIM) (T39/01) [2002] E.C.R. II-5233; [2003] E.T.M.R.
　　98; *Times,* December 28, 2002, CFI (4th Chamber). . . . . 　*Digested,* 03/**2620**:
　　　　　　　　　　　　　　　　　　　　　　　　　　　　　　　　　　　　　　　Applied, 05/2540
Kabushiki Kaisha Sony Computer Entertainment Inc *v.* Ball (Application for Summary
　　Judgment); *sub nom* Sony Computer Entertainment Inc *v.* Ball (Application for
　　Summary Judgment) [2004] EWHC 1738; [2005] E.C.C. 24; [2004] E.C.D.R.
　　33; [2004] Info. T.L.R. 350; [2005] F.S.R. 9; (2004) 27(8) I.P.D. 27086;
　　(2004) 101 (39) L.S.G. 34; *Times,* October 21, 2004; *Independent,* October 11,
　　2004 (C.S), Ch D . . . . 　*Digested,* 04/**2254**
Kabushiki Kaisha Sony Computer Entertainment Inc *v.* Nuplayer Ltd [2005] EWHC 1522;
　　(2005) 28(8) I.P.D. 28061, Ch D
Kadre *v.* France [2005] EWHC 1712; *Times,* August 12, 2005, QBD (Admin) . . . . 　*Digested,* 05/**1489**
Kahn *v.* Inland Revenue Commissioners see Toshoku Finance UK Plc (In Liquidation),
　　Re

Kain v. Hutton (No.1) (2004-05) 7 I.T.E.L.R. 1, HC (NZ) . . . . *Digested*, 05/**4318**
Kain v. Hutton (No.2) [2005] W.T.L.R. 977, HC (NZ)
Kalamazoo (Aust) Pty v. Compact Business Systems Ltd (1985) 5 I.P.R. 213, Sup Ct
   (Qld) . . . . *Considered*, 05/2427
Kalfelis v. Bankhaus Schroder Munchmeyer Hengst & Co (t/a HEMA
   Beteiligungsgesellschaft mbH) (189/87) [1988] E.C.R. 5565; [1989] E.C.C.
   407; *Times*, October 5, 1988, ECJ (5th Chamber) . . . . *Digested*, 91/**3936**:
                   Applied, 91/5161, 94/5038, 96/5344, 97/898, 03/484: *Considered*, 98/3466,
                      99/715, 05/427: *Distinguished*, 96/7098: *Followed*, 94/5036, 96/1085:
                                        Referred to, 97/3890
Kamer van Koophandel en Fabrieken voor Amsterdam v. Inspire Art Ltd (C167/01)
   [2003] E.C.R. I-10155; [2005] 3 C.M.L.R. 34, ECJ
Kanapathiar v. Harrow LBC [2003] I.R.L.R. 571, EAT . . . . *Followed*, 05/1284
Kangol Ltd v. Hay & Robertson Plc see Hay & Robertson Plc v. Kangol Ltd
Kansal v. United Kingdom (21413/02) (2004) 39 E.H.R.R. 31; [2004] B.P.I.R. 740;
   Times, April 29, 2004, ECHR . . . . *Digested*, 05/**2092**:
                                  Previous proceedings, 02/849
Kanssen v. Secretary of State for the Environment, Food and Rural Affairs [2005]
   EWHC 1024; [2005] N.P.C. 76, QBD (Admin)
KAO/External medication (T871/96) [2005] E.P.O.R. 19, EPO (Technical Bd App) . . . . *Digested*, 05/**2467**
KapHag Rendiefonds 35 Spreecenter Berlin-Hellersdorf 3 Tranche GbR v. Finanzamt
   Charlottenburg (C442/01) [2005] S.T.C. 1500; [2003] E.C.R. I-6851; [2005]
   B.T.C. 5535; [2005] B.V.C. 566; [2003] S.T.I. 1147, ECJ (6th Chamber) . . . . *Followed*, 05/4363
Kapniki Michailidis AE v. Idrima Kinonikon Asphaliseon (IKA) (C441/98); *sub nom*
   Kapniki Mikhailidis AE v. Idrima Kinonikon Asphaliseon (IKA) (C441/98) [2000]
   E.C.R. I-7145; [2001] 1 C.M.L.R. 13, ECJ (5th Chamber) . . . . *Digested*, 01/**5211**:
                                        Followed, 05/943
Kapniki Mikhailidis AE v. Idrima Kinonikon Asphaliseon (IKA) (C441/98) see Kapniki
   Michailidis AE v. Idrima Kinonikon Asphaliseon (IKA) (C441/98)
Karanakaran v. Secretary of State for the Home Department [2000] 3 All E.R. 449;
   [2000] Imm. A.R. 271; [2000] I.N.L.R. 122; (2000) 97(5) L.S.G. 34; (2000)
   97(10) L.S.G. 36; (2000) 144 S.J.L.B. 81; *Times*, February 16, 2000;
   Independent, February 4, 2000, CA (Civ Div) . . . . *Digested*, 00/**3307**:
                       Applied, 03/2218, 03/2275, 03/5733: *Considered*, 04/2043:
                           Followed, 02/5874, 02/5877, 05/2182
Karhuvaara v. Finland (53678/00) (2005) 41 E.H.R.R. 51, ECHR
Karling v. Purdue 2004 S.L.T. 1067; 2005 S.C.L.R. 43; [2005] P.N.L.R. 13; 2004
   G.W.D. 30-627; *Times*, October 15, 2004, OH . . . . *Digested*, 04/**4466**
Karner v. Austria (40016/98) [2003] 2 F.L.R. 623; [2004] 2 F.C.R. 563; (2004) 38
   E.H.R.R. 24; 14 B.H.R.C. 674; [2003] Fam. Law 724, ECHR . . . . *Digested*, 04/**1983**:
                                      Considered, 05/2118
Kashmiri v. Secretary of State for the Home Department see Huang v. Secretary of
   State for the Home Department
Kassam v. Touhey [2002] EWHC 675; [2005] B.P.I.R. 1370, Ch D
Kastner v. Jason; Sherman v. Kastner [2004] EWCA Civ 1599; [2005] 1 Lloyd's Rep.
   397; (2004) 148 S.J.L.B. 1436; [2004] N.P.C. 181; *Times*, December 21, 2004,
   CA (Civ Div); affirming [2004] EWHC 592; [2004] 2 Lloyd's Rep. 233; [2004]
   N.P.C. 47; [2004] 2 P. & C.R. DG2; *Times*, April 26, 2004, Ch D . . . . *Digested*, 05/**3384**
Kastor Navigation Co Ltd v. AGF MAT (The Kastor Too); *sub nom* Kastor Navigation Co
   Ltd v. Axa Global Risks (UK) Ltd (The Kastor Too) [2004] EWCA Civ 277;
   [2005] 2 All E.R. (Comm) 720; [2004] 2 Lloyd's Rep. 119; [2004] 2 C.L.C. 68;
   [2004] 4 Costs L.R. 569; [2004] Lloyd's Rep. I.R. 481; *Times*, April 29, 2004,
   CA (Civ Div); reversing in part [2002] EWHC 2601; [2003] 1 All E.R. (Comm)
   277; [2003] 1 Lloyd's Rep. 296; [2003] 2 C.L.C. 489; [2003] Lloyd's Rep. I.R.
   262, QBD (Comm) . . . . *Digested*, 04/**2225**
Kastor Navigation Co Ltd v. Axa Global Risks (UK) Ltd (The Kastor Too) see Kastor
   Navigation Co Ltd v. AGF MAT (The Kastor Too)
Kataria v. Essex Strategic HA [2004] EWHC 641; [2004] 3 All E.R. 572; [2004]
   Lloyd's Rep. Med. 215; (2005) 81 B.M.L.R. 179; (2004) 101(17) L.S.G. 32;
   Times, April 16, 2004, QBD (Admin) . . . . *Digested*, 04/**1626**
Katsikas v. Konstantinidis (C132/91); Skreb v. PCO Stauereibetrieb Paetz & Co
   Nachfolgar GmbH (C138/91); Scholl v. PCO Stauereibetrieb Paetz & Co
   Nachfolgar GmbH (C139/91) [1992] E.C.R. I-6577; [1993] 1 C.M.L.R. 845;
   [1993] I.R.L.R. 179, ECJ . . . . *Digested*, 93/**4280**:
                        Considered, 00/2228: *Followed*, 05/1314
Kaur v. Dhaliwal; *sub nom* Dhaliwal (A Child), Re [2005] EWCA Civ 743; [2005] 2
   F.C.R. 398, CA (Civ Div) . . . . *Digested*, 05/**1577**
Kaur v. MG Rover Group Ltd [2004] EWCA Civ 1507; [2005] I.C.R. 625; [2005]
   I.R.L.R. 40; *Times*, December 6, 2004, CA (Civ Div); reversing [2004] I.R.L.R.
   279, QBD . . . . *Digested*, 05/**1216**
Kausar v. Eagle Star Insurance Co Ltd; *sub nom* Eagle Star Insurance Co Ltd v. Kausar
   [1997] C.L.C. 129; [2000] Lloyd's Rep. I.R. 154; [1996] 5 Re. L.R. 191; (1996)
   140 S.J.L.B. 150; *Times*, July 15, 1996, CA (Civ Div) . . . . *Digested*, 96/**3574**:
                               Applied, 05/2401: *Followed*, 98/3363

Kawthar Consulting Ltd v. Revenue and Customs Commissioners see Netlogic
　　Consulting Ltd v. Revenue and Customs Commissioners
Kay v. Lambeth LBC; *sub nom* Lambeth LBC v. Kay; Gorman v. Lambeth LBC;
　　Constantine v. Lambeth LBC; Barnett v. Lambeth LBC; Cole v. Lambeth LBC;
　　Price v. Leeds City Council; Dymny v. Lambeth LBC; Leeds City Council v. Price;
　　TNS, HL; affirming [2004] EWCA Civ 926; [2005] Q.B. 352; [2004] 3 W.L.R.
　　1396; [2004] H.L.R. 56; *Times*, July 26, 2004, CA (Civ Div) . . . .　*Digested*, 04/**2535**:
　　　　　　　　　　　　　　　　Considered, 05/3424: *Previous proceedings*, 05/3424
Kay v. Whittle [2005] 2 Q.R. 15; [2004] 6 Q.R. 11, CC (Birkenhead) [*Ex rel*. Michael W
　　Halsall, Solicitors, 2 The Parks, Newton-le-Willows] . . . .　*Digested*, 04/**2986**
Kaya v. Haringey LBC [2001] EWCA Civ 677; [2002] H.L.R. 1; (2001) 98(25) L.S.G.
　　46; *Times*, June 14, 2001, CA (Civ Div) . . . .　*Digested*, 01/**3421**:
　　　　　　　　　　　　　　　　　　　　　　　Considered, 03/3944, 05/3882
Kaye v. Bourne [2004] EWHC 3236; [2005] B.P.I.R. 590, Ch D
Kazakhstan v. Istil Group Inc [2005] EWCA Civ 1468; *Times*, November 17, 2005, CA
　　(Civ Div); reversing [2005] EWHC 2309, QBD (Comm)
KE KELIT Kunststoffwerk GmbH v. Commission of the European Communities (C205/
　　02 P) see Dansk Rorindustri A/S v. Commission of the European Communities
　　(C189/02 P)
Keam v. Department for Environment, Food and Rural Affairs see R. (on the
　　application of Keam) v. Department for Environment, Food and Rural Affairs
Kean v. Harker see Harker's Will Trusts, Re
Kearns v. General Council of the Bar [2003] EWCA Civ 331; [2003] 1 W.L.R. 1357;
　　[2003] 2 All E.R. 534; [2003] E.M.L.R. 27; (2003) 153 N.L.J. 482; (2003) 147
　　S.J.L.B. 476, CA (Civ Div); affirming [2002] EWHC 1681; [2002] 4 All E.R.
　　1075; *Independent*, November 4, 2002 (C.S), QBD . . . .　*Digested*, 03/**956**:
　　　　　　　　　　　　　　　　　　　　　　　　　　　　　Applied, 05/976
Kearsley v. Klarfeld; *sub nom* Kearsley v. Klarfield [2005] EWCA Civ 1510;
　　Independent, December 16, 2005, CA (Civ Div)
Kearsley v. Klarfield see Kearsley v. Klarfeld
Keating v. Bromley LBC (No.2) see X (Minors) v. Bedfordshire CC
Kebbell Development Ltd v. First Secretary of State; *sub nom* R. (on the application of
　　Kebbell Development Ltd) v. First Secretary of State [2003] EWCA Civ 1855;
　　[2004] J.P.L. 1710, CA (Civ Div); reversing [2003] EWHC 902; [2003] 2 P.L.R.
　　52; [2004] J.P.L. 353, QBD (Admin) . . . .　*Digested*, 05/**3310**
Kebbell Homes Ltd v. Fareham BC [2005] P.A.D. 77, Planning Inspector
Keedy v. First West Yorkshire Ltd (Unreported, December 20, 2004), CC (Leeds) [*Ex
　　rel*. Tom Nossiter, Barrister, Park Lane Chambers, 19, Westgate, Leeds] . . . .　*Digested*, 05/**3145**
Keeley v. Pashen [2004] EWCA Civ 1491; [2005] 1 W.L.R. 1226; [2005] R.T.R. 10;
　　[2005] Lloyd's Rep. I.R. 289; (2004) 101(45) L.S.G. 32; *Times*, November 17,
　　2004, CA (Civ Div) . . . .　*Digested*, 05/**2376**
Keesoondoyal v. BP Oil UK Ltd [2004] EWCA Civ 708; [2004] C.P. Rep. 40, CA (Civ
　　Div) . . . .　*Digested*, 05/**486**
Kefalas v. Greece (C367/96) [1998] E.C.R. I-2843; [1999] 2 C.M.L.R. 144, ECJ . . . . .　*Digested*, 99/**645**:
　　　　　　　　　　　　　　　　　　　　　　　　　　　　Applied, 05/4380
Kehinde, Re (Unreported, December 19, 2001), IAT . . . .　*Considered*, 02/2594,
　　　　　　　　　　　　　　　　　　　　　　　　　　　　　　　05/2195
Kehoe v. Secretary of State for Work and Pensions see R. (on the application of
　　Kehoe) v. Secretary of State for Work and Pensions
Kehoe v. Williams-Sonoma Inc [2005] E.T.M.R. 74, OHIM (Cancellation Div) . . . .　*Digested*, 05/**2537**
Kellar v. Williams [2004] UKPC 30; [2005] 4 Costs L.R. 559; (2004) 148 S.J.L.B.
　　821, PC (TCI)
Kelly v. Hammersmith LBC see R. (on the application of Kelly) v. Hammersmith and
　　Fulham LBC
Kelly v. Mersey Docks & Harbour Co [2004] EWCA Civ 1676; [2005] O.P.L.R. 341;
　　[2005] Pens. L.R. 133, CA (Civ Div) . . . .　*Digested*, 05/**2969**
Kemble v. Hicks (No.1) see Scientific Investment Pension Plan (No.2), Re
Kemnal Manor Memorial Gardens Ltd v. First Secretary of State [2005] EWCA Civ 835;
　　[2005] J.P.L. 1568, CA (Civ Div); affirming [2004] EWHC 2638; [2005] 2 P.
　　& C.R. 12; [2004] N.P.C. 173, QBD (Admin) . . . .　*Digested*, 05/**3247**
Kempe v. Inland Revenue Commissioners [2004] S.T.C. (S.C.D.) 467; [2004] W.T.L.R.
　　955; [2004] S.T.I. 1941, Sp Comm . . . .　*Digested*, 05/**4119**
Kemsley v. DPP [2004] EWHC 278; [2005] 169 J.P. 148; (2005) 169 J.P.N. 239,
　　QBD (Admin) . . . .　*Digested*, 05/**874**
Kemsley v. Foot [1952] A.C. 345; [1952] 1 All E.R. 501; [1952] 1 T.L.R. 532; 96 S.J.
　　165, HL; affirming [1951] 2 K.B. 34; [1951] 1 All E.R. 331; [1951] 1 T.L.R. 197,
　　CA . . . .　*Digested*, 52/**2002**:
　　　　　　　　　　Applied, 59/1866, 61/4995, 68/2233, 69/2082, 05/982:
　　　　　　　　　　　　　　　　Considered, 91/2323, 92/2789
Kennedy v. Crown Prosecution Service; *sub nom* Kennedy v. DPP [2002] EWHC
　　2297; (2003) 167 J.P. 267; [2004] R.T.R. 6; [2003] Crim. L.R. 120; (2003) 167
　　J.P.N. 412, QBD (Admin) . . . .　*Digested*, 03/**778**:
　　　　　　　　　Applied, 04/733, 04/799: *Considered*, 04/685, 05/739
Kennedy v. DPP see Kennedy v. Crown Prosecution Service

KENNEDY INSTITUTE OF RHEUMATOLOGY/Treatment of autoimmune disorders (T188/04) [2005] E.P.O.R. 51, EPO (Technical Bd App)

Kennemer Golf & Country Club v. Inspecteur Belastingdienst Particulieren/Ondernemingen Haarlem (C174/00) see Kennemer Golf & Country Club v. Staatssecretaris van Financien (C174/00)

Kennemer Golf & Country Club v. Staatssecretaris van Financien (C174/00); *sub nom* Kennemer Golf & Country Club v. Inspecteur Belastingdienst Particulieren/Ondernemingen Haarlem (C174/00) [2002] Q.B. 1252; [2002] 3 W.L.R. 829; [2002] All E.R. (EC) 480; [2002] S.T.C. 502; [2002] E.C.R. I-3293; [2002] 2 C.M.L.R. 12; [2002] C.E.C. 330; [2002] B.T.C. 5205; [2002] B.V.C. 395; [2002] S.T.I. 354; *Times*, April 11, 2002, ECJ (5th Chamber) . . . . *Digested*, 02/**4756**:
                 Considered, 05/4358: *Followed*, 02/4758

Kensington and Chelsea RBC v. Sager House (Chelsea) Ltd [2005] P.A.D. 47, Planning Inspector

Kent v. First Secretary of State see R. (on the application of Kent) v. First Secretary of State

Kent CC v. G see G (A Child) (Interim Care Order: Residential Assessment), Re

Kent CC v. Green see Green v. Victoria Road Primary School Governing Body

Kent Pharmaceuticals Ltd v. Director of the Serious Fraud Office [2002] EWHC 3023, QBD . . . . *Applied*, 05/**930**:
                 Subsequent proceedings, 04/1615

Kenyon-Brown v. Desmond Banks & Co (Undue Influence) (No.2) see Royal Bank of Scotland Plc v. Etridge (No.2)

Keondjian v. Kay [2004] EWHC 2820; [2005] 1 P. & C.R. DG20, Ch D

Kerr v. British Leyland (Staff) Trustees Ltd [2001] W.T.L.R. 1071, CA (Civ Div) . . . . *Digested*, 02/**3366**:
                 Considered, 05/4304

Kerry Foods Ltd v. Lynch [2005] I.R.L.R. 681, EAT

Kershaw v. Thrower & Hammond Electrical & Mechanical Services Ltd [2005] 2 Q.R. 22; [2004] 6 Q.R. 6, CC (Barnstaple) [*Ex rel*. Timothy Briden, Barrister, Lamb Chambers, Lamb Building, Temple, London] . . . . *Digested*, 04/**2860**

Kesko Oy v. Commission of the European Communities (T22/97) [1999] E.C.R. II-3775; [2000] 4 C.M.L.R. 335, CFI (2nd Chamber) . . . . *Digested*, 00/**723**:
                 Applied, 05/582

Kesslar v. Moore & Tibbits (A Firm); *sub nom* Kesslar v. Moore & Tibbs [2004] EWCA Civ 1551; [2005] P.N.L.R. 17; (2004) 148 S.J.L.B. 1316; [2004] N.P.C. 163, CA (Civ Div) . . . . *Digested*, 05/**480**:
                 Considered, 05/315

Ketteman v. Hansel Properties Ltd [1987] A.C. 189; [1987] 2 W.L.R. 312; [1988] 1 All E.R. 38; 36 B.L.R. 1; [1987] 1 F.T.L.R. 284; 85 L.G.R. 409; [1987] 1 E.G.L.R. 237; (1987) 84 L.S.G. 657; (1987) 137 N.L.J. 100; (1987) 131 S.J. 134, HL; affirming [1984] 1 W.L.R. 1274; [1985] 1 All E.R. 352; 27 B.L.R. 1; (1985) 49 P. & C.R. 257; (1984) 271 E.G. 1099; [1984] C.I.L.L. 109; (1984) 81 L.S.G. 3018; (1984) 128 S.J. 800, CA (Civ Div) . . . . *Digested*, 87/**2330**:
      Applied, 86/1993, 89/3048, 00/473, 05/436: *Considered*, 87/229, 88/2158, 89/2093, 90/3623, 92/581, 92/3401, 92/3575, 92/3581, 93/3127, 93/3299, 94/3746, 05/476: *Distinguished*, 93/1760: *Referred to*, 93/2613, 93/3613, 03/2629

Key Finance Ltd v. Revenue and Customs Commissioners [2005] S.T.I. 1730, V&DTr

Keydon Estates Ltd v. Eversheds LLP [2005] EWHC 972; [2005] P.N.L.R. 40; [2005] 21 E.G.C.S. 139; [2005] N.P.C. 69, Ch D . . . . *Digested*, 05/**962**

KF v. Secretary of State for the Home Department; *sub nom* KF (Removal Directions: Statelessness: Iran), Re [2005] UKIAT 109; [2005] Imm. A.R. 458, IAT

KF (Removal Directions: Statelessness: Iran), Re see KF v. Secretary of State for the Home Department

Khalfaoui v. France (34791/97) (2001) 31 E.H.R.R. 42, ECHR . . . . *Digested*, 01/**3499**:
                 Followed, 05/2078

Khan v. Chief Constable of West Yorkshire see Chief Constable of West Yorkshire v. Khan

Khan v. General Medical Council [1996] I.C.R. 1032; [1994] I.R.L.R. 646; *Independent*, April 11, 1994 (C.S.), CA (Civ Div); affirming [1993] I.C.R. 627; [1993] I.R.L.R. 378; *Times*, March 29, 1993; *Independent*, March 24, 1993, EAT . . *Digested*, 95/**2027**:
                 Applied, 05/1293

Khan v. Inland Revenue Commissioners see Toshoku Finance UK Plc (In Liquidation), Re

Khan v. Revenue and Customs Commissioners see Khan (t/a Greyhound Dry Cleaners) v. Customs and Excise Commissioners

Khan v. Royal Air Force Summary Appeal Court [2004] EWHC 2230; [2004] H.R.L.R. 40; [2005] A.C.D. 39; *Times*, October 28, 2004, QBD (Admin) . . . . . . *Digested*, 04/**1925**

Khan v. Trinidad and Tobago [2003] UKPC 79; [2005] 1 A.C. 374; [2004] 2 W.L.R. 692; 16 B.H.R.C. 184; (2004) 101(2) L.S.G. 28; *Times*, November 26, 2003, PC (Trin) . . . . *Digested*, 04/**584**:
                 Considered, 05/773

Khan (t/a Greyhound Dry Cleaners) *v.* Customs and Excise Commissioners; *sub nom* Khan *v.* Revenue and Customs Commissioners; C3/2005/1015, CA (Civ Div); affirming [2005] EWHC 653; [2005] S.T.C. 1271; [2005] B.T.C. 5487; [2005] B.V.C. 518; [2005] S.T.I. 863, Ch D .... *Digested*, 05/**4414**

Khashoggi *v.* IPC Magazines Ltd [1986] 1 W.L.R. 1412; [1986] 3 All E.R. 577; (1986) 83 L.S.G. 3598; (1986) 136 N.L.J. 1111; (1986) 130 S.J. 862, CA (Civ Div) .... *Digested*, 86/**1990**: *Considered*, 89/2250, 05/970

Khatun *v.* Newham LBC see R. (on the application of Khatun) *v.* Newham LBC

Khudados *v.* Leggate [2005] I.C.R. 1013; [2005] I.R.L.R. 540, EAT .... *Digested*, 05/**1242**

Kiam *v.* MGN Ltd (Costs) [2002] EWCA Civ 66; [2002] 1 W.L.R. 2810; [2002] 2 All E.R. 242; [2002] C.P. Rep. 30; [2002] E.M.L.R. 26; *Independent*, March 25, 2002 (CS), CA (Civ Div) .... *Digested*, 02/**347**: *Applied*, 03/342, 05/2728

Kien Tran *v.* Greenwich Vietnam Community Project see Tran *v.* Greenwich Vietnam Community Project

Kigass Aero Components Ltd *v.* Brown see Brown *v.* Kigass Aero Components Ltd

Kilcarne Holdings Ltd *v.* Targetfollow (Birmingham) Ltd [2005] EWCA Civ 1355; [2005] N.P.C. 132, CA (Civ Div); affirming [2004] EWHC 2547; [2005] 2 P. & C.R. 8; [2004] N.P.C. 167, Ch D .... *Digested*, 05/**695**

Kilhey Court Hotels Ltd *v.* Wigan MBC [2004] EWHC 2890; (2005) 169 J.P. 1; [2005] A.C.D. 66; (2005) 169 J.P.N. 58, QBD (Admin) .... *Digested*, 05/**1760**

Kilnoore Ltd (In Liquidation), Re see Unidare Plc *v.* Cohen

Kimber *v.* Brookman Solicitors [2004] 2 F.L.R. 221; [2004] Fam. Law 649, Fam Div .. *Digested*, 05/**1655**

Kinane *v.* Almack Marketing Services Ltd see Kinane *v.* Mackie-Conteh

Kinane *v.* Mackie-Conteh; Kinane *v.* Almack Marketing Services Ltd [2005] EWCA Civ 45; [2005] W.T.L.R. 345; [2005] 6 E.G.C.S. 140; (2005) 149 S.J.L.B. 177; [2005] 2 P. & C.R. DG3, CA (Civ Div); affirming in part [2004] EWHC 998; [2004] 19 E.G.C.S. 164, Ch D

KINDER Trade Marks see Ferrero SpA's Trade Marks

King *v.* Brandywine Reinsurance Co (UK) Ltd (formerly Cigna RE Co (UK) Ltd) [2005] EWCA Civ 235; [2005] 2 All E.R. (Comm) 1; [2005] 1 Lloyd's Rep. 655; [2005] 1 C.L.C. 283; [2005] Env. L.R. 33; [2005] Lloyd's Rep. I.R. 509, CA (Civ Div); affirming [2004] EWHC 1033; [2004] 2 All E.R. (Comm) 443; [2004] 2 Lloyd's Rep. 670; [2004] 2 C.L.C. 981; [2004] Lloyd's Rep. I.R. 554, QBD (Comm) .... *Digested*, 05/**2408**

King *v.* Eaton Ltd (No.2); *sub nom* Eaton Ltd *v.* King 1999 S.L.T. 656; 1998 S.C.L.R. 1017; [1998] I.R.L.R. 686; 1998 G.W.D. 27-1381, IH (2 Div)............... *Digested*, 99/**6048**: *Followed*, 05/1333

King *v.* Lewis; *sub nom* Lewis *v.* King [2004] EWCA Civ 1329; [2005] I.L.Pr. 16; [2005] E.M.L.R. 4; (2004) 148 S.J.L.B. 1248; *Times*, October 26, 2004; *Independent*, November 11, 2004, CA (Civ Div); affirming [2004] EWHC 168; [2004] I.L.Pr. 31, QBD... *Digested*, 05/**611**

King *v.* Telegraph Group Ltd [2004] EWCA Civ 613; [2005] 1 W.L.R. 2282; [2004] C.P. Rep. 35; [2004] 3 Costs L.R. 449; [2004] E.M.L.R. 23; (2004) 101(25) L.S.G. 27; (2004) 154 N.L.J. 823; (2004) 148 S.J.L.B. 664; *Times*, May 21, 2004, CA (Civ Div); affirming [2003] EWHC 1312, QBD .... *Digested*, 04/**326**: *Applied*, 05/354

King *v.* United Kingdom (13881/02) [2005] S.T.C. 438; (2005) 41 E.H.R.R. 2; 76 T.C. 699; 7 I.T.L. Rep. 339; [2004] S.T.I. 2396; *Times*, November 23, 2004, ECHR... *Digested*, 05/**2086**

King's Prosecutor (Brussels) *v.* Cando Armas see Office of the King's Prosecutor (Brussels) *v.* Armas

Kingfisher Plc *v.* Customs and Excise Commissioners [2004] V. & D.R. 206, V&DTr (London) .... *Digested*, 05/**4417**

Kings *v.* Barker (Inspector of Taxes) see Kings *v.* King (Inspector of Taxes)

Kings *v.* King (Inspector of Taxes); Kings *v.* Barker (Inspector of Taxes) [2004] S.T.C. (S.C.D.) 186; [2004] S.T.I. 1030, Sp Comm .... *Digested*, 05/**4064**

Kingscrest Associates Ltd *v.* Customs and Excise Commissioners (C498/03) [2005] S.T.C. 1547; [2005] E.C.R. I-4427; [2005] 2 C.M.L.R. 57; [2005] S.T.I. 1019; *Times*, June 9, 2005, ECJ (3rd Chamber)

Kingston Upon Hull City Council *v.* Dunnachie (No.1) see Dunnachie *v.* Kingston upon Hull City Council

Kiriacoulis Lines SA *v.* Compagnie d'Assurances Maritimes Aeriennes et Terrestres (CAMAT) (The Demetra K) [2002] EWCA Civ 1070; [2002] 2 Lloyd's Rep. 581; [2003] 1 C.L.C. 579; [2002] Lloyd's Rep. I.R. 795, CA (Civ Div); affirming 1197, QBD (Comm) .... *Digested*, 05/**2385**

Kirin-Amgen Inc *v.* Hoechst Marion Roussel Ltd (No.2) see Kirin-Amgen Inc *v.* Transkaryotic Therapies Inc (No.2)

Kirin-Amgen Inc v. Transkaryotic Therapies Inc (No.2); *sub nom* Kirin-Amgen Inc's European Patent (No.148605) (No.2); Kirin-Amgen Inc v. Hoechst Marion Roussel Ltd (No.2) [2004] UKHL 46; [2005] 1 All E.R. 667; [2005] R.P.C. 9; (2005) 28(7) I.P.D. 28049; (2004) 148 S.J.L.B. 1249, HL; affirming [2002] EWCA Civ 1096; [2003] E.N.P.R. 4; [2003] R.P.C. 3; (2002) 25(11) I.P.D. 25076, CA (Civ Div); reversing in part [2002] R.P.C. 2; (2001) 24(8) I.P.D. 24051; (2001) 98(24) L.S.G. 45; *Times*, June 1, 2001, Ch D (Patents Ct) . . . . . .   *Digested*, 05/**2479**:
Considered, 04/363: *Previous proceedings*, 02/2820

Kirin-Amgen Inc v. Transkaryotic Therapies Inc (No.4) see Kirin-Amgen Inc's European Patent (No.148605) (Relief Pending Appeal)

Kirin-Amgen Inc's European Patent (No.148605) (No.2) see Kirin-Amgen Inc v. Transkaryotic Therapies Inc (No.2)

Kirin-Amgen Inc's European Patent (No.148605) (Relief Pending Appeal); *sub nom* Kirin-Amgen Inc v. Transkaryotic Therapies Inc (No.4) [2005] F.S.R. 41; (2001) 24(12) I.P.D. 24080, Ch D (Patents Ct)

Kirker v. Ambitions Personnel (Nottinghamshire) Ltd see Rhys-Harper v. Relaxion Group Plc

Kirker v. British Sugar Plc see Rhys-Harper v. Relaxion Group Plc

Kirklees MBC v. Brook [2004] EWHC 2841; [2005] 2 P. & C.R. 17; [2005] 2 P.L.R. 40, Ch D

Kirklees MBC v. S (Contact to Newborn Babies); *sub nom* S (A Child) (Care Proceedings: Contact), Re [2005] Fam. Law 768; *Times*, September 22, 2005, Fam Div

Kirkman-Moeller, Re [2005] EWHC 381; [2005] B.P.I.R. 1136, Ch D

Kirkup v. DPP [2003] EWHC 2354; (2004) 168 J.P. 255; [2004] Crim. L.R. 230; (2004) 168 J.P.N. 357, QBD (Admin) . . . .   *Digested*, 04/**799**:
Applied, 05/739

Kjartan Asmundsson v. Iceland (60669/00) (2005) 41 E.H.R.R. 42, ECHR

KK v. Secretary of State for the Home Department; *sub nom* KK: Article 1F(C): Turkey, Re [2004] UKIAT 101; [2004] Imm. A.R. 284; [2005] I.N.L.R. 124, IAT . . . .   *Digested*, 05/**2228**

KK: Article 1F(C): Turkey, Re see KK v. Secretary of State for the Home Department

Klamer v. Kyriakides & Braier (A Firm) [2005] B.P.I.R. 1142, Ch D

Klein v. Rhodos Management Ltd [2005] I.L.Pr. 17, OLG (Hamm)

Kleinwort Benson Ltd v. Birmingham City Council see Kleinwort Benson Ltd v. Lincoln City Council

Kleinwort Benson Ltd v. Kensington and Chelsea RLBC see Kleinwort Benson Ltd v. Lincoln City Council

Kleinwort Benson Ltd v. Lincoln City Council; Kleinwort Benson Ltd v. Birmingham City Council; Kleinwort Benson Ltd v. Southwark LBC; Kleinwort Benson Ltd v. Kensington and Chelsea RLBC [1999] 2 A.C. 349; [1998] 3 W.L.R. 1095; [1998] 4 All E.R. 513; [1998] Lloyd's Rep. Bank. 387; [1999] C.L.C. 332; (1999) 1 L.G.L.R. 148; (1999) 11 Admin. L.R. 130; [1998] R.V.R. 315; (1998) 148 N.L.J. 1674; (1998) 142 S.J.L.B. 279; [1998] N.P.C. 145; *Times*, October 30, 1998; *Independent*, November 4, 1998, HL . . . .   *Digested*, 98/**2297**:
Applied, 99/2218, 03/4142, 04/383: *Considered*, 99/532, 03/1579, 05/4129:
Not applied, 04/3173: *Previous proceedings*, 96/425

Kleinwort Benson Ltd v. Sandwell BC see Westdeutsche Landesbank Girozentrale v. Islington LBC

Kleinwort Benson Ltd v. Southwark LBC see Kleinwort Benson Ltd v. Lincoln City Council

Kmetty v. Hungary (57967/00) (2005) 40 E.H.R.R. 6, ECHR . . . .   *Digested*, 05/**2059**

Knapp v. Ecclesiastical Insurance Group Plc [1998] Lloyd's Rep. I.R. 390; [1998] P.N.L.R. 172; *Times*, November 17, 1997, CA (Civ Div) . . . .   *Digested*, 97/**645**:
Applied, 01/4526, 03/3003: *Cited*, 99/3365: *Considered*, 00/2621:
Distinguished, 05/443

Knight v. Harrow LBC; *sub nom* Harrow LBC v. Knight [2003] I.R.L.R. 140, EAT . . . . . .   *Digested*, 03/**1354**:
Considered, 05/1281

Knowles v. Culmer (Superintendent of Fox Hill Prison) [2005] UKPC 17; [2005] 1 W.L.R. 2546, PC (Bah) . . . .   *Digested*, 05/**1483**

Knox v. Dean; *sub nom* Knox v. Deane [2005] UKPC 25; [2005] B.C.C. 884, PC (Bar). . . . .   *Digested*, 05/**536**

Knox v. Deane see Knox v. Dean

Koca v. Secretary of State for the Home Department 2005 S.C. 487; 2005 S.L.T. 838; [2005] I.N.L.R. 506; 2005 G.W.D. 25-488, IH (1 Div); reversing 2002 G.W.D. 38-1263, OH . . . .   *Digested*, 05/**5433**

Kocak v. Landesversicherungsanstalt Oberfranken und Mittelfranken (C102/98); Ors v. Bundesknappschaft (C211/98) [2000] E.C.R. I-1287; [2004] 2 C.M.L.R. 46, ECJ . . . .   *Digested*, 05/**3889**

Kochar v. Commissioner of Police of the Metropolis see Yearwood v. Commissioner of Police of the Metropolis

Koeller v. Coleg Elidyr (Camphill Communities Wales) Ltd; *sub nom* Colleg Elidyr (Camphill Communities Wales) Ltd v. Koeller [2005] EWCA Civ 856; [2005] 2 B.C.L.C. 379; [2005] N.P.C. 90, CA (Civ Div)

Koffiebranderij en Theehandel Drie Mollen Sinds 1818 BV *v.* Office for Harmonisation in the Internal Market (Trade Marks and Designs) (OHIM) (T66/03) [2005] E.T.M.R. 33, CFI . . . . *Digested*, 05/**2538**

Kohler *v.* Finanzamt Dusseldorf-Nord (C58/04) [2005] S.T.I. 1603, ECJ (1st Chamber)

Kolanis *v.* United Kingdom (517/02) (2005) 84 B.M.L.R. 102; *Times*, July 28, 2005, ECHR

Kolomoisky *v.* Shahar see Shahar *v.* Tsitsekkos

Konamaneni *v.* Rolls Royce Industrial Power (India) Ltd [2002] 1 W.L.R. 1269; [2002] 1 All E.R. 979; [2002] 1 All E.R. (Comm) 532; [2003] B.C.C. 790; [2002] 1 B.C.L.C. 336; [2002] I.L.Pr. 40; *Times*, January 31, 2002, Ch D . . . . *Digested*, 02/**619**:
Approved, 05/615

Konami Corp's Patent Application [2004] Info.T.L.R. 241, PO . . . . *Digested*, 05/**2446**

Koninklijke KPN Nederland NV *v.* Benelux-Merkenbureau (C363/99) [2005] 3 W.L.R. 649; [2005] All E.R. (EC) 19; [2005] 2 C.M.L.R. 10; [2005] C.E.C. 216; [2004] E.T.M.R. 57, ECJ (6th Chamber). . . . . *Digested*, 05/**2437**:
Applied, 05/2529: *Considered*, 05/2532

Koninklijke Philips Electronics NV *v.* Rayovac Europe Ltd see Koninklijke Philips Electronics NV *v.* Remington Consumer Products Ltd

Koninklijke Philips Electronics NV *v.* Remington Consumer Products Ltd; Koninklijke Philips Electronics NV *v.* Rayovac Europe Ltd; A3/2004/2448, CA (Civ Div); reversing in part [2004] EWHC 2327; [2005] F.S.R. 17; (2005) 28(1) I.P.D. 27110; *Times*, November 2, 2004, Ch D . . . . *Digested*, 05/**2578**:
Previous proceedings, 02/2903

Koninklijke Philips Electronics NV *v.* Remington Consumer Products Ltd (C299/99); *sub nom* Philips Electronics NV *v.* Remington Consumer Products Ltd (C299/99) [2003] Ch. 159; [2003] 2 W.L.R. 294; [2002] All E.R. (EC) 634; [2002] E.C.R. I-5475; [2002] 2 C.M.L.R. 52; [2002] C.E.C. 525; [2002] E.T.M.R. 81; [2003] R.P.C. 2; (2002) 25(9) I.P.D. 25060; *Times*, June 20, 2002; *Daily Telegraph*, June 27, 2002, ECJ [2002] E.C.R. I-5475; [2001] E.T.M.R. 48; [2001] R.P.C. 38, AGO . . . . *Digested*, 02/**2903**:
Applied, 03/2632, 05/2438, 05/2578: *Considered*, 03/2613, 03/2631, 05/2533: *Followed*, 05/2548

Koninklijke Philips Electronics NV *v.* Rotary Shaver Sweden AB [2005] E.T.M.R. 103, HR (Stockholm)

Konkola Copper Mines Plc *v.* Coromin Ltd A3/2005/1148, CA (Civ Div); affirming [2005] EWHC 898; [2005] 2 All E.R. (Comm) 637; [2005] 2 Lloyd's Rep. 555; [2005] 1 C.L.C. 1021; [2005] I.L.Pr. 39, QBD (Comm) . . . . *Digested*, 05/**2406**

Konttinen *v.* Finland (24949/94) (1996) 87 D. & R. 68, Eur Comm HR . . . . *Applied*, 05/1328

Koonjul *v.* Thameslink Healthcare Services [2000] P.I.Q.R. P123; *Times*, May 19, 2000, CA (Civ Div) . . . . *Digested*, 00/**2983**:
Applied, 00/2970, 02/2222: *Considered*, 05/1957: *Followed*, 01/3305

Kopecky *v.* Slovakia (44912/98) (2005) 41 E.H.R.R. 43, ECHR (Grand Chamber)

Kotke *v.* Saffarini [2005] EWCA Civ 221; [2005] 2 F.L.R. 517; [2005] 1 F.C.R. 642; [2005] P.I.Q.R. P26; [2005] Fam. Law 535; (2005) 155 N.L.J. 414; *Independent*, March 16, 2005, CA (Civ Div) . . . . *Digested*, 05/**55**

Koubi *v.* Office for Harmonisation in the Internal Market (Trade Marks and Designs) (OHIM) (T10/03) [2004] E.C.R. II-719; [2004] E.T.M.R. 61, CFI (4th Chamber) . *Digested*, 05/**2509**

Kovacs *v.* Queen Mary and Westfield College [2002] EWCA Civ 352; [2002] I.C.R. 919; [2002] I.R.L.R. 414; [2002] Emp. L.R. 940; (2002) 99(19) L.S.G. 29; (2002) 146 S.J.L.B. 91; *Times*, April 12, 2002, CA (Civ Div); affirming EAT/1157/99, EAT. . . . . *Digested*, 02/**1348**:
Considered, 05/1220

KPN Telecom BV *v.* Onafhankelijke Post en Telecommunicatie Autoriteit (OPTA) (C109/03) [2004] E.C.R. I-11273; [2005] Info.T.L.R. 271, ECJ (1st Chamber)

KR *v.* Bryn Alyn Community (Holdings) Ltd (In Liquidation); *sub nom* Various Claimants *v.* BACHL; Various Claimants *v.* Bryn Alyn Community (Holdings) Ltd (In Liquidation) [2003] EWCA Civ 85; [2003] 3 W.L.R. 107; [2004] 2 All E.R. 716; [2003] 1 F.L.R. 1203; [2003] 1 F.C.R. 385; [2003] Lloyd's Rep. Med. 175; [2003] Fam. Law 482; *Times*, February 17, 2003, CA (Civ Div); affirming HQ/99/01473, QBD . . . . *Digested*, 03/**432**:
Applied, 05/2859

Kranemann *v.* Land Nordrhein-Westfalen (C109/04) [2005] E.C.R. I-2421; [2005] 2 C.M.L.R. 15; [2005] C.E.C. 707, ECJ (1st Chamber) . . . . *Digested*, 05/**1461**

Krasner *v.* Dennison; *sub nom* Lesser *v.* Lawrence; Dennison *v.* Krasner; Lawrence *v.* Lesser [2001] Ch. 76; [2000] 3 W.L.R. 720; [2000] 3 All E.R. 234; [2000] B.P.I.R. 410; [2000] O.P.L.R. 299; [2000] Pens. L.R. 213; (2000) 97(19) L.S.G. 42; (2000) 150 N.L.J. 543; (2000) 144 S.J.L.B. 205; *Times*, April 18, 2000, CA (Civ Div) . . . . *Digested*, 00/**3444**:
Followed, 03/2364, 05/2278

Krasner *v.* McMath see Huddersfield Fine Worsteds Ltd, Re

Krastanov *v.* Bulgaria (50222/99) (2005) 41 E.H.R.R. 50, ECHR

Kretztechnik AG v. Finanzamt Linz (C465/03) [2005] 1 W.L.R. 3755; [2005] S.T.C.
   1118; [2005] 2 C.M.L.R. 46; [2005] B.T.C. 5823; [2005] S.T.I. 1020; *Times*, June
   21, 2005, ECJ (1st Chamber) . . . .   *Digested*, 05/**4363**:
                              Considered, 05/4371
Krone Verlag GmbH & Co KG v. Austria (40284/98) (2004) 39 E.H.R.R. 42, ECHR . . .   *Digested*, 05/**2047**
Kronhofer v. Maier (C168/02) [2004] All E.R. (EC) 939; [2004] 2 All E.R. (Comm)
   759; [2005] 1 Lloyd's Rep. 284; [2004] I.L.Pr. 27, ECJ (2nd Chamber) . . . .   *Digested*, 05/**603**
Krotov v. Secretary of State for the Home Department [2004] EWCA Civ 69; [2004]
   1 W.L.R. 1825; [2004] I.N.L.R. 304; *Times*, February 26, 2004, CA (Civ Div) . . .   *Digested*, 05/**2178**:
                              Applied, 05/5439
Kruja v. Enfield LBC; *sub nom* Enfield LBC v. Kruja [2004] EWCA Civ 1769; [2005]
   H.L.R. 13, CA (Civ Div) . . . .   *Digested*, 05/**2006**
Krupp Thyssen Stainless GmbH v. Commission of the European Communities (T45/98);
   sub nom Stainless Steel Cartel (T45/98), Re; Acciai Speciali Terni SpA v.
   Commission of the European Communities (T47/98) [2001] E.C.R. II-3757;
   [2002] 4 C.M.L.R. 15, CFI (1st Chamber) . . . .   *Digested*, 02/**574**:
                              Followed, 05/554
KU (A Child) v. Liverpool City Council see U (A Child) v. Liverpool City Council
Kuala Pertang Syndicate v. Inland Revenue Commissioners see Brooklands Selangor
   Holdings v. Inland Revenue Commissioners
Kuddus v. Chief Constable of Leicestershire [2001] UKHL 29; [2002] 2 A.C. 122;
   [2001] 2 W.L.R. 1789; [2001] 3 All E.R. 193; (2001) 3 L.G.L.R. 45; (2001)
   98(28) L.S.G. 43; (2001) 151 N.L.J. 936; (2001) 145 S.J.L.B. 166; *Times*, June
   13, 2001; *Independent*, June 12, 2001; *Daily Telegraph*, June 12, 2001, HL;
   reversing (2000) 2 L.G.L.R. 822; *Times*, March 16, 2000; *Independent*, February
   17, 2000, CA (Civ Div) . . . .   *Digested*, 01/**1512**:
       Applied, 04/2510: *Considered*, 04/1306, 05/956: *Explained*, 05/1263
Kuijer v. Council of the European Union (T188/98) [2000] E.C.R. II-1959; [2000] 2
   C.M.L.R. 400; *Times*, April 14, 2000, CFI (4th Chamber) . . . .   *Digested*, 00/**2392**:
                              Applied, 05/1425
Kuijper v. Netherlands (Admissibility) (64848/01) (2005) 41 E.H.R.R. SE16, ECHR
Kundrath v. Harry Kwatia & Gooding (A Firm) [2004] EWHC 2852; [2005] 2 Costs
   L.R. 279, QBD . . . .   *Digested*, 05/**361**
Kurz v. Land Baden-Wurttemberg (C188/00) [2002] E.C.R. I-10691, ECJ . . . .   *Considered*, 05/2206
Kus v. Landeshauptstadt Wiesbaden (C237/91) [1992] E.C.R. I-6781; [1993] 2
   C.M.L.R. 887, ECJ . . . .   *Digested*, 93/**4348**:
                      Considered, 96/3292, 05/2229
Kutic v. Croatia (48778/99) (Unreported, March 1, 2002), ECHR . . . .   *Considered*, 05/2073
Kutz-Bauer v. Freie und Hansestadt Hamburg (C187/00) [2003] E.C.R. I-2741; [2005]
   2 C.M.L.R. 35; [2003] I.R.L.R. 368; [2003] Pens. L.R. 125, ECJ (6th
   Chamber) . . . .   *Digested*, 03/**1276**
Kuwait Airways Corp v. Iraq Airways Co (No.6) see Kuwait Airways Corp v. Iraqi
   Airways Co (No.6)
Kuwait Airways Corp v. Iraqi Airways Co (Disclosure: Fraud Exception) [2005] EWCA
   Civ 286; [2005] 1 W.L.R. 2734; [2005] C.P. Rep. 32; (2005) 102(21) L.S.G.
   33; (2005) 155 N.L.J. 468; *Times*, April 25, 2005, CA (Civ Div); affirming
   [2005] EWHC 367, QBD (Comm) . . . .   *Digested*, 05/**294**
Kuwait Airways Corp v. Iraqi Airways Co (No.5) see Kuwait Airways Corp v. Iraqi
   Airways Co (No.6)
Kuwait Airways Corp v. Iraqi Airways Co (No.6); *sub nom* Kuwait Airways Corp v. Iraq
   Airways Co (No.6); Kuwait Airways Corp v. Iraqi Airways Co (No.5) [2002]
   UKHL 19; [2002] 2 A.C. 883; [2002] 2 W.L.R. 1353; [2002] 3 All E.R. 209;
   [2002] 1 All E.R. (Comm) 843; [2003] 1 C.L.C. 183; *Times*, May 21, 2002, HL;
   affirming [2001] 3 W.L.R. 1117; [2001] 1 All E.R. (Comm) 557; [2001] 1 Lloyd's
   Rep. 161; [2001] C.L.C. 262; (2000) 97(48) L.S.G. 37; (2001) 145 S.J.L.B. 5;
   Times, November 21, 2000; *Daily Telegraph*, November 21, 2000, CA (Civ Div);
   reversing in part [2000] 2 All E.R. (Comm) 360; (2000) 97(23) L.S.G. 44;
   Times, May 31, 2000, QBD (Comm) . . . .   *Digested*, 02/**4540**:
       Applied, 04/1277: *Considered*, 04/734, 04/2249, 05/212: *Followed*, 04/427:
                      Previous proceedings, 98/3552, 99/723
Kuwait Oil Tanker Co SAK v. Al-Bader (No.3) [2000] 2 All E.R. (Comm) 271; (2000)
   97(23) L.S.G. 44; *Times*, May 30, 2000; *Independent*, June 26, 2000 (C.S), CA
   (Civ Div); affirming *Independent*, January 11, 1999 (C.S), QBD (Comm) . . . .   *Digested*, 00/**5106**:
            Applied, 04/451, 05/4190: *Considered*, 04/7
Kvaerner Warnow Werft GmbH v. Commission of the European Communities (T227/99)
   see Commission of the European Communities v. Kvaerner Warnow Werft
   GmbH (C181/02 P)
Kwamin v. Abbey National Plc; Birmingham City Council v. Mtize; Martin v. Southwark
   LBC; Connex South Eastern Ltd v. Bangs [2004] I.C.R. 841; [2004] I.R.L.R.
   516; (2004) 154 N.L.J. 418, EAT . . . .   *Digested*, 04/**1241**:
                            Overruled in part, 05/1249
Kwik Save Stores Ltd v. Swain [1997] I.C.R. 49, EAT . . . .   *Digested*, 97/**2221**:
       Applied, 05/1250, 05/1297: *Considered*, 99/2048

KWS Saat AG *v.* Office for Harmonisation in the Internal Market (Trade Marks and Designs) (OHIM) (T173/00) see KWS Saat AG *v.* Office for Harmonisation in the Internal Market (Trade Marks and Designs) (OHIM) (C447/02 P)

KWS Saat AG *v.* Office for Harmonisation in the Internal Market (Trade Marks and Designs) (OHIM) (C447/02 P); *sub nom* KWS Saat AG *v.* Office for Harmonisation in the Internal Market (Trade Marks and Designs) (OHIM) (T173/00) [2004] E.C.R. I-10107; [2005] E.T.M.R. 86, ECJ (2nd Chamber); affirming [2002] E.C.R. II-3843; [2003] E.T.M.R. 23, CFI (2nd Chamber) . . . .　*Digested,* 05/**2525**

Kyriakides *v.* Pippas [2004] EWHC 646; [2004] 2 F.C.R. 434; [2004] 2 P. & C.R. DG4, Ch D . . . .　*Digested,* 05/**3398**

Kyrtatos *v.* Greece (41666/98) (2005) 40 E.H.R.R. 16, ECHR . . . .　*Digested,* 05/**2085**

Kyzuna Investments Ltd *v.* Ocean Marine Mutual Insurance Association (Europe) [2000] 1 All E.R. (Comm) 557; [2000] 1 Lloyd's Rep. 505; [2000] C.L.C. 925; [2000] Lloyd's Rep. I.R. 513; (2000) 97(12) L.S.G. 44; (2000) 144 S.J.L.B. 142; *Times,* March 31, 2000, QBD (Comm) . . . .　*Digested,* 00/**3543**: *Followed,* 05/2386

L *v.* Tower Hamlets LBC see S *v.* Gloucestershire CC

L *v.* United Kingdom (45508/99) see HL *v.* United Kingdom (45508/99)

L (A Child) *v.* Stewart (Unreported, June 15, 2004), CC (Hertford) [*Ex rel.* Gurion Taussig, Barrister, 199 Strand, London] . . . .　*Digested,* 05/**3165**

L (A Child) (Care: Assessment: Fair Trial), Re; *sub nom* C (A Child) (Care Proceedings: Disclosure of Local Authority's Decision Making Process), Re [2002] EWHC 1379; [2002] 2 F.L.R. 730; [2002] 2 F.C.R. 673; [2002] Fam. Law 802, Fam Div . . . .　*Digested,* 03/**1522**:
　　　　　　　　　　　　　　Considered, 03/1519, 05/1536: *Distinguished,* 05/318

L (A Child) (Contact: Domestic Violence), Re; V (A Child) (Contact: Domestic Violence), Re; M (A Child) (Contact: Domestic Violence), Re; H (Children) (Contact: Domestic Violence), Re [2001] Fam. 260; [2001] 2 W.L.R. 339; [2000] 4 All E.R. 609; [2000] 2 F.L.R. 334; [2000] 2 F.C.R. 404; [2000] Fam. Law 603; (2000) 164 J.P.N. 918; (2000) 144 S.J.L.B. 222; *Times,* June 21, 2000; *Independent,* June 22, 2000, CA (Civ Div) . . . .　*Digested,* 00/**2475**:
　　　　　　　　　　　　　Applied, 01/2564, 05/1587: *Considered,* 03/1541

L (A Child) (Medical Treatment: Benefit), Re [2004] EWHC 2713; [2005] 1 F.L.R. 491; [2005] Fam. Law 211, Fam Div . . . .　*Digested,* 05/**1677**:
　　　　　　　　　　　　　　　　　　　　　　　　　　　Applied, 05/1794

L (Children) *v.* Bower (Unreported, August 16, 2004), CC (Liverpool) [*Ex rel.* Heather Belbin, Barrister, Oriel Chambers, 14 Water Street, Liverpool] . . . .　*Digested,* 05/**3128**

L (Family Proceedings Court) (Appeal: Jurisdiction), Re [2003] EWHC 1682; [2005] 1 F.L.R. 210; [2005] Fam. Law 23, Fam Div . . . .　*Digested,* 05/**1552**

L (Minors) (Care Proceedings: Appeal), Re see L (Minors) (Sexual Abuse: Standard of Proof), Re

L (Minors) (Sexual Abuse: Standard of Proof), Re; *sub nom* L (Minors) (Care Proceedings: Appeal), Re [1996] 1 F.L.R. 116; [1996] 2 F.C.R. 352; [1996] Fam. Law 73; (1995) 159 J.P.N. 812; *Times,* July 3, 1995, CA (Civ Div) . . . .　*Digested,* 96/**482**:
　　　　　　　　　　　Applied, 05/1566, 05/1570: *Doubted,* 01/2562: *Followed,* 00/2482

L Woolley Jewellers Ltd *v.* A&A Jewellery Ltd (No.2) [2004] F.S.R. 47, PCC . . . .　*Digested,* 05/**2435**

L'OREAL/Skin equivalent (T998/99) [2005] E.P.O.R. 39, EPO (Technical Bd App)

La Francaise des Jeux SA *v.* Ayache (Liquidator of Groupe Telci and Societe Tim) [2005] E.C.C. 28, Cass (F)

La Mer Technology Inc *v.* Laboratoires Goemar SA; *sub nom* LABORATOIRE DE LA MER Trade Mark (No.2); Laboratoires Goemar SA's Trade Marks (Nos.1338514 and 1402537); Laboratoires Goemar SA *v.* La Mer Technology Inc [2005] EWCA Civ 978; [2005] E.T.M.R. 114, CA (Civ Div); reversing [2004] EWHC 2960; [2005] F.S.R. 29; (2005) 28(3) I.P.D. 28014, Ch D . . . .　*Digested,* 05/**2582**:
　　　　　　　　　　　　　　　　　　　　Previous proceedings, 04/2417

La Mer Technology Inc *v.* Laboratoires Goemar SA (C259/02); *sub nom* Laboratoires Goemar SA's Trade Marks (Nos.1338514 and 1402537) (C259/02) [2004] E.C.R. I-1159; [2004] E.T.M.R. 47; [2004] F.S.R. 38, ECJ (3rd Chamber) . . . . .　*Digested,* 04/**2417**:
　　　　　　　　　　　Applied, 05/2518, 05/2582: *Previous proceedings,* 02/2924

La Mer Technology Inc *v.* Laboratoires Goemar SA (Request for Further Reference to ECJ) [2005] EWCA Civ 1109; (2005) 28(9) I.P.D. 28064, CA (Civ Div)

Laara *v.* Kihlakunnansyyttaja (Jyvaskyla) (C124/97) [1999] E.C.R. I-6067; [2001] 2 C.M.L.R. 14; *Times,* October 20, 1999, ECJ . . . .　*Digested,* 99/**2250**:
　　　　　　　　　　　　　　　　　　　　　　　　　　Considered, 05/1467

Labinjo *v.* University of Salford [2005] E.L.R. 1, Visitor (University)

LABORATOIRE DE LA MER Trade Mark (No.1) see Laboratoires Goemar SA's Trade Mark (No.1)

LABORATOIRE DE LA MER Trade Mark (No.2) see La Mer Technology Inc *v.* Laboratoires Goemar SA

Laboratoires Fournier SA *v.* Direction des Verifications Nationales et Internationales (C39/04) [2005] E.C.R. I-2057; [2005] 2 C.M.L.R. 5; [2005] C.E.C. 567; [2005] S.T.I. 367, ECJ (3rd Chamber) . . . .　*Digested,* 05/**4034**

Laboratoires Goemar SA *v.* La Mer Technology Inc see La Mer Technology Inc *v.*
    Laboratoires Goemar SA
Laboratoires Goemar SA's Trade Mark (No.1); *sub nom* LABORATOIRE DE LA MER Trade
    Mark (No.1); Laboratories Goemar SA's Trade Mark [2002] E.T.M.R. 34; [2002]
    F.S.R. 51, Ch D . . . . *Digested*, 02/**2924**:
                              Applied, 05/2575: *Subsequent proceedings*, 04/2417
Laboratoires Goemar SA's Trade Marks (Nos.1338514 and 1402537) see La Mer
    Technology Inc *v.* Laboratoires Goemar SA
Laboratoires Pharmaceutiques Bergaderm SA *v.* Commission of the European
    Communities (C352/98 P); *sub nom* Laboratoires Pharmaceutiques Bergaderm
    SA *v.* Commission of the European Communities (T199/96) [2000] E.C.R. I-
    5291, ECJ [1998] E.C.R. II-2805; (2001) 62 B.M.L.R. 179, CFI . . . . *Digested*, 02/**2215**:
                              Applied, 03/550: *Considered*, 05/1475
Laboratoires Pharmaceutiques Bergaderm SA *v.* Commission of the European
    Communities (T199/96) see Laboratoires Pharmaceutiques Bergaderm SA *v.*
    Commission of the European Communities (C352/98 P)
Laboratoires Goemar SA's Trade Mark see Laboratoires Goemar SA's Trade Mark (No.1)
Laboratories Goemar SA's Trade Marks (Nos.1338514 and 1402537) (C259/02) see La
    Mer Technology Inc *v.* Laboratoires Goemar SA (C259/02)
Labour Party *v.* Ahsan see Carter *v.* Ahsan (No.1)
Laceys (Wholesale) Footwear Ltd *v.* Bowler International Freight Ltd [1997] 2 Lloyd's
    Rep. 369; *Times*, May 12, 1997, CA (Civ Div) . . . . *Digested*, 97/**4287**:
                              Applied, 98/4807, 05/3455
Ladbroke (Football) Ltd *v.* William Hill (Football) Ltd; *sub nom* William Hill (Football)
    Ltd *v.* Ladbroke (Football) Ltd [1964] 1 W.L.R. 273; [1964] 1 All E.R. 465;
    (1964) 108 S.J. 135, HL; affirming [1980] R.P.C. 539; (1963) 107 S.J. 34, CA;
    reversing *Times*, June 27, 1962; *Guardian*, June 27, 1962, Ch D . . . . *Digested*, 64/**611**:
           Applied, 67/657, 77/406, 83/492, 83/2772, 84/434, 84/436, 85/428,
           94/617, 97/1038, 05/2424: *Considered*, 88/502: *Followed*, 95/869,
                                    99/3440, 99/3446
Ladd *v.* Marshall [1954] 1 W.L.R. 1489; [1954] 3 All E.R. 745; (1954) 98 S.J. 870, CA . *Digested*, 54/**2507**:
      Applied, 61/6769, 66/9796, 67/3202, 68/1544, 68/1545, 69/572, 71/3489,
      73/2097, 79/318.u, 84/1737, 88/2128, 91/2927, 91/2928, 92/604,
      92/3384.A, 93/1855, 95/504, 95/3922, 96/654, 96/656, 96/5321,
      97/2869, 98/3200, 00/302, 01/632, 01/633, 02/309, 02/2859, 03/274,
      03/943, 03/2235, 03/4116, 04/255, 05/2208, 05/2224, 05/2494:
                          Considered, 63/1013, 67/1339,
      74/113.u, 74/163.u, 74/199.u, 74/226.u, 74/227.u, 74/252.u, 75/230.u, 75/
      374.u, 79/355.u, 81/2110, 82/2382, 83/2702, 83/3016, 84/1255, 85/1256,
      86/1853, 86/2017, 87/2494, 89/2245, 90/1552, 91/471, 94/2623, 94/3746,
      95/3442, 96/680, 96/2994, 96/3242, 96/5722, 97/2865, 97/4903, 98/322,
      00/305, 00/306, 00/562, 00/3292, 01/634, 01/3621, 02/270, 02/271,
      02/506, 03/2242, 03/2597, 04/2030, 05/290, 05/464:
      Distinguished, 61/2556, 61/6677, 63/603, 90/3542, 92/2059, 96/756,
      97/3366, 99/3546: *Followed*, 59/2147, 83/2860, 92/3290, 97/458:
      Not applied, 97/3000, 00/3710: *Referred to*, 76/470.u, 99/3153, 99/3256,
                                  99/4014
Lady Navigation Inc *v.* LauritzenCool AB see LauritzenCool AB *v.* Lady Navigation Inc
Lady Nuffield Home *v.* Revenue and Customs Commissioners [2005] S.T.I. 1658,
    V&DTr (London)
Laemthong International Lines Co Ltd *v.* Abdullah Mohammed Fahem & Co see
    Laemthong International Lines Co Ltd *v.* Artis (The Laemthong Glory) (No.2)
Laemthong International Lines Co Ltd *v.* Artis (The Laemthong Glory) (No.1) [2004]
    EWHC 2226; [2004] 2 All E.R. (Comm) 797; [2005] 1 Lloyd's Rep. 100; [2005]
    2 C.L.C. 644, QBD (Comm) . . . . *Digested*, 05/**413**
Laemthong International Lines Co Ltd *v.* Artis (The Laemthong Glory) (No.2); *sub nom*
    Laemthong International Lines Co Ltd *v.* Abdullah Mohammed Fahem & Co
    [2005] EWCA Civ 519; [2005] 2 All E.R. (Comm) 167; [2005] 1 Lloyd's Rep.
    688; [2005] 1 C.L.C. 739, CA (Civ Div); affirming [2004] EWHC 2738; [2005]
    1 Lloyd's Rep. 632, QBD (Comm) . . . . *Digested*, 05/**3791**
Lafarge (Aggregates) Ltd *v.* Newham LBC [2005] EWHC 1337; [2005] 2 Lloyd's Rep.
    577, QBD (Comm)
Lafforgue *v.* Sweet Factory International Ltd [2005] I.L.Pr. 43, Cass (F)
Lagardere Active Broadcast SA *v.* Societe pour la Perception de la Remuneration
    Equitable (SPRE) (C192/04) [2005] 3 C.M.L.R. 48, ECJ (3rd Chamber)
Laing the Jeweller Ltd *v.* Customs and Excise Commissioners [2005] S.T.I. 147, V&DTr
Laiqat *v.* Majid [2005] EWHC 1305; [2005] 26 E.G.C.S. 130; [2005] N.P.C. 81, QBD
Lam *v.* Inland Revenue Commissioners [2005] S.T.I. 652, Ch D
Lam *v.* United Kingdom (Admissibility) (41671/98) (Unreported, July 5, 2001), ECHR . *Applied*, 05/3351
Lama *v.* Hope (2005-06) 8 I.T.E.L.R. 49, HC (NZ)
Lamb *v.* Khan (Costs) see Botham *v.* Khan (Costs)
Lamb *v.* Winchester [2005] P.A.D. 10, Planning Inspector
Lambe *v.* 186K Ltd [2004] EWCA Civ 1045; [2005] I.C.R. 307; (2004) 148 S.J.L.B.
    1150, CA (Civ Div) . . . . *Digested*, 05/**1333**

Lambert *v.* Home [1914] 3 K.B. 86, CA . . . . *Applied*, 05/300
Lambert *v.* Travelsphere (Unreported, September 1, 2004), CC (Peterborough) [*Ex rel.*
Sarah Prager, Barrister, 1 Serjeants' Inn, London] . . . . *Digested*, 05/**1977**
Lambeth LBC *v.* Howard [2001] EWCA Civ 468; (2001) 33 H.L.R. 58, CA (Civ Div) . . *Digested*, 01/**4200**:
Applied, 05/298

Lambeth LBC *v.* Kay see Kay *v.* Lambeth LBC
Lambeth LBC *v.* O'Kane; Helena Housing Ltd *v.* Pinder [2005] EWCA Civ 1010;
[2005] 32 E.G.C.S. 67; [2005] N.P.C. 110; *Times*, September 22, 2005, CA (Civ
Div)
Lambeth LBC *v.* S [2005] EWHC 776; [2005] 2 F.L.R. 1171; [2005] Fam. Law 685;
Times, May 19, 2005, Fam Div
Lambretta Clothing Co Ltd *v.* Next Retail Plc see Lambretta Clothing Co Ltd *v.* Teddy
Smith (UK) Ltd
Lambretta Clothing Co Ltd *v.* Teddy Smith (UK) Ltd; Lambretta Clothing Co Ltd *v.* Next
Retail Plc [2004] EWCA Civ 886; [2005] R.P.C. 6; (2004) 148 S.J.L.B. 911;
Times, September 28, 2004, CA (Civ Div); affirming [2003] EWHC 1204;
[2003] R.P.C. 41, Ch D . . . . *Digested*, 04/**2262**:
Applied, 05/2590

Lanarkshire Valuation Joint Board Assessor *v.* Clydesdale Bank Plc; *sub nom* Clydesdale
Bank Plc *v.* Lanarkshire Valuation Joint Board Assessor; Marks & Spencer Plc *v.*
Lanarkshire Valuation Joint Board Assessor; Marks & Spencer Plc *v.*
Renfrewshire Valuation Joint Board Assessor 2005 S.L.T. 167; 2005 S.C.L.R.
415; [2005] R.A. 1; 2004 GW.D. 38-786, LVAC . . . . *Digested*, 05/**5618**
Lancashire CC *v.* Taylor; *sub nom* Taylor *v.* Lancashire CC [2005] EWCA Civ 284;
[2005] 1 W.L.R. 2668; [2005] H.R.L.R. 17; [2005] U.K.H.R.R. 766; [2005] L.
& T.R. 26; [2005] 2 E.G.L.R. 17; [2005] 23 E.G. 142; [2005] N.P.C. 43; *Times*,
March 31, 2005, CA (Civ Div); affirming [2004] EWHC 776; [2005] 1 P. & C.R.
2; [2004] N.P.C. 62; [2004] 2 P. & C.R. DG8, QBD . . . . *Digested*, 05/**2636**:
Previous proceedings, 02/3005
Lancashire Fires Ltd *v.* SA Lyons & Co Ltd [1997] I.R.L.R. 113; [1996] F.S.R. 629;
(1996) 19(8) I.P.D. 19068, CA (Civ Div); reversing (1996) 19(5) I.P.D. 19032,
Ch D . . . . *Digested*, 96/**2519**:
Explained, 05/2416
Lancecrest Ltd *v.* Asiwaju [2005] EWCA Civ 117; [2005] L. & T.R. 22; [2005] 1
E.G.L.R. 40; [2005] 16 E.G. 146; [2005] N.P.C. 21, CA (Civ Div) . . . . *Digested*, 05/**2679**
Lancome *v.* Kecofa (C0200726/MA) [2005] E.C.D.R. 5, Hof (NL)
Lancome Parfums Beaute & Cie *v.* Kruidvat Retail BV [2005] E.T.M.R. 26, Hof
(Amsterdam)
Land Brandenburg *v.* Sass (C284/02) [2004] E.C.R. I-11143; [2005] 1 C.M.L.R. 27;
[2005] C.E.C. 3; [2005] I.R.L.R. 147, ECJ (1st Chamber) . . . . *Digested*, 05/**1266**
Land Nordrhein-Westfalen *v.* Pokrzeptowicz-Meyer (C162/00) [2002] E.C.R. I-1049;
[2002] 2 C.M.L.R. 1, ECJ . . . . *Digested*, 02/**1333**:
Applied, 05/1460
Land Oberosterreich *v.* Cez AS (3 OB 266/03v) [2005] I.L.Pr. 46, OGH (A)
Land Securities Trillium Ltd *v.* Thornley [2005] I.R.L.R. 765, EAT
Landelijke Vereniging tot Behoud van de Waddenzee *v.* Staatssecretaris van Landbouw,
Natuurbeheer en Visserij (C127/02) [2005] All E.R. (EC) 353; [2004] E.C.R. I-
7405; [2005] 2 C.M.L.R. 31; [2005] Env. L.R. 14; [2004] N.P.C. 136, ECJ . . . . *Digested*, 05/**1439**
Landing Fees at Portuguese Airports (C163/99), Re see Portugal *v.* Commission of the
European Communities (C163/99)
Landsman *v.* De Concilio [2005] EWHC 267; [2005] B.P.I.R. 829, Ch D
Lang (Eric) *v.* Lang (Jean Wauchope) [1955] A.C. 402; [1954] 3 W.L.R. 762; [1954]
3 All E.R. 571; (1954) 98 S.J. 803, PC (Aus) . . . . *Digested*, 54/**964**:
Applied, 55/811, 56/2542, 56/2546, 62/978, 64/1074, 65/1266, 65/1564:
Considered, 56/2603, 61/2483: *Explained*, 05/3883
Langley *v.* Bradford MDC see M *v.* Secretary of State for Work and Pensions
Langley *v.* Coal Authority (No.2) [2003] EWCA Civ 204; [2005] R.V.R. 111; *Times*,
March 31, 2003, CA (Civ Div); reversing in part [2002] R.V.R. 233, Lands Tr . . . *Digested*, 03/**2963**
Langley *v.* Liverpool City Council [2005] EWCA Civ 1173; [2005] 3 F.C.R. 303;
Times, October 19, 2005; *Independent*, October 25, 2005, CA (Civ Div) . . . . . . *Digested*, 05/**1567**
Langstane Housing Association Ltd *v.* Revenue and Customs Commissioners [2005]
S.T.I. 1657, V&D Tr
Larusai *v.* Secretary of State for Work and Pensions [2003] EWHC 371, QBD (Admin) . *Considered*, 05/3901
Lassence *v.* Tierney 41 E.R. 1379; (1849) 1 Mac. & G. 551 . . . . *Applied*, 47-51/1173,
47-51/9343, 57/3726, 67/3070, 68/3573, 81/1996: *Considered*, 47-51/10786,
67/410, 67/4081, 05/3972: *Distinguished*, 60/2896, 67/4097:
Followed, 84/1801, 85/3134
Latchmere Properties Ltd *v.* Customs and Excise Commissioners; *sub nom* Customs
and Excise Commissioners *v.* Latchmere Properties Ltd [2005] EWHC 133;
[2005] S.T.C. 731; [2005] B.T.C. 5622; [2005] B.V.C. 653; [2005] S.T.I. 219, Ch
D; affirming [2004] B.V.C. 2132; [2004] V. & D.R. 49; [2004] S.T.I. 1307,
V&D Tr (London) . . . . *Digested*, 05/**4385**
LATCHWAYS/Unlawful applicant (G3/92) [1995] E.P.O.R. 141, EPO (Enlarged Bd App) *Followed*, 05/2463

Lau *v.* DPP [2000] 1 F.L.R. 799; [2000] Crim. L.R. 580; [2000] Fam. Law 610; *Times,*
    March 29, 2000; *Independent,* April 10, 2000 (C.S.), DC . . . . *Digested,* 00/**942**:
                                Applied, 01/1050: *Considered,* 01/1048, 05/734, 05/885
LauritzenCool AB *v.* Lady Navigation Inc; *sub nom* Lady Navigation Inc *v.*
    LauritzenCool AB [2005] EWCA Civ 579; [2005] 1 W.L.R. 3686; [2005] 2 All
    E.R. (Comm) 183; [2005] 2 Lloyd's Rep. 63; [2005] 1 C.L.C. 758; *Times,* May
    26, 2005, CA (Civ Div); affirming [2004] EWHC 2607; [2005] 1 All E.R.
    (Comm) 77; [2005] 1 Lloyd's Rep. 260, QBD (Comm) . . . . *Digested,* 05/**422**
Lavarack *v.* Woods of Colchester [1967] 1 Q.B. 278; [1966] 3 W.L.R. 706; [1966] 3
    All E.R. 683; 1 K.I.R. 312; (1966) 110 S.J. 770, CA. . . . . *Digested,* 66/**4415**:
               Applied, 84/1014, 98/2098: *Distinguished,* 73/1140, 03/1216, 05/1212:
                                            Followed, 97/6006
Laver *v.* Harrogate BC [2005] P.A.D. 3, Planning Inspector
Law Debenture Trust Corp Plc *v.* Acciona SA [2004] EWHC 270, Ch D . . . . *Considered,* 05/263
Law Debenture Trust Corp Plc *v.* Elektrim Finance BV [2005] EWHC 1412; [2005] 2 All
    E.R. 476; [2005] 2 Lloyd's Rep. 755; [2005] 2 C.L.C. 39; *Times,* August 4,
    2005, Ch D . . . . *Digested,* 05/**984**
Law Debenture Trust Corp (Channel Islands) Ltd *v.* Lexington Insurance Co (Application
    for Disclosure) [2003] EWHC 2297; (2003) 153 N.L.J. 1551, QBD (Comm) . . . *Considered,* 05/396
Law on the Posting of Workers, Re (C341/02) see Commission of the European
    Communities *v.* Germany (C341/02)
Law on Work Permits for Foreign Workers Employed by Cross Border Service Providers, Re
    (C445/03) see Commission of the European Communities *v.* Luxembourg
    (C445/03)
Law Prohibiting Employment of Women in Specific Posts, Re (C203/03) see Commission
    of the European Communities *v.* Austria (C203/03)
Law Society *v.* Bultitude see Bultitude *v.* Law Society
Law Society *v.* Master of the Rolls see R. (on the application of the Law Society) *v.*
    Master of the Rolls
Law Society *v.* Sephton & Co TNS, HL; affirming [2004] EWCA Civ 1627; [2005]
    Q.B. 1013; [2005] 3 W.L.R. 212; [2005] P.N.L.R. 21; (2005) 102(5) L.S.G. 29;
    (2005) 149 S.J.L.B. 56; *Times,* January 11, 2005, CA (Civ Div); reversing in
    part [2004] EWHC 544; [2004] P.N.L.R. 27, Ch D . . . . *Digested,* 05/**437**
Law Society *v.* Sritharan see Sritharan *v.* Law Society
Law to Promote Confidence in the Digital Economy, Re [2005] 1 C.M.L.R. 14, Cons Const
    (F)
Law (Deceased), Re (2004-05) 7 I.T.E.L.R. 400, CFI (HK)
Lawal *v.* Northern Spirit Ltd [2003] UKHL 35; [2004] 1 All E.R. 187; [2003] I.C.R.
    856; [2003] I.R.L.R. 538; [2003] H.R.L.R. 29; [2003] U.K.H.R.R. 1024;
    (2003) 100(28) L.S.G. 30; (2003) 153 N.L.J. 1005; (2003) 147 S.J.L.B. 783;
    Times, June 27, 2003, HL; reversing [2002] EWCA Civ 1218; [2003] C.P. Rep.
    21; [2002] I.C.R. 1507; [2002] I.R.L.R. 714; [2002] H.R.L.R. 46; [2003]
    U.K.H.R.R. 238; (2002) 99(46) L.S.G. 33; *Times,* November 7, 2002, CA (Civ
    Div); affirming [2002] I.C.R. 486; [2002] I.R.L.R. 228; *Times,* January 29, 2002,
    EAT . . . . *Digested,* 03/**1251**:
                                  Applied, 05/2908: *Considered,* 04/1904
Lawrence *v.* Lesser see Krasner *v.* Dennison
Lawrence *v.* Regent Office Care Ltd (C320/00) [2002] E.C.R. I-7325; [2002] 3
    C.M.L.R. 27; [2003] I.C.R. 1092; [2002] I.R.L.R. 822; [2002] Emp. L.R. 1248;
    Times, October 10, 2002, ECJ [2002] E.C.R. I-7325, AGO . . . . *Digested,* 02/**1363**:
                               Applied, 05/1258: *Considered,* 04/1253, 04/1258
Lawrie-Blum *v.* Land Baden-Wurttemberg (C66/85) [1986] E.C.R. 2121; [1987] 3
    C.M.L.R. 389; [1987] I.C.R. 483, ECJ . . . . *Digested,* 87/**1569**:
                              Applied, 91/3958, 00/2389, 05/3856
Lawson *v.* Serco Ltd; *sub nom* Serco Ltd *v.* Lawson; Crofts *v.* Veta Ltd; Botham *v.*
    Ministry of Defence; TNS, HL; reversing [2004] EWCA Civ 12; [2004] 2 All E.R.
    200; [2004] I.C.R. 204; [2004] I.R.L.R. 206; (2004) 148 S.J.L.B. 148; *Times,*
    January 30, 2004, CA (Civ Div); reversing EAT/0018/02TM, EAT . . . . *Digested,* 04/**1243**:
                             Applied, 05/1210, 05/1329: *Not followed,* 03/1264:
                                  Previous proceedings, 05/1329
Lay *v.* Ackerman [2004] EWCA Civ 184; [2004] H.L.R. 40; [2004] L. & T.R. 29;
    [2005] 1 E.G.L.R. 139; (2004) 101(15) L.S.G. 28; (2004) 148 S.J.L.B. 299;
    [2004] N.P.C. 37; *Times,* March 24, 2004, CA (Civ Div) . . . . *Digested,* 04/**2497**
Lazarevic *v.* Secretary of State for the Home Department see Adan (Hassan Hussein)
    v. Secretary of State for the Home Department
LB (A Child), Re see U (A Child) (Serious Injury: Standard of Proof), Re
Le Compte *v.* Belgium (A/43); Van Leuven *v.* Belgium (A/43); De Meyere *v.* Belgium
    (A/43) [1982] E.C.C. 240; (1982) 4 E.H.R.R. 1, ECHR; reversing [1980] E.C.C.
    294, Eur Comm HR . . . . *Applied,* 97/2811,
                           98/3120, 98/3156, 00/2212, 05/2734
Le Pen *v.* European Parliament (C208/03 P) [2005] 3 C.M.L.R. 35, ECJ (2nd
    Chamber) . . . . *Previous proceedings,*
                                         03/1452
Le Quilliec *v.* Olivio SA [2004] E.C.C. 31; [2005] E.T.M.R. 53, Cass (F)

Le Serveur Administratif SA v. Erhmann [2004] E.C.C. 35; [2005] E.C.D.R. 14, Cass (F)

Leadenhall Independent Trustees Ltd v. Welham [2004] EWHC 740; [2004] O.P.L.R.
115, Ch D . . . . *Digested*, 05/**3000**

League of Friends of Poole General Hospital v. Customs and Excise Commissioners
Unreported, VAT Tr. . . . . *Distinguished*, 05/4346

Leander International Pet Foods Ltd (t/a Arden Grange) v. Customs and Excise
Commissioners [2005] BV.C. 2273, V&DTr

Lebbink v. Netherlands (45582/99) [2004] 2 F.L.R. 463; [2004] 3 F.C.R. 59; (2005)
40 E.H.R.R. 18; [2004] Fam. Law 643, ECHR . . . . *Digested*, 05/**2123**:
Considered, 04/2067

Lecombe v. Bourotte [2005] I.L.Pr. 9, Cass (F)

Lee v. Barrey [1957] Ch. 251; [1957] 2 W.L.R. 245; [1957] 1 All E.R. 191; (1957) 101
S.J. 129, CA . . . . *Digested*, 57/**1900**:
Followed, 05/3383

Lee v. Sankey (1872-73) L.R. 15 Eq. 204, Ct of Chancery . . . . *Applied*, 05/2325:
Considered, 68/3705

Lee (t/a Hong Kong Chop Suey) v. Inland Revenue Commissioners; Hong Kong Chop
Suey v. Inland Revenue Commissioners [2005] S.T.C. (S.C.D.) 279; [2005] S.T.I.
111, Sp Comm . . . . *Digested*, 05/**334**

Lee-Verhulst (Investments) Ltd v. Harwood Trust [1973] Q.B. 204; [1972] 3 W.L.R.
772; [1972] 3 All E.R. 619; (1972) 24 P. & C.R. 346; (1972) 116 S.J. 801, CA
(Civ Div) . . . . *Digested*, 72/**1981**:
Applied, 76/1538, 94/2726: *Considered*, 83/2109, 84/1885, 85/1855,
86/1837, 86/1875, 87/2134, 92/2699, 05/2648: *Distinguished*, 76/2321,
86/1828, 95/2969: *Explained*, 78/1774

Leeder v. Stevens see Stevens v. Newey

Leeds City Council v. Price see Kay v. Lambeth LBC

Leeds City Council v. Price; *sub nom* Price v. Leeds City Council [2005] EWCA Civ
289; [2005] 1 W.L.R. 1825; [2005] 3 All E.R. 573; [2005] U.K.H.R.R. 413;
[2005] H.L.R. 31; [2005] B.L.G.R. 782; [2005] 2 P. & C.R. 26; [2005] J.P.L.
1241; [2005] 12 E.G.C.S. 218; (2005) 102(19) L.S.G. 33; (2005) 149 S.J.L.B.
359; [2005] N.P.C. 41; *Times*, March 17, 2005; *Independent*, April 5, 2005, CA
(Civ Div) . . . . *Digested*, 05/**3424**

Leeds Permanent Building Society v. United Kingdom (21449/93) see National &
Provincial Building Society v. United Kingdom (21319/93)

Leeson v. General Council of Medical Education and Registration (1890) L.R. 43 Ch.
D. 366, CA . . . . *Applied*, 05/13:
Approved, 67/17: *Considered*, 66/12184, 67/3973, 81/2120:
Distinguished, 52/3361, 52/3505

Legal & General Assurance Society Ltd v. Drake Insurance Co (t/a Drake Motor Policies
at Lloyd's) [1992] Q.B. 887; [1992] 2 W.L.R. 157; [1992] 1 All E.R. 283; [1991]
2 Lloyd's Rep. 36; [1992] R.T.R. 162; (1992) 89(2) L.S.G. 30; *Times*, January
15, 1991; *Financial Times*, January 15, 1991, CA (Civ Div); reversing [1989] 3 All
E.R. 923, QBD. . . . . *Digested*, 92/**2613**:
Applied, 05/2384: *Distinguished*, 04/2228: *Not followed*, 93/2399

Legal & General Assurance Society Ltd v. Financial Services Authority, *Independent*,
January 26, 2005, FSMT

Legal & General Assurance Society Ltd v. Thomas (Inspector of Taxes) (No.1) [2005]
S.T.C. (S.C.D.) 350; 7 I.T.L. Rep. 655; [2005] S.T.I. 225, Sp Comm . . . . *Digested*, 05/**4027**

Legal & General Assurance Society Ltd v. Thomas (Inspector of Taxes) (No.2) [2005]
S.T.C. (S.C.D.) 707; [2005] S.T.I. 1562, Sp Comm

Legends Surf Shops Plc (In Administrative Receivership) v. Sun Life Assurance Society
Plc; *sub nom* Sun Life Assurance Society Plc v. Legends Surf Shops Plc
[2005] EWHC 1438; [2005] B.P.I.R. 1145; [2005] 3 E.G.L.R. 43; [2005] 46
E.G. 178; [2005] N.P.C. 94, Ch D . . . . *Digested*, 05/**2643**

Leica Microsystems (Schweiz) AG v. Carl Zeiss (A Firm) (T1122/01) (Unreported, May
6, 2004), EPO (Technical Bd App) . . . . *Considered*, 05/2470

Leicestershire CC v. Unison [2005] I.R.L.R. 920; (2005) 102(42) L.S.G. 24, EAT

Lemmerz-werke GmbH v. High Authority of the European Coal and Steel Community
(111/63 R) [1965] E.C.R. 883, ECJ . . . . *Followed*, 05/576

Lemos v. Coutts (Cayman) Ltd (2005-06) 8 I.T.E.L.R. 153, Grand Court (CI)

Lennartz v. Finanzamt Munchen III (C97/90) [1995] S.T.C. 514; [1991] E.C.R. I-3795;
[1993] 3 C.M.L.R. 689; [1991] S.T.I. 700, ECJ (6th Chamber) . . . . *Digested*, 95/**5057**:
Applied, 03/4272, 03/4563: *Distinguished*, 96/5860, 03/4553:
Followed, 05/4364, 05/4365

Lennon v. Scottish Daily Record & Sunday Mail Ltd [2004] EWHC 359; [2004]
E.M.L.R. 18, QBD . . . . *Digested*, 05/**978**

Leon Corp v. Atlantic Lines & Navigation Co Inc (The Leon) [1985] 2 Lloyd's Rep.
470, QBD (Comm) . . . . *Digested*, 86/**3107**:
Considered, 05/388

Leonard v. Southern Derbyshire Chamber of Commerce [2001] I.R.L.R. 19, EAT . . . . . . *Digested*, 01/**2235**:
Applied, 01/2242, 05/1147

Les Grands Chais de France SA v. Albert Heijn BV [2005] E.T.M.R. 79, RB (Den Haag)

Les Verts, Parti Ecologiste v. European Parliament (294/83) see Parti Ecologiste Les Verts v. European Parliament (294/83)

Lesotho Highlands Development Authority v. Impregilo SpA [2005] UKHL 43; [2005] 3 W.L.R. 129; [2005] 3 All E.R. 789; [2005] 2 All E.R. (Comm) 265; [2005] 2 Lloyd's Rep. 310; [2005] 2 C.L.C. 1; [2005] B.L.R. 351; 101 Con. L.R. 1; [2005] 27 E.G.C.S. 220; (2005) 155 N.L.J. 1046; *Times*, July 6, 2005, HL; reversing [2003] EWCA Civ 1159; [2004] 1 All E.R. (Comm) 97; [2003] 2 Lloyd's Rep. 497; [2003] B.L.R. 347; (2003) 100(39) L.S.G. 37; (2003) 153 N.L.J. 1239; *Times*, September 15, 2003, CA (Civ Div); affirming [2002] EWHC 2435; [2003] 1 All E.R. (Comm) 22; [2003] B.L.R. 98; *Times*, December 6, 2002, QBD (Comm) . . . . *Digested*, 05/**207**

Less v. Benedict [2005] EWHC 1643; [2005] 4 Costs L.R. 688; (2005) 102(33) L.S.G. 23, Ch D

Lesser v. Lawrence see Krasner v. Dennison

Lester Aldridge (A Firm) v. Customs and Excise Commissioners [2005] B.V.C. 2231; [2004] V. & D.R. 292, V&DTr (London) . . . . *Digested*, 05/**4375**

Level 3 Communications Inc's Application [2005] E.T.M.R. 76, OHIM (2nd Bd App) . . . *Digested*, 05/**2534**

Lever Bros Ltd v. Bell see Bell v. Lever Brothers Ltd

Levi Strauss & Co v. Costco Wholesale UK Ltd (C416/99) see Zino Davidoff SA v. A&G Imports Ltd

Levi Strauss & Co v. Tesco Stores Ltd (C415/99) see Zino Davidoff SA v. A&G Imports Ltd

Levob Verzekeringen BV v. Staatssecretaris van Financien (C41/04) [2005] S.T.I. 1777, ECJ (1st Chamber)

Levolux AT Ltd v. Ferson Contractors Ltd; *sub nom* Ferson Contractors Ltd v. Levolux AT Ltd [2003] EWCA Civ 11; [2003] 1 All E.R. (Comm) 385; [2003] B.L.R. 118; [2003] T.C.L.R. 5; 86 Con. L.R. 98; [2003] 5 E.G.C.S. 145; (2003) 147 S.J.L.B. 115, CA (Civ Div); affirming [2002] B.L.R. 341, QBD (TCC) . . . . *Digested*, 03/**667**: *Distinguished*, 05/666

Levy to Income on Investments, Re (C334/02) see Commission of the European Communities v. France (C334/02)

Lewin v. Purity Soft Drinks Ltd see Northamptonshire CC v. Purity Soft Drinks Ltd

Lewis v. Gibson [2005] EWCA Civ 587; [2005] 2 F.C.R. 241; (2005) 8 C.C.L. Rep. 399, CA (Civ Div) . . . . *Digested*, 05/**2819**

Lewis v. King see King v. Lewis

Lewis v. Luminar Dancing Ltd [2005] 2 Q.R. 18; [2004] 3 Q.R. 10, CC (Chesterfield) [*Ex rel*. Jason Cox, Barrister, 24, The Ropewalk, Nottingham] . . . . *Digested*, 04/**2933**

Lewis v. Motorworld Garages Ltd [1986] I.C.R. 157; [1985] I.R.L.R. 465, CA (Civ Div) . *Digested*, 86/**1261**: *Applied*, 00/2132, 05/1209

Lewis v. Pensions Ombudsman; *sub nom* Nortel Networks UK Pension Plan, Re [2005] EWHC 103; [2005] O.P.L.R. 41; [2005] Pens. L.R. 195, Ch D

Lewis v. United Kingdom (40461/98) see Edwards v. United Kingdom (39647/98)

Lewis v. Williams see Lewis's Will Trusts, Re

Lewis's Will Trusts, Re; *sub nom* Lewis v. Williams [1985] 1 W.L.R. 102; [1984] 3 All E.R. 930; (1984) 128 S.J. 385, Ch D . . . . *Digested*, 85/**3640**: *Applied*, 05/3975

Lewisham LBC v. Hall [2002] EWHC 960; [2003] Env. L.R. 4; [2002] A.C.D. 68; [2002] E.H.L.R. Dig. 9, QBD (Admin) . . . . *Digested*, 03/**3036**: *Applied*, 05/2894

LG Caltex Gas Co Ltd v. China National Petroleum Corp; Contigroup Companies Inc (formerly Continental Grain Co) v. China Petroleum Technology & Development Corp [2001] EWCA Civ 788; [2001] 1 W.L.R. 1892; [2001] 4 All E.R. 875; [2001] 2 All E.R. (Comm) 97; [2001] C.L.C. 1392; [2001] B.L.R. 325; (2001) 3 T.C.L.R. 22; (2001) 98(25) L.S.G. 46; (2001) 145 S.J.L.B. 142; *Times*, June 6, 2001, CA (Civ Div); reversing [2001] B.L.R. 235; *Times*, February 23, 2001; *Independent*, February 26, 2001 (C.S), QBD (Comm) . . . . *Digested*, 01/**336**: *Followed*, 05/202

Libertel Groep BV v. Benelux-Merkenbureau (C104/01) [2004] Ch. 83; [2004] 2 W.L.R. 1081; [2003] E.C.R. I-3793; [2005] 2 C.M.L.R. 45; [2003] E.T.M.R. 63; [2004] F.S.R. 4; *Times*, May 12, 2003, ECJ [2003] E.C.R. I-3793; [2003] E.T.M.R. 41, AGO . . . . *Digested*, 04/**2362**: *Applied*, 04/2370, 05/2529, 05/2533: *Considered*, 05/2532: *Followed*, 05/2553

Lidl Stiftung & Co KG v. Kingsley Foods Ltd (R 508/2003-1) [2005] E.T.M.R. 38, OHIM (1st Bd App) . . . . *Digested*, 05/**2512**

Lidl Stiftung & Co KG v. Office for Harmonisation in the Internal Market (Trade Marks and Designs) (OHIM) (T296/02) [2005] E.T.M.R. 98, CFI

Lightfoot v. Lightfoot-Brown [2005] EWCA Civ 201; [2005] 2 P. & C.R. 22; [2005] W.T.L.R. 1031; [2005] 2 P. & C.R. DG4, CA (Civ Div); affirming [2004] EWHC 840, Ch D . . . . *Digested*, 05/**3378**

Lightly v. Howard [2005] 3 Q.R. 12, CC (York) [*Ex rel*. John Collins, Barrister, Zenith Chambers, 10 Park Square, Leeds] . . . . *Digested*, 05/**3205**

Lilly ICOS LLC v. Pfizer Ltd (No.2) see Lilly ICOS Ltd v. Pfizer Ltd (No.2)

Lilly ICOS Ltd v. Pfizer Ltd (No.2); *sub nom* Lilly ICOS LLC v. Pfizer Ltd (No.2); Lily ICOS Ltd v. Pfizer Ltd (No.2) [2002] EWCA Civ 2; [2002] 1 W.L.R. 2253; [2002] 1 All E.R. 842; [2002] F.S.R. 54; (2002) 25(3) I.P.D. 25016; (2002) 99(10) L.S.G. 33; (2002) 146 S.J.L.B. 29; *Times*, January 28, 2002, CA (Civ Div) . . . . *Digested*, 02/**417**:
Applied, 05/396: *Followed*, 03/404
Lily ICOS Ltd v. Pfizer Ltd (No.2) see Lilly ICOS Ltd v. Pfizer Ltd (No.2)
Limburgse Vinyl Maatschappij NV v. Commission of the European Communities (T305/ 94) see Limburgse Vinyl Maatschappij NV (LVM) v. Commission of the European Communities (C238/99 P)
Limburgse Vinyl Maatschappij NV (LVM) v. Commission of the European Communities (C238/99 P); *sub nom* PVC Cartel II (T305/94), Re; Limburgse Vinyl Maatschappij NV v. Commission of the European Communities (T305/94); DSM Kunststoffen BV v. Commission of the European Communities (C244/99 P) [2002] E.C.R. I-8375; [2003] 4 C.M.L.R. 10, ECJ; affirming [1999] E.C.R. II-931; [1999] 5 C.M.L.R. 303, CFI (3rd Chamber) . . . . *Digested*, 03/**554**:
Applied, 03/558: *Followed*, 05/553
Limit (No.3) Ltd v. PDV Insurance Co Ltd [2005] EWCA Civ 383; [2005] 2 All E.R. (Comm) 347; [2005] 1 C.L.C. 515; [2005] Lloyd's Rep. I.R. 552; *Times*, April 14, 2005, CA (Civ Div); affirming [2003] EWHC 2632, QBD (Comm) . . . . *Digested*, 05/**2403**
Lincoln National Life Insurance Co v. Sun Life Assurance Co of Canada; *sub nom* Sun Life Assurance Co of Canada v. Lincoln National Life Insurance Co [2004] EWCA Civ 1660; [2005] 1 Lloyd's Rep. 606; [2005] 2 C.L.C. 664, CA (Civ Div); reversing [2004] EWHC 343; [2004] 1 Lloyd's Rep. 737; [2004] 2 C.L.C. 36; (2004) 154 N.L.J. 352, QBD (Comm) . . . . *Digested*, 05/**208**
Linde AG v. Deutsches Patent- und Markenamt (C53/01) see Linde AG's Trade Mark Application (C53/01)
Linde AG's Trade Mark Application (C53/01); *sub nom* Linde AG v. Deutsches Patent-und Markenamt (C53/01); Rado Uhren AG's Trade Mark Application (C55/01); Winward Industrie Inc's Trade Mark Application (C54/01) [2003] E.C.R. I-3161; [2005] 2 C.M.L.R. 44; [2003] E.T.M.R. 78; [2003] R.P.C. 45; *Times*, April 24, 2003, ECJ [2003] E.C.R. I-3161; [2003] E.T.M.R. 28, AGO . . . . *Digested*, 03/**2613**:
Applied, 03/2633, 04/2372, 05/2438
Linden Gardens Trust Ltd v. Lenesta Sludge Disposal Ltd; St Martins Property Corp Ltd v. Sir Robert McAlpine & Sons [1994] 1 A.C. 85; [1993] 3 W.L.R. 408; [1993] 3 All E.R. 417; 63 B.L.R. 1; 36 Con. L.R. 1; [1993] E.G.C.S. 139; (1993) 143 N.L.J. 1152; (1993) 137 S.J.L.B. 183; *Times*, July 23, 1993; *Independent*, July 30, 1993, HL; reversing in part 57 B.L.R. 57; 30 Con. L.R. 1; (1992) 8 Const. L.J. 180; *Times*, February 27, 1992; *Independent*, March 6, 1992; *Financial Times*, February 20, 1992, CA (Civ Div); reversing 52 B.L.R. 93; 25 Con. L.R. 28; [1991] E.G.C.S. 11, QBD . . . . *Digested*, 93/**303**:
Applied, 94/319, 95/487, 95/3701, 98/809, 99/832, 02/3042, 05/2372:
Cited, 99/1417: *Considered*, 94/549, 95/771, 95/4162, 99/440, 00/864,
02/726: *Followed*, 98/401, 00/859, 00/5980, 03/2753
Lindex AB v. National Tax Board 8 I.T.L. Rep. 81, Lansratt (Swe)
Lindfors v. Finland (C365/02) see Lindfors (C365/02), Re
Lindfors (C365/02), Re; *sub nom* Lindfors v. Finland (C365/02) [2005] All E.R. (EC) 745; [2004] E.C.R. I-7183; [2004] 3 C.M.L.R. 43, ECJ (1st Chamber) . . . . *Digested*, 05/**4008**
Lindman v. Skatterattelsnamnden (C42/02) see Proceedings brought by Lindman, Re (C42/02)
Lindsay v. Customs and Excise Commissioners [2002] EWCA Civ 267; [2002] 1 W.L.R. 1766; [2002] 3 All E.R. 118; [2002] S.T.C. 588; [2002] R.T.R. 18; [2002] Eu. L.R. 290; [2002] S.T.I. 238; *Times*, February 27, 2002; *Independent*, February 26, 2002, CA (Civ Div); reversing in part [2001] V. & D.R. 219, V&DTr . . . *Digested*, 02/**921**:
Applied, 03/910, 05/945: *Followed*, 03/927, 05/949
Lindsay Cars Ltd v. Customs and Excise Commissioners [2005] B.V.C. 2461; [2005] V. & D.R. 21; [2005] S.T.I. 878, V&DTr (London)
Linea GIG Srl v. Commission of the European Communities (T398/02 R) see Linea GIG Srl (In Liquidation) v. Commission of the European Communities (C233/03 P (R))
Linea GIG Srl (In Liquidation) v. Commission of the European Communities (C233/03 P (R)); *sub nom* Linea GIG Srl v. Commission of the European Communities (T398/02 R) [2003] E.C.R. I-7911; [2005] 5 C.M.L.R. 7, ECJ; affirming [2003] E.C.R. II-1139; [2005] 5 C.M.L.R. 9, CFI
Linelevel Ltd v. Powszechny Zaklad Ubezpieczen SA (The Nore Challenger) [2005] EWHC 421; [2005] 2 Lloyd's Rep. 534, QBD (Comm)
Linfood Cash & Carry Ltd v. Thomson [1989] I.C.R. 518; [1989] I.R.L.R. 235; *Daily Telegraph*, June 8, 1989, EAT . . . . *Digested*, 90/**1949.a**:
Considered, 02/1387: *Not applied*, 05/1317
Lingfield Park (1991) Ltd v. Shove (Inspector of Taxes) see Shove (Inspector of Taxes) v. Lingfield Park 1991 Ltd
Linkin Park LLC's Trade Mark Application [2005] E.T.M.R. 17, TMR . . . . *Digested*, 05/**2588**
Lips v. Older [2004] EWHC 1686; [2005] P.I.Q.R. P14, QBD . . . . *Digested*, 05/**2886**

Lips Maritime Corp *v.* President of India see President of India *v.* Lips Maritime Corp
(The Lips)
List Design Group Ltd *v.* Catley see List Design Group Ltd *v.* Douglas
List Design Group Ltd *v.* Douglas; List Design Group Ltd *v.* Catley [2002] I.C.R. 686;
[2003] I.R.L.R. 14, EAT . . . . *Digested*, 02/**1375**:
Applied, 04/1267: *Overruled*, 05/1273
Lister *v.* Hesley Hall Ltd [2001] UKHL 22; [2002] 1 A.C. 215; [2001] 2 W.L.R. 1311;
[2001] 2 All E.R. 769; [2001] I.C.R. 665; [2001] I.R.L.R. 472; [2001] Emp. L.R.
819; [2001] 2 F.L.R. 307; [2001] 2 F.C.R. 97; (2001) 3 L.G.L.R. 49; [2001]
E.L.R. 422; [2001] Fam. Law 595; (2001) 98(24) L.S.G. 45; (2001) 151 N.L.J.
728; (2001) 145 S.J.L.B. 126; [2001] N.P.C. 89; *Times*, May 10, 2001;
Independent, June 11, 2001 (C.S); *Daily Telegraph*, May 8, 2001, HL; reversing
Times, October 13, 1999; *Independent*, November 22, 1999 (C.S.), CA (Civ Div) . . . *Digested*, 01/**5359**:
Applied, 02/1531, 03/432, 03/3033, 03/3046, 04/655, 05/4199, 05/4200:
Cited, 02/5360, 03/2975: *Considered*, 05/5573
Lister & Co *v.* Stubbs (1890) L.R. 45 Ch. D. 1, CA . . . . *Applied*, 86/1572,
87/3553: *Disapproved*, 93/1834, 94/2083: *Distinguished*, 55/361, 81/2158,
05/3443
LITE Community Trade Mark (T79/00) see Rewe Zentral AG *v.* Office for Harmonisation in
the Internal Market (Trade Marks and Designs) (OHIM) (T79/00)
Littman *v.* Aspen Oil (Broking) Ltd [2005] EWCA Civ 1579; [2005] N.P.C. 150, CA
(Civ Div); affirming [2005] EWHC 1369; [2005] N.P.C. 88; [2005] 2 P. & C.R.
DG19, Ch D
Liu *v.* Secretary of State for the Home Department [2005] EWCA Civ 249; [2005] 1
W.L.R. 2858; [2005] I.N.L.R. 525; (2005) 102(22) L.S.G. 26; *Times*, April 15,
2005, CA (Civ Div) . . . . *Digested*, 05/**2227**
Liverpool City Council *v.* Plemora Distribution Ltd; *sub nom* Liverpool City Council *v.*
Pleroma Distribution Ltd; Liverpool City Council *v.* Pleruma Distribution Ltd
[2002] EWHC 2467; [2003] R.A. 34; (2003) 100(4) L.S.G. 33; *Times*,
December 2, 2002, QBD (Admin) . . . . *Digested*, 03/**37**:
Applied, 05/387: *Considered*, 05/430: *Followed*, 05/3357
Liverpool City Council Trading Standards Office *v.* Somerfield Stores Ltd see Haringey
LBC *v.* Marks & Spencer Plc
Livingstone *v.* Rawyards Coal Co (1879-80) L.R. 5 App. Cas. 25, HL . . . . *Applied*, 79/2776,
86/3195, 87/3551, 88/1051, 89/1199, 90/1522, 91/1322, 92/1533, 03/3023,
05/962: *Cited*, 01/4593: *Considered*, 90/1567, 93/2504, 94/2771, 96/4483:
Referred to, 94/3437
LJP *v.* GRGP see P *v.* P (Financial Relief: Illiquid Assets)
Lloyd *v.* Young [1963] Crim. L.R. 703; 107 S.J. 631, DC . . . . *Digested*, 63/**2138**:
Followed, 05/887
Lloyd Schuhfabrik Meyer & Co GmbH *v.* Klijsen Handel BV (C342/97) [1999] All E.R.
(EC) 587; [1999] E.C.R. I-3819; [1999] 2 C.M.L.R. 1343; [1999] C.E.C. 285;
[1999] E.T.M.R. 690; [2000] F.S.R. 77; (1999) 22(11) I.P.D. 22111; *Times*, June
30, 1999, ECJ [1999] E.C.R. I-3819; [1999] E.T.M.R. 10; [1999] F.S.R. 627,
AGO . . . . *Digested*, 99/**3538**:
Applied, 01/4056, 01/5881, 04/2375: *Considered*, 04/2380, 05/2509,
05/2514: *Followed*, 00/3773
Lloyds Bank *v.* Jones see Taylor, Re
Lloyds Bank Plc *v.* Cassidy, *Times*, January 11, 2005, CA (Civ Div)
Lloyds Bank Plc *v.* Rogers (No.2) [1999] 3 E.G.L.R. 83; [1999] 38 E.G. 187; [1999]
E.G.C.S. 106; (1999) 96(30) L.S.G. 30, CA (Civ Div) . . . . *Digested*, 99/**4383**:
Applied, 05/313
Lloyds Bank Plc *v.* Rosset [1991] 1 A.C. 107; [1990] 2 W.L.R. 867; [1990] 1 All E.R.
1111; [1990] 2 F.L.R. 155; (1990) 22 H.L.R. 349; (1990) 60 P. & C.R. 311; (1990)
140 N.L.J. 478, HL; reversing [1989] Ch. 350; [1988] 3 W.L.R. 1301; [1988] 3
All E.R. 915; [1989] 1 F.L.R. 51; (1989) 57 P. & C.R. 62; [1988] Fam. Law 472;
(1989) 86(1) L.S.G. 39; (1988) 138 N.L.J. Rep. 149; (1988) 132 S.J. 1698;
Times, May 23, 1988; *Independent*, June 3, 1988; *Guardian*, June 9, 1988; *Daily
Telegraph*, June 9, 1988, CA (Civ Div) . . . . *Digested*, 90/**706**:
Applied, 92/2034, 96/4993, 01/5503, 02/1670, 02/1684, 02/3823, 02/4317,
03/3592, 03/4479, 04/3233, 04/3948, 05/3379: *Approved*, 90/707:
Considered, 89/467, 92/2031, 96/4950, 96/4952, 96/4995, 97/4937:
Distinguished, 04/4342: *Followed*, 93/572, 95/2187, 96/4943
Lloyds Investment (Scandinavia) *v.* Ager-Hanssen [2003] EWHC 1740, Ch D . . . . *Applied*, 05/420
Lloyds TSB Bank Plc *v.* Hayward [2002] EWCA Civ 1813, CA (Civ Div); reversing
[2002] EWHC 456, Ch D . . . . *Applied*, 05/292
Lloyds TSB Bank Plc's Trade Mark Application [2005] E.T.M.R. 84, TMR
Lloyds TSB Private Banking Plc (Personal Representative of Antrobus (Deceased)) *v.*
Twiddy [2005] W.T.L.R. 1535, Lands Tr
Lo-Line Electric Motors Ltd, Re [1988] Ch. 477; [1988] 3 W.L.R. 26; [1988] 2 All E.R. 692;
(1988) 4 B.C.C. 415; [1988] B.C.L.C. 698; [1988] P.C.C. 236; [1988] 2 F.T.L.R. 107;
(1988) 138 N.L.J. Rep. 119; (1988) 132 S.J. 851; *Times*, April 7, 1988; *Independent*,
April 20, 1988; *Financial Times*, April 27, 1988, Ch D . . . . *Digested*, 88/**316**:
Approved, 91/401: *Followed*, 05/2294: *Referred to*, 01/714

Loader v. Lucas (1999) 99(5) Q.R. 8, QBD .... *Digested*, 99/**1620**:
Considered, 05/406
Locabail (UK) Ltd v. Bayfield Properties Ltd (Leave to Appeal); Locabail (UK) Ltd v.
Waldorf Investment Corp (Leave to Appeal); Timmins v. Gormley; Williams v.
Inspector of Taxes; R. v. Bristol Betting and Gaming Licensing Committee Ex p.
O'Callaghan [2000] Q.B. 451; [2000] 2 W.L.R. 870; [2000] 1 All E.R. 65;
[2000] I.R.L.R. 96; [2000] H.R.L.R. 290; [2000] U.K.H.R.R. 300; 7 B.H.R.C.
583; (1999) 149 N.L.J. 1793; [1999] N.P.C. 143; *Times*, November 19, 1999 ;
Independent, November 23, 1999, CA (Civ Div) .... *Digested*, 99/**38**:
Applied, 00/52, 00/53, 01/13, 01/2268, 04/30, 05/890:
Considered, 00/4140, 00/6092, 01/334, 02/4828, 03/5169
Locabail (UK) Ltd v. Waldorf Investment Corp (Leave to Appeal) see Locabail (UK) Ltd
v. Bayfield Properties Ltd (Leave to Appeal)
Local Authorities Mutual Investment Trust v. Customs and Excise Commissioners
[2003] EWHC 2766; [2004] S.T.C. 246; [2004] Eu. L.R. 320; [2004] B.T.C.
5319; [2004] B.V.C. 379; [2003] S.T.I. 2184, Ch D; affirming [2004] V. & D.R.
310; [2003] S.T.I. 1081, V&DTr .... *Applied*, 05/**4377**
Lockley v. National Blood Transfusion Service [1992] 1 W.L.R. 492; [1992] 2 All E.R.
589; [1992] 3 Med. L.R. 173; *Times*, November 11, 1991; *Independent*, November
4, 1991, CA (Civ Div) .... *Digested*, 92/**2773**:
Applied, 01/525, 04/310, 05/384: *Considered*, 95/3108
Lodgepower Ltd v. Taylor; *sub nom* Taylor v. Lodgepower Ltd [2004] EWCA Civ 1367;
[2005] 1 E.G.L.R. 1; [2005] 08 E.G. 192; [2004] 44 E.G.C.S. 152; [2004] N.P.C.
156; *Times*, November 3, 2004, CA (Civ Div) .... *Digested*, 05/**2638**
Lodwick v. Southwark LBC [2004] EWCA Civ 306; [2004] I.C.R. 884; [2004]
I.R.L.R. 554; (2004) 148 S.J.L.B. 385; *Times*, April 9, 2004, CA (Civ Div) ..... *Considered*, 05/1220
Loftus (Deceased), Re see Green v. Gaul
Logitext UK Ltd, Re [2004] EWHC 2899; [2005] 1 B.C.L.C. 326, Ch D .... *Digested*, 05/**2257**
Loizidou v. Turkey (15318/89) (1997) 23 E.H.R.R. 513, ECHR. .... *Digested*, 97/**2799**:
Considered, 98/3151, 05/2129: *Distinguished*, 05/2065
Loizidou v. Turkey (Preliminary Objections) (A/310) (1995) 20 E.H.R.R. 99; *Times*,
April 15, 1995, ECHR .... *Digested*, 95/**2655**:
Applied, 05/2069: *Considered*, 97/2771: *Followed*, 97/2769
Lomas v. Parle [2003] EWCA Civ 1804; [2004] 1 W.L.R. 1642; [2004] 1 All E.R. 1173;
[2004] 1 F.L.R. 812; [2004] 1 F.C.R. 97; [2004] Fam. Law 243; *Times*, January
13, 2004, CA (Civ Div) .... *Digested*, 04/**1502**:
Considered, 05/343, 05/1621
Lomotey v. Enfield LBC; *sub nom* Enfield LBC v. Lamotey [2004] EWCA Civ 627;
[2004] H.L.R. 45; [2004] N.P.C. 73, CA (Civ Div) .... *Digested*, 05/**2002**
London & Quadrant Housing Trust v. Morgan see North British Housing Association Ltd
v. Matthews
London & Quadrant Housing Trust v. Root; *sub nom* London Quadrant Housing Trust v.
Root [2005] EWCA Civ 43; [2005] H.L.R. 28; [2005] L. & T.R. 23, CA (Civ
Div) .... *Digested*, 05/**2640**
London Corp v. Eurostar (UK) Ltd see City of London Corp v. Eurostar (UK) Ltd
London Diocesan Fund v. Avonridge Property Co Ltd see Avonridge Property Co Ltd v.
Mashru
London Diocesan Fund v. Phithwa see Avonridge Property Co Ltd v. Mashru
London Fire and Emergency Planning Authority (LFEPA) v. Halcrow Gilbert & Co Ltd;
Halcrow Gilbert & Co Ltd v. Jones [2004] EWHC 2340; [2005] B.L.R. 18, QBD
(TCC) .... *Digested*, 05/**293**
London General Holdings Ltd v. USP Plc; *sub nom* USP Plc v. London General Holdings
Ltd (Damages) [2005] EWCA Civ 931; (2005) 28(10) I.P.D. 28073, CA (Civ
Div)
London International College v. Sen [1993] I.R.L.R. 333, CA (Civ Div); affirming
[1992] I.R.L.R. 292, EAT .... *Digested*, 94/**2031**:
Considered, 05/1336
London Life Association, Re, *Independent*, February 27, 1989 (C.S.), Ch D .... *Applied*, 05/**2362**:
Followed, 98/3370: *Referred to*, 94/2675, 95/2924
London Local Residential Ltd (Assets: Sale at Undervalue), Re [2004] EWHC 504; [2005]
B.P.I.R. 163, Ch D
London North Securities Ltd v. Meadows [2005] EWCA Civ 956, CA (Civ Div);
affirming [2005] 1 P. & C.R. DG16, CC (Liverpool)
London Oratory School v. Schools Adjudicator (No.1) [2004] EWHC 3014; [2005]
E.L.R. 162; [2005] A.C.D. 47, QBD (Admin) .... *Digested*, 05/**1167**
London Oratory School v. Schools Adjudicator (No.2) [2005] EWHC 1842; [2005]
E.L.R. 484; (2005) 102(35) L.S.G. 43, QBD (Admin)
London Probation Board v. Kirkpatrick [2005] I.C.R. 965; [2005] I.R.L.R. 443, EAT .. *Digested*, 05/**1324**
London Quadrant Housing Trust v. Root see London & Quadrant Housing Trust v. Root
London Sephardi Trust v. Baker see Wembley Park Estate Co Ltd's Transfer, Re
London Underground Ltd v. Ferenc-Batchelor; Harding v. London Underground Ltd
[2003] I.C.R. 656; [2003] I.R.L.R. 252, EAT .... *Digested*, 03/**1232**:
Applied, 04/1231: *Followed*, 05/1309

London Underground Ltd *v.* Strouthos; *sub nom* Strouthos *v.* London Underground Ltd
[2004] EWCA Civ 402; [2004] I.R.L.R. 636, CA (Civ Div); reversing EAT/
0016/03/ZT, EAT . . . . *Digested*, 05/**1332**
Lonergan *v.* Lewes Crown Court see R. (on the application of Lonergan) *v.* Lewes
Crown Court
Long *v.* Farrer & Co [2004] EWHC 1774; [2004] B.P.I.R. 1218, Ch D . . . . *Digested*, 05/**2294**
Long *v.* Wiltshire (Unreported, January 19, 2004), CC (Lincoln) [*Ex rel.* Mark Henley,
Barrister, Zenith Chambers, 10 Park Square, Leeds] . . . . *Digested*, 05/**3129**
Long Acre Securities Ltd *v.* Karet [2004] EWHC 442; [2005] Ch. 61; [2004] 3 W.L.R.
866; [2005] 4 All E.R. 413; [2004] L. & T.R. 30; [2004] 2 E.G.L.R. 121;
[2004] 11 E.G.C.S. 138; (2004) 101 (13) L.S.G. 34; *Times*, March 24, 2004,
Ch D . . . . *Digested*, 04/**2541**
Longborough Festival Opera *v.* Revenue and Customs Commissioners CH/2005/APP/
0488, Ch D; reversing [2005] B.V.C. 2650; [2005] S.T.I. 1655, V&D Tr
Longmint Ltd *v.* Marcus [2004] 3 E.G.L.R. 171, Lands Tr. . . . . *Digested*, 05/**2651**
Longstaff International Ltd *v.* Baker & McKenzie [2004] EWHC 1852; [2004] 1 W.L.R.
2917, Ch D . . . . *Digested*, 05/**465**
Lonrho Ltd *v.* Shell Petroleum Co Ltd (No.2) [1982] A.C. 173; [1981] 3 W.L.R. 33;
[1981] 2 All E.R. 456; 125 S.J. 429, HL; affirming [1981] Com. L.R. 74; 125 S.J.
255, CA (Civ Div); affirming [1981] Com. L.R. 6; *Times*, December 2, 1980,
QBD (Comm) . . . . *Digested*, 81/**2649**:
Applied, 82/436, 87/516, 89/3520, 89/3528, 91/2456, 92/1524, 93/1391,
94/2281, 95/2901, 00/5111, 05/2812: *Considered*, 85/2774, 87/501, 87/1315,
88/1324, 88/3405, 92/2547, 92/3651, 92/4130, 93/363, 95/3452,
96/5690, 00/5106: *Distinguished*, 88/3404, 96/7366, 02/3781:
Followed, 96/1085, 04/7: *Referred to*, 85/3384
Lonrho Plc *v.* Al-Fayed (No.1) [1992] 1 A.C. 448; [1991] 3 W.L.R. 188; [1991] 3 All
E.R. 303; [1991] B.C.C. 641; [1991] B.C.L.C. 779; (1991) 141 N.L.J. 927; (1991)
135 S.J.L.B. 68; *Times*, July 3, 1991; *Independent*, July 3, 1991; *Financial Times*,
July 3, 1991; *Guardian*, June 28, 1991, HL; affirming [1990] 2 Q.B. 479; [1989] 3
W.L.R. 631; [1989] 2 All E.R. 65; [1989] B.C.L.C. 485; [1989] P.C.C. 215;
(1989) 139 N.L.J. 539, CA (Civ Div); reversing [1990] 1 Q.B. 490; [1989] 2
W.L.R. 356; (1988) 4 B.C.C. 688; [1989] B.C.L.C. 75; [1989] P.C.C. 173; (1989)
86(10) L.S.G. 43; (1988) 138 N.L.J. Rep. 225; (1989) 133 S.J. 220;
Independent, July 19, 1988, QBD . . . . *Digested*, 92/**4130**:
Applied, 92/2, 03/4357, 05/2812: *Considered*, 98/4069: *Followed*, 94/4040
Lonsdale *v.* Braisby (Inspector of Taxes) [2005] EWCA Civ 709; [2005] S.T.C. 1049;
[2005] Pens. L.R. 409; 77 T.C. 358; [2005] B.T.C. 392; [2005] S.T.I. 1100;
Times, July 7, 2005; *Independent*, June 24, 2005, CA (Civ Div); affirming
[2004] EWHC 1811; [2004] S.T.C. 1606; [2004] Pens. L.R. 367; [2005] B.T.C.
30; [2004] S.T.I. 1726; *Times*, August 10, 2004, Ch D . . . . *Digested*, 05/**4096**
Lonslow *v.* Hennig (formerly Lonslow) [1986] 2 F.L.R. 378; [1986] Fam. Law 303,
CA (Civ Div) . . . . *Digested*, 87/**2487**:
Considered, 05/1574
Lopez *v.* Philibert [2005] E.C.C. 44; [2005] E.C.D.R. 22, Trib Gde Inst (Paris)
Lord Fisher DSC *v.* Customs and Excise Commissioners see Customs and Excise
Commissioners *v.* Lord Fisher
Lord Saville of Newdigate *v.* Widgery Soldiers see R. (on the application of A) *v.* Lord
Saville of Newdigate (Bloody Sunday Inquiry)
Lord (Liquidator of Rosshill Properties Ltd) *v.* Sinai Securities Ltd [2004] EWHC 1764;
[2004] B.C.C. 986; [2005] 1 B.C.L.C. 295; [2004] B.P.I.R. 1244, Ch D . . . . . . *Digested*, 05/**2304**
Loss Relief Group Litigation Order Claimants *v.* Inland Revenue Commissioners see
Autologic Holdings Plc *v.* Inland Revenue Commissioners
Loucks *v.* Standard Oil Co of New York 120 N.E. 198. . . . . *Applied*, 82/**1680**:
Considered, 05/621
Loufrani *v.* FW Woolworth & Co GmbH (R658/2004-1) [2005] E.T.M.R. CN10,
OHIM (1st Bd App)
Lough *v.* First Secretary of State [2004] EWCA Civ 905; [2004] 1 W.L.R. 2557;
[2005] 1 P. & C.R. 5; [2004] J.P.L. 208; [2004] 31 E.G.C.S. 92; (2004) 148
S.J.L.B. 879; [2004] N.P.C. 115; *Times*, July 29, 2004, CA (Civ Div); affirming
[2004] EWHC 23; [2004] 3 P.L.R. 38, QBD (Admin) . . . . *Digested*, 04/**3042**:
Applied, 05/2027, 05/3295
Love & Care Ltd *v.* Kiernan [2005] EWHC 2180; [2005] N.P.C. 117, Ch D
Loveday *v.* Renton (No.1) [1989] 1 Med. L.R. 117; *Times*, March 31, 1988; *Guardian*,
April 2, 1988, QBD . . . . *Digested*, 88/**1599**:
Applied, 01/4454, 04/2696, 05/1559: *Considered*, 90/2896, 91/2313
Low *v.* Revenue and Customs Commissioners (No.1) [2005] S.T.I. 1999, Sp Comm
Lowden *v.* Lowden Guitar Co Ltd see LOWDEN Trade Mark
Lowden Guitar Co Ltd's Application for Revocation (No.81567) see LOWDEN Trade Mark
LOWDEN Trade Mark; *sub nom* Lowden Guitar Co Ltd's Application for Revocation
(No.81567); Lowden *v.* Lowden Guitar Co Ltd [2004] EWHC 2531; [2005]
R.P.C. 18; (2005) 28(2) I.P.D. 28005, Ch D . . . . *Digested*, 05/**2583**

Loweth v. Minister of Housing and Local Government; Loweth v. Minister of Transport
(1971) 22 P. & C.R. 125, QBD . . . . *Digested*, 71/**1531**:
Approved, 76/307: *Followed*, 05/3258
Loweth v. Minister of Transport see Loweth v. Minister of Housing and Local
Government
Lownds v. Home Office; *sub nom* Home Office v. Lownds; Lownds v. Secretary of
State for the Home Department [2002] EWCA Civ 365; [2002] 1 W.L.R. 2450;
[2002] 4 All E.R. 775; [2002] C.P. Rep. 43; [2002] C.P.L.R. 328; [2002] 2
Costs L.R. 279; (2002) 99(19) L.S.G. 28; (2002) 146 S.J.L.B. 86; *Times*, April
5, 2002, CA (Civ Div) . . . . *Digested*, 02/**333**:
Applied, 03/259, 03/347, 04/293, 04/301, 04/303, 04/316, 04/320, 05/331,
05/372: *Considered*, 04/319
Lownds v. Secretary of State for the Home Department see Lownds v. Home Office
Lowsley v. Forbes (t/a LE Design Services) [1999] 1 A.C. 329; [1998] 3 W.L.R. 501;
[1998] 3 All E.R. 897; [1998] 2 Lloyd's Rep. 577; (1998) 95(35) L.S.G. 37;
(1998) 148 N.L.J. 1268; (1998) 142 S.J.L.B. 247; *Times*, August 24, 1998, HL;
reversing in part [1996] C.L.C. 1370; *Times*, April 5, 1996, CA (Civ Div) . . . . *Digested*, 98/**539**:
Applied, 05/497
Loyalty Management UK Ltd v. Customs and Excise Commissioners [2005] B.V.C.
2628, V&DTr
LP's Application for Judicial Review, Re [2005] N.I. 271, CA (NI)
LR af 1998 A/S v. Commission of the European Communities (C206/02 P) see Dansk
Rorindustri A/S v. Commission of the European Communities (C189/02 P)
LR af 1998 (Deutschland) GmbH v. Commission of the European Communities (C208/
02 P) see Dansk Rorindustri A/S v. Commission of the European Communities
(C189/02 P)
LS v. Secretary of State for the Home Department; *sub nom* LS (Post Decision
Evidence: Direction: Appealability: Gambia), Re [2005] UKIAT 85; [2005] Imm.
A.R. 310, IAT
LS (Post Decision Evidence: Direction: Appealability: Gambia), Re see LS v. Secretary of
State for the Home Department
LU (A Child), Re see U (A Child) (Serious Injury: Standard of Proof), Re
Lubenham Fidelities & Investment Co Ltd v. South Pembrokeshire DC and Wigley Fox
Partnership 33 B.L.R. 39; 6 Con. L.R. 85; (1986) 2 Const. L.J. 111; *Times*, April 8,
1986, CA (Civ Div); affirming [1985] C.I.L.L. 214 . . . . *Digested*, 86/**206**:
Applied, 05/656
Lubrizol Corp v. Esso Petroleum Co Ltd (No.5) [1998] R.P.C. 727; (1998) 21(8) I.P.D.
21081, CA (Civ Div); affirming [1997] R.P.C. 195, Ch D (Patents Ct) . . . . *Digested*, 99/**3507**:
Considered, 05/2505
LUBRIZOL/Prior use (T959/00) [2005] E.P.O.R. 44, EPO (Technical Bd App)
Luby v. Newcastle under Lyme Corp [1965] 1 Q.B. 214; [1964] 3 W.L.R. 500; [1964]
3 All E.R. 169; (1964) 128 J.P. 536; 62 L.G.R. 622; [1964] R.V.R. 708; 108 S.J.
541, CA; affirming [1964] 2 Q.B. 64; [1964] 2 W.L.R. 475; [1964] 1 All E.R. 84;
(1964) 128 J.P. 138; 62 L.G.R. 140; (1963) 107 S.J. 983, QBD . . . . *Digested*, 64/**2999**:
Applied, 72/2933, 05/1415: *Considered*, 87/2385
Luc Thiet Thuan v. Queen, The [1997] A.C. 131; [1996] 3 W.L.R. 45; [1996] 2 All E.R.
1033; [1996] 2 Cr. App. R. 178; (1996) 32 B.M.L.R. 112; [1996] Crim. L.R. 820;
(1996) 93(16) L.S.G. 30; (1996) 146 N.L.J. 513; (1996) 140 S.J.L.B. 107;
Times, April 2, 1996, PC (HK) . . . . *Digested*, 96/**1456**:
Applied, 05/807: *Considered*, 97/1127, 00/986: *Not followed*, 98/960
Luca v. Italy (33354/96) (2003) 36 E.H.R.R. 46; [2001] Crim. L.R. 747, ECHR . . . . . . *Digested*, 03/**2125**:
Cited, 05/888
Lucas v. Ministry of Defence see Saggar v. Ministry of Defence
Lucking's Will Trusts, Re; *sub nom* Renwick v. Lucking [1968] 1 W.L.R. 866; [1967] 3
All E.R. 726; (1967) 112 S.J. 444, Ch D . . . . *Digested*, 67/**3554**:
Considered, 05/520
Ludwigshafener Walzmuhle Erling KG v. European Economic Community (197/80)
[1981] E.C.R. 1041, ECJ . . . . *Followed*, 05/576
Luke v. Wansbroughs (A Firm) [2003] EWHC 3151; [2005] P.N.L.R. 2, QBD . . . . *Digested*, 05/**2870**
Lumbermans Mutual Casualty Co v. Bovis Lend Lease Ltd (Preliminary Issues); *sub
nom* Lumbermens Mutual Casualty Co v. Bovis Lend Lease Ltd (Preliminary
Issues) [2004] EWHC 2197; [2005] 2 All E.R. (Comm) 669; [2005] 1 Lloyd's
Rep. 494; [2005] 2 C.L.C. 617; [2005] B.L.R. 47; 98 Con. L.R. 21; [2005]
Lloyd's Rep. I.R. 74; [2004] 42 E.G.C.S. 160, QBD (Comm) . . . . *Digested*, 05/**2393**
Lumley v. Wagner (1852) 1 De G.M. & G. 604 . . . . *Applied*, 55/1094,
67/316, 67/3160, 78/916: *Considered*, 68/3135, 05/422
Lunt v. Merseyside TEC Ltd [1999] I.C.R. 17; [1999] I.R.L.R. 458, EAT . . . . *Digested*, 99/**2137**:
Considered, 05/1207
Luordo v. Italy (32190/96) (2005) 41 E.H.R.R. 26, ECHR
Lux Traffic Controls Ltd v. Faronwise Ltd see Lux Traffic Controls Ltd v. Pike Signals Ltd
Lux Traffic Controls Ltd v. Pike Signals Ltd; Lux Traffic Controls Ltd v. Faronwise Ltd
[1993] R.P.C. 107, Ch D (Patents Ct) . . . . *Applied*, 05/2492:
Considered, 05/2491: *Followed*, 96/4557

Luxembourg v. Vermietungsgesellschaft Objekt Kirchberg Sarl (C269/03) [2005]
  S.T.C.1345; [2004] 3 C.M.L.R. 49; [2004] S.T.I. 2070, ECJ (1st Chamber) . . . .   *Digested,* 05/**4384**
Lyddon v. Moss (1859) 4 De G. & J.104 . . . .   *Applied,* 05/2720
Lynall v. Inland Revenue Commissioners; *sub nom* Lynall (Deceased), Re [1972] A.C.
  680; [1971] 3 W.L.R. 759; [1971] 3 All E.R. 914; 47 T.C. 375; [1971] T.R. 309;
  115 S.J. 872, HL; reversing [1970] Ch. 138; [1969] 3 W.L.R. 711; [1969] 3 All
  E.R. 984; [1969] T.R. 353; 113 S.J. 723, CA (Civ Div); reversing [1969] 1 Ch.
  421; [1968] 3 W.L.R. 1056; [1968] 3 All E.R. 322; [1968] T.R. 283; 112 S.J.
  765, Ch D . . . .   *Digested,* 71/**3309**:
                      Applied, 05/2844: *Considered,* 85/1932, 87/2204, 88/2729, 00/5028:
                                                         Distinguished, 89/2181
Lynall (Deceased), Re see Lynall v. Inland Revenue Commissioners
Lynn v. Nathanson [1931] 2 D.L.R. 457, CA (NS) . . . .   *Distinguished,* 05/2692

M v. B [2005] EWHC 1681; [2005] Fam. Law 860; (2005) 102(34) L.S.G. 31; *Times,*
  August 10, 2005, Fam Div . . . .   *Digested,* 05/**1673**
M v. Islington LBC see R. (on the application of M) v. Islington LBC
M v. M (Breaches of Orders: Committal) [2005] EWCA Civ 1722; *Times,* August 24,
  2005, CA (Civ Div)
M v. M (Short Marriage: Clean Break) see Miller v. Miller
M v. M (Stay of Proceedings: Return of Children) [2005] EWHC 1159; [2005] Fam.
  Law 853, Fam Div
M v. P (Contempt of Court: Committal Order); Butler v. Butler [1993] Fam. 167;
  [1992] 3 W.L.R. 813; [1992] 4 All E.R. 833; [1993] 1 F.L.R. 773; [1993] 1 F.C.R.
  405; [1993] Fam. Law 467; (1992) 142 N.L.J. 1339; *Times,* August 4, 1992,
  CA (Civ Div) . . . .   *Digested,* 93/**3132**:
                          Applied, 03/317, 05/345: *Distinguished,* 95/4145, 96/799
M v. Secretary of State for the Home Department see P v. Secretary of State for the
  Home Department
M v. Secretary of State for the Home Department; *sub nom* DM (Proportionality:
  Article 8: Croatia CG), Re [2004] UKIAT 24; [2004] Imm. A.R. 211; [2004]
  I.N.L.R. 327, IAT . . . .   *Digested,* 05/**2159**:
                                                          Considered, 05/2192
M v. Secretary of State for Work and Pensions; *sub nom* Secretary of State for Work
  and Pensions v. M; Langley v. Bradford MDC; TNS, HL; reversing [2004] EWCA
  Civ 1343; [2005] 2 W.L.R. 740; [2005] 1 F.L.R. 498; [2004] 3 F.C.R. 507;
  [2005] A.C.D. 58; (2004) 101(45) L.S.G. 31; (2004) 148 S.J.L.B. 1244; *Times,*
  November 11, 2004, CA (Civ Div) . . . .   *Digested,* 05/**2118**
M v. Special Educational Needs & Disability Tribunal see M v. SW School
M v. SW School; M v. Special Educational Needs & Disability Tribunal [2004] EWHC
  2586; [2005] E.L.R. 285, QBD (Admin) . . . .   *Digested,* 05/**1061**
M v. United Kingdom (6638/03) see PM v. United Kingdom (6638/03)
M (A Child), Re (Unreported, May 11, 2004), CICAP [*Ex rel.* ASD, Solicitors, 275 Ecclesall
  Road, Sheffield] . . . .   *Digested,* 05/**67**
M (A Child), Re [2005] EWCA Civ 408; (2005) 149 S.J.L.B. 296, CA (Civ Div)
M (A Child) v. Ali (Unreported, June 9, 2004), CC (Birmingham) [*Ex rel.* Stephen
  Garner, Barrister, No.8 Chambers, Fountain Court, Steelhouse Lane,
  Birmingham.] . . . .   *Digested,* 05/**3227**
M (A Child) v. British School of Motoring Ltd (Unreported, September 16, 2004), CC
  (Aldershot & Farnham) [*Ex rel.* Gurion Taussig, Barrister, 199 Strand, London] . .   *Digested,* 05/**3122**
M (A Child) v. Graham [2005] 2 Q.R. 10, CC (Central London) [*Ex rel.* Joanna Kerr,
  Barrister, Lamb Chambers, Lamb Building, Temple, London] . . . .   *Digested,* 04/**2863**
M (A Child) v. Khan (Unreported, August 12, 2004), CC (Birmingham) [*Ex rel.* Stephen
  Garner, Barrister, No.8 Chambers, Fountain Court, Steelhouse Lane,
  Birmingham.] . . . .   *Digested,* 05/**3182**
M (A Child) v. Lemon (Unreported, January 10, 2005), CC (Staines) [*Ex rel.* Joanna
  Kerr, Barrister, Lamb Chambers, Lamb Building, Temple, London] . . . .   *Digested,* 05/**3151**
M (A Child) v. Smith (Unreported, August 27, 2004), CC (Croydon) [*Ex rel.* Thomas
  Wood, Barrister, 199 Strand Chambers, London] . . . .   *Digested,* 05/**3119**
M (A Child) v. Wandsworth LBC Independent Appeal Panel see W (A Child) v.
  Wandsworth LBC Independent Appeal Panel
M (A Child) v. Yates (Unreported, April 1, 2005), CC (Brentford) [*Ex rel.* Joanna Kerr,
  Barrister, Lamb Chambers, Lamb Building, Temple, London] . . . .   *Digested,* 05/**3137**
M (A Child) (Contact: Domestic Violence), Re see L (A Child) (Contact: Domestic
  Violence), Re
M (A Child) (Contact Order: Committal for Contempt), Re; *sub nom* M (Children), Re
  [2005] EWCA Civ 615; [2005] 2 F.L.R. 1006; [2005] Fam. Law 694; *Times,*
  April 18, 2005, CA (Civ Div) . . . .   *Digested,* 05/**3563**
M (A Child) (Contempt of Court), Re [2004] EWCA Civ 1621; [2005] 2 F.L.R. 413; [2005]
  Fam. Law 531, CA (Civ Div) . . . .   *Digested,* 05/**1639**
M (A Minor) v. Newham LBC see X (Minors) v. Bedfordshire CC
M (A Minor) (Contempt of Court: Committal of Court's Own Motion), Re see M (Minors)
  (Breach of Contact Order: Committal), Re

M (Abduction: Habitual Residence: Relocation), Re [2005] Fam. Law 441, Fam Div
M (Afghanistan) *v.* Secretary of State for the Home Department see R (Iran) *v.*
Secretary of State for the Home Department
M (Children), Re see M (A Child) (Contact Order: Committal for Contempt), Re
M (Children) (Contact: LongTerm Best Interests), Re; *sub nom* M (Children) (Intractable
Contact Dispute: Court's Positive Duty), Re [2005] EWCA Civ 1090; [2005]
Fam. Law 938; *Times*, June 27, 2005, CA (Civ Div) . . . .   *Digested*, 05/**1678**
M (Children) (Interim Care Order: Removal), Re [2005] EWCA Civ 1594; (2005) 149
S.J.L.B. 1355; *Times*, November 11, 2005, CA (Civ Div)
M (Children) (Intractable Contact Dispute: Court's Positive Duty, Re see M (Children)
(Contact: LongTerm Best Interests), Re
M (Children) (Residence), Re [2004] EWCA Civ 1574; [2005] 1 F.L.R. 656; [2005] Fam.
Law 216; *Times*, November 5, 2004, CA (Civ Div) . . . .   *Digested*, 05/**1687**
M (Minors) (Breach of Contact Order: Committal), Re; *sub nom* M (A Minor) (Contempt
of Court: Committal of Court's Own Motion), Re [1999] Fam. 263; [1999] 2
W.L.R. 810; [1999] 2 All E.R. 56; [1999] 1 F.L.R. 810; [1999] 1 F.C.R. 683;
[1999] Fam. Law 208; (1999) 96(6) L.S.G. 33; (1999) 143 S.J.L.B. 36; *Times*,
December 31, 1998; *Independent*, January 14, 1999, CA (Civ Div) . . . .   *Digested*, 99/**2365**:
Considered, 05/1639
M (Minors) (Child Abduction: Undertakings), Re [1995] 1 F.L.R.1021; [1995] 3 F.C.R. 745;
Times, August 15, 1994; *Independent*, August 22, 1994 (C.S.), CA (Civ Div) . . . .   *Digested*, 96/**541**:
Distinguished, 05/1544
M Holleran Ltd *v.* Severn Trent Water Ltd [2004] EWHC 2508; [2005] Eu. L.R. 364,
QBD (Comm) . . . .   *Digested*, 05/**3351**
M+M Gesellschaft fur Unternehmensberatung und Informationssysteme mbH *v.* Office
for Harmonisation in the Internal Market (Trade Marks and Designs) (OHIM)
(T317/01) [2005] E.T.M.R. 34, CFI (2nd Chamber) . . . .   *Digested*, 05/**2516**
MA *v.* Secretary of State for the Home Department; *sub nom* MA (Fresh Evidence: Sri
Lanka), Re [2004] UKIAT 161; [2004] Imm. A.R. 460; [2005] I.N.L.R. 13, IAT . .   *Digested*, 05/**2208**
MA *v.* Secretary of State for the Home Department; *sub nom* MA (Seven Year Child
Concession: Pakistan), Re [2005] UKIAT 90; [2005] Imm. A.R. 338, IAT
MA (Fresh Evidence: Sri Lanka), Re see MA *v.* Secretary of State for the Home
Department
MA (Seven Year Child Concession: Pakistan), Re see MA *v.* Secretary of State for the
Home Department
Maatschap MJM Linthorst *v.* Inspecteur der Belastingdienst/Ondernemingen Roermond
(C167/95) [1997] S.T.C. 1287; [1997] E.C.R. I-1195; [1997] 2 C.M.L.R. 478;
[1997] B.T.C. 5366; [1997] B.V.C. 480, ECJ (6th Chamber) . . . .   *Digested*, 97/**5020**:
Followed, 05/4404
Mabon *v.* Mabon [2005] EWCA Civ 634; [2005] Fam. 366; [2005] 3 W.L.R. 460;
[2005] 2 F.L.R. 1011; [2005] 2 F.C.R. 354; [2005] H.R.L.R. 29; (2005) 8
C.C.L. Rep. 412; [2005] Fam. Law 696; *Times*, June 2, 2005, CA (Civ Div) . . . .   *Digested*, 05/**1634**
Maccaba *v.* Lichtenstein (Defamation) [2004] EWHC 1577; [2005] E.M.L.R. 9, QBD . .   *Digested*, 05/**981**
Maccaba *v.* Lichtenstein (Misuse of Private Information) [2004] EWHC 1579; [2005]
E.M.L.R. 6, QBD . . . .   *Digested*, 05/**979**
Machado *v.* Secretary of State for the Home Department [2005] EWCA Civ 597;
[2005] 2 C.M.L.R. 43; [2005] Eu. L.R. 851, CA (Civ Div) . . . .   *Digested*, 05/**2193**
Macklin *v.* Dowsett [2004] EWCA Civ 904; [2004] 2 E.G.L.R. 75; [2004] 34 E.G.
68; [2005] W.T.L.R.1561; [2004] 26 E.G.C.S.193, CA (Civ Div) . . . .   *Digested*, 05/**2673**:
Applied, 05/3402
Maco Door & Window Hardware (UK) Ltd *v.* Revenue and Customs Commissioners
[2005] S.T.I. 1996, Sp Comm
Macro *v.* Thompson (No.3) [1997] 2 B.C.L.C. 36, Ch D . . . .   *Digested*, 97/**843**:
Applied, 05/309
Madden *v.* Preferred Technical Group CHA Ltd [2004] EWCA Civ 1178; [2005]
I.R.L.R. 46; (2004) 148 S.J.L.B. 1064, CA (Civ Div); affirming UKEAT/0668/
03/MAA, EAT . . . .   *Digested*, 05/**1291**
Madden *v.* Quirk [1989] 1 W.L.R. 702; [1989] R.T.R. 304; (1989) 133 S.J. 752, QBD . .   *Digested*, 89/**2555**:
Applied, 05/2833
Maden *v.* Clifford Coppock & Carter [2004] EWCA Civ 1037; [2005] 2 All E.R. 43;
[2005] P.N.L.R. 7; (2004) 101 (38) L.S.G. 29; (2004) 154 N.L.J. 1218, CA (Civ
Div) . . . .   *Digested*, 05/**2880**
Madgett (t/a Howden Court Hotel) *v.* Customs and Excise Commissioners (C308/96);
sub nom Customs and Excise Commissioners *v.* Madgett (t/a Howden Court
Hotel) (C308/96) [1998] S.T.C. 1189; [1998] E.C.R. I-6229; [1999] 2 C.M.L.R.
392; [1998] C.E.C. 1004; [1998] B.T.C. 5440; [1998] B.V.C. 458, ECJ (5th
Chamber) . . . .   *Digested*, 99/**5002**:
Applied, 03/4537: *Explained*, 04/3968: *Followed*, 05/4406
Maersk Olie & Gas A/S *v.* Firma M de Haan en W de Boer (C39/02) [2005] 1 Lloyd's
Rep. 210; [2004] E.C.R. I-9657; [2005] 1 C.L.C. 479, ECJ . . . .   *Digested*, 05/**624**
Maestri *v.* Italy (39748/98) (2004) 39 E.H.R.R. 38, ECHR . . . .   *Digested*, 05/**2039**
Mafin SpA's Design [2005] E.T.M.R. 106; [2005] E.C.D.R. 29, OHIM (Cancellation Div)

Mag Instrument Inc *v.* Office for Harmonisation in the Internal Market (Trade Marks and Designs) (OHIM) (T88/00) see Mag Instrument Inc *v.* Office for Harmonisation in the Internal Market (Trade Marks and Designs) (OHIM) (C136/02 P)

Mag Instrument Inc *v.* Office for Harmonisation in the Internal Market (Trade Marks and Designs) (OHIM) (C136/02 P); *sub nom* Mag Instrument Inc *v.* Office for Harmonisation in the Internal Market (Trade Marks and Designs) (OHIM) (T88/00) [2004] E.C.R. I-9165; [2005] E.T.M.R. 46, ECJ (2nd Chamber); affirming [2002] E.C.R. II-467; [2002] C.E.C. 190; [2002] E.T.M.R. 61, CFI (4th Chamber); affirming. . . . . *Digested,* 05/**2556**:
Applied, 04/2392

Magell Ltd *v.* Dumfries and Galloway Regional Assessor (No.2) 2005 S.L.T. 726; 2005 S.C.L.R. 1118; [2005] R.A. 306; 2005 G.W.D. 25-498, LVAC . . . . *Digested,* 05/**5620**

Magill *v.* Porter see Porter *v.* Magill

Magill *v.* Weeks see Porter *v.* Magill

Magill Case (C241/91 P), Re see Radio Telefis Eireann *v.* Commission of the European Communities (C241/91 P)

Magoke *v.* Sweden (Admissibility) (12611/03) (2005) 41 E.H.R.R. SE10, ECHR

Maguire *v.* Harland & Wolff Plc [2005] EWCA Civ 1; [2005] P.I.Q.R. P21; (2005) 102(12) L.S.G. 26; (2005) 149 S.J.L.B. 144; *Times,* January 27, 2005; *Independent,* January 28, 2005, CA (Civ Div); reversing [2004] EWHC 577; [2004] P.I.Q.R. P29; *Times,* April 29, 2004, QBD . . . . *Digested,* 05/**2864**

Maguire (t/a Skian Mhor) *v.* Customs and Excise Commissioners [2004] V. & D.R. 288; [2004] S.T.I. 2313, V&DTr (London) . . . . *Digested,* 05/**4369**

Mahfouz *v.* General Medical Council see R. (on the application of Mahfouz) *v.* General Medical Council

Mahfouz *v.* Morris see Bank of Credit and Commerce International SA (In Liquidation) (No.9), Re

Mahme Trust Reg *v.* Lloyds TSB Bank Plc [2004] EWHC 1931; [2004] 2 Lloyd's Rep. 637; [2004] I.L.Pr. 43; *Times,* August 25, 2004, Ch D . . . . *Digested,* 05/**601**

Mahmood *v.* Penrose [2004] EWHC 1500; [2005] B.P.I.R. 170, Ch D

Mahmud *v.* Bank of Credit and Commerce International SA (In Liquidation) see Malik *v.* Bank of Credit and Commerce International SA (In Liquidation)

Mahon *v.* Air New Zealand [1984] A.C. 808; [1984] 3 W.L.R. 884; [1984] 3 All E.R. 201; (1984) 81 L.S.G. 3336; (1984) 128 S.J. 752; *Times,* October 21, 1983, PC (NZ) . . . . *Digested,* 84/**2706**:
Applied, 94/1950, 05/1169: *Considered,* 86/3398, 87/3736, 94/1874

Mahon *v.* Sims [2005] 3 E.G.L.R. 67; [2005] 39 E.G. 138; *Times,* June 16, 2005, QBD

Maidment *v.* Southampton City Council [2005] 3 Q.R. 8, CC (Southampton) [*Ex rel.* Stuart McGhee, Barrister, College Chambers, 19 Carlton Crescent, Southampton] . . . . *Digested,* 05/**3093**

Maidstone BC *v.* Draper [2005] P.A.D. 52, Planning Inspector

Maierhofer *v.* Finanzamt Augsburg-Land (C315/00) [2003] S.T.C. 564; [2003] E.C.R. I-563; [2003] 2 C.M.L.R. 37; [2003] C.E.C. 192; [2003] B.T.C. 5269; [2003] B.V.C. 325; [2003] S.T.I. 88, ECJ (5th Chamber). . . . . *Digested,* 03/**4532**:
Applied, 05/4421: *Considered,* 05/4403

Mailer *v.* Austin Rover Group see Austin Rover Group Ltd *v.* HM Inspector of Factories

Main *v.* Swansea City Council; *sub nom* R. *v.* Swansea City Council Ex p. Main (1985) 49 P. & C.R. 26; [1985] J.P.L. 558, CA (Civ Div); affirming *Times,* December 23, 1981, QBD . . . . *Digested,* 85/**3463**:
Considered, 90/4367, 01/4688: *Distinguished,* 05/3305

Mainstream Properties Ltd *v.* Young [2005] EWCA Civ 861; [2005] I.R.L.R. 964; (2005) 102(30) L.S.G. 31; *Times,* July 28, 2005, CA (Civ Div) . . . . *Digested,* 05/**4188**

Mair *v.* Matthews Plant Hire (Unreported, June 25, 2004), CC (Truro) [*Ex rel.* Adrian Posta, Barrister, Albion Chambers, Broad Street, Bristol] . . . . *Digested,* 05/**3186**

Mairs (Inspector of Taxes) *v.* Haughey [1994] 1 A.C. 303; [1993] 3 W.L.R. 393; [1993] 3 All E.R. 801; [1993] S.T.C. 569; [1993] I.R.L.R. 551; 66 T.C. 273; [1993] B.T.C. 339; *Times,* July 23, 1993; *Independent,* August 16, 1993 (C.S.), HL (NI); affirming [1992] S.T.C. 495, CA (NI) . . . . *Digested,* 93/**2275**:
Applied, 05/4071: *Considered,* 99/4729: *Distinguished,* 97/2974

Majrowski *v.* Guy's and St Thomas's NHS Trust; *sub nom* Majorowski *v.* Guy's and St Thomas's NHS Trust [2005] EWCA Civ 251; [2005] Q.B. 848; [2005] 2 W.L.R. 1503; [2005] I.C.R. 977; [2005] I.R.L.R. 340; (2005) 149 S.J.L.B. 358; *Times,* March 21, 2005; *Independent,* April 8, 2005, CA (Civ Div) . . . . *Digested,* 05/**4199**

MAK *v.* Dewsbury Healthcare NHS Trust see JD *v.* East Berkshire Community Health NHS Trust

Makaratzis *v.* Greece (50385/99) (2005) 41 E.H.R.R. 49, ECHR

Makhfi *v.* France (59335/00) (2005) 41 E.H.R.R. 35, ECHR

Malcolm, Re see Malcolm *v.* Mackenzie

Malcolm *v.* Benedict Mackenzie (A Firm) see Malcolm *v.* Mackenzie

Malcolm *v.* Mackenzie; *sub nom* Malcolm, Re; Malcolm *v.* Benedict Mackenzie (A Firm) [2004] EWCA Civ 1748; [2005] 1 W.L.R. 1238; [2005] I.C.R. 611; [2005] B.P.I.R. 176; [2005] O.P.L.R. 301; (2005) 102(3) L.S.G. 30; *Times,* January 4, 2005, CA (Civ Div); affirming [2004] EWHC 339; [2004] 1 W.L.R. 1803; [2004] B.P.I.R. 747; [2004] Pens. L.R. 239; (2004) 101(13) L.S.G. 34, Ch D . . *Digested,* 05/**2278**

Malec v. Westminster City Council [2005] R.V.R. 384, Lands Tr

Malekshad v. Howard de Walden Estates Ltd (No.2); *sub nom* Howard de Walden
Estates Ltd v. Malekshad [2003] EWHC 3106; [2004] 1 W.L.R. 862; [2004] 4
All E.R. 162; [2005] L. & T.R. 4; (2004) 101(3) L.S.G. 35; [2003] N.P.C. 164;
Times, January 14, 2004, Ch D . . . .   *Digested*, 04/**3226**

Malik v. Bank of Credit and Commerce International SA (In Liquidation); *sub nom*
Mahmud v. Bank of Credit and Commerce International SA (In Liquidation);
BCCI SA, Re [1998] A.C. 20; [1997] 3 W.L.R. 95; [1997] 3 All E.R. 1; [1997]
I.C.R. 606; [1997] I.R.L.R. 462; (1997) 94(25) L.S.G. 33; (1997) 147 N.L.J. 917;
Times, June 13, 1997; *Independent*, June 20, 1997, HL; reversing [1995] 3 All
E.R. 545; [1996] I.C.R. 406; [1995] I.R.L.R. 375; (1995) 145 N.L.J. 593; *Times*,
April 12, 1995; *Independent*, March 17, 1995, CA (Civ Div); affirming [1994]
I.R.L.R. 282; *Times*, February 23, 1994; *Independent*, March 21, 1994 (C.S.),
Ch D . . . .   *Digested*, 97/**2192**:
Applied, 99/2010, 01/2305, 03/1216, 04/1193, 04/1196, 04/2215, 05/1209:
Considered, 98/2106, 99/2030, 99/2149, 01/2253, 03/1246:
Explained, 99/2111

Mallia v. Islington LBC (Unreported, November 8, 2002), MCLC [*Ex rel.* Thompsons
Solicitors, Congress House, Great Russell Street, London] . . . .   *Digested*, 04/**337**:
Applied, 05/312

Mallinson (t/a The Hair Team) v. Revenue and Customs Commissioners; Mould (t/a Leon
Jaimes Hair Fashion) v. Revenue and Customs Commissioners [2005] S.T.I.
1653, VAT Tr

Maloney v. St George [2004] EWHC 1724; [2005] B.P.I.R. 190, Ch D

Maltby v. DJ Freeman & Co [1978] 1 W.L.R. 431; [1978] 2 All E.R. 913; 122 S.J. 212,
Ch D . . . .   *Digested*, 78/**2819**:
Applied, 77/2879, 78/2348, 78/2817, 79/2188: *Considered*, 05/352:
Distinguished, 93/3169

Malvern Hills DC v. Secretary of State for the Environment 81 L.G.R. 13; (1983) 46 P. &
C.R. 58; (1982) 262 E.G. 1190; [1982] J.P.L. 439; *Times*, March 25, 1982, CA
(Civ Div) . . . .   *Digested*, 83/**3722**:
Applied, 91/3517, 92/4338, 92/4351: *Followed*, 92/4372, 05/3260

Mamatkulov v. Turkey (46827/99); Askarov v. Turkey (46951/99) (2005) 41 E.H.R.R.
25; 18 B.H.R.C. 203; *Times*, March 8, 2005, ECHR (Grand Chamber) . . . .   *Digested*, 05/**2076**

Man B&W Diesel SE Asia Pte Ltd v. PT Bumi International Tankers (2005) 21 Const. L.J.
126, CA (Sing) . . . .   *Digested*, 05/**2856**

Manchester City Council v. Higgins [2005] EWCA Civ 1423; [2005] 48 E.G.C.S. 222;
(2005) 102(47) L.S.G. 27; *Times*, December 14, 2005; *Independent*, November
30, 2005, CA (Civ Div)

Manchester City Council v. Romano; Manchester City Council v. Samari [2004] EWCA
Civ 834; [2005] 1 W.L.R. 2775; [2004] 4 All E.R. 21; [2004] H.L.R. 47;
[2005] B.L.G.R. 282; (2005) 83 B.M.L.R. 175; [2005] L. & T.R. 13; (2004)
101(27) L.S.G. 32; (2004) 148 S.J.L.B. 824; [2004] N.P.C. 106; *Times*, July 27,
2004, CA (Civ Div) . . . .   *Digested*, 04/**2532**

Manchester City Council v. Samari see Manchester City Council v. Romano

Manchester City Football Club Plc v. Royle; *sub nom* Royle v. Manchester City Football
Club Plc [2005] EWCA Civ 195; *Times*, March 14, 2005, CA (Civ Div) . . . .   *Digested*, 05/**707**

Manchester, Sheffield and Lincolnshire Railway Co v. Anderson [1898] 2 Ch. 394, CA .   *Applied*, 61/7524:
Considered, 05/2644

Mango Sport System Srl Socio Unico Mangone Antonio Vincenzo v. Dikhan SL [2005]
E.T.M.R. 5, OHIM (1st Bd App) . . . .   *Digested*, 05/**2523**

Mangotsfield Cemetery, Downend, Bristol, Re [2005] W.T.L.R. 1381; *Times*, April 26,
2005, Cons Ct

Manifest Shipping Co Ltd v. Uni-Polaris Insurance Co Ltd (The Star Sea); *sub nom*
Manifest Shipping Co Ltd v. Uni-Polaris Shipping Co Ltd (The Star Sea) [2001]
UKHL 1; [2003] 1 A.C. 469; [2001] 2 W.L.R. 170; [2001] 1 All E.R. 743; [2001]
1 All E.R. (Comm) 193; [2001] 1 Lloyd's Rep. 389; [2001] C.L.C. 608; [2001]
Lloyd's Rep. I.R. 247; *Times*, January 23, 2001, HL; affirming [1997] 1 Lloyd's
Rep. 360; [1997] C.L.C. 481; [1997] 6 Re. L.R. 175; *Times*, January 23, 1997, CA
(Civ Div); affirming [1995] 1 Lloyd's Rep. 651, QBD (Comm) . . . .   *Digested*, 01/**3825**:
Applied, 00/4696, 00/4744, 02/2732, 02/2739, 04/471:
Considered, 01/3827, 05/2359

Manley v. Sartori [1927] 1 Ch. 157, Ch D . . . .   *Applied*, 60/898,
66/8954, 95/3746: *Considered*, 05/2899

Mann v. Goldstein [1968] 1 W.L.R. 1091; [1968] 2 All E.R. 769; 112 S.J. 439, Ch D . . . .   *Digested*, 68/**456**:
Applied, 72/387, 78/260, 86/343, 05/2997: *Approved*, 80/294:
Considered, 95/2861

Mannai Investment Co Ltd *v.* Eagle Star Life Assurance Co Ltd [1997] A.C. 749; [1997] 2 W.L.R. 945; [1997] 3 All E.R. 352; [1997] C.L.C. 1124; [1997] 1 E.G.L.R. 57; [1997] 25 E.G. 138; [1997] 24 E.G. 122; (1997) 16 Tr. L.R. 432; [1997] E.G.C.S. 82; (1997) 94(30) L.S.G. 30; (1997) 147 N.L.J. 846; (1997) 141 S.J.L.B. 130; [1997] N.P.C. 81; *Times,* May 26, 1997, HL; reversing [1995] 1 W.L.R. 1508; [1996] 1 All E.R. 55; (1996) 71 P. & C.R. 129; [1996] 1 E.G.L.R. 69; [1996] 06 E.G. 140; [1995] E.G.C.S. 124; (1995) 139 S.J.L.B. 179; [1995] N.P.C. 117; *Times,* July 19, 1995, CA (Civ Div) . . . . *Digested,* 97/**3256**:
Applied, 98/3598, 00/5612, 01/4156, 01/4182, 02/3008, 03/2723, 04/670, 04/2243, 04/2497, 05/523, 05/2646: *Considered,* 03/2758, 05/475: *Distinguished,* 98/3033, 98/3608, 00/3910, 04/2488: *Followed,* 98/3614, 00/3885, 00/4421

Manninen *v.* Finland (C319/02) see Proceedings brought by Manninen (C319/02)
Manninen (C319/02), Re see Proceedings brought by Manninen (C319/02)
Manning *v.* AIG Europe UK Ltd; *sub nom* SSSL Realisations (2002) Ltd (formerly Save Service Stations Ltd) (In Liquidation), Re; Squires *v.* Aig Europe UK Ltd; Save Group Plc (In Liquidation), Re; Robinson *v.* AIG Europe UK Ltd [2004] EWHC 1760; [2005] 1 B.C.L.C. 1; [2004] B.P.I.R. 1334, Ch D (Companies Ct) . . . . *Digested,* 05/**2321**
Mansfield *v.* Leeds City Council [2004] EWHC 3350; [2005] O.P.L.R. 221, Ch D
Manufacture Francaise des Pneumatiques Michelin *v.* Commission of the European Communities (T203/01) [2003] E.C.R. II-4071; [2004] 4 C.M.L.R. 18, CFI (3rd Chamber) . . . . *Digested,* 05/**571**
Mapah *v.* Secretary of State for the Home Department see R. (on the application of Mapah) *v.* Secretary of State for the Home Department
Marc Rich Agriculture Trading SA *v.* Fortis Corporate Insurance NV [2004] EWHC 2632; [2005] Lloyd's Rep. I.R. 396, QBD (Comm)
Marc Rich & Co AG *v.* Societa Italiana Impianti SpA (C190/89) [1992] 1 Lloyd's Rep. 342; [1991] E.C.R. I-3855; [1991] I.L.Pr. 524; *Times,* September 20, 1991; *Financial Times,* October 16, 1991, ECJ . . . . *Digested,* 91/**3930**:
Applied, 97/883, 02/642: *Considered,* 97/4484, 05/599, 05/604: *Followed,* 97/4584
Marchant *v.* Fibernet Group Plc [2005] 3 Q.R. 9, CC (Basingstoke) [*Ex rel.* Marcus Pilgerstorfer, Barrister, Old Square Chambers, 1 Verulam Buildings, Gray's Inn, London] . . . . *Digested,* 05/**3160**
Marcic *v.* Thames Water Utilities Ltd; *sub nom* Thames Water Utilities Ltd *v.* Marcic [2003] UKHL 66; [2004] 2 A.C. 42; [2003] 3 W.L.R. 1603; [2004] 1 All E.R. 135; [2004] B.L.R. 1; 91 Con. L.R. 1; [2004] Env. L.R. 25; [2004] H.R.L.R. 10; [2004] U.K.H.R.R. 253; [2003] 50 E.G.C.S. 95; (2004) 101(4) L.S.G. 32; (2003) 153 N.L.J. 1869; (2003) 147 S.J.L.B. 1429; [2003] N.P.C. 150; *Times,* December 5, 2003; *Independent,* December 9, 2003, HL; reversing [2002] EWCA Civ 64; [2002] Q.B. 929; [2002] 2 W.L.R. 932; [2002] 2 All E.R. 55; [2002] B.L.R. 174; [2002] T.C.L.R. 15; 81 Con. L.R. 193; [2002] Env. L.R. 32; [2003] E.H.L.R. 2; [2002] H.R.L.R. 22; [2002] U.K.H.R.R. 1041; (2002) 18 Const. L.J. 152; [2002] 7 E.G.C.S. 122; (2002) 99(12) L.S.G. 34; (2002) 146 S.J.L.B. 51; [2002] N.P.C. 20; *Times,* February 14, 2002; *Independent,* February 12, 2002, CA (Civ Div); reversing in part [2001] 3 All E.R. 698; (2001) 3 T.C.L.R. 28; 77 Con. L.R. 42; [2002] Env. L.R. 6; [2001] H.R.L.R. 52; [2001] 3 E.G.L.R. 111; [2001] N.P.C. 95; [2001] E.H.L.R. Dig. 6; *Independent,* July 9, 2001 (C.S), QBD (TCC) . . . . *Digested,* 04/**2763**:
Applied, 03/3038, 05/2893: *Distinguished,* 04/1373, 04/2756: *Previous proceedings,* 01/1525
Marckx *v.* Belgium (A/31) (1979-80) 2 E.H.R.R. 330, ECHR . . . . *Applied,* 00/6142, 02/3079, 05/2126: *Followed,* 02/1700
Marconi Communications International Ltd *v.* PT Pan Indonesia Bank TBK; *sub nom* Marconi Communications International Ltd *v.* PT Pan Indonesian Bank Ltd [2005] EWCA Civ 422; [2005] 2 All E.R. (Comm) 325; *Times,* May 18, 2005, CA (Civ Div); affirming [2004] EWHC 129; [2004] 1 Lloyd's Rep. 594; [2004] 2 C.L.C. 570, QBD (Comm) . . . . *Digested,* 05/**628**
Marcus *v.* Institute of Chartered Accountants [2004] EWHC 3010; [2005] B.P.I.R. 413, Ch D . . . . *Digested,* 05/**2273**
Maresca *v.* Motor Insurance Repair Research Centre [2004] 4 All E.R. 254; [2005] I.C.R. 197, EAT. . . . . *Digested,* 04/**1246**
Margaretta Ltd (In Liquidation), Re see Freeman *v.* Customs and Excise Commissioners
Margulead Ltd *v.* Exide Technologies [2004] EWHC 1019; [2004] 2 All E.R. (Comm) 727; [2005] 1 Lloyd's Rep. 324, QBD (Comm)
Mariotte *v.* La Francaise des Jeux [2005] E.T.M.R. 101, C d'A (Paris)
Mark *v.* Mark; *sub nom* Marks *v.* Marks (Divorce: Jurisdiction) [2005] UKHL 42; [2005] 3 W.L.R. 111; [2005] 3 All E.R. 912; [2005] 2 F.L.R. 1193; [2005] 2 F.C.R. 467; [2005] I.N.L.R. 614; [2005] W.T.L.R. 1223; [2005] Fam. Law 857; (2005) 102(28) L.S.G. 32; *Times,* July 5, 2005; *Independent,* July 5, 2005, HL; affirming [2004] EWCA Civ 168; [2005] Fam. 267; [2004] 3 W.L.R. 641; [2004] 1 F.L.R. 1069; [2004] 1 F.C.R. 385; [2004] Fam. Law 402; (2004) 101(13) L.S.G. 33; *Times,* February 27, 2004, CA (Civ Div) . . . . *Digested,* 05/**1627**

Markel International Insurance Co Ltd *v.* La Republica Compania Argentina de Seguros
Generales SA [2004] EWHC 1826; [2005] Lloyd's Rep. I.R. 90, QBD (Comm) . *Digested,* 05/**609**
Markem Corp *v.* Zipher Ltd; Markem Technologies Ltd *v.* Buckby [2005] EWCA Civ
267; [2005] R.P.C. 31; (2005) 28(6) I.P.D. 28042, CA (Civ Div); reversing
(2005) 28(5) I.P.D. 28041, Ch D (Patents Ct) . . . . *Digested,* 05/**2448**:
Previous proceedings, 04/363, 04/2283, 05/2447
Markem Corp *v.* Zipher Ltd (Patent: Findings as to Claims) [2005] R.P.C. 3; (2004)
27(2) I.P.D. 27020, Ch D (Patents Ct) . . . . *Digested,* 05/**2447**:
Subsequent proceedings, 05/2448
Markem Technologies Ltd *v.* Buckby see Markem Corp *v.* Zipher Ltd
Market Investigations Ltd *v.* Minister of Social Security [1969] 2 Q.B. 173; [1969] 2
W.L.R. 1; [1968] 3 All E.R. 732; 112 S.J. 905, QBD . . . . *Digested,* 69/**2337**:
Applied, 72/525, 73/420, 80/891, 81/932, 90/1864, 92/2498, 01/2263,
05/4128: *Approved,* 76/871, 04/1315: *Considered,* 94/2546:
Followed, 72/1758, 73/1680
Marketing of Chocolate, Re (C12/00) see Commission of the European Communities *v.*
Spain (C12/00)
Marketing of Chocolate, Re (C14/00) see Commission of the European Communities *v.*
Italy (C14/00)
Markets South West (Holdings) Ltd *v.* First Secretary of State [2004] EWHC 1917;
[2005] J.P.L. 684, QBD (Admin). . . . . *Digested,* 05/**3304**
Markopoulos *v.* Anaptyxis (C255/01) [2004] E.C.R. I-9077; [2005] 1 C.M.L.R. 11;
[2005] C.E.C. 253, ECJ (1st Chamber) . . . . *Digested,* 05/**4**
Markose *v.* Epsom & St Helier NHS Trust [2004] EWHC 3130; [2005] Lloyd's Rep.
Med. 334, QBD. . . . . *Digested,* 05/**2840**
Marks *v.* Marks (Divorce: Jurisdiction) see Mark *v.* Mark
Marks *v.* McNally (Inspector of Taxes) [2004] S.T.C. (S.C.D.) 503; [2004] S.T.I. 2259,
Sp Comm . . . . *Digested,* 05/**3996**
Marks *v.* Sherred (Inspector of Taxes) [2004] S.T.C. (S.C.D.) 362; [2004] W.T.L.R.
1251; [2004] S.T.I. 1729, Sp Comm. . . . . *Digested,* 05/**4007**
Marks & Spencer Plc *v.* Customs and Excise Commissioners (C62/00) [2003] Q.B.
866; [2003] 2 W.L.R. 665; [2002] S.T.C. 1036; [2002] E.C.R. I-6325; [2002] 3
C.M.L.R. 9; [2002] C.E.C. 572; [2002] B.T.C. 5477; [2002] B.V.C. 622; [2002]
S.T.I. 1009; *Times,* July 20, 2002, ECJ (5th Chamber) [2002] E.C.R. I-6325,
AGO . . . . *Digested,* 02/**4775**:
Applied, 04/3987, 05/4377: *Considered,* 05/4367:
Previous proceedings, 00/5317: *Subsequent proceedings,* 03/4568
Marks & Spencer Plc *v.* Customs and Excise Commissioners (No.5); Sussex University
v. Customs and Excise Commissioners [2005] UKHL 53; [2005] S.T.C. 1254;
[2005] 3 C.M.L.R. 3; [2005] B.T.C. 5472; [2005] B.V.C. 503; [2005] S.T.I.
1338, HL [2003] EWCA Civ 1448; [2004] S.T.C. 1; [2004] 1 C.M.L.R. 8; [2004]
Eu. L.R. 170; [2004] B.T.C. 5091; [2004] B.V.C. 151; [2003] S.T.I. 1848; (2003)
100(45) L.S.G. 30; *Times,* October 27, 2003; *Independent,* October 24, 2003,
CA (Civ Div) . . . . *Digested,* 05/**4399**:
Previous proceedings 02/4775
Marks & Spencer Plc *v.* Freshfields Bruckhaus Deringer [2004] EWCA Civ 741; [2005]
P.N.L.R. 4; (2004) 148 S.J.L.B. 788, CA (Civ Div); affirming [2004] EWHC
1337; [2004] 1 W.L.R. 2331; [2004] 3 All E.R. 773; (2004) 101(27) L.S.G. 31;
Times, June 18, 2004, Ch D . . . . *Digested,* 05/**2724**
Marks & Spencer Plc *v.* Halsey (Inspector of Taxes) (C446/03) 8 I.T.L. Rep. 358; *Times,*
December 15, 2005, ECJ
Marks & Spencer Plc *v.* Lanarkshire Valuation Joint Board Assessor see Lanarkshire
Valuation Joint Board Assessor *v.* Clydesdale Bank Plc
Marks & Spencer Plc *v.* Renfrewshire Valuation Joint Board Assessor see Lanarkshire
Valuation Joint Board Assessor *v.* Clydesdale Bank Plc
Marks & Spencer Plc *v.* Williams-Ryan [2005] EWCA Civ 470; [2005] I.C.R. 1293;
[2005] I.R.L.R. 562, CA (Civ Div); affirming UKEAT/0145/04/SM, EAT . . . . . . *Digested,* 05/**1336**
Marlborough (West End) Ltd *v.* Wilks Head & Eve (Unreported, December 20, 1996) . . *Followed,* 05/3434
Marleasing SA *v.* La Comercial Internacional de Alimentacion SA (C106/89) [1990]
E.C.R. I-4135; [1993] B.C.C. 421; [1992] 1 C.M.L.R. 305, ECJ (6th Chamber) . . *Applied,* 97/2383,
00/5520, 02/4402: *Considered,* 03/2647, 05/4411: *Distinguished,* 94/2098,
95/2938
Marlines SA *v.* Commission of the European Communities (T56/99) [2003] E.C.R. II-
5225; [2005] 5 C.M.L.R. 28, CFI (5th Chamber)
Marlwood Commercial Inc *v.* Kozeny see Omega Group Holdings Ltd *v.* Kozeny
Maroussem *v.* Income Tax Commissioner see De Maroussem *v.* Commissioner of
Income Tax
Marpa Zeeland BV *v.* Netherlands (46300/99) (2005) 40 E.H.R.R. 34, ECHR
Marren *v.* Dawson Bentley & Co [1961] 2 Q.B. 135; [1961] 2 W.L.R. 679; [1961] 2 All
E.R. 270; 105 S.J. 383, Assizes (Leeds) . . . . *Digested,* 61/**5054**:
Applied, 05/892: *Approved,* 72/2037, 73/1964
Mars *v.* Hall (Unreported, June 17, 2004), CC (Tunbridge Wells) [*Ex rel.* Andrew Roy,
Barrister, 12 Kings Bench Walk, Temple, London] . . . . *Digested,* 05/**3173**

Mars UK Ltd *v.* Small (Inspector of Taxes); *sub nom* Small (Inspector of Taxes) *v.* Mars UK Ltd; William Grant & Sons Distillers Ltd *v.* Inland Revenue Commissioners [2005] EWHC 553; [2005] S.T.C. 958; [2005] B.T.C. 236; [2005] S.T.I. 833; *Times,* May 11, 2005, Ch D; reversing [2004] S.T.C. (S.C.D.) 253; [2004] S.T.I. 1282, Sp Comm . . . . *Digested,* 05/**4022**:
Overruled, 05/5692

Mars UK Ltd *v.* Societe des Produits Nestle SA (Three Dimensional Trade Marks); *sub nom* Nestle SA's Trade Mark Application (No.2006992) [2004] EWCA Civ 1008; [2005] R.P.C. 5; (2004) 27(7) I.P.D. 27068; (2004) 148 S.J.L.B. 944; *Times,* August 4, 2004, CA (Civ Div); affirming [2003] EWHC 3052; [2004] R.P.C. 27; (2004) 27(3) I.P.D. 27025, Ch D . . . . *Digested,* 04/**2359**

Marshall *v.* Allotts (A Firm) [2004] EWHC 1964; [2005] P.N.L.R. 11, DR (Leeds)

Marshall *v.* Jarvis Homes Ltd see Jarvis Homes Ltd *v.* Marshall

Marshall *v.* Marshall; *sub nom* Marshall *v.* Toothill [2005] EWCA Civ 641; *Times,* June 17, 2005, CA (Civ Div)

Marshall *v.* NM Financial Management Ltd; *sub nom* NM Financial Management Ltd *v.* Marshall [1997] 1 W.L.R. 1527; [1997] I.C.R. 1065; [1997] I.R.L.R. 449; *Times,* June 24, 1997, CA (Civ Div); affirming [1995] 1 W.L.R. 1461; [1995] 4 All E.R. 785; [1995] I.C.R. 1042; [1996] I.R.L.R. 20; *Times,* July 10, 1995, Ch D . . . . *Digested,* 96/**2600**:
Applied, 04/1199: *Considered,* 05/700

Marshall *v.* Southampton and South West Hampshire AHA (No.1) (152/84) [1986] Q.B. 401; [1986] 2 W.L.R. 780; [1986] 2 All E.R. 584; [1986] E.C.R. 723; [1986] 1 C.M.L.R. 688; [1986] I.C.R. 335; [1986] I.R.L.R. 140; (1986) 83 L.S.G. 1720; (1986) 130 S.J. 340, ECJ [1986] E.C.R. 723, AGO . . . . *Digested,* 86/**1456**:
Applied, 00/4458, 05/358: *Considered,* 87/1370, 87/3084, 88/1244, 88/2159, 90/3417: *Followed,* 88/1879, 89/1984, 90/3990, 96/2625:
Referred to, 87/2623, 88/1325

Marshall *v.* Southampton and South West Hampshire AHA (No.2) (C271/91) [1994] Q.B. 126; [1993] 3 W.L.R. 1054; [1993] 4 All E.R. 586; [1993] E.C.R. I-4367; [1993] 3 C.M.L.R. 293; [1993] I.C.R. 893; [1993] I.R.L.R. 445; *Times,* August 4, 1993; *Independent,* August 4, 1993 ; *Financial Times,* August 10, 1993, ECJ. . . . *Digested,* 94/**4927**:
Applied, 98/2100: *Considered,* 95/2031, 96/2551, 96/2625, 05/3984:
Previous proceedings, 91/4076: *Referred to,* 96/2606, 97/4672:
Subsequent proceedings, 94/1988

Marshall *v.* Toothill see Marshall *v.* Marshall

Marshalls Clay Products Ltd *v.* Caulfield; *sub nom* Caulfield *v.* Marshalls Clay Products Ltd; Pearce *v.* Huw Howatson Ltd; Clarke *v.* Frank Staddon Ltd; Sutton *v.* Potting Construction Ltd; Hoy *v.* Hanlin Construction Ltd [2004] EWCA Civ 422; [2004] 2 C.M.L.R. 45; [2004] I.C.R. 1502; [2004] I.R.L.R. 564; (2004) 148 S.J.L.B. 539, CA (Civ Div) [2004] I.C.R. 436; [2003] I.R.L.R. 552; *Times,* August 25, 2003, EAT. . . . . *Digested,* 04/**1266**:
Applied, 05/1211

MARTEK/Omega-3 highly unsaturated fatty acids (T343/01) [2005] E.P.O.R. 49, EPO (Technical Bd App)

Martin *v.* David Wilson Homes Ltd [2004] EWCA Civ 1027; [2004] 3 E.G.L.R. 77; [2004] 39 E.G. 134; [2004] N.P.C. 105, CA (Civ Div) . . . . *Digested,* 05/**3430**:
Applied, 05/3307

Martin *v.* Kaisary (No.1) [2005] EWCA Civ 594; [2005] C.P. Rep. 35, CA (Civ Div) . . . *Digested,* 05/**307**

Martin *v.* Lancehawk Ltd (t/a European Telecom Solutions) UKEAT/0525/ILB, EAT. . . . *Approved,* 05/1221

Martin *v.* Nicholson [2004] EWHC 2135; [2005] W.T.L.R. 175, Ch D . . . . *Digested,* 05/**3974**

Martin *v.* Southwark LBC see Kwamin *v.* Abbey National Plc

Martinez Sala *v.* Freistaat Bayern (C85/96) [1998] E.C.R. I-2691, ECJ. . . . . *Applied,* 05/3922

Marubeni Hong Kong & South China Ltd *v.* Mongolia [2005] EWCA Civ 395; [2005] 1 W.L.R. 2497; [2005] 2 All E.R. (Comm) 288; [2005] 2 Lloyd's Rep. 231; [2005] 1 C.L.C. 540; *Times,* April 22, 2005, CA (Civ Div); affirming [2004] EWHC 472; [2004] 2 Lloyd's Rep. 198; *Times,* May 14, 2004, QBD (Comm) . . . *Digested,* 05/**703**

Masa Invest Group *v.* Ukraine (Admissibility) (3540/03) 8 I.T.L. Rep. 262, ECHR

Mashru *v.* Avonridge Property Co Ltd see Avonridge Property Co Ltd *v.* Mashru

Masri *v.* Consolidated Contractors Group SAL see Masri *v.* Consolidated Contractors International (UK) Ltd

Masri *v.* Consolidated Contractors International (UK) Ltd; *sub nom* Masri *v.* Consolidated Contractors Group SAL [2005] EWCA Civ 1436; [2005] 2 C.L.C. 704; (2005) 102(43) L.S.G. 28; *Times,* October 27, 2005, CA (Civ Div); affirming [2005] EWHC 944; [2005] 1 C.L.C. 1125, QBD (Comm) . . . . *Digested,* 05/**469**

Massarella *v.* Phee (Unreported, August 6, 2004), CC (Maidstone) [*Ex rel.* Tim Petts, Barrister, 12 King's Bench Walk, London] . . . . *Digested,* 05/**3156**

Masson *v.* Netherlands (A/327) (1996) 22 E.H.R.R. 491, ECHR . . . . *Digested,* 97/**2801**:
Applied, 98/3156: *Considered,* 05/633: *Distinguished,* 98/3121:
Followed, 97/2805

Mastercard International Inc *v.* Hitachi Credit (UK) Plc; *sub nom* CREDITMASTER Trade Mark [2004] EWHC 1623; [2005] E.T.M.R. 10; [2005] R.P.C. 21; (2004) 27(9) I.P.D. 27091, Ch D . . . . *Digested,* 05/**2562**:
Considered, 05/2561

Masterman-Lister *v.* Brutton & Co see Masterman-Lister *v.* Jewell

Masterman-Lister *v.* Jewell; Masterman-Lister *v.* Brutton & Co [2002] EWCA Civ 1889; [2003] 1 W.L.R. 1511; [2003] 3 All E.R. 162; [2003] C.P. Rep. 29; (2004) 7 C.C.L. Rep. 5; [2003] P.I.Q.R. P20; [2003] Lloyd's Rep. Med. 244; (2003) 73 B.M.L.R. 1; [2003] W.T.L.R. 259; (2003) 147 S.J.L.B. 60; *Times,* December 28, 2002, CA (Civ Div); affirming [2002] EWHC 417; [2002] Lloyd's Rep. Med. 239; [2002] W.T.L.R. 563, QBD. . . . . *Digested,* 03/**311**:
Considered, 03/4492: *Followed,* 05/473
Mathew *v.* Canada; *sub nom* Mathew *v.* R. 8 I.T.L. Rep. 306, Sup Ct (Can); affirming CA (Can); affirming 5 I.T.L. Rep. 153, Tax Ct (Can)
Mathew *v.* R. see Mathew *v.* Canada
Mathews *v.* Kent and Medway Towns Fire Authority see Matthews *v.* Kent and Medway Towns Fire Authority
Mattel Inc *v.* RSW Group Plc [2004] EWHC 1610; [2005] F.S.R. 5; (2004) 27(9) I.P.D. 27092, Ch D . . . . *Digested,* 05/**372**:
Considered, 05/367
Matthew *v.* Aitken; *sub nom* Matthew *v.* Procurator Fiscal, Wick 2004 S.C.C.R. 515; [2005] Eu. L.R. 48, HCJ . . . . *Digested,* 05/**5284**
Matthew *v.* Procurator Fiscal, Wick see Matthew *v.* Aitken
Matthew *v.* Trinidad and Tobago; *sub nom* Matthew (Charles) *v.* Queen, The [2004] UKPC 33; [2005] 1 A.C. 433; [2004] 3 W.L.R. 812; (2004) 101(32) L.S.G. 35; *Times,* July 14, 2004, PC (Trin) . . . . *Digested,* 04/**3337**:
Referred to, 04/3335, 04/3336
Matthew (Charles) *v.* Queen, The see Matthew *v.* Trinidad and Tobago
Matthews, Re [2004] EWHC 782; [2005] B.P.I.R. 416, Ch D . . . . *Digested,* 05/**2289**
Matthews *v.* Associated Portland Cement Manufacturers (1978) Ltd see Fairchild *v.* Glenhaven Funeral Services Ltd (t/a GH Dovener & Son)
Matthews *v.* British Uralite Plc see Fairchild *v.* Glenhaven Funeral Services Ltd (t/a GH Dovener & Son)
Matthews *v.* Kent and Medway Towns Fire Authority; *sub nom* Mathews *v.* Kent and Medway Towns Fire Authority; TNS, HL; reversing [2004] EWCA Civ 844; [2004] 3 All E.R. 620; [2005] I.C.R. 84; [2004] I.R.L.R. 697; [2004] Pens. L.R. 313; (2004) 148 S.J.L.B. 876; *Times,* July 8, 2004; *Independent,* July 7, 2004, CA (Civ Div); affirming [2004] I.C.R. 257; [2003] I.R.L.R. 732; [2004] Pens. L.R. 139, EAT . . . . *Digested,* 04/**1260**
Matthews *v.* Ministry of Defence [2003] UKHL 4; [2003] 1 A.C. 1163; [2003] 2 W.L.R. 435; [2003] 1 All E.R. 689; [2003] I.C.R. 247; [2004] H.R.L.R. 2; [2003] U.K.H.R.R. 453; 14 B.H.R.C. 585; [2003] P.I.Q.R. P24; [2003] A.C.D. 42; (2003) 100(13) L.S.G. 26; (2003) 153 N.L.J. 261; (2003) 147 S.J.L.B. 235; *Times,* February 14, 2003, HL; affirming [2002] EWCA Civ 773; [2002] 1 W.L.R. 2621; [2002] 3 All E.R. 513; [2002] I.C.R. 1003; [2002] H.R.L.R. 39; 12 B.H.R.C. 652; [2002] P.I.Q.R. P4; [2002] A.C.D. 77; (2002) 99(27) L.S.G. 33; (2002) 152 N.L.J. 879; (2002) 146 S.J.L.B. 144; *Times,* May 31, 2002; *Independent,* June 11, 2002, CA (Civ Div); reversing [2002] EWHC 13; [2002] C.P. Rep. 26; [2002] P.I.Q.R. P25; [2002] A.C.D. 42; *Times,* January 30, 2002, QBD . . . . *Digested,* 03/**2970**
Mattos Junior *v.* MacDaniels Ltd see Barros Mattos Junior *v.* MacDaniels Ltd
MATUSHITA/Remote control (T244/00) [2005] E.P.O.R. 12, EPO (Technical Bd App) . *Digested,* 05/**2482**
Mauri *v.* Ministero della Giustizia (C250/03 R) [2005] E.C.R. I-1267; [2005] 4 C.M.L.R. 11, ECJ (2nd Chamber) . . . . *Digested,* 05/**1429**
Maurice *v.* France (11810/03) [2005] 3 F.C.R. 365, ECHR (Grand Chamber)
Maurice *v.* Hollow-Ware Products Ltd; *sub nom* Maurice *v.* Holloware Products [2005] EWHC 815; [2005] 2 E.G.L.R. 71; [2005] 26 E.G. 132; (2005) 102(19) L.S.G. 34; *Times,* March 31, 2005, Ch D . . . . *Digested,* 05/**2666**
Maurice *v.* Holloware Products see Maurice *v.* Hollow-Ware Products Ltd
Max.Mobil Telekommunikation Service GmbH *v.* Commission of the European Communities (T54/99) [2002] E.C.R. II-313; [2002] 4 C.M.L.R. 32, CFI (2nd Chamber) . . . . *Digested,* 02/**1540**:
Followed, 04/545: *Overruled,* 05/1473
Maxol Oil Ltd *v.* Department of the Environment for Northern Ireland [2005] R.V.R. 97, Lands Tr (NI)
Maxwell Communications Corp Plc (No.1), Re [1992] B.C.C. 372; [1992] B.C.L.C. 465, Ch D . . . . *Digested,* 92/**2536**:
Applied, 05/2267
May *v.* Ashford BC [2005] P.A.D. 58, Planning Inspector
Mayan *v.* Societe Television Francaise 1 [2005] E.C.C. 23, C d'A (Paris)
Mayariya (t/a Oaktree Lane (Selly Oak) Post Office & Stores) *v.* Customs and Excise Commissioners [2005] S.T.I. 1026, V&DTr
Mayban General Assurance BHD *v.* Alstom Power Plants Ltd [2004] EWHC 1038; [2004] 2 Lloyd's Rep. 609; [2004] 2 C.L.C. 682; [2005] Lloyd's Rep. I.R. 18, QBD (Comm) . . . . *Digested,* 05/**2383**
Mayer Parry Recycling Ltd *v.* Environment Agency [1999] 1 C.M.L.R. 963; [1999] Env. L.R. 489; (1999) 96(6) L.S.G. 32; *Times,* December 3, 1998, Ch D . . . . *Digested,* 99/**2207**:
Considered, 01/573, 02/1520, 05/1362: *Not applied,* 01/2413
Mayes *v.* Beadle see Beadle (Deceased), Re

Mayfair Property Co v. Johnston [1894] 1 Ch. 508, Ch D . . . .   *Considered*, 05/**3239**
Mayne Pharma Pty Ltd v. Pharmacia Italia SpA [2005] EWCA Civ 137; (2005) 28(3) I.P.D. 28011, CA; reversing [2004] EWHC 2458, Ch D
Mayne Pharma Pty Ltd v. Pharmacia Italia SPA (Costs) [2005] EWCA Civ 294; (2005) 28(5) I.P.D. 28034, CA (Civ Div); affirming [2004] EWHC 3066, Ch D (Patents Ct)
Mayo-Deman v. University of Greenwich [2005] I.R.L.R. 845, EAT
Mayor and Commonalty and Citizens of the City of London v. Intercede 1765 Ltd; *sub nom* City of London v. Intercede Ltd; City of London v. Wardens and Commonality of the Mystery of Mercers in the City of London [2005] EWHC 1691; [2005] N.P.C. 103, Ch D
Mayr-melnhof Kartongesellschaft mbh v. Commission of the European Communities (T347/94) [1998] E.C.R. II-1751, CFI . . . .   *Followed*, 01/**768**, 05/**554**
Mazur Media Ltd v. Mazur Media GmbH [2004] EWHC 1566; [2004] 1 W.L.R. 2966; [2005] 1 Lloyd's Rep. 41; [2005] 1 B.C.L.C. 305; [2004] I.L.Pr. 36; [2004] B.P.I.R. 1253; *Times*, July 29, 2004, Ch D . . . .   *Digested*, 05/**620**
MB (A Patient) (Court of Protection: Appeal), Re see B (A Patient) (Court of Protection: Appeal), Re
Mbasogo v. Logo Ltd (No.1) [2005] EWHC 2034; (2005) 102(39) L.S.G. 32, QBD
MC v. Bulgaria (39272/98) (2005) 40 E.H.R.R. 20; 15 B.H.R.C. 627, ECHR . . . .   *Digested*, 04/**1931**
McAdams Homes Ltd v. Robinson [2004] EWCA Civ 214; [2005] 1 P. & C.R. 30; [2004] 3 E.G.L.R. 93; (2004) 101(10) L.S.G. 30; (2004) 148 S.J.L.B. 296; [2004] N.P.C. 33; [2004] 2 P. & C.R. DG3; *Independent*, March 9, 2004, CA (Civ Div) . . . .   *Digested*, 05/**3403**
Macalister Todd Phillips Bodkins v. AMP General Insurance Ltd; *sub nom* AMP General Insurance Ltd v. Macalister Todd Phillips Bodkins (2005-06) 8 I.T.E.L.R. 15, HC (NZ)
McAlpine PPS Pipeline Systems Joint Venture v. Transco Plc [2004] EWHC 2030; [2004] B.L.R. 352; 96 Con. L.R. 69, QBD (TCC) . . . .   *Digested*, 05/**648**
McBride v. Blackburn (Inspector of Taxes) [2003] S.T.C. (S.C.D.) 139; [2003] S.T.I. 269, Sp Comm . . . .   *Digested*, 03/**4232**: *Applied*, 05/4016
McCabe v. Cornwall CC see Eastwood v. Magnox Electric Plc
McCann v. Birmingham City Council; *sub nom* McGann v. Birmingham City Council [2004] EWHC 2156; [2004] N.P.C. 140; [2005] 1 P. & C.R. DG5, QBD (Admin)
McCausland v. Duncan Lawrie Ltd [1997] 1 W.L.R. 38; [1996] 4 All E.R. 995; (1997) 74 P. & C.R. 343; [1996] E.G.C.S. 103; (1996) 93(26) L.S.G. 19; (1996) 146 N.L.J. 1387; [1996] N.P.C. 94; *Times*, June 18, 1996; *Independent*, June 11, 1996, CA (Civ Div); reversing [1995] E.G.C.S. 133, Ch D . . . .   *Digested*, 96/**1256**: *Applied*, 04/3216, 05/695
McClean's Application for Judicial Review (No.1), Re [2005] N.I. 1, CA (NI); affirming QBD (NI)
McClean's Application for Judicial Review (No.2), Re [2005] UKHL 46; [2005] N.I. 490; [2005] U.K.H.R.R. 826; (2005) 102(29) L.S.G. 32, HL (NI); reversing [2005] N.I. 21, CA (NI); reversing QBD (NI)
McCullough (Inspector of Taxes) v. Ahluwalia [2004] EWCA Civ 889; [2004] S.T.C. 1295; [2004] B.T.C. 348; [2004] S.T.I. 1514; *Times*, August 9, 2004, CA (Civ Div) . . . .   *Digested*, 05/**4060**
McDermott Industries (Aust) Pty Ltd v. Commissioner of Taxation 7 I.T.L. Rep. 800, Fed Ct (Aus) (Full Ct) . . . .   *Digested*, 05/**4038**
McDonagh v. Ali see Triesman v. Ali
MacDonald v. Advocate General for Scotland see Advocate General for Scotland v. MacDonald
MacDonald v. Ministry of Defence see Advocate General for Scotland v. MacDonald
MacDonald (Inspector of Taxes) v. Dextra Accessories Ltd see Dextra Accessories Ltd v. MacDonald (Inspector of Taxes)
McDonald's Corp v. Future Enterprises Pte Ltd [2005] F.S.R. 32, CA (Sing)
McDonald's International Property Co Ltd v. Irfan Aydemir [2005] E.T.M.R. 18, OHIM (3rd Bd App) . . . .   *Digested*, 05/**2541**
McDonnell v. Holwerda [2005] EWHC 1081; [2005] Lloyd's Rep. Med. 423; (2005) 155 N.L.J. 903; *Times*, June 2, 2005, QBD . . . .   *Digested*, 05/**2887**
McEwan v. Martin (Inspector of Taxes) [2005] EWHC 714; [2005] S.T.C. 993; [2005] B.T.C. 293; [2005] S.T.I. 140; *Times*, July 1, 2005, Ch D . . . .   *Digested*, 05/**4002**
McEwan v. O'Donoghue (Inspector of Taxes) [2005] S.T.C. (S.C.D.) 437; [2005] S.T.I. 870, Sp Comm . . . .   *Digested*, 05/**4100**
McEwan v. O'Donoghue (Inspector of Taxes) (Costs) [2005] S.T.C. (S.C.D.) 681, Sp Comm
McFadden v. United Kingdom (11365/85) see Brogan v. United Kingdom (A/145-B)
McFarland's Application for Judicial Review, Re [2000] N.I. 403, QBD (NI) . . . .   *Digested*, 01/**5735**: *Considered*, 05/884
McFarlane v. Coggins & Griffiths (Liverpool) Ltd see Mersey Docks and Harbour Board v. Coggins & Griffith (Liverpool) Ltd

MacFarlane v. Glasgow City Council [2001] I.R.L.R. 7, EAT . . . .   *Digested,* 01/**6468**:
                                                              Applied, 03/4030: *Considered,* 05/1325
McFarlane v. McFarlane; Parlour v. Parlour [2004] EWCA Civ 872; [2005] Fam. 171;
    [2004] 3 W.L.R. 1480; [2004] 3 All E.R. 921; [2004] 2 F.L.R. 893; [2004] 2
    F.C.R. 657; [2004] Fam. Law 714; *Times,* July 9, 2004; *Independent,* July 13,
    2004, CA (Civ Div); reversing [2003] EWHC 2410, Fam Div . . . .   *Digested,* 04/**1523**:
                                                                      Applied, 05/1656, 05/1662
McGann v. Birmingham City Council see McCann v. Birmingham City Council
McGee v. South Lanarkshire Council [2005] R.V.R. 218; 2005 Hous. L.R. 41, Lands Tr
    (Scot) . . . .   *Digested,* 05/**5596**
McGhie v. British Telecommunications Plc [2005] EWCA Civ 48; (2005) 149 S.J.L.B.
    114, CA (Civ Div)
McGlashan v. Westminster CC [2005] P.A.D. 31, Planning Inspector
McGlinn v. Waltham Contractors Ltd [2005] EWHC 1419; [2005] 3 All E.R. 1126;
    [2005] B.L.R. 432; [2005] T.C.L.R. 8; 102 Con. L.R. 111, QBD (TCC)
McGowan v. Scottish Water [2005] I.R.L.R. 167, EAT (SC) . . . .   *Digested,* 05/**5219**
McGuinness v. Southwark LBC [2005] R.V.R. 331, Lands Tr
MacKay v. First Secretary of State (2005) 149 S.J.L.B. 771, CA (Civ Div)
McKay v. Rogers; *sub nom* McKay (A Bankrupt) (No.1), Re [2002] EWHC 2825;
    [2004] B.P.I.R. 1272, Ch D . . . .   *Digested,* 05/**2287**
McKay v. Titley; *sub nom* McKay (A Bankrupt) (No.2), Re [2004] EWCA Civ 801;
    [2004] B.P.I.R. 1282, CA (Civ Div) . . . .   *Digested,* 05/**2281**
McKay (A Bankrupt) (No.1), Re see McKay v. Rogers
McKay (A Bankrupt) (No.2), Re see McKay v. Titley
McKeith v. News Group Newspapers Ltd [2005] EWHC 1162; [2005] E.M.L.R. 32,
    QBD . . . .   *Digested,* 05/**973**
McKerr, Re see McKerr's Application for Judicial Review, Re
McKerr's Application for Judicial Review, Re; *sub nom* McKerr, Re [2004] UKHL 12;
    [2004] 1 W.L.R. 807; [2004] 2 All E.R. 409; [2004] N.I. 212; [2004] H.R.L.R.
    26; [2004] U.K.H.R.R. 385; 17 B.H.R.C. 68; [2004] Lloyd's Rep. Med. 263;
    (2004) 101(13) L.S.G. 33; (2004) 148 S.J.L.B. 355; *Times,* March 12, 2004, HL
    (NI); reversing [2003] N.I. 117, CA (NI) . . . .   *Digested,* 04/**1976**:
                                                                      Considered, 05/17
Mackinnon v. Donaldson Lufkin & Jenrette Securities Corp [1986] Ch. 482; [1986] 2
    W.L.R. 453; [1986] 1 All E.R. 653; [1987] E.C.C. 139; [1986] Fin. L.R. 225;
    (1986) 83 L.S.G. 1226; (1985) 130 S.J. 224; *Financial Times,* November 12,
    1985, Ch D . . . .   *Digested,* 86/**1501**:
                    Applied, 87/209: *Considered,* 94/270: *Distinguished,* 05/395, 05/601:
                                                              Referred to, 98/3308
MacKinnon v. Regent Trust Co Ltd [2005] W.T.L.R. 1367, CA (Jer)
Maclaine Watson & Co Ltd v. Department of Trade and Industry see JH Rayner (Mincing
    Lane) Ltd v. Department of Trade and Industry
Maclaine Watson & Co Ltd v. International Tin Council see JH Rayner (Mincing Lane)
    Ltd v. Department of Trade and Industry
McLaren Murdoch & Hamilton Ltd v. Abercromby Motor Group Ltd 2003 S.C.L.R. 323;
    100 Con. L.R. 63; 2002 G.W.D. 38-1242, OH . . . .   *Digested,* 03/**5323**
McLarnon v. Bradford District Care NHS Trust [2005] Lloyd's Rep. Med. 345, QBD
McLoughlin v. O'Brian [1983] 1 A.C. 410; [1982] 2 W.L.R. 982; [1982] 2 All E.R. 298;
    [1982] R.T.R. 209; (1982) 79 L.S.G. 922; 126 S.J. 347, HL; reversing [1981]
    Q.B. 599; [1981] 2 W.L.R. 1014; [1981] 1 All E.R. 809; 125 S.J. 169, CA (Civ
    Div) . . . .   *Digested,* 82/**2153**:
                    Applied, 84/2330, 87/2857, 91/2670, 91/2671, 92/3250, 92/3251, 95/6157,
                    02/3275, 03/3132: *Considered,* 83/2609, 84/2342, 85/2322, 85/2326,
                    86/1069, 87/2580, 87/2608, 88/6, 90/1571, 90/3727, 91/2512, 00/4213,
                    00/4220, 05/2834: *Distinguished,* 98/5723: *Followed,* 03/3028
McManus v. Sharif see Cranfield v. Bridgegrove Ltd
McMeechan v. Secretary of State for Employment [1997] I.C.R. 549; [1997] I.R.L.R.
    353, CA (Civ Div); affirming [1995] I.C.R. 444; [1995] I.R.L.R. 461, EAT . . . . . .   *Digested,* 97/**2195**:
                    Applied, 03/1258: *Considered,* 98/2137, 01/2264: *Distinguished,* 05/1214
McMillan Williams (A Firm) v. Range [2004] EWCA Civ 294; [2004] 1 W.L.R. 1858;
    [2005] E.C.C. 8; (2004) 148 S.J.L.B. 384; *Times,* April 16, 2004, CA (Civ Div) .   *Digested,* 04/**642**
McNicholas Construction Co Ltd v. Customs and Excise Commissioners [2000] S.T.C.
    553; [2000] B.T.C. 5225; [2000] B.V.C. 255; [2000] S.T.I. 889; *Independent,*
    July 24, 2000 (C.S), QBD . . . .   *Digested,* 00/**5348**:
                    Applied, 05/2307: *Approved,* 03/4601: *Considered,* 02/4732:
                                          Subsequent proceedings, 02/290

MacNiven (Inspector of Taxes) v. Westmoreland Investments Ltd; *sub nom* Westmoreland Investments Ltd v. MacNiven (Inspector of Taxes) [2001] UKHL 6; [2003] 1 A.C. 311; [2001] 2 W.L.R. 377; [2001] 1 All E.R. 865; [2001] S.T.C. 237; 73 T.C. 1; [2001] B.T.C. 44; 3 I.T.L. Rep. 342; [2001] S.T.I. 168; (2001) 98(11) L.S.G. 44; (2001) 151 N.L.J. 223; (2001) 145 S.J.L.B. 55; *Times*, February 14, 2001; *Independent*, March 19, 2001 (C.S), HL; affirming [1998] S.T.C. 1131; [1998] B.T.C. 422; 1 I.T.L. Rep. 208; (1998) 95(44) L.S.G. 35; (1998) 142 S.J.L.B. 262; *Times*, October 26, 1998; *Independent*, November 2, 1998 (C.S.), CA (Civ Div); reversing [1997] S.T.C. 1103; [1997] B.T.C. 424; *Times*, August 19, 1997, Ch D . . . . *Digested*, 01/**5199**:
Applied, 01/5205, 03/4173, 03/4185: *Considered*, 02/4352, 02/4498, 03/4145, 05/3988, 05/4084: *Distinguished*, 05/4037
McNulty v. PC Harrinton Ltd see Smith v. AJ Morrisroes & Sons Ltd
McPherson v. BNP Paribas SA (London Branch) [2004] EWCA Civ 569; [2004] 3 All E.R. 266; [2004] 4 Costs L.R. 596; [2004] I.C.R. 1398; [2004] I.R.L.R. 558; *Times*, May 31, 2004; *Independent*, May 20, 2004, CA (Civ Div); reversing EAT/0916/02 ILB, EAT . . . . *Digested*, 04/**1314**:
Applied, 05/1220
MacPherson & Kelley v. Kevin J Prunty & Associates [1983] V.R. 573, Sup Ct (Vic) . . .   *Digested*, 83/**3610**:
Considered, 05/2865
McPherson v. Secretary of State for the Home Department [2001] EWCA Civ 1955; [2002] I.N.L.R. 139, CA (Civ Div) . . . .   *Digested*, 02/**2550**:
Applied, 04/2039, 05/2167
McPhilemy v. Times Newspapers Ltd (Costs) [2001] EWCA Civ 933; [2002] 1 W.L.R. 934; [2001] 4 All E.R. 861; [2002] C.P. Rep. 9; [2001] 2 Costs L.R. 295; [2001] E.M.L.R. 35; *Times*, July 3, 2001, CA (Civ Div) . . . .   *Digested*, 01/**484**:
Applied, 02/349, 03/355: *Considered*, 02/347, 05/369
McQueen v. Glendales Ltd (Unreported, February 12, 2004), CC (Liverpool) [*Ex rel.* David Binns, Barrister, St James's Chambers, 68 Quay Street, Manchester.] . . . .   *Digested*, 05/**3194**
McQUEEN CLOTHING CO Trade Mark see Croom's Trade Mark Application
Macredie v. Thrapston Garage see Brown v. Kigass Aero Components Ltd
McTear v. Imperial Tobacco Ltd; *sub nom* McTear's Executrix v. Imperial Tobacco Ltd 2005 2 S.C. 1; 2005 G.W.D. 20-365; *Times*, June 14, 2005, OH
McTear's Executrix v. Imperial Tobacco Ltd see McTear v. Imperial Tobacco Ltd
McVicar v. United Kingdom (46311/99) (2002) 35 E.H.R.R. 22; 12 B.H.R.C. 567; (2002) 152 N.L.J. 759, ECHR . . . .   *Digested*, 03/**2092**:
Applied, 05/2089
MCI Inc v. Commission of the European Communities (T310/00) [2004] 5 C.M.L.R. 26, CFI (2nd Chamber) . . . .   *Digested*, 05/**582**
MCI WorldCom International Inc v. Primus Telecommunications Inc; *sub nom* Primus Telecommunications Inc v. MCI Worldcom International Inc [2004] EWCA Civ 957; [2004] 2 All E.R. (Comm) 833; [2004] Info. T.L.R. 250, CA (Civ Div); reversing [2003] EWHC 2182; [2004] 1 All E.R. (Comm) 138; [2004] 1 B.C.L.C. 42, QBD (Comm) . . . .   *Digested*, 05/**715**
MD v. Secretary of State for the Home Department; *sub nom* MD (Imprisonment in UK: Article 8: Serbia and Montenegro), Re [2004] UKIAT 292; [2005] Imm. A.R. 153, IAT
MD (Imprisonment in UK: Article 8: Serbia and Montenegro), Re see MD v. Secretary of State for the Home Department
MDA Investment Management (No.1), Re; *sub nom* Whalley v. Doney (No.1) [2003] EWHC 2277; [2005] B.C.C. 783; [2004] 1 B.C.L.C. 217; [2004] B.P.I.R. 75, Ch D . . . .   *Digested*, 04/**2148**
MDA Investment Management (No.2), Re; *sub nom* Whalley v. Doney (No.2) [2004] EWHC 42; [2005] B.C.C. 783, Ch D . . . .   *Digested*, 05/**531**
Mears v. L&SWR Co (1862) 11 C.B. N.S. 1029 . . . .   *Considered*, 05/**3239**
Mears v. RG Carter Ltd see Grieves v. FT Everard & Sons Ltd
Meca-Medina v. Commission of the European Communities (T313/02) [2004] 3 C.M.L.R. 60; [2005] C.E.C. 176; *Times*, October 25, 2004, CFI (4th Chamber) . .   *Digested*, 05/**3963**
Mediakabel BV v. Commissariaat voor de Media (C89/04) [2005] Info. T.L.R. 307; *Times*, June 13, 2005, ECJ (3rd Chamber)
Medical Protection Society v. Sadek see Sadek v. Medical Protection Society
Medicaments and Related Classes of Goods (No.2), Re see Director General of Fair Trading v. Proprietary Association of Great Britain
MEDINOL/Flexible stent (T306/01) [2005] E.P.O.R. 16, EPO (Technical Bd App) . . . . .   *Digested*, 05/**2472**
Medion AG v. Thomson Multimedia Sales Germany & Austria GmbH (C120/04) [2005] C.E.C. 720, ECJ (2nd Chamber)
Meek v. Birmingham City Council see Meek v. Birmingham DC
Meek v. Birmingham DC; *sub nom* Meek v. Birmingham City Council [1987] I.R.L.R. 250, CA (Civ Div) . . . .   *Digested*, 87/**1399**:
Applied, 03/1224: *Followed*, 05/1333
Meerabux v. Attorney General of Belize [2005] UKPC 12; [2005] 2 A.C. 513; [2005] 2 W.L.R. 1307; *Times*, April 20, 2005, PC (Bze) . . . .   *Digested*, 05/**13**
Mega Bloks Inc v. Kirkbi A/S [2005] E.T.M.R. 87, OHIM (Cancellation Div) . . . .   *Digested*, 05/**2533**

Meikle v. Nottinghamshire CC; *sub nom* Nottinghamshire CC v. Meikle [2004] EWCA
   Civ 859; [2004] 4 All E.R. 97; [2005] I.C.R. 1; [2004] I.R.L.R. 703; (2004) 80
   B.M.L.R. 129; (2004) 148 S.J.L.B. 908; *Times*, July 15, 2004; *Independent*, July
   14, 2004, CA (Civ Div); affirming EAT/0033/03 RN, EAT . . . .   *Digested*, 04/**1193**:
                            Applied, 05/1227

Meisels v. Martin [2005] EWHC 845; [2005] B.P.I.R. 1151, Ch D

Melchior v. Vettivel [2002] C.P. Rep. 24, Ch D . . . .   *Digested*, 02/**404**:
                            Considered, 05/379

Melhuish v. Redbridge Citizens Advice Bureau [2005] I.R.L.R. 419, EAT . . . .   *Digested*, 05/**1330**

Melia v. Magna Kansei Ltd [2005] EWCA Civ 1547; *Times*, November 14, 2005, CA
   (Civ Div); reversing [2005] I.C.R. 874; [2005] I.R.L.R. 449, EAT . . . .   *Digested*, 05/**1206**

Melville v. Home Office see Hartman v. South Essex Mental Health and Community
   Care NHS Trust

Melville v. Welsh Development Agency see Waters v. Welsh Development Agency

MEM Bauchemie GmbH v. Montajes de Estructuras Metalicas SCV (2005) 28(4) I.P.D.
   28028, OHIM (1st Bd App)

Memorandum for Third Summit of the Council of Europe (2005) 41 E.H.R.R. SE6, ECHR

Mendip DC v. O'Connor [2005] P.A.D. 39, Planning Inspector

Mendoza v. Ghaidan see Ghaidan v. Godin-Mendoza

Merchant Navy Officers Pension Fund Trustees Ltd v. FT Everard & Sons Ltd see MNOPF
   Trustees Ltd v. FT Everard & Sons Ltd

Merci Convenzionali Porto di Genova SpA v. Siderurgica Gabriella SpA (C179/90)
   [1991] E.C.R. I-5889; [1994] 4 C.M.L.R. 422, ECJ . . . .   *Digested*, 92/**4771**:
                            Considered, 05/578

Merida v. Germany (C400/02) [2004] E.C.R. I-8471; [2004] 3 C.M.L.R. 52, ECJ
   (2nd Chamber) . . . .   *Digested*, 05/**3860**

Meridian Global Funds Management Asia Ltd v. Securities Commission [1995] 2 A.C.
   500; [1995] 3 W.L.R. 413; [1995] 3 All E.R. 918; [1995] B.C.C. 942; [1995] 2
   B.C.L.C. 116; (1995) 92(28) L.S.G. 39; (1995) 139 S.J.L.B. 152; *Times*, June 29,
   1995, PC (NZ) . . . .   *Digested*, 96/**969**:
             Applied, 04/456: *Considered*, 00/980, 05/2307

Merino Gomez v. Continental Industrias del Caucho SA (C342/01) [2004] E.C.R. I-
   2605; [2004] 2 C.M.L.R. 3; [2005] I.C.R. 1040; [2004] I.R.L.R. 407, ECJ (6th
   Chamber) . . . .   *Digested*, 04/**1290**

Merkur Island Shipping Corp v. Laughton (The Hoegh Anapa) [1983] 2 A.C. 570;
   [1983] 2 W.L.R. 778; [1983] 2 All E.R. 189; [1983] 2 Lloyd's Rep. 1; [1983]
   I.C.R. 490; [1983] I.R.L.R. 218; (1983) 133 N.L.J. 577; (1983) 127 S.J. 306,
   HL; affirming [1983] 2 W.L.R. 45; [1982] 1 All E.R. 334; [1983] 1 Lloyd's Rep.
   154; [1983] I.C.R. 178; [1982] I.R.L.R. 26; (1983) 80 L.S.G. 213; (1983) 133
   N.L.J. 186; 126 S.J. 745; *Times*, November 5, 1982, CA (Civ Div) . . . .   *Digested*, 83/**3794**:
        Applied, 84/3553, 85/3384, 86/3443, 87/3769: *Considered*, 87/3759,
                            88/3417, 89/3519, 05/4189

Merrill Lynch Inc's Patent Application [1989] R.P.C. 561; *Times*, April 27, 1989; *Daily
   Telegraph*, April 28, 1989, CA (Civ Div); affirming [1988] R.P.C. 1, Ch D (Patents
   Ct) . . . .   *Digested*, 89/**2798**:
        Applied, 92/3279, 95/3777: *Cited*, 03/2519: *Followed*, 05/2446:
                            Referred to, 02/2846

Mersey Docks and Harbour Board v. Coggins & Griffith (Liverpool) Ltd; *sub nom*
   McFarlane v. Coggins & Griffiths (Liverpool) Ltd [1947] A.C. 1; [1946] 2 All E.R.
   345; (1946) 79 Ll. L. Rep. 569; 62 T.L.R. 533; 115 L.J. K.B. 465; 175 L.T. 270,
   HL; affirming [1945] K.B. 301, CA . . . .   *Digested*, 47-51/**3610**:
        Applied, 47-51/3611, 47-51/6611, 52/1255, 53/962.277, 53/2510, 55/1870,
                56/3165, 57/1277, 57/3371, 58/1209, 58/3760, 01/2267, 05/2889:
               Considered, 75/2342, 05/2890: *Distinguished*, 57/2429, 70/1877:
                            Followed, 47-51/3612

Mersey Docks Property Holdings Ltd v. Birse Construction Ltd [2004] EWHC 3264; 99
   Con. L.R. 122, QBD (TCC) . . . .   *Digested*, 05/**450**

Mersey Docks Property Holdings Ltd v. Kilgour [2004] EWHC 1638; [2004] B.L.R. 412,
   QBD (TCC) . . . .   *Digested*, 05/**466**:
                              Considered, 05/387

Merseyside Fire and Civil Defence Authority v. Bassie [2005] EWCA Civ 1474; (2005)
   149 S.J.L.B. 1352, CA (Civ Div)

Merton LBC v. K (Care: Representation: Public Funding) [2005] EWHC 167; [2005] 2
   F.L.R. 422; [2005] Fam. Law 446, Fam Div

Merton LBC v. Richards [2005] EWCA Civ 639; [2005] H.L.R. 44, CA (Civ Div)

Messe Munchen GmbH v. Office for Harmonisation in the Internal Market (Trade Marks
   and Designs) (OHIM) (T32/00) [2000] E.C.R. II-3829; [2001] C.E.C. 3;
   [2001] E.T.M.R. 13; (2001) 24(1) I.P.D. 24002, CFI (4th Chamber) . . . .   *Digested*, 01/**3993**:
                          Applied, 04/2367, 05/2505

Messenger Leisure Developments Ltd *v.* Customs and Excise Commissioners; *sub nom* Messenger Leisure Developments Ltd *v.* Revenue and Customs Commissioners [2005] EWCA Civ 648; [2005] S.T.C. 1078; [2005] B.T.C. 5332; [2005] B.V.C. 363; [2005] S.T.I. 1022; *Times*, June 14, 2005; *Independent*, June 9, 2005, CA (Civ Div); affirming [2004] EWHC 1761; [2004] S.T.C. 1563; [2004] B.T.C. 5785; [2004] B.V.C. 844; [2004] S.T.I. 1725, Ch D; affirming [2004] B.V.C. 2003; [2003] S.T.I. 2204, V&DTr .... *Digested,* 05/**4358**
Messenger Leisure Developments Ltd *v.* Revenue and Customs Commissioners see Messenger Leisure Developments Ltd *v.* Customs and Excise Commissioners
Messier Dowty Ltd *v.* Sabena SA [2000] 1 W.L.R. 2040; [2001] 1 All E.R. 275; [2000] 1 All E.R. (Comm) 833; [2000] 1 Lloyd's Rep. 428; [2000] C.P. Rep. 72; [2000] C.L.C. 889; [2001] I.L.Pr. 5; (2000) 97(10) L.S.G. 36; (2000) 144 S.J.L.B. 124; *Times*, March 14, 2000; *Independent*, February 29, 2000, CA (Civ Div) .... *Digested,* 00/**778**:
Considered, 05/434: *Followed,* 01/543, 04/566
Messina *v.* Commission of the European Communities (T76/02) [2003] E.C.R. II-3203; [2005] 2 C.M.L.R. 21, CFI (4th Chamber) .... *Digested,* 05/**1427**
Metal Distributors (UK) Ltd *v.* ZCCM Investment Holdings Plc [2005] EWHC 156; [2005] 2 Lloyd's Rep. 37; *Times*, March 9, 2005, QBD (Comm) .... *Digested,* 05/**206**
Metallgesellschaft Ltd *v.* Inland Revenue Commissioners (C397/98); Hoechst AG *v.* Inland Revenue Commissioners (C410/98) [2001] Ch. 620; [2001] 2 W.L.R. 1497; [2001] All E.R. (EC) 496; [2001] S.T.C. 452; [2001] E.C.R. I-1727; [2001] 2 C.M.L.R. 32; [2001] B.T.C. 99; 3 I.T.L. Rep. 385; [2001] S.T.I. 498; *Times*, March 20, 2001, ECJ (5th Chamber) .... *Digested,* 01/**5173**:
Considered, 03/4141, 03/4142, 04/3681, 04/3682, 05/4056, 05/4129, 05/4387: *Followed,* 04/3721
Metropol Treuhand Wirtschaftstreuhand GmbH *v.* Finanzlandesdirektion fur Steiermark (C409/99); Stadler *v.* Finanzlandesdirektion fur Vorarlberg (C409/99) [2002] E.C.R. I-81; [2004] B.T.C. 5364; [2004] B.V.C. 424, ECJ (5th Chamber) ...... *Digested,* 04/**3989**:
Followed, 05/4365
Metropolitan Police District Receiver *v.* Palacegate Properties Ltd [2001] Ch. 131; [2000] 3 W.L.R. 519; [2000] 3 All E.R. 663; (2000) 80 P. & C.R. 32; [2000] L. & T.R. 358; [2000] 1 E.G.L.R. 63; [2000] 13 E.G. 187; (2000) 97(9) L.S.G. 42; (2000) 150 N.L.J. 226; [2000] N.P.C. 13; (2000) 79 P. & C.R. D34; *Times*, March 21, 2000; *Independent*, February 16, 2000, CA (Civ Div) .... *Digested,* 00/**3893**:
Applied, 05/2650
Metropolitan Police Service *v.* Shoebridge [2004] I.C.R. 1690, EAT .... *Digested,* 05/**1302**:
Applied, 05/1229
Mettoy Pension Trustees Ltd *v.* Evans [1990] 1 W.L.R. 1587; [1991] 2 All E.R. 513; *Financial Times*, February 9, 1990, Ch D .... *Digested,* 91/**2726**:
Considered, 04/4626, 05/4304, 05/4305
Meyrick Estate Management Ltd *v.* Secretary of State for the Environment, Food and Rural Affairs [2005] EWHC 2618; [2005] 45 E.G.C.S. 169; [2005] N.P.C. 137, QBD (Admin)
MEZZACORONA Trade Mark see Miguel Torres SA *v.* Cantine Mezzacorona SCARL
MG *v.* Entry Clearance Officer, Kingston; *sub nom* MG (Visit Appeal: Directions: Jamaica), Re [2004] UKIAT 140; [2004] Imm. A.R. 377, IAT .... *Digested,* 05/**2198**
MG *v.* Secretary of State for the Home Department see MM *v.* Secretary of State for the Home Department
MG Rover Espana SA, Re [2005] B.P.I.R. 1162, Ch D
MG (Visit Appeal: Directions: Jamaica), Re see MG *v.* Entry Clearance Officer, Kingston
MH *v.* Sutton and Merton Primary Care Trust see CH *v.* Sutton and Merton Primary Care Trust
MHC (Michael Hammond Partnership) *v.* Customs and Excise Commissioners [2004] V. & D.R. 1; [2004] S.T.I. 1304, V&DTr (Manchester) .... *Digested,* 05/**4389**
MHID Ltd, Re see MHMH Ltd *v.* Carwood Barker Holdings Ltd
MHMH Ltd *v.* Carwood Barker Holdings Ltd; *sub nom* MHID Ltd, Re; Moorgate House Group Ltd, Re [2004] EWHC 3174; [2005] B.C.C. 536; [2005] B.P.I.R. 601, Ch D .... *Digested,* 05/**2344**
Mibanga *v.* Secretary of State for the Home Department [2005] EWCA Civ 367; [2005] I.N.L.R. 377, CA (Civ Div) .... *Digested,* 05/**2187**
Michael *v.* Cansick [2004] EWHC 1684; [2004] W.T.L.R. 961, Ch D .... *Digested,* 05/**3968**
Michael *v.* Pratt (Unreported, October 21, 2004), CC (Southend) [*Ex rel.* Morris Orman Hearle Solicitors, Wynnstay House, St James Square, Cheltenham, Gloucestershire] .... *Digested,* 05/**376**
Michaelek *v.* Wandsworth LBC see Wandsworth LBC *v.* Michalak
Michaelides, Re [2003] EWHC 3029; [2005] 2 Costs L.R. 191; [2004] B.P.I.R. 613, Ch D   *Digested,* 04/**303**
Michalak *v.* Wandsworth LBC see Wandsworth LBC *v.* Michalak
Microsoft Corp *v.* Commission of the European Communities (T201/04 R 1) [2004] 5 C.M.L.R. 21, CFI .... *Digested,* 05/**577**
Microsoft Corp *v.* Commission of the European Communities (T201/04 R 2) [2005] 4 C.M.L.R. 5; [2005] E.C.D.R. 19; [2005] Info. T.L.R. 179, CFI .... *Digested,* 05/**550**
Microsoft Corp *v.* Commission of the European Communities (T201/04 R 3) [2005] 4 C.M.L.R. 18, CFI (4th Chamber) .... *Digested,* 05/**576**

Microsoft Corp *v.* Commission of the European Communities (T201/04 R 4) [2005] 5
C.M.L.R. 4, CFI (4th Chamber)
Mid-Bedfordshire DC *v.* Brown [2004] EWCA Civ 1709; [2005] 1 W.L.R. 1460;
[2005] J.P.L. 1060; (2005) 102(4) L.S.G. 31; *Times,* January 3, 2005;
Independent, January 12, 2005, CA (Civ Div) . . . . *Digested,* 05/**3245**
Midland Bank Plc *v.* Customs and Excise Commissioners (C98/98); *sub nom* Customs
and Excise Commissioners *v.* Midland Bank Plc (C98/98) [2000] 1 W.L.R.
2080; [2000] All E.R. (EC) 673; [2000] S.T.C. 501; [2000] E.C.R. I-4177;
[2000] 3 C.M.L.R. 301; [2000] C.E.C. 441; [2000] B.T.C. 5199; [2000] B.V.C.
229; [2000] S.T.I. 852; *Times,* June 16, 2000, ECJ (2nd Chamber) . . . . *Digested,* 00/**5302**:
Applied, 01/5586, 03/4556, 04/3990, 05/4380: *Considered,* 01/5585,
04/3994

Midland Bank Plc *v.* Wallace see Royal Bank of Scotland Plc *v.* Etridge (No.2)
Midland Bank Plc *v.* Wyatt [1997] 1 B.C.L.C. 242; [1995] 1 F.L.R. 697; [1995] 3 F.C.R.
11; [1996] B.P.I.R. 288; [1994] E.G.C.S. 113, Ch D . . . . *Digested,* 96/**3513**:
Considered, 05/1657
Midland Mainline *v.* Wade (Unreported, November 4, 2002), EAT . . . . *Approved,* 05/1334
Midland Marts Ltd *v.* Hobday [1989] 1 W.L.R. 1143; [1989] 3 All E.R. 246; (1989)
86(27) L.S.G. 41; (1989) 133 S.J. 1109; *Times,* April 25, 1989, Ch D . . . . *Digested,* 89/**2927**:
Applied, 05/2421: *Considered,* 00/494

Midland Packaging Ltd *v.* Clark see Clark *v.* Midland Packaging Ltd
Midlands Cooperative Society Ltd *v.* Revenue and Customs Commissioners [2005]
S.T.I. 1737, V&DTr
Midtown Ltd *v.* City of London Real Property Co Ltd; Joseph *v.* City of London Real
Property Co Ltd [2005] EWHC 33; [2005] 1 E.G.L.R. 65; [2005] 14 E.G. 130;
[2005] J.P.L. 1220; [2005] 4 E.G.C.S. 166; (2005) 102(14) L.S.G. 26; [2005]
N.P.C. 13; *Times,* February 14, 2005, Ch D . . . . *Digested,* 05/**3434**
Miftari *v.* Secretary of State for the Home Department [2005] EWCA Civ 481, CA
(Civ Div) . . . . *Applied,* 05/2213
Miguel Torres SA *v.* Cantine Mezzacorona SCARL; *sub nom* Cantine Mezzacorona
SCARL *v.* Miguel Torres SA; MEZZACORONA Trade Mark [2003] EWCA Civ
1861; [2005] E.T.M.R. 39; [2004] R.P.C. 26; (2004) 148 S.J.L.B. 60, CA (Civ
Div); affirming [2003] EWHC 3359; [2004] R.P.C. 25; (2004) 27(3) I.P.D.
27024, Ch D . . . . *Digested,* 04/**2267**
Mikropolis-Infomedica (formerly Amstrad Hellas SA) *v.* Amstrad Plc (formerly Betacom
Plc) [2005] I.L.Pr. 27, Ar Pag (GR) . . . . *Digested,* 05/**411**
Milchwerke Koln Wuppertal eG *v.* Hauptzollamt Koln-Rheinau (C352/92) [1994] E.C.R.
I-3385, ECJ (3rd Chamber) . . . . *Digested,* 94/**4735**:
Followed, 05/142

Miles *v.* Gilbank A2/2005/2196, CA (Civ Div) *Times,* November 16, 2005, EAT
Miles *v.* Tingley (t/a Tingley Skips) [2005] 3 Q.R. 11, CC (Eastbourne) [*Ex rel.* Nikolas
Clarke, Barrister, Lamb Building, Temple, London] . . . . *Digested,* 05/**3180**
Miliangos *v.* George Frank (Textiles) Ltd (No.1) [1976] A.C. 443; [1975] 3 W.L.R. 758;
[1975] 3 All E.R. 801; [1976] 1 Lloyd's Rep. 201; [1975] 2 C.M.L.R. 585; 119 S.J.
774, HL; affirming [1975] Q.B. 487; [1975] 2 W.L.R. 555; [1975] 1 All E.R.
1076; [1975] 1 Lloyd's Rep. 587; [1975] 1 C.M.L.R. 630; 119 S.J. 322, CA (Civ
Div); reversing [1975] 1 Lloyd's Rep. 436; [1975] 1 C.M.L.R. 121; (1974) 119 S.J.
10; *Times,* December 5, 1974, QBD . . . . *Digested,* 75/**2657**:
Applied, 77/194, 77/735, 78/710, 87/365, 05/330: *Considered,* 76/327,
77/731, 77/1602, 77/2728, 77/3735, 79/155, 81/260, 84/323, 00/1467:
Distinguished, 78/3691, 80/642: *Followed,* 75/3142, 76/675, 77/2334,
77/2354, 77/3625: *Not followed,* 76/273, 82/335
Millar *v.* Galashiels Gas Co Ltd see Galashiels Gas Co Ltd *v.* Millar
Millenium Construction Ltd *v.* Torbay CC [2005] P.A.D. 8, Planning Inspector
Miller *v.* Associated Newspapers Ltd (No.1) [2003] EWHC 2799; [2004] E.M.L.R.
33, QBD . . . . *Digested,* 05/**980**:
Applied, 05/973
Miller *v.* DPP [2004] EWHC 595; [2005] R.T.R. 3; (2004) 101(17) L.S.G. 30; *Times,*
June 7, 2004; *Independent,* May 3, 2004 (C.S), QBD (Admin) . . . . *Digested,* 04/**3439**
Miller *v.* Miller; *sub nom* M *v.* M (Short Marriage: Clean Break) [2005] EWCA Civ
984; [2005] 2 F.C.R. 713; [2005] Fam. Law 766; (2005) 102(33) L.S.G. 24,
CA (Civ Div); affirming [2005] EWHC 528; [2005] 2 F.L.R. 533; [2005] Fam.
Law 537, Fam Div . . . . *Digested,* 05/**1656**
Mills *v.* Barnsley MBC [1992] P.I.Q.R. P291; (1993) 157 J.P.N. 831, CA (Civ Div) . . . . . *Digested,* 93/**2967**:
Applied, 00/4230, 01/4497, 02/3271, 05/2888: *Cited,* 96/4480:
Followed, 99/2891: *Referred to,* 96/5670
Mills-Davies *v.* Royal Society for the Protection of Birds see Mills-Davies *v.* RSPB
Mills-Davies *v.* RSPB; *sub nom* Mills-Davies *v.* Royal Society for the Protection of
Birds; (Unreported, May 21, 2004), QBD [*Ex rel.* Lyons Davidson Solicitors,
Victoria House, 51 Victoria Street, Bristol] . . . . *Digested,* 05/**4196**
Millwood Designer Homes Kent Ltd *v.* Rother DC [2005] P.A.D. 79, Planning Inspector

Milne *v.* Express Newspapers Ltd (No.1) [2004] EWCA Civ 664; [2005] 1 W.L.R. 772; [2005] 1 All E.R. 1021; [2004] E.M.L.R. 24; (2004) 148 S.J.L.B. 696; *Independent*, June 11, 2004, CA (Civ Div); affirming [2002] EWHC 2564; [2003] 1 W.L.R. 927; [2003] 1 All E.R. 482; [2003] E.M.L.R. 22; (2003) 100(5) L.S.G. 32; *Times*, December 9, 2002, QBD . . . . *Digested*, 04/**937**

Milner *v.* Lancashire CC (Unreported, April 27, 2005), CC (Burnley) [*Ex rel.* Karim Sabry, Barrister, 8 King Street, Manchester] . . . . *Digested*, 05/**3203**

Milner's Safe Co Ltd *v.* Great Northern and City Railway Co [1907] 1 Ch. 208, Ch D . . . *Applied*, 89/1297, 91/1509: *Considered*, 05/3403: *Distinguished*, 84/1153

Milton Keynes Development Corp *v.* Cooper (Great Britain) see Commission for the New Towns *v.* Cooper (Great Britain) Ltd (formerly Coopind UK)

Mimran *v.* Russo see Shalson *v.* Russo

Minermet SpA Milan *v.* Luckyfield Shipping Corp SA [2004] EWHC 729; [2004] 2 Lloyd's Rep. 348; [2004] 2 C.L.C. 421, QBD (Comm). . . . . *Digested*, 05/**201**

Minister for Aboriginal Affairs *v.* Peko Wallsend Ltd 162 C.L.R. 24, HC (Aus) . . . . *Applied*, 98/3091: *Considered*, 05/59

Minister for Immigration and Multicultural Affairs *v.* Khawar, HC (Aus) . . . . *Considered*, 05/2223

Minister for Immigration and Multicultural Affairs *v.* Yusuf, HC (Aus) . . . . *Considered*, 05/2223

Minister for Immigration and Multicultural Affairs *v.* Zamora [1998] 85 F.C.R. 458, Fed Ct (Aus) (Full Ct) . . . . *Considered*, 05/2223

Minister for Social Security *v.* Greenham Ready Mixed Concrete Ltd see Ready Mixed Concrete (South East) Ltd *v.* Minister of Pensions and National Insurance

Minister for Social Security *v.* Ready Mixed Concrete (South East) Ltd see Ready Mixed Concrete (South East) Ltd *v.* Minister of Pensions and National Insurance

Minister for the Civil Service *v.* Oakes [2003] EWHC 3314; [2004] O.P.L.R. 235, Ch D . . . . *Digested*, 05/**2954**

Ministere Public *v.* Greenham (C95/01) see Criminal Proceedings against Greenham (C95/01)

Ministere Public *v.* Van de Walle (C1/03) see Criminal Proceedings against Van de Walle (C1/03)

Ministre de l'Economie *v.* Millennium Pharmaceuticals Inc (C252/03) see Novartis AG *v.* Comptroller-General of Patents, Designs and Trade Marks (C207/03)

Ministre de l'Emploi et de la Solidarite *v.* Bourdignon [2005] E.C.C. 26, CE (F)

Ministre de l'Interieur *v.* Oteiza Olazabal (C100/01) [2002] E.C.R. I-10981; [2005] 1 C.M.L.R. 49; (2003) 147 S.J.L.B. 178, ECJ. . . . . *Digested*, 05/**1462**

Ministre des Finances *v.* Weidert (C242/03) [2005] S.T.C. 1241; [2004] 3 C.M.L.R. 18; [2004] S.T.I. 1657, ECJ (1st Chamber) . . . . *Digested*, 05/**4134**

Ministry of Defence *v.* Armstrong [2004] I.R.L.R. 672, EAT . . . . *Digested*, 05/**1260**

Ministry of Defence *v.* Gandiya see Saggar *v.* Ministry of Defence

Ministry of Health *v.* Simpson; *sub nom* Diplock's Estate, Re; Diplock *v.* Wintle; Simpson *v.* Lilburn [1951] A.C. 251; [1950] 2 All E.R. 1137; 66 T.L.R. (Pt. 2) 1015; 94 S.J. 777, HL; affirming [1948] Ch. 465; [1948] 2 All E.R. 318; [1948] L.J.R. 1670; 92 S.J. 484, CA; reversing [1947] Ch. 716; [1947] 1 All E.R. 522; [1947] L.J.R. 1158; 177 L.T. 40; 91 S.J. 248, Ch D . . . . *Digested*, 47-51/**5743**: *Applied*, 66/567, 05/3967: *Approved*, 94/259, 95/2211: *Considered*, 76/274, 90/1993: *Distinguished*, 74/363: *Followed*, 92/2050, 92/2576

Minoan Lines SA *v.* Commission of the European Communities (T66/99) [2003] E.C.R. II-5515; [2005] 5 C.M.L.R. 32, CFI (5th Chamber)

Minter *v.* Julius Baer Investment Management Inc London; Minter *v.* Julius Baer Investments Ltd [2004] EWHC 2472; [2005] Pens. L.R. 73, Ch D . . . . *Digested*, 05/**1213**

Minwalla *v.* Minwalla [2004] EWHC 2823; [2005] 1 F.L.R. 771; (2004-05) 7 I.T.E.L.R. 457; [2005] Fam. Law 357, Fam Div . . . . *Digested*, 05/**1657**

Mirror Group Newspapers Plc *v.* Maxwell (No.1) [1998] B.C.C. 324; [1998] 1 B.C.L.C. 638; *Times*, July 15, 1997, Ch D . . . . *Digested*, 97/**3072**: *Considered*, 05/352

Mirvahedy *v.* Henley [2003] UKHL 16; [2003] 2 A.C. 491; [2003] 2 W.L.R. 882; [2003] 2 All E.R. 401; [2003] R.T.R. 26; [2003] P.I.Q.R. P25; (2003) 100(19) L.S.G. 31; (2003) 153 N.L.J. 483; (2003) 147 S.J.L.B. 352; [2003] N.P.C. 38; *Times*, March 24, 2003, HL; affirming [2001] EWCA Civ 1749; [2002] Q.B. 769; [2002] 2 W.L.R. 566; [2002] P.I.Q.R. P19; (2002) 99(3) L.S.G. 25; (2002) 146 S.J.L.B. 12; *Times*, December 11, 2001; *Daily Telegraph*, November 27, 2001, CA (Civ Div) . . . . *Digested*, 03/**178**: *Applied*, 04/169: *Cited*, 03/59: *Followed*, 05/189

MIT/Optical imaging and measurement (T30/01) [2005] E.P.O.R. 7, EPO (Technical Bd App). . . . . *Digested*, 05/**2459**

Mitchell *v.* Al-Dali see Jones *v.* Saudi Arabia

Mitchell *v.* Alasia [2005] EWHC 11, QBD. . . . . *Not followed*, 05/3071

Mitchell *v.* Centrica Plc [2005] 3 Q.R. 12, CC (Luton) [*Ex rel.* Stephen Garner, Barrister, No.8 Chambers, Fountain Court, Steelhouse Lane, Birmingham.] . . . . . *Digested*, 05/**3209**

Mitchell *v.* Potter [2005] EWCA Civ 88; *Times*, January 24, 2005, CA (Civ Div) . . . . . . *Digested*, 05/**3435**

Mitsubishi Corp *v.* Eastwind Transport Ltd (The Irbenskiy Proliv) [2004] EWHC 2924; [2005] 1 All E.R. (Comm) 328; [2005] 1 Lloyd's Rep. 383, QBD (Comm) . . . . . *Digested*, 05/**3788**

Mitsui & Co Ltd *v.* Nexen Petroleum UK Ltd [2005] EWHC 625; [2005] 3 All E.R. 511; *Times*, May 18, 2005, Ch D . . . . *Digested*, 05/**395**

Mlauzi v. Secretary of State for the Home Department [2005] EWCA Civ 128; *Times*,
February 15, 2005, CA (Civ Div) . . . .   *Digested*, 05/**2217**
MM v. Netherlands (39339/98) (2004) 39 E.H.R.R. 19, ECHR. . . . .   *Digested*, 05/**2115**
MM v. Secretary of State for the Home Department; *sub nom* MM (Out of Time
Appeals: Burundi), Re; CN v. Secretary of State for the Home Department; MG
v. Secretary of State for the Home Department [2004] UKIAT 182; [2004] Imm.
A.R. 515; [2004] I.N.L.R. 482, IAT. . . . .   *Digested*, 05/**322**
MM v. Secretary of State for the Home Department; *sub nom* MM (DRC: Plausibility:
Democratic Republic of Congo), Re [2005] UKIAT 19; [2005] Imm. A.R. 198,
IAT
MM v. Secretary of State for the Home Department; *sub nom* MM (Section 8:
Commencement: Iran), Re [2005] UKIAT 115; [2005] Imm. A.R. 666, IAT
MM (DRC: Plausibility: Democratic Republic of Congo), Re see MM v. Secretary of State
for the Home Department
MM (Out of Time Appeals: Burundi), Re see MM v. Secretary of State for the Home
Department
MM (Section 8: Commencement: Iran), Re see MM v. Secretary of State for the Home
Department
MMR/MR Vaccine Litigation see Horne-Roberts v. SmithKline Beecham Plc
MNM v. Secretary of State for the Home Department [2000] I.N.L.R. 576, IAT . . . .   *Applied*, 05/**323**:
Considered, 05/2153
MNOPF Trustees Ltd v. FT Everard & Sons Ltd; *sub nom* Merchant Navy Officers
Pension Fund Trustees Ltd v. FT Everard & Sons Ltd [2005] EWHC 446; [2005]
O.P.L.R. 315; [2005] Pens. L.R. 225; (2004-05) 7 I.T.E.L.R. 687, Ch D . . . . . .   *Digested*, 05/**2944**
Moat Housing Group-South Ltd v. Harris [2005] EWCA Civ 287; [2005] 3 W.L.R. 691;
[2005] 4 All E.R. 1051; [2005] 2 F.L.R. 551; [2005] 3 F.C.R. 123; [2005]
H.L.R. 33; [2005] Fam. Law 544; [2005] N.P.C. 40; *Times*, March 23, 2005,
CA (Civ Div) . . . .   *Digested*, 05/**324**
Moat Housing Group-South Ltd v. Harris (Application for Stay of Execution) [2004]
EWCA Civ 1852; *Times*, January 13, 2005, CA (Civ Div) . . . .   *Digested*, 05/**2675**
Mobil Exploration & Production UK Ltd v. Lloyds TSB Bank Ltd see BP Oil UK Ltd v.
Lloyds TSB Bank Plc
Mobistar SA v. Commune de Fleron (C544/03); Belgacom Mobile SA v. Commune de
Schaerbeek (C545/03) [2005] 3 C.M.L.R. 46, ECJ (1st Chamber)
Modern Jet Support Centre Ltd, Re see Brenner v. Revenue and Customs Commissioners
Moeliker v. A Reyrolle & Co Ltd [1977] 1 W.L.R. 132; [1976] I.C.R. 253, CA (Civ Div) . .   *Digested*, 76/**1881**:
Applied, 03/3210, 05/955: *Considered*, 77/736, 77/791,
78/46.u, 82/78.u, 83/2584, 94/1487, 96/2137: *Distinguished*, 77/798
Moggs v. Inland Revenue Commissioners [2005] S.T.C. (S.C.D.) 394; [2005] W.T.L.R.
1045; [2005] S.T.I. 725, Sp Comm. . . . .   *Digested*, 05/**4115**
Mohamed v. Hammersmith and Fulham LBC; *sub nom* Mohammed v. Hammersmith
and Fulham LBC; Surdonja v. Ealing LBC; Ealing LBC v. Surdonja [2001] UKHL
57; [2002] 1 A.C. 547; [2001] 3 W.L.R. 1339; [2002] 1 All E.R. 176; [2002] 1
F.C.R. 183; [2002] H.L.R. 7; (2001) 98(45) L.S.G. 26; (2001) 151 N.L.J. 1664;
(2001) 145 S.J.L.B. 253; [2001] N.P.C. 154; *Times*, November 2, 2001;
Independent, November 8, 2001; *Daily Telegraph*, November 6, 2001, HL;
affirming [2001] Q.B. 97; [2000] 3 W.L.R. 481; [2000] 2 All E.R. 597; (2000)
32 H.L.R. 481; [2000] N.P.C. 5; *Times*, February 11, 2000, CA (Civ Div) . . . .   *Digested*, 01/**3419**:
Applied, 05/2008: *Considered*, 03/2050
Mohamed v. Kensington and Chelsea RLBC see Mohamed v. Manek
Mohamed v. Manek; Mohamed v. Kensington and Chelsea RLBC (1995) 27 H.L.R.
439; 94 L.G.R. 211; (1995) 159 L.G. Rev. 869; (1995) 139 S.J.L.B. 130; [1995]
N.P.C. 56; *Times*, April 28, 1995; *Independent*, April 19, 1995, CA (Civ Div) . . . .   *Digested*, 95/**2531**:
Distinguished, 05/2660
Mohamed v. Westminster City Council; *sub nom* Mohammed v. Westminster City
Council [2005] EWCA Civ 796; [2005] H.L.R. 47; (2005) 149 S.J.L.B. 772, CA
(Civ Div)
Mohammed v. Hammersmith and Fulham LBC see Mohamed v. Hammersmith and
Fulham LBC
Mohammed v. Westminster City Council see Mohamed v. Westminster City Council
Mohammed Abdulmohsin Al-Kharafi & Sons WLL v. Big Dig Construction (Proprietary)
Ltd (In Liquidation) see Protech Projects Construction (Pty) Ltd v. Al-Kharafi &
Sons
Mohindra v. DPP; *sub nom* Browne v. DPP; Browne v. Chief Constable of Greater
Manchester [2004] EWHC 490; (2004) 168 J.P. 448; [2005] R.T.R. 7; (2004)
154 N.L.J. 468; *Times*, March 30, 2004, QBD (Admin) . . . .   *Digested*, 04/**775**
Mokrani v. France (52206/99) (2005) 40 E.H.R.R. 5, ECHR . . . .   *Digested*, 05/**2120**
Molenaar v. Allgemeine Ortskrankenkasse Baden-Wurttemberg (C160/96) [1998]
E.C.R. I-843, ECJ . . . .   *Applied*, 05/3859

Molins Plc *v.* GD SpA [2000] 1 W.L.R. 1741; [2000] 2 Lloyd's Rep. 234; [2000] C.P.
Rep. 54; [2000] C.L.C. 1027; [2001] I.L.Pr. 14; [2000] F.S.R. 893; *Times,* March
29, 2000; *Independent,* March 23, 2000, CA (Civ Div); reversing [2001] I.L.Pr.
1; (2000) 23(4) I.P.D. 23027; (2000) 97(8) L.S.G. 35; *Times,* March 1, 2000,
Ch D (Patents Ct) . . . . *Digested,* 00/**567**:
Distinguished, 04/579: *Followed,* 05/468
Molloy *v.* Shell UK Ltd [2001] EWCA Civ 1272; [2002] P.I.Q.R. P7, CA (Civ Div) . . . . . *Applied,* 05/347
Mond *v.* Hammond Suddards (No.1) [1996] 2 B.C.L.C. 470, Ch D . . . . *Digested,* 97/**3095**:
Considered, 05/2345
Monk *v.* Warbey [1935] 1 K.B. 75; (1934) 50 Ll. L. Rep. 33, CA; affirming (1934) 48
Ll. L. Rep. 157, KBD . . . . *Applied,* 47-51/**9111**:
Considered, 69/1897, 70/206, 00/3544, 05/2843: *Distinguished,* 70/1198,
71/11235, 94/2281, 95/2901: *Followed,* 71/3138
Monnell *v.* United Kingdom (9562/81) see Monnell *v.* United Kingdom (A/115)
Monnell *v.* United Kingdom (A/115); *sub nom* Monnell *v.* United Kingdom (9562/81);
Morris *v.* United Kingdom (9818/82); Morris *v.* United Kingdom (A/115) (1988)
10 E.H.R.R. 205; *Times,* March 3, 1987, ECHR (1984) 6 E.H.R.R. CD592;
(1985) 7 E.H.R.R. CD579, Eur Comm HR . . . . *Digested,* 88/**1803**:
Applied, 98/3143: *Considered,* 05/3736
Monopole SpA *v.* Office for Harmonisation in the Internal Market (Trade Marks and
Designs) (OHIM) (T67/04) [2005] E.T.M.R. 109, CFI
Monopole SpA *v.* Office for Harmonisation in the Internal Market (Trade Marks and
Designs) (OHIM) (T186/04) [2005] E.T.M.R. 108, CFI (2nd Chamber)
Monory *v.* Romania (71099/01) (2005) 41 E.H.R.R. 37, ECHR
Montes *v.* Secretary of State for the Home Department [2004] EWCA Civ 404;
[2004] Imm. A.R. 250, CA (Civ Div) . . . . *Digested,* 05/**2224**
Montgomery *v.* Johnson Underwood Ltd; *sub nom* Johnson Underwood Ltd *v.*
Montgomery [2001] EWCA Civ 318; [2001] I.C.R. 819; [2001] I.R.L.R. 269;
[2001] Emp. L.R. 405; (2001) 98(20) L.S.G. 40; *Times,* March 16, 2001;
Independent, May 7, 2001 (C.S), CA (Civ Div); reversing EAT/509/98, EAT . . . *Digested,* 01/**2264**:
Applied, 04/1204, 05/4128
Montlake *v.* Lambert Smith Hampton Group Ltd [2004] EWHC 938; [2004] 3
E.G.L.R. 149; [2004] 20 E.G.C.S. 167, QBD (Comm) . . . . *Digested,* 05/**2882**
Montlake *v.* Lambert Smith Hampton Group Ltd (Costs) [2004] EWHC 1503; [2004]
4 Costs L.R. 650; [2004] N.P.C. 112, QBD (Comm) . . . . *Digested,* 05/**353**
Montracon Ltd *v.* Whalley; *sub nom* Whalley *v.* Montracon Ltd [2005] EWCA Civ
1383; *Independent,* November 24, 2005, CA (Civ Div)
Montrose Investments Ltd *v.* Orion Nominees Ltd (No.2); *sub nom* Montrose
Investment Ltd *v.* Orion Nominees Ltd (No.2) [2004] EWCA Civ 1032; [2004]
W.T.L.R. 1133; (2004-05) 7 I.T.E.L.R. 255; (2004) 148 S.J.L.B. 946, CA (Civ
Div); reversing [2003] EWHC 2100, Ch D . . . . *Digested,* 04/**3939**
Moody *v.* Cox [1917] 2 Ch. 71, CA . . . . *Applied,* 05/2881:
Distinguished, 70/283
Mooney *v.* Cardiff Justices see Mooney *v.* Cardiff Magistrates Court
Mooney *v.* Cardiff Magistrates Court; *sub nom* Mooney *v.* Cardiff Justices (2000) 164
J.P. 220; (2000) 164 J.P.N. 283; (1999) 96(42) L.S.G. 40; *Times,* November 17,
1999 ; *Independent,* December 6, 1999 (C.S.), QBD . . . . *Digested,* 99/**984**:
Considered, 05/871
Moonsar *v.* Fiveways Express Transport Ltd [2005] I.R.L.R. 9, EAT . . . . *Digested,* 05/**1305**
Moorcock, The (1889) L.R. 14 P.D. 64; [1886-90] All E.R. Rep. 530, CA; affirming (1888)
L.R. 13 P.D. 157, PDAD . . . . *Applied,* 83/2064,
93/2407: *Considered,* 76/1532, 86/421, 98/2492, 05/697:
Distinguished, 80/1643: *Doubted,* 47-51/1756: *Referred to,* 84/1935, 85/1929
Moore *v.* Assignment Courier [1977] 1 W.L.R. 638; [1977] 2 All E.R. 842; (1978) 35
P. & C.R. 400; 121 S.J. 155, CA (Civ Div) . . . . *Digested,* 77/**2374**:
Applied, 77/333, 78/2690, 05/4420: *Referred to,* 78/1802, 79/1623
Moore *v.* Care Standards Tribunal see R. (on the application of Moore) *v.* Care
Standards Tribunal
Moore *v.* Cherry Lewis Ltd (In Receivership) see Smith *v.* Cherry Lewis Ltd (In
Receivership)
Moore *v.* Moore [2004] EWCA Civ 1243; [2005] 1 F.L.R. 666; [2004] 3 F.C.R. 461;
[2005] H.L.R. 5, CA (Civ Div) . . . . *Digested,* 04/**1531**
Moore *v.* Welwyn Components Ltd see Hartman *v.* South Essex Mental Health and
Community Care NHS Trust
Moores *v.* Snow Dome Ltd (Unreported, July 20, 2004), CC (Birmingham) [*Ex rel.*
Davies Arnold Cooper Solicitors, 6-7 Bouverie Street, London] . . . . *Digested,* 05/**4195**
Moorgate House Group Ltd, Re see MHMH Ltd *v.* Carwood Barker Holdings Ltd
Mora Shipping Inc *v.* Axa Corporate Solutions Assurance SA [2005] EWCA Civ 1069;
[2005] 2 Lloyd's Rep. 769; [2005] 2 C.L.C. 349, CA (Civ Div); affirming
[2005] EWHC 315; [2005] 1 C.L.C. 339, QBD (Comm) . . . . *Digested,* 05/**605**
Moran, Re see Attorney General's Reference (No.25 of 2001), Re
Morbaine *v.* Lear Management Ltd see Morbaine Ltd *v.* First Secretary of State

Morbaine Ltd v. First Secretary of State; Morbaine Ltd v. Stoke on Trent City Council; Morbaine v. Lear Management Ltd [2004] EWHC 1708; [2005] J.P.L. 377, QBD (Admin)

Morbaine Ltd v. Stoke on Trent City Council see Morbaine Ltd v. First Secretary of State

More OG Romsdal Fylkesbatar AS v. Demise Charterers of the Jotunheim [2004] EWHC 671; [2005] 1 Lloyd's Rep. 181, QBD (Comm) . . . .   *Digested*, 05/**3793**

Moreno Gomez v. Spain (4143/02) (2005) 41 E.H.R.R. 40, ECHR

Morgan v. Middlesbrough BC [2005] EWCA Civ 1432, CA (Civ Div); reversing (2005) 149 S.J.L.B. 922, EAT

Morgan v. Staffordshire University [2002] I.C.R. 475; [2002] I.R.L.R. 190, EAT . . . . . .   *Digested*, 02/**1328**: *Applied*, 05/1224

Morgan Est (Scotland) Ltd v. Hanson Concrete Products Ltd [2005] EWCA Civ 134; [2005] 1 W.L.R. 2557; [2005] 3 All E.R. 135; [2005] C.P. Rep. 23; [2005] B.L.R. 218; (2005) 102(17) L.S.G. 32; *Times*, February 28, 2005, CA (Civ Div); affirming [2004] EWHC 1778, QBD (TCC) . . . .   *Digested*, 05/**315**

Morgan's Executors v. Fellows (Inspector of Taxes) see Fallon (Morgan's Executors) v. Fellows (Inspector of Taxes)

Morgans v. Alpha Plus Security Ltd [2005] 4 All E.R. 655; [2005] I.C.R. 525; [2005] I.R.L.R. 234, EAT . . . .   *Digested*, 05/**1322**

Moriarty v. Regent's Garage & Engineering Co Ltd [1921] 2 K.B. 766, CA; reversing [1921] 1 K.B. 423, KBD . . . .   *Applied*, 05/524

Morley v. United Kingdom (Admissibility) (16084/03) (2005) 40 E.H.R.R. SE8, ECHR

Moroak (t/a Blake Envelopes) v. Cromie [2005] I.C.R. 1226; [2005] I.R.L.R. 353, EAT .   *Digested*, 05/**1297**

Morris v. Agrichemicals Ltd see Bank of Credit and Commerce International SA (In Liquidation) (No.8), Re

Morris v. Bank of India; *sub nom* Bank of Credit and Commerce International SA (In Liquidation) (No.15), Re; Bank of India v. Morris [2005] EWCA Civ 693; [2005] B.C.C. 739; [2005] 2 B.C.L.C. 328; [2005] B.P.I.R. 1067; *Times*, July 19, 2005, CA (Civ Div); affirming [2004] EWHC 528; [2005] 1 All E.R. (Comm) 209; [2004] B.C.C. 404; [2004] 2 B.C.L.C. 279, Ch D (Companies Ct) . . . .   *Digested*, 05/**2307**

Morris v. Baron & Co [1918] A.C. 1, HL; reversing (1856) 18 C.B. 587, CA . . . .   *Applied*, 68/**2502**, 96/1221, 05/695: *Considered*, 65/590, 71/1797: *Followed*, 93/82, 94/129

Morris v. Beardmore [1981] A.C. 446; [1980] 3 W.L.R. 283; [1980] 2 All E.R. 753; (1980) 71 Cr. App. R. 256; [1980] R.T.R. 321; 124 S.J. 512, HL; reversing [1980] Q.B. 105; [1979] 3 W.L.R. 93; [1979] 3 All E.R. 290; [1979] Crim. L.R. 394; (1979) 145 J.P.N. 255; 123 S.J. 300, QBD . . . .   *Digested*, 80/**2310**: *Applied*, 84/3006: *Considered*, 85/3075, 05/810: *Distinguished*, 81/2340, 82/2367, 82/2711, 82/2717, 83/3230, 85/2986, 87/3247

Morris v. London Iron & Steel Co [1988] Q.B. 493; [1987] 3 W.L.R. 836; [1987] 2 All E.R. 496; [1987] I.C.R. 855; [1987] I.R.L.R. 182; (1987) 131 S.J. 1040, CA (Civ Div); reversing [1986] I.C.R. 629, EAT . . . .   *Digested*, 87/**1337**: *Considered*, 04/2745, 05/292

Morris v. Mahfouz see Bank of Credit and Commerce International SA (In Liquidation) (No.9), Re

Morris v. Rayners Enterprises Inc see Bank of Credit and Commerce International SA (In Liquidation) (No.8), Re

Morris v. Revenue and Customs Commissioners see County Pharmacy Ltd v. Revenue and Customs Commissioners

Morris v. Roberts (Inspector of Taxes) (Wasted Costs Order) [2005] EWHC 1040; [2005] P.N.L.R. 41; 77 T.C. 204; [2005] S.T.I. 1014, Ch D . . . .   *Digested*, 05/**496**

Morris v. United Kingdom (38784/97) (2002) 34 E.H.R.R. 52; [2002] Crim. L.R. 494, ECHR . . . .   *Digested*, 02/**2411**: *Considered*, 02/227, 04/1945, 05/234

Morris v. United Kingdom (68416/01) see Steel v. United Kingdom (68416/01)

Morris v. United Kingdom (9818/82) see Monnell v. United Kingdom (A/115)

Morris v. United Kingdom (A/115) see Monnell v. United Kingdom (A/115)

Mortgage Corp v. Lewis Silkin (A Firm) see Mortgage Corp v. Shaire

Mortgage Corp v. Shaire; Mortgage Corp v. Lewis Silkin (A Firm) [2001] Ch. 743; [2001] 3 W.L.R. 639; [2001] 4 All E.R. 364; [2000] 1 F.L.R. 973; [2000] 2 F.C.R. 222; [2000] B.P.I.R. 483; (2000) 80 P. & C.R. 280; [2000] 3 E.G.L.R. 131; [2000] W.T.L.R. 357; [2000] Fam. Law 402; [2000] E.G.C.S. 35; (2000) 97(11) L.S.G. 37; *Times*, March 21, 2000, Ch D . . . .   *Digested*, 00/**4659**: *Considered*, 05/278, 05/3380

Mortgage Express v. Mardner [2004] EWCA Civ 1859, CA (Civ Div) . . . .   *Applied*, 05/3428

Mortimer v. Bailey [2004] EWCA Civ 1514; [2005] B.L.R. 85; [2005] 2 P. & C.R. 9; [2005] 1 E.G.L.R. 75; [2005] 02 E.G. 102; [2004] N.P.C. 162, CA (Civ Div) . . .   *Digested*, 05/**3410**

Mortimer Investments Ltd v. Mount Eden Land Ltd (Unreported, March 26, 1997) . . . .   *Considered*, 05/2668

Moscow City Council v. Bankers Trust Co see Department of Economic Policy and Development of the City of Moscow v. Bankers Trust Co

Moses v. Leahy (Valuation Officer) [2005] R.A. 315, Lands Tr

Moss v. Bassetlaw DC [2005] P.A.D. 60, Planning Inspector

Moss *v.* McLachlan (1985) 149 J.P. 167; [1985] I.R.L.R. 76; (1985) 149 J.P.N. 149,
DC . . . . *Digested*, 85/**647**:
Applied, 04/3144: *Approved*, 05/3341
Mothew *v.* Bristol and West Building Society see Bristol and West Building Society *v.*
Mothew (t/a Stapley & Co)
Mould (t/a Leon Jaimes Hair Fashion) *v.* Revenue and Customs Commissioners see
Mallinson (t/a The Hair Team) *v.* Revenue and Customs Commissioners
Mount *v.* Barker Austin [1998] P.N.L.R. 493, CA (Civ Div) . . . . *Digested*, 98/**4023**:
Applied, 02/947, 04/913, 05/957
Mount Carmel Investments Ltd *v.* Peter Thurlow Ltd see Mount Carmel Investments Ltd
v. Thurlow
Mount Carmel Investments Ltd *v.* Thurlow; *sub nom* Mount Carmel Investments Ltd *v.*
Peter Thurlow Ltd [1988] 1 W.L.R. 1078; [1988] 3 All E.R. 129; (1989) 57 P. &
C.R. 396, CA (Civ Div) . . . . *Digested*, 89/**2278**:
Applied, 01/4842, 05/3376
Mount Cook Land Ltd *v.* Joint London Holdings Ltd see Joint London Holdings Ltd *v.*
Mount Cook Land Ltd
Mount Cook Land Ltd *v.* Westminster City Council see R. (on the application of Mount
Cook Land Ltd) *v.* Westminster City Council
Mouvement contre le Racisme, l'Antisemitisme et la Xenophobie ASBL (MRAX) *v.* Belgium
(C459/99) [2003] 1 W.L.R. 1073; [2002] E.C.R. I-6591; [2002] 3 C.M.L.R.
25, ECJ [2002] E.C.R. I-6591, AGO . . . . *Digested*, 03/**1446**:
Applied, 05/1480
MOVIESTAR Trade Mark see Applied Technologies Manufacturing Ltd's Trade Mark
Application (No.2149359)
Mowlem Plc *v.* Phi Group Ltd [2004] B.L.R. 421, QBD (TCC) . . . . *Digested*, 05/**658**
Moy *v.* Pettman Smith (A Firm) [2005] UKHL 7; [2005] 1 W.L.R. 581; [2005] 1 All
E.R. 903; [2005] Lloyd's Rep. Med. 293; [2005] P.N.L.R. 24; (2005) 102(11)
L.S.G. 31; (2005) 155 N.L.J. 218; (2005) 149 S.J.L.B. 180; [2005] N.P.C. 15;
Times, February 4, 2005, HL; reversing [2002] EWCA Civ 875; [2002] C.P.L.R.
619; [2002] Lloyd's Rep. P.N. 513; [2002] P.N.L.R. 44; *Independent*, June 28,
2002, CA (Civ Div); reversing HQ 99026934, QBD . . . . *Digested*, 05/**2869**
Moyna *v.* Secretary of State for Social Security see Moyna *v.* Secretary of State for
Work and Pensions
Moyna *v.* Secretary of State for Work and Pensions; *sub nom* Moyna *v.* Secretary of
State for Social Security [2003] UKHL 44; [2003] 1 W.L.R. 1929; [2003] 4 All
E.R. 162; (2003) 73 B.M.L.R. 201; *Times*, August 11, 2003; *Independent*,
October 2, 2003, HL; reversing [2002] EWCA Civ 408, CA (Civ Div) . . . . *Digested*, 03/**4000**:
Applied, 05/796
Moyse *v.* Regal Mortgages Ltd Partnership [2004] EWCA Civ 1269; [2005] C.P. Rep.
9, CA (Civ Div) . . . . *Digested*, 05/**452**
MS *v.* Sweden (1999) 28 E.H.R.R. 313; 3 B.H.R.C. 248; (1999) 45 B.M.L.R. 133,
ECHR . . . . *Digested*, 98/**3105**:
Referred to, 05/1785
Mubarak *v.* Mubarik [2004] EWCA Civ 1573, CA (Civ Div); affirming [2004] EWHC
1158; [2004] 2 F.L.R. 932; [2005] Fam. Law 355, Fam Div . . . . *Digested*, 05/**1664**
Muck It Ltd *v.* Secretary of State for Transport [2005] EWCA Civ 1124; (2005) 102(37)
L.S.G. 33; *Times*, October 13, 2005, CA (Civ Div) . . . . *Digested*, 05/**3454**
Muhlens GmbH & Co KG *v.* Office for Harmonisation in the Internal Market (Trade
Marks and Designs) (OHIM) (T355/02) [2004] E.C.R. II-791; [2004] E.T.M.R.
101, CFI (4th Chamber) . . . . *Digested*, 05/**2510**
Muhlens GMBH & Co KG *v.* Zirh International Corp [2005] E.T.M.R. 55, LG (Hamburg)
Muir *v.* Inland Revenue Commissioner 7 I.T.L. Rep. 324, CA (NZ) . . . . *Digested*, 05/**4157**
Mulder, Re [1943] 2 All E.R. 150, CA . . . . *Applied*, 05/3975:
Distinguished, 84/3661, 85/3640, 01/5164
Mulhearn (t/a Sandancer Amusements) *v.* Revenue and Customs Commissioners
[2005] S.T.I. 2035, V&DTr
Muller-Faure *v.* Onderlinge Waarborgmaatschappij OZ Zorgverzekeringen UA (C385/
99); Van Riet *v.* Onderlinge Waarborgmaatschappij OZ Zorgverzekeringen UA
(C385/99) [2004] Q.B. 1081; [2004] 3 W.L.R. 374; [2005] All E.R. (EC) 62;
[2003] E.C.R. I-4509; [2004] 2 C.M.L.R. 33; (2004) 80 B.M.L.R. 68, ECJ . . . *Digested*, 05/**1849**:
Considered, 03/1799, 04/1688
Mullins *v.* Phillips (Unreported, April 18, 2005), CC (Uxbridge) [*Ex rel.* Joanna Kerr,
Barrister, Lamb Chambers, Temple, London] . . . . *Digested*, 05/**963**
Multigroup Bulgaria Holding AD *v.* Oxford Analytica Ltd [2001] E.M.L.R. 28, QBD . . . . *Digested*, 01/**1835**:
Considered, 05/974
Multiple Claimants *v.* TUI UK Ltd (2005) 102(39) L.S.G. 29, Sup Ct Costs Office
Multiplex *v.* Croatia (58112/00) (Unreported, July 10, 2003), ECHR . . . . *Considered*, 05/2073
Mumbray *v.* Lapper [2005] EWHC 1152; [2005] B.C.C. 990; *Times*, May 31, 2005, Ch
D
Munchener Ruckversicherungs-Gesellschaft AG (t/a Munich Reinsurance Co) *v.*
Commonwealth Insurance Co [2004] EWHC 914; [2004] 2 C.L.C. 665; [2005]
Lloyd's Rep. I.R. 99, QBD (Comm) . . . . *Digested*, 05/**610**

Munchener Ruckversicherungs-Gesellschaft AG (t/a Munich Reinsurance Co) *v.* Office for Harmonisation in the Internal Market (Trade Marks and Designs) (OHIM) (T316/03) [2005] C.E.C. 653, CFI (5th Chamber)

Munjaz *v.* Mersey Care NHS Trust see R. (on the application of Munjaz) *v.* Mersey Care NHS Trust

Murad *v.* Al-Saraj; Murad *v.* Westwood Business Inc [2005] EWCA Civ 959; [2005] W.T.L.R. 1573; (2005) 102(32) L.S.G. 31, CA (Civ Div); affirming [2004] EWHC 1235, Ch D

Murad *v.* Westwood Business Inc see Murad *v.* Al-Saraj

Murat *v.* Inland Revenue Commissioners; *sub nom* Murat *v.* Ornoch (Inspector of Taxes); R. (on the application of Murat) *v.* Inland Revenue Commissioners [2004] EWHC 3123; [2005] S.T.C. 184; 77 T.C. 122; [2005] B.T.C. 83; [2004] S.T.I. 2300, QBD (Admin); affirming [2004] S.T.C. (S.C.D.) 115; [2004] S.T.I. 559, Sp Comm . . . . *Digested,* 05/**4138**: *Considered,* 05/4164

Murat *v.* Ornoch (Inspector of Taxes) see Murat *v.* Inland Revenue Commissioners

MURATA MANUFACTURING/Acousto-optic deflector (T970/00) [2005] E.P.O.R. 23, EPO (Technical Bd App) . . . . *Digested,* 05/**2462**

Murphy *v.* A Birrell & Sons Ltd [1978] I.R.L.R. 458, EAT . . . . *Digested,* 78/**1008**: *Applied,* 98/2231: *Considered,* 05/1324: *Distinguished,* 84/1197

Murphy *v.* Brentwood DC [1991] 1 A.C. 398; [1990] 3 W.L.R. 414; [1990] 2 All E.R. 908; [1990] 2 Lloyd's Rep. 467; 50 B.L.R. 1; 21 Con. L.R. 1; (1990) 22 H.L.R. 502; 89 L.G.R. 24; (1991) 3 Admin. L.R. 37; (1990) 6 Const. L.J. 304; (1990) 154 L.G. Rev. 1010; [1990] E.G.C.S. 105; (1990) 87(30) L.S.G. 15; (1990) 134 S.J. 1076; *Times,* July 27, 1990; *Independent,* July 27, 1990, HL; reversing [1990] 2 W.L.R. 944; [1990] 2 All E.R. 269; 88 L.G.R. 333; (1990) 87(5) L.S.G. 42; (1990) 134 S.J. 458; *Times,* December 27, 1989; *Independent,* January 26, 1990, CA (Civ Div); affirming 13 Con. L.R. 96, OR. . . . . *Digested,* 91/**2661**: *Applied,* 90/3290, 91/2660, 94/2881, 96/4433, 00/4227, 01/4509, 02/3291, 03/2995, 04/600: *Considered,* 92/3219, 93/2997, 94/3749, 94/4517, 95/2496, 95/3648, 95/3667, 95/4189, 96/2993, 96/4438, 96/4448, 96/7223, 97/3816, 05/436: *Distinguished,* 92/3199, 96/1156, 97/1752, 97/3776, 99/1409: *Followed,* 98/3955: *Not followed,* 98/3924: *Referred to,* 94/6386

Murphy *v.* Burrows [2004] EWHC 1900; (2004-05) 7 I.T.E.L.R. 116; [2005] 1 P. & C.R. DG3, Ch D

Murphy *v.* Ethical Standards Officer of the Standards Board for England [2004] EWHC 2377; [2005] B.L.G.R. 161; [2004] N.P.C. 160, QBD (Admin)

Murphy *v.* Gowers (Inspector of Taxes) [2005] S.T.C. (S.C.D.) 44; [2004] S.T.I. 2267, Sp Comm . . . . *Digested,* 05/**4087**

Murphy *v.* Slough BC [2005] EWCA Civ 122; [2005] I.C.R. 721; [2005] I.R.L.R. 382; *Times,* April 6, 2005, CA (Civ Div); affirming [2004] I.C.R. 1163, EAT . . . . *Digested,* 05/**1223**

Murphy *v.* Staples UK Ltd see Cranfield *v.* Bridgegrove Ltd

Murray *v.* Leisureplay Plc [2005] EWCA Civ 963; [2005] I.R.L.R. 946, CA (Civ Div); reversing [2004] EWHC 1927, QBD

Murray *v.* Robinson see Robinson *v.* Murray

Murray (Deceased) *v.* British Shipbuilders (Hydrodynamics) Ltd see Barker *v.* Saint Gobain Pipelines Plc

Murria *v.* Lord Chancellor [2000] 2 All E.R. 941; [2000] 1 Costs L.R. 81; (2000) 97(3) L.S.G. 35; (2000) 150 N.L.J. 59; (2000) 144 S.J.L.B. 36; *Times,* January 11, 2000; *Independent,* February 7, 2000 (C.S.), QBD . . . . *Digested,* 00/**3973**: *Applied,* 05/2711

Murry *v.* Blackburn, Hyndburn and Ribble Valley Healthcare NHS Trust see Crouch *v.* King's Healthcare NHS Trust

Murthy *v.* Sivajothi [1999] 1 W.L.R. 467; [1999] 1 All E.R. 721; [1999] I.L.Pr. 320; *Times,* November 11, 1998; *Independent,* November 11, 1998, CA (Civ Div) . . . . . *Digested,* 98/**753**: *Applied,* 05/1568

Musashi Autoparts Europe Ltd (formerly TAP Manufacturing Ltd) *v.* Customs and Excise Commissioners; *sub nom* Customs and Excise Commissioners *v.* Musashi Autoparts Europe Ltd [2003] EWCA Civ 1738; [2004] S.T.C. 220; [2004] B.T.C. 5067; [2004] B.V.C. 127; [2004] S.T.I. 231, CA (Civ Div); affirming [2003] EWHC 343; [2003] S.T.C. 449; [2003] B.T.C. 5470; [2003] B.V.C. 526; [2003] S.T.I. 296; (2003) 100(17) L.S.G. 28; *Times,* April 1, 2003, Ch D; reversing [2003] S.T.I. 310, V&DTr . . . . *Digested,* 04/**4019**: *Applied,* 05/4085 *Applied,* 05/4300

Muschinski *v.* Dodds 160 C.L.R. 583, HC (Aus). . . . . *Applied,* 05/4300

Musisi *v.* Secretary of State for the Home Department see Bugdaycay *v.* Secretary of State for the Home Department

Mustad *v.* Dosen; *sub nom* O Mustad & Son *v.* S Allcock & Co [1964] 1 W.L.R. 109 (Note); [1963] 3 All E.R. 416; [1963] R.P.C. 41, HL. *Digested,* 63/**3338**: *Considered,* 05/2416, 05/2812: *Distinguished,* 64/1306

Muys en de Winter's Bouw- en Aannemingsbedrijf BV v. Staatssecretaris van Financien (C281/91) [1997] S.T.C. 665; [1993] E.C.R. I-5405; [1995] 1 C.M.L.R. 126, ECJ (5th Chamber) [1993] E.C.R. I-5405, AGO . . . .   *Digested*, 94/**4959**:
                   Considered, 05/4419

MY v. Secretary of State for the Home Department; *sub nom* MY (Disputed Somali Nationality: Somalia), Re [2004] UKIAT 174; [2004] Imm. A.R. 359, IAT . . . . . .   *Digested*, 05/**2148**

My v. Office National des Pensions (ONP) (C293/03) [2004] E.C.R. I-12013; [2005] 1 C.M.L.R. 37; [2005] C.E.C. 437, ECJ (2nd Chamber). . . . .   *Digested*, 05/**1452**

MY (Disputed Somali Nationality: Somalia), Re see MY v. Secretary of State for the Home Department

Myers v. Myers; *sub nom* Myers, In the Estate of [2004] EWHC 1944; [2005] W.T.L.R. 851, Fam Div

Myers v. South Lakeland DC [2004] R.V.R. 279, Lands Tr. . . . .   *Digested*, 05/**3251**

Myers v. South Lakeland DC (Application for Permission to Appeal) [2005] EWCA Civ 498; [2005] R.V.R. 300, CA (Civ Div)

Myers, In the Estate of see Myers v. Myers

Myles v. DPP [2004] EWHC 594; [2004] 2 All E.R. 902; [2005] R.T.R. 1; *Independent*, May 3, 2004 (C.S), QBD (Admin) . . . .   *Digested*, 04/**733**:
                   Considered, 05/739

MyTravel Group Plc, Re [2004] EWCA Civ 1734; [2005] 2 B.C.L.C. 123, CA (Civ Div); reversing in part [2004] EWHC 2741; [2005] 1 W.L.R. 2365; [2005] B.C.C. 457; *Times*, November 30, 2004, Ch D . . . .   *Digested*, 05/**2335**

MyTravel Group Plc v. Customs and Excise Commissioners (C291/03) [2005] S.T.C. 1617; [2005] C.E.C. 782; [2005] S.T.I. 1679, ECJ (3rd Chamber)

MyTravel Group Plc (formerly Airtours Plc) v. Customs and Excise Commissioners [2005] B.V.C. 2431; [2005] S.T.I. 818, V&DTr

N v. Secretary of State for the Home Department [2005] UKHL 31; [2005] 2 A.C. 296; [2005] 2 W.L.R. 1124; [2005] 4 All E.R. 1017; [2005] H.R.L.R. 22; [2005] U.K.H.R.R. 862; [2005] Imm. A.R. 353; [2005] I.N.L.R. 388; (2005) 84 B.M.L.R. 126; (2005) 102(24) L.S.G. 35; (2005) 155 N.L.J. 748; *Times*, May 9, 2005, HL; affirming [2003] EWCA Civ 1369; [2004] 1 W.L.R. 1182; [2004] U.K.H.R.R. 49; [2004] I.N.L.R. 10; *Times*, October 23, 2003, CA (Civ Div) . . . . .   *Digested*, 05/**2160**:
                   Distinguished, 04/2041

N (A Child) v. Charteris (Unreported, May 28, 2004), CC (Milton Keynes) [*Ex rel.* Gurion Taussig, Barrister, 199 The Strand, London] . . . .   *Digested*, 05/**3170**

N (Sexual Abuse Allegations: Professionals Not Abiding by Findings of Fact), Re [2005] 2 F.L.R. 340; [2005] Fam. Law 529, Fam Div . . . .   *Digested*, 05/**1620**

Nabb Bros Ltd v. Lloyds Bank International (Guernsey) Ltd [2005] EWHC 405; [2005] I.L.Pr. 37, Ch D . . . .   *Digested*, 05/**471**

Nachova v. Bulgaria (43577/98) 19 B.H.R.C. 1, ECHR (Grand Chamber) . . . .   *Previous proceedings*,
                   05/2112

Nachova v. Bulgaria (43577/98) (2004) 39 E.H.R.R. 37, ECHR . . . .   *Digested*, 05/**2112**

Nadarajah v. Secretary of State for the Home Department see R. (on the application of Nadarajah) v. Secretary of State for the Home Department

Nadim Khouri Klinik v. Verrieres Brosse [2005] E.T.M.R. 51, C d'A (Paris)

Nagarajan v. London Regional Transport; *sub nom* Swiggs v. Nagarajan (No.2); Nagarajan v. Swiggs (No.2) [2000] 1 A.C. 501; [1999] 3 W.L.R. 425; [1999] 4 All E.R. 65; [1999] I.C.R. 877; [1999] I.R.L.R. 572; (1999) 96(31) L.S.G. 36; (1999) 149 N.L.J. 1109; (1999) 143 S.J.L.B. 219; *Times*, July 19, 1999 ; *Independent*, October 11, 1999 (C.S.), HL; reversing [1998] I.R.L.R. 73, CA (Civ Div) . . . .   *Digested*, 99/**2093**:
      Applied, 02/1332, 02/1415, 05/1290, 05/2162: *Considered*, 01/2301:
                   Followed, 03/1354

Nagarajan v. Swiggs (No.2) see Nagarajan v. London Regional Transport

Nagulananthan v. Secretary of State for the Home Department see Subesh v. Secretary of State for the Home Department

Naidike v. Attorney General of Trinidad and Tobago [2004] UKPC 49; [2005] 1 A.C. 538; [2004] 3 W.L.R. 1430, PC (Trin) . . . .   *Digested*, 05/**2236**

Nail v. Jones see Nail v. News Group Newspapers Ltd

Nail v. News Group Newspapers Ltd; Nail v. Jones [2004] EWCA Civ 1708; [2005] 1 All E.R. 1040; [2005] E.M.L.R. 12; (2005) 155 N.L.J. 111; *Times*, January 6, 2005; *Independent*, January 14, 2005, CA (Civ Div); affirming [2004] EWHC 647; [2004] E.M.L.R. 20, QBD . . . .   *Digested*, 05/**971**:
         Applied, 05/834, 05/969, 05/972

Napier v. Scottish Ministers 2005 S.C. 307; 2005 S.L.T. 379; [2005] U.K.H.R.R. 268; 2005 G.W.D. 9-136, IH (1 Div); affirming 2005 S.C. 229; 2004 S.L.T. 555; 2004 S.C.L.R. 558; [2004] U.K.H.R.R. 881; 2004 G.W.D. 14-316; *Times*, May 13, 2004, OH . . . .   *Digested*, 05/**5430**:
       Considered, 05/4964: *Previous proceedings*, 01/6834

Napier v. Secretary of State for the Home Department see R. (on the application of Napier) v. Secretary of State for the Home Department

Napijalo v. Croatia (66485/01) (2005) 40 E.H.R.R. 30; 15 B.H.R.C. 422, ECHR . . . . . .   *Digested*, 04/**1954**

Napp Pharmaceutical Holdings Ltd v. Director General of Fair Trading (No.3) [2001]
CAT 3; [2001] Comp. A.R. 33; [2002] E.C.C. 3, CCAT . . . . *Digested*, 02/**585**:
Considered, 04/515: *Followed*, 05/565
Napp Pharmaceutical Holdings Ltd v. Director General of Fair Trading (No.4) [2002]
CAT 1; [2002] Comp. A.R. 13; [2002] E.C.C. 13; (2002) 64 B.M.L.R. 165,
CCAT . . . . *Digested*, 02/**597**:
Applied, 04/542, 05/570: *Followed*, 05/572
Narey v. Customs and Excise Commissioners [2005] EWHC 784; [2005] A.C.D. 85,
QBD (Admin)
Narinen v. Finland (45027/98) [2004] B.P.I.R. 914, ECHR . . . . *Digested*, 05/**2331**
Nash v. Birmingham Crown Court [2005] EWHC 338; (2005) 169 J.P. 157; (2005)
169 J.P.N. 457, QBD (Admin) . . . . *Digested*, 05/**168**
Nash v. Paragon Finance Plc see Paragon Finance Plc (formerly National Home Loans
Corp) v. Nash
Nasser v. United Bank of Kuwait (Security for Costs) [2001] EWCA Civ 556; [2002]
1 W.L.R. 1868; [2002] 1 All E.R. 401; [2001] C.P. Rep. 105, CA (Civ Div) . . . . . . *Digested*, 02/**385**:
Applied, 04/330, 05/465: *Considered*, 02/384, 04/274
NAT SHIPPING BAGGING SERVICES/Material distribution (T636/88); *sub nom* NAT/
Bagging plant (T636/88) [2003] E.P.O.R. 2; [1993] E.P.O.R. 517, EPO
(Technical Bd App) . . . . *Considered*, 05/**2491**
NAT/Bagging plant (T636/88) see NAT SHIPPING BAGGING SERVICES/Material
distribution (T636/88)
National & Provincial Building Society v. United Kingdom (21319/93); Leeds Permanent
Building Society v. United Kingdom (21449/93); Yorkshire Building Society v.
United Kingdom (21675/93) [1997] S.T.C. 1466; (1998) 25 E.H.R.R. 127; 69 T.C.
540; [1997] B.T.C. 624; [1998] H.R.C.D. 34; *Times*, November 6, 1997, ECHR
(1995) 19 E.H.R.R. CD56, Eur Comm HR . . . . *Digested*, 97/**2756**:
Applied, 05/2084
National Association of Health Stores v. Department of Health see R. (on the application
of National Association of Health Stores) v. Secretary of State for Health
National Association of Software and Service Companies v. Sood [2005] F.S.R. 38, HC
(Ind)
National Bank Ltd, Re [1966] 1 W.L.R. 819; [1966] 1 All E.R. 1006; 110 S.J. 226, Ch D . *Digested*, 66/**1305**:
Applied, 00/683, 02/2715, 05/2334: *Considered*, 00/684
National Car Parks Ltd v. Baird (Valuation Officer) [2004] EWCA Civ 967; [2005] 1 All
E.R. 53; [2004] R.A. 245; (2004) 148 S.J.L.B. 942; [2004] N.P.C. 126; *Times*,
September 9, 2004, CA (Civ Div); affirming [2003] R.A. 289, Lands Tr . . . . *Digested*, 04/**3178**
National Coal Board v. National Union of Mineworkers [1986] I.C.R. 736; [1986]
I.R.L.R. 439, Ch D . . . . *Digested*, 87/**3762**:
Applied, 97/2188, 01/2332, 05/1216: *Considered*, 91/1622
National Greyhound Racing Club Ltd v. Flaherty see Flaherty v. National Greyhound
Racing Club Ltd
National Insurance & Guarantee Corp Ltd v. M Young Legal Services Ltd [2004] EWHC
2972; [2005] 2 Lloyd's Rep. 46, QBD . . . . *Considered*, 05/325
National Organisation Systems SA's Application, Re [2005] I.L.Pr. 52, Protodikeio
(Athens)
National Paintball Parks v. North Warwickshire BC [2005] P.A.D. 30, Planning
Inspector
National Power Plc, Re (C151/97 P (I)); *sub nom* British Coal Corp v. Commission of the
European Communities (T367/94); PowerGen Plc, Re (C157/97 P (I)) [1997]
All E.R. (E.C.) 673; [1997] E.C.R. I-3491; [1998] 4 C.M.L.R. 502, ECJ . . . . *Digested*, 98/**2306**:
Followed, 01/2472, 05/576, 05/577
National Provident Institution v. Customs and Excise Commissioners [2005] B.V.C.
2398; [2005] S.T.I. 821, V&DTr (London)
National Trust v. Chilcott [2005] R.A. 266, VT
National Vulcan Engineering Insurance Group Ltd v. Pentax Pty Ltd (t/a Lif-Rig) [2005]
B.L.R. 287, Sup Ct (NSW)
National Westminster Bank Plc v. Gill see Royal Bank of Scotland Plc v. Etridge (No.2)
National Westminster Bank Plc v. Jones; *sub nom* Jones v. National Westminster Bank
Plc [2001] EWCA Civ 1541; [2002] 1 B.C.L.C. 55; [2002] B.P.I.R. 361; (2001)
98(44) L.S.G. 35; (2001) 145 S.J.L.B. 246; [2002] 1 P. & C.R. DG12; *Times*,
November 19, 2001; *Independent*, December 10, 2001 (C.S), CA (Civ Div);
affirming [2001] 1 B.C.L.C. 98; [2000] B.P.I.R. 1092; [2000] E.G.C.S. 82;
(2000) 97(28) L.S.G. 31; [2000] N.P.C. 73; *Times*, July 7, 2000, Ch D . . . . *Digested*, 01/**3785**:
Applied, 05/2341, 05/2898: *Considered*, 01/896
National Westminster Bank Plc v. Parry see Parry v. National Westminster Bank Plc
National Westminster Bank Plc v. Spectrum Plus Ltd (In Creditors Voluntary Liquidation)
see Spectrum Plus Ltd (In Liquidation), Re
Naturally Yours Cosmetics Ltd v. Customs and Excise Commissioners (C230/87)
[1988] S.T.C. 879; [1988] E.C.R. 6365; [1989] 1 C.M.L.R. 797; *Times*,
November 29, 1988; *Daily Telegraph*, December 31, 1988, ECJ. . . . . *Digested*, 89/**1683**:
Applied, 90/4622, 91/3668, 97/4975, 97/4976, 98/4936, 00/5319, 01/5597,
05/4347: *Considered*, 00/5347, 01/5556, 01/5598, 01/5599:
Followed, 05/4406

Navigation Maritime Bulgare v. Rustal Trading Ltd (The Ivan Zagubanski) [2002] 1
Lloyd's Rep. 106, QBD (Comm) . . . . *Digested*, 02/**642**:
Approved, 05/599: *Followed*, 04/560
Navigazione Alta Italia SpA v. Concordia Maritime Chartering AB (The Stena Pacifica)
[1990] 2 Lloyd's Rep. 234, QBD (Comm). . . . . *Digested*, 91/**182**:
Followed, 05/3816
Navimprex Centrala Navala v. George Moundreas & Co SA (1983) 127 S.J. 392, CA
(Civ Div). . . . . *Digested*, 83/**2958**:
Doubted, 05/208
Navitaire Inc v. EasyJet Airline Co Ltd (No.3) [2004] EWHC 1725; [2005] E.C.C. 30;
[2005] E.C.D.R. 17; [2005] Info. T.L.R. 1, Ch D . . . . *Digested*, 05/**2427**
NB Three Shipping Ltd v. Harebell Shipping Ltd [2004] EWHC 2001; [2005] 1 All E.R.
(Comm) 200; [2005] 1 Lloyd's Rep. 509; [2005] 2 C.L.C. 29, QBD (Comm) . . *Digested*, 05/**3792**
NBTY Europe Ltd (formerly Holland & Barrett Europe Ltd) v. Nutricia International BV
[2005] EWHC 734; [2005] 2 Lloyd's Rep. 350, QBD (Comm) . . . . *Digested*, 05/**718**
NCR Ltd v. Riverland Portfolio No.1 Ltd (No.1) [2004] EWHC 921; [2005] 1 P. & C.R.
3; [2004] L. & T.R. 31; [2004] 16 E.G.C.S. 110; (2004) 101(15) L.S.G. 29, Ch D
. . . . *Digested*, 05/**2694**
NCR Ltd v. Riverland Portfolio No.1 Ltd (No.2) [2005] EWCA Civ 312; [2005] 2 P. &
C.R. 27; [2005] L. & T.R. 25; [2005] 2 E.G.L.R. 42; [2005] 22 E.G. 134;
[2005] 13 E.G.C.S. 135; [2005] N.P.C. 46; [2005] 2 P. & C.R. DG11, CA (Civ
Div); reversing [2004] EWHC 2073; [2005] L. & T.R. 6, Ch D . . . . *Digested*, 05/**2689**
Ndangoya v. Sweden (17868/03), ECHR . . . . *Considered*, 05/2160
Nederlandsche Banden Industrie Michelin NV v. Commission of the European
Communities (322/81) [1983] E.C.R. 3461; [1985] 1 C.M.L.R. 282; [1985]
F.S.R. 250, ECJ. . . . . *Digested*, 85/**1319**:
Applied, 02/597: *Considered*, 05/571, 05/575: *Followed*, 00/715
Nederlandse Federatieve Vereniging voor de Groothandel op Elektrotechnisch Gebied v.
Commission of the European Communities (C7/01 P (R)); *sub nom*
Electrotechnical Fittings Cartel (C7/01 P (R)), Re ; Nederlandse Federatieve
Vereniging voor de Groothandel op Elektrotechnisch Gebied v. Commission of
the European Communities (T5/00 R) [2001] E.C.R. I-2559; [2004] 5 C.M.L.R.
18, ECJ; affirming [2000] E.C.R. II-4121; [2004] 5 C.M.L.R. 19, CFI . . . . *Digested*, 05/**544**
Nederlandse Federatieve Vereniging voor de Groothandel op Elektrotechnisch Gebied v.
Commission of the European Communities (T5/00) [2003] E.C.R. II-5761;
[2004] 5 C.M.L.R. 20, CFI (1st Chamber)
Nelidow Santis v. Secretary of State for the Home Department see Bugdaycay v.
Secretary of State for the Home Department
Nelson v. Nelson [1997] 1 W.L.R. 233; [1997] 1 All E.R. 970; [1997] B.P.I.R. 702;
[1997] P.N.L.R. 413; (1997) 94(2) L.S.G. 26; (1997) 147 N.L.J. 126; (1997) 141
S.J.L.B. 30; *Times*, January 8, 1997, CA (Civ Div) . . . . *Digested*, 97/**576**:
Applied, 05/89: *Considered*, 02/409
Nestle SA's Trade Mark Application (No.2006992) see Mars UK Ltd v. Societe des
Produits Nestle SA (Three Dimensional Trade Marks)
Nethercoat v. PMI Construction Ltd (Unreported, October 4, 2004), CC (Barnet) [*Ex
rel*. Gurion Taussig, Barrister, 199 The Strand, Temple, London] . . . . *Digested*, 05/**3107**
Netherlands v. Commission of the European Communities (59/70) [1971] E.C.R. 639,
ECJ . . . . *Followed*, 05/584
Netherlands v. Ten Kate Holding Musselkanaal BV (C511/03), *Times*, November 8,
2005, ECJ (3rd Chamber)
Netherlands Antilles v. Commission of the European Communities (T32/98); *sub nom*
Netherlands Antilles v. Commission of the European Communities (T41/98)
[2000] E.C.R. II-201; [2002] 1 C.M.L.R. 10, CFI (3rd Chamber). . . . . *Digested*, 02/**1543**:
Overruled, 05/1474
Netherlands Antilles v. Commission of the European Communities (T41/98) see
Netherlands Antilles v. Commission of the European Communities (T32/98)
Netherlane Ltd v. York [2005] S.T.C. (S.C.D.) 305; [2005] S.T.I. 165, Sp Comm. . . . . . . *Digested*, 05/**4127**
Netlogic Consulting Ltd v. Revenue and Customs Commissioners; Kawthar Consulting
Ltd v. Revenue and Customs Commissioners [2005] S.T.C. (S.C.D.) 524, Sp
Comm
Nevmerzhitsky v. Ukraine (54825/00) 19 B.H.R.C. 177, ECHR
New Bullas Trading Ltd, Re [1994] B.C.C. 36; [1994] 1 B.C.L.C. 485; *Times*, January 12,
1994, CA (Civ Div); reversing [1993] B.C.C. 251; [1993] B.C.L.C. 1389, Ch D
(Companies Ct) . . . . *Digested*, 94/**2601**:
Applied, 04/227: *Considered*, 95/567, 01/733: *Disapproved*, 01/732:
Distinguished, 00/3483: *Overruled*, 05/2320
New Cap Reinsurance Corp Ltd v. General Cologne Re Australia Ltd (2004-05) 7
I.T.E.L.R. 295, Sup Ct (NSW). . . . . *Digested*, 05/**522**
New Century Cleaning Co v. Church [2000] I.R.L.R. 27; *Independent*, April 23, 1999,
CA (Civ Div) . . . . *Digested*, 99/**2148**:
Applied, 05/1196
New Charter Housing (North) Ltd v. Ashcroft [2004] EWCA Civ 310; [2004] H.L.R.
36; (2004) 148 S.J.L.B. 352, CA (Civ Div). . . . . *Digested*, 05/**2642**

New Fashion (London) Ltd *v.* Revenue and Customs Commissioners see New Fashions (London) Ltd *v.* Revenue and Customs Commissioners

New Fashions (London) Ltd *v.* Revenue and Customs Commissioners; *sub nom* New Fashion (London) Ltd *v.* Revenue and Customs Commissioners [2005] EWHC 1628; [2005] S.T.I. 1317, Ch D

New Gadget Shop Ltd, Re see Wilkinson *v.* West Coast Capital (Pre-Trial Review)

New Look Ltd *v.* Newman (R 20/2003-1) [2005] E.T.M.R. 36, OHIM (1st Bd App) . . .   *Digested*, 05/**2539**

New Look Ltd *v.* Office for Harmonisation in the Internal Market (Trade Marks and Designs) (OHIM) (T117/03) [2005] E.T.M.R. 35, CFI (2nd Chamber) . . . .   *Digested*, 05/**2535**

New Southern Railway Ltd *v.* Rodway see South Central Trains Ltd *v.* Rodway

Newbury DC *v.* International Synthetic Rubber Co Ltd see Newbury DC *v.* Secretary of State for the Environment

Newbury DC *v.* Secretary of State for the Environment; Newbury DC *v.* International Synthetic Rubber Co Ltd [1981] A.C. 578; [1980] 2 W.L.R. 379; [1980] 1 All E.R. 731; 78 L.G.R. 306; (1980) 40 P. & C.R. 148; [1980] J.P.L. 325; 124 S.J. 186, HL; reversing [1978] 1 W.L.R. 1241; [1979] 1 All E.R. 243; 77 L.G.R. 60; (1979) 37 P. & C.R. 73; (1978) 248 E.G. 223; (1978) 248 E.G. 1017; [1979] J.P.L. 26; 122 S.J. 524, CA (Civ Div); reversing 75 L.G.R. 608; (1978) 35 P. & C.R. 170; (1977) 242 E.G. 377; [1977] J.P.L. 373; 121 S.J. 254, QBD . . . .   *Digested*, 80/**2667**:
    Applied, 82/3185, 84/3413, 84/3465, 88/3530, 89/3541, 92/4363, 93/3936, 93/3948, 94/4435, 94/4462, 98/4212, 99/4221, 99/4243, 00/4418, 00/4479, 00/4511, 00/4515, 02/3695: *Considered*, 83/3719, 84/3478, 84/4734, 89/3643, 90/4452, 94/4331, 95/4784: *Distinguished*, 82/3169, 01/4699: *Followed*, 05/3304: *Referred to*, 83/3716, 90/4362, 90/4438, 91/3524, 91/5757

Newcastle upon Tyne City Council *v.* Allan; Degnan *v.* Redcar and Cleveland BC [2005] I.C.R. 1170; [2005] I.R.L.R. 504, EAT . . . .   *Digested*, 05/**1263**

Newcastle upon Tyne City Council *v.* Barns (NE) Ltd; *sub nom* Barns (NE) Ltd *v.* Newcastle upon Tyne City Council [2005] EWCA Civ 1274; (2005) 102(44) L.S.G. 31, CA (Civ Div)

Newcastle upon Tyne City Council *v.* Le Quelenec see R. (on the application of Newcastle upon Tyne City Council) *v.* Le Quelenec

Newfield Construction Ltd *v.* Tomlinson [2004] EWHC 3051; 97 Con. L.R. 148, QBD (TCC) . . . .   *Digested*, 05/**205**

Newham LBC *v.* Hawkins see Hawkins *v.* Newham LBC

Newham LBC *v.* Khatun see R. (on the application of Khatun) *v.* Newham LBC

Newham LBC *v.* Takavarasha (Permission to Appeal) [2005] EWCA Civ 850; [2005] R.V.R. 324, CA (Civ Div)

Newnham *v.* Clatworthy (Inspector of Taxes) 76 T.C. 772, Ch D

Newnham College, Cambridge *v.* Customs and Excise Commissioners; *sub nom* Newnham College, Cambridge *v.* Revenue and Customs Commissioners; C3/2005/1283, CA (Civ Div); reversing [2005] B.V.C. 2374; [2005] V. & D.R. 36; [2005] S.T.I. 816, V&DTr (London)

Newnham College, Cambridge *v.* Revenue and Customs Commissioners see Newnham College, Cambridge *v.* Customs and Excise Commissioners

Newsum *v.* National Assembly for Wales see R. (on the application of Newsum) *v.* Welsh Assembly (No.1)

Newsum *v.* Welsh Assembly see R. (on the application of Newsum) *v.* Welsh Assembly (No.1)

Nexus Communications Group Ltd *v.* Lambert [2005] EWHC 345; (2005) 102(13) L.S.G. 28; *Times*, March 3, 2005, Ch D . . . .   *Digested*, 05/**702**

NHS Pensions Agency *v.* Suggett C3/2005/1018/CHANF, CA (Civ Div); affirming [2005] EWHC 1265; [2005] O.P.L.R. 287, Ch D

NIC Instruments Ltd's Licence of Right (Design Right) Application [2005] R.P.C. 1, PO .   *Digested*, 05/**2436**

Nicholas *v.* Soundcraft Electronics Ltd; *sub nom* Soundcraft Magnetics, Re [1993] B.C.L.C. 360; *Times*, July 10, 1992, CA (Civ Div) . . . .   *Digested*, 93/**390**:
    Applied, 05/530

Nicholls *v.* Nicholls [1997] 1 W.L.R. 314; [1997] 2 All E.R. 97; [1997] 1 F.L.R. 649; [1997] 3 F.C.R. 14; [1997] Fam. Law 321; (1997) 147 N.L.J. 61; *Times*, January 21, 1997, CA (Civ Div) . . . .   *Digested*, 97/**2447**:
    Applied, 03/317, 05/345: *Considered*, 01/451

Nichols Plc *v.* Registrar of Trade Marks (C404/02) [2005] 1 W.L.R. 1418; [2005] All E.R. (EC) 1; [2005] C.E.C. 160; [2005] E.T.M.R. 21; [2005] R.P.C. 12; *Times*, October 20, 2004, ECJ (2nd Chamber) [2004] E.T.M.R. 48, AGO . . . .   *Digested*, 05/**2438**:
    Applied, 05/2565: *Considered*, 05/2563

Nicol *v.* National Coal Board (1952) 102 L.J. 357 . . . .   *Applied*, 54/2076:
    Considered, 05/4199

Niemietz *v.* Germany (A/251-B) (1993) 16 E.H.R.R. 97, ECHR . . . .   *Digested*, 93/**2157**:
    Applied, 98/3154: *Considered*, 00/3248, 04/1304, 05/2116

Niersmans *v.* Pesticcio see Pesticcio *v.* Huet

Nikitin *v.* Russia (50178/99) (2005) 41 E.H.R.R. 10, ECHR . . . .   *Digested*, 05/**2087**

Nikken Kosakusho Works *v.* Pioneer Trading Co [2004] EWHC 2246; [2005] F.S.R. 15; (2005) 28(2) I.P.D. 28004, Ch D . . . .   *Digested*, 05/**2489**

Nikoloudi v. Organismos Tilepikinonion Ellados (OTE) AE (C196/02) [2005] E.C.R. I-1789; [2005] 1 C.M.L.R. 54, ECJ (1st Chamber). . . . . *Digested,* 05/**1268**
Nilsen v. Full Sutton Prison Governor see R. (on the application of Nilsen) v. Full Sutton Prison Governor
Nimz v. Freie und Hansestadt Hamburg (C184/89) [1991] E.C.R. I-297; [1992] 3 C.M.L.R. 699; [1991] I.R.L.R. 222, ECJ (6th Chamber) . . . . *Considered,* 95/2052, 96/2629, 05/1261: *Distinguished,* 04/1254
Ninni-Orasche v. Bundesminister fur Wissenschaft, Verkehr und Kunst (C413/01) [2004] All E.R. (EC) 765; [2004] 1 C.M.L.R. 19, ECJ (6th Chamber) . . . . *Digested,* 04/**1263**: *Considered,* 05/3856
Nippon Yusen Kaisha Ltd v. Scindia Steam Navigation Co Ltd (The Jalagouri; *sub nom* Scindia Steamship Navigation Co Ltd Bombay v. Nippon Yusen Kaisha Ltd (The Jalagouri) [2000] 2 All E.R. (Comm) 700; [2000] 1 Lloyd's Rep. 515; [2000] C.L.C. 1051; *Independent,* April 7, 2000, CA (Civ Div); affirming [1999] 1 Lloyd's Rep. 903; [1998] C.L.C. 1054, QBD (Comm) . . . . *Digested,* 00/**4703**: *Applied,* 05/3812
NKK CORP/Iron-zinc alloy plating (T241/02) [2005] E.P.O.R. 28, EPO (Technical Bd App)
NM Financial Management Ltd v. Marshall see Marshall v. NM Financial Management Ltd
NN/Time limit definition (J24/03) [2004] E.P.O.R. 53, EPO (Legal Bd App) . . . . *Digested,* 05/**2457**
Nokia Corp v. InterDigital Technology Corp [2005] EWCA Civ 614, CA (Civ Div); affirming [2004] EWHC 2920; (2005) 28(5) I.P.D. 28039, Ch D (Patents Ct)
Nokia Corp v. InterDigital Technology Corp [2005] EWHC 2134; (2005) 28(10) I.P.D. 28079, Ch D (Patents Ct)
Nolan v. Nolan [2004] W.T.L.R. 1261, CA (Vic) . . . . *Digested,* 05/**4289**
Nolte v. Landesversicherungsanstalt Hannover (C317/93) [1995] E.C.R. I-4625, AGO . *Applied,* 05/3886
Nomad Developments Ltd v. Gateshead BC [2005] R.V.R. 187, Lands Tr . . . . *Digested,* 05/**3250**
Non-payment of Cheque, Re [2005] I.L.Pr. 14, BGH (Ger)
Nooh v. Secretary of State for the Home Department see Adan (Hassan Hussein) v. Secretary of State for the Home Department
Noonan v. Ealing LBC [2005] P.A.D. 46, Planning Inspector
Noranda Inc v. Barton (Time Charter) Ltd (The Marinor) [1996] 1 Lloyd's Rep. 301; [1996] C.L.C. 337, QBD (Comm) . . . . *Applied,* 97/4514: *Distinguished,* 05/3816
Norberg v. Wynrib [1992] 2 S.C.R. 226, Sup Ct (Can) . . . . *Applied,* 05/4299
Nordsee Deutsche Hochseefischerei GmbH v. Reederei Mond Hochseefischerei Nordstern AG & Co KG (102/81) [1982] E.C.R. 1095; [1982] Com. L.R. 154, ECJ . . . . *Digested,* 82/**102**: *Applied,* 05/1478
Norfolk Capital Group Ltd v. Cadogan Estates Ltd [2004] EWHC 384; [2004] 1 W.L.R. 1458; [2004] 3 All E.R. 889; [2004] L. & T.R. 33; [2004] 2 E.G.L.R. 50; [2004] 32 E.G. 64; *Times,* March 12, 2004, Ch D . . . . *Digested,* 05/**2649**
Norma Lebensmittelfilialbetrieb GmbH & Co KG v. Office for Harmonisation in the Internal Market (Trade Marks and Designs) (OHIM) (T281/02) [2005] E.T.M.R. 49, CFI (4th Chamber) . . . . *Digested,* 05/**2558**: *Followed,* 05/2581
Norman, Re (1885-86) L.R. 16 Q.B.D. 673, CA . . . . *Considered,* 05/361
Norman v. Ali (Limitation Period); Aziz v. Norman [2000] R.T.R. 107; [2000] Lloyd's Rep. I.R. 395; [2000] P.I.Q.R. P72; (2000) 97(2) L.S.G. 30; (2000) 144 S.J.L.B. 18; *Times,* February 25, 2000; *Independent,* February 7, 2000 (C.S.), CA (Civ Div) . . . . *Digested,* 00/**3548**: *Considered,* 05/2843
Norman v. Federal Commissioner of Taxation 109 C.L.R. 9 . . . . *Considered,* 05/844
Norman v. Secretary of State for the Home Department see Bugdaycay v. Secretary of State for the Home Department
Normans Bay Ltd (formerly Illingworth Morris Ltd) v. Coudert Bros [2004] EWCA Civ 215; (2004) 101(13) L.S.G. 36; (2004) 148 S.J.L.B. 296; *Times,* March 24, 2004, CA (Civ Div); reversing in part [2003] EWHC 191, QBD. . . . . *Applied,* 05/1319
Normhurst Ltd v. Dornoch Ltd [2004] EWHC 567; [2005] Lloyd's Rep. I.R. 27, QBD (Comm) . . . . *Digested,* 05/**2358**
Norris v. Norris; Haskins v. Haskins [2003] EWCA Civ 1084; [2003] 1 W.L.R. 2960; [2003] 4 Costs L.R. 591; [2003] 2 F.L.R. 1124; [2003] 3 F.C.R. 136; [2003] Fam. Law 721; (2003) 100(36) L.S.G. 37; *Times,* August 26, 2003, CA (Civ Div); affirming [2002] EWHC 2996; [2003] 1 F.L.R. 1142; [2003] 2 F.C.R. 245; [2003] Fam. Law 301, Fam Div . . . . *Digested,* 03/**1571**: *Applied,* 05/1625: *Followed,* 05/1688
Norris v. W Moss & Sons [1954] 1 W.L.R. 346; [1954] 1 All E.R. 324; 52 L.G.R. 140; 98 S.J. 110, CA . . . . *Digested,* 54/**352**: *Applied,* 05/1955
Nortel Networks UK Pension Plan, Re see Lewis v. Pensions Ombudsman
North & South Trust Co v. Berkeley; *sub nom* Berkeley v. North & South Trust Co [1971] 1 W.L.R. 470; [1971] 1 All E.R. 980; [1970] 2 Lloyd's Rep. 467; (1970) 115 S.J. 244, QBD (Comm) . . . . *Digested,* 71/**111**: *Applied,* 05/2355: *Distinguished,* 93/72

North Atlantic Insurance Co Ltd *v.* Nationwide General Insurance Co Ltd [2004] EWCA Civ 423; [2004] 2 All E.R. (Comm) 351; [2004] 1 C.L.C. 1131; [2004] Lloyd's Rep. I.R. 466; (2004) 148 S.J.L.B. 508, CA (Civ Div); affirming [2003] EWHC 449; [2003] 2 C.L.C. 731, QBD (Comm) .... *Digested,* 05/**2407**

North British Housing Association Ltd *v.* Masood see North British Housing Association Ltd *v.* Matthews

North British Housing Association Ltd *v.* Matthews; North British Housing Association Ltd *v.* Snaith; North British Housing Association Ltd *v.* Masood; London & Quadrant Housing Trust *v.* Morgan [2004] EWCA Civ 1736; [2005] 1 W.L.R. 3133; [2005] 2 All E.R. 667; [2005] C.P. Rep. 16; [2005] H.L.R. 17; [2005] 2 P. & C.R. 13; [2005] 1 E.G.L.R. 31; [2005] 13 E.G. 136; [2005] 2 E.G.C.S. 101; *Times,* January 11, 2005, CA (Civ Div) .... *Digested,* 05/**2674**

North British Housing Association Ltd *v.* Snaith see North British Housing Association Ltd *v.* Matthews

North Dorset DC *v.* Miller [2005] P.A.D. 83, Planning Inspector

North East Derbyshire DC *v.* PPW & P Calvert [2005] P.A.D. 12, Planning Inspector

North East Lincolnshire DC *v.* Parker [2005] P.A.D. 26, Planning Inspector

North Kesteven DC *v.* Gentle [2005] P.A.D. 57, Planning Inspector

North Norfolk DC *v.* Miles [2005] P.A.D. 61, Planning Inspector

North Star Shipping Ltd *v.* Sphere Drake Insurance Plc [2004] EWHC 2457; [2005] 1 All E.R. (Comm) 112; [2005] Lloyd's Rep. I.R. 404, QBD (Comm) .... *Digested,* 05/**451**

North Star Shipping Ltd *v.* Sphere Drake Insurance Plc A3/2005/1022, CA (Civ Div); affirming [2005] EWHC 665; [2005] 2 Lloyd's Rep. 76; [2005] 2 C.L.C. 238, QBD (Comm) .... *Digested,* 05/**2390**

North Western Health Board *v.* McKenna (C191/03) [2005] I.R.L.R. 895, ECJ (2nd Chamber)

North Wiltshire DC *v.* Beattie see North Wiltshire DC *v.* Ward

North Wiltshire DC *v.* Ward; North Wiltshire DC *v.* Beattie [2005] P.A.D. 27, Planning Inspector

North Wiltshire DC *v.* Ward [2005] P.A.D. 53, Planning Inspector

Northampton BC *v.* First Secretary of State see Northampton BC *v.* Secretary of State for the Home Department

Northampton BC *v.* Secretary of State for the Home Department; *sub nom* Northampton BC *v.* First Secretary of State [2005] EWHC 168; [2005] J.P.L. 1213; [2005] 7 E.G.C.S. 142; (2005) 149 S.J.L.B. 356, QBD (Admin)

Northamptonshire CC *v.* Purity Soft Drinks Ltd; *sub nom* Lewin *v.* Purity Soft Drinks Ltd [2004] EWHC 3119; (2005) 169 J.P. 84; [2005] A.C.D. 81; (2005) 169 J.P.N. 119; *Times,* December 27, 2004, QBD (Admin) .... *Digested,* 05/**690**

Northstar Systems Ltd (In Liquidation) *v.* Fielding see Ultraframe (UK) Ltd *v.* Fielding

Norton *v.* Thompson (Inspector of Taxes) [2004] S.T.C. (S.C.D.) 163; [2004] S.T.I. 897, Sp Comm .... *Digested,* 05/**4085**

Norton Tool Co Ltd *v.* Tewson [1973] 1 W.L.R. 45; [1973] 1 All E.R. 183; [1972] I.C.R. 501; [1972] I.R.L.R. 86; (1972) 13 K.I.R. 328; [1973] I.T.R. 23; 117 S.J. 33, NIRC. .... *Digested,* 73/**1136**:
Applied, 73/1132, 73/1137, 73/1186, 74/1294, 74/1305, 74/1312, 74/1346, 75/1145, 75/1165, 75/2702, 76/963, 76/965, 84/1289, 03/1333, 05/1331:
Approved, 04/1303: *Considered,* 73/1143, 81/935, 97/2190, 98/2238:
Followed, 74/1287, 74/1290, 76/960, 87/1388: *Referred to,* 88/1336

Norwegian American Cruises A/S *v.* Paul Mundy Ltd (The Vistafjord) [1988] 2 Lloyd's Rep. 343; *Times,* April 22, 1988, CA (Civ Div) .... *Digested,* 89/**1531**:
Applied, 05/538

Norwich City Council *v.* Famuyiwa [2004] EWCA Civ 1770; *Times,* January 24, 2005, CA (Civ Div) .... *Digested,* 05/**2687**

Norwich Corp *v.* Sagnata Investments Ltd see Sagnata Investments Ltd *v.* Norwich Corp

Norwich Union Fire Insurance Co *v.* Colonial Mutual Fire Insurance Co Ltd; *sub nom* Norwich Union Fire Insurance Society Ltd *v.* Colonial Mutual Fire Insurance Co Ltd [1922] 2 K.B. 461; (1922) 12 Ll. L. Rep. 215, KBD .... *Applied,* 05/2405

Norwich Union Fire Insurance Society Ltd *v.* Colonial Mutual Fire Insurance Co Ltd see Norwich Union Fire Insurance Co *v.* Colonial Mutual Fire Insurance Co Ltd

Norwich Union Life Insurance Society *v.* Shopmoor Ltd [1999] 1 W.L.R. 531; [1998] 3 All E.R. 32; [1998] 2 E.G.L.R. 167, Ch D .... *Digested,* 97/**3250**:
Applied, 98/3617: *Approved,* 03/2752

Norwich Union Linked Life Assurance Ltd, Re [2004] EWHC 2802; [2005] B.C.C. 586, Ch D (Companies Ct) .... *Digested,* 05/**2361**:
Followed, 05/2362

Norwood *v.* United Kingdom (Admissibility) (23131/03) (2005) 40 E.H.R.R. SE11, ECHR

Nottingham CC *v.* Hardy & Hansons Plc [2005] P.A.D. 1, Planning Inspector

Nottinghamshire CC *v.* Meikle see Meikle *v.* Nottinghamshire CC

Nottinghamshire Healthcare NHS Trust *v.* News Group Newspapers Ltd [2002] EWHC 409; [2002] E.M.L.R. 33; [2002] R.P.C. 49; (2002) 99(18) L.S.G. 36; (2002) 146 S.J.L.B. 92; [2002] E.C.D.R. CN5; *Times,* April 1, 2002, Ch D .... *Digested,* 02/**2763**:
Applied, 05/2421

Nouri *v.* Marvi [2005] EWHC 2996; [2005] 43 E.G.C.S. 188, Ch D

Novartis AG *v.* Comptroller-General of Patents, Designs and Trade Marks (C207/03); Ministre de l'Economie *v.* Millennium Pharmaceuticals Inc (C252/03) [2005] R.P.C. 33, ECJ (2nd Chamber)

NOVARTIS/Purified polyactide compositon (T803/01) [2005] E.P.O.R. 26, EPO (Technical Bd App)

Novello & Co Ltd *v.* Keith Prowse Music Publishing Co Ltd [2004] EWCA Civ 1776; [2005] E.M.L.R. 21; [2005] R.P.C. 23; (2005) 28(3) I.P.D. 28012; *Times,* January 10, 2005, CA (Civ Div); affirming [2004] EWHC 766; [2004] E.M.L.R. 16; [2004] R.P.C. 48; *Times,* May 20, 2004, Ch D . . . . *Digested,* 05/**2426**

Nowell *v.* Flannery see Hodgson, Re

NP *v.* South Gloucestershire CC see C (A Child) (Care Order: Application to Discharge), Re

NPower Direct Ltd *v.* South of Scotland Power Ltd [2005] EWHC 2123; (2005) 102(43) L.S.G. 29, QBD (Comm)

Numast *v.* P&O Scottish Ferries [2005] I.C.R. 1270, EAT (SC) . . . . *Digested,* 05/**5215**

Nunes *v.* Davies Laing & Dick Ltd (1986) 51 P. & C.R. 310; [1986] 1 E.G.L.R. 106; (1985) 277 E.G. 416, Ch D . . . . *Digested,* 86/**1923**:
Applied, 90/651, 05/2679: *Considered,* 86/1917, 88/2067, 89/2159, 90/118, 90/2862, 92/106, 92/2732, 92/2733, 93/2526, 93/2536:
Distinguished, 89/2181

Nunneley *v.* Nunneley (1890) L.R. 15 P.D. 186, PDAD . . . . *Considered,* 85/1055:
Followed, 05/1682

Nurkowski, Re see Hill *v.* Spread Trustee Co Ltd

Nurnberger Allgemeine Versicherungs AG *v.* Portbridge Transport International BV (C148/03) [2005] 1 Lloyd's Rep. 592; [2004] E.C.R. I-10327; [2004] C.E.C. 480; [2005] I.L.Pr. 1, ECJ (3rd Chamber)

Nuttall *v.* Vehicle Inspectorate see Vehicle Inspectorate *v.* Nuttall

Nutting *v.* Southern Housing Group Ltd [2004] EWHC 2982; [2005] 1 F.L.R. 1066; [2005] H.L.R. 25; [2005] 2 P. & C.R. 14; [2005] Fam. Law 210; (2005) 102(6) L.S.G. 32; [2005] 1 P. & C.R. DG22; *Times,* January 5, 2005, Ch D . . . . *Digested,* 05/**2641**

O (Children) (Hearing in Private: Assistance), Re; *sub nom* O (Children) (Representation: McKenzie Friend), Re; WR (A Child) (Representation: McKenzie Friend), Re; W (Children) (Representation: McKenzie Friend), Re [2005] EWCA Civ 759; [2005] 3 W.L.R. 1191; [2005] 2 F.L.R. 967; [2005] 2 F.C.R. 563; [2005] H.R.L.R. 37; [2005] Fam. Law 773; *Times,* June 27, 2005; *Independent,* July 1, 2005, CA (Civ Div) . . . . *Digested,* 05/**1646**

O (Children) (Representation: McKenzie Friend), Re see O (Children) (Hearing in Private: Assistance), Re

O and N (Children) (Care: Preliminary Hearing), Re see O and N (Children) (Non-Accidental Injury: Burden of Proof), Re

O and N (Children) (Non-Accidental Injury: Burden of Proof), Re; *sub nom* O and N (Children) (Care: Preliminary Hearing), Re; B (Children), Re; B (A Child) (Non-Accidental Injury: Compelling Medical Evidence), Re [2003] UKHL 18; [2004] 1 A.C. 523; [2003] 2 W.L.R. 1075; [2003] 2 All E.R. 305; [2003] 1 F.L.R. 1169; [2003] 1 F.C.R. 673; [2003] Fam. Law 464; (2003) 100(23) L.S.G. 36; *Times,* April 4, 2003; *Independent,* April 8, 2003, HL; reversing [2002] EWCA Civ 1271; [2002] 2 F.L.R. 1167; [2002] 3 F.C.R. 418; [2002] Fam. Law 881, CA (Civ Div) . . . . *Digested,* 03/**1517**:
Applied, 03/1516, 05/1559: *Previous proceedings,* 03/1532

O Mustad & Son *v.* S Allcock & Co see Mustad *v.* Dosen

O'Brien *v.* Barnet Magistrates Court [2005] EWCA Civ 4; [2005] R.V.R. 134, CA (Civ Div)

O'Brien *v.* Chief Constable of South Wales [2005] UKHL 26; [2005] 2 A.C. 534; [2005] 2 W.L.R. 1038; [2005] 2 All E.R. 931; *Times,* April 29, 2005; *Independent,* May 4, 2005, HL; affirming [2003] EWCA Civ 1085; [2004] C.P. Rep. 5; (2003) 100(37) L.S.G. 32; *Times,* August 22, 2003, CA (Civ Div) . . . . . *Digested,* 05/**302**

O'Brien *v.* Leahy (Valuation Officer) [2005] R.A. 324, Lands Tr

O'Brien *v.* Royal Society for Mentally Handicapped Children and Adults [2001] 1 Q.R. 9, CC (Clerkenwell) [*Ex rel.* David McHugh, Barrister, Bracton Chambers, 95A Chancery Lane, London] . . . . *Digested,* 01/**1642**:
Considered, 05/3160

O'Carroll *v.* Diamond [2005] P.N.L.R. 34, Sup Ct (Irl)

O'Carroll *v.* United Kingdom (Admissibility) (35557/03) (2005) 41 E.H.R.R. SE1, ECHR

O'Connor's Application for Judicial Review, Re [2005] Eu. L.R. 719, QBD (NI) . . . . *Digested,* 05/**4984**

O'Dea *v.* ISC Chemicals Ltd [1996] I.C.R. 222; [1995] I.R.L.R. 799; *Times,* August 4, 1995; *Independent,* August 24, 1995, CA (Civ Div) . . . . *Digested,* 96/**2668**:
Followed, 05/1333

O'Donoghue (James Keith), Re [2004] EWCA Civ 1800; (2004) 148 S.J.L.B. 1316, CA (Civ Div); affirming [2004] EWHC 176, QBD (Admin) . . . . *Followed,* 05/844

O'Flynn *v.* Adjudication Officer (C237/94) [1996] All E.R. (EC) 541; [1996] E.C.R. I-2617; [1996] 3 C.M.L.R. 103; [1998] I.C.R. 608; (1997) 33 B.M.L.R. 54; *Times*, June 7, 1996; *Independent*, July 8, 1996 (C.S.), ECJ (5th Chamber) [1996] E.C.R. I-2617, AGO . . . . *Digested*, 96/**5517**: *Considered*, 05/3827

O'Gallagher *v.* Lambeth LBC [2005] 2 Q.R. 8; [2004] 3 Q.R. 6, CC (Central London) [*Ex rel.* Scott Matthewson, Barrister, 22 Old Buildings, Lincoln's Inn, London] . .   *Digested*, 04/**2866**

O'Hara *v.* Liverpool City Council (Unreported, April 21, 2004), CC (Liverpool) [*Ex rel.* Justin Valentine, Barrister, Atlantic Chambers, 4-6 Cook Street, Liverpool] . . . . .   *Digested*, 05/**381**

O'Hara *v.* McDougal (2005) 102(48) L.S.G. 20, CA (Civ Div)

O'Kane *v.* Jones (The Martin P) [2003] EWHC 3470; [2004] 1 Lloyd's Rep. 389; [2005] Lloyd's Rep. I.R. 174, QBD (Comm) . . . .   *Digested*, 05/**2384**: *Considered*, 05/2390

O'Neill *v.* DSG Retail Ltd; *sub nom* O'Neil *v.* DSG Retail Ltd [2002] EWCA Civ 1139; [2003] I.C.R. 222; (2002) 99(40) L.S.G. 32; *Times*, September 9, 2002, CA (Civ Div). . . . .   *Digested*, 02/**2222**: *Considered*, 05/1957

O'Neill *v.* Phillips; *sub nom* Company (No.000709 of 1992), Re; Pectel Ltd, Re [1999] 1 W.L.R. 1092; [1999] 2 All E.R. 961; [1999] B.C.C. 600; [1999] 2 B.C.L.C. 1; (1999) 96(23) L.S.G. 33; (1999) 149 N.L.J. 805; *Times*, May 21, 1999, HL; affirming [1998] B.C.C. 417; [1997] 2 B.C.L.C. 739, CA (Civ Div) . . . .   *Digested*, 99/**634**: *Applied*, 00/691, 01/747, 02/5375, 05/39: *Considered*, 04/477, 04/478: *Distinguished*, 03/545

O'Neill *v.* Vauxhall Ltd [2005] 3 Q.R. 10, CC (Luton) [*Ex rel.* Paul McGrath, Barrister, 1 Temple Gardens, Temple, London] . . . .   *Digested*, 05/**3193**

O'Reilly *v.* Ireland (54725/00) (2005) 40 E.H.R.R. 40, ECHR

O'Riordan *v.* DPP [2005] EWHC 1240; *Times*, May 31, 2005, QBD (Admin) . . . .   *Digested*, 05/**815**

O'Sullivan *v.* Inland Revenue Commissioners see O'Sullivan *v.* Philip (Inspector of Taxes)

O'Sullivan *v.* Philip (Inspector of Taxes); *sub nom* O'Sullivan *v.* Inland Revenue Commissioners [2005] EWHC 2130; [2005] S.T.C. 1712; [2005] B.T.C. 544; [2005] S.T.I. 1681; *Times*, October 13, 2005, Ch D; affirming [2005] S.T.C. (S.C.D.) 51; [2004] S.T.I. 2437, Sp Comm. . . . .   *Digested*, 05/**4006**

O2 Holdings Ltd *v.* Hutchison 3G UK Ltd; *sub nom* O2 (UK) Ltd *v.* Hutchinson 3G UK Ltd [2004] EWHC 2571; [2005] E.T.M.R. 61, Ch D . . . .   *Digested*, 05/**2570**

O2 Holdings Ltd *v.* Hutchison 3G UK Ltd; *sub nom* O2 (UK) Ltd *v.* Hutchinson 3G UK Ltd [2005] EWHC 344; [2005] Eu. L.R. 745; [2005] E.T.M.R. 62; (2005) 28(6) I.P.D. 28045, Ch D . . . .   *Digested*, 05/**2569**

O2 (UK) Ltd *v.* Hutchison 3G UK Ltd see O2 Holdings Ltd *v.* Hutchison 3G UK Ltd

O2 (UK) Ltd *v.* Hutchinson 3G UK Ltd see O2 Holdings Ltd *v.* Hutchison 3G UK Ltd

Oakes *v.* Hopcroft [2000] Lloyd's Rep. Med. 394; (2000) 56 B.M.L.R. 136; [2000] Lloyd's Rep. P.N. 946; *Independent*, October 30, 2000 (C.S), CA (Civ Div) . . . .   *Digested*, 00/**4197**: *Considered*, 04/379, 05/433

Oakley *v.* Inland Revenue Commissioners [2005] S.T.C. (S.C.D.) 343; [2005] W.T.L.R. 181; [2005] S.T.I. 224, Sp Comm . . . .   *Digested*, 05/**4308**

Oakley *v.* Ultra Vehicle Design Ltd (In Liquidation); *sub nom* Ultra Motorhomes International Ltd, Re [2005] EWHC 872; [2005] I.L.Pr. 55, Ch D

Oakley Inc *v.* Animal Ltd [2005] EWCA Civ 1191; *Times*, November 7, 2005, CA (Civ Div); reversing [2005] EWHC 419; [2005] Eu. L.R. 713, Ch D (Patents Ct) . . . .   *Digested*, 05/**2501**

Oakley Inc *v.* Animal Ltd (Preliminary Issue) [2005] EWHC 210; [2005] 1 C.M.L.R. 51; [2005] Eu. L.R. 657; [2005] E.C.D.R. 25; [2005] R.P.C. 30; (2005) 28(4) I.P.D. 28020; *Times*, March 10, 2005, Ch D (Patents Ct) . . . .   *Digested*, 05/**2502**

Oakley-Smith *v.* Greenberg; *sub nom* TBL Realisations Plc, Re [2002] EWCA Civ 1217; [2004] B.C.C. 81; [2005] 2 B.C.L.C. 74; [2003] B.P.I.R. 709, CA (Civ Div); affirming 6087/2000, HQ0000460, Ch D . . . .   *Digested*, 04/**2145**

Oberhauser *v.* Office for Harmonisation in the Internal Market (Trade Marks and Designs) (OHIM) (T104/01) [2002] E.C.R. II-4359; [2003] E.T.M.R. 58, CFI (4th Chamber) . . . .   *Digested*, 04/**2380**: *Considered*, 05/2509

OBG Ltd *v.* Allan; *sub nom* OBG Ltd *v.* Allen [2005] EWCA Civ 106; [2005] Q.B. 762; [2005] 2 W.L.R. 1174; [2005] 2 All E.R. 602; [2005] 1 All E.R. (Comm) 639; [2005] 1 B.C.L.C. 711; [2005] B.L.R. 245; [2005] B.P.I.R. 928; [2005] P.N.L.R. 27; (2005) 102(14) L.S.G. 27; *Times*, February 24, 2005; *Independent*, February 18, 2005, CA (Civ Div) . . . .   *Digested*, 05/**4189**

OBG Ltd *v.* Allen see OBG Ltd *v.* Allan

Ocalan *v.* Turkey (46221/99) (2005) 41 E.H.R.R. 45; 18 B.H.R.C. 293, ECHR (Grand Chamber)

Occidental Exploration & Production Co *v.* Ecuador see Ecuador *v.* Occidental Exploration & Production Co

Occidental Petroleum Corp *v.* Buttes Gas & Oil Co (No.2) see Buttes Gas & Oil Co *v.* Hammer (No.3)

Ocean Leisure Ltd v. Westminster City Council; *sub nom* Westminster City Council v. Ocean Leisure Ltd [2004] EWCA Civ 970; [2004] B.L.R. 393; [2005] 1 P. & C.R. 25; [2004] 3 E.G.L.R. 9; [2004] 43 E.G. 144; [2004] R.V.R. 219; (2004) 101(33) L.S.G. 36; (2004) 148 S.J.L.B. 940; [2004] N.P.C. 124; *Times*, September 2, 2004, CA (Civ Div); affirming [2004] R.V.R. 145, Lands Tr . . . . .   *Digested*, 04/**3234**

Odfjell Seachem A/S v. Continentale des Petroles et d'Investissements; *sub nom* Odfjfell Seachem A/S v. Continentale des Petroles et d'Investissements [2004] EWHC 2929; [2005] 1 All E.R. (Comm) 421; [2005] 1 Lloyd's Rep. 275, QBD (Comm) . . . .   *Digested*, 05/**3790**

Odhams Press Ltd v. Cook [1940] 3 All E.R. 15; 23 T.C. 233, HL. . . . .   *Considered*, 05/3986: *Distinguished*, 64/1831

Offer-Hoar v. Larkstore Ltd [2005] EWHC 2742; [2005] 50 E.G.C.S. 90, QBD (TCC)

Office & Commercial Developments Ltd v. Cox see Overseas & Commercial Developments Ltd v. Cox

Office Angels v. Rainer-Thomas [1991] I.R.L.R. 214; *Times*, April 15, 1991; *Independent*, May 14, 1991; *Financial Times*, March 27, 1991, CA (Civ Div); reversing *Independent*, February 4, 1991 (C.S.), QBD . . . .   *Digested*, 91/**447**: *Applied*, 98/2193: *Considered*, 97/2257, 97/2258, 05/700

Office for Harmonisation in the Internal Market (Trade Marks and Designs) (OHIM) v. Erpo Mobelwerk (C64/02 P) [2004] E.C.R. I-10031; [2005] E.T.M.R. 58, ECJ . . . . . .   *Digested*, 05/**2544**: *Previous proceedings*, 03/2602

Office for Harmonisation in the Internal Market (Trade Marks and Designs) (OHIM) v. Wm Wrigley Jr Co (C191/01 P); *sub nom* Wm Wrigley Jr Co v. Office for Harmonisation in the Internal Market (Trade Marks and Designs) (OHIM) (T193/99) [2004] 1 W.L.R. 1728; [2004] All E.R. (EC) 1040; [2003] E.C.R. I-12447; [2005] 3 C.M.L.R. 21; [2004] E.T.M.R. 9; [2004] R.P.C. 18; *Times*, November 10, 2003, ECJ; reversing [2001] E.C.R. II-417; [2001] E.T.M.R. 58; (2001) 24(5) I.P.D. 24033; [2003] E.C.R. I-12447; [2003] E.T.M.R. 88; (2003) 26(8) I.P.D. 26049, AGO . . . .   *Digested*, 04/**2372**: *Applied*, 05/2543

Office for Harmonisation in the Internal Market (Trade Marks and Designs) (OHIM) v. Zapf Creation AG (C498/01 P) [2004] E.C.R. I-11349; [2005] E.T.M.R. 68, ECJ (2nd Chamber) [2004] E.C.R. I-11349; [2004] E.T.M.R. 67, AGO . . . .   *Digested*, 05/**2549**: *Considered*, 05/2588: *Previous proceedings*, 02/2880

Office National de l'Emploi v. Ioannidis (C258/04) [2005] 3 C.M.L.R. 47, ECJ (1st Chamber)

Office of Fair Trading v. IBA Healthcare Ltd see IBA Health Ltd v. Office of Fair Trading

Office of Fair Trading v. Lloyds TSB Bank Plc A3/2004/2720, CA (Civ Div); reversing [2004] EWHC 2600; [2005] 1 All E.R. 843; [2005] 1 All E.R. (Comm) 354; [2005] E.C.C. 27; (2004) 154 N.L.J. 1728, QBD (Comm) . . . .   *Digested*, 05/**685**

Office of Fair Trading v. MB Designs (Scotland) Ltd 2005 S.L.T. 691; 2005 S.C.L.R. 894; 2005 G.W.D. 22-393; *Times*, August 11, 2005, OH . . . .   *Digested*, 05/**5074**

Office of National Statistics v. Ali see Ali v. Office of National Statistics

Office of the King's Prosecutor (Brussels) v. Armas; *sub nom* King's Prosecutor (Brussels) v. Cando Armas [2005] UKHL 67; [2005] 3 W.L.R. 1079; (2005) 155 N.L.J. 1809; *Times*, November 18, 2005; *Independent*, November 22, 2005, HL; affirming [2004] EWHC 2019; [2005] 1 W.L.R. 1389; [2005] 2 All E.R. 181; (2004) 154 N.L.J. 1498; *Times*, October 8, 2004, QBD (Admin) . . . .   *Digested*, 04/**1436**

Official Receiver as Trustee of the Estate of Izon (A Bankrupt) v. Tailby see Tailby v. Official Receiver

Officier van Justitie v. Sandoz BV (174/82) [1983] E.C.R. 2445; [1984] 3 C.M.L.R. 43, ECJ (5th Chamber) . . . .   *Considered*, 04/1600: *Followed*, 05/1450, 05/1732

Oguntunde-Smith v. Treharne; *sub nom* Ogutunde-Smith v. Treharne [2004] EWHC 1105; [2004] B.P.I.R. 925, Ch D . . . .   *Digested*, 05/**10**

OIOI Trade Mark Unreported, App Person . . . .   *Doubted*, 05/2584

Olatawura v. Abiloye [2002] EWCA Civ 998; [2003] 1 W.L.R. 275; [2002] 4 All E.R. 903; [2002] C.P. Rep. 73; [2002] C.P.L.R. 778; (2002) 99(36) L.S.G. 39; (2002) 152 N.L.J. 1204; (2002) 146 S.J.L.B. 197; *Times*, July 24, 2002; *Independent*, October 14, 2002 (C.S), CA (Civ Div) . . . .   *Digested*, 02/**386**: *Applied*, 05/482

Olbena SA v. Psara Maritime Inc (The Thanassis A) (Unreported, March 22, 1982) . . . .   *Applied*, 05/3784: *Considered*, 04/3489

Oldershaw (t/a Oldershaw Brewery) v. Customs and Excise Commissioners [2005] S.T.I. 898, V&D Tr

Olding v. North Wiltshire [2005] P.A.D. 90, Planning Inspector

Olivebank A/S v. Dansk Svovlsyre Fabrik; *sub nom* Aktieselskabet Olivebank v. Danck Svovlsyre Fabrik [1919] 2 K.B. 162, CA; affirming [1919] 1 K.B. 388, KBD . . . . .   *Considered*, 87/455, 88/3165: *Distinguished*, 05/267

Oliver v. Chief Constable of Northumbria (Pre-Trial Review) [2003] EWHC 2417; [2004] E.M.L.R. 32, QBD . . . .   *Digested*, 05/**982**

Oliveri v. Land Baden-Wurttemberg (C493/01) see Orfanopoulos v. Land Baden-Wurttemberg (C482/01)

Olszanecki v. Hillocks [2002] EWHC 1997; [2004] W.T.L.R. 975, Ch D . . . .   *Digested*, 05/**4320**

Omar v. Secretary of State for the Home Department see R. (on the application of
　　Omar) v. Secretary of State for the Home Department
Ombull v. Sherrards Solicitors see Woolwich Plc v. Jones-Dunross
Omega Engineering Inc v. Omega SA [2004] EWHC 2315; [2005] F.S.R. 12, Ch D　...　　Digested, 05/**483**
Omega Group Holdings Ltd v. Kozeny; Marlwood Commercial Inc v. Kozeny [2004]
　　EWCA Civ 798; [2005] 1 W.L.R. 104; [2004] 3 All E.R. 648; [2004] 2 C.L.C.
　　166; (2004) 148 S.J.L.B. 822, CA (Civ Div); affirming [2004] EWHC 189, QBD
　　(Comm) . . . . 　　Digested, 04/**344**
Omega Spielhallen- und Automatenaufstellungs GmbH v. Bundesstadt Bonn (C36/02)
　　[2004] E.C.R. I-9609; [2005] 1 C.M.L.R. 5; [2005] C.E.C. 391; Times, October
　　20, 2004, ECJ (1st Chamber). . . . .　·　Digested, 05/**1467**
Omilaju v. Waltham Forest LBC (No.2); sub nom Waltham Forest LBC v. Omilaju (No.2)
　　[2004] EWCA Civ 1493; [2005] 1 All E.R. 75; [2005] I.C.R. 481; [2005]
　　I.R.L.R. 35; (2004) 148 S.J.L.B. 1370; Times, November 26, 2004, CA (Civ Div);
　　reversing [2004] 3 All E.R. 129, EAT. . . . .　　Digested, 05/**1209**
On Demand Information Plc (In Administrative Receivership) v. Michael Gerson (Finance)
　　Plc [2002] UKHL 13; [2003] 1 A.C. 368; [2002] 2 W.L.R. 919; [2002] 2 All
　　E.R. 949; [2002] 1 All E.R. (Comm) 641; [2002] B.C.C. 673; [2002] C.L.C.
　　1140; (2002) 99(21) L.S.G. 31; (2002) 146 S.J.L.B. 110; Times, May 2, 2002,
　　HL; reversing [2001] 1 W.L.R. 155; [2000] 4 All E.R. 734; [2000] 2 All E.R.
　　(Comm) 513; [2002] B.C.C. 122; (2000) 150 N.L.J. 1300; Times, September 19,
　　2000, CA (Civ Div); affirming [1999] 2 All E.R. 811; [1999] 1 All E.R. (Comm.)
　　512; [2000] B.C.C. 289; Times, April 28, 1999, Ch D . . . .　　Digested, 02/**448**:
　　　　　　　　　　　　　　　　　　　　　　　　　　　　　　　Considered, 05/**3793**
On Fire Restaurants Ltd's Community Trade Mark Application [2005] E.T.M.R. 19, OHIM
　　(2nd Bd App) . . . . 　　Digested, 05/**2530**
Oneryildiz v. Turkey (48939/99) (No.1) (2004) 39 E.H.R.R. 12, ECHR. . . . . 　　Digested, 05/**2113**
Oneryildiz v. Turkey (48939/99) (No.2) (2005) 41 E.H.R.R. 20; 18 B.H.R.C. 145, ECHR
　　(Grand Chamber)
Onwuka v. Relq Europe Ltd see Onwuka v. Spherion Technology UK Ltd
Onwuka v. Spherion Technology UK Ltd; Onwuka v. Relq Europe Ltd; Onwuka v.
　　Systems Testing Associates Ltd; Onwuka v. Thompson [2005] I.C.R. 567, EAT. . 　　Digested, 05/**1327**
Onwuka v. Systems Testing Associates Ltd see Onwuka v. Spherion Technology UK Ltd
Onwuka v. Thompson see Onwuka v. Spherion Technology UK Ltd
Openbaar Ministerie v. Van Lent (C232/01) see Criminal Proceedings against Van Lent
　　(C232/01)
Opening of Insolvency Proceedings, Re (IX ZB 418/02) [2005] I.L.Pr. 4, BGH (Ger)
Ophthalmic Innovations International (UK) Ltd v. Ophthalmic Innovations International
　　Inc [2004] EWHC 2948; [2005] I.L.Pr. 10, Ch D . . . . 　　Digested, 05/**602**
Optical Express (Southern) Ltd v. Birmingham City Council [2005] 2 E.G.L.R. 141;
　　[2005] R.V.R. 230, Lands Tr . . . . 　　Digested, 05/**3252**
OPTISCAN/Scanning confocal endoscope (T74/00) [2005] E.P.O.R. 43, EPO (Technical
　　Bd App)
Optiver BV v. Stichting Autoriteit Financiele Markten (C22/03) [2005] S.T.C. 1393;
　　[2005] E.C.R. I-1839; [2005] S.T.I. 369, ECJ
Opuku-Donker v. Newham LBC see Hughes v. Newham LBC
Orange Personal Communications Services Ltd v. First Secretary of State see T Mobile
　　(UK) Ltd v. First Secretary of State
Orchard v. South Eastern Electricity Board [1987] Q.B. 565; [1987] 2 W.L.R. 102;
　　[1987] 1 All E.R. 95; (1986) 130 S.J. 956, CA (Civ Div) . . . . 　　Digested, 87/**3547**:
　　　　　　　　　　　　Applied, 87/3555, 03/382, 05/363: Cited, 93/3174, 93/3177, 93/3180,
　　　　　　　　　　　　95/4033: Considered, 90/3615, 91/2823, 93/3153, 93/3894, 93/3895,
　　　　　　　　　　　　　　　　　　　　　　　　　　　　　　　94/3623, 95/135
Orfanopoulos v. Land Baden-Wurttemberg (C482/01); Oliveri v. Land Baden-
　　Wurttemberg (C493/01) [2004] E.C.R. I-5257; [2005] 1 C.M.L.R. 18, ECJ (5th
　　Chamber) . . . . 　　Digested, 05/**1456**
Organ Retention Group Litigation, Re see A v. Leeds Teaching Hospital NHS Trust
Organic Labelling, Re (C135/03) see Commission of the European Communities v. Spain
　　(C135/03)
Organic Peroxides Cartel, Re (Comp/E2/37.857) [2005] 5 C.M.L.R. 14, CEC
Orphanos v. Queen Mary College [1985] A.C. 761; [1985] 2 W.L.R. 703; [1985] 2 All
　　E.R. 233; [1986] 2 C.M.L.R. 73; [1985] I.R.L.R. 349; (1985) 82 L.S.G. 1787;
　　(1985) 129 S.J. 284, HL . . . . 　　Digested, 85/**3550**:
　　　　　　　　　　　　　　　　　　　　　　　　　　　　　　　　　Applied, 05/85
Ors v. Bundesknappschaft (C211/98) see Kocak v. Landesversicherungsanstalt
　　Oberfranken und Mittelfranken (C102/98)
Orthet Ltd v. Vince-Cain see Vince-Cain v. Orthet Ltd
OS v. DS (Oral Disclosure: Preliminary Hearing) see S v. S (Ancillary Relief: Preliminary
　　Hearing of Oral Evidence)
Oscar Bronner GmbH & Co KG v. Mediaprint Zeitungs- und Zeitschriftenverlag GmbH &
　　Co KG (C7/97) [1998] E.C.R. I-7791; [1999] 4 C.M.L.R. 112; [1999] C.E.C. 53,
　　ECJ (6th Chamber) . . . . 　　Digested, 99/**674**:
　　　　　　　　　　　　Applied, 05/578: Considered, 05/574: Followed, 04/523
Osea Road Camp Sites Ltd, Re see Bamber v. Eaton

Oska's Ltd's Trade Mark Application [2005] R.P.C. 20, App Person . . . .   *Digested,* 05/**2565**
Osman v. Elasha; *sub nom* E (Abduction: Non Convention Country), Re [2000] Fam.
62; [2000] 2 W.L.R. 1036; [1999] 2 F.L.R. 642; [1999] 3 F.C.R. 497; [1999]
Fam. Law 610; (1999) 96(30) L.S.G. 29; *Times,* July 7, 1999, CA (Civ Div) . . . .   *Digested,* 99/**2332**:
                                            Considered, 02/1634: *Disapproved,* 05/1569
Osmani v. Camden LBC [2004] EWCA Civ 1706; [2005] H.L.R. 22; (2005) 149
S.J.L.B. 61, CA (Civ Div) . . . .   *Digested,* 05/**1989**
Ospelt v. Schlossle Weissenberg Familienstiftung (C452/01) see Ospelt v.
Unabhangiger Verwaltungssenat des Landes Vorarlberg (C452/01)
Ospelt v. Unabhangiger Verwaltungssenat des Landes Vorarlberg (C452/01); *sub nom*
Ospelt v. Schlossle Weissenberg Familienstiftung (C452/01) [2003] E.C.R. I-
9743; [2005] 3 C.M.L.R. 40; [2003] N.P.C. 109, ECJ
Osterreichischer Gewerkschaftsbund (Gewerkschaft der Privatangestellten) v.
Wirtschaftskammer Osterreich (C220/02) [2004] E.C.R. I-5907; [2004] 3
C.M.L.R. 37; [2005] C.E.C. 307, ECJ . . . .   *Digested,* 05/**1282**
Oswald Tillotson Ltd v. Inland Revenue Commissioners [1933] 1 K.B. 134, CA . . . .   *Applied,* 94/2538,
                                               05/2335: *Considered,* 70/2715
OT Africa Line Ltd v. Magic Sportswear Corp [2005] EWCA Civ 710; [2005] 2 Lloyd's
Rep. 170; [2005] 1 C.L.C. 923; 2005 A.M.C. 2179; *Times,* June 21, 2005;
Independent, June 16, 2005, CA (Civ Div); affirming [2004] EWHC 2441;
[2005] 1 Lloyd's Rep. 252, QBD (Comm) . . . .   *Digested,* 05/**627**
Oulane v. Minister voor Vreemdelingenzaken en Integratie (C215/03) [2005] Q.B.
1055; [2005] 3 W.L.R. 543; [2005] E.C.R. I-1215; *Times,* February 21, 2005,
ECJ
Ove Arup & Partners International Ltd v. Mirant Asia-Pacific Construction (Hong Kong)
Ltd (No.2) [2005] EWCA Civ 1585, CA (Civ Div); affirming [2004] EWHC
1750; 97 Con. L.R. 1; [2005] P.N.L.R. 10, QBD (TCC) . . . .   *Digested,* 05/**667**
Overseas & Commercial Developments Ltd v. Cox; *sub nom* Office & Commercial
Developments Ltd v. Cox [2002] EWCA Civ 635; [2002] B.P.I.R. 1150; (2002)
99(20) L.S.G. 34, CA (Civ Div) . . . .   *Digested,* 03/**468**:
                                               Explained, 05/306
Overseas Aviation Engineering (GB), Re [1963] Ch. 24; [1962] 3 W.L.R. 594; [1962] 3 All
E.R. 12, CA; affirming [1962] Ch. 738; [1962] 2 W.L.R. 968; [1962] 1 All E.R. 930;
106 S.J. 243, Ch D . . . .   *Digested,* 62/**2420**:
                             Applied, 05/2343: *Considered,* 94/2854, 95/3104
Overton v. Cape Industrial Services Ltd [2005] 3 Q.R. 13, QBD [*Ex rel.* Joel Donovan,
Barrister, Cloisters, 1 Pump Court, London] . . . .   *Digested,* 05/**3215**
Owen v. IMI Yorkshire Copper Tube (Unreported, June 15, 1995) . . . .   *Considered,* 05/2864
OWENS-BROCKWAY/Extension agreements (J9/04) [2005] E.P.O.R. 48, EPO (Legal Bd
App)
Owners of Cargo Lately Laden on Board the Eleftheria v. Owners of the Eleftheria [1970]
P. 94; [1969] 2 W.L.R. 1073; [1969] 2 All E.R. 641; [1969] 1 Lloyd's Rep. 237;
113 S.J. 407, PDAD . . . .   *Digested,* 69/**3293**:
         Applied, 81/2198, 01/4902: *Considered,* 79/308, 79/311, 80/317, 00/4685,
                                                      05/625
Owners of Cargo Lately Laden on Board the River Gurara v. Nigerian National Shipping
Line Ltd [1998] Q.B. 610; [1997] 3 W.L.R. 1128; [1997] 4 All E.R. 498; [1998]
1 Lloyd's Rep. 225; [1997] C.L.C. 1322; (1997) 94(33) L.S.G. 27; (1997) 141
S.J.L.B. 175; *Times,* July 29, 1997, CA (Civ Div); affirming [1996] 2 Lloyd's Rep.
53; [1996] C.L.C. 927; *Times,* March 6, 1996, QBD (Admlty) . . . .   *Digested,* 98/**4405**:
                                               Followed, 05/3786
Owners of Cargo Lately Laden on Board the Tatry v. Owners of the Maciej Rataj (C406/
92) [1999] Q.B. 515; [1999] 2 W.L.R. 181; [1995] All E.R. (E.C.) 229; [1995] 1
Lloyd's Rep. 302; [1994] E.C.R. I-5439; [1995] I.L.Pr. 81; *Times,* December 28,
1994; *Financial Times,* December 13, 1994, ECJ. . . . .   *Digested,* 95/**704**:
        Applied, 96/7098, 99/732, 00/738, 00/776, 05/624: *Considered,* 97/900,
            99/715, 00/5442, 05/604: *Followed,* 96/1089, 02/5366, 05/622
Owners of the Bow Spring v. Owners of the Manzanillo II [2004] EWCA Civ 1007;
[2005] 1 W.L.R. 144; [2004] 4 All E.R. 899; [2005] 1 All E.R. (Comm) 53;
[2005] 1 Lloyd's Rep. 1; [2005] 1 C.L.C. 394; *Times,* August 19, 2004;
Independent, October 8, 2004, CA (Civ Div); affirming [2003] EWHC 1802;
[2004] 1 Lloyd's Rep. 647, QBD (Admlty) . . . .   *Digested,* 04/**3495**:
                                               Considered, 05/3794
Owners of the Denise v. Charterers of the Denise see Vessel SA v. CP Ships (UK) Ltd
Owners of the Global Mariner v. Owners of the Atlantic Crusader [2005] EWHC 380;
[2005] 2 All E.R. (Comm) 389; [2005] 1 Lloyd's Rep. 699; [2005] 1 C.L.C. 413;
(2005) 155 N.L.J. 594, QBD (Admlty) . . . .   *Digested,* 05/**3794**
Owners of the Maridive VII, Maridive XIII, Maridive 85 and Maridive 94 v. Owners and
Demise Charterers of the Key Singapore [2004] EWHC 2227; [2005] 1 All E.R.
(Comm) 99; [2005] 1 Lloyd's Rep. 91, QBD (Comm) . . . .   *Digested,* 05/**3810**
Owners of the Sardinia Sulcis v. Owners of the Al Tawwab [1991] 1 Lloyd's Rep. 201;
Times, November 21, 1990; *Independent,* December 3, 1990 (C.S.); *Financial
Times,* November 13, 1990, CA (Civ Div) . . . .   *Digested,* 91/**3204**:
             Applied, 99/494, 05/89: *Followed,* 96/890: *Not followed,* 05/315

Owners of the Steamship Mediana v. Owners of the Lightship Comet [1900] A.C. 113, HL; affirming [1899] P. 127, CA . . . . *Applied*, 47-51/2554,
　　　　　　　　　　　　　　　　　47/2554, 03/943, 05/4193: *Considered*, 52/893, 78/44.u
Owners of the Western Regent v. Charterers of the Western Regent see Seismic
　Shipping Inc v. Total E&P UK Plc (The Western Regent)
Owusu v. Jackson (t/a Villa Holidays Bal Inn Villas) (C281/02) [2005] Q.B. 801;
　[2005] 2 W.L.R. 942; [2005] 2 All E.R. (Comm) 577; [2005] 1 Lloyd's Rep.
　452; [2005] E.C.R. I-1383; [2005] 1 C.L.C. 246; [2005] I.L.Pr. 25; *Times*,
　March 9, 2005, ECJ . . . . *Digested*, 05/**604**:
　　　　　　　　　　　　　　　　　　　　　　　　　　　　　Distinguished, 05/2406
Oxford City Council v. RA Property Developers [2005] P.A.D. 66, Planning Inspector
Oxfordshire CC v. DP; *sub nom* A County Council v. DP [2005] EWHC 1593; [2005]
　2 F.L.R. 1031; [2005] Fam. Law 769, Fam Div
Oxfordshire CC v. Oxford City Council [2005] EWCA Civ 175; [2005] 3 W.L.R. 1043;
　[2005] 3 All E.R. 961; [2005] B.L.G.R. 664; [2005] 2 P. & C.R. 28; [2005] 2
　P.L.R. 75; [2005] 2 E.G.L.R. 91; [2005] 9 E.G.C.S. 189; (2005) 149 S.J.L.B.
　267; [2005] N.P.C. 28; *Independent*, March 2, 2005, CA (Civ Div); reversing in
　part [2004] EWHC 12; [2004] Ch. 253; [2004] 2 W.L.R. 1291; [2004] 2 P. &
　C.R. 19; [2004] 2 P.L.R. 65; [2004] 1 E.G.L.R. 105; [2004] 6 E.G.C.S. 144;
　(2004) 101(6) L.S.G. 32; [2004] N.P.C. 6; *Times*, January 30, 2004, Ch D . . . . *Digested*, 05/**3440**:
　　　　　　　　　　　　　　　　　　　　　　　　　　　　　Considered, 04/3262
Oxley v. Hiscock; *sub nom* Hiscock v. Oxley [2004] EWCA Civ 546; [2005] Fam. 211;
　[2004] 3 W.L.R. 715; [2004] 3 All E.R. 703; [2004] 2 F.L.R. 669; [2004] 2
　F.C.R. 295; [2004] W.T.L.R. 709; (2003-04) 6 I.T.E.L.R. 1091; [2004] Fam. Law
　569; [2004] 20 E.G.C.S. 166; (2004) 101(21) L.S.G. 35; (2004) 148 S.J.L.B.
　571; [2004] N.P.C. 70; [2004] 2 P. & C.R. DG14; *Times*, July 14, 2004, CA (Civ
　Div) . . . . *Digested*, 04/**3196**:
　　　　　　　　Applied, 05/3379, 05/3380, 05/3391: *Considered*, 05/3378
Oystertec Plc v. Davidson (No.3) [2004] EWHC 2563; [2005] B.P.I.R. 401, Ch D . . . . *Digested*, 05/**414**
Ozcan v. Turkey (Admissibility) (41557/98) (2005) 40 E.H.R.R. SE12, ECHR
Ozturk v. Pensionsversicherungsanstalt der Arbeiter (C373/02) [2004] E.C.R. I-3605;
　[2004] 2 C.M.L.R. 47, ECJ . . . . *Digested*, 05/**3888**
Ozturk v. Secretary of State for the Home Department see R. (on the application of
　Ozturk) v. Secretary of State for the Home Department

P v. DPP [2005] EWHC 1485; *Times*, June 20, 2005, QBD (Admin) . . . . *Digested*, 05/**291**
P v. Leeds Teaching Hospitals NHS Trust; *sub nom* P v. Leeds Teaching Hospital NHS
　Trust [2004] EWHC 1392; [2004] Lloyd's Rep. Med. 537, QBD . . . . *Digested*, 05/**2836**
P v. Liverpool Daily Post and Echo see Pickering v. Liverpool Daily Post and Echo
P v. P (Ancillary Relief: Proceeds of Crime); *sub nom* P v. P (Divorce: Ancillary Relief)
　[2003] EWHC 2260; [2004] Fam. 1; [2003] 3 W.L.R. 1350; [2003] 4 All E.R.
　843; [2004] 1 F.L.R. 193; [2003] 3 F.C.R. 459; [2003] W.T.L.R. 1449; [2004]
　Fam. Law 9; (2003) 100(41) L.S.G. 33; (2003) 153 N.L.J. 1550; (2003) 147
　S.J.L.B. 1206; *Times*, October 14, 2003, Fam Div. . . . . *Digested*, 03/**1598**:
　　　　　　　　　　　　　　　　　　　　　　　　　　　　　Disapproved, 05/811
P v. P (Divorce: Ancillary Relief) see P v. P (Ancillary Relief: Proceeds of Crime)
P v. P (Financial Relief: Illiquid Assets); *sub nom* LJP v. GRGP [2004] EWHC 2277;
　[2005] 1 F.L.R. 548; [2005] Fam. Law 207, Fam Div . . . . *Digested*, 05/**1654**
P v. P (Inherited Property) [2004] EWHC 1364; [2005] 1 F.L.R. 576, Fam Div . . . . *Digested*, 05/**1625**
P v. P (Removal of Child to New Zealand) see Payne v. Payne
P v. Secretary of State for the Home Department; M v. Secretary of State for the
　Home Department [2004] EWCA Civ 1640; [2005] Imm. A.R. 84; [2005]
　I.N.L.R. 167; *Times*, December 14, 2004; *Independent*, December 15, 2004, CA
　(Civ Div) . . . . *Digested*, 05/**2150**
P v. T see P (A Child) (Financial Provision), Re
P (A Barrister) v. General Council of the Bar [2005] 1 W.L.R. 3019; [2005] P.N.L.R.
　32, Visitors (Inns of Ct)
P (A Child) v. Coggins (Unreported, April 8, 2004), CC (Medway) [*Ex rel.* Gurion
　Taussig, Barrister, 199 The Strand, London] . . . . *Digested*, 05/**3118**
P (A Child) v. Doncaster MBC [2005] 2 Q.R. 19; [2004] 6 Q.R. 12, CC (Doncaster)
　[*Ex rel.* Frank Allen Pennington Solicitors, 5/7 Regent Terrace, South Parade,
　Doncaster] . . . . *Digested*, 04/**3009**
P (A Child) v. Hallam Housing Society Ltd [2005] 3 Q.R. 8, CC (Doncaster) [*Ex rel.*
　Frank Allen Pennington Solicitors, 5-7 Regent Terrace, South Parade,
　Doncaster] . . . . *Digested*, 05/**3098**
P (A Child) v. Kumar (Unreported, February 15, 2005), CC (Romford) [*Ex rel.* Joanna
　Kerr, Barrister, Lamb Chambers, Lamb Building, Temple, London]. . . . . *Digested*, 05/**3120**
P (A Child) v. Nashayman Housing Association [2005] 2 Q.R. 19; [2004] 6 Q.R. 9, CC
　(Maidstone) [*Ex rel.* Gurion Taussig, Lamb Chambers, Chancery Lane, London] . *Digested*, 04/**2932**
P (A Child) v. Parker [2005] 3 Q.R. 14, CC (West London) [*Ex rel.* Joanna Kerr,
　Barrister, Lamb Chambers, Lamb Building, Temple, London] . . . . *Digested*, 05/**3225**
P (A Child) v. Pemberton (Unreported, October 14, 2004), CC (Horsham) [*Ex rel.*
　Gurion Taussig, Lamb Chambers, Chancery Lane, London] . . . . *Digested*, 05/**3126**

P (A Child) *v.* Penny (Unreported, March 26, 2004), CC (Chelmsford) [*Ex rel.* Adam
    Walker, Barrister, Lamb Chambers, Lamb Building, Elm Court, Temple, London] .   *Digested,* 05/**3220**
P (A Child) (Abduction: Acquiescence), Re see P (A Child) (Abduction: Custody Rights),
    Re
P (A Child) (Abduction: Consent), Re see P (A Child) (Abduction: Custody Rights), Re
P (A Child) (Abduction: Custody Rights), Re; *sub nom* P (A Child) (Abduction:
    Consent), Re; P (A Child) (Abduction: Acquiescence), Re [2004] EWCA Civ
    971; [2005] Fam. 293; [2005] 2 W.L.R. 201; [2004] 2 F.L.R. 1057; [2004] 2
    F.C.R. 698; [2004] Fam. Law 711; (2004) 101 (35) L.S.G. 33; *Times,* August 19,
    2004, CA (Civ Div) . . . .   *Digested,* 04/**1470**:
                                         Followed, 05/1541
P (A Child) (Financial Provision), Re; *sub nom* P *v.* T [2003] EWCA Civ 837; [2003] 2
    F.L.R. 865; [2003] 2 F.C.R. 481; [2003] Fam. Law 717; (2003) 100(33)
    L.S.G. 27; *Times,* July 24, 2003; *Independent,* July 3, 2003, CA (Civ Div);
    reversing [2003] Fam. Law 303; *Independent,* December 11, 2002, Fam Div . . .   *Digested,* 03/**1577**:
                        Applied, 05/**1666**: *Distinguished,* 05/1652
P (A Minor) (Residence Order: Child's Welfare), Re; *sub nom* P (Section 91(14)
    Guidelines: Residence and Religious Heritage), Re [2000] Fam. 15; [1999] 3
    W.L.R. 1164; [1999] 3 All E.R. 734; [1999] 2 F.L.R. 573; [1999] 2 F.C.R. 289;
    [1999] Fam. Law 531; (1999) 163 J.P.N. 712; (1999) 96(21) L.S.G. 38; (1999)
    149 N.L.J. 719; (1999) 143 S.J.L.B. 141; *Times,* May 11, 1999, CA (Civ Div) . . . . .   *Digested,* 99/**2389**:
                        Applied, 05/**1587**: *Considered,* 02/1664, 03/47
P (Adoption), Re [2004] EWHC 1954; [2005] 1 F.L.R. 303, Fam Div . . . .   *Digested,* 05/**1509**
P (Adoption: Breach of Care Plan), Re [2004] EWCA Civ 355; [2004] 2 F.L.R.1109; [2004]
    Fam. Law 708, CA (Civ Div) . . . .   *Digested,* 05/**1497**
P (Medical Treatment: Best Interests), Re [2003] EWHC 2327; [2004] 2 F.L.R.1117; [2004]
    Fam. Law 716, Fam Div . . . .   *Digested,* 05/**1793**
P (Section 91(14) Guidelines: Residence and Religious Heritage), Re see P (A Minor)
    (Residence Order: Child's Welfare), Re
P&O Nedlloyd BV *v.* Arab Metals Co (The UB Tiger) [2005] EWHC 1276; [2005] 1
    W.L.R. 3733; *Times,* August 3, 2005, QBD (Comm) . . . .   *Digested,* 05/**314**
P1 International Ltd *v.* Llewellyn [2005] EWHC 407; [2005] U.K.C.L.R. 530, QBD
Pabari *v.* Secretary of State for Work and Pensions [2004] EWCA Civ 1480; [2005] 1
    All E.R. 287; *Independent,* November 17, 2004, CA (Civ Div) . . . .   *Digested,* 05/**1555**
Pabo Ltd *v.* Liverpool City Council see Interfact Ltd *v.* Liverpool City Council
PACE Aerospace Engineering & Information Technology GmbH's Community Trade Mark
    (1033/2003) Unreported, OHIM (Opposition Div) . . . .   *Considered,* 05/2568
Paco Holdings Ltd's Registered Trade Mark Application (Nos.2101219 and 2101220) see
    PACO/PACO LIFE IN COLOUR Trade Marks
PACO/PACO LIFE IN COLOUR Trade Marks; *sub nom* Paco Holdings Ltd's Registered
    Trade Mark Application (Nos.2101219 and 2101220) [2000] R.P.C. 451; (2000)
    23(4) I.P.D. 23032, TMR . . . .   *Digested,* 00/**3775**:
                                          Approved, 05/2563
Padden *v.* Arbuthnot Pensions & Investments Ltd; *sub nom* Arbuthnot Pensions &
    Investments Ltd *v.* Padden [2004] EWCA Civ 582; [2004] C.P. Rep. 36; (2004)
    101(24) L.S.G. 32; (2004) 148 S.J.L.B. 631, CA (Civ Div) . . . .   *Digested,* 05/**1237**
Paddle *v.* Cumbria CC [2005] N.P.C. 105, HC
Padfield *v.* Minister of Agriculture, Fisheries and Food; *sub nom* R. *v.* Minister of
    Agriculture and Fisheries Ex p. Padfield [1968] A.C. 997; [1968] 2 W.L.R. 924;
    [1968] 1 All E.R. 694; 112 S.J. 171, HL; reversing (1966) 110 S.J. 604; *Times,* July
    28, 1966, CA; reversing *Times,* February 4, 1966, DC . . . .   *Digested,* 68/**1667**:
          Applied, 71/11754, 75/17, 76/22, 80/1341, 83/2228, 84/3439, 86/21, 87/29,
                        87/3188, 92/2084, 92/3828, 93/590, 93/1871, 05/2752:
              Considered, 70/568, 76/1349, 79/25, 79/2243, 83/29, 85/2791, 85/3376,
                     90/2585, 91/1981, 94/1866, 95/1911: *Distinguished,* 69/3447, 89/41, 90/4
Page *v.* Plymouth Hospitals NHS Trust [2004] EWHC 1154; [2004] 3 All E.R. 367;
    [2004] P.I.Q.R. Q6; [2004] Lloyd's Rep. Med. 337; (2005) 82 B.M.L.R. 1;
    (2004) 101(26) L.S.G. 27; (2004) 154 N.L.J. 853, QBD . . . .   *Digested,* 04/**910**
Page *v.* Sheerness Steel Co Plc see Wells *v.* Wells
Paglieri SpA *v.* Gabbiano SpA [2005] E.T.M.R.16, It Cass (I)
Pagnan SpA *v.* Tradax Ocean Transportation SA; *sub nom* Tradax Ocean Transportation
    SA *v.* Pagnan [1987] 3 All E.R. 565; [1987] 2 Lloyd's Rep. 342, CA (Civ Div);
    affirming [1987] 1 All E.R. 81; [1986] 2 Lloyd's Rep. 646; *Financial Times,* July 8,
    1986, QBD (Comm) . . . .   *Digested,* 88/**3174**:
                                           Followed, 05/2867
Paine *v.* Catlins [2004] EWHC 3054; 98 Con. L.R. 107; [2005] Lloyd's Rep. I.R. 665,
    QBD (TCC) . . . .   *Digested,* 05/**2395**
Painting *v.* Oxford University [2005] EWCA Civ 161; [2005] 3 Costs L.R. 394;
    [2005] P.I.Q.R. Q5; (2005) 102(14) L.S.G. 26; (2005) 149 S.J.L.B. 183; *Times,*
    February 15, 2005, CA (Civ Div) . . . .   *Digested,* 05/**347**
Palau-Martinez *v.* France (64927/01) [2004] 2 F.L.R. 810; (2005) 41 E.H.R.R. 9;
    [2004] Fam. Law 413, ECHR . . . .   *Digested,* 04/**1998**
Palfrey *v.* Transco Plc [2004] I.R.L.R. 916, EAT . . . .   *Digested,* 05/**1306**

Palin Granit Oy v. Lounais-Suomen Ymparistokeskus (C9/00); *sub nom* Palin Granit Oy v. Vehmassalon Kansanterveystyon Kuntayhtyman Hallitus (C9/00); Palin Granit Oy's Application (C9/00), Re [2002] 1 W.L.R. 2644; [2003] All E.R. (EC) 366; [2002] E.C.R. I-3533; [2002] 2 C.M.L.R. 24; [2002] Env. L.R. 35, ECJ (6th Chamber) [2002] E.C.R. I-3533, AGO . . . . *Digested,* 02/**1521**: *Considered,* 04/1350: *Followed,* 05/1414

Palin Granit Oy v. Vehmassalon Kansanterveystyon Kuntayhtyman Hallitus (C9/00) see Palin Granit Oy v. Lounais-Suomen Ymparistokeskus (C9/00)

Palin Granit Oy's Application (C9/00), Re see Palin Granit Oy v. Lounais-Suomen Ymparistokeskus (C9/00)

Pallant v. Morgan [1953] Ch. 43; [1952] 2 All E.R. 951; [1952] 2 T.L.R. 813, Ch D . . . . *Digested,* 52/**3571**: *Applied,* 00/2317: *Approved,* 00/2327: *Considered,* 05/695

Palmac Contracting Ltd v. Park Lane Estates Ltd [2005] EWHC 919; [2005] B.L.R. 301, QBD (TCC)

Palmer v. Richardson (Inspector of Taxes) [2005] S.T.C. (S.C.D.) 418; [2005] S.T.I. 837, Sp Comm . . . . *Digested,* 05/**4000**

Palmer v. Southend on Sea BC [1984] 1 W.L.R. 1129; [1984] 1 All E.R. 945; [1984] I.C.R. 372; [1984] I.R.L.R. 119; (1984) 81 L.S.G. 893; (1984) 134 N.L.J. 148; (1984) 128 S.J. 262, CA (Civ Div) . . . . *Digested,* 84/**1238**: *Considered,* 96/2667, 99/2051, 99/2146, 05/1336: *Followed,* 89/4302

Palmer v. United Kingdom (30671/96) see Wilson v. United Kingdom (30668/96)

Pan Ocean Shipping Co v. Creditcorp (The Trident Beauty) [1994] 1 W.L.R. 161; [1994] 1 All E.R. 470; [1994] 1 Lloyd's Rep. 365; (1994) 144 N.L.J. 1203; *Times,* February 1, 1994; *Independent,* February 1, 1994, HL; affirming [1993] 1 Lloyd's Rep. 443; (1993) 137 S.J.L.B. 53; *Times,* January 28, 1993, CA (Civ Div) . . . . . *Digested,* 94/**529**: *Applied,* 05/3789

PanAmSat International Systems Inc, Re 7 I.T.L. Rep. 419

Panayiotou v. Sony Music Entertainment (UK) Ltd [1994] Ch. 142; [1994] 2 W.L.R. 241; [1994] 1 All E.R. 755; [1994] I.L.Pr. 241; (1993) 143 N.L.J. 1065; *Times,* August 2, 1993; *Independent,* July 21, 1993, Ch D . . . . *Digested,* 94/**2120**: *Applied,* 05/209

Panayotova v. Minister voor Vreemdelingenzaken en Integratie (C327/02) [2004] E.C.R. I-11055; [2005] 1 C.M.L.R. 24; [2005] C.E.C. 278, ECJ . . . . *Digested,* 05/**1453**

Panchal v. Maguire (Unreported, December 3, 2004), CC (Edmonton) [*Ex rel.* Nigel Ffitch, Barrister, Phoenix Chambers, Gray's Inn Chambers, Gray's Inn, London] . *Digested,* 05/**3185**

Panrico SA v. Rogers [2005] E.T.M.R. 73, OHIM (Cancellation Div) . . . . *Digested,* 05/**2559**

Pantea v. Romania (33343/96) (2005) 40 E.H.R.R. 26, ECHR . . . . *Digested,* 05/**2060**

Papadimitriou, Petitioner [2004] W.T.L.R. 1141, HC (IoM) . . . . *Digested,* 05/**4306**

Papamichalopoulos v. Greece (A/260-B) (1993) 16 E.H.R.R. 440, ECHR . . . . *Applied,* 05/1410: *Distinguished,* 98/3133

Papanagiotou v. Greece [2005] E.C.D.R. 24, Ar Pag (GR)

Papanicola v. Humphreys [2005] EWHC 335; [2005] 2 All E.R. 418; (2005) 102(19) L.S.G. 33; *Times,* April 28, 2005, Ch D (Bankruptcy Ct) . . . . *Digested,* 05/**2277**

Papastavrou v. Greece (46372/99) (2005) 40 E.H.R.R. 14, ECHR . . . . *Digested,* 05/**2072**

Pape v. Minister van Landbouw, Natuurbeheer en Visserij (C175/02) [2005] E.C.R. I-127; [2005] S.T.I. 136, ECJ (1st Chamber)

PAPERBOY site (I ZR 259/00) [2005] E.C.D.R. 7, BGH (Ger)

Papon v. France (54210/00) (2004) 39 E.H.R.R. 10, ECHR . . . . *Digested,* 05/**2078**

Papouis v. Gibson-West; *sub nom* Bennett (Florence Lilian), In the Estate of [2004] EWHC 396; [2004] W.T.L.R. 485, Ch D . . . . *Digested,* 05/**3970**: *Applied,* 05/3968

Paragon Finance Plc v. Banks see Bristol & West Plc v. Bartlett

Paragon Finance Plc v. Staunton see Paragon Finance Plc (formerly National Home Loans Corp) v. Nash

Paragon Finance Plc (formerly National Home Loans Corp) v. Nash; *sub nom* Nash v. Paragon Finance Plc; Staunton v. Paragon Finance Plc; Paragon Finance Plc v. Staunton [2001] EWCA Civ 1466; [2002] 1 W.L.R. 685; [2002] 2 All E.R. 248; [2001] 2 All E.R. (Comm) 1025; [2002] 2 P. & C.R. 20; (2001) 98(44) L.S.G. 36; (2001) 145 S.J.L.B. 244; [2002] 1 P. & C.R. DG13; *Times,* October 25, 2001, CA (Civ Div) . . . . *Digested,* 01/**4874**: *Applied,* 05/1212, 05/3421: *Followed,* 02/694

Paragon Finance Plc (formerly National Home Loans Corp) v. Pender [2005] EWCA Civ 760; [2005] 1 W.L.R. 3412; [2005] N.P.C. 84; [2005] 2 P. & C.R. DG18; *Times,* July 19, 2005, CA (Civ Div); affirming [2003] EWHC 2834; [2003] 49 E.G.C.S. 128, Ch D . . . . *Digested,* 05/**3421**

Paramount Kitchens Ltd, Re see Anglorom Trans (UK) Ltd, Re

Paranova Lakemedel AB v. Lakemedelsverket (C15/01) [2005] All E.R. (EC) 104; [2003] E.C.R. I-4175; [2003] 2 C.M.L.R. 27; (2004) 78 B.M.L.R. 37, ECJ (6th Chamber) . . . . *Digested,* 03/**1444**

Parental Leave, Re (C519/03) see Commission of the European Communities v. Luxembourg (C519/03)

Park v. Chief Constable of Greater Manchester see Calveley v. Chief Constable of Merseyside

Parker *v.* Allsop (Unreported, June 24, 2004), CC (Derby) [*Ex rel.* Jonathan Hand, Barrister, Outer Temple Chambers, Outer Temple, 222 The Strand, London] ....   *Digested*, 05/**3092**
Parlour *v.* Parlour see McFarlane *v.* McFarlane
Parnall *v.* Hurst (Application for Withdrawal of Judgment) [2003] EWHC 2164; [2005] W.T.L.R. 1241, Ch D
Parry *v.* DPP [2004] EWHC 3112; [2005] A.C.D. 64, QBD (Admin)
Parry *v.* National Westminster Bank Plc; *sub nom* National Westminster Bank Plc *v.* Parry [2004] EWCA Civ 1563; [2005] I.C.R. 396; [2005] I.R.L.R. 193; (2004) 101 (44) L.S.G. 31; (2004) 148 S.J.L.B. 1314; *Times*, November 4, 2004, CA (Civ Div); affirming UKEAT/0977/03/ILB, EAT . . . .   *Digested*, 05/**1334**
Parsons *v.* George [2004] EWCA Civ 912; [2004] 1 W.L.R. 3264; [2004] 3 All E.R. 633; [2005] C.P. Rep. 3; [2004] 3 E.G.L.R. 49; [2004] 40 E.G. 150; [2004] 31 E.G.C.S. 93; (2004) 101 (33) L.S.G. 36; (2004) 148 S.J.L.B. 879; [2004] N.P.C. 117; [2005] 1 P. & C.R. DG1; *Times*, July 28, 2004, CA (Civ Div) . . . .   *Digested*, 04/**286**:
            Applied, 05/480: *Considered*, 05/315
Parti Ecologiste Les Verts *v.* European Parliament (294/83); *sub nom* Les Verts, Parti Ecologiste *v.* European Parliament (294/83) [1986] E.C.R. 1339; [1987] 2 C.M.L.R. 343; *Times*, April 24, 1986, ECJ . . . .   *Digested*, 87/**1555**:
           Distinguished, 02/1556, 05/1445: *Followed*, 02/1555
Partridge *v.* Lawrence [2003] EWCA Civ 1121; [2004] 1 P. & C.R. 14, CA (Civ Div) . . . .   *Digested*, 04/**3255**:
            Followed, 05/3383
Pasquantino *v.* United States 7 I.T.L. Rep. 774, US Ct
Pastouna *v.* Black see Black *v.* Pastouna
Patchett's Patent (No.2) [1967] F.S.R. 249; [1967] R.P.C. 237, CA (Civ Div); reversing [1966] F.S.R. 237; [1967] R.P.C. 77; *Times*, June 22, 1966, Ch D . . . .   *Digested*, 67/**2976**:
            Applied, 05/2436
Patel *v.* Brent LBC (No.3) [2005] EWCA Civ 644; [2005] 3 P.L.R. 114; [2005] 2 E.G.L.R. 85; [2005] 31 E.G. 82; [2005] J.P.L. 1515; [2005] 22 E.G.C.S. 133; [2005] N.P.C. 73, CA (Civ Div); reversing in part [2004] EWHC 763; [2005] 1 P. & C.R. 20; [2004] 3 P.L.R. 74; [2004] 17 E.G.C.S. 129; (2004) 101 (16) L.S.G. 29, Ch D . . . .   *Digested*, 05/**3289**
Patel *v.* Earlspring Properties Ltd [1991] 2 E.G.L.R. 131; [1991] 46 E.G. 153, CA (Civ Div) . . . .   *Digested*, 92/**2742**:
            Considered, 05/2679
Patel *v.* Jones; *sub nom* Jones *v.* Patel [2001] EWCA Civ 779; [2001] B.P.I.R. 919; (2001) 3 L.G.L.R. 44; [2001] Pens. L.R. 217; *Times*, May 29, 2001, CA (Civ Div); affirming [1999] B.P.I.R. 509; [1999] Pens. L.R. 203, Ch D . . . .   *Digested*, 01/**3734**:
           Considered, 05/2278: *Followed*, 03/2364
Patel *v.* Shah [2005] EWCA Civ 157; [2005] W.T.L.R. 359; [2005] 8 E.G.C.S. 190, CA (Civ Div); affirming [2004] EWHC 1683, Ch D . . . .   *Digested*, 05/**3381**
Pathak *v.* Secretary of State for Health see Chaudhary *v.* Specialist Training Authority Appeal Panel
Pathe Screen Entertainments Ltd *v.* Hand Made Films Ltd see Cannon Screen Entertainment Ltd *v.* Handmade Films (Distributors) Ltd
Pathirana *v.* Pathirana [1967] 1 A.C. 233; [1966] 3 W.L.R. 666; 110 S.J. 547, PC (Cey) .   *Digested*, 66/**8954**:
           Cited, 05/2899: *Considered*, 99/4092
Patrick *v.* Royal London Mutual Insurance Society Ltd see Ronson International Ltd *v.* Patrick
Patterson *v.* Ministry of Defence (Unreported, July 29, 1986) . . . .   *Digested*, 87/**1194**:
           Considered, 03/3131, 05/955
Patterson (Deceased) *v.* Smiths Dock Ltd see Barker *v.* Saint Gobain Pipelines Plc
Paulin *v.* Secretary of State for Trade and Industry see Secretary of State for Trade and Industry *v.* Paulin
Pauling's Settlement Trusts (No.1), Re; *sub nom* Younghusband *v.* Coutts & Co (No.1) [1964] Ch. 303; [1963] 3 W.L.R. 742; [1963] 3 All E.R. 1; 107 S.J. 492, CA; affirming in part [1962] 1 W.L.R. 86; [1961] 3 All E.R. 713; 106 S.J. 135, Ch D . .   *Digested*, 63/**3167**:
       Applied, 68/1572, 05/3967: *Followed*, 66/150, 66/4986:
            Subsequent proceedings, 63/3140
Payir *v.* Secretary of State for the Home Department see R. (on the application of Payir) *v.* Secretary of State for the Home Department
Payne *v.* Payne; *sub nom* P *v.* P (Removal of Child to New Zealand) [2001] EWCA Civ 166; [2001] Fam. 473; [2001] 2 W.L.R. 1826; [2001] 1 F.L.R. 1052; [2001] 1 F.C.R. 425; [2001] H.R.L.R. 28; [2001] U.K.H.R.R. 484; (2001) 165 J.P.N. 466; (2001) 98(10) L.S.G. 41; (2001) 145 S.J.L.B. 61; *Times*, March 9, 2001; *Independent*, February 22, 2001; *Daily Telegraph*, February 27, 2001, CA (Civ Div) . . . .   *Digested*, 01/**2596**:
      Applied, 01/2597, 03/1545, 01/1590: *Considered*, 05/1572, 05/1574,
           05/1635: *Distinguished*, 05/1575
Payne *v.* Pensions Ombudsman [2003] EWHC 3218; [2004] O.P.L.R. 185, Ch D . . . . .   *Digested*, 05/**3064**
Payne *v.* Royal & Sun Alliance Insurance Group Plc see Royal & Sun Alliance Insurance Group Plc *v.* Payne
Payroll Data Services (Italy) Srl, Re (C79/01) [2002] E.C.R. I-8923; [2004] 3 C.M.L.R. 36, ECJ (5th Chamber) [2002] E.C.R. I-8923, AGO. . . . .   *Digested*, 05/**1468**:
            Applied, 05/3856

PB *v.* Secretary of State for the Home Department; *sub nom* PB (Goa: EEA Discretionary Permit: Interpretation: India), Re [2005] UKIAT 82; [2005] Imm. A.R. 586, IAT

PB (Goa: EEA Discretionary Permit: Interpretation: India), Re see PB *v.* Secretary of State for the Home Department

PBS PARTNERSHIP/Controlling pension benefits systems (T931/95) [2002] E.P.O.R. 52, EPO (Technical Bd App) . . . . *Digested,* 03/**2515**:
Distinguished, 05/2460: *Followed,* 04/2329

Peach and Dolphin Trust (1988), Re (2004-05) 7 I.T.E.L.R. 570, Royal Ct (Jer) . . . . *Digested,* 05/**4302**

Peak Construction (Liverpool) Ltd *v.* McKinney Foundations Ltd 1 B.L.R. 111; 69 L.G.R. 1, CA (Civ Div) . . . . *Digested,* 71/**999**:
Applied, 84/2715, 86/233, 05/653: *Considered,* 84/228

Peak Holding AB *v.* Axolin-Elinor AB (C16/03) [2005] Ch. 261; [2005] 2 W.L.R. 650; [2005] All E.R. (EC) 723; [2004] E.C.R. I-11313; [2005] 1 C.M.L.R. 45; [2005] C.E.C. 481; [2005] E.T.M.R. 28; *Times,* December 6, 2004, ECJ . . . . *Digested,* 05/**2567**

Peak Land Ltd *v.* Canterbury City Council [2005] P.A.D. 72, Planning Inspector

Pearce *v.* European Reinsurance Consultants & Run-Off Ltd [2005] EWHC 1493; [2005] 2 B.C.L.C. 366, Ch D

Pearce *v.* Huw Howatson Ltd see Marshalls Clay Products Ltd *v.* Caulfield

Pearce *v.* Mayfield Secondary School Governing Body see Advocate General for Scotland *v.* MacDonald

Pearce & High Ltd *v.* Baxter [1999] C.L.C. 749; [1999] B.L.R. 101; (1999) 1 T.C.L.R. 157; 66 Con. L.R. 110; *Times,* March 24, 1999; *Independent,* March 4, 1999, CA (Civ Div) . . . . *Digested,* 99/**792**:
Applied, 02/671, 05/654

Pearson *v.* HM Coroner for Inner London North [2005] EWHC 833; [2005] U.K.H.R.R. 896, QBD (Admin) . . . . *Distinguished,* 05/17

Pearson *v.* Inland Revenue Commissioners; *sub nom* Pilkington Trustees *v.* Inland Revenue Commissioners [1981] A.C. 753; [1980] 2 W.L.R. 872; [1980] 2 All E.R. 479; [1980] S.T.C. 318; [1980] T.R. 177; 124 S.J. 377, HL; reversing [1980] Ch. 1; [1979] 3 W.L.R. 112; [1979] 3 All E.R. 7; [1979] S.T.C. 516; [1979] T.R. 195; 123 S.J. 490, CA (Civ Div); affirming [1979] 2 W.L.R. 353; [1979] 1 All E.R. 273; [1978] S.T.C. 627; [1978] T.R. 349; 123 S.J. 185, Ch D . . . . *Digested,* 80/**228**:
Applied, 84/260, 01/5282, 05/4308: *Considered,* 81/1374

Pectel Ltd, Re see O'Neill *v.* Phillips

Pedicel AS *v.* Sosial- og Helsedirektoratet (Directorate for Health and Social Affairs) (E4/04) [2005] 2 C.M.L.R. 7, EFTA

Peek *v.* Towle [1945] K.B. 458, KBD . . . . *Followed,* 05/782

Peekay Intermark Ltd *v.* Australia & New Zealand Banking Group Ltd A3/2005/1263, CA (Civ Div); reversing [2005] EWHC 830; [2005] 2 C.L.C. 111; [2005] P.N.L.R. 42; *Times,* June 10, 2005, QBD (Comm) . . . . *Digested,* 05/**714**

Peer Freeholds Ltd *v.* Clean Wash International Ltd [2005] EWHC 179; [2005] 1 E.G.L.R. 47; [2005] 17 E.G. 124; [2005] N.P.C. 26; [2005] 2 P. & C.R. DG6, Ch D . . . . *Digested,* 05/**2646**

Peer International Corp *v.* Termidor Music Publishers Ltd (No.3) [2005] EWHC 1048; (2005) 28(7) I.P.D. 28050; *Times,* June 2, 2005, Ch D . . . . *Digested,* 05/**301**

Peerbooms *v.* Stichting CZ Groep Zorgverzekeringen (C157/99) see Geraets-Smits *v.* Stichting Ziekenfonds VGZ (C157/99)

Pelissier *v.* France (2000) 30 E.H.R.R. 715, ECHR . . . . *Digested,* 01/**3510**:
Applied, 05/2086: *Considered,* 03/2127

Pena *v.* Coyne (No.1) [2004] EWHC 2684; [2004] 2 B.C.L.C. 703; [2004] B.P.I.R. 1286, Ch D . . . . *Digested,* 05/**2322**

Pena *v.* Coyne (No.2) [2004] EWHC 2685; [2004] 2 B.C.L.C. 730; [2004] B.P.I.R. 1286, Ch D . . . . *Digested,* 05/**2323**

Pena *v.* Dale [2003] EWHC 1065; [2004] 2 B.C.L.C. 508, Ch D . . . . *Digested,* 05/**529**

Pendleton *v.* Stone & Webster Engineering Ltd see Fairchild *v.* Glenhaven Funeral Services Ltd (t/a GH Dovener & Son)

Pendragon Plc (t/a CD Bramall Bradford) *v.* Copus [2005] I.C.R. 1671, EAT . . . . *Digested,* 05/**1250**

Penk *v.* Wright see Alcock *v.* Chief Constable of South Yorkshire

Pennington *v.* Crampton [2003] EWHC 2691; [2004] B.C.C. 611; [2005] W.T.L.R. 559, Ch D . . . . *Digested,* 04/**474**

Pennycook *v.* Shaws (EAL) Ltd; *sub nom* Pennycook *v.* Shuns (EAL) Ltd; Shaws (EAL) Ltd *v.* Pennycook [2004] EWCA Civ 100; [2004] Ch. 296; [2004] 2 W.L.R. 1331; [2004] 2 All E.R. 665; [2004] L. & T.R. 34; [2004] 2 E.G.L.R. 55; [2004] 18 E.G. 102; [2004] 8 E.G.C.S. 135; (2004) 101 (11) L.S.G. 35; (2004) 148 S.J.L.B. 235; [2004] N.P.C. 21; [2004] 1 P. & C.R. DG25; *Times,* February 20, 2004; *Independent,* February 19, 2004, CA (Civ Div); reversing [2002] EWHC 2769; [2003] Ch. 399; [2003] 2 W.L.R. 1265; [2003] 3 All E.R. 1316; [2003] 2 P. & C.R. 8; [2003] L. & T.R. 16; [2003] 3 E.G.L.R. 28; [2003] 45 E.G. 176; [2002] 50 E.G.C.S. 113; (2002) 99(49) L.S.G. 20; [2002] N.P.C. 157; [2003] 1 P. & C.R. DG24; *Times,* December 9, 2002, Ch D . . . . *Digested,* 04/**2494**:
Applied, 05/3376

Pennycook *v.* Shuns (EAL) Ltd see Pennycook *v.* Shaws (EAL) Ltd

Pentiacova *v.* Moldova (Admissibility) (14462/03) (2005) 40 E.H.R.R. SE23, ECHR

Penwith DC *v.* VP Developments Ltd [2005] EWHC 259; [2005] B.C.C. 393; [2005] 2 B.C.L.C. 607; [2005] T.C.L.R. 4; 102 Con. L.R. 117; [2005] B.P.I.R. 607; [2005] N.P.C. 32, Ch D (Companies Ct) .... *Digested,* 05/**2346**
Pepe Textiles Espana SA *v.* Liwe Espanola SA [2005] E.T.M.R. CN12, Trib Sup (Sp)
Pepper (Inspector of Taxes) *v.* Hart [1993] A.C. 593; [1992] 3 W.L.R. 1032; [1993] 1 All E.R. 42; [1992] S.T.C. 898; [1993] I.C.R. 291; [1993] I.R.L.R. 33; [1993] R.V.R. 127; (1993) 143 N.L.J. 17; [1992] N.P.C. 154; *Times,* November 30, 1992; *Independent,* November 26, 1992, HL; reversing [1991] Ch. 203; [1991] 2 W.L.R. 483; [1990] S.T.C. 786; [1991] I.C.R. 681; [1991] I.R.L.R. 125; (1990) 134 S.J. 1478; *Times,* November 15, 1990; *Financial Times,* November 16, 1990; *Guardian,* November 21, 1990; *Daily Telegraph,* November 19, 1990, CA (Civ Div); affirming [1990] 1 W.L.R. 204; [1990] S.T.C. 6; (1989) 86(46) L.S.G. 41, Ch D
.... *Digested,* 93/**459**:
Applied, 93/3714, 94/2514, 98/321, 98/966, 01/4489, 03/3600, 05/4063: *Cited,* 00/5239: *Considered,* 93/426, 93/1866, 93/2260, 93/3860, 94/968, 94/3413, 94/3900, 95/881, 96/1297, 96/1606, 96/3928, 01/5174, 04/628, 05/2742: *Distinguished,* 94/125, 95/181, 95/2520, 97/4657, 00/2122, 01/4284: *Followed,* 96/4190: *Not applied,* 01/4206: *Referred to,* 93/486, 94/353, 94/2723, 94/2729, 94/3445, 94/5459, 94/5899, 95/522, 95/861
Percy *v.* Church of Scotland Board of National Mission [2005] UKHL 73; *Times,* December 16, 2005; *Independent,* December 20, 2005, HL; reversing 2001 S.C. 757; 2001 S.L.T. 497; 2001 G.W.D. 12-434, IH (1 Div).................... *Digested,* 02/**5576**
Percy *v.* DPP see Ayliffe *v.* DPP
Peregrine Systems Ltd *v.* Steria Ltd [2005] EWCA Civ 239; [2005] Info. T.L.R. 294, CA (Civ Div); affirming [2004] EWHC 275; [2004] Masons C.L.R. 20, QBD (TCC)
Perez *v.* France (47287/99) (2005) 40 E.H.R.R. 39, ECHR
Peri *v.* Engel see Engel *v.* Peri
Perkin *v.* St George's Healthcare NHS Trust [2005] EWCA Civ 1174; [2005] I.R.L.R. 934, CA (Civ Div); affirming UKEAT/0293/04/MAA, EAT
Perks *v.* United Kingdom (25277/94) (2000) 30 E.H.R.R. 33; [2000] R.A. 487, ECHR (1997) 24 E.H.R.R. CD35, Eur Comm HR.......................... *Digested,* 00/**3221**:
Considered, 05/2100
Perlman *v.* Rayden [2004] EWHC 2192; [2004] 43 E.G.C.S. 142; [2005] 1 P. & C.R. DG10, Ch D
Pernod-Ricard SA *v.* Office of Fair Trading (Appeal: Procedure) [2004] CAT 10; [2004] Comp. A.R. 707, CAT.. *Digested,* 05/**586**:
Considered, 05/561
Pernod-Ricard SA *v.* Office of Fair Trading (Costs) [2005] CAT 9; [2005] Comp. A.R. 894, CAT
Perotti, Re see Perotti *v.* Collyer-Bristow (A Firm) (Right to Legal Representation)
Perotti *v.* Collyer-Bristow (A Firm) (Right to Legal Representation); *sub nom* Perotti, Re [2003] EWCA Civ 1521; [2004] 2 All E.R. 189; *Times,* November 27, 2003; *Independent,* November 6, 2003, CA (Civ Div)...................... *Digested,* 04/**2560**:
Applied, 05/308
Perotti *v.* Collyer-Bristow (A Firm) (Vexatious Litigant: Directions) [2004] EWCA Civ 639; [2004] 4 All E.R. 53, CA (Civ Div).......................... *Digested,* 05/**494**
Perotti *v.* Collyer-Bristow (A Firm) (Vexatious Litigant: Directions: Corrections) [2004] EWCA Civ 1019; [2004] 4 All E.R. 72, CA (Civ Div).................... *Digested,* 05/**426**
Perotti *v.* Westminster City Council (Application for Permission to Appeal) [2005] EWCA Civ 581; [2005] C.P. Rep. 38; [2005] R.V.R. 321; [2005] N.P.C. 67; *Times,* May 30, 2005, CA (Civ Div)............................ *Digested,* 05/**417**
Perpetual Trust Ltd *v.* Roman Catholic Bishop of the Diocese of Christchurch; *sub nom* Armstrong (Deceased), Re (2005-06) 8 I.T.E.L.R. 222, HC (NZ)
Perrett *v.* Collins [1998] 2 Lloyd's Rep. 255; [1999] P.N.L.R. 77; *Times,* June 23, 1998, CA (Civ Div).. *Digested,* 98/**3923**:
Applied, 05/2858: *Followed,* 04/2710
Perry *v.* Day [2004] EWHC 1398; [2005] B.C.C. 375, Ch D .... *Digested,* 05/**533**
Perry *v.* Day [2004] EWHC 3372; [2005] 2 B.C.L.C. 405, Ch D
Perry *v.* Inland Revenue Commissioners [2005] S.T.C. (S.C.D.) 474; [2005] W.T.L.R. 1077, Sp Comm
Persimmon Homes (Thames Valley) Ltd *v.* North Hertfordshire DC see R. (on the application of Persimmon Homes (Thames Valley) Ltd) *v.* North Hertfordshire DC
Persimmon Homes (Thames Valley) Ltd *v.* Stevenage BC; *sub nom* Persimmon Homes (Thames Valley) Ltd *v.* Taylor Woodrow Homes Ltd [2005] EWCA Civ 1365; [2005] N.P.C. 136, CA (Civ Div); affirming [2005] EWHC 957; [2005] 23 E.G.C.S. 141; [2005] N.P.C. 71, QBD (Admin)
Persimmon Homes (Thames Valley) Ltd *v.* Taylor Woodrow Homes Ltd see Persimmon Homes (Thames Valley) Ltd *v.* Stevenage BC
Persimmon Homes (Wales) Ltd *v.* Rhondda Cynon Taff CBC [2005] R.V.R. 59, Lands Tr. *Digested,* 05/**3254**
Personal Protective Equipment for Firefighters, Re (C103/01) see Commission of the European Communities *v.* Germany (C103/01)
Pervaiz *v.* Revenue and Customs Commissioners [2005] S.T.I. 1731, V&DTr

Pesticcio v. Huet; *sub nom* Niersmans v. Pesticcio [2004] EWCA Civ 372; [2004]
   W.T.L.R. 699; (2004) 154 N.L.J. 653; (2004) 148 S.J.L.B. 420; [2004] N.P.C.
   55; *Independent*, April 7, 2004, CA (Civ Div); affirming [2003] EWHC 2293;
   (2003) 73 B.M.L.R. 57; [2003] W.T.L.R.1327; [2003] 2 P. & C.R. DG8, Ch D .   *Digested*, 05/**3401**
Petch v. Gurney (Inspector of Taxes); *sub nom* Gurney (Inspector of Taxes) v. Petch
   [1994] 3 All E.R. 731; [1994] S.T.C. 689; 66 T.C. 743; [1994] S.T.I. 678; (1994)
   91(27) L.S.G. 37; *Times*, June 8, 1994; *Independent*, July 11, 1994 (C.S.), CA
   (Civ Div); affirming [1992] S.T.C. 892, Ch D . . . .   *Digested*, 94/**2529**:
                                        Applied, 95/2750, 05/2652: *Considered*, 03/501
Peterson v. Inland Revenue Commissioner [2005] UKPC 5; [2005] S.T.C. 448; 7 I.T.L.
   Rep. 603; [2005] S.T.I. 358, PC (NZ). . . . .   *Digested*, 05/**4105**
Petroalliance Services Co Ltd v. Yukos Oil Co see Dardana Ltd v. Yukos Oil Co (No.1)
Petroleo Brasiliero SA v. Mellitus Shipping Inc (The Baltic Flame) [2001] EWCA Civ
   418; [2001] 1 All E.R. (Comm) 993; [2001] 2 Lloyd's Rep. 203; [2001] C.L.C.
   1151; *Times*, April 5, 2001, CA (Civ Div) . . . .   *Digested*, 01/**610**:
                                                                Applied, 05/2396
Petromec Inc v. Petroleo Brasileiro SA Petrobras (No.3) [2004] EWHC 1180; [2005] 1
   Lloyd's Rep. 219, QBD (Comm) . . . .   *Digested*, 05/**2389**
Petrotrade Inc v. Texaco Ltd [2002] 1 W.L.R. 947 (Note); [2001] 4 All E.R. 853;
   [2001] C.P. Rep. 29; [2000] C.L.C. 1341; [2002] 1 Costs L.R. 60; *Times*, June
   14, 2000; *Independent*, July 10, 2000 (C.S), CA (Civ Div); affirming 1998 Folio
   1348, QBD (Comm) . . . .   *Digested*, 00/**539**:
                       Applied, 01/484, 02/346, 02/349, 02/356: *Considered*, 02/347, 05/369
Pettkus v. Becker [1980] 2 S.C.R. 834, Sup Ct (Can). . . . .   *Considered*, 05/4310
Petursson v. Hutchison 3G UK Ltd (No.1) [2005] B.L.R. 210, QBD (TCC). . . . .   *Digested*, 05/**327**
Peugeot Citroen Automobiles Ltd v. Customs and Excise Commissioners [2004] V. &
   D.R. 157; [2004] S.T.I. 2353, V&DTr (Manchester) . . . .   *Digested*, 05/**4361**
Peugeot Motor Co Plc v. Customs and Excise Commissioners (Employee Incentive
   Scheme) [2000] S.T.I. 1554, V&DTr . . . .   *Applied*, 05/4361
Pewter v. United Kingdom (48906/99) see Whitfield v. United Kingdom (46387/99)
Pfeiffer v. Deutsches Rotes Kreuz Kreisverband Waldshut eV (C397/01) [2004] E.C.R.
   I-8835; [2005] 1 C.M.L.R. 44; [2005] I.C.R. 1307; [2005] I.R.L.R.137, ECJ . . .   *Digested*, 05/**1275**:
                                                                Applied, 05/358
Pfeiffer Grosshandel GmbH v. Lowa Warenhandel GmbH (C255/97) [1999] E.C.R. I-
   2835; [2001] 1 C.M.L.R. 7; [1999] E.T.M.R. 603, ECJ. . . . .   *Digested*, 00/**3799**:
                                        Applied, 05/3856: *Followed*, 05/1468
Pharma Intranet Information AG v. IMS Health GmbH & Co OHG (11 U 67/2000)
   [2005] E.C.C.12, OLG (Frankfurt Am Main)
Pharmacia & Upjohn Co LLC's Community Trade Mark Application (R694/2004-1) [2005]
   E.T.M.R. CN11, OHIM (1st Bd App)
Pharmacia Italia SpA v. Deutsches Patentamt (C31/03) [2005] R.P.C. 27, ECJ (5th
   Chamber) . . . .   *Digested*, 05/**2503**
Pharmedica GmbH's International Trade Mark Application (No.649380) [2000] R.P.C.
   536; (2000) 23(3) I.P.D. 23024; *Independent*, March 6, 2000 (C.S.), Ch D . . .   *Digested*, 00/**3697**:
                                                        Applied, 02/2787, 05/2583
Pharos SA v. Commission of the European Communities (C151/98 P (R)) [1998]
   E.C.R. I-5441, ECJ . . . .   *Followed*, 05/576,
                                                                05/577
Phelps v. Hillingdon LBC; *sub nom* G (A Child), Re; Anderton v. Clwyd CC; G (A
   Child) v. Bromley LBC; Jarvis v. Hampshire CC [2001] 2 A.C. 619; [2000] 3
   W.L.R. 776; [2000] 4 All E.R. 504; [2000] 3 F.C.R. 102; (2001) 3 L.G.L.R. 5;
   [2000] B.L.G.R. 651; [2000] Ed. C.R. 700; [2000] E.L.R. 499; (2000) 3 C.C.L.
   Rep. 156; (2000) 56 B.M.L.R. 1; (2000) 150 N.L.J. 1198; (2000) 144 S.J.L.B.
   241; *Times*, July 28, 2000; *Independent*, November 13, 2000 (C.S), HL;
   reversing [1999] 1 W.L.R. 500; [1999] 1 All E.R. 421; [1999] 1 F.C.R. 440;
   (1999) 1 L.G.L.R. 246; [1999] B.L.G.R. 103; [1999] Ed. C.R. 368; [1998] E.L.R.
   587; (1999) 46 B.M.L.R. 100; (1998) 95(45) L.S.G. 41; (1998) 148 N.L.J.
   1710; (1999) 143 S.J.L.B. 11; *Times*, November 9, 1998, CA (Civ Div); reversing
   [1997] 3 F.C.R. 621; (1997) 9 Admin. L.R. 657; [1998] Ed. C.R. 47; [1998]
   E.L.R. 38; (1998) 39 B.M.L.R. 51; (1997) 94(39) L.S.G. 39; (1997) 147 N.L.J.
   1421; (1997) 141 S.J.L.B. 214; *Times*, October 10, 1997, QBD . . . .   *Digested*, 00/**1947**:
             Applied, 99/1889, 99/4010, 01/4540, 03/2972, 05/1042, 05/1140, 05/2845,
             05/2861: *Considered*, 99/3966, 99/3968, 04/996, 04/1818, 04/2719,
             05/2891: *Distinguished*, 99/3967: *Explained*, 03/1118: *Followed*, 05/2871:
                                        Previous proceedings, 99/1889, 99/3967, 99/4010
Philex Plc v. Golban see Ridehalgh v. Horsefield
Philips Electronics NV v. Remington Consumer Products Ltd (C299/99) see Koninklijke
   Philips Electronics NV v. Remington Consumer Products Ltd (C299/99)

Philips Electronics NV v. Remington Consumer Products Ltd (No.1) [1999] E.T.M.R.
816; [1999] R.P.C. 809; (1999) 22(9) I.P.D. 22084, CA (Civ Div) [1998]
E.T.M.R. 124; [1998] R.P.C. 283; (1998) 21(3) I.P.D. 21023; *Times*, February 2,
1998, Ch D (Patents Ct) . . . . *Digested*, 99/**3564**:
Applied, 99/3583, 00/3793, 05/2578: *Considered*, 99/3567, 01/4041,
04/2398: *Followed*, 00/3758: *Referred to*, 99/3593, 01/4026, 01/4030:
Subsequent proceedings, 02/2903
Philis v. Greece (No.1) (A/209) (1991) 13 E.H.R.R. 741; *Times*, December 23, 1991,
ECHR . . . . *Considered*, 97/2810:
Distinguished, 05/1553
Phillips v. Avena [2005] EWHC 3333; *Times*, November 22, 2005, Ch D
Phillips v. Camden LBC see Cramp v. Hastings BC
Phillips v. Magill see Porter v. Magill
Phillips v. Peace [2004] EWHC 3180; [2005] 1 W.L.R. 3246; [2005] 2 All E.R. 752;
[2005] 2 F.L.R. 1212; [2005] 2 F.C.R. 265; [2005] Fam. Law 692, Fam Div . . . *Digested*, 05/**1666**
Phillips v. Symes (A Bankrupt) (Expert Witnesses: Costs) [2004] EWHC 2330;
[2005] 1 W.L.R. 2043; [2005] 4 All E.R. 519; [2005] 2 All E.R. (Comm) 538;
[2005] C.P. Rep. 12; [2005] 2 Costs L.R. 224; (2005) 83 B.M.L.R. 115; (2004)
101(44) L.S.G. 29; (2004) 154 N.L.J. 1615; *Times*, November 5, 2004, Ch D . . *Digested*, 05/**363**
Phillips v. Symes (A Bankrupt) [2005] EWCA Civ 533; [2005] 1 W.L.R. 2986;
Independent, May 13, 2005, CA (Civ Div); reversing [2005] EWHC 90, Ch D . . *Digested*, 05/**344**
Phillips v. United Kingdom (41087/98) 11 B.H.R.C. 280; [2001] Crim. L.R. 817; *Times*,
August 13, 2001, ECHR . . . . *Digested*, 01/**3537**:
Applied, 02/3896: *Followed*, 05/3568
Phillips Van Heusen Corp v. Office for Harmonisation in the Internal Market (Trade Marks
and Designs) (OHIM) (T292/01) [2003] E.C.R. II-4335; [2004] E.T.M.R. 60;
(2003) 26(11) I.P.D. 26074, CFI (2nd Chamber). . . . . *Digested*, 05/**2514**:
Applied, 05/2510
Phipps v. Boardman see Boardman v. Phipps
Phoenix General Insurance Co of Greece SA v. Administratia Asigurarilor de Stat see
Phoenix General Insurance Co of Greece SA v. Halvanon Insurance Co Ltd
Phoenix General Insurance Co of Greece SA v. Halvanon Insurance Co Ltd; *sub nom*
Phoenix General Insurance Co of Greece SA v. Administratia Asigurarilor de Stat
[1988] Q.B. 216; [1987] 2 W.L.R. 512; [1987] 2 All E.R. 152; [1986] 2 Lloyd's
Rep. 552; [1987] Fin. L.R. 48; (1987) 84 L.S.G. 1055; (1987) 131 S.J. 257;
Financial Times, October 15, 1986, CA (Civ Div); reversing [1986] 1 All E.R. 908;
[1985] 2 Lloyd's Rep. 599; [1985] Fin. L.R. 368; (1985) 135 N.L.J. 1081;
Financial Times, August 20, 1985, QBD (Comm) . . . . *Digested*, 87/**2050**:
Applied, 96/3566: *Considered*, 92/182, 99/110: *Distinguished*, 05/2397:
Followed, 93/2415
Phoenix Venture Holdings Ltd v. Independent Trustee Services Ltd [2005] EWHC 1379;
[2005] Pens. L.R. 379, Ch D (Companies Ct) . . . . *Digested*, 05/**2997**
Phonographic Performance Ltd v. AEI Rediffusion Music Ltd (Costs) see AEI
Rediffusion Music Ltd v. Phonographic Performance Ltd (Costs)
Phonographic Performance Ltd v. Department of Trade and Industry [2004] EWHC
1795; [2004] 1 W.L.R. 2893; [2005] 1 All E.R. 369; [2004] 3 C.M.L.R. 31;
[2004] Eu. L.R. 1003; [2004] E.M.L.R. 30; [2005] R.P.C. 8; (2004) 27(8)
I.P.D. 27085; (2004) 101(34) L.S.G. 31; *Times*, August 27, 2004, Ch D . . . . . . *Digested*, 05/**2497**
Phonographic Performance Ltd v. Reader [2005] EWHC 416; [2005] E.M.L.R. 26;
[2005] F.S.R. 42, Ch D . . . . *Digested*, 05/**2421**
Photo Production Ltd v. Securicor Transport Ltd [1980] A.C. 827; [1980] 2 W.L.R.
283; [1980] 1 All E.R. 556; [1980] 1 Lloyd's Rep. 545; 124 S.J. 147, HL;
reversing [1978] 1 W.L.R. 856; [1978] 3 All E.R. 146; [1978] 2 Lloyd's Rep. 172;
122 S.J. 315, CA (Civ Div) . . . . *Digested*, 80/**353**:
Applied, 81/301, 81/303, 81/2994, 82/3501, 83/3330, 83/3440, 88/2388,
92/317, 05/2356: *Considered*, 82/403, 83/3314, 89/415, 94/540, 94/2705,
95/179, 95/778, 02/4098: *Distinguished*, 84/1902, 85/1863
Piau v. Commission of the European Communities (T193/02) [2005] 5 C.M.L.R. 2,
CFI (4th Chamber)
Piazza v. Paul Schurte AG (E10/04) [2005] 2 C.M.L.R. 59, EFTA
Pibernik v. Croatia (75139/01) (2005) 40 E.H.R.R. 28, ECHR . . . . *Digested*, 05/**2099**
Pickering v. Liverpool Daily Post and Echo; *sub nom* P v. Liverpool Daily Post and
Echo [1991] 2 A.C. 370; [1991] 2 W.L.R. 513; [1991] 1 All E.R. 622; (1991) 3
Admin. L.R. 397; [1991] 2 Med. L.R. 240; (1991) 141 N.L.J. 166; 135 S.J.L.B.
166, HL; reversing [1990] 2 W.L.R. 494; [1990] 1 All E.R. 335; (1990) 2 Admin.
L.R. 403; (1990) 87(14) L.S.G. 44; 134 S.J. 786, CA (Civ Div) . . . . *Digested*, 91/**2456**:
Considered, 02/3231, 05/2822: *Followed*, 03/5
Pierson v. Secretary of State for the Home Department see R. v. Secretary of State for
the Home Department Ex p. Pierson
Pilkington Trustees v. Inland Revenue Commissioners see Pearson v. Inland Revenue
Commissioners
Pilkington UK Ltd v. CGU Insurance Plc [2004] EWCA Civ 23; [2005] 1 All E.R.
(Comm) 283; [2004] 1 C.L.C. 1059; [2004] B.L.R. 97; [2004] T.C.L.R. 5;
[2004] Lloyd's Rep. I.R. 891; [2004] N.P.C. 10, CA (Civ Div) . . . . *Digested*, 05/**2378**

Pinder v. United Kingdom (10096/82) (1985) 7 E.H.R.R. CD464, Eur Comm HR . . . . . *Applied*, 05/1553:
Doubted, 02/3259

Pinfield v. Eagles [2005] EWHC 477; [2005] 2 P. & C.R. DG10, Ch D
Pini v. Romania (78028/01) [2005] 2 F.L.R. 596; (2005) 40 E.H.R.R. 13; [2005]
Fam. Law 697, ECHR. . . . . *Digested*, 05/**2124**:
Considered, 04/2067

Pinnington v. Swansea City Council [2005] EWCA Civ 135; [2005] I.C.R. 685; *Times*,
March 9, 2005, CA (Civ Div); reversing UKEAT/0561/03/MAA, EAT. . . . . *Digested*, 05/**1286**

Pinochet Ugarte (No.2), Re see R. v. Bow Street Metropolitan Stipendiary Magistrate Ex
p. Pinochet Ugarte (No.2)

Pinsent Curtis v. Capital Cranfield Trustees Ltd; *sub nom* Capital Cranfield Trustees Ltd
v. Pinsent Curtis (A Firm); Capital Cranfield Trustees Ltd v. Walsh; K&J Holdings
Ltd, Re [2005] EWCA Civ 860; [2005] 4 All E.R. 449; [2005] I.C.R. 1767;
Independent, July 20, 2005, CA (Civ Div); affirming [2004] EWHC 2874;
[2005] Pens. L.R. 251, Ch D (Companies Ct). . . . . *Digested*, 05/**2957**

Pinto v. Lim; *sub nom* Pinton v. Lim [2005] EWHC 630; *Times*, June 8, 2005, Ch D
Pinton v. Lim see Pinto v. Lim

Pioneer Aggregates (UK) Ltd v. Secretary of State for the Environment [1985] A.C. 132;
[1984] 3 W.L.R. 32; [1984] 2 All E.R. 358; 82 L.G.R. 488; (1984) 48 P. &
C.R. 95; (1984) 272 E.G. 425; [1984] J.P.L. 651; (1984) 81 L.S.G. 2148; (1984)
128 S.J. 416, HL; affirming 82 L.G.R. 112; (1983) 46 P. & C.R. 313; (1983) 267
E.G. 941; [1983] J.P.L. 733, CA (Civ Div); affirming (1983) 46 P. & C.R. 113;
[1982] J.P.L. 371, QBD . . . . *Digested*, 84/**3465**:
Applied, 85/3476, 86/3348, 92/4357, 00/4515, 05/3269:
Approved, 99/4255: *Considered*, 89/3569, 90/3917, 90/4435, 91/3457,
92/4272, 92/4373, 93/3956, 95/4770, 98/6136: *Distinguished*, 86/3337,
87/3710: *Followed*, 88/3517, 89/3553

Piraiki-Patraiki Cotton Industry AE v. Commission of the European Communities (11/82)
[1985] E.C.R. 207; [1985] 2 C.M.L.R. 4; [1985] 2 C.M.L.R. 461, ECJ (1st
Chamber) . . . . *Digested*, 85/**1438**:
Distinguished, 02/1541, 05/1471

PIRELLI & CAMBIENTE/Disapproval of the text proposed for grant (T1181/04) [2005]
E.P.O.R. 37, EPO (Technical Bd App)

Pirelli General Cable Works Ltd v. Oscar Faber & Partners [1983] 2 A.C. 1; [1983] 2
W.L.R. 6; [1983] 1 All E.R. 65; (1983) 265 E.G. 979; *Times*, December 11, 1982,
HL; reversing (1982) 262 E.G. 879, CA (Civ Div) . . . . *Digested*, 83/**2216**:
Applied, 83/2215, 84/212, 84/2284, 84/2675, 85/208, 85/212, 87/229,
87/2330, 88/2158, 96/1156, 01/4511, 01/4907, 05/436: *Considered*, 84/214,
85/189, 89/2585, 89/3516, 90/3290, 91/2660, 93/2997:
Disapproved, 96/4438: *Distinguished*, 85/228, 86/1993, 87/2321, 92/3219:
Followed, 88/2154, 94/6161: *Not followed*, 85/2303: *Referred to*, 84/240

Pirelli General Plc v. Gaca see Gaca v. Pirelli General Plc
Pirtek (UK) Ltd v. Deanswood Ltd [2005] EWHC 2301; [2005] 2 Lloyd's Rep. 728,
QBD (Comm)

Pitmans Trustees Ltd v. Telecommunications Group Plc [2004] EWHC 181; [2005]
O.P.L.R. 1; [2004] Pens. L.R. 213; *Independent*, March 29, 2004 (C.S), Ch D . . *Digested*, 04/**2818**:
Considered, 05/2950

PJG Developments Ltd v. Revenue and Customs Commissioners [2005] B.V.C. 2681;
[2005] V. & D.R. 215; [2005] S.T.I. 1656, V&DTr

Pla v. Andorra (69498/01) [2004] 2 F.C.R. 630; 18 B.H.R.C. 120, ECHR . . . . *Digested*, 05/**2126**

Plantiflor Ltd v. Customs and Excise Commissioners see Customs and Excise
Commissioners v. Plantiflor Ltd

Plato Plastik Robert Frank GmbH v. Caropack Handelsgesellschaft mbH (C341/01)
[2004] E.C.R. I-4883; [2004] 3 C.M.L.R. 30; [2005] Env. L.R. 9, ECJ (5th
Chamber) . . . . *Digested*, 05/**1408**

Platt v. Chaudhary (Appeal: Multiple Application) see British Medical Association v.
Chaudhary (No.1)

Plaumann & Co v. Commission of the European Economic Community (25/62) [1963]
E.C.R. 95; [1964] C.M.L.R. 29, ECJ [1963] E.C.R. 95; [1963] E.C.R. 199, AGO . *Digested*, 64/**1440**:
Applied, 65/1518, 98/735, 98/2311, 05/1470: *Considered*, 02/1588:
Followed, 02/1543

Play It Ltd v. Digital Bridges Ltd [2005] EWHC 1001; (2005) 28(7) I.P.D. 28051, Ch D
Plumex v. Young Sports NV [2005] I.L.Pr. 47, HvC (B)
Plummer, Re [2004] B.P.I.R. 767, Ch D (Bankruptcy Ct) . . . . *Digested*, 05/**2275**

Plymouth City Airport Ltd v. Secretary of State for the Environment, Transport and the
Regions see R. (on the application of Plymouth City Airport Ltd) v. Secretary of
State for the Environment, Transport and the Regions

Plymouth City Council v. County of Devon Coroner see R. (on the application of
Plymouth City Council) v. HM Coroner for Devon

PM v. United Kingdom (6638/03) (Admissibility) [2005] S.T.I. 1480; (2004) 39
E.H.R.R. SE21, ECHR

PM v. United Kingdom (6638/03); *sub nom* M v. United Kingdom (6638/03) [2005]
S.T.C. 1566; [2005] 3 F.C.R. 101; 18 B.H.R.C. 668; 7 I.T.L. Rep. 970; *Times*,
September 15, 2005, ECHR

PMS International Group Plc *v.* North East Lincolnshire Council see In the Pink Ltd *v.* North East Lincolnshire Council

Poel *v.* Poel [1970] 1 W.L.R. 1469; 114 S.J. 720, CA (Civ Div) . . . . *Digested,* 70/**777**:
Applied, 87/2487, 94/3210, 94/3281, 95/3971, 96/543, 01/2596, 03/1545, 05/1590: *Considered,* 80/1836, 83/2447, 93/2824, 94/2166, 95/3482, 95/3483, 96/644, 01/2588: *Followed,* 87/2492, 88/2340

Pointstar Shipping & Finance Ltd *v.* 7 Strathray Gardens Ltd see 7 Strathray Gardens Ltd *v.* Pointstar Shipping & Finance Ltd

Poirrez *v.* France (40892/98) (2005) 40 E.H.R.R. 2, ECHR . . . . *Digested,* 05/**2035**

Polanski *v.* Conde Nast Publications Ltd [2005] UKHL 10; [2005] 1 W.L.R. 637; [2005] 1 All E.R. 945; [2005] C.P. Rep. 22; [2005] E.M.L.R. 14; [2005] H.R.L.R. 11; [2005] U.K.H.R.R. 277; (2005) 102(10) L.S.G. 29; (2005) 155 N.L.J. 245; *Times,* February 11, 2005; *Independent,* February 16, 2005, HL; reversing [2003] EWCA Civ 1573; [2004] 1 W.L.R. 387; [2004] 1 All E.R. 1220; [2004] C.P. Rep. 13; [2004] E.M.L.R. 7; [2004] U.K.H.R.R. 278; (2003) 100(46) L.S.G. 24; (2003) 153 N.L.J. 1760; (2003) 147 S.J.L.B. 1363; *Times,* November 18, 2003, CA (Civ Div) . . . . *Digested,* 05/**303**

Police Service of Northern Ireland *v.* McCaughey [2005] N.I. 344, CA (NI)

Polkey *v.* AE Dayton Services Ltd; *sub nom* Polkey *v.* Edmund Walker (Holdings) Ltd [1988] A.C. 344; [1987] 3 W.L.R. 1153; [1987] 3 All E.R. 974; [1988] I.C.R. 142; [1987] I.R.L.R. 503; (1987) 137 N.L.J. 1109; (1988) 138 N.L.J. Rep. 33; (1987) 131 S.J. 1624, HL; reversing [1987] 1 W.L.R. 1147; [1987] 1 All E.R. 984; [1987] I.C.R. 301; [1987] I.R.L.R. 13; (1987) 84 L.S.G. 2690; (1987) 131 S.J. 1062, CA (Civ Div) . . . . *Digested,* 88/**1353**:
Applied, 89/1500, 90/1927, 92/1985, 96/2655, 98/2238, 99/2115, 99/2135, 00/2190: *Considered,* 89/1440, 90/1895, 92/1946, 92/1988, 94/2022, 94/2025, 94/2026, 95/2079, 95/2098, 96/2664, 97/2283, 01/2313, 05/1333: *Explained,* 99/6048: *Referred to,* 91/1704

Polkey *v.* Edmund Walker (Holdings) Ltd see Polkey *v.* AE Dayton Services Ltd

Pollard *v.* Ashurst see Ashurst *v.* Pollard

Polskiego *v.* Poland (42049/98) (2005) 41 E.H.R.R. 21, ECHR

Poltoratskiy *v.* Ukraine (38812/97) (2004) 39 E.H.R.R. 43, ECHR . . . . *Digested,* 05/**2062**

Polypropylene Cartel (T7/89), Re see Hercules Chemicals NV *v.* Commission of the European Communities (C51/92 P)

Poole *v.* Smith (Unreported, May 24, 2004), CC (Birkenhead) [*Ex rel.* Chris Middleton, Barrister, Oriel Chambers, 14 Water Street, Liverpool] . . . . *Digested,* 05/**3189**

Popat *v.* Shonchhatra [1997] 1 W.L.R. 1367; [1997] 3 All E.R. 800; (1997) 94(27) L.S.G. 22; (1997) 141 S.J.L.B. 163; *Times,* July 4, 1997, CA (Civ Div); reversing [1995] 1 W.L.R. 908; [1995] 4 All E.R. 646; *Times,* May 4, 1995, Ch D . . . . *Digested,* 97/**3874**:
Applied, 04/2766: *Cited,* 05/2899

Popowski *v.* Popowski [2004] EWHC 668; [2004] 2 P. & C.R. DG10, Ch D . . . . *Considered,* 05/**4301**

Port of Tilbury (London) Ltd *v.* Beck see Port of Tilbury (London) Ltd *v.* Birch

Port of Tilbury (London) Ltd *v.* Birch; Port of Tilbury (London) Ltd *v.* Talbot; Port of Tilbury (London) Ltd *v.* Hall; Port of Tilbury (London) Ltd *v.* Beck [2005] I.R.L.R. 92; [2005] O.P.L.R. 335; (2004) 101(45) L.S.G. 31; *Times,* November 3, 2004, EAT . . . . *Digested,* 05/**1205**

Port of Tilbury (London) Ltd *v.* Hall see Port of Tilbury (London) Ltd *v.* Birch

Port of Tilbury (London) Ltd *v.* Talbot see Port of Tilbury (London) Ltd *v.* Birch

Porter *v.* Magill; *sub nom* Magill *v.* Porter; Magill *v.* Weeks; Weeks *v.* Magill; Hartley *v.* Magill; England *v.* Magill; Phillips *v.* Magill [2001] UKHL 67; [2002] 2 A.C. 357; [2002] 2 W.L.R. 37; [2002] 1 All E.R. 465; [2002] H.R.L.R. 16; [2002] H.L.R. 16; [2002] B.L.G.R. 51; (2001) 151 N.L.J. 1886; [2001] N.P.C. 184; *Times,* December 14, 2001; *Independent,* February 4, 2002 (C.S.); *Daily Telegraph,* December 20, 2001, HL; reversing [2000] 2 W.L.R. 1420; (1999) 31 H.L.R. 823; (1999) 1 L.G.L.R. 523; [1999] B.L.G.R. 375; (1999) 11 Admin. L.R. 661; (1999) 163 J.P.N. 1025; (1999) 96(21) L.S.G. 39; (1999) 143 S.J.L.B. 147; *Times,* May 6, 1999, CA (Civ Div); reversing (1998) 30 H.L.R. 997, QBD . . . . . . *Digested,* 02/**3185**:
Applied, 03/319, 03/1251, 03/1261, 04/30, 04/2652, 05/13, 05/894, 05/2153, 05/2908, 05/3279: *Considered,* 02/294, 02/451, 05/646: *Followed,* 03/5397, 04/1904, 04/4467: *Subsequent proceedings,* 02/3161

Porter *v.* Revenue and Customs Commissioners [2005] S.T.C. (S.C.D.) 803; [2005] S.T.I. 1684, Sp Comm

Portfolios of Distinction Ltd *v.* Laird [2004] EWHC 2071; [2005] B.C.C. 216; [2004] 2 B.C.L.C. 741, Ch D . . . . *Digested,* 05/**393**

Portolana Compania Naviera Ltd *v.* Vitol SA Inc (The Afrapearl) [2004] EWCA Civ 864; [2004] 1 W.L.R. 3111; [2004] 2 All E.R. (Comm) 578; [2004] 2 Lloyd's Rep. 305; [2004] 2 C.L.C. 199; (2004) 101(33) L.S.G. 37; *Times,* August 24, 2004, CA (Civ Div); reversing [2003] EWHC 1904; [2004] 1 All E.R. (Comm) 269; [2003] 2 Lloyd's Rep. 671, QBD (Comm) . . . . *Digested,* 05/**3784**

Portsmouth *v.* Alldays Franchising Ltd [2005] EWHC 1006; [2005] B.P.I.R. 1394, Ch D

Portsmouth City Council *v.* Quietlynn Ltd see Portsmouth City Council *v.* Richards

Portsmouth City Council *v.* Richards; Portsmouth City Council *v.* Quietlynn Ltd [1989] 1 C.M.L.R. 673; 87 L.G.R. 757; *Times*, November 21, 1988; *Independent*, November 25, 1988; *Daily Telegraph*, December 12, 1988, CA (Civ Div); reversing (1989) 153 L.G. Rev. 4, DC . . . . *Digested*, 90/**3704**: *Applied*, 05/2804

Portsmouth NHS Trust *v.* W [2005] EWHC 2293; [2005] 4 All E.R. 1325; (2005) 155 N.L.J. 1634; *Independent*, October 27, 2005, Fam Div

Portsmouth NHS Trust *v.* Wyatt (No.1); *sub nom* Wyatt (A Child) (Medical Treatment: Parents Consent), Re [2004] EWHC 2247; [2005] 1 F.L.R. 21; (2005) 84 B.M.L.R. 206; [2004] Fam. Law 866; (2004) 154 N.L.J. 1526; *Independent*, October 13, 2004, Fam Div . . . . *Digested*, 05/**1848**: *Applied*, 05/1677

Portsmouth NHS Trust *v.* Wyatt (No.2); *sub nom* Wyatt (A Child) (Medical Treatment: Continuation of Order), Re [2005] EWCA Civ 1181; [2005] 1 W.L.R. 3995; [2005] 3 F.C.R. 263; [2005] Lloyd's Rep. Med. 474; (2005) 86 B.M.L.R. 173, CA (Civ Div); affirming [2005] EWHC 693; [2005] 2 F.L.R. 480; [2005] Fam. Law 614, Fam Div . . . . *Digested*, 05/**1794**: *Previous proceedings*, 05/1848

Portugaia Construcoes Lda *v.* Urlaubs- und Lohnausgleichskasse der Bauwirtschaft (C70/98) see Finalarte Sociedade de Construcao Civil Lda *v.* Urlaubs- und Lohnausgleichskasse der Bauwirtschaft (C49/98)

Portugaia Construcoes Lda (C164/99), Re [2002] E.C.R. I-787; [2003] 2 C.M.L.R. 35, ECJ (5th Chamber) . . . . *Considered*, 05/1465

Portugal *v.* Commission of the European Communities (C163/99); *sub nom* Landing Fees at Portuguese Airports (C163/99), Re [2001] E.C.R. I-2613; [2002] 4 C.M.L.R. 31, ECJ (6th Chamber) . . . . *Digested*, 02/**584**: *Considered*, 05/571

Portugal *v.* Commission of the European Communities (C42/01) [2004] E.C.R. I-6079; [2004] 5 C.M.L.R. 9, ECJ . . . . *Digested*, 05/**585**

Positive Locations Ltd *v.* Macclesfield BC [2005] P.A.D. 5, Planning Inspector

Posokhov *v.* Russia (63486/00) (2004) 39 E.H.R.R. 21, ECHR . . . . *Digested*, 05/**2101**

Post Office *v.* Jones see Jones *v.* Post Office

Postal Service of a Claim Form, Re [2005] I.L.Pr. 13, OLG (Ger)

Poste Italiane SpA *v.* Commission of the European Communities (T53/01 R) [2001] E.C.R. II-1479, CFI . . . . *Followed*, 05/550

Postlethwaite, Re see Belgium *v.* Postlethwaite

Potter *v.* Potter [2004] UKPC 41; [2004] W.T.L.R. 1331; [2004] 2 P. & C.R. DG23, PC (NZ) . . . . *Digested*, 05/**4292**

Potts *v.* Hickman; *sub nom* Hickman *v.* Potts [1941] A.C. 212, HL; affirming [1940] 1 K.B. 29, CA . . . . *Applied*, 05/2343: *Considered*, 89/3148, 93/3391

Pountney *v.* Griffiths; *sub nom* R. *v.* Bracknell Justices Ex p. Griffiths [1976] A.C. 314; [1975] 3 W.L.R. 140; [1975] 2 All E.R. 881; [1975] Crim. L.R. 702; 119 S.J. 493, HL; affirming [1975] 2 W.L.R. 291; [1975] 1 All E.R. 900; 119 S.J. 114, DC . . . . . *Digested*, 75/**2128**: *Considered*, 81/175.u, 05/2826

Pour *v.* Westminster City Council see Feld *v.* Barnet LBC

Powell *v.* Revenue and Customs Commissioners [2005] V. & D.R. 1, V&DTr (London)

Powell *v.* United Kingdom (Admissibility) (45305/99) (2000) 30 E.H.R.R. CD362, ECHR . . . . *Applied*, 05/34

Powell *v.* Whitman Breed Abbot & Morgan (A Firm) [2003] EWHC 1169; [2005] P.N.L.R. 1, QBD . . . . *Digested*, 05/**2879**

Powell *v.* Wiltshire; *sub nom* Wiltshire *v.* Powell [2004] EWCA Civ 534; [2005] Q.B. 117; [2004] 3 W.L.R. 666; [2004] 3 All E.R. 235; (2004) 148 S.J.L.B. 573; *Times*, June 3, 2004, CA (Civ Div) . . . . *Digested*, 04/**3271**

PowerGen Plc, Re (C157/97 P (I)) see National Power Plc, Re (C151/97 P (I))

Powerhouse Retail Ltd *v.* Burroughs; *sub nom* Preston *v.* Wolverhampton Healthcare NHS Trust (No.3); Fletcher *v.* Midland Bank Plc (No.3); TNS, HL; affirming [2004] EWCA Civ 1281; [2005] I.C.R. 222; [2004] I.R.L.R. 979; [2004] O.P.L.R. 363; [2004] Pens. L.R. 377; (2004) 148 S.J.L.B. 1212; *Times*, October 27, 2004; *Independent*, October 14, 2004, CA (Civ Div) . . . . *Digested*, 05/**1217**: *Previous proceedings*, 04/1256

Poyiadjis, Re [2004] W.T.L.R. 1169, HC (IoM) . . . . *Digested*, 05/**4314**

PPG Industries Ohio Inc *v.* Saint-Gobain Glass France (G1/03) see PPG/Disclaimer (G1/03)

PPG/Disclaimer (G1/03); *sub nom* Genetic Systems/Disclaimer (G2/03); PPG Industries Ohio Inc *v.* Saint-Gobain Glass France (G1/03); Genetic Systems *v.* Roche Diagnostics GmbH (G2/03) [2004] E.P.O.R. 33, EPO (Enlarged Bd App) . . . . *Applied*, 05/2466, 05/2468

Practice Direction (CA (Crim Div): Criminal Proceedings: Consolidation); *sub nom*
Practice Statement (CA (Crim Div): Consolidated Criminal Practice Direction)
[2002] 1 W.L.R. 2870; [2002] 3 All E.R. 904; [2002] 2 Cr. App. R. 35, CA
(Crim Div)... *Digested*, 02/**899**:
      Cited, 04/856, 05/3678: *Considered*, 05/913: *Followed*, 03/3780:
      Superseded in part, 03/899, 04/877, 04/879, 05/914, 05/3708, 05/3710
Practice Direction (CA (Crim Div): Custodial Sentences: Explanations); *sub nom* Practice
Direction (Sup Ct: Custodial Sentences) [1998] 1 W.L.R. 278; [1998] 1 All
E.R. 733; [1998] 1 Cr. App. R. 397; (1998) 148 N.L.J. 158; (1998) 142 S.J.L.B.
52; *Times*, January 24, 1998, CA (Crim Div) .... *Digested*, 98/**1333**:
      Cited, 05/3708, 05/3710
Practice Direction (CA (Crim Div): Minimum Periods: Life Imprisonment) see Practice
Statement (Sup Ct: Crime: Life Sentences)
Practice Direction (Ch D: Hearing of Insolvency Proceedings) [2005] B.C.C. 456; [2005]
B.P.I.R. 688, Ch D .... *Digested*, 05/**2327**
Practice Direction (Ch D: Insolvency Proceedings) (No.1) [1999] B.C.C. 727; [1999]
B.P.I.R. 441, Ch D .... *Digested*, 99/**3318**:
      Cited, 01/3775, 05/2280: *Considered*, 02/2670
Practice Direction (Ch D: Insolvency Proceedings) (No.2) [2000] B.C.C. 927; [2000]
B.P.I.R. 647, Ch D .... *Digested*, 01/**3775**:
      Applied, 05/10, 05/2327, 05/2337
Practice Direction (Criminal Proceedings: Consolidation (Amendment) see Practice
Direction (Sup Ct: Crime: Mandatory Life Sentences) (No.1)
Practice Direction (Crown Ct: Classification and Allocation of Business); *sub nom*
Consolidated Criminal Practice Direction (Amendment No.12) (Classification
and Allocation of Business) [2005] 1 W.L.R. 2215; [2005] 2 Cr. App. R. 33;
Times, June 7, 2005, Sup Ct .... *Digested*, 05/**914**
Practice Direction (Crown Ct: Guidance to Jurors); *sub nom* Consolidated Criminal
Practice Direction (Amendment No.4) (Guidance to Jurors) [2004] 1 W.L.R.
665; [2004] 2 Cr. App. R. 1; *Times*, February 27, 2004, CA (Crim Div) .... *Digested*, 04/**856**:
      Considered, 05/849
Practice Direction (Crown Ct: Jury Service) see Practice Direction (Sup Ct: Jury Service:
Excusal)
Practice Direction (EAT: Appeal Procedure) [2003] I.C.R. 122; [2003] I.R.L.R. 65, EAT   *Digested*, 03/**1291**:
      Cited, 05/1242: *Superseded*, 05/1285
Practice Direction (EAT: Appeal Procedure) [2005] I.C.R. 637; [2005] I.R.L.R. 94, EAT   *Digested*, 05/**1285**:
      Followed, 05/1284
Practice Direction (EAT: Procedure: Lodging Documents with Notice to Appeal) [2005]
I.C.R. 660, EAT .... *Digested*, 05/**1284**:
      Cited, 05/1244
Practice Direction (ECJ: Direct Actions and Appeals) [2005] 1 C.M.L.R. 7, ECJ ...... *Digested*, 05/**1442**
Practice Direction (Fam Div: Applications for Reporting Restriction Orders) [2005] 2 F.L.R.
120, Fam Div.. *Digested*, 05/**1683**
Practice Direction (Fam Div: Family Procedure: Adoptions), *Times*, November 21, 2005,
Fam Div
Practice Direction (Fam Div: Gender Recognition Act 2004: Procedure) [2005] 2 F.L.R.
122, Fam Div.. *Digested*, 05/**1684**
Practice Direction (IAT: Appeal and Immigration Tribunal); *sub nom* Practice Direction
(IAT: Asylum and Immigration Tribunal) [2005] Imm. A.R. 1; [2005] I.N.L.R. 357,
IAT... *Digested*, 05/**2225**
Practice Direction (IAT: Asylum and Immigration Tribunal) see Practice Direction (IAT:
Appeal and Immigration Tribunal)
Practice Direction (Lands Tr: Procedure) [2005] R.V.R. 9, Lands Tr .... *Digested*, 05/**3417**
Practice Direction (QBD: Judgment: Foreign Currency) (No.1) [1976] 1 W.L.R. 83; [1976] 1
All E.R. 669; [1976] 1 Lloyd's Rep. 282, QBD .... *Digested*, 76/**2177**:
      Considered, 05/330: *Explained*, 77/194
Practice Direction (Sup Ct: Amendments No.9, 10 and 11 to Consolidated Criminal Practice
Direction) TNS, Sup Ct .... *Digested*, 05/**913**
Practice Direction (Sup Ct: Civil Litigation: Procedure); *sub nom* Practice Directions
(Civil Procedure Rules) [1999] 1 W.L.R. 1124; [1999] 3 All E.R. 380; *Times*, April
26, 1999, Sup Ct .... *Digested*, 99/**513**:
      Applied, 99/512, 99/1410, 00/349, 00/424, 03/468, 04/250, 05/477:
      Cited, 99/408, 00/239, 00/240, 00/314, 00/340, 00/358, 00/368, 00/369,
      00/370, 00/393, 00/400, 00/419, 00/449, 00/450, 00/470, 00/492, 00/545,
      00/564, 00/2551, 00/3915, 01/423, 01/441, 01/515, 01/521, 01/524, 01/529,
      01/535, 01/558, 01/563, 01/564, 01/572, 01/620, 01/624, 01/653, 01/662,
      01/667, 01/672, 01/4890, 02/10, 02/218, 02/302, 02/307, 02/316, 02/330,
      02/334, 02/336, 02/340, 02/368, 02/386, 02/390, 02/431, 02/432,
      02/486, 02/488, 02/501, 02/642, 02/2768, 02/3115, 03/317, 03/323,
      03/334, 03/336, 03/340, 03/344, 03/467, 03/473, 03/848, 04/420,
      04/423, 04/603, 04/939, 04/2356, 04/3671, 05/303, 05/332, 05/353,
      05/376, 05/377, 05/2860: *Considered*, 99/561, 99/640, 00/324, 01/426,
      01/664, 02/3638: *Explained*, 99/505, 99/1419: *Referred to*, 99/343, 99/357,
      00/392, 00/567, 02/210, 02/361: *Superseded in part*, 02/475

Practice Direction (Sup Ct: Crime: Case Management) see Practice Direction (Sup Ct: Criminal Proceedings: Case Management)

Practice Direction (Sup Ct: Crime: Mandatory Life Sentences) (No.1); *sub nom* Practice Direction (Criminal Proceedings: Consolidation (Amendment); Consolidated Criminal Practice Direction (Amendment No.6) (Mandatory Life Sentences) [2004] 1 W.L.R. 1874; [2004] 2 Cr. App. R. 24; *Times*, May 20, 2004, Sup Ct . . *Digested*, 05/**3710**:
Cited, 04/3401: *Superseded*, 05/3709

Practice Direction (Sup Ct: Crime: Mandatory Life Sentences) (No.2) [2004] 1 W.L.R. 2551; [2005] 1 Cr. App. R. 8; *Times*, August 2, 2004, Sup Ct. . . . . *Digested*, 05/**3709**:
Cited, 05/3679

Practice Direction (Sup Ct: Criminal Proceedings: Case Management); *sub nom* Amendment No.11 to the Consolidated Criminal Practice Direction (Case Management); Practice Direction (Sup Ct: Crime: Case Management) [2005] 1 W.L.R. 1491; [2005] 3 All E.R. 91; [2005] 2 Cr. App. R. 18; *Times*, March 28, 2005, Sup Ct

Practice Direction (Sup Ct: Criminal Proceedings: Forms); *sub nom* Amendment No.10 to the Consolidated Criminal Practice Direction (Forms for use in Criminal Proceedings); Practice Direction (Sup Ct: Forms for use in Criminal Proceedings) [2005] 1 W.L.R. 1479; [2005] 2 All E.R. 916; [2005] 2 Cr. App. R. 17; *Times*, March 28, 2005, Sup Ct

Practice Direction (Sup Ct: Custodial Sentences) see Practice Direction (CA (Crim Div): Custodial Sentences: Explanations)

Practice Direction (Sup Ct: Custodial Sentences: Explanations); *sub nom* Consolidated Criminal Practice Direction (Amendment No.7) (Explanations for the Imposition of Custodial Sentences) [2004] 1 W.L.R. 1878; [2004] 2 Cr. App. R. 25, Sup Ct. . . . . *Digested*, 05/**3708**

Practice Direction (Sup Ct: Forms for use in Criminal Proceedings) see Practice Direction (Sup Ct: Criminal Proceedings: Forms)

Practice Direction (Sup Ct: Jury Service: Excusal); *sub nom* Practice Direction (Crown Ct: Jury Service); Amendment No.9 to the Consolidated Criminal Practice Direction (Jury Service) [2005] 1 W.L.R. 1361; [2005] 3 All E.R. 89; [2005] 2 Cr. App. R. 16; *Times*, March 24, 2005, Sup Ct

Practice Directions (Civil Procedure Rules) see Practice Direction (Sup Ct: Civil Litigation: Procedure)

Practice Note (Official Solicitor: Deputy Director of Legal Services: CAFCASS: Applications for Reporting Restriction Orders) [2005] 2 F.L.R. 111, Fam Div. . . . *Digested*, 05/**1685**

Practice Statement (CA (Crim Div): Consolidated Criminal Practice Direction) see Practice Direction (CA (Crim Div): Criminal Proceedings: Consolidation)

Practice Statement (CA (Crim Div): Juveniles: Murder Tariff) [2000] 1 W.L.R. 1655; [2000] 4 All E.R. 831; [2000] 2 Cr. App. R. 457; *Times*, August 9, 2000, CA (Crim Div) . *Digested*, 00/**1095**:
Cited, 00/1331, 02/4004, 03/3774: *Considered*, 05/3775:
Superseded, 02/901

Practice Statement (CA (Crim Div): Life Sentences) see Practice Statement (Sup Ct: Crime: Life Sentences)

Practice Statement (Ch D: Fixing and Approval of Remuneration of Appointees) [2004] B.C.C. 912; [2004] B.P.I.R. 953, Ch D . . . . *Digested*, 05/**2328**

Practice Statement (Ch D: Schemes of Arrangements with Creditors) [2002] 1 W.L.R. 1345; [2002] 3 All E.R. 96; [2002] B.C.C. 355; (2002) 146 S.J.L.B. 99, Ch D . *Digested*, 02/**2705**:
Followed, 05/2333

Practice Statement (QBD (TCC): Arrangements) see Practice Statement (QBD (TCC): Case Management: Arrangements)

Practice Statement (QBD (TCC): Case Management: Arrangements); *sub nom* Practice Statement (QBD (TCC): Arrangements) [2005] 3 All E.R. 289; 100 Con. L.R. 209; *Times*, June 14, 2005, QBD (TCC)

Practice Statement (Sup Ct: Crime: Life Sentences); *sub nom* Practice Statement (CA (Crim Div): Life Sentences); Practice Direction (CA (Crim Div): Minimum Periods: Life Imprisonment) [2002] 1 W.L.R. 1789; [2002] 3 All E.R. 412; [2002] 2 Cr. App. R. 18; [2003] 1 Cr. App. R. (S.) 46; (2002) 146 S.J.L.B. 132; *Times*, June 4, 2002, Sup Ct . . . . *Digested*, 02/**901**:
Applied, 05/3679: *Cited*, 03/3757, 04/3401, 04/3472, 04/3473, 04/3474, 05/3677, 05/3683

Practice Statement (Sup Ct: Judgments) (No.1) [1998] 1 W.L.R. 825; [1998] 2 All E.R. 667; [1998] 2 Cr. App. R. 144; [1998] 1 F.L.R. 1102; [1998] 2 F.C.R. 1; (1998) 148 N.L.J. 631; *Times*, April 23, 1998, Sup Ct . . . . *Digested*, 98/**71**:
Cited, 00/504, 05/426: *Superseded in part*, 99/73

Praktiker Bau- und Heimwerkermarkte AG v. Deutsches Patent- und Markenamt (C418/02) [2005] E.T.M.R. 88, ECJ (2nd Chamber)

Pratt v. Bull see Hollins v. Russell

Pratt v. DPP [2001] EWHC Admin 483; (2001) 165 J.P. 800; [2002] A.C.D. 2; (2001) 165 J.P.N. 750; *Times*, August 22, 2001, DC . . . . *Digested*, 01/**1048**:
Considered, 02/797, 05/885

Pratt v. Smith (Quantum) [2005] 2 Q.R. 5; [2004] 3 Q.R. 6, QBD [*Ex rel.* Andrew Granville Stafford, Barrister, 4 King's Bench Walk, Temple, London] . . . . *Digested*, 04/**2855**

Pratt Contractors Ltd *v.* Transit New Zealand [2003] UKPC 83; [2004] B.L.R. 143; 100
     Con. L.R. 29, PC (NZ) . . . .   *Digested,* 04/**3164**
Precis (521) Plc *v.* William M Mercer Ltd [2005] EWCA Civ 114; [2005] P.N.L.R. 28;
     [2005] O.P.L.R. 89; (2005) 102(17) L.S.G. 33; *Times,* February 24, 2005, CA
     (Civ Div); affirming [2004] EWHC 838, Ch D . . . .   *Digested,* 05/**2868**
Preferred Mortgages Ltd *v.* Countrywide Surveyors Ltd [2005] EWHC 2820; [2005]
     31 E.G.C.S. 81, Ch D
Preiss *v.* General Dental Council; *sub nom* Preiss *v.* General Medical Council [2001]
     UKPC 36; [2001] 1 W.L.R. 1926; [2001] I.R.L.R. 696; [2001] H.R.L.R. 56;
     [2001] Lloyd's Rep. Med. 491; (2001) 98(33) L.S.G. 31; *Times,* August 14, 2001,
     PC (UK) . . . .   *Digested,* 01/**2891**:
              Applied, 03/1730, 05/1802: *Cited,* 02/1837: *Distinguished,* 02/1838
Preiss *v.* General Medical Council see Preiss *v.* General Dental Council
Prengate Properties Ltd *v.* Secretary of State for the Environment 71 L.G.R. 373; (1973)
     25 P. & C.R. 311, DC . . . .   *Digested,* 73/**3234**:
                                                     Considered, 05/3271
Prenn *v.* Simmonds [1971] 1 W.L.R. 1381; [1971] 3 All E.R. 237; 115 S.J. 654, HL . . . . . .   *Digested,* 71/**1711**:
            Applied, 92/311, 01/3835, 03/3557, 04/273, 04/670, 05/288:
                     Considered, 86/9, 05/1213: *Referred to,* 94/3430
Presbyterian Church Fund of New Zealand *v.* Inland Revenue Commissioner [1994] 3
     N.Z.L.R. 363, HC (NZ) . . . .   *Considered,* 05/282
Prescott (otherwise Fellowes) *v.* Fellowes [1958] P. 260; [1958] 3 W.L.R. 288; [1958]
     3 All E.R. 55; 102 S.J. 581, CA; reversing [1958] 2 W.L.R. 679; [1958] 1 All
     E.R. 824; 102 S.J. 271, PDAD . . . .   *Digested,* 58/**1094**:
                             Distinguished, 59/1056: *Followed,* 05/1682
Preservatrice Fonciere Assurances *v.* Caisse Regionale de Credit Agricole Mutuel
     [2005] E.C.C. 17, Cass (F)
President of India *v.* La Pintada Compania Navigacion SA (The La Pintada) [1985]
     A.C. 104; [1984] 3 W.L.R. 10; [1984] 2 All E.R. 773; [1984] 2 Lloyd's Rep. 9;
     [1984] C.I.L.L. 110; (1984) 81 L.S.G. 1999; (1984) 128 S.J. 414, HL; reversing
     [1983] 1 Lloyd's Rep. 37; [1982] Com. L.R. 250; *Times,* November 1, 1982, QBD
     (Comm) . . . .   *Digested,* 84/**123**:
            Applied, 84/120, 85/3160: *Cited,* 00/1453: *Considered,* 84/2346, 86/2760,
                           87/2429, 97/3839, 98/1433, 05/3984: *Followed,* 98/231
President of India *v.* Lips Maritime Corp (The Lips); *sub nom* Lips Maritime Corp *v.*
     President of India [1988] A.C. 395; [1987] 3 W.L.R. 572; [1987] 3 All E.R. 110;
     [1987] 2 Lloyd's Rep. 311; [1987] 2 F.T.L.R. 477; [1987] Fin. L.R. 313; (1987)
     84 L.S.G. 2765; (1987) 137 N.L.J. 734; (1987) 131 S.J. 1085, HL; reversing
     [1987] 2 W.L.R. 906; [1987] 1 All E.R. 957; [1987] 1 Lloyd's Rep. 131; [1987] 1
     F.T.L.R. 50; [1987] Fin. L.R. 91; (1987) 84 L.S.G. 1333; (1987) 131 S.J. 422;
     Financial Times, November 4, 1986, CA (Civ Div); reversing [1985] 2 Lloyd's
     Rep. 180; (1984) 134 N.L.J. 969, QBD (Comm) . . . .   *Digested,* 87/**3399**:
                          Applied, 92/3972, 93/3619: *Followed,* 05/2358
Presidential Party of Mordovia *v.* Russia (65659/01) (2005) 41 E.H.R.R. 34, ECHR
Preston *v.* Wolverhampton Healthcare NHS Trust (No.2); Fletcher *v.* Midland Bank Plc
     (No.2) [2001] UKHL 5; [2001] 2 A.C. 455; [2001] 2 W.L.R. 448; [2001] 3 All
     E.R. 947; [2001] 1 C.M.L.R. 46; [2001] I.C.R. 217; [2001] I.R.L.R. 237; [2001]
     Emp. L.R. 256; [2001] O.P.L.R. 1; [2001] Pens. L.R. 39; (2001) 98(10) L.S.G.
     41; (2001) 145 S.J.L.B. 55; *Times,* February 9, 2001, HL . . . .   *Digested,* 01/**2279**:
                       Applied, 05/1263: *Previous proceedings,* 00/2162:
                                  Subsequent proceedings, 03/3095
Preston *v.* Wolverhampton Healthcare NHS Trust (No.3) see Powerhouse Retail Ltd *v.*
     Burroughs
Preston *v.* Wolverhampton Healthcare NHS Trust (No.3); Fletcher *v.* Midland Bank Plc
     (No.3) [2004] I.C.R. 993; [2004] I.R.L.R. 96; [2004] O.P.L.R. 33; [2004]
     Pens. L.R. 97, EAT; reversing in part [2002] O.P.L.R. 323; [2002] Pens. L.R.
     389, ET . . . .   *Digested,* 04/**1256**:
                          Applied, 05/1263: *Overruled in part,* 05/1217
Preston Meats Ltd *v.* Hammond (Inspector of Taxes) [2005] S.T.C. (S.C.D.) 90; [2004]
     S.T.I. 2340, Sp Comm . . . .   *Digested,* 05/**3983**
Price *v.* Caerphilly CBC [2005] 1 E.G.L.R. 157; [2005] R.V.R. 103, Lands Tr
Price *v.* Leeds City Council see Kay *v.* Lambeth LBC
Price *v.* Leeds City Council see Leeds City Council *v.* Price
Price *v.* Thomson (Unreported, June 7, 2004), CC (Southampton) [*Ex rel.* James
     Counsell, Barrister, Outer Temple Chambers, Outer Temple, 222 Strand, London]   *Digested,* 05/**3154**
Priestley *v.* Demaine (Unreported, March 4, 2004), CC (Sheffield) [*Ex rel.* Andrew
     Hogan, Barrister, 24, The Ropewalk, Nottingham] . . . .   *Digested,* 05/**3103**
Prifti *v.* Musini Sociedad Anonima de Seguros y Reaseguros [2003] EWHC 2796;
     [2004] I.L.Pr. 517; [2004] Lloyd's Rep. I.R. 528, QBD (Admin) . . . .   *Digested,* 05/**614**
Primback Ltd *v.* Customs and Excise Commissioners (C34/99) see Customs and
     Excise Commissioners *v.* Primback Ltd (C34/99)
Primetrade AG *v.* Ythan Ltd [2005] EWHC 2399; [2005] 2 C.L.C. 911, QBD (Comm)
Primus Telecommunications Inc *v.* MCI Worldcom International Inc see MCI WorldCom
     International Inc *v.* Primus Telecommunications Inc

Prince Albert v. Strange (1849) 1 Mac. & G. 25; (1849) 18 L.J. Ch. 120 . . . .   *Applied,* 64/1353,
    65/1483, 75/2714: *Considered,* 05/2812: *Distinguished,* 68/3133
Prison Service v. Beart (No.2) [2005] EWCA Civ 467; [2005] I.C.R. 1206; [2005]
    I.R.L.R. 568, CA (Civ Div); affirming [2005] I.R.L.R. 171, EAT . . . .   *Digested,* 05/**1319**
Pritchard Englefield (A Firm) v. Steinberg [2004] EWHC 1908; [2005] 1 P. & C.R. DG2,
    Ch D
Pritchard Englefield (A Firm) v. Steinberg [2005] EWCA Civ 288; (2005) 149 S.J.L.B.
    300, CA (Civ Div)
Pro Sieben Media AG v. Carlton UK Television Ltd [1999] 1 W.L.R. 605; [2000]
    E.C.D.R. 110; [1999] E.M.L.R. 109; [1999] I.T.C.L.R. 332; [1999] F.S.R. 610;
    (1999) 22(3) I.P.D. 22029; (1999) 96(5) L.S.G. 35; (1999) 143 S.J.L.B. 37;
    Times, January 7, 1999; *Independent,* January 22, 1999, CA (Civ Div); reversing
    [1998] E.C.C. 112; [1997] E.M.L.R. 509; [1998] F.S.R. 43; (1997) 20(10) I.P.D.
    20101; *Times,* September 24, 1997, Ch D . . . .   *Digested,* 99/**3438**:
    Applied, 01/3851, 05/2420
Probert v. Dudley MBC see R. v. Dudley Magistrates Court Ex p. Hollis
Proceedings brought by Lindman, Re (C42/02); *sub nom* Lindman v.
    Skatterattelsnamnden (C42/02) [2005] S.T.C. 873; [2004] 1 C.M.L.R. 38;
    [2003] S.T.I. 2120, ECJ (5th Chamber) . . . .   *Digested,* 04/**3773**
Proceedings brought by Manninen (C319/02); *sub nom* Manninen v. Finland (C319/02);
    Manninen (C319/02), Re [2005] Ch. 236; [2005] 2 W.L.R. 670; [2005] All
    E.R. (EC) 465; [2004] S.T.C. 1444; [2004] E.C.R. I-7477; [2004] 3 C.M.L.R.
    40; [2005] C.E.C. 507; 7 I.T.L. Rep. 119; [2004] S.T.I. 2068, ECJ . . . .   *Digested,* 05/**4028**
Procter & Gamble Co v. Office for Harmonisation in the Internal Market (Trade Marks
    and Designs) (OHIM) (T163/98) see Procter & Gamble Co v. Office for
    Harmonisation in the Internal Market (Trade Marks and Designs) (OHIM) (C383/
    99 P)
Procter & Gamble Co v. Office for Harmonisation in the Internal Market (Trade Marks
    and Designs) (OHIM) (C383/99 P); *sub nom* Procter & Gamble Co v. Office for
    Harmonisation in the Internal Market (Trade Marks and Designs) (OHIM)
    (T163/98) [2002] Ch. 82; [2002] 2 W.L.R. 485; [2002] All E.R. (EC) 29;
    [2001] E.C.R. I-6251; [2001] C.E.C. 325; [2002] E.T.M.R. 3; [2002] R.P.C. 17;
    (2001) 24(12) I.P.D. 24076; *Times,* October 3, 2001, ECJ; reversing [2000] 1
    W.L.R. 91; [1999] All E.R. (EC) 648; [1999] E.C.R. II-2383; [1999] 2 C.M.L.R.
    1442; [1999] C.E.C. 329; [1999] E.T.M.R. 767; *Times,* July 29, 1999, CFI (2nd
    Chamber); reversing in part [1999] E.T.M.R. 240, OHIM (1st Bd App) . . . .   *Digested,* 01/**4003**:
    Applied, 01/4004, 01/4016, 03/2633: *Considered,* 03/2626, 03/2631,
    03/2651, 05/2530: *Distinguished,* 04/2395: *Followed,* 00/3715, 03/2610:
    Not applied, 05/2545: *Referred to,* 00/3717, 01/3994
Procureur du Roi v. Dassonville (8/74); *sub nom* Dassonville v. Commission of the
    European Communities (8/74) [1974] E.C.R. 837; [1974] 2 C.M.L.R. 436;
    [1975] F.S.R. 191, ECJ . . . .   *Digested,* 75/**1285**:
    Applied, 98/728, 05/1450: *Considered,* 94/4885: *Followed,* 80/1160,
    80/1193.a, 95/9, 96/4865, 01/2489, 01/2508
Product Liability Directive, Re (C300/95) see Commission of the European Communities
    v. United Kingdom (C300/95)
Profile Software Ltd v. Becogent Ltd [2005] E.C.D.R. 26, OH
Prohibition of Marketing of Enriched Foods (C192/01), Re see Commission of the European
    Communities v. Denmark (C192/01)
Project Blue Sky Inc v. Australian Broadcasting Authority 194 C.L.R. 355, HC (Aus) . . .   *Considered,* 05/842
Property Co v. Inspector of Taxes [2005] S.T.C. (S.C.D.) 59; [2004] S.T.I. 2300, Sp
    Comm . . . .   *Digested,* 05/**3982**
Protech Projects Construction (Pty) Ltd v. Al-Kharafi & Sons; Mohammed Abdulmohsin
    Al-Kharafi & Sons WLL v. Big Dig Construction (Proprietary) Ltd (In
    Liquidation) [2005] EWHC 2165; [2005] 2 Lloyd's Rep. 779, QBD (Comm)
Proteome Inc v. Office for Harmonisation in the Internal Market (Trade Marks and
    Designs) (OHIM) (T387/03) [2005] Info. T.L.R. 283; [2005] E.T.M.R. CN4, CFI
    (3rd Chamber)
Protocol for the Control and Management of Heavy Fraud and Other Complex Criminal
    Cases [2005] 2 All E.R. 429, CA (Crim Div)
Provimi Ltd v. Aventis Animal Nutrition SA; Trouw (UK) Ltd v. Rhodia Ltd; Provimi Ltd
    v. Roche Products Ltd; Trouw (UK) Ltd v. Roche Products Ltd [2003] EWHC
    961; [2003] 2 All E.R. (Comm) 683; [2003] U.K.C.L.R. 493; [2003] E.C.C. 29;
    [2003] Eu. L.R. 517, QBD (Comm) . . . .   *Digested,* 03/**625**:
    Considered, 05/626
Provimi Ltd v. Roche Products Ltd see Provimi Ltd v. Aventis Animal Nutrition SA
Prudential Assurance Co Ltd v. Chatterley-Whitfield Collieries Ltd; *sub nom* Chatterley-
    Whitfield Collieries Ltd, Re [1949] A.C. 512; [1949] 1 All E.R. 1094, HL;
    affirming [1948] 2 All E.R. 593; [1948] W.N. 367, CA; reversing [1948] 1 All
    E.R. 911, Chancery Ct of Lancaster . . . .   *Digested,* 47-51/**1250**:
    Applied, 47-51/1249, 68/401, 05/532: *Distinguished,* 54/438
Pryke v. Gibbs Hartley Cooper Ltd; Excess Insurance Co Ltd v. Gibbs Hartley Cooper
    Ltd [1991] 1 Lloyd's Rep. 602, QBD (Comm) . . . .   *Digested,* 92/**2594**:
    Applied, 96/3588, 05/2355

Pub Estate Co Ltd *v.* Harding see Harding *v.* Pub Estate Co Ltd
Public Employees (No.1) (149/79), Re see Commission of the European Communities *v.*
    Belgium (No.1) (149/79)
Public Trustee *v.* Bennett (2004-05) 7 I.T.E.L.R. 392, Sup Ct (NSW) . . . .   *Digested*, 05/**3972**
Publivia SAE *v.* Departmento de Sanidad y Seguridad Social de la Generalitat de
    Cataluna (C176/90) see Aragonesa de Publicidad Exterior SA *v.* Departmento de
    Sanidad y Seguridad Social de la Generalitat de Cataluna (C1/90)
Puglia *v.* C James & Sons [1996] I.C.R. 301; [1996] I.R.L.R. 70, EAT . . . .   *Digested*, 96/**2654**:
                                   Distinguished, 96/2653: *Followed*, 05/1322
Puhlhofer *v.* Hillingdon LBC see R. *v.* Hillingdon LBC Ex p. Puhlhofer
Purple Parking *v.* Hillingdon LBC [2005] P.A.D. 85, Planning Inspector
Pusa *v.* Osuuspankkien Keskinainen Vakuutusyhtio (C224/02) [2004] All E.R. (EC)
    797; [2004] S.T.C. 1066; [2004] E.C.R. I-5763; [2004] 2 C.M.L.R. 23; [2004]
    S.T.I. 1167, ECJ (5th Chamber) . . . .   *Digested*, 05/**3002**
Puttock *v.* Bexley LBC [2004] R.V.R. 216, Lands Tr. . . . .   *Digested*, 05/**3248**
PVC Cartel II (T305/94), Re see Limburgse Vinyl Maatschappij NV (LVM) *v.* Commission
    of the European Communities (C238/99 P)
PW & Co *v.* Milton Gate Investments Ltd [2003] EWHC 1994; [2004] Ch. 142; [2004]
    2 W.L.R. 443; [2004] L. & T.R. 8; [2004] 3 E.G.L.R. 103; (2003) 100(38)
    L.S.G. 36; (2003) 153 N.L.J. 1347, Ch D . . . .   *Digested*, 04/**2539**:
                                         Distinguished, 05/3384
Pyrene Co Ltd *v.* Scindia Steam Navigation Co Ltd [1954] 2 Q.B. 402; [1954] 2
    W.L.R. 1005; [1954] 2 All E.R. 158; [1954] 1 Lloyd's Rep. 321; 98 S.J. 354,
    QBD . . . .   *Digested*, 54/**3197**:
               Applied, 57/3300, 59/3031, 79/2434, 81/215, 82/389, 93/3573:
                Considered, 59/3029, 74/3545, 80/2667, 81/2538, 05/3787:
                                          Followed, 84/3160
Pyx Granite Co Ltd *v.* Ministry of Housing and Local Government [1960] A.C. 260;
    [1959] 3 W.L.R. 346; [1959] 3 All E.R. 1; 123 J.P. 429; 58 L.G.R. 1; (1959) 10 P.
    & C.R. 319; 103 S.J. 633, HL; reversing [1958] 1 Q.B. 554; [1958] 2 W.L.R.
    371; [1958] 1 All E.R. 625; 122 J.P. 182; 56 L.G.R. 171; (1958) 9 P. & C.R. 204;
    102 S.J. 175, CA . . . .   *Digested*, 59/**3260**:
               Applied, 59/3229, 60/3110, 63/2259, 63/3426, 64/3556, 64/3600,
               64/3601, 69/1168, 70/711, 70/836, 71/5152, 71/6934, 72/3358, 73/2055,
               76/2727, 77/2973, 77/2976, 78/2889, 79/2634, 80/308, 82/2396, 83/2108,
               84/10, 85/9, 98/281: *Considered*, 63/3429, 63/8429, 68/3837, 69/2896,
               70/1757, 80/2667, 82/2489, 87/3097, 90/120, 90/2829, 90/3908, 91/119,
                     05/2685: *Distinguished*, 64/2433, 70/2778, 82/1264, 82/2928:
                                         Not applied, 75/2865

Q *v.* Q [2005] EWHC 402; [2005] 2 F.L.R. 640; [2005] Fam. Law 539, Fam Div . . . .   *Digested*, 05/**1662**
Qaisar *v.* Customs and Excise Commissioners [2004] EWHC 506; [2005] S.T.C. 119;
    [2005] B.T.C. 5311; [2005] B.V.C. 342; [2004] S.T.I. 556, Ch D; affirming
    [2003] S.T.I. 1430, V&DTr . . . .   *Digested*, 05/**4416**
Qazi *v.* Harrow LBC; *sub nom* Harrow LBC *v.* Quazi; Harrow LBC *v.* Qazi [2003]
    UKHL 43; [2004] 1 A.C. 983; [2003] 3 W.L.R. 792; [2003] 4 All E.R. 461;
    [2003] 2 F.L.R. 973; [2003] 3 F.C.R. 43; [2003] H.R.L.R. 40; [2003]
    U.K.H.R.R. 974; [2003] H.L.R. 75; [2004] 1 P. & C.R. 19; [2004] L. & T.R. 9;
    [2003] 3 E.G.L.R. 109; [2003] Fam. Law 875; (2003) 100(38) L.S.G. 34;
    (2003) 147 S.J.L.B. 937; [2003] N.P.C. 101; *Times*, August 1, 2003;
    Independent, October 3, 2003, HL; reversing [2001] EWCA Civ 1834; [2002]
    U.K.H.R.R. 316; [2002] H.L.R. 14; [2002] L. & T.R. 23; *Independent*, January
    14, 2002 (C.S), CA (Civ Div) . . . .   *Digested*, 03/**2786**:
                       Applied, 02/3060, 04/2519, 04/3042, 05/190: *Followed*, 05/3424
QDQ Media SA *v.* Omedas Lecha (C235/03) [2005] E.C.R. I-1937; [2005] 1 C.M.L.R.
    55, ECJ (6th Chamber) . . . .   *Digested*, 05/**358**
QR Sciences Ltd *v.* BTG International Ltd; *sub nom* QRS Sciences Ltd *v.* BTG
    International Ltd [2005] EWHC 670; [2005] F.S.R. 43, Ch D . . . .   *Digested*, 05/**696**
QRS Sciences Ltd *v.* BTG International Ltd see QR Sciences Ltd *v.* BTG International
    Ltd
Qua *v.* John Ford Morrison Solicitors [2003] I.C.R. 482; [2003] I.R.L.R. 184; (2003)
    153 N.L.J. 95; *Times*, February 6, 2003; *Independent*, February 24, 2003 (C.S),
    EAT . . . .   *Digested*, 03/**1351**:
                                       Applied, 04/1313, 05/1308
Qualifying Insurers Subscribing to the ARP *v.* Ross & Co [2004] EWHC 1181; [2004]
    U.K.C.L.R. 1483; [2004] Eu. L.R. 879, Ch D . . . .   *Digested*, 05/**2733**
Quantrill *v.* South Tyneside Health Care NHS Trust (Unreported, September 27, 2004),
    CC (Newcastle) [*Ex rel.* Thompsons, Solicitors, St. Nicholas Building, St.
    Nicholas Street, Newcastle] . . . .   *Digested*, 05/**3147**
Quantum Learning Curve *v.* Revenue and Customs Commissioners [2005] S.T.I. 2033,
    V&DTr (London)
Quarcoopome *v.* Sock Shop Holdings Ltd [1995] I.R.L.R. 353, EAT . . . .   *Digested*, 95/**2025**:
                                 Considered, 00/2207: *Doubted*, 05/1278

Quarter Master UK Ltd (In Liquidation) *v.* Pyke [2004] EWHC 1815; [2005] 1 B.C.L.C.
　245, Ch D . . . . 　*Digested,* 05/**523**
Queens Moat Houses Plc *v.* Capita IRG Trustees Ltd [2004] EWHC 868; [2005] B.C.C.
　347; [2005] 2 B.C.L.C. 199; [2004] N.P.C. 67, Ch D . . . . 　*Digested,* 05/**264**
Queens Moat Houses Plc (No.2), Re see Secretary of State for Trade and Industry *v.*
　Bairstow (No.2)
Questore di Verona *v.* Zenatti (C67/98) [1999] E.C.R. I-7289; [2000] 1 C.M.L.R. 201,
　ECJ [1999] E.C.R. I-7289, AGO. . . . . 　*Digested,* 00/**2397**:
　　　　　　　　　　　　　　　　　　　　Considered, 05/1467: *Followed,* 02/1581
Quicksons (South & West) Ltd *v.* Katz (No.1); *sub nom* Buildlead Ltd (In Creditors
　Voluntary Liquidation) (No.1), Re [2003] EWHC 1981; [2003] 4 All E.R. 864;
　[2005] B.C.C. 133; [2004] 1 B.C.L.C. 83; (2003) 153 N.L.J. 1309, Ch D
　(Companies Ct) . . . . 　*Digested,* 03/**2406**
Quicksons (South & West) Ltd *v.* Katz (No.2); *sub nom* Buildlead Ltd (In Creditors
　Voluntary Liquidation) (No.2), Re [2004] EWHC 2443; [2005] B.C.C. 138;
　[2004] B.P.I.R. 1139, Ch D (Companies Ct) . . . . 　*Digested,* 05/**2324**
Quiksilver Pty Ltd *v.* Charles Robertson (Developments) Ltd (t/a Trago Mills) [2004]
　EWHC 2010; [2005] 1 C.M.L.R. 36; [2005] F.S.R. 8; (2004) 27(9) I.P.D.
　27093, Ch D . . . . 　*Digested,* 05/**2572**
Quinn *v.* George Clark & Nem Ltd see Grieves *v.* FT Everard & Sons Ltd
Quintain Estates Development Plc *v.* Customs and Excise Commissioners [2005] B.V.C.
　2298; [2005] V. & D.R. 123, V&DTr (London)
Quintavalle *v.* Human Fertilisation and Embryology Authority see R. (on the application
　of Quintavalle) *v.* Human Fertilisation and Embryology Authority
Quistclose Investments Ltd *v.* Rolls Razor Ltd (In Voluntary Liquidation) see Barclays
　Bank Ltd *v.* Quistclose Investments Ltd
Quorn Hunt *v.* Marlow Foods Ltd [2005] E.T.M.R. 11, TMR. . . . . 　*Digested,* 05/**2561**
Quorum A/S *v.* Schramm (Damage) [2002] 2 All E.R. (Comm) 147; [2002] 1 Lloyd's
　Rep. 249; [2002] C.L.C. 77; [2002] Lloyd's Rep. I.R. 292, QBD (Comm) . . . . . 　*Digested,* 02/**2741**:
　　　　　　　　　　　　　　　　　　　　　　　　　　　　　Followed, 05/2386

R *v.* Crown Prosecution Service see Hughes *v.* Customs and Excise Commissioners
R *v.* DPP see Hughes *v.* Customs and Excise Commissioners
R *v.* Holden (Inspector of Taxes) see Wood *v.* Holden (Inspector of Taxes)
R *v.* Leeds Magistrates Court; *sub nom* R. (on the application of R) *v.* Leeds
　Magistrates Court [2005] EWHC 1479; [2005] E.L.R. 589, QBD (Admin)
R *v.* R (Company Valuation and Liquidity) see R *v.* R (Financial Relief: Company
　Valuation)
R *v.* R (Divorce: Hemain Injunction) [2003] EWHC 2113; [2005] 1 F.L.R. 386; [2005]
　Fam. Law 17, Fam Div . . . . 　*Digested,* 05/**1623**
R *v.* R (Divorce: Jurisdiction: Domicile) [2005] Fam. Law 941, Fam Div
R *v.* R (Financial Relief: Company Valuation); *sub nom* R *v.* R (Company Valuation and
　Liquidity) [2005] 2 F.L.R. 365; [2005] Fam. Law 608, Fam Div . . . . 　*Digested,* 05/**1650**
R *v.* R (Leave to Remove); *sub nom* R (Emma) *v.* R (Edward) [2004] EWHC 2572;
　[2005] 1 F.L.R. 687, Fam Div. . . . . 　*Digested,* 05/**1590**
R *v.* Secretary of State for Scotland; *sub nom* AHLR, Petitioner [1999] 2 A.C. 512;
　[1999] 2 W.L.R. 28; [1999] 1 All E.R. 481; 1999 S.C. (H.L.) 17; 1999 S.L.T. 279;
　1999 S.C.L.R. 74; (1999) 96(4) L.S.G. 37; 1998 G.W.D. 40-2075; *Times,*
　December 7, 1998; *Independent,* December 8, 1998, HL; reversing 1998 S.C. 49;
　1998 S.L.T. 162; 1997 S.C.L.R. 1056; 1997 G.W.D. 35-1793, IH (2 Div);
　reversing 1997 S.L.T. 555, OH . . . . 　*Digested,* 99/**6363**:
　　　　　　　　　Applied, 00/4174: *Considered,* 99/6361, 00/6472: *Followed,* 05/2825
R *v.* Secretary of State for the Home Department see E *v.* Secretary of State for the
　Home Department
R (A Child) *v.* Fuller (Unreported, February 22, 2005), CC (Dartford) [*Ex rel.* Joanna
　Kerr, Barrister, Lamb Chambers, Lamb Building, Temple, London]. . . . . 　*Digested,* 05/**3099**
R (A Child) *v.* Nurse (Unreported, August 18, 2004), CC (Ipswich) [*Ex rel.* Gurion
　Taussig, Barrister, 199 Strand, London]. . . . . 　*Digested,* 05/**3229**
R (A Child) *v.* Patel (Unreported, July 27, 2004), CC (Bow) [*Ex rel.* David McHugh,
　Barrister, 1, Essex Court Chambers, 1st Floor, Temple, London] . . . . 　*Digested,* 05/**3136**
R (A Child) *v.* Popat (Unreported, August 31, 2004), CC (Watford) [*Ex rel.* Thomas
　Wood, Barrister, 199 Strand Chambers, London] . . . . 　*Digested,* 05/**3138**
R (A Child) (Adoption: Contact Orders), Re [2005] EWCA Civ 1128; *Times,* September 15,
　2005, CA (Civ Div)
R (A Child) (Contact: Human Fertilisation and Embryology Act 1990) (No.2), Re see R (A
　Child) (IVF: Paternity of Child), Re

R (A Child) (IVF: Paternity of Child), Re; *sub nom* R (A Child) (Contact: Human Fertilisation and Embryology Act 1990) (No.2), Re; D (A Child) (IVF: Paternity of Child), Re; R (A Child) (Parental Responsibility: IVF Baby), Re; B v. R [2005] UKHL 33; [2005] 2 A.C. 621; [2005] 2 W.L.R. 1158; [2005] 4 All E.R. 433; [2005] 2 F.L.R. 843; [2005] 2 F.C.R. 223; [2005] Fam. Law 701; (2005) 102(21) L.S.G. 33; (2005) 155 N.L.J. 797; *Times*, May 13, 2005; *Independent*, May 17, 2005, HL; affirming [2003] EWCA Civ 182; [2003] Fam. 129; [2003] 2 W.L.R. 1485; [2003] 2 All E.R. 131; [2003] 1 F.L.R. 1183; [2003] 1 F.C.R. 481; (2003) 71 B.M.L.R. 157; [2003] Fam. Law 394; (2003) 100(13) L.S.G. 27; (2003) 153 N.L.J. 317; *Times*, February 20, 2003; *Independent*, February 25, 2003, CA (Civ Div); reversing [2002] 2 F.L.R. 843, Fam Div . . . .   *Digested*, 05/**1681**:
Applied, 04/1673

R (A Child) (Parental Responsibility: IVF Baby), Re see R (A Child) (IVF: Paternity of Child), Re

R (Abduction: Immigration Concerns), Re [2004] EWHC 2042; [2005] 1 F.L.R. 33; [2004] Fam. Law 862, Fam Div . . . .   *Digested*, 05/**1543**

R (Emma) v. R (Edward) see R v. R (Leave to Remove)

R (Iran) v. Secretary of State for the Home Department; *sub nom* R. (on the application of R) v. Secretary of State for the Home Department; A (Afghanistan) v. Secretary of State for the Home Department; M (Afghanistan) v. Secretary of State for the Home Department; T (Afghanistan) v. Secretary of State for the Home Department; T (Eritrea) v. Secretary of State for the Home Department [2005] EWCA Civ 982; [2005] Imm. A.R. 535; [2005] I.N.L.R. 633; *Times*, August 19, 2005, CA (Civ Div) . . . .   *Digested*, 05/**2213**

R (Minors: Child Abduction), Re [1995] 1 F.L.R. 716; [1995] 2 F.C.R. 609; *Times*, December 5, 1994, CA (Civ Div) . . . .   *Digested*, 94/**3149**:
Applied, 05/1538, 05/1652

R Griggs Group Ltd v. Evans (No.1); *sub nom* Griggs Group Ltd v. Evans [2005] EWCA Civ 11; [2005] E.C.D.R. 30; [2005] F.S.R. 31; (2005) 28(5) I.P.D. 28033, CA (Civ Div); affirming [2003] EWHC 2914; [2004] E.C.D.R. 15; [2004] F.S.R. 31, Ch D . . . .   *Digested*, 05/**2425**:
Considered, 04/2255

R Griggs Group Ltd v. Evans (No.2) [2004] EWHC 1088; [2005] Ch. 153; [2005] 2 W.L.R. 513; [2005] E.C.D.R. 12; [2004] F.S.R. 48; (2004) 27(9) I.P.D. 27095; *Times*, May 27, 2004, Ch D . . . .   *Digested*, 04/**2255**

R-B (A Patient) v. Official Solicitor see A (Mental Patient: Sterilisation), Re

R. v. A see R. v. AA

R. v. A [2005] EWCA Crim 2598; (2005) 149 S.J.L.B. 1350, CA (Crim Div)

R. v. A (Complainant's Sexual History); *sub nom* R. v. Y (Sexual Offence: Complainant's Sexual History); R. v. A (No.2) [2001] UKHL 25; [2002] 1 A.C. 45; [2001] 2 W.L.R. 1546; [2001] 3 All E.R. 1; [2001] 2 Cr. App. R. 21; (2001) 165 J.P. 609; [2001] H.R.L.R. 48; [2001] U.K.H.R.R. 825; 11 B.H.R.C. 225; [2001] Crim. L.R. 908; (2001) 165 J.P.N. 750; *Times*, May 24, 2001; *Independent*, May 22, 2001; *Daily Telegraph*, May 29, 2001, HL; affirming [2001] EWCA Crim 4; [2001] Crim. L.R. 389; (2001) 145 S.J.L.B. 43; *Times*, February 13, 2001, CA (Crim Div) . . . .   *Digested*, 01/**977**:
Applied, 02/487: *Considered*, 02/753, 03/5019, 05/799

R. v. A (No.2) see R. v. A (Complainant's Sexual History)

R. v. AA; *sub nom* R. v. A [2005] EWCA Crim 1564; (2005) 149 S.J.L.B. 772, CA (Crim Div)

R. v. Abdelrahman (Samir) [2005] EWCA Crim 1367; *Times*, June 15, 2005, CA (Crim Div)

R. v. Abdi (Hassan) see R. v. Lang (Stephen Howard)

R. v. Abdroikov (Nurlon); R. v. Green (Richard John); R. v. Williamson (Kenneth Joseph) [2005] EWCA Crim 1986; [2005] 1 W.L.R. 3538; [2005] 4 All E.R. 869; *Times*, August 18, 2005, CA (Crim Div) . . . .   *Digested*, 05/**894**

R. v. AC see Attorney General's Reference (Nos.31, 42, 43, 45, 50 and 51 of 2003), Re

R. v. AC see Attorney General's Reference (Nos.37, 38, 44, 54, 51, 53, 35, 40, 43, 45, 41 and 42 of 2003), Re

R. v. Acott (Brian Gordon) [1997] 1 W.L.R. 306; [1997] 1 All E.R. 706; [1997] 2 Cr. App. R. 94; (1997) 161 J.P. 368; [1997] Crim. L.R. 514; (1997) 161 J.P.N. 285; (1997) 94(10) L.S.G. 31; (1997) 147 N.L.J. 290; (1997) 141 S.J.L.B. 65; *Times*, February 21, 1997; *Independent*, March 11, 1997, HL; affirming [1996] 4 All E.R. 443; [1996] 2 Cr. App. R. 290; (1996) 160 J.P. 655; [1996] Crim. L.R. 664; (1996) 160 J.P.N. 608; *Times*, April 5, 1996, CA (Crim Div) . . . .   *Digested*, 97/**1337**:
Considered, 05/900: *Followed*, 04/871

R. v. Adams (David Anthony); R. v. Harding (William Henry) [2000] 2 Cr. App. R. (S.) 274, CA (Crim Div) . . . .   *Digested*, 00/**1352**:
Applied, 02/4016: *Considered*, 05/3730: *Followed*, 03/3775

R. v. Adamson (Michael Joseph) see R. v. Nazari (Fazlollah)

R. v. Adaway (Glen) [2004] EWCA Crim 2831; (2004) 168 J.P. 645; (2004) 168 J.P.N. 956; *Times*, November 22, 2004, CA (Crim Div) . . . .   *Digested*, 05/**936**

R. v. Adcock (Deric James) [2000] 1 Cr. App. R. (S.) 563, CA (Crim Div) . . . .   *Digested*, 00/**1302**:
Applied, 05/3745

R. v. Admiralty Board of the Defence Council Ex p. Beckett see R. v. Ministry of
Defence Ex p. Smith
R. v. Admiralty Board of the Defence Council Ex p. Lustig-Prean see R. v. Ministry of
Defence Ex p. Smith
R. v. Adomako (John Asare); R. v. Sullman (Barry); R. v. Prentice (Michael Charles); R.
v. Holloway (Stephen John) [1995] 1 A.C. 171; [1994] 3 W.L.R. 288; [1994] 3
All E.R. 79; (1994) 99 Cr. App. R. 362; (1994) 158 J.P. 653; [1994] 5 Med. L.R.
277; [1994] Crim. L.R. 757; (1994) 158 J.P.N. 507; (1994) 144 N.L.J. 936;
Times, July 4, 1994; Independent, July 1, 1994, HL; affirming [1994] Q.B. 302;
[1993] 3 W.L.R. 927; [1993] 4 All E.R. 935; (1994) 98 Cr. App. R. 262; Times,
May 21, 1993; Independent, May 21, 1993, CA (Crim Div) . . . .   Digested, 94/**1124**:
                      Applied, 95/875, 05/804: Considered, 94/637, 96/47, 05/805:
                                           Distinguished, 95/923: Followed, 01/1052
R. v. Adu (Peter); R. v. Yeboah (Mustafa) [2005] EWCA Crim 647; [2005] 2 Cr. App.
R. (S.) 93, CA (Crim Div)
R. v. AF (A Juvenile) see Attorney General's Reference (No.121 of 2002), Re
R. v. Afonso (Americo Practicio); R. v. Sajid (Mohammed); R. v. Andrews (Douglas)
[2004] EWCA Crim 2342; [2005] 1 Cr. App. R. (S.) 99; [2005] Crim. L.R. 73;
(2004) 148 S.J.L.B. 1120; Times, October 14, 2004, CA (Crim Div) . . . .   Digested, 04/**3454**:
                      Considered, 05/3700, 05/3748, 05/3751: Distinguished, 05/3752
R. v. Afzal (Mohammed) see Attorney General's Reference (Nos.83 and 85 of 2004),
Re
R. v. Ahemed (Lukman Yakub) [2005] EWCA Crim 1954; [2005] Crim. L.R. 974, CA
(Crim Div)
R. v. Ahmed (Mumtaz); sub nom R. v. Ahmed (Muntaz); R. v. Qureshi (Ghulam)
[2004] EWCA Crim 2599; [2005] 1 W.L.R. 122; [2005] 1 All E.R. 128; [2005] 1
Cr. App. R. (S.) 123; [2005] 1 F.L.R. 679; [2005] Crim. L.R. 240; (2004)
101(44) L.S.G. 29; (2004) 148 S.J.L.B. 1313; Times, November 3, 2004, CA
(Crim Div) . . . .   Digested, 05/**3571**:
                                                                   Applied, 05/840
R. v. Ahmed (Muntaz) see R. v. Ahmed (Mumtaz)
R. v. Akram (Adil) see R. v. Renda (Raymond)
R. v. Aksu (Ali) see R. v. Kaynak (Hussein)
R. v. Akuffo (Andrew Frank) see Attorney General's Reference (No.3 of 2004), Re
R. v. Akyeah (Christiana) [2003] EWCA Crim 1988; [2004] 1 Cr. App. R. (S.) 36, CA
(Crim Div) . . . .   Digested, 04/**3341**:
                                                                  Followed, 05/3589
R. v. Al-Khawaja (Imad) [2005] EWCA Crim 2697; Times, November 15, 2005;
Independent, November 9, 2005, CA (Crim Div)
R. v. Alagbala (Michael); sub nom R. v. Alagobola (Michael) [2004] EWCA Crim 89;
[2004] 2 Cr. App. R. (S.) 48; [2004] Crim. L.R. 384, CA (Crim Div) . . . .   Digested, 05/**3570**
R. v. Alagobola (Michael) see R. v. Alagbala (Michael)
R. v. Alexander (Adrian Stephen) [1997] 2 Cr. App. R. (S.) 74, CA (Crim Div) . . . .   Digested, 97/**1576**:
                                                                Considered, 05/3556
R. v. Alexander (James) [2004] EWCA Crim 3398; [2005] 2 Cr. App. R. (S.) 49, CA
(Crim Div) . . . .   Digested, 05/**3521**
R. v. Alger (James Terrance) [2004] EWCA Crim 1868; [2005] 1 Cr. App. R. (S.) 69,
CA (Crim Div) . . . .   Digested, 05/**3592**
R. v. Ali (Idris) [1998] 2 Cr. App. R. (S.) 123, CA (Crim Div) . . . .   Digested, 98/**1237**:
                                                                  Followed, 05/3711
R. v. Ali (Liaquat); R. v. Hussein (Akhtar); R. v. Khan (Mohsan); R. v. Bhatti (Shahid)
[2005] EWCA Crim 87; [2005] Crim. L.R. 864; (2005) 149 S.J.L.B. 770, CA
(Crim Div)
R. v. Ali (Mudassir Mohammed) see R. v. Lambert (Steven)
R. v. Ali (Zuber Makbul); R. v. Lotay (Anadeep) [2004] EWCA Crim 2735; [2005] 2
Cr. App. R. (S.) 2, CA (Crim Div) . . . .   Digested, 05/**3758**
R. v. Allan (Richard Roy) [2004] EWCA Crim 2236; [2005] Crim. L.R. 716; (2004)
148 S.J.L.B. 1032, CA (Crim Div)
R. v. Allen (Brian Roger) (Appeals against Sentence) see R. v. Dimsey (Dermot
Jeremy) (Appeals against Sentence)
R. v. Allen (Craig Michael) [2004] EWCA Crim 1030; [2005] 1 Cr. App. R. (S.) 2, CA
(Crim Div) . . . .   Digested, 05/**3648**
R. v. Allen (Wesley) [2005] EWCA Crim 667; [2005] 2 Cr. App. R. (S.) 95, CA (Crim
Div) . . . .   Digested, 05/**3778**
R. v. Alleyne (Carl Anthony) see R. v. Jordan (Andrew James)
R. v. Allsopp (Michael Nevin); R. v. Kelly (Anthony Joseph); R. v. Wolf (Karl Christian);
R. v. West (Melvin) [2005] EWCA Crim 703; (2005) 149 S.J.L.B. 388, CA
(Crim Div)
R. v. Alwan (Hisham) [2000] 2 Costs L.R. 326, Sup Ct Costs Office . . . .   Digested, 01/**1114**:
                                                                Considered, 05/2711
R. v. Anderson (Norman) [2005] EWCA Crim 75; [2005] 2 Cr. App. R. (S.) 54, CA
(Crim Div) . . . .   Digested, 05/**3597**

R. v. Anderson (William Ronald) [1986] A.C. 27; [1985] 3 W.L.R. 268; [1985] 2 All
E.R. 961; (1985) 81 Cr. App. R. 253; [1985] Crim. L.R. 651, HL; affirming (1985)
80 Cr. App. R. 64; [1984] Crim. L.R. 550, CA (Crim Div) . . . . *Digested*, 85/**528**:
Applied, 05/767: *Distinguished*, 94/1080: *Explained*, 90/1118
R. v. Andrews (Douglas) see R. v. Afonso (Americo Practicio)
R. v. Angel (Robert Charles) [1968] 1 W.L.R. 669; [1968] 2 All E.R. 607 (Note);
(1968) 52 Cr. App. R. 280; (1968) 112 S.J. 310, CA (Crim Div) . . . . *Digested*, 68/**892**:
Considered, 05/2826
R. v. Anwar (Kamran) see R. v. Spruce (Ronald Arthur)
R. v. Anyanwu (Ebenezer Chuwuma) see R. v. Nazari (Fazlollah)
R. v. Aramah (John Uzu) (1983) 76 Cr. App. R. 190; (1982) 4 Cr. App. R. (S.) 407;
[1983] Crim. L.R. 271, CA (Crim Div) . . . . *Digested*, 83/**764**.19:
Applied, 84/868, 85/703, 86/812, 86/834, 87/954, 87/1076, 88/871,
88/1007, 89/839, 89/939, 90/1185, 90/1284, 90/1285, 91/1097, 92/1227,
93/1108, 00/5487: *Considered*, 84/852, 86/719, 86/823, 86/845,
86/0734.a, 87/897, 87/898, 87/926, 87/940, 87/942, 87/952, 87/953,
88/872, 88/911, 88/922, 88/929, 88/930, 89/938, 89/949, 89/1011,
89/1028, 90/1290, 90/1291, 90/1297, 91/1103, 92/1247, 92/1248, 93/1328,
97/1510, 97/1517, 97/1518, 97/1522, 98/1177, 98/1180, 98/1181, 98/1183,
98/1195, 98/1197, 99/1127, 99/1129, 99/1134, 99/1140, 99/1145, 99/1148,
00/1206, 00/1207, 00/1211, 00/1218, 00/1233, 01/1282, 02/3926, 03/3686,
03/3695, 04/3343, 05/3588, 05/3596, 05/3597, 05/3751:
Distinguished, 83/764.25: *Doubted*, 99/5226: *Explained*, 84/835, 85/727,
86/833: *Followed*, 84/904, 96/1857, 96/1863, 96/1873, 97/1512:
Not followed, 87/1022, 88/969, 89/991, 89/1030, 90/1289:
Referred to, 83/820, 84/853, 86/757, 87/1054, 88/907, 89/993, 89/1027,
89/1033, 90/1268, 90/1292, 90/1301, 91/1046, 91/1092, 91/1093, 91/1112,
92/1242, 92/1245, 92/1257, 93/1123, 93/1127, 93/1130, 93/1131, 93/1137,
93/1139, 94/1403, 95/1360, 95/1367
R. v. Aranguren (Jose de Jesus); R. v. Aroyewumi (Bisi); R. v. Bioshogun (Nimota); R.
v. Littlefield (John); R. v. Gould (Robert Sidney) (1994) 99 Cr. App. R. 347;
(1995) 16 Cr. App. R. (S.) 211; [1994] Crim. L.R. 695; (1994) 144 N.L.J. 864;
Times, June 23, 1994; *Independent*, June 30, 1994, CA (Crim Div) . . . . *Digested*, 95/**1364**:
Considered, 96/1872, 96/1875, 96/1879, 98/1191, 99/1124, 99/1129, 00/1211,
00/1233, 03/3695, 05/3591, 05/3598, 05/3754: *Distinguished*, 96/1873:
Followed, 97/1522, 04/3343, 05/3589
R. v. Archer (Patrick John); R. v. Purnell (Danny Lee); R. v. Eaton (Craig Keith) [1998]
2 Cr. App. R. (S.) 76, CA (Crim Div) . . . . *Digested*, 98/**1304**:
Considered, 05/3658
R. v. Armana Ltd [2004] EWCA Crim 1069; [2005] 1 Cr. App. R. (S.) 7, CA (Crim
Div) . . . . *Digested*, 05/**3606**
R. v. Armitage (Lewis) see R. v. Lang (Stephen Howard)
R. v. Arnold (Kenneth) [2004] EWCA Crim 1293; [2005] Crim. L.R. 56; (2004) 148
S.J.L.B. 660, CA (Crim Div). . . . . *Considered*, 05/888
R. v. Arobieke (Akinwale) see R. v. Underwood (Kevin John)
R. v. Aroyewumi (Bisi) see R. v. Aranguren (Jose de Jesus)
R. v. Artry (Marcus) see R. v. Carroll (Jerome)
R. v. AS 200000239 X5, CA (Crim Div) . . . . *Considered*, 05/3562
R. v. Aslam (Mohammed) [2004] EWCA Crim 2801; [2005] 1 Cr. App. R. (S.) 116;
[2005] Crim. L.R. 145, CA (Crim Div) . . . . *Digested*, 05/**3569**
R. v. Atkinson (Glynn); *sub nom* R. v. Atkinson (Glynn); R. v. Smith (Paul) [2004]
EWCA Crim 3223; [2005] 2 Cr. App. R. (S.) 34, CA (Crim Div). . . . . *Digested*, 05/**3730**
R. v. Atkinson (Michael Frederick) (1993) 14 Cr. App. R. (S.) 182; [1992] Crim. L.R.
749, CA (Crim Div) . . . . *Digested*, 93/**1074**:
Considered, 93/1151, 94/1260: *Distinguished*, 05/840
R. v. Atlan (Oren) [2004] EWCA Crim 1798; [2005] Crim. L.R. 63, CA (Crim Div)
R. v. Attiq (Mohammed) see Attorney General's Reference (No.81 of 2003), Re
R. v. Attuh-Benson (Irene Cynthia) [2004] EWCA Crim 3032; [2005] 2 Cr. App. R.
(S.) 11; [2005] Crim. L.R. 243, CA (Crim Div). . . . . *Digested*, 05/**3596**
R. v. Avis (Tony); R. v. Barton (Richard); R. v. Thomas (Gerald John); R. v. Torrington
(Richard Edward); R. v. Marquez (Shaun); R. v. Goldsmith (Harold Egan) [1998]
1 Cr. App. R. 420; [1998] 2 Cr. App. R. (S.) 178; [1998] Crim. L.R. 428; *Times*,
December 19, 1997, CA (Crim Div) . . . . *Digested*, 98/**1214**:
Applied, 01/1299, 01/1308, 02/3873, 04/876, 04/3350, 04/3409:
Considered, 99/1158, 99/1160, 99/1161, 99/1162, 99/1164, 99/1165, 00/1242,
00/1244, 00/1245, 00/1247, 00/1250, 00/1252, 00/1253, 01/1298, 01/1304,
01/1312, 01/1313, 02/3941, 02/3947, 02/3948, 02/4057, 04/3411, 05/3690,
05/3692, 05/3696, 05/3759: *Followed*, 99/1168, 05/3675:
Referred to, 99/1110

R. *v.* Aziz (Kazim); R. *v.* Tosun (Ali Yener); R. *v.* Yorganci (Metin) [1996] A.C. 41; [1995] 3 W.L.R. 53; [1995] 3 All E.R. 149; [1995] 2 Cr. App. R. 478; (1995) 159 J.P. 669; [1995] Crim. L.R. 897; (1995) 159 J.P.N. 756; (1995) 92(28) L.S.G. 41; (1995) 145 N.L.J. 921; [1995] 139 S.J.L.B. 158; *Times*, June 16, 1995; *Independent*, June 16, 1995, HL . . . . *Digested*, 95/**1044**
Applied, 05/**937**: *Considered*, 98/**1050**
R. *v.* B see Attorney General's Reference (No.3 of 1999), Re
R. *v.* B [2005] EWCA Crim 312; [2005] 2 Cr. App. R. (S.) 87; [2005] Crim. L.R. 488; (2005) 102(15) L.S.G. 32; *Times*, March 3, 2005, CA (Crim Div) . . . . *Digested*, 05/**3600**
R. *v.* B (Colin) see Attorney General's Reference (No.76 of 2004), Re
R. *v.* B (David) [2005] EWCA Crim 158; [2005] 2 Cr. App. R. (S.) 65, CA (Crim Div) . . *Digested*, 05/**3738**
R. *v.* B (Ejaz) [2005] EWCA Crim 805; *Times*, May 3, 2005, CA (Crim Div) . . . . *Digested*, 05/**837**
R. *v.* B (Michael) [2005] EWCA Crim 3174; (2005) 149 S.J.L.B. 1353, CA (Crim Div)
R. *v.* B (Ray) [2004] EWCA Crim 3216; *Times*, December 10, 2004, CA (Crim Div) . . . . *Digested*, 05/**3601**
R. *v.* B&Q Plc [2005] EWCA Crim 2297; (2005) 102(39) L.S.G. 29; *Times*, November 3, 2005, CA (Crim Div)
R. *v.* Bailey (William) [2004] EWCA Crim 3058; [2005] 2 Cr. App. R. (S.) 16; [2005] Crim. L.R. 317, CA (Crim Div). . . . . *Digested*, 05/**3559**
R. *v.* Bain (Steven William) [2005] EWCA Crim 7; [2005] 2 Cr. App. R. (S.) 53; (2005) 149 S.J.L.B. 113, CA (Crim Div) . . . . *Digested*, 05/**3582**
R. *v.* Bajwa (Narip Singh) see R. *v.* Early (John)
R. *v.* Baker (Costs); R. *v.* Fowler (Costs) [2004] 4 Costs L.R. 693, Sup Ct Costs Office . . . . *Digested*, 05/**855**
R. *v.* Baker (Robert John) see R. *v.* Cheetham (David Edward)
R. *v.* Baker (Tony) (No.1); R. *v.* Ward (Alan) [1999] 2 Cr. App. R. 335; *Times*, April 28, 1999, CA (Crim Div) . . . . *Digested*, 99/**1020**
Cited, 99/931: *Overruled*, 05/765
R. *v.* Balasubramaniam (Ravindran); *sub nom* R. *v.* Balasubramaniam (Ravidran) [2001] EWCA Crim 2680; [2002] 2 Cr. App. R. (S.) 17, CA (Crim Div) . . . . *Digested*, 04/**3351**
Considered, 05/911: *Doubted*, 05/**3610**
R. *v.* Baldwin (Leslie) see R. *v.* Oliver (Mark David)
R. *v.* Ball (Nathan) see R. *v.* Renda (Raymond)
R. *v.* Ballard (Russ Francois) [2004] EWCA Crim 3305; [2005] 2 Cr. App. R. (S.) 31; [2005] Crim. L.R. 323, CA (Crim Div) . . . . *Digested*, 05/**3772**
R. *v.* Ballinger (Paul) [2005] EWCA Crim 1060; [2005] 2 Cr. App. R. 29, CA (Crim Div) . . . . *Digested*, 05/**859**
R. *v.* Barber (Kenneth Leslie) see R. *v.* Pepper (Jeremy Paul)
R. *v.* Baria (Peter) see Attorney General's Reference (Nos.13, 14, 15, 16, 17 and 18 of 2004), Re
R. *v.* Barker (Daniel) see Attorney General's Reference (No.20 of 2004), Re
R. *v.* Barnard (Shaun) [2005] EWCA Crim 268; [2005] 2 Cr. App. R. (S.) 81, CA (Crim Div)
R. *v.* Barnes (Mark) [2004] EWCA Crim 3246; [2005] 1 W.L.R. 910; [2005] 2 All E.R. 113; [2005] 1 Cr. App. R. 30; [2005] Crim. L.R. 381; (2005) 102(4) L.S.G. 30; *Times*, January 10, 2005, CA (Crim Div) . . . . *Digested*, 05/**795**
Applied, 05/766, 05/3618
R. *v.* Barnet LBC Ex p. Shah (Nilish); Akbarali *v.* Brent LBC; Abdullah *v.* Shropshire CC; Shabpar *v.* Barnet LBC; Shah (Jitendra) *v.* Barnet LBC; Ablack *v.* Inner London Education Authority; R. *v.* Shropshire CC Ex p. Abdullah [1983] 2 A.C. 309; [1983] 2 W.L.R. 16; [1983] 1 All E.R. 226; 81 L.G.R. 305; (1983) 133 N.L.J. 61; (1983) 127 S.J. 36, HL; reversing [1982] Q.B. 688; [1982] 2 W.L.R. 474; [1982] 1 All E.R. 698; 80 L.G.R. 571; *Times*, November 12, 1981, CA (Civ Div); affirming [1981] 2 W.L.R. 86; [1980] 3 All E.R. 679; 79 L.G.R. 210; 125 S.J. 64, QBD . . . . *Digested*, 83/**1157**
Applied, 80/853, 84/1138, 84/3033, 85/1074, 85/1732, 85/1737, 86/703, 86/1692, 87/3489, 98/3007, 01/2612, 01/2617, 03/1127, 03/1556, 05/1627:
Considered, 82/973, 83/1815, 84/1173, 84/1645, 85/1107, 85/1108, 85/1127, 85/2165, 86/1136, 90/11, 91/2371, 91/2372, 95/3206, 99/4564, 00/2778:
Distinguished, 83/1800, 04/1885: *Followed*, 85/1735, 87/1928:
Referred to, 91/2373
R. *v.* Barnham (John Thomas) [2005] EWCA Crim 1049; [2005] Crim. L.R. 657, CA (Crim Div)
R. *v.* Barrett (Michael) see Attorney General's Reference (No.118 of 2004), Re
R. *v.* Barrick (John) (1985) 81 Cr. App. R. 78; (1985) 7 Cr. App. R. (S.) 142; (1985) 149 J.P. 705; (1985) 129 S.J. 416, CA (Crim Div) . . . . *Digested*, 85/**765**
Applied, 86/884, 86/885, 86/889, 03/3870: *Cited*, 88/999, 88/1001, 89/1123, 90/1429, 91/1228, 91/1230, 92/1442, 93/1294, 94/1366:
Considered, 86/759, 87/457, 87/1013, 87/1015, 88/1056, 87/1057, 87/1061, 87/1063, 87/1828, 88/925, 88/934, 88/1002, 88/1713, 89/1046, 89/1121, 91/1173, 91/1225, 92/1167, 95/1385, 96/1752, 97/1549, 98/1316, 98/1391, 98/1392, 99/1174, 99/1277, 99/1359, 99/1362, 00/1436, 03/3670, 05/3611:
Distinguished, 86/760, 87/1058, 03/3811: *Followed*, 04/3353:
Referred to, 86/711, 87/1055, 87/1064

R. *v.* Bartle Ex p. Pinochet Ugarte (No.2) see R. *v.* Bow Street Metropolitan
    Stipendiary Magistrate Ex p. Pinochet Ugarte (No.2)

R. *v.* Barton (Richard) see R. *v.* Avis (Tony)

R. *v.* Basra (Ajaib Singh) [2002] EWCA Crim 541; [2002] 2 Cr. App. R. (S.) 100;
    Times, April 1, 2002, CA (Crim Div) . . . .   *Digested*, 02/**4036**:
                                          Considered, 03/3806, 05/3673

R. *v.* Bates (Alan Roy) see Attorney General's Reference (No.70 of 2003), Re

R. *v.* Batty (Christopher Andrew) see Attorney General's Reference (Nos.148, 149, 150,
    151, 152, 153, 154 and 155 of 2001), Re

R. *v.* Baxter (Robert Peter) [2002] EWCA Crim 1516; [2003] 1 Cr. App. R. (S.) 50, CA
    (Crim Div) . . . .   *Digested*, 03/**3746**:
                                          Considered, 05/3689

R. *v.* Beard (Gary Colin) see Attorney General's Reference (Nos.120 and 121 of 2004),
    Re

R. *v.* Beard (Peter) see Attorney General's Reference (No.59 of 2004), Re

R. *v.* Bebbington (Shaun Anthony) see R. *v.* Boness (Dean)

R. *v.* Beckett (Guy Philip) [2005] EWCA Crim 274; [2005] 2 Cr. App. R. (S.) 71, CA
    (Crim Div) . . . .   *Digested*, 05/**3674**

R. *v.* Beckles (Keith Anderson) [2004] EWCA Crim 2766; [2005] 1 W.L.R. 2829;
    [2005] 1 All E.R. 705; [2005] 1 Cr. App. R. 23; [2005] Crim. L.R. 560; (2005)
    102(1) L.S.G. 16; (2004) 148 S.J.L.B. 1432; *Times*, November 17, 2004, CA
    (Crim Div) . . . .   *Digested*, 05/**901**:
                                       Previous proceedings, 02/2461

R. *v.* Becouarn (Darren) [2005] UKHL 55; [2005] 1 W.L.R. 2589; [2005] 4 All E.R.
    673; (2005) 155 N.L.J. 1416; *Times*, August 1, 2005, HL; affirming [2003]
    EWCA Crim 1154, CA (Crim Div) . . . .   *Digested*, 05/**748**

R. *v.* Benabbas (Ahmed) [2005] EWCA Crim 2113; [2005] Crim. L.R. 976, CA (Crim
    Div)

R. *v.* Benfield (Anthony John); R. *v.* Sobers (Leon Anderson) [2003] EWCA Crim
    2223; [2004] 1 Cr. App. R. 8; [2004] 1 Cr. App. R. (S.) 52; [2003] Crim. L.R.
    811; (2003) 100(36) L.S.G. 38; (2003) 147 S.J.L.B. 906; *Times*, September 9,
    2003, CA (Crim Div) . . . .   *Digested*, 03/**3778**:
                                 Applied, 05/3650: *Distinguished*, 05/3608

R. *v.* Benjafield (Karl Robert) (Confiscation Order); R. *v.* Leal (Manoj) (Confiscation
    Order); R. *v.* Milford (David John); R. *v.* Rezvi (Syed) [2002] UKHL 2; [2003] 1
    A.C. 1099; [2002] 2 W.L.R. 235; [2002] 1 All E.R. 815; [2002] 2 Cr. App. R.
    3; [2002] 2 Cr. App. R. (S.) 71; [2002] H.R.L.R. 20; [2002] Crim. L.R. 337;
    (2002) 99(10) L.S.G. 29; (2002) 146 S.J.L.B. 37; *Times*, January 28, 2002, HL;
    affirming [2001] 3 W.L.R. 75; [2001] 2 All E.R. 609; [2001] 2 Cr. App. R. 7;
    [2001] 2 Cr. App. R. (S.) 47; [2001] H.R.L.R. 25; 10 B.H.R.C. 19; [2001] Crim.
    L.R. 245; (2001) 98(12) L.S.G. 41; *Times*, December 28, 2000; *Independent*,
    January 31, 2001, CA (Crim Div) . . . .   *Digested*, 02/**3897**:
               Considered, 01/6327, 02/849, 05/3557: *Followed*, 02/2663, 05/3749:
                  Referred to, 02/3892: *Subsequent proceedings*, 02/3896

R. *v.* Bennett (Andrew) [2005] EWCA Crim 603; [2005] 2 Cr. App. R. (S.) 59, CA
    (Crim Div) . . . .   *Digested*, 05/**3629**

R. *v.* Bennett (John) [1998] 1 Cr. App. R. (S.) 429, CA (Crim Div) . . . .   *Digested*, 98/**1193**:
                                         Considered, 00/1205, 05/3578

R. *v.* Bennett (Michael) [2003] EWCA Crim 2446; [2004] 1 Cr. App. R. (S.) 65, CA
    (Crim Div) . . . .   *Digested*, 04/**3392**:
                                          Considered, 05/3661

R. *v.* Bentham (Peter) [2005] UKHL 18; [2005] 1 W.L.R. 1057; [2005] 2 All E.R. 65;
    [2005] 2 Cr. App. R. 11; (2005) 169 J.P. 181; [2005] Crim. L.R. 648; (2005)
    169 J.P.N. 299; (2005) 155 N.L.J. 545; (2005) 149 S.J.L.B. 358; *Times*, March
    11, 2005; *Independent*, March 15, 2005, HL; reversing [2003] EWCA Crim
    3751; [2004] 2 All E.R. 549; [2004] 1 Cr. App. R. 37; (2004) 168 J.P. 278;
    (2004) 168 J.P.N. 400; (2004) 101(3) L.S.G. 32; *Times*, December 10, 2003,
    CA (Crim Div) . . . .   *Digested*, 05/**798**

R. *v.* Berry (James William) see R. *v.* Dalby (Christopher John)

R. *v.* Betts (Raymond Christopher); R. *v.* Hall (John Anthony) [2001] EWCA Crim
    224; [2001] 2 Cr. App. R. 16; [2001] Crim. L.R. 754, CA (Crim Div) . . . .   *Digested*, 01/**997**:
                        Applied, 05/749, 05/901: *Not followed*, 05/927

R. *v.* Bhatti (Shahid) see R. *v.* Ali (Liaquat)

R. *v.* Bhuller (Surinder Singh) see R. *v.* Kalia (Daya)

R. v. Billam (Keith) [1986] 1 W.L.R. 349; [1986] 1 All E.R. 985; (1986) 82 Cr. App. R.
347; (1986) 8 Cr. App. R. (S.) 48; [1986] Crim. L.R. 347, CA (Crim Div) . . . . . .   *Digested,* 86/**868**:
     Applied, 91/1192, 92/1374, 92/1376, 92/1379, 93/1265, 94/3837, 95/1411,
     96/1976, 96/1992, 96/2052, 99/1314, 00/1333, 03/3827, 03/3833,
     04/3424, 05/3718: *Cited,* 94/1411: *Considered,* 87/1032, 87/1033, 87/1036,
     87/1076, 88/867, 88/868, 88/975, 88/976, 88/978, 88/980, 88/1007,
     90/1395, 90/1398, 92/1370, 93/1031, 93/1033, 93/1262, 93/1267, 93/1269,
     94/1181, 94/1183, 94/1326, 94/1335, 94/1340, 95/1456, 95/1462, 96/1939,
     96/2039, 96/2044, 96/2045, 96/2047, 96/2048, 96/2051, 97/1432,
     97/1452, 97/1454, 98/1143, 98/1286, 98/1292, 98/1339, 98/1343, 98/1346,
     98/1347, 98/1349, 98/1351, 98/1352, 98/1354, 99/869, 99/1298, 99/1304,
     99/1306, 99/1311, 00/1311, 00/1392, 00/1395, 00/1401, 00/1402, 01/1455,
     01/1463, 02/4054, 03/3834, 04/3422: *Followed,* 97/1645, 99/1297,
     99/1312: *Referred to,* 89/1105, 89/1213, 90/1220, 90/1392, 90/1487, 91/1194,
     91/1196, 92/1154, 92/1163, 92/1375, 92/1377, 93/1014, 93/1214, 93/1257,
     93/1260, 93/1261, 93/1264, 94/1307, 97/1646, 97/1648
R. v. Binstead (David Charles) [2005] EWCA Crim 164; [2005] 2 Cr. App. R. (S.) 62,
CA (Crim Div) . . . .   *Digested,* 05/**3662**
R. v. Bioshogun (Nimota) see R. v. Aranguren (Jose de Jesus)
R. v. Birch (Beulah) (1990) 90 Cr. App. R. 78; (1989) 11 Cr. App. R. (S.) 202; [1990]
2 Med. L.R. 77; [1989] Crim. L.R. 757; *Times,* May 4, 1989, CA (Crim Div) . . . . .   *Digested,* 91/**1136**:
     Approved, 03/3773: *Considered,* 95/1429, 96/2001, 98/1356:
     Distinguished, 05/3632
R. v. Blackall (Neal) [2005] EWCA Crim 1128; [2005] Crim. L.R. 875, CA (Crim Div)
R. v. Blackburn (Paul) [2005] EWCA Crim 1349; [2005] 2 Cr. App. R. 30; *Times,* June
10, 2005, CA (Crim Div) . . . .   *Digested,* 05/**730**
R. v. Blake (Michael) see R. v. Hounsham (Robin Edward)
R. v. Blastland (Douglas) [1986] A.C. 41; [1985] 3 W.L.R. 345; [1985] 2 All E.R.
1095; (1985) 81 Cr. App. R. 266; [1985] Crim. L.R. 727, HL; affirming *Times,*
January 22, 1985, CA (Crim Div) . . . .   *Digested,* 85/**578**:
     Applied, 92/852, 93/651, 05/735: *Considered,* 87/659, 92/850:
     Followed, 96/1412
R. v. Blewitt (Kevin Stanley) (1994) 15 Cr. App. R. (S.) 132, CA (Crim Div) . . . .   *Considered,* 05/3523
R. v. Blight (1903) 22 N.Z.L.R. 837, CA (NZ) . . . .   *Considered,* 05/921
R. v. Board of Trade Ex p. St Martin Preserving Co Ltd [1965] 1 Q.B. 603; [1964] 3
W.L.R. 262; [1964] 2 All E.R. 561; 108 S.J. 602, QBD . . . .   *Digested,* 64/**455**:
     Applied, 80/275, 05/530: *Considered,* 92/394
R. v. Bolton (Stephen George) (Costs) [2005] 2 Costs L.R. 334, Sup Ct Costs Office
R. v. Bond (Michael) (Costs) [2005] 3 Costs L.R. 532, Sup Ct Costs Office
R. v. Boness (Dean); R. v. Bebbington (Shaun Anthony) [2005] EWCA Crim 2395;
(2005) 169 J.P. 621; (2005) 169 J.P.N. 937; *Times,* October 24, 2005, CA (Crim
Div)
R. v. Bore (Larry) [2004] EWCA Crim 1452; (2005) 169 J.P. 245; (2005) 169 J.P.N.
360, CA (Crim Div) . . . .   *Digested,* 05/**3602**
R. v. Bossom see R. v. Joy
R. v. Bott-Walters (John Anthony) [2005] EWCA Crim 243; [2005] 2 Cr. App. R. (S.)
70, CA (Crim Div) . . . .   *Digested,* 05/**910**
R. v. Bouchereau (Pierre Roger) (30/77) [1978] Q.B. 732; [1978] 2 W.L.R. 251;
[1981] 2 All E.R. 924; [1978] E.C.R. 1999; (1978) 66 Cr. App. R. 202; [1977] 2
C.M.L.R. 800; 122 S.J. 79, ECJ . . . .   *Digested,* 78/**629**:
     Applied, 87/1938, 88/982, 89/1108, 00/3345: *Considered,* 83/1895,
     93/5141, 97/2902: *Followed,* 05/1462: *Referred to,* 82/684.34, 83/806,
     89/797, 90/1405, 92/1227, 93/1108
R. v. Boujettif (Moussin) see Attorney General's Reference (No.66 of 2003), Re
R. v. Boulter (Andrew Paul) [1996] 2 Cr. App. R. (S.) 428, CA (Crim Div) . . . .   *Digested,* 97/**1555**:
     Considered, 05/3619
R. v. Bovell (Kelvin Anthony); R. v. Dowds (Peter Andrew) [2005] EWCA Crim 1091;
[2005] 2 Cr. App. R. 27; [2005] Crim. L.R. 790; *Times,* May 13, 2005, CA (Crim
Div) . . . .   *Digested,* 05/**725**
R. v. Bow County Court Ex p. Pelling (No.1) [1999] 1 W.L.R. 1807; [1999] 4 All E.R.
751; [1999] 2 F.L.R. 1126; [1999] 3 F.C.R. 97; [1999] Fam. Law 698; (1999)
96(32) L.S.G. 33; (1999) 149 N.L.J. 1369; *Times,* August 18, 1999 ;
Independent, October 1, 1999, CA (Civ Div); affirming [1999] 2 All E.R. 582;
[1999] 2 F.L.R. 149; [1999] 2 F.C.R. 97; [1999] C.O.D. 277; [1999] Fam. Law
384; *Times,* March 8, 1999; *Independent,* March 11, 1999, QBD . . . .   *Digested,* 99/**46**:
     Explained, 05/1646
R. v. Bow Street Metropolitan Stipendiary Magistrate Ex p. Pinochet Ugarte (No.2);
sub nom Pinochet Ugarte (No.2), Re; R. v. Evans Ex p. Pinochet Ugarte (No.2);
R. v. Bartle Ex p. Pinochet Ugarte (No.2) [2000] 1 A.C. 119; [1999] 2 W.L.R.
272; [1999] 1 All E.R. 577; 6 B.H.R.C. 1; (1999) 11 Admin. L.R. 57; (1999) 96(6)
L.S.G. 33; (1999) 149 N.L.J. 88; *Times,* January 18, 1999; *Independent,*
January 19, 1999, HL . . . .   *Digested,* 99/**39**:
     Applied, 99/38, 04/30: *Considered,* 00/4140, 00/6092, 01/6705, 05/13

R. *v.* Bowers (Aran) [2004] EWCA Crim 1247; [2005] 1 Cr. App. R. (S.) 28, CA (Crim Div) . . . . *Digested*, 05/**3523**
R. *v.* Bracknell Justices Ex p. Griffiths see Pountney *v.* Griffiths
R. *v.* Bradley (David Benjamin) [2005] EWCA Crim 20; [2005] 1 Cr. App. R. 24; (2005) 169 J.P. 73; [2005] Crim. L.R. 411; (2005) 169 J.P.N. 200; (2005) 102(8) L.S.G. 29; *Times*, January 17, 2005, CA (Crim Div). . . . . *Digested*, 05/**731**:
Considered, 05/**915**
R. *v.* Brady (Paul Clement) [2004] EWCA Crim 1763; [2004] 1 W.L.R. 3240; [2004] 3 All E.R. 520; [2005] B.C.C. 357; [2005] 1 Cr. App. R. 5; [2004] B.P.I.R. 962; [2005] Crim. L.R. 224; (2004) 101(29) L.S.G. 29; (2004) 148 S.J.L.B. 1149; *Times*, July 9, 2004, CA (Crim Div) . . . . *Digested*, 05/**838**
R. *v.* Branchflower (Paul Lee) [2004] EWCA Crim 2042; [2005] 1 Cr. App. R. 10; [2005] R.T.R. 13; [2005] Crim. L.R. 388, CA (Crim Div) . . . . *Digested*, 05/**755**
R. *v.* Bravard (Jacques) see R. *v.* May (Raymond George)
R. *v.* Braxton (Curtis) (Application for Leave to Appeal) [2004] EWCA Crim 1374; [2005] 1 Cr. App. R. (S.) 36, CA (Crim Div) . . . . *Digested*, 05/**3528**
R. *v.* Briers (Michael) (Costs) [2005] 1 Costs L.R. 146, Sup Ct Costs Office . . . . *Digested*, 05/**881**
R. *v.* Briggs (David Michael) see Attorney General's Reference (No.127 of 2004), Re
R. *v.* Bright (Barry James) see R. *v.* Whiteman (Mark)
R. *v.* Bristol Betting and Gaming Licensing Committee Ex p. O'Callaghan see Locabail (UK) Ltd *v.* Bayfield Properties Ltd (Leave to Appeal)
R. *v.* Bristol City Council Ex p. Everett [1999] 1 W.L.R. 1170; [1999] 2 All E.R. 193; [1999] Env. L.R. 587; [1999] E.H.L.R. 265; (1999) 31 H.L.R. 1102; [1999] B.L.G.R. 513; [1999] 3 P.L.R. 14; [1999] E.G.C.S. 33; (1999) 96(13) L.S.G. 31; (1999) 96(10) L.S.G. 32; (1999) 149 N.L.J. 370; (1999) 143 S.J.L.B. 104; [1999] N.P.C. 28; *Times*, March 9, 1999, CA (Civ Div); affirming [1999] 1 W.L.R. 92; [1998] 3 All E.R. 603; [1999] Env. L.R. 256; [1999] E.H.L.R. 59; (1999) 31 H.L.R. 292; (1999) 77 P. & C.R. 216; [1998] 3 E.G.L.R. 25; [1998] 42 E.G. 166; (1998) 95(23) L.S.G. 26; (1998) 148 N.L.J. 836; (1998) 142 S.J.L.B. 173; [1998] N.P.C. 86; *Times*, May 27, 1998, QBD . . . . *Digested*, 99/**4074**:
Considered, 05/333
R. *v.* Britton (Gary Michael) see Attorney General's Reference (No.64 of 2003), Re
R. *v.* Brixton Prison Governor Ex p. Atkinson see Atkinson *v.* United States
R. *v.* Broad (Simon Ronald) see Attorney General's Reference (Nos.86, 87 and 88 of 2004), Re
R. *v.* Broadbent (Timothy Charles) see R. *v.* Rawlings (Royston George)
R. *v.* Brook (Costs) [2004] 1 Costs L.R. 178, Sup Ct Costs Office. . . . . *Digested*, 04/**810**:
Followed, 05/855
R. *v.* Brown (Anthony Joseph); R. *v.* Laskey (Colin); R. *v.* Jaggard (Roland Leonard); R. *v.* Lucas (Saxon); R. *v.* Carter (Christopher Robert); R. *v.* Cadman (Graham William) [1994] 1 A.C. 212; [1993] 2 W.L.R. 556; [1993] 2 All E.R. 75; (1993) 97 Cr. App. R. 44; (1993) 157 J.P. 337; (1993) 157 J.P.N. 233; (1993) 143 N.L.J. 399; *Times*, March 12, 1993; *Independent*, March 12, 1993, HL; affirming [1992] Q.B. 491; [1992] 2 W.L.R. 441; [1992] 2 All E.R. 552; (1992) 94 Cr. App. R. 302; (1992) 156 J.P. 396; (1992) 142 N.L.J. 275; (1992) 136 S.J.L.B. 90; *Times*, February 21, 1992; *Independent*, February 20, 1992; *Guardian*, March 4, 1992, CA (Crim Div) . . . . *Digested*, 93/**920**:
Applied, 00/28: *Considered*, 99/961, 04/749, 05/766, 05/795:
Distinguished, 96/1436
R. *v.* Brown (Billy) see R. *v.* Whiteman (Mark)
R. *v.* Brown (Kevin) (1984) 79 Cr. App. R. 115; [1984] Crim. L.R. 167, CA (Crim Div) . . . *Digested*, 84/**624**:
Applied, 95/1091, 97/1179, 01/1149: *Considered*, 86/667, 87/725, 87/791,
87/864, 88/659, 88/786, 88/864, 92/785, 93/777, 93/778, 94/814,
94/830, 94/1040, 94/1137, 95/1063, 96/1633, 96/1674, 97/1187:
Distinguished, 86/606, 99/1059, 05/793
R. *v.* Brown (Uriah) see Brown (Uriah) *v.* Queen, The
R. *v.* Bryan (Gary David) [2005] EWCA Crim 765; [2005] 2 Cr. App. R. (S.) 106, CA (Crim Div)
R. *v.* Bullen (David) see R. *v.* Everson (Louis) (Appeal against Sentence)
R. *v.* Bullen (David Frederick) see R. *v.* Soneji (Kamlesh Kumar)
R. *v.* Burden (Sarah) see Attorney General's Reference (Nos.132 and 133 of 2004), Re
R. *v.* Burgess (Daniel) see Attorney General's Reference (Nos.31, 42, 43, 45, 50 and 51 of 2003), Re
R. *v.* Burrows (David John) [2004] EWCA Crim 677; [2004] 2 Cr. App. R. (S.) 89, CA (Crim Div) . . . . *Digested*, 05/**3691**
R. *v.* Burrows (Lorraine Shirley) [1998] 2 Cr. App. R. (S.) 407, CA (Crim Div) . . . . *Digested*, 99/**1097**:
Considered, 05/3562
R. *v.* Burt (Gavin) [2004] EWCA Crim 2826; *Independent*, December 3, 2004, CA (Crim Div). . . . . *Digested*, 05/**826**
R. *v.* Burt (Scott-Rab John) see R. *v.* S
R. *v.* Burton on Trent Justices Ex p. Woolley (1995) 159 J.P. 165; [1995] R.T.R. 139; [1996] Crim. L.R. 340; *Times*, November 17, 1994; *Independent*, January 27, 1995; *Independent*, December 29, 1994, DC. . . . . *Digested*, 95/**4413**:
Considered, 95/4411: *Distinguished*, 01/990: *Followed*, 05/781

R. v. Burwood (James) see Attorney General's Reference (Nos.148, 149, 150, 151, 152, 153, 154 and 155 of 2001), Re

R. v. Butler (Joe) [2004] EWCA Crim 2767; [2005] 1 Cr. App. R. (S.) 124, CA (Crim Div)

R. v. Button (Christina Marina) (No.1); R. v. Tannahill (Simon David) [2005] EWCA Crim 516; [2005] Crim. L.R. 571, CA (Crim Div)

R. v. Byrne (Alan) see Attorney General's Reference (Nos.19, 20 and 21 of 2001), Re

R. v. C see R. v. H

R. v. C (Barry) [2004] EWCA Crim 292; [2004] 1 W.L.R. 2098; [2004] 3 All E.R. 1; [2004] 2 Cr. App. R. 15; [2004] 1 F.C.R. 759; [2005] Crim. L.R. 238; (2004) 101 (15) L.S.G. 27; Times, March 25, 2004, CA (Crim Div)..................... *Digested*, 04/**780**

R. v. C (Craig) (A Juvenile) see Attorney General's Reference (Nos.19, 20 and 21 of 2001), Re

R. v. C (David Alexander) [2005] EWCA Crim 2827; Times, November 29, 2005, CA (Crim Div)

R. v. C (James) (A Juvenile) see R. v. Enright (Georgina)

R. v. Cadman (Graham William) see R. v. Brown (Anthony Joseph)

R. v. Cadman-Smith (David) see R. v. Smith (David Cadman)

R. v. Camden and Islington HA Ex p. K see R. (on the application of K) v. Camden and Islington HA

R. v. Camden LBC Ex p. Pereira (1999) 31 H.L.R. 317; [1998] N.P.C. 94, CA (Civ Div); reversing [1998] C.O.D. 318, QBD .... *Digested*, 99/**3062**:
Applied, 05/1989, 05/1991: *Considered*, 05/1990, 05/2006:
Followed, 04/1894

R. v. Cameron (David) see Attorney General's Reference (No.42 of 2005), Re

R. v. Campbell (Michael George) [2004] EWCA Crim 2333; [2005] 1 Cr. App. R. (S.) 92, CA (Crim Div) .... *Digested*, 05/**3588**

R. v. Campbell (Shantelle Jamie) see R. v. Peters (Benjamin)

R. v. Camplin (Paul); sub nom DPP v. Camplin [1978] A.C. 705; [1978] 2 W.L.R. 679; [1978] 2 All E.R. 168; (1978) 67 Cr. App. R. 14; [1978] Crim. L.R. 432; 122 S.J. 280; Times, April 11, 1978, HL; affirming [1978] Q.B. 254; [1977] 3 W.L.R. 929; [1978] 1 All E.R. 1236; (1978) 66 Cr. App. R. 37; [1977] Crim. L.R. 748; 121 S.J. 676, CA (Crim Div) .... *Digested*, 78/**558**:
Applied, 82/676, 87/799, 89/859, 90/850, 05/807: *Considered*, 87/803,
90/920, 93/968, 94/681, 94/1127, 95/1280, 95/1281, 98/960, 00/986:
Distinguished, 84/501, 85/503, 90/1132: *Referred to*, 00/1017

R. v. Canavan (Darren Anthony) see R. v. Kidd (Philip Richard)

R. v. Cann (Jackson) [2004] EWCA Crim 1075; [2005] 1 Cr. App. R. (S.) 12, CA (Crim Div)... *Digested*, 05/**3541**

R. v. Cannings (Angela) [2004] EWCA Crim 1; [2004] 1 W.L.R. 2607; [2004] 1 All E.R. 725; [2004] 2 Cr. App. R. 7; [2004] 1 F.C.R. 193; [2005] Crim. L.R. 126; (2004) 101 (5) L.S.G. 27; (2004) 148 S.J.L.B. 114; Times, January 23, 2004, CA (Crim Div)... *Digested*, 04/**714**:
Considered, 04/1458: *Distinguished*, 05/747: *Referred to*, 05/3659

R. v. Carasco (Charles) see R. v. Lang (Stephen Howard)

R. v. Carp (Anthony Mark) see R. v. Highton (Edward Paul)

R. v. Carr (Craig Edward) see R. v. S

R. v. Carroll Unreported, HC (Aus) .... *Considered*, 05/733

R. v. Carroll (Jerome); R. v. Artry (Marcus) [2004] EWCA Crim 1367; [2005] 1 Cr. App. R. (S.) 10, CA (Crim Div)

R. v. Carroll (Matthew) see R. v. Rees (Louis)

R. v. Carter (Christopher Robert) see R. v. Brown (Anthony Joseph)

R. v. Cassidy (Thomas Joseph) [2004] EWCA Crim 1480; [2005] 1 Cr. App. R. (S.) 44, CA (Crim Div) .... *Digested*, 05/**3598**

R. v. CCE see Attorney General's Reference (Nos.91, 119 and 120 of 2002), Re

R. v. Celaire (Mario Rolando) see R. v. Poulton (Sarah Jane)

R. v. Central Criminal Court Ex p. Director of the Serious Fraud Office [1993] 1 W.L.R. 949; [1993] 2 All E.R. 399; (1993) 96 Cr. App. R. 248; [1993] C.O.D. 59; Times, September 8, 1992; Independent, September 3, 1992, QBD................ *Digested*, 93/**12**:
Considered, 94/8: *Doubted*, 05/71

R. v. Chaaban (Khodr); sub nom R. v. Chabaan (Khodr) [2003] EWCA Crim 1012; [2003] Crim. L.R. 658; Times, May 9, 2003; Independent, May 6, 2003, CA (Crim Div)... *Digested*, 03/**816**:
Applied, 05/837: *Followed*, 04/889

R. v. Chabaan (Khodr) see R. v. Chaaban (Khodr)

R. v. Chambers (Stephen Paul) see Attorney General's Reference (No.90 of 2004), Re

R. v. Chapman (Andrew Edward) [2002] EWCA Crim 2346; (2002) 146 S.J.L.B. 242, CA (Crim Div).. *Considered*, 05/3761

R. v. Chappell (Edwin John) see Attorney General's Reference (No.147 of 2004), Re

R. v. Charles (Anthony Roger) [2004] EWCA Crim 1977; [2005] 1 Cr. App. R. (S.) 56, CA (Crim Div) .... *Digested*, 05/**3698**

R. v. Charlton (Brett) see Attorney General's Reference (No.19 of 2004), Re

R. *v.* Cheema (Gurmit Singh) [2002] EWCA Crim 325; [2002] 2 Cr. App. R. (S.) 79,
CA (Crim Div) . . . . *Digested,* 02/**3950**:
Applied, 05/3610: *Considered,* 05/3605
R. *v.* Cheetham (David Edward); R. *v.* Baker (Robert John) [2004] EWCA Crim 409;
[2004] 2 Cr. App. R. (S.) 53, CA (Crim Div) . . . . *Considered,* 05/3663
R. *v.* Chellouj (Tariq) see Attorney General's Reference (Nos.27, 28, 29 and 30 of
2005), Re
R. *v.* Cherry (Alan Barry) see R. *v.* Harris (Lorraine)
R. *v.* Chichester Crown Court Ex p. Moss see DPP *v.* O'Connor
R. *v.* Chief Constable of Devon and Cornwall Ex p. Hay; R. *v.* Chief Constable of
Devon and Cornwall Ex p. Police Complaints Authority [1996] 2 All E.R. 711;
Times, February 19, 1996, QBD . . . . *Digested,* 96/**4859**:
Applied, 05/3334
R. *v.* Chief Constable of Devon and Cornwall Ex p. Police Complaints Authority see R.
v. Chief Constable of Devon and Cornwall Ex p. Hay
R. *v.* Chief Constable of Thames Valley Ex p. Cotton; *sub nom* R. *v.* Deputy Chief
Constable of Thames Valley Ex p. Cotton [1990] I.R.L.R. 344; *Times,* December
28, 1989; *Independent,* December 22, 1989, CA (Civ Div); affirming [1989]
C.O.D. 318, QBD . . . . *Digested,* 91/**95**:
Considered, 92/955, 94/43, 98/3025, 05/75: *Followed,* 99/97
R. *v.* Chirila (Adina Ramova) see R. *v.* Chirila (Remus Tenistocle)
R. *v.* Chirila (Remus Tenistocle); R. *v.* Monteanu (Adrian); R. *v.* Chirila (Adina Ramova)
[2004] EWCA Crim 2200; [2005] 1 Cr. App. R. (S.) 93, CA (Crim Div) . . . . *Digested,* 05/**3614**
R. *v.* Chisti (Pirzada) see R. *v.* Rizvi (Zafar)
R. *v.* Chohan (Naveed Nasir) see R. *v.* Edwards (Karl Adrian)
R. *v.* Chuni (Narinder) [2000] 2 Cr. App. R. (S.) 64, CA (Crim Div) . . . . *Digested,* 00/**1191**:
Applied, 05/3728
R. *v.* Cioffo (Antonio) [1996] 1 Cr. App. R. (S.) 427, CA (Crim Div) . . . . *Digested,* 96/**1730**:
Considered, 05/3696: *Distinguished,* 03/3630
R. *v.* City of London Corp Ex p. Mystery of the Barbers of London; *sub nom* R. *v.*
Mayor and Commonality and the Citizens of London Ex p. Mystery of the
Barbers of London (1997) 73 P. & C.R. 59; [1996] 2 E.G.L.R. 128; [1996] 42
E.G. 156; [1996] E.G.C.S. 101; [1996] N.P.C. 91; *Times,* June 28, 1996, QBD . . . . *Digested,* 96/**4750**:
Considered, 05/3434
R. *v.* Clark (Brian James) [2001] EWCA Crim 884; [2002] 1 Cr. App. R. 14; [2001]
Crim. L.R. 572, CA (Crim Div) . . . . *Digested,* 02/**809**:
Followed, 05/850
R. *v.* Clark (Raymond Dennis) [1996] 2 Cr. App. R. 282; [1996] 2 Cr. App. R. (S.) 351;
[1996] Crim. L.R. 448; *Times,* April 10, 1996, CA (Crim Div) . . . . *Digested,* 96/**1944**:
Applied, 98/1123, 98/1387, 05/3737, 05/3742: *Approved,* 97/1492:
Considered, 99/1351: *Disapproved,* 97/1103: *Distinguished,* 97/1493:
Followed, 99/1352
R. *v.* Clark (Trevor) [1998] 2 Cr. App. R. 137; [1998] 2 Cr. App. R. (S.) 95; [1998]
Crim. L.R. 227; (1998) 95(2) L.S.G. 22; (1998) 142 S.J.L.B. 27; *Times,*
December 4, 1997, CA (Crim Div) . . . . *Digested,* 98/**1392**:
Applied, 00/1237, 01/1491, 03/3870, 04/858, 04/3318: *Considered,* 98/1316,
98/1394, 99/1121, 99/1174, 99/1277, 99/1359, 99/1362, 99/1364, 00/1436,
02/4038, 02/4039, 05/3611: *Distinguished,* 03/3811: *Followed,* 04/3353
R. *v.* Clements (Paul) see Attorney General's Reference (Nos.148, 149, 150, 151, 152,
153, 154 and 155 of 2001), Re
R. *v.* Cliff (Oliver Lewis) [2004] EWCA Crim 3139; [2005] 2 Cr. App. R. (S.) 22;
[2005] R.T.R. 11; [2005] Crim. L.R. 250; *Times,* December 1, 2004, CA (Crim
Div) . . . . *Digested,* 05/**3584**
R. *v.* Clugston (John) [2004] EWCA Crim 1324; [2005] 1 Cr. App. R. (S.) 30, CA
(Crim Div) . . . . *Digested,* 05/**3685**
R. *v.* Clwyd CC Ex p. A [1994] 1 F.C.R. 334; [1993] C.O.D. 35; (1993) 157 L.G. Rev.
567; *Times,* August 26, 1992, QBD . . . . *Digested,* 94/**1875**:
Considered, 05/1145
R. *v.* Coates (Victor Henry); R. *v.* Graves (Martin John); R. *v.* Terry (Wayne Michael); R.
v. Colman (Robert Luke) [2004] EWCA Crim 2253; [2004] 1 W.L.R. 3043;
[2004] 4 All E.R. 1150; [2005] 1 Cr. App. R. 14; [2005] Crim. L.R. 308; (2004)
101(36) L.S.G. 33; (2004) 148 S.J.L.B. 1118; *Times,* August 24, 2004, CA
(Crim Div) . . . . *Digested,* 04/**39**
R. *v.* Coleman (Anthony Neville) (1992) 95 Cr. App. R. 159; (1992) 13 Cr. App. R. (S.)
508; [1992] Crim. L.R. 315; *Times,* December 10, 1991, CA (Crim Div) . . . . *Digested,* 93/**1224**:
Cited, 01/1427: *Considered,* 97/1554, 99/1261, 00/1362, 04/3470, 05/3662,
05/3667: *Referred to,* 94/1306, 95/1434, 97/1620
R. *v.* Coleman (George Romero) see R. *v.* Petch (Thomas)
R. *v.* Coles (Dean) see Attorney General's Reference (Nos.37, 38, 44, 54, 51, 53, 35,
40, 43, 45, 41 and 42 of 2003), Re
R. *v.* Collard (Jonathan Richard) [2004] EWCA Crim 1664; [2005] 1 Cr. App. R. (S.)
34; [2004] Crim. L.R. 757; (2004) 148 S.J.L.B. 663; *Times,* June 7, 2004, CA
(Crim Div) . . . . *Digested,* 04/**3378**
R. *v.* Collier (Edward) see R. *v.* Lang (Stephen Howard)

R. *v.* Collier (Edward John) [2004] EWCA Crim 1411; [2005] 1 W.L.R. 843; [2005] 1
Cr. App. R. 9; (2004) 101 (27) L.S.G. 29; *Times,* July 13, 2004, CA (Crim Div) . .   *Digested,* 05/**800**
R. *v.* Collier (Michael Anthony) see Attorney General's Reference (Nos.60 and 61 of
1995), Re
R. *v.* Collins (Justin) see R. *v.* Woods (David Reginald)
R. *v.* Collins (Kerrie Jane) [2004] EWCA Crim 1269; [2005] 1 Cr. App. R. (S.) 22, CA
(Crim Div). . . . .   *Digested,* 05/**3688**
R. *v.* Colman (Robert Luke) see R. *v.* Coates (Victor Henry)
R. *v.* Colman (Robert Luke) see R. *v.* Terry (Wayne Michael)
R. *v.* Colthrop Board Mills Ltd [2002] EWCA Crim 520; [2002] 2 Cr. App. R. (S.) 80,
CA (Crim Div). . . . .   *Digested,* 02/**3968**:
                                              Considered, 03/1923, 03/3715, 05/3630
R. *v.* Comerford (Thomas Anthony) see R. *v.* Healey (Bernard)
R. *v.* Commissioner for Local Administration Ex p. Croydon LBC [1989] 1 All E.R.
1033; 87 L.G.R. 221; [1989] C.O.D. 226; (1989) 153 L.G. Rev. 131; *Times,* June
9, 1988; *Independent,* June 9, 1988; *Guardian,* June 17, 1988, QBD . . . .   *Digested,* 89/**2328**:
                          Applied, 94/1866, 95/1911: *Considered,* 94/1858, 97/2108, 98/1915, 00/1921,
                                             05/402: *Referred to,* 90/42, 92/1852
R. *v.* Connell (Tom) see Attorney General's Reference (Nos.99, 100, 101 and 102 of
2004), Re
R. *v.* Connor (Ben) see R. *v.* Mirza (Shabbir Ali)
R. *v.* Connors (James) see R. *v.* Underwood (Kevin John)
R. *v.* Cook (Jordan) see R. *v.* Docking (Jason)
R. *v.* Cook (Neil Terence) see Attorney General's Reference (No.152 of 2002), Re
R. *v.* Cooksley (Robert Charles) see Attorney General's Reference (No.152 of 2002),
Re
R. *v.* Coombes (Jeffrey Ian) see Attorney General's Reference (Nos.115 and 116 of
2004), Re
R. *v.* Cooper (Mark Anthony) [1996] 1 Cr. App. R. (S.) 303, CA (Crim Div). . . . .   *Digested,* 96/**1970**:
                                                 Considered, 05/3619
R. *v.* Cornwall CC Ex p. Huntington; R. *v.* Devon CC Ex p. Isaac [1994] 1 All E.R. 694,
CA (Civ Div); affirming [1992] 3 All E.R. 566; [1992] C.O.D. 223; (1992) 142
N.L.J. 348; *Times,* March 5, 1992, QBD . . . .   *Digested,* 94/**65**:
                          Applied, 96/4839, 97/4132, 99/4227, 01/4676: *Considered,* 05/3459
R. *v.* Corran (Ben); R. *v.* Cutler (Jason); R. *v.* Heard (Kevin Phillip); R. *v.* Williams
(Anthony Michael) [2005] EWCA Crim 192; [2005] 2 Cr. App. R. (S.) 73;
[2005] Crim. L.R. 404; *Times,* March 8, 2005, CA (Crim Div) . . . .   *Digested,* 05/**3734**:
                                                 Approved, 05/3776
R. *v.* Corriette (Jean-Yves) see Attorney General's Reference (No.21 of 2005), Re
R. *v.* Cosco (Michael Nicola) [2005] EWCA Crim 207; [2005] 2 Cr. App. R. (S.) 66,
CA (Crim Div). . . . .   *Digested,* 05/**3686**
R. *v.* Costen (Sharon Elizabeth) (1989) 11 Cr. App. R. (S.) 182; [1989] Crim. L.R. 601,
CA (Crim Div). . . . .   *Digested,* 91/**1134**:
                          Considered, 96/1717, 99/1168, 01/1468: *Followed,* 05/3607:
                                              Referred to, 92/1293, 93/1048
R. *v.* Cotton (1896) 60 J.P. 824 . . . .   *Considered,* 05/921
R. *v.* Court (Robert Christopher) [1989] A.C. 28; [1988] 2 W.L.R. 1071; [1988] 2 All
E.R. 221; (1988) 87 Cr. App. R. 144; (1988) 152 J.P. 422; [1988] Crim. L.R. 537;
(1988) 152 J.P.N. 414; (1988) 138 N.L.J. Rep. 128; *Times,* May 3, 1988;
Independent, May 4, 1988; *Guardian,* May 6, 1988, HL; affirming [1987] Q.B.
156; [1986] 3 W.L.R. 1029; [1987] 1 All E.R. 120; (1987) 84 Cr. App. R. 210;
[1987] Crim. L.R. 134, CA (Crim Div) . . . .   *Digested,* 88/**793**:
                        Applied, 90/1111: *Considered,* 94/855, 05/819: *Distinguished,* 88/796,
                                                      89/836, 93/959
R. *v.* Coutts (Graham James) [2005] EWCA Crim 52; [2005] 1 W.L.R. 1605; [2005]
1 Cr. App. R. 31; [2005] Crim. L.R. 784; (2005) 102(9) L.S.G. 28; *Times,*
January 26, 2005, CA (Crim Div). . . . .   *Digested,* 05/**896**
R. *v.* Cova Products Ltd [2005] EWCA Crim 95; [2005] Crim. L.R. 667, CA (Crim
Div)
R. *v.* Coventry DC Housing Benefit Review Board Ex p. Bodden see R. *v.* Sheffield
Housing Benefit Review Board Ex p. Smith
R. *v.* Cowan (Donald); R. *v.* Gayle (Ricky); R. *v.* Ricciardi (Carmine) [1996] Q.B. 373;
[1995] 3 W.L.R. 818; [1995] 4 All E.R. 939; [1996] 1 Cr. App. R. 1; (1996) 160
J.P. 165; [1996] Crim. L.R. 409; (1996) 160 J.P.N. 14; (1995) 92(38) L.S.G.
26; (1995) 145 N.L.J. 1611; (1995) 139 S.J.L.B. 215; *Times,* October 13, 1995;
Independent, October 25, 1995, CA (Crim Div). . . . .   *Digested,* 96/**1511**:
                          Applied, 98/1059, 00/1076, 04/858: *Considered,* 97/1320, 97/4364, 05/748:
                                                 Followed, 00/1074
R. *v.* Cox (Alan David) [2004] EWCA Crim 2637; [2005] 1 Cr. App. R. (S.) 105, CA
(Crim Div)
R. *v.* Cox (Earl Webster) see Attorney General's Reference (No.89 of 2004), Re
R. *v.* Cox (Jacqueline) [2004] EWCA Crim 282; [2004] 2 Cr. App. R. (S.) 54; *Times,*
February 20, 2004, CA (Crim Div) . . . .   *Digested,* 05/**3580**

R. v. Cox (Richard Cobden); R. v. Railton (Richard Johnson) (1884-85) L.R. 14 Q.B.D.
153; [1881-85] All E.R. Rep. 68, Crown Cases Reserved . . . . *Applied,* 72/2732:
Considered, 70/1039, 87/3059, 89/694, 91/781, 91/2859, 01/399, 05/744:
Explained, 88/845, 89/898, 90/1175: *Followed,* 80/2138
R. v. Coyne (Timothy Malcolm) see R. v. S
R. v. Crane (Sara) see R. v. Last (Emma)
R. v. Craven (Adrian) see R. v. Meredith (Christopher)
R. v. Crawley (Alexander Steven) see Attorney General's Reference (Nos.3 and 4 of
2005), Re
R. v. Cronshaw (Michael George) [2004] EWCA Crim 2057; [2005] 1 Cr. App. R. (S.)
89, CA (Crim Div) . . . . *Applied,* 05/3644
R. v. Crow (William John); R. v. Pennington (Derek) (1995) 16 Cr. App. R. (S.) 409;
[1994] Crim. L.R. 958, CA (Crim Div) . . . . *Considered,* 94/1300,
96/1698, 96/1905, 98/1248, 99/1335, 00/1284, 03/3878, 05/3648
R. v. Crowley (Helen) see Attorney General's Reference (No.1 of 2004), Re
R. v. Croydon Youth Court Ex p. DPP [1997] 2 Cr. App. R. 411; [1997] C.O.D. 419,
QBD . . . . *Digested,* 98/**1069**:
Considered, 05/3635
R. v. Crump (Richard James) see Attorney General's Reference (No.152 of 2002), Re
R. v. Cummins (Dominic John) see R. v. Mason (Nicholas)
R. v. Customs and Excise Commissioners Ex p. Kilroy Television Co Ltd see Customs
and Excise Commissioners v. Kilroy Television Co Ltd
R. v. Customs and Excise Commissioners Ex p. Lunn Poly Ltd [1999] S.T.C. 350;
[1999] 1 C.M.L.R. 1357; [1999] Eu. L.R. 653; (1999) 96(13) L.S.G. 32; (1999)
143 S.J.L.B. 104; *Times,* March 11, 1999, CA (Civ Div); affirming [1998] S.T.C.
649; [1998] 2 C.M.L.R. 560; [1998] Eu. L.R. 438; *Times,* April 8, 1998, DC . . . . *Digested,* 99/**4743**:
Applied, 01/5316, 01/5346, 02/4462: *Followed,* 01/118, 02/4420:
Referred to, 05/2380
R. v. Customs and Excise Commissioners Ex p. Strangewood [1987] S.T.C. 502, QBD . *Digested,* 87/**3832**:
Applied, 05/4373: *Distinguished,* 04/4032
R. v. Customs and Excise Commissioners Ex p. Tattersalls Ltd (10/87) [1988] S.T.C.
630; [1988] E.C.R. 3281; [1988] 3 C.M.L.R. 113; *Times,* June 22, 1988, ECJ . . . *Digested,* 89/**1677**:
Considered, 05/4396
R. v. Cutler (Jason) see R. v. Corran (Ben)
R. v. Cutler (Saul Roland) see Attorney General's Reference (No.18 of 1997), Re
R. v. D see R. v. Lang (Stephen Howard)
R. v. D [2005] EWCA Crim 3660; *Independent,* December 21, 2005, CA (Crim Div)
R. v. D (Adam George) see R. v. K (Patrick Joseph)
R. v. D (Hollie Louise) [2005] EWCA Crim 2292; (2005) 169 J.P. 662; (2005) 169
J.P.N. 979, CA (Crim Div)
R. v. D (Joined Charges: Evidence) [2003] EWCA Crim 2424; [2004] 1 Cr. App. R.
19; [2005] Crim. L.R. 163; (2003) 147 S.J.L.B. 1088; *Times,* October 9, 2003,
CA (Crim Div) . . . . *Digested,* 04/**857**
R. v. Dad (Arif Mahmood) see Attorney General's Reference (No.311 of 2004), Re
R. v. Dadley (Andrew Mark) [2004] EWCA Crim 2216; [2005] 1 Cr. App. R. (S.) 87,
CA (Crim Div) . . . . *Digested,* 05/**3628**
R. v. Dalby (Christopher John); R. v. Berry (James William) [2005] EWCA Crim 1292;
[2005] Crim. L.R. 731, CA (Crim Div)
R. v. Dalby (Derek Shaun) [1982] 1 W.L.R. 425; [1982] 1 All E.R. 916; (1982) 74 Cr.
App. R. 348; [1982] Crim. L.R. 439, CA (Crim Div) . . . . *Digested,* 82/**639**:
Cited, 92/1335, 93/1223: *Considered,* 89/847, 90/1114:
Distinguished, 05/803: *Explained,* 86/635
R. v. Dale (Adam) see Attorney General's Reference (Nos.39, 40 and 41 of 2005)
R. v. Dale (Andrew Peter) [2004] EWCA Crim 231; [2004] 2 Cr. App. R. (S.) 58, CA
(Crim Div). . . . . *Digested,* 05/**3566**
R. v. Daventry DC Ex p. Thornby Farms see R. (on the application of Thornby Farms
Ltd) v. Daventry DC
R. v. Davey (Mark Andrew) see R. v. Lowe (Paul)
R. v. Davies (Craig Darren) [2003] EWCA Crim 850; [2003] 2 Cr. App. R. (S.) 104,
CA (Crim Div) . . . . *Digested,* 03/**3854**:
Considered, 05/3733
R. v. Davies (David Patrick) [1996] 1 Cr. App. R. (S.) 28, CA (Crim Div) . . . . *Considered,* 96/2017,
97/1622, 99/1267, 05/3664
R. v. Davis (Reginald) [1998] Crim. L.R. 564, CA (Crim Div) . . . . *Considered,* 05/797
R. v. Davy (Leonard Francis) [1997] 1 Cr. App. R. (S.) 17, CA (Crim Div) . . . . *Digested,* 97/**1517**:
Considered, 05/3578
R. v. Dawn (Andrew Stephen) (1994) 15 Cr. App. R. (S.) 720, CA (Crim Div) . . . . *Digested,* 95/**1444**:
Considered, 05/3556
R. v. Dawson (James Anthony) see Attorney General's Reference (No.37 of 2004), Re
R. v. De Qun He see R. v. Weir (Antony Albert)
R. v. Deb (Peter) see R. v. Din (Ameen)
R. v. Dekson (Rasheed) [2004] EWCA Crim 3205; [2005] 1 Cr. App. R. (S.) 114, CA
(Crim Div). . . . . *Digested,* 05/**911**
R. v. Demers (Rejean) 19 B.H.R.C. 247, Sup Ct (Can)

R. *v.* Denton (Errol) see Attorney General's Reference (No.1 of 2004), Re
R. *v.* Denton (Vincent) see R. *v.* S
R. *v.* Deo (Sarwan Singh) see R. *v.* Saini (Jarnail Singh)
R. *v.* Deputy Chief Constable of Thames Valley Ex p. Cotton see R. *v.* Chief Constable
　　of Thames Valley Ex p. Cotton
R. *v.* Deputy Governor of Parkhurst Prison Ex p. Hague; *sub nom* Hague *v.* Deputy
　　Governor of Parkhurst Prison; Weldon *v.* Home Office [1992] 1 A.C. 58; [1991] 3
　　W.L.R. 340; [1991] 3 All E.R. 733; (1993) 5 Admin. L.R. 425; [1992] C.O.D.
　　69; (1991) 135 S.J.L.B. 102; *Times*, July 25, 1991; *Independent*, September 4,
　　1991; *Guardian*, July 31, 1991, HL; affirming [1990] 3 W.L.R. 1210; [1990] 3 All
　　E.R. 687; (1991) 3 Admin. L.R. 581; [1990] C.O.D. 459; (1990) 140 N.L.J. 1036;
　　Times, June 22, 1990; *Independent*, June 15, 1990; *Guardian*, June 5, 1990, CA
　　(Civ Div); reversing in part [1990] C.O.D. 67, QBD . . . . 　*Digested*, 92/**3651**:
　　　　　　　　　　　　Applied, 93/2983, 00/5662, 02/3240: *Distinguished*, 94/4284, 05/2917:
　　　　　　　　　　　　Followed, 92/3210, 92/3657: *Previous proceedings*, 90/4313
R. *v.* Derbyshire CC Ex p. Woods [1998] Env. L.R. 277; [1997] J.P.L. 958, CA (Civ
　　Div) . . . . 　*Digested*, 97/**4106**:
　　　　　　　　　　　Applied, 99/4256, 00/4504, 01/4763, 05/3295: *Considered*, 00/4491:
　　　　　　　　　　　　　　　　　　　　　　　　　　　　　　　　　　　Referred to, 00/4520
R. *v.* Derekis (Theresa Anne) [2004] EWCA Crim 2729; [2005] 2 Cr. App. R. (S.) 1,
　　CA (Crim Div) . . . . 　*Digested*, 05/**3664**
R. *v.* Dervishi (Markel) see Attorney General's Reference (Nos.135, 136 and 137), Re
R. *v.* Despres (Costs) [2005] 4 Costs L.R. 750, Sup Ct Costs Office
R. *v.* Devon CC Ex p. Isaac see R. *v.* Cornwall CC Ex p. Huntington
R. *v.* Dhaliwal (Costs) [2004] 4 Costs L.R. 689, Sup Ct Costs Office . . . . 　*Digested*, 05/**852**
R. *v.* Dhillon (Pritpal Sineh) [2005] EWCA Crim 2996; *Times*, November 29, 2005, CA
　　(Crim Div)
R. *v.* Dhnoay (Gurdev Singh) see R. *v.* Knights (Richard Michael)
R. *v.* Diani Unreported, Sup Ct (Gib) . . . . 　*Considered*, 05/633
R. *v.* Dias (Fernando Augusto) [2001] EWCA Crim 2986; [2002] 2 Cr. App. R. 5;
　　[2002] Crim. L.R. 490, CA (Crim Div) . . . . 　*Digested*, 02/**801**:
　　　　　　　　　　　　　　　　　　　　Applied, 03/794: *Considered*, 05/803
R. *v.* Dica (Mohammed) [2004] EWCA Crim 1103; [2004] Q.B. 1257; [2004] 3
　　W.L.R. 213; [2004] 3 All E.R. 593; [2004] 2 Cr. App. R. 28; (2004) 77 B.M.L.R.
　　243; (2004) 101(21) L.S.G. 35; (2004) 148 S.J.L.B. 570; *Times*, May 11, 2004,
　　CA (Crim Div) . . . . 　*Digested*, 04/**749**:
　　　　　　　　　　　　　　　　　　　　Applied, 05/766: *Considered*, 05/795
R. *v.* Dica (Mohammed) [2005] EWCA Crim 2304; *Times*, September 7, 2005, CA
　　(Crim Div) . . . . 　*Digested*, 05/**3618**
R. *v.* Dickinson (Neville) [2005] EWCA Crim 289; [2005] 2 Cr. App. R. (S.) 78, CA
　　(Crim Div) . . . . 　*Digested*, 05/**3527**
R. *v.* Dickson (Robert Leslie) see Attorney General's Reference (Nos.3, 4, 8, 9, 10, 11,
　　14 and 16 of 1990), Re
R. *v.* Dillon (Matthew James) see R. *v.* Pick (Martin James)
R. *v.* Dimsey (Dermot Jeremy) (Appeals against Sentence); R. *v.* Allen (Brian Roger)
　　(Appeals against Sentence) [2000] 2 All E.R. 142; [2000] 1 Cr. App. R. (S.)
　　497; [2000] Crim. L.R. 199; *Times*, October 13, 1999, CA (Crim Div) . . . . 　*Digested*, 99/**910**:
　　　　　　　　　　　　　　　Considered, 01/1111, 05/840: *Distinguished*, 00/1162
R. *v.* Din (Ameen); R. *v.* Deb (Peter); R. *v.* Zaheer (Mohammed); R. *v.* Din (Yasin); R. *v.*
　　Najib (Parvaz); R. *v.* Hussain (Sajid) [2004] EWCA Crim 3364; [2005] 2 Cr.
　　App. R. (S.) 40, CA (Crim Div) . . . . 　*Digested*, 05/**3613**
R. *v.* Din (Yasin) see R. *v.* Din (Ameen)
R. *v.* Dissanayake (Rohan Shivantha) see R. *v.* Nazari (Fazlollah)
R. *v.* Ditchfield (Jeffrey) see R. *v.* Quayle (Barry)
R. *v.* Djahit (Turkesh) [1999] 2 Cr. App. R. (S.) 142, CA (Crim Div) . . . . 　*Digested*, 99/**1137**:
　　　　　　　　　　Applied, 01/1282: *Considered*, 00/1225, 02/3928, 03/3695, 04/3412,
　　　　　　　　　　04/3450, 04/3452, 05/3590, 05/3707, 05/3748, 05/3751, 05/3753:
　　　　　　　　　　　　　　　　　　　　　　　　　　　　　Distinguished, 04/3454
R. *v.* Docking (Jason); R. *v.* Wild (James Matthew); R. *v.* Lewis (Leroy Marvin); R. *v.*
　　Cook (Jordan) [2004] EWCA Crim 2675; [2005] 1 Cr. App. R. (S.) 119, CA
　　(Crim Div) . . . . 　*Digested*, 05/**3675**
R. *v.* Dodds (Raymond) [2002] EWCA Crim 1328; [2003] 1 Cr. App. R. 3; [2002]
　　Crim. L.R. 735, CA (Crim Div) . . . . 　*Digested*, 03/**875**:
　　　　　　　　　　　　　　　　　　　　　　　　　　　　　　　　Considered, 05/847
R. *v.* Doidge (Carl) [2005] EWCA Crim 273; *Times*, March 10, 2005, CA (Crim Div) . . . 　*Digested*, 05/**3780**
R. *v.* Donaghue (Troy) see Attorney General's Reference (Nos.38 and 39 of 2004), Re
R. *v.* Donnelly (Miles) see R. *v.* Kelly (Lewis)
R. *v.* Donovan (Terrence Mark); *sub nom* R. *v.* Donovan (Terence Mark) [2004] EWCA
　　Crim 1237; [2005] 1 Cr. App. R. (S.) 16, CA (Crim Div) . . . . 　*Digested*, 05/**3704**:
　　　　　　　　　　　　　　　　　　　　　　　　　　　　　　　　Followed, 05/3578
R. *v.* Dooley (Michael) (Appeal against Conviction) [2005] EWCA Crim 3093; *Times*,
　　November 10, 2005, CA (Crim Div)
R. *v.* Doubtfire (Robert Henry) (No.1) see R. *v.* Van Tattenhove (Frans Willem)
R. *v.* Dowds (Peter Andrew) see R. *v.* Bovell (Kelvin Anthony)

R. *v.* Dowell (Richard Alexander) see R. *v.* Early (John)

R. *v.* Downes (Rawle Colin) [2005] EWCA Crim 457; (2005) 149 S.J.L.B. 265, CA (Crim Div)

R. *v.* Doyle (Kevin) [1996] 1 Cr. App. R. (S.) 449, CA (Crim Div) . . . .   *Digested,* 96/**1857**: *Considered,* 05/3704

R. *v.* DPP Ex p. Bull see R. *v.* Lord Chancellor Ex p. Child Poverty Action Group

R. *v.* Draper [1962] Crim. L.R. 107, CCA . . . .   *Digested,* 62/**647**: *Disapproved,* 05/902

R. *v.* Draper (James Thomas) see R. *v.* Whiteman (Mark)

R. *v.* Drayton (Alan Clark) [2005] EWCA Crim 2013; (2005) 169 J.P. 593; (2005) 169 J.P.N. 877; *Times,* September 14, 2005, CA (Crim Div)

R. *v.* DS see Attorney General's Reference (Nos.37, 38, 44, 54, 51, 53, 35, 40, 43, 45, 41 and 42 of 2003), Re

R. *v.* Dudley Magistrates Court Ex p. Hollis; Hollis *v.* Dudley MBC; Probert *v.* Dudley MBC [1999] 1 W.L.R. 642; [1998] 1 All E.R. 759; [1998] Env. L.R. 354; [1998] E.H.L.R. 42; (1998) 30 H.L.R. 902; [1998] 2 E.G.L.R. 19; [1998] 18 E.G. 133; [1998] J.P.L. 652; [1998] C.O.D. 186; [1997] N.P.C. 169; *Times,* December 12, 1997, DC . . . .   *Digested,* 98/**4048**: *Applied,* 05/342: *Considered,* 05/1486

R. *v.* Duffy (Nicholas Thomas) [2004] EWCA Crim 2054; [2005] 1 Cr. App. R. (S.) 75, CA (Crim Div) . . . .   *Digested,* 05/**3607**

R. *v.* Duffy (Warren Edward) see Attorney General's Reference (Nos.3, 4, 8, 9, 10, 11, 14 and 16 of 1990), Re

R. *v.* Duggan (James Edward) see R. *v.* Edwards (Karl Adrian)

R. *v.* Dundon (Richard John) [2004] EWCA Crim 621; [2004] U.K.H.R.R. 717; (2004) 148 S.J.L.B. 536; *Times,* April 28, 2004, CMAC . . . .   *Digested,* 04/**202**: *Considered,* 05/859

R. *v.* Dunraven School Governors Ex p. B (A Child) [2000] B.L.G.R. 494; [2000] Ed. C.R. 291; [2000] E.L.R. 156; (2000) 97(4) L.S.G. 32; (2000) 144 S.J.L.B. 51; *Times,* February 3, 2000, CA (Civ Div); reversing *Times,* November 10, 1999, QBD . . . .   *Digested,* 00/**1925**: *Applied,* 01/1975, 03/1058: *Considered,* 05/1071: *Distinguished,* 03/1055, 04/1065

R. *v.* Dwyer (Monique Zoe) [2004] EWCA Crim 2982; [2005] 2 Cr. App. R. (S.) 9; [2005] Crim. L.R. 320, CA (Civ Div) . . . .   *Digested,* 05/**3774**

R. *v.* Dytham (Philip Thomas) [1979] Q.B. 722; [1979] 3 W.L.R. 467; [1979] 3 All E.R. 641; (1979) 69 Cr. App. R. 387; [1979] Crim. L.R. 666, CA (Crim Div) . . . .   *Digested,* 79/**2085**: *Applied,* 04/753, 05/898: *Considered,* 95/165: *Distinguished,* 93/2958

R. *v.* E; *sub nom* R. *v.* TE [2004] EWCA Crim 1441; [2004] 2 Cr. App. R. 36; [2005] Crim. L.R. 74, CA (Crim Div)

R. *v.* E (Dennis Andrew) [2004] EWCA Crim 1313; [2005] Crim. L.R. 227, CA (Crim Div)

R. *v.* E (Keith) see Attorney General's Reference (No.44 of 2004), Re

R. *v.* Ealing LBC Ex p. McBain [1985] 1 W.L.R. 1351; [1986] 1 All E.R. 13; [1986] 1 F.L.R. 479; (1986) 18 H.L.R. 59; 84 L.G.R. 278; [1986] Fam. Law 77; (1985) 135 N.L.J. 120; (1985) 129 S.J. 870; *Times,* October 10, 1985, CA (Civ Div); reversing (1985) 17 H.L.R. 465 . . . .   *Digested,* 86/**1628**: *Considered,* 94/2345, 95/2580, 05/1986: *Distinguished,* 93/2047

R. *v.* Early (John); R. *v.* Bajwa (Narip Singh); R. *v.* Vickers (Royston Gary); R. *v.* Dowell (Richard Alexander); R. *v.* Patel (Rahul); R. *v.* Patel (Nilam); R. *v.* Pearcy (Colin); R. *v.* Patel (Madhusudan Maganbhai) [2002] EWCA Crim 1904; [2003] 1 Cr. App. R. 19; (2002) 99(39) L.S.G. 38; *Times,* August 2, 2002, CA (Crim Div) . . .   *Digested,* 02/**904**: *Distinguished,* 05/875

R. *v.* Eastwood [1961] Crim. L.R. 414, CCA . . . .   *Digested,* 61/**2167**: *Disapproved,* 05/902

R. *v.* Eaton (Craig Keith) see R. *v.* Archer (Patrick John)

R. *v.* Edwards (Anthony Glen) [1998] 2 Cr. App. R. (S.) 213; [1998] Crim. L.R. 298, CA (Crim Div) . . . .   *Digested,* 98/**665**: *Considered,* 05/910: *Followed,* 99/1156

R. *v.* Edwards (Brynley Maldwin) [2001] EWCA Crim 862; [2001] 2 Cr. App. R. (S.) 125, CA (Crim Div) . . . .   *Digested,* 01/**1425**: *Considered,* 05/3662

R. *v.* Edwards (Caroline Patricia) see Attorney General's Reference (No.1 of 2004), Re

R. *v.* Edwards (Costs) [2004] 4 Costs L.R. 679, Sup Ct Costs Office . . . .   *Digested,* 05/**853**

R. *v.* Edwards (Glyn) [2004] EWCA Crim 2923; [2005] 2 Cr. App. R. (S.) 29; (2004) 148 S.J.L.B. 1433, CA (Crim Div) . . . .   *Digested,* 05/**794**

R. *v.* Edwards (Karl Adrian); R. *v.* Fysh (Stephen John); R. *v.* Duggan (James Edward); R. *v.* Chohan (Naveed Nasir) [2005] EWCA Crim 1813; *Times,* September 9, 2005, CA (Crim Div) . . . .   *Digested,* 05/**835**: *Followed,* 05/726

R. *v.* Edwards (Kyle Frederick) see R. *v.* Lang (Stephen Howard)

R. *v.* EE see Attorney General's Reference (Nos.37, 38, 44, 54, 51, 53, 35, 40, 43, 45, 41 and 42 of 2003), Re

R. *v.* Elener (Barry) see R. *v.* Sullivan (Melvin Terrence)

R. v. Elener (Derek) see R. v. Sullivan (Melvin Terrence)
R. v. Ellingham (Paul Robert) [2004] EWCA Crim 3446; [2005] 2 Cr. App. R. (S.) 32,
   CA (Crim Div) . . . . *Digested*, 05/**3616**
R. v. Ellis (Anthony) see R. v. Lowe (Paul)
R. v. Ellis (Anthony Daniel); *sub nom* R. v. Ellis (Antony Daniel) [2004] EWCA Crim
   1355; [2005] 1 Cr. App. R. (S.) 31, CA (Crim Div)
R. v. Ellis (Antony Daniel) see R. v. Ellis (Anthony Daniel)
R. v. Ellis (Russell John) see Attorney General's Reference (No.158 of 2004), Re
R. v. Ellis (Ruth) [2003] EWCA Crim 3556, CA (Crim Div). *Followed*, 05/850
R. v. EM see Attorney General's Reference (Nos.37, 38, 44, 54, 51, 53, 35, 40, 43, 45,
   41 and 42 of 2003), Re
R. v. Embaye (Senait Tekie) see R. v. Navabi (Fraydon)
R. v. Enright (Georgina); R. v. C (James) (A Juvenile) [2001] EWCA Crim 62, CA
   (Crim Div) . . . . *Considered*, 05/3541
R. v. Environment Agency Ex p. Mayer Parry Recycling Ltd (C444/00) see R. (on the
   application of Mayer Parry Recycling Ltd) v. Environment Agency (C444/00)
R. v. ESB Hotels Ltd [2005] EWCA Crim 132; [2005] 2 Cr. App. R. (S.) 56; (2005)
   149 S.J.L.B. 117, CA (Crim Div) . . . . *Digested*, 05/**3630**
R. v. Eubank (Winston) [2001] EWCA Crim 891; [2002] 1 Cr. App. R. (S.) 4; [2001]
   Crim. L.R. 495; *Times*, May 3, 2001, CA (Crim Div) . . . . *Digested*, 01/**1140**:
                      Applied, 05/3650: *Considered*, 03/3776: *Distinguished*, 03/3777
R. v. Evans (Alan Roy) [2004] EWCA Crim 632; *Times*, March 22, 2004, CA (Crim
   Div) . . . . *Digested*, 04/**838**:
                                          Considered, 05/3743
R. v. Evans (Daniel John) [1998] 2 Cr. App. R. (S.) 72, CA (Crim Div). . . . . *Digested*, 98/**1325**:
                                          Considered, 05/3688
R. v. Evans (Dorothy Gertrude) [2004] EWCA Crim 3102; [2005] 1 W.L.R. 1435;
   [2005] 1 Cr. App. R. 32; (2005) 169 J.P. 129; [2005] Crim. L.R. 654; (2005)
   169 J.P.N. 222; (2005) 102(7) L.S.G. 26; *Times*, December 10, 2004, CA (Crim
   Div) . . . . *Digested*, 05/**796**
R. v. Evans (Glenn Clifford) [2000] 1 Cr. App. R. (S.) 454, CA (Crim Div) . . . . *Digested*, 00/**1424**:
                                          Considered, 05/3727
R. v. Evans (Jacqueline) [2005] EWCA Crim 3080; *Times*, November 22, 2005, CA
   (Crim Div)
R. v. Evans (Peter) [2005] EWCA Crim 1811; [2005] Crim. L.R. 876, CA (Crim Div)
R. v. Evans (Roger Paul) [2000] 1 Cr. App. R. (S.) 107, CA (Crim Div) . . . . *Digested*, 00/**1205**:
                                          Considered, 05/3578
R. v. Evans Ex p. Pinochet Ugarte (No.2) see R. v. Bow Street Metropolitan
   Stipendiary Magistrate Ex p. Pinochet Ugarte (No.2)
R. v. Everson (Louis) (Appeal against Sentence); R. v. Soneji (Kamalesh); R. v. Bullen
   (David) [2001] EWCA Crim 2262; [2002] 1 Cr. App. R. (S.) 132, CA (Crim
   Div) . . . . *Considered*, 04/3399,
                           05/3673: *Subsequent proceedings*, 05/842
R. v. Eyre (Christopher Peter) [2004] EWCA Crim 1114; [2005] 1 Cr. App. R. (S.) 4,
   CA (Crim Div) . . . . *Digested*, 05/**3520**
R. v. Eyre (Nathan Oliver) see Attorney General's Reference (No.122 and 123 of 2004),
   Re
R. v. F [2005] EWCA Crim 493; [2005] 1 W.L.R. 2848; [2005] 2 Cr. App. R. 13;
   [2005] Crim. L.R. 564; (2005) 102(18) L.S.G. 22; *Times*, March 16, 2005, CA
   (Crim Div) . . . . *Digested*, 05/**737**
R. v. F Howe & Son (Engineers) Ltd [1999] 2 All E.R. 249; [1999] 2 Cr. App. R. (S.)
   37; (1999) 163 J.P. 359; [1999] I.R.L.R. 434; [1999] Crim. L.R. 238; (1999)
   163 J.P.N. 693; (1998) 95(46) L.S.G. 34; *Times*, November 27, 1998;
   Independent, November 13, 1998, CA (Crim Div) . . . . *Digested*, 98/**2839**:
              Applied, 99/2860, 01/3296, 03/1922, 03/1923: *Considered*, 00/2968,
                  01/1348, 01/1350, 02/3968, 03/3715, 05/1945, 05/3630:
                                    Followed, 99/2858
R. v. Fairbanks (John) [1986] 1 W.L.R. 1202; (1986) 83 Cr. App. R. 251; [1986] R.T.R.
   309; (1986) 130 S.J. 1202, CA (Crim Div) . . . . *Digested*, 86/**473**:
              Applied, 05/792: *Approved*, 90/846: *Considered*, 91/3155, 95/1145, 97/1384,
                     05/896: *Disapproved*, 88/676: *Followed*, 95/1025
R. v. Fairhurst (David) [1996] 1 Cr. App. R. (S.) 242, CA (Crim Div) . . . . *Digested*, 96/**2001**:
                                         Distinguished, 05/3632
R. v. Falconer-Atlee (Joan Olive) (1974) 58 Cr. App. R. 348, CA (Crim Div) . . . . *Digested*, 74/**699**:
                   Applied, 84/970, 05/898: *Considered*, 94/1055, 95/1088:
                                   Distinguished, 96/1635
R. v. Faulder (Michael Ian) see R. v. Harris (Lorraine)
R. v. Fawcett (Kenneth John) (1983) 5 Cr. App. R. (S.) 158, CA (Crim Div). . . . . *Digested*, 84/**836**:
            Applied, 00/1335, 03/3818: *Cited*, 93/1025, 96/1866: *Considered*, 96/1926,
             97/1511, 98/1172, 04/785, 05/3764: *Followed*, 01/1385
R. v. Fazal (Mohammed Mazar) [2004] EWCA Crim 2811; [2005] 1 Cr. App. R. (S.)
   106, CA (Crim Div)
R. v. Feihn (Steven) see R. v. Lang (Stephen Howard)

R. *v.* Ferguson (Frank) (1970) 54 Cr. App. R. 415; [1970] Crim. L.R. 652; 114 S.J. 621,
   CA (Crim Div) . . . . *Digested,* 71/**2542**:
                   Applied, 79/2319, 89/3261: *Disapproved,* 05/902: *Distinguished,* 73/471,
                                                            74/3297
R. *v.* Fernandez (Joseph) see R. *v.* Nazari (Fazlollah)
R. *v.* Field (Jason) see Attorney General's Reference (Nos.19, 20 and 21 of 2001), Re
R. *v.* Fielding (Ian Thomas) [2004] EWCA Crim 502, CA (Crim Div) . . . . *Considered,* 05/3692
R. *v.* Finlay (Paul Anthony) [2003] EWCA Crim 3868, CA (Crim Div). . . . . *Considered,* 05/803
R. *v.* FK see Attorney General's Reference (No.97 of 2004), Re
R. *v.* Flamson (Lee Andrew) [2001] EWCA Crim 3030; [2002] 2 Cr. App. R. (S.) 48;
   [2002] Crim. L.R. 339, CA (Crim Div) . . . . *Digested,* 03/**3777**:
                         Considered, 03/3778, 05/3650: *Followed,* 04/3288
R. *v.* Fleming (Paul Eric) [2004] EWCA Crim 2471; [2005] 1 Cr. App. R. (S.) 103, CA
   (Crim Div)
R. *v.* Fletcher (Francis Royston) see R. *v.* Smith (Ruben)
R. *v.* Fletcher (Raymond) [2004] EWCA Crim 2959; [2005] 2 Cr. App. R. (S.) 4, CA
   (Crim Div) . . . . *Digested,* 05/**3625**
R. *v.* Flynn (Brendan Gerard) see R. *v.* Stockdale (Rae)
R. *v.* Follows (Dean John) see Attorney General's Reference (No.113 of 2004), Re
R. *v.* Foot (Costs) [2004] 3 Costs L.R. 525, Sup Ct Costs Office . . . . *Digested,* 05/**2698**
R. *v.* Foote (Terry Andrew) [2004] EWCA Crim 2820; [2005] 2 Cr. App. R. (S.) 5, CA
   (Crim Div) . . . . *Digested,* 05/**3624**
R. *v.* Ford (Kevin) [2005] EWCA Crim 1358; [2005] Crim. L.R. 807, CA (Crim Div)
R. *v.* Foster (Barry Arthur) [1985] Q.B. 115; [1984] 3 W.L.R. 401; [1984] 2 All E.R.
   679; (1984) 79 Cr. App. R. 61; (1984) 148 J.P. 747; [1984] Crim. L.R. 423, CA
   (Crim Div) . . . . *Digested,* 84/**496**:
                                                     Followed, 05/850
R. *v.* Foster (John) see R. *v.* Gordon (Neil)
R. *v.* Fowler (Costs) see R. *v.* Baker (Costs)
R. *v.* Fowles (Herbert) see R. *v.* May (Raymond George)
R. *v.* Frampton (Costs) [2005] 3 Costs L.R. 527, Sup Ct Costs Office
R. *v.* Franks (Jamie John) [2004] EWCA Crim 1241; [2005] 1 Cr. App. R. (S.) 13, CA
   (Crim Div) . . . . *Digested,* 05/**3771**
R. *v.* Frederick (Carl Emerson) see R. *v.* Lowe (Paul)
R. *v.* Freeman (John) [1997] 2 Cr. App. R. (S.) 224, CA (Crim Div) . . . . *Digested,* 97/**1518**:
                                          Distinguished, 05/3592
R. *v.* Fresha Bakeries Ltd; R. *v.* Harvestime Ltd [2002] EWCA Crim 1451; [2003] 1 Cr.
   App. R. (S.) 44, CA (Crim Div) . . . . *Digested,* 03/**1923**:
                                  Considered, 03/3715, 05/3630
R. *v.* Friskies Petcare (UK) Ltd [2000] 2 Cr. App. R. (S.) 401, CA (Crim Div) . . . . *Digested,* 01/**3296**:
                            Considered, 03/1923, 03/3715, 05/3630
R. *v.* Fysh (Stephen John) see R. *v.* Edwards (Karl Adrian)
R. *v.* G see R. *v.* K
R. *v.* G see R. *v.* Pepper (Jeremy Paul)
R. *v.* G; R. *v.* R [2003] UKHL 50; [2004] 1 A.C. 1034; [2003] 3 W.L.R. 1060; [2003]
   4 All E.R. 765; [2004] 1 Cr. App. R. 21; (2003) 167 J.P. 621; [2004] Crim. L.R.
   369; (2003) 167 J.P.N. 955; (2003) 100(43) L.S.G. 31; *Times,* October 17,
   2003, HL; reversing [2002] EWCA Crim 1992; [2003] 3 All E.R. 206; [2003] 1
   Cr. App. R. 23; [2002] Crim. L.R. 926; *Times,* August 1, 2002; *Independent,*
   October 21, 2002 (C.S), CA (Crim Div) . . . . *Digested,* 03/**775**:
                                 Applied, 03/1692, 04/753, 05/3787
R. *v.* G (Entrapment) see Attorney General's Reference (No.3 of 2000), Re
R. *v.* G (Michael) [2005] EWCA Crim 1300; [2005] Crim. L.R. 800, CA (Crim Div)
R. *v.* G (Richard Shane) see Attorney General's Reference (No.142 of 2004), Re
R. *v.* Gale (Carmello) [2005] EWCA Crim 286; (2005) 169 J.P. 166; (2005) 169
   J.P.N. 417, CA (Crim Div) . . . . *Digested,* 05/**922**
R. *v.* Gantz (Ramon) [2004] EWCA Crim 2862; [2005] 1 Cr. App. R. (S.) 104, CA
   (Crim Div)
R. *v.* Garaxo (Shino) [2005] EWCA Crim 1170; [2005] Crim. L.R. 883, CA (Crim Div)
R. *v.* Gardner (Haroon) see R. *v.* Taj (Kamran)
R. *v.* Gardner (Matthew) see Attorney General's Reference (Nos.83 and 85 of 2004),
   Re
R. *v.* Garvey (Wayne) see Attorney General's Reference (No.104 of 2004), Re
R. *v.* Gault (Michael Paul) (1995) 16 Cr. App. R. (S.) 1013; [1996] R.T.R. 348; [1995]
   Crim. L.R. 581, CA (Crim Div) . . . . *Considered,* 00/1364,
                                          04/3389, 05/3771, 05/3774
R. *v.* Gay (Alan Thomas) see Attorney General's Reference (No.25 of 2004), Re
R. *v.* Gayle (Ricky) see R. *v.* Cowan (Donald)
R. *v.* Gearing (Jack William) [1968] 1 W.L.R. 344 (Note); (1966) 50 Cr. App. R. 18;
   [1966] Crim. L.R. 438; 109 S.J. 872; *Times,* October 26, 1965, CCA . . . . *Digested,* 66/**2903**:
                        Applied, 72/620, 72/1936: *Considered,* 05/832
R. *v.* George [1956] Crim. L.R. 52, Assizes (Lincoln) . . . . *Digested,* 56/**1903**:
                                     Considered, 84/639, 05/819

R. *v.* Geraghty (Desmond) see Attorney General's Reference (Nos.48, 49, 50 and 51 of 2002), Re

R. *v.* Gerrard (Brian) see R. *v.* Grundy (Brian)

R. *v.* GGM see Attorney General's Reference (No.43 of 1999), Re

R. *v.* Ghafoor (Imran Hussain) [2002] EWCA Crim 1857; [2003] 1 Cr. App. R. (S.) 84; (2002) 166 J.P. 601; [2002] Crim. L.R. 739; (2002) 166 J.P.N. 744, CA (Crim Div) . . . . *Digested,* 02/**4047**:
Applied, 04/3380: *Considered,* 05/3765

R. *v.* Gibbs (Martin Godwin) see R. *v.* Sullivan (Melvin Terrence)

R. *v.* Gibson (Karl Mark) [2004] EWCA Crim 593; [2004] 2 Cr. App. R. (S.) 84; [2004] Crim. L.R. 592, CA (Crim Div) . . . . *Digested,* 05/**3544**

R. *v.* Gilbert (Martin Roy) [2005] EWCA Crim 789; [2005] 2 Cr. App. R. (S.) 108, CA (Crim Div)

R. *v.* Gilbert (Raymond Sidney) (1978) 66 Cr. App. R. 237; [1978] Crim. L.R. 216, CA (Crim Div). . . . . *Digested,* 78/**559**:
Considered, 85/567, 86/563, 94/1045, 05/724: *Followed,* 87/2103:
Referred to, 94/1043

R. *v.* Gill (Paramjit Singh) see R. *v.* Gill (Sewa Singh)

R. *v.* Gill (Sewa Singh); R. *v.* Gill (Paramjit Singh) [2003] EWCA Crim 2256; [2004] 1 W.L.R. 469; [2003] 4 All E.R. 681; [2003] S.T.C. 1229; [2004] 1 Cr. App. R. 20; [2003] B.T.C. 404; [2003] Crim. L.R. 883; [2003] S.T.I. 1421; (2003) 100(37) L.S.G. 31; (2003) 147 S.J.L.B. 993; *Times,* August 29, 2003, CA (Crim Div) . . . *Digested,* 03/**744**:
Distinguished, 05/4414

R. *v.* Gillam (Leslie George); *sub nom* R. *v.* Gillan (1980) 2 Cr. App. R. (S.) 267; [1981] Crim. L.R. 55, CA (Crim Div) . . . . *Digested,* 81/**525.41**:
Applied, 87/855, 87/856, 88/859, 89/913, 05/3544: *Cited,* 89/912, 90/1187,
91/991: *Considered,* 83/764.2, 84/874, 89/914, 94/1226, 96/1805, 00/1029:
Distinguished, 84/723, 86/703: *Followed,* 83/761, 87/1037, 88/860, 01/1441

R. *v.* Gillan see R. *v.* Gillam (Leslie George)

R. *v.* Gilmore (Vincent Martin) see R. *v.* Hanson (Nicky)

R. *v.* Girt (Stuart Barry) see Attorney General's Reference (No.35 of 2001), Re

R. *v.* Glave (Heathcliffe) see R. *v.* Lang (Stephen Howard)

R. *v.* Gloucestershire CC Ex p. Barry; *sub nom* R. *v.* Gloucestershire CC Ex p. Mahfood; R. *v.* Lancashire CC Ex p. Royal Association for Disability and Rehabilitation; R. *v.* Islington LBC Ex p. McMillan; R. *v.* Gloucestershire CC Ex p. Grinham; R. *v.* Gloucestershire CC Ex p. Dartnell [1997] A.C. 584; [1997] 2 W.L.R. 459; [1997] 2 All E.R. 1; (1997) 9 Admin. L.R. 209; (1997-98) 1 C.C.L. Rep. 40; (1997) 36 B.M.L.R. 92; [1997] C.O.D. 304; (1997) 94(14) L.S.G. 25; (1997) 147 N.L.J. 453; (1997) 141 S.J.L.B. 91; *Times,* March 21, 1997; *Independent,* April 9, 1997, HL; reversing [1996] 4 All E.R. 421; [1997] 4 Admin. L.R. 69; (1997-98) 1 C.C.L. Rep. 19; (1997) 36 B.M.L.R. 69; [1996] C.O.D. 387; (1996) 93(33) L.S.G. 25; (1996) 140 S.J.L.B. 177; *Times,* July 12, 1996; *Independent,* July 10, 1996, CA (Civ Div); reversing 94 L.G.R. 593; (1996) 8 Admin. L.R. 181; (1997-98) 1 C.C.L. Rep. 7; (1996) 30 B.M.L.R. 20; [1996] C.O.D. 67; (1996) 160 L.G. Rev. 321; *Times,* June 21, 1995; *Independent,* June 20, 1995, DC . . . . *Digested,* 97/**4714**:
Applied, 97/2089, 97/4721, 98/2853, 05/3928: *Considered,* 96/5528,
99/3052, 99/4623: *Followed,* 95/3225, 96/3029, 96/5530, 97/4711,
98/1674

R. *v.* Gloucestershire CC Ex p. Dartnell see R. *v.* Gloucestershire CC Ex p. Barry

R. *v.* Gloucestershire CC Ex p. Grinham see R. *v.* Gloucestershire CC Ex p. Barry

R. *v.* Gloucestershire CC Ex p. Mahfood see R. *v.* Gloucestershire CC Ex p. Barry

R. *v.* Goad (William Alexander) see Attorney General's Reference (No.131 of 2004), Re

R. *v.* Goldrick (Valerie May) (1988) 10 Cr. App. R. (S.) 346, CA (Crim Div) . . . . *Digested,* 90/**1430**:
Considered, 05/3746

R. *v.* Goldsmith (Harold Egan) see R. *v.* Avis (Tony)

R. *v.* Goldstein (Harry Chaim) see R. *v.* Rimmington (Anthony)

R. *v.* Goodenough (Alan John) [2004] EWCA Crim 2260; [2005] 1 Cr. App. R. (S.) 88; [2005] Crim. L.R. 71, CA (Crim Div). . . . . *Digested,* 05/**3568**

R. *v.* Goodwin (Frankie) see Attorney General's Reference (Nos.59, 60 and 63 of 1998), Re

R. *v.* Goodwin (Mark) [2005] EWCA Crim 3184; [2005] 2 C.L.C. 1066; *Independent,* December 9, 2005, CA (Crim Div)

R. *v.* Goodyear (Karl) [2005] EWCA Crim 888; [2005] 1 W.L.R. 2532; [2005] 3 All E.R. 117; [2005] 2 Cr. App. R. 20; [2005] Crim. L.R. 659; *Times,* April 21, 2005, CA (Crim Div) . . . . *Digested,* 05/**893**

R. *v.* Gordon (Neil); R. *v.* Foster (John) [2001] 1 Cr. App. R. (S.) 58, CA (Crim Div) . . . . *Digested,* 01/**1207**:
Considered, 01/1477, 05/3777

R. *v.* Gormanly (Fraser) see Attorney General's Reference (No.66 of 2005), Re

R. *v.* Gornall (Paul) [2005] EWCA Crim 668; (2005) 149 S.J.L.B. 300, CA (Crim Div)

R. *v.* Goss (Dennis Anthony) [2003] EWCA Crim 3208; [2005] Crim. L.R. 61; *Times,* October 27, 2003, CA (Crim Div). . . . . *Digested,* 04/**876**

R. *v.* Gould (Robert Sidney) see R. *v.* Aranguren (Jose de Jesus)

R. *v.* Goult (Raymond Arthur) (1983) 76 Cr. App. R. 140; (1982) 4 Cr. App. R. (S.) 355; [1983] Crim. L.R.103, CA (Crim Div) . . . . *Digested*, 83/**582**: *Considered*, 83/764.13, 84/844, 98/1162, 05/3689

R. *v.* Gourzoilidis (Anastasios) see R. *v.* Loizou (Lisa)

R. *v.* Governor of Ashford Remand Centre Ex p. Postlethwaite see Belgium *v.* Postlethwaite

R. *v.* Governor of Brixton Prison Ex p. Evans see Evans, Re

R. *v.* Governor of Brixton Prison Ex p. Saifi see R. (on the application of Saifi) *v.* Governor of Brixton Prison

R. *v.* Governor of Brixton Prison Ex p. Servini [1914] 1 K.B. 77, KBD . . . . *Applied*, 69/1455, 05/1486

R. *v.* Governor of Brockhill Prison Ex p. Evans (No.2); *sub nom* Evans *v.* Governor of Brockhill Prison [2001] 2 A.C. 19; [2000] 3 W.L.R. 843; [2000] 4 All E.R. 15; [2000] U.K.H.R.R. 836; (2000) 97(32) L.S.G. 38; (2000) 144 S.J.L.B. 241; *Times*, August 2, 2000; *Independent*, November 6, 2000 (C.S), HL; affirming [1999] Q.B.1043; [1999] 1 W.L.R. 103; [1998] 4 All E.R. 993; (1999) 11 Admin. L.R. 6; [1998] C.O.D. 378; (1999) 163 J.P.N. 51; (1998) 95(33) L.S.G. 35; (1998) 142 S.J.L.B. 196; *Times*, July 6, 1998; *Independent*, June 24, 1998, CA (Civ Div); reversing CO 2955-96, QBD . . . . *Digested*, 00/**5113**: *Applied*, 01/1091, 02/4543: *Considered*, 01/1524, 04/2776, 05/2163

R. *v.* Governor of Durham Prison Ex p. Singh (Hardial); *sub nom* R. *v.* Secretary of State for the Home Department Ex p. Singh (Hardial) [1984] 1 W.L.R. 704; [1984] 1 All E.R. 983; [1983] Imm. A.R. 983; (1984) 128 S.J. 349, QBD . . . . . . *Digested*, 84/**1726**: *Approved*, 03/2236: *Considered*, 95/2726, 96/3278, 05/2161: *Distinguished*, 00/3347

R. *v.* Governor of Whitemoor Prison Ex p. Main see R. *v.* Secretary of State for the Home Department Ex p. Simms

R. *v.* Grad (David Karl) [2004] EWCA Crim 44; [2004] 2 Cr. App. R. (S.) 43, CA (Crim Div) . . . . *Considered*, 05/3663

R. *v.* Graham (Cheryl Angela); R. *v.* Whatley (Albert John) [2004] EWCA Crim 2755; [2005] 1 Cr. App. R. (S.) 115; [2005] Crim. L.R. 247, CA (Crim Div)

R. *v.* Graham (Joseph); R. *v.* Watson (Robert James); R. *v.* Marshall (Lee); R. *v.* McNee (John) [2004] EWCA Crim 2762; [2005] 1 Cr. App. R. (S.) 110, CA (Crim Div)

R. *v.* Grant (Edward) [2005] EWCA Crim 1089; [2005] 3 W.L.R. 437; [2005] 2 Cr. App. R. 28; [2005] Crim. L.R. 955; *Times*, May 12, 2005, CA (Crim Div) . . . . . . *Digested*, 05/**834**

R. *v.* Graves (Martin John) see R. *v.* Coates (Victor Henry)

R. *v.* Gray (John) [2004] EWCA Crim 1074; [2004] 2 Cr. App. R. 30; (2004) 148 S.J.L.B. 665, CA (Crim Div) . . . . *Digested*, 05/**937**

R. *v.* Green (Anthony) see Attorney General's Reference (No.59 of 2004), Re

R. *v.* Green (Edward Lloyd) [2005] EWCA Crim 2513; (2005) 149 S.J.L.B. 1350, CA (Crim Div)

R. *v.* Green (Joseph) see Attorney General's Reference (No.4 of 2004), Re

R. *v.* Green (Richard John) see R. *v.* Abdroikov (Nurlon)

R. *v.* Green (Ryan Keith) see Attorney General's Reference (No.157 of 2004), Re

R. *v.* Greenall (William) [2004] EWCA Crim 3430; [2005] 2 Cr. App. R. (S.) 46, CA (Crim Div) . . . . *Digested*, 05/**3573**

R. *v.* Greenland (Jason) [2002] EWCA Crim 1748; [2003] 1 Cr. App. R. (S.) 74, CA (Crim Div) . . . . *Digested*, 03/**3852**: *Distinguished*, 04/3432: *Not applied*, 05/3735

R. *v.* Greenwood (Andrew Philip) [2004] EWCA Crim 1388; [2005] 1 Cr. App. R. 7; [2005] Crim. L.R. 59; (2004) 148 S.J.L.B. 788, CA (Crim Div) . . . . *Digested*, 05/**735**

R. *v.* Greet (Michael Hugh) [2005] EWCA Crim 205; [2005] B.P.I.R. 1409, CA (Crim Div)

R. *v.* Grierson (Ernest Roy) see Attorney General's Reference (No.77 of 2003), Re

R. *v.* Griffin (Joseph) (1989) 88 Cr. App. R. 63; [1988] Crim. L.R. 680; *Times*, March 1, 1988, CA (Crim Div). . . . . *Digested*, 89/**623**: *Considered*, 96/1564, 05/847

R. *v.* Griffith (Tennyson Winston) see Griffith *v.* Queen, The

R. *v.* Griffiths (Jonathan) [2004] EWCA Crim 2656; [2005] 1 Cr. App. R. (S.) 108, CA (Crim Div)

R. *v.* Grimwood (David Thomas) [2005] EWCA Crim 1411; (2005) 169 J.P. 373; (2005) 169 J.P.N. 616, CA (Crim Div) . . . . *Digested*, 05/**728**

R. *v.* Grossman (Joseph Henry) (1981) 73 Cr. App. R. 302; [1981] Crim. L.R. 396, CA (Civ Div). . . . . *Digested*, 81/**2306**: *Applied*, 85/155, 86/1501: *Distinguished*, 05/601: *Not followed*, 85/2596

R. *v.* Grundy [1977] Crim. L.R. 543, CA (Crim Div) . . . . *Digested*, 77/**486**: *Applied*, 83/560, 84/524: *Considered*, 05/899

R. *v.* Grundy (Brian); R. *v.* Gerrard (Brian); R. *v.* Patterson (John) (1989) 89 Cr. App. R. 333; [1989] Crim. L.R. 502, CA (Crim Div) . . . . *Digested*, 90/**1185**: *Distinguished*, 03/878, 05/899

R. *v.* GS see Attorney General's Reference (Nos.37, 38, 44, 54, 51, 53, 35, 40, 43, 45, 41 and 42 of 2003), Re

R. *v.* Guidera (Michael) see R. *v.* Lang (Stephen Howard)

R. *v.* Guirdham (Daniel) see Attorney General's Reference (No.44 of 2005), Re

R. v. Gupta (Surinder Mohan) see R. v. Raviraj (Thaneran)
R. v. Gusman (Costs) (Unreported, September 6, 1999) . . . . *Considered*, 05/882
R. v. H see Attorney General's Reference (No.105 of 2004), Re
R. v. H   *Applied*, 05/937
R. v. H see R. v. S
R. v. H; R. v. C [2004] UKHL 3; [2004] 2 A.C. 134; [2004] 2 W.L.R. 335; [2004] 1
    All E.R. 1269; [2004] 2 Cr. App. R. 10; [2004] H.R.L.R. 20; 16 B.H.R.C. 332;
    (2004) 101(8) L.S.G. 29; (2004) 148 S.J.L.B. 183; *Times*, February 6, 2004;
    Independent, February 10, 2004, HL; affirming [2003] EWCA Crim 2847;
    [2003] 1 W.L.R. 3006; [2004] 1 Cr. App. R. 17; (2003) 100(43) L.S.G. 31;
    Times, October 24, 2003; *Independent*, November 14, 2003, CA (Crim Div). . . . *Digested*, 04/**798**:
        Applied, 05/840: *Followed*, 05/875
R. v. H (Childhood Amnesia); *sub nom* R. v. JRH; R. v. TG (Deceased); R. v. X
    (Childhood Amnesia) [2005] EWCA Crim 1828; *Times*, August 5, 2005, CA
    (Crim Div). . . . . *Digested*, 05/**742**
R. v. H (Cyril Arthur) see Attorney General's Reference (No.3 of 1995), Re
R. v. H (Evidence: Admissibility); *sub nom* R. v. PGH [2005] EWCA Crim 2083; *Times*,
    August 22, 2005, CA (Crim Div) . . . . *Digested*, 05/**915**
R. v. H (Karl Anthony) [2005] EWCA Crim 732; [2005] 1 W.L.R. 2005; [2005] 2 All
    E.R. 859; [2005] 2 Cr. App. R. 9; [2005] Crim. L.R. 735; (2005) 102(14) L.S.G.
    26, CA (Crim Div) . . . . *Digested*, 05/**819**
R. v. H (Sexual Assault: Touching) (2005) 149 S.J.L.B. 179; *Times*, February 8, 2005,
    CA (Crim Div)
R. v. H (Special Measures), *Times*, April 15, 2003, CA (Crim Div) . . . . *Considered*, 05/751
R. v. H (Terence) see Attorney General's Reference (No.35 of 1994), Re
R. v. Hadley (Costs) [2005] 3 Costs L.R. 548, Sup Ct Costs Office
R. v. Hall [2003] EWCA Crim 1714, CA (Crim Div) . . . . *Considered*, 05/3541
R. v. Hall (Billy Paul) [2004] EWCA Crim 2671; [2005] 1 Cr. App. R. (S.) 118; [2005]
    Crim. L.R. 152, CA (Crim Div) . . . . *Considered*, 05/3585
R. v. Hall (Darren David) [1997] 1 Cr. App. R. (S.) 62, CA (Crim Div) . . . . *Digested*, 97/**1569**:
        Considered, 05/3619
R. v. Hall (John Anthony) see R. v. Betts (Raymond Christopher)
R. v. Hampson (Anthony); R. v. Hampson (David James) [2004] EWCA Crim 2011;
    [2005] 1 Cr. App. R. (S.) 51, CA (Crim Div) . . . . *Digested*, 05/**3572**
R. v. Hampson (David James) see R. v. Hampson (Anthony)
R. v. Hanley (Kevin) see R. v. Soares (Ronald)
R. v. Hanratty (James) (Deceased) [2002] EWCA Crim 1141; [2002] 3 All E.R. 534;
    [2002] 2 Cr. App. R. 30; [2002] Crim. L.R. 650; (2002) 99(24) L.S.G. 34;
    (2002) 146 S.J.L.B. 136; *Times*, May 16, 2002; *Daily Telegraph*, May 16, 2002,
    CA (Crim Div) . . . . *Digested*, 02/**735**:
        Considered, 02/845: *Followed*, 05/850
R. v. Hanson (Nicky); R. v. Gilmore (Vincent Martin); R. v. Pickstone (Robert Alan)
    [2005] EWCA Crim 824; [2005] 1 W.L.R. 3169; [2005] 2 Cr. App. R. 21;
    (2005) 169 J.P. 250; [2005] Crim. L.R. 787; (2005) 169 J.P.N. 380; (2005)
    149 S.J.L.B. 392; *Times*, March 24, 2005, CA (Crim Div) . . . . *Digested*, 05/**736**:
        Considered, 05/725, 05/835: *Followed*, 05/726
R. v. Harding (William Henry) see R. v. Adams (David Anthony)
R. v. Hardy (Gary) [2004] EWCA Crim 3397; [2005] 2 Cr. App. R. (S.) 48, CA (Crim
    Div) . . . . *Digested*, 05/**3689**
R. v. Hargreaves (Stephen Lee) see R. v. S
R. v. Harmer (Roy Peter) [2005] EWCA Crim 1; [2005] 2 Cr. App. R. 2; [2005] Crim.
    L.R. 482, CA (Crim Div) . . . . *Digested*, 05/**768**:
R. v. Harrington (Robert) 00/1780/X2, CA (Crim Div) . . . . *Applied*, 05/802
R. v. Harris (Adrian) see Attorney General's Reference (No.80 of 2003), Re
R. v. Harris (Lorraine); R. v. Rock (Raymond Charles); R. v. Cherry (Alan Barry); R. v.
    Faulder (Michael Ian) [2005] EWCA Crim 1980; (2005) 85 B.M.L.R. 75, CA
    (Crim Div). . . . . *Digested*, 05/**745**
R. v. Harris (Phillip Geoffrey) [2005] EWCA Crim 775; [2005] 2 Cr. App. R. (S.) 103,
    CA (Crim Div) . . . . *Digested*, 05/**3599**
R. v. Harrison (Christopher Arthur) [1997] 2 Cr. App. R. (S.) 174, CA (Crim Div) . . . . . . *Digested*, 97/**1713**:
        Considered, 05/3599
R. v. Harrison (John) see Attorney General's Reference (No.66 of 2003), Re
R. v. Harrison (Simon) [2001] EWCA Crim 2117; [2002] 1 Cr. App. R. (S.) 107, CA
    (Crim Div). . . . . *Digested*, 02/**3874**:
        Applied, 04/3282: *Considered*, 05/3525: *Referred to*, 03/3622
R. v. Harrow LBC Ex p. Fahia [1998] 1 W.L.R. 1396; [1998] 4 All E.R. 137; [1998] 3
    F.C.R. 363; (1998) 30 H.L.R. 1124; (1998) 95(35) L.S.G. 38; (1998) 148 N.L.J.
    1354; (1998) 142 S.J.L.B. 226; [1998] N.P.C. 122; *Times*, July 24, 1998, HL;
    affirming (1997) 29 H.L.R. 974, CA (Civ Div); affirming (1997) 29 H.L.R. 94,
    QBD . . . . *Digested*, 98/**3014**:
        Applied, 05/1986, 05/1988: *Considered*, 97/2666: *Followed*, 98/3011
R. v. Hartley (Russell) see Attorney General's Reference (No.35 of 1995), Re
R. v. Hartrey (Michael Patrick) see R. v. Oliver (Mark David)
R. v. Harvestime Ltd see R. v. Fresha Bakeries Ltd

R. *v.* Harvey (Michael) see Attorney General's Reference (No.38 of 1995), Re

R. *v.* Harvey (Winston George) [2000] 1 Cr. App. R. (S.) 368; [1999] Crim. L.R. 849, CA (Crim Div) . . . . *Digested*, 00/**1228**:
Applied, 05/3702

R. *v.* Hasan (Aytach); *sub nom* R. *v.* Z [2005] UKHL 22; [2005] 2 A.C. 467; [2005] 2 W.L.R. 709; [2005] 4 All E.R. 685; [2005] 2 Cr. App. R. 22; (2005) 149 S.J.L.B. 360; *Times*, March 21, 2005; *Independent*, March 22, 2005, HL; reversing [2003] EWCA Crim 191; [2003] 1 W.L.R. 1489; [2003] 2 Cr. App. R. 12; [2003] Crim. L.R. 627; *Times*, March 26, 2003, CA (Crim Div) . . . . *Digested*, 05/**765**:
Considered, 05/772

R. *v.* Hasan (Miriwan Ali) see Attorney General's Reference (No.143 of 2004), Re

R. *v.* Hatton (Jonathan) [2005] EWCA Crim 2951; (2005) 102(44) L.S.G. 30; *Times*, November 10, 2005, CA (Crim Div)

R. *v.* Hawkins (Paul Nigel) [1997] 1 Cr. App. R. 234; [1997] Crim. L.R. 134; (1996) 93(36) L.S.G. 35; (1996) 140 S.J.L.B. 214; *Times*, August 6, 1996, CA (Crim Div) . . . . *Digested*, 96/**1548**:
Applied, 05/859: *Considered*, 01/1113: *Followed*, 97/1260

R. *v.* Hawthorne (Raymond Colin) see Attorney General's Reference (No.122 and 123 of 2004), Re

R. *v.* Hay (Christopher Paul) (1983) 77 Cr. App. R. 70; [1983] Crim. L.R. 390, CA (Crim Div) . . . . *Digested*, 83/**660**:
Distinguished, 89/756, 90/796, 90/797, 05/733

R. *v.* Hayes (Andrew Michael) see R. *v.* Liddle (Mark) (Appeal against Sentence)

R. *v.* Hayes (Justin) [2004] EWCA Crim 2844; [2005] 1 Cr. App. R. 33, CA (Crim Div) . . . . *Digested*, 05/**732**

R. *v.* Hayter (Paul Ali) [2005] UKHL 6; [2005] 1 W.L.R. 605; [2005] 2 All E.R. 209; [2005] 2 Cr. App. R. 3; [2005] Crim. L.R. 720; (2005) 149 S.J.L.B. 180; *Times*, February 7, 2005; *Independent*, February 8, 2005, HL; affirming [2003] EWCA Crim 1048; [2003] 1 W.L.R. 1910; [2003] 2 Cr. App. R. 27; [2003] Crim. L.R. 887; (2003) 100(25) L.S.G. 45; (2003) 147 S.J.L.B. 537; *Times*, April 18, 2003, CA (Crim Div) . . . . *Digested*, 05/**741**

R. *v.* Hayward (John Victor) (No.2) see R. *v.* Jones (Anthony William)

R. *v.* Haywood (John Victor) see R. *v.* Jones (Anthony William)

R. *v.* Healey (Bernard); R. *v.* Comerford (Thomas Anthony); R. *v.* Owens (John Anthony); R. *v.* Smith (George William) [1965] 1 W.L.R. 1059; [1965] 1 All E.R. 365; (1965) 49 Cr. App. R. 77; 129 J.P. 157; 109 S.J. 572; *Guardian*, December 9, 1964, CCA . . . . *Digested*, 65/**939**:
Disapproved, 05/902: *Distinguished*, 73/2933

R. *v.* Heard (Kevin Phillip) see R. *v.* Corran (Ben)

R. *v.* Heighton (Mark Kristian) see Attorney General's Reference (No.88 of 2000), Re

R. *v.* Hembling (Leoni Jayne) [2005] EWCA Crim 200; [2005] Crim. L.R. 586, CA (Crim Div)

R. *v.* Hendley (Ian) see Attorney General's Reference (No.1 of 2004), Re

R. *v.* Henry (Andrew John) see Attorney General's Reference (No.154 of 2004), Re

R. *v.* Henry (Carl Anthony) see R. *v.* Miller (Stephen)

R. *v.* Henry (Errol George) (1988) 10 Cr. App. R. (S.) 327; [1989] Crim. L.R. 78, CA (Crim Div) . . . . *Digested*, 89/**1070**:
Applied, 05/3718: *Cited*, 94/1297: *Considered*, 98/1343

R. *v.* Herbert (Stephen Ronald) see Attorney General's Reference (Nos.120 and 121 of 2004), Re

R. *v.* Herridge (Matthew John) [2005] EWCA Crim 1410; [2005] Crim. L.R. 806; *Times*, June 7, 2005, CA (Crim Div) . . . . *Digested*, 05/**3578**

R. *v.* Hibbard (Terence) see Attorney General's Reference (Nos.64 and 65 of 1997), Re

R. *v.* Highton (Edward Paul); R. *v.* Van Nguyen (Dong); R. *v.* Carp (Anthony Mark) [2005] EWCA Crim 1985; [2005] 1 W.L.R. 3472; *Times*, September 2, 2005; *Times*, August 9, 2005, CA (Crim Div) . . . . *Digested*, 05/**726**

R. *v.* Hill (Debra) see Attorney General's Reference (Nos.132 and 133 of 2004), Re

R. *v.* Hillhands (Brian) see R. *v.* Lowe (Paul)

R. *v.* Hillingdon LBC Ex p. Puhlhofer; *sub nom* Puhlhofer *v.* Hillingdon LBC [1986] A.C. 484; [1986] 2 W.L.R. 259; [1986] 1 All E.R. 467; [1986] 1 F.L.R. 22; (1986) 18 H.L.R. 158; [1986] Fam. Law 218; (1986) 83 L.S.G. 785; (1986) 136 N.L.J. 140; (1986) 130 S.J. 143, HL; affirming [1985] 3 All E.R. 734; [1986] 2 F.L.R. 5; [1986] 1 F.L.R. 5; (1985) 17 H.L.R. 588; (1985) 82 L.S.G. 3701; (1985) 135 N.L.J. 983, CA (Civ Div); reversing (1985) 17 H.L.R. 278; (1985) 82 L.S.G. 1336; (1987) 137 N.L.J. 731; (1987) 137 N.L.J. 1045, QBD . . . . *Digested*, 86/**1619**:
Applied, 97/6114, 05/1415, 05/1987, 05/3872: *Considered*, 86/1621, 87/173, 87/1878, 87/2385, 89/3547, 89/3586, 91/1901, 94/3973, 94/5918, 95/155, 95/2569, 96/3065, 96/4700, 97/2661: *Distinguished*, 04/1895:
Referred to, 91/3495

R. *v.* Hinchliffe (Allen Patrick) see Attorney General's Reference (No.49 of 1999), Re

R. *v.* Hind (Jodie Thomas) see R. *v.* Johnson (James Gordon)

R. *v.* Hiscock (Christopher) see Attorney General's Reference (Nos.115 and 116 of 2004), Re

R. v. HM Coroner for North Humberside and Scunthorpe Ex p. Jamieson [1995] Q.B.
1; [1994] 3 W.L.R. 82; [1994] 3 All E.R. 972; (1994) 158 J.P. 1011; [1994] 5
Med. L.R. 217; [1994] C.O.D. 455; *Times*, April 28, 1994; *Independent*, April 27,
1994, CA (Civ Div); affirming [1994] C.O.D. 173; *Times*, July 23, 1993;
Independent, October 18, 1993 (C.S.); *Independent*, October 4, 1993 (C.S.);
Guardian, July 12, 1993, QBD . . . . *Digested*, 94/**631**:
Applied, 00/50, 01/26, 02/26, 03/13, 04/36: *Cited*, 00/49:
Considered, 94/629, 94/630, 95/872, 95/873, 96/42, 96/44, 96/49, 97/39,
01/27, 02/25, 04/12, 04/38, 05/17: *Disapproved*, 04/37
R. v. HM Coroner for Western Somerset Ex p. Middleton see R. (on the application of
Middleton) v. HM Coroner for Western Somerset
R. v. HN see Attorney General's Reference (Nos.37, 38, 44, 54, 51, 53, 35, 40, 43, 45,
41 and 42 of 2003), Re
R. v. Hoare (Jamie Matthew) [2004] EWCA Crim 191; [2004] 2 Cr. App. R. (S.) 50;
[2004] Crim. L.R. 594, CA (Crim Div) . . . . *Digested*, 05/**3545**
R. v. Hoare (Kevin); R. v. Pierce (Graham) [2004] EWCA Crim 784; [2005] 1 W.L.R.
1804; [2005] 1 Cr. App. R. 22; [2005] Crim. L.R. 567; (2004) 148 S.J.L.B. 473,
CA (Crim Div) . . . . *Digested*, 05/**749**:
Applied, 05/901
R. v. Hodgkins (Barry Kenneth) see Attorney General's Reference (Nos.3, 4, 8, 9, 10, 11,
14 and 16 of 1990), Re
R. v. Hodgkins (Daniel) see Attorney General's Reference (Nos.37, 38, 44, 54, 51, 53,
35, 40, 43, 45, 41 and 42 of 2003), Re
R. v. Holbrook (Lee David) see R. v. Last (Emma)
R. v. Holliday (Paul); R. v. Leboutillier (Paul) [2004] EWCA Crim 1847; [2005] 1 Cr.
App. R. (S.) 70, CA (Crim Div) . . . . *Digested*, 05/**3713**
R. v. Holloway (Stephen John) see R. v. Adomako (John Asare)
R. v. Holmes (Anthony James) see Attorney General's Reference (Nos.74 and 75 of
2004), Re
R. v. Holmes (Christopher) (Unreported, May 22, 1997), CA (Crim Div) . . . . *Considered*, 05/3530
R. v. Holness (Peter Phillip) see Attorney General's Reference (No.128 of 2004), Re
R. v. Hong Qiang He see R. v. Weir (Antony Albert)
R. v. Honz (Tomas) see R. v. Kaynak (Hussein)
R. v. Horrocks (Terrence Alan) [2004] EWCA Crim 2129; [2005] 1 Cr. App. R. (S.) 80,
CA (Crim Div) . . . . *Digested*, 05/**3626**
R. v. Horseferry Road Magistrates Court Ex p. Bennett (No.1); *sub nom* Bennett v.
Horseferry Road Magistrates Court [1994] 1 A.C. 42; [1993] 3 W.L.R. 90;
[1993] 3 All E.R. 138; (1994) 98 Cr. App. R. 114; [1994] C.O.D. 123; (1993) 157
J.P.N. 506; (1993) 143 N.L.J. 955; (1993) 137 S.J.L.B. 159; *Times*, June 25,
1993; *Independent*, July 1, 1993, HL; reversing [1993] 2 All E.R. 474; (1993) 97
Cr. App. R. 29; (1993) 157 J.P. 713; [1993] C.O.D. 22; (1993) 157 J.P.N. 189;
(1993) 137 S.J.L.B. 159; *Times*, September 1, 1992; *Independent*, September 14,
1992 (C.S.), QBD . . . . *Digested*, 93/**1867**:
Applied, 94/658, 98/984, 99/5205: *Considered*, 94/85, 95/906, 95/2287,
95/5744, 96/1541, 96/1599, 97/1256, 97/1257, 97/1375, 99/485, 99/881,
99/5215, 05/3343: *Distinguished*, 94/2137, 98/260, 98/2353, 02/1593
R. v. Hounsham (Robin Edward); R. v. Mayes (Richard); R. v. Blake (Michael) [2005]
EWCA Crim 1366; [2005] 1 Crim. L.R. 991; *Times*, June 16, 2005, CA (Crim Div) . *Digested*, 05/**3343**
R. v. Howard (John) (1992) 13 Cr. App. R. (S.) 720, CA (Crim Div) . . . . *Digested*, 93/**1010**:
Considered, 05/3562
R. v. Howell (Jeffrey John) [2003] EWCA Crim 1; [2005] 1 Cr. App. R. 1; [2003] Crim.
L.R. 405, CA (Crim Div) . . . . *Digested*, 05/**927**:
Applied, 05/749: *Approved*, 03/763
R. v. Howell (Seymour Joseph) (1985) 7 Cr. App. R. (S.) 360, CA (Crim Div) . . . . *Digested*, 87/**913**:
Cited, 89/2397, 90/1364, 91/1136, 93/1227: *Considered*, 87/992, 96/2001,
97/1644: *Distinguished*, 05/3632
R. v. Humphris (Andrew James) [2005] EWCA Crim 2030; (2005) 169 J.P. 441;
(2005) 169 J.P.N. 718; *Times*, September 19, 2005, CA (Crim Div)
R. v. Humphrys (Bruce Edward) see DPP v. Humphrys (Bruce Edward)
R. v. Hunstanton Justices Ex p. Clayton see Chief Constable of Norfolk v. Clayton
R. v. Hunter (Neil Peter) [2004] EWCA Crim 3240; [2005] 2 Cr. App. R. (S.) 36, CA
(Crim Div) . . . . *Digested*, 05/**3525**
R. v. Huntroyd (Sean) [2004] EWCA Crim 2182; [2005] 1 Cr. App. R. (S.) 85, CA
(Crim Div) . . . . *Digested*, 05/**3619**
R. v. Husain (Syed) see Attorney General's Reference (No.79 of 2004), Re
R. v. Hussain (Mohammed) [2005] EWCA Crim 1866; *Times*, July 7, 2005, CA (Crim
Div) . . . . *Digested*, 05/**3615**
R. v. Hussain (Nazar) [2004] EWCA Crim 763; [2004] 2 Cr. App. R. (S.) 93, CA
(Crim Div) . . . . *Digested*, 05/**3658**
R. v. Hussain (Sajid) see R. v. Din (Ameen)
R. v. Hussain (Syed) see Attorney General's Reference (No.79 of 2004), Re
R. v. Hussein (Akhtar) see R. v. Ali (Liaquat)
R. v. Hutchinson (Carlos) [2005] EWCA Crim 78; (2005) 149 S.J.L.B. 116, CA (Crim
Div)

R. v. Hylands (Robert Stanford) [2004] EWCA Crim 2999; [2005] 2 Cr. App. R. (S.)
25; [2005] Crim. L.R. 154; (2004) 148 S.J.L.B. 1406; *Times,* December 21,
2004, CA (Crim Div) .... *Digested,* 05/**3650**
R. v. Ibrahima (Thomas) [2005] EWCA Crim 1436; [2005] Crim. L.R. 887, CA (Crim
Div)
R. v. Immigration Appeal Tribunal Ex p. Jeyeanthan see R. v. Secretary of State for the
Home Department Ex p. Jeyeanthan
R. v. Immigration Appeal Tribunal Ex p. Mehta (No.1) [1976] Imm. A.R. 38, CA (Civ
Div) .... *Digested,* 77/**13**:
Distinguished, 05/2221: *Referred to,* 97/2843
R. v. Immigration Appeal Tribunal Ex p. Rajendrakumar see R. v. Secretary of State for
the Home Department Ex p. Ravichandran (No.1)
R. v. Immigration Appeal Tribunal Ex p. Sandralingam (No.1) see R. v. Secretary of
State for the Home Department Ex p. Ravichandran (No.1)
R. v. Independent Television Commission Ex p. TSW Broadcasting Ltd [1996] E.M.L.R.
291; *Times,* March 30, 1992; *Independent,* March 27, 1992; *Guardian,* April 2,
1992, HL; affirming *Times,* February 7, 1992; *Independent,* February 6, 1992;
Guardian, February 12, 1992, CA (Civ Div) .... *Digested,* 92/**65**:
Applied, 05/1415: *Considered,* 94/79, 95/137
R. v. Inland Revenue Commissioners Ex p. Matteson's Walls Ltd see R. v. Inland
Revenue Commissioners Ex p. Unilever Plc
R. v. Inland Revenue Commissioners Ex p. Unilever Plc; R. v. Inland Revenue
Commissioners Ex p. Matteson's Walls Ltd [1996] S.T.C. 681; 68 T.C. 205;
[1996] C.O.D. 421, CA (Civ Div); affirming [1994] S.T.C. 841; [1994] S.T.I. 1023;
Independent, September 12, 1994 (C.S.), QBD .... *Digested,* 95/**895**:
Applied, 00/4072: *Considered,* 01/5605: *Distinguished,* 04/3786, 05/4121
R. v. Inns (Terry Michael) (1974) 60 Cr. App. R. 231; [1975] Crim. L.R. 182; 119 S.J.
150, CA (Crim Div) .... *Digested,* 75/**669**:
Applied, 78/575: *Considered,* 05/883
R. v. IP [2004] EWCA Crim 2646; [2005] 1 Cr. App. R. (S.) 102; [2005] Crim. L.R.
152, CA (Crim Div) .... *Digested,* 05/**3744**
R. v. Islington LBC Ex p. McMillan see R. v. Gloucestershire CC Ex p. Barry
R. v. Ismail (Abokar Ahmed); *sub nom* R. v. Ismail (Abokor Ahmed) [2005] EWCA
Crim 397; [2005] 2 Cr. App. R. (S.) 88; [2005] Crim. L.R. 491; *Times,* March 4,
2005, CA (Crim Div) .... *Digested,* 05/**3776**
R. v. J; *sub nom* R. v. MJ [2004] UKHL 42; [2005] 1 A.C. 562; [2004] 3 W.L.R.
1019; [2005] 1 All E.R. 1; [2005] 1 Cr. App. R. 19; (2004) 101(40) L.S.G. 28;
(2004) 148 S.J.L.B. 1216; *Times,* October 15, 2004; *Independent,* October 20,
2004, HL; reversing [2002] EWCA Crim 2983; [2003] 1 W.L.R. 1590; [2003] 1
All E.R. 518; [2003] 2 Cr. App. R. 8; (2003) 167 J.P. 108; [2003] Crim. L.R.
391; (2003) 167 J.P.N. 191; *Times,* February 7, 2003, CA (Crim Div) .... *Digested,* 05/**921**:
Considered, 03/3864
R. v. J (Patricia); R. v. M (Christopher Michael) [2004] EWCA Crim 2002; [2005] 1
Cr. App. R. (S.) 63, CA (Crim Div)
R. v. J (Unreasonable Delay) see Attorney General's Reference (No.2 of 2001), Re
R. v. Jackson (Leanna) see Attorney General's Reference (No.119 of 2004), Re
R. v. Jackson (Ruth) see Attorney General's Reference (No.1 of 2004), Re
R. v. Jaggard (Roland Leonard) see R. v. Brown (Anthony Joseph)
R. v. James (Michael Harold) [2005] EWCA Crim 110; [2005] 2 Cr. App. R. 4; [2005]
Crim. L.R. 642, CA (Crim Div) .... *Digested,* 05/**723**
R. v. Jarvis Facilities Ltd [2005] EWCA Crim 1409; (2005) 149 S.J.L.B. 769; *Times,*
June 6, 2005, CA (Crim Div) .... *Digested,* 05/**1945**
R. v. Jary (Stephen) see Attorney General's Reference (Nos.148, 149, 150, 151, 152,
153, 154 and 155 of 2001), Re
R. v. JC see Attorney General's Reference (Nos.37, 38, 44, 54, 51, 53, 35, 40, 43, 45,
41 and 42 of 2003), Re
R. v. Jeffrey (Wayne Peter) [2003] EWCA Crim 2098; [2004] 1 Cr. App. R. (S.) 25,
CA (Crim Div) .... *Digested,* 04/**3354**:
Considered, 05/3624
R. v. Jisl (Jan); R. v. Tekin (Gungor); R. v. Konakli (Yucel) [2004] EWCA Crim 696;
Times, April 19, 2004, CA (Crim Div) .... *Digested,* 04/**889**:
Considered, 05/740
R. v. JO'B (A Juvenile) see Attorney General's Reference (Nos.59, 60 and 63 of 1998),
Re
R. v. Johnson (Brian) see R. v. Sinclair (James)
R. v. Johnson (Costs) [2005] 1 Costs L.R. 153, Sup Ct Costs Office .... *Digested,* 05/**880**
R. v. Johnson (James Gordon); R. v. Hind (Jodie Thomas) [2005] EWCA Crim 971;
Times, May 3, 2005, CA (Crim Div) .... *Digested,* 05/**724**
R. v. Johnson (Martin Clive) see Attorney General's Reference (No.48 of 2000), Re
R. v. Johnson Partnership Solicitors [2004] EWCA Crim 2343; [2005] P.N.L.R. 12,
CA (Crim Div)
R. v. Johnston (George) see Attorney General's Reference (Nos.144 and 145 of 2004),
Re

R. v. Jones (Anthony William); *sub nom* R. v. Haywood (John Victor); R. v. Hayward (John Victor) (No.2); R. v. Purvis (Paul Nigel) [2002] UKHL 5; [2003] 1 A.C. 1; [2002] 2 W.L.R. 524; [2002] 2 All E.R. 113; [2002] 2 Cr. App. R. 9; (2002) 166 J.P. 333; [2002] H.R.L.R. 23; (2002) 166 J.P.N. 431; (2002) 99(13) L.S.G. 26; (2002) 146 S.J.L.B. 61; *Times*, February 21, 2002; *Independent*, February 27, 2002, HL; affirming [2001] EWCA Crim 168; [2001] Q.B. 862; [2001] 3 W.L.R. 125; [2001] 2 Cr. App. R. 11; (2001) 165 J.P. 281; [2001] Crim. L.R. 502; (2001) 165 J.P.N. 665; (2001) 98(9) L.S.G. 38; (2001) 145 S.J.L.B. 53; *Times*, February 14, 2001; *Independent*, February 8, 2001, CA (Crim Div) . . . .   *Digested*, 02/**913**:
                                             Considered, 05/1488: *Followed*, 04/877
R. v. Jones (Gail Lesley) [1996] 2 Cr. App. R. (S.) 134, CA (Crim Div) . . . .   *Digested*, 96/**1852**:
                                             Considered, 05/3587
R. v. Jones (Jason) see Attorney General's Reference (No.78 of 2000), Re
R. v. Jones (Leon) see Attorney General's Reference (Nos.13, 14, 15, 16, 17 and 18 of 2004), Re
R. v. Jones (Margaret); R. v. Milling (Arthur Paul); R. v. Olditch (Toby); R. v. Pritchard (Philip); R. v. Richards (Josh); Ayliffe v. DPP; Swain v. DPP; TNS, HL; affirming [2004] EWCA Crim 1981; [2005] Q.B. 259; [2004] 3 W.L.R. 1362; [2004] 4 All E.R. 955; [2005] 1 Cr. App. R. 12; [2005] Crim. L.R. 122; [2005] A.C.D. 5; (2004) 148 S.J.L.B. 1149; *Times*, July 30, 2004, CA (Crim Div); affirming in part (Unreported, May 12, 2004), Crown Ct (Bristol) . . . .   *Digested*, 04/**734**:
                                             Applied, 05/754: *Previous proceedings*, 05/754
R. v. Jones (Neil Andrew) see Attorney General's Reference (No.89 of 2000), Re
R. v. Jordan (Andrew James); R. v. Alleyne (Carl Anthony); R. v. Redfern (David Christopher) [2004] EWCA Crim 3291; [2005] 2 Cr. App. R. (S.) 44; [2005] Crim. L.R. 312, CA (Crim Div) . . . .   *Digested*, 05/**3690**:
                                             Considered, 05/3694
R. v. Jordan (Shirley) see R. v. Lambert (Steven)
R. v. Joy; R. v. Bossom [2005] Eu. L.R. 765, CC (Lewes)
R. v. JRH see R. v. H (Childhood Amnesia)
R. v. K; R. v. G; R. v. M [2005] EWCA Crim 145; [2005] 4 Costs L.R. 571; *Times*, February 15, 2005, CA (Crim Div) . . . .   *Digested*, 05/**924**
R. v. K [2005] EWCA Crim 619; *Times*, March 15, 2005, CA (Crim Div)
R. v. K (Age of Consent: Reasonable Belief); *sub nom* Crown Prosecution Service v. K (Age of Consent: Reasonable Belief) [2001] UKHL 41; [2002] 1 A.C. 462; [2001] 3 W.L.R. 471; [2001] 3 All E.R. 897; [2002] 1 Cr. App. R. 13; [2001] 3 F.C.R. 115; [2001] Crim. L.R. 993; (2001) 98(34) L.S.G. 39; (2001) 145 S.J.L.B. 202; *Times*, July 26, 2001; *Independent*, July 27, 2001; *Daily Telegraph*, July 31, 2001, HL; reversing [2001] 1 Cr. App. R. 35; [2001] Crim. L.R. 134; (2000) 97(44) L.S.G. 44; (2000) 144 S.J.L.B. 272; *Times*, November 7, 2000; *Independent*, November 8, 2000, CA (Crim Div). . . . .   *Digested*, 01/**1070**:
                                             Applied, 02/800: *Followed*, 05/758
R. v. K (Herbert) [2005] EWCA Crim 955; *Times*, May 17, 2005, CA (Crim Div) . . . . . .   *Digested*, 05/**3736**
R. v. K (Patrick Joseph); R. v. M (Mark Anthony); R. v. D (Adam George) [2004] EWCA Crim 2685; [2005] 1 Cr. App. R. 25; [2005] Crim. L.R. 298, CA (Crim Div) . . . .   *Digested*, 05/**793**
R. v. Kabir (Shahajan) see Attorney General's Reference (No.106 of 2004), Re
R. v. Kai-Whitewind (Chaha'oh Niyol) [2005] EWCA Crim 1092; [2005] 2 Cr. App. R. 31; *Times*, May 11, 2005, CA (Crim Div) . . . .   *Digested*, 05/**747**
R. v. Kalemi (Alban) see Attorney General's Reference (Nos.135, 136 and 137), Re
R. v. Kalia (Daya); R. v. Kalia (Jagan Nath); R. v. Bhuller (Surinder Singh); R. v. Sahi (Harinder Singh); R. v. Sidhu (Joginder Singh); R. v. Sharma (Ramlok); R. v. Sharma (Balbir Chandra) (1974) 60 Cr. App. R. 200; [1975] Crim. L.R. 181, CA (Crim Div). . . . .   *Digested*, 75/**529**:
                                             Applied, 05/837
R. v. Kalia (Jagan Nath) see R. v. Kalia (Daya)
R. v. Kalyan (Sohan Lal) see R. v. Saini (Jarnail Singh)
R. v. Kamel (Izem) see Attorney General's Reference (Nos.27, 28, 29 and 30 of 2005), Re
R. v. Kandhari (Unreported, April 24, 1979), CA (Crim Div) . . . .   *Cited*, 92/1224,
                                             92/1226, 93/1105, 93/1106: *Considered*, 05/3768
R. v. Kansal (Maden Lal) see R. v. Raviraj (Thaneran)
R. v. Kansal (Raj Kumar) see R. v. Raviraj (Thaneran)
R. v. Kansal (Yash Pal) (No.2) see R. v. Kansal (Yash Pal) (Change of Law)

R. v. Kansal (Yash Pal) (Change of Law); *sub nom* R. v. Kansal (Yash Pal) (No.2)
[2001] UKHL 62; [2002] 2 A.C. 69; [2001] 3 W.L.R. 1562; [2002] 1 All E.R.
257; [2002] 1 Cr. App. R. 36; [2002] H.R.L.R. 9; [2002] U.K.H.R.R. 169;
[2002] B.P.I.R. 370; [2002] Crim. L.R. 498; (2002) 99(3) L.S.G. 25; (2001)
145 S.J.L.B. 275; *Times*, December 4, 2001; *Independent*, December 4, 2001;
Daily Telegraph, December 6, 2001, HL; reversing [2001] EWCA Crim 1260;
[2001] 3 W.L.R. 751; [2001] 2 Cr. App. R. 30; (2001) 98(28) L.S.G. 43; (2001)
145 S.J.L.B. 157; *Times*, June 11, 2001; *Independent*, June 6, 2001, CA (Crim
Div) . . . . *Digested*, 02/**849**:
         Applied, 02/3896, 02/3897, 05/875: *Followed*, 02/844, 02/2663:
         Previous proceedings, 92/979: *Subsequent proceedings*, 05/2092
R. v. Karakaya (Adem) [2005] EWCA Crim 346; [2005] 2 Cr. App. R. 5; [2005] Crim.
L.R. 574; *Times*, February 28, 2005, CA (Crim Div) . . . . *Digested*, 05/**832**
R. v. Karim (Imran Abid) [2005] EWCA Crim 533; (2005) 149 S.J.L.B. 269, CA (Crim
Div)
R. v. Kayar (Sakir) [1998] 2 Cr. App. R. (S.) 355, CA (Crim Div) . . . . *Digested*, 99/**1129**:
         Considered, 05/3597
R. v. Kaynak (Hussein); R. v. Honz (Tomas); R. v. Simsek (Muslum); R. v. Aksu (Ali)
[1998] 2 Cr. App. R. (S.) 283, CA (Crim Div) . . . . *Digested*, 98/**1185**:
         Distinguished, 05/3597
R. v. KC [2004] EWCA Crim 2361; [2005] 1 Cr. App. R. (S.) 97, CA (Crim Div) . . . . *Digested*, 05/**3770**
R. v. Keane (Michael) see Attorney General's Reference (No.31 of 2005), Re
R. v. Keating (Stephen James) see R. v. McInerney (William Patrick)
R. v. Keenan (Martin Thomas) see Attorney General's Reference (No.96 of 2004), Re
R. v. Kelleher (Paul) [2003] EWCA Crim 3525; (2003) 147 S.J.L.B. 1395, CA (Crim
Div) . . . . *Applied*, 05/902
R. v. Kelly (Anthony Joseph) see R. v. Allsopp (Michael Nevin)
R. v. Kelly (Francis William) [1970] 1 W.L.R. 1050; [1970] 2 All E.R. 198; (1970) 54 Cr.
App. R. 334; 114 S.J. 357, CA (Crim Div) . . . . *Digested*, 70/**2519**:
         Applied, 70/2522, 71/10236: *Considered*, 71/10223, 73/2929:
         Disapproved, 05/902: *Distinguished*, 73/2931, 73/2933: *Followed*, 73/2930
R. v. Kelly (James Stephen) [2004] EWCA Crim 1629; [2005] 1 Cr. App. R. (S.) 39,
CA (Crim Div) . . . . *Digested*, 05/**3766**
R. v. Kelly (Lewis); R. v. Donnelly (Miles) [2001] EWCA Crim 170; [2001] 2 Cr. App.
R. (S.) 73; [2001] Crim. L.R. 411, CA (Crim Div) . . . . *Digested*, 01/**1191**:
         Applied, 04/3469: *Considered*, 04/3417, 05/3651: *Distinguished*, 04/3300:
         Followed, 03/3824, 05/3521, 05/3760
R. v. Kennedy (Karen Mary) see R. v. Khan (Bajlu Islam)
R. v. Kennedy (Simon) [2005] EWCA Crim 685; [2005] 1 W.L.R. 2159; [2005] 2 Cr.
App. R. 23; *Times*, April 6, 2005, CA (Crim Div) . . . . *Digested*, 05/**803**
R. v. Kenny (Graham Jack) see R. v. Quayle (Barry)
R. v. Kensington and Chelsea RLBC Ex p. Lawrie Plantation Services Ltd [1999] 1
W.L.R. 1415; [1999] 3 All E.R. 929; (2000) 79 P. & C.R. 467; [1999] 3 P.L.R.
138; [2000] J.P.L. 181; [1999] E.G.C.S. 100; [1999] N.P.C. 86; *Times*, July 12,
1999 ; *Independent*, July 13, 1999, HL; reversing [1998] 1 P.L.R. 109; [1998]
E.G.C.S. 3; [1998] N.P.C. 2; *Times*, January 21, 1998, CA (Civ Div); affirming
(1997) 74 P. & C.R. 270; [1997] J.P.L. 997; [1997] N.P.C. 30, QBD . . . . *Digested*, 99/**4180**:
         Considered, 05/3263
R. v. Kent CC Ex p. C [1998] E.L.R. 108, QBD . . . . *Digested*, 98/**1913**:
         Followed, 05/1078
R. v. Kenyon (Margaret Rose) [2005] EWCA Crim 424; (2005) 149 S.J.L.B. 265, CA
(Crim Div)
R. v. Keogh (Brian) (1994) 15 Cr. App. R. (S.) 279; [1993] Crim. L.R. 895, CA (Crim
Div) . . . . *Digested*, 94/**1318**:
         Disapproved, 05/3746
R. v. Kerr (Vincent Kirk) [2005] EWCA Crim 2037; (2005) 102(29) L.S.G. 32, CA
(Crim Div)
R. v. Khair (Lee) (Costs) [2005] 3 Costs L.R. 542, Sup Ct Costs Office
R. v. Khair (Lee Michael) [2004] EWCA Crim 1296; [2005] 1 Cr. App. R. (S.) 29, CA
(Crim Div) . . . . *Digested*, 05/**3661**
R. v. Khan (Bajlu Islam); R. v. Kennedy (Karen Mary) [2004] EWCA Crim 3316;
[2005] 2 Cr. App. R. (S.) 45, CA (Crim Div) . . . . *Digested*, 05/**3540**
R. v. Khan (Jameel) see Attorney General's Reference (No.26 of 2004), Re
R. v. Khan (Mohammed Iftiyaz) see R. v. Underwood (Kevin John)
R. v. Khan (Mohsan) see R. v. Ali (Liaquat)
R. v. Khan (Rungzabe); R. v. Khan (Tahir) [1998] Crim. L.R. 830; *Times*, April 7, 1998;
Independent, March 25, 1998, CA (Crim Div) . . . . *Digested*, 98/**958**:
         Considered, 05/805
R. v. Khan (Tahir) see R. v. Khan (Rungzabe)
R. v. Khan (Zulfi Al) (Costs) [2005] 1 Costs L.R. 157, Sup Ct Costs Office . . . . *Digested*, 05/**882**
R. v. Khela (Dalbir Singh); R. v. Smith (Tina) [2005] EWCA Crim 3446; *Times*,
December 6, 2005, CA (Crim Div)

R. *v.* Kidd (Philip Richard); R. *v.* Canavan (Darren Anthony); R. *v.* Shaw (Dennis) [1998] 1 W.L.R. 604; [1998] 1 All E.R. 42; [1998] 1 Cr. App. R. 79; [1998] 1 Cr. App. R. (S.) 243; (1997) 161 J.P. 709; [1997] Crim. L.R. 766; (1997) 161 J.P.N. 838; (1997) 94(35) L.S.G. 33; (1997) 147 N.L.J. 1457; (1997) 141 S.J.L.B. 169; *Times,* July 21, 1997, CA (Crim Div) . . . . *Digested,* 97/**1492**:
Applied, 04/3376, 05/3742: *Considered,* 98/1387, 99/1351, 99/1352:
Distinguished, 03/3826

R. *v.* Kiernan (Ian Donald) see R. *v.* Soares (Ronald)
R. *v.* Killick (Bill George) see R. *v.* Rees (Louis)
R. *v.* Kirby (Lee) [2005] EWCA Crim 1228; [2005] Crim. L.R. 732, CA (Crim Div) . . . .   *Followed,* 05/3585
R. *v.* Kirk (Craig); R. *v.* Russell (Steven John) [2002] EWCA Crim 1580; [2002] Crim. L.R. 756; (2002) 99(30) L.S.G. 37; (2002) 146 S.J.L.B. 154; *Times,* June 26, 2002, CA (Crim Div) . . . .   *Digested,* 02/**831**:
Considered, 05/2102

R. *v.* Kirkham (Gary) see Attorney General's Reference (No.76 of 1998), Re
R. *v.* Kishientine (Micheline Bulankay) [2004] EWCA Crim 3352; [2005] 2 Cr. App. R. (S.) 28; *Times,* December 9, 2004, CA (Crim Div) . . . .   *Digested,* 05/**3684**
R. *v.* Kitchener (Marvine Wayne) see Attorney General's Reference (No.19 of 1999), Re
R. *v.* Knight (Philip) [2003] EWCA Crim 1977; [2004] 1 W.L.R. 340; [2004] 1 Cr. App. R. 9; [2003] Crim. L.R. 799; (2003) 100(37) L.S.G. 31; *Times,* August 20, 2003, CA (Crim Div) . . . .   *Digested,* 03/**763**:
Applied, 05/749: *Considered,* 04/886

R. *v.* Knights (Richard Michael); R. *v.* Singh (Shangara); R. *v.* Sekhon (Daljit Singh); R. *v.* Singh (Satnam); R. *v.* Dhnoay (Gurdev Singh); R. *v.* Maguire (Kevin); R. *v.* McFaul (Kevin) [2005] UKHL 50; [2005] 3 W.L.R. 330; [2005] 4 All E.R. 347; (2005) 155 N.L.J. 1316; *Times,* July 27, 2005; *Independent,* July 27, 2005, HL; affirming [2002] EWCA Crim 2954; [2003] 1 W.L.R. 1655; [2003] 3 All E.R. 508; [2003] 1 Cr. App. R. 34; [2003] 2 Cr. App. R. (S.) 38; [2003] Crim. L.R. 642; (2003) 100(8) L.S.G. 29; (2003) 147 S.J.L.B. 148; *Times,* December 27, 2002, CA (Crim Div) . . . .   *Digested,* 05/**841**:
Applied, 03/900, 03/3662, 03/3663, 04/806, 04/3330:
Considered, 03/846, 05/2826

R. *v.* Kolawole (David Oladotun) [2004] EWCA Crim 3047; [2005] 2 Cr. App. R. (S.) 14; [2005] Crim. L.R. 245; (2004) 148 S.J.L.B. 1370; *Times,* November 16, 2004, CA (Crim Div) . . . .   *Digested,* 05/**3610**
R. *v.* Konakli (Yucel) see R. *v.* Jisl (Jan)
R. *v.* Konzani (Feston) [2005] EWCA Crim 706; [2005] 2 Cr. App. R. 14; (2005) 149 S.J.L.B. 389, CA (Crim Div) . . . .   *Digested,* 05/**766**:
Applied, 05/3618

R. *v.* Kumar (Aman) [2004] EWCA Crim 3207; [2005] 1 W.L.R. 1352; [2005] 1 Cr. App. R. 34; [2005] Crim. L.R. 470; *Times,* January 10, 2005, CA (Crim Div) . . .   *Digested,* 05/**758**
R. *v.* Kuosmanen (Paavo Topias) [2004] EWCA Crim 1861; [2005] 1 Cr. App. R. (S.) 71, CA (Crim Div)
R. *v.* KV; *sub nom* R. *v.* V [2005] EWCA Crim 581; (2005) 149 S.J.L.B. 301, CA (Crim Div)
R. *v.* L (Indecent Assault: Sentencing) [1999] 1 Cr. App. R. 117; [1999] 1 Cr. App. R. (S.) 19; (1998) 95(26) L.S.G. 31; (1998) 142 S.J.L.B. 156; *Times,* April 28, 1998; *Independent,* April 28, 1998, CA (Crim Div) . . . .   *Digested,* 98/**1257**:
Applied, 99/1196: *Considered,* 99/1194, 99/1199, 99/1203, 99/1302,
00/1288, 01/1354, 05/3637: *Followed,* 99/1207, 01/1484

R. *v.* L (Young Offender: Time in Custody on Remand) see R. *v.* M (Young Offender: Time in Custody on Remand)
R. *v.* Lacey (Steven Lloyd) see Attorney General's Reference (No.9 of 1989), Re
R. *v.* Lackenby (Ian Stuart) see R. *v.* Millberry (William Christopher)
R. *v.* Lahaye (Dean John) [2005] EWCA Crim 2847; *Times,* October 25, 2005, CA (Crim Div)
R. *v.* Lahbib (Hassan) [2004] EWCA Crim 1877; [2005] 1 Cr. App. R. (S.) 68, CA (Crim Div) . . . .   *Digested,* 05/**3669**
R. *v.* Lamb (Christopher) [2005] EWCA Crim 3000; *Times,* December 1, 2005, CA (Crim Div)
R. *v.* Lambert (Steven); R. *v.* Ali (Mudassir Mohammed); R. *v.* Jordan (Shirley) [2001] UKHL 37; [2002] 2 A.C. 545; [2001] 3 W.L.R. 206; [2002] 1 All E.R. 2; [2001] 3 All E.R. 577; [2001] 2 Cr. App. R. 28; [2001] H.R.L.R. 55; [2001] U.K.H.R.R. 1074; [2001] Crim. L.R. 806; (2001) 98(33) L.S.G. 29; (2001) 145 S.J.L.B. 174; *Times,* July 6, 2001; *Independent,* July 19, 2001; *Daily Telegraph,* July 17, 2001, HL; affirming [2002] Q.B. 1112; [2001] 2 W.L.R. 211; [2001] 1 All E.R. 1014; [2001] 1 Cr. App. R. 14; [2001] H.R.L.R. 4; [2000] U.K.H.R.R. 864; (2000) 97(35) L.S.G. 36; *Times,* September 5, 2000, CA (Crim Div) . . . .   *Digested,* 01/**3504**:
Applied, 01/2315, 03/780, 03/4064, 05/875: *Considered,* 02/785, 02/795,
03/761, 03/802, 04/707, 04/800, 04/4066, 05/5111: *Distinguished,* 02/813,
03/814: *Followed,* 01/1193, 01/5271, 02/844, 02/849, 02/1526, 02/2663

R. *v.* Lamont (Martin) see R. *v.* Pepper (Jeremy Paul)
R. *v.* Lamoon (Johnathon Joe) see Attorney General's Reference (No.52 of 2001), Re

R. _v._ Lancashire CC Ex p. Royal Association for Disability and Rehabilitation see R. _v._ Gloucestershire CC Ex p. Barry

R. _v._ Land (Michael) [1999] Q.B. 65; [1998] 3 W.L.R. 322; [1998] 1 All E.R. 403; [1998] 1 Cr. App. R. 301; (1998) 162 J.P. 29; [1998] 1 F.L.R. 438; [1998] Crim. L.R. 70; [1998] Fam. Law 133; (1997) 161 J.P.N. 1173; (1997) 94(42) L.S.G. 32; _Times_, November 4, 1997; _Independent_, October 16, 1997, CA (Crim Div) . . .   _Digested_, 97/**1160**:
Considered, 05/800: _Followed_, 05/5095

R. _v._ Lang (Stephen Howard); R. _v._ Abdi (Hassan); R. _v._ Winters (Keith); R. _v._ Carasco (Charles); R. _v._ Feihn (Steven); R. _v._ Wright (Robert); R. _v._ Smith (Gary); R. _v._ Armitage (Lewis); R. _v._ Glave (Heathcliffe); R. _v._ Collier (Edward); R. _v._ Sheppard (James); R. _v._ Guidera (Michael); R. _v._ Edwards (Kyle Frederick); R. _v._ D [2005] EWCA Crim 2864; _Times_, November 10, 2005, CA (Crim Div)

R. _v._ Larkin [1943] K.B. 174; [1943] 1 All E.R. 217, CCA . . . .   _Applied_, 59/**735**,
61/2167, 70/1368, 71/6012, 76/496: _Considered_, 63/865:
Disapproved, 05/902: _Followed_, 62/669, 65/848

R. _v._ Lashley (Angela) [2005] EWCA Crim 2016; _Times_, September 28, 2005, CA (Crim Div). . . . .   _Digested_, 05/**891**

R. _v._ Lashley (Mark) (1988) 10 Cr. App. R. (S.) 396, CA (Crim Div) . . . .   _Digested_, 90/**1349**:
Applied, 05/743: _Considered_, 96/1887

R. _v._ Laskey (Colin) see R. _v._ Brown (Anthony Joseph)

R. _v._ Last (Emma); R. _v._ Crane (Sara); R. _v._ Quillan (Edward Steven); R. _v._ Quillan (James Angus); R. _v._ Holbrook (Lee David) [2005] EWCA Crim 106; [2005] 2 Cr. App. R. (S.) 64; [2005] Crim. L.R. 407; (2005) 149 S.J.L.B. 147; _Times_, January 31, 2005, CA (Crim Div) . . . .   _Digested_, 05/**3680**:
Applied, 05/3682, 05/3735

R. _v._ Lawrence (Daniel Kent) [2004] EWCA Crim 2219; [2005] 1 Cr. App. R. (S.) 83, CA (Crim Div) . . . .   _Digested_, 05/**3756**

R. _v._ Lawrence (Steven) see R. _v._ May (Raymond George)

R. _v._ Lawson (Adam) [2005] EWCA Crim 1840; [2005] Crim. L.R. 871, CA (Crim Div)

R. _v._ Lazarus (Tony Jason) [2004] EWCA Crim 2297; [2005] 1 Cr. App. R. (S.) 98; [2005] Crim. L.R. 64, CA (Crim Div) . . . .   _Digested_, 05/**843**

R. _v._ Le (Van Binh); R. _v._ Stark (Rudi) [1999] 1 Cr. App. R. (S.) 422; [1998] I.N.L.R. 677; [1999] Crim. L.R. 96; _Times_, October 15, 1998, CA (Crim Div) . . . .   _Digested_, 98/**1245**:
Applied, 03/3678, 05/3534: _Considered_, 00/1275, 05/3535, 05/3605:
Followed, 05/3536

R. _v._ Leal (Manoj) (Confiscation Order) see R. _v._ Benjafield (Karl Robert) (Confiscation Order)

R. _v._ Leather (John Holdsworth) (1994) 98 Cr. App. R. 179; [1993] 2 F.L.R. 770; [1994] 1 F.C.R. 877; [1993] Crim. L.R. 516; [1994] Fam. Law 70; (1993) 137 S.J.L.B. 54; _Times_, January 21, 1993, CA (Crim Div) . . . .   _Digested_, 94/**3164**:
Considered, 05/760

R. _v._ Leboutillier (Paul) see R. _v._ Holliday (Paul)

R. _v._ Lee (May Po) see R. _v._ Quayle (Barry)

R. _v._ Leer (Nicholas) see Attorney General's Reference (No.87 of 2003), Re

R. _v._ Legal Aid Board Ex p. Kaim Todner; _sub nom_ R. _v._ Legal Aid Board Ex p. T (A Firm of Solicitors) [1999] Q.B. 966; [1998] 3 W.L.R. 925; [1998] 3 All E.R. 541; (1998) 95(26) L.S.G. 31; (1998) 148 N.L.J. 941; (1998) 142 S.J.L.B. 189; _Times_, June 15, 1998; _Independent_, June 12, 1998, CA (Civ Div); affirming CO-330-97, QBD . . . .   _Digested_, 98/**83**:
Considered, 05/2121

R. _v._ Legal Aid Board Ex p. T (A Firm of Solicitors) see R. _v._ Legal Aid Board Ex p. Kaim Todner

R. _v._ Lehal (Bhupinder) see Attorney General's Reference (Nos.31, 42, 43, 45, 50 and 51 of 2003), Re

R. _v._ Lehal (Surinder) see Attorney General's Reference (Nos.31, 42, 43, 45, 50 and 51 of 2003), Re

R. _v._ Leiger (George) see R. _v._ Leigers (George)

R. _v._ Leigers (George); _sub nom_ R. _v._ Leiger (George) [2005] EWCA Crim 802; [2005] 2 Cr. App. R. (S.) 104; [2005] Crim. L.R. 584; (2005) 149 S.J.L.B. 389, CA (Crim Div) . . . .   _Digested_, 05/**3653**

R. _v._ Leng (Darren Shaun) see Attorney General's Reference (Nos.148, 149, 150, 151, 152, 153, 154 and 155 of 2001), Re

R. _v._ Leominster DC Ex p. Pothecary (1998) 10 Admin. L.R. 484; (1998) 76 P. & C.R. 346; [1998] 3 P.L.R. 91; [1998] J.P.L. 335; (1997) 94(45) L.S.G. 28; [1997] N.P.C. 151; _Times_, November 18, 1997, CA (Civ Div); reversing [1997] J.P.L. 835; [1997] E.G.C.S. 2, QBD . . . .   _Digested_, 97/**4116**:
Applied, 05/3292

R. _v._ Lewis (Leroy Marvin) see R. _v._ Docking (Jason)

R. _v._ Lewis (Michael William) [2005] EWCA Crim 859; [2005] Crim. L.R. 796; _Times_, May 19, 2005, CA (Crim Div). . . . .   _Digested_, 05/**875**

R. *v.* Liddle (Mark) (Appeal against Sentence); R. *v.* Hayes (Andrew Michael) [1999] 3 All E.R. 816; [2000] 1 Cr. App. R. (S.) 131; [1999] Crim. L.R. 847; (1999) 96(23) L.S.G. 34; *Times,* May 26, 1999; *Independent,* June 16, 1999, CA (Crim Div) . . . . *Digested,* 99/**1188**:
Applied, 01/1344: *Considered,* 01/1346, 02/3967, 05/3628, 05/3629, 05/3722: *Distinguished,* 04/3359

R. *v.* Limani (Beher) see R. *v.* Momodou (Henry)

R. *v.* Little (David) see Attorney General's Reference (No.64 of 2001), Re

R. *v.* Littlefield (John) see R. *v.* Aranguren (Jose de Jesus)

R. *v.* Lizziemore (Bryan Roger) see Attorney General's Reference (Nos.48, 49, 50 and 51 of 2002), Re

R. *v.* Llewellyn (David Stephen) see Attorney General's Reference (Nos.3 and 4 of 2005), Re

R. *v.* Llewellyn-Jones (Hopkin Alfred); R. *v.* Lougher (William Layton Pritchard) [1968] 1 Q.B. 429; [1967] 3 W.L.R. 1298; [1967] 3 All E.R. 225; (1967) 51 Cr. App. R. 204; 111 S.J. 112, CA (Crim Div); affirming (1967) 51 Cr. App. R. 4, Assizes (Cardiff) . . . . *Digested,* 67/**841**:
Considered, 79/2085, 95/165, 05/898: *Distinguished,* 81/506, 82/665

R. *v.* LM Unreported, Sup Ct (Qld) . . . . *Applied,* 05/1559

R. *v.* LM [2002] EWCA Crim 3047; [2003] 2 Cr. App. R. (S.) 26; [2003] Crim. L.R. 205, CA (Crim Div) . . . . *Digested,* 03/**3751**:
Considered, 05/3765

R. *v.* Lobban (Adrian Michael) see Attorney General's Reference (Nos.4 and 7 of 2002), Re

R. *v.* Local Commissioner for Administration for England Ex p. Eastleigh BC; *sub nom* R. *v.* Local Commissioner for Administration for the South, the West, the West Midlands, Leicestershire, Lincolnshire and Cambridgeshire Ex p. Eastleigh BC [1988] Q.B. 855; [1988] 3 W.L.R. 113; [1988] 3 All E.R. 151; 86 L.G.R. 491; (1988) 152 L.G. Rev. 890; [1988] E.G.C.S. 28; (1988) 132 S.J. 564, CA (Civ Div); reversing 86 L.G.R. 145; *Times,* July 14, 1987, DC . . . . *Digested,* 88/**2200**:
Applied, 05/3054: *Considered,* 97/4646

R. *v.* Local Commissioner for Administration for the South, the West, the West Midlands, Leicestershire, Lincolnshire and Cambridgeshire Ex p. Eastleigh BC see R. *v.* Local Commissioner for Administration for England Ex p. Eastleigh BC

R. *v.* Loizou (Lisa); R. *v.* Gourzoilidis (Anastasios); R. *v.* Quilligan (James); R. *v.* McCarthy (John) [2005] EWCA Crim 1579; [2005] 2 Cr. App. R. 37; [2005] Crim. L.R. 885; *Times,* June 23, 2005, CA (Crim Div) . . . . *Digested,* 05/**812**

R. *v.* Long (James) see Attorney General's Reference (Nos.99, 100, 101 and 102 of 2004), Re

R. *v.* Longworth (Gary Dean) TNS, HL; reversing [2004] EWCA Crim 2145; [2005] 1 Cr. App. R. (S.) 81; *Times,* August 17, 2004, CA (Crim Div). . . . . *Digested,* 05/**3567**

R. *v.* Looseley (Grant Spencer) (No.2) see Attorney General's Reference (No.3 of 2000), Re

R. *v.* Loosely (Grant Spencer) see Attorney General's Reference (No.3 of 2000), Re

R. *v.* Loosley (Grant Spencer) (No.2) see Attorney General's Reference (No.3 of 2000), Re

R. *v.* Lopez (Michael) see Attorney General's Reference (Nos.11 and 12 of 2005), Re

R. *v.* Lord Chancellor Ex p. Child Poverty Action Group; R. *v.* DPP Ex p. Bull [1999] 1 W.L.R. 347; [1998] 2 All E.R. 755; [1998] C.O.D. 267; (1998) 148 N.L.J. 20; *Times,* February 27, 1998; *Independent,* February 11, 1998, QBD . . . . *Digested,* 98/**412**:
Applied, 00/430: *Considered,* 03/358, 05/354

R. *v.* Lord Saville of Newdigate Ex p. A see R. *v.* Lord Saville of Newdigate Ex p. B (No.2)

R. *v.* Lord Saville of Newdigate Ex p. B (No.2); *sub nom* R. *v.* Lord Saville of Newdigate Ex p. A [2000] 1 W.L.R. 1855; [1999] 4 All E.R. 860; [1999] C.O.D. 436; (1999) 149 N.L.J. 1201; *Times,* July 29, 1999, CA (Civ Div); affirming (1999) 149 N.L.J. 965; *Times,* June 22, 1999 ; *Independent,* June 22, 1999, QBD . . . . *Digested,* 99/**80**:
Applied, 01/82, 04/35: *Considered,* 01/3684, 05/33: *Followed,* 00/47

R. *v.* Lord Spens (No.2) see R. *v.* Spens (No.2)

R. *v.* Lotay (Anadeep) see R. *v.* Ali (Zuber Makbul)

R. *v.* Lougher (William Layton Pritchard) see R. *v.* Llewellyn-Jones (Hopkin Alfred)

R. *v.* Lowe (Allan) see Attorney General's Reference (No.53 of 2004), Re

R. *v.* Lowe (Paul); R. *v.* Parkinson (Anthony); R. *v.* Neary (Martin Desmond); R. *v.* Davey (Mark Andrew); R. *v.* Ellis (Anthony); R. *v.* Smith (Stephen Paul); R. *v.* Frederick (Carl Emerson); R. *v.* Hillhands (Brian); R. *v.* Smith (Jason Giles) [2003] EWCA Crim 3182, CA (Crim Div) . . . . *Considered,* 05/3750

R. *v.* Lowrie (Robin Jason) [2004] EWCA Crim 2325; [2005] 1 Cr. App. R. (S.) 95, CA (Crim Div) . . . . *Digested,* 05/**3712**

R. *v.* Lucas (Lyabode Ruth) [1981] Q.B. 720; [1981] 3 W.L.R. 120; [1981] 2 All E.R.
1008; (1981) 73 Cr. App. R. 159; [1981] Crim. L.R. 624, CA (Crim Div) . . . .   *Digested,* 81/**400**:
                  Applied, 84/710, 85/565.6, 85/566, 86/562, 92/658, 93/770, 93/788,
                  94/820, 94/826, 95/1072, 95/1073, 95/1075, 02/880: *Considered,* 94/814,
                  94/825, 95/1047, 95/1074, 96/1364, 96/1674, 96/1908, 97/1142, 97/1233,
                  05/1529: *Followed,* 83/652

R. *v.* Lucas (Saxon) see R. *v.* Brown (Anthony Joseph)

R. *v.* Lumsden (George Arthur) [2004] EWCA Crim 3187; [2005] 2 Cr. App. R. (S.)
27, CA (Crim Div) . . . .   *Digested,* 05/**3663**

R. *v.* Lunnon (Henry Joseph) [2004] EWCA Crim 1125; [2005] 1 Cr. App. R. (S.) 24;
[2004] Crim. L.R. 678; (2004) 148 S.J.L.B. 570, CA (Crim Div) . . . .   *Digested,* 05/**3749**

R. *v.* Luton Justices Ex p. Abecasis (2000) 164 J.P. 265; (2000) 164 J.P.N. 344;
(2000) 97(13) L.S.G. 43; *Times,* March 30, 2000, CA (Civ Div); affirming
(1999) 163 J.P. 828, QBD . . . .   *Digested,* 00/**1055**:
                  Followed, 05/892

R. *v.* Lyon (Clayton) [2005] EWCA Crim 1365; *Times,* May 19, 2005, CA (Crim Div) . . .   *Digested,* 05/**3530**

R. *v.* Lyons (Isidore Jack) (No.3); R. *v.* Parnes (Anthony Keith) (No.3); R. *v.* Ronson
(Gerald Maurice) (No.3); R. *v.* Saunders (Ernest Walter) (No.3) [2002] UKHL
44; [2003] 1 A.C. 976; [2002] 3 W.L.R. 1562; [2002] 4 All E.R. 1028; [2002]
B.C.C. 968; [2003] 1 Cr. App. R. 24; [2003] H.R.L.R. 6; [2003] Crim. L.R. 623;
(2002) 146 S.J.L.B. 264; *Times,* November 15, 2002; *Independent,* November
20, 2002, HL; affirming [2001] EWCA Crim 2860; [2002] 2 Cr. App. R. 15;
[2002] H.R.L.R. 18; [2002] A.C.D. 55; *Times,* February 1, 2002; *Daily Telegraph,*
January 17, 2002, CA (Crim Div) . . . .   *Digested,* 02/**844**:
              Applied, 05/875: *Considered,* 03/2676, 04/2088:
              Previous proceedings, 97/2816, 00/3234

R. *v.* M see R. *v.* K

R. *v.* M (Christopher Michael) see R. *v.* J (Patricia)

R. *v.* M (Discretionary Life Sentence) see R. *v.* M (Young Offender: Time in Custody
on Remand)

R. *v.* M (John) [1996] 2 Cr. App. R. 56; (1996) 140 S.J.L.B. 37; *Times,* November 29,
1995; *Independent,* January 15, 1996 (C.S.), CA (Crim Div) . . . .   *Digested,* 96/**1422**:
                  Considered, 05/752

R. *v.* M (Mark Anthony) see R. *v.* K (Patrick Joseph)

R. *v.* M (Patrick) [2004] EWCA Crim 1679; [2005] 1 Cr. App. R. (S.) 49, CA (Crim
Div) . . . .   *Digested,* 05/**3719**

R. *v.* M (Sarah Ruth) (A Juvenile) see Attorney General's Reference (Nos.78, 79 and
85 of 1998), Re

R. *v.* M (Witness Statement) [2003] EWCA Crim 357; [2003] 2 Cr. App. R. 21; *Times,*
May 2, 2003, CA (Crim Div) . . . .   *Digested,* 03/**865**:
                  Considered, 05/888

R. *v.* M (Young Offender: Time in Custody on Remand); *sub nom* R. *v.* M
(Discretionary Life Sentence); R. *v.* L (Young Offender: Time in Custody on
Remand) [1999] 1 W.L.R. 485; [1998] 2 All E.R. 939; [1999] 1 Cr. App. R. (S.)
6; [1998] Crim. L.R. 512; *Times,* April 7, 1998, CA (Crim Div) . . . .   *Digested,* 98/**1269**:
              Applied, 99/5949, 00/1356, 01/1353, 01/1439, 02/3943, 03/3774, 05/3654,
              05/3718: *Considered,* 99/1079, 99/1248, 99/1255, 99/1268, 00/1351,
              00/1352, 00/1354, 00/1355, 00/1360, 01/1298, 05/3717: *Followed,* 99/1241,
              99/1252, 99/1257

R. *v.* MacDonagh (Brian) [1974] Q.B. 448; [1974] 2 W.L.R. 529; [1974] 2 All E.R.
257; (1974) 59 Cr. App. R. 55; [1974] R.T.R. 372; [1974] Crim. L.R. 317; 118 S.J.
222, CA (Crim Div) . . . .   *Digested,* 74/**3384**:
              Applied, 75/3006, 80/2323, 81/2345, 87/3291, 04/739, 05/817:
              Considered, 75/2969: *Disapproved,* 90/5752: *Distinguished,* 79/3387,
              94/3990

R. *v.* MacLeod (Donald Gerrard) (1981) 3 Cr. App. R. (S.) 247; [1982] Crim. L.R. 61,
CA (Crim Div) . . . .   *Digested,* 82/**684.76**:
              Considered, 94/1318: *Disapproved,* 05/3746

R. *v.* MacNicol (Andrew Brian) [2003] EWCA Crim 3093; [2004] 2 Cr. App. R. (S.)
2; (2003) 147 S.J.L.B. 1275, CA (Crim Div) . . . .   *Digested,* 04/**3446**:
              Distinguished, 05/3520

R. *v.* Magalhaes (Elisiu) [2004] EWCA Crim 2976; [2005] 2 Cr. App. R. (S.) 13;
[2005] Crim. L.R. 144, CA (Crim Div) . . . .   *Digested,* 05/**3539**

R. *v.* Maguire (Kevin) see R. *v.* Knights (Richard Michael)

R. *v.* Maguire (Thomas) [2004] EWCA Crim 2220; [2005] 1 Cr. App. R. (S.) 84, CA
(Crim Div) . . . .   *Digested,* 05/**3654**

R. *v.* Maher (Gerrard Martin) see R. *v.* Page (Cyril Edward)

R. *v.* Mahmood see R. *v.* Najeeb (Parvais)

R. *v.* Mainprize (Craig) see R. *v.* Wilson (Ian)

R. *v.* Manchester Crown Court Ex p. DPP see Ashton, Re

R. v. Manchester Crown Court Ex p. DPP; *sub nom* Huckfield, Re [1993] 1 W.L.R.
1524; [1993] 4 All E.R. 928; (1994) 98 Cr. App. R. 461; [1994] 1 C.M.L.R. 457;
(1993) 143 N.L.J. 1711; *Times,* November 26, 1993; *Independent,* December 7,
1993, HL; reversing [1993] 1 W.L.R. 693; [1993] 1 All E.R. 801; (1993) 96 Cr.
App. R. 210; [1992] 3 C.M.L.R. 329; [1993] Crim. L.R. 377; [1993] C.O.D. 123;
(1992) 136 S.J.L.B. 235; *Times,* July 29, 1992; *Independent,* July 3, 1992, QBD .   *Digested,* 94/**19**:
Applied, 05/71: *Considered,* 94/35, 95/969: *Followed,* 96/1550, 98/96

R. v. Manchester Crown Court Ex p. M (A Child) see R. (on the application of
McCann) v. Manchester Crown Court

R. v. Manister (Simon) see R. v. Weir (Antony Albert)

R. v. Mann (Keith) see Attorney General's Reference (No.54 of 2005), Re

R. v. Marcus (Ruel) [2004] EWCA Crim 3387; [2005] Crim. L.R. 384; *Times,*
December 3, 2004, CA (Crim Div) . . . .   *Digested,* 05/**738**

R. v. Mariconda (Liana) (1988) 10 Cr. App. R. (S.) 356, CA (Crim Div) . . . .   *Digested,* 90/**1428**:
Considered, 05/3746

R. v. Marples (Christopher) [1998] 1 Cr. App. R. (S.) 335, CA (Crim Div) . . . .   *Digested,* 98/**1106**:
Considered, 05/3523

R. v. Marquez (Shaun) see R. v. Avis (Tony)

R. v. Marshall (Lee) see R. v. Graham (Joseph)

R. v. Martin (Colin) [1989] 1 All E.R. 652; (1989) 88 Cr. App. R. 343; (1989) 153 J.P.
231; [1989] R.T.R. 63; [1989] Crim. L.R. 284, CA (Crim Div) . . . .   *Digested,* 89/**860**:
Considered, 94/1129, 94/3841, 95/1256, 95/4407, 99/922, 99/1021, 03/877,
05/772

R. v. Martin (Deborah) see Attorney General's Reference (No.155 of 2004), Re

R. v. Martin (Durwayne Nathan) [2004] EWCA Crim 916; [2004] 2 Cr. App. R. 22;
Times, June 8, 2004, CA (Crim Div) . . . .   *Digested,* 05/**799**

R. v. Martin (Justin Thomas) [2005] EWCA Crim 748; [2005] 2 Cr. App. R. (S.) 99,
CA (Crim Div) . . . .   *Digested,* 05/**3550**

R. v. Martin (Mark Anthony) see Attorney General's Reference (Nos.32 and 33 of
1995), Re

R. v. Maskin see R. v. Najeeb (Parvais)

R. v. Mason (Auburn) [2001] EWCA Crim 1138; [2002] 1 Cr. App. R. (S.) 29, CA
(Crim Div) . . . .   *Digested,* 02/**3969**:
Considered, 05/3599

R. v. Mason (Nicholas); R. v. Cummins (Dominic John) [2004] EWCA Crim 2173;
[2005] 1 Cr. App. R. 11; [2005] Crim. L.R. 140, CA (Crim Div) . . . .   *Digested,* 05/**917**

R. v. Matthews (Jamie Lee) see Attorney General's Reference (Nos.86, 87 and 88 of
2004), Re

R. v. Matthews (Paul) [1998] 1 Cr. App. R. (S.) 220, CA (Crim Div) . . . .   *Digested,* 98/**1339**:
Considered, 05/3721

R. v. May (Michael Anthony) see Attorney General's Reference (No.20 of 2005), Re

R. v. May (Raymond George); R. v. Bravard (Jacques); R. v. Stapleton (Vincent); R. v.
Lawrence (Steven); R. v. Fowles (Herbert) [2005] EWCA Crim 97; [2005] 1
W.L.R. 2902; [2005] 3 All E.R. 523; [2005] 2 Cr. App. R. (S.) 67; (2005) 149
S.J.L.B. 176; *Times,* February 15, 2005, CA (Crim Div) . . . .   *Digested,* 05/**840**:
Applied, 05/926, 05/3901

R. v. Mayes (Richard) see R. v. Hounsham (Robin Edward)

R. v. Mayor and Commonality and the Citizens of London Ex p. Mystery of the
Barbers of London see R. v. City of London Corp Ex p. Mystery of the Barbers of
London

R. v. Mbatha (Vermet) (1985) 7 Cr. App. R. (S.) 373, CA (Crim Div) . . . .   *Digested,* 87/**992**:
Cited, 89/2397, 90/1364, 91/1136, 93/1227: *Considered,* 96/2001, 97/1644:
Distinguished, 05/3632: *Followed,* 04/3387

R. v. McCarthy (Denis Lewis) [2002] EWCA Crim 2579; [2003] 1 Cr. App. R. (S.)
119, CA (Crim Div) . . . .   *Considered,* 05/3733

R. v. McCarthy (John) see R. v. Loizou (Lisa)

R. v. McClean (Costs) [2005] 4 Costs L.R. 740, Sup Ct Costs Office

R. v. McCluskie (George) see Attorney General's Reference (No.28 of 2004), Re

R. v. McCourt (Richard Joseph) [2004] EWCA Crim 3294; [2005] 2 Cr. App. R. (S.)
41, CA (Crim Div) . . . .   *Digested,* 05/**3707**

R. v. McDonald (Michael Christopher) [2004] EWCA Crim 2614; (2004) 148 S.J.L.B.
1218; *Times,* November 8, 2004, CA (Crim Div) . . . .   *Digested,* 05/**860**

R. v. McDowell (Steven) see Attorney General's Reference (No.114 of 2004), Re

R. v. McElroy (Sean James) see R. v. Rees (Louis)

R. v. McEneaney (John Paul) [2005] EWCA Crim 431; [2005] 2 Cr. App. R. (S.) 86;
[2005] Crim. L.R. 579, CA (Crim Div) . . . .   *Digested,* 05/**3694**

R. v. McFaul (Kevin) see R. v. Knights (Richard Michael)

R. v. McGilliard (Peter Wilson) see R. v. Offen (Matthew Barry) (No.2)

R. v. McGillivray (Atholl) [2005] EWCA Crim 604; [2005] 2 Cr. App. R. (S.) 60;
[2005] Crim. L.R. 484, CA (Crim Div) . . . .   *Digested,* 05/**3522**

R. v. McGrath (Jamie Paul) [2005] EWCA Crim 353; [2005] 2 Cr. App. R. (S.) 85,
CA (Crim Div) . . . .   *Digested,* 05/**830**

R. v. McGunigle (Thomas) (Costs) [2005] 3 Costs L.R. 537, Sup Ct Costs Office

R. *v.* McInerney (Thomas) see Attorney General's Reference (Nos.31, 42, 43, 45, 50 and 51 of 2003), Re

R. *v.* McInerney (William Patrick); R. *v.* Keating (Stephen James) [2002] EWCA Crim 3003; [2003] 1 All E.R. 1089; [2003] 1 Cr. App. R. 36; [2003] 2 Cr. App. R. (S.) 39; [2003] Crim. L.R. 209; (2003) 100(6) L.S.G. 25; *Times*, December 20, 2002, CA (Crim Div) . . . . *Digested*, 03/**3636**:
Applied, 05/3702: *Considered*, 03/835, 05/3525, 05/3545

R. *v.* McKendrick (Gary Gordon) [2005] EWCA Crim 180; [2005] 2 Cr. App. R. (S.) 68, CA (Crim Div) . . . . *Digested*, 05/**3721**

R. *v.* McKeown (Clifford) [2005] N.I. 301, CA (Crim Div) (NI)

R. *v.* McKeown (Darren) see R. *v.* Offen (Matthew Barry) (No.2)

R. *v.* McKeown (Jason) see Attorney General's Reference (Nos.13, 14, 15, 16, 17 and 18 of 2004), Re

R. *v.* McKeown (Nigel) see Attorney General's Reference (Nos.13, 14, 15, 16, 17 and 18 of 2004), Re

R. *v.* McKeown (Sharon Ann) see Attorney General's Reference (Nos.13, 14, 15, 16, 17 and 18 of 2004), Re

R. *v.* McLean (Adele) see Attorney General's Reference (Nos.31, 42, 43, 45, 50 and 51 of 2003), Re

R. *v.* McMilan (Paul); *sub nom* R. *v.* McMillan [2005] EWCA Crim 222; [2005] 2 Cr. App. R. (S.) 63, CA (Crim Div) . . . . *Digested*, 05/**3538**

R. *v.* McMillan see R. *v.* McMilan (Paul)

R. *v.* McNee (John) see R. *v.* Graham (Joseph)

R. *v.* McQuade (Joseph) [2005] N.I. 331, CA (Crim Div) (NI)

R. *v.* McShefferty (Jason) see Attorney General's Reference (Nos.144 and 145 of 2004), Re

R. *v.* Meakin (Joel) see Attorney General's Reference (No.98 of 2004), Re

R. *v.* Medway (Andrew George) [1976] Q.B. 779; [1976] 2 W.L.R. 528; [1976] 1 All E.R. 527; (1976) 62 Cr. App. R. 85; [1976] Crim. L.R. 118, CA (Crim Div) . . . . . . *Digested*, 76/**399**:
Applied, 82/504, 05/826: *Considered*, 95/1433, 97/288:
Distinguished, 86/476: *Followed*, 97/1260

R. *v.* Mee (Jason David) [2004] EWCA Crim 629; [2004] 2 Cr. App. R. (S.) 81; [2004] Crim. L.R. 487; (2004) 148 S.J.L.B. 267; *Times*, April 1, 2004, CA (Crim Div) . . . . *Digested*, 04/**3458**:
Considered, 05/3588

R. *v.* Mehmet (Mustafa) [2005] EWCA Crim 2074; [2005] Crim. L.R. 877, CA (Crim Div)

R. *v.* Mendy (Alphonse Francis) see Attorney General's Reference (Nos.3, 4, 8, 9, 10, 11, 14 and 16 of 1990), Re

R. *v.* Mentor (Steven) [2004] EWCA Crim 3104; [2005] 2 Cr. App. R. (S.) 33; [2005] Crim. L.R. 472, CA (Crim Div) . . . . *Digested*, 05/**743**

R. *v.* Mercieca (Joseph) see R. *v.* Smith (Patrick)

R. *v.* Meredith (Christopher); R. *v.* Craven (Adrian) [2000] 1 Cr. App. R. (S.) 508, CA (Crim Div) . . . . *Digested*, 00/**1267**:
Considered, 05/3651

R. *v.* Merrin (Charles William) see R. *v.* Skitt (Harry)

R. *v.* Mertens (Jan Paul) [2004] EWCA Crim 2252; [2005] Crim. L.R. 301, CA (Crim Div)

R. *v.* Metcalfe (Carl James) (Appeal against Confiscation Orders); R. *v.* Metcalfe (Valerie) [2004] EWCA Crim 3253; [2005] 2 Cr. App. R. (S.) 50; [2005] Crim. L.R. 315; *Times*, January 12, 2005, CA (Crim Div) . . . . *Digested*, 05/**3595**

R. *v.* Metcalfe (Valerie) see R. *v.* Metcalfe (Carl James) (Appeal against Confiscation Orders)

R. *v.* Miao (Hui) [2003] EWCA Crim 3486; (2004) 101(5) L.S.G. 28; *Times*, November 26, 2003, CA (Crim Div) . . . . *Digested*, 04/**871**:
Considered, 05/900

R. *v.* Middleton (John Dicketts) [2004] EWCA Crim 1487; [2005] 1 Cr. App. R. (S.) 42, CA (Crim Div) . . . . *Digested*, 05/**3656**

R. *v.* Mighty (Daniel Ivor) see Attorney General's Reference (No.29 of 1995), Re

R. *v.* Milford (David John) see R. *v.* Benjafield (Karl Robert) (Confiscation Order)

R. *v.* Millard (Ray) (1994) 15 Cr. App. R. (S.) 445; [1994] Crim. L.R. 146, CA (Crim Div) . . . . *Considered*, 98/665,
05/910

R. *v.* Millberry (William Christopher); R. *v.* Morgan (Paul Robert); R. *v.* Lackenby (Ian Stuart) [2002] EWCA Crim 2891; [2003] 1 W.L.R. 546; [2003] 2 All E.R. 939; [2003] 1 Cr. App. R. 25; [2003] 2 Cr. App. R. (S.) 31; [2003] Crim. L.R. 207; (2003) 100(7) L.S.G. 34; (2003) 147 S.J.L.B. 28; *Times*, December 11, 2002, CA (Crim Div) . . . . *Digested*, 03/**3829**:
Applied, 03/3826, 03/3827, 03/3835, 03/3866, 04/3285, 04/3373,
04/3443, 05/3718, 05/3721, 05/3734: *Cited*, 04/3444:
Considered, 03/3828, 04/3422, 04/3423, 04/3426, 05/3638, 05/3714,
05/3717, 05/3719, 05/3739, 05/3741, 05/3776: *Followed*, 03/3825,
03/3836, 04/3421, 04/3427, 05/3536

R. *v.* Miller (Christopher Richard) see Attorney General's Reference (Nos.148, 149, 150, 151, 152, 153, 154 and 155 of 2001), Re

R. *v.* Miller (Stephen); R. *v.* Henry (Carl Anthony) [2004] EWCA Crim 3323; [2005] 2 Cr. App. R. (S.) 43, CA (Crim Div) . . . . *Digested,* 05/**3733**

R. *v.* Milling (Arthur Paul) see R. *v.* Jones (Margaret)

R. *v.* Mills (Brett Mark) [2004] EWCA Crim 3506; *Times,* December 3, 2004, CA (Crim Div) . . . . *Digested,* 05/**3652**

R. *v.* Mills (Gary) [2004] EWCA Crim 1466; [2005] 1 Cr. App. R. (S.) 38, CA (Crim Div) . . . . *Digested,* 05/**3706**

R. *v.* Minister of Agriculture and Fisheries Ex p. Padfield see Padfield *v.* Minister of Agriculture, Fisheries and Food

R. *v.* Ministry of Defence Ex p. Grady see R. *v.* Ministry of Defence Ex p. Smith

R. *v.* Ministry of Defence Ex p. Smith; R. *v.* Admiralty Board of the Defence Council Ex p. Lustig-Prean; R. *v.* Admiralty Board of the Defence Council Ex p. Beckett; R. *v.* Ministry of Defence Ex p. Grady [1996] Q.B. 517; [1996] 2 W.L.R. 305; [1996] 1 All E.R. 257; [1996] I.C.R. 740; [1996] I.R.L.R. 100; (1996) 8 Admin. L.R. 29; [1996] C.O.D. 237; (1995) 145 N.L.J. 1689; *Times,* November 6, 1995; *Independent,* November 7, 1995, CA (Civ Div); affirming [1995] 4 All E.R. 427; [1995] I.R.L.R. 585; [1995] C.O.D. 423; (1995) 145 N.L.J. 887; *Times,* June 13, 1995; *Independent,* June 8, 1995, DC . . . . *Digested,* 96/**383**: *Applied,* 97/4111, 00/7, 00/4172, 00/5325, 01/5879, 02/3711, 05/3340: *Considered,* 96/2535, 97/299, 97/3559, 99/3181, 99/3715, 01/3661, 01/3684, 03/2934: *Followed,* 96/249, 96/3256

R. *v.* Mirza (Shabbir Ali); R. *v.* Connor (Ben); R. *v.* Rollock (Ashley Kenneth) [2004] UKHL 2; [2004] 1 A.C. 1118; [2004] 2 W.L.R. 201; [2004] 1 All E.R. 925; [2004] 2 Cr. App. R. 8; [2004] H.R.L.R. 11; 16 B.H.R.C. 279; (2004) 101(7) L.S.G. 34; (2004) 154 N.L.J. 145; (2004) 148 S.J.L.B. 117; *Times,* January 23, 2004, HL; affirming [2002] EWCA Crim 1235; [2002] Crim. L.R. 921, CA (Crim Div) . . . . *Digested,* 04/**694**: *Applied,* 05/827, 05/832, 05/849: *Explained,* 05/895

R. *v.* Misra (Amit); R. *v.* Srivastava (Rajeev) [2004] EWCA Crim 2375; [2005] 1 Cr. App. R. 21; [2005] Crim. L.R. 234; (2004) 101(41) L.S.G. 35; (2004) 148 S.J.L.B. 1213; *Times,* October 13, 2004, CA (Crim Div) . . . . *Digested,* 05/**804**

R. *v.* Mitchell (Clive); R. *v.* Mitchell (Jennifer) [2001] 2 Cr. App. R. (S.) 29; [2001] Crim. L.R. 239; *Times,* January 9, 2001, CA (Crim Div) . . . . *Digested,* 01/**1238**: *Applied,* 03/3660: *Considered,* 05/3568

R. *v.* Mitchell (Jennifer) see R. *v.* Mitchell (Clive)

R. *v.* Mitchell (Natalie) [2004] EWCA Crim 2945, CA (Crim Div) . . . . *Followed,* 05/**3578**

R. *v.* Mitchell (Roy) [2004] EWCA Crim 1516; [2005] 1 Cr. App. R. (S.) 41, CA (Crim Div) . . . . *Digested,* 05/**3687**

R. *v.* MJ see R. *v.* J

R. *v.* Momodou (Henry); R. *v.* Limani (Beher) [2005] EWCA Crim 177; [2005] 1 W.L.R. 3442; [2005] 2 All E.R. 571; [2005] 2 Cr. App. R. 6; (2005) 169 J.P. 186; [2005] Crim. L.R. 588; (2005) 169 J.P.N. 276; (2005) 149 S.J.L.B. 178; *Times,* February 9, 2005; *Independent,* February 11, 2005, CA (Crim Div) . . . . . *Digested,* 05/**827**

R. *v.* Monteanu (Adrian) see R. *v.* Chirila (Remus Tenistocle)

R. *v.* Montila (Steven William); *sub nom* R. *v.* Montilla (Steven William) [2004] UKHL 50; [2004] 1 W.L.R. 3141; [2005] 1 All E.R. 113; [2005] 1 Cr. App. R. 26; [2005] Crim. L.R. 479; (2005) 102(3) L.S.G. 30; (2004) 148 S.J.L.B. 1403; *Times,* November 26, 2004; *Independent,* November 30, 2004, HL; reversing [2003] EWCA Crim 3082; [2004] 1 W.L.R. 624; [2004] 1 All E.R. 877; [2004] 1 Cr. App. R. 32; (2003) 100(46) L.S.G. 24; (2003) 147 S.J.L.B. 1305; *Times,* November 12, 2003, CA (Crim Div) . . . . *Digested,* 05/**806**: *Applied,* 05/768

R. *v.* Montilla (Steven William) see R. *v.* Montila (Steven William)

R. *v.* Monument (Andrew) [2005] EWCA Crim 30; [2005] 2 Cr. App. R. (S.) 57; [2005] Crim. L.R. 401; *Times,* March 3, 2005, CA (Crim Div) . . . . *Digested,* 05/**3723**

R. *v.* Moore (Andrew Neish) [2004] EWCA Crim 2574; [2005] 1 Cr. App. R. (S.) 101, CA (Crim Div)

R. *v.* Moran (Frank Adam) see Attorney General's Reference (No.25 of 2001), Re

R. *v.* Morgan (Paul Robert) see R. *v.* Millberry (William Christopher)

R. *v.* Morris (Kenneth Morleen) [1972] 1 W.L.R. 228; [1972] 1 All E.R. 384; (1972) 56 Cr. App. R. 175; [1972] R.T.R. 201; [1972] Crim. L.R. 116; [1971] 116 S.J. 17; *Times,* November 23, 1971, CA (Crim Div) . . . . *Digested,* 72/**3015**: *Applied,* 79/2311: *Disapproved,* 05/902: *Distinguished,* 73/2933

R. *v.* Morris-Brooks (Stuart) see R. *v.* Rees (Louis)

R. *v.* Morrison (Jamie Joe) [2001] 1 Cr. App. R. (S.) 5; [2000] Crim. L.R. 605, CA (Crim Div) . . . . *Digested,* 01/**1221**: *Considered,* 05/3651

R. *v.* Moss (Linda) (1986) 8 Cr. App. R. (S.) 276, CA (Crim Div) . . . . *Digested,* 87/**1059**: *Considered,* 05/3746

R. *v.* Moulden (Leslie James) see R. *v.* Mouldon (Leslie James)

R. *v.* Mouldon (Leslie James); *sub nom* R. *v.* Moulden (Leslie James) [2004] EWCA Crim 2715; [2005] 1 Cr. App. R. (S.) 121, CA (Crim Div) . . . . *Digested,* 05/**3593**

R. *v.* Mousir [1987] Crim. L.R. 561; (1987) 84 L.S.G. 1328, CA (Crim Div) . . . .   *Digested*, 87/**765**:
                                                               Considered, 05/760
R. *v.* Mullen (James Arthur) [2004] EWCA Crim 602; [2004] 2 Cr. App. R. 18;
    [2005] Crim. L.R. 76; (2004) 148 S.J.L.B. 386; *Times*, April 19, 2004, CA (Crim
    Div) . . . .   *Digested*, 05/**752**
R. *v.* Mullen (Nicholas Robert) (No.2) [2000] Q.B. 520; [1999] 3 W.L.R. 777; [1999]
    2 Cr. App. R. 143; [1999] Crim. L.R. 561; *Times*, February 15, 1999, CA (Crim
    Div) . . . .   *Digested*, 99/**972**:
                Applied, 00/1026, 00/1056, 01/5733, 02/904: *Considered*, 00/1025, 05/838,
                          05/3343: *Distinguished*, 05/875: *Subsequent proceedings*, 02/892
R. *v.* Muller (Roland) [2003] EWCA Crim 2499, CA (Crim Div) . . . .   *Considered*, 05/3605
R. *v.* Murphy (Brendan William) [2002] EWCA Crim 1624; [2003] 1 Cr. App. R. (S.)
    39; [2002] Crim. L.R. 674, CA (Crim Div) . . . .   *Digested*, 03/**3776**:
                                  Applied, 05/3650: *Not followed*, 04/3288
R. *v.* Murray (Arthur Alan) [2004] EWCA Crim 2211; [2005] Crim. L.R. 387, CA (Crim
    Div)
R. *v.* Murray (Richard Alexander) see R. *v.* Pepper (Jeremy Paul)
R. *v.* Murrell (John David) [2005] EWCA Crim 382; [2005] Crim. L.R. 869, CA (Crim
    Div)
R. *v.* Mushtaq (Ashfaq Ahmed) [2005] UKHL 25; [2005] 1 W.L.R. 1513; [2005] 3 All
    E.R. 885; [2005] 2 Cr. App. R. 32; (2005) 169 J.P. 277; [2005] H.R.L.R. 28; 18
    B.H.R.C. 474; (2005) 169 J.P.N. 397; (2005) 102(22) L.S.G. 26; *Times*, April
    28, 2005; *Independent*, April 26, 2005, HL; affirming [2002] EWCA Crim 1943,
    CA (Crim Div) . . . .   *Digested*, 05/**897**
R. *v.* N (James) (Unduly Lenient Sentence) see Attorney General's Reference (No.6 of
    2005) (Unduly Lenient Sentence), Re
R. *v.* N (James) see Attorney General's Reference (No.6 of 2005), Re
R. *v.* Nadarajah (Milroy) see Attorney General's Reference (Nos.99, 100, 101 and 102 of
    2004), Re
R. *v.* Nafei (Abdelkhalek) [2004] EWCA Crim 3238; [2005] 2 Cr. App. R. (S.) 24;
    [2005] Crim. L.R. 409, CA (Crim Div) . . . .   *Digested*, 05/**3632**
R. *v.* Najeeb (Parvais); R. *v.* Qazi (Shakeel); R. *v.* Mahmood; R. *v.* Raja; R. *v.* Maskin
    [2003] EWCA Crim 194; [2003] 2 Cr. App. R. (S.) 69; *Times*, February 5, 2003,
    CA (Crim Div) . . . .   *Digested*, 03/**3837**:
                                                 Considered, 05/3573
R. *v.* Najib (Parvaz) see R. *v.* Din (Ameen)
R. *v.* Napper (Barry) (1997) 161 J.P. 16; [1996] Crim. L.R. 591; (1997) 161 J.P.N. 62,
    CA (Crim Div) . . . .   *Considered*, 05/748
R. *v.* Nash (Paul Brian) [2004] EWCA Crim 2696; [2005] Crim. L.R. 232; (2004) 148
    S.J.L.B. 1249, CA (Crim Div)
R. *v.* Navabi (Fraydon); R. *v.* Embaye (Senait Tekie) [2005] EWCA Crim 2865; *Times*,
    December 5, 2005, CA (Crim Div)
R. *v.* Nazari (Fazlollah); R. *v.* Fernandez (Joseph); R. *v.* Dissanayake (Rohan
    Shivantha); R. *v.* Anyanwu (Ebenezer Chuwuma); R. *v.* Adamson (Michael
    Joseph) [1980] 1 W.L.R. 1366; [1980] 3 All E.R. 880; (1980) 71 Cr. App. R. 87;
    (1980) 2 Cr. App. R. (S.) 84; [1980] Crim. L.R. 447, CA (Crim Div) . . . .   *Digested*, 80/**581**:
                Applied, 05/3589: *Cited*, 88/982, 89/977, 89/1108, 90/1405, 92/1224,
                      92/1225, 92/1226, 92/1227, 93/1105, 93/1106, 93/1108, 93/1109:
                Considered, 80/1422, 84/1755, 87/1996, 97/2907, 99/1129, 03/2232,
                                    05/3768: *Referred to*, 85/1714
R. *v.* Neary (Martin Desmond) see R. *v.* Lowe (Paul)
R. *v.* Nedrick (Ransford Delroy) [1986] 1 W.L.R. 1025; [1986] 3 All E.R. 1; (1986) 83
    Cr. App. R. 267; (1986) 8 Cr. App. R. (S.) 179; (1986) 150 J.P. 589; [1986]
    Crim. L.R. 792; (1986) 150 J.P.N. 637, CA (Crim Div) . . . .   *Digested*, 86/**651**:
              Applied, 90/1116, 90/1121: *Approved*, 98/1052: *Considered*, 90/1122, 91/953,
                              94/811, 95/1064, 00/1069, 03/800, 05/3658
R. *v.* Nelson (Patrick Alan) [2001] EWCA Crim 2264; [2002] 1 Cr. App. R. (S.) 134;
    [2001] Crim. L.R. 999; *Times*, December 10, 2001; *Independent*, October 30,
    2001, CA (Crim Div) . . . .   *Digested*, 01/**1369**:
              Applied, 05/3743: *Considered*, 02/3984, 03/3840, 04/3367, 05/3648,
                                      05/3741
R. *v.* Neville (Daniel John) see Attorney General's Reference (No.2 of 2004), Re
R. *v.* Newbon [2005] Crim. L.R. 738, CC (Stoke on Trent)
R. *v.* Newham LBC Ex p. Al-Nashed see R. (on the application of Bibi) *v.* Newham
    LBC (No.1)
R. *v.* Newham LBC Ex p. Bibi see R. (on the application of Bibi) *v.* Newham LBC
    (No.1)
R. *v.* Newham LBC Ex p. Sacupima see R. (on the application of Sacupima) *v.*
    Newham LBC
R. *v.* Newmarch (Jennifer Leslie) see Attorney General's Reference (Nos.48, 49, 50
    and 51 of 2002), Re
R. *v.* Newsome (Peter Alan) [1997] 2 Cr. App. R. (S.) 69; [1997] Crim. L.R. 237, CA
    (Crim Div) . . . .   *Digested*, 97/**1428**:
                            Applied, 01/1231: *Distinguished*, 05/3559

R. *v.* Nixon (Tyrone Carlos) see Attorney General's Reference (No.71 of 2001), Re
R. *v.* NJK see Attorney General's Reference (Nos.91, 119 and 120 of 2002), Re
R. *v.* North and East Devon HA Ex p. Coughlan [2001] Q.B. 213; [2000] 2 W.L.R.
    622; [2000] 3 All E.R. 850; (2000) 2 L.G.L.R. 1; [1999] B.L.G.R. 703; (1999) 2
    C.C.L. Rep. 285; [1999] Lloyd's Rep. Med. 306; (2000) 51 B.M.L.R. 1; [1999]
    C.O.D. 340; (1999) 96(31) L.S.G. 39; (1999) 143 S.J.L.B. 213; *Times*, July 20,
    1999 ; *Independent*, July 20, 1999, CA (Civ Div); affirming (1999) 2 C.C.L. Rep.
    27; (1999) 47 B.M.L.R. 27; [1999] C.O.D. 174; *Times*, December 29, 1998,
    QBD . . . . *Digested*, 99/**2643**:
                 Applied, 00/4526, 01/5879, 02/46, 02/4293, 03/1917, 03/2837, 03/3399,
                                  03/4101, 03/4713, 04/1905, 04/2643, 04/3859, 05/1837:
                   Considered, 05/2154: *Distinguished*, 03/4091, 05/4121: *Followed*, 99/3931,
                                                                                     00/1915
R. *v.* Northallerton Magistrates Court Ex p. Dove [2000] 1 Cr. App. R. (S.) 136; (1999)
    163 J.P. 657; [1999] Crim. L.R. 760; [1999] C.O.D. 598; (1999) 163 J.P.N.
    894; *Times*, June 17, 1999, QBD . . . . *Digested*, 99/**985**:
                                              Cited, 00/4296: *Considered*, 05/729
R. *v.* Nwoko (Roseline); R. *v.* Olukunle (Albert) (1995) 16 Cr. App. R. (S.) 612, CA
    (Crim Div). . . . . *Followed*, 05/3589
R. *v.* Nyanteh (Michael) [2005] EWCA Crim 686; [2005] Crim. L.R. 651, CA (Crim
    Div)
R. *v.* O (Jason Patrick) (A Juvenile) see Attorney General's Reference (Nos.78, 79 and
    85 of 1998), Re
R. *v.* O (Stevie Jack) [2005] EWCA Crim 3082; *Times*, November 17, 2005, CA (Crim
    Div)
R. *v.* O (Tina Donna) [2004] EWCA Crim 1750; [2005] 1 Cr. App. R. (S.) 47, CA
    (Crim Div). . . . . *Digested*, 05/**3561**
R. *v.* O'Brien (Michael) [2005] EWCA Crim 173; [2005] 2 Cr. App. R. (S.) 58, CA
    (Crim Div). . . . . *Digested*, 05/**3679**
R. *v.* O'Brien (Ronan Stephen) [2003] EWCA Crim 302; [2003] 2 Cr. App. R. (S.) 66,
    CA (Crim Div) . . . . *Digested*, 03/**3673**:
                                                                       Considered, 05/3742
R. *v.* O'Callaghan (Patrick) [2005] EWCA Crim 317; [2005] 2 Cr. App. R. (S.) 83;
    [2005] Crim. L.R. 486, CA (Crim Div) . . . . *Digested*, 05/**3737**
R. *v.* O'Connor (Michael Joseph) (1994) 15 Cr. App. R. (S.) 473; [1994] Crim. L.R.
    227, CA (Crim Div) . . . . *Applied*, 02/3943,
             05/3718: *Considered*, 96/1989, 96/2003, 98/1342, 04/3425:
                                                          Followed, 96/2004, 96/2005
R. *v.* O'Flaherty (Errol Carlton); R. *v.* Ryan (Phillip Junior); R. *v.* Toussaint (Mitchell
    Paris) [2004] EWCA Crim 526; [2004] 2 Cr. App. R. 20; [2004] Crim. L.R. 751;
    (2004) 148 S.J.L.B. 353, CA (Crim Div) . . . . *Digested*, 05/**899**
R. *v.* O'Gorman (John) see Attorney General's Reference (Nos.64 and 65 of 1997), Re
R. *v.* O'Leary (Daniel Christopher) see R. *v.* Palmer (Justin Anthony)
R. *v.* O'Rourke (Stephen Michael) [2004] EWCA Crim 1808; [2005] 1 Cr. App. R. (S.)
    53, CA (Crim Div) . . . . *Digested*, 05/**3553**
R. *v.* Odewale (Ayodele Oluseye); R. *v.* Oshungbure (Kazeem Ladie) [2005] EWCA
    Crim 709; [2005] 2 Cr. App. R. (S.) 102; [2005] Crim. L.R. 581; *Times*, March
    14, 2005, CA (Crim Div) . . . . *Digested*, 05/**890**
R. *v.* Offen (Matthew Barry) (No.2); R. *v.* McGilliard (Peter Wilson); R. *v.* McKeown
    (Darren); R. *v.* Okwuegbunam (Kristova); R. *v.* S (Stephen) [2001] 1 W.L.R. 253;
    [2001] 2 All E.R. 154; [2001] 1 Cr. App. R. 24; [2001] 2 Cr. App. R. (S.) 10;
    [2001] Crim. L.R. 63; (2001) 98(1) L.S.G. 23; (2000) 144 S.J.L.B. 288; *Times*,
    November 10, 2000; *Independent*, November 17, 2000, CA (Crim Div) . . . . *Digested*, 00/**1347**:
                       Applied, 01/1413, 01/1414, 02/4014, 02/4034, 02/4035, 03/3777, 04/3287:
                          Approved, 03/3773: *Cited*, 02/4020: *Considered*, 02/4019, 03/3771,
                         03/3772, 05/3539, 05/3693: *Followed*, 02/4052: *Not followed*, 01/1412
R. *v.* Okwuegbunam (Kristova) see R. *v.* Offen (Matthew Barry) (No.2)
R. *v.* Olditch (Toby) see R. *v.* Jones (Margaret)
R. *v.* Oliver (Mark David); R. *v.* Hartrey (Michael Patrick); R. *v.* Baldwin (Leslie) [2002]
    EWCA Crim 2766; [2003] 1 Cr. App. R. 28; [2003] 2 Cr. App. R. (S.) 15; [2003]
    Crim. L.R. 127; *Times*, December 6, 2002, CA (Crim Div). . . . . *Digested*, 03/**3745**:
                   Applied, 04/3376, 05/3349: *Considered*, 04/838, 04/3377, 05/3645,
                                                          05/3647: *Followed*, 04/849, 05/3646
R. *v.* Ollis (Thomas Edwin) [1900] 2 Q.B. 758, Crown Cases Reserved. . . . . *Applied*, 05/733:
                        Considered, 63/632, 64/665, 64/768: *Distinguished*, 66/2286, 67/739
R. *v.* Olubitan (Ayodele Olusegun) [2003] EWCA Crim 2940; [2004] 2 Cr. App. R.
    (S.) 14; [2004] Crim. L.R. 155; *Times*, November 14, 2003, CA (Crim Div) . . . . . *Digested*, 04/**3309**:
                                                                           Applied, 05/840
R. *v.* Olukunle (Albert) see R. *v.* Nwoko (Roseline)
R. *v.* Omar (Bassam) [2004] EWCA Crim 2320; [2005] 1 Cr. App. R. (S.) 86, CA
    (Crim Div). . . . . *Digested*, 05/**3557**
R. *v.* Onley (Haley Nicola) [2004] EWCA Crim 1383; [2005] 1 Cr. App. R. (S.) 26, CA
    (Crim Div). . . . . *Digested*, 05/**3672**

R. v. Oosthuizen (Lee) [2005] EWCA Crim 1978; [2005] Crim. L.R. 979; *Times,*
September 5, 2005, CA (Crim Div) . . . .   *Digested,* 05/**3735**
R. v. Orr (Robert Horatio) see Attorney General's Reference (No.5 of 2005), Re
R. v. Osbourne (Lee) see R. v. Renda (Raymond)
R. v. Oshungbure (Kazeem Ladie) see R. v. Odewale (Ayodele Oluseye)
R. v. Owen (John) [1952] 2 Q.B. 362; [1952] 1 All E.R. 1040; [1952] 1 T.L.R. 1220;
(1952) 36 Cr. App. R. 16; 116 J.P. 244; 96 S.J. 281, CCA . . . .   *Digested,* 52/**760**:
Applied, 69/628, 72/619, 72/620, 72/1936, 84/609, 85/830:
Considered, 62/783, 91/836, 92/897, 93/676, 05/832:
Distinguished, 53/779, 58/700: *Followed,* 57/740, 58/701
R. v. Owens (John Anthony) see R. v. Healey (Bernard)
R. v. Oxfordshire CC Ex p. Sunningwell Parish Council [2000] 1 A.C. 335; [1999] 3
W.L.R. 160; [1999] 3 All E.R. 385; [1999] B.L.G.R. 651; (2000) 79 P. & C.R.
199; [1999] 2 E.G.L.R. 94; [1999] 31 E.G. 85; [2000] J.P.L. 384; [1999]
E.G.C.S. 91; (1999) 96(29) L.S.G. 29; (1999) 149 N.L.J. 1038; (1999) 143
S.J.L.B. 205; [1999] N.P.C. 74; *Times,* June 25, 1999 ; *Independent,* June 29,
1999, HL; reversing FC3 97/6534/D, CA (Civ Div); affirming CO 2744-96,
QBD . . . .   *Digested,* 99/**4393**:
Applied, 04/3205: *Considered,* 04/3203, 05/3440
R. v. P (A Father) see DPP v. P
R. v. P (Shane Tony) [2004] EWCA Crim 287; [2004] 2 Cr. App. R. (S.) 63; [2004]
Crim. L.R. 490; *Times,* February 19, 2004, CA (Crim Div). . . . .   *Digested,* 04/**3283**:
Considered, 05/3529
R. v. P&O European Ferries (Irish Sea) Ltd see R. v. P&O Ferries (Irish Sea) Ltd
R. v. P&O Ferries (Irish Sea) Ltd; *sub nom* R. v. P&O European Ferries (Irish Sea) Ltd
[2004] EWCA Crim 3236; [2005] 2 Cr. App. R. (S.) 21, CA (Crim Div)
R. v. Pace (David Paul) [2004] EWCA Crim 2018; [2005] 1 Cr. App. R. (S.) 74, CA
(Crim Div) . . . .   *Digested,* 05/**3627**
R. v. Packer (Peter) see Attorney General's Reference (No.152 of 2004), Re
R. v. Page (Cyril Edward); R. v. Maher (Gerrard Martin); R. v. Stewart (David Ian)
[2004] EWCA Crim 3358; [2005] 2 Cr. App. R. (S.) 37; (2005) 149 S.J.L.B.
26; *Times,* December 23, 2004, CA (Crim Div) . . . .   *Digested,* 05/**3746**
R. v. Palma (Aniello) (1986) 8 Cr. App. R. (S.) 148, CA (Crim Div) . . . .   *Digested,* 87/**1006**:
Considered, 05/3658
R. v. Palmer (Daniel Roy) see R. v. Peters (Benjamin)
R. v. Palmer (Jason Lee) [2004] EWCA Crim 2631; [2005] 1 Cr. App. R. (S.) 109, CA
(Crim Div)
R. v. Palmer (Justin Anthony); R. v. O'Leary (Daniel Christopher); R. v. Wooden (James
Ray) [2004] EWCA Crim 1039; [2004] 2 Cr. App. R. (S.) 97, CA (Crim Div) . . .   *Digested,* 05/**3765**
R. v. Parfitt (David Andrew) [2004] EWCA Crim 1755; [2005] 1 Cr. App. R. (S.) 50,
CA (Crim Div) . . . .   *Digested,* 05/**3668**
R. v. Park (Randy Alyan) (1994) 99 Cr. App. R. 270; (1994) 158 J.P. 144; (1994) 158
L.G. Rev. 92; *Times,* July 30, 1993, CA (Crim Div) . . . .   *Digested,* 94/**967**:
Approved, 05/765: *Considered,* 97/1360
R. v. Parkinson (Anthony) see R. v. Lowe (Paul)
R. v. Parnell (Brian Michael) [2004] EWCA Crim 2523; [2005] 1 W.L.R. 853; *Times,*
November 8, 2004, CA (Crim Div) . . . .   *Digested,* 04/**3447**
R. v. Parnes (Anthony Keith) (No.3) see R. v. Lyons (Isidore Jack) (No.3)
R. v. Parsons (Adam) see Attorney General's Reference (Nos.13, 14, 15, 16, 17 and 18 of
2004), Re
R. v. Parsons (John David) see R. v. S
R. v. Patel (Assesh) [2000] 2 Cr. App. R. (S.) 10; [2000] Crim. L.R. 201, CA (Crim
Div) . . . .   *Digested,* 00/**1165**:
Applied, 05/926: *Considered,* 05/840
R. v. Patel (Madhusudan Maganbhai) see R. v. Early (John)
R. v. Patel (Nilam) see R. v. Early (John)
R. v. Patel (Nitin) [2004] EWCA Crim 3284; [2005] 1 Cr. App. R. 27; (2005) 169 J.P.
93; [2005] 1 F.L.R. 803; [2005] Crim. L.R. 649; [2005] Fam. Law 209; (2004)
101 (46) L.S.G. 33; *Times,* November 29, 2004, CA (Crim Div) . . . .   *Digested,* 05/**885**
R. v. Patel (Rahul) see R. v. Early (John)
R. v. Patrascu (Andrew) [2004] EWCA Crim 2417; [2005] 1 W.L.R. 3344; [2004] 4
All E.R. 1066; [2005] 1 Cr. App. R. 35; (2004) 168 J.P. 589; [2005] Crim. L.R.
593; (2004) 168 J.P.N. 897, CA (Crim Div) . . . .   *Digested,* 04/**752**
R. v. Patterson (John) see R. v. Grundy (Brian)
R. v. Paulssen (Hans Constantin) see Attorney General's Reference (Nos.48, 49, 50
and 51 of 2002), Re
R. v. Pearce (Lisa Jayne) [2004] EWCA Crim 2029; [2005] 1 Cr. App. R. (S.) 73, CA
(Crim Div) . . . .   *Digested,* 05/**3702**
R. v. Pearcy (Colin) see R. v. Early (John)
R. v. Pegg (Shane Robin) see Attorney General's Reference (Nos.32 and 33 of 1995),
Re
R. v. Pennington (Derek) see R. v. Crow (William John)

R. *v.* Pepper (Jeremy Paul); R. *v.* Barber (Kenneth Leslie); R. *v.* Lamont (Martin); R. *v.*
G; R. *v.* Murray (Richard Alexander) [2005] EWCA Crim 1181; *Times*, May 10,
2005, CA (Crim Div) . . . . *Digested,* 05/**3743**
R. *v.* Perkins (James) see R. *v.* Skitt (Harry)
R. *v.* Perman (Sam) [1996] 1 Cr. App. R. 24; [1995] Crim. L.R. 736, CA (Crim Div) . . . .   *Digested,* 96/**1482**:
                                                             Considered, 05/**899**
R. *v.* Petch (Thomas); R. *v.* Coleman (George Romero) [2005] EWCA Crim 1883;
[2005] 2 Cr. App. R. 40, CA (Crim Div) . . . . *Digested,* 05/**909**
R. *v.* Peters (Benjamin); R. *v.* Palmer (Daniel Roy); R. *v.* Campbell (Shantelle Jamie)
[2005] EWCA Crim 605; [2005] 2 Cr. App. R. (S.) 101; [2005] Crim. L.R. 492;
Times, March 29, 2005, CA (Crim Div). . . . . *Digested,* 05/**3682**:
                                 Applied, 05/3735: *Considered,* 05/3764
R. *v.* PGH see R. *v.* H (Evidence: Admissibility)
R. *v.* Phillips (Brian) [2004] EWCA Crim 2651; [2005] 1 Cr. App. R. (S.) 113, CA
(Crim Div)
R. *v.* Pick (Martin James); R. *v.* Dillon (Matthew James) [2005] EWCA Crim 1853;
[2005] Crim. L.R. 873, CA (Crim Div)
R. *v.* Pickett (Costs) [2004] 3 Costs L.R. 529, Sup Ct Costs Office . . . . *Digested,* 05/**2797**
R. *v.* Pickstone (Robert Alan) see R. *v.* Hanson (Nicky)
R. *v.* Pico [1971] R.T.R. 500, CA (Crim Div) . . . . *Digested,* 71/**10223**:
                                                       Disapproved, 05/902
R. *v.* Pielesz (Mark) [2005] EWCA Crim 230; [2005] 2 Cr. App. R. (S.) 72, CA (Crim
Div) . . . . *Digested,* 05/**3548**
R. *v.* Pierce (Graham) see R. *v.* Hoare (Kevin)
R. *v.* Pitchforth (Costs) [2005] 4 Costs L.R. 721, Sup Ct Costs Office
R. *v.* Plakici (Luan) see Attorney General's Reference (No.6 of 2004), Re
R. *v.* Pleydell (Michael Aaron) [2005] EWCA Crim 1447; (2005) 169 J.P. 400, CA
(Crim Div) . . . . *Digested,* 05/**727**
R. *v.* Plymouth City Airport Ltd see R. (on the application of Plymouth City Airport
Ltd) *v.* Secretary of State for the Environment, Transport and the Regions
R. *v.* Portillo (Jose) see Attorney General's Reference (No.126 of 2004), Re
R. *v.* Poulton (Sarah Jane); R. *v.* Celaire (Mario Rolando) [2002] EWCA Crim 2487;
[2003] 4 All E.R. 869; [2003] 1 Cr. App. R. (S.) 116; [2003] Crim. L.R. 124;
Times, November 1, 2002, CA (Crim Div) . . . . *Digested,* 02/**4042**:
                                               Applied, 05/3698
R. *v.* Pound (Guy) see Attorney General's Reference (No.59 of 2004), Re
R. *v.* Powell (Ashna George) [2001] 1 Cr. App. R. (S.) 76; *Times*, August 15, 2000, CA
(Crim Div). . . . . *Digested,* 00/**1385**:
                                               Followed, 05/3536
R. *v.* Prenga (Costs) [2004] 4 Costs L.R. 699, Sup Ct Costs Office . . . . *Digested,* 05/**851**
R. *v.* Prentice (Michael Charles) see R. *v.* Adomako (John Asare)
R. *v.* Price (Kevin) [2005] EWCA Crim 1757; *Times*, July 25, 2005, CA (Crim Div). . . . . *Digested,* 05/**3633**
R. *v.* Price (Richard Lyn) [2004] EWCA Crim 1359; [2005] Crim. L.R. 304, CA (Crim
Div)
R. *v.* Prime (Roy Vincent) [2004] EWCA Crim 2009; [2005] 1 Cr. App. R. (S.) 45;
(2004) 148 S.J.L.B. 759, CA (Crim Div). . . . . *Digested,* 05/**3560**
R. *v.* Prince (James Peter) [1996] 1 Cr. App. R. (S.) 335, CA (Crim Div) . . . . *Digested,* 96/**1853**:
                        Considered, 99/1136, 99/1141, 00/1221, 04/3416, 05/3706
R. *v.* Pritchard (Philip) see R. *v.* Jones (Margaret)
R. *v.* Purnell (Danny Lee) see R. *v.* Archer (Patrick John)
R. *v.* Purvis (Paul Nigel) see R. *v.* Jones (Anthony William)
R. *v.* Pylle (Kenneth Thomas) [2005] EWCA Crim 467; [2005] 2 Cr. App. R. (S.) 89,
CA (Crim Div)
R. *v.* Q (Steven James) (A Juvenile) see Attorney General's Reference (Nos.4 and 7 of
2002), Re
R. *v.* Qadar (Mohammed) [2004] EWCA Crim 2881; [2005] 2 Cr. App. R. (S.) 7, CA
(Crim Div). . . . . *Digested,* 05/**3683**
R. *v.* Qazi (Shakeel) see R. *v.* Najeeb (Parvais)
R. *v.* Quayle (Barry); *sub nom* Attorney General's Reference (No.2 of 2004), Re; R. *v.*
Wales (Reay James); R. *v.* Kenny (Graham Jack); R. *v.* Taylor (Anthony); R. *v.* Lee
(May Po); R. *v.* Ditchfield (Jeffrey) [2005] EWCA Crim 1415; [2005] 1 W.L.R.
3642; [2005] 2 Cr. App. R. 34; *Times*, June 22, 2005, CA (Crim Div) . . . . *Digested,* 05/**772**
R. *v.* Quillan (Edward Steven) see R. *v.* Last (Emma)
R. *v.* Quillan (James Angus) see R. *v.* Last (Emma)
R. *v.* Quilligan (James) see R. *v.* Loizou (Lisa)
R. *v.* Quinn (Kieran James) see Attorney General's Reference (No.49 of 2004), Re
R. *v.* Qureshi (Ghulam) see R. *v.* Ahmed (Mumtaz)
R. *v.* R see R. *v.* G
R. *v.* Rafiq (Mohammed) [2005] EWCA Crim 1423; [2005] Crim. L.R. 963, CA (Crim
Div)
R. *v.* Railton (Richard Johnson) see R. *v.* Cox (Richard Cobden)
R. *v.* Raja see R. *v.* Najeeb (Parvais)
R. *v.* Ramosa Ltd [2004] EWCA Crim 2170; [2005] 1 Cr. App. R. (S.) 77, CA (Crim
Div)

R. v. Randall (Aaron) see Attorney General's Reference (Nos.38 and 39 of 2004), Re

R. v. Ranganathan (Umaharan) see Attorney General's Reference (No.73 of 2003), Re

R. v. Rattigan (Philip) [2005] EWCA Crim 162; [2005] 2 Cr. App. R. (S.) 61, CA (Crim Div) .... *Digested,* 05/**3692**

R. v. Raviraj (Thaneran); R. v. Kansal (Maden Lal); R. v. Kansal (Raj Kumar); R. v. Gupta (Surinder Mohan) (1987) 85 Cr. App. R. 93, CA (Crim Div) .... *Digested,* 87/**2103**: *Considered,* 05/724

R. v. Rawlings (Royston George); R. v. Broadbent (Timothy Charles) [1995] 1 W.L.R. 178; [1995] 1 All E.R. 580; [1995] 2 Cr. App. R. 222; (1995) 92(2) L.S.G. 36; (1994) 144 N.L.J. 1626; (1994) 138 S.J.L.B. 223; *Times,* October 19, 1994; *Independent,* October 18, 1994, CA (Crim Div) .... *Digested,* 95/**2955**: *Considered,* 95/1220, 96/1339, 96/1391, 96/1393, 96/1422, 05/752: *Distinguished,* 96/1390

R. v. Razaq (Abdul) see R. v. Renda (Raymond)

R. v. Razaq (Ajaz) see R. v. Renda (Raymond)

R. v. RD see Attorney General's Reference (Nos.37, 38, 44, 54, 51, 53, 35, 40, 43, 45, 41 and 42 of 2003), Re

R. v. Redfern (David Christopher) see R. v. Jordan (Andrew James)

R. v. Reece (Paul Michael) [2004] EWCA Crim 1387; [2005] 1 Cr. App. R. (S.) 21, CA (Crim Div)

R. v. Rees (Louis); R. v. McElroy (Sean James); R. v. Carroll (Matthew); R. v. Killick (Bill George); R. v. Morris-Brooks (Stuart) [2005] EWCA Crim 1857; *Times,* July 22, 2005, CA (Crim Div) .... *Digested,* 05/**3761**: *Considered,* 05/3732

R. v. Reeves (Audrey Doris) (1980) 2 Cr. App. R. (S.) 35; [1980] Crim. L.R. 316, CA (Crim Div) .... *Digested,* 80/**571.72**: *Disapproved,* 05/3746

R. v. Registered Designs Appeal Tribunal Ex p. Ford Motor Co Ltd; *sub nom* Ford Motor Co Ltd's Design Application, Re [1995] 1 W.L.R. 18; [1995] R.T.R. 68; [1995] R.P.C. 167; (1995) 92(8) L.S.G. 39; (1995) 139 S.J.L.B. 42; *Times,* December 16, 1994, HL; affirming [1995] R.T.R. 68; [1994] R.P.C. 545; [1994] C.O.D. 333; *Times,* March 9, 1994, QBD .... *Digested,* 95/**3793**: *Considered,* 05/2589

R. v. Rehman (Zakir); R. v. Wood (Gary Dominic) [2005] EWCA Crim 2056; [2005] Crim. L.R. 878; *Times,* September 27, 2005, CA (Crim Div) .... *Digested,* 05/**3693**

R. v. Reichwald (Stephen Howard) see R. v. Sakavickas (Rolandas)

R. v. Reid (David William) [2004] EWCA Crim 2930; [2005] 2 Cr. App. R. (S.) 12; [2005] Crim. L.R. 161, CA (Crim Div) .... *Digested,* 05/**3681**

R. v. Reid (Ian) (1982) 4 Cr. App. R. (S.) 280, CA (Crim Div) .... *Digested,* 83/**855**: *Considered,* 05/3556

R. v. Reid (John Joseph) [1992] 1 W.L.R. 793; [1992] 3 All E.R. 673; (1992) 95 Cr. App. R. 391; (1994) 158 J.P. 517; [1992] R.T.R. 341; (1994) 158 J.P.N. 452; (1992) 89(34) L.S.G. 40; (1992) 136 S.J.L.B. 253, HL; affirming (1990) 91 Cr. App. R. 263; [1990] R.T.R. 276; [1991] Crim. L.R. 269, CA (Crim Div) .... *Digested,* 92/**3844**: *Applied,* 05/757: *Considered,* 90/4006, 93/3530, 96/1710: *Distinguished,* 95/923

R. v. Renda (Raymond); R. v. Ball (Nathan); R. v. Akram (Adil); R. v. Osbourne (Lee); R. v. Razaq (Ajaz); R. v. Razaq (Abdul) [2005] EWCA Crim 2826; *Times,* November 16, 2005, CA (Crim Div)

R. v. Rezvi (Syed) see R. v. Benjafield (Karl Robert) (Confiscation Order)

R. v. Rezvi (Syed) [2002] UKHL 1; [2003] 1 A.C. 1099; [2002] 2 W.L.R. 235; [2002] 1 All E.R. 801; [2002] 2 Cr. App. R. 2; [2002] 2 Cr. App. R. (S.) 70; [2002] H.R.L.R. 19; [2002] U.K.H.R.R. 374; [2002] Crim. L.R. 335; (2002) 99(10) L.S.G. 29; (2002) 146 S.J.L.B. 37; *Times,* January 28, 2002, HL .... *Digested,* 02/**3896**: *Applied,* 04/3311: *Followed,* 05/3568: *Previous proceedings,* 01/1237

R. v. Rhodes (George Cecil) (1960) 44 Cr. App. R. 23, CCA .... *Digested,* 60/**651**: *Considered,* 05/741: *Distinguished,* 03/741

R. v. Ricciardi (Carmine) see R. v. Cowan (Donald)

R. v. Richards (Darrell) (No.1) [2001] EWCA Crim 2712; [2002] 2 Cr. App. R. (S.) 26; [2002] Crim. L.R. 144, CA (Crim Div) .... *Digested,* 02/**4035**: *Considered,* 05/3539

R. v. Richards (Josh) see R. v. Jones (Margaret)

R. v. Richards (Michael); *sub nom* Department for Work and Pensions v. Richards [2005] EWCA Crim 491; [2005] 2 Cr. App. R. (S.) 97; [2005] Crim. L.R. 582; (2005) 149 S.J.L.B. 357; *Times,* March 11, 2005, CA (Crim Div) .... *Digested,* 05/**3901**

R. v. Richardson (Adam) [2005] EWCA Crim 1408; [2005] Crim. L.R. 804, CA (Crim Div)

R. v. Ridley (John Hamilton) [2004] EWCA Crim 2275; [2005] 1 Cr. App. R. (S.) 94, CA (Crim Div) .... *Digested,* 05/**3651**

R. v. Rimmer (Martin) [1999] 1 Cr. App. R. (S.) 234, CA (Crim Div) .... *Digested,* 99/**1125**: *Considered,* 05/3597

R. v. Rimmington (Anthony); R. v. Goldstein (Harry Chaim) [2005] UKHL 63; [2005] 3 W.L.R. 982; (2005) 102(43) L.S.G. 28; (2005) 155 N.L.J. 1685; *Times*, October 28, 2005; *Independent*, November 1, 2005, HL; reversing [2003] EWCA Crim 3450; [2004] 1 W.L.R. 2878; [2004] 2 All E.R. 589; [2004] 1 Cr. App. R. 27; [2004] U.K.H.R.R. 296; [2004] Crim. L.R. 303; *Times*, December 17, 2003, CA (Crim Div) .... *Digested*, 04/**768**

R. v. Ripley (Samuel) [1997] 1 Cr. App. R. (S.) 19, CA (Crim Div) .... *Considered*, 00/1364, 05/3771

R. v. Rizvi (Zafar); R. v. Chisti (Pirzada) [2003] EWCA Crim 3575, CA (Crim Div) ..... *Applied*, 05/767, 05/883

R. v. Roberts (Ian); *sub nom* R. v. Roberts (James) [2004] EWCA Crim 1445; [2005] 1 Cr. App. R. (S.) 40, CA (Crim Div) .... *Digested*, 05/**3549**

R. v. Roberts (James) see R. v. Roberts (Ian)

R. v. Robinson (Timothy Morgan) [2002] EWCA Crim 2489; [2003] Crim. L.R. 284; (2003) 100(2) L.S.G. 31; (2002) 146 S.J.L.B. 256; *Times*, November 13, 2002, CA (Crim Div) .... *Digested*, 02/**876**: *Considered*, 05/895

R. v. Rock (Raymond Charles) see R. v. Harris (Lorraine)

R. v. Rodger (Andrew); R. v. Rose (Keith John) [1998] 1 Cr. App. R. 143; *Times*, July 30, 1997, CA (Crim Div) .... *Digested*, 97/**1195**: *Considered*, 05/772

R. v. Rodgers (Paul Anthony) see R. v. Soares (Ronald)

R. v. Rodgers (Stanley John) [2004] EWCA Crim 3115; [2005] 2 Cr. App. R. (S.) 19, CA (Crim Div) .... *Digested*, 05/**3660**

R. v. Rogers (Philip) [2005] EWCA Crim 2863; *Times*, November 22, 2005, CA (Crim Div)

R. v. Rollock (Ashley Kenneth) see R. v. Mirza (Shabbir Ali)

R. v. Ronson (Gerald Maurice) (No.3) see R. v. Lyons (Isidore Jack) (No.3)

R. v. Rose (Keith John) see R. v. Rodger (Andrew)

R. v. Roth (Alfred) (1980) 2 Cr. App. R. (S.) 65, CA (Crim Div) .... *Digested*, 81/**525.183**: *Considered*, 94/1318: *Disapproved*, 05/3746

R. v. Rousseau (Nicholas James) [2002] EWCA Crim 1252; [2003] 1 Cr. App. R. (S.) 15, CA (Crim Div) .... *Digested*, 03/**3784**: *Considered*, 05/3656

R. v. Rouvier (Delphine) see Attorney General's Reference (Nos.27, 28, 29 and 30 of 2005), Re

R. v. Rowe [2005] Crim. L.R. 559, Central Crim Ct

R. v. Royle (Eifion Wyn) [2005] EWCA Crim 279; [2005] 2 Cr. App. R. (S.) 76, CA (Crim Div)

R. v. Rugby BC Housing Benefit Review Board Ex p. Harrison see R. v. Sheffield Housing Benefit Review Board Ex p. Smith

R. v. Russell (Graham) see Attorney General's Reference (Nos.148, 149, 150, 151, 152, 153, 154 and 155 of 2001), Re

R. v. Russell (Robert John) see Attorney General's Reference (Nos.78, 79 and 85 of 1998), Re

R. v. Russell (Steven John) see R. v. Kirk (Craig)

R. v. Ryan (James Francis) see Attorney General's Reference (Nos.3, 4, 8, 9, 10, 11, 14 and 16 of 1990), Re

R. v. Ryan (Phillip Junior) see R. v. O'Flaherty (Errol Carlton)

R. v. S [2005] EWCA Crim 819; (2005) 149 S.J.L.B. 390, CA (Crim Div)

R. v. S; R. v. Burt (Scott-Rab John); R. v. Parsons (John David); R. v. Carr (Craig Edward); R. v. Hargreaves (Stephen Lee); R. v. Denton (Vincent); R. v. Taylor (Timothy Nicholas); R. v. Coyne (Timothy Malcolm); R. v. H [2005] EWCA Crim 3616; *Times*, December 30, 2005, CA (Crim Div)

R. v. S (Christopher) see Attorney General's Reference (No.156 of 2004), Re

R. v. S (Graham) [2001] 1 Cr. App. R. 7; [2001] 1 Cr. App. R. (S.) 97; (2000) 97(36) L.S.G. 41; *Times*, August 29, 2000, CA (Crim Div) .... *Digested*, 00/**1301**: *Doubted*, 05/3640

R. v. S (Stephen) see R. v. Offen (Matthew Barry) (No.2)

R. v. Sackey (Alex Quayson) [2004] EWCA Crim 566; [2004] 2 Cr. App. R. (S.) 85, CA (Crim Div) .... *Digested*, 05/**3534**

R. v. Saha (Tapah Kumar); *sub nom* R. v. Saha (Tapash Kumar) [2005] EWCA Crim 324; [2005] 2 Cr. App. R. (S.) 80, CA (Crim Div)

R. v. Sahi (Harinder Singh) see R. v. Kalia (Daya)

R. v. Saik (Abdul Rahman) TNS, HL; reversing [2004] EWCA Crim 2936; *Times*, November 29, 2004, CA (Crim Div) .... *Digested*, 05/**883**

R. v. Saini (Jarnail Singh); *sub nom* R. v. Saini (Jarneil Singh); R. v. Kalyan (Sohan Lal); R. v. Deo (Sarwan Singh) [2004] EWCA Crim 1900; [2005] 1 Cr. App. R. (S.) 62, CA (Crim Div) .... *Digested*, 05/**3535**

R. v. Sajid (Mohammed) see R. v. Afonso (Americo Practicio)

R. v. Sakavickas (Rolandas); R. v. Reichwald (Stephen Howard) [2004] EWCA Crim 2686; [2005] 1 W.L.R. 857; [2005] 1 Cr. App. R. 36; [2005] Crim. L.R. 293; (2004) 101(44) L.S.G. 29; *Times*, November 18, 2004, CA (Crim Div) .... *Digested*, 05/**767**

R. v. Salmon (Rena) (2005) 149 S.J.L.B. 113, CA (Crim Div)

R. *v.* Samuel (Joel Nirushan) see R. *v.* Taj (Kamran)
R. *v.* Samuels-Furness (Anthony) [2005] EWCA Crim 265; [2005] 2 Cr. App. R. (S.)
    84, CA (Crim Div) . . . .   *Digested,* 05/**3623**
R. *v.* Sandasi (Unity) [2005] EWCA Crim 505; [2005] 2 Cr. App. R. (S.) 92, CA
    (Crim Div)
R. *v.* Sanderson (Andrew John) [1953] 1 W.L.R. 392; [1953] 1 All E.R. 485; (1953)
    37 Cr. App. R. 32; 97 S.J. 136, CCA; affirming (Unreported, November 19, 1952),
    Central Crim Ct . . . .   *Digested,* 53/**779**:
                             Considered, 05/832: *Distinguished,* 68/731
R. *v.* Santiago (Steven Anthony) [2005] EWCA Crim 556; [2005] 2 Cr. App. R. 24;
    [2005] Crim. L.R. 714; (2005) 102(18) L.S.G. 22; *Times,* March 16, 2005, CA
    (Crim Div) . . . .   *Digested,* 05/**847**
R. *v.* Saraswati (1989) 18 N.SW.L.R. 143, CCA (NSW) . . . .   *Considered,* 05/**921**
R. *v.* Sat-Bhambra (Ajit Singh) (1989) 88 Cr. App. R. 55; (1988) 152 J.P. 365; [1988]
    Crim. L.R. 453; (1988) 152 J.P.N. 383; (1988) 132 S.J. 896, CA (Crim Div) . . .   *Digested,* 89/**553**:
                                    Approved, 05/765: *Referred to,* 89/552
R. *v.* Saunders (Ernest Walter) (No.3) see R. *v.* Lyons (Isidore Jack) (No.3)
R. *v.* Saunders (Joseph Brian) [2000] 1 Cr. App. R. 458; [2000] 2 Cr. App. R. (S.) 71;
    [2000] Crim. L.R. 314; (1999) 96(47) L.S.G. 30; (2000) 144 S.J.L.B. 10; *Times,*
    January 28, 2000; *Independent,* December 17, 1999, CA (Crim Div) . . . .   *Digested,* 00/**1388**:
                 Considered, 01/1221, 03/3673, 04/3417, 04/3418: *Followed,* 05/3760
R. *v.* Saunders (Richard) [2004] EWCA Crim 777; [2004] 2 Cr. App. R. (S.) 86, CA
    (Crim Div) . . . .   *Digested,* 05/**3647**
R. *v.* Sawyers (Christopher) see Attorney General's Reference (Nos.4 and 7 of 2002),
    Re
R. *v.* Schilling (Rae) (also known as Newlands) see R. *v.* Schilling (Rae)
R. *v.* Schilling (Rae); *sub nom* R. *v.* Schilling (Rae) (also known as Newlands) [2002]
    EWCA Crim 3198; [2003] 2 Cr. App. R. (S.) 45, CA (Crim Div) . . . .   *Considered,* 05/3713
R. *v.* Schultz (Karl) [1996] 1 Cr. App. R. (S.) 451, CA (Crim Div) . . . .   *Digested,* 96/**2059**:
                      Applied, 00/1352: *Considered,* 97/1700, 05/3730
R. *v.* Scotney (Stephen Reginald) see Attorney General's Reference (No.77 of 2002),
    Re
R. *v.* Scott (Mark Raymond) see Attorney General's Reference (Nos.74 and 75 of
    2004), Re
R. *v.* Scriven (Geoffrey Harold) see Scriven (No.2), Re
R. *v.* Scunthorpe Justices Ex p. M (1998) 162 J.P. 635; *Times,* March 10, 1998, DC . . . .   *Digested,* 98/**1038**:
                   Applied, 00/1047, 05/828: *Followed,* 98/1037, 00/1048
R. *v.* Secretary of State for Defence Ex p. Hayman see DPP *v.* Hutchinson
R. *v.* Secretary of State for Defence Ex p. Parker see DPP *v.* Hutchinson
R. *v.* Secretary of State for Employment Ex p. Seymour-Smith (C167/97) [1999] 2
    A.C. 554; [1999] 3 W.L.R. 460; [1999] All E.R. (E.C.) 97; [1999] E.C.R. I-623;
    [1999] 2 C.M.L.R. 273; [1999] C.E.C. 79; [1999] I.C.R. 447; [1999] I.R.L.R.
    253; *Times,* February 25, 1999, ECJ [1999] E.C.R. I-623, AGO   *Digested,* 99/**2141**:
                Applied, 04/1268, 05/1268, 05/3886: *Considered,* 01/2319, 05/1265:
              Followed, 00/2160, 03/1307, 03/1341: *Previous proceedings,* 97/2265:
                                 Subsequent proceedings, 00/2210
R. *v.* Secretary of State for Health Ex p. British American Tobacco (Investments) Ltd
    (C491/01) see R. (on the application of British American Tobacco (Investments)
    Ltd) *v.* Secretary of State for Health (C491/01)
R. *v.* Secretary of State for Health Ex p. Gallagher (C11/92) [1993] E.C.R. I-3545;
    Times, June 28, 1993; *Financial Times,* June 29, 1993, ECJ . . . .   *Digested,* 93/**4330**:
                                          Followed, 05/1401
R. *v.* Secretary of State for Social Services Ex p. Britnell; *sub nom* Britnell *v.* Secretary
    of State for Social Services [1991] 1 W.L.R. 198; [1991] 2 All E.R. 726; (1991)
    135 S.J. 412; *Times,* March 15, 1991; *Independent,* April 4, 1991, HL; affirming
    Times, February 16, 1990; *Independent,* March 2, 1990, CA (Civ Div); affirming
    [1989] C.O.D. 487; *Times,* January 27, 1989; *Independent,* January 30, 1989
    (C.S.), QBD . . . .   *Digested,* 91/**3366**:
                             Considered, 95/4887, 96/4844, 05/2742
R. *v.* Secretary of State for the Environment Ex p. Brent LBC [1982] Q.B. 593; [1982]
    2 W.L.R. 693; [1983] 3 All E.R. 321; 80 L.G.R. 357; 126 S.J. 118; *Times,* October
    29, 1981, DC . . . .   *Digested,* 83/**3147**:
                   Applied, 84/23: *Considered,* 87/3159, 87/3189, 05/75
R. *v.* Secretary of State for the Environment Ex p. Islington LBC [1992] C.O.D. 67;
    [1991] N.P.C. 90; *Independent,* September 6, 1991, CA (Civ Div) . . . .   *Digested,* 92/**3493**:
                                     Applied, 00/5402, 05/1671
R. *v.* Secretary of State for the Environment Ex p. North Tyneside BC [1990] C.O.D.
    195, DC . . . .   *Digested,* 91/**65**
R. *v.* Secretary of State for the Environment Ex p. Ostler; *sub nom* R. *v.* Secretary of
    State for the Home Department Ex p. Ostler [1977] Q.B. 122; [1976] 3 W.L.R.
    288; [1976] 3 All E.R. 90; 75 L.G.R. 45; (1976) 32 P. & C.R. 166; (1976) 238
    E.G. 971; [1976] J.P.L. 301; 120 S.J. 332, CA (Civ Div) . . . .   *Digested,* 76/**19**:
         Applied, 84/3464.A, 84/3483, 88/3418, 89/3626, 90/4424, 92/163, 93/63:
                                   Considered, 05/3459

R. *v.* Secretary of State for the Environment, Transport and the Regions Ex p. Holdings & Barnes Plc see R. (on the application of Holding & Barnes Plc) *v.* Secretary of State for the Environment, Transport and the Regions

R. *v.* Secretary of State for the Environment, Transport and the Regions Ex p. Plymouth City Airport Ltd see R. (on the application of Plymouth City Airport Ltd) *v.* Secretary of State for the Environment, Transport and the Regions

R. *v.* Secretary of State for the Foreign and Commonwealth Office Ex p. Bancoult see R. (on the application of Bancoult) *v.* Secretary of State for the Foreign and Commonwealth Office

R. *v.* Secretary of State for the Home Department Ex p. Adan (Hassan Hussein) see Adan (Hassan Hussein) *v.* Secretary of State for the Home Department

R. *v.* Secretary of State for the Home Department Ex p. Ahmed (Mohammed Hussain); R. *v.* Secretary of State for the Home Department Ex p. Patel (Idris Ibrahim) [1999] Imm. A.R. 22; [1998] I.N.L.R. 570; [1999] C.O.D. 69; *Times*, October 15, 1998, CA (Civ Div); affirming [1998] Imm. A.R. 375; [1998] I.N.L.R. 546, QBD .   *Digested*, 98/**3238**:
Applied, 05/2154: *Considered*, 00/3301

R. *v.* Secretary of State for the Home Department Ex p. Al-Mehdawi; *sub nom* Al-Mehdawi *v.* Secretary of State for the Home Department [1990] 1 A.C. 876; [1989] 3 W.L.R. 1294; [1989] 3 All E.R. 843; [1990] Imm. A.R. 140; (1990) 2 Admin. L.R. 367; [1990] C.O.D. 188; (1990) 134 S.J. 50, HL; reversing [1989] 2 W.L.R. 603; [1989] 1 All E.R. 777; [1989] Imm. A.R. 125; [1989] C.O.D. 280; (1989) 86(10) L.S.G. 42; (1988) 138 N.L.J. Rep. 351; (1989) 133 S.J. 185; *Times*, November 26, 1988; *Independent*, December 6, 1988; *Independent*, November 28, 1988 (C.S.); *Daily Telegraph*, December 2, 1988, CA (Civ Div) . . .   *Digested*, 90/**66**:
Applied, 90/938, 91/3108, 94/2467, 95/2677, 95/2710, 02/285, 05/430:
Considered, 92/4240, 94/3974, 95/4413, 97/6141: *Distinguished*, 02/2583:
Followed, 95/2284

R. *v.* Secretary of State for the Home Department Ex p. Bagga [1991] 1 Q.B. 485; [1990] 3 W.L.R. 1013; [1991] 1 All E.R. 777; [1990] Imm. A.R. 413; (1990) 134 S.J. 860, CA (Civ Div); reversing *Times*, May 24, 1989, DC . . . .   *Digested*, 91/**2062**:
Applied, 95/2742, 96/2631, 05/4072

R. *v.* Secretary of State for the Home Department Ex p. Bamber see R. *v.* Secretary of State for the Home Department Ex p. Hickey (No.2)

R. *v.* Secretary of State for the Home Department Ex p. Barkoci (C257/99) see R. (on the application of Barkoci) *v.* Secretary of State for the Home Department (C257/99)

R. *v.* Secretary of State for the Home Department Ex p. Bugdaycay see Bugdaycay *v.* Secretary of State for the Home Department

R. *v.* Secretary of State for the Home Department Ex p. Carroll see R. (on the application of Carroll) *v.* Secretary of State for the Home Department

R. *v.* Secretary of State for the Home Department Ex p. Daly see R. (on the application of Daly) *v.* Secretary of State for the Home Department

R. *v.* Secretary of State for the Home Department Ex p. Davis see R. *v.* Secretary of State for the Home Department Ex p. Hickey (No.2)

R. *v.* Secretary of State for the Home Department Ex p. Doody; R. *v.* Secretary of State for the Home Department Ex p. Pierson; R. *v.* Secretary of State for the Home Department Ex p. Smart; R. *v.* Secretary of State for the Home Department Ex p. Pegg [1994] 1 A.C. 531; [1993] 3 W.L.R. 154; [1993] 3 All E.R. 92; (1995) 7 Admin. L.R. 1; [1993] 143 N.L.J. 991; *Times*, June 29, 1993; *Independent*, June 25, 1993, HL; affirming [1993] Q.B. 157; [1992] 3 W.L.R. 956; [1993] 1 All E.R. 151; (1993) 5 Admin. L.R. 93; [1992] C.O.D. 458; *Times*, May 8, 1992; *Independent*, May 7, 1992; *Guardian*, May 13, 1992, CA (Civ Div); reversing [1991] C.O.D. 256, QBD . . . .   *Digested*, 93/**1213**:
Applied, 94/768, 94/3848, 95/960, 97/1335, 97/3929, 99/5437, 03/2058, 04/2772, 05/1785, 05/4967: *Considered*, 93/1679, 94/44, 94/49, 94/3841, 95/42, 95/162, 95/2534, 96/1954, 96/4579, 96/6855, 97/1595, 97/2443, 98/4079, 00/3334, 00/4326, 02/3234, 04/1904: *Followed*, 95/81, 95/3228, 96/1953, 96/3981, 97/1626, 97/2672, 97/2678, 99/5212:
Referred to, 95/1314

R. *v.* Secretary of State for the Home Department Ex p. Fininvest SpA [1997] 1 W.L.R. 743; [1997] 1 All E.R. 942; [1995] 2 B.C.L.C. 585; [1997] 1 Cr. App. R. 257; [1997] Crim. L.R. 213; [1997] C.O.D. 94; *Times*, November 11, 1996, DC . . . . . .   *Digested*, 96/**1669**:
Applied, 02/754, 05/930

R. *v.* Secretary of State for the Home Department Ex p. H (No.1); *sub nom* R. *v.* Secretary of State for the Home Department Ex p. T; R. *v.* Secretary of State for the Home Department Ex p. Hickey (No.1) [1995] Q.B. 43; [1994] 3 W.L.R. 1110; [1995] 1 All E.R. 479; [1994] 138 S.J.L.B. 237; *Times*, July 29, 1994; *Independent*, August 2, 1994, CA (Civ Div); reversing [1994] Q.B. 378; [1994] 2 W.L.R. 190; [1994] 1 All E.R. 794; (1994) 6 Admin. L.R. 487; [1994] C.O.D. 127; (1994) 91(7) L.S.G. 31; *Times*, October 28, 1993; *Independent*, November 16, 1993, DC . . . .   *Digested*, 95/**4256**:
Considered, 03/3052, 05/2912

R. *v.* Secretary of State for the Home Department Ex p. Hepworth (Parole) [1998] C.O.D. 146, QBD

R. *v.* Secretary of State for the Home Department Ex p. Hickey (No.1) see R. *v.* Secretary of State for the Home Department Ex p. H (No.1)

R. *v.* Secretary of State for the Home Department Ex p. Hickey (No.2); R. *v.* Secretary of State for the Home Department Ex p. Malone; R. *v.* Secretary of State for the Home Department Ex p. Bamber; R. *v.* Secretary of State for the Home Department Ex p. Davis [1995] 1 W.L.R. 734; [1995] 1 All E.R. 490; (1995) 7 Admin. L.R. 549; (1994) 144 N.L.J. 1732; *Times*, December 2, 1994; *Independent*, November 29, 1994, DC . . . . *Digested*, 95/**960**:
Applied, 05/2917: *Considered*, 96/1366: *Referred to*, 96/1549

R. *v.* Secretary of State for the Home Department Ex p. Jeyeanthan; *sub nom* R. *v.* Immigration Appeal Tribunal Ex p. Jeyeanthan; Secretary of State for the Home Department *v.* Ravichandran; Ravichandran *v.* Secretary of State for the Home Department [2000] 1 W.L.R. 354; [1999] 3 All E.R. 231; [2000] Imm. A.R. 10; [1999] I.N.L.R. 241; (1999) 11 Admin. L.R. 824; [1999] C.O.D. 349; *Times*, May 26, 1999; *Independent*, June 8, 1999, CA (Civ Div); affirming [1998] Imm. A.R. 369; [1998] I.N.L.R. 540; *Times*, April 23, 1998, QBD . . . . *Digested*, 99/**3162**:
Applied, 01/4380, 02/858, 04/4156: *Considered*, 04/2012, 05/2826:
Distinguished, 02/4216: *Referred to*, 01/4713

R. *v.* Secretary of State for the Home Department Ex p. Khawaja; R. *v.* Secretary of State for the Home Department Ex p. Khera [1984] A.C. 74; [1983] 2 W.L.R. 321; [1983] 1 All E.R. 765; [1982] Imm. A.R. 139; 127 S.J. 137, HL; affirming [1982] 1 W.L.R. 625; [1982] 2 All E.R. 523; 126 S.J. 294, CA (Civ Div) . . . . *Digested*, 83/**1908**:
Applied, 84/1737, 90/744, 91/580, 91/2004, 91/2024, 91/2037, 92/2270, 92/2400, 93/2188, 93/2194, 94/2490, 94/2499, 94/2521, 96/606, 96/3295, 96/3305, 97/2927, 99/2167, 02/2934, 03/2248, 05/2163:
Approved, 91/1956: *Considered*, 83/26, 84/1548, 84/1723, 84/1751, 85/1732, 86/1690, 86/1692, 86/1986, 87/1933, 87/1944, 87/1989, 88/23, 88/1838, 88/1853, 89/525, 90/2597, 90/2605, 91/2001, 91/2006, 91/2007, 92/2396, 92/2854, 93/2053, 93/2233, 93/2991, 94/2448, 96/3278, 03/2283, 04/1437: *Distinguished*, 85/1725, 86/1696, 88/1837, 88/1875, 91/1974, 00/4172, 00/5472: *Followed*, 83/1910, 95/4243, 96/3300, 97/2929, 00/3288: *Not followed*, 88/1882: *Referred to*, 85/1714, 86/2595, 87/1941, 87/1958, 87/2937, 88/1867

R. *v.* Secretary of State for the Home Department Ex p. Khera see R. *v.* Secretary of State for the Home Department Ex p. Khawaja

R. *v.* Secretary of State for the Home Department Ex p. Kondova (C235/99) see R. (on the application of Kondova) *v.* Secretary of State for the Home Department (C235/99)

R. *v.* Secretary of State for the Home Department Ex p. Leech (No.2) [1994] Q.B. 198; [1993] 3 W.L.R. 1125; [1993] 4 All E.R. 539; (1993) 137 S.J.L.B. 173; *Times*, May 20, 1993; *Independent*, May 20, 1993, CA (Civ Div); reversing [1992] C.O.D. 168 . . . . *Digested*, 94/**3849**:
Applied, 98/3899, 05/4193: *Considered*, 96/3219, 97/2782, 99/335, 03/2223

R. *v.* Secretary of State for the Home Department Ex p. Main see R. *v.* Secretary of State for the Home Department Ex p. Simms

R. *v.* Secretary of State for the Home Department Ex p. Malone see R. *v.* Secretary of State for the Home Department Ex p. Hickey (No.2)

R. *v.* Secretary of State for the Home Department Ex p. Mellor see R. (on the application of Mellor) *v.* Secretary of State for the Home Department

R. *v.* Secretary of State for the Home Department Ex p. O'Brien see R. *v.* Secretary of State for the Home Department Ex p. Simms

R. *v.* Secretary of State for the Home Department Ex p. Ostler see R. *v.* Secretary of State for the Environment Ex p. Ostler

R. *v.* Secretary of State for the Home Department Ex p. Patel (Idris Ibrahim) see R. *v.* Secretary of State for the Home Department Ex p. Ahmed (Mohammed Hussain)

R. *v.* Secretary of State for the Home Department Ex p. Pegg see R. *v.* Secretary of State for the Home Department Ex p. Doody

R. *v.* Secretary of State for the Home Department Ex p. Pierson see R. *v.* Secretary of State for the Home Department Ex p. Doody

R. *v.* Secretary of State for the Home Department Ex p. Pierson; *sub nom* Pierson *v.* Secretary of State for the Home Department [1998] A.C. 539; [1997] 3 W.L.R. 492; [1997] 3 All E.R. 577; (1997) 94(37) L.S.G. 41; (1997) 147 N.L.J. 1238; (1997) 141 S.J.L.B. 212; *Times*, July 28, 1997; *Independent*, July 31, 1997, HL; reversing [1996] 3 W.L.R. 547; [1996] 1 All E.R. 837; [1996] C.O.D. 362; *Times*, December 8, 1995; *Independent*, December 12, 1995, CA (Civ Div); reversing [1996] C.O.D. 255; *Times*, November 29, 1995; *Independent*, November 14, 1995, QBD . . . . *Digested*, 97/**1627**:
Applied, 04/2772: *Considered*, 96/1954, 05/3635: *Distinguished*, 98/4074

R. *v.* Secretary of State for the Home Department Ex p. Radiom (C111/95) see R. *v.* Secretary of State for the Home Department Ex p. Shingara (C65/95)

R. *v.* Secretary of State for the Home Department Ex p. Ravichandran (No.1); *sub nom* R. *v.* Immigration Appeal Tribunal Ex p. Sandralingam (No.1); R. *v.* Secretary of State for the Home Department Ex p. Sandralingham (No.1); R. *v.* Immigration Appeal Tribunal Ex p. Rajendrakumar [1996] Imm. A.R. 97; *Times,* October 30, 1995, CA (Civ Div) . . . . *Digested,* 96/**3216:** *Applied,* 98/3174, 03/2234: *Cited,* 99/3202: *Considered,* 96/3225, 97/2862, 98/3227, 99/3168, 05/2154: *Followed,* 97/2863, 00/3322, 05/2215

R. *v.* Secretary of State for the Home Department Ex p. Samaroo see R. (on the application of Samaroo) *v.* Secretary of State for the Home Department

R. *v.* Secretary of State for the Home Department Ex p. Sandralingham (No.1) see R. *v.* Secretary of State for the Home Department Ex p. Ravichandran (No.1)

R. *v.* Secretary of State for the Home Department Ex p. Shah see Islam *v.* Secretary of State for the Home Department

R. *v.* Secretary of State for the Home Department Ex p. Shingara (C65/95); R. *v.* Secretary of State for the Home Department Ex p. Radiom (C111/95) [1997] All E.R. (EC) 577; [1997] E.C.R. I-3343; [1997] 3 C.M.L.R. 703; *Times,* June 23, 1997, ECJ . . . . *Digested,* 97/**2913:** *Followed,* 05/1462: *Subsequent proceedings,* 99/3196

R. *v.* Secretary of State for the Home Department Ex p. Simms; *sub nom* R. *v.* Secretary of State for the Home Department Ex p. Main; R. *v.* Secretary of State for the Home Department Ex p. O'Brien; R. *v.* Governor of Whitemoor Prison Ex p. Main [2000] 2 A.C. 115; [1999] 3 W.L.R. 328; [1999] 3 All E.R. 400; [1999] E.M.L.R. 689; 7 B.H.R.C. 411; (1999) 11 Admin. L.R. 961; [1999] C.O.D. 520; (1999) 96(30) L.S.G. 28; (1999) 149 N.L.J. 1073; (1999) 143 S.J.L.B. 212; *Times,* July 9, 1999, HL; reversing [1999] Q.B. 349; [1998] 3 W.L.R. 1169; [1998] 2 All E.R. 491; [1998] E.M.L.R. 431; (1998) 95(1) L.S.G. 23; (1998) 142 S.J.L.B. 38; *Times,* December 9, 1997; *Independent,* December 10, 1997, CA (Civ Div); reversing [1997] E.M.L.R. 261; [1997] C.O.D. 217; *Times,* January 17, 1997, QBD . . . . *Digested,* 99/**4105:** *Applied,* 02/4505: *Considered,* 99/335, 01/4578, 03/2223: *Distinguished,* 05/2914: *Followed,* 99/4100

R. *v.* Secretary of State for the Home Department Ex p. Singh, *Times,* March 28, 1988; *Independent,* April 11, 1988 (C.S.), CA (Civ Div); affirming [1987] Imm. A.R. 489, QBD . . . . *Digested,* 88/**2834:** *Considered,* 05/2199

R. *v.* Secretary of State for the Home Department Ex p. Singh (Hardial) see R. *v.* Governor of Durham Prison Ex p. Singh (Hardial)

R. *v.* Secretary of State for the Home Department Ex p. Smart see R. *v.* Secretary of State for the Home Department Ex p. Doody

R. *v.* Secretary of State for the Home Department Ex p. T see R. *v.* Secretary of State for the Home Department Ex p. H (No.1)

R. *v.* Secretary of State for the Home Department Ex p. T see T *v.* Secretary of State for the Home Department

R. *v.* Secretary of State for the Home Department Ex p. Thompson see R. *v.* Secretary of State for the Home Department Ex p. Venables

R. *v.* Secretary of State for the Home Department Ex p. Ullah (Mohammed); *sub nom* Ullah (Mohammed) *v.* Secretary of State for the Home Department [1995] Imm. A.R. 166; *Independent,* July 5, 1994, CA (Civ Div) . . . . *Digested,* 96/**3261:** *Applied,* 96/3262: *Not followed,* 05/2163

R. *v.* Secretary of State for the Home Department Ex p. Venables; R. *v.* Secretary of State for the Home Department Ex p. Thompson [1998] A.C. 407; [1997] 3 W.L.R. 23; [1997] 3 All E.R. 97; [1997] 2 F.L.R. 471; (1997) 9 Admin. L.R. 413; [1997] Fam. Law 789; (1997) 94(34) L.S.G. 27; (1997) 147 N.L.J. 955; *Times,* June 13, 1997; *Independent,* June 18, 1997, HL; affirming [1997] 2 W.L.R. 67; [1997] 1 All E.R. 327; (1997) 9 Admin. L.R. 281; [1997] C.O.D. 100; *Times,* August 7, 1996, CA (Civ Div); affirming [1996] C.O.D. 365; (1996) 93(18) L.S.G. 37; (1996) 146 N.L.J. 786; (1996) 140 S.J.L.B. 127; *Times,* May 7, 1996; *Independent,* June 10, 1996 (C.S.), QBD . . . . *Digested,* 97/**1595:** *Applied,* 97/1593, 99/781, 01/89, 03/3054: *Considered,* 05/2923: *Followed,* 04/3471

R. *v.* Sed (Ali Dahir) [2004] EWCA Crim 1294; [2004] 1 W.L.R. 3218; [2005] 1 Cr. App. R. 4; (2004) 148 S.J.L.B. 756; *Times,* July 8, 2004, CA (Crim Div) . . . . . . *Digested,* 04/**701**

R. *v.* Sefton MBC Ex p. Help the Aged [1997] 4 All E.R. 532; [1997] 3 F.C.R. 573; (1997-98) 1 C.C.L. Rep. 57; (1997) 38 B.M.L.R. 135; [1998] C.O.D. 69; *Times,* August 23, 1997; *Independent,* October 3, 1997, CA (Civ Div); reversing [1997] 3 F.C.R. 392; (1997) 36 B.M.L.R. 110; [1997] C.O.D. 387; (1997) 147 N.L.J. 490; *Times,* March 27, 1997; *Independent,* April 18, 1997, QBD . . . . *Digested,* 97/**4721:** *Applied,* 99/4622, 02/4257, 05/3947: *Considered,* 99/3052, 02/949

R. *v.* Sejdial (Gentian) see Attorney General's Reference (Nos.135, 136 and 137), Re

R. *v.* Sekhon (Daljit Singh) see R. *v.* Knights (Richard Michael)

R. *v.* Selby DC Ex p. Oxton Farms [1997] E.G.C.S. 60, CA (Civ Div) . . . . *Digested,* 97/**4114:** *Applied,* 05/3279

R. *v.* Sellars (Dylan Brian) see Attorney General's Reference (Nos.86, 87 and 88 of 2004), Re

R. _v._ Sellick (Carlo) see R. _v._ Sellick (Santino)
R. _v._ Sellick (Santino); R. _v._ Sellick (Carlo) [2005] EWCA Crim 651; [2005] 1 W.L.R. 3257; [2005] 2 Cr. App. R. 15; [2005] Crim. L.R. 722; (2005) 102(19) L.S.G. 33; _Times,_ March 22, 2005, CA (Crim Div) . . . . _Digested,_ 05/**888**
R. _v._ Sentence (Unreported, April 1, 2004), Crown Ct (Lincoln) . . . . _Considered,_ 05/834
R. _v._ Serdeiro (Roberto Newton) [1996] 1 Cr. App. R. (S.) 251, CA (Crim Div) . . . . _Digested,_ 96/**1871**:
                                                         Considered, 98/1185, 05/3597
R. _v._ Serumaga (Peter) [2005] EWCA Crim 370; [2005] 1 W.L.R. 3366; [2005] 2 All E.R. 160; [2005] 2 Cr. App. R. 12; [2005] Crim. L.R. 638; _Times,_ February 28, 2005, CA (Crim Div) . . . . _Digested,_ 05/**846**
R. _v._ Seymour (Edward John) [1983] 2 A.C. 493; [1983] 3 W.L.R. 349; [1983] 2 All E.R. 1058; (1983) 77 Cr. App. R. 215; (1984) 148 J.P. 530; [1983] R.T.R. 455; [1983] Crim. L.R. 742; (1984) 148 J.P.N. 331; (1983) 127 S.J. 522, HL; affirming (1983) 76 Cr. App. R. 211; [1983] R.T.R. 202; [1983] Crim. L.R. 260, CA (Crim Div) . . . . _Digested,_ 84/**525**:
             Applied, 85/627, 86/636, 05/757: _Cited,_ 91/1160, 92/1333:
                         Considered, 90/1126: _Disapproved,_ 94/1124
R. _v._ Shacklady (Andrew) (Costs) [2005] 4 Costs L.R. 716, Sup Ct Costs Office
R. _v._ Shannon (Paul) see R. _v._ Soares (Ronald)
R. _v._ Sharma (Balbir Chandra) see R. _v._ Kalia (Daya)
R. _v._ Sharma (Ramlok) see R. _v._ Kalia (Daya)
R. _v._ Sharp (John Wilson) see Attorney General's Reference (Nos.148, 149, 150, 151, 152, 153, 154 and 155 of 2001), Re
R. _v._ Shaw (Carl William) [1998] 2 Cr. App. R. (S.) 233, CA (Crim Div) . . . . _Digested,_ 98/**1377**:
                                              Considered, 05/3728
R. _v._ Shaw (Dennis) see R. _v._ Kidd (Philip Richard)
R. _v._ Shaw (James Edward) CARC 3417, CA (Crim Div) (NI) . . . . _Considered,_ 05/896
R. _v._ Shaw (Mark Anthony) (Costs) [2005] 2 Costs L.R. 326, Sup Ct Costs Office
R. _v._ Shearman (Peter) see Attorney General's Reference (Nos.39, 40 and 41 of 2005)
R. _v._ Sheffield Housing Benefit Review Board Ex p. Smith; R. _v._ Rugby BC Housing Benefit Review Board Ex p. Harrison; R. _v._ Coventry DC Housing Benefit Review Board Ex p. Bodden (1996) 28 H.L.R. 36; 93 L.G.R. 139; _Times,_ December 28, 1994, QBD . . . . _Digested,_ 95/**2601**:
                                         Considered, 01/5028, 05/3873
R. _v._ Sheikh (Hafeez); _sub nom_ R. _v._ Sheik (Hafeez); R. _v._ Sheikh (Saqeb); R. _v._ Sheikh (Junaid) [2004] EWCA Crim 492; [2004] 2 Cr. App. R. 13; [2004] 2 Cr. App. R. (S.) 90; [2004] Crim. L.R. 484; (2004) 148 S.J.L.B. 352, CA (Crim Div). . . . . . _Digested,_ 05/**884**
R. _v._ Sheikh (Junaid) see R. _v._ Sheikh (Hafeez)
R. _v._ Sheikh (Saqeb) see R. _v._ Sheikh (Hafeez)
R. _v._ Shepherd (Peter James) see Attorney General's Reference (Nos.14 and 24 of 1993), Re
R. _v._ Sheppard (James) see R. _v._ Lang (Stephen Howard)
R. _v._ Shropshire CC Ex p. Abdullah see R. _v._ Barnet LBC Ex p. Shah (Nilish)
R. _v._ Sidhu (Joginder Singh) see R. _v._ Kalia (Daya)
R. _v._ Siliavski (Boyan Yossifov) [2000] 1 Cr. App. R. (S.) 23, CA (Crim Div). . . . . _Digested,_ 00/**1255**:
                      Applied, 04/3352: _Considered,_ 02/3950: _Doubted,_ 05/3610
R. _v._ Silver (Michael) (1994) 15 Cr. App. R. (S.) 836, CA (Crim Div) . . . . _Digested,_ 95/**1431**:
                      Considered, 99/1265, 00/1366, 05/3666: _Referred to,_ 97/1616
R. _v._ Simpson (Ian McDonald) [2003] EWCA Crim 1499; [2004] Q.B. 118; [2003] 3 W.L.R. 337; [2003] 3 All E.R. 531; [2003] 2 Cr. App. R. 36; [2004] 1 Cr. App. R. (S.) 24; [2003] Crim. L.R. 652; (2003) 100(27) L.S.G. 34; (2003) 147 S.J.L.B. 694; _Times,_ May 26, 2003, CA (Crim Div) . . . . _Digested,_ 03/**900**:
                                              Followed, 05/3569
R. _v._ Simsek (Muslum) see R. _v._ Kaynak (Hussein)
R. _v._ Sinclair (James); R. _v._ Johnson (Brian); R. _v._ Smith (Ian) (1998) 148 N.L.J. 1353, CA (Crim Div) . . . . _Considered,_ 05/805
R. _v._ Singh (Daljit) [1999] 1 Cr. App. R. (S.) 490; [1999] Crim. L.R. 236; (1998) 95(45) L.S.G. 40; _Times,_ November 5, 1998; _Independent,_ November 12, 1998, CA (Crim Div) . . . . _Digested,_ 98/**1227**:
                    Considered, 00/1255, 02/3950, 05/911, 05/3610
R. _v._ Singh (Gurphal) [1999] Crim. L.R. 582; _Times,_ April 17, 1999, CA (Crim Div) . . . . . _Digested,_ 99/**945**:
                                              Considered, 05/805
R. _v._ Singh (Mark) [2005] EWCA Crim 90, CA (Crim Div) . . . . _Applied,_ 05/812
R. _v._ Singh (Satnam) see R. _v._ Knights (Richard Michael)
R. _v._ Singh (Satvir) (1988) 10 Cr. App. R. (S.) 402, CA (Crim Div) . . . . _Digested,_ 90/**1290**:
             Cited, 93/1139: _Considered,_ 98/1191, 99/1137, 99/1148, 00/1233, 05/3587,
                                                      05/3751
R. _v._ Singh (Shangara) see R. _v._ Knights (Richard Michael)
R. _v._ Singleton (Edward) see Attorney General's Reference (Nos.3, 4, 8, 9, 10, 11, 14 and 16 of 1990), Re
R. _v._ Skitt (Harry); R. _v._ Merrin (Charles William); R. _v._ Wright (John); R. _v._ Perkins (James) [2004] EWCA Crim 3141; [2005] 2 Cr. App. R. (S.) 23; [2005] Crim. L.R. 252, CA (Crim Div)

R. v. S

R. v. Slocombe (Nicholas) [2005] EWCA Crim 2997; *Times*, December 6, 2005, CA
(Crim Div)
R. v. Smaine (Moumen) see Attorney General's Reference (Nos.27, 28, 29 and 30 of
2005), Re
R. v. Smith (Costs) [2004] 2 Costs L.R. 348, Sup Ct Costs Office . . . .   *Applied*, 05/851
R. v. Smith (Craig Ashley) [2004] EWCA Crim 2867; [2005] 2 Cr. App. R. (S.) 8, CA
(Crim Div) . . . .   *Digested*, 05/**3552**
R. v. Smith (David) [2004] EWCA Crim 1040; [2004] 2 Cr. App. R. (S.) 92, CA (Crim
Div) . . . .   *Digested*, 05/**3718**
R. v. Smith (David Cadman); *sub nom* R. v. Cadman-Smith (David) [2001] UKHL 68;
[2002] 1 W.L.R. 54; [2002] 1 All E.R. 366; [2002] 1 Cr. App. R. 35; [2002] 2
Cr. App. R. (S.) 37; [2002] Crim. L.R. 396; (2002) 99(7) L.S.G. 34; (2002) 146
S.J.L.B. 20; *Times*, December 17, 2001; *Independent*, December 18, 2001; *Daily
Telegraph*, December 20, 2001, HL; reversing [2001] 1 Cr. App. R. (S.) 61;
(2000) 164 J.P. 575; (2001) 165 J.P.N. 66; *Times*, July 26, 2000, CA (Crim
Div) . . . .   *Digested*, 02/**3898**:
   Applied, 04/3310, 05/3616, 05/3901: *Distinguished*, 03/3659:
   Followed, 03/3658, 05/794
R. v. Smith (Donald Sydney) [1973] Q.B. 924; [1973] 3 W.L.R. 88; [1973] 2 All E.R.
1161; (1973) 57 Cr. App. R. 737; [1973] Crim. L.R. 516; 117 S.J. 564, CA (Crim
Div) . . . .   *Digested*, 73/**512**:
   Applied, 74/568: *Considered*, 05/794
R. v. Smith (Gary) see R. v. Lang (Stephen Howard)
R. v. Smith (George William) see R. v. Healey (Bernard)
R. v. Smith (Ian) see R. v. Sinclair (James)
R. v. Smith (Jason Giles) see R. v. Lowe (Paul)
R. v. Smith (Morgan James) [2001] 1 A.C. 146; [2000] 3 W.L.R. 654; [2000] 4 All
E.R. 289; [2001] 1 Cr. App. R. 5; [2000] Crim. L.R. 1004; (2000) 97(37) L.S.G.
39; (2000) 150 N.L.J. 1199; (2000) 144 S.J.L.B. 251; *Times*, August 4, 2000;
Independent, October 4, 2000, HL; affirming [1999] Q.B. 1079; [1999] 2 W.L.R.
610; [1998] 4 All E.R. 387; [1999] 1 Cr. App. R. 256; (1999) 45 B.M.L.R. 146;
[1998] Crim. L.R. 896; (1998) 148 N.L.J. 1086; *Times*, July 29, 1998;
Independent, July 15, 1998, CA (Crim Div) . . . .   *Digested*, 00/**986**:
   Applied, 04/755: *Cited*, 03/879: *Considered*, 03/3801, 04/860:
   Distinguished, 01/1054: *Followed*, 01/5729: *Not followed*, 05/807
R. v. Smith (Patrick); R. v. Mercieca (Joseph) [2005] UKHL 12; [2005] 1 W.L.R. 704;
[2005] 2 All E.R. 29; [2005] 2 Cr. App. R. 10; [2005] Crim. L.R. 476; *Times*,
February 17, 2005; *Independent*, February 23, 2005, HL; reversing [2003]
EWCA Crim 3847, CA (Crim Div) . . . .   *Digested*, 05/**895**
R. v. Smith (Paul) see R. v. Atkinson (Glynn)
R. v. Smith (Peter John) see R. v. Tovey (David)
R. v. Smith (Robert John) see Attorney General's Reference (No.47 of 1994), Re
R. v. Smith (Ruben); R. v. Fletcher (Francis Royston) [2001] EWCA Crim 1700; [2002]
1 Cr. App. R. (S.) 82; [2001] Crim. L.R. 833, CA (Crim Div) . . . .   *Digested*, 02/**4020**:
   Considered, 05/3539
R. v. Smith (Stephen Paul) see R. v. Lowe (Paul)
R. v. Smith (Stuart) [2002] EWCA Crim 1946, CA (Crim Div) . . . .   *Considered*, 05/3541
R. v. Smith (Tina) see R. v. Khela (Dalbir Singh)
R. v. Smitheringale (Keith) [2004] EWCA Crim 1974; [2005] 1 Cr. App. R. (S.) 58, CA
(Crim Div) . . . .   *Digested*, 05/**3591**
R. v. Snaresbrook Crown Court Ex p. DPP [1988] Q.B. 532; [1987] 3 W.L.R. 1054;
[1988] 1 All E.R. 315; (1988) 86 Cr. App. R. 227; [1987] Crim. L.R. 824; (1987)
131 S.J. 1487, QBD . . . .   *Digested*, 88/**727**:
   Considered, 91/781, 05/744: *Doubted*, 88/668
R. v. Soares (Ronald); R. v. Shannon (Paul); R. v. Wright (Brian Antony); R. v. Kiernan
(Ian Donald); R. v. Rodgers (Paul Anthony); R. v. Hanley (Kevin) [2003] EWCA
Crim 2488, CA (Crim Div) . . . .   *Considered*, 05/3750
R. v. Sobers (Leon Anderson) see R. v. Benfield (Anthony John)
R. v. Sofroniou (Leon Florenzous) [2003] EWCA Crim 3681; [2004] Q.B. 1218;
[2004] 3 W.L.R. 161; [2004] 1 Cr. App. R. 35; [2004] Crim. L.R. 381; (2004)
101 (6) L.S.G. 31; *Times*, January 5, 2004, CA (Crim Div) . . . .   *Digested*, 04/**756**:
   Applied, 05/911
R. v. Somanathan (Ramanathan) see R. v. Weir (Antony Albert)
R. v. Soneji (Kamalesh Kumar) see R. v. Soneji (Kamlesh Kumar)
R. v. Soneji (Kamalesh) see R. v. Everson (Louis) (Appeal against Sentence)
R. v. Soneji (Kamlesh Kumar); *sub nom* R. v. Soneji (Kamalesh Kumar); R. v. Bullen
(David Frederick) [2005] UKHL 49; [2005] 3 W.L.R. 303; [2005] 4 All E.R.
321; (2005) 102(31) L.S.G. 26; (2005) 155 N.L.J. 1315; (2005) 149 S.J.L.B.
924; *Times*, July 22, 2005; *Independent*, July 26, 2005, HL; reversing [2003]
EWCA Crim 1765; [2004] 1 Cr. App. R. (S.) 34; [2003] Crim. L.R. 738; (2003)
100(33) L.S.G. 27; (2003) 147 S.J.L.B. 817; *Times*, July 1, 2003, CA (Crim
Div) . . . .   *Digested*, 05/**842**:
   Applied, 04/806: *Followed*, 05/841
R. v. Sood (Anurag) (Costs) [2004] 3 Costs L.R. 520, Sup Ct Costs Office . . . .   *Digested*, 05/**2711**

R. *v.* Southwark Crown Court Ex p. Associated Newspapers see R. *v.* Southwark Crown Court Ex p. Godwin

R. *v.* Southwark Crown Court Ex p. Daily Telegraph see R. *v.* Southwark Crown Court Ex p. Godwin

R. *v.* Southwark Crown Court Ex p. Godwin; *sub nom* Godwin, Re; R. *v.* Southwark Crown Court Ex p. Daily Telegraph; R. *v.* Southwark Crown Court Ex p. MGN Ltd; R. *v.* Southwark Crown Court Ex p. Associated Newspapers; R. *v.* Southwark Crown Court Ex p. Newspaper Publishing [1992] Q.B. 190; [1991] 3 W.L.R. 689; [1991] 3 All E.R. 818; (1992) 94 Cr. App. R. 34; (1992) 156 J.P. 86; [1991] Crim. L.R. 302; (1991) 155 J.P.N. 834; (1991) 141 N.L.J. 963; (1991) 135 S.J.L.B. 28; *Times,* May 30, 1991; *Independent,* July 9, 1991; *Guardian,* June 6, 1991, CA (Civ Div). . . . . *Digested,* 92/**970**: *Applied,* 94/3245, 95/3546, 05/923

R. *v.* Southwark Crown Court Ex p. MGN Ltd see R. *v.* Southwark Crown Court Ex p. Godwin

R. *v.* Southwark Crown Court Ex p. Newspaper Publishing see R. *v.* Southwark Crown Court Ex p. Godwin

R. *v.* Southwark LBC Ex p. Campisi (1999) 31 H.L.R. 560, CA (Civ Div) . . . . *Digested,* 99/**3064**: *Considered,* 05/1986, 05/1988

R. *v.* Speechley (William James) [2004] EWCA Crim 3067; [2005] 2 Cr. App. R. (S.) 15; [2005] Crim. L.R. 811; (2004) 148 S.J.L.B. 1374; *Times,* December 1, 2004, CA (Crim Div). . . . . *Digested,* 05/**898**

R. *v.* Spence (Clinton Everton); R. *v.* Thomas (Vernon Walter) (1983) 5 Cr. App. R. (S.) 413; [1984] Crim. L.R. 372, CA (Crim Div) . . . . *Digested,* 84/**876**: *Applied,* 03/3770: *Cited,* 91/1146, 94/1292: *Considered,* 86/741, 86/742, 87/986, 87/988, 92/1445, 96/1888, 96/1889, 97/1540, 04/3322, 04/3384, 05/3604, 05/3649: *Distinguished,* 85/728, 86/842: *Followed,* 97/1604, 05/3536: *Referred to,* 00/1262

R. *v.* Spencer (Paul) (Unreported, June 29, 1998), CA (Crim Div). . . . . *Considered,* 05/3541

R. *v.* Spens (No.2); *sub nom* R. *v.* Lord Spens (No.2) (1992) 142 N.L.J. 528; *Independent,* March 18, 1992; *Financial Times,* March 31, 1992; *Guardian,* April 2, 1992. . . . . *Digested,* 92/**625**: *Applied,* 05/871

R. *v.* Spinks (Mark Lee) [1982] 1 All E.R. 587; (1982) 74 Cr. App. R. 263; [1982] Crim. L.R. 231, CA (Crim Div) . . . . *Digested,* 82/**503**: *Considered,* 05/741: *Distinguished,* 03/741

R. *v.* Spokes (Paul George) see R. *v.* Whiteman (Mark)

R. *v.* Spruce (Ronald Arthur); R. *v.* Anwar (Kamran) [2005] EWCA Crim 1090; *Times,* May 5, 2005, CA (Crim Div) . . . . *Digested,* 05/**3531**

R. *v.* Srivastava (Rajeev) see R. *v.* Misra (Amit)

R. *v.* Ssan (Archit) see Attorney General's Reference (No.129 of 2004), Re

R. *v.* Stacey (Lester John) [2004] EWCA Crim 564; [2004] 2 Cr. App. R. (S.) 87, CA (Crim Div). . . . . *Digested,* 05/**3603**

R. *v.* Standing (Colin Frederick) [2002] EWCA Crim 1547; [2003] 1 Cr. App. R. (S.) 52, CA (Crim Div) . . . . *Digested,* 03/**3728**: *Considered,* 05/3625

R. *v.* Staniland (Craig) (Costs) [2005] 2 Costs L.R. 337, Sup Ct Costs Office

R. *v.* Stannard (Michael Richard) [2005] EWCA Crim 2717; [2005] B.T.C. 558, CA (Crim Div)

R. *v.* Stapleton (Vincent) see R. *v.* May (Raymond George)

R. *v.* Stark (Barry John) [2002] EWCA Crim 542; [2002] 2 Cr. App. R. (S.) 104; [2002] Crim. L.R. 592, CA (Crim Div) . . . . *Digested,* 02/**4052**: *Considered,* 05/3539

R. *v.* Stark (Rudi) see R. *v.* Le (Van Binh)

R. *v.* Stephenson (Malcolm) see R. *v.* Vye (John Arthur)

R. *v.* Stephenson (Matthew John) see Attorney General's Reference (No.46 of 2005), Re

R. *v.* Steward (William) [2004] EWCA Crim 1093; [2005] 1 Cr. App. R. (S.) 5, CA (Crim Div). . . . . *Digested,* 05/**3714**

R. *v.* Stewart (Christopher) (Costs) [2004] 3 Costs L.R. 501, Crown Ct (Middlesex) . . *Digested,* 05/**871**

R. *v.* Stewart (David Ian) see R. *v.* Page (Cyril Edward)

R. *v.* Stewart (Robert) see Attorney General's Reference (No.146 of 2002), Re

R. *v.* Stockdale (Rae); R. *v.* Flynn (Brendan Gerard); R. *v.* Tankard (Julie Dawn) [2005] EWCA Crim 1582, CA (Crim Div) . . . . *Doubted,* 05/**3735**

R. *v.* Stone (Michael John) [2005] EWCA Crim 105; [2005] Crim. L.R. 569, CA (Crim Div)

R. *v.* Storey (Stephen David) (1984) 6 Cr. App. R. (S.) 104; [1984] Crim. L.R. 438, CA (Crim Div). . . . . *Digested,* 85/**810**: *Applied,* 86/771, 86/772: *Considered,* 86/740, 87/971, 88/1018, 89/794, 89/925, 89/1101, 89/1150, 90/1054, 90/1446, 90/1478.b, 96/1749, 96/1958, 96/1959, 97/1558, 98/1275, 99/1240, 00/1310, 00/1328, 05/3765: *Referred to,* 87/972, 87/973, 89/1057, 90/1447, 90/1478, 90/1480, 92/1432, 93/1337

R. *v.* Stow (Matthew Gary) [2005] EWCA Crim 1157; [2005] U.K.H.R.R. 754, CMAC . *Digested,* 05/**234**

R. *v.* Strange (Kevin Martin) [2005] EWCA Crim 80; (2005) 149 S.J.L.B. 116, CA (Crim Div)
R. *v.* Stride (Ian Paul) see Attorney General's Reference (No.152 of 2002), Re
R. *v.* Suchedina (Hasnain Mohammed) see Attorney General's Reference (No.4 of 2003), Re
R. *v.* Suffolk CC Ex p. Steed; *sub nom* Steed *v.* Suffolk CC (1998) 75 P. & C.R. 102; [1997] 1 E.G.L.R. 131; [1997] 10 E.G. 146; [1996] E.G.C.S. 122; [1996] N.P.C. 117; *Times*, November 11, 1996; *Times*, August 2, 1996, CA (Civ Div); affirming (1996) 71 P. & C.R. 463; (1995) 70 P. & C.R. 487; [1995] E.G.C.S. 80; [1995] N.P.C. 82, QBD . . . . *Digested*, 96/**4936**:
Applied, 97/4227: *Considered*, 00/4616, 05/3440: *Disapproved*, 99/4393
R. *v.* Sullivan (Melvin Terrence); R. *v.* Gibbs (Martin Godwin); R. *v.* Elener (Barry); R. *v.* Elener (Derek) [2004] EWCA Crim 1762; [2005] 1 Cr. App. R. 3; [2005] 1 Cr. App. R. (S.) 67; (2004) 148 S.J.L.B. 1029; *Times*, July 14, 2004, CA (Crim Div) . *Digested*, 04/**3401**:
Applied, 05/3677, 05/3678, 05/3679, 05/3682: *Considered*, 05/3653, 05/3681, 05/3709
R. *v.* Sullman (Barry) see R. *v.* Adomako (John Asare)
R. *v.* Sunderland (Kevin Thomas) see Attorney General's Reference (Nos.60 and 61 of 1995), Re
R. *v.* Sutherland (Unreported, January 29, 2002), Crown Ct (Nottingham) . . . . *Considered*, 05/834
R. *v.* Swansea City Council Ex p. Main see Main *v.* Swansea City Council
R. *v.* Syed (Costs) [2004] 4 Costs L.R. 686, Sup Ct Costs Office . . . . *Digested*, 05/**856**
R. *v.* Szlukovinyi (June Elizabeth) [2004] EWCA Crim 1788; [2005] 1 Cr. App. R. (S.) 55, CA (Crim Div) . . . . *Digested*, 05/**3555**
R. *v.* TAG see Attorney General's Reference (Nos.91, 119 and 120 of 2002), Re
R. *v.* Taj (Kamran); R. *v.* Gardner (Haroon); R. *v.* Samuel (Joel Nirushan) [2003] EWCA Crim 2633, CA (Crim Div) . . . . *Applied*, 04/3320:
Considered, 05/3613
R. *v.* Tankard (Julie Dawn) see R. *v.* Stockdale (Rae)
R. *v.* Tannahill (Simon David) see R. *v.* Button (Christina Marina) (No.1)
R. *v.* Tapken (Christopher) see Attorney General's Reference (Nos.148, 149, 150, 151, 152, 153, 154 and 155 of 2001), Re
R. *v.* Taroni (Ross Paul) see Attorney General's Reference (No.30 of 2004), Re
R. *v.* Tatam (Andrew) [2004] EWCA Crim 1856; [2005] 1 Cr. App. R. (S.) 57, CA (Crim Div). . . . . *Digested*, 05/**3646**
R. *v.* Taylor (Anthony) see R. *v.* Quayle (Barry)
R. *v.* Taylor (Costs) [2005] 4 Costs L.R. 712, Sup Ct Costs Office
R. *v.* Taylor (Timothy Nicholas) see R. *v.* S
R. *v.* TC see Attorney General's Reference (Nos.37, 38, 44, 54, 51, 53, 35, 40, 43, 45, 41 and 42 of 2003), Re
R. *v.* TE see R. *v.* E
R. *v.* Teale (Joseph Michael) see Attorney General's Reference (No.311 of 2004), Re
R. *v.* Teesdale (Simon Walker) see Attorney General's Reference (No.10 of 2004), Re
R. *v.* Tekin (Gungor) see R. *v.* Jisl (Jan)
R. *v.* Terry (Wayne Michael) see R. *v.* Coates (Victor Henry)
R. *v.* Terry (Wayne Michael); R. *v.* Colman (Robert Luke) [2004] EWCA Crim 3252; [2005] Q.B. 996; [2005] 3 W.L.R. 379; [2005] 2 Cr. App. R. 7; (2005) 102(8) L.S.G. 29; *Times*, December 28, 2004, CA (Crim Div) . . . . *Digested*, 05/**733**
R. *v.* Tetley (John) [2004] EWCA Crim 3228; [2005] 2 Cr. App. R. (S.) 35, CA (Crim Div) . . . . *Digested*, 05/**3722**
R. *v.* TG see Attorney General's Reference (Nos.37, 38, 44, 54, 51, 53, 35, 40, 43, 45, 41 and 42 of 2003), Re
R. *v.* TG (Deceased) see R. *v.* H (Childhood Amnesia)
R. *v.* TH (A Juvenile) see Attorney General's Reference (Nos.59, 60 and 63 of 1998), Re
R. *v.* TH (A Juvenile) see Attorney General's Reference (Nos.41 and 42 of 2001), Re
R. *v.* Thomas (Corey) [2005] EWCA Crim 2023; *Times*, October 20, 2005, CA (Crim Div)
R. *v.* Thomas (Gerald John) see R. *v.* Avis (Tony)
R. *v.* Thomas (Jahmarl) [2004] EWCA Crim 2199; [2005] 1 Cr. App. R. (S.) 96, CA (Crim Div)
R. *v.* Thomas (John Anthony) [2004] EWCA Crim 1173; [2005] 1 Cr. App. R. (S.) 9, CA (Crim Div) . . . . *Digested*, 05/**3526**
R. *v.* Thomas (Kenneth Kince) see Attorney General's Reference (No.141 of 2004), Re
R. *v.* Thomas (Nigel Wynn) see Attorney General's Reference (No.68 of 1999), Re
R. *v.* Thomas (Stephen Francis) [2004] EWCA Crim 3092; [2005] 2 Cr. App. R. (S.) 10; *Times*, November 12, 2004, CA (Crim Div). . . . . *Digested*, 05/**3701**
R. *v.* Thomas (Vernon Walter) see R. *v.* Spence (Clinton Everton)
R. *v.* Thompson (Jaime Ian) see Attorney General's Reference (No.81 of 2004), Re
R. *v.* Thompson (Richard) [2004] EWCA Crim 669; [2004] 2 Cr. App. R. 16; [2005] 1 Cr. App. R. (S.) 1; (2004) 148 S.J.L.B. 417; *Times*, April 16, 2004; *Independent*, March 31, 2004, CA (Crim Div) . . . . *Digested*, 04/**849**
R. *v.* Thornhill (Leigh James) see Attorney General's Reference (No.130 of 2004), Re

R. v. Timmins (Mark) [2005] EWCA Crim 2909; *Times*, November 29, 2005, CA (Crim Div)
R. v. TL (A Juvenile) see Attorney General's Reference (Nos.41 and 42 of 2001), Re
R. v. Tonks (William) [2004] EWCA Crim 1392; (2004) 148 S.J.L.B. 789, CA (Crim Div) . . . . *Considered*, 05/3539
R. v. Torkoniak (Dmytro) [2004] EWCA Crim 1402; [2005] 1 Cr. App. R. (S.) 27, CA (Crim Div)
R. v. Torrington (Richard Edward) see R. v. Avis (Tony)
R. v. Tosun (Ali Yener) see R. v. Aziz (Kazim)
R. v. Toussaint (Mitchell Paris) see R. v. O'Flaherty (Errol Carlton)
R. v. Tovey (David); R. v. Smith (Peter John) [2005] EWCA Crim 530; [2005] 2 Cr. App. R. (S.) 100; [2005] Crim. L.R. 575; *Times*, April 19, 2005, CA (Crim Div) . .   *Digested*, 05/**3742**
R. v. Tower Hamlets LBC Ex p. Tower Hamlets Combined Traders Association [1994] C.O.D. 325, QBD. . . . .   *Digested*, 95/**89**:
                                                          Applied, 05/2805
R. v. Turner (Bryan James) (1975) 61 Cr. App. R. 67; [1975] Crim. L.R. 525; [1975] Crim. L.R. 451; (1975) 119 S.J. 422; (1975) 119 S.J. 575, CA (Crim Div). . . . . . .   *Digested*, 75/**559**:
                            Applied, 83/649, 83/691, 84/584, 86/769, 04/854, 05/3733:
            Considered, 76/567, 79/550, 83/1700, 83/2647, 84/790, 84/2254, 85/2258,
                 86/624, 86/747, 86/753, 87/1001, 87/1044, 90/1408, 92/850, 92/1394,
               93/1277, 95/1338, 96/1977, 98/1213, 98/1374, 98/1375, 00/1340,
            00/1352, 05/3730: *Explained*, 77/678, 78/476: *Followed*, 89/921, 90/1406,
                                                91/1208, 97/1702
R. v. Turner (Frank Richard) (No.1) [1970] 2 Q.B. 321; [1970] 2 W.L.R. 1093; [1970] 2 All E.R. 281; (1970) 54 Cr. App. R. 352; 114 S.J. 337, CA (Crim Div)   *Digested*, 70/**479**:
               Applied, 75/717, 77/652, 78/573, 78/595.50, 78/621, 78/625, 79/527,
          80/547, 90/1229, 91/794, 93/754, 99/3800: *Considered*, 84/655, 85/670,
               90/1230, 91/1041, 05/883: *Explained*, 76/541: *Followed*, 76/615, 96/1678:
                                          Overruled in part, 05/893
R. v. Turner (Terence Stuart) [1975] Q.B. 834; [1975] 2 W.L.R. 56; [1975] 1 All E.R. 70; (1974) 60 Cr. App. R. 80; [1975] Crim. L.R. 98; 118 S.J. 848; *Times*, October 23, 1974, CA (Crim Div). . . . .   *Digested*, 75/**562**:
              Applied, 85/645, 90/826, 91/667, 95/932, 96/1373, 05/742:
          Approved, 02/5426: *Considered*, 90/801, 91/666, 91/687, 93/657, 93/723,
                            94/898, 94/899, 94/914, 94/3835, 00/906
R. v. TW [2004] EWCA Crim 3103; [2005] Crim. L.R. 965, CA (Crim Div)
R. v. Twisse (Michael James) [2001] 2 Cr. App. R. (S.) 9; [2001] Crim. L.R. 151; *Times*, November 30, 2000, CA (Crim Div) . . . .   *Digested*, 01/**1282**:
         Applied, 02/3922, 02/3932: *Considered*, 01/1279, 03/3695, 04/3412,
           04/3450, 04/3452, 05/3700, 05/3707, 05/3748: *Distinguished*, 04/3454:
                                             Followed, 01/1490
R. v. Twumasi (Daniel) [2005] EWCA Crim 793; [2005] 2 Cr. App. R. (S.) 107, CA (Crim Div)
R. v. Tzambazles (Christos) [1997] 1 Cr. App. R. (S.) 87, CA (Crim Div) . . . .   *Digested*, 97/**1158**:
                                       Considered, 99/1265, 05/3666
R. v. Uddin (Alim) see Attorney General's Reference (No.9 of 2004), Re
R. v. Ukoh (Chibo) [2004] EWCA Crim 3270; [2005] 2 Cr. App. R. (S.) 38; [2005] Crim. L.R. 314; *Times*, December 28, 2004, CA (Crim Div) . . . .   *Digested*, 05/**3589**
R. v. Underwood (Anthony) [2004] EWCA Crim 1816; [2005] 1 Cr. App. R. (S.) 54, CA (Crim Div) . . . .   *Digested*, 05/**3581**
R. v. Underwood (Kevin John); R. v. Arobieke (Akinwale); R. v. Khan (Mohammed Iftiyaz); R. v. Connors (James) [2004] EWCA Crim 2256; [2005] 1 Cr. App. R. 13; [2005] 1 Cr. App. R. (S.) 90; (2004) 148 S.J.L.B. 974; *Times*, September 1, 2004, CA (Crim Div) . . . .   *Considered*, 05/3699
R. v. Unlu (Ali) [2002] EWCA Crim 2220; [2003] 1 Cr. App. R. (S.) 101, CA (Crim Div) . . . .   *Considered*, 05/3597
R. v. V see R. v. KV
R. v. Van Dongen (Anthony Gerrard) (Appeal against Conviction); R. v. Van Dongen (Mitchell) (Appeal against Conviction) [2005] EWCA Crim 1728; [2005] 2 Cr. App. R. 38; [2005] Crim. L.R. 971, CA (Crim Div). . . . .   *Digested*, 05/**900**
R. v. Van Dongen (Mitchell) (Appeal against Conviction) see R. v. Van Dongen (Anthony Gerrard) (Appeal against Conviction)
R. v. Van Nguyen (Dong) see R. v. Highton (Edward Paul)
R. v. Van Tattenhove (Frans Willem); R. v. Doubtfire (Robert Henry) (No.1) [1996] 1 Cr. App. R. 408; [1996] 2 Cr. App. R. (S.) 91, CA (Crim Div) . . . .   *Considered*, 00/1229,
                                               04/3341: *Followed*, 05/3589
R. v. Verdi (Charan) [2004] EWCA Crim 1485; [2005] 1 Cr. App. R. (S.) 43; (2004) 148 S.J.L.B. 789, CA (Crim Div). . . . .   *Digested*, 05/**3767**
R. v. Versluis (Pieter Willem) [2004] EWCA Crim 3168; [2005] 2 Cr. App. R. (S.) 26; [2005] Crim. L.R. 253, CA (Crim Div) . . . .   *Digested*, 05/**3594**
R. v. Vickers (Royston Gary) see R. v. Early (John)
R. v. Villiers (Costs) [2005] 4 Costs L.R. 732, Sup Ct Costs Office
R. v. Vittles (Anthony Malcolm) [2004] EWCA Crim 1089; [2005] 1 Cr. App. R. (S.) 8, CA (Crim Div) . . . .   *Digested*, 05/**3529**

R. v. Vye (John Arthur); R. v. Wise (Frederick James); R. v. Stephenson (Malcolm) [1993] 1 W.L.R. 471; [1993] 3 All E.R. 241; (1993) 97 Cr. App. R. 134; (1993) 157 J.P. 953; (1993) 12 Tr. L.R. 62; (1993) 157 J.P.N. 380; (1993) 143 N.L.J. 400; *Times*, February 22, 1993, CA (Crim Div) . . . . *Digested,* 93/**769**:
Applied, 93/772, 95/1091, 96/1635, 05/937: *Considered,* 94/818, 94/821, 95/1042, 95/1043, 95/1044, 96/1632, 96/1929
R. v. W see Attorney General's Reference (No.5 of 2002), Re
R. v. W see Attorney General's Reference (Nos.39, 40 and 41 of 2005)
R. v. W (Michael Paul) (A Juvenile) see Attorney General's Reference (No.54 of 1998), Re
R. v. Wacker (Perry) [2002] EWCA Crim 1944; [2003] Q.B. 1207; [2003] 2 W.L.R. 374; [2003] 4 All E.R. 295; [2003] 1 Cr. App. R. 22; [2003] 1 Cr. App. R. (S.) 92; [2003] Crim. L.R. 108; [2002] Crim. L.R. 839; (2002) 99(39) L.S.G. 37; *Times*, September 5, 2002, CA (Crim Div) . . . . *Digested,* 02/**802**:
Approved, 05/805: *Distinguished,* 05/3658
R. v. Wade (Scott Patrick) [2005] EWCA Crim 183; [2005] 2 Cr. App. R. (S.) 69, CA (Crim Div) . . . . *Digested,* 05/**3751**
R. v. Wales (Reay James) see R. v. Quayle (Barry)
R. v. Walker (John Owen) [2005] EWCA Crim 82; [2005] 2 Cr. App. R. (S.) 55, CA (Crim Div) . . . . *Digested,* 05/**3678**
R. v. Walsall Justices Ex p. W [1990] 1 Q.B. 253; [1989] 3 W.L.R. 1311; [1989] 3 All E.R. 460; (1990) 90 Cr. App. R. 186; (1989) 153 J.P. 624; (1989) 1 Admin. L.R. 89; (1989) 86(46) L.S.G. 39; (1989) 139 N.L.J. 682; (1990) 134 S.J. 114, QBD . . . . *Digested,* 90/**774**:
Applied, 05/2674
R. v. Walsh (Martin Peter Andrew) see Attorney General's Reference (Nos.3, 4, 8, 9, 10, 11, 14 and 16 of 1990), Re
R. v. Walters (Alexander Farrar) [2002] EWCA Crim 1114, CA (Crim Div) . . . . *Considered,* 05/3541
R. v. Walters (Daniel) [2004] EWCA Crim 2587; [2005] 1 Cr. App. R. (S.) 100, CA (Crim Div) . . . . *Digested,* 05/**3773**
R. v. Wang (Bei Bei) [2005] EWCA Crim 293; [2005] 2 Cr. App. R. (S.) 79, CA (Crim Div) . . . . *Digested,* 05/**3768**
R. v. Wang (Cheong) [2005] UKHL 9; [2005] 1 W.L.R. 661; [2005] 1 All E.R. 782; [2005] 2 Cr. App. R. 8; (2005) 169 J.P. 224; [2005] Crim. L.R. 645; (2005) 169 J.P.N. 339; (2005) 102(10) L.S.G. 29; *Times*, February 11, 2005; *Independent*, February 15, 2005, HL; reversing [2003] EWCA Crim 3228; (2004) 168 J.P. 224; (2004) 168 J.P.N. 294, CA (Crim Div) . . . . *Digested,* 05/**902**
R. v. Ward (Alan) see R. v. Baker (Tony) (No.1)
R. v. Ward (Mark Richard) see Attorney General's Reference (No.4 of 1998), Re
R. v. Ward-Allen (Costs) [2005] 4 Costs L.R. 745, Sup Ct Costs Office
R. v. Warren (Ashley Leon) see Attorney General's Reference (Nos.150 and 151 of 2002), Re
R. v. Warsame (Abdiaziz) [2004] EWCA Crim 2770; [2005] 1 Cr. App. R. (S.) 122; [2005] Crim. L.R. 159, CA (Crim Div)
R. v. Warwick Crown Court Ex p. Smalley (No.1) see Smalley, Re
R. v. Watson (Robert James) see R. v. Graham (Joseph)
R. v. Webb (Ian David) see Attorney General's Reference (No.52 of 2003), Re
R. v. Webb (Michael John) see Attorney General's Reference (No.34 of 2004), Re
R. v. Weekes (Alfred Washington) see Attorney General's Reference (No.12 of 2004), Re
R. v. Weeks (David Alexander) [1999] 2 Cr. App. R. (S.) 16, CA (Crim Div) . . . . *Digested,* 99/**1148**:
Considered, 05/3707
R. v. Weir (Antony Albert); R. v. Somanathan (Ramanathan); R. v. Yaxley-Lennon (Stephen); R. v. Manister (Simon); R. v. Hong Qiang He; R. v. De Qun He [2005] EWCA Crim 2866; *Times*, November 18, 2005, CA (Crim Div)
R. v. Wenman (Frank Samuel) [2004] EWCA Crim 2995; [2005] 2 Cr. App. R. (S.) 3, CA (Crim Div) . . . . *Digested,* 05/**3556**
R. v. Wernet (Robert Stewart) see Attorney General's Reference (Nos.14 and 24 of 1993), Re
R. v. West (Melvin) see R. v. Allsopp (Michael Nevin)
R. v. Westminster City Council Ex p. Chorion Plc see R. (on the application of Chorion Plc) v. Westminster City Council (No.1)
R. v. Westminster City Council Ex p. Ermakov [1996] 2 All E.R. 302; [1996] 2 F.C.R. 208; (1996) 28 H.L.R. 819; (1996) 8 Admin. L.R. 389; [1996] C.O.D. 391; (1996) 160 J.P. Rep. 814; (1996) 140 S.J.L.B. 23; *Times*, November 20, 1995, CA (Civ Div); reversing (1995) 27 H.L.R. 168; [1995] C.O.D. 123, QBD . . . . *Digested,* 95/**2568**:
Applied, 97/3923, 01/3425, 02/2039, 03/4463, 05/1138, 05/1991, 05/3281, 05/3300, 05/3459: *Considered,* 97/2688, 01/95: *Distinguished,* 97/2659, 99/2167: *Followed,* 96/5448, 04/1901
R. v. Whatley (Albert John) see R. v. Graham (Cheryl Angela)
R. v. Wheaton (David George) [2004] EWCA Crim 2270; [2005] 1 Cr. App. R. (S.) 82; [2005] Crim. L.R. 68, CA (Crim Div) . . . . *Digested,* 05/**3717**
R. v. Wheeler (Michael Anthony) see Attorney General's Reference (No.42 of 2003), Re

R. v. Whellams (Kyrt Anthony) see Attorney General's Reference (Nos.150 and 151 of 2002), Re

R. v. Whenman (Andrew Henry) [2001] EWCA Crim 328; [2001] 2 Cr. App. R. (S.) 87, CA (Crim Div) .... *Digested*, 01/**1281**: *Considered*, 03/3692, 05/3706

R. v. White (Edward) (1992) 13 Cr. App. R. (S.) 108, CA (Crim Div) .... *Digested*, 92/**1152**: *Applied*, 04/3286: *Considered*, 98/1306, 00/1267, 00/1369, 03/3808: *Not followed*, 05/3675

R. v. White (Shane) see Attorney General's Reference (No.138 of 2004), Re

R. v. Whitehead (Patricia Anne) [1996] 1 Cr. App. R. (S.) 111; [1995] Crim. L.R. 755, CA (Crim Div) .... *Digested*, 96/**1709**: *Considered*, 98/1393, 05/3596

R. v. Whiteman (Mark); R. v. Brown (Billy); R. v. Spokes (Paul George); R. v. Draper (James Thomas); R. v. Bright (Barry James) [2004] EWCA Crim 569; [2004] 2 Cr. App. R. (S.) 59, CA (Crim Div) .... *Digested*, 05/**3711**

R. v. Whiteway (Jules Devere) see Attorney General's Reference (Nos.99, 100, 101 and 102 of 2004), Re

R. v. Whyte (Lincoln) see Attorney General's Reference (No.34 of 2005), Re

R. v. Wild (James Matthew) see R. v. Docking (Jason)

R. v. Wiles (Alan Ralph) [2004] EWCA Crim 836; [2004] 2 Cr. App. R. (S.) 88; [2004] Crim. L.R. 596, CA (Crim Div) .... *Digested*, 05/**3640**

R. v. Williams (Anthony Michael) see R. v. Corran (Ben)

R. v. Williams (Mark) [1997] 2 Cr. App. R. (S.) 221, CA (Crim Div) .... *Digested*, 97/**1641**: *Considered*, 99/1289, 05/3689

R. v. Williams (Theo Yestin) [2005] EWCA Crim 1796; (2005) 169 J.P. 588; [2005] Crim. L.R. 872; *Times*, July 15, 2005, CA (Crim Div) .... *Digested*, 05/**3585**

R. v. Williamson (Kenneth Joseph) see R. v. Abdroikov (Nurlon)

R. v. Willoughby (Keith Calverley) [2004] EWCA Crim 3365; [2005] 1 W.L.R. 1880; [2005] 1 Cr. App. R. 29; [2005] Crim. L.R. 389; (2005) 102(5) L.S.G. 26; *Times*, December 21, 2004, CA (Crim Div) .... *Digested*, 05/**805**

R. v. Wilson (Daniel) see Attorney General's Reference (No.38 of 2005), Re

R. v. Wilson (Ian); R. v. Mainprize (Craig) [2004] EWCA Crim 2086; [2005] 1 Cr. App. R. (S.) 64, CA (Crim Div) .... *Digested*, 05/**3631**

R. v. Wilson (Joseph) (1957) 41 Cr. App. R. 226, CCA .... *Digested*, 58/**701**: *Applied*, 72/620, 72/1936: *Considered*, 05/832: *Doubted*, 76/480: *Followed*, 65/923, 66/2903

R. v. Wilson (Mark) see Attorney General's Reference (Nos.148, 149, 150, 151, 152, 153, 154 and 155 of 2001), Re

R. v. Wilson (Rebecca) see Attorney General's Reference (No.16 of 2005), Re

R. v. Winslow (Terence Edward); *sub nom* R. v. Winslow (Terrence Edward) [2004] EWCA Crim 3417; [2005] 2 Cr. App. R. (S.) 51, CA (Crim Div) .... *Digested*, 05/**3649**

R. v. Winters (Keith) see R. v. Lang (Stephen Howard)

R. v. Wise (Frederick James) see R. v. Vye (John Arthur)

R. v. Wisniewski (Mariuzs); *sub nom* R. v. Wisniewski (Mariusz) [2004] EWCA Crim 3361; [2005] 2 Cr. App. R. (S.) 39; [2005] Crim. L.R. 403; *Times*, December 20, 2004, CA (Crim Div) .... *Digested*, 05/**3741**

R. v. Wolf (Karl Christian) see R. v. Allsopp (Michael Nevin)

R. v. Wood (Gary Dominic) see R. v. Rehman (Zakir)

R. v. Wooden (James Ray) see R. v. Palmer (Justin Anthony)

R. v. Woods (David Reginald); R. v. Collins (Justin) [2005] EWCA Crim 2065; [2005] Crim. L.R. 982, CA (Crim Div)

R. v. Woodward (Terence) [1995] 1 W.L.R. 375; [1995] 3 All E.R. 79; [1995] 2 Cr. App. R. 388; (1995) 159 J.P. 349; [1995] R.T.R. 130; [1995] Crim. L.R. 487; (1995) 139 S.J.L.B. 18; *Times*, December 7, 1994, CA (Crim Div) .... *Digested*, 96/**1356**: *Considered*, 96/1451: *Distinguished*, 05/727

R. v. Worth (Duncan) see Attorney General's Reference (No.139 of 2004), Re

R. v. Wrench (Peter) [1996] 1 Cr. App. R. 340; [1996] 1 Cr. App. R. (S.) 145; [1995] Crim. L.R. 265, CA (Crim Div) .... *Digested*, 96/**1566**: *Applied*, 05/3559: *Disapproved*, 01/1125: *Distinguished*, 97/1428

R. v. Wright (Brian Antony) see R. v. Soares (Ronald)

R. v. Wright (John) see R. v. Skitt (Harry)

R. v. Wright (John Steven) (1995) 16 Cr. App. R. (S.) 877, CA (Crim Div) .... *Considered*, 05/3664

R. v. Wright (Robert) see R. v. Lang (Stephen Howard)

R. v. X (Childhood Amnesia) see R. v. H (Childhood Amnesia)

R. v. X (Prior Acquittal) see R. v. Z (Prior Acquittal)

R. v. XY, *Times*, July 25, 2005, CA (Crim Div)

R. v. Y (Sexual Offence: Complainant's Sexual History) see R. v. A (Complainant's Sexual History)

R. v. Yates (Paul Joseph) [2001] 1 Cr. App. R. (S.) 124, CA (Crim Div) .... *Digested*, 01/**1416**: *Considered*, 05/3661

R. v. Yaxley-Lennon (Stephen) see R. v. Weir (Antony Albert)

R. v. Yeboah (Mustafa) see R. v. Adu (Peter)

R. v. Yemm (Andrew Neil) see Attorney General's Reference (No. 112 of 2004), Re

R. *v.* Yoonus (Naushad) [2004] EWCA Crim 1734; [2005] 1 Cr. App. R. (S.) 46, CA
(Crim Div). . . . . *Digested,* 05/**3673**
R. *v.* Yorganci (Metin) see R. *v.* Aziz (Kazim)
R. *v.* Young (Robert) [2004] EWCA Crim 1183; [2005] 1 Cr. App. R. (S.) 11, CA (Crim
Div) . . . . *Digested,* 05/**3745**
R. *v.* Z see R. *v.* Hasan (Aytach)
R. *v.* Z; *sub nom* Z (Attorney General for Northern Ireland's Reference), Re [2005]
UKHL 35; [2005] 2 A.C. 645; [2005] 2 W.L.R. 1286; [2005] 3 All E.R. 95;
[2005] N.I. 468; [2005] Crim. L.R. 985; *Times,* May 20, 2005; *Independent,*
May 25, 2005, HL (NI); affirming [2005] N.I. 106, CA (NI) . . . . *Digested,* 05/**823**
R. *v.* Z (Prior Acquittal); *sub nom* R. *v.* X (Prior Acquittal) [2000] 2 A.C. 483; [2000]
3 W.L.R. 117; [2000] 3 All E.R. 385; [2000] 2 Cr. App. R. 281; (2000) 164 J.P.
533; (2000) 164 J.P.N. 824; (2000) 97(28) L.S.G. 31; (2000) 150 N.L.J. 984;
Times, June 23, 2000; *Independent,* June 27, 2000, HL; reversing (2000) 164
J.P. 240; [2000] Crim. L.R. 293; (2000) 164 J.P.N. 206; (2000) 97(1) L.S.G.
22; (2000) 144 S.J.L.B. 26; *Times,* December 14, 1999 ; *Independent,* December
8, 1999, CA (Crim Div) . . . . *Digested,* 00/**924**:
                                                 Applied, 03/278, 05/733
R. *v.* Zaheer (Mohammed) see R. *v.* Din (Ameen)
R. Matthews (David George) see Attorney General's Reference (Nos.11 and 12 of 2005), Re
R. Roberts (Michael John) see Attorney General's Reference (No.134 of 2004), Re
R. (on the application of A) *v.* DPP [2004] EWHC 2454; [2005] A.C.D. 61, QBD
(Admin)
R. (on the application of A) *v.* East Sussex CC [2005] EWHC 585; (2005) 8 C.C.L.
Rep. 228, QBD (Admin) . . . . *Digested,* 05/**348**
R. (on the application of A) *v.* HM Coroner for Inner South London; *sub nom* A *v.* Inner
South London Coroner; Bennett *v.* A [2004] EWCA Civ 1439; [2005]
U.K.H.R.R. 44; (2004) 148 S.J.L.B. 1315; *Times,* November 11, 2004, CA (Civ
Div); affirming [2004] EWHC 1592; (2004) 168 J.P. 511; [2005] A.C.D. 3;
(2004) 101(30) L.S.G. 29; *Times,* July 12, 2004, QBD (Admin). . . . . *Digested,* 05/**33**
R. (on the application of A) *v.* Lambeth LBC see R. (on the application of G) *v.* Barnet
LBC
R. (on the application of A) *v.* Lord Saville of Newdigate (Bloody Sunday Inquiry); *sub
nom* R. (on the application of Widgery Soldiers) *v.* Lord Saville of Newdigate;
Lord Saville of Newdigate *v.* Widgery Soldiers [2001] EWCA Civ 2048; [2002] 1
W.L.R. 1249; [2002] A.C.D. 22; *Times,* December 21, 2001; *Independent,*
January 11, 2002; *Daily Telegraph,* January 11, 2002, CA (Civ Div); affirming
[2001] EWHC Admin 888; (2001) 98(48) L.S.G. 29; (2001) 145 S.J.L.B. 262;
Times, November 21, 2001; *Daily Telegraph,* November 20, 2001, DC . . . . *Digested,* 02/**38**:
                                          Applied, 03/2238, 04/35, 05/33
R. (on the application of A (A Child)) *v.* Leeds Magistrates Court [2004] EWHC 554;
Times, March 31, 2004, QBD (Admin) . . . . *Digested,* 04/**793**:
                                          Considered, 05/3357
R. (on the application of Aaalamini) *v.* Thames Magistrates Court [2005] EWHC 1617;
[2005] R.V.R. 373, QBD (Admin)
R. (on the application of Abdi) *v.* Secretary of State for the Home Department see R. (on
the application of Nadarajah) *v.* Secretary of State for the Home Department
R. (on the application of Adam) *v.* Secretary of State for the Home Department see R.
(on the application of Limbuela) *v.* Secretary of State for the Home Department
R. (on the application of Aerlink Leisure Ltd (In Liquidation)) *v.* First Secretary of State see
Aerlink Leisure Ltd (In Liquidation) *v.* First Secretary of State
R. (on the application of Afzal) *v.* Election Court [2005] EWCA Civ 647; [2005]
B.L.G.R. 823; *Times,* June 7, 2005; *Independent,* June 10, 2005, CA (Civ Div) . . *Digested,* 05/**1169**
R. (on the application of Akyuz) *v.* Secretary of State for the Home Department see R.
(on the application of Ozturk) *v.* Secretary of State for the Home Department
R. (on the application of AL) *v.* Secretary of State for the Home Department see R. (on
the application of L) *v.* Secretary of State for the Home Department
R. (on the application of Al-Hasan) *v.* Secretary of State for the Home Department see
R. (on the application of Carroll) *v.* Secretary of State for the Home Department
R. (on the application of Al-Jedda) *v.* Secretary of State for Defence C1/2005/2251, CA
(Civ Div); affirming [2005] EWHC 1809; [2005] H.R.L.R. 39; *Times,*
September 12, 2005, QBD (Admin) . . . . *Digested,* 05/**2106**
R. (on the application of Al-Nashed) *v.* Newham LBC see R. (on the application of Bibi)
v. Newham LBC (No.1)
R. (on the application of Al-Skeini) *v.* Secretary of State for Defence [2005] EWCA Civ
1609, CA (Civ Div); affirming [2004] EWHC 2911; [2005] 2 W.L.R. 1401;
[2005] H.R.L.R. 3; [2005] U.K.H.R.R. 427; [2005] A.C.D. 51; (2005) 102(3)
L.S.G. 30; (2005) 155 N.L.J. 58; *Times,* December 20, 2004, QBD (Admin) . . . *Digested,* 05/**2129**
R. (on the application of Alconbury Developments Ltd) *v.* Secretary of State for the
Environment, Transport and the Regions see R. (on the application of Holding &
Barnes Plc) *v.* Secretary of State for the Environment, Transport and the
Regions

R. (on the application of Alliance for Natural Health) v. Secretary of State for Health (C154/04); R. (on the application of National Association of Health Stores) v. Secretary of State for Health (C155/04) [2005] 2 C.M.L.R. 61; *Times*, July 15, 2005, ECJ

R. (on the application of Alloway) v. Bromley LBC [2004] EWHC 2108; (2005) 8 C.C.L. Rep. 61, QBD (Admin) . . . . *Digested*, 05/**3953**

R. (on the application of AN) v. Mental Health Review Tribunal (Northern Region) see R. (on the application of N) v. Mental Health Review Tribunal (Northern Region)

R. (on the application of Anderson) v. Customs and Excise Commissioners see Hughes v. Customs and Excise Commissioners

R. (on the application of Anderson) v. HM Coroner for Inner North Greater London [2004] EWHC 2729; [2005] A.C.D. 68, QBD (Admin)

R. (on the application of Anton) v. Secretary of State for the Home Department [2004] EWHC 2730; [2005] 2 F.L.R. 818; [2005] Fam. Law 442, QBD (Admin)

R. (on the application of Anufrijeva) v. Southwark LBC see Anufrijeva v. Southwark LBC

R. (on the application of Arthur) v. RSPCA [2005] EWHC 2616; (2005) 169 J.P. 676; (2005) 169 J.P.N. 1001, QBD (Admin)

R. (on the application of Arun DC) v. First Secretary of State see Arun DC v. First Secretary of State

R. (on the application of Ashbrook) v. Secretary of State for the Environment, Food and Rural Affairs [2004] EWHC 2387; [2005] 1 W.L.R. 1764; [2005] 1 All E.R. 166; [2005] 2 P. & C.R. 7; [2004] 4 P.L.R. 107; [2005] 1 E.G.L.R. 99; *Times*, November 3, 2004, QBD (Admin) . . . . *Digested*, 05/**1356**

R. (on the application of Ashworth Hospital Authority) v. Mental Health Review Tribunal for West Midlands and North West Region see R. (on the application of H) v. Ashworth Hospital Authority

R. (on the application of Awan) v. Immigration Appeal Tribunal [2004] EWCA Civ 922; [2005] C.P. Rep. 1; [2005] A.C.D. 18; *Times*, June 24, 2004, CA (Civ Div) . . . . . *Digested*, 04/**2046**

R. (on the application of B) v. Ashworth Hospital Authority [2005] UKHL 20; [2005] 2 A.C. 278; [2005] 2 W.L.R. 695; [2005] 2 All E.R. 289; (2005) 8 C.C.L. Rep. 287; (2005) 83 B.M.L.R. 160; (2005) 155 N.L.J. 546; (2005) 149 S.J.L.B. 359; *Times*, March 18, 2005, HL; reversing [2003] EWCA Civ 547; [2003] 1 W.L.R. 1886; [2003] 4 All E.R. 319; (2003) 74 B.M.L.R. 58; (2003) 100(25) L.S.G. 47; (2003) 147 S.J.L.B. 504; *Times*, April 24, 2003, CA (Civ Div); reversing [2002] EWHC 1442, QBD (Admin) . . . . *Digested*, 05/**2820**:
Distinguished, 05/2817: *Followed*, 05/2830

R. (on the application of B) v. Asylum Support Adjudicator [2005] EWHC 2017; (2005) 102(38) L.S.G. 28; *Times*, October 5, 2005, QBD (Admin)

R. (on the application of B) v. Camden LBC [2005] EWHC 1366; (2005) 8 C.C.L. Rep. 422; (2005) 85 B.M.L.R. 28, QBD (Admin) . . . . *Digested*, 05/**2824**

R. (on the application of B) v. Haddock [2005] EWHC 921; (2005) 85 B.M.L.R. 57, QBD (Admin) . . . . *Digested*, 05/**2830**

R. (on the application of B) v. Hertfordshire CC [2004] EWHC 2324; [2005] E.L.R. 17, QBD (Admin) . . . . *Digested*, 05/**1069**

R. (on the application of B) v. Immigration Appeal Tribunal see R. (on the application of Hoxha) v. Special Adjudicator

R. (on the application of B) v. Medway Council; *sub nom* R. (on the application of BG) v. Medway Council [2005] EWHC 1932; [2005] 3 F.C.R. 199; (2005) 8 C.C.L. Rep. 448, QBD (Admin) . . . . *Digested*, 05/**3945**

R. (on the application of B) v. Merton LBC [2003] EWHC 1689; [2003] 4 All E.R. 280; [2003] 2 F.L.R. 888; [2005] 3 F.C.R. 69; (2003) 6 C.C.L. Rep. 457; [2003] Fam. Law 813; *Times*, July 18, 2003, QBD (Admin) . . . . *Digested*, 03/**2895**:
Followed, 05/2146

R. (on the application of B) v. S (Responsible Medical Officer, Broadmoor Hospital) C1/ 2005/2080, CA (Civ Div); affirming [2005] EWHC 1936; [2005] H.R.L.R. 40; (2005) 102(37) L.S.G. 32, QBD (Admin). . . . . *Digested*, 05/**2823**

R. (on the application of B) v. Secretary of State for Foreign and Commonwealth Affairs [2004] EWCA Civ 1344; [2005] Q.B. 643; [2005] 2 W.L.R. 618; [2004] H.R.L.R. 41; [2005] Imm. A.R. 32; [2005] I.N.L.R. 36; [2005] A.C.D. 72; (2004) 101(42) L.S.G. 30; (2004) 148 S.J.L.B. 1247; *Times*, October 25, 2004; *Independent*, November 10, 2004, CA (Civ Div) . . . . *Digested*, 04/**2008**

R. (on the application of B) v. Secretary of State for the Home Department see R. (on the application of Q) v. Secretary of State for the Home Department

R. (on the application of B) v. SS [2005] EWHC 86; [2005] A.C.D. 55; [2005] A.C.D. 91, QBD (Admin)

R. (on the application of Badu) v. Lambeth LBC see R. (on the application of Morris) v. Westminster City Council (No.3)

R. (on the application of Bagdanavicius) v. Secretary of State for the Home Department [2005] UKHL 38; [2005] 2 A.C. 668; [2005] 2 W.L.R. 1359; [2005] 4 All E.R. 263; [2005] H.R.L.R. 24; [2005] U.K.H.R.R. 907; [2005] Imm. A.R. 430; [2005] I.N.L.R. 422; *Times*, May 30, 2005; *Independent*, June 15, 2005, HL; affirming [2003] EWCA Civ 1605; [2004] 1 W.L.R. 1207; [2004] Imm. A.R. 36; [2004] I.N.L.R. 163; [2004] A.C.D. 6; (2004) 101(2) L.S.G. 29; *Times*, November 21, 2003; *Independent*, November 21, 2003, CA (Civ Div); affirming [2003] EWHC 854, QBD (Admin) . . . .   *Digested*, 05/**2167**

R. (on the application of Bancoult) v. Secretary of State for Foreign and Commonwealth Affairs see R. (on the application of Bancoult) v. Secretary of State for the Foreign and Commonwealth Office

R. (on the application of Bancoult) v. Secretary of State for the Foreign and Commonwealth Office; *sub nom* R. v. Secretary of State for the Foreign and Commonwealth Office Ex p. Bancoult; R. (on the application of Bancoult) v. Secretary of State for Foreign and Commonwealth Affairs [2001] Q.B. 1067; [2001] 2 W.L.R. 1219; [2001] A.C.D. 18; (2000) 97(47) L.S.G. 39; *Times*, November 10, 2000, QBD (Admin) . . . .   *Digested*, 00/**96**: *Considered*, 05/4197

R. (on the application of Bancroft) v. Secretary of State for Culture, Media and Sport [2004] EWHC 1822; [2005] 2 P. & C.R. 10; [2005] J.P.L. 477, QBD (Admin) . .   *Digested*, 05/**3267**

R. (on the application of Barkoci) v. Secretary of State for the Home Department (C257/99); *sub nom* R. v. Secretary of State for the Home Department Ex p. Barkoci (C257/99) [2001] All E.R. (EC) 903; [2001] E.C.R. I-6557; [2001] 3 C.M.L.R. 48; [2002] I.N.L.R. 152; *Times*, November 13, 2001, ECJ . . . .   *Digested*, 02/**1574**: *Considered*, 05/1453

R. (on the application of Barrington) v. Preston Crown Court [2001] EWHC Admin 599, QBD (Admin) . . . .   *Considered*, 05/871

R. (on the application of Basildon DC) v. First Secretary of State [2004] EWHC 2759; [2005] J.P.L. 942, QBD (Admin) . . . .   *Digested*, 05/**3264**

R. (on the application of Begum (Shabina)) v. Denbigh High School Governors; *sub nom* R. (on the application of SB) v. Denbigh High School Governors; TNS, HL; reversing [2005] EWCA Civ 199; [2005] 1 W.L.R. 3372; [2005] 2 All E.R. 396; [2005] 1 F.C.R. 530; [2005] H.R.L.R. 16; [2005] U.K.H.R.R. 681; 19 B.H.R.C. 126; [2005] E.L.R. 198; (2005) 102(17) L.S.G. 31; (2005) 155 N.L.J. 383; (2005) 149 S.J.L.B. 300; *Times*, March 4, 2005; *Independent*, March 8, 2005, CA (Civ Div); reversing [2004] EWHC 1389; [2004] E.L.R. 374; [2004] A.C.D. 66; (2004) 101(27) L.S.G. 29; *Times*, June 18, 2004, QBD (Admin) . . . .   *Digested*, 05/**1131**

R. (on the application of Bevan) v. General Medical Council [2005] EWHC 174; [2005] Lloyd's Rep. Med. 321, QBD (Admin) . . . .   *Digested*, 05/**1807**

R. (on the application of BG) v. Medway Council see R. (on the application of B) v. Medway Council

R. (on the application of Bibi) v. Camden LBC [2004] EWHC 2527; [2005] 1 F.L.R. 413; [2005] H.L.R. 18; [2005] A.C.D. 53; *Times*, October 25, 2004, QBD (Admin) . .   *Digested*, 05/**2007**

R. (on the application of Bibi) v. Immigration Appeal Tribunal; *sub nom* Bibi v. Immigration Appeal Tribunal [2005] EWHC 386; [2005] 1 W.L.R. 3214; [2005] Imm. A.R. 221, QBD (Admin) . . . .   *Digested*, 05/**2200**

R. (on the application of Bibi) v. Newham LBC (No.1); *sub nom* R. v. Newham LBC Ex p. Bibi; R. v. Newham LBC Ex p. Al-Nashed; R. (on the application of Al-Nashed) v. Newham LBC [2001] EWCA Civ 607; [2002] 1 W.L.R. 237; (2001) 33 H.L.R. 84; (2001) 98(23) L.S.G. 38; [2001] N.P.C. 83; *Times*, May 10, 2001, CA (Civ Div); reversing in part CO/1748/0159/99, QBD . . . .   *Digested*, 01/**3426**: *Applied*, 02/1204, 03/1126, 03/2061, 03/3601: *Considered*, 05/2154: *Followed*, 02/1701

R. (on the application of Bidar) v. Ealing LBC (C209/03) [2005] Q.B. 812; [2005] 2 W.L.R. 1078; [2005] All E.R. (EC) 687; [2005] E.C.R. I-2119; [2005] 2 C.M.L.R. 3; [2005] C.E.C. 607; [2005] E.L.R. 404; *Times*, March 29, 2005, ECJ . . . .   *Digested*, 05/**3922**

R. (on the application of Bleta) v. Secretary of State for the Home Department [2004] EWHC 2034; [2005] 1 W.L.R. 3194; [2005] 1 All E.R. 810, QBD (Admin) . . . . .   *Digested*, 05/**1490**

R. (on the application of Blewett) v. Derbyshire CC; *sub nom* Blewitt v. Derbyshire Waste Ltd; Derbyshire Waste Ltd v. Blewett [2004] EWCA Civ 1508; [2005] Env. L.R. 15; [2005] 1 P.L.R. 54; [2005] J.P.L. 620; (2004) 148 S.J.L.B. 1369; [2004] N.P.C. 171; *Times*, November 12, 2004; *Independent*, November 19, 2004, CA (Civ Div); affirming [2003] EWHC 2775; [2004] Env. L.R. 29; [2004] J.P.L. 751, QBD (Admin) . . . .   *Digested*, 05/**1402**: *Followed*, 05/3298

R. (on the application of Bonner) v. DPP see Bonner v. DPP

R. (on the application of Borak) v. Secretary of State for the Home Department [2005] EWCA Civ 110; [2004] Imm. A.R. 768; [2005] I.N.L.R. 318; (2005) 149 S.J.L.B. 117, CA (Civ Div); affirming [2004] EWHC 1861; [2004] 1 W.L.R. 3129; [2005] A.C.D. 29; *Times*, September 15, 2004, QBD (Admin) . . . .   *Digested*, 05/**2158**

R. (on the application of Bosombanguwa) v. Immigration Appeal Tribunal [2004] EWHC 1656; [2004] Imm. A.R. 616, QBD (Admin) . . . .   *Digested*, 05/**323**

R. (on the application of Boucher) v. Luton Crown Court see R. (on the application of
  Salubi) v. Bow Street Magistrates Court
R. (on the application of Boxall) v. Waltham Forest LBC (2001) 4 C.C.L. Rep. 258, QBD
  (Admin) . . . .   *Digested*, 03/**348**:
                                                                Applied, 01/3596, 03/368, 05/348
R. (on the application of Brannan) v. Secretary of State for the Home Department see R.
  (on the application of Murphy) v. Secretary of State for the Home Department
R. (on the application of Brehony) v. Chief Constable of Greater Manchester [2005]
  EWHC 640; (2005) 149 S.J.L.B. 393; *Times*, April 15, 2005, QBD (Admin) . . . .   *Digested*, 05/**3340**
R. (on the application of Brighton and Hove City Council) v. Brighton and Hove Justices
  [2004] EWHC 1800; [2004] R.A. 277; [2005] A.C.D. 38, QBD (Admin) . . . . .   *Digested*, 05/**3357**:
                                                                                          Applied, 05/387
R. (on the application of Britannic Asset Management Ltd) v. Pensions Ombudsman; *sub*
  nom R. (on the application of Brittannic Asset Management Ltd) v. Pensions
  Ombudsman; Britannic Asset Management Ltd v. Pensions Ombudsman [2002]
  EWCA Civ 1405; [2002] 4 All E.R. 860; [2003] I.C.R. 99; [2003] O.P.L.R. 93;
  [2002] Pens. L.R. 527; (2002) 99(44) L.S.G. 33; *Times*, October 22, 2002, CA
  (Civ Div); affirming [2002] EWHC 441; [2002] O.P.L.R. 175; (2002) 99(20)
  L.S.G. 32; *Times*, April 16, 2002, QBD (Admin) . . . .   *Digested*, 02/**3400**:
                                                                                         Applied, 05/3054
R. (on the application of British American Tobacco UK Ltd) v. Secretary of State for Health
  [2004] EWHC 2493; [2005] A.C.D. 27; (2004) 101(45) L.S.G. 33; *Times*,
  November 11, 2004, QBD (Admin) . . . .   *Digested*, 05/**2740**
R. (on the application of British American Tobacco (Investments) Ltd) v. Secretary of State
  for Health (C491/01); *sub nom* R. v. Secretary of State for Health Ex p. British
  American Tobacco (Investments) Ltd (C491/01) [2003] All E.R. (EC) 604;
  [2002] E.C.R. I-11453; [2003] 1 C.M.L.R. 14; [2003] C.E.C. 53; [2003]
  E.T.M.R. CN5; [2003] E.T.M.R. CN10; *Times*, December 13, 2002, ECJ [2002]
  E.C.R. I-11453; [2002] E.T.M.R. CN13, AGO . . . .   *Digested*, 03/**1455**:
                                                                                        Considered, 05/1448
R. (on the application of British Telecommunications Plc) v. Revenue and Customs
  Commissioners [2005] EWHC 1043; [2005] S.T.C. 1148; [2005] 2 C.M.L.R. 64;
  [2005] Eu. L.R. 914; [2005] B.T.C. 5371; [2005] B.V.C. 402; [2005] S.T.I.
  1015, QBD (Admin). . . . .   *Digested*, 05/**4387**
R. (on the application of Brittannic Asset Management Ltd) v. Pensions Ombudsman see
  R. (on the application of Britannic Asset Management Ltd) v. Pensions
  Ombudsman
R. (on the application of Broadbent) v. Parole Board; *sub nom* Broadbent v. Parole
  Board [2005] EWHC 1207; *Times*, June 22, 2005, QBD (Admin) . . . .   *Digested*, 05/**2907**
R. (on the application of Brooks) v. Parole Board [2004] EWCA Civ 80; (2004) 148
  S.J.L.B. 233, CA (Civ Div); affirming [2003] EWHC 1458, QBD (Admin) . . . . .   *Considered*, 05/2907
R. (on the application of Buddington) v. Secretary of State for the Home Department;
  sub nom Buddington v. Secretary of State for the Home Department; C1/2005/
  2413, CA (Civ Div); affirming [2005] EWHC 2198; *Times*, October 20, 2005,
  QBD
R. (on the application of Bulbul) v. Secretary of State for the Home Department see
  Sepet v. Secretary of State for the Home Department
R. (on the application of Burke) v. General Medical Council [2005] EWCA Civ 1003;
  [2005] 3 W.L.R. 1132; [2005] 2 F.L.R. 1223; [2005] 3 F.C.R. 169; [2005]
  H.R.L.R. 35; (2005) 8 C.C.L. Rep. 463; [2005] Lloyd's Rep. Med. 403; (2005)
  85 B.M.L.R. 1; [2005] Fam. Law 776; (2005) 155 N.L.J. 1457, CA (Civ Div);
  reversing [2004] EWHC 1879; [2005] Q.B. 424; [2005] 2 W.L.R. 431; [2004]
  2 F.L.R. 1121; [2004] 3 F.C.R. 579; (2004) 7 C.C.L. Rep. 609; [2004] Lloyd's
  Rep. Med. 451; (2004) 79 B.M.L.R. 126; [2004] A.C.D. 84; *Times*, August 6,
  2004, QBD (Admin) . . . .   *Digested*, 05/**1812**:
                                                        Considered, 05/1850: *Doubted*, 05/1794
R. (on the application of Burkett) v. Hammersmith and Fulham LBC (Costs) [2004]
  EWCA Civ 1342; [2005] C.P. Rep. 11; [2005] 1 Costs L.R. 104; [2005] J.P.L.
  525; [2005] A.C.D. 73; (2004) 101(42) L.S.G. 30; (2004) 148 S.J.L.B. 1245;
  Times, October 20, 2004, CA (Civ Div) . . . .   *Digested*, 05/**384**
R. (on the application of Bushell) v. Newcastle upon Tyne Licensing Justices TNS, HL;
  reversing [2004] EWCA Civ 767; [2005] 1 W.L.R. 1732; [2004] 3 All E.R. 493;
  (2004) 168 J.P. 437; (2004) 168 J.P.N. 660; (2004) 148 S.J.L.B. 794; *Times*,
  July 9, 2004, CA (Civ Div); affirming [2004] EWHC 446; [2004] N.P.C. 44,
  QBD (Admin) . . . .   *Digested*, 04/**2584**
R. (on the application of Buxton) v. Parole Board [2004] EWHC 1930; [2005] A.C.D. 6,
  QBD (Admin)
R. (on the application of C) v. Admission Panel of Nottinghamshire CC [2004] EWHC
  2988; [2005] E.L.R. 182, QBD (Admin). . . . .   *Digested*, 05/**1068**
R. (on the application of C) v. Enfield LBC see R. (on the application of T) v. Enfield LBC
R. (on the application of C) v. Grimsby and Cleethorpes Magistrates Court [2004]
  EWHC 2240; (2004) 168 J.P. 569; (2004) 168 J.P.N. 856, QBD (Admin) . . . . .   *Digested*, 05/**906**

R. (on the application of C) v. London South and South West Region Mental Health Review Tribunal see R. (on the application of C) v. Mental Health Review Tribunal

R. (on the application of C) v. Mental Health Review Tribunal; *sub nom* R. (on the application of C) v. London South and South West Region Mental Health Review Tribunal [2001] EWCA Civ 1110; [2002] 1 W.L.R. 176; [2002] 2 F.C.R. 181; (2001) 4 C.C.L. Rep. 284; [2001] Lloyd's Rep. Med. 450; (2001) 98(29) L.S.G. 39; (2001) 145 S.J.L.B. 167; *Times,* July 11, 2001; *Independent,* July 10, 2001, CA (Civ Div); reversing [2001] A.C.D. 63, QBD (Admin) . . . . 　*Digested,* 01/**4424**: *Considered,* 05/2921

R. (on the application of C) v. Mental Health Review Tribunal; *sub nom* R. (on the application of SC) v. Mental Health Review Tribunal [2005] EWHC 17; [2005] A.C.D. 89; [2005] A.C.D. 102; (2005) 102(9) L.S.G. 30; *Times,* January 24, 2005, QBD (Admin) . . . . 　*Digested,* 05/**2817**

R. (on the application of C) v. Merton LBC [2005] EWHC 1753; [2005] 3 F.C.R. 42, QBD (Admin) . . . . 　*Digested,* 05/**2803**

R. (on the application of C) v. Sheffield Youth Court see R. (on the application of D) v. Sheffield Youth Court

R. (on the application of Caine) v. Cavendish [2001] EWHC Admin 18, QBD (Admin) . . 　*Approved,* 05/3332

R. (on the application of Calgin) v. Enfield LBC [2005] EWHC 1716; *Times,* September 27, 2005, QBD (Admin) . . . . 　*Digested,* 05/**1987**

R. (on the application of Camacho) v. Law Society (No.2) see Camacho v. Law Society (No.2)

R. (on the application of Campbell) v. General Medical Council [2005] EWCA Civ 250; [2005] 1 W.L.R. 3488; [2005] 2 All E.R. 970; [2005] Lloyd's Rep. Med. 353; (2005) 83 B.M.L.R. 30; *Times,* April 18, 2005; *Independent,* April 12, 2005, CA (Civ Div); reversing [2004] EWHC 1301, QBD (Admin) . . . . 　*Digested,* 05/**1802**

R. (on the application of Candlish) v. Hastings BC [2005] EWHC 1539; [2005] 29 E.G.C.S. 98; [2005] N.P.C. 102, QBD (Admin)

R. (on the application of Capenhurst) v. Leicester City Council [2004] EWHC 2124; (2004) 7 C.C.L. Rep. 557; [2004] A.C.D. 93, QBD (Admin) . . . . 　*Digested,* 05/**75**

R. (on the application of Carroll) v. Secretary of State for the Home Department; *sub nom* R. v. Secretary of State for the Home Department Ex p. Carroll; R. (on the application of Greenfield) v. Secretary of State for the Home Department; R. (on the application of Al-Hasan) v. Secretary of State for the Home Department [2005] UKHL 13; [2005] 1 W.L.R. 688; [2005] 1 All E.R. 927; [2005] H.R.L.R. 12; 19 B.H.R.C. 282; (2005) 102(15) L.S.G. 35; *Times,* February 18, 2005, HL; reversing [2001] EWCA Civ 1224; [2002] 1 W.L.R. 545; [2001] H.R.L.R. 58; *Times,* August 16, 2001, CA (Civ Div); affirming [2001] EWHC Admin 110; [2001] H.R.L.R. 34, QBD (Admin) . . . . 　*Digested,* 05/**2908**: *Considered,* 03/4961: *Overruled,* 05/2066: *Previous proceedings,* 01/4572

R. (on the application of Carson) v. Secretary of State for Work and Pensions; *sub nom* Carson v. Secretary of State for Work and Pensions; R. (on the application of Reynolds) v. Secretary of State for Work and Pensions [2005] UKHL 37; [2005] 2 W.L.R. 1369; [2005] 4 All E.R. 545; [2005] H.R.L.R. 23; [2005] U.K.H.R.R. 1185; 18 B.H.R.C. 677; *Times,* May 27, 2005, HL; affirming [2003] EWCA Civ 797; [2003] 3 All E.R. 577; [2003] H.R.L.R. 36; [2003] Pens. L.R. 215; [2003] A.C.D. 76; (2003) 100(34) L.S.G. 32; (2003) 147 S.J.L.B. 780; *Times,* June 28, 2003, CA (Civ Div); affirming [2002] EWHC 978; [2002] 3 All E.R. 994; (2002) 99(26) L.S.G. 39; *Times,* May 24, 2002; *Daily Telegraph,* May 30, 2002, QBD (Admin) . . . . 　*Digested,* 05/**3835**: *Applied,* 04/2821, 04/3579, 05/1139: *Considered,* 04/1889

R. (on the application of Castillo) v. Spain; *sub nom* Castillo v. Spain [2004] EWHC 1676; [2005] 1 W.L.R. 1043, QBD (Admin) . . . . 　*Digested,* 05/**1491**

R. (on the application of CD) v. Isle of Anglesey CC; *sub nom* CD (A Child) v. Isle of Anglesey CC [2004] EWHC 1635; [2005] 1 F.L.R. 59; [2004] 3 F.C.R. 171; (2004) 7 C.C.L. Rep. 589; [2004] Fam. Law 865, QBD (Admin) . . . . 　*Digested,* 04/**3623**

R. (on the application of Charlton Thomson) v. Secretary of State for Education and Skills see R. (on the application of Thomson) v. Minister of State for Children

R. (on the application of Chelmsford BC) v. First Secretary of State; *sub nom* Chelmsford BC v. First Secretary of State [2003] EWHC 2978; [2004] 2 P. & C.R. 34; [2004] 2 P.L.R. 34, QBD (Admin) . . . . 　*Considered,* 05/3264

R. (on the application of Chelmsford Car & Commercials Ltd) v. Chelmsford BC [2005] EWHC 1705; [2005] 28 E.G.C.S. 121, QBD (Admin)

R. (on the application of Cherwell DC) v. First Secretary of State [2004] EWCA Civ 1420; [2005] 1 W.L.R. 1128; [2005] 1 P. & C.R. 22; [2005] 1 P.L.R. 11; [2005] J.P.L. 768; [2004] 45 E.G.C.S. 125; (2004) 101(45) L.S.G. 32; (2004) 148 S.J.L.B. 1284; [2004] N.P.C. 159; *Times,* November 4, 2004, CA (Civ Div); affirming [2004] EWHC 724; [2004] 2 P. & C.R. 27; [2004] 16 E.G.C.S. 111; [2004] N.P.C. 58, QBD (Admin) . . . . 　*Digested,* 05/**3261**

R. (on the application of Chisnell) v. Richmond upon Thames LBC [2005] EWHC 134; [2005] 5 E.G.C.S. 203, QBD (Admin)

R. (on the application of Chorion Plc) v. Westminster City Council (No.1); *sub nom* R. v. Westminster City Council Ex p. Chorion Plc [2001] EWHC Admin 754, QBD (Admin) . . . . *Considered*, 05/2752

R. (on the application of Clarke) v. Secretary of State for the Home Department see R. (on the application of Francis) v. Secretary of State for the Home Department

R. (on the application of Clays Lane Housing Cooperative Ltd) v. Housing Corp [2004] EWCA Civ 1658; [2005] 1 W.L.R. 2229; [2005] H.L.R. 15; [2004] N.P.C. 184; *Times*, December 27, 2004, CA (Civ Div); affirming [2004] EWHC 1084; [2004] H.L.R. 51, QBD (Admin) . . . . *Digested*, 05/**2027**

R. (on the application of Cobbledick) v. First Secretary of State [2004] EWHC 1341; [2005] 1 P.L.R. 1, QBD (Admin)

R. (on the application of Coghlan) v. Chief Constable of Greater Manchester [2004] EWHC 2801; [2005] 2 All E.R. 890; [2005] A.C.D. 34, QBD (Admin) . . . . *Digested*, 05/**3334**

R. (on the application of Colonel M) v. Ashworth Hospital Authority (now Mersey Care NHS Trust) see R. (on the application of Munjaz) v. Mersey Care NHS Trust

R. (on the application of Compassion in World Farming Ltd) v. Secretary of State for the Environment, Food and Rural Affairs; *sub nom* Compassion in World Farming Ltd v. Secretary of State for the Environment, Food and Rural Affairs [2004] EWCA Civ 1009; [2004] Eu. L.R. 1021; *Times*, August 9, 2004, CA (Civ Div); affirming [2003] EWHC 2850; [2004] Eu. L.R. 382; [2004] A.C.D. 52; [2003] N.P.C. 144; *Times*, December 5, 2003, QBD (Admin) . . . . *Digested*, 05/**170**

R. (on the application of Conde) v. Lambeth LBC [2005] EWHC 62; [2005] 2 F.L.R. 198; [2005] 1 F.C.R. 189; [2005] H.L.R. 29; (2005) 8 C.C.L. Rep. 486; [2005] Fam. Law 455, QBD (Admin) . . . . *Digested*, 05/**2004**

R. (on the application of Corbett) v. First Secretary of State [2005] EWHC 2433; [2005] 30 E.G.C.S. 88, QBD (Admin)

R. (on the application of Corner House Research) v. Secretary of State for Trade and Industry [2005] EWCA Civ 192; [2005] 1 W.L.R. 2600; [2005] 4 All E.R. 1; [2005] C.P. Rep. 28; [2005] 3 Costs L.R. 455; [2005] A.C.D. 100; (2005) 102(17) L.S.G. 31; (2005) 149 S.J.L.B. 297; *Times*, March 7, 2005; *Independent*, March 4, 2005, CA (Civ Div); reversing [2004] EWHC 3011, QBD (Admin) . . . . *Digested*, 05/**354**: *Applied*, 05/373: *Considered*, 05/366

R. (on the application of Council for National Parks Ltd) v. Pembrokeshire Coast National Park Authority see Council for National Parks Ltd v. Pembrokeshire Coast National Park Authority

R. (on the application of Crown Castle UK Ltd) v. Islington LBC see R. (on the application of Orange PCS Ltd) v. Islington LBC

R. (on the application of Crown Prosecution Service) v. Blaydon Youth Court [2004] EWHC 2296; (2004) 168 J.P. 638; [2005] Crim. L.R. 495; (2004) 168 J.P.N. 917, QBD (Admin) . . . . *Digested*, 05/**905**

R. (on the application of Crown Prosecution Service) v. Bolton Magistrates Court; *sub nom* R. (on the application of Crown Prosecution Service) v. Bolton Justices [2003] EWHC 2697; [2004] 1 W.L.R. 835; [2005] 2 All E.R. 848; [2004] 1 Cr. App. R. 33; (2004) 168 J.P. 10; [2004] Crim. L.R. 379; (2004) 168 J.P.N. 52; *Times*, November 7, 2003, QBD (Admin) . . . . *Digested*, 04/**846**

R. (on the application of CS) v. Mental Health Review Tribunal [2004] EWHC 2958; [2005] A.C.D. 54, QBD (Admin)

R. (on the application of D) v. Camberwell Green Youth Court; R. (on the application of R) v. Balham Youth Court; R. (on the application of N) v. Camberwell Green Youth Court; R. (on the application of DPP) v. Camberwell Green Youth Court; R. (on the application of G) v. Camberwell Green Youth Court [2005] UKHL 4; [2005] 1 W.L.R. 393; [2005] 1 All E.R. 999; [2005] 2 Cr. App. R. 1; (2005) 169 J.P. 105; [2005] 1 F.C.R. 365; [2005] H.R.L.R. 9; [2005] U.K.H.R.R. 302; 17 B.H.R.C. 625; [2005] Crim. L.R. 497; (2005) 169 J.P.N. 257; (2005) 102(13) L.S.G. 27; (2005) 149 S.J.L.B. 146; *Times*, February 1, 2005, HL; affirming [2003] EWHC 227; [2003] 2 Cr. App. R. 16; (2003) 167 J.P. 210; [2003] Crim. L.R. 659; (2003) 167 J.P.N. 317; *Times*, February 13, 2003, QBD (Admin) . . . . . *Digested*, 05/**751**

R. (on the application of D) v. Manchester City Youth Court [2001] EWHC Admin 860; [2002] 1 Cr. App. R. (S.) 135; (2002) 166 J.P. 15; [2002] Crim. L.R. 149, QBD (Admin) . . . . *Digested*, 02/**895**: *Applied*, 03/882, 04/894, 05/940: *Considered*, 03/3756, 04/3295

R. (on the application of D) v. Secretary of State for the Home Department see D v. Secretary of State for the Home Department

R. (on the application of D) v. Secretary of State for the Home Department see R. (on the application of Q) v. Secretary of State for the Home Department

R. (on the application of D) v. Secretary of State for the Home Department see R. (on the application of S) v. Secretary of State for the Home Department

R. (on the application of D) v. Secretary of State for the Home Department C1/2005/1064, C1/2005/1064(B), CA (Civ Div); affirming in part [2005] EWHC 728; [2005] U.K.H.R.R. 917, QBD (Admin)

R. (on the application of D) *v.* Sheffield Youth Court; *sub nom* R. (on the application of C) *v.* Sheffield Youth Court; R. (on the application of N) *v.* Sheffield Youth Court [2003] EWHC 35; (2003) 167 J.P. 159; [2003] A.C.D. 22; (2003) 167 J.P.N. 251; (2003) 100(12) L.S.G. 29; *Times*, February 3, 2003, QBD (Admin) . .   *Digested*, 03/**881**:
             Applied, 04/895, 05/940

R. (on the application of D) *v.* Stratford Youth Court [2005] EWHC 2562; (2005) 169 J.P. 656; (2005) 169 J.P.N. 959, QBD (Admin)

R. (on the application of D (A Child)) *v.* Plymouth High School for Girls Governing Body; *sub nom* D (A Child) *v.* S (Education: Discrimination) [2004] EWHC 1923; [2004] E.L.R. 591, QBD (Admin) . . . .   *Digested*, 05/**1062**

R. (on the application of Daly) *v.* Secretary of State for the Home Department; *sub nom* R. *v.* Secretary of State for the Home Department Ex p. Daly [2001] UKHL 26; [2001] 2 A.C. 532; [2001] 2 W.L.R. 1622; [2001] 3 All E.R. 433; [2001] H.R.L.R. 49; [2001] U.K.H.R.R. 887; [2001] A.C.D. 79; (2001) 98(26) L.S.G. 43; (2001) 145 S.J.L.B. 156; *Times*, May 25, 2001; *Daily Telegraph*, May 29, 2001, HL; reversing [1999] C.O.D. 388, CA (Civ Div) . . . .   *Digested*, 01/**4578**:
         Applied, 03/3481, 04/2778, 05/2027, 05/2192, 05/2193, 05/2917:
            Considered, 01/426, 01/3660, 01/4574, 03/2934

R. (on the application of Dari) *v.* Secretary of State for the Home Department see R. (on the application of Tum) *v.* Secretary of State for the Home Department

R. (on the application of Davies) *v.* Birmingham Deputy Coroner (Costs) see R. (on the application of Davies) *v.* HM Deputy Coroner for Birmingham (Costs)

R. (on the application of Davies) *v.* Financial Services Authority; *sub nom* R. (on the application of Davis) *v.* Financial Services Authority [2003] EWCA Civ 1128; [2004] 1 W.L.R. 185; [2003] 4 All E.R. 1196; [2004] 1 All E.R. (Comm) 88; [2005] 1 B.C.L.C. 286; [2003] A.C.D. 83; (2003) 100(38) L.S.G. 34; *Times*, October 6, 2003, CA (Civ Div); affirming [2002] EWHC 2997; [2003] 1 W.L.R. 1284; [2003] 1 All E.R. 859; *Independent*, February 24, 2003 (C.S), QBD (Admin) . . . .   *Digested*, 03/**1630**

R. (on the application of Davies) *v.* HM Deputy Coroner for Birmingham (Costs); *sub nom* R. (on the application of Davies) *v.* Birmingham Deputy Coroner (Costs) [2004] EWCA Civ 207; [2004] 1 W.L.R. 2739; [2004] 3 All E.R. 543; [2004] 4 Costs L.R. 545; (2004) 80 B.M.L.R. 48; (2004) 148 S.J.L.B. 297; *Times*, March 10, 2004; *Independent*, March 18, 2004, CA (Civ Div) . . . .   *Digested*, 04/**300**:
             Applied, 05/387

R. (on the application of Davis) *v.* Financial Services Authority see R. (on the application of Davies) *v.* Financial Services Authority

R. (on the application of Dawes) *v.* Nottingham Crown Court (2005) 102(9) L.S.G. 30; *Times*, January 19, 2005, QBD (Admin)

R. (on the application of De Beer) *v.* Balabanoff; *sub nom* R. (on the application of De Beer) *v.* Returning Officer for Harrow LBC [2002] EWHC 670; [2002] A.C.D. 83; *Times*, April 25, 2002, QBD (Admin). . . . .   *Digested*, 02/**1270**:
             Applied, 05/1175

R. (on the application of De Beer) *v.* Returning Officer for Harrow LBC see R. (on the application of De Beer) *v.* Balabanoff

R. (on the application of Deluni Mobile Ltd) *v.* Customs and Excise Commissioners [2004] EWHC 1030, QBD (Admin) . . . .   *Applied*, 05/4373

R. (on the application of Deman) *v.* Lord Chancellor's Department; *sub nom* Deman *v.* Lord Chancellor's Department [2004] EWHC 930; [2004] E.L.R. 484, QBD (Admin) . . . .   *Digested*, 05/**1165**

R. (on the application of Dennis) *v.* Sevenoaks DC [2004] EWHC 2758; [2005] 2 P. & C.R. 4; [2005] J.P.L. 791, QBD (Admin). . . . .   *Digested*, 05/**3271**

R. (on the application of Denny) *v.* Acton Youth Court [2004] EWHC 948; [2004] 1 W.L.R. 3051; [2004] 2 All E.R. 961; [2005] 1 Cr. App. R. (S.) 6; (2004) 168 J.P. 388; (2004) 168 J.P.N. 556; (2004) 101(21) L.S.G. 35; *Times*, June 3, 2004, QBD (Admin) . . . .   *Digested*, 04/**892**

R. (on the application of Derwin) *v.* Attorney General see R. (on the application of the Countryside Alliance) *v.* Attorney General

R. (on the application of Dirshe) *v.* Secretary of State for the Home Department [2005] EWCA Civ 421; [2005] 1 W.L.R. 2685; [2005] Imm. A.R. 319; [2005] I.N.L.R. 432; *Times*, May 5, 2005; *Independent*, April 28, 2005, CA (Civ Div); reversing [2004] EWHC 2127, QBD (Admin) . . . .   *Digested*, 05/**2169**

R. (on the application of Dixon) *v.* Secretary of State for the Environment, Food and Rural Affairs [2002] EWHC 831; [2002] A.C.D. 65; *Times*, April 22, 2002, QBD (Admin) . . . .   *Digested*, 02/**70**:
             Followed, 05/135

R. (on the application of DJ) *v.* Mental Health Review Tribunal see R. (on the application of N) *v.* Mental Health Review Tribunal (Northern Region)

R. (on the application of Doka) *v.* Immigration Appeal Tribunal [2004] EWHC 3072; [2005] 1 F.C.R. 180, QBD (Admin)

R. (on the application of Dolatabadi) *v.* Transport for London [2005] EWHC 1942; (2005) 102(34) L.S.G. 31, QBD (Admin)

R. (on the application of DPP) *v.* Camberwell Green Youth Court see R. (on the application of D) *v.* Camberwell Green Youth Court

R. (on the application of DPP) *v.* Camberwell Green Youth Court [2003] EWHC 3217; (2004) 168 J.P. 157; [2004] A.C.D. 21; (2004) 168 J.P.N. 233; *Times,* January 9, 2004, QBD (Admin) . . . . *Digested,* 04/**870**:
Applied, 04/802, 05/906

R. (on the application of DPP) *v.* Camberwell Youth Court; R. (on the application of H) *v.* Camberwell Youth Court [2004] EWHC 1805; [2005] 1 W.L.R. 810; [2004] 4 All E.R. 699; [2005] 1 Cr. App. R. 6; (2004) 168 J.P. 481; [2005] Crim. L.R. 165; [2005] A.C.D. 25; (2004) 168 J.P.N. 738; *Times,* August 12, 2004, QBD (Admin) . . . . *Digested,* 04/**895**

R. (on the application of DPP) *v.* Everest see DPP *v.* Everest

R. (on the application of DPP) *v.* Glendinning see DPP *v.* Glendinning

R. (on the application of DPP) *v.* Sharma see DPP *v.* Sharma

R. (on the application of Drain) *v.* Secretary of State for the Environment, Food and Rural Affairs see R. (on the application of Godmanchester Town Council) *v.* Secretary of State for the Environment, Food and Rural Affairs

R. (on the application of Dudson) *v.* Secretary of State for the Home Department see R. (on the application of Smith) *v.* Secretary of State for the Home Department

R. (on the application of Dudson) *v.* Secretary of State for the Home Department [2005] UKHL 52; [2005] 3 W.L.R. 422; [2005] H.R.L.R. 34; [2005] U.K.H.R.R. 1216; (2005) 155 N.L.J. 1246; *Times,* July 29, 2005, HL . . . . *Digested,* 05/**3775**:
Previous proceedings, 04/3471

R. (on the application of E) *v.* Newham LBC see E *v.* Newham LBC

R. (on the application of Ealing LBC) *v.* Audit Commission; *sub nom* Ealing LBC *v.* Audit Commission; Audit Commission for England and Wales *v.* Ealing LBC [2005] EWCA Civ 556; (2005) 8 C.C.L. Rep. 317; *Times,* May 26, 2005, CA (Civ Div); reversing in part [2005] EWHC 195; (2005) 102(16) L.S.G. 28; *Times,* March 2, 2005, QBD (Admin) . . . . *Digested,* 05/**2796**

R. (on the application of Edwards) *v.* Environment Agency (No.2) [2005] EWHC 657; [2005] J.P.L. 1576; [2005] N.P.C. 53, QBD (Admin)

R. (on the application of Elias) *v.* Secretary of State for Defence [2005] EWHC 1435; [2005] I.R.L.R. 788; (2005) 102(30) L.S.G. 30; *Times,* August 25, 2005, QBD (Admin) . . . . *Digested,* 05/**85**

R. (on the application of Elite Mobile Plc) *v.* Customs and Excise Commissioners [2004] EWHC 2923; [2005] S.T.C. 275; [2005] B.T.C. 5113; [2005] B.V.C. 144; [2005] S.T.I. 21, QBD (Admin) . . . . *Digested,* 05/**4374**

R. (on the application of Energy Financing Team Ltd) *v.* Bow Street Magistrates' Court see Energy Financing Team Ltd *v.* Director of the Serious Fraud Office

R. (on the application of Epping Forest DC) *v.* Secretary of State for Transport, Local Government and the Regions [2005] EWHC 424; [2005] N.P.C. 44, QBD (Admin)

R. (on the application of Erdogan) *v.* Secretary of State for the Home Department (Application to Appeal Out of Time) [2004] EWCA Civ 1087; [2004] I.N.L.R. 503, CA (Civ Div); reversing [2004] EWHC 541, QBD (Admin). . . . . *Digested,* 05/**2156**

R. (on the application of Essex CC) *v.* Secretary of State for Transport see R. (on the application of Wandsworth LBC) *v.* Secretary of State for Transport

R. (on the application of European Low Fares Airline Association *v.* Department of Transport) see R. (on the application of International Air Transport Association) *v.* Department of Transport

R. (on the application of European Roma Rights Centre) *v.* Immigration Officer, Prague Airport; *sub nom* R. (on the application of European Roma Rights Centre) *v.* Secretary of State for the Home Department; European Roma Rights Centre *v.* Immigration Officer, Prague Airport [2004] UKHL 55; [2005] 2 A.C. 1; [2005] 2 W.L.R. 1; [2005] 1 All E.R. 527; [2005] I.R.L.R. 115; [2005] H.R.L.R. 4; [2005] U.K.H.R.R. 530; 18 B.H.R.C. 1; [2005] Imm. A.R. 100; [2005] I.N.L.R. 182; (2004) 154 N.L.J. 1893; (2005) 149 S.J.L.B. 26; *Times,* December 10, 2004; *Independent,* December 17, 2004, HL; reversing [2003] EWCA Civ 666; [2004] Q.B. 811; [2004] 2 W.L.R. 147; [2003] 4 All E.R. 247; [2003] I.R.L.R. 577; 15 B.H.R.C. 51; [2003] I.N.L.R. 374; [2003] A.C.D. 64; (2003) 100(29) L.S.G. 35; *Times,* May 22, 2003, CA (Civ Div); affirming [2002] EWHC 1989; [2003] A.C.D. 15, QBD (Admin) . . . . *Digested,* 05/**2162**

R. (on the application of European Roma Rights Centre) *v.* Secretary of State for the Home Department see R. (on the application of European Roma Rights Centre) *v.* Immigration Officer, Prague Airport

R. (on the application of Evans) *v.* First Secretary of State [2005] EWHC 149; [2005] J.P.L. 1343, QBD (Admin)

R. (on the application of Exmouth Marina Ltd) *v.* First Secretary of State see Exmouth Marina Ltd *v.* First Secretary of State

R. (on the application of F) *v.* Secretary of State for the Home Department see R. (on the application of Q) *v.* Secretary of State for the Home Department

R. (on the application of Fairstate Ltd) *v.* First Secretary of State see Fairstate Ltd *v.* First Secretary of State

R. (on the application of Federation of Technological Industries) v. Customs and Excise Commissioners; *sub nom* Customs and Excise Commissioners v. Federation of Technological Industries [2004] EWCA Civ 1020; [2004] S.T.C. 1424; [2004] 3 C.M.L.R. 41; [2005] Eu. L.R. 110; [2004] B.T.C. 5623; [2004] B.V.C. 682; [2004] S.T.I. 1763; (2004) 101(36) L.S.G. 35; (2004) 148 S.J.L.B. 977, CA (Civ Div); affirming [2004] EWHC 254; [2004] S.T.C. 1008; [2004] S.T.I. 441; *Independent*, March 29, 2004 (C.S), QBD (Admin) . . . .   *Digested*, 04/**403**

R. (on the application of Fisher) v. English Nature; *sub nom* Fisher v. English Nature [2004] EWCA Civ 663; [2005] 1 W.L.R. 147; [2004] 4 All E.R. 861; [2005] Env. L.R. 10; [2004] 2 P. & C.R. 32; [2004] 3 P.L.R. 98; [2005] J.P.L. 83; [2004] 23 E.G.C.S. 121; [2004] N.P.C. 84; *Times*, June 4, 2004; *Independent*, June 17, 2004, CA (Civ Div); affirming [2003] EWHC 1599; [2004] 1 W.L.R. 503; [2003] 4 All E.R. 366; [2004] Env. L.R. 7; [2003] 4 P.L.R. 41; [2004] J.P.L. 217; [2003] N.P.C. 84; *Times*, September 15, 2003; *Independent*, October 6, 2003 (C.S), QBD (Admin) . . . .   *Digested*, 04/**1351**: *Considered*, 04/1376

R. (on the application of Ford (t/a David Sayers) v. Leasehold Valuation Tribunal [2005] EWHC 503; [2005] H.L.R. 36, QBD (Admin). . . . .   *Digested*, 05/**3387**

R. (on the application of Francis) v. Secretary of State for the Home Department; R. (on the application of Clarke) v. Secretary of State for the Home Department [2004] EWHC 2143; [2005] 1 W.L.R. 186; *Times*, October 12, 2004, QBD (Admin) . . . .   *Digested*, 04/**2786**

R. (on the application of Friend) v. Attorney General see R. (on the application of the Countryside Alliance) v. Attorney General

R. (on the application of G) v. Barnet LBC; R. (on the application of W) v. Lambeth LBC; R. (on the application of A) v. Lambeth LBC [2003] UKHL 57; [2004] 2 A.C. 208; [2003] 3 W.L.R. 1194; [2004] 1 All E.R. 97; [2004] 1 F.L.R. 454; [2003] 3 F.C.R. 419; [2004] H.R.L.R. 4; [2004] H.L.R. 10; [2003] B.L.G.R. 569; (2003) 6 C.C.L. Rep. 500; [2004] Fam. Law 21; (2003) 100(45) L.S.G. 29; [2003] N.P.C. 123; *Times*, October 24, 2003; *Independent*, October 29, 2003, HL; affirming [2001] EWCA Civ 540; [2001] 2 F.L.R. 877; [2001] 2 F.C.R. 193; (2001) 33 H.L.R. 59; [2002] B.L.G.R. 34; (2001) 4 C.C.L. Rep. 128; [2001] Fam. Law 662; (2001) 98(24) L.S.G. 43; *Times*, June 5, 2001; *Independent*, April 25, 2001, CA (Civ Div); reversing [2001] EWHC Admin 5; [2001] 1 F.C.R. 743; (2001) 4 C.C.L. Rep. 33; [2001] A.C.D. 59, QBD (Admin) . . . .   *Digested*, 04/**3643**: *Applied*, 05/2004: *Followed*, 04/3636: *Previous proceedings*, 01/3434, 02/2339

R. (on the application of G) v. Camberwell Green Youth Court see R. (on the application of D) v. Camberwell Green Youth Court

R. (on the application of G) v. Immigration Appeal Tribunal; R. (on the application of M) v. Immigration Appeal Tribunal [2004] EWCA Civ 1731; [2005] 1 W.L.R. 1445; [2005] 2 All E.R. 165; [2005] Imm. A.R. 106; [2005] I.N.L.R. 329; (2005) 102(6) L.S.G. 32; (2005) 149 S.J.L.B. 59; *Times*, December 23, 2004; *Independent*, January 11, 2005, CA (Civ Div); affirming [2004] EWHC 588; [2004] 1 W.L.R. 2953; [2004] 3 All E.R. 286; [2004] A.C.D. 85; *Times*, May 13, 2004, QBD (Admin) . . . .   *Digested*, 05/**2170**

R. (on the application of G) v. Mental Health Review Tribunal [2004] EWHC 2193; [2005] A.C.D. 74, QBD (Admin)

R. (on the application of G) v. Secretary of State for the Home Department [2005] EWCA Civ 546; *Times*, May 3, 2005, CA (Civ Div); affirming [2004] EWHC 2848; (2005) 102(2) L.S.G. 29; *Times*, December 15, 2004, QBD (Admin) . . . .   *Digested*, 05/**2181**

R. (on the application of G (A Child)) v. Westminster City Council [2004] EWCA Civ 45; [2004] 1 W.L.R. 1113; [2004] 4 All E.R. 572; [2005] B.L.G.R. 64; [2004] E.L.R. 135; (2004) 101(7) L.S.G. 35; (2004) 148 S.J.L.B. 179; *Times*, February 5, 2004; *Independent*, February 3, 2004, CA (Civ Div) . . . .   *Digested*, 04/**999**

R. (on the application of Gazette Media Co Ltd) v. Teesside Crown Court; *sub nom* Gazette Media Co Ltd, Re [2005] EWCA Crim 1983; [2005] E.M.L.R. 34; *Times*, August 8, 2005, CA (Crim Div) . . . .   *Digested*, 05/**923**

R. (on the application of Georgiou) v. Enfield LBC see Georgiou v. Enfield LBC

R. (on the application of Gezer) v. Secretary of State for the Home Department; *sub nom* Gezer v. Secretary of State for the Home Department [2004] EWCA Civ 1730; [2005] H.R.L.R. 7; [2005] Imm. A.R. 131; [2005] H.L.R. 16; (2005) 102(7) L.S.G. 26; *Times*, December 23, 2004, CA (Civ Div); affirming [2003] EWHC 860; [2003] H.L.R. 64; [2003] A.C.D. 80, QBD (Admin) . . . .   *Digested*, 05/**2157**

R. (on the application of Gillan) v. Commissioner of Police of the Metropolis; R. (on the application of Quinton) v. Commissioner of Police of the Metropolis; TNS, HL; affirming [2004] EWCA Civ 1067; [2005] Q.B. 388; [2004] 3 W.L.R. 1144; [2005] 1 All E.R. 970; [2004] U.K.H.R.R. 1108; [2005] Crim. L.R. 414; [2004] A.C.D. 94; (2004) 101(35) L.S.G. 35; *Times*, August 12, 2004; *Independent*, October 5, 2004, CA (Civ Div); affirming [2003] EWHC 2545; *Times*, November 5, 2003, QBD (Admin) . . . .   *Digested*, 04/**3152**

R. (on the application of Gillespie) v. First Secretary of State see Gillespie v. First Secretary of State

R. (on the application of Gilman) *v.* Rutland CC [2004] EWHC 2792; [2005] J.P.L. 970; [2004] N.P.C.183, QBD (Admin).. *Digested*, 05/**3319**

R. (on the application of Gladstone Plc) *v.* Manchester City Magistrates Court [2004] EWHC 2806; [2005] 1 W.L.R.1987; [2005] 2 All E.R. 56; *Times*, November 26, 2004, QBD (Admin) .... *Digested*, 05/**919**

R. (on the application of Gleaves) *v.* Secretary of State for the Home Department [2004] EWHC 2522; *Times*, November 15, 2004, QBD (Admin) .... *Digested*, 05/**2910**

R. (on the application of Godmanchester Town Council) *v.* Secretary of State for the Environment, Food and Rural Affairs; R. (on the application of Drain) *v.* Secretary of State for the Environment, Food and Rural Affairs [2005] EWCA Civ 1597; [2005] N.P.C. 149; *Times*, December 27, 2005, CA (Civ Div); affirming [2004] EWHC 1217; [2005] 1 W.L.R. 926; [2004] 4 All E.R. 342; [2005] A.C.D. 28; [2004] N.P.C.127; *Independent*, October 11, 2004 (C.S), QBD (Admin) ...... *Digested*, 04/**1817**

R. (on the application of Goldsmith) *v.* Wandsworth LBC [2004] EWCA Civ 1170; (2004) 7 C.C.L. Rep. 472; (2004) 148 S.J.L.B.1065, CA (Civ Div).......... *Digested*, 05/**3948**

R. (on the application of Goodson) *v.* HM Coroner for Bedfordshire and Luton; *sub nom* Goodson *v.* Bedfordshire and Luton Coroner [2004] EWHC 2931; [2005] 2 All E.R. 791; [2005] Lloyd's Rep. Med. 202; (2005) 84 B.M.L.R. 72; [2005] A.C.D. 42, QBD (Admin) .... *Digested*, 05/**34**

R. (on the application of Goodson) *v.* HM Coroner for Bedfordshire and Luton (Protective Costs) see Goodson *v.* HM Coroner for Bedfordshire and Luton (Protective Costs)

R. (on the application of Grant) *v.* Lambeth LBC; *sub nom* Grant *v.* Lambeth LBC [2004] EWCA Civ 1711; [2005] 1 W.L.R. 1781; [2005] 1 F.C.R. 1; [2005] H.L.R. 27; [2005] B.L.G.R. 81; (2005) 102(8) L.S.G. 30; *Times*, January 5, 2005, CA (Civ Div); reversing [2004] EWHC 1524; [2004] 3 F.C.R. 494; [2004] B.L.G.R. 867, QBD (Admin) .... *Digested*, 05/**2210**

R. (on the application of Greenfield) *v.* Secretary of State for the Home Department see R. (on the application of Carroll) *v.* Secretary of State for the Home Department

R. (on the application of Greenfield) *v.* Secretary of State for the Home Department [2005] UKHL 14; [2005] 1 W.L.R. 673; [2005] 2 All E.R. 240; [2005] H.R.L.R. 13; [2005] U.K.H.R.R. 323; 18 B.H.R.C. 252; (2005) 102(16) L.S.G. 30; (2005) 155 N.L.J. 298; *Times*, February 18, 2005, HL.................. *Digested*, 05/**2066**: *Previous proceedings*, 01/4571

R. (on the application of Greenpeace Ltd) *v.* Secretary of State for the Environment, Food and Rural Affairs see Greenpeace Ltd *v.* Secretary of State for the Environment, Food and Rural Affairs

R. (on the application of Grierson) *v.* Office of Communications (OFCOM) [2005] EWHC 1899; [2005] E.M.L.R. 37; (2005) 102(35) L.S.G. 41, QBD (Admin)

R. (on the application of Griffin) *v.* Southwark LBC [2004] EWHC 2463; [2005] H.L.R. 12; *Times*, January 3, 2005, QBD (Admin) .... *Digested*, 05/**1988**

R. (on the application of Gunter) *v.* South Western Staffordshire Primary Care Trust; *sub nom* Gunter *v.* South Western Staffordshire Primary Care Trust [2005] EWHC 1894; (2005) 86 B.M.L.R. 60; (2005) 102(36) L.S.G. 30, QBD (Admin)

R. (on the application of H) *v.* Ashworth Hospital Authority; R. (on the application of Ashworth Hospital Authority) *v.* Mental Health Review Tribunal for West Midlands and North West Region [2002] EWCA Civ 923; [2003] 1 W.L.R. 127; (2002) 5 C.C.L. Rep. 390; (2003) 70 B.M.L.R. 40; [2002] A.C.D. 102; (2002) 99(34) L.S.G. 29; (2002) 146 S.J.L.B. 198; *Times*, July 10, 2002; *Daily Telegraph*, July 11, 2002, CA (Civ Div); affirming in part [2001] EWHC Admin 901; (2002) 5 C.C.L. Rep. 78, QBD (Admin)........................... *Digested*, 02/**3230**: *Applied*, 03/2953, 05/2822

R. (on the application of H) *v.* Camberwell Youth Court see R. (on the application of DPP) *v.* Camberwell Youth Court

R. (on the application of H) *v.* Mental Health Review Tribunal for North and East London Region; *sub nom* R. (on the application of H) *v.* North and East London Regional Mental Health Review Tribunal; R. (on the application of H) *v.* London North and East Region Mental Health Review Tribunal [2001] EWCA Civ 415; [2002] Q.B. 1; [2001] 3 W.L.R. 512; [2001] H.R.L.R. 36; [2001] U.K.H.R.R. 717; (2001) 4 C.C.L. Rep. 119; [2001] Lloyd's Rep. Med. 302; (2001) 61 B.M.L.R. 163; [2001] A.C.D. 78; (2001) 98(21) L.S.G. 40; (2001) 145 S.J.L.B.108; *Times*, April 2, 2001; *Independent*, April 3, 2001, CA (Civ Div); reversing CO 2120/ 2000, QBD (Admin) .... *Digested*, 01/**4432**: *Followed*, 05/2825

R. (on the application of H) *v.* North and East London Regional Mental Health Review Tribunal see R. (on the application of H) *v.* Mental Health Review Tribunal for North and East London Region

R. (on the application of H) *v.* Secretary of State for Health; *sub nom* R. (on the application of MH) *v.* Secretary of State for Health; H *v.* Secretary of State for Health [2005] UKHL 60; [2005] 3 W.L.R. 867; [2005] 4 All E.R. 1311; (2005) 86 B.M.L.R. 71; *Times*, October 25, 2005; *Independent*, October 26, 2005, HL; reversing [2004] EWCA Civ 1609; [2005] 1 W.L.R. 1209; [2005] 3 All E.R. 468; (2005) 8 C.C.L. Rep. 75; (2005) 82 B.M.L.R. 168; (2004) 101(48) L.S.G. 26; (2004) 148 S.J.L.B. 1437; *Times*, December 8, 2004; *Independent*, December 7, 2004, CA (Civ Div); reversing [2004] EWHC 56, QBD (Admin) . . . ⸺ *Digested*, 05/**2818**

R. (on the application of H) *v.* Southampton Youth Court [2004] EWHC 2912; [2005] 2 Cr. App. R. (S.) 30; (2005) 169 J.P. 37; [2005] Crim. L.R. 395; [2005] A.C.D. 45; (2005) 169 J.P.N. 159, QBD (Admin) . . . . *Digested*, 05/**939**: *Applied*, 05/940

R. (on the application of H) *v.* Special Educational Needs Tribunal; *sub nom* H *v.* R School [2004] EWHC 981; [2005] E.L.R. 67, QBD (Admin) . . . . *Digested*, 05/**1147**

R. (on the application of H) *v.* Y College Independent Panel [2004] EWHC 1193; [2005] E.L.R. 25, QBD (Admin) . . . . *Digested*, 05/**1073**

R. (on the application of Hallinan Blackburn-Gittings & Nott (A Firm)) *v.* Middlesex Guildhall Crown Court [2004] EWHC 2726; [2005] 1 W.L.R. 766; *Times*, November 29, 2004, QBD (Admin) . . . . *Digested*, 05/**744**: *Approved*, 05/294

R. (on the application of Hammia) *v.* Wandsworth LBC [2005] EWHC 1127; [2005] H.L.R. 45, QBD (Admin)

R. (on the application of Hammond) *v.* Secretary of State for the Home Department [2005] UKHL 69; [2005] 3 W.L.R. 1229; (2005) 155 N.L.J. 1886; *Times*, December 2, 2005, HL; affirming [2004] EWHC 2753; [2005] 4 All E.R. 1127; [2005] A.C.D. 31; *Times*, December 6, 2004, QBD (Admin) . . . . *Digested*, 05/**3657**

R. (on the application of Hampstead Heath Winter Swimming Club) *v.* London Corp; *sub nom* Hampstead Heath Winter Swimming Club *v.* London Corp [2005] EWHC 713; [2005] 1 W.L.R. 2930; [2005] B.L.G.R. 481; [2005] A.C.D. 90; [2005] N.P.C. 57; *Times*, May 19, 2005, QBD (Admin) . . . . *Digested*, 05/**1955**

R. (on the application of Hamsher) *v.* First Secretary of State see Hamsher *v.* First Secretary of State

R. (on the application of Handa) *v.* Bow Street Magistrates Court see Handa *v.* High Instance Court of Paris

R. (on the application of Harmer) *v.* Customs and Excise Commissioners see R. (on the application of Salubi) *v.* Bow Street Magistrates Court

R. (on the application of Harrison) *v.* Flintshire Magistrates Court [2004] EWHC 2456; (2004) 168 J.P. 653; (2004) 168 J.P.N. 981, QBD (Admin) . . . . *Digested*, 05/**935**

R. (on the application of Harrop) *v.* General Teaching Council for England Returning Officer [2004] EWHC 3204; [2005] B.L.G.R. 384, QBD (Admin). . . . . *Digested*, 05/**1175**

R. (on the application of Hart Aggregates Ltd) *v.* Hartlepool BC [2005] EWHC 840; [2005] 2 P. & C.R. 31; [2005] J.P.L. 1602, QBD (Admin)

R. (on the application of Hastings BC) *v.* Jones see Hastings BC *v.* Jones

R. (on the application of Haw) *v.* Secretary of State for the Home Department C1/2005/1915, CA (Civ Div) [2005] EWHC 2061; *Times*, August 4, 2005, QBD (Admin) . *Digested*, 05/**2742**

R. (on the application of Hawkes) *v.* DPP; *sub nom* Hawkes *v.* DPP [2005] EWHC 3046; *Times*, November 29, 2005, QBD (Admin)

R. (on the application of Headley) *v.* Secretary of State for the Home Department see R. (on the application of Hindawi) *v.* Secretary of State for the Home Department

R. (on the application of Heath) *v.* Home Office Policy and Advisory Board for Forensic Pathology [2005] EWHC 1793; *Times*, October 18, 2005, QBD (Admin)

R. (on the application of Heffernan) *v.* Sheffield City Council [2004] EWHC 1377; (2004) 7 C.C.L. Rep. 350, QBD (Admin) . . . . *Digested*, 05/**3931**

R. (on the application of Hereford Waste Watchers Ltd) *v.* Herefordshire CC; *sub nom* Hereford Waste Watchers Ltd *v.* Hereford Council [2005] EWHC 191; [2005] Env. L.R. 29; [2005] J.P.L. 1469; [2005] 9 E.G.C.S. 188, QBD (Admin) . . . . . . *Digested*, 05/**3281**

R. (on the application of Hertfordshire CC) *v.* Department of Environment, Food and Rural Affairs [2005] EWHC 2363; [2005] N.P.C. 129, QBD (Admin)

R. (on the application of Hickey (Michael)) *v.* Independent Assessor see R. (on the application of O'Brien) *v.* Independent Assessor

R. (on the application of Hickey (Vincent)) *v.* Independent Assessor see R. (on the application of O'Brien) *v.* Independent Assessor

R. (on the application of Hill) *v.* First Secretary of State [2005] EWHC 1128; [2005] J.P.L. 1531, QBD (Admin)

R. (on the application of Hindawi) *v.* Secretary of State for the Home Department; *sub nom* Hindawi *v.* Secretary of State for the Home Department; Secretary of State for the Home Department *v.* Hindawi; R. (on the application of Headley) *v.* Secretary of State for the Home Department [2004] EWCA Civ 1309; [2005] 1 W.L.R. 1102; [2004] U.K.H.R.R. 1146; [2005] A.C.D. 88; (2004) 101(43) L.S.G. 33; (2004) 148 S.J.L.B. 1214; *Times*, October 26, 2004, CA (Civ Div); reversing [2004] EWHC 78; *Times*, February 5, 2004, QBD (Admin) . . . . *Digested*, 04/**2776**

R. (on the application of Hirst) *v.* Secretary of State for the Home Department [2005] EWHC 1480; (2005) 102(40) L.S.G. 27; *Times*, July 4, 2005, QBD (Admin) . . . *Digested*, 05/**2921**

R. (on the application of Hitch) v. Oliver (Special Commissioner of Income Tax) see R. (on the application of Hitch) v. Special Commissioners

R. (on the application of Hitch) v. Special Commissioners; *sub nom* R. (on the application of Hitch) v. Oliver (Special Commissioner of Income Tax) [2005] EWHC 291; [2005] 1 W.L.R. 1651; [2005] S.T.C. 474; 77 T.C. 70; [2005] B.T.C. 219; [2005] S.T.I. 365; (2005) 102(18) L.S.G. 23; (2005) 155 N.L.J. 384; [2005] N.P.C. 34; *Times*, March 14, 2005, QBD (Admin) . . . . *Digested*, 05/**3986**

R. (on the application of Holding & Barnes Plc) v. Secretary of State for the Environment, Transport and the Regions; *sub nom* R. v. Secretary of State for the Environment, Transport and the Regions Ex p. Holdings & Barnes Plc; R. (on the application of Premier Leisure UK Ltd) v. Secretary of State for the Environment, Transport and the Regions; R. (on the application of Alconbury Developments Ltd) v. Secretary of State for the Environment, Transport and the Regions; Secretary of State for the Environment, Transport and the Regions v. Legal & General Assurance Society Ltd [2001] UKHL 23; [2003] 2 A.C. 295; [2001] 2 W.L.R. 1389; [2001] 2 All E.R. 929; [2002] Env. L.R. 12; [2001] H.R.L.R. 45; [2001] U.K.H.R.R. 728; (2001) 3 L.G.L.R. 38; (2001) 82 P. & C.R. 40; [2001] 2 P.L.R. 76; [2001] J.P.L. 920; [2001] 20 E.G.C.S. 228; (2001) 98(24) L.S.G. 45; (2001) 151 N.L.J. 727; (2001) 145 S.J.L.B. 140; [2001] N.P.C. 90; *Times*, May 10, 2001; *Independent*, June 25, 2001 (C.S); *Daily Telegraph*, May 15, 2001, HL; reversing [2001] H.R.L.R. 2; [2001] U.K.H.R.R. 270; (2001) 3 L.G.L.R. 21; [2001] 1 P.L.R. 58; [2001] 1 E.G.L.R. 33; [2001] 05 E.G. 170; [2001] J.P.L. 291; [2001] 4 E.G.C.S. 141; (2001) 151 N.L.J. 135; (2001) 145 S.J.L.B. 84; *Times*, January 24, 2001; *Independent*, January 22, 2001 (C.S), DC . . . . *Digested*, 01/**4761**:
Applied, 02/2337, 02/3700, 02/4191, 05/1410: *Cited*, 01/6853, 02/1647:
Considered, 02/3696, 02/3699, 03/55, 04/790, 04/1529:
Followed, 02/1526, 03/3446

R. (on the application of Holme) v. Liverpool Magistrates Court; *sub nom* Holme v. Liverpool City Justices [2004] EWHC 3131; (2005) 169 J.P. 306; [2005] A.C.D. 37; (2005) 169 J.P.N. 417, QBD (Admin) . . . . *Digested*, 05/**3635**

R. (on the application of Hooper) v. Secretary of State for Work and Pensions; *sub nom* Hooper v. Secretary of State for Work and Pensions; R. (on the application of Withey) v. Secretary of State for Work and Pensions; R. (on the application of Naylor) v. Secretary of State for Work and Pensions; R. (on the application of Martin) v. Secretary of State for Work and Pensions [2005] UKHL 29; [2005] 1 W.L.R. 1681; [2005] 2 F.C.R. 183; [2005] H.R.L.R. 21; [2005] U.K.H.R.R. 717; [2005] Pens. L.R. 337; *Times*, May 6, 2005; *Independent*, May 10, 2005, HL; reversing [2003] EWCA Civ 813; [2003] 1 W.L.R. 2623; [2003] 3 All E.R. 673; [2003] 2 F.C.R. 504; [2003] U.K.H.R.R. 1268; 14 B.H.R.C. 626; (2003) 100(29) L.S.G. 35; *Times*, June 28, 2003; *Independent*, June 25, 2003, CA (Civ Div); affirming [2002] EWHC 191; [2002] U.K.H.R.R. 785, QBD (Admin) . . . . . *Digested*, 05/**3926**

R. (on the application of Horne & Meredith Properties Ltd) v. Bridgnorth DC [2005] EWHC 2251; [2005] N.P.C. 123, QBD (Admin)

R. (on the application of Howe) v. South Durham Magistrates Court [2004] EWHC 362; (2004) 168 J.P. 424; [2005] R.T.R. 4; (2004) 168 J.P.N. 637; *Times*, February 26, 2004, QBD (Admin) . . . . *Digested*, 04/**719**

R. (on the application of Hoxa) v. Special Adjudicator see R. (on the application of Hoxha) v. Special Adjudicator

R. (on the application of Hoxha) v. Special Adjudicator; *sub nom* Hoxha v. Secretary of State for the Home Department; B v. Secretary of State for the Home Department; R. (on the application of Hoxha) v. Special Adjudicator; B, Re; R. (on the application of B) v. Immigration Appeal Tribunal [2005] UKHL 19; [2005] 1 W.L.R. 1063; [2005] 4 All E.R. 580; 19 B.H.R.C. 676; [2005] Imm. A.R. 272; [2005] I.N.L.R. 440; (2005) 149 S.J.L.B. 358; *Times*, March 11, 2005, HL; affirming [2002] EWCA Civ 1403; [2003] 1 W.L.R. 241; [2003] Imm. A.R. 211; [2002] I.N.L.R. 559; (2002) 99(44) L.S.G. 32; *Times*, October 31, 2002, CA (Civ Div); affirming [2001] EWHC Admin 708, QBD (Admin) . . . . *Digested*, 05/**2177**

R. (on the application of HP) v. Islington LBC [2004] EWHC 7; (2005) 82 B.M.L.R. 113, QBD (Admin)

R. (on the application of Hughes) v. Customs and Excise Commissioners see Hughes v. Customs and Excise Commissioners

R. (on the application of Hughes) v. Liverpool City Council [2005] EWHC 428; [2005] B.L.G.R. 531; (2005) 8 C.C.L. Rep. 243, QBD (Admin) . . . . *Digested*, 05/**3947**

R. (on the application of Hurst) v. HM Coroner for Northern District London; *sub nom* Commissioner of Police of the Metropolis v. Hurst; R. (on the application of Hurst) v. Northern District of London Coroner [2005] EWCA Civ 890; [2005] 1 W.L.R. 3892; [2005] H.R.L.R. 31; [2005] U.K.H.R.R. 1259; (2005) 102(31) L.S.G. 27; (2005) 155 N.L.J. 1207; *Times*, August 11, 2005; *Independent*, July 28, 2005, CA (Civ Div); affirming [2003] EWHC 1721; [2004] U.K.H.R.R. 139; [2003] A.C.D. 88, QBD (Admin) . . . . *Digested*, 05/**17**:
Disapproved, 04/1976

R. (on the application of Hurst) v. Northern District of London Coroner see R. (on the application of Hurst) v. HM Coroner for Northern District London

R. (on the application of Husan) *v.* Secretary of State for the Home Department [2005] EWHC 189; (2005) 102(16) L.S.G. 28; *Times*, March 1, 2005, QBD (Admin) . . .   *Digested*, 05/**2222**

R. (on the application of Hutchinson 3G (UK) Ltd) *v.* Islington LBC see R. (on the application of Orange PCS Ltd) *v.* Islington LBC

R. (on the application of Hwez) *v.* Secretary of State for the Home Department see R. (on the application of Khadir) *v.* Secretary of State for the Home Department

R. (on the application of I) *v.* Independent Appeal Panel for G [2005] EWHC 558; [2005] E.L.R. 490, QBD (Admin)

R. (on the application of I) *v.* Secretary of State for the Home Department; R. (on the application of O) *v.* Secretary of State for the Home Department [2005] EWHC 1025; *Times*, June 10, 2005, QBD (Admin) . . . .   *Digested*, 05/**2145**

R. (on the application of I'm Your Man Ltd) *v.* North Somerset Council [2004] EWHC 342; [2004] 4 P.L.R. 1; [2004] J.P.L. 1563; [2004] N.P.C. 31, QBD (Admin) . . .   *Digested*, 05/**3246**

R. (on the application of IDT Card Services Ireland Ltd) *v.* Customs and Excise Commissioners; *sub nom* Revenue and Customs Commissioners *v.* IDT Card Services Ireland Ltd; C1/2005/0183, CA (Civ Div); reversing [2004] EWHC 3188; [2005] S.T.C. 314; [2005] B.T.C. 5163; [2005] B.V.C. 194; [2005] S.T.I. 22, QBD (Admin) . . . .   *Digested*, 05/**4405**

R. (on the application of Inland Revenue Commissioners) *v.* Aberdeen General Commissioners of Income Tax see Revenue and Customs Commissioners, Petitioners

R. (on the application of International Air Transport Association) *v.* Department of Transport; R. (on the application of European Low Fares Airline Association *v.* Department of Transport) [2004] EWHC 1721; [2004] 3 C.M.L.R. 20; [2004] Eu. L.R. 998, QBD (Admin) . . . .   *Digested*, 05/**1475**

R. (on the application of International Air Transport Association) *v.* Department of Transport (C344/04), *Times*, January 16, 2005, ECJ . . . .   *Previous proceedings*, 05/1475

R. (on the application of International Transport Roth GmbH) *v.* Secretary of State for the Home Department see International Transport Roth GmbH *v.* Secretary of State for the Home Department

R. (on the application of Iqbal) *v.* Newham LBC see R. (on the application of Khatun) *v.* Newham LBC

R. (on the application of Isle of Anglesey CC) *v.* Secretary of State for Work and Pensions [2003] EWHC 2518; [2004] B.L.G.R. 614; [2003] N.P.C. 130, QBD (Admin) . .   *Digested*, 04/**3581**: *Applied*, 05/3876

R. (on the application of J) *v.* Caerphilly CBC [2005] EWHC 586; [2005] 2 F.L.R. 860; [2005] 2 F.C.R. 153; (2005) 8 C.C.L. Rep. 255; [2005] A.C.D. 80; [2005] Fam. Law 528; [2005] Fam. Law 611; *Times*, April 21, 2005, QBD (Admin) . . . .   *Digested*, 05/**3930**

R. (on the application of J) *v.* Secretary of State for the Home Department see R. (on the application of Q) *v.* Secretary of State for the Home Department

R. (on the application of J) *v.* Southend BC (2005) 102(33) L.S.G. 25, QBD (Admin)

R. (on the application of Jackson) *v.* Attorney General; *sub nom* Jackson *v.* Attorney General [2005] UKHL 56; [2005] 3 W.L.R. 733; [2005] 4 All E.R. 1253; (2005) 155 N.L.J. 1600; [2005] N.P.C. 116; *Times*, October 14, 2005; *Independent*, October 20, 2005, HL; affirming [2005] EWCA Civ 126; [2005] Q.B. 579; [2005] 2 W.L.R. 866; (2005) 102(15) L.S.G. 32; (2005) 155 N.L.J. 297; [2005] N.P.C. 24; *Times*, February 17, 2005; *Independent*, February 22, 2005, CA (Civ Div); affirming [2005] EWHC 94; (2005) 102(13) L.S.G. 27; (2005) 149 S.J.L.B. 177; *Times*, January 31, 2005; *Independent*, February 1, 2005, QBD (Admin) . . . .   *Digested*, 05/**638**

R. (on the application of Jeyapragash) *v.* Immigration Appeal Tribunal see Jeyapragash *v.* Secretary of State for the Home Department

R. (on the application of Jones) *v.* Ceredigion CC; *sub nom* R. (on the application of Jones) *v.* Ceredigon CC [2004] EWHC 1376; [2005] 1 W.L.R. 3626; [2004] B.L.G.R. 881; [2004] E.L.R. 506; *Times*, July 8, 2004, QBD (Admin) . . . .   *Digested*, 05/**1078**

R. (on the application of Jones) *v.* Ceredigion CC (No.2) see R. (on the application of Jones) *v.* Ceredigion CC (Permission to Appeal)

R. (on the application of Jones) *v.* Ceredigion CC (Permission to Appeal); *sub nom* R. (on the application of Jones) *v.* Ceredigion CC (No.2) [2005] EWCA Civ 986; [2005] C.P. Rep. 48; [2005] E.L.R. 565; *Times*, September 16, 2005, CA (Civ Div)

R. (on the application of Jones) *v.* Chief Constable of Cheshire [2005] EWHC 2457; *Times*, November 4, 2005, QBD (Admin)

R. (on the application of Jones) *v.* Mansfield DC [2003] EWCA Civ 1408; [2004] Env. L.R. 21; [2004] 2 P. & C.R. 14; (2003) 147 S.J.L.B. 1209; [2003] N.P.C. 119; *Times*, October 31, 2003, CA (Civ Div); affirming [2003] EWHC 7; [2003] Env. L.R. 26; [2003] 1 P. & C.R. 31; [2003] J.P.L. 1148; [2003] N.P.C. 5, QBD (Admin) . . . .   *Digested*, 03/**3421**: *Applied*, 05/3270, 05/3298: *Considered*, 04/3084

R. (on the application of K) *v.* Bow Street Magistrates Court see R. (on the application of M) *v.* Bow Street Magistrates Court

R. (on the application of K) *v.* Camden and Islington HA; *sub nom* R. *v.* Camden and Islington HA Ex p. K [2001] EWCA Civ 240; [2002] Q.B. 198; [2001] 3 W.L.R. 553; [2001] U.K.H.R.R. 1378; (2001) 4 C.C.L. Rep. 170; [2001] Lloyd's Rep. Med. 152; (2001) 61 B.M.L.R. 173; (2001) 98(16) L.S.G. 34; (2001) 145 S.J.L.B. 69; *Times*, March 15, 2001; *Independent*, February 28, 2001, CA (Civ Div); affirming (2000) 3 C.C.L. Rep. 256; [2000] C.O.D. 483, QBD . . . . *Digested*, 01/**4430**:
Applied, 05/2824: *Considered*, 02/3239, 03/2956

R. (on the application of K) *v.* Croydon Crown Court; *sub nom* K *v.* Croydon Crown Court [2005] EWHC 478; [2005] 2 Cr. App. R. (S.) 96, QBD (Admin) . . . . *Digested*, 05/**2171**

R. (on the application of K) *v.* Knowsley MBC see K *v.* Knowsley MBC

R. (on the application of K) *v.* Tamworth Manor High School Governors [2004] EWHC 2564; [2005] E.L.R. 192; [2005] A.C.D. 71, QBD (Admin) . . . . *Digested*, 05/**1074**

R. (on the application of K) *v.* West London Mental Health NHS Trust C1/2005/1538, CA (Civ Div); affirming [2005] EWHC 1454; (2005) 102(36) L.S.G. 32, QBD (Admin)

R. (on the application of K) *v.* Wirral Borough Magistrates Court see R. (on the application of W) *v.* Southampton Youth Court

R. (on the application of Keam) *v.* DEFRA see R. (on the application of Keam) *v.* Department for Environment, Food and Rural Affairs

R. (on the application of Keam) *v.* Department for Environment, Food and Rural Affairs; *sub nom* Keam *v.* Department for Environment, Food and Rural Affairs; R. (on the application of Keam) *v.* DEFRA [2005] EWHC 1582; (2005) 169 J.P. 512; (2005) 169 J.P.N. 761, QBD (Admin)

R. (on the application of Keating) *v.* Cardiff Local Health Board [2005] EWCA Civ 847; [2005] 3 All E.R. 1000; (2005) 8 C.C.L. Rep. 504; (2005) 85 B.M.L.R. 190; *Times*, September 6, 2005, CA (Civ Div); reversing [2005] EWHC 559, QBD (Admin) . . . . *Digested*, 05/**1829**

R. (on the application of Kebbell Development Ltd) *v.* First Secretary of State see Kebbell Development Ltd *v.* First Secretary of State

R. (on the application of Kehoe) *v.* Secretary of State for Work and Pensions; *sub nom* Secretary of State for Work and Pensions *v.* Kehoe; Kehoe *v.* Secretary of State for Work and Pensions [2005] UKHL 48; [2005] 3 W.L.R. 252; [2005] 4 All E.R. 905; [2005] 2 F.L.R. 1249; [2005] 2 F.C.R. 683; [2005] H.R.L.R. 30; [2005] Fam. Law 850; (2005) 155 N.L.J. 1123; (2005) 149 S.J.L.B. 921; *Times*, July 15, 2005; *Independent*, July 19, 2005, HL; affirming [2004] EWCA Civ 225; [2004] Q.B. 1378; [2004] 2 W.L.R. 1481; [2004] 1 F.L.R. 1132; [2004] 1 F.C.R. 511; [2004] U.K.H.R.R. 443; [2004] Fam. Law 399; (2004) 101(13) L.S.G. 33; (2004) 148 S.J.L.B. 301; *Times*, March 10, 2004; *Independent*, March 19, 2004, CA (Civ Div); reversing [2003] EWHC 1021; [2003] 2 F.L.R. 578; [2003] 3 F.C.R. 481; [2003] U.K.H.R.R. 702; [2003] Fam. Law 718; (2003) 100(26) L.S.G. 37; *Times*, May 21, 2003, QBD (Admin) . . . . *Digested*, 05/**1553**

R. (on the application of Kelly) *v.* Hammersmith and Fulham LBC; *sub nom* Kelly *v.* Hammersmith LBC [2004] EWHC 435; (2004) 7 C.C.L. Rep. 542, QBD (Admin) . . . . *Digested*, 05/**3407**

R. (on the application of Kenny) *v.* Leeds Magistrates Court see R. (on the application of M) *v.* Secretary of State for Constitutional Affairs

R. (on the application of Kent) *v.* First Secretary of State; *sub nom* Kent *v.* First Secretary of State [2004] EWHC 2953; [2005] Env. L.R. 30; [2005] 2 P. & C.R. 16; [2005] J.P.L. 951; *Times*, January 6, 2005, QBD (Admin) . . . . *Digested*, 05/**3298**

R. (on the application of Kent Pharmaceuticals Ltd) *v.* Director of the Serious Fraud Office [2004] EWCA Civ 1494; [2005] 1 W.L.R. 1302; [2005] 1 All E.R. 449; (2004) 101(48) L.S.G. 26; *Times*, November 18, 2004, CA (Civ Div); affirming [2003] EWHC 3002; [2004] A.C.D. 23; *Times*, January 6, 2004, QBD (Admin) . . . . *Digested*, 05/**1785**

R. (on the application of Khadir) *v.* Secretary of State for the Home Department; R. (on the application of Hwez) *v.* Secretary of State for the Home Department [2005] UKHL 39; [2005] 3 W.L.R. 1; [2005] 4 All E.R. 114; [2005] I.N.L.R. 538; (2005) 155 N.L.J. 971; (2005) 149 S.J.L.B. 773; *Times*, June 17, 2005, HL; affirming [2003] EWCA Civ 475; [2003] I.N.L.R. 426; (2003) 100(23) L.S.G. 37, CA (Civ Div); reversing [2002] EWHC 1597, QBD (Admin) . . . . *Digested*, 05/**2161**

R. (on the application of Khan (Mohammed Farooq)) *v.* Secretary of State for Health [2003] EWCA Civ 1129; [2004] 1 W.L.R. 971; [2003] 4 All E.R. 1239; [2003] 3 F.C.R. 341; (2004) 7 C.C.L. Rep. 361; [2004] Lloyd's Rep. Med. 159; (2004) 76 B.M.L.R. 118; [2003] A.C.D. 89; (2003) 100(44) L.S.G. 30; (2003) 147 S.J.L.B. 1207; *Times*, October 15, 2003, CA (Civ Div); reversing [2003] EWHC 1414; [2003] Lloyd's Rep. Med. 429, QBD (Admin) . . . . *Digested*, 03/**2810**:
Considered, 05/34: *Disapproved*, 04/1976: *Overruled*, 04/13

R. (on the application of Khatun) *v.* Newham LBC; *sub nom* Khatun *v.* Newham LBC; Newham LBC *v.* Khatun; R. (on the application of Zeb) *v.* Newham LBC; R. (on the application of Iqbal) *v.* Newham LBC [2004] EWCA Civ 55; [2005] Q.B. 37; [2004] 3 W.L.R. 417; [2004] Eu. L.R. 628; [2004] H.L.R. 29; [2004] B.L.G.R. 696; [2004] L. & T.R. 18; (2004) 148 S.J.L.B. 268; [2004] N.P.C. 28; *Times*, February 27, 2004; *Independent*, March 4, 2004, CA (Civ Div); reversing in part [2003] EWHC 2326; [2004] Eu. L.R. 116; [2004] 1 E.G.L.R. 34; [2004] 08 E.G. 136; [2003] N.P.C. 114, QBD (Admin) . . . .   *Digested*, 04/**1907**

R. (on the application of Kind) *v.* Secretary of State for the Environment, Food and Rural Affairs [2005] EWHC 1324; [2005] 3 W.L.R. 616; [2005] R.T.R. 24; [2005] N.P.C. 83; *Times*, August 30, 2005, QBD (Admin) . . . .   *Digested*, 05/**3425**

R. (on the application of Kondova) *v.* Secretary of State for the Home Department (C235/99); *sub nom* R. *v.* Secretary of State for the Home Department Ex p. Kondova (C235/99) [2001] E.C.R. I-6427; [2001] 3 C.M.L.R. 47; *Times*, November 13, 2001, ECJ . . . .   *Digested*, 02/**1575**: *Applied*, 05/2199

R. (on the application of Kpangni) *v.* Secretary of State for the Home Department [2005] EWHC 881; *Times*, May 3, 2005, QBD (Admin) . . . .   *Digested*, 05/**2166**

R. (on the application of L) *v.* Secretary of State for the Home Department; *sub nom* R. (on the application of AL) *v.* Secretary of State for the Home Department [2005] EWCA Civ 2; (2005) 155 N.L.J. 140; (2005) 149 S.J.L.B. 144; *Times*, January 27, 2005; *Independent*, January 27, 2005, CA (Civ Div); affirming [2004] EWHC 1025, QBD (Admin) . . . .   *Digested*, 05/**2831**: *Applied*, 05/2817

R. (on the application of L) *v.* Waltham Forest LBC [2003] EWHC 2907; [2004] E.L.R. 161, QBD (Admin) . . . .   *Digested*, 04/**1087**: *Applied*, 05/1061

R. (on the application of L (A Child)) *v.* St Edward's College Independent Appeal Panel [2001] EWHC Admin 108; [2001] E.L.R. 542, QBD (Admin) . . . .   *Digested*, 01/**1974**: *Considered*, 05/1068

R. (on the application of Lambeth LBC) *v.* Secretary of State for Work and Pensions [2005] EWHC 637; [2005] B.L.G.R. 764; [2005] N.P.C. 54; *Times*, May 13, 2005, QBD (Admin) . . . .   *Digested*, 05/**3876**

R. (on the application of Lampkin) *v.* Horseferry Road Magistrates Court [2005] EWHC 312; [2005] R.A. 233, QBD (Admin)

R. (on the application of Laporte) *v.* Chief Constable of Gloucestershire [2004] EWCA Civ 1639; [2005] Q.B. 678; [2005] 2 W.L.R. 789; [2005] 1 All E.R. 473; [2005] H.R.L.R. 6; [2005] Crim. L.R. 467; [2005] A.C.D. 57; (2005) 102(6) L.S.G. 32; *Times*, December 13, 2004; *Independent*, December 14, 2004, CA (Civ Div); affirming [2004] EWHC 253; [2004] 2 All E.R. 874; [2004] U.K.H.R.R. 484; [2004] A.C.D. 34; (2004) 154 N.L.J. 308; *Times*, February 26, 2004, QBD (Admin) . . . .   *Digested*, 05/**3341**

R. (on the application of Lebus) *v.* South Cambridgeshire DC [2002] EWHC 2009; [2003] Env. L.R. 17; [2003] 2 P. & C.R. 5; [2003] J.P.L. 466; (2002) 99(36) L.S.G. 42, QBD (Admin) . . . .   *Digested*, 03/**3422**: *Considered*, 05/3308

R. (on the application of Lee) *v.* Nuneaton and Bedworth BC [2004] EWHC 950; [2004] J.P.L. 1698; [2004] A.C.D. 96; [2004] 18 E.G.C.S. 101, QBD (Admin) . .   *Digested*, 05/**3283**

R. (on the application of Legal & General Assurance Society Ltd) *v.* Rushmoor BC [2004] EWHC 2094; [2005] 1 P. & C.R. 26, QBD (Admin) . . . .   *Digested*, 05/**3307**

R. (on the application of Limbuela) *v.* Secretary of State for the Home Department; R. (on the application of Tesema) *v.* Secretary of State for the Home Department; R. (on the application of Adam) *v.* Secretary of State for the Home Department [2005] UKHL 66; [2005] 3 W.L.R. 1014; (2005) 102(46) L.S.G. 25; (2005) 149 S.J.L.B. 1354; *Times*, November 4, 2005, HL; affirming [2004] EWCA Civ 540; [2004] Q.B. 1440; [2004] 3 W.L.R. 561; [2005] 3 All E.R. 29; [2004] H.L.R. 38; (2004) 7 C.C.L. Rep. 267; [2004] A.C.D. 70; (2004) 101(23) L.S.G. 32; *Times*, May 26, 2004; *Independent*, May 25, 2004, CA (Civ Div); affirming [2004] EWHC 219; *Times*, February 9, 2004, QBD . . . .   *Digested*, 04/**2026**: *Considered*, 05/2157

R. (on the application of London Corp) *v.* Secretary of State for the Environment, Food and Rural Affairs; *sub nom* City of London Corp *v.* Secretary of State for the Environment, Food and Rural Affairs [2004] EWCA Civ 1765; [2005] 1 W.L.R. 1286; *Times*, December 27, 2004; *Independent*, January 18, 2005, CA (Civ Div) . . . .   *Digested*, 05/**60**

R. (on the application of Lonergan) *v.* Lewes Crown Court; *sub nom* Lonergan *v.* Lewes Crown Court [2005] EWHC 457; [2005] 1 W.L.R. 2570; [2005] 2 All E.R. 362; (2005) 169 J.P. 324; [2005] A.C.D. 84; (2005) 169 J.P.N. 477; (2005) 102(23) L.S.G. 27; *Times*, April 25, 2005, QBD (Admin) . . . .   *Digested*, 05/**319**

R. (on the application of Loutchansky) *v.* First Secretary of State [2005] EWHC 1779; [2005] 3 C.M.L.R. 15, QBD (Admin) . . . .   *Digested*, 05/**351**

R. (on the application of Lunn) *v.* Governor of Moorland Prison [2005] EWHC 2558; *Times*, November 2, 2005, QBD

R. (on the application of M) *v.* Bow Street Magistrates Court; *sub nom* R. (on the application of K) *v.* Bow Street Magistrates Court [2005] EWHC 2271; *Times,* July 27, 2005, QBD (Admin)

R. (on the application of M) *v.* Criminal Injuries Compensation Appeals Panel [2004] EWHC 1701; [2005] P.I.Q.R. P4; [2005] A.C.D. 24; (2004) 101 (30) L.S.G. 29; *Times,* July 8, 2004, QBD . . . . *Digested,* 04/**63**

R. (on the application of M) *v.* Immigration Appeal Tribunal see R. (on the application of G) *v.* Immigration Appeal Tribunal

R. (on the application of M) *v.* Immigration Appeal Tribunal [2005] EWHC 251; [2005] Imm. A.R. 213, QBD (Admin)

R. (on the application of M) *v.* Independent Appeal Panel [2004] EWHC 1831; [2005] E.L.R. 38, QBD (Admin) . . . . *Digested,* 05/**1071**

R. (on the application of M) *v.* Islington LBC; *sub nom* M *v.* Islington LBC [2004] EWCA Civ 235; [2005] 1 W.L.R. 884; [2004] 4 All E.R. 709; [2004] 2 F.L.R. 867; [2004] 2 F.C.R. 363; [2004] B.L.G.R. 815; (2004) 7 C.C.L. Rep. 230; [2004] Fam. Law 645; *Times,* April 22, 2004, CA (Civ Div); reversing [2003] EWHC 1388; [2003] 2 F.L.R. 903; [2003] H.L.R. 73; [2004] A.C.D. 8; [2003] Fam. Law 729; (2003) 100 (31) L.S.G. 32; *Times,* June 12, 2003, QBD (Admin) .   *Digested,* 04/**2072**: *Applied,* 04/2076

R. (on the application of M) *v.* Secretary of State for Constitutional Affairs; R. (on the application of Kenny) *v.* Leeds Magistrates Court [2004] EWCA Civ 312; [2004] 1 W.L.R. 2298; [2004] 2 All E.R. 531; (2004) 168 J.P. 529; [2004] B.L.G.R. 417; (2004) 168 J.P.N. 818; (2004) 101 (15) L.S.G. 27; (2004) 148 S.J.L.B. 385; *Times,* March 31, 2004; *Independent,* March 25, 2004, CA (Civ Div); affirming [2003] EWHC 2963; [2004] 1 All E.R. 1333; (2004) 168 J.P. 125; (2004) 168 J.P.N. 274, QBD (Admin) . . . .   *Digested,* 04/**790**: *Applied,* 05/316

R. (on the application of M) *v.* Secretary of State for the Home Department see Anufrijeva *v.* Southwark LBC

R. (on the application of M) *v.* Secretary of State for the Home Department see R. (on the application of Q) *v.* Secretary of State for the Home Department

R. (on the application of M) *v.* Special Educational Needs Tribunal [2004] EWHC 422; [2004] E.L.R. 599; [2004] A.C.D. 80, QBD (Admin) . . . . *Digested,* 05/**1144**

R. (on the application of M) *v.* Waltham Forest Youth Court see R. (on the application of W) *v.* Thetford Youth Court

R. (on the application of M) *v.* West London Youth Court; R. (on the application of W) *v.* West London Youth Court [2004] EWHC 1144; [2005] A.C.D. 4, QBD (Admin) .   *Applied,* 04/895

R. (on the application of M) *v.* Worcestershire CC [2004] EWHC 1045; [2005] E.L.R. 48, QBD (Admin) . . . . *Digested,* 05/**1137**

R. (on the application of M (A Child)) *v.* Manchester Crown Court see R. (on the application of McCann) *v.* Manchester Crown Court

R. (on the application of M (A Child)) *v.* Sheffield Magistrates Court [2004] EWHC 1830; (2005) 169 J.P. 557; [2005] 1 F.L.R. 81; [2004] 3 F.C.R. 281; [2005] B.L.G.R. 126; [2005] A.C.D. 43; [2004] Fam. Law 790; (2005) 169 J.P.N. 818; (2004) 101 (39) L.S.G. 34; (2004) 154 N.L.J. 1410; *Times,* August 30, 2004, QBD (Admin) . . . .   *Digested,* 05/**317**: *Considered,* 05/319

R. (on the application of Maged) *v.* Secretary of State for the Home Department see R. (on the application of Saadi) *v.* Secretary of State for the Home Department

R. (on the application of Maheshwaran) *v.* Secretary of State for the Home Department; *sub nom* Secretary of State for the Home Department *v.* Maheshwaran [2002] EWCA Civ 173; [2004] Imm. A.R. 176; *Independent,* February 20, 2002, CA (Civ Div); reversing [2001] EWHC Admin 562, QBD (Admin) . . . . *Considered,* 05/2153

R. (on the application of Mahfouz) *v.* General Medical Council; *sub nom* Mahfouz *v.* General Medical Council [2004] EWCA Civ 233; [2004] Lloyd's Rep. Med. 377; (2004) 80 B.M.L.R. 113; (2004) 101 (13) L.S.G. 35; *Times,* March 19, 2004, CA (Civ Div); reversing in part [2003] EWHC 1695, QBD (Admin) . . . .   *Digested,* 04/**1629**: *Applied,* 05/1800

R. (on the application of Majead) *v.* Immigration Appeal Tribunal see R. (on the application of Majead) *v.* Secretary of State for the Home Department

R. (on the application of Majead) *v.* Secretary of State for the Home Department; *sub nom* R. (on the application of Majead) *v.* Immigration Appeal Tribunal [2003] EWCA Civ 615; [2003] A.C.D. 70; (2003) 100 (23) L.S.G. 38; (2003) 147 S.J.L.B. 539; *Times,* April 24, 2003, CA (Civ Div) . . . .   *Digested,* 03/**2215**: *Applied,* 05/401: *Considered,* 04/4482: *Followed,* 04/4481

R. (on the application of Makke) *v.* Immigration Appeal Tribunal see R. (on the application of Makke) *v.* Secretary of State for the Home Department

R. (on the application of Makke) *v.* Secretary of State for the Home Department; *sub nom* R. (on the application of Makke) *v.* Immigration Appeal Tribunal; Secretary of State for the Home Department *v.* Makke [2005] EWCA Civ 176; [2005] Imm. A.R. 231; *Times,* April 5, 2005; *Independent,* March 3, 2005, CA (Civ Div) . . . .   *Digested,* 05/**2151**

R. (on the application of Malekout) v. Secretary of State for Health [2005] EWCA Civ
1170, CA (Civ Div); affirming [2004] EWHC 2879; *Times*, January 4, 2005, QBD
(Admin) . . . . *Digested*, 05/**3075**

R. (on the application of Manchester City Council) v. Manchester Magistrates Court
[2005] EWHC 253; *Times*, March 8, 2005, QBD (Admin) . . . . *Digested*, 05/**316**

R. (on the application of Mapah) v. Secretary of State for the Home Department; *sub
nom* Mapah v. Secretary of State for the Home Department [2003] EWHC 306;
[2003] Imm. A.R. 395; [2003] A.C.D. 49; (2003) 100(17) L.S.G. 28; *Times*,
March 5, 2003, QBD (Admin) . . . . *Digested*, 03/**2251**:
Distinguished, 05/2169

R. (on the application of Marper) v. Chief Constable of South Yorkshire see R. (on the
application of S) v. Chief Constable of South Yorkshire

R. (on the application of Martin) v. Secretary of State for Work and Pensions see R. (on
the application of Hooper) v. Secretary of State for Work and Pensions

R. (on the application of Martin Grant Homes Ltd) v. Wealden DC; *sub nom* Wealdon DC
v. Martin Grant Homes Ltd [2005] EWCA Civ 1221; (2005) 149 S.J.L.B. 1351;
[2005] N.P.C. 124; *Times*, November 11, 2005, CA (Civ Div); reversing [2005]
EWHC 453; [2005] 2 P.L.R. 113; [2005] J.P.L. 1349; [2005] 11 E.G.C.S. 180;
[2005] N.P.C. 56; *Times*, March 18, 2005, QBD (Admin) . . . . *Digested*, 05/**3269**

R. (on the application of Martiner) v. DPP [2004] EWHC 2484; [2005] A.C.D. 65, QBD
(Admin)

R. (on the application of Matara) v. Brent Magistrates Court [2005] EWHC 1829;
(2005) 169 J.P. 576; (2005) 169 J.P.N. 836, QBD (Admin) . . . . *Digested*, 05/**2710**

R. (on the application of Mathialagan) v. Camberwell Green Justices see R. (on the
application of Mathialagan) v. Southwark LBC

R. (on the application of Mathialagan) v. Southwark LBC; *sub nom* R. (on the
application of Mathialagan) v. Camberwell Green Justices [2004] EWCA Civ
1689; [2005] R.A. 43; [2005] A.C.D. 60; (2005) 102(4) L.S.G. 31; *Times*,
December 21, 2004, CA (Civ Div); affirming [2004] EWHC 929; [2004] R.V.R.
212, QBD (Admin) . . . . *Digested*, 05/**430**

R. (on the application of Mayer Parry Recycling Ltd) v. Environment Agency (C444/00);
sub nom R. v. Environment Agency Ex p. Mayer Parry Recycling Ltd (C444/
00) [2004] 1 W.L.R. 538; [2005] All E.R. (EC) 647; [2003] E.C.R. I-6163;
[2003] 3 C.M.L.R. 8; [2004] Env. L.R. 6; *Times*, July 14, 2003, ECJ (5th
Chamber)

R. (on the application of McCann) v. Manchester Crown Court; *sub nom* R. v.
Manchester Crown Court Ex p. M (A Child); R. (on the application of M (A
Child)) v. Manchester Crown Court; Clingham v. Kensington and Chelsea RLBC
[2002] UKHL 39; [2003] 1 A.C. 787; [2002] 3 W.L.R. 1313; [2002] 4 All E.R.
593; [2003] 1 Cr. App. R. 27; (2002) 166 J.P. 657; [2002] U.K.H.R.R. 1286; 13
B.H.R.C. 482; [2003] H.L.R. 17; [2003] B.L.G.R. 57; [2003] Crim. L.R. 269;
(2002) 166 J.P.N. 850; (2002) 146 S.J.L.B. 239; *Times*, October 21, 2002;
Independent, October 23, 2002, HL; affirming [2001] EWCA Civ 281; [2001] 1
W.L.R. 1084; [2001] 4 All E.R. 264; (2001) 165 J.P. 545; [2001] H.R.L.R. 37;
(2002) 166 J.P.N. 150; *Times*, March 9, 2001; *Independent*, March 20, 2001, CA
(Civ Div); affirming [2001] 1 W.L.R. 358; (2001) 165 J.P. 225; (2001) 165
J.P.N. 204; (2001) 98(2) L.S.G. 40; (2000) 144 S.J.L.B. 287; *Times*, December
22, 2000; *Daily Telegraph*, December 12, 2000, DC. . . . . *Digested*, 02/**3**:
Applied, 01/41, 02/1579, 04/366, 04/1020: *Considered*, 03/831, 04/790,
05/1073: *Distinguished*, 04/1458: *Followed*, 05/342:
Previous proceedings, 01/396

R. (on the application of McGinley) v. Medical Referee see R. (on the application of
McGinley) v. Schilling (Medical Referee)

R. (on the application of McGinley) v. Schilling (Medical Referee); *sub nom* R. (on the
application of McGinley) v. Medical Referee; R. (on the application of
Metropolitan Police Service) v. Beck (Medical Referee) [2005] EWCA Civ 567;
[2005] I.C.R. 1282; *Times*, May 25, 2005, CA (Civ Div); affirming [2004] EWHC
1617, QBD (Admin) . . . . *Digested*, 05/**3332**

R. (on the application of McKay) v. First Secretary of State [2005] EWCA Civ 774;
[2005] 24 E.G.C.S. 178, CA (Civ Div); reversing [2004] EWHC 2778, QBD
(Admin)

R. (on the application of Mellor) v. Secretary of State for the Home Department; *sub
nom* R. v. Secretary of State for the Home Department Ex p. Mellor [2001]
EWCA Civ 472; [2002] Q.B. 13; [2001] 3 W.L.R. 533; [2001] 2 F.L.R. 1158;
[2001] 2 F.C.R. 153; [2001] H.R.L.R. 38; (2001) 59 B.M.L.R. 1; [2001] Fam.
Law 736; (2001) 98(22) L.S.G. 35; (2001) 145 S.J.L.B. 117; *Times*, May 1, 2001;
Independent, April 6, 2001, CA (Civ Div); affirming [2000] 2 F.L.R. 951;
[2000] 3 F.C.R. 148; [2000] H.R.L.R. 846; (2001) 4 C.C.L. Rep. 71; [2000]
C.O.D. 497; [2000] Fam. Law 881; *Times*, September 5, 2000, QBD . . . . *Digested*, 01/**4579**:
Applied, 05/2914: *Considered*, 01/1520, 01/4575

R. (on the application of Merck Sharp & Dohme Ltd) v. Licensing Authority [2005]
EWHC 710; [2005] Eu. L.R. 797, QBD (Admin)

R. (on the application of Mersey Care NHS Trust) *v.* Mental Health ReviewTribunal [2004]
    EWHC 1749; [2005] 1 W.L.R. 2469; [2005] 2 All E.R. 820; (2005) 83
    B.M.L.R. 1, QBD (Admin) . . . . *Digested,* 05/**2822**

R. (on the application of Metropolitan Police Authority) *v.* Medical Referee (No.1) [2001]
    EWHC Admin 753, QBD (Admin) . . . . *Approved,* 05/3332

R. (on the application of Metropolitan Police Service) *v.* Beck (Medical Referee) see R.
    (on the application of McGinley) *v.* Schilling (Medical Referee)

R. (on the application of MH) *v.* Secretary of State for Health see R. (on the application
    of H) *v.* Secretary of State for Health

R. (on the application of MH) *v.* Special Educational Needs and Disability Tribunal; *sub*
    nom H *v.* Special Educational Needs and Disability Tribunal [2004] EWCA Civ
    770; [2004] B.L.G.R. 844; [2004] E.L.R. 424; (2004) 101(29) L.S.G. 29;
    (2004) 148 S.J.L.B. 792; *Times,* July 8, 2004, CA (Civ Div); reversing [2004]
    EWHC 462, QBD (Admin) . . . . *Digested,* 04/**1079**:
                                      Considered, 04/1085, 05/1145

R. (on the application of Miah) *v.* Secretary of State for the Home Department [2004]
    EWHC 2569; [2005] A.C.D. 33; *Times,* September 10, 2004, QBD (Admin) . . .   *Digested,* 05/**2912**

R. (on the application of Middleton) *v.* HM Coroner forWestern Somerset; *sub nom* R. *v.*
    HM Coroner for Western Somerset Ex p. Middleton; R. (on the application of
    Middleton) *v.* West Somerset Coroner [2004] UKHL 10; [2004] 2 A.C. 182;
    [2004] 2 W.L.R. 800; [2004] 2 All E.R. 465; (2004) 168 J.P. 329; [2004]
    H.R.L.R. 29; [2004] U.K.H.R.R. 501; 17 B.H.R.C. 49; [2004] Lloyd's Rep. Med.
    288; (2004) 79 B.M.L.R. 51; (2004) 168 J.P.N. 479; (2004) 101(15) L.S.G.
    27; (2004) 154 N.L.J. 417; (2004) 148 S.J.L.B. 354; *Times,* March 12, 2004;
    Independent, March 16, 2004, HL . . . .   *Digested,* 04/**37**:
                      Applied, 05/34: *Explained,* 05/17: *Followed,* 04/38:
                                        Previous proceedings, 02/25

R. (on the application of Middleton) *v.*West Somerset Coroner see R. (on the application
    of Middleton) *v.* HM Coroner forWestern Somerset

R. (on the application of Mohammed (Rizgan)) *v.* Secretary of State for the Home
    Department see R. (on the application of Saadi) *v.* Secretary of State for the
    Home Department

R. (on the application of Montpeliers and Trevors Association) *v.* City of Westminster
    [2005] EWHC 16; [2005] 3 E.G.C.S. 117, QBD (Admin)

R. (on the application of Moore) *v.* Care Standards Tribunal; *sub nom* Moore *v.* Care
    Standards Tribunal [2005] EWCA Civ 627; [2005] 1 W.L.R. 2979; [2005] 3 All
    E.R. 428; (2005) 8 C.C.L. Rep. 354; *Times,* May 30, 2005, CA (Civ Div);
    affirming [2004] EWHC 2481; [2005] B.L.G.R. 179; (2005) 8 C.C.L. Rep. 91,
    QBD (Admin) . . . . *Digested,* 05/**3952**

R. (on the application of Morris) *v.* Westminster City Council (No.3); *sub nom*
    Westminster City Council *v.* Morris; R. (on the application of Badu) *v.* Lambeth
    LBC [2005] EWCA Civ 1184; [2005] H.R.L.R. 43; *Times,* October 19, 2005;
    Independent, October 21, 2005, CA (Civ Div); affirming [2004] EWHC 2191;
    [2005] 1 W.L.R. 865; [2005] 1 All E.R. 351; [2005] 1 F.L.R. 429; [2004]
    H.R.L.R. 43; [2004] U.K.H.R.R. 1126; [2005] H.L.R. 7; [2005] B.L.G.R. 191;
    [2005] Fam. Law 18; (2004) 101(41) L.S.G. 35; *Times,* October 20, 2004, QBD
    (Admin) . . . . *Digested,* 04/**1889**

R. (on the application of Mount Cook Land Ltd) *v.* Westminster City Council; *sub nom*
    Mount Cook Land Ltd *v.* Westminster City Council [2003] EWCA Civ 1346;
    [2004] C.P. Rep. 12; [2004] 2 Costs L.R. 211; [2004] 2 P. & C.R. 22; [2004] 1
    P.L.R. 29; [2004] J.P.L. 470; [2003] 43 E.G.C.S. 137; (2003) 147 S.J.L.B.
    1272; [2003] N.P.C. 117; *Times,* October 16, 2003, CA (Civ Div); affirming
    [2002] EWHC 2125, QBD (Admin) . . . . *Digested,* 04/**367**:
                            Applied, 04/1387: *Considered,* 05/3307

R. (on the application of Mullen) *v.* Secretary of State for the Home Department [2004]
    UKHL 18; [2005] 1 A.C. 1; [2004] 2 W.L.R. 1140; [2004] 3 All E.R. 65; [2004]
    U.K.H.R.R. 745; 16 B.H.R.C. 469; (2004) 154 N.L.J. 706; (2004) 148 S.J.L.B.
    542; *Times,* May 3, 2004, HL; reversing [2002] EWCA Civ 1882; [2003] Q.B.
    993; [2003] 2 W.L.R. 835; [2003] 1 All E.R. 613; (2003) 100(10) L.S.G. 27;
    Times, December 31, 2002; *Independent,* January 21, 2003, CA (Civ Div);
    reversing [2002] EWHC 230; [2002] 1 W.L.R. 1857; [2002] 3 All E.R. 293;
    (2002) 99(13) L.S.G. 26; (2002) 146 S.J.L.B. 62; *Times,* February 27, 2002,
    QBD (Admin) . . . . *Digested,* 04/**869**:
                      Applied, 05/908: *Considered,* 02/893: *Previous proceedings,* 99/972

R. (on the application of Mullins) *v.* Jockey Club Appeal Board (No.1) [2005] EWHC
    2197; *Times,* October 24, 2005, QBD (Admin)

R. (on the application of Munjaz) *v.* Ashworth Hospital Authority (now Mersey Care
    NHS Trust) see R. (on the application of Munjaz) *v.* Mersey Care NHS Trust

R. (on the application of Munjaz) v. Mersey Care NHS Trust; *sub nom* R. (on the application of Colonel M) v. Ashworth Hospital Authority (now Mersey Care NHS Trust); Munjaz v. Mersey Care NHS Trust; S v. Airedale NHS Trust; R. (on the application of Munjaz) v. Ashworth Hospital Authority (now Mersey Care NHS Trust); R. (on the application of S) v. Airedale NHS Trust (Appeal) [2005] UKHL 58; [2005] 3 W.L.R. 793; [2005] H.R.L.R. 42; (2005) 86 B.M.L.R. 84; *Times*, October 18, 2005; *Independent*, October 18, 2005, HL; reversing [2003] EWCA Civ 1036; [2004] Q.B. 395; [2003] 3 W.L.R. 1505; [2003] H.R.L.R. 38; [2003] Lloyd's Rep. Med. 534; (2003) 74 B.M.L.R. 178; (2003) 147 S.J.L.B. 903; *Times*, July 25, 2003; *Independent*, July 23, 2003, CA (Civ Div); reversing [2002] EWHC 1521, QBD (Admin) . . . . *Digested*, 05/**2829**:
Applied, 02/3240: *Previous proceedings*, 02/3240

R. (on the application of Murat) v. Inland Revenue Commissioners see Murat v. Inland Revenue Commissioners

R. (on the application of Murphy) v. Secretary of State for the Home Department; R. (on the application of Brannan) v. Secretary of State for the Home Department [2005] EWHC 140; [2005] 1 W.L.R. 3516; [2005] 2 All E.R. 763; (2005) 102(16) L.S.G. 27; *Times*, February 28, 2005, QBD (Admin) . . . . *Digested*, 05/**908**

R. (on the application of Murray) v. Derbyshire CC see R. (on the application of Thornby Farms Ltd) v. Daventry DC

R. (on the application of N) v. Camberwell Green Youth Court see R. (on the application of D) v. Camberwell Green Youth Court

R. (on the application of N) v. M [2002] EWCA Civ 1789; [2003] 1 W.L.R. 562; [2003] 1 F.L.R. 667; [2003] 1 F.C.R. 124; [2003] Lloyd's Rep. Med. 81; (2003) 72 B.M.L.R. 81; [2003] Fam. Law 160; (2003) 100(8) L.S.G. 29; *Times*, December 12, 2002; *Independent*, December 13, 2002, CA (Civ Div); affirming [2002] EWHC 1911; [2003] A.C.D. 17, QBD (Admin) . . . . *Digested*, 03/**2958**:
Applied, 05/2830: *Considered*, 05/2818

R. (on the application of N) v. Mental Health Review Tribunal (Northern Region); *sub nom* R. (on the application of AN) v. Mental Health Review Tribunal (Northern Region); R. (on the application of DJ) v. Mental Health Review Tribunal [2005] EWCA Civ 1605, CA (Civ Div); affirming [2005] EWHC 587; [2005] A.C.D. 92; *Times*, April 18, 2005, QBD (Admin). . . . . *Digested*, 05/**2825**

R. (on the application of N) v. Secretary of State for the Home Department see Anufrijeva v. Southwark LBC

R. (on the application of N) v. Sheffield Youth Court see R. (on the application of D) v. Sheffield Youth Court

R. (on the application of Nadarajah) v. Secretary of State for the Home Department see R. (on the application of Razgar) v. Secretary of State for the Home Department (No.2)

R. (on the application of Nadarajah) v. Secretary of State for the Home Department; *sub nom* Nadarajah v. Secretary of State for the Home Department; Abdi v. Secretary of State for the Home Department; R. (on the application of Abdi) v. Secretary of State for the Home Department [2005] EWCA Civ 1363; *Times*, December 14, 2005, CA (Civ Div) . . . . *Previous proceedings*, 03/2234

R. (on the application of Napier) v. Secretary of State for the Home Department; *sub nom* Napier v. Secretary of State for the Home Department [2004] EWHC 936; [2004] 1 W.L.R. 3056; [2005] 3 All E.R. 76; [2004] A.C.D. 61; (2004) 101(22) L.S.G. 33; *Times*, May 27, 2004, QBD (Admin) . . . . *Digested*, 04/**2777**

R. (on the application of Nash) v. Chelsea College of Art and Design [2001] EWHC Admin 538; *Times*, July 25, 2001, QBD (Admin) . . . . *Digested*, 01/**95**:
Applied, 05/3281: *Considered*, 05/2910

R. (on the application of National Association of Health Stores) v. Secretary of State for Health; *sub nom* National Association of Health Stores v. Department of Health [2005] EWCA Civ 154; *Times*, March 9, 2005, CA (Civ Div); affirming [2003] EWHC 3133, QBD . . . . *Digested*, 05/**59**

R. (on the application of National Association of Health Stores) v. Secretary of State for Health (C155/04) see R. (on the application of Alliance for Natural Health) v. Secretary of State for Health (C154/04)

R. (on the application of National Care Standards Commission) v. Jones see Jones v. Commission for Social Care Inspection

R. (on the application of National Union of Journalists) v. Central Arbitration Committee [2005] EWCA Civ 1309; *Times*, July 29, 2005, CA (Civ Div); affirming [2004] EWHC 2612; [2005] I.C.R. 493; [2005] I.R.L.R. 28; (2005) 102(1) L.S.G. 16; *Times*, November 25, 2004, QBD (Admin) . . . . *Digested*, 05/**1310**

R. (on the application of Naylor) v. Secretary of State for Work and Pensions see R. (on the application of Hooper) v. Secretary of State for Work and Pensions

R. (on the application of Newcastle upon Tyne City Council) v. Le Quelenec; *sub nom* Newcastle upon Tyne City Council v. Le Quelenec [2005] EWHC 45; (2005) 102(8) L.S.G. 30; *Times*, January 17, 2005, QBD. . . . . *Digested*, 05/**3489**

R. (on the application of Newham LBC) v. Stratford Magistrates Court [2004] EWHC 2506; (2004) 168 J.P. 658; (2004) 168 J.P.N. 1002, QBD (Admin) . . . . *Digested*, 05/**445**

R. (on the application of Newsum) v. Welsh Assembly (No.1); *sub nom* Newsum v. Welsh Assembly; Newsum v. National Assembly for Wales [2004] EWCA Civ 1565; [2005] Env. L.R. 16; [2005] 1 P.L.R. 107; [2005] J.P.L. 935; [2004] 49 E.G.C.S. 134; (2004) 148 S.J.L.B. 1402; [2004] N.P.C. 174; *Times*, December 7, 2004, CA (Civ Div); reversing [2004] EWHC 50; [2004] Env. L.R. 39; [2004] J.P.L. 1537; [2004] 7 E.G.C.S. 130; [2004] N.P.C. 11, QBD (Admin) . . . .   *Digested*, 05/**1359**

R. (on the application of Newsum) v. Welsh Assembly (No.2) [2005] EWHC 538; [2005] 2 P. & C.R. 32; [2005] J.P.L. 1486; [2005] 16 E.G.C.S. 144; [2005] N.P.C. 50, QBD (Admin)

R. (on the application of Nilsen) v. Full Sutton Prison Governor; *sub nom* Nilsen v. Full Sutton Prison Governor [2004] EWCA Civ 1540; [2005] 1 W.L.R. 1028; [2005] E.M.L.R. 11; (2005) 102(2) L.S.G. 29; (2004) 154 N.L.J. 1788; (2004) 148 S.J.L.B. 1372; *Times*, November 23, 2004, CA (Civ Div); affirming [2003] EWHC 3160; [2004] E.M.L.R. 9; [2004] A.C.D. 59; *Times*, January 2, 2004, QBD (Admin) . . . .   *Digested*, 05/**2914**

R. (on the application of Noble Organisation Ltd) v. Thanet DC [2005] EWCA Civ 782; [2005] N.P.C. 86; *Times*, August 26, 2005, CA (Civ Div); affirming [2004] EWHC 2576; [2005] Env. L.R. 25; [2005] 1 P. & C.R. 27; [2005] A.C.D. 35; [2004] N.P.C. 172, QBD (Admin) . . . .   *Digested*, 05/**3270**

R. (on the application of Noorkoiv) v. Secretary of State for the Home Department (No.2) [2002] EWCA Civ 770; [2002] 1 W.L.R. 3284; [2002] 4 All E.R. 515; [2002] H.R.L.R. 36; [2002] A.C.D. 66; (2002) 99(27) L.S.G. 34; (2002) 146 S.J.L.B. 145; *Times*, May 31, 2002; *Independent*, June 14, 2002; *Daily Telegraph*, June 13, 2002, CA (Civ Div); reversing in part [2001] EWHC Admin 345; *Independent*, July 2, 2001 (C.S), QBD (Admin) . . . .   *Digested*, 02/**3339**:
                                             Applied, 04/2783: *Considered*, 05/2921

R. (on the application of Norfolk CC) v. Secretary of State for the Environment, Food and Rural Affairs [2005] EWHC 119; [2005] 4 All E.R. 994; [2005] N.P.C. 22, QBD (Admin)

R. (on the application of North Cyprus Tourism Centre Ltd) v. Transport for London [2005] EWHC 1698; [2005] U.K.H.R.R. 1231; [2005] A.C.D. 101; *Times*, August 24, 2005, QBD (Admin) . . . .   *Digested*, 05/**72**

R. (on the application of Novartis Pharmaceuticals UK Ltd) v. Licensing Authority (C106/01) [2005] All E.R. (EC) 192; [2004] E.C.R. I-4403; [2004] 2 C.M.L.R. 26; (2005) 81 B.M.L.R. 200, ECJ (6th Chamber) . . . .   *Digested*, 04/**1697**

R. (on the application of Nunn) v. First Secretary of State [2005] EWCA Civ 101; [2005] 2 All E.R. 987; [2005] Env. L.R. 32; [2005] 2 P.L.R. 61; [2005] 7 E.G.C.S. 143; [2005] N.P.C. 16; *Times*, February 23, 2005, CA (Civ Div) . . . .   *Digested*, 05/**3309**

R. (on the application of O) v. Secretary of State for the Home Department see R. (on the application of I) v. Secretary of State for the Home Department

R. (on the application of O'Brien) v. Independent Assessor; *sub nom* Independent Assessor v. O'Brien; R. (on the application of Hickey (Vincent)) v. Independent Assessor; R. (on the application of Hickey (Michael)) v. Independent Assessor [2004] EWCA Civ 1035; [2005] P.I.Q.R. Q7; *Times*, September 7, 2004, CA (Civ Div); reversing [2003] EWHC 855; (2003) 100(26) L.S.G. 36; (2003) 153 N.L.J. 668; *Times*, May 5, 2003, QBD (Admin) . . . .   *Digested*, 05/**49**

R. (on the application of O'Connell) v. Fareham Magistrates Court (Permission to Appeal) [2005] EWCA Civ 212; [2005] R.V.R. 373, CA (Civ Div)

R. (on the application of O'Connell) v. Gosport BC [2004] EWHC 3088; [2005] R.V.R. 96, QBD (Admin)

R. (on the application of O'Reilly) v. First Secretary of State [2005] EWHC 1286; [2005] 24 E.G.C.S. 179, QBD (Admin)

R. (on the application of Ojutaleyo) v. Bournemouth Crown Court see R. (on the application of Salubi) v. Bow Street Magistrates Court

R. (on the application of Okandeji) v. Bow Street Magistrates Court [2005] EWHC 2925; *Times*, November 23, 2005, QBD (Admin)

R. (on the application of Omar) v. Secretary of State for the Home Department; *sub nom* Omar v. Secretary of State for the Home Department [2005] EWCA Civ 285; [2005] I.N.L.R. 470, CA (Civ Div); affirming [2004] EWHC 1427; [2004] A.C.D. 87, QBD (Admin) . . . .   *Digested*, 05/**2180**

R. (on the application of Orange PCS Ltd) v. Islington LBC; *sub nom* R. (on the application of Orange Personal Communications Services Ltd) v. Islington LBC; R. (on the application of Crown Castle UK Ltd) v. Islington LBC; R. (on the application of Hutchinson 3G (UK) Ltd) v. Islington LBC; C1/2005/1126, CA (Civ Div); affirming [2005] EWHC 963; [2005] 3 P.L.R. 101; [2005] 20 E.G.C.S. 261, QBD (Admin)

R. (on the application of Orange Personal Communications Services Ltd) v. Islington LBC see R. (on the application of Orange PCS Ltd) v. Islington LBC

R. (on the application of Osman (Dilshad)) v. Secretary of State for the Home Department see R. (on the application of Saadi) v. Secretary of State for the Home Department

R. (on the application of Ozturk) *v.* Secretary of State for the Home Department; *sub nom* Ozturk *v.* Secretary of State for the Home Department; Akyuz *v.* Secretary of State for the Home Department; R. (on the application of Akyuz) *v.* Secretary of State for the Home Department [2005] EWHC 1433; [2005] 3 C.M.L.R. 26; [2005] Imm. A.R. 677; *Times,* July 20, 2005, QBD (Admin) . . . .   *Digested,* 05/**2229**

R. (on the application of P) *v.* Newham LBC [2004] EWHC 2210; [2005] 2 F.C.R. 171; (2004) 7 C.C.L. Rep. 553, QBD (Admin) . . . .   *Digested,* 05/**3932**

R. (on the application of P) *v.* Secretary of State for the Home Department; *sub nom* R. (on the application of SP) *v.* Secretary of State for the Home Department; Secretary of State for the Home Department *v.* SP [2004] EWCA Civ 1750; (2005) 102(7) L.S.G. 27; *Times,* January 21, 2005, CA (Civ Div); affirming [2004] EWHC 1418; [2004] A.C.D. 75; *Times,* October 13, 2004, QBD (Admin).   *Digested,* 05/**2917**

R. (on the application of Paterson) *v.* First Secretary of State [2004] EWHC 185; [2005] 1 P. & C.R. 21, QBD (Admin) . . . .   *Digested,* 05/**3288**

R. (on the application of Paul Rackham Ltd) *v.* Swaffham Magistrates Court [2004] EWHC 1417; [2005] J.P.L. 224, QBD (Admin) . . . .   *Digested,* 05/**1362**

R. (on the application of Payir) *v.* Secretary of State for the Home Department; *sub nom* Payir *v.* Secretary of State for the Home Department [2005] EWHC 1426; [2005] 1 W.L.R. 3609; [2005] 3 C.M.L.R. 27; *Times,* July 20, 2005, QBD (Admin) . . . .   *Digested,* 05/**2206**

R. (on the application of Persimmon Homes (South East) Ltd) *v.* Secretary of State for Transport [2005] EWHC 96; [2005] 2 P. & C.R. 24; [2005] J.P.L. 1202; [2005] 4 E.G.C.S. 167, QBD (Admin) . . . .   *Digested,* 05/**3294**

R. (on the application of Persimmon Homes (Thames Valley) Ltd) *v.* North Hertfordshire DC; *sub nom* Persimmon Homes (Thames Valley) Ltd *v.* North Hertfordshire DC [2001] EWHC Admin 565; [2001] 1 W.L.R. 2393; [2002] J.P.L. 460; [2001] 31 E.G.C.S. 102; (2001) 98(34) L.S.G. 41; [2001] N.P.C. 122; *Times,* September 18, 2001, QBD (Admin). . . . .   *Digested,* 01/**4718**: *Considered,* 05/3269

R. (on the application of Phillips) *v.* General Medical Council [2004] EWHC 1858; (2005) 82 B.M.L.R. 135, QBD (Admin) . . . .   *Digested,* 05/**1804**

R. (on the application of Plymouth City Airport Ltd) *v.* Secretary of State for the Environment, Transport and the Regions; *sub nom* Plymouth City Airport Ltd *v.* Secretary of State for the Environment, Transport and the Regions; R. *v.* Plymouth City Airport Ltd; R. *v.* Secretary of State for the Environment, Transport and the Regions Ex p. Plymouth City Airport Ltd [2001] EWCA Civ 144; (2001) 82 P. & C.R. 20; (2001) 98(8) L.S.G. 48, CA (Civ Div); affirming (2000) 97(7) L.S.G. 42, QBD . . . .   *Digested,* 01/**4681**: *Considered,* 04/214, 05/3390

R. (on the application of Plymouth City Council) *v.* HM Coroner for Devon; *sub nom* Plymouth City Council *v.* County of Devon Coroner [2005] EWHC 1014; [2005] 2 F.L.R. 1279; [2005] 2 F.C.R. 428; [2005] A.C.D. 83; [2005] Fam. Law 699, QBD (Admin) . . . .   *Digested,* 05/**16**

R. (on the application of Premier Leisure UK Ltd) *v.* Secretary of State for the Environment, Transport and the Regions see R. (on the application of Holding & Barnes Plc) *v.* Secretary of State for the Environment, Transport and the Regions

R. (on the application of Pridmore) *v.* Salisbury DC [2004] EWHC 2511; [2005] 1 P. & C.R. 32; [2005] 1 P.L.R. 39; [2005] J.P.L. 655; [2004] 47 E.G.C.S. 165, QBD (Admin) . . . .   *Digested,* 05/**3305**

R. (on the application of Purja) *v.* Ministry of Defence [2003] EWCA Civ 1345; [2004] 1 W.L.R. 289; [2004] U.K.H.R.R. 309; (2003) 100(41) L.S.G. 33; *Times,* October 16, 2003, CA (Civ Div); affirming [2003] EWHC 445; [2003] A.C.D. 45; *Times,* March 10, 2003, QBD (Admin). . . . .   *Digested,* 03/**2084**: *Distinguished,* 05/2118

R. (on the application of Q) *v.* Secretary of State for the Home Department; R. (on the application of D) *v.* Secretary of State for the Home Department; R. (on the application of J) *v.* Secretary of State for the Home Department; R. (on the application of M) *v.* Secretary of State for the Home Department; R. (on the application of F) *v.* Secretary of State for the Home Department; R. (on the application of B) *v.* Secretary of State for the Home Department [2003] EWCA Civ 364; [2004] Q.B. 36; [2003] 3 W.L.R. 365; [2003] 2 All E.R. 905; [2003] H.R.L.R. 21; [2003] U.K.H.R.R. 607; 14 B.H.R.C. 262; [2003] H.L.R. 57; (2003) 6 C.C.L. Rep. 136; [2003] A.C.D. 46; (2003) 100(21) L.S.G. 29; *Times,* March 19, 2003; *Independent,* March 21, 2003, CA (Civ Div); affirming [2003] EWHC 195; (2003) 100(15) L.S.G. 26; *Times,* February 20, 2003, QBD (Admin) . . . .   *Digested,* 03/**4070**: *Considered,* 05/2171: *Followed,* 04/2026

R. (on the application of Q) *v.* Wolverhampton City Council Independent Appeal Panel [2005] EWHC 277; [2005] E.L.R. 501, QBD (Admin)

R. (on the application of Quark Fishing Ltd) *v.* Secretary of State for Foreign and Commonwealth Affairs (No.2) [2005] UKHL 57; [2005] 3 W.L.R. 837; [2005] H.R.L.R. 41; *Times,* October 17, 2005, HL; reversing in part [2004] EWCA Civ 527; [2005] Q.B. 93; [2004] 3 W.L.R. 1; [2004] H.R.L.R. 28; *Times,* May 10, 2004, CA (Civ Div); affirming [2003] EWHC 1743; [2003] A.C.D. 96, QBD (Admin) . . . .   *Digested,* 04/**1917**

R. (on the application of Quintavalle) *v.* Human Fertilisation and Embryology Authority; *sub nom* Quintavalle *v.* Human Fertilisation and Embryology Authority [2005] UKHL 28; [2005] 2 A.C. 561; [2005] 2 W.L.R. 1061; [2005] 2 All E.R. 555; [2005] 2 F.L.R. 349; [2005] 2 F.C.R. 135; (2005) 83 B.M.L.R. 143; [2005] Fam. Law 613; (2005) 155 N.L.J. 691; *Times,* April 29, 2005; *Independent,* May 3, 2005, HL; affirming [2003] EWCA Civ 667; [2004] Q.B. 168; [2003] 3 W.L.R. 878; [2003] 3 All E.R. 257; [2003] 2 F.L.R. 335; [2003] 2 F.C.R. 193; [2003] Lloyd's Rep. Med. 294; (2003) 73 B.M.L.R. 116; [2003] A.C.D. 75; [2003] Fam. Law 565; (2003) 100(27) L.S.G. 37; (2003) 153 N.L.J. 824; (2003) 147 S.J.L.B. 598; *Times,* May 20, 2003; *Independent,* May 20, 2003, CA (Civ Div); reversing [2002] EWHC 3000; [2003] 2 All E.R. 105; [2003] 1 F.C.R. 664; (2003) 70 B.M.L.R. 236; (2003) 153 N.L.J. 57; *Times,* January 20, 2003; *Independent,* January 14, 2003, QBD (Admin) . . . .   *Digested,* 05/**1809**:
       Applied, 04/1673

R. (on the application of Quintavalle) *v.* Secretary of State for Health [2003] UKHL 13; [2003] 2 A.C. 687; [2003] 2 W.L.R. 692; [2003] 2 All E.R. 113; [2003] 1 F.C.R. 577; (2003) 71 B.M.L.R. 209; (2003) 153 N.L.J. 439; *Times,* March 14, 2003; *Independent,* March 18, 2003, HL; affirming [2002] EWCA Civ 29; [2002] Q.B. 628; [2002] 2 W.L.R. 550; [2002] 2 All E.R. 625; [2002] 2 F.C.R. 140; (2002) 64 B.M.L.R. 72; (2002) 99(10) L.S.G. 32; (2002) 146 S.J.L.B. 30; *Times,* January 25, 2002; *Independent,* January 22, 2002; *Daily Telegraph,* January 24, 2002, CA (Civ Div); reversing [2001] EWHC Admin 918; [2001] 4 All E.R. 1013; (2002) 63 B.M.L.R. 167; (2001) 151 N.L.J. 1732; *Times,* December 5, 2001, QBD (Admin). . . . .   *Digested,* 04/**3274**:
       Applied, 05/823

R. (on the application of Quinton) *v.* Commissioner of Police of the Metropolis see R. (on the application of Gillan) *v.* Commissioner of Police of the Metropolis

R. (on the application of R) *v.* Balham Youth Court see R. (on the application of D) *v.* Camberwell Green Youth Court

R. (on the application of R) *v.* Durham Constabulary; R. (on the application of U) *v.* Commissioner of Police of the Metropolis [2005] UKHL 21; [2005] 1 W.L.R. 1184; [2005] 2 All E.R. 369; [2005] H.R.L.R. 18; [2005] U.K.H.R.R. 584; (2005) 155 N.L.J. 467; (2005) 149 S.J.L.B. 360; *Times,* March 18, 2005, HL; reversing [2002] EWHC 2486; [2003] 1 W.L.R. 897; [2003] 3 All E.R. 419; [2003] 1 Cr. App. R. 29; [2003] H.R.L.R. 13; [2003] U.K.H.R.R. 287; [2003] Crim. L.R. 349; *Times,* December 10, 2002, QBD (Admin) . . . .   *Digested,* 05/**925**

R. (on the application of R) *v.* Hackney LBC see R. (on the application of SR) *v.* Huntercombe Maidenhead Hospital

R. (on the application of R) *v.* Leeds Magistrates Court see R *v.* Leeds Magistrates Court

R. (on the application of R) *v.* Secretary of State for the Home Department see R (Iran) *v.* Secretary of State for the Home Department

R. (on the application of Rashid) *v.* Secretary of State for the Home Department; *sub nom* Rashid *v.* Secretary of State for the Home Department [2005] EWCA Civ 744; [2005] Imm. A.R. 608; [2005] I.N.L.R. 550; *Times,* July 12, 2005; *Independent,* June 21, 2005, CA (Civ Div); affirming [2004] EWHC 2465; *Times,* November 17, 2004, QBD (Admin). . . . .   *Digested,* 05/**2154**

R. (on the application of Razgar) *v.* Secretary of State for the Home Department (No.2); *sub nom* Secretary of State for the Home Department *v.* Razgar; R. (on the application of Soumahoro) *v.* Secretary of State for the Home Department; R. (on the application of Nadarajah) *v.* Secretary of State for the Home Department [2004] UKHL 27; [2004] 2 A.C. 368; [2004] 3 W.L.R. 58; [2004] 3 All E.R. 821; [2004] H.R.L.R. 32; [2004] Imm. A.R. 381; [2004] I.N.L.R. 349; [2004] A.C.D. 83; (2004) 101(28) L.S.G. 33; (2004) 154 N.L.J. 986; (2004) 148 S.J.L.B. 761; *Times,* June 21, 2004; *Independent,* June 23, 2004, HL; affirming [2003] EWCA Civ 840; [2003] Imm. A.R. 529; [2003] I.N.L.R. 543; [2003] A.C.D. 81, CA (Civ Div); affirming [2002] EWHC 2554; [2003] Imm. A.R. 269, QBD (Admin) . . . .   *Digested,* 04/**2029**:
       Applied, 04/2032, 04/2041, 04/2052, 05/2159, 05/2181, 05/2192:
       Considered, 04/839, 05/2179, 05/2213, 05/5431:
       Previous proceedings, 03/2234

R. (on the application of Redgrave) *v.* Commissioner of Police of the Metropolis [2003] EWCA Civ 4; [2003] 1 W.L.R. 1136; (2003) 100(11) L.S.G. 34; (2003) 147 S.J.L.B. 116; *Times,* January 30, 2003, CA (Civ Div); affirming [2002] EWHC 1074, QBD (Admin). . . . .   *Applied,* 05/1804

R. (on the application of Redrow Homes Ltd) *v.* First Secretary of State see Redrow Homes Ltd *v.* First Secretary of State

R. (on the application of Refugee Legal Centre) *v.* Secretary of State for the Home Department [2004] EWCA Civ 1481; [2005] 1 W.L.R. 2219; [2005] I.N.L.R. 236; [2005] A.C.D. 52; (2005) 102(1) L.S.G. 16; *Times*, November 24, 2004, CA (Civ Div); affirming [2004] EWHC 684; [2004] Imm. A.R. 142, QBD (Admin) . . . . *Digested*, 05/**2155**

R. (on the application of Revenue and Customs Commissioners) *v.* Machell [2005] EWHC 2593; (2005) 155 N.L.J. 1847; *Times*, November 30, 2005, QBD (Admin)

R. (on the application of Reynolds) *v.* Secretary of State for Work and Pensions see R. (on the application of Carson) *v.* Secretary of State for Work and Pensions

R. (on the application of Richards) *v.* Pembrokeshire CC [2004] EWCA Civ 1000; [2005] B.L.G.R. 105, CA (Civ Div); reversing [2003] EWHC 2532; (2003) 100(40) L.S.G. 32, QBD (Admin) . . . . *Digested*, 05/**3459**

R. (on the application of Richardson) *v.* North Yorkshire CC; *sub nom* Richardson *v.* North Yorkshire CC [2003] EWCA Civ 1860; [2004] 1 W.L.R. 1920; [2004] 2 All E.R. 31; [2004] Env. L.R. 34; [2004] B.L.G.R. 351; [2004] 2 P. & C.R. 15; [2004] J.P.L. 911; [2004] A.C.D. 62; [2004] 2 E.G.C.S. 93; (2004) 101(2) L.S.G. 31; (2004) 101(6) L.S.G. 32; (2004) 148 S.J.L.B. 58; *Times*, January 19, 2004, CA (Civ Div); affirming [2003] EWHC 764; [2004] Env. L.R. 13; [2004] 1 P. & C.R. 23; [2003] 18 E.G.C.S.113, QBD (Admin) . . . . *Digested*, 04/**3092**:
Distinguished, 05/3300: *Explained*, 05/2785

R. (on the application of Ridehalgh) *v.* DPP see Ridehalgh *v.* DPP

R. (on the application of Roberts) *v.* Parole Board; *sub nom* Roberts *v.* Parole Board [2005] UKHL 45; [2005] 2 A.C. 738; [2005] 3 W.L.R. 152; [2005] H.R.L.R. 38; [2005] U.K.H.R.R. 939; (2005) 155 N.L.J. 1096; *Times*, July 8, 2005; *Independent*, July 12, 2005, HL; affirming [2004] EWCA Civ 1031; [2005] Q.B. 410; [2005] 2 W.L.R. 54; [2004] 4 All E.R. 1136; [2004] A.C.D. 79; (2004) 148 S.J.L.B. 1150; *Times*, September 6, 2004; *Independent*, October 7, 2004, CA (Civ Div); affirming [2003] EWHC 3120; [2004] 2 All E.R. 776; [2004] A.C.D. 60, QBD (Admin) . . . . *Digested*, 05/**2916**

R. (on the application of Rockware Glass Ltd) *v.* Chester City Council [2005] EWHC 2250; [2005] N.P.C.120, QBD (Admin)

R. (on the application of Rodriguez-Bannister) *v.* Somerset Partnership NHS and Social Care Trust; *sub nom* Rodriguez-Bannister *v.* Somerset Partnership NHS and Social Care Trust [2003] EWHC 2184; (2004) 7 C.C.L. Rep. 385, QBD (Admin) . . . . *Digested*, 05/**3950**

R. (on the application of Rodriguez-Torres) *v.* Secretary of State for the Home Department; *sub nom* Torres *v.* Secretary of State for the Home Department [2005] EWCA Civ 1328; *Times*, December 6, 2005, CA (Civ Div)

R. (on the application of Rosen) *v.* Transport for London [2004] EWHC 1218; [2005] A.C.D.12, QBD (Admin)

R. (on the application of Rubin) *v.* First Secretary of State see Rubin *v.* First Secretary of State

R. (on the application of S) *v.* Airedale NHS Trust (Appeal) see R. (on the application of Munjaz) *v.* Mersey Care NHS Trust

R. (on the application of S) *v.* Almondbury Junior School Head Teacher and Governing Body [2004] EWCA Civ 1041; [2004] E.L.R. 612, CA (Civ Div) . . . . *Digested*, 05/**1141**

R. (on the application of S) *v.* Chief Constable of South Yorkshire; R. (on the application of Marper) *v.* Chief Constable of South Yorkshire [2004] UKHL 39; [2004] 1 W.L.R. 2196; [2004] 4 All E.R. 193; [2004] H.R.L.R. 35; [2004] U.K.H.R.R. 967; [2005] Crim. L.R.136; (2004) 101(34) L.S.G. 29; (2004) 154 N.L.J. 1183; (2004) 148 S.J.L.B. 914; *Times*, July 23, 2004; *Independent*, July 29, 2004, HL; affirming [2002] EWCA Civ 1275; [2002] 1 W.L.R. 3223; [2003] 1 All E.R. 148; [2003] 1 Cr. App. R. 16; [2003] H.R.L.R. 1; 13 B.H.R.C. 569; [2003] Crim. L.R. 39; [2003] A.C.D. 42; (2002) 99(40) L.S.G. 32; (2002) 152 N.L.J. 1483; (2002) 146 S.J.L.B. 207; *Times*, October 3, 2002; *Independent*, October 1, 2002, CA (Civ Div); affirming [2002] EWHC 478; *Times*, April 4, 2002; *Daily Telegraph*, April 11, 2002, QBD (Admin) . . . . *Digested*, 04/**710**:
Applied, 05/3835: *Considered*, 05/190

R. (on the application of S) *v.* Secretary of State for the Home Department; R. (on the application of D) *v.* Secretary of State for the Home Department; R. (on the application of T) *v.* Secretary of State for the Home Department [2003] EWCA Civ 1285; [2003] U.K.H.R.R. 1321; [2004] H.L.R. 17; (2004) 7 C.C.L. Rep. 53; (2003) 153 N.L.J. 1474; (2003) 147 S.J.L.B. 1121; *Times*, October 9, 2003, CA (Civ Div); reversing [2003] EWHC 1941; [2004] H.L.R. 16; (2004) 7 C.C.L. Rep. 32; (2003) 100(36) L.S.G. 39; *Times*, August 6, 2003, QBD (Admin) . . . . *Digested*, 04/**2027**:
Considered, 04/2026, 05/2171

R. (on the application of S) *v.* YP School [2003] EWCA Civ 1306; [2004] E.L.R. 37, CA (Civ Div); reversing [2002] EWHC 2975; [2003] E.L.R. 578, QBD (Admin) . . . *Digested*, 04/**1020**:
Considered, 05/1071, 05/1073

R. (on the application of S (A Child)) *v.* Oxfordshire CC [2004] EWHC 133; [2004] E.L.R. 489; [2005] A.C.D. 8; *Times*, March 3, 2004, QBD (Admin) . . . . *Digested*, 04/**995**

R. (on the application of Saadi) *v.* Secretary of State for the Home Department; R. (on the application of Maged) *v.* Secretary of State for the Home Department; R. (on the application of Osman (Dilshad)) *v.* Secretary of State for the Home Department; R. (on the application of Mohammed (Rizgan)) *v.* Secretary of State for the Home Department [2002] UKHL 41; [2002] 1 W.L.R. 3131; [2002] 4 All E.R. 785; [2003] U.K.H.R.R. 173; [2002] I.N.L.R. 523; [2003] A.C.D. 11; (2002) 146 S.J.L.B. 250; *Times,* November 5, 2002; *Independent,* November 5, 2002, HL; affirming [2001] EWCA Civ 1512; [2002] 1 W.L.R. 356; [2001] 4 All E.R. 961; [2002] H.R.L.R. 7; [2002] Imm. A.R. 121; [2002] A.C.D. 7; (2001) 98(44) L.S.G. 35; (2001) 151 N.L.J. 1573; (2001) 145 S.J.L.B. 246; *Times,* October 22, 2001; *Independent,* October 23, 2001; *Daily Telegraph,* October 23, 2001, CA (Civ Div); reversing [2001] EWHC Admin 670; (2001) 151 N.L.J. 1407; *Daily Telegraph,* September 11, 2001, QBD (Admin) . . . . *Digested,* 02/**2578**: *Considered,* 05/2163

R. (on the application of Sacupima) *v.* Newham LBC; *sub nom* R. *v.* Newham LBC Ex p. Sacupima [2001] 1 W.L.R. 563; (2001) 33 H.L.R. 2; [2000] N.P.C. 127; *Times,* December 1, 2000; *Independent,* November 28, 2000, CA (Civ Div); reversing in part (2001) 33 H.L.R. 1; [2000] C.O.D. 133; *Times,* January 12, 2000 ; *Independent,* December 2, 1999, QBD . . . . *Digested,* 01/**3428**: *Applied,* 05/1987: *Approved,* 04/1890: *Disapproved,* 00/3147

R. (on the application of Saifi) *v.* Governor of Brixton Prison; *sub nom* Saifi *v.* Governor of Brixton Prison; R. *v.* Governor of Brixton Prison Ex p. Saifi [2001] 1 W.L.R. 1134; [2001] 4 All E.R. 168; [2001] Crim. L.R. 653; *Times,* January 24, 2001, DC . . . . *Digested,* 01/**2525**: *Considered,* 05/1491

R. (on the application of Sainsbury's Supermarkets Ltd) *v.* Cherwell DC see R. (on the application of Sainsbury's Supermarkets Ltd) *v.* First Secretary of State

R. (on the application of Sainsbury's Supermarkets Ltd) *v.* First Secretary of State; *sub nom* First Secretary of State *v.* Sainsbury's Supermarkets Ltd; R. (on the application of Sainsbury's Supermarkets Ltd) *v.* Cherwell DC [2005] EWCA Civ 520; [2005] N.P.C. 60, CA (Civ Div); reversing [2004] EWHC 1726; [2004] N.P.C. 107, QBD (Admin)

R. (on the application of Salman) *v.* Barking and Dagenham LBC [2005] EWHC 731; [2005] E.L.R. 514, QBD (Admin)

R. (on the application of Salubi) *v.* Bow Street Magistrates Court; R. (on the application of Wanogho) *v.* Bow Street Magistrates Court; R. (on the application of Harmer) *v.* Customs and Excise Commissioners; R. (on the application of Ojutaleyo) *v.* Bournemouth Crown Court; R. (on the application of Boucher) *v.* Luton Crown Court [2002] EWHC 919; [2002] 1 W.L.R. 3073; [2002] 2 Cr. App. R. 40; [2003] Crim. L.R. 111; (2002) 146 S.J.L.B. 152; *Times,* June 4, 2002, QBD (Admin) . . . . *Digested,* 02/**857**: *Applied,* 05/71

R. (on the application of Samaroo) *v.* Secretary of State for the Home Department; *sub nom* R. *v.* Secretary of State for the Home Department Ex p. Samaroo; Samaroo *v.* Secretary of State for the Home Department; Sezek *v.* Secretary of State for the Home Department [2001] EWCA Civ 1139; [2001] U.K.H.R.R. 1150; [2002] I.N.L.R. 55; (2001) 98(34) L.S.G. 40; (2001) 145 S.J.L.B. 208; *Times,* September 18, 2001, CA (Civ Div); affirming [2001] Imm. A.R. 324; *Daily Telegraph,* January 23, 2001, QBD (Admin) . . . . *Digested,* 01/**3660**: *Applied,* 04/3040, 05/3340: *Considered,* 03/2232, 03/3068, 04/3042: *Distinguished,* 05/2027: *Followed,* 04/2051

R. (on the application of SB) *v.* Denbigh High School Governors see R. (on the application of Begum (Shabina)) *v.* Denbigh High School Governors

R. (on the application of SC) *v.* Mental Health Review Tribunal see R. (on the application of C) *v.* Mental Health Review Tribunal

R. (on the application of Secretary of State for the Home Department) *v.* Mental Health Review Tribunal [2004] EWHC 1029, QBD (Admin) . . . . *Followed,* 05/2817

R. (on the application of Septet) *v.* Secretary of State for the Home Department see Sepet *v.* Secretary of State for the Home Department

R. (on the application of Sevenoaks DC) *v.* First Secretary of State see Sevenoaks DC *v.* First Secretary of State

R. (on the application of Shah) *v.* Immigration Appeal Tribunal; *sub nom* Shah *v.* Immigration Appeal Tribunal [2004] EWCA Civ 1665; *Times,* December 9, 2004, CA (Civ Div) . . . . *Digested,* 05/**401**

R. (on the application of Sharman) *v.* HM Coroner for Inner North London; *sub nom* Sharman *v.* HM Coroner for Inner North London [2005] EWCA Civ 967, CA (Civ Div); affirming [2005] EWHC 857; [2005] A.C.D. 96, QBD (Admin)

R. (on the application of Simeer) *v.* Immigration Appeal Tribunal [2003] EWHC 2683, QBD (Admin) . . . . *Applied,* 05/2151

R. (on the application of Sinclair Gardens Investments (Kensington) Ltd) v. Lands Tribunal; *sub nom* Sinclair Gardens Investments (Kensington) Ltd v. Lands Tribunal [2005] EWCA Civ 1305; (2005) 102(46) L.S.G. 27; [2005] N.P.C. 128; *Times*, November 28, 2005; *Independent*, November 11, 2005, CA (Civ Div); affirming [2004] EWHC 1910; [2004] 3 E.G.L.R. 15; [2004] 47 E.G. 166; [2004] R.V.R. 230; [2005] A.C.D. 32; *Times*, November 2, 2004, QBD (Admin) . . . .   *Digested*, 05/**2661**

R. (on the application of Sissen) v. Newcastle upon Tyne Crown Court [2004] EWHC 1905; [2005] Env. L.R. 17, QBD (Admin) . . . .   *Digested*, 05/**949**

R. (on the application of Sivasubramaniam) v. Guildford College of Further & Higher Education see R. (on the application of Sivasubramaniam) v. Wandsworth County Court

R. (on the application of Sivasubramaniam) v. Kingston upon Thames County Court see R. (on the application of Sivasubramaniam) v. Wandsworth County Court

R. (on the application of Sivasubramaniam) v. Wandsworth County Court; *sub nom* Sivasubramaniam v. Wandsworth County Court; R. (on the application of Sivasubramaniam) v. Guildford College of Further & Higher Education; R. (on the application of Sivasubramaniam) v. Kingston upon Thames County Court [2002] EWCA Civ 1738; [2003] 1 W.L.R. 475; [2003] 2 All E.R. 160; [2003] C.P. Rep. 27; (2003) 100(3) L.S.G. 34; *Times*, November 30, 2002, CA (Civ Div) . . . .   *Digested*, 03/**66**:
Applied, 04/1634, 05/73, 05/2661: *Considered*, 05/2170: *Followed*, 04/2083

R. (on the application of Smith) v. East Kent Hospital NHS Trust [2002] EWHC 2640; (2003) 6 C.C.L. Rep. 251, QBD (Admin) . . . .   *Digested*, 03/**1917**:
Applied, 05/58

R. (on the application of Smith) v. Parole Board; *sub nom* Smith v. Parole Board; R. (on the application of West) v. Parole Board [2005] UKHL 1; [2005] 1 W.L.R. 350; [2005] 1 All E.R. 755; [2005] H.R.L.R. 8; 18 B.H.R.C. 267; (2005) 102(12) L.S.G. 26; (2005) 149 S.J.L.B. 145; *Times*, January 28, 2005; *Independent*, February 2, 2005, HL; reversing [2003] EWCA Civ 1269; [2004] 1 W.L.R. 421; (2003) 100(38) L.S.G. 34; (2003) 153 N.L.J. 1427; *Times*, September 2, 2003, CA (Civ Div) . . . .   *Digested*, 05/**2920**:
Applied, 04/2776, 05/2734: *Considered*, 05/2907: *Distinguished*, 04/3349:
Followed, 04/2782: *Previous proceedings*, 02/3349

R. (on the application of Smith) v. Secretary of State for Defence [2004] EWCA Civ 1664, CA (Civ Div); affirming [2004] EWHC 1797; [2005] 1 F.L.R. 97; [2004] Pens. L.R. 323; [2005] A.C.D. 15; [2004] Fam. Law 868; (2004) 101(34) L.S.G. 30; *Times*, July 30, 2004, QBD (Admin) . . . .   *Digested*, 04/**2821**

R. (on the application of Smith) v. Secretary of State for the Environment, Transport and Regions see Smith v. Secretary of State for the Environment, Transport and the Regions

R. (on the application of Smith) v. Secretary of State for the Home Department; *sub nom* Secretary of State for the Home Department v. Smith; Dudson v. Secretary of State; R. (on the application of Dudson) v. Secretary of State for the Home Department [2005] UKHL 51; [2005] 3 W.L.R. 410; [2005] H.R.L.R. 33; (2005) 155 N.L.J. 1415; *Times*, July 29, 2005, HL; affirming [2004] EWCA Civ 99; [2004] Q.B. 1341; [2004] 3 W.L.R. 341; [2004] H.R.L.R. 21; [2004] U.K.H.R.R. 532; (2004) 101(10) L.S.G. 29; (2004) 148 S.J.L.B. 233; *Times*, February 18, 2004, CA (Civ Div); affirming [2003] EWHC 692; [2003] 1 W.L.R. 2176; (2003) 100(24) L.S.G. 35; *Times*, April 11, 2003, QBD (Admin) . . . .   *Digested*, 05/**2923**:
Considered, 04/3475: *Previous proceedings*, 04/3475:
Subsequent proceedings, 05/3775

R. (on the application of Snelgrove) v. Woolwich Crown Court [2004] EWHC 2172; [2005] 1 W.L.R. 3223; [2005] 1 Cr. App. R. 18, QBD (Admin) . . . .   *Digested*, 05/**71**

R. (on the application of Soumahoro) v. Secretary of State for the Home Department see R. (on the application of Razgar) v. Secretary of State for the Home Department (No.2)

R. (on the application of South Cambridgeshire DC) v. First Secretary of State [2005] EWHC 1746; [2005] R.V.R. 369, QBD (Admin)

R. (on the application of SP) v. Secretary of State for the Home Department see R. (on the application of P) v. Secretary of State for the Home Department

R. (on the application of Spink) v. Wandsworth LBC [2005] EWCA Civ 302; [2005] 1 W.L.R. 2884; [2005] 2 All E.R. 954; [2005] 1 F.C.R. 608; [2005] H.L.R. 41; [2005] B.L.G.R. 561; (2005) 8 C.C.L. Rep. 272; (2005) 84 B.M.L.R. 169; (2005) 102(19) L.S.G. 34; (2005) 149 S.J.L.B. 390; *Times*, April 5, 2005; *Independent*, March 23, 2005, CA (Civ Div); affirming [2004] EWHC 2314; [2005] 1 W.L.R. 258; [2005] 1 F.L.R. 448; [2004] 3 F.C.R. 471; [2005] B.L.G.R. 1; [2005] A.C.D. 30; [2005] Fam. Law 22; *Times*, November 2, 2004, QBD (Admin) . . . .   *Digested*, 05/**3928**

R. (on the application of Spinks) v. Secretary of State for the Home Department [2005] EWCA Civ 275, CA (Civ Div); affirming [2004] EWHC 2916; [2005] A.C.D. 75, QBD (Admin)

R. (on the application of Spring Salmon & Seafood Ltd) v. Inland Revenue Commissioners see Spring Salmon & Seafood Ltd v. Advocate General for Scotland

R. (on the application of SR) *v.* Hackney LBC see R. (on the application of SR) *v.* Huntercombe Maidenhead Hospital

R. (on the application of SR) *v.* Huntercombe Maidenhead Hospital; *sub nom* R. (on the application of R) *v.* Hackney LBC; R. (on the application of SR) *v.* Hackney LBC [2005] EWHC 2361; (2005) 102(39) L.S.G. 31, QBD (Admin)

R. (on the application of Stanley) *v.* Commissioner of Police of the Metropolis [2004] EWHC 2229; (2004) 168 J.P. 623; [2005] E.M.L.R. 3; [2005] U.K.H.R.R. 115; [2005] H.L.R. 8; [2005] Crim. L.R. 292; [2005] A.C.D. 13; (2004) 168 J.P.N. 937; (2004) 101(40) L.S.G. 28; (2004) 154 N.L.J. 1525; *Times*, October 22, 2004, QBD (Admin)   *Digested*, 04/**272**

R. (on the application of Steele) *v.* Birmingham City Council [2005] EWCA Civ 1824, CA (Civ Div); reversing [2005] EWHC 783; [2005] R.V.R. 374, QBD (Admin)

R. (on the application of Stephenson) *v.* Stockton on Tees BC [2005] EWCA Civ 960; [2005] 3 F.C.R. 248; (2005) 8 C.C.L. Rep. 517; *Times*, September 5, 2005, CA (Civ Div); reversing [2004] EWHC 2228; [2005] 1 F.C.R. 165; (2004) 7 C.C.L. Rep. 459, QBD (Admin)   *Digested*, 05/**3937**

R. (on the application of Stoddard) *v.* Oxford Magistrates Court [2005] EWHC 2733; (2005) 169 J.P. 683, QBD (Admin)

R. (on the application of Swedish Match AB) *v.* Secretary of State for Health (C210/03); *sub nom* Swedish Match AB *v.* Secretary of State for Health (C210/03) [2004] E.C.R. I-11893; [2005] 1 C.M.L.R. 26, ECJ   *Digested*, 05/**1448**: *Followed*, 05/3354

R. (on the application of Sweet) *v.* English Nature see R. (on the application of Sweet) *v.* First Secretary of State

R. (on the application of Sweet) *v.* First Secretary of State; R. (on the application of Sweet) *v.* Somerset CC; R. (on the application of Sweet) *v.* English Nature; R. (on the application of Sweet) *v.* Somerset Wildlife Trust [2004] EWHC 2565; [2005] A.C.D. 78, QBD (Admin)

R. (on the application of Sweet) *v.* Somerset CC see R. (on the application of Sweet) *v.* First Secretary of State

R. (on the application of Sweet) *v.* Somerset Wildlife Trust see R. (on the application of Sweet) *v.* First Secretary of State

R. (on the application of Szuluk) *v.* Governor of Full Sutton Prison [2004] EWCA Civ 1426; [2005] A.C.D. 62; (2004) 148 S.J.L.B. 1314; *Independent*, November 4, 2004, CA (Civ Div); reversing [2004] EWHC 514; [2004] A.C.D. 45, QBD (Admin)   *Digested*, 05/**2913**

R. (on the application of T) *v.* Calderdale MBC [2004] EWHC 1998; (2005) 8 C.C.L. Rep. 101; [2005] A.C.D. 2, QBD (Admin)   *Digested*, 05/**3949**

R. (on the application of T) *v.* Enfield LBC; *sub nom* R. (on the application of C) *v.* Enfield LBC [2004] EWHC 2297; [2005] 3 F.C.R. 55, QBD (Admin)   *Digested*, 05/**2146**

R. (on the application of T) *v.* OL Primary School Governing Body [2005] EWHC 753; [2005] E.L.R. 522, QBD (Admin)

R. (on the application of T) *v.* Secretary of State for the Home Department see R. (on the application of S) *v.* Secretary of State for the Home Department

R. (on the application of T) *v.* St Albans Crown Court; Chief Constable of Surrey *v.* JHG [2002] EWHC 1129, QBD (Admin)   *Applied*, 05/831

R. (on the application of Takoushis) *v.* HM Coroner for Inner North London [2005] EWCA Civ 1440; *Times*, December 8, 2005, CA (Civ Div); reversing [2004] EWHC 2922, QBD (Admin)

R. (on the application of Tangney) *v.* Secretary of State for the Home Department see Tangney *v.* Governor of Elmley Prison

R. (on the application of Teleos Plc) *v.* Customs and Excise Commissioners [2004] EWHC 1035; [2004] Eu. L.R. 798; [2005] B.T.C. 5062; [2005] B.V.C. 93, QBD (Admin)   *Digested*, 04/**4038**

R. (on the application of Teleos Plc) *v.* Customs and Excise Commissioners (Interim Relief) [2005] EWCA Civ 200; [2005] 1 W.L.R. 3007; [2005] S.T.C. 1471; [2005] 2 C.M.L.R. 8; [2005] B.T.C. 5222; [2005] B.V.C. 253; [2005] S.T.I. 359; (2005) 102(18) L.S.G. 24; (2005) 149 S.J.L.B. 298; *Times*, March 9, 2005; *Independent*, March 17, 2005, CA (Civ Div); affirming [2004] EWHC 2350, QBD (Admin)   *Digested*, 05/**4420**

R. (on the application of Tesema) *v.* Secretary of State for the Home Department see R. (on the application of Limbuela) *v.* Secretary of State for the Home Department

R. (on the application of the Countryside Alliance) *v.* Attorney General; R. (on the application of Derwin) *v.* Attorney General; R. (on the application of Friend) *v.* Attorney General [2005] EWHC 1677; (2005) 102(36) L.S.G. 29; (2005) 155 N.L.J. 1245; [2005] N.P.C. 107; *Times*, August 3, 2005, QBD (Admin)   *Digested*, 05/**190**

R. (on the application of the Crown Prosecution Service) *v.* Redbridge Youth Court [2005] EWHC 1390; (2005) 169 J.P. 393; (2005) 169 J.P.N. 557; *Times*, July 13, 2005, QBD (Admin)   *Digested*, 05/**940**

R. (on the application of the Director of the Assets Recovery Agency) *v.* Creaven see Director of the Assets Recovery Agency *v.* Creaven

R. (on the application of the Law Society) *v.* Master of the Rolls; *sub nom* Law Society *v.* Master of the Rolls [2005] EWHC 146; [2005] 1 W.L.R. 2033; [2005] 2 All E.R. 640; (2005) 155 N.L.J. 246; *Times*, February 21, 2005, QBD (Admin)   *Digested*, 05/**2723**

R. (on the application of the Lord Chancellor) *v.* Chief Land Registrar [2005] EWHC 1706; [2005] 4 All E.R. 643; (2005) 169 J.P. 497; (2005) 169 J.P.N. 798; [2005] 29 E.G.C.S. 99; (2005) 102(34) L.S.G. 32; *Times*, August 31, 2005; *Times*, August 9, 2005, QBD (Admin) . . . .   *Digested*, 05/**3399**

R. (on the application of the Ministry of Defence) *v.* Wiltshire and Swindon Coroner [2005] EWHC 889; [2005] 4 All E.R. 40; *Times*, May 5, 2005, QBD (Admin) . .   *Digested*, 05/**366**

R. (on the application of Thomas Bates & Son Ltd) *v.* Secretary of State for Transport, Local Government and the Regions [2004] EWHC 1818; [2005] 2 P. & C.R. 11; [2005] J.P.L. 343; (2004) 101(32) L.S.G. 30; [2004] N.P.C. 113, QBD (Admin) . . . .   *Digested*, 05/**3313**

R. (on the application of Thompson) *v.* Law Society [2004] EWCA Civ 167; [2004] 1 W.L.R. 2522; [2004] 2 All E.R. 113; (2004) 101(13) L.S.G. 35; (2004) 154 N.L.J. 307; (2004) 148 S.J.L.B. 265; *Times*, April 1, 2004; *Independent*, March 29, 2004 (C.S), CA (Civ Div). . . . .   *Digested*, 05/**2734**

R. (on the application of Thomson) *v.* Minister of State for Children; *sub nom* R. (on the application of Charlton Thomson) *v.* Secretary of State for Education and Skills [2005] EWHC 1378; [2005] 2 F.C.R. 603; [2005] Fam. Law 861; *Times*, August 12, 2005, QBD (Admin) . . . .   *Digested*, 05/**1671**

R. (on the application of Thornby Farms Ltd) *v.* Daventry DC; *sub nom* Thornby Farms Ltd *v.* Daventry DC; R. *v.* Daventry DC Ex p. Thornby Farms; R. (on the application of Murray) *v.* Derbyshire DC; R. (on the application of Murray) *v.* Derbyshire CC [2002] EWCA Civ 31; [2003] Q.B. 503; [2002] 3 W.L.R. 875; [2002] Env. L.R. 28; [2003] E.H.L.R. 4; [2002] 2 P.L.R. 21; [2002] J.P.L. 937; [2002] A.C.D. 53; [2002] 5 E.G.C.S. 131; [2002] 5 E.G.C.S. 132; (2002) 99(11) L.S.G. 35; (2002) 146 S.J.L.B. 52; [2002] N.P.C. 13; *Times*, February 1, 2002, CA (Civ Div); affirming [2001] Env. L.R. 20; [2001] E.H.L.R. 6; [2001] J.P.L. 228 (Note); (2000) 97(35) L.S.G. 39; [2000] N.P.C. 91; *Times*, October 5, 2000, QBD . . . .   *Digested*, 02/**1514**:
   Applied, 04/3088, 05/1402: *Previous proceedings*, 00/4505:
   Referred to, 03/1410

R. (on the application of Tower of Refuge Ministry) *v.* Highbury Corner Magistrates Court [2004] EWHC 2372; [2004] R.V.R. 269, QBD (Admin) . . . .   *Digested*, 05/**3365**

R. (on the application of Trailer & Marina (Leven) Ltd) *v.* Secretary of State for the Environment, Food and Rural Affairs; *sub nom* Trailer & Marina (Leven) Ltd *v.* Secretary of State for the Environment, Food and Rural Affairs [2004] EWCA Civ 1580; [2005] 1 W.L.R. 1267; [2005] Env. L.R. 27; [2005] 1 P. & C.R. 28; [2005] J.P.L. 1086; (2005) 102(5) L.S.G. 26; (2005) 149 S.J.L.B. 60; *Times*, December 28, 2004, CA (Civ Div); affirming [2004] EWHC 153; [2004] Env. L.R. 40; [2004] J.P.L. 1512; (2004) 101(7) L.S.G. 37; [2004] N.P.C. 14; *Times*, February 19, 2004, QBD (Admin). . . . .   *Digested*, 05/**1410**

R. (on the application of Traves) *v.* DPP [2005] EWHC 1482; (2005) 169 J.P. 421; (2005) 169 J.P.N. 659, QBD (Admin) . . . .   *Digested*, 05/**817**

R. (on the application of Trend Properties Ltd) *v.* Islington LBC [2005] EWHC 906; [2005] N.P.C. 70, QBD

R. (on the application of Tromans) *v.* Cannock Chase DC [2004] EWCA Civ 1036; [2004] B.L.G.R. 735; [2005] J.P.L. 338; [2004] N.P.C. 132; *Times*, August 25, 2004, CA (Civ Div); reversing [2003] EWHC 3037, QBD (Admin)

R. (on the application of Tull) *v.* Camberwell Green Magistrates Court [2004] EWHC 2780; [2005] R.A. 31, QBD (Admin) . . . .   *Digested*, 05/**387**

R. (on the application of Tum) *v.* Secretary of State for the Home Department; *sub nom* Tum *v.* Secretary of State for the Home Department; Dari *v.* Secretary of State for the Home Department; R. (on the application of Dari) *v.* Secretary of State for the Home Department [2004] EWCA Civ 788; [2004] 2 C.M.L.R. 48; [2004] I.N.L.R. 442; *Independent*, June 18, 2004, CA (Civ Div); affirming [2003] EWHC 2745; [2004] 1 C.M.L.R. 33; [2004] Eu. L.R. 298; *Times*, November 27, 2003, QBD (Admin) . . . .   *Digested*, 04/**2036**:
   Applied, 05/2199

R. (on the application of Turner) *v.* Highbury Corner Magistrates Court; *sub nom* Turner *v.* Highbury Corner Magistrates Court [2005] EWHC 2568; *Times*, October 26, 2005, QBD (Admin)

R. (on the application of U) *v.* Commissioner of Police of the Metropolis see R. (on the application of R) *v.* Durham Constabulary

R. (on the application of UK Tradecorp Ltd) *v.* Customs and Excise Commissioners [2004] EWHC 2515; [2005] S.T.C. 138; [2005] B.T.C. 5097; [2005] B.V.C. 128; [2004] S.T.I. 2376; *Times*, November 17, 2004, QBD (Admin) . . . .   *Digested*, 05/**4373**

R. (on the application of Ullah) v. Special Adjudicator; *sub nom* Ullah (Ahsan) v. Special
Adjudicator; Do v. Secretary of State for the Home Department; R. (on the
application of Ullah (Ahsan)) v. Secretary of State for the Home Department; Do
v. Immigration Appeal Tribunal [2004] UKHL 26; [2004] 2 A.C. 323; [2004] 3
W.L.R. 23; [2004] 3 All E.R. 785; [2004] H.R.L.R. 33; [2004] U.K.H.R.R. 995;
[2004] Imm. A.R. 419; [2004] I.N.L.R. 381; (2004) 101(28) L.S.G. 33;
(2004) 154 N.L.J. 985; (2004) 148 S.J.L.B. 762; *Times*, June 18, 2004;
Independent, June 22, 2004, HL; affirming [2002] EWCA Civ 1856; [2003] 1
W.L.R. 770; [2003] 3 All E.R. 1174; [2003] H.R.L.R. 12; [2003] U.K.H.R.R. 302;
[2003] Imm. A.R. 304; [2003] I.N.L.R. 74; [2003] A.C.D. 30; (2003) 100(10)
L.S.G. 28; (2003) 147 S.J.L.B. 28; *Times*, December 18, 2002; *Independent*,
December 20, 2002, CA (Civ Div); affirming [2002] EWHC 1584; [2002] Imm.
A.R. 601; *Times*, September 5, 2002; *Independent*, October 14, 2002 (C.S),
QBD (Admin) . . . .   *Digested*, 04/**2009**:
Applied, 04/2052, 05/401, 05/2195: *Considered*, 04/839, 04/2038, 05/2140,
05/5431

R. (on the application of Ullah (Ahsan)) v. Secretary of State for the Home Department
see R. (on the application of Ullah) v. Special Adjudicator

R. (on the application of Ultraframe (UK) Ltd) v. Central Arbitration Committee; *sub nom*
Central Arbitration Committee v. Ultraframe (UK) Ltd [2005] EWCA Civ 560;
[2005] I.C.R. 1194; [2005] I.R.L.R. 641; *Times*, May 11, 2005, CA (Civ Div);
reversing [2005] EWHC 112; *Times*, April 12, 2005, QBD (Admin) . . . .   *Digested*, 05/**1201**

R. (on the application of Uttley) v. Secretary of State for the Home Department [2004]
UKHL 38; [2004] 1 W.L.R. 2278; [2004] 4 All E.R. 1; [2005] 1 Cr. App. R. 15;
[2005] 1 Cr. App. R. (S.) 91; [2004] H.R.L.R. 42; [2004] U.K.H.R.R. 1031; 17
B.H.R.C. 379; (2004) 101(35) L.S.G. 33; (2004) 154 N.L.J. 1255; (2004) 148
S.J.L.B. 977; *Times*, August 13, 2004, HL; reversing [2003] EWCA Civ 1130;
[2003] 1 W.L.R. 2590; [2003] 4 All E.R. 891; [2004] 1 Cr. App. R. (S.) 61;
[2003] H.R.L.R. 39; [2003] U.K.H.R.R. 1332; [2003] Crim. L.R. 900; *Times*,
August 4, 2003, CA (Civ Div); reversing [2003] EWHC 950, QBD (Admin) . . .   *Digested*, 04/**3428**

R. (on the application of Vella) v. Lambeth LBC; *sub nom* Vella v. Lambeth LBC [2005]
EWHC 2473; [2005] 47 E.G.C.S. 144; *Times*, November 23, 2005, QBD
(Admin)

R. (on the application of W) v. Commissioner of Police of the Metropolis C1/2005/1798,
CA (Civ Div); reversing [2005] EWHC 1586; [2005] 1 W.L.R. 3706; [2005] 3
All E.R. 749; (2005) 169 J.P. 473; (2005) 169 J.P.N. 718; (2005) 155 N.L.J.
1184; *Times*, July 21, 2005; *Independent*, July 22, 2005, QBD (Admin) . . . .   *Digested*, 05/**810**

R. (on the application of W) v. Doncaster MBC; *sub nom* W v. Doncaster MBC [2004]
EWCA Civ 378; [2004] B.L.G.R. 743; (2004) 101(22) L.S.G. 32; (2004) 148
S.J.L.B. 572; *Times*, May 13, 2004, CA (Civ Div); affirming [2003] EWHC 192;
(2003) 6 C.C.L. Rep. 301; *Times*, March 12, 2003, QBD (Admin) . . . .   *Digested*, 04/**2686**:
Applied, 05/2824

R. (on the application of W) v. DPP see W v. DPP

R. (on the application of W) v. Lambeth LBC see R. (on the application of G) v. Barnet
LBC

R. (on the application of W) v. Southampton Youth Court; *sub nom* R. (on the
application of K) v. Wirral Borough Magistrates Court [2002] EWHC 1640;
[2003] 1 Cr. App. R. (S.) 87; (2002) 166 J.P. 569; [2002] Crim. L.R. 750;
(2002) 166 J.P.N. 709, QBD (Admin) . . . .   *Digested*, 03/**882**:
Applied, 03/881, 04/894, 04/895: *Followed*, 05/939

R. (on the application of W) v. Special Educational Needs and Disability Tribunal [2005]
EWHC 1580; [2005] E.L.R. 599, QBD (Admin)

R. (on the application of W) v. Thetford Youth Court; R. (on the application of M) v.
Waltham Forest Youth Court [2002] EWHC 1252; [2003] 1 Cr. App. R. (S.) 67;
(2002) 166 J.P. 453; [2002] Crim. L.R. 681; (2002) 166 J.P.N. 573, QBD
(Admin) . . . .   *Digested*, 03/**3756**:
Applied, 03/881, 05/940: *Considered*, 04/3476

R. (on the application of W) v. West London Youth Court see R. (on the application of M)
v. West London Youth Court

R. (on the application of Wahid) v. Tower Hamlets LBC [2002] EWCA Civ 287; [2003]
H.L.R. 2; [2002] B.L.G.R. 545; (2002) 5 C.C.L. Rep. 239, CA (Civ Div);
affirming [2001] EWHC Admin 641; (2001) 4 C.C.L. Rep. 455, QBD (Admin) . .   *Digested*, 03/**2046**:
Considered, 05/3947

R. (on the application of Wall) v. Brighton and Hove City Council [2004] EWHC 2582;
[2005] 1 P. & C.R. 33; [2004] 4 P.L.R. 115; [2005] J.P.L. 807; [2004] 46
E.G.C.S. 150; (2004) 101(44) L.S.G. 33; *Times*, November 16, 2004, QBD
(Admin) . . . .   *Digested*, 05/**3300**

R. (on the application of Walmsley) v. Lane; *sub nom* Walmsley v. Transport for London
[2005] EWCA Civ 1540; *Times*, November 28, 2005, CA (Civ Div); affirming
[2005] EWHC 896; [2005] R.T.R. 28; *Times*, May 25, 2005, QBD (Admin) . . . .   *Digested*, 05/**3452**

R. (on the application of Wandsworth LBC) v. Secretary of State for Transport; R. (on the
application of Essex CC) v. Secretary of State for Transport [2005] EWHC 20;
[2005] 8 E.G.C.S. 191; *Times*, February 22, 2005, QBD (Admin) . . . .   *Digested*, 05/**58**

R. (on the application of Wandsworth LBC) *v.* Secretary of State for Transport (Summary of Judgment) [2005] J.P.L.1635, QBD (Admin)

R. (on the application of Wanogho) *v.* Bow Street Magistrates Court see R. (on the application of Salubi) *v.* Bow Street Magistrates Court

R. (on the application of Watford Grammar School for Girls) *v.* Adjudicator for Schools [2003] EWHC 2480; [2004] E.L.R. 40; *Times*, October 27, 2003, QBD (Admin) . . . . *Digested*, 04/**1019**:
Applied, 05/1167

R. (on the application of Wells) *v.* Secretary of State for Transport, Local Government and the Regions (C201/02); *sub nom* Wells *v.* Secretary of State for Transport, Local Government and the Regions (C201/02) [2005] All E.R. (EC) 323; [2004] E.C.R. I-723; [2004] 1 C.M.L.R. 31; [2004] Env. L.R. 27; [2004] N.P.C. 1, ECJ (5th Chamber) . . . . *Digested*, 04/**1397**

R. (on the application of West) *v.* Parole Board see R. (on the application of Smith) *v.* Parole Board

R. (on the application of West) *v.* Parole Board [2002] EWCA Civ 1641; [2003] 1 W.L.R. 705; (2003) 100(3) L.S.G. 31; (2002) 146 S.J.L.B. 265; *Times*, November 21, 2002, CA (Civ Div); affirming [2002] EWHC 769, QBD (Admin) . . . . *Digested*, 02/**3349**:
Applied, 03/2144: *Overruled*, 05/2920

R. (on the application of West End Street Traders Association) *v.* Westminster City Council [2004] EWHC 1167; [2005] B.L.G.R. 143; [2004] A.C.D. 73, QBD (Admin) . . . *Digested*, 05/**2805**

R. (on the application of Western Riverside Waste Authority) *v.* Wandsworth LBC [2005] EWHC 536; [2005] Env. L.R. 41; [2005] B.L.G.R. 846, QBD (Admin). . . . . *Digested*, 05/**1415**

R. (on the application of Westlake) *v.* Criminal Cases Review Commission [2004] EWHC 2779; *Times*, November 19, 2004, QBD (Admin) . . . . *Digested*, 05/**850**

R. (on the application of Westminster City Council) *v.* Middlesex Crown Court [2002] EWHC 1104, QBD (Admin) . . . . *Followed*, 05/2754

R. (on the application of Whitmey) *v.* Commons Commissioners [2004] EWCA Civ 951; [2005] Q.B. 282; [2004] 3 W.L.R. 1343; [2005] 1 P. & C.R. 24; [2004] 4 P.L.R. 68; [2004] 3 E.G.L.R. 1; [2004] 45 E.G. 126; [2004] 32 E.G.C.S. 63; (2004) 101(34) L.S.G. 30; (2004) 148 S.J.L.B. 940; [2004] N.P.C. 125; *Times*, August 10, 2004, CA (Civ Div) . . . . *Digested*, 04/**3262**

R. (on the application of Widgery Soldiers) *v.* Lord Saville of Newdigate see R. (on the application of A) *v.* Lord Saville of Newdigate (Bloody Sunday Inquiry)

R. (on the application of Wildman) *v.* Office of Communications [2005] EWHC 1573; *Times*, September 28, 2005, QBD (Admin)

R. (on the application of Wilkinson) *v.* Broadmoor Hospital; *sub nom* R. (on the application of Wilkinson) *v.* Broadmoor Special Hospital Authority; R. (on the application of Wilkinson) *v.* Responsible Medical Officer Broadmoor Hospital [2001] EWCA Civ 1545; [2002] 1 W.L.R. 419; [2002] U.K.H.R.R. 390; (2002) 5 C.C.L. Rep. 121; [2002] Lloyd's Rep. Med. 41; (2002) 65 B.M.L.R. 15; [2002] A.C.D. 47; (2001) 98(44) L.S.G. 36; (2001) 145 S.J.L.B. 247; *Times*, November 2, 2001; *Independent*, December 10, 2001 (C.S); *Daily Telegraph*, October 30, 2001, CA (Civ Div) . . . . *Digested*, 01/**4431**:
Applied, 05/1837, 05/2830: *Considered*, 02/51, 02/3234

R. (on the application of Wilkinson) *v.* Broadmoor Special Hospital Authority see R. (on the application of Wilkinson) *v.* Broadmoor Hospital

R. (on the application of Wilkinson) *v.* Inland Revenue Commissioners; *sub nom* Wilkinson *v.* Inland Revenue Commissioners [2005] UKHL 30; [2005] 1 W.L.R. 1718; [2005] U.K.H.R.R. 704; 77 T.C. 78; [2005] S.T.I. 904; (2005) 102(25) L.S.G. 33; *Times*, May 6, 2005; *Independent*, May 11, 2005, HL; affirming [2003] EWCA Civ 814; [2003] 1 W.L.R. 2683; [2003] 3 All E.R. 719; [2003] S.T.C. 1113; [2003] 2 F.C.R. 558; [2003] U.K.H.R.R. 1068; [2003] B.T.C. 282; [2003] S.T.I. 1125; (2003) 100(33) L.S.G. 27; (2003) 147 S.J.L.B. 781; *Times*, June 28, 2003; *Independent*, June 26, 2003, CA (Civ Div); affirming [2002] EWHC 182; [2002] S.T.C. 347; [2002] B.T.C. 97; [2002] S.T.I. 234; (2002) 152 N.L.J. 282, QBD (Admin) . . . . *Digested*, 05/**3985**

R. (on the application of Wilkinson) *v.* Responsible Medical Officer Broadmoor Hospital see R. (on the application of Wilkinson) *v.* Broadmoor Hospital

R. (on the application of Williamson) *v.* Secretary of State for Education and Employment; *sub nom* Williamson *v.* Secretary of State for Education and Employment [2005] UKHL 15; [2005] 2 A.C. 246; [2005] 2 W.L.R. 590; [2005] 2 All E.R. 1; [2005] 2 F.L.R. 374; [2005] 1 F.C.R. 498; [2005] H.R.L.R. 14; [2005] U.K.H.R.R. 339; 19 B.H.R.C. 99; [2005] E.L.R. 291; [2005] Fam. Law 456; (2005) 102(16) L.S.G. 27; (2005) 155 N.L.J. 324; (2005) 149 S.J.L.B. 266; *Times*, February 25, 2005; *Independent*, March 1, 2005, HL; affirming [2002] EWCA Civ 1926; [2003] Q.B. 1300; [2003] 3 W.L.R. 482; [2003] 1 All E.R. 385; [2003] 1 F.L.R. 726; [2003] 1 F.C.R. 1; [2003] H.R.L.R. 10; [2003] U.K.H.R.R. 800; [2003] E.L.R. 176; [2003] Fam. Law 227; (2003) 100(9) L.S.G. 27; *Times*, December 18, 2002; *Independent*, December 19, 2002, CA (Civ Div); affirming [2001] EWHC Admin 960; [2002] 1 F.L.R. 493; [2002] H.R.L.R. 14; [2002] E.L.R. 214; [2002] A.C.D. 32; [2002] Fam. Law 257; *Times*, December 12, 2001, QBD (Admin) . . . . *Digested*, 05/**1019**:
Applied, 04/4349: *Considered*, 03/1114, 04/1925

R. (on the application of Wirral MBC) *v.* Chief Schools Adjudicator [2001] E.L.R. 574, QBD (Admin) . . . . *Digested*, 01/**1971**:
Considered, 05/1167

R. (on the application of Withey) *v.* Secretary of State for Work and Pensions see R. (on the application of Hooper) *v.* Secretary of State for Work and Pensions

R. (on the application of X) *v.* Chief Constable of the West Midlands; *sub nom* X *v.* Chief Constable of the West Midlands [2004] EWCA Civ 1068; [2005] 1 W.L.R. 65; [2005] 1 All E.R. 610; (2004) 101(35) L.S.G. 34; (2004) 148 S.J.L.B. 1119; *Times*, August 18, 2004; *Independent*, October 1, 2004, CA (Civ Div); reversing [2004] EWHC 61; [2004] 1 W.L.R. 1518; [2004] 2 All E.R. 1; (2004) 101(6) L.S.G. 31; (2004) 154 N.L.J. 146; *Times*, February 2, 2004, QBD (Admin) . . . . . *Digested*, 05/**3324**

R. (on the application of Yilmaz) *v.* Secretary of State for the Home Department; *sub nom* Yilmaz *v.* Secretary of State for the Home Department [2005] EWHC 1068; [2005] 1 W.L.R. 3944; *Times*, July 27, 2005, QBD (Admin) . . . . *Digested*, 05/**2199**

R. (on the application of Zeb) *v.* Newham LBC see R. (on the application of Khatun) *v.* Newham LBC

Rabahallah *v.* British Telecommunications Plc; *sub nom* Rabahallah *v.* BT Group Plc [2005] I.C.R. 440; [2005] I.R.L.R. 184, EAT . . . . *Digested*, 05/**1253**

Rabahallah *v.* BT Group Plc see Rabahallah *v.* British Telecommunications Plc

Rackind *v.* Gross see Gross *v.* Rackind

Radcliffe, Re [2005] W.T.L.R. 1395, Sup Ct Costs Office

Radclyffe *v.* Royal Mail Group Plc (Unreported, August 12, 2004), CC (High Wycombe) [*Ex rel.* Marc Beaumont, Barrister, Windsor Chambers, Royal Albert House, Sheet Street, Windsor, Berkshire] . . . . *Digested*, 05/**287**

Radio France *v.* France (53984/00) (2005) 40 E.H.R.R. 29, ECHR . . . . *Digested*, 05/**2043**

Radio Telefis Eireann *v.* Commission of the European Communities (C241/91 P); *sub nom* Magill Case (C241/91 P), Re; Radio Telefis Eireann *v.* Commission of the European Communities (T69/89); Independent Television Publications Ltd *v.* Commission of the European Communities (C242/91 P) [1995] All E.R. (E.C.) 416; [1995] E.C.R. I-743; [1995] 4 C.M.L.R. 718; [1995] E.M.L.R. 337; [1995] F.S.R. 530; [1998] Masons C.L.R. Rep. 58; *Times*, April 17, 1995; *Financial Times*, April 11, 1995, ECJ; affirming [1991] E.C.R. II-485; [1991] 4 C.M.L.R. 586; *Times*, October 21, 1991, CFI (2nd Chamber) . . . . *Digested*, 95/**639**:
Applied, 98/724: *Considered*, 94/3525, 01/3847, 02/589, 03/2528:
Distinguished, 98/3426, 02/590: *Followed*, 04/523, 05/550:
Previous proceedings, 90/2070, 90/2123: *Referred to*, 00/702

Radio Telefis Eireann *v.* Commission of the European Communities (T69/89) see Radio Telefis Eireann *v.* Commission of the European Communities (C241/91 P)

Radivojevic *v.* Secretary of State for the Home Department see Adan (Hassan Hussein) *v.* Secretary of State for the Home Department

Radlberger Getrankegesellschaft mbH & Co *v.* Land Baden-Wurttemberg (C309/02); *sub nom* Verpack V, Re (C309/02) [2005] All E.R. (EC) 1001; [2004] E.C.R. I-11763; [2005] 1 C.M.L.R. 35, ECJ . . . . *Digested*, 05/**1477**

Rado Uhren AG's Trade Mark Application (C55/01) see Linde AG's Trade Mark Application (C53/01)

Radovanovic *v.* Austria (42703/98) (2005) 41 E.H.R.R. 6, ECHR . . . . *Digested*, 05/**2122**

Rafferty *v.* Revenue and Customs Commissioners [2005] S.T.C. (S.C.D.) 484, Sp Comm

Raffile *v.* United States of America [2004] EWHC 2913; [2005] 1 All E.R. 889, QBD (Admin) . . . . *Digested*, 05/**1485**

Raffles *v.* Wichelhaus (1864) 2 Hurl. & C. 906 . . . . *Considered*, 71/11921:
Distinguished, 05/718

Raja *v.* Austin Gray (A Firm) [2002] EWCA Civ 1965; [2003] B.P.I.R. 725; [2003] Lloyd's Rep. P.N. 126; [2003] 1 E.G.L.R. 91; [2003] 13 E.G. 117; [2003] 4 E.G.C.S. 151, CA (Civ Div); reversing [2002] EWHC 1607; [2003] B.P.I.R. 120; [2003] P.N.L.R. 5; [2002] 3 E.G.L.R. 61; [2002] 43 E.G. 210; [2002] 33 E.G.C.S. 98; [2002] N.P.C. 114, QBD . . . . *Digested*, 03/**2993**:
Followed, 05/3419

Raja *v.* Van Hoogstraten (Application to Strike Out) [2004] EWCA Civ 968; [2004] 4 All E.R. 793; [2005] C.P. Rep. 6; *Times*, July 27, 2004; *Independent*, July 27, 2004, CA (Civ Div); reversing [2002] EWHC 2729, Ch D . . . . *Digested*, 04/**287**

Rajcoomar *v.* United Kingdom (Admissibility) (59457/00) (2005) 40 E.H.R.R. SE20, ECHR

RAL (Channel Islands) Ltd *v.* Customs and Excise Commissioners (C452/03) [2005] S.T.C. 1025; [2005] 2 C.M.L.R. 50; [2005] S.T.I. 919; *Times*, May 30, 2005, ECJ (1st Chamber) . . . . *Digested*, 05/**4404**

Ram *v.* Ram (No.1) [2004] EWCA Civ 1452; [2005] 2 B.C.L.C. 476; [2005] 2 F.L.R. 63; [2004] B.P.I.R. 616; [2005] Fam. Law 274; (2004) 148 S.J.L.B. 1317, CA (Civ Div) . . . . *Digested*, 04/**2122**

Ram *v.* Ram (No.2) [2004] EWCA Civ 1684; [2005] 2 F.L.R. 75; [2004] 3 F.C.R. 673; [2005] B.P.I.R. 628; [2005] Fam. Law 348; (2004) 148 S.J.L.B. 1371, CA (Civ Div) . . . . *Digested*, 05/**1653**

Rambus Inc v. Hynix Semiconductor UK Ltd (formerly Hyundai Electronics UK Ltd);
Rambus Inc v. Micron Europe Ltd [2004] EWHC 2313; [2005] F.S.R. 19;
(2005) 28(1) I.P.D. 27114, Ch D (Patents Ct) . . . . *Digested*, 05/**355**
Rambus Inc v. Micron Europe Ltd see Rambus Inc v. Hynix Semiconductor UK Ltd
(formerly Hyundai Electronics UK Ltd)
Ramdoolar v. Bycity Ltd [2005] I.C.R. 368, EAT . . . . *Digested*, 05/**1193**
Ramlort Ltd v. Reid see Reid v. Ramlort Ltd
Ramondin SA v. Commission of the European Communities (C186/02 P) [2004]
E.C.R. I-10653; [2005] 1 C.M.L.R. 32, ECJ (2nd Chamber) . . . . *Digested*, 05/**593**
Ramsamy v. Babar [2003] EWCA Civ 1253; [2005] 1 F.L.R. 113; [2005] Fam. Law
461, CA (Civ Div) . . . . *Digested*, 05/**1675**
Ramsarran v. Attorney General of Trinidad and Tobago [2005] UKPC 8; [2005] 2 A.C.
614; [2005] 2 W.L.R. 936, PC (Trin) . . . . *Digested*, 05/**872**
Ramsey v. Walkers Snack Foods Ltd; Hamblet v. Walkers Snack Foods Ltd [2004]
I.R.L.R. 754, EAT. . . . . *Digested*, 05/**1317**
Ranbaxy (UK) Ltd v. Warner-Lambert Co [2005] EWHC 1908; (2005) 28(10) I.P.D.
28080, Ch D (Patents Ct)
Randall v. Randall [2004] EWHC 2258; [2005] W.T.L.R. 119; (2004-05) 7 I.T.E.L.R.
340; [2005] 1 P. & C.R. DG4, Ch D . . . . *Digested*, 05/**1423**
Rangers Football Club Plc v. Revenue and Customs Commissioners [2005] S.T.I. 1733,
V&DTr
Rao v. General Medical Council [2002] UKPC 65; [2003] Lloyd's Rep. Med. 62;
(2003) 147 S.J.L.B. 113, PC (UK). . . . . *Digested*, 03/**1730**:
Applied, 03/1726: *Disapproved*, 05/1802
Rashid v. Secretary of State for the Home Department see R. (on the application of
Rashid) v. Secretary of State for the Home Department
Rasmussen v. Total E&P Norge AS (E2/04) [2005] 1 C.M.L.R. 19, EFTA . . . . *Digested*, 05/**1314**
Ratiu v. Conway; *sub nom* Conway v. Ratiu [2005] EWCA Civ 1302; [2005] 46
E.G.C.S. 177; *Times*, November 29, 2005, CA (Civ Div)
Ratners Group, Re (1988) 4 B.C.C. 293; [1988] B.C.L.C. 685, DC . . . . *Digested*, 88/**345**:
Applied, 05/532
Ravichandran, Re [2004] B.P.I.R. 814, Ch D (Bankruptcy Ct). . . . . *Digested*, 05/**2276**
Ravichandran v. Secretary of State for the Home Department see R. v. Secretary of
State for the Home Department Ex p. Jeyeanthan
Ray v. Classic FM Plc [1998] E.C.C. 488; [1999] I.T.C.L.R. 256; [1998] F.S.R. 622;
(1998) 21(5) I.P.D. 21047; (1998) 95(17) L.S.G. 32; (1998) 148 N.L.J. 445;
Times, April 8, 1998, Ch D . . . . *Digested*, 98/**3431**:
Applied, 04/2252, 05/2425: *Approved*, 03/2502
Raymond v. Honey [1983] 1 A.C. 1; [1982] 2 W.L.R. 465; [1982] 1 All E.R. 756;
(1982) 75 Cr. App. R. 16, HL; affirming [1981] Q.B. 874; [1981] 3 W.L.R. 218;
[1981] 2 All E.R. 1084; (1981) 73 Cr. App. R. 242; *Times*, April 8, 1981, QBD . . . *Digested*, 82/**2613**:
Applied, 88/2976, 94/735, 95/1033: *Considered*, 83/3080, 84/2762,
86/2678, 01/4582, 03/2223: *Distinguished*, 84/2754, 91/5481, 92/3632,
05/2914: *Followed*, 94/3849, 99/4104: *Referred to*, 92/6216
RB (Male Patient: Sterilisation), Re see A (Mental Patient: Sterilisation), Re
RBG Resources Plc, Re see Shierson v. Rastogi
RBG Resources Plc v. Rastogi [2005] EWHC 994; [2005] 2 B.C.L.C. 592, Ch D
RBS Deutschland Holdings GmbH v. Customs and Excise Commissioners [2004] V. &
D.R. 447; [2005] S.T.I. 123, V&DTr (Edinburgh)
RCI (Europe) Ltd v. Woods (Inspector of Taxes) [2003] EWHC 3129; [2004] S.T.C.
315; 76 T.C. 390; [2004] B.T.C. 285; [2004] S.T.I. 45; *Times*, January 9, 2004,
Ch D; affirming [2003] S.T.C. (S.C.D.) 128; [2003] S.T.I. 247, Sp Comm . . . . . . *Digested*, 04/**3801**
RD v. Poland (29692/96) (2004) 39 E.H.R.R. 11, ECHR . . . . *Digested*, 05/**2079**
Re-Source America International Ltd v. Platt Site Services Ltd [2004] EWCA Civ 665;
95 Con. L.R. 1; [2004] N.P.C. 89, CA (Civ Div); affirming [2003] EWHC 1142;
90 Con. L.R. 139, QBD (TCC) . . . . *Digested*, 05/**663**:
Followed, 05/2833
Re-Source America International Ltd v. Platt Site Services Ltd (Damages); *sub nom*
Barkin Construction Ltd v. Re-Source America International Ltd [2005] EWCA
Civ 97; [2005] 2 Lloyd's Rep. 50; [2005] N.P.C. 19, CA (Civ Div); reversing in
part [2004] EWHC 1405; 95 Con. L.R. 24, QBD (TCC). . . . . *Digested*, 05/**958**
Read v. Edmed [2004] EWHC 3274; [2005] P.I.Q.R. P16; *Times*, December 13, 2004,
QBD . . . . *Digested*, 05/**369**
Reading BC v. Fisher [2005] P.A.D. 71, Planning Inspector
Ready Mixed Concrete (South East) Ltd v. Minister of Pensions and National Insurance;
Minister for Social Security v. Greenham Ready Mixed Concrete Ltd; Minister
for Social Security v. Ready Mixed Concrete (South East) Ltd [1968] 2 Q.B.
497; [1968] 2 W.L.R. 775; [1968] 1 All E.R. 433; 4 K.I.R. 132; (1967) 112 S.J. 14;
Times, December 11, 1967, QBD . . . . *Digested*, 68/**2550**:
Applied, 77/1124, 82/1010, 01/2263, 01/2264, 04/2263, 05/1330:
Approved, 76/871, 78/1116, 04/1315: *Considered*, 69/2338, 82/1011, 01/6467,
01/6468, 05/4128: *Followed*, 71/3945, 76/878

Reardon Smith Line Ltd *v.* Hansen-Tangen (The Diana Prosperity); Hansen-Tangen *v.* Sanko Steamship Co Ltd [1976] 1 W.L.R. 989; [1976] 3 All E.R. 570; [1976] 2 Lloyd's Rep. 621; 120 S.J. 719, HL; affirming [1976] 2 Lloyd's Rep. 60; 120 S.J. 329, CA (Civ Div) . . . . *Digested,* 77/**2816**:
Applied, 78/338, 83/2127, 92/311, 01/2287, 01/4950, 02/671, 05/288:
Approved, 97/2189: *Considered,* 76/1204, 80/2458, 81/16, 86/1513, 93/2519, 94/332, 94/3430, 95/1974, 98/2300: *Followed,* 76/333, 77/2668, 79/813
Reckitt Benckiser (UK) Ltd *v.* Home Pairfum Ltd; *sub nom* Reckitt Benkiser (UK) Ltd *v.* Home Pairfum Ltd [2004] EWHC 302; [2005] E.T.M.R. 94; [2004] F.S.R. 37; (2004) 27(7) I.P.D. 27074, Ch D . . . . *Digested,* 04/**426**
Recogniton of a Default Judgment, Re (C16 W12/02) [2005] I.L.Pr. 23, OLG (Koln)
Recot Inc's Design [2005] E.C.D.R. 13, OHIM (Cancellation Div) . . . . *Digested,* 05/**2413**
Recruitment of Teaching Staff, Re (C278/03) see Commission of the European Communities *v.* Italy (C278/03)
Red Discretionary Trustees *v.* Inspector of Taxes see Howell *v.* Trippier (Inspector of Taxes)
Reda *v.* Flag Ltd [2002] UKPC 38; [2002] I.R.L.R. 747, PC (Ber) . . . . *Digested,* 03/**1317**:
Distinguished, 05/1212
Redcar and Cleveland BC *v.* Degnan; *sub nom* Degnan *v.* Redcar and Cleveland BC [2005] EWCA Civ 726; [2005] I.R.L.R. 615; [2005] E.L.R. 475, CA (Civ Div); [2005] EWCA Civ 726; [2005] I.R.L.R. 615; [2005] E.L.R. 475, CA (Civ Div); . . . . *Digested,* 05/**1259**
Redfearn *v.* Serco Ltd (t/a West Yorkshire Transport Service) [2005] I.R.L.R. 744, EAT . . *Digested,* 05/**1290**
Redfish Quotas, Re (C62/89) see Commission of the European Communities *v.* France (C62/89)
Redrow Homes Ltd *v.* First Secretary of State; *sub nom* R. (on the application of Redrow Homes Ltd) *v.* First Secretary of State; First Secretary of State *v.* Redrow Homes Ltd [2004] EWCA Civ 1375; [2005] J.P.L. 502; [2004] N.P.C. 143, CA (Civ Div); affirming [2003] EWHC 3094; [2004] 2 P.L.R. 51; [2004] J.P.L. 1273; [2003] 50 E.G.C.S. 94; [2003] N.P.C. 149, QBD (Admin) . . . . *Digested,* 05/**3293**
Redundant Employee *v.* McNally (Inspector of Taxes) see Ibe *v.* McNally (Inspector of Taxes)
Reed *v.* Oury (No.2) [2002] EWHC 369, Ch D; reversing in part . . . . *Considered,* 05/482
Reed Executive Plc *v.* Reed Business Information Ltd (Costs: Alternative Dispute Resolution) [2004] EWCA Civ 887; [2004] 1 W.L.R. 3026; [2004] 4 All E.R. 942; [2005] C.P. Rep. 4; [2004] 4 Costs L.R. 662; [2005] F.S.R. 3; (2004) 27(7) I.P.D. 27067; (2004) 148 S.J.L.B. 881; *Times,* July 16, 2004, CA (Civ Div) . . . . *Digested,* 04/**266**
REEF Trade Mark; *sub nom* South Cone Inc *v.* Bessant (t/a REEF); Bessant *v.* South Cone Inc [2002] EWCA Civ 763; [2003] R.P.C. 5; *Times,* May 31, 2002, CA (Civ Div); reversing [2002] R.P.C. 19; (2001) 24(11) I.P.D. 24072; (2001) 98(38) L.S.G. 39; [2001] E.T.M.R. CN19; *Times,* October 9, 2001, Ch D . . . . . . *Digested,* 02/**2897**:
Applied, 02/2859, 05/2568: *Followed,* 02/2861
Refugee Appeal No.74665/03 [2005] I.N.L.R. 68, Refugees Status Apps
Regazzoni *v.* KC Sethia (1944) Ltd; *sub nom* Regazzoni *v.* Sethia (KC) (1944) [1958] A.C. 301; [1957] 3 W.L.R. 752; [1957] 3 All E.R. 286; [1957] 2 Lloyd's Rep. 289; 101 S.J. 848, HL; affirming [1956] 2 Q.B. 490; [1956] 3 W.L.R. 79; [1956] 2 All E.R. 487; [1956] 1 Lloyd's Rep. 435; 100 S.J. 417, CA; affirming [1956] 2 W.L.R. 204; [1956] 1 All E.R. 229; [1955] 2 Lloyd's Rep. 766; 100 S.J. 55, QBD . . . . *Digested,* 57/**585**:
Applied, 59/1474, 97/689: *Considered,* 66/541, 82/1680, 87/201, 88/182, 89/376: *Distinguished,* 71/1886, 72/532, 05/196
Regent International Hotels (UK) *v.* Pageguide, *Times,* May 13, 1985, CA (Civ Div) . . . . . *Digested,* 85/**404**:
Applied, 05/422
Regie Dauphinoise-Cabinet A Forest Sarl *v.* Ministre du Budget (C306/94) [1996] S.T.C. 1176; [1996] E.C.R. I-3695; [1996] 3 C.M.L.R. 193; [1996] C.E.C. 817, ECJ (5th Chamber) . . . . *Applied,* 05/**4345**
Rehman *v.* Boardman (No.1) [2004] B.P.I.R. 820, Ch D . . . . *Digested,* 05/**2286**
Rehman *v.* Boardman (No.2) [2004] EWHC 605; [2004] B.P.I.R. 1020, Ch D . . . . *Digested,* 05/**2291**
Rehman *v.* Secretary of State for the Home Department see Secretary of State for the Home Department *v.* Rehman
Reichert *v.* Dresdner Bank (C261/90) [1992] E.C.R. I-2149; [1992] I.L.Pr. 404; [1999] B.P.I.R. 946, ECJ (5th Chamber) . . . . *Digested,* 92/**4824**:
Considered, 01/820, 03/1585: *Followed,* 05/428
Reid *v.* Ramlort Ltd; *sub nom* Thoars (Deceased), Re; Ramlort Ltd *v.* Reid [2004] EWCA Civ 800; [2005] 1 B.C.L.C. 331; [2004] B.P.I.R. 985; (2004) 148 S.J.L.B. 877, CA (Civ Div); affirming [2003] EWHC 1999; [2005] 1 B.C.L.C. 331; [2003] B.P.I.R. 1444, Ch D . . . . *Digested,* 04/**2187**:
Previous proceedings, 98/6002, 02/2669
Reisch Montage AG *v.* Kiesel Baumaschinen Handels GmbH [2005] I.L.Pr. 44, OGH (A)
Relaxion Group Plc *v.* Rhys-Harper see Rhys-Harper *v.* Relaxion Group Plc
Relkobrook Ltd *v.* Mapstone (Inspector of Taxes) [2005] S.T.C. (S.C.D.) 272; [2005] S.T.I. 158, Sp Comm. . . . . *Digested,* 05/**4033**

Remia BV *v.* Commission of the European Communities (42/84) [1985] E.C.R. 2545; [1987] 1 C.M.L.R. 1; [1987] F.S.R. 190, ECJ (5th Chamber) . . . . *Digested*, 87/**1503**:
Applied, 05/549
Remy *v.* Germany (Admissibility) (70826/01) 7 I.T.L. Rep. 270, ECHR . . . . *Digested*, 05/**2084**
Renault *v.* d'Amato [2005] E.C.C. 15, Cass (F)
Rendall *v.* Blair (1890) L.R. 45 Ch. D. 139, CA . . . . *Applied*, 66/1,240,
67/412: *Considered*, 05/2826
Rendall *v.* Combined Insurance Co of America [2005] EWHC 678; [2005] 1 C.L.C. 565, QBD (Comm) . . . . *Digested*, 05/**2400**
Rene Lancry SA *v.* Direction Generale des Douanes (C363/93) [1994] E.C.R. I-3957, ECJ . . . . *Digested*, 94/**4863**:
Followed, 05/943
Renwick *v.* Lucking see Lucking's Will Trusts, Re
Representative Body for the Church in Wales *v.* Newton [2005] EWHC 631; [2005] 16 E.G.C.S. 145, QBD
Research Establishment *v.* Revenue and Customs Commissioners [2005] S.T.I. 1654, V&DTr
Research In Motion UK Ltd *v.* Inpro Licensing Sarl [2005] EWHC 1292; (2005) 28(7) I.P.D. 28052; (2005) 102(40) L.S.G. 27, Ch D (Patents Ct)
Research in Motion UK Ltd *v.* Inpro Licensing Sarl (Application to Reopen Order) [2005] EWHC 1907; (2005) 28(9) I.P.D. 28065, Ch D
Residence Visas, Re (C157/03) see Commission of the European Communities *v.* Spain (C157/03)
Reunion Europeenne SA *v.* Spliethoff's Bevrachtingskantoor BV (C51/97) [2000] Q.B. 690; [2000] 3 W.L.R. 1213; [1998] E.C.R. I-6511; [1999] C.L.C. 282; [1999] I.L.Pr. 205; *Times*, November 16, 1998, ECJ (3rd Chamber) . . . . *Digested*, 98/**769**:
Applied, 04/559, 05/470: *Followed*, 01/4290
Revenue and Customs Commissioners, Petitioners; *sub nom* R. (on the application of Inland Revenue Commissioners) *v.* Aberdeen General Commissioners of Income Tax; Inland Revenue Commissioners, Petitioners 2005 S.L.T. 1061; [2005] S.T.I. 1755; 2005 G.W.D. 33-634, OH
Revenue and Customs Commissioners *v.* Debenhams Retail Plc see Debenhams Retail Plc *v.* Customs and Excise Commissioners
Revenue and Customs Commissioners *v.* Fenwood Developments Ltd see Fenwood Developments Ltd *v.* Customs and Excise Commissioners
Revenue and Customs Commissioners *v.* IDT Card Services Ireland Ltd see R. (on the application of IDT Card Services Ireland Ltd) *v.* Customs and Excise Commissioners
Revenue and Customs Commissioners *v.* Jacobs see Jacobs *v.* Customs and Excise Commissioners
Revenue and Customs Commissioners *v.* Jeancharm Ltd (t/a Beaver International) see Jeancharm Ltd (t/a Beaver International) *v.* Customs and Excise Commissioners
Revenue and Customs Commissioners *v.* K&L Childcare Service Ltd [2005] EWHC 2414; [2005] S.T.I. 1811, Ch D
Revenue and Customs Commissioners *v.* Robertson's Electrical Ltd see Robertson's Electrical Ltd *v.* Customs and Excise Commissioners
Revenue and Customs Commissioners *v.* Salaried Persons Postal Loans Ltd see Salaried Persons Postal Loans Ltd *v.* Revenue and Customs Commissioners
Revenue and Customs Commissioners *v.* Thompson [2005] S.T.I. 1812, Ch D
Revenue and Customs Commissioners *v.* Tinsley see Tinsley *v.* Customs and Excise Commissioners
Revenue and Customs Commissioners *v.* Vodafone 2 see Vodafone 2 *v.* Revenue and Customs Commissioners
Revenue and Customs Commissioners *v.* Walsh [2005] EWCA Civ 1291, CA (Civ Div); affirming [2005] EWHC 1304; [2005] 2 B.C.L.C. 455; [2005] B.P.I.R. 1105, Ch D . . . . *Digested*, 05/**2300**
Revenue and Customs Commissioners *v.* William Grant & Sons Distillers Ltd; *sub nom* William Grant & Sons Distillers Ltd *v.* Inland Revenue Commissioners; Inland Revenue Commissioners *v.* William Grant & Sons Distillers Ltd 2005 S.L.T. 888; [2005] B.T.C. 483; [2005] S.T.I. 1647; 2005 G.W.D. 29-536, IH (Ex Div) . . . . . . *Digested*, 05/**5692**:
Previous proceedings, 04/3712
Revenue and Customs Commissioners *v.* Zurich Insurance Co see Zurich Insurance Co *v.* Revenue and Customs Commissioners
Revenue and Customs Prosecutions Office *v.* Hill [2005] EWCA Crim 3271; *Times*, December 27, 2005, CA (Crim Div)
Revival Properties Ltd *v.* Edinburgh City Council see Edinburgh City Council *v.* Secretary of State for Scotland
Rewah France *v.* Liquidator of Societe Europeenne d'Humidite [2005] I.L.Pr. 36, Cass (F)
Rewe Zentral AG *v.* Office for Harmonisation in the Internal Market (Trade Marks and Designs) (OHIM) (T79/00); *sub nom* LITE Community Trade Mark (T79/00) [2002] E.C.R. II-705; [2002] E.T.M.R. 91, CFI (4th Chamber) . . . . *Digested*, 03/**2617**:
Followed, 05/2528

Rexodan International Ltd *v.* Commercial Union Assurance Co Plc; *sub nom* Rodan International Ltd *v.* Commercial Union Assurance Co Plc [1999] Lloyd's Rep. I.R. 495, CA (Civ Div) . . . . *Applied*, 05/2375

Rey *v.* Graham & Oldham [2000] B.P.I.R. 354, QBD . . . . *Digested*, 00/**4266**: *Applied*, 05/960

Reynolds *v.* Commissioner of Police of the Metropolis [1985] Q.B. 881; [1985] 2 W.L.R. 93; [1984] 3 All E.R. 649; (1985) 80 Cr. App. R. 125; [1984] Crim. L.R. 688; (1984) 81 L.S.G. 2856; (1984) 128 S.J. 736, CA (Civ Div) . . . . *Digested*, 84/**2533**: *Applied*, 97/1167, 99/901, 05/4165: *Considered*, 99/900

Reynolds *v.* Times Newspapers Ltd [2001] 2 A.C. 127; [1999] 3 W.L.R. 1010; [1999] 4 All E.R. 609; [2000] E.M.L.R. 1; [2000] H.R.L.R. 134; 7 B.H.R.C. 289; (1999) 96(45) L.S.G. 34; (1999) 149 N.L.J. 1697; (1999) 143 S.J.L.B. 270; *Times*, October 29, 1999; *Independent*, November 3, 1999, HL; affirming [1998] 3 W.L.R. 862; [1998] 3 All E.R. 961; [1998] E.M.L.R. 723; (1998) 95(32) L.S.G. 30; (1998) 148 N.L.J. 1051; (1998) 142 S.J.L.B. 218; *Times*, July 9, 1998; *Independent*, July 14, 1998, CA (Civ Div) . . . . *Digested*, 99/**1630**: *Applied*, 99/1625, 00/1761, 00/1763, 01/1823, 01/1829, 01/1831, 02/953, 02/959, 04/935, 05/980: *Considered*, 01/1824, 01/1832, 01/1834, 05/973, 05/977: *Followed*, 99/1626, 02/960

Rhesa Shipping Co SA *v.* Edmunds (The Popi M); Rhesa Shipping Co SA *v.* Fenton Insurance Co Ltd [1985] 1 W.L.R. 948; [1985] 2 All E.R. 712; [1985] 2 Lloyd's Rep. 1; (1985) 82 L.S.G. 2995; (1985) 129 S.J. 503, HL; reversing [1984] 2 Lloyd's Rep. 555, CA (Civ Div); reversing in part [1983] 2 Lloyd's Rep. 235, QBD (Comm) . . . . *Digested*, 85/**3207**: *Applied*, 90/3232, 90/3252, 92/3975, 95/4534, 02/349: *Considered*, 05/292: *Distinguished*, 00/2984: *Followed*, 02/4123

Rhesa Shipping Co SA *v.* Fenton Insurance Co Ltd see Rhesa Shipping Co SA *v.* Edmunds (The Popi M)

Rhind *v.* Astbury Water Park Ltd [2004] EWCA Civ 756; (2004) 148 S.J.L.B. 759; [2004] N.P.C. 95; *Independent*, June 25, 2004, CA (Civ Div); affirming [2003] EWHC 1029, QBD . . . . *Digested*, 05/**4194**

Rhys-Harper *v.* Relaxion Group Plc; *sub nom* Relaxion Group Plc *v.* Rhys-Harper; Kirker *v.* British Sugar Plc; Jones *v.* 3M Healthcare Ltd (No.1); D'Souza *v.* Lambeth LBC (No.2); Kirker *v.* Ambitions Personnel (Nottinghamshire) Ltd; Angel *v.* New Possibilities NHS Trust; Bond *v.* Hackney Citizens Advice Bureau [2003] UKHL 33; [2003] 4 All E.R. 1113; [2003] 2 C.M.L.R. 44; [2003] I.C.R. 867; [2003] I.R.L.R. 484; (2003) 74 B.M.L.R. 109; (2003) 100(30) L.S.G. 30; (2003) 147 S.J.L.B. 782; *Times*, June 23, 2003; *Independent*, June 24, 2003, HL; reversing [2001] EWCA Civ 634; [2001] 2 C.M.L.R. 44; [2001] I.C.R. 1176; [2001] I.R.L.R. 460; [2001] Emp. L.R. 646; (2001) 98(24) L.S.G. 43; *Times*, June 12, 2001; *Independent*, May 11, 2001; *Daily Telegraph*, May 15, 2001, CA (Civ Div); affirming [2000] I.R.L.R. 810, EAT . . . . *Digested*, 03/**1315**: *Applied*, 02/1401, 05/1229, 05/1302: *Previous proceedings*, 02/1331

Rialas *v.* Mitchell (1984) 128 S.J. 704, CA (Civ Div) . . . . *Digested*, 84/**1013**: *Applied*, 05/3072

Richard W Price (Roofing Contractors) Ltd *v.* Office of Fair Trading [2005] CAT 5; [2005] Comp. A.R. 801, CAT

Richard W Price (Roofing Contractors) Ltd *v.* Office of Fair Trading (Interest and Costs) [2005] CAT 12; [2005] Comp. A.R. 901, CAT

Richardson *v.* Ealing LBC see Ealing LBC *v.* Richardson

Richardson *v.* Howie [2004] EWCA Civ 1127; [2005] P.I.Q.R. Q3; (2004) 101(37) L.S.G. 36; (2004) 154 N.L.J. 1361; (2004) 148 S.J.L.B. 1030; *Times*, September 10, 2004, CA (Civ Div) . . . . *Digested*, 04/**914**

Richardson *v.* North Yorkshire CC see R. (on the application of Richardson) *v.* North Yorkshire CC

Richardson *v.* U Mole Ltd [2005] I.C.R. 1664; [2005] I.R.L.R. 668, EAT

Richert *v.* Stewards Charitable Foundation [2005] W.T.L.R. 371, Sup Ct (BC)

Richmond Housing Partnership Ltd *v.* Brick Farm Management Ltd see Brick Farm Management Ltd *v.* Richmond Housing Partnership Ltd

Richmondshire DC *v.* Merewood Homes [2005] P.A.D. 74, Planning Inspector

Ricketts *v.* Ad Valorem Factors Ltd [2003] EWCA Civ 1706; [2004] 1 All E.R. 894; [2004] B.C.C. 164; [2004] 1 B.C.L.C. 1; [2004] B.P.I.R. 825; (2003) 153 N.L.J. 1841, CA (Civ Div) . . . . *Digested*, 04/**2152**: *Followed*, 05/2300

Ricoh Co Ltd's Community Trade Mark (R 516/2004-1) (2005) 28(4) I.P.D. 28026, OHIM (1st Bd App)

Ridehalgh *v.* DPP; *sub nom* R. (on the application of Ridehalgh) *v.* DPP [2005] EWHC 1100; [2005] R.T.R. 26, QBD (Admin) . . . . *Digested*, 05/**912**

Ridehalgh v. Horsefield; Allen v. Unigate Dairies Ltd; Antonelli v. Wade Gery Farr (A Firm); Philex Plc v. Golban; Roberts v. Coverite (Asphalters) Ltd; Watson v. Watson (Wasted Costs Orders) [1994] Ch. 205; [1994] 3 W.L.R. 462; [1994] 3 All E.R. 848; [1994] B.C.C. 390; [1994] 2 F.L.R. 194; [1955-95] P.N.L.R. 636; [1994] Fam. Law 560; [1994] E.G.C.S. 15; (1994) 144 N.L.J. 231; [1994] N.P.C. 7; *Times*, January 28, 1994; *Independent*, February 4, 1994, CA (Civ Div) . . . . . .   *Digested*, 94/**3623**: *Applied*, 95/4028, 95/4030, 95/4031, 95/4034, 96/936, 96/939, 96/3524, 97/602, 99/988, 00/470, 00/471, 00/4001, 01/4516, 02/408, 02/409, 03/382, 03/383, 04/323, 04/325, 05/496: *Approved*, 00/469: *Considered*, 94/3620, 95/2273, 95/4673, 96/940, 96/3899, 96/4508, 97/605, 97/607, 97/610, 97/1387, 98/497, 99/422, 99/989, 00/2466, 01/537, 01/589, 04/324: *Followed*, 98/496, 98/499, 00/1043: *Previous proceedings*, 92/2709, 93/3176, 93/3177

Ridgeway Motors (Isleworth) Ltd v. Altis Ltd see Ridgeway Motors (Isleworth) Ltd v. ALTS Ltd

Ridgeway Motors (Isleworth) Ltd v. ALTS Ltd; *sub nom* Ridgeway Motors (Isleworth) Ltd v. Altis Ltd [2005] EWCA Civ 92; [2005] 1 W.L.R. 2871; [2005] 2 All E.R. 304; [2005] C.P. Rep. 34; [2005] B.C.C. 496; [2005] 2 B.C.L.C. 61; [2005] B.P.I.R. 423; [2005] R.V.R. 173; [2005] N.P.C. 27; *Times*, February 24, 2005, CA (Civ Div); affirming [2004] EWHC 1535; [2004] B.P.I.R. 1323, Ch D . . . .   *Digested*, 05/**497**

Ridgewood Investments Ltd v. Haringey LBC [2005] P.A.D. 65; [2004] P.A.D. 109, Planning Inspector

Rihal v. Ealing LBC; *sub nom* Ealing LBC v. Rihal [2004] EWCA Civ 623; [2004] I.R.L.R. 642, CA (Civ Div); affirming EAT/0987/01/SM, EAT . . . .   *Digested*, 05/**1295**

RII Diffusion Relais Informatique Internationale Diffusion Sarl v. Compain [2005] E.C.C. 21, Cass (F)

Riley v. Tesco Stores Ltd [1980] I.C.R. 323; [1980] I.R.L.R. 103, CA (Civ Div); affirming [1979] I.C.R. 223; [1979] I.R.L.R. 49; *Times*, November 13, 1978, EAT .   *Digested*, 80/**999**: *Considered*, 05/1336: *Distinguished*, 90/1896, 91/1649

Rindberg Holding Co Ltd v. Newcastle upon Tyne Justices [2004] EWHC 1903; (2005) 169 J.P. 20; [2005] A.C.D. 14; (2005) 169 J.P.N. 39, QBD (Admin) . . . .   *Digested*, 05/**2756**

Ringside Refreshments v. Customs and Excise Commissioners [2003] EWHC 3043; [2004] S.T.C. 426; [2004] B.T.C. 5265; [2004] B.V.C. 325; [2004] S.T.I. 46, Ch D; reversing (2003) 147 S.J.L.B. 542, V&D Tr (Manchester) . . . .   *Digested*, 04/**4017**: *Applied*, 05/4417

Rinner-Kuhn v. FWW Spezial-Gebaudereinigung GmbH & Co KG (171/88) [1989] E.C.R. 2743; [1993] 2 C.M.L.R. 932; [1989] I.R.L.R. 493; *Times*, September 29, 1989, ECJ (6th Chamber) . . . .   *Digested*, 90/**2203**.a: *Applied*, 94/1981, 98/2240, 05/1268: *Considered*, 95/2052, 96/2629, 04/1258: *Followed*, 96/2574, 96/5389, 96/5390

Ritchie Brothers (PWC) Ltd v. David Philp (Commercials) Ltd 2005 S.C. 384; 2005 S.L.T. 341; 2005 S.C.L.R. 829; [2005] B.L.R. 384; 2005 G.W.D. 11-169; *Times*, May 24, 2005, IH (2 Div); reversing 2004 S.L.T. 471; [2004] B.L.R. 379; 2004 G.W.D. 13-282, OH . . . .   *Digested*, 05/**5068**

Rivas v. France (59584/00) [2005] Crim. L.R. 305, ECHR

Riverside Housing Association Ltd v. White see White v. Riverside Housing Association Ltd

Riverside Property Investments Ltd v. Blackhawk Automotive [2004] EWHC 3052; [2005] 1 E.G.L.R. 114; [2005] 1 E.G.C.S. 94, QBD (TCC) . . . .   *Digested*, 05/**2684**

Riyad Bank v. Ahli United Bank (UK) Plc [2005] EWHC 279; [2005] 2 Lloyd's Rep. 409, QBD (Comm) . . . .   *Digested*, 05/**268**

Riyad Bank v. Ahli United Bank (UK) Plc (Permission to Appeal and Amend) [2005] EWCA Civ 1419; *Times*, December 16, 2005, CA (Civ Div)

RK v. Oldham NHS Trust see JD v. East Berkshire Community Health NHS Trust

RL v. France (44568/98) [2005] Crim. L.R. 307, ECHR

RL v. Gloucestershire CC see S v. Gloucestershire CC

RL v. Tower Hamlets LBC see S v. Gloucestershire CC

RMC (UK) Ltd v. Greenwich LBC [2005] R.V.R. 140, Lands Tr

RO Somerton Ltd v. Customs and Excise Commissioners [2005] S.T.I. 119, V&D Tr

Roads v. Central Trains Ltd [2004] EWCA Civ 1541; (2005) 21 Const. L.J. 456, CA (Civ Div) . . . .   *Applied*, 05/249

Robbins v. Customs and Excise Commissioners; *sub nom* Customs and Excise Commissioners v. Robbins [2004] EWHC 3373; [2005] S.T.C. 1103; [2005] B.T.C. 5379; [2004] B.V.C. 410; [2004] S.T.I. 1118, Ch D; reversing [2003] S.T.I. 2207, V&D Tr . . . .   *Digested*, 05/**4362**

Robert Hitchins Ltd v. Kennet DC [2005] P.A.D. 75, Planning Inspector

Robert McBride Ltd's Trade Mark Application [2005] E.T.M.R. 85, App Person . . . .   *Digested*, 05/**2504**

Roberti (CICA: Quantum: 2004), Re [2005] 2 Q.R. 6, CICA (London) [*Ex rel*. G Mott, Barrister, 5th Floor, Gray's Inn Chambers, Gray's Inn, London] . . . .   *Digested*, 04/**2859**

Roberts v. Ashford BC [2005] R.V.R. 388, Lands Tr

Roberts v. Coverite (Asphalters) Ltd see Ridehalgh v. Horsefield

Roberts v. Maclachlan [2005] 2 Q.R. 14, CC (Cardiff) [*Ex rel*. Andrew Arentsen, Barrister, 33 Park Place, Cardiff] . . . .   *Digested*, 04/**2883**

Roberts v. MacLaren see Figgis, Re

Roberts v. Parole Board see R. (on the application of Roberts) v. Parole Board

Roberts v. Secretary of State for the Home Department [2005] EWCA Civ 1663; *Times*, December 2, 2005, CA (Civ Div)

Roberts v. West Coast Trains Ltd [2004] EWCA Civ 900; [2005] I.C.R. 254; [2004] I.R.L.R. 788; (2004) 101(28) L.S.G. 33; *Times*, June 25, 2004, CA (Civ Div); affirming EAT/0312/03/ZT, EAT. . . . . *Digested*, 04/**1310**

Roberts v. Williams [2005] EWCA Civ 1086; [2005] C.P. Rep. 44, CA (Civ Div)

Roberts v. Wrexham City Council (Unreported, April 4, 2005), CC (Wrexham) [*Ex rel.* Karim Sabry, Barrister, 8 King Street Chambers, 8 King Street, Third Floor, Manchester] . . . . *Digested*, 05/**3091**

Robertson v. Department for the Environment, Food and Rural Affairs; *sub nom* Department for the Environment, Food and Rural Affairs v. Robertson [2005] EWCA Civ 138; [2005] I.C.R. 750; [2005] I.R.L.R. 363; (2005) 102(15) L.S.G. 33; *Times*, March 2, 2005; *Independent*, February 24, 2005, CA (Civ Div); affirming [2004] I.C.R. 1289, EAT . . . . *Digested*, 05/**1258**

Robertson v. Revenue and Customs Commissioners [2005] S.T.C. (S.C.D.) 723; [2005] W.T.L.R. 1413; [2005] S.T.I. 1565, Sp Comm

Robertson v. Robertson (1983) 4 F.L.R. 387; (1982) 12 Fam. Law 181, Fam Div . . . . . . *Digested*, 82/**941**: *Doubted*, 05/**1656**

Robertson Group (Construction) Ltd v. Amey-Miller (Edinburgh) Joint Venture 2005 S.C.L.R. 854; [2005] B.L.R. 491, OH

Robertson's Electrical Ltd v. Customs and Excise Commissioners; *sub nom* Revenue and Customs Commissioners v. Robertson's Electrical Ltd 2005 S.L.T. 1149; [2005] S.T.I. 1813; 2005 G.W.D. 37-699, IH (2 Div); reversing [2005] B.V.C. 2070; [2004] V. & D.R. 481; [2004] S.T.I. 2570, V&DTr (Edinburgh)

Robins Application, Re [2005] R.V.R. 217, Lands Tr . . . . *Digested*, 05/**3416**

Robinson v. AIG Europe UK Ltd see Manning v. AIG Europe UK Ltd

Robinson v. Bird; *sub nom* Robinson v. Fernsby; Scott-Kilvert's Estate, Re [2003] EWCA Civ 1820; [2004] W.T.L.R. 257; (2004) 101(7) L.S.G. 36; (2004) 148 S.J.L.B. 59; *Times*, January 20, 2004, CA (Civ Div); affirming [2003] EWHC 30; [2003] W.T.L.R. 529, Ch D . . . . *Digested*, 03/**4123**: *Applied*, 05/2693

Robinson v. Fernsby see Robinson v. Bird

Robinson v. Murray; *sub nom* Murray v. Robinson [2005] EWCA Civ 935; [2005] 3 F.C.R. 504; [2005] Fam. Law 859; *Times*, August 19, 2005, CA (Civ Div) . . . . . *Digested*, 05/**343**

Robinson v. Queen, The see Dunkley v. Queen, The

Robinson Jarvis & Rolf v. Cave see Cave v. Robinson Jarvis & Rolf

Robinson (Frank) v. Queen, The [1985] A.C. 956; [1985] 3 W.L.R. 84; [1985] 2 All E.R. 594; [1985] Crim. L.R. 448, PC (Jam) . . . . *Digested*, 85/**182**: *Applied*, 94/665, 95/2634, 05/903

Robson v. Mitchell (Inspector of Taxes) [2005] EWCA Civ 585; [2005] S.T.C. 893; [2005] B.T.C. 321; [2005] S.T.I. 990; [2005] N.P.C. 66; *Times*, June 6, 2005, CA (Civ Div); affirming [2004] EWHC 1596; [2004] S.T.C. 1544; [2005] B.T.C. 13; [2004] S.T.I. 1605; *Times*, July 22, 2004, Ch D . . . . *Digested*, 05/**3998**

Roche v. Chief Constable of Greater Manchester [2005] EWCA Civ 1454; *Times*, November 10, 2005, CA (Civ Div)

Roche v. Secretary of State for Defence [2004] EWHC 2344; [2005] A.C.D. 16, QBD (Admin)

Roche v. United Kingdom (32555/96), *Times*, October 27, 2005, ECHR (Grand Chamber)

Roche Consumer Health (Worldwide) Ltd v. Vitabalans Oy [2005] E.T.M.R. 14, KKO (Fin)

Rochead v. Airtours Holidays Ltd Unreported . . . . *Considered*, 05/1980

Rodan International Ltd v. Commercial Union Assurance Co Plc see Rexodan International Ltd v. Commercial Union Assurance Co Plc

Rodgers (t/a LJR Transport) v. Customs and Excise Commissioners [2004] V. & D.R. 5, V&DTr (London) . . . . *Digested*, 05/**945**

Rodriguez-Bannister v. Somerset Partnership NHS and Social Care Trust see R. (on the application of Rodriguez-Bannister) v. Somerset Partnership NHS and Social Care Trust

Rodway v. South Central Trains Ltd see South Central Trains Ltd v. Rodway

Rodway v. Southern Railways Ltd (formerly South Central Trains Ltd) see South Central Trains Ltd v. Rodway

Roerig v. Valiant Trawlers Ltd [2002] EWCA Civ 21; [2002] 1 W.L.R. 2304; [2002] 1 All E.R. 961; [2002] 1 Lloyd's Rep. 681; [2002] C.L.C. 629; [2002] P.I.Q.R. Q8; (2002) 152 N.L.J. 171, CA (Civ Div) . . . . *Digested*, 02/**634**: *Not followed*, 05/608

Rogers-Headicar v. Headicar [2004] EWCA Civ 1867; [2005] 2 F.C.R. 1, CA (Civ Div) . *Digested*, 05/**1628**

Rogerson v. Wigan MBC [2004] EWHC 1677; [2005] 2 All E.R. 1000; [2005] H.L.R. 10; [2005] B.L.G.R. 549; [2004] 2 P. & C.R. DG21, QBD . . . . *Digested*, 05/**2660**

ROHM & HAAS COMPANY/Polymer (T500/00) [2005] E.P.O.R. 3, EPO (Technical Bd App) . . . . *Digested*, 05/**2455**

Rolex Internet Auction (1ZR 304/01), Re see Internet Auctions of Counterfeit Watches, Re (I ZR 304/01)

Rollerson *v.* Clark (Unreported, February 5, 2004), CC (Cambridge) [*Ex rel.* Joanna
　　Kerr, Barrister, Lamb Chambers, Lamb Building, Temple, London] . . . .　　*Digested*, 05/**3109**
Rolls Royce Power Engineering Plc *v.* Ricardo Consulting Engineers Ltd [2003] EWHC
　　2871; [2004] 2 All E.R. (Comm) 129; 98 Con. L.R. 169, QBD (TCC) . . . .　　*Digested*, 04/**657**
Roman O PM's Trade Mark [2005] E.T.M.R. 112, Sad Najwyzszy (PL)
Romer-Ormiston *v.* Claygreen Ltd; *sub nom* Claygreen Ltd, Re [2005] EWHC 2032;
　　(2005) 102(38) L.S.G. 28, Ch D (Companies Ct)
Rompelman *v.* Minister van Financien (268/83) [1985] E.C.R. 655; [1985] 3
　　C.M.L.R. 202, ECJ (2nd Chamber) . . . .　　*Digested*, 85/**1499**:
　　　　　　　　　　　　　Applied, 91/3631, 05/4380: *Considered*, 91/4147, 91/4148:
　　　　　　　　　　　　　Followed, 86/1498, 91/4145, 02/4737, 05/4363, 05/4364:
　　　　　　　　　　　　　Not followed, 91/3648: *Referred to*, 94/4554, 95/5056
Ronly Holdings Ltd *v.* JSC Zestafoni G Nikoladze Ferroalloy Plant [2004] EWHC 1354;
　　[2004] 1 C.L.C. 1168; [2004] B.L.R. 323, QBD (Comm) . . . .　　*Digested*, 05/**204**:
　　　　　　　　　　　　　　　　　　　　　　　　　　　　　　　　　　Considered, 05/206
Ronson International Ltd *v.* Patrick; *sub nom* Patrick *v.* Royal London Mutual Insurance
　　Society Ltd; A2/2005/1513, CA (Civ Div); affirming [2005] EWHC 1767;
　　[2005] 2 All E.R. (Comm) 453, QBD
Roodal *v.* Trinidad and Tobago [2003] UKPC 78; [2005] 1 A.C. 328; [2004] 2 W.L.R.
　　652; 16 B.H.R.C. 147; (2004) 101(5) L.S.G. 27; (2004) 101(2) L.S.G. 28;
　　(2003) 147 S.J.L.B. 1395; *Times*, November 26, 2003, PC (Trin) . . . .　　*Digested*, 04/**3334**:
　　　　　　　　　　　　　　　　Applied, 04/584: *Considered*, 04/3335: *Overruled*, 04/3337
Rookes *v.* Barnard (No.1) [1964] A.C. 1129; [1964] 2 W.L.R. 269; [1964] 1 All E.R.
　　367; [1964] 1 Lloyd's Rep. 28; 108 S.J. 93, HL; reversing [1963] 1 Q.B. 623;
　　[1962] 3 W.L.R. 260; [1962] 2 All E.R. 579; 106 S.J. 371, CA; reversing [1961]
　　3 W.L.R. 438; [1961] 2 All E.R. 825; 105 S.J. 530, QBD . . . .　　*Digested*, 64/**3703**:
　　　　　　　　　　　Applied, 64/2120, 65/1022, 65/2254, 65/2255, 65/2260, 67/2275, 67/2276,
　　　　　　　　　　　67/3981, 70/1143, 71/9438, 77/336, 77/1768, 78/284, 78/1822, 79/399,
　　　　　　　　　　　84/1098, 87/1144, 90/2995, 92/1941, 94/5067, 97/3798, 98/5150, 00/5118,
　　　　　　　　　　　01/1512, 04/2510, 05/956: *Considered*, 65/834, 65/3967, 67/3276, 69/295,
　　　　　　　　　　　70/2739, 72/2705, 75/397.u, 75/779, 86/3443, 87/3769, 88/1295, 93/1392,
　　　　　　　　　　　93/1607, 96/2606, 96/3821, 97/2754, 04/914: *Distinguished*, 64/3702,
　　　　　　　　　　　68/3954, 74/3867, 92/1526, 93/1598: *Explained*, 79/198:
　　　　　　　　　　　Followed, 72/2745, 97/3286, 00/5112: *Not followed*, 71/6742
Rose *v.* Dodd (formerly t/a Reynolds & Dodds Solicitors) [2005] EWCA Civ 957;
　　[2005] I.C.R. 1776; [2005] I.R.L.R. 977; *Times*, August 16, 2005; *Independent*,
　　October 4, 2005, CA (Civ Div); affirming UKEAT/0517/04/ILB, EAT . . . .　　*Digested*, 05/**1307**
Rosenquist *v.* Sweden (Admissibility) (60619/00) 7 I.T.L. Rep. 257; (2005) 40
　　E.H.R.R. SE24, ECHR. . . . .　　*Digested*, 05/**2036**
Rosewood Trucking Ltd *v.* Balaam [2005] EWCA Civ 1461; [2005] 2 C.L.C. 959, CA
　　(Civ Div)
Rosewood Trust Ltd *v.* Schmidt see Schmidt *v.* Rosewood Trust Ltd
Rosling King *v.* Rothschild Trust [2002] EWHC 1346; [2005] 2 Costs L.R. 165, Ch D
Ross *v.* Perrin-Hughes; *sub nom* Ross (Deceased), Re [2004] EWHC 2559; [2005]
　　W.T.L.R. 191; (2004-05) 7 I.T.E.L.R. 405; [2004] N.P.C. 170; [2005] 1 P. & C.R.
　　DG14; *Times*, November 24, 2004, Ch D . . . .　　*Digested*, 05/**3969**
Ross *v.* Ryanair Ltd [2004] EWCA Civ 1751; [2005] 1 W.L.R. 2447; (2005) 8 C.C.L.
　　Rep. 360; (2005) 155 N.L.J. 112; *Times*, January 11, 2005, CA (Civ Div);
　　affirming in part(Unreported, January 30, 2004), CC (Central London) . . . .　　*Digested*, 05/**249**
Ross *v.* Stonewood Securities Ltd [2004] EWHC 2235; [2005] 1 Costs L.R. 89;
　　[2005] B.P.I.R. 197, Ch D . . . .　　*Previous proceedings*,
　　　　　　　　　　　　　　　　　　　　　　　　　　　　　　　　　　　　00/3435
Ross Hillman Ltd *v.* Bond [1974] Q.B. 435; [1974] 2 W.L.R. 436; [1974] 2 All E.R. 287;
　　(1974) 59 Cr. App. R. 42; [1974] R.T.R. 279; 118 S.J. 243, DC . . . .　　*Digested*, 74/**3246**:
　　　　　　　　　　　　　　　　　　　　　　　　　　　　　　Applied, 75/2911, 05/818
Ross (Deceased), Re see Ross *v.* Perrin-Hughes
Rosshill Properties Ltd (In Administration), Re see Sinai Securities Ltd *v.* Hooper
Rothley *v.* European Parliament (C167/02 P); *sub nom* Rothley *v.* European Parliament
　　(T17/00) [2004] E.C.R. I-3149; [2004] 2 C.M.L.R. 11, ECJ; affirming [2002]
　　E.C.R. II-579; [2002] 2 C.M.L.R. 30, CFI (5th Chamber). . . . .　　*Digested*, 05/**1471**
Rothley *v.* European Parliament (T17/00) see Rothley *v.* European Parliament (C167/02
　　P)
Rothmans International BV *v.* Commission of the European Communities (T188/97)
　　[1999] E.C.R. II-2463; [1999] 3 C.M.L.R. 66, CFI (1st Chamber) . . . .　　*Digested*, 99/**2255**:
　　　　　　　　　　　　　　　　　　　　　　　　　　　　　　　　　　　Applied, 05/1426
Rothwell *v.* Chemical & Insulating Co Ltd see Grieves *v.* FT Everard & Sons Ltd
Rotsart de Hertaing *v.* J Benoidt SA (In Liquidation) (C305/94) [1997] All E.R. (E.C.)
　　40; [1996] E.C.R. I-5927; [1997] 1 C.M.L.R. 329; [1997] I.R.L.R. 127; *Times*,
　　November 25, 1996, ECJ (2nd Chamber) . . . .　　*Digested*, 96/**2640**:
　　　　　　　　　　　　　　　　　　　　　　　　　　　　　　　　　　　Followed, 05/1314
Roux *v.* Belgium (C363/89) [1991] E.C.R. I-273; [1993] 1 C.M.L.R. 3, ECJ (3rd
　　Chamber) . . . .　　*Followed*, 05/**1462**

Rowland v. Bock [2002] EWHC 692; [2002] 4 All E.R. 370; *Daily Telegraph*, May 13, 2002, QBD . . . .   *Digested*, 02/**274**:
                                           Approved, 05/303: *Considered*, 04/259

Rowland v. Environment Agency [2003] EWCA Civ 1885; [2005] Ch. 1; [2004] 3 W.L.R. 249; [2004] 2 Lloyd's Rep. 55; (2004) 101(8) L.S.G. 30; [2003] N.P.C. 165; *Times*, January 20, 2004, CA (Civ Div); affirming [2002] EWHC 2785; [2003] Ch. 581; [2003] 2 W.L.R. 1233; [2003] 1 All E.R. 625; [2003] 1 Lloyd's Rep. 427; (2003) 100(9) L.S.G. 28; *Times*, December 28, 2002, Ch D . . . .   *Digested*, 04/**3256**

Royal & Sun Alliance Insurance Group Plc v. Payne; *sub nom* Payne v. Royal & Sun Alliance Insurance Group Plc [2005] I.R.L.R. 848; *Times*, October 12, 2005, EAT . . . .   *Digested*, 05/**1241**

Royal & Sun Alliance Insurance Plc v. Dornoch Ltd; *sub nom* Dornoch Ltd v. Royal & Sun Alliance Insurance Plc [2005] EWCA Civ 238; [2005] 1 All E.R. (Comm) 590; [2005] 1 C.L.C. 466; [2005] Lloyd's Rep. I.R. 544, CA (Civ Div); affirming [2004] EWHC 803; [2004] 2 C.L.C. 133; [2004] Lloyd's Rep. I.R. 826, QBD (Comm) . . . .   *Digested*, 05/**2402**

Royal & Sun Alliance Insurance Plc v. MK Digital FZE (Cyprus) Ltd [2005] EWHC 1408; [2005] 2 Lloyd's Rep. 679; [2005] 2 C.L.C. 146; [2005] I.L.Pr. 51, QBD (Comm) . . . .   *Digested*, 05/**618**

Royal & Sun Alliance Insurance Plc v. Retail Brand Alliance Inc [2004] EWHC 2139; [2005] Lloyd's Rep. I.R. 110, QBD (Comm)

Royal & Sun Alliance Plc v. Customs and Excise Commissioners [2005] B.V.C. 2216; [2005] S.T.I. 147, V&DTr

Royal Bank of Canada v. Cooperatieve Centrale Raiffeisen-Boerenleenbank BA [2004] EWCA Civ 7; [2004] 2 All E.R. (Comm) 847; [2004] 1 Lloyd's Rep. 471; [2004] 1 C.L.C. 170; (2004) 148 S.J.L.B. 147, CA (Civ Div); affirming [2003] EWHC 2913, QBD (Comm) . . . .   *Digested*, 04/**573**:
                                                Considered, 05/3801

Royal Bank of Scotland Plc v. Bannerman Johnstone Maclay 2005 S.C. 437; 2005 S.L.T. 579; [2005] P.N.L.R. 43; 2005 Rep. L.R. 66; 2005 G.W.D. 17-309, IH (2 Div); reversing in part 2003 S.C. 125; 2003 S.L.T. 181; [2005] B.C.C. 235; [2003] P.N.L.R. 6; 2002 G.W.D. 26-917; *Times*, August 1, 2002, OH . . . .   *Digested*, 05/**5572**

Royal Bank of Scotland Plc v. Etridge (No.2); Barclays Bank Plc v. Coleman; Barclays Bank Plc v. Harris; Midland Bank Plc v. Wallace; National Westminster Bank Plc v. Gill; UCB Home Loans Corp Ltd v. Moore; Bank of Scotland v. Bennett; Kenyon-Brown v. Desmond Banks & Co (Undue Influence) (No.2) [2001] UKHL 44; [2002] 2 A.C. 773; [2001] 3 W.L.R. 1021; [2001] 4 All E.R. 449; [2001] 2 All E.R. (Comm) 1061; [2002] 1 Lloyd's Rep. 343; [2001] 2 F.L.R. 1364; [2001] 3 F.C.R. 481; [2002] H.L.R. 4; [2001] Fam. Law 880; [2001] 43 E.G.C.S. 184; (2001) 151 N.L.J. 1538; [2001] N.P.C. 147; [2002] 1 P. & C.R. DG14; *Times*, October 17, 2001; *Daily Telegraph*, October 23, 2001, HL; affirming in part [1998] 4 All E.R. 705; [1998] 2 F.L.R. 843; [1998] 3 F.C.R. 675; (1999) 31 H.L.R. 575; [1998] Fam. Law 665; (1998) 95(32) L.S.G. 31; (2001) 151 N.L.J. 1538; (1998) 148 N.L.J. 1390; [1998] N.P.C. 130; (1998) 76 P. & C.R. D39; *Times*, August 17, 1998, CA (Civ Div) . . . .   *Digested*, 01/**4880**:
                 Applied, 00/4664, 01/4879, 03/2379, 03/3556, 03/3587, 03/3588,
            03/3612, 03/4118, 03/4122, 03/4124, 04/3671, 05/1423, 05/2673, 05/3402,
               05/3438, 05/3442, 05/3968: *Considered*, 00/2333, 01/4878, 02/3840,
                    02/3841, 02/5794, 03/233, 03/5680, 04/1526, 05/4291, 05/4301:
                Followed, 00/2334, 00/4273, 04/3246: *Previous proceedings*, 99/4391,
                           00/4273, 00/4662: *Referred to*, 99/4030

Royal Bank of Scotland Plc v. Jennings (1998) 75 P. & C.R. 458; [1997] 1 E.G.L.R. 101; [1997] 19 E.G. 152; [1996] E.G.C.S. 168; [1996] N.P.C. 145, CA (Civ Div); affirming (1995) 70 P. & C.R. 459; [1995] 2 E.G.L.R. 87; [1995] 35 E.G. 140, Ch D . . . .   *Digested*, 97/**3320**:
                                       Distinguished, 97/3319, 05/2667

Royal Club Liegois SA v. Bosman (C415/93) see Union Royale Belge des Societes de Football Association (ASBL) v. Bosman (C415/93)

Royal National Lifeboat Institution v. Bushaway [2005] I.R.L.R. 675, EAT

Royal National Theatre Board Ltd v. Collins see Collins v. Royal National Theatre Board Ltd

Royal Philips Electronics NV v. Commission of the European Communities (T119/02) [2003] E.C.R. II-1433; [2003] 5 C.M.L.R. 2, CFI (3rd Chamber) . . . .   *Digested*, 04/**529**:
                                                   Applied, 05/583

Royle v. Manchester City Football Club Plc see Manchester City Football Club Plc v. Royle

RP Ltd v. Customs and Excise Commissioners [2004] V. & D.R. 452; [2005] S.T.I. 816, V&DTr (London)

RP Wallace Inc v. United States (2005) 21 Const. L.J. 378, US Ct

RS v. Secretary of State for the Home Department; *sub nom* RS (Funding: Meaning of Significant Prospect: Iran), Re [2005] UKIAT 138; [2005] Imm. A.R. 726, IAT

RS (A Child) v. Entry Clearance Officer, New Delhi see S (A Child) v. Entry Clearance Officer, New Delhi

RS (Funding: Meaning of Significant Prospect: Iran), Re see RS *v.* Secretary of State for the Home Department
RSP Architects Planners and Engineers *v.* Ocean Front Pte Ltd (1998) 14 Const. L.J. 139, CA (Sing) . . . . *Digested*, 98/**3924**:
    Considered, 05/2856
Rubenstein (t/a McGuffies Dispensing Chemists) *v.* McGloughlin (No.2) [1997] I.C.R. 318; [1996] I.R.L.R. 557, EAT . . . . *Digested*, 96/**2653**:
    Not followed, 05/1322
Rubin *v.* First Secretary of State; *sub nom* R. (on the application of Rubin) *v.* First Secretary of State [2004] EWHC 266; [2004] 3 P.L.R. 53; [2005] J.P.L. 234, QBD (Admin) . . . . *Digested*, 05/**3291**
Rudolph Roock Transeuropa Haus-Haus Speditions KG *v.* Boulanger Belgique [2005] I.L.Pr. 21, Cass (F)
Rugby Joinery UK Ltd *v.* Whitfield; *sub nom* Rugby Joinery UK Ltd *v.* Whitford [2005] EWCA Civ 561; *Times*, May 31, 2005, CA (Civ Div) . . . . *Digested*, 05/**965**
Rugby Joinery UK Ltd *v.* Whitford see Rugby Joinery UK Ltd *v.* Whitfield
Ruiz-Picasso *v.* Office for Harmonisation in the Internal Market (Trade Marks and Designs) (OHIM) (T185/02) [2005] E.T.M.R. 22, CFI (2nd Chamber) . . . . *Digested*, 05/**2551**
Rupert Morgan Building Services (LLC) Ltd *v.* Jervis [2003] EWCA Civ 1563; [2004] 1 W.L.R. 1867; [2004] 1 All E.R. 529; [2004] B.L.R. 18; [2004] T.C.L.R. 3; 91 Con. L.R. 81; (2003) 153 N.L.J. 1761; *Times*, November 26, 2003; *Independent*, November 20, 2003, CA (Civ Div) . . . . *Digested*, 04/**607**:
    Distinguished, 05/198
Ruscillo *v.* Council for the Regulation of Health Care Professionals see Council for the Regulation of Health Care Professionals *v.* General Medical Council
Rush Portuguesa Lda *v.* Office National d'Immigration (C113/89) [1990] E.C.R. I-1417; [1991] 2 C.M.L.R. 818; *Times*, April 12, 1990, ECJ (6th Chamber) . . . . *Digested*, 91/**4005**:
    Considered, 05/351, 05/1466
Russell *v.* Pal Pak Corrugated Ltd (No.1) see Callery *v.* Gray (No.1)
Russell Grant Ltd *v.* Scott Equipment Co; *sub nom* Scott Equipment Co *v.* Russell Grant Ltd [2005] EWCA Civ 156; (2005) 149 S.J.L.B. 266, CA (Civ Div); reversing in part [2004] EWHC 1229, QBD
Russell-Cooke Trust Co *v.* Elliott HC/000 1425, Ch D . . . . *Applied*, 03/253,
    05/1708
Rustal Trading Ltd *v.* Gill & Duffus SA [2000] 1 Lloyd's Rep. 14; [2000] C.L.C. 231, QBD (Comm) . . . . *Digested*, 00/**224**:
    Applied, 05/199
Rutherford *v.* DPP see Foster *v.* DPP
Rutherford *v.* Harvest Towncircle Ltd (In Liquidation) see Rutherford *v.* Secretary of State for Trade and Industry
Rutherford *v.* Secretary of State for Trade and Industry; *sub nom* Rutherford *v.* Harvest Towncircle Ltd (In Liquidation); Secretary of State for Trade and Industry *v.* Rutherford; Bentley *v.* Secretary of State for Trade and Industry; TNS, HL; affirming [2004] EWCA Civ 1186; [2004] 3 C.M.L.R. 53; [2005] I.C.R. 119; [2004] I.R.L.R. 892; (2004) 148 S.J.L.B. 1065; *Times*, November 4, 2004, CA (Civ Div); affirming [2003] 3 C.M.L.R. 27; [2003] I.R.L.R. 858; [2004] Pens. L.R. 1; (2003) 100(42) L.S.G. 31; (2003) 153 N.L.J. 1633; *Times*, October 8, 2003, EAT; reversing [2003] 2 C.M.L.R. 28; [2002] I.R.L.R. 768, ET . . . . *Digested*, 04/**1268**:
    Previous proceedings, 01/2308
Rutili *v.* Ministre de l'interieur (36/75) [1975] E.C.R. 1219; [1976] 1 C.M.L.R. 140; *Times*, November 10, 1975, ECJ . . . . *Digested*, 76/**1088**:
    Distinguished, 05/1462
Ryabykh *v.* Russia (52854/99) (2005) 40 E.H.R.R. 25, ECHR . . . . *Digested*, 05/**2094**
Ryan *v.* Imperial Brewing & Leisure see Courage Group's Pension Schemes, Re
Ryde International Plc *v.* London Regional Transport [2004] EWCA Civ 232; [2004] 2 E.G.L.R. 1; [2004] 30 E.G. 108; [2004] R.V.R. 60; [2004] 12 E.G.C.S. 170; (2004) 101(12) L.S.G. 38; (2004) 148 S.J.L.B. 301; [2004] N.P.C. 36, CA (Civ Div); affirming [2003] R.V.R. 49, Lands Tr . . . . *Digested*, 05/**3256**:
    Previous proceedings, 01/4662

S *v.* A Health Authority see ES *v.* Chesterfield and North Derbyshire Royal Hospital NHS Trust
S *v.* Airedale NHS Trust see R. (on the application of Munjaz) *v.* Mersey Care NHS Trust
S *v.* B (Abduction: Human Rights) [2005] EWHC 733; [2005] 2 F.L.R. 878; [2005] Fam. Law 610; *Times*, May 17, 2005, Fam Div . . . . *Digested*, 05/**1545**
S *v.* B (Ancillary Relief: Costs) [2004] EWHC 2089; [2005] 1 F.L.R. 474, Fam Div . . . . *Digested*, 05/**1626**
S *v.* Balfour Beatty Rail Maintenance (Unreported, May 17, 2004), CC (Newcastle) [*Ex rel.* Bruce Silvester, Barrister, Devereux Chambers, Devereux Court, London] . . . *Digested*, 05/**3088**
S *v.* Commission of the European Communities (C206/89 R) [1989] E.C.R. 2841, ECJ . . . . *Applied*, 05/**1443**
S *v.* Customs and Excise Commissioners see S (Restraint Order: Release of Assets for Legal Representation), Re

S v. Gloucestershire CC; *sub nom* RL v. Gloucestershire CC; DS v. Gloucestershire CC; RL v. Tower Hamlets LBC; L v. Tower Hamlets LBC [2001] Fam. 313; [2001] 2 W.L.R. 909; [2000] 3 All E.R. 346; [2000] 1 F.L.R. 825; [2000] 2 F.C.R. 345; (2000) 2 L.G.L.R. 848; (2000) 3 C.C.L. Rep. 294; [2000] Fam. Law 474; *Independent*, March 24, 2000, CA (Civ Div)........................ *Digested*, 00/**4212**:
     Considered, 01/589, 02/3316, 05/2852
S v. Miller (No.1); *sub nom* S v. Principal Reporter (No.1) 2001 S.C. 977; 2001 S.L.T. 531; [2001] U.K.H.R.R. 514; 2001 G.W.D. 13-458, IH (1 Div) .... *Digested*, 01/**6506**:
     Applied, 05/925: *Cited*, 01/6507
S v. Minister for Immigration and Multicultural Affairs [2004] I.N.L.R. 558, HC (Aus). . .   *Digested*, 05/**2223**
S v. Oxfordshire School Admission Appeals Panel; *sub nom* S v. Oxfordshire School Exclusion Appeals Panel [2005] EWHC 53; [2005] E.L.R. 533; *Times*, February 11, 2005, QBD (Admin) .... *Digested*, 05/**1072**
S v. Oxfordshire School Exclusion Appeals Panel see S v. Oxfordshire School Admission Appeals Panel
S v. Principal Reporter (No.1) see S v. Miller (No.1)
S v. S (Ancillary Relief: Preliminary Hearing of Oral Evidence); *sub nom* OS v. DS (Oral Disclosure: Preliminary Hearing) [2004] EWHC 2376; [2005] 1 F.L.R. 675; [2005] 1 F.C.R. 494; [2005] Fam. Law 11, Fam Div .... *Digested*, 05/**1651**
S v. Secretary of State for the Home Department [2002] UKIAT 5613, IAT .... *Followed*, 05/2215
S v. Special Educational Needs and Disability Tribunal [2005] EWHC 196; [2005] E.L.R. 443, QBD (Admin) .... *Digested*, 05/**1139**
S (A Child) v. Entry Clearance Officer, New Delhi; *sub nom* RS (A Child) v. Entry Clearance Officer, New Delhi [2005] EWCA Civ 89; [2005] 2 F.L.R. 219; [2005] Imm. A.R. 175; [2005] I.N.L.R. 564; [2005] Fam. Law 458; *Times*, February 23, 2005, CA (Civ Div) .... *Digested*, 05/**2196**
S (A Child) v. Goldstraw (Unreported, April 22, 2005), CC (Oldham) [*Ex rel.* Weightmans Solicitors, India Buildings, Water Street, Liverpool] .... *Digested*, 05/**2353**
S (A Child) v. Gurnani [2002] 6 Q.R. 17, CC (Coventry) [*Ex rel.* Stephen Garner, Barrister, No.8 Chambers, Fountain Court, Steelhouse Lane, Birmingham.] ..... *Digested*, 02/**3598**:
     Considered, 05/3131
S (A Child) v. Islington LBC (Unreported, June 25, 2004), CC (Clerkenwell) [*Ex rel.* J David Cook, Barrister, Chambers of Ami Feder, Lamb Building, Temple, London] .... *Digested*, 05/**3082**
S (A Child) v. Lewis (Unreported, June 3, 2004), CC (Kingston on Thames) [*Ex rel.* Joanna Kerr, Barrister, Lamb Chambers, Lamb Building, Temple, London]...... *Digested*, 05/**3149**
S (A Child) v. Sanmartin (Unreported, June 22, 2004), CC (Epsom) [*Ex rel.* Gurion Taussig, Barrister, 199 Strand, London]............................ *Digested*, 05/**3164**
S (A Child) v. United Steels & Sections Plc [2005] 2 Q.R. 17; [2004] 6 Q.R. 8, CC (Birmingham) [*Ex rel.* Stephen Garner, Barrister, No.8 Chambers, Fountain Court, Steelhouse Lane, Birmingham.] .... *Digested*, 04/**2907**
S (A Child) v. Warwick DC (Unreported, March 3, 2004), CC (Warwick) [*Ex rel.* Stephen Garner, Barrister, No.8 Chambers, Fountain Court, Steelhouse Lane, Birmingham.]... *Digested*, 05/**3208**
S (A Child) (Care: Parenting Skills: Personality Tests), Re [2004] EWCA Civ 1029; [2005] 2 F.L.R. 658; [2005] Fam. Law 452, CA (Civ Div)
S (A Child) (Care Proceedings: Contact), Re see Kirklees MBC v. S (Contact to Newborn Babies)
S (A Child) (Contact Dispute: Committal), Re [2004] EWCA Civ 1790; [2005] 1 F.L.R. 812; [2005] Fam. Law 206; *Times*, December 9, 2004, CA (Civ Div) .... *Digested*, 05/**1571**
S (A Child) (Financial Provision), Re [2004] EWCA Civ 1685; [2005] Fam. 316; [2005] 2 W.L.R. 895; [2005] 2 F.L.R. 94; [2005] Fam. Law 203; *Times*, November 15, 2004, CA (Civ Div) .... *Digested*, 05/**1663**
S (A Child) (Identification: Restrictions on Publication), Re; *sub nom* S (A Child) (Identification: Restriction on Publication), Re [2004] UKHL 47; [2005] 1 A.C. 593; [2004] 3 W.L.R. 1129; [2004] 4 All E.R. 683; [2005] E.M.L.R. 2; [2005] 1 F.L.R. 591; [2004] 3 F.C.R. 407; [2005] H.R.L.R. 5; [2005] U.K.H.R.R. 129; 17 B.H.R.C. 646; [2005] Crim. L.R. 310; (2004) 154 N.L.J. 1654; (2004) 148 S.J.L.B. 1285; *Times*, October 29, 2004; *Independent*, November 2, 2004, HL; affirming [2003] EWCA Civ 963; [2004] Fam. 43; [2004] 3 W.L.R. 1425; [2003] 2 F.L.R. 1253; [2003] 2 F.C.R. 577; [2003] H.R.L.R. 30; [2003] Fam. Law 818; (2003) 100(34) L.S.G. 29; (2003) 153 N.L.J. 1120; (2003) 147 S.J.L.B. 873; *Times*, July 21, 2003; *Independent*, July 15, 2003, CA (Civ Div); affirming [2003] EWHC 254, Fam Div .... *Digested*, 05/**2121**:
     Applied, 05/1686, 05/2049, 05/4191: *Considered*, 05/923
S (A Child) (Residence Order: Condition) (No.1), Re [2001] EWCA Civ 847; [2001] 3 F.C.R. 154, CA (Civ Div) .... *Digested*, 01/**2667**:
     Followed, 05/1576
S (A Minor) (Independent Representation), Re [1993] Fam. 263; [1993] 2 W.L.R. 801; [1993] 3 All E.R. 36; [1993] 2 F.L.R. 437; [1993] 2 F.C.R.1; [1993] Fam. Law 465; (1993) 143 N.L.J. 435; *Times*, March 2, 1993; *Independent*, March 2, 1993; *Guardian*, March 1, 1993, CA (Civ Div) .... *Digested*, 93/**2845**:
     Applied, 94/3208: *Considered*, 93/2844, 05/1634: *Referred to*, 95/3429
S (An Infant) v. Manchester City Recorder see S (An Infant) v. Recorder of Manchester

S (An Infant) *v.* Recorder of Manchester; *sub nom* S (An Infant) *v.* Manchester City
Recorder [1971] A.C. 481; [1970] 2 W.L.R. 21; [1969] 3 All E.R. 1230; 113 S.J.
872, HL. . . . . *Digested*, 69/**2189**:
Applied, 73/2099, 74/724, 78/1926, 82/736, 83/548, 85/608, 87/562,
92/687, 93/702: *Considered*, 70/1669, 79/1715, 84/2105, 88/894, 96/1640,
05/884: *Distinguished*, 84/630: *Followed*, 70/1672, 71/7150
S (Children) *v.* Turney (Unreported, September 7, 2004), CC (Staines) [*Ex rel.* Gurion
Taussig, Barrister, 199 Strand, London] . . . . *Digested*, 05/**3234**
S (Children) (Application for Removal from Jurisdiction), Re [2004] EWCA Civ 1724;
[2005] 1 F.C.R. 471, CA (Civ Div)
S (Children) (Care: Parental Contact), Re; *sub nom* S (Children) (Termination of
Contact), Re [2004] EWCA Civ 1397; [2005] 1 F.L.R. 469; [2005] 1 F.C.R. 489;
[2005] Fam. Law 14, CA (Civ Div) . . . . *Digested*, 05/**1570**:
Applied, 05/1566
S (Children) (Specific Issue Order: Religion: Circumcision), Re [2004] EWHC 1282;
[2005] 1 F.L.R. 236; [2004] Fam. Law 869, Fam Div . . . . *Digested*, 05/**1580**
S (Children) (Termination of Contact), Re see S (Children) (Care: Parental Contact), Re
S (Minors) (Child Abduction: Child's Views: Non Convention Country), Re [2005] N.I. 399,
Fam Div (NI)
S (Restraint Order: Release of Assets for Legal Representation), Re; *sub nom* S *v.*
Customs and Excise Commissioners [2004] EWCA Crim 2374; [2005] 1 W.L.R.
1338; [2005] 1 Cr. App. R. 17; (2004) 148 S.J.L.B. 1153; *Times*, October 8,
2004, CA (Crim Div) . . . . *Digested*, 04/**405**
S LBC *v.* S; *sub nom* S LBC *v.* K (A Child) [2004] EWHC 2876; [2005] E.L.R. 276;
Times, November 1, 2004, QBD (Admin) . . . . *Digested*, 05/**792**
Saarland *v.* Ministry for Industry, Posts, Telecommunications and Tourism (187/87); *sub
nom* Saarland *v.* Minister of Industry (187/87) [1988] E.C.R. 5013; [1989] 1
C.M.L.R. 529; *Times*, September 24, 1988, ECJ . . . . *Digested*, 90/**2106**:
Followed, 05/1406

Sabaf SpA *v.* Meneghetti SpA see Sabaf SpA *v.* MFI Furniture Centres Ltd
Sabaf SpA *v.* MFI Furniture Centres Ltd; *sub nom* Sabaf SpA *v.* Meneghetti SpA
[2004] UKHL 45; [2005] R.P.C. 10; (2004) 148 S.J.L.B. 1217, HL; reversing
[2002] EWCA Civ 976; [2003] R.P.C. 14; *Times*, July 24, 2002, CA (Civ Div);
reversing (2001) 24(10) I.P.D. 24069, Ch D (Patents Ct) . . . . *Digested*, 05/**2480**:
Distinguished, 05/2481

Sabel BV *v.* Puma AG (C251/95) [1997] E.C.R. I-6191; [1998] 1 C.M.L.R. 445; [1998]
C.E.C. 315; [1998] E.T.M.R. 1; [1998] R.P.C. 199, ECJ [1997] E.C.R. I-6191;
[1997] E.T.M.R. 283, AGO . . . . *Digested*, 98/**3512**:
Applied, 00/3777, 00/3778, 01/4025, 01/4036, 02/2870, 04/2379, 04/2414,
05/2562: *Considered*, 98/3501, 98/3509, 00/3701, 03/2657, 05/2509:
Followed, 99/3539, 99/3541: *Referred to*, 99/3542, 99/3562, 99/3568,
99/3581, 99/3587, 01/3987, 01/4024

SACMI Cooperative Meccanici Imola *v.* Chi Kok Tam (2004-05) 7 I.T.E.L.R. 861, CFI
(HK)
Sadek *v.* Medical Protection Society; *sub nom* Medical Protection Society *v.* Sadek
[2004] EWCA Civ 865; [2004] 4 All E.R. 118; [2004] I.C.R. 1263; [2005]
I.R.L.R. 57; (2004) 101(32) L.S.G. 36; (2004) 148 S.J.L.B. 878; *Times*,
September 2, 2004; *Independent*, July 15, 2004, CA (Civ Div); affirming
UKEAT/0594/03/DM, EAT . . . . *Digested*, 04/**1281**
Sadler *v.* General Medical Council [2003] UKPC 59; [2003] 1 W.L.R. 2259; [2004]
H.R.L.R. 8; [2004] Lloyd's Rep. Med. 44; *Times*, September 29, 2003, PC
(UK) . . . . *Digested*, 03/**1721**:
Considered, 05/1807
Sadler *v.* Whittaker 162 E.G. 404; [1953] C.P.L. 652, CA . . . . *Digested*, 53/**33**:
Considered, 05/90
Safalero Srl *v.* Prefetto di Genova (C13/01) [2003] E.C.R. I-8679; [2003] Info. T.L.R.
431, ECJ . . . . *Digested*, 05/**4179**
Safar *v.* Bergin & Wolstenholme (t/a Bellsure Motor Co) (Unreported, July 12, 2004),
CC (Manchester) [*Ex rel.* James Hurd, Barrister, St James's Chambers, 68 Quay
Street, Manchester.] . . . . *Digested*, 05/**3155**
Safeway Stores Plc *v.* Legal and General Assurance Society Ltd [2004] EWHC 415;
[2005] 1 P. & C.R. 9, Ch D . . . . *Digested*, 05/**2681**
Saffil Pension Scheme Trustees *v.* Curzon [2005] EWHC 293; [2005] O.P.L.R. 113;
[2005] Pens. L.R. 267, Ch D . . . . *Digested*, 05/**3033**
Saga Holidays Ltd *v.* Customs and Excise Commissioners [2004] B.V.C. 2200; [2004]
V. & D.R. 94; [2004] S.T.I. 1563, V&DTr (London) . . . . *Digested*, 05/**4406**
Sage *v.* Maidstone BC see Sage *v.* Secretary of State for the Environment, Transport
and the Regions

Sage v. Secretary of State for the Environment, Transport and the Regions; *sub nom*
Sage v. Maidstone BC [2003] UKHL 22; [2003] 1 W.L.R. 983; [2003] 2 All E.R.
689; [2003] 2 P. & C.R. 26; [2003] 1 P.L.R. 121; [2003] J.P.L. 1299; [2003]
16 E.G.C.S. 102; (2003) 147 S.J.L.B. 472; [2003] N.P.C. 51; *Times*, April 11,
2003; *Independent*, June 9, 2003 (C.S), HL; reversing [2001] EWCA Civ 1100;
[2002] 1 P. & C.R. 38; [2001] 3 P.L.R. 107; [2002] J.P.L. 352; [2001] 27
E.G.C.S. 133; *Times*, October 23, 2001, CA (Civ Div); affirming [2001] J.P.L.
986; [2000] E.G.C.S. 112; *Daily Telegraph*, November 14, 2000, QBD (Admin) . .   *Digested*, 03/**3386**:
                                                                Considered, 04/3047, 05/3271
Saggar v. Ministry of Defence; Lucas v. Ministry of Defence; Ministry of Defence v.
Gandiya [2005] EWCA Civ 413; [2005] I.C.R. 1073; [2005] I.R.L.R. 618;
(2005) 102(23) L.S.G. 27; *Times*, May 9, 2005, CA (Civ Div); reversing [2004]
I.C.R. 1708, EAT   *Digested*, 05/**1252**
Saggar (Confiscation Order: Delay), Re [2005] EWCA Civ 174; [2005] 1 W.L.R. 2693;
(2005) 102(17) L.S.G. 31; (2005) 149 S.J.L.B. 268; *Times*, March 14, 2005, CA
(Civ Div). . . . .   *Digested*, 05/**845**
Sagnata Investments Ltd v. Norwich Corp; *sub nom* Norwich Corp v. Sagnata
Investments Ltd [1971] 2 Q.B. 614; [1971] 3 W.L.R. 133; [1971] 2 All E.R. 1441;
69 L.G.R. 471; 115 S.J. 406, CA (Civ Div) . . . .   *Digested*, 71/**5081**:
                    Applied, 00/5658, 05/2754: *Considered*, 82/1906, 83/3147
Sahardid v. Camden LBC [2004] EWCA Civ 1485; [2005] H.L.R. 11; (2004) 148
S.J.L.B. 1283; [2004] N.P.C. 157, CA (Civ Div); reversing (Unreported, May 27,
2004), CC (Central London) . . . .   *Digested*, 05/**2008**
Sahin v. Turkey (44774/98) (2005) 41 E.H.R.R. 8; [2004] E.L.R. 520, ECHR . . . .   *Digested*, 05/**2050**:
                              Considered, 04/1925: *Distinguished*, 05/1131
Saif Ali v. Sydney Mitchell & Co [1980] A.C. 198; [1978] 3 W.L.R. 849; [1978] 3 All
E.R. 1033; [1955-95] P.N.L.R. 151; 122 S.J. 761, HL; reversing [1978] Q.B. 95;
[1977] 3 W.L.R. 421; [1977] 3 All E.R. 744; 121 S.J. 336, CA (Civ Div). . . . .   *Digested*, 78/**2323**:
                    Applied, 80/2609, 91/2869, 92/3499, 93/3180, 94/2687, 94/3623,
                    95/4033, 98/4011, 99/4034, 03/3008, 05/2870: *Considered*, 90/3264,
                    96/3580, 98/4012, 99/4021: *Distinguished*, 79/2293, 88/2768, 89/3073,
                    01/42: *Followed*, 96/4509, 97/3815, 00/4001: *Referred to*, 79/2110, 79/2111,
                                                                81/2184, 92/3212, 97/3825
Saifi v. Governor of Brixton Prison see R. (on the application of Saifi) v. Governor of
Brixton Prison
Sainsbury's Supermarkets Ltd v. Olympia Homes Ltd [2005] EWHC 1235; [2005] 25
E.G.C.S. 193; [2005] N.P.C. 79, Ch D
Saint-Gobain Pam SA v. Fusion Provida Ltd [2005] EWCA Civ 177; (2005) 28(6)
I.P.D. 28043, CA (Civ Div); affirming [2004] EWHC 2469; (2005) 28(1) I.P.D.
27113, Ch D
Sajid v. Chowdhury see Sajid v. Sussex Muslim Society
Sajid v. Sussex Muslim Society; *sub nom* Sajid v. Chowdhury [2001] EWCA Civ 1684;
[2002] I.R.L.R. 113, CA (Civ Div) . . . .   *Digested*, 02/**1357**:
                                                                Distinguished, 05/1316
Salaried Persons Postal Loans Ltd v. Revenue and Customs Commissioners; *sub nom*
Revenue and Customs Commissioners v. Salaried Persons Postal Loans Ltd;
CH/2005/APP/0839, Ch D; affirming [2005] S.T.C. (S.C.D.) 851; [2005] S.T.I.
1797, Sp Comm
Sale of Postage Stamps, Re (16 OK 14/03) [2005] E.C.C. 5, OGH (A)
Salford City Council v. Torkington [2004] EWCA Civ 1646; [2004] 51 E.G.C.S. 89;
(2005) 149 S.J.L.B. 28, CA (Civ Div)
Salinas v. Bear Stearns International Holdings Inc [2005] I.C.R. 1117, EAT . . . .   *Digested*, 05/**1220**
Salter Ltd v. Inland Revenue Commissioners see Slater Ltd v. Beacontree General
Commissioners (No.2)
Saltman Engineering Co v. Campbell Engineering Co (1948) [1963] 3 All E.R. 413
(Note); (1948) 65 R.P.C. 203, CA . . . .   *Digested*, 47-51/**7033**:
                    Applied, 77/2162: *Considered*, 84/440, 86/972, 05/2812:
                              Distinguished, 68/1458: *Followed*, 63/2607, 63/3337
Samaroo v. Secretary of State for the Home Department see R. (on the application of
Samaroo) v. Secretary of State for the Home Department
Sambasivam v. Public Prosecutor, Malaya [1950] A.C. 458; 66 T.L.R. (Pt. 2) 254, PC
(FMS) . . . .   *Digested*, 47-51/**7972**:
                    Applied, 83/660: *Considered*, 78/464: *Distinguished*, 64/665, 64/768,
                    89/756, 90/796, 90/7921, 00/924, 05/733: *Followed*, 63/632
Samonini v. London General Transport Services Ltd [2005] P.I.Q.R. P20, Sup Ct
Costs Office . . . .   *Digested*, 05/**2701**
Sampson, Re; *sub nom* Sampson's Application, Re; Sampson v. Croydon Crown Court
[1987] 1 W.L.R. 194; [1987] 1 All E.R. 609; (1987) 84 Cr. App. R. 376; [1987]
Crim. L.R. 570; (1987) 84 L.S.G. 825; (1987) 137 N.L.J. 169; (1987) 131 S.J.
225, HL . . . .   *Digested*, 87/**2282**:
                    Applied, 92/33, 92/39, 93/12, 93/15, 05/71: *Considered*, 90/766, 91/613,
                                                                93/10: *Followed*, 01/3539: *Referred to*, 93/11
Sampson v. Croydon Crown Court see Sampson, Re
Sampson's Application, Re see Sampson, Re

Samuels *v.* My Travel Tour Operations Ltd (t/a Cresta Holidays) (Unreported, February 27, 2004), CC (Barnet) [*Ex rel.* Milkovics & Co, Solicitors Ref: Mark Milkovics, 15 Charing Cross, Norwich, Norfolk] . . . . *Digested*, 05/**1979**
Samuels & Samuels Ltd *v.* Richardson (Inspector of Taxes) [2005] S.T.C. (S.C.D.) 1; [2004] S.T.I. 2242, Sp Comm . . . . *Digested*, 05/**3892**
Sanders *v.* Isaacs [1971] 1 W.L.R. 240; [1971] 1 All E.R. 755; (1970) 115 S.J. 95, Ch D . *Digested*, 71/**11121**: *Considered*, 05/361
Sanders *v.* Kingston (No.1) [2005] EWHC 1145; [2005] B.L.G.R. 719; *Times*, June 16, 2005, QBD (Admin) . . . . *Digested*, 05/**2786**
Sanders *v.* Kingston (No.2) [2005] EWHC 2132; (2005) 102(44) L.S.G. 33; *Times*, November 14, 2005, QBD (Admin)
Sanders BVBA *v.* Belgium (C47/96) see Garage Molenheide BVBA *v.* Belgium (C286/94)
Sandhar *v.* Department of Transport, Environment and the Regions; *sub nom* Sandhar *v.* Department of Transport, Local Government and the Regions [2004] EWCA Civ 1440; [2005] 1 W.L.R. 1632; [2005] R.T.R. 9; [2005] P.I.Q.R. P13; [2004] 46 E.G.C.S. 151; (2004) 101(45) L.S.G. 32; (2004) 148 S.J.L.B. 1317; *Times*, November 15, 2004, CA (Civ Div); affirming [2004] EWHC 28; (2004) 101(5) L.S.G. 30; (2004) 148 S.J.L.B. 145, QBD . . . . *Digested*, 04/**1818**
Sandhu *v.* Gill; *sub nom* Gill *v.* Sandhu [2005] EWCA Civ 1297; (2005) 155 N.L.J. 1713; (2005) 149 S.J.L.B. 1353; [2005] N.P.C. 125; *Times*, November 8, 2005; *Independent*, November 4, 2005, CA (Civ Div); reversing [2005] EWHC 43; [2005] 1 W.L.R. 1979; [2005] 1 All E.R. 990; (2005) 102(11) L.S.G. 29; [2005] N.P.C. 9; *Times*, February 7, 2005, Ch D . . . . *Digested*, 05/**2899**
Sandwell MBC *v.* Jones see Barber *v.* Somerset CC
Sangster *v.* Biddulphs; *sub nom* Sangster *v.* Biddulph [2005] EWHC 658; [2005] P.N.L.R. 33, Ch D . . . . *Digested*, 05/**2897**
Sankyo Pharma UK Ltd *v.* Stop Huntingdon Animal Cruelty see Daiichi Pharmaceuticals UK Ltd *v.* Stop Huntingdon Animal Cruelty
Sanofi Synthelabo SA *v.* Directeur des Services Fiscaux du Val-de-Marne (C181/99) see Ampafrance SA *v.* Directeur des Services Fiscaux de Maine-et-Loire (C177/99)
Sanofi-Synthelabo Canada Inc *v.* Apotex Inc [2005] R.P.C. 34, Fed Ct (Can)
Santambrogio *v.* Italy (61945/00) (2005) 41 E.H.R.R. 48, ECHR
Sargent *v.* Long (Long's Executor) [2005] 2 Q.R. 6; [2004] 5 Q.R. 3, CC (Nottingham) [*Ex rel.* Barratt Goff & Tomlinson, Solicitors, The Old Dairy, 67a Melton Road, West Bridgford, Nottingham] . . . . *Digested*, 04/**2856**
Sarkisov *v.* United States of America 7 I.T.L. Rep. 469, US Ct
SAT.1 Satellitenfernsehen GmbH *v.* Office for Harmonisation in the Internal Market (Trade Marks and Designs) (OHIM) (T323/00) [2002] E.C.R. II-2839; [2003] E.T.M.R. 49, CFI . . . . *Overruled*, 05/2542
SAT.1 Satellitenfernsehen GmbH *v.* Office for Harmonisation in the Internal Market (Trade Marks and Designs) (OHIM) (C329/02 P) [2005] 1 C.M.L.R. 57; [2005] E.T.M.R. 20, ECJ (2nd Chamber) [2004] E.T.M.R. 80, AGO . . . . *Digested*, 05/**2542**
Saudi Arabian Monetary Agency *v.* Dresdner Bank AG [2004] EWCA Civ 1074; [2005] 1 Lloyd's Rep. 12; [2005] 1 C.L.C. 905, CA (Civ Div); affirming [2003] EWHC 3271; [2004] 2 Lloyd's Rep. 19, Ch D . . . . *Digested*, 05/**258**
Saunders *v.* Garrett [2005] W.T.L.R. 749, Ch D
Saunders *v.* United Kingdom (19187/91) [1997] B.C.C. 872; [1998] 1 B.C.L.C. 362; (1997) 23 E.H.R.R. 313; 2 B.H.R.C. 358; *Times*, December 18, 1996; *Independent*, January 14, 1997, ECHR; affirming (1994) 18 E.H.R.R. CD23; *Independent*, September 30, 1994, Eur Comm HR. . . . . *Digested*, 97/**2816**:
Applied, 01/1047, 05/2092: *Considered*, 97/2818, 98/3150, 00/5473, 00/6043, 01/974, 01/6319, 02/849, 02/2664: *Distinguished*, 00/667, 00/2300, 04/1951, 05/765: *Followed*, 97/817, 00/3234: *Not applied*, 98/682
Saunders (A Bankrupt), Re; *sub nom* Bristol and West Building Society *v.* Saunders; Bearman (A Bankrupt), Re [1997] Ch. 60; [1996] 3 W.L.R. 473; [1997] 3 All E.R. 992; [1997] B.C.C. 83; [1996] B.P.I.R. 355, Ch D . . . . *Digested*, 96/**3444**:
Considered, 05/2826: *Followed*, 98/3319
Save Group Plc (In Liquidation), Re see Manning *v.* AIG Europe UK Ltd
Saville *v.* Gerrard [2004] EWHC 1363; [2005] B.C.C. 433; [2004] B.P.I.R. 1332, Ch D (Companies Ct) . . . . *Digested*, 05/**2314**
Savva *v.* Galway-Cooper [2005] EWCA Civ 1068; [2005] 3 E.G.L.R. 40; [2005] 45 E.G. 170; [2005] 28 E.G.C.S. 120; (2005) 102(29) L.S.G. 31, CA (Civ Div)
Sawden *v.* Sawden [2004] EWCA Civ 339; [2004] 1 F.C.R. 776, CA (Civ Div). . . . . . . *Digested*, 05/**1658**
Sawkins *v.* Hyperion Records Ltd; *sub nom* Hyperion Records Ltd *v.* Sawkins [2005] EWCA Civ 565; [2005] 1 W.L.R. 3281; [2005] 3 All E.R. 636; [2005] E.C.D.R. 33; [2005] E.M.L.R. 29; [2005] R.P.C. 32; (2005) 28(6) I.P.D. 28044; *Times*, May 23, 2005, CA (Civ Div); affirming [2004] EWHC 1530; [2004] 4 All E.R. 418; [2005] E.C.D.R. 10; [2004] E.M.L.R. 27; [2005] R.P.C. 4; (2004) 101(35) L.S.G. 35; *Times*, July 26, 2004, Ch D . . . . *Digested*, 05/**2424**
Saxon *v.* Moore; *sub nom* Saxon *v.* Warnesmoore [2005] EWHC 27; (2005) 102(10) L.S.G. 232, Ch D
Saxon *v.* Warnesmoore see Saxon *v.* Moore

Sayers v. SmithKline Beecham Plc (Withdrawal of Funding for Group Personal Injury
    Action) [2004] EWHC 1899; [2005] P.I.Q.R. P8; *Times*, October 22, 2004,
    QBD . . . . *Digested*, 05/**398**
SC v. United Kingdom (60958/00) [2005] 1 F.C.R. 347; (2005) 40 E.H.R.R. 10; 17
    B.H.R.C. 607; [2005] Crim. L.R. 130; *Times*, June 29, 2004, ECHR . . . . *Digested*, 05/**2082**
Scales v. Thames Water Utilities Plc [2005] R.V.R. 263, LandsTr
Scammell v. Dicker see Dicker v. Scammell
Scandinavian Airlines System AB v. Commission of the European Communities (T241/
    01) [2005] 5 C.M.L.R. 18, CFI (3rd Chamber)
Scandinavian Trading Tanker Co AB v. Flota Petrolera Ecuatoriana (The Scaptrade)
    [1983] 2 A.C. 694; [1983] 3 W.L.R. 203; [1983] 2 All E.R. 763; [1983] 2
    Lloyd's Rep. 253, HL; affirming [1983] Q.B. 529; [1983] 2 W.L.R. 248; [1983]
    1 All E.R. 301; [1983] 1 Lloyd's Rep. 146; (1983) 133 N.L.J. 133; 126 S.J. 853;
    Times, November 30, 1982, CA (Civ Div); affirming [1981] 2 Lloyd's Rep. 425;
    [1981] Com. L.R. 214, QBD (Comm) . . . . *Digested*, 83/**3405**:
               Considered, 83/421, 84/1326, 93/2495, 05/3793: *Distinguished*, 85/2604,
                                                    05/422
Scarborough BC v. Truman [2005] P.A.D. 50, Planning Inspector
Schaal v. Luxembourg (51773/99) (2005) 41 E.H.R.R. 47, ECHR
Schalit v. Joseph Nadler Ltd [1933] 2 K.B. 79, KBD . . . . *Considered*, 05/**2657**
Scharsach v. Austria (39394/98) (2005) 40 E.H.R.R. 22, ECHR . . . . *Digested*, 05/**2046**
Schemmer v. Property Resources Ltd [1975] Ch. 273; [1974] 3 W.L.R. 406; [1974] 3
    All E.R. 451; 118 S.J. 716, Ch D . . . . *Digested*, 74/**403**:
             Applied, 81/1204: *Considered*, 88/408, 88/1605, 89/1715, 94/436:
                                       Distinguished, 05/621
Schempp v. Finanzamt Munchen (C403/03) [2005] S.T.C. 1792; [2005] 3 C.M.L.R.
    37; [2005] S.T.I. 1255, ECJ
Schengen Implementing System, Re (C257/01) see Commission of the European
    Communities v. Council of the European Union (C257/01)
Schepens v. Belgium (C340/95) see Garage Molenheide BVBA v. Belgium (C286/94)
Schering Corp v. Cipla Ltd [2004] EWHC 2587; [2005] F.S.R. 25; (2005) 28(2)
    I.P.D. 28009; (2004) 101(47) L.S.G. 30; *Times*, December 2, 2004, Ch D . . . . *Digested*, 05/**295**
Schiffahrtsgesellschaft Detlev Von Appen GmbH v. Voest Alpine Intertrading GmbH;
    Schiffahrtsgesellschaft Detlev Von Appen GmbH v. Weiner Allianz Versicherungs
    AG [1997] 2 Lloyd's Rep. 279, CA (Civ Div); reversing [1997] 1 Lloyd's Rep. 179,
    QBD (Comm) . . . . *Digested*, 97/**4597**:
                                     Applied, 05/200, 05/2357
Schiffahrtsgesellschaft Detlev Von Appen GmbH v. Weiner Allianz Versicherungs AG see
    Schiffahrtsgesellschaft Detlev Von Appen GmbH v. Voest Alpine Intertrading
    GmbH
Schilling v. Finanzamt Nurnberg Sud (C209/01) [2005] S.T.C. 1756; [2003] E.C.R. I-
    13389; [2003] S.T.I. 2121, ECJ (5th Chamber)
Schirmer v. Poland (68880/01) (2005) 40 E.H.R.R. 47, ECHR . . . . *Digested*, 05/**2070**
Schlusselverlag JS Moser GmbH v. Commission of the European Communities (C170/
    02 P); *sub nom* Schlusselverlag JS Moser GmbH v. Commission of the European
    Communities (T3/02) [2003] E.C.R. I-9889; [2004] 4 C.M.L.R. 27, ECJ (6th
    Chamber); affirming [2002] E.C.R. II-1473; [2004] 4 C.M.L.R. 29, CFI (3rd
    Chamber) . . . . *Digested*, 05/**584**
Schlusselverlag JS Moser GmbH v. Commission of the European Communities (T3/02)
    see Schlusselverlag JS Moser GmbH v. Commission of the European
    Communities (C170/02 P)
Schmidt v. Rosewood Trust Ltd; *sub nom* Angora Trust, Re; Everest Trust, Re;
    Rosewood Trust Ltd v. Schmidt [2003] UKPC 26; [2003] 2 A.C. 709; [2003] 2
    W.L.R. 1442; [2003] 3 All E.R. 76; [2003] Pens. L.R. 145; [2003] W.T.L.R.
    565; (2002-03) 5 I.T.E.L.R. 715; (2003) 100(22) L.S.G. 31; *Times*, March 29,
    2003, PC (IoM); reversing [2001] W.T.L.R. 1081; (2000-01) 3 I.T.E.L.R. 734, HC
    (IoM) . . . . *Digested*, 03/**4485**:
               Applied, 04/2815, 04/3950, 05/4303: *Followed*, 05/4293
Schmidt v. Wong [2005] EWCA Civ 1506; [2005] N.P.C. 143; *Times*, December 13,
    2005; *Independent*, December 15, 2005, CA (Civ Div)
Schoning-Kougebetopoulou v. Freie und Hansestadt Hamburg (C15/96) [1998] All
    E.R. (E.C.) 97; [1998] E.C.R. I-47; [1998] 1 C.M.L.R. 931; [1998] C.E.C. 280,
    ECJ . . . . *Digested*, 98/**2155**:
                                 Followed, 02/1411, 05/3860
Schroll v. PCO Stauereibetrieb Paetz & Co Nachfolgar GmbH (C139/91) see Katsikas
    v. Konstantinidis (C132/91)
Schulin v. Saatgut-Treuhandverwaltungs GmbH (C305/00) [2003] E.C.R. I-3525;
    [2005] 1 C.M.L.R. 17, ECJ (5th Chamber) . . . . *Digested*, 05/**152**
Scientific Investment Pension Plan (No.2), Re; *sub nom* Kemble v. Hicks (No.1); Trusts of
    the Scientific Investment Pension Plan, Re [1999] Ch. 53; [1998] 3 W.L.R.
    1191; [1998] 3 All E.R. 154; [1998] 2 B.C.L.C. 360; [1998] 2 F.L.R. 761; [1998]
    B.P.I.R. 410; [1998] O.P.L.R. 41; [1998] Pens. L.R. 141; [1998] Fam. Law 582;
    Times, March 5, 1998, Ch D . . . . *Digested*, 98/**3279**:
                                   Considered, 05/2278

Scindia Steamship Navigation Co Ltd Bombay *v.* Nippon Yusen Kaisha Ltd (The Jalagouri) see Nippon Yusen Kaisha Ltd *v.* Scindia Steam Navigation Co Ltd (The Jalagouri)

SCIP-r-NOSCO Trade Mark [2005] E.T.M.R. CN2, TMR

Scippacercola *v.* Commission of the European Communities (T187/03) [2005] 2 C.M.L.R. 54, CFI (3rd Chamber) . . . . *Digested*, 05/**1436**

SCLAVO/Bordetella pertussis toxin (T900/02) [2005] E.P.O.R. 4, EPO (Technical Bd App) *Digested*, 05/**2469**

Scott, Petitioner see Davidson *v.* Scottish Ministers (No.1)

Scott *v.* Inland Revenue Commissioners [2004] EWCA Civ 400; [2004] I.C.R. 1410; [2004] I.R.L.R. 713; (2004) 148 S.J.L.B. 474; *Times*, April 19, 2004, CA (Civ Div); reversing UKEAT/0068/03/ZT, EAT . . . . *Digested*, 05/**1318**

Scott *v.* Jelf [1974] R.T.R. 256; [1974] Crim. L.R. 191, DC . . . . *Digested*, 74/**3271**: *Followed*, 05/780

Scott *v.* Scottish Ministers see Davidson *v.* Scottish Ministers (No.1)

Scott Equipment Co *v.* Russell Grant Ltd see Russell Grant Ltd *v.* Scott Equipment Co

Scott (t/a Farthings Steak House) *v.* McDonald (Inspector of Taxes) [1996] S.T.C. (S.C.D.) 381, Sp Comm . . . . *Digested*, 96/**3328**: *Distinguished*, 05/4083

Scott-Kilvert's Estate, Re see Robinson *v.* Bird

Scottish Equitable Plc *v.* Miller Construction Ltd 2002 S.C.L.R. 10; 83 Con. L.R. 183; 2001 G.W.D. 28-1119, IH (Ex Div) . . . . *Digested*, 02/**6055**: *Considered*, 05/656

Scottish Exhibition Centre Ltd *v.* Customs and Excise Commissioners [2005] B.V.C. 2529; [2005] S.T.I. 896, V&DTr

Scottish Power Generation Ltd *v.* Scottish Environment Protection Agency (No.1) 2005 S.L.T. 98; [2005] Eu. L.R. 449; [2005] Env. L.R. 38; 2005 G.W.D. 1-1, OH . . . . . *Digested*, 05/**4970**

Scottish Provident Institution *v.* Inland Revenue Commissioners; *sub nom* Inland Revenue Commissioners *v.* Scottish Provident Institution [2004] UKHL 52; [2004] 1 W.L.R. 3172; [2005] 1 All E.R. 325; [2005] S.T.C. 15; 2005 S.C. (H.L.) 33; 76 T.C. 538; [2004] B.T.C. 426; 7 I.T.L. Rep. 403; [2004] S.T.I. 2433; (2004) 148 S.J.L.B. 1404; *Times*, November 26, 2004; *Independent*, December 1, 2004, HL; reversing [2003] S.T.C. 1035; 2004 S.C. 135; 2003 S.C.L.R. 867; [2004] B.T.C. 105; [2003] S.T.I. 1416; 2003 G.W.D. 24-699, IH (1 Div); affirming [2002] S.T.C. (S.C.D.) 252; [2002] S.T.I. 901, Sp Comm . . . . *Digested*, 05/**4158**: *Considered*, 05/4084

Scout Association Trust Corp *v.* Secretary of State for the Environment; *sub nom* Scouts Association Trust Corp *v.* Secretary of State for the Environment [2005] EWCA Civ 980; [2005] S.T.C. 1808; [2005] R.V.R. 303; [2005] S.T.I. 1339; [2005] N.P.C. 106, CA (Civ Div); affirming (Unreported, September 10, 2004), Lands Tr . *Digested*, 05/**4343**

Scribes West Ltd *v.* Anstalt (No.1) see Scribes West Ltd *v.* Relsa Anstalt (No.1)

Scribes West Ltd *v.* Anstalt (No.2) see Scribes West Ltd *v.* Relsa Anstalt (No.2)

Scribes West Ltd *v.* Anstalt (No.3) see Scribes West Ltd *v.* Relsa Anstalt (No.3)

Scribes West Ltd *v.* Relsa Anstalt (No.1); *sub nom* Scribes West Ltd *v.* Anstalt (No.1) [2004] EWCA Civ 835; [2005] C.P. Rep. 2; [2005] 1 Costs L.R. 18; *Times*, July 8, 2004, CA (Civ Div) . . . . *Digested*, 05/**455**

Scribes West Ltd *v.* Relsa Anstalt (No.2); *sub nom* Scribes West Ltd *v.* Anstalt (No.2) [2004] EWCA Civ 965; [2005] 1 W.L.R. 1839; [2004] 4 All E.R. 653; [2005] C.P. Rep. 5, CA (Civ Div) . . . . *Digested*, 04/**276**

Scribes West Ltd *v.* Relsa Anstalt (No.3); *sub nom* Scribes West Ltd *v.* Anstalt (No.3) [2004] EWCA Civ 1744; [2005] 1 W.L.R. 1847; [2005] 2 All E.R. 690; [2005] 2 P. & C.R. 3; [2005] L. & T.R. 14; [2005] 1 E.G.L.R. 22; [2005] 09 E.G. 190; [2005] 2 E.G.C.S. 100; [2005] 1 P. & C.R. DG21, CA (Civ Div) . . . . *Digested*, 05/**2657**

Scriven (No.2), Re; *sub nom* R. *v.* Scriven (Geoffrey Harold) [2004] EWCA Civ 683; [2004] B.P.I.R. 972; (2004) 148 S.J.L.B. 757, CA (Civ Div) . . . . *Digested*, 05/**345**

Scrivens *v.* Ethical Standards Officer [2005] EWHC 529; [2005] B.L.G.R. 641; [2005] N.P.C. 51, QBD (Admin) . . . . *Digested*, 05/**2785**

SDLO/Mystery swine disease (T15/01) [2005] E.P.O.R. 45, EPO (Technical Bd App)

Sea Success Maritime Inc *v.* African Maritime Carriers Ltd [2005] EWHC 1542; [2005] 2 All E.R. (Comm) 445; [2005] 2 Lloyd's Rep. 692; [2005] 2 C.L.C. 167; *Times*, September 6, 2005, QBD (Comm) . . . . *Digested*, 05/**3815**

Seaconsar (Far East) Ltd *v.* Bank Markazi Jomhouri Islami Iran (Service Outside Jurisdiction) [1994] 1 A.C. 438; [1993] 3 W.L.R. 756; [1993] 4 All E.R. 456; [1994] 1 Lloyd's Rep. 1; [1994] I.L.Pr. 678; (1993) 143 N.L.J. 1479; (1993) 137 S.J.L.B. 239; *Times*, October 15, 1993; *Independent*, October 20, 1993, HL; reversing [1993] 1 Lloyd's Rep. 236; *Times*, November 25, 1992, CA (Civ Div) . . *Digested*, 94/**3763**: *Applied*, 95/398, 98/582, 03/310, 04/566, 05/2293: *Considered*, 95/703: *Referred to*, 95/399 *Followed*, 98/4394:

Seager *v.* Copydex Ltd (No.1) [1967] 1 W.L.R. 923; [1967] 2 All E.R. 415; 2 K.I.R. 828; [1967] F.S.R. 211; [1967] R.P.C. 349; 111 S.J. 335, CA (Civ Div) . . . . *Digested*, 67/**1486**: *Applied*, 72/364, 01/4265: *Considered*, 86/412, 87/1294, 88/2859, 88/2862, 89/3103, 96/1219, 96/2519, 05/2416: *Distinguished*, 96/4556: *Followed*, 68/1458

Seal v. Chief Constable of South Wales [2005] EWCA Civ 586; [2005] 1 W.L.R. 3183; [2005] B.P.I.R. 993; (2005) 8 C.C.L. Rep. 372; *Times*, May 31, 2005, CA (Civ Div) . . . . *Digested*, 05/**2826**

Sealey v. Trinidad and Tobago; Headley v. Trinidad and Tobago [2002] UKPC 52; *Times*, November 5, 2002, PC (Trin) . . . . *Digested*, 02/**878**: *Applied*, 05/**938**

Sealy v. Consignia Plc see Consignia Plc v. Sealy

Search Guarantees Ltd v. Earl Cadogan see Earl Cadogan v. Search Guarantees Plc

Searson v. Brioland Ltd; *sub nom* Brioland Ltd v. Searson [2005] EWCA Civ 55; [2005] 5 E.G.C.S. 202; [2005] N.P.C. 12, CA (Civ Div)

Seawind Tankers Corp v. Bayoil SA see Bayoil SA, Re

SEB Trygg Holding AB v. Manches; *sub nom* AMB Generali Holding AG v. SEB Trygg Liv Holding AB; AMB Generali Holding AG v. Manches [2005] EWCA Civ 1237; (2005) 102(45) L.S.G. 28; (2005) 155 N.L.J. 1781; *Times*, December 1, 2005, CA (Civ Div); reversing in part [2005] EWHC 35; [2005] 2 Lloyd's Rep. 129, QBD (Comm) . . . . *Digested*, 05/**89**

Seco SA v. Etablissement d'Assurance contre la Vieillesse et l'Invalidite (62/81) [1982] E.C.R. 223, ECJ . . . . *Digested*, 83/**1622**: *Followed*, 05/1468

Secretarial & Nominee Co Ltd v. Thomas [2005] EWCA Civ 1008; [2005] 3 E.G.L.R. 37; [2005] 44 E.G. 136; *Times*, September 20, 2005, CA (Civ Div) . . . . *Digested*, 05/**2676**

Secretary of State for Constitutional Affairs v. Stork [2005] EWHC 1763; *Times*, October 7, 2005, QBD . . . . *Digested*, 05/**879**

Secretary of State for Defence v. MacDonald see Advocate General for Scotland v. MacDonald

Secretary of State for Education and Skills v. Farley [2004] EWHC 1768; [2004] O.P.L.R. 353; [2004] Pens. L.R. 359, Ch D . . . . *Digested*, 05/**3055**

Secretary of State for Education and Skills v. Frontline Technology Ltd (No.3) [2005] EWHC 37; (2005) 28(5) I.P.D. 28040, Ch D (Patents Ct)

Secretary of State for Education and Skills v. Mairs [2005] EWHC 996; [2005] I.C.R. 1714; [2005] A.C.D. 93; *Times*, June 15, 2005, QBD (Admin) . . . . *Digested*, 05/**11**

Secretary of State for Environment, Food and Rural Affairs v. Feakins; *sub nom* Department for Environment, Food and Rural Affairs v. Feakins [2005] EWCA Civ 1513; *Times*, December 22, 2005, CA (Civ Div); reversing in part [2004] EWHC 2735; [2005] Eu. L.R. 207; [2005] B.P.I.R. 292; [2004] 49 E.G.C.S. 135; (2005) 102(5) L.S.G. 28; *Times*, December 29, 2004, Ch D . . . . *Digested*, 05/**135**

Secretary of State for Health v. Norton Healthcare Ltd (No.3) [2004] EWHC 609; [2005] Eu. L.R. 135, Ch D . . . . *Digested*, 05/**394**

Secretary of State for Scotland v. Revival Properties Ltd see Edinburgh City Council v. Secretary of State for Scotland

Secretary of State for Social Security v. Thomas (C328/91); *sub nom* Thomas v. Chief Adjudication Officer (C328/91) [1993] Q.B. 747; [1993] 3 W.L.R. 581; [1993] 4 All E.R. 556; [1993] E.C.R. I-1247; [1993] 3 C.M.L.R. 880; [1993] I.C.R. 673; [1993] I.R.L.R. 292; *Times*, April 5, 1993, ECJ (6th Chamber) . . . . *Digested*, 93/**4386**:
Applied, 05/1268: *Considered*, 95/3641: *Followed*, 01/4604, 02/4202: *Previous proceedings*, 90/4174, 91/4087: *Referred to*, 00/4819

Secretary of State for the Environment, Food and Rural Affairs v. Alford see Alford v. Secretary of State for the Environment, Food and Rural Affairs

Secretary of State for the Environment, Transport and the Regions v. Legal & General Assurance Society Ltd see R. (on the application of Holding & Barnes Plc) v. Secretary of State for the Environment, Transport and the Regions

Secretary of State for the Home Department v. Adan (Hassan Hussein) see Adan (Hassan Hussein) v. Secretary of State for the Home Department

Secretary of State for the Home Department v. Ahmed (Iftikhar) see Ahmed (Iftikhar) v. Secretary of State for the Home Department

Secretary of State for the Home Department v. Akaeke see Akaeke v. Secretary of State for the Home Department

Secretary of State for the Home Department v. Hindawi see R. (on the application of Hindawi) v. Secretary of State for the Home Department

Secretary of State for the Home Department v. International Transport Roth GmbH see International Transport Roth GmbH v. Secretary of State for the Home Department

Secretary of State for the Home Department v. Maheshwaran see R. (on the application of Maheshwaran) v. Secretary of State for the Home Department

Secretary of State for the Home Department v. Makke see R. (on the application of Makke) v. Secretary of State for the Home Department

Secretary of State for the Home Department v. Ravichandran see R. v. Secretary of State for the Home Department Ex p. Jeyeanthan

Secretary of State for the Home Department v. Razgar see R. (on the application of Razgar) v. Secretary of State for the Home Department (No.2)

Secretary of State for the Home Department *v.* Rehman; *sub nom* Rehman *v.* Secretary of State for the Home Department [2001] UKHL 47; [2003] 1 A.C. 153; [2001] 3 W.L.R. 877; [2002] 1 All E.R. 122; 11 B.H.R.C. 413; [2002] Imm. A.R. 98; [2002] I.N.L.R. 92; [2002] A.C.D. 6; (2001) 98(42) L.S.G. 37; (2001) 145 S.J.L.B. 238; *Times*, October 15, 2001; *Independent*, October 17, 2001, HL; affirming [2000] 3 W.L.R. 1240; [2000] 3 All E.R. 778; [2001] Imm. A.R. 30; [2000] I.N.L.R. 531; (2000) 97(24) L.S.G. 40; *Times*, May 31, 2000; *Independent*, May 26, 2000, CA (Civ Div); reversing [1999] I.N.L.R. 517, Sp Imm App Comm . . . . *Digested*, 01/**3662**:
Considered, 04/2004: *Followed*, 05/2825

Secretary of State for the Home Department *v.* Smith see R. (on the application of Smith) *v.* Secretary of State for the Home Department

Secretary of State for the Home Department *v.* SP see R. (on the application of P) *v.* Secretary of State for the Home Department

Secretary of State for the Home Department *v.* Zeqaj see Zeqaj *v.* Secretary of State for the Home Department

Secretary of State for Trade and Industry *v.* Bairstow (No.2); *sub nom* Queens Moat Houses Plc (No.2), Re [2004] EWHC 1730; [2005] 1 B.C.L.C. 136, Ch D (Companies Ct) . . . . *Digested*, 05/**521**

Secretary of State for Trade and Industry *v.* Baker (No.6); *sub nom* Barings Plc (No.6), Re [2001] B.C.C. 273; [2000] 1 B.C.L.C. 523; *Independent*, March 9, 2000, CA (Civ Div); affirming [1999] 1 B.C.L.C 433, Ch D (Companies Ct). . . . . *Digested*, 00/**660**:
Applied, 05/521: *Followed*, 03/513

Secretary of State for Trade and Industry *v.* Bell Davies Trading Ltd; *sub nom* Bell Davies Trading Ltd *v.* Secretary of State for Trade and Industry [2004] EWCA Civ 1066; [2005] 1 All E.R. 324 (Note); [2005] B.C.C. 564; [2005] 1 B.C.L.C. 516; (2004) 101(36) L.S.G. 33; *Times*, September 21, 2004, CA (Civ Div); affirming [2004] EWHC 20, Ch D (Companies Ct) . . . . *Digested*, 04/**2197**

Secretary of State for Trade and Industry *v.* Blackwood 2003 S.L.T. 120; [2005] B.C.C. 366; 2002 G.W.D. 27-930, IH (1 Div) . . . . *Digested*, 03/**5303**

Secretary of State for Trade and Industry *v.* Blunt [2005] 2 B.C.L.C. 463, Ch D

Secretary of State for Trade and Industry *v.* Collins; *sub nom* TLL Realisations Ltd, Re [2000] B.C.C. 998; [2000] 2 B.C.L.C. 223; (2000) 97(2) L.S.G. 29; *Times*, January 25, 2000, CA (Civ Div). . . . . *Digested*, 00/**672**:
Applied, 01/716, 05/519

Secretary of State for Trade and Industry *v.* Gill [2004] EWHC 175; [2005] B.C.C. 24, Ch D

Secretary of State for Trade and Industry *v.* Paulin; *sub nom* Paulin *v.* Secretary of State for Trade and Industry [2005] EWHC 888; [2005] B.C.C. 927; [2005] 2 B.C.L.C. 667; [2005] B.P.I.R. 968; *Times*, May 26, 2005, Ch D . . . . *Digested*, 05/**2306**

Secretary of State for Trade and Industry *v.* Rutherford see Rutherford *v.* Secretary of State for Trade and Industry

Secretary of State for Trade and Industry *v.* Shakespeare [2005] B.C.C. 891; [2005] 2 B.C.L.C. 471, Ch D

Secretary of State for Trade and Industry *v.* Swan [2005] EWHC 603; [2005] B.C.C. 596, Ch D . . . . *Digested*, 05/**518**

Secretary of State for Transport *v.* Birse-Farr Joint Venture 62 B.L.R. 36; 35 Con. L.R. 8; (1993) 9 Const. L.J. 213, QBD. . . . . *Digested*, 94/**330**:
Considered, 05/656: *Followed*, 95/489, 96/1144

Secretary of State for Transport *v.* Nuttall (t/a Redline Coaches) see Vehicle Inspectorate *v.* Nuttall

Secretary of State for Work and Pensions *v.* Ahmed see Ahmed *v.* Secretary of State for Work and Pensions

Secretary of State for Work and Pensions *v.* Bobezes [2005] EWCA Civ 111; [2005] 3 All E.R. 497; *Times*, March 14, 2005, CA (Civ Div) . . . . *Digested*, 05/**3827**

Secretary of State for Work and Pensions *v.* Kehoe see R. (on the application of Kehoe) *v.* Secretary of State for Work and Pensions

Secretary of State for Work and Pensions *v.* M see M *v.* Secretary of State for Work and Pensions

Secretary of State for Work and Pensions *v.* Perkins [2004] EWCA Civ 1671; [2005] H.L.R. 19; (2005) 102(2) L.S.G. 28; *Times*, December 16, 2004, CA (Civ Div) . . *Digested*, 05/**3871**

Secretary of State for Work and Pensions *v.* W [2005] EWCA Civ 570; *Times*, June 10, 2005, CA (Civ Div) . . . . *Digested*, 05/**3883**

Secretary of State for Work and Pensions *v.* Walker-Fox [2005] EWCA Civ 1441; *Times*, December 8, 2005, CA (Civ Div)

Securum Finance Ltd *v.* Ashton (No.1); *sub nom* Ashton *v.* Securum Finance Ltd [2001] Ch. 291; [2000] 3 W.L.R. 1400; (2000) 97(27) L.S.G. 38; *Times*, July 5, 2000; *Independent*, June 30, 2000, CA (Civ Div); affirming [1999] 2 All E.R. (Comm) 331; (1999) 96(26) L.S.G. 28; (1999) 143 S.J.L.B. 182; *Times*, June 18, 1999 ; *Independent*, June 28, 1999 (C.S.), Ch D . . . . *Digested*, 00/**348**:
Applied, 03/468, 05/413, 05/1316: *Considered*, 02/2652:
Distinguished, 02/504: *Referred to*, 01/668

Seddon v. Binions; Stork v. Binions [1978] 1 Lloyd's Rep. 381; [1978] R.T.R. 163; 122
     S.J. 34, CA (Civ Div) .... *Digested,* 78/**2592**:
                                                   Applied, 00/3522, 05/2376
Seddon Properties Ltd v. Secretary of State for the Environment (1981) 42 P. & C.R.
     26; (1978) 248 E.G. 951; [1978] J.P.L. 835, QBD .... *Digested,* 81/**2730**:
          Applied, 83/3693, 05/3310: *Cited,* 93/3921, 94/4427: *Considered,* 86/3259,
                              87/2898, 88/3442: *Followed,* 93/3925
Seegert (Deceased), Re (2005-06) 8 I.T.E.L.R. 1, Royal Ct (Jer)
Sehgal v. Union of India [2005] F.S.R. 39, HC (Ind)
SEIKO/Image forming apparatus (T904/97) [2000] E.P.O.R. 343, EPO (Technical Bd App)   *Digested,* 00/**3620**:
                                                 Considered, 05/2439
Seismic Shipping Inc v. Total E&P UK Plc (The Western Regent); *sub nom* Owners of
     the Western Regent v. Charterers of the Western Regent [2005] EWCA Civ 985;
     [2005] 2 All E.R. (Comm) 515; [2005] 2 Lloyd's Rep. 359; [2005] 2 C.L.C.
     182, CA (Civ Div); affirming [2005] EWHC 460; [2005] 2 All E.R. (Comm) 51;
     [2005] 2 Lloyd's Rep. 54; *Times,* May 4, 2005, QBD (Admlty) .... *Digested,* 05/**3801**
Selfridges Ltd v. Malik [1998] I.C.R. 268; [1997] I.R.L.R. 577, EAT. .... *Digested,* 98/**2225**:
                                                 Approved, 05/1334
Selisto v. Finland (56767/00) [2005] E.M.L.R. 8, ECHR .... *Digested,* 05/**2044**
Selkent Bus Co Ltd v. Moore [1996] I.C.R. 836; [1996] I.R.L.R. 661, EAT. .... *Digested,* 96/**2661**:
                                 Applied, 00/2207: *Considered,* 05/1278
Sempra Metals Ltd (formerly Metallgesellschaft Ltd) v. Inland Revenue Commissioners
     [2005] EWCA Civ 389; [2005] 3 W.L.R. 521; [2005] S.T.C. 687; [2005] 2
     C.M.L.R. 30; [2005] Eu. L.R. 773; [2005] B.T.C. 202; [2005] S.T.I. 831; [2005]
     N.P.C. 52; *Times,* April 26, 2005; *Independent,* April 22, 2005, CA (Civ Div);
     affirming [2004] EWHC 2387; [2004] S.T.C. 1178; [2004] Eu. L.R. 939; [2004]
     B.T.C. 358; [2004] S.T.I. 1495; *Times,* June 25, 2004, Ch D .... *Digested,* 05/**3984**
Sengupta v. Holmes [2002] EWCA Civ 1104; (2002) 99(39) L.S.G. 39; *Times,* August
     19, 2002; *Independent,* October 3, 2002, CA (Civ Div). .... *Digested,* 02/**452**:
          Applied, 02/1347: *Considered,* 05/2170: *Previous proceedings,* 01/2897
Seniaray v. Rose (Unreported, October 18, 2004), CC (Birmingham) [*Ex rel.* Andrew
     Granville Stafford, Barrister, 4, King's Bench Walk, Temple, London] .... *Digested,* 05/**3174**
Sentges v. Netherlands (Admissibility) (27677/02) (2004) 7 C.C.L. Rep. 400, ECHR .. *Digested,* 05/**1831**
Senthuran v. Secretary of State for the Home Department [2004] EWCA Civ 950;
     [2004] 4 All E.R. 365; [2005] 1 F.L.R. 229; [2004] 3 F.C.R. 273; [2004]
     A.C.D. 90; [2004] Fam. Law 864; *Times,* August 3, 2004, CA (Civ Div) ...... *Digested,* 04/**2050**:
                                                 Applied, 05/2211
Sepet v. Secretary of State for the Home Department; *sub nom* R. (on the application
     of Septet) v. Secretary of State for the Home Department; R. (on the application
     of Bulbul) v. Secretary of State for the Home Department; Bulbul v. Secretary
     of State for the Home Department [2003] UKHL 15; [2003] 1 W.L.R. 856;
     [2003] 3 All E.R. 304; 14 B.H.R.C. 238; [2003] Imm. A.R. 428; [2003] I.N.L.R.
     322; (2003) 100(18) L.S.G. 35; (2003) 147 S.J.L.B. 389; *Times,* March 21,
     2003; *Independent,* March 25, 2003, HL; affirming [2001] EWCA Civ 681;
     [2001] Imm. A.R. 452; [2001] I.N.L.R. 376; *Times,* July 12, 2001; *Independent,*
     May 18, 2001, CA (Civ Div); affirming [2000] Imm. A.R. 445, IAT .... *Digested,* 03/**2229**:
                    Applied, 05/5439: *Considered,* 03/5732, 04/1925, 05/2178
Serco Ltd v. Lawson see Lawson v. Serco Ltd
Set v. Robinson (Inspector of Taxes) see Agassi v. Robinson (Inspector of Taxes)
Sevenoaks DC v. First Secretary of State; *sub nom* R. (on the application of Sevenoaks
     DC) v. First Secretary of State [2004] EWHC 771; [2005] 1 P. & C.R. 13;
     [2005] J.P.L. 116; [2004] 14 E.G.C.S. 141, QBD (Admin) .... *Digested,* 05/**3303**
Sevenoaks DC v. Franz [2005] P.A.D. 44, Planning Inspector
Sevenoaks Stationers (Retail) Ltd, Re [1991] Ch. 164; [1990] 3 W.L.R. 1165; [1991] 3 All
     E.R. 578; [1990] B.C.C. 765; [1991] B.C.L.C. 325; (1990) 134 S.J. 1367, CA (Civ
     Div); reversing [1990] B.C.L.C. 668, Ch D .... *Digested,* 91/**401**:
          Applied, 93/360, 00/662, 00/2243, 02/547, 05/518: *Cited,* 93/359, 93/374:
          Considered, 92/390, 98/670, 98/671: *Followed,* 01/712: *Referred to,* 01/706
Severn Trent Water Ltd v. Barnes [2004] EWCA Civ 570; [2004] 2 E.G.L.R. 95; [2004]
     26 E.G. 194; [2005] R.V.R. 181; (2004) 148 S.J.L.B. 693; [2004] N.P.C. 76, CA
     (Civ Div) .... *Digested,* 04/**912**
Severn Trent Water Ltd v. Coal Authority [2005] R.V.R. 21, Lands Tr. .... *Digested,* 05/**4331**
Seymour v. Caroline Ockwell & Co; *sub nom* Seymour v. Ockwell [2005] EWHC 1137;
     [2005] P.N.L.R. 39, QBD (Merc) .... *Digested,* 05/**2851**
Seymour v. Ockwell see Seymour v. Caroline Ockwell & Co
Seymour (Ninth Marquess of Hertford) v. Inland Revenue Commissioners [2005] S.T.C.
     (S.C.D.) 177; [2005] W.T.L.R. 85; [2005] S.T.I. 2546, Sp Comm .... *Digested,* 05/**4113**
Sezek v. Secretary of State for the Home Department see R. (on the application of
     Samaroo) v. Secretary of State for the Home Department
SG Embiricos Ltd v. Tradax Internacional SA (The Azuero) [1967] 1 Lloyd's Rep. 464;
     117 N.L.J. 680, QBD (Comm) .... *Digested,* 67/**3622**:
                                                 Applied, 05/3813

Shabpar v. Barnet LBC see R. v. Barnet LBC Ex p. Shah (Nilish)
Shackleton v. Eddy Henderson see Snowden, Re

Shackleton *v.* Methodist Missionary Society see Snowden, Re
Shah *v.* Haden Building Management Ltd, *Times*, November 2, 2005, EAT
Shah *v.* Immigration Appeal Tribunal see R. (on the application of Shah) *v.* Immigration
    Appeal Tribunal
Shah *v.* Oliver (Unreported, June 7, 2004), CC (Ashford) [*Ex rel.* Andrew Hammond,
    Barrister, Plowden Buildings, Temple, London] . . . . *Digested*, 05/**364**
Shah *v.* Secretary of State for Social Security [2002] EWCA Civ 285, CA (Civ Div) . . . *Considered*, 05/**2233**
Shah (Jitendra) *v.* Barnet LBC see R. *v.* Barnet LBC Ex p. Shah (Nilish)
Shahar *v.* Tsitsekkos; Kolomoisky *v.* Shahar [2004] EWHC 2659; *Times*, November 30,
    2004, Ch D . . . . *Digested*, 05/**470**
Shaker *v.* Al-Bedrawi; Shaker *v.* Masry; Shaker *v.* Steggles Palmer (A Firm) [2002]
    EWCA Civ 1452; [2003] Ch. 350; [2003] 2 W.L.R. 922; [2002] 4 All E.R. 835;
    [2003] B.C.C. 465; [2003] 1 B.C.L.C. 157; [2003] W.T.L.R. 105; (2002-03) 5
    I.T.E.L.R. 429; *Independent*, October 25, 2002, CA (Civ Div); reversing CH 1991
    S 00242, HC 99 04520, HC 00 00627, Ch D . . . . *Digested*, 02/**566**:
                                Applied, 05/533: *Followed*, 05/520
Shaker *v.* Masry see Shaker *v.* Al-Bedrawi
Shaker *v.* Steggles Palmer (A Firm) see Shaker *v.* Al-Bedrawi
Shala *v.* Secretary of State for the Home Department [2003] EWCA Civ 233; [2003]
    I.N.L.R. 349, CA (Civ Div) . . . . *Digested*, 03/**2270**:
                 Considered, 04/2049: *Distinguished*, 04/2048, 05/2159
Shalson *v.* John Lyon's Free Grammar School; *sub nom* John Lyon's Charity *v.*
    Shalson; Shalson *v.* Keepers and Governors of the Free Grammar School of John
    Lyon [2003] UKHL 32; [2004] 1 A.C. 802; [2003] 3 W.L.R. 1; [2003] 3 All
    E.R. 975; [2003] H.L.R. 74; [2003] L. & T.R. 28; [2003] 2 E.G.L.R. 49; [2003]
    27 E.G. 139; [2004] R.V.R. 184; [2003] 25 E.G.C.S. 142; (2003) 100(30)
    L.S.G. 30; (2003) 153 N.L.J. 949; (2003) 147 S.J.L.B. 752; [2003] N.P.C. 74;
    Times, June 16, 2003; *Independent*, July 28, 2003 (C.S); *Independent*, June 18,
    2003, HL; reversing [2002] EWCA Civ 538; [2003] Ch. 110; [2002] 3 W.L.R.
    1664; [2002] 3 All E.R. 1119; [2003] H.L.R. 4; [2002] L. & T.R. 34; [2002] 2
    E.G.L.R. 55; [2002] 26 E.G. 141; [2002] R.V.R. 276; [2002] 17 E.G.C.S. 156, CA
    (Civ Div) . . . . *Digested*, 03/**2746**:
                                     Applied, 05/3405
Shalson *v.* Keepers and Governors of the Free Grammar School of John Lyon see
    Shalson *v.* John Lyon's Free Grammar School
Shalson *v.* Russo; *sub nom* Mimran *v.* Russo [2003] EWHC 1637; [2005] Ch. 281;
    [2005] 2 W.L.R. 1213; [2003] W.T.L.R. 1165; (2005-06) 8 I.T.E.L.R. 435;
    (2003) 100(35) L.S.G. 37; *Times*, September 3, 2003, Ch D . . . . *Digested*, 03/**3611**
Shamoon *v.* Chief Constable of the Royal Ulster Constabulary [2003] UKHL 11;
    [2003] 2 All E.R. 26; [2003] N.I. 174; [2003] I.C.R. 337; [2003] I.R.L.R. 285;
    (2003) 147 S.J.L.B. 268; *Times*, March 4, 2003, HL (NI); affirming [2001]
    I.R.L.R. 520, CA (NI) . . . . *Digested*, 03/**4767**:
                Applied, 03/1297, 05/1337: *Considered*, 04/1275, 05/1291
Shannon *v.* United Kingdom (6563/03), *Times*, October 12, 2005, ECHR
Shannon *v.* United Kingdom (Admissibility) (67537/01) [2005] Crim. L.R. 133, ECHR
Sharif *v.* Garrett & Co; *sub nom* Sharif *v.* Garret & Co [2001] EWCA Civ 1269; [2002]
    1 W.L.R. 3118; [2002] 3 All E.R. 195; [2002] Lloyd's Rep. I.R. 11; (2001) 151
    N.L.J. 1371, CA (Civ Div) . . . . *Digested*, 02/**947**:
                                      Applied, 05/957
Sharifee (t/a Cafe Flutist) *v.* Wood (Inspector of Taxes) [2004] S.T.C. (S.C.D.) 446, Sp
    Comm . . . . *Digested*, 05/**4090**
Sharkey *v.* De Cross (Inspector of Taxes); *sub nom* Sharkey *v.* De Croos (Inspector of
    Taxes) [2005] S.T.C. (S.C.D.) 336; [2005] S.T.I. 223, Sp Comm . . . . *Digested*, 05/**4164**
Sharman *v.* HM Coroner for Inner North London see R. (on the application of
    Sharman) *v.* HM Coroner for Inner North London
Sharratt *v.* London Central Bus Co Ltd (No.3) see Hollins *v.* Russell
Shaw *v.* Redbridge LBC [2005] EWHC 150; [2005] E.L.R. 320, QBD
Shaw *v.* Tofari (Unreported, March 17, 2005), CC (Reading) [*Ex rel.* Colin Nugent,
    Barrister, Hardwicke Building, New Square, Lincoln's Inn, London] . . . . *Digested*, 05/**3197**
Shaw (Inspector of Taxes) *v.* Vicky Construction Ltd; *sub nom* Vicky Construction Ltd *v.*
    Shaw (Inspector of Taxes) [2002] EWHC 2659; [2002] S.T.C. 1544; 75 T.C.
    26; [2003] B.T.C. 68; [2002] S.T.I. 1689; *Times*, December 27, 2002, Ch D . . . . *Digested*, 03/**4251**:
                            Applied, 05/4036: *Considered*, 05/4017
Shawnee Processors Inc *v.* Granadex SA see Camilla Cotton Oil Co *v.* Granadex SA
Shaws (EAL) Ltd *v.* Pennycook see Pennycook *v.* Shaws (EAL) Ltd
Shawton Engineering Ltd *v.* DGP International Ltd [2003] EWCA Civ 1956; [2004]
    C.P. Rep. 23, CA (Civ Div) . . . . *Digested*, 05/**492**
Sheffield City Council *v.* E; *sub nom* E (Alleged Patient), Re [2004] EWHC 2808;
    [2005] Fam. 326; [2005] 2 W.L.R. 953; [2005] 1 F.L.R. 965; [2005] Lloyd's
    Rep. Med. 223; [2005] Fam. Law 279; (2005) 102(9) L.S.G. 30; *Times*,
    January 20, 2005, Fam Div . . . . *Applied*, 05/**1673**

Sheffield City Council *v.* Smart; *sub nom* Smart *v.* Sheffield City Council; Wilson *v.* Central Sunderland Housing Co; Central Sunderland Housing Co Ltd *v.* Wilson [2002] EWCA Civ 4; [2002] H.L.R. 34; [2002] B.L.G.R. 467; [2002] A.C.D. 56; (2002) 99(11) L.S.G. 36; [2002] N.P.C. 15; *Times*, February 20, 2002; *Independent*, February 1, 2002, CA (Civ Div) . . . .   *Digested*, 02/**2353**:
Applied, 03/2079: *Considered*, 03/2786, 05/190: *Followed*, 02/3060
Sheikh *v.* Law Society [2005] EWHC 1409; [2005] 4 All E.R. 717; (2005) 102(30) L.S.G. 30; (2005) 155 N.L.J. 1095, Ch D . . . .   *Digested*, 05/**2730**
Shekar *v.* Satyam Computer Services Ltd [2005] I.C.R. 737, EAT. . . . .   *Digested*, 05/**1210**
Sheldrake *v.* DPP; Attorney General's Reference (No.4 of 2002), Re [2004] UKHL 43; [2005] 1 A.C. 264; [2004] 3 W.L.R. 976; [2005] 1 All E.R. 237; [2005] 1 Cr. App. R. 28; (2004) 168 J.P. 669; [2005] R.T.R. 2; [2004] H.R.L.R. 44; [2005] U.K.H.R.R. 1; 17 B.H.R.C. 339; [2005] Crim. L.R. 215; (2005) 169 J.P.N. 19; (2004) 101 (43) L.S.G. 33; (2004) 148 S.J.L.B. 1216; *Times*, October 15, 2004, HL; reversing [2003] EWHC 273; [2004] Q.B. 487; [2003] 2 W.L.R. 1629; [2003] 2 All E.R. 497; [2003] 2 Cr. App. R. 14; (2003) 167 J.P. 333; [2004] R.T.R. 3; (2003) 167 J.P.N. 514; (2003) 100(13) L.S.G. 29; *Times*, February 25, 2003, QBD (Admin) . . . .   *Digested*, 04/**707**:
Applied, 03/1692, 05/780: *Approved*, 04/737: *Previous proceedings*, 03/812
Shell Tankers UK Ltd *v.* Dawson see Shell Tankers UK Ltd *v.* Jeromson
Shell Tankers UK Ltd *v.* Jeromson; *sub nom* Jeromson *v.* Shell Tankers UK Ltd; Dawson *v.* Cherry Tree Machine Co Ltd; Cherry Tree Machine Co Ltd *v.* Dawson; Shell Tankers UK Ltd *v.* Dawson [2001] EWCA Civ 101; [2001] I.C.R. 1223; [2001] P.I.Q.R. P19; *Times*, March 2, 2001; *Daily Telegraph*, February 27, 2001, CA (Civ Div) . . . .   *Digested*, 01/**4492**:
Considered, 05/2864
Shelley Films Ltd *v.* Rex Features Ltd [1994] E.M.L.R. 134, Ch D . . . .   *Considered*, 05/2812
Shendish Manor Ltd *v.* Customs and Excise Commissioners [2004] V. & D.R. 64, V&DTr (London) . . . .   *Digested*, 05/**4413**
Shepherd *v.* Revenue and Customs Commissioners [2005] S.T.C. (S.C.D.) 644, Sp Comm
Sheriff *v.* Klyne Tugs (Lowestoft) Ltd [1999] I.C.R. 1170; [1999] I.R.L.R. 481; (1999) 96(27) L.S.G. 34; (1999) 143 S.J.L.B. 189; *Times*, July 8, 1999, CA (Civ Div) . .   *Digested*, 99/**2056**:
Applied, 01/4494, 05/1316: *Considered*, 03/1293, 04/1277:
Distinguished, 00/575
Sherlock & Neal Ltd *v.* Customs and Excise Commissioners [2005] S.T.I. 114, V&DTr
Sherman *v.* Kastner see Kastner *v.* Jason
Sherrington *v.* Sherrington [2005] EWCA Civ 326; [2005] 3 F.C.R. 538; [2005] W.T.L.R. 587; (2004-05) 7 I.T.E.L.R. 711; (2005) 102(19) L.S.G. 34; (2005) 149 S.J.L.B. 392; *Times*, March 24, 2005, CA (Civ Div); reversing [2004] EWHC 1613; [2004] W.T.L.R. 895; (2004-05) 7 I.T.E.L.R. 96, Ch D . . . .   *Digested*, 05/**3980**
Shevill *v.* Presse Alliance SA [1996] A.C. 959; [1996] 3 W.L.R. 420; [1996] 3 All E.R. 929; [1996] I.L.Pr. 798; [1996] E.M.L.R. 533; (1996) 93(38) L.S.G. 42; (1996) 140 S.J.L.B. 208; *Times*, July 26, 1996, HL; affirming [1992] 2 W.L.R. 1; [1992] 1 All E.R. 409; [1991] I.L.Pr. 568; *Times*, March 13, 1991; *Independent*, March 13, 1991; *Financial Times*, March 20, 1991, CA (Civ Div) . . . .   *Digested*, 96/**1083**:
Applied, 05/974: *Considered*, 05/5046: *Distinguished*, 98/748:
Followed, 01/1835: *Previous proceedings*, 95/3127:
Subsequent proceedings, 95/3127
Shibi *v.* Sithole see Bhe *v.* Magistrate of Khayelitsha
Shiblaq *v.* Sadikoglu (Application to Set Aside) (No.1) [2003] EWHC 2128; [2005] 2 C.L.C. 380, QBD (Comm)
Shiblaq *v.* Sadikoglu (Application to Set Aside) (No.2) [2004] EWHC 1890; [2004] 2 All E.R. (Comm) 596; [2004] C.P. Rep. 41; [2005] 2 C.L.C. 380; [2004] I.L.Pr. 51, QBD (Comm) . . . .   *Digested*, 04/**411**
Shield Mark BV *v.* Kist (t/a Memex) (C283/01) [2004] Ch. 97; [2004] 2 W.L.R. 1117; [2004] All E.R. (EC) 277; [2003] E.C.R. I-14313; [2005] 1 C.M.L.R. 41; [2004] C.E.C. 228; [2004] E.T.M.R. 33; [2004] R.P.C. 17; *Times*, December 4, 2003, ECJ (6th Chamber) [2003] E.T.M.R. 64, AGO . . . .   *Digested*, 04/**2420**
Shierson *v.* Rastogi; *sub nom* RBG Resources Plc, Re [2002] EWCA Civ 1624; [2003] 1 W.L.R. 586; [2002] B.C.C. 1005; [2003] B.P.I.R. 148; (2003) 100(2) L.S.G. 31; *Times*, November 20, 2002; *Independent*, November 13, 2002, CA (Civ Div); affirming [2002] EWHC 1612, Ch D . . . .   *Digested*, 02/**2687**:
Applied, 05/2302
Shierson *v.* Vlieland-Boddy [2005] EWCA Civ 974; [2005] 1 W.L.R. 3966; [2005] B.C.C. 949; [2005] B.P.I.R. 1170; *Times*, September 26, 2005, CA (Civ Div); reversing [2004] EWHC 2752; [2005] B.C.C. 416, Ch D . . . .   *Digested*, 05/**2293**
Shiloh Spinners Ltd *v.* Harding [1973] A.C. 691; [1973] 2 W.L.R. 28; [1973] 1 All E.R. 90; (1973) 25 P. & C.R. 48; (1972) 117 S.J. 34, HL; reversing [1972] Ch. 326; [1971] 3 W.L.R. 34; [1971] 2 All E.R. 307; (1971) 22 P. & C.R. 447; 115 S.J. 248, CA (Civ Div) . . . .   *Digested*, 73/**1867**:
Applied, 85/1878, 99/3290: *Considered*, 74/2023, 81/1503, 83/421, 83/3405, 84/1326, 84/1901, 84/1931, 86/1841, 87/2959, 89/2126, 89/2128, 91/2226, 91/2232, 97/3293, 00/2326, 05/3793: *Distinguished*, 00/4658

Shilton v. Wilmshurst (Inspector of Taxes) [1991] 1 A.C. 684; [1991] 2 W.L.R. 530;
[1991] 3 All E.R. 148; [1991] S.T.C. 88; 64 T.C. 78; (1991) 135 S.J. 250; *Times,*
February 13, 1991; *Independent,* February 20, 1991; *Financial Times,* February 12,
1991; *Guardian,* February 12, 1991, HL; reversing [1990] 1 W.L.R. 373; [1990]
S.T.C. 55; (1990) 87(4) L.S.G. 43; (1990) 134 S.J. 50, CA (Civ Div); affirming
[1989] 1 W.L.R.179; [1988] S.T.C. 868; (1988) 132 S.J. 1755, Ch D . . . . *Digested,* 91/**2092**:
Applied, 93/2275, 99/4729, 05/4071
Shine v. English Churches Housing Group see English Churches Housing Group v.
Shine
Shinedean Ltd v. Alldown Demolition (London) Ltd (In Liquidation) [2005] EWHC
2319; [2005] 2 C.L.C.1159, QBD (TCC)
Shirayama Shokusan Co Ltd v. Danovo Ltd (No.2) [2004] EWHC 390; [2004] 1
W.L.R. 2985; (2004) 101(13) L.S.G. 34; *Times,* March 22, 2004, Ch D . . . . . . *Digested,* 05/**985**
Shirayama Shokusan Co Ltd v. Danovo Ltd (No.3) [2004] EWHC 2288; [2005] L. &
T.R.15, Ch D
Shirayama Shokusan Co Ltd v. Danovo Ltd (No.4) [2005] EWHC 2589; [2005] 44
E.G.C.S.134, Ch D
Shofman v. Russia (74826/01) [2005] 3 F.C.R. 581, ECHR
Short v. Birmingham City Council [2004] EWHC 2112; [2005] H.L.R. 6, QBD . . . . *Digested,* 05/**321**
Shove (Inspector of Taxes) v. Lingfield Park 1991 Ltd; *sub nom* Lingfield Park (1991) Ltd
v. Shove (Inspector of Taxes) [2004] EWCA Civ 391; [2004] S.T.C. 805; 76
T.C. 363; [2005] B.T.C. 89; [2004] S.T.I. 987; (2004) 101(18) L.S.G. 35;
(2004) 148 S.J.L.B. 537; *Times,* April 26, 2004; *Independent,* April 20, 2004,
CA (Civ Div); affirming [2003] EWHC 1684; [2003] S.T.C. 1003; [2003] B.T.C.
422; [2003] S.T.I.1146; (2003) 100(35) L.S.G. 38; *Times,* August 11, 2003,
Ch D . . . . *Digested,* 04/**3691**:
Distinguished, 05/5691
Showboat Entertainment Centre v. Owens [1984] 1 W.L.R. 384; [1984] 1 All E.R. 836;
[1984] I.C.R. 65; [1984] I.R.L.R. 7; (1983) 80 L.S.G. 3002; (1984) 134 N.L.J.
37; (1984) 128 S.J.152, EAT . . . . *Digested,* 83/**1265**:
Applied, 05/1290: *Considered,* 92/1955, 98/2180
Shruth Ltd (In Liquidation), Re see International Brands USA Inc v. Goldstein
Shuttari v. Solicitors Indemnity Fund [2005] B.P.I.R.1004, Ch D
Shuttleworth v. Secretary of State for Trade and Industry see Dawes & Henderson
(Agencies) Ltd (In Liquidation) (No.2), Re
SHV Gas Supply & Trading SAS v. Naftomar Shipping & Trading Co Ltd Inc (The Azur
Gaz) [2005] EWHC 2528; [2005] 2 C.L.C. 815, QBD (Comm)
SIAC Construction Ltd v. National Roads Authority [2005] Eu. L.R. 65, HC (Irl)
SIB International Srl v. Metallgesellschaft Corp (The Noel Bay) [1989] 1 Lloyd's Rep.
361, CA (Civ Div) . . . . *Digested,* 90/**4121**:
Distinguished, 05/3790
Sidabras v. Lithuania (55480/2000). . . . . *Considered,* 05/190
Siebe Gorman & Co Ltd v. Barclays Bank Ltd; *sub nom* Siebe Gorman & Co Ltd v. RH
McDonald Ltd [1979] 2 Lloyd's Rep.142, Ch D . . . . *Digested,* 79/**169**:
Applied, 01/732: *Considered,* 88/325, 93/2331, 00/3483, 04/227, 05/2324:
Distinguished, 88/306: *Overruled,* 05/2320
Siebe Gorman & Co Ltd v. RH McDonald Ltd see Siebe Gorman & Co Ltd v. Barclays
Bank Ltd
Sieckmann v. Deutsches Patent- und Markenamt (C273/00) [2003] Ch. 487; [2003]
3 W.L.R. 424; [2004] All E.R. (EC) 253; [2002] E.C.R. I-11737; [2005] 1
C.M.L.R. 40; [2004] C.E.C. 404; [2003] E.T.M.R. 37; [2003] R.P.C. 38; *Times,*
December 27, 2002, ECJ [2002] E.C.R. I-11737, AGO . . . . *Digested,* 03/**2637**:
Applied, 04/2370, 05/2536: *Considered,* 04/2420
Sieff v. Fox; *sub nom* Bedford Estates, Re [2005] EWHC 1312; [2005] 1 W.L.R. 3811;
[2005] 3 All E.R. 693; [2005] B.T.C. 452; [2005] W.T.L.R. 891; (2005-06) 8
I.T.E.L.R. 93; [2005] N.P.C. 80, Ch D . . . . *Digested,* 05/**4304**
Siemens AG Osterreich v. Hauptverband der Osterreichischen Sozialversicherungstrager
(C314/01) [2004] E.C.R. I-2549; [2004] 2 C.M.L.R. 27, ECJ (6th Chamber) . . *Digested,* 05/**3352**
Sieminska v. Poland (37602/97) (Unreported, March 29, 2001), ECHR . . . . *Considered,* 05/34
Significant Ltd v. Farrel (Inspector of taxes) [2005] S.T.I.1097, Ch D
Sigurdsson v. Iceland (39731/98) (2005) 40 E.H.R.R.15, ECHR . . . . *Digested,* 05/**2103**
Sigurthor Arnarsson v. Iceland (44671/98) (2004) 39 E.H.R.R. 20, ECHR . . . . *Digested,* 05/**2095**
Sihra's Trade Mark Application (No.2028015) see Intel Corp v. Sihra
Silk v. Fletcher (Inspector of Taxes) [2000] S.T.C. (S.C.D.) 565; [2000] S.T.I. 1655, Sp
Comm . . . . *Digested,* 01/**5299**:
Considered, 05/4103
Sillars v. Inland Revenue Commissioners [2004] S.T.C. (S.C.D.) 180; [2004] W.T.L.R.
591; [2004] S.T.I. 900; (2004) 148 S.J.L.B. 536, Sp Comm . . . . *Digested,* 05/**4118**
Sillitoe v. McGraw-Hill Book Co (UK) Ltd [1983] F.S.R. 545; *Times,* January 18, 1982,
Ch D . . . . *Digested,* 83/**494**:
Applied, 05/2420: *Considered,* 97/1055: *Distinguished,* 95/860
Silver v. General Medical Council [2003] UKPC 33; [2003] Lloyd's Rep. Med. 333;
Times, May 9, 2003, PC (UK) . . . . *Digested,* 03/**1726**:
Disapproved, 05/1802

Simkin's Trustees *v.* Inland Revenue Commissioner; *sub nom* Trustees in the CB Simkin Trust *v.* Inland Revenue Commissioner [2004] UKPC 55; [2005] S.T.C. 268; [2005] F.S.R. 18; [2005] S.T.I. 96; (2005) 149 S.J.L.B. 57, PC (NZ) . . . . *Digested,* 05/**3991**

Simmon Box (Diamonds) Ltd, Re see Cohen *v.* Selby

Simmons *v.* Dresden [2004] EWHC 993; 97 Con. L.R. 81, QBD (TCC) . . . . *Digested,* 05/**2682**

Simmons *v.* First Secretary of State; *sub nom* First Secretary of State *v.* Simmons [2005] EWCA Civ 1295; (2005) 149 S.J.L.B. 1354; [2005] N.P.C. 127, CA (Civ Div); reversing [2005] EWHC 287; [2005] 2 P. & C.R. 25; [2005] 3 P.L.R. 87; (2005) 149 S.J.L.B. 356; [2005] N.P.C. 33; *Times,* April 15, 2005, QBD (Admin) . . . . *Digested,* 05/**3297**

Simmons *v.* Mole Valley DC [2004] EWHC 475; [2004] B.P.I.R. 1022, Ch D . . . . *Digested,* 05/**2271**

Simms *v.* Law Society [2005] EWCA Civ 849; [2005] A.C.D. 98; (2005) 155 N.L.J. 1124; *Independent,* July 14, 2005, CA (Civ Div); reversing in part [2004] EWHC 1706, Ch D . . . . *Digested,* 05/**2728**

Simplex GE (Holdings) Ltd *v.* Secretary of State for the Environment (1989) 57 P. & C.R. 306; [1988] 3 P.L.R. 25; [1988] J.P.L. 809; [1988] E.G.C.S. 65; *Times,* June 2, 1988; *Daily Telegraph,* May 13, 1988, CA (Civ Div) . . . . *Digested,* 89/**3578**: *Applied,* 01/4728, 02/3726, 05/3307: *Considered,* 99/4230

Simpson *v.* Lilburn see Ministry of Health *v.* Simpson

Simpson *v.* Norwest Holst Southern Ltd [1980] 1 W.L.R. 968; [1980] 2 All E.R. 471; 124 S.J. 313, CA (Civ Div) . . . . *Digested,* 80/**1682**: *Applied,* 86/1996, 05/439: *Referred to,* 90/2961

Simpson *v.* Prescott Thomas Ltd (Unreported, February 25, 2005), CC (Barnet) [*Ex rel.* Joanna Kerr, Barrister, Lamb Chambers, Lamb Building, Temple, London] . . . *Digested,* 05/**3171**

Simutenkov *v.* Ministerio de Educacion y Cultura (C265/03) [2005] E.C.R. I-2579; [2005] 2 C.M.L.R. 11, ECJ

Sinai Securities Ltd *v.* Hooper; *sub nom* Rosshill Properties Ltd (In Administration), Re [2003] EWHC 910; [2004] B.C.C. 973; [2004] 2 B.C.L.C. 575, Ch D . . . . *Digested,* 05/**2298**

Sinclair *v.* Woods of Winchester Ltd [2005] EWHC 1631; 102 Con. L.R. 127, QBD

Sinclair Gardens Investments (Kensington) Ltd *v.* Lands Tribunal see R. (on the application of Sinclair Gardens Investments (Kensington) Ltd) *v.* Lands Tribunal

Sinclair Gardens Investments (Kensington) Ltd *v.* Oak Investments RTM Co Ltd [2005] R.V.R. 426, Lands Tr

Sinclair Gardens Investments (Kensington) Ltd *v.* Walsh see Escalus Properties Ltd *v.* Robinson

Sinclair Roche & Temperley *v.* Heard (No.1) [2004] I.R.L.R. 763, EAT . . . . *Digested,* 05/**1274**: *Applied,* 05/1292

Sinclair (Alvin Lee) *v.* HM Advocate [2005] UKPC D2; 2005 S.C. (P.C.) 28; 2005 S.L.T. 553; 2005 S.C.C.R. 446; [2005] H.R.L.R. 26; 18 B.H.R.C. 527; 2005 G.W.D. 17-306; *Times,* June 1, 2005, PC (Sc); reversing 2004 S.L.T. 794; 2004 S.C.C.R. 499; 2004 G.W.D. 23-503, HCJ . . . . *Digested,* 05/**5136**

Sindicato de Medicos de Asistencia Publica (SIMAP) *v.* Conselleria de Sanidad y Consumo de la Generalidad Valenciana (C303/98) [2001] All E.R. (EC) 609; [2000] E.C.R. I-7963; [2001] 3 C.M.L.R. 42; [2001] I.C.R. 1116; [2000] I.R.L.R. 845; *Times,* October 18, 2000, ECJ . . . . *Digested,* 00/**2716**: *Considered,* 05/1275: *Followed,* 04/1316

Singh (Balwinder) *v.* Secretary of State for the Home Department [2001] EWHC Admin 925, QBD (Admin) . . . . *Distinguished,* 05/**2222**

Singh (Jagdeo) *v.* Trinidad and Tobago [2005] UKPC 35; [2005] 4 All E.R. 781, PC (Trin) . . . . *Digested,* 05/**802**

Singh (Pawandeep) *v.* Entry Clearance Officer, New Delhi [2004] EWCA Civ 1075; [2005] Q.B. 608; [2005] 2 W.L.R. 325; [2005] 1 F.L.R. 308; [2004] 3 F.C.R. 72; [2004] Imm. A.R. 672; [2004] I.N.L.R. 515; [2005] Fam. Law 9; (2004) 101 (36) L.S.G. 33; *Times,* September 15, 2004; *Independent,* October 6, 2004, CA (Civ Div) . . . . *Digested,* 04/**2067**

Singh (Ravinder Mehat) *v.* HM Advocate 2004 S.C.C.R. 651, HCJ . . . . *Digested,* 05/**750**

Sinn Fein's Application for Judicial Review, Re [2005] N.I. 412, QBD (NI)

Sintesi SpA *v.* Autorita per la Vigilanza sui Lavori Pubblici (C247/02) [2004] E.C.R. I-9215; [2005] 1 C.M.L.R. 12; [2004] C.E.C. 465, ECJ (2nd Chamber)

Siomab SA *v.* Institut Bruxellois pour la Gestion de l'Environnement (IBGE) (C472/02) [2004] E.C.R. I-9971; [2005] Env. L.R. D2, ECJ

Siplast SA *v.* Delbouw Roermond BV [2005] I.L.Pr. 6, HR (NL)

Siporex Trade SA *v.* Banque Indosuez [1986] 2 Lloyd's Rep. 146, QBD (Comm) . . . . *Digested,* 86/**168**: *Applied,* 01/379: *Considered,* 90/269, 91/256: *Distinguished,* 05/703

Sirius International Insurance Co (Publ) *v.* FAI General Insurance Ltd; *sub nom* Sirius International Insurance Corp Ltd *v.* FAI General Insurance Co Ltd [2004] UKHL 54; [2004] 1 W.L.R. 3251; [2005] 1 All E.R. 191; [2005] 1 All E.R. (Comm) 117; [2005] 1 Lloyd's Rep. 461; [2005] 1 C.L.C. 451; [2005] Lloyd's Rep. I.R. 294; (2004) 101 (48) L.S.G. 25; (2004) 148 S.J.L.B. 1435; *Times,* December 3, 2004, HL; reversing [2003] EWCA Civ 470; [2003] 1 W.L.R. 2214; [2004] 1 All E.R. 308; [2003] 1 All E.R. (Comm) 865; [2003] 1 C.L.C. 1124; [2004] Lloyd's Rep. I.R. 47; (2003) 147 S.J.L.B. 477, CA (Civ Div); reversing in part [2002] EWHC 1611; [2003] 1 W.L.R. 87; [2002] 2 All E.R. (Comm) 745; (2002) 99(39) L.S.G. 37; *Times,* August 26, 2002, Ch D (Companies Ct) . . . . *Digested,* 05/**475**

Sirius International Insurance Corp Ltd v. FAI General Insurance Co Ltd see Sirius International Insurance Co (Publ) v. FAI General Insurance Ltd
Sison v. Council of the European Union (T110/03) [2005] 2 C.M.L.R. 29, CFI (2nd Chamber) .... *Digested*, 05/**1425**
Sisu Capital Fund Ltd v. Tucker (Costs); Sisu Capital Fund Ltd v. Wallace [2005] EWHC 2321; (2005) 155 N.L.J. 1686; *Times*, November 4, 2005, Ch D (Companies Ct)
Sisu Capital Fund Ltd v. Wallace see Sisu Capital Fund Ltd v. Tucker (Costs)
Sivanandan v. Enfield LBC; *sub nom* Enfield LBC v. Sivanandan [2005] EWCA Civ 10; (2005) 102(8) L.S.G. 30; *Times*, January 25, 2005, CA (Civ Div); reversing [2004] EWHC 672, QBD. .... *Digested*, 05/**1316**
Sivasubramaniam v. Wandsworth County Court see R. (on the application of Sivasubramaniam) v. Wandsworth County Court
Siwek v. Inland Revenue Commissioners (Application to Set Aside Decision) [2005] S.T.C. (S.C.D.) 163; [2004] S.T.I. 2503, Sp Comm .... *Digested*, 05/**418**
Siwek v. Inland Revenue Commissioners (Notice of Determination) [2004] S.T.C. (S.C.D.) 493; [2004] S.T.I. 2258, Sp Comm .... *Digested*, 05/**4099**
SK (An Adult) (Forced Marriage: Appropriate Relief), Re; *sub nom* SK (Proposed Plaintiff), Re [2004] EWHC 3202; [2005] 3 All E.R. 421; [2005] 2 F.L.R. 230; [2005] 2 F.C.R. 459; [2005] Fam. Law 460, Fam Div .... *Digested*, 05/**1667**
SK (CICA: Quantum: 2001), Re [2005] 2 Q.R. 7, CICA (London) [*Ex rel.* Geoffrey Mott, Barrister, Renaissance Chambers, Gray's Inn, London] .... *Digested*, 04/**2864**
SK (Proposed Plaintiff), Re see SK (An Adult) (Forced Marriage: Appropriate Relief), Re
Skelly's Application for Judicial Review, Re [2005] N.I. 135, QBD (NI)
Skiggs v. South West Trains Ltd [2005] I.R.L.R. 459, EAT. .... *Digested*, 05/**1309**
Skinner v. DPP [2004] EWHC 2914; [2005] R.T.R. 17, QBD (Admin) .... *Digested*, 05/**740**
Skinner v. Scottish Ambulance Service 2004 S.C. 790; 2004 S.L.T. 834; [2005] Eu. L.R. 54; 2004 Rep. L.R. 103; 2004 G.W.D. 23-498, IH (Ex Div); reversing 2004 G.W.D. 9-196, OH .... *Digested*, 04/**4903**
Skipper v. Perry (Unreported, March 27, 1995), CC (Evesham) [*Ex rel.* Tayntons, Solicitors] .... *Digested*, 95/**1627**:
Considered, 05/**2855**
Skreb v. PCO Stauereibetrieb Paetz & Co Nachfolgar GmbH (C138/91) see Katsikas v. Konstantinidis (C132/91)
Skupinski's Application, Re [2005] R.V.R. 269, Lands Tr
Skuse v. Granada Television Ltd [1996] E.M.L.R. 278; *Independent*, April 2, 1993, CA (Civ Div). .... *Digested*, 93/**2584**:
Applied, 01/1830, 05/982: *Considered*, 02/953, 02/955: *Followed*, 95/3131
Skylight Maritime SA v. Ascot Underwriting Ltd [2005] EWHC 15; [2005] P.N.L.R. 25; (2005) 155 N.L.J. 139, QBD (Comm) .... *Digested*, 05/**489**
SL (Adoption: Home in Jurisdiction), Re [2004] EWHC 1283; [2005] 1 F.L.R. 118; [2004] Fam. Law 860, Fam Div. .... *Digested*, 05/**1670**
Slamon v. Planchon [2004] EWCA Civ 799; [2005] Ch. 142; [2005] 2 W.L.R. 257; [2004] 4 All E.R. 407; [2004] H.L.R. 55; [2005] L. & T.R. 8; (2004) 148 S.J.L.B. 822; *Times*, July 28, 2004, CA (Civ Div) .... *Digested*, 04/**3228**
Slater v. General Commissioners of Income Tax for Beacontree (No.2) see Slater Ltd v. Beacontree General Commissioners (No.2)
Slater Ltd v. Beacontree General Commissioners (No.1) [2002] S.T.C. 246; 74 T.C. 471; [2002] B.T.C. 42; [2001] S.T.I. 1699; (2002) 99(6) L.S.G. 31; *Times*, December 18, 2001, Ch D .... *Digested*, 02/**4506**:
Applied, 05/4031
Slater Ltd v. Beacontree General Commissioners (No.2); *sub nom* Slater Ltd v. Inland Revenue Commissioners; Salter Ltd v. Inland Revenue Commissioners; Slater v. General Commissioners of Income Tax for Beacontree (No.2) [2002] EWHC 2676; [2004] S.T.C. 1342; [2004] B.T.C. 398; [2002] S.T.I. 1539, Ch D .... *Digested*, 05/**4031**
Slater Ltd v. Inland Revenue Commissioners see Slater Ltd v. Beacontree General Commissioners (No.2)
Slavic University in Bulgaria v. Bulgaria (Admissibility) (60781/00) (2005) 40 E.H.R.R. SE13, ECHR
Sleebush v. Gordon [2004] EWHC 2287; [2005] 1 P. & C.R. DG6, Ch D
SLEPIAN/Cellular therapy (T611/01) [2005] E.P.O.R. 15, EPO (Technical Bd App) .... *Digested*, 05/**2474**
Slough BC v. C [2004] EWHC 1759; [2005] B.L.G.R. 368; [2004] E.L.R. 546; [2005] A.C.D. 9; (2004) 101(34) L.S.G. 30; *Times*, August 27, 2004, QBD (Admin) .... *Digested*, 04/**1085**
SM v. Secretary of State for the Home Department; *sub nom* SM (Section 8: Judge's Process: Iran), Re [2005] UKIAT 116; [2005] Imm. A.R. 673, IAT
SM Goldstein & Co (Pty) Ltd v. Cathkin Park Hotel (Pty) Ltd [2004] B.L.R. 369, Sup Ct (SA). .... *Digested*, 05/**2846**
SM (Section 8: Judge's Process: Iran), Re see SM v. Secretary of State for the Home Department
Small (Inspector of Taxes) v. Mars UK Ltd see Mars UK Ltd v. Small (Inspector of Taxes)

Smalley, Re; *sub nom* Smalley *v.* Warwick Crown Court; R. *v.* Warwick Crown Court Ex
    p. Smalley (No.1) [1985] A.C. 622; [1985] 2 W.L.R. 538; [1985] 1 All E.R.
    769; (1985) 80 Cr. App. R. 205; (1985) 149 J.P. 319; [1985] Crim. L.R. 371;
    (1985) 82 L.S.G. 1638; (1985) 135 N.L.J. 229; (1985) 129 S.J. 172, HL;
    reversing (1984) 148 J.P. 708, DC .... *Digested*, 85/**555**:
                                    Applied, 86/604, 86/625, 87/599, 88/587, 92/33, 92/39, 93/12, 93/15,
                                    05/71: *Considered*, 87/2282, 90/766, 91/613, 93/10, 93/1082, 93/2556,
                                    95/3098: *Distinguished*, 93/11: *Followed*, 93/14
Smalley *v.* Warwick Crown Court see Smalley, Re
Smallwood *v.* Revenue and Customs Commissioners [2005] S.T.I. 1998, Sp Comm
Smart *v.* East Cheshire NHS Trust [2003] EWHC 2806; [2004] 1 Costs L.R. 124;
    (2004) 80 B.M.L.R. 175, QBD .... *Followed*, 05/**327**
Smart *v.* Sheffield City Council see Sheffield City Council *v.* Smart
Smirnova (Irina) *v.* Russia (48183/99) see Smirnova (Yelena) *v.* Russia
Smirnova (Yelena) *v.* Russia (46133/99); Smirnova (Irina) *v.* Russia (48183/99)
    (2004) 39 E.H.R.R. 22, ECHR .... *Digested*, 05/**2110**
Smith *v.* AJ Morrisroes & Sons Ltd; JJ Cafferkey & Co Ltd *v.* Byrne; Wiggins *v.* North
    Yorkshire CC; McNulty *v.* PC Harrinton Ltd [2005] I.C.R. 596; [2005] I.R.L.R.
    72, EAT. .... *Digested*, 05/**1211**
Smith *v.* Charles Building Services Ltd A3/2005/1075, CA (Civ Div); affirming [2005]
    EWHC 654; [2005] B.C.C. 513, Ch D .... *Digested*, 05/**534**
Smith *v.* Cherry Lewis Ltd (In Receivership); Moore *v.* Cherry Lewis Ltd (In
    Receivership) [2005] I.R.L.R. 86, EAT............................. *Digested*, 05/**1287**
Smith *v.* Clerical Medical and General Life Assurance Society [1993] 1 F.L.R. 47;
    [1992] F.C.R. 262, CA (Civ Div) .... *Digested*, 93/**4137**:
                                    Applied, 04/3194: *Considered*, 05/3969
Smith *v.* First Secretary of State; Smith *v.* Mid-Bedfordshire DC [2005] EWCA Civ
    859; (2005) 102(31) L.S.G. 28; (2005) 149 S.J.L.B. 295; [2005] N.P.C. 99, CA
    (Civ Div); reversing [2004] EWHC 2583, QBD (Admin)
Smith *v.* Havering LBC [2004] EWHC 599; [2004] E.L.R. 629, QBD .... *Digested*, 05/**1140**
Smith *v.* Hughes see Cranfield *v.* Bridgegrove Ltd
Smith *v.* Jenkins (Unreported, March 9, 2004), CC (Salford) [*Ex rel.* Jonathan
    Thompson, Barrister, King Street Chambers, 8, King Street, Manchester] ...... *Digested*, 05/**3161**
Smith *v.* Malvern Hills DC [2005] P.A.D. 2, Planning Inspector
Smith *v.* Mid-Bedfordshire DC see Smith *v.* First Secretary of State
Smith *v.* Parole Board see R. (on the application of Smith) *v.* Parole Board
Smith *v.* Revenue and Customs Commissioners [2005] S.T.C. (S.C.D.) 772; [2005]
    S.T.I. 1634, Sp Comm
Smith *v.* Secretary of State for the Environment, Transport and the Regions; *sub nom*
    R. (on the application of Smith) *v.* Secretary of State for the Environment,
    Transport and Regions [2003] EWCA Civ 262; [2003] Env. L.R. 32; [2003] 2 P.
    & C.R. 11; [2003] J.P.L. 1316; (2003) 147 S.J.L.B. 298; [2003] N.P.C. 31;
    Independent, March 19, 2003, CA (Civ Div); affirming [2001] EWHC Admin
    1170; [2002] Env. L.R. D11, QBD (Admin) .... *Digested*, 03/**3420**:
                                    Applied, 04/3088, 05/3281, 05/3298: *Followed*, 04/3053
Smith *v.* Secretary of State for Work and Pensions see Smith *v.* Smith
Smith *v.* Sheridan [2005] EWHC 614; [2005] 2 F.C.R. 18, QBD
Smith *v.* Smith 1962 (3) S.A. 930 .... *Doubted*, 05/**1627**
Smith *v.* Smith; *sub nom* Smith *v.* Secretary of State for Work and Pensions [2004]
    EWCA Civ 1318; [2005] 1 W.L.R. 1318; [2005] 1 F.L.R. 606; [2005] Fam. Law
    204; (2004) 101(43) L.S.G. 34; *Times*, November 2, 2004; *Independent*,
    October 26, 2004, CA (Civ Div) .... *Digested*, 05/**1556**
Smith *v.* Thompson (Unreported, April 20, 2004), CC (Birmingham) [*Ex rel.* Adam
    Farrer, Barrister, 5, Fountain Court, Birmingham] .... *Digested*, 05/**3179**
Smith *v.* Titanate Ltd [2005] 2 E.G.L.R. 63; [2005] 20 E.G. 262, CC (Central
    London) .... *Digested*, 05/**2648**
Smith *v.* Tyne and Wear Autistic Society see Tyne and Wear Autistic Society *v.* Smith
Smith International Inc *v.* Specialised Petroleum Services Group Ltd (Permission to
    Appeal) [2005] EWCA Civ 1357; (2005) 102(48) L.S.G. 19; *Independent*,
    November 23, 2005, CA (Civ Div)
Smith (Letitia) *v.* Smith (Richard) [2000] 3 F.C.R. 374, CA (Civ Div) .... *Digested*, 00/**2519**:
                                    Considered, 05/1688
SMITHKLEIN BEECHAM CONSUMER HEALTHCARE/Toothbrush (T725/00) see
    SMITHKLINE BEECHAM CONSUMER HEALTHCARE/Toothbrush (T725/00)
SMITHKLINE BEECHAM CONSUMER HEALTHCARE/Toothbrush (T725/00); *sub nom*
    SMITHKLEIN BEECHAM CONSUMER HEALTHCARE/Toothbrush (T725/00)
    [2005] E.P.O.R. 2, EPO (Technical Bd App) .... *Digested*, 05/**2456**
Smithkline Beecham Plc *v.* Apotex (Reformulation of Claim) [2005] EWHC 1759;
    (2005) 28(10) I.P.D. 28078, Ch D (Patents Ct)
SmithKline Beecham Plc *v.* Apotex Europe Ltd see Apotex Europe Ltd *v.* SmithKline
    Beecham Plc
SmithKline Beecham Plc *v.* Apotex Europe Ltd [2005] EWHC 1655; [2005] F.S.R. 44;
    (2005) 28(10) I.P.D. 28077; *Times*, August 10, 2005, Ch D .... *Digested*, 05/**476**

SmithKline Beecham Plc *v.* Apotex Europe Ltd (Costs) (No.2) [2004] EWCA Civ 1703; [2005] 2 Costs L.R. 293; [2005] F.S.R. 24; *Times,* January 12, 2005, CA (Civ Div); reversing . . . . *Digested,* 05/**370**

Smithkline Beecham Plc *v.* Dowelhurst Ltd (Form of Reference to ECJ) see Boehringer Ingelheim KG *v.* Swingward Ltd (Form of Reference to ECJ)

SmithKline Beecham Plc *v.* H (A Child) see Horne-Roberts *v.* SmithKline Beecham Plc

Smithkline Beecham Plc *v.* Horne-Roberts see Horne-Roberts *v.* SmithKline Beecham Plc

SmithKline Beecham Plc's (Paroxetine Methanesulfonate) Patent (No.2) see Synthon BV *v.* SmithKline Beecham Plc (No.2)

Smiths Dock Ltd *v.* Edwards [2004] EWHC 1116; [2004] 3 Costs L.R. 440, QBD . . . . . *Digested,* 05/**2703**

SN *v.* Sweden (34209/96) (2004) 39 E.H.R.R. 13; [2002] Crim. L.R. 831, ECHR . . . . . *Digested,* 05/**2083**

Sniace SA *v.* Commission of the European Communities (T88/01) [2005] All E.R. (EC) 925; [2005] 3 C.M.L.R. 7; [2005] C.E.C. 808, CFI (5th Chamber)

Snook *v.* London and West Riding Investments Ltd [1967] 2 Q.B. 786; [1967] 2 W.L.R. 1020; [1967] 1 All E.R. 518; 111 S.J. 71, CA (Civ Div) . . . . *Digested,* 67/**1836**:
Applied, 99/4764, 00/3879, 01/5319, 04/3954: *Considered,* 84/1915, 87/2162, 88/2026, 88/2043, 89/2112, 89/2145: *Followed,* 99/2485, 02/5841, 05/4313

Snook *v.* Somerset CC [2005] 1 E.G.L.R. 147; [2004] R.V.R. 254, Lands Tr . . . . *Digested,* 05/**3257**

Snowden, Re; *sub nom* Shackleton *v.* Eddy Henderson; Henderson *v.* Attorney General; Snowden *v.* Eddy Henderson; Shackleton *v.* Methodist Missionary Society; Henderson, Re [1970] Ch. 700; [1969] 3 W.L.R. 273; [1969] 3 All E.R. 208; 113 S.J. 545, Ch D . . . . *Digested,* 69/**344**:
Considered, 05/241

Snowden *v.* Eddy Henderson see Snowden, Re

Soar *v.* Ashwell [1893] 2 Q.B. 390, CA . . . . *Applied,* 47-51/1281, 47-51/1335, 05/2325

Social Security Commissioner's Decision (R (IS) 12/99), Re Unreported, SS Comm . . . *Explained,* 05/3883

Societe Brasserie Fischer SA *v.* Societe Interbrew France SAS [2005] E.T.M.R. 65, C d'A (Paris)

Societe Colas Est *v.* France (37971/97) (2004) 39 E.H.R.R. 17, ECHR . . . . *Digested,* 05/**2116**

Societe Commerciale des Potasses et de l'Azote (SCPA) *v.* Commission of the European Communities (C30/95) see France *v.* Commission of the European Communities (C68/94)

Societe d'Investissements Financiers Industriels et Miniers (SOFEMI) *v.* Comilog SA [2005] E.C.C. 20, Cass (F)

Societe des Participants du Commissariat a l'Energie Atomique SA (SPCEA) *v.* Greenpeace France [2005] E.T.M.R. 78, Trib Gde Inst (Paris)

Societe des Produits Nestle SA *v.* Mars Inc (R 0506/2003-2) [2005] E.T.M.R. 37, OHIM (2nd Bd App) . . . . *Digested,* 05/**2554**

Societe des Produits Nestle SA *v.* Mars UK Ltd (C353/03) [2005] 3 C.M.L.R. 12; [2005] E.T.M.R. 96; (2005) 28(10) I.P.D. 28071; *Times,* July 20, 2005, ECJ (2nd Chamber)

Societe Financiere et Industrielle du Peloux *v.* Axa Belgium (C112/03) [2005] 2 All E.R. (Comm) 419; [2005] E.C.R. I-3707; [2005] I.L.Pr. 32, ECJ . . . . *Digested,* 05/**2368**

Societe Generale SA *v.* Montaurier [2005] E.C.C. 37, Cass (F)

Societe GPS, Re [2005] I.L.Pr. 48, Cass (F)

Societe Italiana Dragaggi SpA *v.* Ministero delle Infrastrutture e dei Trasporti (C117/03) [2005] E.C.R. I-167; [2005] 2 C.M.L.R. 56; [2005] Env. L.R. 31, ECJ (2nd Chamber)

Societe Nationale Industrielle Aerospatiale (SNIA) *v.* Lee Kui Jak [1987] A.C. 871; [1987] 3 W.L.R. 59; [1987] 3 All E.R. 510; (1987) 84 L.S.G. 2048, PC (Bru) . . . *Digested,* 87/**3024**:
Applied, 97/879, 97/4597, 98/757, 02/643, 04/573: *Considered,* 88/1620, 89/1729, 92/3516, 93/1978, 94/3708, 96/5344, 00/747, 02/641, 05/1623:
Distinguished, 95/4149: *Followed,* 88/2884, 89/381, 91/5405, 95/6052, 97/885

Societe Provencale d'Achat et de Gestion (SPAG) SA *v.* Office for Harmonisation in the Internal Market (Trade Marks and Designs) (OHIM) (T57/03) [2005] E.T.M.R. 116, CFI (2nd Chamber)

Society of Lloyd's *v.* Longtin [2005] EWHC 2491; [2005] 2 C.L.C. 774, QBD (Comm)

Society of Lloyd's *v.* Surman [2004] EWHC 2967; [2005] 2 C.L.C. 1119, Ch D

Socony Mobil Oil Co Inc *v.* West of England Shipowners Mutual Insurance Association (London) Ltd (The Padre Island) (No.2) see Firma C-Trade SA *v.* Newcastle Protection and Indemnity Association (The Fanti)

Sodexho Ltd *v.* Gibbons [2005] I.C.R. 1647; [2005] I.R.L.R. 836, EAT . . . . *Digested,* 05/**1251**

Soering *v.* United Kingdom (A/161) (1989) 11 E.H.R.R. 439; *Times,* July 8, 1989; *Independent,* July 11, 1989; *Guardian,* July 13, 1989; *Daily Telegraph,* October 2, 1989, ECHR . . . . *Digested,* 89/**1712**:
Applied, 97/2764, 02/2577, 05/2167: *Considered,* 03/2162, 03/2256, 04/839, 04/2009, 05/2058, 05/2076: *Followed,* 02/2514:
Previous proceedings, 88/1609: *Subsequent proceedings,* 91/1747

Sofrimport Sarl *v.* Commission of the European Communities (C152/88) [1990] E.C.R.
I-2477; [1990] 3 C.M.L.R. 80; *Times*, July 23, 1990, ECJ (5th Chamber) . . . . . .   *Digested*, 91/**3775**:
Distinguished, 05/1471

SOHEI/General purpose management system (T769/92) [1996] E.P.O.R. 253, EPO
(Technical Bd App) . . . .   *Doubted*, 05/2492

Soleh Boneh International *v.* Uganda and National Housing Corp [1993] 2 Lloyd's Rep.
208; *Times*, March 18, 1993, CA (Civ Div) . . . .   *Digested*, 94/**3758**:
Applied, 01/342: *Considered*, 05/213: *Distinguished*, 03/196:
Followed, 02/219

Solicitor, Re [1993] Q.B. 69; [1992] 2 W.L.R. 552; [1992] 2 All E.R. 335; (1991) 141 N.L.J.
1447; *Times*, September 24, 1991; *Independent*, July 12, 1991, QBD . . . .   *Digested*, 92/**4089**:
Applied, 97/3380: *Considered*, 05/2727

Sollitt *v.* DJ Broady Ltd [2000] C.P.L.R. 259, CA (Civ Div) . . . .   *Digested*, 00/**355**:
Considered, 03/295, 05/312: *Followed*, 04/267

Solon South West Housing Association Ltd *v.* James [2004] EWCA Civ 1847; [2005]
H.L.R. 24, CA (Civ Div) . . . .   *Digested*, 05/**298**

Solutia UK Ltd (formerly Monsanto Chemicals UK Ltd) *v.* Griffiths see Griffiths *v.* Solutia
UK Ltd

Solvay et Cie *v.* Commission of the European Communities (No.1) (T30/91) see Solvay
et Cie SA *v.* Commission of the European Communities (C287/95)

Solvay et Cie SA *v.* Commission of the European Communities (C287/95); *sub nom*
Solvay et Cie *v.* Commission of the European Communities (No.1) (T30/91); ICI
Plc *v.* Commission of the European Communities (T36/91); Solvay et Cie SA *v.*
Commission of the European Communities (T32/91) [2001] All E.R. (EC) 439;
[2000] E.C.R. I-2391; [2000] 5 C.M.L.R. 454; *Times*, April 14, 2000, ECJ (5th
Chamber); affirming [1995] All E.R. (E.C.) 600; [1995] E.C.R. II-1775; [1996] 5
C.M.L.R. 57; [1996] C.E.C. 137; [1996] C.E.C. 196, CFI (1st Chamber) . . . .   *Digested*, 00/**2370**:
Considered, 00/719: *Followed*, 05/1435: *Joined proceedings*, 00/2369

Solvay et Cie SA *v.* Commission of the European Communities (T32/91) see Solvay et
Cie SA *v.* Commission of the European Communities (C287/95)

Somerset CC *v.* Barber see Barber *v.* Somerset CC

Sommer *v.* Sweet see Sweet *v.* Sommer

Sony Computer Entertainment *v.* Owen see Kabushi Kaisha Sony Computer
Entertainment Inc *v.* Owen (t/a Neo Technologies)

Sony Computer Entertainment Europe Ltd *v.* Customs and Excise Commissioners
[2005] EWHC 1644, Ch D; affirming [2004] V. & D.R. 104, V&DTr (London) . . .   *Digested*, 05/**944**

Sony Computer Entertainment Inc *v.* Ball (Application for Summary Judgment) see
Kabushiki Kaisha Sony Computer Entertainment Inc *v.* Ball (Application for
Summary Judgment)

Sookraj *v.* Samaroo [2004] UKPC 50; (2004) 148 S.J.L.B. 1244; [2005] 1 P. & C.R.
DG11, PC (Trin)

Sorata Ltd *v.* Gardex Ltd [1984] R.P.C. 317, CA (Civ Div); affirming [1984] F.S.R. 81,
Ch D (Patents Ct). . . . .   *Digested*, 84/**2494**:
Applied, 05/2476: *Considered*, 92/3611

Sorsbie v. Tea Corp see Tea Corp, Re

Soundcraft Magnetics, Re see Nicholas *v.* Soundcraft Electronics Ltd

South African Breweries International (Finance) BV *v.* Laugh It Off Promotions CC
[2005] F.S.R. 30, Sup Ct (SA)

South African Human Rights Commission *v.* President of South Africa see Bhe *v.*
Magistrate of Khayelitsha

South African Supply and Cold Storage Co, Re; *sub nom* Wild v. South African Supply &
Cold Storage Co [1904] 2 Ch. 268, Ch D . . . .   *Applied*, 70/2715,
91/3390, 01/5183, 05/2335

South Bedfordshire DC *v.* Price A2 2005/2241, CA (Civ Div) [2005] EWHC 2031;
(2005) 102(40) L.S.G. 28, QBD

South Buckinghamshire DC *v.* Coates; *sub nom* Coates *v.* South Buckinghamshire DC;
South Buckinghamshire DC *v.* Cooper [2004] EWCA Civ 1378; [2005] B.L.G.R.
626; [2004] 4 P.L.R. 93; [2005] J.P.L. 668; [2005] A.C.D. 59; (2004) 148
S.J.L.B. 1282; [2004] N.P.C. 155; *Times*, October 27, 2004; *Independent*,
October 29, 2004, CA (Civ Div); affirming [2004] EWHC 155, QBD . . . .   *Digested*, 04/**3055**

South Buckinghamshire DC *v.* Cooper see South Buckinghamshire DC *v.* Coates

South Buckinghamshire DC *v.* Porter (No.1); *sub nom* South Bucks DC *v.* Porter;
Chichester DC *v.* Searle; Wrexham CBC *v.* Berry; Hertsmere BC *v.* Harty [2003]
UKHL 26; [2003] 2 A.C. 558; [2003] 2 W.L.R. 1547; [2003] 3 All E.R. 1;
[2003] H.R.L.R. 27; [2003] U.K.H.R.R. 1344; [2003] B.L.G.R. 449; [2003] 2
P.L.R. 101; [2003] J.P.L. 1412; [2003] 23 E.G.C.S. 135; (2003) 100(22) L.S.G.
32; (2003) 147 S.J.L.B. 626; [2003] N.P.C. 70; *Times*, May 23, 2003, HL;
affirming [2001] EWCA Civ 1549; [2002] 1 W.L.R. 1359; [2002] 1 All E.R. 425;
[2002] B.L.G.R. 443; [2002] 2 P. & C.R. 16; [2002] 3 P.L.R. 1; [2002] J.P.L.
608; (2001) 98(46) L.S.G. 35; *Times*, November 9, 2001, CA (Civ Div) . . . .   *Digested*, 03/**3381**:
Applied, 02/3675, 03/3384, 05/3285: *Considered*, 03/3382, 03/3485,
05/3283

South Buckinghamshire DC *v.* Porter (No.2); *sub nom* South Buckinghamshire DC *v.* Secretary of State for Transport, Local Government and the Regions [2004] UKHL 33; [2004] 1 W.L.R. 1953; [2004] 4 All E.R. 775; [2005] 1 P. & C.R. 6; [2004] 4 P.L.R. 50; [2004] 28 E.G.C.S. 177; (2004) 101(31) L.S.G. 25; (2004) 148 S.J.L.B. 825; [2004] N.P.C. 108; *Times*, July 2, 2004; *Independent*, July 6, 2004, HL; reversing [2003] EWCA Civ 687; [2004] 1 P. & C.R. 8; [2004] J.P.L. 207; (2003) 147 S.J.L.B. 628; [2003] N.P.C. 68; *Times*, May 23, 2003; *Independent*, May 23, 2003, CA (Civ Div); reversing [2002] EWHC 2136, QBD (Admin) . . . . *Digested*, 04/**3087**: *Applied*, 05/3296: *Followed*, 05/3304

South Buckinghamshire DC *v.* Secretary of State for Transport, Local Government and the Regions see South Buckinghamshire DC *v.* Porter (No.2)

South Bucks DC *v.* Porter see South Buckinghamshire DC *v.* Porter (No.1)

South Cambridgeshire DC *v.* Gammell; Bromley LBC *v.* Maughan [2005] EWCA Civ 1429; *Times*, November 3, 2005, CA (Civ Div)

South Cambridgeshire DC *v.* Heddon Management [2005] P.A.D. 37, Planning Inspector

South Cambridgeshire DC *v.* Persons Unknown [2004] EWCA Civ 1280; [2004] 4 P.L.R. 88; [2005] J.P.L. 680; (2004) 148 S.J.L.B. 1121; [2004] N.P.C. 138; *Times*, November 11, 2004, CA (Civ Div) . . . . *Digested*, 05/**3284**

South Caribbean Trading Ltd *v.* Trafigura Beheer BV [2004] EWHC 2676; [2005] 1 Lloyd's Rep. 128, QBD (Comm) . . . . *Digested*, 05/**697**

South Central Trains Ltd *v.* Rodway; *sub nom* Rodway *v.* South Central Trains Ltd; Rodway *v.* Southern Railways Ltd (formerly South Central Trains Ltd); New Southern Railway Ltd *v.* Rodway [2005] EWCA Civ 443; [2005] I.C.R. 1162; [2005] I.R.L.R. 583; *Times*, April 21, 2005, CA (Civ Div); affirming [2005] I.C.R. 75; [2004] I.R.L.R. 777, EAT . . . . *Digested*, 05/**1281**

South Cone Inc *v.* Bessant (t/a REEF) see REEF Trade Mark

South Glamorgan CC *v.* Griffiths (1992) 24 H.L.R. 334; [1992] 2 E.G.L.R. 232; [1992] N.P.C. 13, CA (Civ Div) . . . . *Digested*, 92/**2329**: *Considered*, 93/2107, 96/3833, 05/2688

South Liverpool Housing Ltd *v.* Customs and Excise Commissioners [2005] B.V.C. 2049; [2004] S.T.I. 2568, V&DTr

South Northants DC *v.* Whittlebury Park Golf and Country Club [2005] P.A.D. 18, Planning Inspector

South Shropshire DC *v.* Amos [1986] 1 W.L.R. 1271; [1987] 1 All E.R. 340; [1986] 2 E.G.L.R. 194; (1986) 280 E.G. 635; [1986] R.V.R. 235; (1986) 83 L.S.G. 3513; (1986) 136 N.L.J. 800; (1986) 130 S.J. 803, CA (Civ Div) . . . . *Digested*, 86/**1517**: *Applied*, 03/293: *Considered*, 88/2729, 95/840, 05/295: *Distinguished*, 89/449

South Staffordshire DC *v.* Secretary of State for the Environment (1988) 55 P. & C.R. 258; [1987] J.P.L. 635, QBD . . . . *Digested*, 88/**3436**: *Considered*, 88/3438, 05/3304

South Tyneside Healthcare NHS Trust *v.* Awotona see Awotona *v.* South Tyneside Healthcare NHS Trust

Southampton Container Terminals Ltd *v.* Hansa Schiffahrts GmbH (The Maersk Colombo); *sub nom* Southampton Container Terminals Ltd *v.* Schiffahrtsgesellschaft Hansa Australia MGH & Co [2001] EWCA Civ 717; [2001] 2 Lloyd's Rep. 275; (2001) 98(24) L.S.G. 43; (2001) 145 S.J.L.B. 149; *Times*, June 13, 2001, CA (Civ Div); affirming [1999] 2 Lloyd's Rep. 491; [1999] C.L.C. 1814, QBD (Admlty) . . . . *Digested*, 01/**4501**: *Considered*, 05/374: *Followed*, 03/939

Southampton Container Terminals Ltd *v.* Schiffahrtsgesellschaft Hansa Australia MGH & Co see Southampton Container Terminals Ltd *v.* Hansa Schiffahrts GmbH (The Maersk Colombo)

Southampton University *v.* Revenue and Customs Commissioners see University of Southampton *v.* Revenue and Customs Commissioners

Southern Cross Group Plc *v.* Deka Immobilien Investment GmbH [2005] B.P.I.R. 1010, Ch D

Southlong East Midlands Ltd *v.* Customs and Excise Commissioners [2005] B.V.C. 2387; [2005] S.T.I. 820, V&DTr (London)

Southwark LBC *v.* Adelekun (Unreported, November 11, 2004), CC (Central London) [*Ex rel.* Samuel Waritay, Barrister, Arden Chambers, 2 John Street, London,]. . . . *Digested*, 05/**2644**

Sovereign Life Assurance Co (In Liquidation) *v.* Dodd [1892] 2 Q.B. 573, CA; affirming [1892] 1 Q.B. 405, QBD . . . . *Applied*, 01/3748, 04/2192, 05/2333: *Considered*, 86/390, 02/2714

Sowden *v.* Lodge; *sub nom* Crookdake *v.* Drury [2004] EWCA Civ 1370; [2005] 1 W.L.R. 2129; [2005] 1 All E.R. 581; [2005] Lloyd's Rep. Med. 86; (2004) 148 S.J.L.B. 1282, CA (Civ Div); reversing in part [2003] EWHC 588, QBD . . . . *Digested*, 05/**3072**: *Applied*, 05/3071: *Considered*, 04/2845: *Previous proceedings*, 04/2845

SP *v.* Belguim 7 I.T.L. Rep. 453, Cass (B)

Spa Monopole SA *v.* Spa Finders Travel Arrangements Ltd [2005] E.T.M.R. 9, OHIM (1st Bd App) . . . . *Digested*, 05/**2520**

Spain v. Commission of the European Communities (C276/02) [2004] 3 C.M.L.R. 47,
ECJ (2nd Chamber) .... *Digested*, 05/**591**
Spain v. Commission of the European Communities (C278/92) [1994] E.C.R. I-4103,
ECJ .... *Digested*, 95/**656**:
Applied, 00/729: *Followed*, 05/590
Special Commissioner's Decision (CIS/2790/1998), Re Unreported, Sp Comm ...... *Considered*, 05/3883
Specialist Ceiling Services Northern Ltd v. ZVI Construction (UK) Ltd [2004] B.L.R.
403, QBD (TCC) .... *Digested*, 05/**647**
Specialist Group International Ltd v. Deakin see Deakin v. Faulding
Spectrum Plus Ltd (In Liquidation), Re; *sub nom* National Westminster Bank Plc v.
Spectrum Plus Ltd (In Creditors Voluntary Liquidation) [2005] UKHL 41; [2005]
2 A.C. 680; [2005] 3 W.L.R. 58; [2005] 4 All E.R. 209; [2005] 2 Lloyd's Rep.
275; [2005] B.C.C. 694; [2005] 2 B.C.L.C. 269; (2005) 155 N.L.J. 1045;
Times, July 1, 2005; *Independent*, July 6, 2005, HL; reversing [2004] EWCA Civ
670; [2004] Ch. 337; [2004] 3 W.L.R. 503; [2004] 4 All E.R. 995; [2004]
B.C.C. 660; [2005] 2 B.C.L.C. 30; (2004) 101(23) L.S.G. 32; (2004) 154
N.L.J. 890; (2004) 148 S.J.L.B. 694; *Times*, June 4, 2004; *Independent*, June 8,
2004, CA (Civ Div); reversing [2004] EWHC 9; [2004] 2 W.L.R. 783; [2004]
1 All E.R. 981; [2004] B.C.C. 51; [2004] 1 B.C.L.C. 335; (2004) 154 N.L.J. 93;
Times, January 23, 2004, Ch D (Companies Ct) .... *Digested*, 05/**2320**
Speed Investments Ltd v. Formula One Holdings Ltd (No.1) [2004] EWHC 1772;
[2005] 1 W.L.R. 1233; (2004) 101(33) L.S.G. 37; *Times*, September 10, 2004,
Ch D .... *Digested*, 05/**487**
Speed Investments Ltd v. Formula One Holdings Ltd (No.2); *sub nom* Bambino
Holdings Ltd v. Speed Investments Ltd [2004] EWCA Civ 1512; [2005] 1 W.L.R.
1936; [2005] 1 B.C.L.C. 455; [2005] I.L.Pr. 5; (2005) 102(2) L.S.G. 28;
(2004) 148 S.J.L.B. 1401; *Times*, November 18, 2004, CA (Civ Div); affirming
[2004] EWHC 1827; [2004] I.L.Pr. 46; *Times*, August 13, 2004, Ch D .... *Digested*, 05/**619**
Spelthorne BC v. Englemere Homes [2005] P.A.D. 82; [2004] P.A.D. 76, Planning
Inspector
Spencer v. First West Yorkshire Ltd (Unreported, December 9, 2004), CC (Leeds) [*Ex
rel.* Tom Nossiter, Barrister, Park Lane Chambers, 19, Westgate, Leeds] .... *Digested*, 05/**3087**
Spencer v. Wood (t/a Gordon's Tyres) [2004] EWCA Civ 352; [2004] 3 Costs L.R.
372; (2004) 148 S.J.L.B. 356; *Times*, March 30, 2004, CA (Civ Div) .... *Digested*, 05/**2705**
Sphere Drake Insurance Ltd v. Euro International Underwriting Ltd [2003] EWHC 1636;
[2003] Lloyd's Rep. I.R. 525; *Times*, August 11, 2003, QBD (Comm) .... *Digested*, 03/**2484**:
Followed, 05/2397
Spicer v. Spain [2004] EWCA Civ 1046; [2005] I.C.R. 213; *Times*, September 10,
2004, CA (Civ Div); reversing EAT/0516/03 RN, EAT .... *Digested*, 05/**1294**
Spijkers v. Gebroeders Benedik Abattoir CV (24/85) [1986] E.C.R. 1119; [1986] 2
C.M.L.R. 296, ECJ (5th Chamber) .... *Digested*, 86/**1362**:
Applied, 94/2001, 94/4832, 94/5110, 95/2071, 95/2073, 99/2133, 99/6043,
00/2229, 00/2231, 00/2232, 05/1313: *Considered*, 95/2072, 96/2649,
97/2274, 97/2278, 02/1429
Spiliada Maritime Corp v. Cansulex Ltd (The Spiliada) [1987] A.C. 460; [1986] 3
W.L.R. 972; [1986] 3 All E.R. 843; [1987] 1 Lloyd's Rep. 1; [1987] E.C.C. 168;
[1987] 1 F.T.L.R. 103; (1987) 84 L.S.G. 113; (1986) 136 N.L.J. 1137; (1986) 130
S.J. 925; *Financial Times*, November 25, 1986, HL; reversing [1985] 2 Lloyd's
Rep. 116; (1985) 82 L.S.G. 1416, CA (Civ Div) .... *Digested*, 87/**3135**:
Applied, 85/2597, 86/2705, 89/1722, 89/3095, 89/3394, 90/3768, 91/475,
91/476, 92/475, 93/3571, 93/5876, 94/483, 94/4040, 95/696, 96/846,
97/908, 98/4398, 99/717, 99/719, 99/750, 99/2405, 00/775, 01/815,
03/599, 04/1493, 05/622: *Considered*, 87/3095, 88/2911, 89/2725,
89/3042, 92/3072, 94/3252, 94/3256, 95/3484, 96/1089, 96/1091,
98/764, 02/477, 02/2756, 05/611: *Distinguished*, 87/3024, 03/2215:
Explained, 00/769: *Followed*, 91/5142, 95/690, 95/6052, 97/2453, 98/748,
98/749, 05/978
Spinnato v. Governor of Brixton Prison [2001] EWHC Admin 1124, DC .... *Considered*, 05/**1488**
Sporrong & Lonnroth v. Sweden (A/52) (1983) 5 E.H.R.R. 35, ECHR .... *Applied*, 98/3133:
Considered, 97/2796, 03/2824, 03/4413, 03/4975, 04/1376, 05/2893:
Distinguished, 98/3128
Sport in Desford v. Customs and Excise Commissioners [2005] B.V.C. 2338, V&DTr
Sporting Options Plc, Re [2004] EWHC 3128; [2005] B.C.C. 88; [2005] B.P.I.R. 435, Ch D *Digested*, 05/**2269**
Sportswear Co SpA v. Ghattaura (t/a GS3) see Sportswear Co SpA v. Stonestyle Ltd
Sportswear Co SpA v. Stonestyle Ltd; *sub nom* Sportswear Co SpA v. Ghattaura (t/a
GS3); A3 2005/2316, CA (Civ Div); reversing [2005] EWHC 2087; (2005)
28(10) I.P.D. 28076; (2005) 102(40) L.S.G. 26, Ch D
Spriggs v. Wessington Court School Ltd [2004] EWHC 1432; [2005] Lloyd's Rep. I.R.
474, QBD

Spring v. Guardian Assurance Plc [1995] 2 A.C. 296; [1994] 3 W.L.R. 354; [1994] 3
All E.R. 129; [1994] I.C.R. 596; [1994] I.R.L.R. 460; (1994) 91 (40) L.S.G. 36;
(1994) 144 N.L.J. 971; (1994) 138 S.J.L.B. 183; *Times*, July 8, 1994;
Independent, July 12, 1994, HL; reversing [1993] 2 All E.R. 273; [1993] I.C.R.
412; [1993] I.R.L.R. 122; (1993) 12 Tr. L.R. 33; (1993) 143 N.L.J. 365; (1993)
137 S.J.L.B. 47; *Times*, December 22, 1992; *Independent*, January 26, 1993, CA
(Civ Div); reversing [1992] I.R.L.R. 173; (1992) 11 Tr. L.R. 100; *Times*, February
10, 1992, QBD . . . . *Digested*, 94/**1918**:
       Applied, 94/1930, 94/3383, 94/3514, 95/4838, 99/2108, 00/2108, 02/3277,
       04/1203, 04/2706: *Cited*, 05/976: *Considered*, 94/3345, 95/3652, 00/4219,
       02/1318: *Distinguished*, 98/3935: *Followed*, 01/2254
Spring Salmon & Seafood Ltd v. Advocate General for Scotland; *sub nom* Spring
Salmon & Seafood Ltd, Petitioners; R. (on the application of Spring Salmon &
Seafood Ltd) v. Inland Revenue Commissioners [2004] S.T.C. 444; 2004 S.L.T.
501; 76 T.C. 609; [2004] S.T.I. 889; 2004 G.W.D. 8-194; *Times*, March 22, 2004,
OH . . . . *Digested*, 04/**5147**
Spring Salmon & Seafood Ltd v. Revenue and Customs Commissioners [2005] S.T.C.
(S.C.D.) 830; [2005] S.T.I. 1759, Sp Comm
Springette v. Defoe [1992] 2 F.L.R. 388; [1992] 2 F.C.R. 561; (1992) 24 H.L.R. 552;
(1993) 65 P. & C.R. 1; [1992] Fam. Law 489; [1992] N.P.C. 34; *Independent*,
March 24, 1992; *Guardian*, April 29, 1992, CA (Civ Div) . . . . *Digested*, 92/**2031**:
       Considered, 96/4996, 00/3941, 05/3378, 05/3407: *Followed*, 93/1876,
       95/2188, 96/2887
Sprung v. Royal Insurance (UK) Ltd [1997] C.L.C. 70; [1999] 1 Lloyd's Rep. I.R. 111,
CA (Civ Div) . . . . *Digested*, 97/**3121**:
       Followed, 05/2358
Squires v. Aig Europe UK Ltd see Manning v. AIG Europe UK Ltd
Squirrel v. Revenue and Customs Commissioners see Squirrell v. Revenue and
Customs Commissioners
Squirrell v. Revenue and Customs Commissioners; *sub nom* Squirrel v. Revenue and
Customs Commissioners [2005] S.T.C. (S.C.D.) 717; [2005] S.T.I. 1563, Sp
Comm
Squirrell Ltd v. National Westminster Bank Plc [2005] EWHC 664; [2005] 2 All E.R.
784; [2005] 1 All E.R. (Comm) 749; [2005] 2 Lloyd's Rep. 374; *Times*, May 25,
2005, Ch D . . . . *Digested*, 05/**459**
Sritharan v. Law Society; *sub nom* Law Society v. Sritharan [2005] EWCA Civ 476;
[2005] 1 W.L.R. 2708; [2005] 4 All E.R. 1105; (2005) 102(22) L.S.G. 27;
(2005) 155 N.L.J. 798; *Times*, May 11, 2005; *Independent*, May 5, 2005, CA
(Civ Div); affirming [2004] EWHC 2932, Ch D . . . . *Digested*, 05/**2725**
SS v. Secretary of State for the Home Department; *sub nom* SS (False Nationality
Appeal: Somalia), Re [2005] UKIAT 59; [2005] Imm. A.R. 303, IAT
SS (False Nationality Appeal: Somalia), Re see SS v. Secretary of State for the Home
Department
SS (Malaysian Citizen) v. Secretary of State for the Home Department [2004] UKIAT
91; [2004] Imm. A.R. 153, IAT . . . . *Digested*, 05/**2195**
SS (Sri Lankan Citizen) v. Secretary of State for the Home Department [2004] UKIAT
39; [2004] Imm. A.R. 95, IAT . . . . *Digested*, 05/**2152**
SSAFA Forces Help v. McClymont see Dickie v. Cathay Pacific Airways Ltd
SSC v. Sweden (46553/93) (2000) 29 E.H.R.R. CD245, ECHR . . . . *Considered*, 05/2160
SSSL Realisations (2002) Ltd (formerly Save Service Stations Ltd) (In Liquidation), Re see
Manning v. AIG Europe UK Ltd
ST v. Secretary of State for the Home Department; *sub nom* ST (NS Case: Scope of
Appeal: Sri Lanka), Re [2005] UKIAT 6; [2005] Imm. A.R. 163, IAT
St Albans Cathedral (Chapter of the Abbey Church) v. Booth (Valuation Officer) [2004]
R.A. 309, VT . . . . *Digested*, 05/**3367**
St Andrew, Trent, Re Unreported . . . . *Considered*, 05/990
St Barbe Green v. Inland Revenue Commissioners; *sub nom* Green v. Inland Revenue
Commissioners [2005] EWHC 14; [2005] 1 W.L.R. 1772; [2005] S.T.C. 288;
[2005] B.P.I.R. 1218; [2005] B.T.C. 8003; [2005] W.T.L.R. 75; [2005] S.T.I. 106;
(2005) 102(7) L.S.G. 26; [2005] N.P.C. 6; *Times*, January 14, 2005, Ch D . . . . *Digested*, 05/**4117**
ST Dupont v. El Du Pont de Nemours & Co; *sub nom* El Du Pont de Nemours & Co v.
ST Dupont; DU PONT Trade Mark [2003] EWCA Civ 1368; [2004] F.S.R. 15;
(2004) 27(2) I.P.D. 27009; (2003) 147 S.J.L.B. 1207, CA (Civ Div); reversing
[2002] EWHC 2455; (2003) 100(5) L.S.G. 32; *Times*, November 28, 2002,
Ch D . . . . *Digested*, 04/**2399**:
       Considered, 05/2563
St George South London Ltd v. Southwark LBC [2005] P.A.D. 80, Planning Inspector
St George's Investment Co v. Gemini Consulting Ltd [2004] EWHC 2353; [2005] 1
E.G.L.R. 5; [2005] 01 E.G. 96; [2005] 1 P. & C.R. DG12, Ch D . . . . *Digested*, 05/**2678**
St Gregory's, Tredington, Re; *sub nom* St Gregory Tredington, Re [1972] Fam. 236;
[1971] 2 W.L.R. 796; [1971] 3 All E.R. 269; 115 S.J. 284, Arches Ct . . . . *Digested*, 71/**3773**:
       Applied, 76/820, 76/822, 85/1094, 87/1241: *Considered*, 95/1868, 05/990

St Helens MBC v. Derbyshire; *sub nom* Derbyshire v. St Helens MBC [2005] EWCA
 Civ 977; [2005] I.R.L.R. 801; *Times*, August 26, 2005, CA (Civ Div); reversing
 [2004] I.R.L.R. 851, EAT . . . .   *Digested*, 05/**1235**
St John the Baptist, Halifax, Re (Unreported, December 2000), Cons Ct (Wakefield) . .   *Considered*, 05/**990**
St Lawrence, Stratford-sub-Castle, Re, *Times*, March 10, 2005, Cons Ct
St Leger-Davey v. First Secretary of State [2004] EWCA Civ 1612; [2005] 2 P. & C.R.
 6; [2005] 1 P.L.R. 117; (2004) 148 S.J.L.B. 1434; [2004] N.P.C. 178; *Times*,
 December 3, 2004; *Independent*, December 9, 2004, CA (Civ Div); affirming
 [2004] EWHC 512; [2004] J.P.L. 1581; [2004] A.C.D. 46, QBD (Admin) . . . . .   *Digested*, 05/**3280**
St Martins Property Corp Ltd v. Sir Robert McAlpine & Sons see Linden Gardens Trust
 Ltd v. Lenesta Sludge Disposal Ltd
St Mary the Virgin, East Chinnock, Re, *Times*, December 1, 2005, Cons Ct (Bath & Wells)
St Mary, Longstock, Re, *Times*, November 17, 2005, Cons Ct (Winchester)
St Nicholas, Sevenoaks, Re [2005] 1 W.L.R. 1011; (2004) 101 (44) L.S.G. 31; *Times*,
 October 29, 2004, Arches Ct . . . .   *Digested*, 05/**993**
St Paul Dairy Industries NV v. Unibel Exser BVBA (C104/03) [2005] E.C.R. I-3481;
 [2005] I.L.Pr. 31, ECJ (1st Chamber) . . . .   *Digested*, 05/**428**
St Paul's Community Project Ltd v. Customs and Excise Commissioners see Customs
 and Excise Commissioners v. St Paul's Community Project Ltd
ST Shipping & Transport Inc v. Vyzantio Shipping Ltd (The Byzantio) [2004] EWHC
 3067; [2005] 1 Lloyd's Rep. 531, QBD (Comm) . . . .   *Digested*, 05/**341**
ST (NS Case: Scope of Appeal: Sri Lanka), Re see ST v. Secretary of State for the Home
 Department
Staatsanwaltschaft Frankenthal (Pfalz) v. Kapper (C476/01) see Criminal Proceedings
 against Kapper (C476/01)
Staatssecretaris van Financien v. Arthur Andersen & Co Accountants CS (C472/03)
 [2005] S.T.C. 508; [2005] E.C.R. I-1719; [2005] 2 C.M.L.R. 51; [2005] S.T.I.
 363, ECJ (1st Chamber) . . . .   *Digested*, 05/**4350**
Staatssecretaris van Financien v. Lipjes (C68/03) [2004] S.T.C. 1592; [2004] E.C.R. I-
 5879; [2004] 2 C.M.L.R. 43; [2004] S.T.I. 1322, ECJ (1st Chamber) . . . .   *Digested*, 05/**4402**
Staatssecretaris van Financien v. Shipping and Forwarding Enterprise Safe BV (C320/
 88) [1991] S.T.C. 627; [1990] E.C.R. I-285; [1993] 3 C.M.L.R. 547; *Times*,
 March 21, 1990, ECJ (6th Chamber) . . . .   *Digested*, 90/**2242**:
                                                              Applied, 05/4395
Staatssecretaris van Financien v. Verkooijen (C35/98) [2002] S.T.C. 654; [2000]
 E.C.R. I-4071; [2002] 1 C.M.L.R. 48; 2 I.T.L. Rep. 727; [2000] S.T.I. 884, ECJ
 [2000] E.C.R. I-4071, AGO . . . .   *Digested*, 02/**4433**:
                                 Applied, 05/4028: *Considered*, 05/4134
Stacey v. Player see Stacy v. Player
Stacey-Kemp v. Maplewell Hall School Governors [2005] 2 Q.R. 9, CC (Leicester) [*Ex
 rel.* Robert CD Rees, Barrister, 27, New Walk, Leicester] . . . .   *Digested*, 04/**2862**
Stack v. Dowden; *sub nom* Dowden v. Stack [2005] EWCA Civ 857; [2005] 2 F.C.R.
 739; (2005-06) 8 I.T.E.L.R. 174; [2005] Fam. Law 864; [2005] N.P.C. 93, CA
 (Civ Div) . . . .   *Digested*, 05/**3391**
Stacy v. Player; *sub nom* Stacey v. Player [2004] EWCA Civ 241; [2004] 4 Costs L.R.
 585, CA (Civ Div); reversing (2001) 98(10) L.S.G. 43; *Times*, February 23,
 2001, Ch D . . . .   *Digested*, 05/**2699**
Stadler v. Finanzlandesdirektion fur Vorarlberg (C409/99) see Metropol Treuhand
 Wirtschaftstreuhand GmbH v. Finanzlandesdirektion fur Steiermark (C409/99)
Stafford v. United Kingdom (46295/99) (2002) 35 E.H.R.R. 32; 13 B.H.R.C. 260;
 [2002] Crim. L.R. 828; (2002) 152 N.L.J. 880; *Times*, May 31, 2002, ECHR . . .   *Digested*, 02/**3338**:
             Applied, 04/2784: *Considered*, 03/3059, 03/3064: *Followed*, 03/3782,
                                        05/2107: *Previous proceedings*, 98/4074
Stafford BC v. Leadbetter [2005] P.A.D. 94, Planning Inspector
Staffordshire Sentinel Newspapers Ltd v. Potter [2004] I.R.L.R. 752, EAT . . . .   *Digested*, 05/**1325**
Staghold Ltd v. Takeda [2005] 3 E.G.L.R. 45; [2005] 47 E.G. 146, CC (London)
Stainless Steel Cartel (T45/98), Re see Krupp Thyssen Stainless GmbH v. Commission of
 the European Communities (T45/98)
Stamp Commissioner v. Carreras Group Ltd see Carreras Group Ltd v. Stamp
 Commissioner
Stancliffe Stone Co Ltd v. Peak District National Park Authority [2005] EWCA Civ 747;
 [2005] A.C.D. 104; [2005] N.P.C. 78; *Times*, July 14, 2005, CA (Civ Div);
 affirming [2004] EWHC 1475; [2005] Env. L.R. 4; [2004] N.P.C. 101, QBD . . . .   *Digested*, 05/**3306**
Standard Life Assurance Co v. Scottish Ministers [2005] 15 E.G.C.S. 123, IH (Ex Div)
Standard Steamship Owners Protection & Indemnity Association (Bermuda) Ltd v. GIE
 Vision Bail [2004] EWHC 2919; [2005] 1 All E.R. (Comm) 618; [2005] 2 C.L.C.
 1135; [2005] Lloyd's Rep. I.R. 407, QBD (Comm) . . . .   *Digested*, 05/**2388**
Stanelco Fibre Optics Ltd v. Bioprogress Technology Ltd; *sub nom* Stanelco Fibre
 Optics Ltd's Patent Applications (No.1) [2004] EWHC 2263; [2005] R.P.C. 15,
 Ch D (Patents Ct) . . . .   *Digested*, 05/**2486**:
                                                              Approved, 05/2448

Stanelco Fibre Optics Ltd v. Bioprogress Technology Ltd (Application to Adduce Fresh Evidence); *sub nom* Stanelco Fibre Optics Ltd's Patent Applications (Application to Adduce Fresh Evidence) [2005] R.P.C. 16; (2005) 28(3) I.P.D. 28019, Ch D (Patents Ct) .... *Digested*, 05/**2494**

Stanelco Fibre Optics Ltd's Patent Applications (Application to Adduce Fresh Evidence) see Stanelco Fibre Optics Ltd v. Bioprogress Technology Ltd (Application to Adduce Fresh Evidence)

Stanelco Fibre Optics Ltd's Patent Applications (No.1) see Stanelco Fibre Optics Ltd v. Bioprogress Technology Ltd

Stanford v. Kingston upon Hull City Council (Unreported, February 1, 2005), CC (Kingston upon Hull) [*Ex rel.* Craig Moore, Barrister, Park Lane Chambers, 19 Westgate, Leeds] .... *Digested*, 05/**3196**

Stanley House Logistics Ltd v. Customs and Excise Commissioners [2005] V. & D.R. 176, V&D Tr (London)

Stannard v. Fisons Pension Trust Ltd [1992] I.R.L.R. 27; *Times*, November 19, 1991, CA (Civ Div) .... *Digested*, 92/**3332**: *Considered*, 05/**4304**

Stansell Ltd (formerly Stansell (Builders) Ltd v. Co-operative Group (CWS) Ltd; *sub nom* Co-operative Group (CWS) Ltd v. Stansell Ltd (formerly Stansell (Builders) Ltd; A3/2005/1866, CA (Civ Div); reversing [2005] EWHC 1601; [2005] N.P.C. 101, Ch D

Stanton v. Callaghan [2000] Q.B. 75; [1999] 2 W.L.R. 745; [1998] 4 All E.R. 961; [1999] C.P.L.R. 31; [1999] B.L.R. 172; (1999) 1 T.C.L.R. 50; 62 Con. L.R. 1; [1999] P.N.L.R. 116; [1998] 3 E.G.L.R. 165; (1999) 15 Const. L.J. 50; [1998] E.G.C.S. 115; (1998) 95(28) L.S.G. 32; (1998) 95(33) L.S.G. 33; (1998) 148 N.L.J. 1355; (1998) 142 S.J.L.B. 220; [1998] N.P.C. 113; *Times*, July 25, 1998; *Independent*, July 16, 1998, CA (Civ Div) .... *Digested*, 98/**520**: *Applied*, 01/401, 05/363

Stark v. West Berkshire DC [2005] P.A.D. 42, Planning Inspector

Starr v. Revenue and Customs Commissioners [2005] S.T.I. 1736, V&D Tr (Manchester)

State Aid to Bug-Alutechnik GmbH (C5/89), Re see Commission of the European Communities v. Germany (C5/89)

Staunton v. Paragon Finance Plc see Paragon Finance Plc (formerly National Home Loans Corp) v. Nash

Steamship Mutual Underwriting Association Trustees (Bermuda) Ltd v. Baring Asset Management Ltd [2004] EWHC 202; [2004] 2 C.L.C. 628, QBD (Comm) .... *Digested*, 05/**456**

Stec v. United Kingdom (Admissibility) (65731/01) (2005) 41 E.H.R.R. SE18, ECHR

Stedman v. United Kingdom (Admissibility) (29107/95) (1997) 23 E.H.R.R. CD168, Eur Comm HR .... *Applied*, 05/1328

Steed v. Suffolk CC see R. v. Suffolk CC Ex p. Steed

Steeds v. Peverel Management Services Ltd [2001] EWCA Civ 419; *Times*, May 16, 2001; *Daily Telegraph*, April 10, 2001, CA (Civ Div) .... *Digested*, 01/**601**: *Followed*, 05/1301

Steel v. Joy see Halsey v. Milton Keynes General NHS Trust

Steel v. United Kingdom (68416/01); Morris v. United Kingdom (68416/01) [2005] E.M.L.R. 15; (2005) 41 E.H.R.R. 22; 18 B.H.R.C. 545; *Times*, February 16, 2005, ECHR .... *Digested*, 05/**2089**

Steele v. Mooney [2005] EWCA Civ 96; [2005] 1 W.L.R. 2819; [2005] 2 All E.R. 256; [2005] C.P. Rep. 26; *Times*, February 15, 2005, CA (Civ Div) .... *Digested*, 05/**340**

Stefcom SpA's Trade Mark [2005] E.T.M.R. 82, PO (Irl)

Steliou v. Compton see Woodhouse v. Consignia Plc

Stephens v. Cannon [2005] EWCA Civ 222; [2005] C.P. Rep. 31; *Times*, May 3, 2005, CA (Civ Div) .... *Digested*, 05/**292**

Stephenson v. Leathbond Ltd [2005] 3 E.G.L.R. 79; [2005] 40 E.G. 184, Lands Tr

Stepton v. Wolseley (Unreported, January 17, 2005), CC (Southampton) [*Ex rel.* James Counsell, Barrister, Outer Temple Chambers, 222 Strand, London]...... *Digested*, 05/**3198**

Stevens v. Bell; *sub nom* Airways Pension Scheme, Re; British Airways Pension Trustees Ltd v. British Airways Plc [2002] EWCA Civ 672; [2002] O.P.L.R. 207; [2002] Pens. L.R. 247, CA (Civ Div); affirming in part [2001] O.P.L.R. 135; [2001] Pens. L.R. 99, Ch D .... *Digested*, 02/**3390**: *Applied*, 05/2944

Stevens v. Blaenau Gwent CBC [2004] EWCA Civ 715; [2004] H.L.R. 54; [2004] N.P.C. 94; *Times*, June 29, 2004, CA (Civ Div) .... *Digested*, 05/**2853**

Stevens v. Head 176 C.L.R. 433, HC (Aus) .... *Considered*, 05/608

Stevens v. Leeder see Stevens v. Newey

Stevens v. Newey; *sub nom* Stevens v. Leeder; Leeder v. Stevens [2005] EWCA Civ 50; (2005) 149 S.J.L.B. 112; *Times*, January 14, 2005, CA (Civ Div).......... *Digested*, 05/**3442**

Stevens v. Peacock see Heath v. Tang

Stichting Certificatie Kraanverhuurbedrijf (SCK) v. Commission of the European Communities (C268/96 P (R)) [1996] E.C.R. I-4971; [1997] 5 C.M.L.R. 157, ECJ .... *Followed*, 05/544

Stichting Goed Wonen v. Staatssecretaris van Financien (C326/99) [2003] S.T.C. 1137; [2001] E.C.R. I-6831; [2001] 3 C.M.L.R. 54; [2002] C.E.C. 213; [2001] B.T.C. 5583; [2002] B.V.C. 46; [2003] S.T.I. 1068, ECJ (5th Chamber) . . . . *Digested,* 02/**4786:** *Considered,* 05/4351, 05/4403

Stichting Goed Wonen v. Staatssecretaris van Financien (C376/02) [2005] E.C.R. I-3445; [2005] 2 C.M.L.R. 41; [2005] S.T.I. 890, ECJ

Stichting ter Exploitatie van Naburige Rechten (SENA) v. Nederlandse Omroep Stichting (NOS) (C245/00) [2003] E.C.R. I-1251; [2005] 3 C.M.L.R. 36; [2003] E.C.D.R. 12; [2003] E.M.L.R. 17; [2003] R.P.C. 42, ECJ (6th Chamber) (Unreported, September 26, 2002), AGO . . . . *Digested,* 03/**2589**

Stock v. London Underground Ltd, *Times,* August 13, 1999, CA (Civ Div) . . . . *Digested,* 99/**3944:** *Applied,* 05/313

Stockley v. Knowsley MBC [1986] 2 E.G.L.R. 141; (1986) 279 E.G. 677, CA (Civ Div) . . *Digested,* 86/**2249:** *Not applied,* 05/2853

Stoeckert v. Geddes (No.2); *sub nom* Stoekert v. Geddes (No.2) [2004] UKPC 54; (2004-05) 7 I.T.E.L.R. 506; (2005) 149 S.J.L.B. 57, PC (Jam) . . . . *Digested,* 05/**256**

Stoekert v. Geddes (No.2) see Stoeckert v. Geddes (No.2)

Stoke on Trent City Council v. B&Q (Retail) Ltd; Wolverhampton BC v. B&Q (Retail) Ltd; Barking and Dagenham LBC v. Home Charm Retail [1984] A.C. 754; [1984] 2 W.L.R. 929; [1984] 2 All E.R. 332; 82 L.G.R. 473; 128 S.J. 364; (1985) 4 Tr. L. 9, HL; affirming [1984] Ch. 1; [1983] 3 W.L.R. 78; [1983] 2 All E.R. 787; 82 L.G.R. 10; (1983) 2 Tr. L.R. 66; 127 S.J. 426, CA (Civ Div) . . . . *Digested,* 84/**3231:** *Applied,* 85/2042, 85/3431, 86/3390.c, 89/2990, 90/3704, 90/4127, 92/2904, 97/3862: *Considered,* 85/3406, 86/3390.d, 91/3463, 01/4400: *Followed,* 05/2804

Stoke on Trent City Council v. Wood Mitchell & Co Ltd; *sub nom* Wood Mitchell & Co Ltd v. Stoke on Trent City Council [1980] 1 W.L.R. 254; [1979] 2 All E.R. 65; [1979] S.T.C. 197; (1979) 38 P. & C.R. 126; (1978) 248 E.G. 871; [1978] T.R. 471; [1979] J.P.L. 230; 124 S.J. 168, CA (Civ Div); affirming (1977) 33 P. & C.R. 516; (1976) 241 E.G. 855, Lands Tr . . . . *Digested,* 79/**301:** *Considered,* 89/3639: *Distinguished,* 05/4343

Stokes Pension Fund Trustees v. Western Power Distribution (South West) Plc; *sub nom* Trustees of the Stokes Pension Fund v. Western Power Distribution (South West) Plc [2005] EWCA Civ 854; [2005] 1 W.L.R. 3595; [2005] 3 All E.R. 775; [2005] C.P. Rep. 40; [2005] B.L.R. 497; (2005) 102(30) L.S.G. 28; *Times,* July 28, 2005; *Independent,* July 15, 2005, CA (Civ Div) . . . . *Digested,* 05/**374**

Stokke Gruppen AS v. Trip Trap Denmark A/S [2005] E.T.M.R. 90, BG (Swi)

Stolzenberg v. Daimler Chrysler Canada Inc [2005] I.L.Pr. 24, Cass (F)

Stone v. Harrow LBC [2005] P.A.D. 15, Planning Inspector

Stone Court Shipping Co SA v. Spain (55524/00) (2005) 40 E.H.R.R. 31, ECHR . . . . . *Digested,* 05/**2080**

Stone (Inspector of Taxes) v. Hitch see Hitch v. Stone (Inspector of Taxes)

Stonegate Securities Ltd v. Gregory [1980] Ch. 576; [1980] 3 W.L.R. 168; [1980] 1 All E.R. 241; 124 S.J. 495, CA (Civ Div) . . . . *Digested,* 80/**294:** *Applied,* 05/2997: *Considered,* 92/2590: *Followed,* 84/329

Storey v. Clellands Shipbuilders Ltd see Grieves v. FT Everard & Sons Ltd

Stork v. Binions see Seddon v. Binions

Stovin v. Wise [1996] A.C. 923; [1996] 3 W.L.R. 388; [1996] 3 All E.R. 801; [1996] R.T.R. 354; (1996) 93(35) L.S.G. 33; (1996) 146 N.L.J. 1185; (1996) 140 S.J.L.B. 201; *Times,* July 26, 1996; *Independent,* July 31, 1996, HL; reversing [1994] 1 W.L.R. 1124; [1994] 3 All E.R. 467; [1994] R.T.R. 225; 92 L.G.R. 577; 159 J.P.N. 722; (1994) 91(14) L.S.G. 48; 138 S.J.L.B. 60; *Times,* March 8, 1994, CA (Civ Div) . . . . *Digested,* 96/**4058:** *Applied,* 97/3778, 01/4483, 01/4499, 04/1442, 04/2752, 05/2891: *Considered,* 97/4087: *Distinguished,* 00/4232, 01/4495: *Followed,* 99/2889

Strachan v. Gleaner Co Ltd [2005] UKPC 33; [2005] 1 W.L.R. 3204, PC (Jam) . . . . . . *Digested,* 05/**400**

Strathclyde RC v. Wallace; *sub nom* West Dunbartonshire Council v. Wallace [1998] 1 W.L.R. 259; [1998] 1 All E.R. 394; 1998 S.C. (H.L.) 72; 1998 S.L.T. 421; 1998 S.C.L.R. 340; [1998] I.C.R. 205; [1998] I.R.L.R. 146; (1998) 95(7) L.S.G. 31; (1998) 142 S.J.L.B. 83; 1998 G.W.D. 4-181; *Times,* January 24, 1998, HL; affirming 1996 S.C. 535; 1997 S.L.T. 315; 1996 S.C.L.R. 1046; [1996] I.R.L.R. 670, IH (2 Div) . . . . *Digested,* 98/**5807:** *Applied,* 00/6214: *Considered,* 05/1263

Strbac v. Secretary of State for the Home Department [2005] EWCA Civ 848; [2005] Imm. A.R. 504, CA (Civ Div)

Streames v. Copping [1985] Q.B. 920; [1985] 2 W.L.R. 993; [1985] 2 All E.R. 122; (1985) 81 Cr. App. R. 1; (1985) 149 J.P. 305; [1985] R.T.R. 264; (1985) 82 L.S.G. 1709; (1985) 129 S.J. 299, DC . . . . *Digested,* 85/**2128:** *Applied,* 04/867, 05/1362: *Considered,* 87/582, 89/583, 90/856, 94/1115: *Distinguished,* 86/2074, 87/1758: *Followed,* 90/803

Streamserve Inc v. Office for Harmonisation in the Internal Market (Trade Marks and Designs) (OHIM) (T106/00) [2002] E.C.R. II-723; [2003] E.T.M.R. 59; (2002) 25(4) I.P.D. 25026, CFI (4th Chamber) . . . . *Digested,* 04/**2368:** *Applied,* 05/2506: *Subsequent proceedings,* 05/2546

Streamserve Inc v. Office for Harmonisation in the Internal Market (Trade Marks and
Designs) (OHIM) (C150/02 P) [2005] E.T.M.R. 57, ECJ . . . . *Digested,* 05/**2546:**
Previous proceedings, 04/2368
Streekgewest Westelijk Noord-Brabant v. Staatssecretaris van Financien (C174/02)
[2005] E.C.R. I-85; [2005] S.T.I. 136, ECJ (1st Chamber)
Street v. Coombes [2005] EWHC 2290; (2005) 102(42) L.S.G. 23, Ch D
Street v. Derbyshire Unemployed Workers Centre [2004] EWCA Civ 964; [2004] 4 All
E.R. 839; [2005] I.C.R. 97; [2004] I.R.L.R. 687; *Times,* September 6, 2004,
CA (Civ Div); affirming [2004] I.C.R. 213; (2004) 101(2) L.S.G. 29; *Times,*
December 1, 2003, EAT . . . . *Digested,* 04/**1308**
Street v. Mountford [1985] A.C. 809; [1985] 2 W.L.R. 877; [1985] 2 All E.R. 289;
(1985) 17 H.L.R. 402; (1985) 50 P. & C.R. 258; [1985] 1 E.G.L.R. 128; (1985)
274 E.G. 821; (1985) 82 L.S.G. 2087; (1985) 135 N.L.J. 460; (1985) 129 S.J.
348, HL; reversing (1984) 16 H.L.R. 27; (1985) 49 P. & C.R. 324; (1984) 271
E.G. 1153; (1984) 271 E.G. 1261; (1984) 81 L.S.G. 1844; (1984) 128 S.J. 483, CA
(Civ Div) . . . . *Digested,* 85/**1893:**
Applied, 85/1871, 86/1931, 87/2163, 87/2247, 88/2042, 88/2061, 89/2146,
92/2290, 93/2073, 93/2538, 95/1979, 01/4146, 01/4157, 05/2670:
Cited, 00/311: *Considered,* 86/1896, 86/2306, 87/2162, 87/2244, 87/2252,
88/66, 88/2043, 88/2047, 89/2100, 89/2148, 89/2150, 89/2163, 89/2165,
90/2809, 90/2811, 90/2813, 90/2815, 91/545, 91/2243, 91/2262, 92/100,
93/426, 95/3045, 96/3764, 96/3765, 97/3305, 99/3699, 05/2648:
Distinguished, 88/2026, 89/2112, 89/2145, 92/2752, 98/3599:
Followed, 86/1873, 86/1881, 99/3698, 00/2584: *Referred to,* 86/1874,
87/2159, 87/2176
Strickland v. Fogg (Unreported, June 22, 2004), CC (Manchester) [*Ex rel.* Christopher
Taft, Barrister, St James's Chambers, 68 Quay Street, Manchester.] . . . . *Digested,* 05/**3078**
Strintzis Lines Shipping SA v. Commission of the European Communities (T65/99)
[2005] 5 C.M.L.R. 31, CFI (5th Chamber)
Stroude v. Beazer Homes Ltd [2005] EWCA Civ 265; [2005] N.P.C. 45; *Times,* April
28, 2005, CA (Civ Div); affirming [2004] EWHC 676, Ch D . . . . *Digested,* 05/**288**
Stroude v. Beazer Homes Ltd [2005] EWHC 2686; [2005] 48 E.G.C.S. 223, Ch D
Strouthos v. London Underground Ltd see London Underground Ltd v. Strouthos
Strover v. Strover [2005] EWHC 860; [2005] W.T.L.R. 1245; [2005] N.P.C. 64; *Times,*
May 30, 2005, Ch D . . . . *Digested,* 05/**2392**
Stubbings v. United Kingdom (22083/93) [1997] 1 F.L.R. 105; [1997] 3 F.C.R. 157;
(1997) 23 E.H.R.R. 213; 1 B.H.R.C. 316; [1997] Fam. Law 241; *Times,* October
24, 1996; *Independent,* October 24, 1996, ECHR (1994) 18 E.H.R.R. CD185;
(1995) 19 E.H.R.R. CD32, Eur Comm HR . . . . *Digested,* 96/**3156:**
Applied, 01/1897, 03/922: *Considered,* 04/2719, 05/432
Stubbings v. Webb [1993] A.C. 498; [1993] 2 W.L.R. 120; [1993] 1 All E.R. 322;
[1993] 1 F.L.R. 714; [1993] P.I.Q.R. P86; [1993] Fam. Law 342; (1993) 137
S.J.L.B. 32; *Times,* December 17, 1992; *Independent,* January 19, 1993, HL;
reversing [1992] Q.B. 197; [1991] 3 W.L.R. 383; [1991] 3 All E.R. 949; [1992] 1
F.L.R. 296; [1992] Fam. Law 61; *Times,* April 3, 1991; *Daily Telegraph,* May 14,
1991, CA (Civ Div) . . . . *Digested,* 93/**2608:**
Applied, 02/464, 05/432, 05/2859: *Cited,* 03/2975: *Considered,* 95/3180,
96/838, 03/432
Stubbs v. Gonzales [2005] UKPC 22; [2005] 1 W.L.R. 2730; [2005] B.P.I.R. 1227,
PC (Bah) . . . . *Digested,* 05/**2288**
Subesh v. Secretary of State for the Home Department; Suthan v. Secretary of State
for the Home Department; Nagulananthan v. Secretary of State for the Home
Department; Vanniyasingam v. Secretary of State for the Home Department
[2004] EWCA Civ 56; [2004] Imm. A.R. 112; [2004] I.N.L.R. 417, CA (Civ
Div) . . . . *Digested,* 04/**2079:**
Applied, 05/2184: *Followed,* 04/2044, 05/2150
Suckler Cows (8/88), Re see Germany v. Commission of the European Communities (8/
88)
Sue Ryder Care v. Customs and Excise Commissioners [2005] S.T.I. 121, V&DTr
Suffolk CC v. Wallis [2004] EWHC 788; [2004] O.P.L.R. 301; [2004] Pens. L.R. 255,
Ch D . . . . *Digested,* 05/**3054**
Suffolk Coastal DC v. Parochial Church Council [2005] P.A.D. 36, Planning Inspector
Suffolk Coastal DC v. Shand [2005] P.A.D. 13, Planning Inspector
Suffolk Coastal DC v. Suffolk Wildlife Trust [2005] P.A.D. 19, Planning Inspector
Sugden v. B&Q Plc (Unreported, January 14, 2004), CC (Exeter) [*Ex rel.* Adrian Posta,
Barrister, Albion Chambers, Broad Street, Bristol] . . . . *Digested,* 05/**3148**
Suiker Unie v. Commission of the European Communities (40/73) see Cooperatieve
Vereniging Suiker Unie UA v. Commission of the European Communities (40/
73)
Sullivan v. Moody 207 C.L.R. 562, HC (Aus) . . . . *Considered,* 05/2848
Summer Palace Ltd v. Customs and Excise Commissioners [2004] EWHC 2804;
[2005] S.T.C. 564; [2005] B.T.C. 5032; [2005] B.V.C. 63; [2004] S.T.I. 2501;
[2004] N.P.C. 180, Ch D . . . . *Digested,* 05/**368**

Sun Alliance & London Insurance Co Ltd v. Debenhams Retail Plc see Debenhams Retail
    Plc v. Sun Alliance & London Assurance Co Ltd
Sun Life Assurance Co of Canada v. Lincoln National Life Insurance Co see Lincoln
    National Life Insurance Co v. Sun Life Assurance Co of Canada
Sun Life Assurance Plc v. Thales Tracs Ltd (formerly Racal Tracs Ltd) [2001] EWCA Civ
    704; [2001] 1 W.L.R. 1562; [2002] 1 All E.R. 64; [2002] 1 P. & C.R. 12; [2001]
    L. & T.R. 39; [2001] 2 E.G.L.R. 57; [2001] 34 E.G. 100; [2001] 20 E.G.C.S.
    230; (2001) 98(21) L.S.G. 41; (2001) 82 P. & C.R. DG16; *Times,* June 25, 2001;
    Independent, July 2, 2001 (C.S), CA (Civ Div); reversing [2000] 1 E.G.L.R.
    138; [1999] N.P.C. 154; (2000) 80 P. & C.R. D7, QBD . . . .   *Digested,* 01/**4158**:
                                             Considered, 05/3386
Sun Life Assurance Society Plc v. Legends Surf Shops Plc see Legends Surf Shops Plc
    (In Administrative Receivership) v. Sun Life Assurance Society Plc
Sun Myung Moon v. Secretary of State for the Home Department; *sub nom* Sun
    Myung Moon (Human Rights: Entry Clearance: Proportionality: USA), Re
    [2005] UKIAT 112; [2005] Imm. A.R. 624, IAT
Sun Myung Moon (Human Rights: Entry Clearance: Proportionality: USA), Re see Sun
    Myung Moon v. Secretary of State for the Home Department
Sunrider Corp v. Office for Harmonisation in the Internal Market (Trade Marks and
    Designs) (OHIM) (T203/02) [2004] C.E.C. 424, CFI (2nd Chamber) . . . .   *Digested,* 05/**2540**
Sunrider Corp v. Office for Harmonisation in the Internal Market (Trade Marks and
    Designs) (OHIM) (T242/02) [2005] E.T.M.R. CN6, CFI
Supperstone v. Hurst see Hurst v. Supperstone
Supporting Link Alliance Ltd, Re [2004] EWHC 523; [2004] 1 W.L.R. 1549; [2005] 1 All
    E.R. 303; [2004] B.C.C. 764; [2004] 2 B.C.L.C. 486; (2004) 101(14) L.S.G. 25;
    Times, April 28, 2004, Ch D . . . .   *Digested,* 04/**2147**:
                                             Considered, 04/2197
Supreme Holy Council of the Muslim Community v. Bulgaria (39023/97) (2005) 41
    E.H.R.R. 3, ECHR. . . . .   *Digested,* 05/**2051**
Surdonja v. Ealing LBC see Mohamed v. Hammersmith and Fulham LBC
Surefire Systems Ltd v. Guardian ECL Ltd [2005] EWHC 1860; [2005] B.L.R. 534,
    QBD (TCC)
Surrey Heath BC v. Complex UK Ltd [2005] P.A.D. 23, Planning Inspector
Susie Radin Ltd v. GMB [2004] EWCA Civ 180; [2004] 2 All E.R. 279; [2004] I.C.R.
    893; [2004] I.R.L.R. 400; (2004) 101(11) L.S.G. 34; (2004) 148 S.J.L.B. 266;
    Times, March 16, 2004, CA (Civ Div); affirming EAT/0712/02 RN, EAT . . . .   *Digested,* 04/**1285**:
                           Considered, 05/1296: *Followed,* 05/1204, 05/1287
Suss v. Germany (40324/98) [2005] 3 F.C.R. 666, ECHR
Sussex University v. Customs and Excise Commissioners see Marks & Spencer Plc v.
    Customs and Excise Commissioners (No.5)
Suthan v. Secretary of State for the Home Department see Subesh v. Secretary of
    State for the Home Department
Sutherland v. Hatton see Barber v. Somerset CC
Sutradhar v. Natural Environment Research Council [2004] EWCA Civ 175; [2004]
    P.N.L.R. 30; (2004) 101(13) L.S.G. 36; [2004] Env. L.R. D8; *Times,* March 19,
    2004, CA (Civ Div); reversing [2003] EWHC 1046; [2003] P.I.Q.R. P34;
    [2003] N.P.C. 61, QBD . . . .   *Digested,* 05/**2858**
Sutton v. Glendales Ltd (Unreported, October 31, 2003), CC (Liverpool) [*Ex rel.* David
    Binns, Barrister, St James's Chambers, 68 Quay Street, Manchester.] . . . .   *Digested,* 05/**3195**
Sutton v. Horsham DC [2005] 2 Costs L.R. 344, Sup Ct Costs Office
Sutton v. Potting Construction Ltd see Marshalls Clay Products Ltd v. Caulfield
Sutton LBC v. Davis (No.2) [1994] 1 W.L.R. 1317; [1995] 1 All E.R. 65; [1994] 2 F.L.R.
    569; 92 L.G.R. 746; [1994] Fam. Law 616; (1994) 158 J.P.N. 747; (1994)
    91(31) L.S.G. 36; (1994) 138 S.J.L.B. 140; *Times,* June 5, 1994; *Independent,*
    July 8, 1994, Fam Div . . . .   *Digested,* 95/**4005**:
                  Applied, 95/3381, 05/1540: *Considered,* 94/3210, 95/3971
Sutton LBC v. Phenomenal Ltd [2005] P.A.D. 76, Planning Inspector
Suzen v. Zehnacker Gebaudereinigung GmbH Krankenhausservice (C13/95) [1997] All
    E.R. (EC) 289; [1997] E.C.R. I-1259; [1997] 1 C.M.L.R. 768; [1997] I.C.R. 662;
    [1997] I.R.L.R. 255; (1997) 16 Tr. L.R. 365; *Times,* March 26, 1997, ECJ [1997]
    E.C.R. I-1259, AGO . . . .   *Digested,* 97/**2278**:
             Applied, 97/2270, 00/2229, 00/2231, 03/5479: *Considered,* 98/2220,
             02/1429, 04/1294: *Distinguished,* 99/2133: *Followed,* 05/1314:
                                           Not applied, 01/2333
Svenska Handelsbanken AB v. Dandridge see Handelsbanken ASA v. Dandridge (The
    Aliza Glacial)
Svenska Petroleum Exploration AB v. Lithuania (No.1) [2005] EWHC 9; [2005] 1 All
    E.R. (Comm) 515; [2005] 1 Lloyd's Rep. 515, QBD (Comm) . . . .   *Digested,* 05/**463**
Svenska Petroleum Exploration AB v. Lithuania (No.2) [2005] EWHC 2437; [2005] 2
    C.L.C. 965; (2005) 102(47) L.S.G. 26, QBD (Comm)
Swain v. DPP see Ayliffe v. DPP
Swain v. DPP see R. v. Jones (Margaret)

Swainston v. Hetton Victory Club Ltd; *sub nom* Hetton Victory Club Ltd v. Swainston
  [1983] 1 All E.R. 1179; [1983] I.C.R. 341; [1983] I.R.L.R. 164; (1983) 127 S.J.
  171, CA (Civ Div); affirming [1983] I.C.R. 139; (1982) 126 S.J. 673, EAT . . . . . .   *Digested*, 83/**1311**:
                                         Applied, 87/1385, 88/1337, 05/1248: *Cited*, 02/2344
Swale BC v. First Secretary of State [2005] EWCA Civ 1568, CA (Civ Div); reversing
  [2005] EWHC 290; [2005] J.P.L. 1523; [2005] N.P.C. 38, QBD (Admin)
Swedish Match AB v. Secretary of State for Health (C210/03) see R. (on the
  application of Swedish Match AB) v. Secretary of State for Health (C210/03)
Sweet v. Sommer; *sub nom* Sommer v. Sweet [2005] EWCA Civ 227; [2005] 2 All
  E.R. 64 (Note), CA (Civ Div); affirming [2004] EWHC 1504; [2004] 4 All E.R.
  288 (Note); (2004) 101(35) L.S.G. 34; [2004] 2 P. & C.R. DG24; *Times*,
  August 25, 2004, Ch D . . . .   *Digested*, 05/**3437**
Swiftcall Long Distance Ltd's Trade Mark Application [2005] E.T.M.R. 83, PO (Irl)
Swiggs v. Nagarajan (No.2) see Nagarajan v. London Regional Transport
Swinton v. Annabel's (Berkeley Square) Ltd (Unreported, July 8, 2004), CC
  (Lambeth) [*Ex rel.* Tim Petts, Barrister, 12 King's Bench Walk, London] . . . .   *Digested*, 05/**2842**
Swiss Reinsurance Co v. United India Insurance Co Ltd [2005] EWHC 237; [2005] 2
  All E.R. (Comm) 367; [2005] 1 C.L.C. 203; [2005] Lloyd's Rep. I.R. 341, QBD
  (Comm) . . . .   *Digested*, 05/**2401**
Swissair Schweizerische Luftverkehr AG, Re see Flightline Ltd v. Edwards
Swissport International Ltd v. Holco [2005] I.L.Pr. 40, Cass (F)
Sykes v. Patel (Unreported, May 4, 2004), CC (Birmingham) [*Ex rel.* Levenes
  Solicitors, 35 Dale End, Birmingham] . . . .   *Digested*, 05/**3102**
Syme (Deceased), Re [1980] V.R. 109 . . . .   *Followed*, 05/**3978**
Symons v. Revenue and Customs Commissioners [2005] S.T.I. 1735, V&DTr
Symphony Group Plc v. Hodgson [1994] Q.B. 179; [1993] 3 W.L.R. 830; [1993] 4 All
  E.R. 143; (1993) 143 N.L.J. 725; (1993) 137 S.J.L.B. 134; *Times*, May 4, 1993;
  Independent, May 14, 1993, CA (Civ Div) . . . .   *Digested*, 93/**3153**:
            Applied, 95/3994, 95/3995, 96/710, 99/389, 00/416, 00/423, 00/455,
            01/474, 05/363: *Approved*, 99/749: *Considered*, 94/3623, 96/701, 97/3113,
            97/3343, 99/390, 99/391, 02/393, 02/394: *Followed*, 96/3464, 99/387,
                                                 99/392
Synaptek Ltd v. Young (Inspector of Taxes) [2003] EWHC 645; [2003] S.T.C. 543;
  [2003] I.C.R. 1149; 75 T.C. 51; [2003] B.T.C. 8044; [2003] S.T.I. 529; (2003)
  100(22) L.S.G. 31; *Times*, April 7, 2003, Ch D . . . .   *Digested*, 03/**4030**:
                                         Considered, 05/4128
Syndicat des Agreges de l'Enseignement Superieur (SAGES) v. France (26/2004)
  (2005) 41 E.H.R.R. SE21, ECSR
Syndicat des Professionels Europeens de l'Automobile (SPEA) v. Groupement des
  Concessionnaires Automobiles Peugeot (GCAP) [2005] E.C.C. 49, C d'A
  (Paris)
Syndicat Occitan de l'Education v. France (23/2003) (2005) 40 E.H.R.R. SE15, ECSR
Syndicat Professionnel Coordination des Pecheurs de l'Etang de Berre et de la Region v.
  Electricite de France (EDF) (C213/03) [2004] 3 C.M.L.R. 19; [2005] Env. L.R.
  13, ECJ (2nd Chamber) . . . .   *Digested*, 05/**1377**
Synetairismos Farmakopoion Aitolias & Akarnanias (SYFAIT) v. Glaxosmithkline Plc
  (C53/03) [2005] E.C.R. I-4609; [2005] 5 C.M.L.R. 1, ECJ
SYNGENTA/Transgenic Zea mays plants (T161/02) [2005] E.P.O.R. 11, EPO (Technical Bd
  App) . . . .   *Digested*, 05/**2475**
Synthon BV v. SmithKline Beecham Plc (No.2); *sub nom* SmithKline Beecham Plc's
  (Paroxetine Methanesulfonate) Patent (No.2) [2005] UKHL 59; (2005) 86
  B.M.L.R. 130, HL; reversing [2003] EWCA Civ 861; [2003] R.P.C. 43; (2003)
  147 S.J.L.B. 814, CA (Civ Div); reversing [2002] EWHC 2573; [2003] E.N.P.R.
  10; [2003] R.P.C. 33; (2003) 26(1) I.P.D. 26004, Ch D (Patents Ct) . . . .   *Digested*, 04/**2347**
SYNTRON BIORESEARCH INC/Monitoring system (J10/04) [2005] E.P.O.R. 6, EPO
  (Legal Bd App) . . . .   *Digested*, 05/**2471**
Sysdeco Ireland Ltd v. Sysdeco Northern Ireland Ltd see Dickie v. Cathay Pacific
  Airways Ltd
SYSTRAN/Translating natural languages (T1177/97) [2005] E.P.O.R. 13, EPO (Technical
  Bd App) . . . .   *Digested*, 05/**2484**
Szekeres v. Alan Smeath & Co [2005] EWHC 1733; [2005] 4 Costs L.R. 707; (2005)
  102(32) L.S.G. 31, Ch D
Szoma v. Secretary of State for Work and Pensions [2005] UKHL 64; [2005] 3 W.L.R.
  955; (2005) 102(43) L.S.G. 31; *Times*, November 1, 2005, HL; reversing
  [2003] EWCA Civ 1131; *Times*, August 22, 2003, CA (Civ Div) . . . .   *Digested*, 05/**3882**

T v. DPP [2003] EWHC 2408; (2004) 168 J.P. 194; [2005] Crim. L.R. 739; (2004)
  168 J.P.N. 186; *Times*, October 13, 2003, QBD (Admin) . . . .   *Digested*, 03/**884**
T v. Hungary (2/2003) 18 B.H.R.C. 579
T v. Immigration Officer see T v. Secretary of State for the Home Department

T v. Secretary of State for the Home Department; *sub nom* R. v. Secretary of State for
   the Home Department Ex p. T; T v. Immigration Officer [1996] A.C. 742; [1996] 2
   W.L.R. 766; [1996] 2 All E.R. 865; [1996] Imm. A.R. 443; (1996) 146 N.L.J.
   785; (1996) 140 S.J.L.B. 136; *Times*, May 23, 1996; *Independent*, June 4, 1996,
   HL; affirming [1995] 1 W.L.R. 545; [1995] 2 All E.R. 1042; [1995] Imm. A.R.
   142; *Times*, November 9, 1994; *Independent*, November 4, 1994; *Guardian*,
   November 21, 1994, CA (Civ Div) . . . . *Digested*, 96/**3244**:
                              Considered, 98/3205, 00/3352: *Followed*, 05/2228
T v. United Kingdom (24724/94); V v. United Kingdom (24888/94) [2000] 2 All E.R.
   1024 (Note); (2000) 30 E.H.R.R. 121; 7 B.H.R.C. 659; 12 Fed. Sent. R. 266;
   [2000] Crim. L.R. 187; *Times*, December 17, 1999, ECHR [1999] Crim. L.R. 579,
   Eur Comm HR . . . . *Digested*, 00/**3198**:
            Applied, 03/882: *Cited*, 00/1078, 00/1331: *Considered*, 01/1410, 05/2082,
                    05/2923: *Distinguished*, 03/3781: *Referred to*, 00/1090, 00/1095
T (A Child) v. Wackett (Unreported, July 6, 2004), CC (Maidstone) [*Ex rel*. Joanna
   Kerr, Barrister, Lamb Chambers, Lamb Building, Temple, London] . . . . *Digested*, 05/**3222**
T (A Child) v Hertfordshire CC v. Hertfordshire CC [2004] EWCA Civ 927; [2005]
   B.L.G.R. 262, CA (Civ Div); affirming [2003] EWHC 1725; [2003] E.L.R. 763,
   QBD (Admin) . . . . *Digested*, 04/**1080**
T (A Child) (CICAP: Quantum: 2004: Severe Brain Damage), Re [2005] 3 Q.R. 6, CICAP
   [*Ex rel*. Colin Mendoza, Barrister, Devereux Chambers, Devereux Court,
   London] . . . . *Digested*, 05/**3081**
T (A Child) (Order for Costs), Re [2005] EWCA Civ 311; [2005] 2 F.L.R. 681; [2005] 1
   F.C.R. 625; [2005] Fam. Law 534, CA (Civ Div) . . . . *Digested*, 05/**1619**
T (Adult: Refusal of Treatment), Re; *sub nom* T (Consent to Medical Treatment) (Adult
   Patient), Re [1993] Fam. 95; [1992] 3 W.L.R. 782; [1992] 4 All E.R. 649; [1992]
   2 F.L.R. 458; [1992] 2 F.C.R. 861; [1992] 3 Med. L.R. 306; [1993] Fam. Law
   27; (1992) 142 N.L.J. 1125; *Times*, August 21, 1992; *Independent*, July 31, 1992;
   Guardian, August 5, 1992, CA (Civ Div) . . . . *Digested*, 92/**2918**:
            Applied, 94/3063, 94/3850, 95/4266, 03/58: *Considered*, 95/3535,
                            95/4104, 95/4105, 05/1850: *Referred to*, 94/3803
T (Afghanistan) v. Secretary of State for the Home Department see R (Iran) v.
   Secretary of State for the Home Department
T (Children) v. Megicks (Unreported, September 10, 2004), CC (Edmonton) [*Ex rel*.
   Joanna Kerr, Barrister, Lamb Chambers, Lamb Building, Temple, London] . . . . . . *Digested*, 05/**3121**
T (Children in Care: Contact), Re see T (Minors) (Termination of Contact: Discharge of
   Order), Re
T (Consent to Medical Treatment) (Adult Patient), Re see T (Adult: Refusal of Treatment), Re
T (Eritrea) v. Secretary of State for the Home Department see R (Iran) v. Secretary of
   State for the Home Department
T (Minors) (Termination of Contact: Discharge of Order), Re; *sub nom* T (Children in Care:
   Contact), Re [1997] 1 W.L.R. 393; [1997] 1 All E.R. 65; [1997] 1 F.L.R. 517;
   [1997] 3 F.C.R. 73; [1997] Fam. Law 230; (1997) 161 J.P.N. 236; *Times*, January
   1, 1997, CA (Civ Div) . . . . *Digested*, 97/**438**:
                                                           Applied, 05/1566
T Mobile (UK) Ltd v. First Secretary of State; Hutchinson 3G UK Ltd v. First Secretary
   of State; Orange Personal Communications Services Ltd v. First Secretary of
   State [2004] EWCA Civ 1763; [2005] Env. L.R. 18; [2005] 1 P.L.R. 97; (2004)
   148 S.J.L.B. 1371; *Times*, November 16, 2004, CA (Civ Div); affirming [2004]
   EWHC 1713; [2005] J.P.L. 332; [2005] A.C.D. 17; (2004) 101(26) L.S.G. 29;
   [2004] N.P.C. 103; *Times*, July 8, 2004, QBD (Admin) . . . . *Digested*, 05/**3314**
T&N Ltd, Re [2004] EWHC 1680; [2004] O.P.L.R. 343; [2004] Pens. L.R. 351, Ch D
   (Companies Ct) . . . . *Digested*, 05/**2261**
T&N Ltd, Re [2004] EWHC 2361; [2005] 2 B.C.L.C. 488; [2005] Pens. L.R. 1, Ch D
   (Companies Ct) . . . . *Digested*, 05/**2342**
T&N Ltd, Re [2004] EWHC 2878; [2005] B.C.C. 982, Ch D
T&N Ltd (In Administration) v. Royal & Sun Alliance Plc [2003] EWHC 1016; [2003] 2
   All E.R. (Comm) 939; [2004] Lloyd's Rep. I.R. 106; (2003) 153 N.L.J. 750,
   Ch D . . . . *Digested*, 04/**2215**:
                                       Considered, 05/264: *Doubted*, 04/2217
T&N Retirement Benefits Scheme (1989), Re see Alexander Forbes Trustee Services Ltd v.
   Jackson
TA King (Services) Ltd, Re see Cottrell v. King
Tableau Holdings v. Williams see Cenlon Finance Co Ltd v. Ellwood (Inspector of Taxes)
Tailby v. Official Receiver; *sub nom* Official Receiver as Trustee of the Estate of Izon (A
   Bankrupt) v. Tailby (1888) L.R. 13 App. Cas. 523, HL; reversing (1887) L.R. 18
   Q.B.D. 25, CA; reversing (1886) L.R. 17 Q.B.D. 88, QBD . . . . *Applied*, 52/256,
                    91/2601, 05/2320: *Considered*, 94/2601: *Followed*, 62/354
Tajik Aluminium Plant v. Hydro Aluminium AS [2005] EWCA Civ 1218; [2005] 4 All
   E.R. 1232; [2005] 2 C.L.C. 604; *Independent*, October 28, 2005, CA (Civ Div)
Takeda Pharmaceutical Co Ltd v. Teva Pharmaceutical Industries Ltd [2005] EWHC
   2191; (2005) 28(10) I.P.D. 28081, Ch D (Patents Ct)
Talbot Underwriting Ltd v. Nausch Hogan & Murray [2005] EWHC 2359; [2005] 2
   C.L.C. 868, QBD (Comm)

alisman Property Co (UK) Ltd *v.* Norton Rose (A Firm) [2005] EWHC 85; [2005] 2 P. & C.R. DG2, Ch D

angney *v.* Governor of Elmley Prison; *sub nom* R. (on the application of Tangney) *v.* Secretary of State for the Home Department [2005] EWCA Civ 1009; [2005] H.R.L.R. 36; *Times,* August 30, 2005, CA (Civ Div) . . . . *Digested,* 05/**2909**

anner *v.* Everitt [2004] EWHC 1130; [2004] B.P.I.R. 1026, Ch D . . . . *Digested,* 05/**2308**

apecrown Ltd *v.* First Secretary of State [2005] EWHC 1026; [2005] 2 P. & C.R. 33, QBD (Admin)

aree *v.* Bold Transmission Parts Ltd see Brown *v.* Kigass Aero Components Ltd

arnesby *v.* Kensington, Chelsea and Westminster AHA (Teaching) [1981] I.C.R. 615; [1981] I.R.L.R. 369; 125 S.J. 464, HL; affirming [1980] I.C.R. 475; 124 S.J. 377, CA (Civ Div); affirming (1978) 123 S.J. 49, QBD . . . . *Digested,* 81/**1728**:
Cited, 03/1155: *Considered,* 05/1307

asmanian Seafoods Pty Ltd *v.* MacQueen (2004-05) 7 I.T.E.L.R. 887, Sup Ct (Tas) (Full Ct)

avistock Golf Club *v.* West Devon Valuation Officer [2004] R.A. 289, VT . . . . *Digested,* 05/**3370**

avoulareas *v.* Alexander G Tsavliris & Sons Maritime Co (No.2) [2005] EWHC 2643; [2005] 2 C.L.C. 848, QBD (Comm)

avoulareas *v.* Tsavliris (The Atlas Pride) [2004] EWCA Civ 48; [2004] 2 All E.R. (Comm) 221; [2004] 1 Lloyd's Rep. 445; [2004] 1 C.L.C. 423; [2004] I.L.Pr. 29, CA (Civ Div); reversing [2003] EWHC 550; [2004] I.L.Pr. 3, QBD (Comm) . *Digested,* 05/**468**

axation of Wine, Re (106/84) see Commission of the European Communities *v.* Denmark (106/84)

ayeb *v.* HSBC Bank Plc [2004] EWHC 1529; [2004] 4 All E.R. 1024; [2004] 2 All E.R. (Comm) 880; [2005] 1 C.L.C. 866; (2004) 154 N.L.J. 1217, QBD (Comm) . . . . *Digested,* 05/**259**

aylor, Re; *sub nom* Lloyds Bank *v.* Jones [1957] 1 W.L.R. 1043; [1957] 3 All E.R. 56; 101 S.J. 816, Ch D . . . . *Digested,* 57/**3690**:
Applied, 75/3571: *Considered,* 71/12095: *Distinguished,* 66/10940, 05/3978

aylor *v.* Bratherton (Inspector of Taxes) [2005] S.T.C. (S.C.D.) 230; [2005] S.T.I. 107, Sp Comm . . . . *Digested,* 05/**4070**

aylor *v.* Grier (No.3) (Unreported, May 12, 2003) . . . . *Not followed,* 05/2899

aylor *v.* Lancashire CC see Lancashire CC *v.* Taylor

aylor *v.* Lawrence (Appeal: Jurisdiction to Reopen) [2002] EWCA Civ 90; [2003] Q.B. 528; [2002] 3 W.L.R. 640; [2002] 2 All E.R. 353; [2002] C.P. Rep. 29; (2002) 99(12) L.S.G. 35; (2002) 152 N.L.J. 221; (2002) 146 S.J.L.B. 50; *Times,* February 8, 2002; *Independent,* February 14, 2002; *Daily Telegraph,* February 14, 2002, CA (Civ Div) . . . . *Digested,* 02/**294**:
Applied, 02/296, 03/443, 04/255, 05/464: *Considered,* 03/453:
Explained, 04/870: *Followed,* 03/842

aylor *v.* Lodgepower Ltd see Lodgepower Ltd *v.* Taylor

B *v.* JB (formerly JH) (Abduction: Grave Risk of Harm) [2001] 2 F.L.R. 515; [2001] 2 F.C.R. 497; [2001] Fam. Law 576, CA (Civ Div) . . . . *Digested,* 01/**2546**:
Applied, 03/1503, 05/1545: *Considered,* 02/1632

BL Realisations Plc, Re see Oakley-Smith *v.* Greenberg

Cl Trans Commodities AG *v.* Islamic Solidarity Shipping Co Jordan Inc see Jindal Iron & Steel Co Ltd *v.* Islamic Solidarity Shipping Co Jordan Inc

ea Corp, Re; *sub nom* Sorsbie v. Tea Corp; Tea Corp Ltd, Re [1904] 1 Ch. 12, CA . . . . . *Applied,* 05/**2335**:
Considered, 92/2532

echnip-Coflexip SA *v.* Tube Tech International Ltd see Tube Tech International Ltd *v.* Technip-Coflexip SA

echnocrats International Inc *v.* Fredic Ltd (No.3) [2004] EWHC 2674; [2005] 1 B.C.L.C. 467, QBD . . . . *Digested,* 05/**709**

ee *v.* Inspector of Taxes see West (Inspector of Taxes) *v.* Trennery

eeluck *v.* Queen, The see Teeluck *v.* Trinidad and Tobago

eeluck *v.* Trinidad and Tobago; *sub nom* Teeluck *v.* Queen, The; John *v.* Trinidad and Tobago [2005] UKPC 14; [2005] 1 W.L.R. 2421; [2005] 2 Cr. App. R. 25; [2005] Crim. L.R. 728; *Times,* May 4, 2005, PC (Trin) . . . . *Digested,* 05/**938**

ektrol Ltd (formerly Atto Power Controls Ltd) *v.* International Insurance Co of Hanover Ltd [2005] EWCA Civ 845; [2005] 2 Lloyd's Rep. 701; [2005] 2 C.L.C. 339, CA (Civ Div); reversing [2004] EWHC 2473; [2005] 1 All E.R. (Comm) 132; [2005] Info. T.L.R. 130; [2005] Lloyd's Rep. I.R. 358, QBD (Comm) . . . . *Digested,* 05/**2352**

elefon & Buch Verlags Gmbh *v.* Office for Harmonisation in the Internal Market (Trade Marks and Designs) (OHIM) (C326/01) [2004] E.C.R. I-1371; [2005] E.T.M.R. 50, ECJ (4th Chamber) . . . . *Digested,* 05/**2557**

elekom Austria, Re (16 OK 11/03) [2005] E.C.C. 48, OGH (A)

elewest Communications Plc *v.* Customs and Excise Commissioners [2005] EWCA Civ 102; [2005] S.T.C. 481; [2005] B.T.C. 5125; [2005] B.V.C. 156; [2005] S.T.I. 220; (2005) 102(17) L.S.G. 33; *Times,* February 21, 2005, CA (Civ Div); reversing [2003] EWHC 3176; [2004] S.T.C. 517; [2004] B.T.C. 5282; [2004] B.V.C. 342; [2004] S.T.I. 54, Ch D; affirming [2003] B.V.C. 2296; [2003] V. & D.R. 54; [2003] S.T.I. 982, V&DTr (London) . . . . *Digested,* 05/**4419**

Telewest Communications Plc (No.1), Re [2004] EWCA Civ 728; [2005] B.C.C. 29; [2005] 1 B.C.L.C. 752, CA (Civ Div); affirming [2004] EWHC 924; [2004] B.C.C. 342; *Times*, May 27, 2004, Ch D (Companies Ct) . . . .   *Digested*, 05/**2333**
                                                             Applied, 05/233**5**

Telewest Communications Plc (No.2), Re [2004] EWHC 1466; [2005] B.C.C. 36; [2005] 1 B.C.L.C. 772, Ch D (Companies Ct) . . . .   *Digested*, 05/**233**4

Templeton (Inspector of Taxes) *v.* Transform Shop Office & Bar Fitters Ltd [2005] EWHC 1558; 77 T.C. 229; [2005] S.T.I. 1261; *Times*, September 20, 2005, Ch D . . . .   *Digested*, 05/**401**7

Ten Holder *v.* Nieuwe Algemene Bedrijfsvereniging (302/84) [1986] E.C.R. 1821; [1987] 2 C.M.L.R. 208, ECJ (3rd Chamber) . . . .   *Followed*, 05/390**0**

Tendring DC *v.* Hodges [2005] P.A.D. 11, Planning Inspector

Tendring DC *v.* Orrin [2005] P.A.D. 33, Planning Inspector

Tene *v.* Trader Com France SA [2005] E.C.C. 33, Cass (F)

Tenenbaum (also known as Ferrat) *v.* Petraco Distribution Sarl [2005] E.C.C. 14, Cass (F)

Tennant *v.* Adamczyk [2005] 41 E.G.C.S. 205, CA (Civ Div)

Terra Baubedarf-Handel GmbH *v.* Finanzamt Osterholz-Scharmbeck (C152/02) [2005] S.T.C. 525; [2004] E.C.R. I-5583; [2004] 3 C.M.L.R. 46; [2004] S.T.I. 1169, ECJ (5th Chamber) . . . .   *Digested*, 05/**436**5

Terry *v.* Tower Hamlets LBC [2005] EWHC 2783; [2005] N.P.C. 144, QBD

Terry (t/a C&J Terry & Sons) *v.* Revenue and Customs Commissioners [2005] S.T.C. (S.C.D.) 629, Sp Comm

Tesco Plc *v.* Customs and Excise Commissioners [2003] EWCA Civ 1367; [2003] S.T.C. 1561; [2003] B.T.C. 5608; [2003] S.T.I. 1820; (2003) 100(42) L.S.G. 32; *Times*, October 16, 2003; *Independent*, October 17, 2003, CA (Civ Div); affirming [2002] EWHC 2131; [2002] S.T.C. 1332; [2003] 1 C.M.L.R. 5; [2002] B.T.C. 5613; [2003] B.V.C. 39; [2002] S.T.I. 1393, Ch D; reversing in part [2001] B.V.C. 2416; [2001] V. & D.R. 366; [2002] S.T.I. 363, V&DTr . . . .   *Digested*, 04/**4015**
                                                             Applied, 05/439**4**

Tesco Stores Ltd *v.* Harrow LBC [2003] EWHC 2919; (2003) 167 J.P. 657, QBD (Admin) . . . .   *Digested*, 04/**1599**
                                                             Applied, 05/92**3**

Tesco Stores Ltd's Trade Mark Applications, Re [2005] R.P.C. 17, App Person . . . .   *Digested*, 05/**2581**

Test Claimants in Loss Relief Group Litigation *v.* Inland Revenue Commissioners see Autologic Holdings Plc *v.* Inland Revenue Commissioners

Test Valley BC *v.* Minilec Engineering Ltd (In Liquidation) [2005] 2 E.G.L.R. 113, Ch D

Tetsall, Re; *sub nom* Foyster *v.* Tetsall [1961] 1 W.L.R. 938; [1961] 2 All E.R. 801; 105 S.J. 444, Ch D . . . .   *Digested*, 61/**9182**
                           Applied, 84/3661, 85/3640, 05/397**5**

Tetteh *v.* Kingston upon Thames RLBC [2004] EWCA Civ 1775; [2005] H.L.R. 21, CA (Civ Div) . . . .   *Digested*, 05/**199**0

Tewkesbury BC *v.* Keeley [2004] EWHC 2594; [2005] J.P.L. 831, QBD . . . .   *Digested*, 05/**324**4

Texuna International Ltd *v.* Cairn Energy Plc [2004] EWHC 1102; [2005] 1 B.C.L.C. 579, QBD (Comm)

TFS Derivatives Ltd *v.* Morgan [2004] EWHC 3181; [2005] I.R.L.R. 246, QBD . . . .   *Digested*, 05/**70**0

Thakerar *v.* Lynch Hall & Hornby (Civil Restraint Order), *Times*, November 30, 2005, Ch D

Thaler *v.* Austria (58141/00) (2005) 41 E.H.R.R. 33, ECHR

Thames Water Utilities Ltd *v.* Marcic see Marcic *v.* Thames Water Utilities Ltd

Thanet DC *v.* Collins [2005] P.A.D. 29, Planning Inspector

Thibault *v.* Caisse Nationale d'Assurance Vieillesse des Travailleurs Salaries (C136/95) see Caisse Nationale d'Assurance Vieillesse des Travailleurs Salaries (CNAVTS) *v.* Thibault (C136/95)

Thirkell *v.* Carillion Housing (Unreported, September 7, 2004), CC (Middlesbrough) [*Ex rel.* Monica Whyte, Barrister, 22 Old Buildings, Lincoln's Inn, London] . . . . .   *Digested*, 05/**321**1

Thoars (Deceased), Re see Reid *v.* Ramlort Ltd

Thomas *v.* Brighton HA see Wells *v.* Wells

Thomas *v.* Chief Adjudication Officer (C328/91) see Secretary of State for Social Security *v.* Thomas (C328/91)

Thomas *v.* Hughes see Thomas *v.* News Group Newspapers Ltd

Thomas *v.* News Group International Ltd see Thomas *v.* News Group Newspapers Ltd

Thomas *v.* News Group Newspapers Ltd; *sub nom* Thomas *v.* Hughes; Thomas *v.* News Group International Ltd [2001] EWCA Civ 1233; [2002] E.M.L.R. 4; (2001) 98(34) L.S.G. 43; (2001) 145 S.J.L.B. 207; *Times*, July 25, 2001; *Independent*, November 12, 2001 (C.S); *Daily Telegraph*, July 24, 2001, CA (Civ Div) . . . .   *Digested*, 01/**4418**
                           Applied, 05/4191: *Considered*, 05/419**5**

Thomas v. Thomas [1947] A.C. 484; [1947] 1 All E.R. 582; 1947 S.C. (H.L.) 45; 1948
    S.L.T. 2; 1947 S.L.T. (Notes) 53; 63 T.L.R. 314; [1948] L.J.R. 515; 176 L.T. 498,
    HL; reversing 1946 S.C. 81; 1946 S.L.T. 63, IH (2 Div) . . . .   *Digested*, 48/**4277**:
                Applied, 47-51/2723, 47-51/2829, 47-51/2837, 47-51/5995, 47-51/7495,
                    47-51/9902, 47-51/10957, 52/987, 55/2078, 59/431, 70/3157, 76/338,
                97/5959, 98/5439, 98/6102, 01/6217, 03/3539: *Considered*, 74/1069,
                91/5082, 94/3280, 94/3439, 03/5285, 05/10: *Distinguished*, 89/5013,
                90/4099: *Followed*, 86/4416, 88/4930: *Not applied*, 47-51/3869
Thomas v. United Kingdom (Admissibility) (19354/02) (2005) 41 E.H.R.R. SE11,
    ECHR
Thomas Bates & Son Ltd v. Wyndham's (Lingerie) Ltd [1981] 1 W.L.R. 505; [1981] 1 All
    E.R. 1077; (1981) 41 P. & C.R. 345; (1980) 257 E.G. 381; 125 S.J. 32, CA (Civ
    Div); affirming (1980) 39 P. & C.R. 517, Ch D . . . .   *Digested*, 81/**1584**:
                Applied, 83/417, 84/1932, 89/2140, 96/3756, 00/4382, 01/5510, 05/3974:
                    Cited, 95/780: *Considered*, 96/5784: *Distinguished*, 90/2833, 92/5952:
                    Not followed, 80/1629, 81/1574
Thomas Cook (New Zealand) Ltd v. Inland Revenue Commissioner [2004] UKPC 53;
    [2005] S.T.C. 297; 77 T.C. 197; [2004] S.T.I. 2378, PC (NZ) . . . .   *Digested*, 05/**262**
Thomas's London Day School v. Jorgensen (Valuation Officer) [2005] R.A. 222, Lands
    Tr
Thomas v. Braintree DC see Braintree DC v. Thompson
Thompson v. Commissioner of Police of the Metropolis; Hsu v. Commissioner of
    Police of the Metropolis [1998] Q.B. 498; [1997] 3 W.L.R. 403; [1997] 2 All
    E.R. 762; (1998) 10 Admin. L.R. 363; (1997) 147 N.L.J. 341; *Times*, February 20,
    1997; *Independent*, February 28, 1997, CA (Civ Div) . . . .   *Digested*, 97/**1765**:
                Applied, 98/1451, 00/5118, 03/893: *Approved*, 97/4856:
                Considered, 99/5229, 01/1524: *Distinguished*, 05/4193: *Followed*, 99/1392
Thompson v. Hampshire CC [2004] EWCA Civ 1016; [2005] B.L.G.R. 467; (2004)
    148 S.J.L.B. 944; [2004] N.P.C. 130; *Times*, October 14, 2004, CA (Civ Div)
Thompson v. Inland Revenue Commissioners [2005] S.T.C. (S.C.D.) 320; [2005] S.T.I.
    222, Sp Comm . . . .   *Digested*, 05/**4062**
Thompson v. News Group International see Venables v. News Group International
    (Breach of Injunction)
Thompson v. United Kingdom (36256/97) (2005) 40 E.H.R.R. 11; *Times*, June 24,
    2004, ECHR . . . .   *Digested*, 05/**2104**
Thompson (Eversley) v. Queen, The [1998] A.C. 811; [1998] 2 W.L.R. 927; (1998) 142
    S.J.L.B. 102, PC (StV) . . . .   *Digested*, 98/**868**:
                Applied, 05/938: *Distinguished*, 98/1050
Thompson (t/a Thompson (HAS) & Co) v. Customs and Excise Commissioners [2005]
    EWHC 342; [2005] S.T.C. 1777; [2005] S.T.I. 369, Ch D
Thomson v. Christie Manson & Woods Ltd [2005] EWCA Civ 555; [2005] P.N.L.R.
    38, CA (Civ Div); affirming in part [2004] EWHC 1101; [2004] P.N.L.R. 42,
    QBD . . . .   *Digested*, 05/**2844**
Thomson v. Inland Revenue Commissioners [2004] S.T.C. (S.C.D.) 520; [2004] S.T.I.
    2240, Sp Comm . . . .   *Digested*, 05/**4120**
Thor Navigation Inc v. Ingosstrakh Insurance Co Ltd [2005] EWHC 19; [2005] 1
    Lloyd's Rep. 547; [2005] 1 C.L.C. 12; [2005] Lloyd's Rep. I.R. 490, QBD
    (Comm) . . . .   *Digested*, 05/**2386**
Thorn v. City Rice Mills (1889) L.R. 40 Ch. D. 357, Ch D . . . .   *Distinguished*, 05/605
Thornby Farms Ltd v. Daventry DC see R. (on the application of Thornby Farms Ltd) v.
    Daventry DC
Thornhill (Trustee in Bankruptcy) v. Atherton [2004] EWCA Civ 1858; [2005] B.P.I.R.
    437, CA (Civ Div) . . . .   *Digested*, 05/**2270**
Thornton v. Newham LBC see Hughes v. Newham LBC
Thorogood v. Revenue and Customs Commissioners [2005] EWHC 1517; [2005]
    S.T.I. 920, Ch D
Thorpe v. Dul; Thorpe v. McGrath; UKEAT/0041/04, UKEAT/0042/04/SM, EAT . . . . . .   *Considered*, 05/1219:
                Previous proceedings, 04/1180
Thorpe v. Dul [2003] I.C.R. 1556, EAT . . . .   *Digested*, 04/**1180**:
                Considered, 05/1219
Thorpe v. McGrath see Thorpe v. Dul
Three Rivers DC v. Bank of England (Application for Judgment in Private) [2005]
    EWCA Civ 933; [2005] C.P. Rep. 47, CA (Civ Div)
Three Rivers DC v. Bank of England (Disclosure) (No.4) [2004] UKHL 48; [2005] 1
    A.C. 610; [2004] 3 W.L.R. 1274; [2005] 4 All E.R. 948; (2004) 101 (46) L.S.G.
    34; (2004) 154 N.L.J. 1727; (2004) 148 S.J.L.B. 1369; *Times*, November 12,
    2004; *Independent*, November 16, 2004, HL; reversing [2004] EWCA Civ 218;
    [2004] Q.B. 916; [2004] 2 W.L.R. 1065; [2004] 3 All E.R. 168; (2004) 101 (11)
    L.S.G. 36; (2004) 154 N.L.J. 382; (2004) 148 S.J.L.B. 297; *Times*, March 3,
    2004; *Independent*, March 10, 2004, CA (Civ Div); affirming [2003] EWHC
    2565, QBD (Comm) . . . .   *Digested*, 05/**299**:
                Considered, 04/257

Three Rivers DC *v.* Bank of England (No.1) [1996] Q.B. 292; [1995] 3 W.L.R. 650; [1995] 4 All E.R. 312; *Times,* December 6, 1994; *Independent,* December 13, CA (Civ Div) . . . . *Digested,* 96/**2780**: *Applied,* 05/315, 05/564

Three Rivers DC *v.* Bank of England (No.3) (Summary Judgment) [2001] UKHL 16; [2003] 2 A.C. 1; [2001] 2 All E.R. 513; [2001] Lloyd's Rep. Bank. 125; (2001) 3 L.G.L.R. 36; *Times,* March 23, 2001, HL . . . . *Digested,* 01/**5355**: *Applied,* 03/509, 05/578: *Considered,* 01/669, 02/505, 03/2462: *Distinguished,* 05/461: *Followed,* 03/478: *Previous proceedings,* 99/4854

Three Rivers DC *v.* Bank of England (No.3) [2003] 2 A.C. 1; [2000] 2 W.L.R. 1220; [2000] 3 All E.R. 1; [2000] Lloyd's Rep. Bank. 235; [2000] 3 C.M.L.R. 205; [2000] Eu. L.R. 583; (2000) 2 L.G.L.R. 769; (2000) 97(23) L.S.G. 41; *Times,* May 19, 2000, HL; affirming in part [2000] 2 W.L.R. 15; [1999] 4 All E.R. 800 (Note); [1999] Lloyd's Rep. Bank. 283; [2000] 3 C.M.L.R. 1; [1999] Eu. L.R. 211; (1999) 1 L.G.L.R. 645; (1999) 11 Admin. L.R. 281; (1999) 163 J.P.N. 314; *Times,* December 10, 1998, CA (Civ Div); affirming [1996] 3 All E.R. 558; [1997] 3 C.M.L.R. 429; *Times,* April 22, 1996, QBD . . . . *Digested,* 00/**270**: *Applied,* 03/4357, 05/4193: *Considered,* 00/5317, 02/4546, 04/753, 05/4197: *Overruled,* 01/5355

Three Rivers DC *v.* Bank of England (Restriction on Cross Examination) [2005] EWCA Civ 889; [2005] C.P. Rep. 46, CA (Civ Div)

Threlfall *v.* General Optical Council [2004] EWHC 2683; [2005] Lloyd's Rep. Med. 250; [2005] A.C.D. 70; (2004) 101(48) L.S.G. 25; *Times,* December 2, 2004, QBD (Admin) . . . . *Digested,* 05/**1917**

Thrells Ltd *v.* Lomas [1993] 1 W.L.R. 456; [1993] 2 All E.R. 546; [1993] B.C.C. 441, Ch D . . . . *Digested,* 93/**3064**: *Applied,* 05/3000

Thrift Rent-a-Car System Inc *v.* Thrift Rent-a-Car Sdn Bhd [2005] F.S.R. 11, HC (Mal) . *Digested,* 05/**2577**

Through Transport Mutual Insurance Association (Eurasia) Ltd *v.* New India Assurance Co Ltd (The Hari Bhum) (No.1) [2004] EWCA Civ 1598; [2005] 1 All E.R. (Comm) 715; [2005] 1 Lloyd's Rep. 67; [2004] 2 C.L.C. 1189; [2005] I.L.Pr. 30; (2004) 148 S.J.L.B. 1435, CA (Civ Div); reversing in part [2003] EWHC 3158; [2004] 1 Lloyd's Rep. 206; [2004] 1 C.L.C. 794, QBD (Comm) . . . . *Digested,* 05/**599**: *Applied,* 05/2357

Through Transport Mutual Insurance Association (Eurasia) Ltd *v.* New India Assurance Co Ltd (The Hari Bhum) (No.2) [2005] EWHC 455; [2005] 2 Lloyd's Rep. 378; [2005] 1 C.L.C. 376, QBD (Comm) . . . . *Digested,* 05/**200**

Thyssen Canada Ltd *v.* Mariana Maritime SA [2005] EWHC 219; [2005] 1 Lloyd's Rep. 640, QBD (Comm) . . . . *Digested,* 05/**199**

Thyssenkrupp Stainless GmbH *v.* Commission of the European Communities (C65/02 P) [2005] 5 C.M.L.R. 16, ECJ (1st Chamber) . . . . *Previous proceedings,* 02/574

Tichband *v.* Hurdman see Hollins *v.* Russell

Tillack *v.* Commission of the European Communities (C521/04); *sub nom* Tillack *v.* Commission of the European Communities (T193/04 R) [2005] 2 C.M.L.R. 37, ECJ [2004] 3 C.M.L.R. 44, CFI . . . . *Digested,* 05/**1441**

Tillack *v.* Commission of the European Communities (T193/04 R) see Tillack *v.* Commission of the European Communities (C521/04)

Tillery Valley Foods *v.* Channel Four Television Corp [2004] EWHC 1075; (2004) 101(22) L.S.G. 31; *Times,* May 21, 2004, Ch D . . . . *Digested,* 05/**2813**

Time Inc *v.* Srivastava [2005] F.S.R. 33, HC (Ind)

Timmins *v.* Conn [2004] EWCA Civ 1761; [2005] B.P.I.R. 647; (2004) 148 S.J.L.B. 1403, CA (Civ Div) . . . . *Digested,* 05/**2310**

Timmins *v.* Gormley see Locabail (UK) Ltd *v.* Bayfield Properties Ltd (Leave to Appeal)

Timofeyev *v.* Russia (58263/00) (2005) 40 E.H.R.R. 38, ECHR

Tinsley *v.* Customs and Excise Commissioners; *sub nom* Revenue and Customs Commissioners *v.* Tinsley; Customs and Excise Commissioners *v.* Tinsley [2005] EWHC 1508; [2005] S.T.C. 1612; [2005] B.T.C. 5576; [2005] B.V.C. 607; [2005] S.T.I. 1063, Ch D; reversing [2002] S.T.I. 1038, V&DTr

Tioxide Europe Ltd *v.* CGU International Insurance Plc [2005] EWCA Civ 928; [2005] 2 C.L.C. 329, CA (Civ Div); affirming [2004] EWHC 2116; [2005] Lloyd's Rep. I.R. 114, QBD (Comm) . . . . *Digested,* 05/**2354**

Tipper *v.* Duggins see Huddersfield Fine Worsteds Ltd, Re

Tkaczuk (Deceased), Re see Dobryden *v.* Wagner

TLL Realisations Ltd, Re see Secretary of State for Trade and Industry *v.* Collins

Tlumaczenie [2005] E.C.D.R. 18, Sad Najwyzszy (PL)

TM Noten BV *v.* Harding [1990] 2 Lloyd's Rep. 283, CA (Civ Div); reversing [1989] 2 Lloyd's Rep. 527, QBD (Comm) . . . . *Digested,* 91/**3252**: *Considered,* 05/2383

Tod's SpA *v.* Heyraud SA (C28/04) [2005] 3 C.M.L.R. 28; [2005] E.C.D.R. 32, ECJ (2nd Chamber)

Todd v. British Midland Airways Ltd [1978] I.C.R. 959; [1978] I.R.L.R. 370; (1978) 13
I.T.R. 553; 122 S.J. 661, CA (Civ Div) . . . . *Digested*, 78/**1138**:
Applied, 05/1329: *Considered*, 89/1490, 99/2055
Todd v. Fawcett (Inspector of Taxes) [2005] S.T.C. (S.C.D.) 97; [2005] W.T.L.R. 377;
[2004] S.T.I. 2402, Sp Comm . . . . *Digested*, 05/**3999**
Todd v. Secretary of State for the Environment, Food and Rural Affairs [2004] EWHC
1450; [2004] 1 W.L.R. 2471; [2004] 4 All E.R. 497; [2005] 1 P. & C.R. 16;
[2005] 2 P.L.R. 1; (2004) 101(26) L.S.G. 29; (2004) 101(28) L.S.G. 34; *Times*,
July 6, 2004, QBD (Admin) . . . . *Digested*, 04/**3247**
Toepfer v. Cremer see Alfred C Toepfer v. Peter Cremer GmbH & Co
Tokai Carbon Co Ltd v. Commission of the European Communities (T236/01) [2004]
E.C.R. II-1181; [2004] 5 C.M.L.R. 28, CFI (2nd Chamber) . . . . *Digested*, 05/**552**
Tokai Carbon Co Ltd v. Commission of the European Communities (T71/03) [2005] 5
C.M.L.R. 13, CFI
Tolstoy Miloslavsky v. Aldington [1996] 1 W.L.R. 736; [1996] 2 All E.R. 556; [1996]
P.N.L.R. 335; (1996) 93(1) L.S.G. 22; (1996) 140 S.J.L.B. 26; *Times*, December
27, 1995; *Independent*, January 3, 1996, CA (Civ Div) . . . . *Digested*, 96/**3899**:
Considered, 02/393: *Followed*, 98/415, 02/363, 03/339, 05/496
Tombs v. Wilson Connolly Ltd (formerly Wilcon Homes Ltd) [2004] EWHC 2809; 98
Con. L.R. 44, QBD (TCC) . . . . *Digested*, 05/**654**
Tomlinson v. Congleton BC [2003] UKHL 47; [2004] 1 A.C. 46; [2003] 3 W.L.R. 705;
[2003] 3 All E.R. 1122; [2004] P.I.Q.R. P8; [2003] 32 E.G.C.S. 68; (2003)
100(34) L.S.G. 33; (2003) 153 N.L.J. 1238; (2003) 147 S.J.L.B. 937; [2003]
N.P.C. 102; *Times*, August 1, 2003; *Independent*, October 7, 2003, HL; reversing
[2002] EWCA Civ 309; [2003] 2 W.L.R. 1120; [2002] P.I.Q.R. P30; [2002]
12 E.G.C.S. 136; (2002) 99(18) L.S.G. 38; (2002) 146 S.J.L.B. 92; [2002]
N.P.C. 42; *Times*, March 22, 2002; *Independent*, March 21, 2002, CA (Civ Div) . *Digested*, 03/**4360**:
Applied, 03/2980, 05/1955: *Considered*, 03/4361, 05/4194, 05/4196
Tonbridge and Malling BC v. Davis; *sub nom* Davis v. Tonbridge and Malling BC [2004]
EWCA Civ 194; (2004) 101(10) L.S.G. 30; (2004) 148 S.J.L.B. 270; [2004]
N.P.C. 30; *Times*, March 5, 2004; *Independent*, March 5, 2004, CA (Civ Div);
affirming [2003] EWHC 1069; [2003] N.P.C. 63, QBD . . . . *Digested*, 05/**3285**
Tongue v. Dugger (Unreported, October 11, 2004), CC (Birmingham) [*Ex rel.* Stephen
Garner, Barrister, No.8 Chambers, Fountain Court, Steelhouse Lane,
Birmingham.] . . . . *Digested*, 05/**3144**
Tonicstar Ltd (t/a Lloyds Syndicate 1861) v. American Home Assurance Co [2004]
EWHC 1234; [2005] Lloyd's Rep. I.R. 32, QBD (Comm) . . . . *Digested*, 05/**600**
Tonnelier v. Smith (1897) 2 Com. Cas. 258 . . . . *Applied*, 80/2450,
05/3789
Toomey v. Banco Vitalicio de Espana SA de Seguros y Reaseguros [2004] EWCA Civ
622; [2004] 1 C.L.C. 965; [2005] Lloyd's Rep. I.R. 423; (2004) 148 S.J.L.B.
633, CA (Civ Div); affirming [2003] EWHC 1102; [2004] Lloyd's Rep. I.R. 354,
QBD (Comm) . . . . *Digested*, 05/**2398**
Tootal Clothing Ltd v. Guinea Properties Management Ltd (1992) 64 P. & C.R. 452;
[1992] 41 E.G. 117; [1992] E.G.C.S. 80; [1992] N.P.C. 75; *Times*, June 8, 1992;
Independent, June 8, 1992, CA (Civ Div) . . . . *Digested*, 93/**2491**:
Considered, 94/3513: *Distinguished*, 97/1005, 05/695: *Doubted*, 01/4852
Top Deck Maintenance v. Repair Centre see Hanning v. Top Deck Travel Group Ltd
Topping v. Benchtown Ltd (formerly Jones Bros (Preston) Ltd) see Grieves v. FT
Everard & Sons Ltd
Topplan Estates Ltd v. Townley [2004] EWCA Civ 1369; [2005] 1 E.G.L.R. 89; (2004)
148 S.J.L.B. 1284; [2004] N.P.C. 158; *Times*, November 15, 2004; *Independent*,
November 5, 2004, CA (Civ Div) . . . . *Digested*, 05/**3422**
Torfaen Voluntary Alliance v. Customs and Excise Commissioners [2005] S.T.I. 115,
V&DTr
Toronto Blue Jays Baseball Club v. Ontario 7 I.T.L. Rep. 591, CA (Ont)
Torquay Hotel Co Ltd v. Cousins [1969] 2 Ch. 106; [1969] 2 W.L.R. 289; [1969] 1 All
E.R. 522; 6 K.I.R. 15; (1968) 113 S.J. 52; *Times*, December 18, 1968, CA (Civ
Div); affirming [1968] 3 W.L.R. 540; [1968] 3 All E.R. 43; 4 K.I.R. 635; (1968)
112 S.J. 688, Ch D . . . . *Digested*, 69/**3574**:
Applied, 73/2661, 78/1025, 83/3704: *Considered*, 70/2739, 82/3276,
87/3771, 05/4189
Torres v. Secretary of State for the Home Department see R. (on the application of
Rodriguez-Torres) v. Secretary of State for the Home Department
TOSHIBA/I C card (T273/02) [2005] E.P.O.R. 52, EPO (Technical Bd App)

Toshoku Finance UK Plc (In Liquidation), Re; *sub nom* Inland Revenue Commissioners *v.*
Kahn; Kahn *v.* Inland Revenue Commissioners; Khan *v.* Inland Revenue
Commissioners [2002] UKHL 6; [2002] 1 W.L.R. 671; [2002] 3 All E.R. 961;
[2002] S.T.C. 368; [2002] B.C.C. 110; [2002] 1 B.C.L.C. 598; [2002] B.P.I.R.
790; [2003] R.V.R. 106; [2002] B.T.C. 69; [2002] S.T.I. 237; (2002) 99(12)
L.S.G. 33; (2002) 146 S.J.L.B. 55; *Times*, February 25, 2002, HL; affirming
[2000] 1 W.L.R. 2478; [2000] 3 All E.R. 938; [2000] S.T.C. 301; [2001] B.C.C.
373; [2000] 1 B.C.L.C. 683; [2000] B.T.C. 96; [2000] S.T.I. 503; (2000)
97(15) L.S.G. 39; (2000) 144 S.J.L.B. 165; *Times*, March 29, 2000, CA (Civ
Div); reversing [1999] S.T.C. 922; [1999] 2 B.C.L.C. 777; [1999] B.T.C. 367,
Ch D .... *Digested*, 02/**2718**:
Distinguished, 05/2260
Tovell *v.* Suffolk CC [2005] 2 Q.R. 20; [2004] 6 Q.R. 10, CC (Southend) [*Ex rel.*
Victoria Seifert, Pupil Barrister, Tanfield Chambers, 2nd Floor, Francis Taylor
Building, Temple, London] .... *Digested*, 04/**2951**
Tower Hamlets LBC *v.* Barrett; *sub nom* Barrett *v.* Tower Hamlets LBC [2005] EWCA
Civ 923; (2005) 149 S.J.L.B. 922; [2005] N.P.C. 95, CA (Civ Div)
Tower Hamlets LBC *v.* Begum (Rahanara) [2005] EWCA Civ 116; [2005] B.L.G.R.
580; [2005] N.P.C. 23; *Times*, February 22, 2005, CA (Civ Div) .... *Digested*, 05/**2009**
Tower Hamlets LBC *v.* Begum (Rikha) see Begum (Rikha) *v.* Tower Hamlets LBC
Townend (t/a Johns Radio) *v.* Goodall (Valuation Officer) [2005] R.A. 209, Lands Tr
Townends Group Ltd *v.* Cobb; *sub nom* Townends Grove Ltd *v.* Cobb [2004] EWHC
3432; (2005) 102(4) L.S.G. 30; *Times*, December 1, 2004, Ch D
Townends Grove Ltd *v.* Cobb see Townends Group Ltd *v.* Cobb
Townsend *v.* Stone Toms & Partners (No.2) 27 B.L.R. 26; (1984) 81 L.S.G. 2293;
(1984) 128 S.J. 659, CA (Civ Div) .... *Digested*, 85/**2701**:
Cited, 05/474: *Considered*, 97/681
Townsend *v.* United Kingdom (42039/98) [2005] R.V.R. 58; *Times*, January 27, 2005,
ECHR .... *Digested*, 05/**2098**
Tracey *v.* United Kingdom see Brogan *v.* United Kingdom (A/145-B)
Tradax Ocean Transportation SA *v.* Pagnan see Pagnan SpA *v.* Tradax Ocean
Transportation SA
Trade Indemnity Co Ltd *v.* Workington Harbour and Dock Board (No.1); *sub nom*
Workington Harbour and Dock Board *v.* Trade Indemnity Co Ltd [1937] A.C. 1;
(1936) 54 Ll. L. Rep. 103, HL; affirming (1934) 49 Ll. L. Rep. 430, CA; reversing
(1933) 47 Ll. L. Rep. 305, KBD .... *Applied*, 95/768,
05/275: *Distinguished*, 95/767
Tradigrain SA *v.* State Trading Corp of India [2005] EWHC 2206; [2005] 2 C.L.C. 589,
QBD (Comm)
Trailer & Marina (Leven) Ltd *v.* Secretary of State for the Environment, Food and Rural
Affairs see R. (on the application of Trailer & Marina (Leven) Ltd) *v.* Secretary of
State for the Environment, Food and Rural Affairs
Tran *v.* Greenwich Vietnam Community Project; *sub nom* Kien Tran *v.* Greenwich
Vietnam Community Project [2002] EWCA Civ 553; [2002] I.C.R. 1101; [2002]
I.R.L.R. 735; (2002) 99(21) L.S.G. 31, CA (Civ Div); affirming EAT/185/00,
EAT .... *Digested*, 03/**1346**:
Applied, 05/1256
Transco Plc *v.* HM Advocate (No.1) 2004 J.C. 29; 2004 S.L.T. 41; 2004 S.C.C.R. 1;
[2005] B.C.C. 296; 2003 G.W.D. 38-1039, HCJ. .... *Digested*, 04/**4634**
Transmetro Corp Ltd *v.* Real Investments Pty Ltd [1999] 17 A.C.L.C. 1314, Sup Ct
(Qld) .... *Applied*, 05/2321
Transport and General Workers Union *v.* Asda [2004] I.R.L.R. 836, CAC .... *Digested*, 05/**1202**
Travel Group Plc, Re (2005) 102(2) L.S.G. 28, Ch D
Travelers Casualty & Surety Co of Europe Ltd *v.* Customs and Excise Commissioners
[2005] V. & D.R. 230, V&DTr (London)
Travelers Casualty & Surety Co of Europe Ltd *v.* Sun Life Assurance Co of Canada (UK)
Ltd [2004] EWHC 1704; [2004] I.L.Pr. 50; [2004] Lloyd's Rep. I.R. 846, QBD
(Comm) .... *Digested*, 05/**606**
Travell *v.* Customs and Excise Commissioners (1998) 162 J.P. 181; [1998] C.O.D. 92;
Independent, November 4, 1997, DC .... *Digested*, 97/**1741**:
Followed, 05/949
Treasury Solicitor *v.* Regester [1978] 1 W.L.R. 446; [1978] 2 All E.R. 920; 122 S.J. 163,
QBD .... *Digested*, 78/**2817**:
Considered, 05/352
Treharne *v.* Brabon see Brabon, Re
Trend Properties Ltd *v.* Crutchfield (Inspector of Taxes) [2005] S.T.C. (S.C.D.) 534, Sp
Comm
Trennery *v.* West (Inspector of Taxes) see West (Inspector of Taxes) *v.* Trennery
Triad Shipping Co *v.* Stellar Chartering and Brokerage Inc (The Island Archon) [1995] 1
All E.R. 595; [1994] 2 Lloyd's Rep. 227; *Times*, July 8, 1994; *Independent*, July
20, 1994, CA (Civ Div); affirming [1993] 2 Lloyd's Rep. 388, QBD (Comm) .... *Digested*, 94/**4059**:
Applied, 05/3814

TRIDONIC/Divisional of a divisional application (T1158/01); *sub nom* TridonicAtco GmbH
& Co KG, Re (T1158/01) [2005] E.P.O.R. 32; (2005) 28(4) I.P.D. 28031, EPO
(Technical Bd App) .... *Digested,* 05/**2439**
TridonicAtco GmbH & Co KG, Re (T1158/01) see TRIDONIC/Divisional of a divisional
application (T1158/01)
Triesman *v.* Ali; *sub nom* McDonagh *v.* Ali; Ali *v.* McDonagh [2002] EWCA Civ 93;
[2002] I.C.R. 1026; [2002] I.R.L.R. 489; *Times,* March 11, 2002; *Independent,*
February 15, 2002, CA (Civ Div); reversing (2001) 151 N.L.J. 610, EAT .... *Digested,* 02/**1395**:
Applied, 05/429
Trinidad and Tobago News Centre Ltd *v.* Attorney General of Trinidad and Tobago see
Independent Publishing Co Ltd *v.* Attorney General of Trinidad and Tobago
Triodos Bank NV *v.* Dobbs; *sub nom* Triodosbank NV *v.* Dobbs [2005] EWCA Civ 630;
[2005] 2 Lloyd's Rep. 588; [2005] 2 C.L.C. 95; *Times,* May 30, 2005, CA
(Civ Div) .... *Digested,* 05/**275**
Triodos Bank NV *v.* Dobbs (Application for Stay of Appeal) [2005] EWCA Civ 468;
(2005) 105(36) L.S.G. 29; *Times,* May 11, 2005, CA (Civ Div) .... *Digested,* 05/**35**
Triodosbank NV *v.* Dobbs see Triodos Bank NV *v.* Dobbs
Trojani *v.* Centre Public d'Aide Sociale de Bruxelles (CPAS) (C456/02) [2004] All E.R.
(EC) 1065; [2004] E.C.R. I-7573; [2004] 3 C.M.L.R. 38; [2005] C.E.C. 139,
ECJ .... *Digested,* 05/**3856**
Trollope & Colls Ltd *v.* North West Metropolitan Regional Hospital Board [1973] 1
W.L.R. 601; [1973] 2 All E.R. 260; 9 B.L.R. 60; 117 S.J. 355, HL .... *Digested,* 73/**270**:
Applied, 82/2940, 92/314, 05/655: *Considered,* 80/17, 90/401, 96/1218,
00/4640: *Distinguished,* 81/828: *Followed,* 80/357
Trouw (UK) Ltd *v.* Rhodia Ltd see Provimi Ltd *v.* Aventis Animal Nutrition SA
Trouw (UK) Ltd *v.* Roche Products Ltd see Provimi Ltd *v.* Aventis Animal Nutrition SA
Truelove *v.* Safeway Stores Plc [2005] I.C.R. 589, EAT .... *Digested,* 05/**1308**
Truscott *v.* Truscott see Wraith *v.* Sheffield Forgemasters Ltd
Trustee *v.* Inland Revenue Commissioners see Hurren (A Bankrupt), Re
Trustees in the CB Simkin Trust *v.* Inland Revenue Commissioner see Simkin's Trustees *v.*
Inland Revenue Commissioner
TRUSTEES OF DARTMOUTH COLLEGE/Divisional application (J2/01) [2004] E.P.O.R.
54; (2005) 28(4) I.P.D. 28030, EPO (Legal Bd App) .... *Digested,* 05/**2463**
Trustees of the Crawford Settlement *v.* Revenue and Customs Commissioners see
Crawford Settlement Trustees *v.* Revenue and Customs Commissioners
Trustees of the Duke of Westminster's Estate *v.* United Kingdom (8793/79) see James *v.*
United Kingdom (A/98)
Trustees of the Stokes Pension Fund *v.* Western Power Distribution (South West) Plc see
Stokes Pension Fund Trustees *v.* Western Power Distribution (South West) Plc
Trustees of Walton on Thames Charities *v.* Walton and Weybridge Urban DC 68 L.G.R.
488; (1970) 21 P. & C.R. 411, CA (Civ Div); affirming (1969) 20 P. & C.R. 250;
[1969] R.V.R. 124, Lands Tr .... *Digested,* 70/**2785**:
Considered, 05/3303
Trusts of the Scientific Investment Pension Plan, Re see Scientific Investment Pension Plan
(No.2), Re
TRUTAC/Entitlement to appeal (T981/01) [2005] E.P.O.R. 24, EPO (Technical Bd App)   *Digested,* 05/**2451**
Tryg Baltica International (UK) Ltd *v.* Boston Compania de Seguros SA [2004] EWHC
1186; [2005] Lloyd's Rep. I.R. 40, QBD (Comm) .... *Digested,* 05/**2379**
Tsagaan *v.* Secretary of State for the Home Department [2004] EWCA Civ 1506, CA
(Civ Div) .... *Followed,* 05/2150
TSB England and Wales *v.* Department of Trade and Industry see JH Rayner (Mincing
Lane) Ltd *v.* Department of Trade and Industry
TSP Group Ltd *v.* Globemark (UK) Ltd [2005] EWHC 2396; *Times,* November 30,
2005, QBD
Tube Tech International Ltd *v.* Technip-Coflexip SA; *sub nom* Technip-Coflexip SA *v.* Tube
Tech International Ltd [2005] EWCA Civ 1369, CA (Civ Div); affirming [2005]
EWHC 2; 99 Con. L.R. 136, QBD (TCC) .... *Digested,* 05/**699**
Tum *v.* Secretary of State for the Home Department see R. (on the application of Tum)
v. Secretary of State for the Home Department
Tuquabo-Tekle *v.* Netherlands (60665/00) [2005] 3 F.C.R. 649, ECHR
Turkey *v.* Awadh [2005] EWCA Civ 382; [2005] 2 F.C.R. 7; [2005] 2 P. & C.R. 29,
CA (Civ Div) .... *Digested,* 05/**3402**
Turner *v.* Grovit (C159/02); *sub nom* Turner (C159/02), Re [2005] 1 A.C. 101; [2004] 3
W.L.R. 1193; [2004] All E.R. (EC) 485; [2004] 2 All E.R. (Comm) 381; [2004]
2 Lloyd's Rep. 169; [2004] E.C.R. I-3565; [2004] 1 C.L.C. 864; [2004] I.L.Pr.
25; [2005] I.C.R. 23; [2004] I.R.L.R. 899; *Times,* April 29, 2004, ECJ [2004] 1
Lloyd's Rep. 216; [2004] E.C.R. I-3565, AGO .... *Digested,* 04/**1393**:
Considered, 05/599, 05/2357, 05/5032: *Previous proceedings,* 02/641
Turner *v.* Grovit (Reference to ECJ) [2001] UKHL 65; [2002] 1 W.L.R. 107; [2002] 1
All E.R. 960 (Note); [2002] 1 All E.R. (Comm) 320 (Note); [2002] C.L.C. 463;
[2002] I.L.Pr. 28; [2002] I.C.R. 94; [2002] I.R.L.R. 358; (2002) 99(7) L.S.G.
34; (2002) 146 S.J.L.B. 20, HL .... *Digested,* 02/**641**:
Applied, 05/627: *Previous proceedings,* 99/709:
Subsequent proceedings, 04/1393

Turner v. Highbury Corner Magistrates Court see R. (on the application of Turner) v. Highbury Corner Magistrates Court

Turner v. News Group Newspapers Ltd [2005] EWHC 892; [2005] E.M.L.R. 25, QBD . *Digested*, 05/**969**

Turner v. Royal Bank of Scotland Plc (Relitigation) [2000] B.P.I.R. 683, CA (Civ Div) . . *Digested*, 00/**3434**:
Applied, 01/374, 03/2350, 05/2336: *Considered*, 05/2279:
Distinguished, 03/2347

Turner v. Turner (Unreported, July 30, 2004), ET [*Ex rel*. David Calvert, Barrister, St James's Chambers, 68 Quay Street, Manchester.] . . . . *Digested*, 05/**1304**

Turner v. Walsh [1909] 2 K.B. 484, CA. . . . . *Considered*, 88/2084, 89/2162, 05/2657

Turner Corp Ltd v. Austotel Pty Ltd UNRREPORTED . . . . *Distinguished*, 05/**653**

Turner (C159/02), Re see Turner v. Grovit (C159/02)

Turner, In the Estate of [2004] W.T.L.R. 1467, Sup Ct (BC) . . . . *Digested*, 05/**3979**

Turnstem Ltd, Re see Bhanderi v. Customs and Excise Commissioners

Twinsectra Ltd v. Yardley [2002] UKHL 12; [2002] 2 A.C. 164; [2002] 2 W.L.R. 802;
[2002] 2 All E.R. 377; [2002] P.N.L.R. 30; [2002] W.T.L.R. 423; [2002] 38
E.G.C.S. 204; (2002) 99(19) L.S.G. 32; (2002) 152 N.L.J. 469; (2002) 146
S.J.L.B. 84; [2002] N.P.C. 47; *Times*, March 25, 2002, HL; reversing [1999]
Lloyd's Rep. Bank. 438; [2000] Lloyd's Rep. P.N. 239; [2000] W.T.L.R. 527, CA
(Civ Div) . . . . *Digested*, 02/**249**:
Applied, 04/3940, 05/2732: *Considered*, 04/2408, 05/2325:
Distinguished, 03/1421: *Followed*, 99/278, 05/2731

TXU Europe German Finance BV, Re; TXU Europe Ireland 1, Re [2005] B.C.C. 90; [2005]
B.P.I.R. 209, Ch D

TXU Europe Ireland 1, Re see TXU Europe German Finance BV, Re

Tye v. Kirkby (Tyres) Ltd (Unreported, May 25, 2004), CC (Birmingham) [*Ex rel*. Adam
Farrer, Barrister, 5 Fountain Court, Steelhouse Lane, Birmingham] . . . . *Digested*, 05/**3157**

Tyne and Wear Autistic Society v. Smith; *sub nom* Smith v. Tyne and Wear Autistic
Society [2005] 4 All E.R. 1336; [2005] I.C.R. 663; [2005] I.R.L.R. 336, EAT . . *Digested*, 05/**1248**

U (A Child) v. Liverpool City Council; *sub nom* KU (A Child) v. Liverpool City Council
[2005] EWCA Civ 475; [2005] 1 W.L.R. 2657; [2005] 4 Costs L.R. 600; *Times*,
May 16, 2005, CA (Civ Div)

U (A Child) (Serious Injury: Standard of Proof), Re; *sub nom* LU (A Child), Re; LB (A
Child), Re; B (A Child) (Serious Injury: Standard of Proof), Re [2004] EWCA Civ
567; [2005] Fam. 134; [2004] 3 W.L.R. 753; [2004] 2 F.L.R. 263; [2004] 2
F.C.R. 257; [2004] Fam. Law 565; (2004) 101(22) L.S.G. 31; (2004) 154
N.L.J. 824; *Times*, May 27, 2004; *Independent*, May 18, 2004, CA (Civ Div) . . . *Digested*, 04/**1458**:
Applied, 05/1559, 05/1560: *Considered*, 05/4191:
Subsequent proceedings, 05/464

U (A Child) (Serious Injury: Standard of Proof) (Permission to Reopen Appeal), Re; *sub
nom* U (Re-Opening of Appeal), Re [2005] EWCA Civ 52; [2005] 1 W.L.R.
2398; [2005] 3 All E.R. 550; [2005] 2 F.L.R. 444; [2005] 1 F.C.R. 583; [2005]
Fam. Law 449; (2005) 102(16) L.S.G. 30; (2005) 155 N.L.J. 325; (2005) 149
S.J.L.B. 266; *Times*, March 31, 2005, CA (Civ Div) . . . . *Digested*, 05/**464**:
Previous proceedings, 04/1458

U (Children) (Application for Direct Contact), Re [2004] EWCA Civ 71; [2004] 1 F.C.R. 768,
CA (Civ Div) . . . . *Digested*, 05/**1679**

U (Re-Opening of Appeal), Re see U (A Child) (Serious Injury: Standard of Proof)
(Permission to Reopen Appeal), Re

Uberseering BV v. Nordic Construction Co Baumanagement GmbH (NCC) (C208/00)
[2005] 1 W.L.R. 315; [2002] E.C.R. I-9919; [2005] 1 C.M.L.R. 1, ECJ

UBS AG v. Revenue and Customs Commissioners; *sub nom* USB AG v. Revenue and
Customs Commissioners 8 I.T.L. Rep. 595, Ch D; reversing [2005] S.T.C.
(S.C.D.) 589; 7 I.T.L. Rep. 893, Sp Comm

UCB Corporate Services Ltd v. Thomason [2005] EWCA Civ 225; [2005] 1 All E.R.
(Comm) 601, CA (Civ Div); affirming [2004] EWHC 1164; [2004] 2 All E.R.
(Comm) 774, Ch D . . . . *Digested*, 05/**274**

UCB Home Loans Corp Ltd v. Moore see Royal Bank of Scotland Plc v. Etridge (No.2)

Ufficio Distrettuale delle Imposte Dirette di Fiorenzuola d'Arda v. Comune di Carpaneto
Piacentino (231/87) [1991] S.T.C. 205; [1989] E.C.R. 3233; *Times*, November
15, 1989, ECJ . . . . *Digested*, 91/**3661**:
Applied, 02/4739: *Considered*, 01/5579, 01/5609: *Followed*, 05/4411

UIC Insurance Co Ltd (In Provisional Liquidation), Re see Jacob v. Equitas Ltd

Ujah (A Bankrupt), Re [2004] EWHC 367; [2005] B.P.I.R. 216, Ch D

UK Tradecorp Ltd v. Customs and Excise Commissioners (No.1) [2004] V. & D.R. 195;
[2004] S.T.I. 2358, V&DTr (London) . . . . *Digested*, 05/**4376**

UK Tradecorp Ltd v. Customs and Excise Commissioners (No.3) [2005] V. & D.R. 82;
[2005] S.T.I. 896, V&DTr (London)

Ullah (Ahsan) v. Special Adjudicator see R. (on the application of Ullah) v. Special
Adjudicator

Ullah (Mohammed) v. Secretary of State for the Home Department see R. v. Secretary
of State for the Home Department Ex p. Ullah (Mohammed)

Ulrich v. Treasury Solicitor [2005] EWHC 67; [2005] 1 All E.R. 1059; [2005] W.T.L.R. 385; (2004-05) 7 I.T.E.L.R. 552; (2005) 102(16) L.S.G. 27; [2005] 2 P. & C.R. DG9; *Times*, March 23, 2005, Ch D

Ulster Independent Clinic Ltd v. Customs and Excise Commissioners [2004] V. & D.R. 32; [2004] S.T.I. 1307, V&DTr (Belfast) . . . . *Digested*, 05/**4355**

Ultra Motorhomes International Ltd, Re see Oakley v. Ultra Vehicle Design Ltd (In Liquidation)

Ultraframe (UK) Ltd v. Clayton (No.3) [2002] EWHC 2697, Ch D . . . . *Applied*, 05/2589

Ultraframe (UK) Ltd v. Eurocell Building Plastics Ltd [2005] EWCA Civ 761; [2005] R.P.C. 36; (2005) 28(8) I.P.D. 28058, CA (Civ Div); affirming [2004] EWHC 1785; [2005] R.P.C. 7; (2004) 27(10) I.P.D. 27081, Ch D (Patents Ct) . . . . *Digested*, 05/**2590**

Ultraframe (UK) Ltd v. Eurocell Building Plastics Ltd [2005] EWHC 2111; (2005) 28(10) I.P.D. 28074, Ch D . . . . *Previous proceedings*, 05/2590

Ultraframe (UK) Ltd v. Eurocell Building Plastics Ltd (Disclosure) [2003] EWHC 3258; [2005] F.S.R. 2, Ch D . . . . *Digested*, 05/**2434**

Ultraframe (UK) Ltd v. Fielding see Ultraframe (UK) Ltd v. Rigby

Ultraframe (UK) Ltd v. Fielding; Northstar Systems Ltd (In Liquidation) v. Fielding; Burnden Group Plc v. Northstar Systems Ltd (In Liquidation) [2005] EWHC 1638; (2005) 28(9) I.P.D. 28069, Ch D

Ultraframe (UK) Ltd v. Rigby; *sub nom* Ultraframe (UK) Ltd v. Fielding [2005] EWCA Civ 276; (2005) 149 S.J.L.B. 116, CA (Civ Div)

Ultraframe (UK) Ltd v. Tailored Roofing Systems Ltd [2004] EWCA Civ 585; [2004] 2 All E.R. (Comm) 692; [2004] B.L.R. 341, CA (Civ Div); affirming (Unreported, August 6, 2003), QBD (Merc) . . . . *Digested*, 05/**706**

Ultraworth Ltd v. General Accident Fire & Life Assurance Corp Plc [2000] L. & T.R. 495; [2000] 2 E.G.L.R. 115; [2000] E.G.C.S. 19, QBD (TCC) . . . . *Digested*, 01/**4191**: *Considered*, 05/2684

Umbro Holdings Ltd v. Office of Fair Trading (Application for Leniency: Confidentiality) [2003] CAT 26; [2004] Comp. A.R. 217, CAT . . . . *Digested*, 04/**507**: *Considered*, 05/580

Umbro Holdings Ltd v. Office of Fair Trading (Costs) [2005] CAT 26; [2005] Comp. A.R. 1232, CAT

Umbro Holdings Ltd v. Office of Fair Trading (Judgment on Penalty) [2005] CAT 22; [2005] Comp. A.R. 1060, CAT

Unal v. Sicherheitsdirektion fur das Bundesland Vorarlberg (C136/03) see Dorr v. Sicherheitsdirektion fur das Bundesland Karnten (C136/03)

Unal Tekeli v. Turkey (29865/96) [2005] 1 F.C.R. 663, ECHR . . . . *Digested*, 05/**2128**

Uner v. Netherlands (46410/99) [2005] 3 F.C.R. 111, ECHR

Unichem Ltd v. Office of Fair Trading [2005] CAT 8; [2005] 2 All E.R. 440; [2005] Comp. A.R. 907, CAT

Unichem Ltd v. Office of Fair Trading (Confidential Guidance: Disclosure) [2005] CAT 3; [2005] Comp. A.R. 499, CAT . . . . *Digested*, 05/**587**

Unidare Plc v. Cohen; *sub nom* Kilnoore Ltd (In Liquidation), Re [2005] EWHC 1410; [2005] 3 All E.R. 730; [2005] B.P.I.R. 1472, Ch D (Companies Ct) . . . . *Digested*, 05/**2299**

Unigreg Ltd (In Administration), Re [2005] B.P.I.R. 220, Ch D

Unilever Plc v. Procter & Gamble Co [2000] 1 W.L.R. 2436; [2001] 1 All E.R. 783; [2000] F.S.R. 344; (2000) 23(1) I.P.D. 23001; (1999) 96(44) L.S.G. 40; (1999) 143 S.J.L.B. 268; *Times*, November 4, 1999 ; *Independent*, November 5, 1999, CA (Civ Div); affirming [1999] 1 W.L.R. 1630; [1999] 2 All E.R. 691; [1999] F.S.R. 849; (1999) 22(5) I.P.D. 22042; (1999) 149 N.L.J. 370; *Times*, March 18, 1999, Ch D (Patents Ct) . . . . *Digested*, 99/**349**: *Applied*, 00/334, 02/276, 03/277, 03/293, 04/251, 04/261, 05/289: *Considered*, 01/397, 01/3966, 03/288: *Followed*, 00/337

UNILEVER/Dissolution aid (T285/00) [2005] E.P.O.R. 20, EPO (Technical Bd App) . . . *Digested*, 05/**2468**

UNILEVER/Reduced dye release (T14/01) [2005] E.P.O.R. 21, EPO (Technical Bd App) *Digested*, 05/**2466**

Unilin Beheer BV v. B&Q Plc see Unilin Beheer BV v. Berry Floor NV

Unilin Beheer BV v. Berry Floor NV; Unilin Beheer BV v. Information Management Consultancy Ltd; Unilin Beheer BV v. B&Q Plc [2004] EWCA Civ 1021; [2005] F.S.R. 6; (2004) 27(8) I.P.D. 27082; (2004) 148 S.J.L.B. 975, CA (Civ Div); affirming [2004] F.S.R. 14, PCC . . . . *Digested*, 04/**2308**

Unilin Beheer BV v. Berry Floor NV [2005] EWCA Civ 1292; (2005) 149 S.J.L.B. 1355, CA (Civ Div); affirming (2005) 28(6) I.P.D. 28048, PCC

Unilin Beheer BV v. Information Management Consultancy Ltd see Unilin Beheer BV v. Berry Floor NV

Union de Pequenos Agricultores v. Council of the European Union (C50/00 P); *sub nom* Union de Pequenos Agricultores (UPA) v. Council of the European Union (T173/98) [2003] Q.B. 893; [2003] 2 W.L.R. 795; [2002] All E.R. (EC) 893; [2002] E.C.R. I-6677; [2002] 3 C.M.L.R. 1; *Times*, August 16, 2002, ECJ . . . . . *Digested*, 02/**1589**: *Followed*, 05/942, 05/1470

Union de Pequenos Agricultores (UPA) v. Council of the European Union (T173/98) see Union de Pequenos Agricultores v. Council of the European Union (C50/00 P)

Union des Associations Europeennes de Football (UEFA) *v.* Bosman (C415/93) see Union Royale Belge des Societes de Football Association (ASBL) *v.* Bosman (C415/93)

Union Nationale des Industries de Carrieres et des Materiaux de Construction (UNICEM)'s Application [2005] E.C.C. 10, CE (F)

Union of Clerical and Commercial Employees *v.* Danish Employers Association Ex p. Danfoss A/S (109/88) see Handels- og Kontorfunktionaerernes Forbund i Danmark *v.* Dansk Arbejdsgiverforening Ex p. Danfoss A/S (109/88)

Union Royale Belge des Societes de Football Association (ASBL) *v.* Bosman (C415/93); *sub nom* Royal Club Liegois SA *v.* Bosman (C415/93); Union des Associations Europeennes de Football (UEFA) *v.* Bosman (C415/93) [1996] All E.R. (EC) 97; [1995] E.C.R. I-4921; [1996] 1 C.M.L.R. 645; [1996] C.E.C. 38; *Times*, January 17, 1996, ECJ . . . . *Digested*, 96/**3149**:
Applied, 00/2383, 05/1454: *Considered*, 00/2175, 05/1460:
Distinguished, 00/4049

Unipart Group Ltd *v.* O2 (UK) Ltd (formerly BT Cellnet Ltd) [2004] EWCA Civ 1034; [2004] U.K.C.L.R. 1453; [2005] E.C.C. 9; [2004] Eu. L.R. 969; [2004] Info. T.L.R. 267; (2004) 148 S.J.L.B. 1119, CA (Civ Div); affirming [2002] EWHC 2459; [2003] U.K.C.L.R. 12; [2003] E.C.C. 22; [2002] Eu. L.R. 794, Ch D . . . . *Digested*, 04/**487**

UNIQ Group Plc *v.* Revenue and Customs Commissioners [2005] S.T.I. 1659, VAT Tr

Unique Pub Properties Ltd *v.* Beer Barrels & Minerals (Wales) Ltd [2004] EWCA Civ 586; [2005] 1 All E.R. (Comm) 181; [2004] N.P.C. 77, CA (Civ Div) . . . . *Digested*, 05/**4198**

Unisoft Group (No.2), Re [1993] B.C.L.C. 532, Ch D (Companies Ct) . . . . *Digested*, 93/**3165**:
Applied, 05/465

United Arab Emirates *v.* Abdelghafar [1995] I.C.R. 65; [1995] I.R.L.R. 243, EAT . . . . . . *Digested*, 95/**1988**:
Applied, 05/1242: *Approved*, 99/2038: *Considered*, 02/1351, 03/1250:
Followed, 04/1293

United Biscuits (UK) Ltd *v.* Customs and Excise Commissioners [2004] V. & D.R. 201; [2004] S.T.I. 1943, V&DTr (Manchester) . . . . *Digested*, 05/**4418**

United Scientific Holdings Ltd *v.* Burnley BC; Cheapside Land Development Co Ltd *v.* Messels Service Co [1978] A.C. 904; [1977] 2 W.L.R. 806; [1977] 2 All E.R. 62; 75 L.G.R. 407; (1977) 33 P. & C.R. 220; (1977) 243 E.G. 43; 121 S.J. 223, HL; reversing [1976] Ch. 128; [1976] 2 W.L.R. 686; [1976] 2 All E.R. 220; 74 L.G.R. 316; (1976) 32 P. & C.R. 183; (1976) 238 E.G. 487; 120 S.J. 183, CA (Civ Div); affirming (1974) 231 E.G. 1543, Ch D . . . . *Digested*, 77/**1758**:
Applied, 79/1638, 80/1637, 81/1573, 83/2126, 83/2131, 83/2138, 83/2139, 84/1947, 84/1950, 84/1951, 84/1952, 84/1956, 85/1935, 85/1937, 86/1908, 87/2202, 87/4626, 88/2075, 92/2743, 96/3814, 01/4208, 05/2679:
Considered, 77/119, 77/1757, 78/101, 80/1635, 81/1582, 81/2433, 82/1801, 83/2080, 83/2128, 83/2130, 83/2132, 83/2135, 83/2137, 85/1918, 85/1920, 85/1927, 86/1913, 87/2206, 89/2151, 89/2153, 89/2155, 90/2855, 90/2859, 90/2861, 91/557, 91/2271, 92/2746, 93/182, 93/2462, 93/2536, 95/2965, 95/3068, 00/3914, 05/2667: *Distinguished*, 77/1726, 86/405, 97/3320:
Followed, 77/1759, 78/1810, 81/1580, 81/1585, 81/1588, 83/2140, 91/5178, 01/4207

United States *v.* Atkinson see Atkinson *v.* United States

United States *v.* BDO Seidman LLP 7 I.T.L. Rep. 718, US Ct

United States *v.* Norris [2005] U.K.C.L.R. 1205, MC

United States Tobacco International Inc *v.* BBC [1998] E.M.L.R. 816; *Independent*, March 15, 1988; *Guardian*, March 16, 1988, CA (Civ Div) . . . . *Digested*, 88/**2124**:
Considered, 02/954, 05/973: *Followed*, 98/1769

UNITED VIDEO PROPERTIES/Program guide (T482/02) [2005] E.P.O.R. 42, EPO (Technical Bd App)

Universal General Insurance Co (UGIC) *v.* Group Josi Reinsurance Co SA (C412/98); *sub nom* Group Josi Reinsurance Co SA *v.* Compagnie d'Assurances Universal General Insurance Co (UGIC) (C412/98) [2001] Q.B. 68; [2000] 3 W.L.R. 1625; [2000] All E.R. (EC) 653; [2000] 2 All E.R. (Comm) 467; [2000] E.C.R. I-5925; [2001] C.L.C. 893; [2000] C.E.C. 462; [2000] I.L.Pr. 549; [2001] Lloyd's Rep. I.R. 483; *Times*, August 9, 2000, ECJ (6th Chamber) . . . . *Digested*, 00/**774**:
Considered, 05/604: *Followed*, 05/2369

Universal Information Technology Group Ltd *v.* Unitech Complete Computing Ltd [2004] EWHC 3419; (2005) 28(10) I.P.D. 28075, Ch D

Universities Superannuation Scheme Ltd, Re see Universities Superannuation Scheme Ltd *v.* Simpson

Universities Superannuation Scheme Ltd *v.* McAdoo see Universities Superannuation Scheme Ltd *v.* Simpson

Universities Superannuation Scheme Ltd *v.* Simpson; *sub nom* Universities Superannuation Scheme Ltd, Re; Universities Superannuation Scheme Ltd *v.* McAdoo; Universities Superannuation Scheme Ltd *v.* University of London [2004] EWHC 935; [2004] I.C.R. 1426; [2004] O.P.L.R. 311; [2004] Pens. L.R. 395; *Times*, May 27, 2004, Ch D . . . . *Digested*, 05/**2938**

Universities Superannuation Scheme Ltd *v.* University of London see Universities Superannuation Scheme Ltd *v.* Simpson

University College of Swansea *v.* Cornelius [1988] I.C.R. 735, EAT. . . . .   *Digested,* 89/**1434**:
    Applied, 05/1235

University Court of the University of Glasgow *v.* Customs and Excise Commissioners see
    University of Glasgow *v.* Customs and Excise Commissioners
University Court of the University of Glasgow *v.* Customs and Excise Commissioners see
    University of Glasgow *v.* Customs and Excise Commissioners
University Court of the University of St Andrews *v.* Customs and Excise Commissioners
    [2005] B.V.C. 2621, V&DTr (Edinburgh)
UNIVERSITY OF CALIFORNIA/Neoplastic phenotype (T347/02) [2004] E.P.O.R. 57, EPO
    (Technical Bd App) . . . .   *Digested,* 05/**2450**
University of East London *v.* Hinton see Hinton *v.* University of East London
University of East London Higher Education Corp *v.* Barking and Dagenham LBC [2004]
    EWHC 2710; [2005] Ch. 354; [2005] 2 W.L.R. 1334; [2005] 3 All E.R. 398;
    [2005] 1 P. & C.R. 31; [2004] N.P.C. 186; *Times,* January 3, 2005, Ch D . . . . . .   *Digested,* 05/**3431**
University of East London Higher Education Corp *v.* Barking and Dagenham LBC (Costs)
    [2004] EWHC 2908; [2005] Ch. 354; [2005] 2 W.L.R. 1334; [2005] 3 All
    E.R. 416; [2005] 2 Costs L.R. 287; *Times,* January 3, 2005, Ch D . . . .   *Digested,* 05/**357**
University of Glasgow *v.* Customs and Excise Commissioners; *sub nom* University
    Court of the University of Glasgow *v.* Customs and Excise Commissioners
    [2003] S.T.C. 495; 2003 S.C. 355; 2003 S.L.T. 472; [2003] B.T.C. 5445;
    [2003] B.V.C. 501; [2003] S.T.I. 420; 2003 G.W.D. 8-238, IH (1 Div); affirming
    [2002] S.T.I. 218, V&DTr . . . .   *Digested,* 03/**5945**:
    Applied, 05/4340

University of Glasgow *v.* Customs and Excise Commissioners; *sub nom* University
    Court of the University of Glasgow *v.* Customs and Excise Commissioners
    [2005] B.V.C. 2583; [2005] V. & D.R. 198, V&DTr (Edinburgh)
University of Keele *v.* Price Waterhouse [2004] EWCA Civ 583; [2004] P.N.L.R. 43,
    CA (Civ Div); affirming [2003] EWHC 1595; [2004] P.N.L.R. 8, Ch D . . . .   *Digested,* 05/**2867**
University of Kent *v.* Customs and Excise Commissioners [2004] B.V.C. 2215; [2004]
    V. & D.R. 372; [2004] S.T.I. 1948, V&DTr (London) . . . .   *Digested,* 05/**4421**
University of Southampton *v.* Customs and Excise Commissioners see University of
    Southampton *v.* Revenue and Customs Commissioners
University of Southampton *v.* Revenue and Customs Commissioners; *sub nom*
    Southampton University *v.* Revenue and Customs Commissioners; University of
    Southampton *v.* Customs and Excise Commissioners; CH/2005/APP/0286, Ch
    D; affirming [2005] B.V.C. 2474; [2005] S.T.I. 908, V&DTr
University of Southampton's Patent Applications see IDA Ltd *v.* University of
    Southampton
Untelrab Ltd *v.* McGregor [1996] S.T.C. (S.C.D.) 1, Sp Comm. . . . .   *Considered,* 05/4156
Unterpertinger *v.* Pensionsversicherungsanstalt der Arbeiter (C212/01) [2004] Q.B.
    1179; [2004] 3 W.L.R. 174; [2005] S.T.C. 650; [2003] E.C.R. I-13859; [2004] 2
    C.M.L.R. 17; [2004] C.E.C. 22; [2004] Pens. L.R. 65; [2005] B.T.C. 5685;
    [2005] B.V.C. 716; [2003] S.T.I. 2181; *Times,* November 27, 2003, ECJ (5th
    Chamber) . . . .   *Digested,* 04/**3980**
Uphill *v.* BRB (Residuary) Ltd [2005] EWCA Civ 60; [2005] 1 W.L.R. 2070; [2005] 3
    All E.R. 264; [2005] C.P. Rep. 20; (2005) 102(15) L.S.G. 35; (2005) 149
    S.J.L.B. 181; *Times,* February 8, 2005; *Independent,* February 17, 2005, CA (Civ
    Div) . . . .   *Digested,* 05/**403**
Upton *v.* National Westminster Bank Plc [2004] EWHC 1962; [2004] W.T.L.R. 1339,
    Ch D . . . .   *Digested,* 05/**3976**
Uratemp Ventures Ltd *v.* Carrell see Uratemp Ventures Ltd *v.* Collins
Uratemp Ventures Ltd *v.* Collins; Uratemp Ventures Ltd *v.* Carrell [2001] UKHL 43;
    [2002] 1 A.C. 301; [2001] 3 W.L.R. 806; [2002] 1 All E.R. 46; (2001) 33 H.L.R.
    85; [2002] L. & T.R. 15; [2001] 3 E.G.L.R. 93; [2002] R.V.R. 162; 2001 Hous.
    L.R. 133; [2001] 43 E.G.C.S. 186; (2001) 98(41) L.S.G. 35; [2001] N.P.C. 145;
    [2002] 1 P. & C.R. DG15; *Times,* October 18, 2001; *Independent,* December 3,
    2001; *Daily Telegraph,* October 16, 2001, HL; reversing (2001) 33 H.L.R. 4;
    [2000] L. & T.R. 369; [2000] 1 E.G.L.R. 156; (2000) 97(1) L.S.G. 23; [1999]
    N.P.C. 153; (2000) 79 P. & C.R. D18; *Times,* December 10, 1999, CA (Civ Div) . .   *Digested,* 01/**4148**:
    Applied, 05/2660

Urbing *v.* Administration de l'Enregistrement et des Domaines (C267/99) see Adam *v.*
    Administration de l'Enregistrement et des Domaines (C267/99)
Uren *v.* First National Home Finance Ltd [2005] EWHC 2529; *Times,* November 17,
    2005, Ch D
Urlaubs- und Lohnausgleichskasse der Bauwirtschaft *v.* Amilcar Oliveira Rocha (C50/
    98) see Finalarte Sociedade de Construcao Civil Lda *v.* Urlaubs- und
    Lohnausgleichskasse der Bauwirtschaft (C49/98)
Urlaubs- und Lohnausgleichskasse der Bauwirtschaft *v.* Duarte dos Santos Sousa
    (C68/98) see Finalarte Sociedade de Construcao Civil Lda *v.* Urlaubs- und
    Lohnausgleichskasse der Bauwirtschaft (C49/98)
Urlaubs- und Lohnausgleichskasse der Bauwirtschaft *v.* Santos & Kewitz Construcoes
    Lda (C69/98) see Finalarte Sociedade de Construcao Civil Lda *v.* Urlaubs- und
    Lohnausgleichskasse der Bauwirtschaft (C49/98)

Urlaubs- und Lohnausgleichskasse der Bauwirtschaft *v.* Tecnamb-Tecnologia do Ambiante Lda (C53/98) see Finalarte Sociedade de Construcao Civil Lda *v.* Urlaubs- und Lohnausgleichskasse der Bauwirtschaft (C49/98)

Urlaubs- und Lohnausgleichskasse der Bauwirtschaft *v.* Tudor Stone Ltd (C52/98) see Finalarte Sociedade de Construcao Civil Lda *v.* Urlaubs- und Lohnausgleichskasse der Bauwirtschaft (C49/98)

Urlaubs- und Lohnausgleichskasse der Bauwirtschaft *v.* Turiprata Construcoes Civil SA (C54/98) see Finalarte Sociedade de Construcao Civil Lda *v.* Urlaubs- und Lohnausgleichskasse der Bauwirtschaft (C49/98)

USB AG *v.* Revenue and Customs Commissioners see UBS AG *v.* Revenue and Customs Commissioners

Usetech Ltd *v.* Young (Inspector of Taxes) [2004] EWHC 2248; [2004] S.T.C. 1671; 76 T.C. 811; [2005] B.T.C. 48; [2004] S.T.I. 2220; (2004) 101 (40) L.S.G. 29; *Times,* October 22, 2004, Ch D; affirming [2004] S.T.C. (S.C.D.) 213; [2004] S.T.I. 993, Sp Comm . . . . *Digested,* 04/**3766**

USP Plc *v.* London General Holdings Ltd (Damages) see London General Holdings Ltd *v.* USP Plc

Utah Construction & Engineering Pty *v.* Pataky [1966] A.C. 629; [1966] 2 W.L.R. 197; [1965] 3 All E.R. 650, PC (Aus). . . . . *Digested,* 65/**376**: *Considered,* 05/2742

Uttamchandani *v.* Central Bank of India (1989) 86(10) L.S.G. 41; (1989) 139 N.L.J. 222; (1989) 133 S.J. 262, CA (Civ Div) . . . . *Digested,* 89/**162**: *Applied,* 05/258

Uyanwa-Odu *v.* Schools Offices Services Ltd; *sub nom* Uyamnwa-Odu *v.* Schools Offices Services Ltd *Independent,* December 1, 2005, EAT

V *v.* United Kingdom (24888/94) see T *v.* United Kingdom (24724/94)

V *v.* V (Financial Relief) [2005] 2 F.L.R. 697; [2005] Fam. Law 684, Fam Div

V (A Child) *v.* Trujillo (Unreported, January 11, 2005), CC (Watford) [*Ex rel.* Joanna Kerr, Barrister, Lamb Chambers, Lamb Building, Temple, London]. . . . . *Digested,* 05/**3152**

V (A Child) (Care: Pre Birth Actions), Re [2004] EWCA Civ 1575; [2005] 1 F.L.R. 627; [2005] U.K.H.R.R. 144; [2005] Fam. Law 201; *Times,* December 1, 2004, CA (Civ Div). . . . . *Digested,* 05/**1536**

V (A Child) (Contact: Domestic Violence), Re see L (A Child) (Contact: Domestic Violence), Re

V (Forum Conveniens), Re [2004] EWHC 2663; [2005] 1 F.L.R. 718; [2005] Fam. Law 205, Fam Div

V-B (Abduction: Rights of Custody), Re; B (A Minor), Re [1999] 2 F.L.R. 192; [1999] 2 F.C.R. 371; [1999] Fam. Law 372, CA (Civ Div) . . . . *Digested,* 99/**2334**: *Followed,* 05/1541

Vahidi *v.* Fairstead House School Trust Ltd; *sub nom* Validi *v.* Fairstead House School Trust Ltd [2005] EWCA Civ 765; [2005] E.L.R. 607; *Times,* June 24, 2005, CA (Civ Div); affirming [2004] EWHC 2102; [2005] P.I.Q.R. P9, QBD . . . . *Digested,* 05/**2862**

Vajpeyi *v.* Yijsaf see Vajpeyi *v.* Yusaf

Vajpeyi *v.* Yusaf; *sub nom* Vajpeyi *v.* Yijsaf [2003] EWHC 2339; [2004] W.T.L.R. 989; (2003) 147 S.J.L.B. 1120; [2003] N.P.C. 108; [2004] 1 P. & C.R. DG1, Ch D . . . *Digested,* 05/**4311**

Vakante *v.* Addey and Stanhope School Governing Body; *sub nom* Addey and Stanhope School *v.* Vakante [2004] EWCA Civ 1065; [2004] 4 All E.R. 1056; [2005] 1 C.M.L.R. 3; [2005] I.C.R. 231; (2004) 101(36) L.S.G. 33; *Times,* September 28, 2004, CA (Civ Div); affirming [2004] I.C.R. 279, EAT . . . . *Digested,* 04/**1278**: *Previous proceedings,* 03/1218

Vale *v.* Armstrong [2004] EWHC 1160; [2004] W.T.L.R. 1471; [2004] 24 E.G.C.S. 148, Ch D . . . . *Digested,* 05/**3438**

Validi *v.* Fairstead House School Trust Ltd see Vahidi *v.* Fairstead House School Trust Ltd

Valmont Nederland BV *v.* Commission of the European Communities (T274/01) [2005] All E.R. (EC) 880; [2005] 3 C.M.L.R. 25, CFI (4th Chamber)

Van De Walle *v.* Texaco Belgium SA (C1/03) see Criminal Proceedings against Van de Walle (C1/03)

Van den Bergh Foods Ltd *v.* Commission of the European Communities (T65/98) [2005] All E.R. (EC) 418; [2003] E.C.R. II-4653; [2004] 4 C.M.L.R. 1; *Times,* November 7, 2003, CFI (5th Chamber) . . . . *Digested,* 04/**489**

Van Duyn *v.* Home Office (41/74) [1975] Ch. 358; [1975] 2 W.L.R. 760; [1975] 3 All E.R. 190; [1974] E.C.R. 1337; [1975] 1 C.M.L.R. 1; (1974) 119 S.J. 302, ECJ . . . . *Digested,* 75/**1290**: *Applied,* 05/1467: *Followed,* 05/1462

Van Kuck *v.* Germany (35968/97) [2003] 2 F.C.R. 421; (2003) 37 E.H.R.R. 51; (2005) 8 C.C.L. Rep. 121, ECHR. . . . . *Digested,* 03/**2196**

Van Laethem *v.* Brooker [2005] EWHC 1478; [2005] N.P.C. 91, Ch D

Van Leuven *v.* Belgium (A/43) see Le Compte *v.* Belgium (A/43)

Van Pommeren-Bourgondien *v.* Raad van Bestuur van de Sociale Verzekeringsbank (C227/03) [2005] 3 C.M.L.R. 24, ECJ

Van Raalte *v.* Netherlands (1997) 24 E.H.R.R. 503, ECHR. . . . . *Digested,* 98/**3076**: *Considered,* 05/3985

Van Riet *v.* Onderlinge Waarborgmaatschappij OZ Zorgverzekeringen UA (C385/99)
　　see Muller-Faure *v.* Onderlinge Waarborgmaatschappij OZ Zorgverzekeringen UA
　　(C385/99)
Van Uden Maritime BV (t/a Van Uden Africa Line) *v.* Kommanditgesellschaft in Firma
　　Deco-Line (C391/95) [1999] Q.B. 1225; [1999] 2 W.L.R. 1181; [1999] All E.R.
　　(E.C.) 258; [1999] 1 All E.R. (Comm.) 385; [1998] E.C.R. I-7091; [1999] I.L.Pr.
　　73; *Times,* December 1, 1998, ECJ .... *Digested,* 99/**739**:
　　　　　　　　　　　　　　　　　　　　　　　　　　　　　Followed, 04/576, 05/428
Vancouver Sun, Re 18 B.H.R.C. 407, Sup Ct (Can)
Vander Elst *v.* Office des Migrations Internationales (OMI) (C43/93) [1994] E.C.R. I-
　　3803; [1995] 1 C.M.L.R. 513, ECJ .... *Digested,* 94/**4909**:
　　　　　　　　　　　　　　　　　　　　Considered, 05/351: *Followed,* 02/1582
Vandervell's Trusts (No.1), Re; *sub nom* White *v.* Vandervell Trustees [1971] A.C. 912;
　　[1970] 3 W.L.R. 452; [1970] 3 All E.R. 16; 46 T.C. 341; [1970] T.R. 129; 114 S.J.
　　652, HL; reversing [1970] Ch. 44; [1969] 3 W.L.R. 458; [1969] 3 All E.R. 496;
　　[1969] T.R. 393; 113 S.J. 449, CA (Civ Div); reversing [1969] 1 W.L.R. 437;
　　[1969] 1 All E.R. 1056, Ch D .... *Digested,* 70/**2324**:
　　　　　Applied, 71/9385, 05/4056: *Considered,* 70/628, 70/1366, 92/612, 93/604:
　　　　　　　Not followed, 96/1313: *Previous proceedings,* 66/6148, 67/1975:
　　　　　　　　　　　　　　　　　　　　　　　　　　　　　Referred to, 76/409.u
Vanniyasingam *v.* Secretary of State for the Home Department see Subesh *v.* Secretary
　　of State for the Home Department
Varas Cruz *v.* Sweden see Cruz Varas *v.* Sweden
Various Claimants *v.* BACHL see KR *v.* Bryn Alyn Community (Holdings) Ltd (In
　　Liquidation)
Various Claimants *v.* Bryn Alyn Community (Holdings) Ltd (In Liquidation) see KR *v.*
　　Bryn Alyn Community (Holdings) Ltd (In Liquidation)
Various Ledward Claimants *v.* Kent and Medway HA [2003] EWHC 2551; [2004] 1
　　Costs L.R. 101, QBD .... *Digested,* 04/**301**:
　　　　　　　　　　　　　　　　　　　　　　　　　　　　　Followed, 05/327
Vasileva *v.* Denmark (52792/99) (2005) 40 E.H.R.R. 27; 15 B.H.R.C. 246, ECHR ..... *Digested,* 04/**1968**
Vasiliou *v.* Hajigeorgiou; *sub nom* Hajigeorgiou *v.* Vasiliou [2005] EWCA Civ 236;
　　[2005] 1 W.L.R. 2195; [2005] 3 All E.R. 17; [2005] C.P. Rep. 27; (2005)
　　102(18) L.S.G. 22; [2005] N.P.C. 39; *Times,* March 22, 2005, CA (Civ Div) ... *Digested,* 05/**296**
Vatcher *v.* Paull [1915] A.C. 372, PC (Jer) .... *Applied,* 47-51/7417,
　　　　　　　47-51/10817, 53/2696, 53/2697, 53/2698, 54/2481, 54/2482, 54/2486,
　　　　　　　　54/3031: *Considered,* 05/2997: *Followed,* 52/261, 52/2614
Vaughan *v.* Barlow Clowes International Ltd see Barlow Clowes International Ltd (In
　　Liquidation) *v.* Vaughan
Vaughan *v.* Emmott Harrison [2005] P.N.L.R. 8, Ch D .... *Digested,* 05/**441**
Vaughan *v.* Vaughan [2002] EWHC 699; [2005] W.T.L.R. 401, Ch D
Vectone Entertainment Holding Ltd *v.* South Entertainment Ltd [2004] EWHC 744;
　　[2005] B.C.C. 123; [2004] 2 B.C.L.C. 224, Ch D
Vedial SA *v.* Office for Harmonisation in the Internal Market (Trade Marks and Designs)
　　(OHIM) (T110/01) [2002] E.C.R. II-5275; [2004] E.T.M.R. 102, CFI .... *Digested,* 05/**2517**:
　　　　　　　　　　　　　　　　　　　　　Subsequent proceedings, 05/2507
Vedial SA *v.* Office for Harmonisation in the Internal Market (Trade Marks and Designs)
　　(OHIM) (C106/03 P) [2004] E.C.R. I-9573; [2005] E.T.M.R. 23, ECJ (2nd
　　Chamber) .... *Digested,* 05/**2507**:
　　　　　　　　　　　　　　　　　　　　　Previous proceedings, 05/2517
Vee Networks Ltd *v.* Econet Wireless International Ltd [2004] EWHC 2909; [2005] 1
　　All E.R. (Comm) 303; [2005] 1 Lloyd's Rep. 192, QBD (Comm) .... *Digested,* 05/**202**
Vehicle and Operator Services Agency *v.* Jones [2005] EWHC 2278; (2005) 169 J.P.
　　611; (2005) 169 J.P.N. 901; *Times,* October 13, 2005, QBD (Admin) .... *Digested,* 05/**4280**
Vehicle Inspectorate *v.* Nuttall; *sub nom* Secretary of State for Transport *v.* Nuttall (t/a
　　Redline Coaches); Wing *v.* Nuttall; Nuttall *v.* Vehicle Inspectorate [1999] 1 W.L.R.
　　629; [1999] 3 All E.R. 833; [1999] R.T.R. 264; [1999] I.R.L.R. 656; [1999]
　　Crim. L.R. 674; (1999) 96(16) L.S.G. 36; (1999) 149 N.L.J. 521; (1999) 143
　　S.J.L.B. 111; *Times,* March 19, 1999; *Independent,* March 24, 1999, HL; reversing
　　(1997) 161 J.P. 701; [1998] R.T.R. 321; (1997) 94(18) L.S.G. 31; (1997) 141
　　S.J.L.B. 98; *Times,* April 30, 1997, QBD.............................. *Digested,* 99/**4945**:
　　　　　　　　　　　　　　　　　　　　　　　　　　　　　Applied, 05/818
Vehicle Operators Services Agency *v.* Law Fertilisers Ltd [2004] EWHC 3000; [2005]
　　R.T.R. 21, QBD (Admin) .... *Digested,* 05/**756**
Vella *v.* Lambeth LBC see R. (on the application of Vella) *v.* Lambeth LBC
Venables *v.* News Group International (Breach of Injunction); *sub nom* Attorney
　　General *v.* Greater Manchester Newspapers Ltd; Thompson *v.* News Group
　　International (2002) 99(6) L.S.G. 30; (2001) 145 S.J.L.B. 279; *Times,*
　　December 7, 2001; *Daily Telegraph,* December 13, 2001, QBD .... *Digested,* 02/**445**:
　　　　　　　　　　　　　　　　　　　　　　　　　　　　　Considered, 05/815
Venema *v.* Netherlands (35731/97) [2003] 1 F.L.R. 552; [2003] 1 F.C.R. 153; (2004)
　　39 E.H.R.R. 5; [2003] Fam. Law 233, ECHR .... *Applied,* 05/1567
Venticinque Ltd *v.* Oakley Inc [2005] E.T.M.R. 115, OHIM (Cancellation Div)

Vento *v.* Chief Constable of West Yorkshire; *sub nom* Chief Constable of West Yorkshire
   v. Vento (No.2) [2002] EWCA Civ 1871; [2003] I.C.R. 318; [2003] I.R.L.R. 102;
   (2003) 100(10) L.S.G. 28; (2003) 147 S.J.L.B. 181; *Times*, December 27,
   2002, CA (Civ Div); affirming [2002] I.R.L.R. 177; [2002] Emp. L.R. 111, EAT . .   *Digested*, 03/**1306**:
                 Considered, 04/917, 04/1276: *Followed*, 04/1306, 05/1318
Ventouris *v.* Mountain (The Italia Express) (No.3) [1992] 2 Lloyd's Rep. 281; *Financial*
   Times, February 12, 1992, QBD (Comm) . . . .   *Digested*, 93/**3619**:
                 Followed, 97/3139, 05/2358: *Referred to*, 97/3121
Ventouris Group Enterprises SA *v.* Commission of the European Communities (T59/99)
   [2005] 5 C.M.L.R. 29, CFI (5th Chamber)
Ventouris Group Enterprises SA *v.* Commission of the European Communities (T59/99
   R) [1999] E.C.R. II-2519, CFI
Venuebest Ltd *v.* Customs and Excise Commissioners [2005] V. & D.R. 92, V&DTr
   (Manchester)
Verderers of the New Forest *v.* Young (No.2) [2004] EWHC 2954; [2005] A.C.D. 22,
   QBD (Admin)
Verein fur Konsumenteninformation *v.* Commission of the European Communities (T2/
   03) [2005] 1 W.L.R. 3302; [2005] All E.R. (EC) 813; [2005] 4 C.M.L.R. 21;
   Times, May 20, 2005, CFI (1st Chamber)
Vereniging Dorpsbelang Hees *v.* Directeur van de dienst Milieu en Water van de
   provincie Gelderland (C419/97) see ARCO Chemie Nederland Ltd *v.* Minister van
   Volkshuisvesting, Ruimtelijke Ordening en Milieubeheer (C418/97)
Vereniging voor Energie Milieu en Water *v.* Directeur van de Dienst Uitvoering en Toezicht
   Energie (C17/03) [2005] 5 C.M.L.R. 8, ECJ
Vergos *v.* Greece (65501/01) (2005) 41 E.H.R.R. 41, ECHR
Verpack V, Re (C309/02) see Radlberger Getrankegesellschaft mbH & Co *v.* Land Baden-
   Wurttemberg (C309/02)
Verpack V, Re (C463/01) see Commission of the European Communities *v.* Germany
   (C463/01)
Verrechia (t/a Freightmaster Commercials) *v.* Commissioner of Police of the Metropolis
   see English *v.* Emery Reimbold & Strick Ltd
Vessel SA *v.* CP Ships (UK) Ltd; *sub nom* Owners of the Denise *v.* Charterers of the
   Denise [2004] EWHC 3305; [2005] 2 All E.R. (Comm) 47, QBD (Admlty) . . . .   *Approved*, 05/3801
Veta Ltd *v.* Crofts see Dickie *v.* Cathay Pacific Airways Ltd
Viasystems (Tyneside) Ltd *v.* Thermal Transfer (Northern) Ltd [2005] EWCA Civ 1151;
   [2005] 4 All E.R. 1181; [2005] I.R.L.R. 983; [2005] 42 E.G.C.S. 235; (2005)
   102(44) L.S.G. 31; [2005] N.P.C. 114; *Independent*, October 12, 2005, CA (Civ
   Div) . . . .   *Digested*, 05/**2890**
Vicky Construction Ltd *v.* Shaw (Inspector of Taxes) see Shaw (Inspector of Taxes) *v.*
   Vicky Construction Ltd
VICOM/Computer-related invention (T208/84) [1987] E.P.O.R. 74, EPO (Technical Bd
   App) . . . .   *Applied*, 05/2492:
                 Considered, 96/4570, 97/3915, 99/3488
Victor Chandler (International) Ltd *v.* BHB Enterprises Plc see BHB Enterprises Plc *v.*
   Victor Chandler (International) Ltd
Vidhani Brothers Ltd *v.* Custom and Excise Commissioners [2005] S.T.I. 897, V&DTr
Vidyarthi *v.* Clifford [2004] EWHC 2084; [2005] 2 F.L.R. 104; [2005] B.P.I.R. 233;
   [2005] Fam. Law 445, Ch D
Viking Line Abp *v.* International Transport Workers Federation; *sub nom* International
   Transport Workers Federation *v.* Viking Line Abp [2005] EWCA Civ 1299; [2005]
   2 C.L.C. 720, CA (Civ Div); reversing [2005] EWHC 1222; [2005] 1 C.L.C.
   951; [2005] 3 C.M.L.R. 29; [2005] Eu. L.R. 1036; *Times*, June 22, 2005, QBD
   (Comm) . . . .   *Digested*, 05/**1454**
Villiers *v.* Villiers [1994] 1 W.L.R. 493; [1994] 2 All E.R. 149; [1994] 1 F.L.R. 647;
   [1994] 2 F.C.R. 702; [1994] Fam. Law 317; (1994) 144 N.L.J. 159; *Independent*,
   December 27, 1993 (C.S.), CA (Civ Div) . . . .   *Digested*, 94/**3553**:
                 Considered, 01/19: *Followed*, 05/344
Vince-Cain *v.* Orthet Ltd; *sub nom* Orthet Ltd *v.* Vince-Cain [2005] I.C.R. 374; [2004]
   I.R.L.R. 857, EAT . . . .   *Digested*, 04/**1186**
Vinos *v.* Marks & Spencer Plc [2001] 3 All E.R. 784; [2001] C.P. Rep. 12; [2000]
   C.P.L.R. 570; *Independent*, July 17, 2000 (C.S), CA (Civ Div) . . . .   *Applied*, 00/535,
       01/641, 01/645, 04/391, 05/466: *Cited*, 03/456: *Considered*, 01/643, 01/644:
                 Distinguished, 01/654, 05/340: *Followed*, 02/479
Virani *v.* Guernsey International Trustees Ltd (No.1) [2004] W.T.L.R. 1007, CA (Gue) . . .   *Digested*, 05/**4315**
Virani *v.* Guernsey International Trustees Ltd (No.2) [2004] W.T.L.R. 1035, Royal Ct
   (Gue) . . . .   *Digested*, 05/**4316**
Viscount Chelsea *v.* Morris; Cadogan Estates Ltd *v.* Morris; Earl Cadogan *v.* Morris
   (1999) 31 H.L.R. 732; (1999) 77 P. & C.R. 336; [1999] L. & T.R. 154; [1999] 1
   E.G.L.R. 59; [1999] 04 E.G. 155; [1998] E.G.C.S. 156; (1998) 95(45) L.S.G.
   40; (1999) 143 S.J.L.B. 11; [1998] N.P.C. 146; (1999) 77 P. & C.R. D13; *Times*,
   November 24, 1998; *Independent*, November 23, 1998 (C.S.), CA (Civ Div);
   reversing [1997] 2 E.G.L.R. 100; [1997] 46 E.G. 159, CC (West London) . . . . . .   *Digested*, 98/**3657**:
                 Applied, 03/2759: *Considered*, 01/4158, 05/3386
Vision Golf *v.* Weightmans [2005] EWHC 1675; [2005] 32 E.G.C.S. 66, Ch D

Vitakraft-Werke Wuhrmann & Sohn GmbH & Co KG *v.* Office for Harmonisation in the
        Internal Market (Trade Marks and Designs) (OHIM) (T356/02) (2005) 28(4)
        I.P.D. 28021, CFI
VK *v.* Norfolk CC [2004] EWHC 2921; [2005] E.L.R. 342; *Times*, January 6, 2005,
        QBD (Admin) . . . .   *Digested*, 05/**1138**
VK HellasTrade in BeveragesTourism and Construction Enterprises SA *v.* GBL International
        Ltd [2005] E.C.C. 41, Protodikeio (Athens)
Vo *v.* France (53924/00) [2004] 2 F.C.R. 577; (2005) 40 E.H.R.R. 12; 17 B.H.R.C. 1;
        (2004) 79 B.M.L.R. 71, ECHR (Grand Chamber). . . . .   *Digested*, 05/**2114**
Vodafone 2 *v.* Revenue and Customs Commissioners; *sub nom* Revenue and Customs
        Commissioners *v.* Vodafone 2 [2005] EWHC 3040; [2005] S.T.I. 1841, Ch D;
        affirming [2005] S.T.C. (S.C.D.) 549; 8 I.T.L. Rep. 27, Sp Comm
Vodafone Cellular Ltd *v.* Shaw (Inspector of Taxes) [1997] S.T.C. 734; 69 T.C. 376;
        [1997] B.T.C. 247; (1997) 141 S.J.L.B. 93; *Times*, March 31, 1997, CA (Civ Div);
        reversing [1995] S.T.C. 353; [1995] S.T.I. 219; (1995) 92(10) L.S.G. 39; *Times*,
        February 8, 1995; *Independent*, March 20, 1995 (C.S.), Ch D . . . .   *Digested*, 97/**1062**:
                            Applied, 00/4932, 00/4934, 00/4935, 03/4174, 04/3700, 05/4016:
                                                                Considered, 98/4630
VoithTurbo Ltd *v.* Stowe [2005] I.C.R. 543; [2005] I.R.L.R. 228, EAT . . . .   *Digested*, 05/**1331**
Volks NO *v.* Robinson 18 B.H.R.C. 593, Const Ct (SA)
Volkswagen's Foreign Distribution System, Re (KZR 24/02) [2005] E.C.C. 47, BGH (Ger)
Volvo Personvagnar AB *v.* Scan Tech USA/Sweden AB [2005] E.T.M.R. CN13, HD
        (Swe)
Von Bulow *v.* United Kingdom (75362/01) (2004) 39 E.H.R.R. 16, ECHR. . . . .   *Digested*, 05/**2107**
Von Hannover *v.* Germany (59320/00) [2004] E.M.L.R. 21; (2005) 40 E.H.R.R. 1; 16
        B.H.R.C. 545, ECHR
Von Horn *v.* Cinnamond (C163/95) [1998] Q.B. 214; [1998] 2 W.L.R. 104; [1997] All
        E.R. (EC) 913; [1997] E.C.R. I-5451; [1997] I.L.Pr. 784; *Times*, November 26,
        1997, ECJ (6th Chamber) . . . .   *Digested*, 97/**903**:
                                Considered, 05/420: *Not applied*, 98/760
Von Starck *v.* Queen, The [2000] 1 W.L.R. 1270; *Times*, March 16, 2000, PC (Jam) . . . .   *Digested*, 00/**1101**:
                                                                Distinguished, 05/896
Vos (Deceased), Re see Dick *v.* Kendall Freeman
Vrbia Inc, Re [2005] E.T.M.R. 81, US Ct

W *v.* A see A (A Child) (Temporary Removal from Jurisdiction), Re
W *v.* Doncaster MBC see R. (on the application of W) *v.* Doncaster MBC
W *v.* DPP; *sub nom* R. (on the application of W) *v.* DPP [2005] EWHC 1333; (2005)
        169 J.P. 435; (2005) 169 J.P.N. 635; *Times*, June 20, 2005, QBD (Admin) . . . .   *Digested*, 05/**829**
W *v.* Home Office [1997] Imm. A.R. 302; *Times*, March 14, 1997; *Independent*, March
        19, 1997, CA (Civ Div) . . . .   *Digested*, 97/**2879**:
                                                                Explained, 05/2163
W *v.* J (A Child) (Variation of Financial Provision) [2003] EWHC 2657; [2004] 2
        F.L.R. 300; [2004] Fam. Law 568, Fam Div. . . . . *Distinguished*, 05/**1663**
W *v.* Leeds City Council [2005] EWCA Civ 988; [2005] E.L.R. 617, CA (Civ Div);
        affirming [2004] EWHC 2513; [2005] E.L.R. 459, QBD (Admin) . . . .   *Digested*, 05/**1146**
W *v.* Oldham MBC; *sub nom* W (A Child) (Non-accidental Injury: Expert Evidence),
        Re; GW *v.* Oldham MBC [2005] EWCA Civ 1247; [2005] 3 F.C.R. 513; (2005)
        149 S.J.L.B. 1351; *Times*, November 7, 2005; *Independent*, November 3, 2005,
        CA (Civ Div)
W *v.* Westminster City Council [2004] EWHC 2866; [2005] 1 F.L.R. 816; [2005] 1
        F.C.R. 39; [2005] Fam. Law 458; *Times*, January 7, 2005, QBD
W *v.* Westminster City Council [2005] EWHC 102; [2005] 4 All E.R. 96 (Note), QBD . .   *Digested*, 05/**976**
W (A Child) *v.* Hopcraft (Unreported, July 1, 2004), CC (Wellingborough) [*Ex rel.*
        GurionTaussig, Barrister, 199, Strand, London] . . . .   *Digested*, 05/**3124**
W (A Child) *v.* Hussein (Unreported, April 4, 2005), CC (Barnet) [*Ex rel.* Adam Walker,
        Barrister, Lamb Chambers, Elm Court,Temple, London] . . . .   *Digested*, 05/**3130**
W (A Child) *v.* Tesco Stores Ltd (Unreported, October 18, 2004), CC (St Albans) [*Ex
        rel.* Gurion Taussig, Barrister, 199 Strand, London] . . . .   *Digested*, 05/**3097**
W (A Child) *v.* Wandsworth LBC Independent Appeal Panel; *sub nom* M (A Child) *v.*
        Wandsworth LBC Independent Appeal Panel [2004] EWCA Civ 1819; [2005]
        E.L.R. 223, CA (Civ Div); affirming [2004] EWHC 1239; [2005] E.L.R. 55, QBD
        (Admin) . . . .   *Digested*, 05/**1070**
W (A Child) (Abduction: Conditions for Return), Re; *sub nom* W (Abduction: Domestic
        Violence), Re [2004] EWCA Civ 1366; [2005] 1 F.L.R. 727; [2004] 3 F.C.R.
        559; [2005] Fam. Law 200, CA (Civ Div); affirming [2004] EWHC 1247;
        [2004] 2 F.L.R. 499; [2004] Fam. Law 785, Fam Div. . . . .   *Digested*, 05/**1547**
W (A Child) (Care Order), Re [2005] EWCA Civ 649; [2005] 2 F.C.R. 277, CA (Civ Div)   *Digested*, 05/**1532**
W (A Child) (Care Proceedings: Leave to Apply), Re [2004] EWHC 3342; [2005] 2 F.L.R.
        468; [2005] Fam. Law 527; *Times*, November 22, 2004, Fam Div
W (A Child) (Non-accidental Injury: Expert Evidence), Re see W *v.* Oldham MBC

W (A Minor) (Medical Treatment: Court's Jurisdiction), Re; *sub nom* J (A Minor) (Consent to Medical Treatment), Re [1993] Fam. 64; [1992] 3 W.L.R. 758; [1992] 4 All E.R. 627; [1992] 3 Med. L.R. 317; (1992) 142 N.L.J. 1124; *Times,* July 15, 1992; *Independent,* July 14, 1992; *Guardian,* July 22, 1992, CA (Civ Div); affirming [1992] 2 F.C.R. 785; (1992) 136 S.J.L.B. 165; *Times,* May 14, 1992; *Independent,* May 18, 1992 (C.S.), Fam Div. . . . . *Digested,* 92/**2919**:
Applied, 04/1924: *Considered,* 95/3578, 05/1793
W (Abduction: Domestic Violence), Re see W (A Child) (Abduction: Conditions for Return), Re
W (Children) (Identification: Restrictions on Publication), Re; *sub nom* A Local Authority *v.* W [2005] EWHC 1564; [2005] Fam. Law 868; *Times,* July 21, 2005, Fam Div . . . . *Digested,* 05/**1686**
W (Children) (Representation: McKenzie Friend), Re see O (Children) (Hearing in Private: Assistance), Re
W (Children: Removal into Care), Re [2005] EWCA Civ 642; [2005] 2 F.L.R.1022; [2005] Fam. Law 767; *Times,* May 25, 2005, CA (Civ Div) . . . . *Digested,* 05/**1534**
W (CICA: Quantum: 2004), Re [2005] 2 Q.R. 10; [2004] 6 Q.R. 5, CICA (York) [*Ex rel.* Dermot Hughes, Barrister, 26, Paradise Square, Sheffield]
W Devis & Sons Ltd *v.* Atkins [1977] A.C. 931; [1977] 3 W.L.R. 214; [1977] 3 All E.R. 40; 8 B.L.R. 57; [1977] I.C.R. 662; [1977] I.R.L.R. 314; (1978) 13 I.T.R. 71; 121 S.J. 512, HL; affirming [1977] 2 W.L.R. 70; [1977] 2 All E.R. 321; [1977] I.C.R. 377; [1976] I.R.L.R. 428; (1976) 12 I.T.R. 12; 121 S.J. 52, CA (Civ Div); affirming [1976] 1 W.L.R. 393; [1976] 2 All E.R. 822; [1976] I.C.R. 196; [1976] I.R.L.R. 16; (1976) 10 I.T.R. 15; 120 S.J. 62, QBD . . . . *Digested,* 77/**1160**:
Applied, 76/991, 78/1059, 81/951, 81/972, 85/1270, 88/1353, 93/1815, 05/1206: *Considered,* 76/986, 77/1137, 79/1017, 97/2290, 04/1303: *Distinguished,* 76/979, 84/1310, 85/1238, 86/1280, 86/1285, 98/2232
W Healthcare NHS Trust *v.* H [2004] EWCA Civ 1324; [2005] 1 W.L.R. 834; *Times,* December 9, 2004; *Independent,* January 21, 2005, CA (Civ Div) . . . . *Digested,* 05/**1850**:
Distinguished, 05/1794
Wabl *v.* Austria (24773/94) (2001) 31 E.H.R.R. 51, ECHR . . . . *Digested,* 01/**3469**:
Distinguished, 05/2046
Wade *v.* Grimwood [2004] EWCA Civ 999; [2004] W.T.L.R. 1195; [2004] 2 P. & C.R. DG20, CA (Civ Div); affirming [2003] EWHC 3030, Ch D . . . . *Digested,* 05/**4298**
Wahlergruppe Gemeinsam Zajedno/Birlikte Alternative und Grune GewerkschafterInnen/ UG (C171/01) [2003] E.C.R. I-4301; [2003] 2 C.M.L.R. 29, ECJ . . . . *Followed,* 05/1234, 05/2204
Waite *v.* GCHQ; *sub nom* Waite *v.* Government Communications Headquarters [1983] 2 A.C. 714; [1983] 3 W.L.R. 389; [1983] 2 All E.R. 1013; [1983] I.C.R. 653; [1983] I.R.L.R. 341; 81 L.G.R. 769; (1983) 133 N.L.J. 745, HL; affirming [1983] I.C.R. 359; [1983] I.R.L.R. 161, CA (Civ Div). . . . . *Digested,* 83/**1327**:
Applied, 84/266, 84/1295, 84/1296, 85/246, 86/1271, 86/1272, 87/1415, 95/2110, 03/1347, 03/1348, 05/1241: *Considered,* 86/1270, 86/4033, 96/2604, 04/1311: *Distinguished,* 03/1285: *Referred to,* 88/1352, 95/2109
Waite *v.* Government Communications Headquarters see Waite *v.* GCHQ
Waite *v.* United Kingdom (53236/99) (2003) 36 E.H.R.R. 54; *Times,* December 31, 2002, ECHR . . . . *Digested,* 03/**2160**:
Considered, 05/2107
Wakefield *v.* Inspector of Taxes [2005] S.T.C. (S.C.D.) 439, Sp Comm . . . . *Digested,* 05/**4001**
Wakelin *v.* Read [2000] O.P.L.R. 277; [2000] Pens. L.R. 319; *Times,* April 10, 2000, CA (Civ Div); reversing [1998] O.P.L.R. 147, Ch D . . . . *Digested,* 00/**4393**:
Applied, 05/2976
Walden *v.* Liechtenstein (Admissibility) (33916/96) UNREPORTED, ECHR . . . . *Considered,* 03/3059, 05/3926
Walford *v.* Miles [1992] 2 A.C. 128; [1992] 2 W.L.R. 174; [1992] 1 All E.R. 453; (1992) 64 P. & C.R. 166; [1992] 1 E.G.L.R. 207; [1992] 11 E.G. 115; [1992] N.P.C. 4; *Times,* January 27, 1992; *Independent,* January 29, 1992, HL; affirming (1991) 62 P. & C.R. 410; [1991] 2 E.G.L.R. 185; [1991] 28 E.G. 81; [1991] 27 E.G. 114; [1990] E.G.C.S. 158; *Independent,* January 15, 1991, CA (Civ Div); reversing [1990] 1 E.G.L.R. 212; [1990] 12 E.G. 107, QBD . . . . *Digested,* 92/**514**:
Applied, 05/309: *Considered,* 93/531, 94/570: *Distinguished,* 97/4535
Walker *v.* D (A Child) see D (A Child) *v.* Walker
Walker *v.* Stones [2001] Q.B. 902; [2001] 2 W.L.R. 623; [2000] 4 All E.R. 412; [2001] B.C.C. 757; [2000] Lloyd's Rep. P.N. 864; [2000] W.T.L.R. 975; (1999-2000) 2 I.T.E.L.R. 848; (2000) 97(35) L.S.G. 36; *Times,* September 26, 2000; *Independent,* July 27, 2000, CA (Civ Div); reversing in part [2000] W.T.L.R. 79, Ch D . . . . *Digested,* 00/**5268**:
Not followed, 05/520
Walker *v.* Walker [2005] EWCA Civ 247; [2005] 1 All E.R. 272; [2005] C.P. Rep. 33; [2005] 3 Costs L.R. 363; [2005] B.P.I.R. 454; *Times,* March 3, 2005, CA (Civ Div) . . . . *Digested,* 05/**362**

Wall v. British Compressed Air Society; *sub nom* British Compressed Air Society v. Wall [2003] EWCA Civ 1762; [2004] I.C.R. 408; [2004] I.R.L.R. 147; [2004] Pens. L.R. 87; (2004) 101(5) L.S.G. 28; (2003) 153 N.L.J. 1903; *Times,* January 9, 2004, CA (Civ Div); affirming [2003] I.R.L.R. 836; *Independent,* July 21, 2003 (C.S), EAT . . . . *Digested,* 04/**1311**: *Considered,* 05/1241

Wall's Meat Co Ltd v. Khan [1979] I.C.R. 52; [1978] I.R.L.R. 499; 122 S.J. 759, CA (Civ Div); affirming [1978] I.R.L.R. 74; (1977) 12 I.T.R. 497, EAT . . . . *Digested,* 79/**979**: *Applied,* 97/2294: *Considered,* 84/1238, 99/2051, 99/2146, 01/2307, 03/4070, 05/1336: *Followed,* 80/999, 89/4302

Wallace v. CA Roofing Services Ltd [1996] I.R.L.R. 435, QBD . . . . *Digested,* 96/**2518**: *Considered,* 03/1330, 05/1219: *Distinguished,* 04/1180

Wallace v. Manchester City Council (1998) 30 H.L.R. 1111; [1998] L. & T.R. 279; [1998] 3 E.G.L.R. 38; [1998] 41 E.G. 223; [1998] E.G.C.S. 114; [1998] N.P.C. 115; *Times,* July 23, 1998; *Independent,* July 17, 1998, CA (Civ Div) . . . . *Digested,* 98/**3678**: *Applied,* 03/2074, 05/2683: *Considered,* 99/3674, 00/4290

Wallace v. Smith [2005] 2 Q.R. 23; [2004] 5 Q.R. 7, CC (Leeds) [*Ex rel.* Tom Nossiter, Barrister, Park Lane Chambers, Leeds] . . . . *Digested,* 04/**2964**

Wallentin v. Riksskatteverket (C169/03) [2004] 3 C.M.L.R. 24, ECJ (1st Chamber) . . . *Digested,* 05/**1469**

Waller v. Cornwall CC [2005] EWHC 1166; [2005] O.P.L.R. 263, Ch D

Walley v. Walley [2005] EWCA Civ 910; [2005] 3 F.C.R. 35; *Times,* July 13, 2005, CA (Civ Div) . . . . *Digested,* 05/**1544**

Wallington v. Montgomeryshire DC see Wallington v. Secretary of State for Wales

Wallington v. Secretary of State for Wales; Wallington v. Montgomeryshire DC (1991) 62 P. & C.R. 150; [1991] 1 P.L.R. 87; [1991] J.P.L. 942; [1990] E.G.C.S. 134; *Times,* November 12, 1990, CA (Civ Div); affirming [1990] J.P.L. 112, DC . . . . . . *Digested,* 92/**4162**: *Applied,* 02/1524, 05/3262

Wallis Retail Ltd's Community Trade Mark (1978/2004) Unreported, OHIM (Opposition Div) . . . . *Considered,* 05/2568

Walmsley v. Transport for London see R. (on the application of Walmsley) v. Lane

Walsh v. Director of the Assets Recovery Agency; *sub nom* Director of the Assets Recovery Agency v. Walsh [2005] N.I. 383, CA (NI); affirming Unreported, QBD (NI)

Walsh v. Secretary of State for Social Security (Unreported, March 28, 1994), QBD . . . *Followed,* 05/3893

Walter v. Lane [1900] A.C. 539, HL; reversing [1899] 2 Ch. 749, CA . . . . *Applied,* 05/2424: *Considered,* 90/3803, 91/2978

Walter L Jacob & Co Ltd, Re (1989) 5 B.C.C. 244; [1989] B.C.L.C. 345; [1989] P.C.C. 47, CA (Civ Div); reversing (1987) 3 B.C.C. 532, DC . . . . *Digested,* 89/**350**: *Applied,* 96/3552, 02/2725, 05/2305: *Followed,* 99/589

Waltham Forest LBC v. Omilaju (No.2) see Omilaju v. Waltham Forest LBC (No.2)

Waltham Forest LBC v. Roberts [2004] EWCA Civ 940; [2005] H.L.R. 2; (2004) 148 S.J.L.B. 910; [2004] N.P.C. 118, CA (Civ Div) . . . . *Digested,* 05/**2685**

Walton v. Calderdale Healthcare NHS Trust [2005] EWHC 1053; [2005] Lloyd's Rep. Med. 398, QBD

Wanadoo (UK) Plc (formerly Freeserve.com Plc) v. Office of Communications (Parallel Investigation: Disclosure) [2004] CAT 15; [2005] Comp. A.R. 286, CAT . . . . . . *Digested,* 05/**562**

Wanadoo (UK) Plc (formerly Freeserve.com Plc) v. Office of Communications (Procedure: Adjournment) [2005] CAT 24; [2005] Comp. A.R. 1241, CAT

Wanadoo (UK) Plc (formerly Freeserve.com Plc) v. Office of Communications (Publication of Judgment) [2004] CAT 20; [2005] Comp. A.R. 430, CAT . . . . . *Digested,* 05/**561**

Wanadoo (UK) Plc (formerly Freeserve.com Plc) v. Office of Communications (Timing of Appeal) [2005] CAT 7; [2005] Comp. A.R. 986, CAT

Wandsworth LBC v. Michalak; *sub nom* Michaelek v. Wandsworth LBC; Michalak v. Wandsworth LBC [2002] EWCA Civ 271; [2003] 1 W.L.R. 617; [2002] 4 All E.R. 1136; [2003] 1 F.C.R. 713; [2002] H.L.R. 39; [2002] N.P.C. 34, CA (Civ Div) . . . . *Digested,* 03/**2789**: *Applied,* 03/2079, 03/4265, 04/710, 04/1889, 04/2782, 04/3731: *Considered,* 03/2171, 04/2534, 04/2776, 04/4738, 05/3835: *Followed,* 02/3079, 04/1898

Wandsworth LBC v. Winder (No.1) [1985] A.C. 461; [1984] 3 W.L.R. 1254; [1984] 3 All E.R. 976; (1985) 17 H.L.R. 196; 83 L.G.R. 143; (1985) 82 L.S.G. 201; (1985) 135 N.L.J. 381; (1984) 128 S.J. 838, HL; affirming [1984] 3 W.L.R. 563; [1984] 3 All E.R. 83; (1984) 15 H.L.R. 1; 82 L.G.R. 509; (1984) 81 L.S.G. 1684; (1984) 128 S.J. 384, CA (Civ Div) . . . . *Digested,* 85/**9**: *Applied,* 87/678, 88/593, 92/30, 92/79, 99/4749, 03/3548, 05/3951: *Considered,* 84/1344, 87/2378, 87/3052, 87/3097, 88/3432, 96/3087, 97/2691: *Distinguished,* 87/3609.a, 88/1, 88/2211, 88/2226, 89/35, 92/394, 93/2048: *Followed,* 00/5126, 03/5265: *Referred to,* 87/2385

Wang v. Inland Revenue Commissioner [1994] 1 W.L.R. 1286; [1995] 1 All E.R. 637; [1994] S.T.C. 753; [1994] S.T.I. 1017; (1994) 91(38) L.S.G. 45; (1994) 138 S.J.L.B. 195, PC (HK) . . . . *Digested,* 95/**4375**: *Applied,* 05/842

Warborough Investments Ltd v. Berry [2003] EWHC 3153; [2005] L. & T.R. 17; (2004) 101(3) L.S.G. 35; [2003] N.P.C. 162, Ch D

Warborough Investments Ltd *v.* S Robinson & Sons (Holdings) Ltd [2003] EWCA Civ 751; [2004] 2 P. & C.R. 6; [2003] 2 E.G.L.R. 149; (2003) 100(24) L.S.G. 38; (2003) 147 S.J.L.B. 748; [2003] N.P.C. 75; *Times,* July 9, 2003, CA (Civ Div); affirming [2002] EWHC 2502, Ch D .... *Digested,* 03/**2778**: *Considered,* 05/2678

Ward *v.* Batten & Stamford Asphalt Co Ltd (Unreported, June 13, 1997), CC (Basingstoke) [*Ex rel.* Mark Gayler, Amery-Parkes Solicitors, Bristol] .... *Digested,* 97/**1935**: *Considered,* 05/3160

Ward *v.* Commissioner of Police of the Metropolis [2005] UKHL 32; [2005] 2 W.L.R. 1114; [2005] 3 All E.R. 1013; (2005) 84 B.M.L.R. 185; (2005) 102(24) L.S.G. 35; (2005) 155 N.L.J. 747; *Times,* May 9, 2005, HL; reversing [2003] EWCA Civ 1152; [2003] 1 W.L.R. 2413; (2003) 74 B.M.L.R. 211; (2003) 100(37) L.S.G. 34; *Times,* September 2, 2003, CA (Civ Div) .... *Digested,* 05/**2828**

Ward *v.* Leeds Teaching Hospitals NHS Trust [2004] EWHC 2106; [2004] Lloyd's Rep. Med. 530, DR (Leeds)....................................... *Digested,* 05/**2834**

Ward *v.* United Kingdom (Admissibility) (31888/03) (2005) 40 E.H.R.R. SE14, ECHR

Wareham *v.* Purbeck DC [2005] EWHC 358; (2005) 169 J.P. 217; [2005] H.L.R. 39; (2005) 169 J.P.N. 319; (2005) 149 S.J.L.B. 388; *Times,* March 28, 2005, QBD (Admin) .... *Digested,* 05/**318**

Warren *v.* Mendy [1989] 1 W.L.R. 853; [1989] 3 All E.R. 103; [1989] I.C.R. 525; [1989] I.R.L.R. 210; (1989) 133 S.J. 1261, CA (Civ Div) .... *Digested,* 90/**649**: *Distinguished,* 05/422

Warren (t/a Sports Network Europe) *v.* Revenue and Customs Commissioners [2005] S.T.I. 2038, V&DTr (London)

Warrington-Shaw *v.* Windsor and Maidenhead RBC [2005] P.A.D. 45, Planning Inspector

Warsame *v.* Hounslow LBC [2000] 1 W.L.R. 696; (2000) 32 H.L.R. 335; (1999) 96(28) L.S.G. 26; (1999) 143 S.J.L.B. 197; *Times,* July 21, 1999 ; *Independent,* July 2, 1999, CA (Civ Div) .... *Digested,* 99/**3047**: *Applied,* 05/2009

Waters *v.* Welsh Development Agency; *sub nom* Melville *v.* Welsh Development Agency [2004] UKHL 19; [2004] 1 W.L.R. 1304; [2004] 2 All E.R. 915; [2005] Env. L.R. 23; [2004] 2 P. & C.R. 29; [2004] 2 E.G.L.R. 103; [2004] R.V.R. 153; [2004] 19 E.G.C.S. 165; (2004) 101(19) L.S.G. 29; (2004) 154 N.L.J. 706; (2004) 148 S.J.L.B. 540; [2004] N.P.C. 68; *Times,* May 5, 2004; *Independent,* May 4, 2004, HL; affirming [2002] EWCA Civ 924; [2003] 4 All E.R. 384; [2003] Env. L.R. 15; [2002] 2 E.G.L.R. 107; [2002] R.V.R. 298; [2002] J.P.L. 1481; [2002] 28 E.G.C.S. 126; (2002) 99(35) L.S.G. 38; [2002] N.P.C. 90; *Independent,* July 5, 2002, CA (Civ Div); affirming [2001] 1 E.G.L.R. 185, Lands Tr .... *Digested,* 04/**3033**

Waterschap Zeeuws Vlaanderen *v.* Staatssecretaris van Financien (C378/02) [2005] S.T.C. 1298; [2005] S.T.I. 1036, ECJ (3rd Chamber) (Unreported, November 18, 2004), AGO

Wathan *v.* Neath and Port Talbot CBC [2002] EWHC 1634, QBD (Admin).......... *Distinguished,* 05/2754

Watkin Jones & Son Ltd *v.* Lidl UK GmbH [2002] EWHC 183; 86 Con. L.R. 155; [2002] C.I.L.L. 1847, QBD (TCC)..................................... *Digested,* 03/**676**: *Distinguished,* 05/642

Watkins *v.* Home Office see Watkins *v.* Secretary of State for the Home Department

Watkins *v.* Secretary of State for the Home Department; *sub nom* Watkins *v.* Home Office; TNS, HL; reversing [2004] EWCA Civ 966; [2005] Q.B. 883; [2005] 2 W.L.R. 1538; [2004] 4 All E.R. 1158; (2004) 101(34) L.S.G. 30; (2004) 148 S.J.L.B. 912; *Times,* August 5, 2004, CA (Civ Div) .... *Digested,* 05/**4193**

Watson *v.* British Boxing Board of Control Ltd [2001] Q.B. 1134; [2001] 2 W.L.R. 1256; [2001] P.I.Q.R. P16; (2001) 98(12) L.S.G. 44; (2001) 145 S.J.L.B. 31; *Times,* February 2, 2001; *Independent,* January 11, 2001; *Daily Telegraph,* January 16, 2001, CA (Civ Div); affirming [2000] E.C.C. 141; (1999) 96(39) L.S.G. 38; (1999) 143 S.J.L.B. 235; *Times,* October 12, 1999, QBD .... *Applied,* 05/2858: *Followed,* 04/2710 *Digested,* 01/**4468**:

Watson *v.* Farmer (Unreported, February 18, 2005), CC (Nuneaton) [*Ex rel.* Stephen Garner, Barrister, No.8 Chambers, Fountain Court, Steelhouse Lane, Birmingham.]... *Digested,* 05/**3113**

Watson *v.* General Medical Council [2005] EWHC 1896; [2005] Lloyd's Rep. Med. 435; (2005) 86 B.M.L.R. 152; (2005) 155 N.L.J. 1356; *Times,* October 7, 2005, QBD (Admin) .... *Digested,* 05/**1800**

Watson *v.* Hackney LBC see Harrison *v.* Hammersmith and Fulham LBC

Watson *v.* Hillingdon (Unreported, October 28, 2004), CC (Uxbridge) [*Ex rel.* Pankaj Pathak, Barrister, 2, Paper Buildings, Temple, London] .... *Digested,* 05/**3207**

Watson *v.* Watson (Wasted Costs Orders) see Ridehalgh *v.* Horsefield

Watson (Lambert) *v.* Queen, The [2004] UKPC 34; [2005] 1 A.C. 472; [2004] 3 W.L.R. 841; 17 B.H.R.C. 95; (2004) 101(32) L.S.G. 35; *Times,* July 14, 2004, PC (Jam) .... *Digested,* 04/**3336**

Watts *v.* Morrow [1991] 1 W.L.R. 1421; [1991] 4 All E.R. 937; 54 B.L.R. 86; 26 Con.
　　L.R. 98; (1991) 23 H.L.R. 608; [1991] 2 E.G.L.R. 152; [1991] 43 E.G. 121; (1992)
　　8 Const. L.J. 73; [1991] E.G.C.S. 88; (1992) 89(14) L.S.G. 33; (1991) 141
　　N.L.J. 1331; [1991] N.P.C. 98; *Independent*, August 20, 1991; *Guardian*,
　　September 4, 1991, CA (Civ Div); reversing 24 Con. L.R. 125; [1991] 15 E.G. 113;
　　[1991] 14 E.G. 111; *Independent*, November 19, 1990 (C.S.), QBD (OR) . . . .　*Digested*, 92/**1548**:
　　　　　　　　　Applied, 94/1762, 94/3395, 95/1565, 95/3706, 96/1211, 96/1882, 96/4499,
　　　　　　　　　96/4518, 00/1480, 00/1485, 00/4276, 02/3311, 03/946, 03/3026, 04/923,
　　　　　　　　　05/1263: *Considered*, 92/1514, 94/1445, 97/3839, 97/6307, 98/2106,
　　　　　　　　　01/4539: *Followed*, 93/1386, 96/4514, 99/1375
Waugh *v.* British Railways Board [1980] A.C. 521; [1979] 3 W.L.R. 150; [1979] 2 All
　　E.R. 1169; [1979] I.R.L.R. 364; 123 S.J. 506, HL; reversing 122 S.J. 730; *Times*,
　　July 29, 1978, CA (Civ Div) . . . .　*Digested*, 79/**2172**:
　　　　　　　　　Applied, 84/1527, 85/2665, 86/2622, 87/3060, 89/3020, 90/3665,
　　　　　　　　　92/3478: *Considered*, 82/2551, 88/1593, 89/2721, 91/2860, 92/3479,
　　　　　　　　　03/403: *Followed*, 05/293: *Referred to*, 80/2131, 81/2142
Waveney DC *v.* Wood [2005] P.A.D. 64, Planning Inspector
Waxman *v.* Waxman (2004-05) 7 I.T.E.L.R. 162, CA (Ont) . . . .　*Digested*, 05/**4299**
Way *v.* Crouch [2005] I.C.R. 1362; [2005] I.R.L.R. 603; (2005) 155 N.L.J. 937, EAT . .　*Digested*, 05/**1231**
Wayne Tank & Pump Co Ltd *v.* Employers Liability Assurance Corp Ltd [1974] Q.B. 57;
　　[1973] 3 W.L.R. 483; [1973] 3 All E.R. 825; [1973] 2 Lloyd's Rep. 237; 117 S.J.
　　564, CA (Civ Div); reversing [1972] 2 Lloyd's Rep. 141, QBD (Comm) . . . .　*Digested*, 73/**395**:
　　　　　　　　　Applied, 04/2204, 05/2352: *Considered*, 86/3086, 87/3409
Wealdon DC *v.* Martin Grant Homes Ltd see R. (on the application of Martin Grant
　　Homes Ltd) *v.* Wealden DC
Weathersfield Ltd (t/a Van & Truck Rentals) *v.* Sargent [1999] I.C.R. 425; [1999] I.R.L.R.
　　94; [1999] Disc. L.R. 290; (1999) 96(5) L.S.G. 35; (1999) 143 S.J.L.B. 39;
　　Times, December 31, 1998, CA (Civ Div); affirming [1998] I.C.R. 198; [1998]
　　I.R.L.R. 14, EAT . . . .　*Digested*, 99/**2091**:
　　　　　　　　　Applied, 05/1290: *Distinguished*, 00/2184
Webb *v.* EMO Air Cargo (UK) Ltd [1995] 1 W.L.R. 1454; [1995] 4 All E.R. 577; [1996]
　　2 C.M.L.R. 990; [1995] I.C.R. 1021; [1995] I.R.L.R. 645; *Times*, October 20,
　　1995; *Independent*, October 26, 1995, HL; reversing [1992] 2 All E.R. 43;
　　[1992] 1 C.M.L.R. 793; [1992] I.C.R. 445; [1992] I.R.L.R. 116; (1992) 89(10)
　　L.S.G. 33; (1992) 142 N.L.J. 16; (1992) 136 S.J.L.B. 32; *Times*, December 30,
　　1991; *Independent*, January 22, 1992; *Guardian*, January 8, 1992, CA (Civ Div);
　　affirming [1990] I.C.R. 442; [1990] I.R.L.R. 124, EAT . . . .　*Digested*, 96/**2622**:
　　　　　　　　　Applied, 92/1971, 92/1972, 96/2623, 98/2194, 02/1418, 05/1262:
　　　　　　　　　Considered, 96/2617, 97/2237: *Distinguished*, 00/2004: *Followed*, 96/2621:
　　　　　　　　　Previous proceedings, 94/4825: *Referred to*, 96/2615:
　　　　　　　　　Subsequent proceedings, 92/1970, 93/1789
Webb *v.* Leadbetter [1966] 1 W.L.R. 245; [1966] 2 All E.R. 114; 130 J.P. 277; 110 S.J.
　　90, QBD . . . .　*Digested*, 66/**7529**:
　　　　　　　　　Applied, 71/9564, 72/621, 73/2106, 05/817: *Considered*, 83/2321, 84/2079
Weber *v.* Universal Ogden Services Ltd [2005] I.L.Pr. 18, HR (NL)
Weber's Wine World Handels GmbH *v.* Abgabenberufungskommission Wien (C147/01)
　　[2005] All E.R. (EC) 224; [2003] E.C.R. I-11365; [2004] 1 C.M.L.R. 7; [2003]
　　C.E.C. 501; [2004] B.T.C. 8019, ECJ (5th Chamber) (Unreported, March 20,
　　2003), AGO . . . .　*Digested*, 04/**908**:
　　　　　　　　　Applied, 03/4569
Webley *v.* Department for Work and Pensions; *sub nom* Department for Work and
　　Pensions *v.* Webley [2004] EWCA Civ 1745; [2005] I.R.L.R.
　　288; (2005) 102(8) L.S.G. 30; *Times*, January 17, 2005; *Independent*, January
　　13, 2005, CA (Civ Div); reversing UKEAT/0033/04/DM, EAT . . . .　*Digested*, 05/**1270**:
Webster *v.* Brunel University (Unreported, December 14, 2004), EAT . . . .　*Overruled*, 05/1221
Webster *v.* Brunel University see Wong *v.* Igen Ltd (formerly Leeds Careers Guidance)
Webster *v.* United Kingdom (A/44) see Young *v.* United Kingdom (A/44)
Wedding Photographs [2005] E.C.D.R. 16
Weeks *v.* Magill see Porter *v.* Magill
Weh *v.* Austria (38544/97) (2005) 40 E.H.R.R. 37, ECHR
Weigel *v.* Finanzlandesdirektion fur Vorarlberg (C387/01) [2004] E.C.R. I-4981;
　　[2004] 3 C.M.L.R. 42, ECJ (6th Chamber) . . . .　*Digested*, 05/**4009**:
　　　　　　　　　Followed, 05/4008
Weinstock *v.* Sarnat (2005-06) 8 I.T.E.L.R. 141, Sup Ct (NSW)
Weir *v.* Secretary of State for Transport see Jeffrey *v.* Secretary of State for Transport
Weldon *v.* Home Office see R. *v.* Deputy Governor of Parkhurst Prison Ex p. Hague
Weldon Plant Ltd *v.* Commission for the New Towns [2001] 1 All E.R. (Comm) 264;
　　[2000] B.L.R. 496; (2000) 2 T.C.L.R. 785; 77 Con. L.R. 1, QBD (TCC) . . . .　*Digested*, 01/**343**:
　　　　　　　　　Considered, 05/205
Well Barn Farming Ltd *v.* Backhouse [2005] EWHC 1520; [2005] 3 E.G.L.R. 109, Ch D
Wellcome Trust Ltd *v.* Customs and Excise Commissioners (C155/94) [1996] All E.R.
　　(EC) 589; [1996] S.T.C. 945; [1996] E.C.R. I-3013; [1996] 2 C.M.L.R. 909;
　　[1996] C.E.C. 611; *Times*, July 10, 1996, ECJ (5th Chamber) . . . .　*Digested*, 96/**5893**:
　　　　　　　　　Followed, 05/4345

WELLCOME/Pigs I (T116/85) [1988] E.P.O.R.1, EPO (Technical Bd App). . . . .   *Considered*, 05/2445

Wells v. Secretary of State for Transport, Local Government and the Regions (C201/02) see R. (on the application of Wells) v. Secretary of State for Transport, Local Government and the Regions (C201/02)

Wells v. Wells; Thomas v. Brighton HA; Page v. Sheerness Steel Co Plc [1999] 1 A.C. 345; [1998] 3 W.L.R. 329; [1998] 3 All E.R. 481; [1998] I.R.L.R. 536; [1998] 2 F.L.R. 507; [1998] P.I.Q.R. Q56; (1998) 43 B.M.L.R. 99; [1998] Fam. Law 593; (1998) 95(35) L.S.G. 35; (1998) 148 N.L.J. 1087; (1998) 142 S.J.L.B. 245; *Times*, July 20, 1998; *Independent*, July 27, 1998 (C.S.), HL; reversing [1997] 1 W.L.R. 652; [1997] 1 All E.R. 673; [1997] P.I.Q.R. Q1; (1997) 37 B.M.L.R. 111; (1996) 93(40) L.S.G. 25; (1996) 140 S.J.L.B. 239; *Times*, October 24, 1996; *Independent*, November 13, 1996, CA (Civ Div); reversing [1996] P.I.Q.R. Q62, QBD. . . . .   *Digested*, 98/**1446**:
    Applied, 98/1478, 98/1573, 00/1479, 00/1503, 01/1546, 03/3125, 04/2847, 05/3072: *Cited*, 00/1489, 00/6430: *Considered*, 98/1474, 99/1397, 99/5671, 04/910: *Distinguished*, 00/1470, 01/6222: *Followed*, 97/1833, 99/1422, 99/5950, 99/5972, 99/5974, 00/1464, 00/1490, 00/1492, 00/5905, 00/6161, 00/6164, 02/928

Welsh Development Agency v. Redpath Dorman Long Ltd [1994] 1 W.L.R. 1409; [1994] 4 All E.R. 10; 67 B.L.R. 1; 38 Con. L.R. 106; (1994) 10 Const. L.J. 325; (1994) 91(21) L.S.G. 42; (1994) 138 S.J.L.B. 87; *Times*, April 4, 1994; *Independent*, May 2, 1994 (C.S.), CA (Civ Div) . . . .   *Digested*, 95/**4191**:
    Applied, 97/1047: *Considered*, 96/859, 97/2719, 99/481, 05/479:
    Distinguished, 96/820, 99/542

Wembley Park Estate Co Ltd's Transfer, Re; London Sephardi Trust v. Baker [1968] Ch. 491; [1968] 2 W.L.R. 500; [1968] 1 All E.R. 457; 112 S.J. 152, Ch D . . . .   *Digested*, 68/**3334**:
    Considered, 89/456, 91/3550, 05/357

Wemhoff v. Germany (A/7) (1979-80) 1 E.H.R.R. 55, ECHR. . . . .   *Digested*, 80/**1384**:
    Considered, 05/2110

Wendt v. Orr (2005-06) 8 I.T.E.L.R. 523, Sup Ct (WA) (Full Ct); reversing [2005] W.T.L.R. 223; (2003-04) 6 I.T.E.L.R. 989, Sup Ct (WA) (Sgl judge)

Wendt v. Orr (Costs) [2005] W.T.L.R. 423, Sup Ct (WA) (Sgl judge)

Wentzel v. General Medical Council [2004] EWHC 381; (2005) 82 B.M.L.R. 127, QBD (Admin) . . . .   *Digested*, 05/**1805**

Wessex Reserve Forces and Cadets Association v. White [2005] EWCA Civ 1744; [2005] 49 E.G.C.S. 89, CA (Civ Div); affirming [2005] EWHC 983; [2005] 3 E.G.L.R. 127; [2005] 22 E.G.C.S. 132; [2005] 2 P. & C.R. DG17, QBD

West v. First Secretary of State [2005] EWHC 729; [2005] N.P.C. 58, QBD (Admin)

West Bromwich Building Society v. Crammer (Application for Permission to Appeal) [2002] EWCA Civ 1924, CA (Civ Div) . . . .   *Applied*, 03/2347:
    Considered, 05/2279

West Bromwich Building Society v. Wilkinson; *sub nom* Wilkinson v. West Bromwich Building Society [2005] UKHL 44; [2005] 1 W.L.R. 2303; [2005] 4 All E.R. 97; [2005] 27 E.G.C.S. 221; (2005) 102(28) L.S.G. 32; [2005] 2 P. & C.R. DG20; *Times*, July 4, 2005; *Independent*, July 7, 2005, HL; affirming [2004] EWCA Civ 1063; [2004] C.P. Rep. 42; (2004) 101(36) L.S.G. 34; (2004) 148 S.J.L.B. 975; [2004] N.P.C. 134; [2004] 2 P. & C.R. DG22; *Times*, October 5, 2004, CA (Civ Div) . . . .   *Digested*, 05/**435**

West Dunbartonshire Council v. Wallace see Strathclyde RC v. Wallace

West Herts College v. Customs and Excise Commissioners see Customs and Excise Commissioners v. West Herts College

West Kent Housing Association Ltd v. Davies (1999) 31 H.L.R. 415; [1998] E.G.C.S. 103, CA (Civ Div) . . . .   *Digested*, 99/**3708**:
    Applied, 00/3923: *Followed*, 05/2642

West Norwood Cemetery, Re [2005] 1 W.L.R. 2176; (2005) 102(18) L.S.G. 22; *Times*, April 20, 2005, Cons Ct. . . . .   *Digested*, 05/**987**

West Oxfordshire DC v. PA Turney Ltd [2005] P.A.D. 22, Planning Inspector

West Tankers Inc v. RAS Riunione Adriatica di Sicurta SpA (The Front Comor) [2005] EWHC 454; [2005] 2 All E.R. (Comm) 240; [2005] 2 Lloyd's Rep. 257; [2005] 1 C.L.C. 347, QBD (Comm) . . . .   *Digested*, 05/**2357**

West Yorkshire Probation Board v. Boulter [2005] EWHC 2342; (2005) 169 J.P. 601; (2005) 169 J.P.N. 920; (2005) 102(42) L.S.G. 24; *Times*, October 11, 2005, QBD (Admin)

West Yorkshire Trading Standards Service v. Lex Vehicle Leasing Ltd [1996] R.T.R. 70, QBD . . . .   *Considered*, 05/818

West (Inspector of Taxes) v. Trennery; *sub nom* Tee v. Inspector of Taxes; Trennery v. West (Inspector of Taxes) [2005] UKHL 5; [2005] 1 All E.R. 827; [2005] S.T.C. 214; 76 T.C. 713; [2005] B.T.C. 69; [2005] W.T.L.R. 205; [2005] S.T.I. 157; (2005) 149 S.J.L.B. 147; [2005] N.P.C. 10; *Times*, February 1, 2005, HL; reversing [2003] EWCA Civ 1792; [2004] S.T.C. 170; [2004] B.T.C. 3; [2004] W.T.L.R. 293; [2004] S.T.I. 51; (2004) 148 S.J.L.B. 56; *Times*, January 23, 2004, CA (Civ Div); reversing [2003] EWHC 676; [2003] S.T.C. 580; [2003] B.T.C. 317; [2003] W.T.L.R. 739; [2003] S.T.I. 585; (2003) 100(23) L.S.G. 39; *Times*, April 18, 2003, Ch D; reversing [2002] S.T.C. (S.C.D.) 370; [2002] W.T.L.R. 1231; [2002] S.T.I. 1257, Sp Comm . . . . *Digested*, 05/**4004**
Westdeutsche Landesbank Girozentrale v. Islington LBC; Kleinwort Benson Ltd v. Sandwell BC [1996] A.C. 669; [1996] 2 W.L.R. 802; [1996] 2 All E.R. 961; [1996] 5 Bank. L.R. 341; [1996] C.L.C. 990; 95 L.G.R. 1; (1996) 160 J.P. Rep. 1130; (1996) 146 N.L.J. 877; (1996) 140 S.J.L.B. 136; *Times*, May 30, 1996, HL; reversing [1994] 1 W.L.R. 938; [1994] 4 All E.R. 890; 92 L.G.R. 405; (1994) 158 L.G. Rev. 981; (1994) 91(8) L.S.G. 29; (1994) 138 S.J.L.B. 26; *Times*, December 30, 1993; *Independent*, January 5, 1994, CA (Civ Div); affirming 91 L.G.R. 323; *Times*, February 23, 1993, QBD . . . . *Digested*, 96/**4149**:
Applied, 98/304, 00/2320, 02/4666, 03/1421, 03/2374, 04/1932, 05/3444:
Considered, 97/712, 98/1433, 02/3386: *Distinguished*, 95/4151, 04/480:
Followed, 98/231, 99/278
Western Bulk Carriers K/S v. Li Hai Maritime Inc [2005] EWHC 735; [2005] 2 Lloyd's Rep. 389; [2005] 1 C.L.C. 704, QBD (Comm) . . . . *Digested*, 05/**3789**
Westland Helicopters Ltd v. Al-Hejailan [2004] EWHC 1625; [2004] 2 Lloyd's Rep. 523, QBD (Comm) . . . . *Digested*, 05/**203**
Westland Helicopters Ltd v. Al-Hejailan (Costs) [2004] EWHC 1688; [2004] 2 Lloyd's Rep. 535, QBD (Comm) . . . . *Digested*, 05/**365**
Westminster Bank Ltd v. Brinkley see Brinkley's Will Trusts, Re
Westminster City Council v. Beechwood Ltd [2005] P.A.D. 93, Planning Inspector
Westminster City Council v. French Connection Retail Ltd [2005] EWHC 933; (2005) 169 J.P. 321; [2005] Env. L.R. 42; (2005) 169 J.P.N. 438, QBD . . . . *Digested*, 05/**790**
Westminster City Council v. McDonald [2003] EWHC 2698; [2005] Env. L.R. 1, QBD (Admin) . . . . *Digested*, 05/**2894**
Westminster City Council v. Morris see R. (on the application of Morris) v. Westminster City Council (No.3)
Westminster City Council v. Ocean Leisure Ltd see Ocean Leisure Ltd v. Westminster City Council
Westminster City Council v. Porter (Third Party Disclosure: Costs Basis) [2003] EWHC 2373; [2005] 2 Costs L.R. 186, Ch D
Westminster City Council v. RA [2005] EWHC 970; [2005] 2 F.L.R. 1309; [2005] Fam. Law 687; *Times*, June 6, 2005, Fam Div . . . . *Digested*, 05/**1528**
Westmoreland Investments Ltd v. MacNiven (Inspector of Taxes) see MacNiven (Inspector of Taxes) v. Westmoreland Investments Ltd
Weston v. Garnett (Inspector of Taxes); *sub nom* Businessman v. Inspector of Taxes [2005] EWCA Civ 742; [2005] S.T.C. 1134; [2005] B.T.C. 342; [2005] S.T.I. 1098; (2005) 149 S.J.L.B. 774; *Times*, June 29, 2005, CA (Civ Div); affirming [2004] EWHC 1607; [2005] S.T.C. 617; [2005] B.T.C. 113; [2004] S.T.I. 1587; *Times*, July 7, 2004, Ch D; affirming [2003] S.T.C. (S.C.D.) 403, Sp Comm . . . . *Digested*, 05/**3997**
Wethered Estate Ltd v. Davis [2005] EWHC 1903; (2005) 102(39) L.S.G. 29, Ch D
Whalley v. Doney (No.1) see MDA Investment Management Ltd (No.1), Re
Whalley v. Doney (No.2) see MDA Investment Management Ltd (No.2), Re
Whalley v. Montracon Ltd see Montracon Ltd v. Whalley
Wheeldon v. Burrows (1879) L.R. 12 Ch. D. 31; [1874-90] All E.R. Rep. 669; (1879) 48 L.J. Ch. 853; (1879) 41 L.T. 327, CA . . . . *Applied*, 69/1153,
69/1158, 00/4631, 05/3403: *Considered*, 70/823, 72/1109, 77/333,
80/93.u, 81/743, 83/224, 87/1231, 88/1181, 88/2088, 95/3740, 00/4640:
Distinguished, 68/1313: *Followed*, 47-51/3227, 93/3007:
Not followed, 66/4174, 66/4176
Wheeldon v. HSBC Bank Ltd see Hartman v. South Essex Mental Health and Community Care NHS Trust
Wheeler v. Quality Deep Ltd (t/a Thai Royale Restaurant); *sub nom* Wheeler v. Qualitydeep Ltd (t/a Thai Royale Restaurant) [2004] EWCA Civ 1085; [2005] I.C.R. 265; (2004) 101(35) L.S.G. 33; *Times*, August 30, 2004, CA (Civ Div); reversing UKEAT/0998/03/TM, EAT . . . . *Digested*, 04/**1201**
Whelehan v. DPP [1995] R.T.R. 177, DC . . . . *Digested*, 95/**1000**:
Considered, 05/912
Whibberley v. Bartlett (Unreported, June 4, 2004), CC (Reading) [*Ex rel*. Joanna Kerr, Barrister, Lamb Chambers, Lamb Building, Temple, London] . . . . *Digested*, 05/**3112**
Whiffen v. Milham Ford Girls School; Whiffen v. Oxfordshire CC [2001] EWCA Civ 385; [2001] I.C.R. 1023; [2001] I.R.L.R. 468; [2001] Emp. L.R. 541; [2001] B.L.G.R. 309; (2001) 98(23) L.S.G. 36; *Times*, April 3, 2001, CA (Civ Div); reversing (Unreported, February 12, 1998), EAT . . . . *Digested*, 01/**2321**:
Distinguished, 05/1270
Whiffen v. Oxfordshire CC see Whiffen v. Milham Ford Girls School

Whiffen (Opticians) *v.* Customs and Excise Commissioners [2005] S.T.I. 877,V&DTr
Whillis *v.* Bodman [2005] 2 Q.R. 19; [2004] 3 Q.R. 12, CC (Truro) [*Ex rel.* Adrian
    Posta, Barrister, Albion Chambers, Broad Street, Bristol] . . . . *Digested*, 04/**2945**
Whitbread Group Plc *v.* Customs and Excise Commissioners [2005] EWHC 418;
    [2005] S.T.C. 539; [2005] B.T.C. 5207; [2005] B.V.C. 238; [2005] S.T.I. 653,
    Ch D; affirming [2004] V. & D.R. 490; [2004] S.T.I. 2356,V&DTr . . . . *Digested*, 05/**4393**
White *v.* Chief Constable of South Yorkshire; Frost *v.* Chief Constable of South
    Yorkshire; Duncan *v.* British Coal Corp [1999] 2 A.C. 455; [1998] 3 W.L.R.
    1509; [1999] 1 All E.R. 1; [1999] I.C.R. 216; [1999] I.R.L.R. 110; (1999) 45
    B.M.L.R. 1; (1999) 96(2) L.S.G. 28; (1998) 148 N.L.J. 1844; (1999) 143
    S.J.L.B. 51; *Times*, December 4, 1998; *Independent*, December 9, 1998, HL;
    reversing [1998] Q.B. 254; [1997] 3 W.L.R. 1194; [1997] 1 All E.R. 540; [1997]
    I.R.L.R. 173; (1997) 33 B.M.L.R. 108; (1996) 146 N.L.J. 1651; *Times*, November
    6, 1996; *Independent*, November 5, 1996, CA (Civ Div); reversing *Times*, July 3,
    1995, QBD . . . . *Digested*, 99/**4059**:
                     Applied, 01/4462, 03/5828, 05/2884: *Considered*, 97/2615, 00/4213,
                        00/4220, 02/948, 02/3307: *Followed*, 99/3980: *Referred to*, 00/6598
White *v.* Paul Davidson & Taylor [2004] EWCA Civ 1511; [2005] P.N.L.R. 15; (2004)
    148 S.J.L.B. 1373, CA (Civ Div) . . . . *Digested*, 05/**2873**
White *v.* Riverside Housing Association Ltd; *sub nom* Riverside Housing Association
    Ltd *v.* White [2005] EWCA Civ 1385; [2005] 50 E.G.C.S. 91; [2005] N.P.C. 142,
    CA (Civ Div)
White *v.* Vandervell Trustees see Vandervell's Trusts (No.1), Re
White (Pamela) *v.* White (Martin) [2001] 1 A.C. 596; [2000] 3 W.L.R. 1571; [2001] 1
    All E.R. 1; [2000] 2 F.L.R. 981; [2000] 3 F.C.R. 555; [2001] Fam. Law 12;
    (2000) 97(43) L.S.G. 38; (2000) 150 N.L.J. 1716; (2000) 144 S.J.L.B. 266;
    [2000] N.P.C. 111; *Times*, October 31, 2000; *Independent*, November 1, 2000;
    Daily Telegraph, November 7, 2000, HL; affirming [1999] Fam. 304; [1999] 2
    W.L.R. 1213; [1998] 4 All E.R. 659; [1998] 2 F.L.R. 310; [1998] 3 F.C.R. 45;
    [1998] Fam. Law 522; *Times*, July 13, 1998; *Independent*, June 29, 1998 (C.S.),
    CA (Civ Div) . . . . *Digested*, 00/**2530**:
             Applied, 01/2634, 01/5156, 02/1678, 02/1679, 02/1682, 02/1687, 02/1690,
                   03/1581, 03/1589, 05/1656: *Considered*, 01/2632, 01/2635, 01/2639,
                   03/1579, 04/1515, 04/4216, 05/1688: *Followed*, 01/2633
Whitely *v.* Marton Electrical Ltd [2003] I.C.R. 495; [2003] I.R.L.R. 197; *Times*,
    January 2, 2003, EAT . . . . *Digested*, 03/**1330**:
                                               Considered, 05/1219
Whitfield *v.* DPP [1998] Crim. L.R. 349, DC. . . . . *Applied*, 05/**817**
Whitfield *v.* United Kingdom (46387/99); Pewter *v.* United Kingdom (48906/99);
    Gaskin *v.* United Kingdom (57410/00); Clarke *v.* United Kingdom (57419/00)
    (2005) 41 E.H.R.R. 44; *Times*, April 27, 2005, ECHR
Whitlam *v.* Lloyds Syndicate 260 (t/a KGM Motor Policies at Lloyds) see Hazel (for
    Lloyd's Syndicate 260) *v.* Whitlam
Whittaker *v.* BBA Groups (Unreported, April 5, 1995) [*Ex rel.* Philip Hamer & Co
    Solicitors, 9/11 Scale Lane, Hull] . . . . *Digested*, 95/**1825**:
                                               Considered, 05/406
Whyte *v.* Whyte [2005] EWCA Civ 858; [2005] 3 F.C.R. 21; [2005] Fam. Law 863;
    (2005) 102(31) L.S.G. 26; *Times*, August 23, 2005, CA (Civ Div) . . . . *Digested*, 05/**1568**
Wielockx *v.* Inspecteur der Directe Belastingen (C80/94) [1996] 1 W.L.R. 84; [1995]
    All E.R. (E.C.) 769; [1995] S.T.C. 876; [1995] E.C.R. I-2493; [1995] 3 C.M.L.R.
    85; *Times*, October 3, 1995, ECJ [1995] E.C.R. I-2493, AGO . . . . *Digested*, 95/**2786**:
                            Applied, 03/4226, 05/4028: *Considered*, 96/3341
Wiener SI GmbH *v.* Hauptzollamt Emmerich (C338/95) [1997] E.C.R. I-6495; [1998]
    1 C.M.L.R. 1110, ECJ . . . . *Applied*, 03/**913**,
                                               05/**2569**
Wiggins *v.* North Yorkshire CC see Smith *v.* AJ Morrisroes & Sons Ltd
Wightman *v.* Bennett [2005] B.P.I.R. 470, Ch D . . . . *Digested*, 05/**2296**
Wilcock *v.* Duckworth [2005] B.P.I.R. 682, Ch D
Wild *v.* South African Supply & Cold Storage Co see South African Supply and Cold Storage
    Co, Re
Wildacre Ltd *v.* Greenwich LBC [2005] P.A.D. 16, Planning Inspector
Wilderbrook Ltd *v.* Olowu; *sub nom* Wilderbrook Ltd *v.* Oluwu [2005] EWCA Civ 1361;
    [2005] N.P.C. 133, CA (Civ Div); affirming 4LB02223, CC (Lambeth)
Wilfling *v.* Austria (6306/02) see Woditschka *v.* Austria (69756/01)
Wilkinson *v.* Inland Revenue Commissioners see R. (on the application of Wilkinson) *v.*
    Inland Revenue Commissioners
Wilkinson *v.* Lord Chancellor's Department; *sub nom* Wilkinson *v.* Official Solicitor;
    Wilkinson *v.* S [2003] EWCA Civ 95; [2003] 1 W.L.R. 1254; [2003] 2 All E.R.
    184; [2003] C.P. Rep. 37; [2003] 1 F.C.R. 741; (2003) 100(12) L.S.G. 29;
    (2003) 147 S.J.L.B. 178; *Times*, February 7, 2003; *Independent*, February 12,
    2003, CA (Civ Div) . . . . *Digested*, 03/**319**:
                                            Applied, 05/846, 05/847
Wilkinson *v.* Official Solicitor see Wilkinson *v.* Lord Chancellor's Department
Wilkinson *v.* S see Wilkinson *v.* Lord Chancellor's Department

Wilkinson v. West Bromwich Building Society see West Bromwich Building Society v. Wilkinson

Wilkinson v. West Coast Capital (Pre-Trial Review); *sub nom* New Gadget Shop Ltd, Re; Gadget Shop Ltd, Re [2005] EWHC 1606, Ch D . . . . *Digested,* 05/**289**

Willcox v. Tucker [2004] R.V.R. 302, Lands Tr . . . . *Digested,* 05/**3404**

William Grant & Sons Distillers Ltd v. Inland Revenue Commissioners see Mars UK Ltd v. Small (Inspector of Taxes)

William Grant & Sons Distillers Ltd v. Inland Revenue Commissioners see Revenue and Customs Commissioners v. William Grant & Sons Distillers Ltd

William Hill (Football) Ltd v. Ladbroke (Football) Ltd see Ladbroke (Football) Ltd v. William Hill (Football) Ltd

William Smith (Wakefield) Ltd v. Parisride Ltd [2005] EWHC 462; [2005] 2 E.G.L.R. 22; [2005] 24 E.G. 180; (2005) 102(22) L.S.G. 27; *Times,* April 8, 2005, QBD (Admin) . . . . *Digested,* 05/**2637**

William Tomkinson & Sons Ltd v. Parochial Church Council of St Michael (1990) 6 Const. L.J. 319 . . . . *Digested,* 91/**337**:
Applied, 05/654: *Considered,* 99/792: *Followed,* 96/1153

William Verry Ltd v. North West London Communal Mikvah [2004] EWHC 1300; [2004] B.L.R. 308; 96 Con. L.R. 96; [2004] 26 E.G.C.S. 192, QBD (TCC) . . . . *Digested,* 05/**666**

Williams v. Ferrosan Ltd [2004] I.R.L.R. 607, EAT . . . . *Applied,* 05/1251

Williams v. Inspector of Taxes see Locabail (UK) Ltd v. Bayfield Properties Ltd (Leave to Appeal)

Williams v. J Walter Thompson Group Ltd; *sub nom* J Walter Thompson Group Ltd v. Williams [2005] EWCA Civ 133; [2005] I.R.L.R. 376; (2005) 102(16) L.S.G. 30; *Times,* April 5, 2005; *Independent,* February 25, 2005, CA (Civ Div); reversing UKEAT/0299/03/ILB, EAT . . . . *Digested,* 05/**1227**

Williams v. Lindley [2005] EWCA Civ 103; [2005] 2 F.L.R. 710; [2005] 1 F.C.R. 269; [2005] Fam. Law 541; *Times,* March 23, 2005, CA (Civ Div) . . . . *Digested,* 05/**1660**

Williams v. Natural Life Health Foods Ltd [1998] 1 W.L.R. 830; [1998] 2 All E.R. 577; [1998] B.C.C. 428; [1998] 1 B.C.L.C. 689; (1998) 17 Tr. L.R. 152; (1998) 95(21) L.S.G. 37; (1998) 148 N.L.J. 657; (1998) 142 S.J.L.B. 166; *Times,* May 1, 1998, HL; reversing [1997] B.C.C. 605; [1997] 1 B.C.L.C. 131; *Times,* January 9, 1997; *Independent,* December 13, 1996, CA (Civ Div); affirming [1996] B.C.C. 376; [1996] 1 B.C.L.C. 288; (1996) 140 S.J.L.B. 43; *Independent,* January 18, 1996, QBD . . . . *Digested,* 98/**3920**:
Applied, 99/4014, 99/4019, 00/4218, 02/4542, 03/2475, 05/2868:
Cited, 99/3311: *Followed,* 99/4405, 02/493

Williams v. Revenue and Customs Commissioners [2005] S.T.C. (S.C.D.) 782; [2005] W.T.L.R. 1421; [2005] S.T.I. 1682, Sp Comm

Williams v. South Gloucestershire Council [2005] P.A.D. 62, Planning Inspector

Williams v. Southampton Institute see Dunnachie v. Kingston upon Hull City Council

Williams v. Trinidad and Tobago [2005] UKPC 11; [2005] 1 W.L.R. 1948, PC (Trin) . . . . . *Digested,* 05/**3634**

Williams (Inspector of Taxes) v. Grundy's Trustees [1934] 1 K.B. 524, KBD . . . . *Applied,* 05/3996:
Followed, 47-51/4619

Williamson v. Secretary of State for Education and Employment see R. (on the application of Williamson) v. Secretary of State for Education and Employment

Willingale v. Globalgrange Ltd; *sub nom* Willingale v. Global Grange Ltd (2001) 33 H.L.R. 17; (2000) 80 P. & C.R. 448; [2000] L. & T.R. 549; [2000] 2 E.G.L.R. 55; [2000] 18 E.G. 152; (2000) 97(12) L.S.G. 44; (2000) 80 P. & C.R. D12; *Times,* March 29, 2000; *Independent,* April 17, 2000 (C.S.), CA (Civ Div) . . . . . . *Digested,* 00/**3899**:
Considered, 05/3386

Willis Management (Isle of Man) Ltd v. Cable & Wireless Plc; *sub nom* Cable & Wireless Plc v. Valentine [2005] EWCA Civ 806; [2005] 2 Lloyd's Rep. 597, CA (Civ Div); reversing [2005] EWHC 409, QBD (Comm)

Willis Pension Trustees Ltd v. Revenue and Customs Commissioners [2005] S.T.I. 2034, V&D Tr (London)

Wilson v. Central Sunderland Housing Co see Sheffield City Council v. Smart

Wilson v. DM Hall & Sons [2005] P.N.L.R. 22, OH . . . . *Digested,* 05/**5577**

Wilson v. First County Trust Ltd (No.2); *sub nom* Wilson v. Secretary of State for Trade and Industry [2003] UKHL 40; [2004] 1 A.C. 816; [2003] 3 W.L.R. 568; [2003] 4 All E.R. 97; [2003] 2 All E.R. (Comm) 491; [2003] H.R.L.R. 33; [2003] U.K.H.R.R. 1085; (2003) 100(35) L.S.G. 39; (2003) 147 S.J.L.B. 872; *Times,* July 11, 2003; *Independent,* November 3, 2003 (C.S), HL; reversing [2001] EWCA Civ 633; [2002] Q.B. 74; [2001] 3 W.L.R. 42; [2001] 3 All E.R. 229; [2001] 2 All E.R. (Comm) 134; [2001] E.C.C. 37; [2001] H.R.L.R. 44; [2001] U.K.H.R.R. 1175; (2001) 98(24) L.S.G. 44; (2001) 145 S.J.L.B. 125; *Times,* May 16, 2001; *Independent,* May 8, 2001; *Daily Telegraph,* May 8, 2001, CA (Civ Div) . . . . *Digested,* 04/**628**:
Applied, 01/2315, 04/2222, 05/190, 05/672, 05/1410, 05/3376:
Considered, 01/100, 01/3504, 04/1312, 04/3581, 05/17

Wilson v. Robertsons (London) Ltd [2005] EWHC 1425; [2005] 3 All E.R. 873; (2005) 102(30) L.S.G. 29; *Times,* July 28, 2005, Ch D . . . . *Digested,* 05/**672**

Wilson v. Secretary of State for Trade and Industry see Wilson v. First County Trust Ltd (No.2)

Wilson v. United Kingdom (30668/96); Palmer v. United Kingdom (30671/96); Doolan v. United Kingdom (30678/96) [2002] I.R.L.R. 568; (2002) 35 E.H.R.R. 20; 13 B.H.R.C. 39; *Times,* July 5, 2002, ECHR . . . .   *Digested,* 02/**2375**:
Applied, 05/1310

Wilson v. Wychavon DC [2005] EWHC 2970; [2005] N.P.C. 151, QBD (Admin)

Wilson (Inspector of Taxes) v. Clayton [2004] EWCA Civ 1657; [2005] S.T.C. 157; [2005] I.R.L.R. 108; 77 T.C. 1; [2004] B.T.C. 477; [2004] S.T.I. 2543; (2005) 102(2) L.S.G. 30; (2005) 149 S.J.L.B. 24; *Times,* January 12, 2005, CA (Civ Div); affirming [2004] EWHC 898; [2004] S.T.C. 1022; [2004] I.R.L.R. 611; [2004] S.T.I. 1121; (2004) 101 (19) L.S.G. 29; *Times,* June 7, 2004, Ch D . . . . . .   *Digested,* 05/**4071**

Wiltshire v. Powell see Powell v. Wiltshire

Wiltshire CC v. Crest Estates Ltd [2005] EWCA Civ 1087; [2005] B.L.R. 458; [2005] 3 E.G.L.R. 19; [2005] 41 E.G. 206; [2005] R.V.R. 325; *Times,* September 22, 2005, CA (Civ Div); affirming [2005] EWHC 2980, QBD . . . .   *Digested,* 05/**712**

Wiltshire Police Authority v. Wynn [1981] Q.B. 95; [1980] 3 W.L.R. 445; [1980] I.C.R. 649; 78 L.G.R. 591; 124 S.J. 463, CA (Civ Div); reversing [1980] I.C.R. 401, EAT . . . .   *Digested,* 80/**2081**:
Applied, 83/1264, 05/1219

Wimbledon and Putney Commons Conservators v. Dixon (1875-76) L.R. 1 Ch. D. 362, CA . . . .   *Applied,* 53/1162,
64/1204, 82/366.13, 84/341.14: *Considered,* 05/3403

Wimbledon Construction Co 2000 Ltd v. Vago [2005] EWHC 1086; [2005] B.L.R. 374; 101 Con. L.R. 99, QBD (TCC)

Winchester CC v. Linden Homes Southern Ltd [2005] P.A.D. 70, Planning Inspector

Windsurfing Chiemsee Produktions und Vertriebs GmbH v. Attenberger (C109/97) see Windsurfing Chiemsee Produktions- und Vertriebs GmbH v. Boots- und Segelzubehor Walter Huber (C108/97)

Windsurfing Chiemsee Produktions- und Vertriebs GmbH v. Boots- und Segelzubehor Walter Huber (C108/97); Windsurfing Chiemsee Produktions und Vertriebs GmbH v. Attenberger (C109/97) [2000] Ch. 523; [2000] 2 W.L.R. 205; [1999] E.C.R. I-2779; [1999] E.T.M.R. 585; *Times,* May 18, 1999, ECJ . . . .   *Digested,* 99/**3530**:
Applied, 00/3705, 00/3718, 04/2372: *Considered,* 00/3724, 00/3758, 02/2885, 03/2651, 04/2398: *Followed,* 05/2557

Windsurfing International Inc v. Tabur Marine (Great Britain) Ltd [1985] R.P.C. 59, CA (Civ Div) . . . .   *Applied,* 92/3291,
92/3319, 93/3041, 95/3758, 95/3777, 95/3778, 96/4568, 97/3902, 98/3477, 99/3506, 99/3519, 00/3639, 01/3902, 02/2816, 02/2840, 04/2273, 04/2308, 04/2341, 04/2346, 05/2481: *Considered,* 94/2766, 01/3963, 02/2845, 03/5748, 04/2340: *Followed,* 96/4543, 97/3901, 00/3678, 01/3967:
Referred to, 94/3438, 99/3480, 99/3514

Wing v. Nuttall see Vehicle Inspectorate v. Nuttall

Wingrove v. United Kingdom (17419/90) (1997) 24 E.H.R.R. 1; 1 B.H.R.C. 509; *Times,* December 5, 1996; *Independent,* November 28, 1996, ECHR (1994) 18 E.H.R.R. CD54, Eur Comm HR . . . .   *Digested,* 96/**3143**:
Considered, 05/692: *Referred to,* 01/3479

Winward Industrie Inc's Trade Mark Application (C54/01) see Linde AG's Trade Mark Application (C53/01)

Wippel v. Peek & Cloppenburg GmbH & Co KG (C313/02) [2004] E.C.R. I-9483; [2005] 1 C.M.L.R. 9; [2005] I.C.R. 1604; [2005] I.R.L.R. 211, ECJ . . . .   *Digested,* 05/**1197**

Wireless Group Plc v. Radio Joint Audience Research Ltd [2004] EWHC 2925; [2005] U.K.C.L.R. 203; [2005] E.C.C. 19; [2005] Eu. L.R. 307; [2005] E.M.L.R. 27, Ch D . . . .   *Digested,* 05/**578**

Wirral BC v. Brock Plc [2004] EWCA Civ 1611; [2005] Env. L.R. 26; [2005] 2 P. & C.R. 18; [2005] J.P.L. 1067; (2005) 149 S.J.L.B. 24, CA (Civ Div) . . . .   *Digested,* 05/**3282**

Wise Group v. Mitchell [2005] I.C.R. 896, EAT . . . .   *Digested,* 05/**1340**

Wiszniewski v. Central Manchester HA; *sub nom* Wisniewski v. Central Manchester HA [1998] P.I.Q.R. P324; [1998] Lloyd's Rep. Med. 223, CA (Civ Div); affirming [1996] 7 Med. L.R. 248, QBD . . . .   *Digested,* 98/**3961**:
Applied, 00/3517: *Considered,* 05/493

Wittek v. Germany (37290/97) (2005) 41 E.H.R.R. 46, ECHR

WM Management & Marketing Ltd v. Customs and Excise Commissioners [2005] V. & D.R. 242, V&DTr (London)

Wm Wrigley Jr Co v. Office for Harmonisation in the Internal Market (Trade Marks and Designs) (OHIM) (T193/99) see Office for Harmonisation in the Internal Market (Trade Marks and Designs) (OHIM) v. Wm Wrigley Jr Co (C191/01 P)

WN v. Secretary of State for the Home Department; *sub nom* WN (Surendran: Credibility: New Evidence: Democratic Republic of Congo), Re [2004] UKIAT 213; [2005] I.N.L.R. 340, IAT . . . .   *Digested,* 05/**2153**

WN (Surendran: Credibility: New Evidence: Democratic Republic of Congo), Re see WN v. Secretary of State for the Home Department

Woditschka v. Austria (69756/01); Wilfling v. Austria (6306/02) (2005) 41 E.H.R.R. 32, ECHR

Wolff v. Wolff [2004] EWHC 2110; [2004] S.T.C. 1633; [2004] W.T.L.R. 1349; [2004] S.T.I. 2068; [2004] N.P.C. 135, Ch D . . . .   *Digested,* 05/**3420**

Wolff & Muller GmbH & Co KG v. Pereira Felix (C60/03) [2004] E.C.R. I-9553; [2005]
   1 C.M.L.R. 21; [2005] C.E.C. 498, ECJ (2nd Chamber).................   *Digested,* 05/**1465**
Wolverhampton BC v. B&Q (Retail) Ltd see Stoke on Trent City Council v. B&Q
   (Retail) Ltd
Wong v. BAE Systems Operations Ltd see Gill v. Ford Motor Co Ltd
Wong v. Igen Ltd (formerly Leeds Careers Guidance); *sub nom* Igen Ltd (formerly
   Leeds Careers Guidance) v. Wong; Brunel University v. Webster; Chambelin
   Solicitors v. Emokpae; Emokpae v. Chamberlin Solicitors; Webster v. Brunel
   University [2005] EWCA Civ 142; [2005] 3 All E.R. 812; [2005] I.C.R. 931;
   [2005] I.R.L.R. 258; (2005) 102(13) L.S.G. 28; (2005) 149 S.J.L.B. 264;
   Times, March 3, 2005, CA (Civ Div); affirming UKEAT/0944/03/RN, EAT.....   *Digested,* 05/**1221**
Wong Liu Sheung v. Burt [2005] W.T.L.R. 291; (2004-05) 7 I.T.E.L.R. 263, CA (NZ) ..   *Digested,* 05/**4317**
Wong Mee Wan v. Kwan Kin Travel Services Ltd [1996] 1 W.L.R. 38; [1995] 4 All E.R.
   745; [1995] C.L.C. 1593; (1996) 93(3) L.S.G. 28; (1995) 139 S.J.L.B. 246, PC
   (HK)...   *Digested,* 96/**1239**:
                                 Applied, 97/3858: *Considered,* 05/1980
Wood v. AFX Engineering see Airfreight Express (UK) Ltd (In Liquidation), Re
Wood v. Chief Constable of the West Midlands [2004] EWCA Civ 1638; [2005]
   E.M.L.R. 20; (2005) 149 S.J.L.B. 25; *Times,* December 13, 2004, CA (Civ Div);
   affirming [2003] EWHC 2971; [2004] E.M.L.R. 17, QBD.................   *Digested,* 05/**975**
Wood v. Holden (Inspector of Taxes); *sub nom* R v. Holden (Inspector of Taxes) 8 I.T.L.
   Rep. 468, CA (Civ Div); affirming [2005] EWHC 547; [2005] S.T.C. 789;
   [2005] B.T.C. 253; 7 I.T.L. Rep. 725; [2005] S.T.I. 801; *Times,* May 10, 2005, Ch
   D; affirming [2004] S.T.C. (S.C.D.) 416; [2004] S.T.I. 1868, Sp Comm........   *Digested,* 05/**4156**
Wood v. Perfection Travel Ltd [1996] L.R.L.R. 233; [1996] C.L.C. 1121; *Lloyd's List,*
   April 23, 1996 (I.D.), CA (Civ Div) ....   *Digested,* 96/**3576**:
                                        Applied, 05/424
Wood Mitchell & Co Ltd v. Stoke on Trent City Council see Stoke on Trent City Council
   v. Wood Mitchell & Co Ltd
Woodhouse v. Consignia Plc; Steliou v. Compton [2002] EWCA Civ 275; [2002] 1
   W.L.R. 2558; [2002] 2 All E.R. 737; [2002] C.P. Rep. 42; (2002) 99(16) L.S.G.
   38; (2002) 152 N.L.J. 517; (2002) 146 S.J.L.B. 76; *Times,* April 5, 2002;
   Independent, March 13, 2002, CA (Civ Div) ....   *Digested,* 02/**307**:
                             Applied, 02/455, 05/413
Woods v. Sevenoaks DC [2004] EWHC 1511; [2005] Env. L.R. 11; [2004] N.P.C. 97,
   QBD (Admin) ....   *Digested,* 05/**333**
Woods (Inspector of Taxes) v. Lightpower Ltd [2005] EWHC 1799; [2005] S.T.I. 1169,
   Ch D
Woodward v. Abbey National Plc (No.1) [2005] I.C.R. 1750, EAT
Woodward v. Abbey National Plc (No.2); JP Garrett Electrical Ltd v. Cotton [2005] 4
   All E.R. 1346; [2005] I.C.R. 1702; [2005] I.R.L.R. 782, EAT ....   *Digested,* 05/**1244**
Woolcock Street Investments Pty Ltd v. CDG Pty Ltd (formerly Cardno & Davies
   Australia Pty Ltd) [2005] B.L.R. 92; 101 Con. L.R. 113; (2005) 21 Const. L.J.
   141, HC (Aus)...   *Digested,* 05/**2847**
Wooldridge v. Canelhas Comercio Importacao e Exportacao Ltda see Canelhas
   Comercio Importacao e Exportacao Ltd v. Wooldridge
Woolhouse v. Barnsley MBC [2005] R.V.R. 178, Lands Tr ....   *Digested,* 05/**3253**
Woollam v. Cleanaway Ltd (Unreported, July 26, 2004), CC (Chester) [*Ex rel.*
   Ricksons Solicitors, The Stock Exchange Building, 4 Norfolk St, Manchester] ...   *Digested,* 05/**377**
Woolwich Building Society (formerly Woolwich Equitable Building Society) v. Inland
   Revenue Commissioners [1993] A.C. 70; [1992] 3 W.L.R. 366; [1992] 3 All E.R.
   737; [1992] S.T.C. 657; (1993) 5 Admin. L.R. 265; 65 T.C. 265; (1992) 142
   N.L.J. 1196; (1992) 136 S.J.L.B. 230; *Times,* July 22, 1992; *Independent,* August
   13, 1992; *Guardian,* August 19, 1992, HL; affirming [1991] 3 W.L.R. 790; [1991]
   4 All E.R. 577; [1991] S.T.C. 364; (1991) 135 S.J.L.B. 46; *Times,* May 27, 1991,
   CA (Civ Div); reversing [1989] 1 W.L.R. 137; [1989] S.T.C. 111; (1989) 133 S.J.
   291, QBD ....   *Digested,* 92/**2508**:
                   Applied, 94/4567: *Considered,* 94/3900, 94/6018, 05/4129:
                   Distinguished, 96/5578, 01/5024: *Followed,* 97/1735
Woolwich Plc v. Jones-Dunross; *sub nom* Ombull v. Sherrards Solicitors [2005]
   EWHC 1488; [2005] N.P.C. 92, Ch D
Worby v. Inland Revenue Commissioners [2005] EWHC 835; [2005] B.P.I.R. 1249,
   Ch D
Worcestershire CC v. Tongue [2004] EWCA Civ 140; [2004] Ch. 236; [2004] 2
   W.L.R. 1193; (2004) 168 J.P. 548; [2004] B.L.G.R. 436; (2004) 168 J.P.N. 797;
   (2004) 101(11) L.S.G. 35; [2004] N.P.C. 23; *Times,* February 26, 2004, CA
   (Civ Div); affirming (2003) 100(39) L.S.G. 39; *Times,* October 1, 2003, Ch D ..   *Digested,* 04/**359**:
                                      Applied, 05/2804
Workington Harbour and Dock Board v. Trade Indemnity Co Ltd see Trade Indemnity Co
   Ltd v. Workington Harbour and Dock Board (No.1)
World Class Homes Ltd, Re [2004] EWHC 2906; [2005] 2 B.C.L.C. 1; (2005) 102(39)
   L.S.G. 30, Ch D ....   *Digested,* 05/**2267**
World Organisation against Torture v. Italy (17/2003) (2005) 41 E.H.R.R. SE7, ECSR

World Trade Corp Ltd *v.* C Czarnikow Sugar Ltd [2004] EWHC 2332; [2004] 2 All E.R.
(Comm) 813; [2005] 1 Lloyd's Rep. 422, QBD (Comm) . . . .   *Digested,* 05/**210**
Worldlingo.Com Pty Ltd's Application [2004] Info. T.L.R. 188, PO . . . .   *Digested,* 05/**2490**
Wormall *v.* Wormall [2004] EWCA Civ 1643; (2005) 102(5) L.S.G. 28; *Times,*
December 1, 2004, CA (Civ Div)
Worrall *v.* Chief Constable of Merseyside see Calveley *v.* Chief Constable of
Merseyside
Worth *v.* McKenna see Hollins *v.* Russell
Wouters *v.* Algemene Raad van de Nederlandse Orde van Advocaten (C309/99)
[2002] All E.R. (EC) 193; [2002] E.C.R. I-1577; [2002] 4 C.M.L.R. 27; [2002]   *Distinguished,*
C.E.C. 250, ECJ 05/**3963**
WP *v.* Poland (Admissibility) (42264/98) (2005) 40 E.H.R.R. SE1, ECHR
WR (A Child) (Representation) (McKenzie Friend), Re see O (Children) (Hearing in Private:
Assistance), Re
Wraith *v.* Sheffield Forgemasters Ltd; Truscott *v.* Truscott [1998] 1 W.L.R. 132; [1998]
1 All E.R. 82; [1997] 2 Costs L.R. 74; [1998] 1 F.L.R. 265; [1998] 1 F.C.R. 270;
[1998] Fam. Law 74; *Times,* October 15, 1997, CA (Civ Div); reversing [1996] 1
W.L.R. 617; [1996] 2 All E.R. 527; [1997] 1 Costs L.R. 23; (1996) 146 N.L.J.
590; (1996) 140 S.J.L.B. 64; *Times,* February 20, 1996, QBD . . . .   *Digested,* 97/**540**:
   Applied, 03/329, 04/301: *Considered,* 05/367, 05/372:
   Distinguished, 01/524: *Followed,* 99/414, 99/415
Wretham *v.* Ross [2005] EWHC 1259; [2005] N.P.C. 87, Ch D
Wrexham CBC *v.* Berry see South Buckinghamshire DC *v.* Porter (No.1)
Wright *v.* Hodgkinson [2004] EWHC 3091; [2005] W.T.L.R. 435, Ch D . . . .   *Digested,* 05/**3400**
Wright *v.* Sullivan [2005] EWCA Civ 656; [2005] C.P. Rep. 37; (2005) 84 B.M.L.R.
196; (2005) 155 N.L.J. 938; *Times,* June 24, 2005; *Independent,* June 8, 2005,
CA (Civ Div) . . . .   *Digested,* 05/**328**
Wrightson *v.* Southern Cross Healthcare Ltd (Unreported, June 17, 2004), CC
(Sheffield) [*Ex rel.* Gordon Stables, Barrister, Paradise Chambers, 26 Paradise
Square, Sheffield] . . . .   *Digested,* 05/**3212**
WT Lamb & Sons *v.* Rider [1948] 2 K.B. 331; [1948] 2 All E.R. 402; 64 T.L.R. 530;
[1949] L.J.R. 258; 92 S.J. 556, CA . . . .   *Digested,* 47-51/**7678**:
   Approved, 98/539: *Considered,* 88/2155, 05/497
WT Ramsay Ltd *v.* Inland Revenue Commissioners; Eilbeck (Inspector of Taxes) *v.*
Rawling [1982] A.C. 300; [1981] 2 W.L.R. 449; [1981] 1 All E.R. 865; [1981]
S.T.C. 174; 54 T.C. 101; [1982] T.R. 123; (1981) 11 A.T.R. 752; 125 S.J. 220, HL;
affirming [1979] 1 W.L.R. 974; [1979] 3 All E.R. 213; [1979] S.T.C. 582; 123 S.J.
456, CA (Civ Div); affirming [1978] 1 W.L.R. 1313; [1978] 2 All E.R. 321; 8
B.L.R. 169; [1978] T.R. 113; 122 S.J. 249, Ch D . . . .   *Digested,* 81/**1385**:
   Applied, 82/1576, 83/1980, 84/270, 85/3364, 85/3407, 86/258, 86/2203,
   86/3204, 88/257, 91/2090, 92/2518, 95/876, 96/1310, 97/2975, 97/2979,
   00/4942, 00/5043, 01/5237, 03/4233, 05/4037, 05/4084, 05/4158:
   Cited, 97/1073: *Considered,* 85/1909, 86/262, 87/274, 87/2036, 90/2685,
   90/3943.a, 91/2115, 92/611, 92/2505, 96/428, 96/3958, 00/4916, 01/5199,
   02/4457: *Distinguished,* 82/1582, 83/1955, 87/270, 87/282, 92/2519,
   95/2750, 98/4631, 99/4709: *Followed,* 03/4145: *Not applied,* 98/4627:
   Referred to, 82/485, 85/456, 95/527
WWF UK (World Wide Fund for Nature) *v.* Commission of the European Communities
(T105/95) [1997] All E.R. (EC) 300; [1997] E.C.R. II-313; [1997] 2 C.M.L.R.
55; [1997] Env. L.R. 242; *Times,* March 26, 1997, CFI (4th Chamber) . . . .   *Digested,* 97/**2386**:
   Applied, 99/2239, 05/1425: *Followed,* 02/1545, 02/1546
Wyatt (A Child) (Medical Treatment: Continuation of Order), Re see Portsmouth NHS Trust
v. Wyatt (No.2)
Wyatt (A Child) (Medical Treatment: Parents Consent), Re see Portsmouth NHS Trust *v.*
Wyatt (No.1)
Wyatt-Jones *v.* Goldsmith see G *v.* G (Financial Provision: Separation Agreement)
Wychavon DC *v.* Doe [2005] P.A.D. 51, Planning Inspector
Wychavon DC *v.* Midland Enterprises (Special Event) Ltd [1988] 1 C.M.L.R. 397; 86
L.G.R. 83; (1987) 151 L.G. Rev. 671; *Times,* February 28, 1987, Ch D . . . .   *Digested,* 88/**3271**:
   Applied, 88/2994, 89/3133, 05/2804
Wycombe DC *v.* National Leisure Ltd [2005] P.A.D. 24, Planning Inspector
Wycombe DC *v.* Wells [2005] EWHC 1012; [2005] J.P.L. 1640; [2005] N.P.C. 75,
QBD (Admin)
Wylie's Application for Judicial Review, Re [2005] N.I. 359, QBD (NI)

X *v.* Caerphilly CBC [2004] EWHC 2140; [2005] E.L.R. 78, QBD (Admin) . . . .   *Digested,* 05/**1043**
X *v.* Chief Constable of the West Midlands see R. (on the application of X) *v.* Chief
Constable of the West Midlands
X *v.* Secretary of State for the Home Department see A *v.* Secretary of State for the
Home Department
X *v.* Wandsworth LBC see A *v.* Hoare
X *v.* X [2005] EWHC 296; [2005] 2 F.L.R. 487; [2005] Fam. Law 543, Fam Div

X NHS Trust *v.* T (Adult Patient: Refusal of Medical Treatment) [2004] EWHC 1279;
  [2005] 1 All E.R. 387; [2004] 3 F.C.R. 297; (2005) 8 C.C.L. Rep. 38; [2004]
  Lloyd's Rep. Med. 433; (2004) 80 B.M.L.R. 184, Fam Div.......................... *Digested*, 04/**1690**
X (Minors) *v.* Bedfordshire CC; M (A Minor) *v.* Newham LBC; E (A Minor) *v.* Dorset
  CC (Appeal); Christmas *v.* Hampshire CC (Duty of Care); Keating *v.* Bromley LBC
  (No.2) [1995] 2 A.C. 633; [1995] 3 W.L.R. 152; [1995] 3 All E.R. 353; [1995]
  2 F.L.R. 276; [1995] 3 F.C.R. 337; 94 L.G.R. 313; (1995) 7 Admin. L.R. 705;
  [1995] Fam. Law 537; (1996) 160 L.G. Rev. 103; (1996) 160 L.G. Rev. 123;
  (1995) 145 N.L.J. 993; *Times*, June 30, 1995; *Independent*, June 30, 1995, HL;
  affirming [1994] 2 W.L.R. 554; [1994] 4 All E.R. 602; [1994] 1 F.L.R. 431; 92
  L.G.R. 427; [1994] Fam. Law 434; (1994) 144 N.L.J. 357; *Times*, March 3, 1994;
  Independent, February 24, 1994; *Guardian*, February 28, 1994, CA (Civ Div);
  affirming [1993] 2 F.L.R. 575; [1994] P.I.Q.R. P515; [1993] Fam. Law 575;
  (1993) 143 N.L.J. 1783; *Times*, November 24, 1993; *Independent*, December 23,
  1993, QBD .... *Digested*, 95/**3452**:
    Applied, 98/2570, 98/3935, 98/3944, 98/3945, 99/1765, 99/1889,
    99/3968, 99/5435, 00/5662, 01/4470, 03/364, 05/976:
    Considered, 96/4140, 96/4441, 97/2692, 97/2879, 97/3775, 98/3931,
    98/3937, 98/3942, 99/5434, 03/1118, 03/3004: *Distinguished*, 99/3966,
    05/2858: *Doubted*, 00/1947: *Followed*, 96/3913, 97/424, 97/2142, 97/4087,
    97/4860, 98/1965, 99/3967: *Previous proceedings*, 94/1878, 95/1927:
    Subsequent proceedings, 98/3943
X (Restraint Order: Payment Out), Re see X (Restraint Order: Variation), Re
X (Restraint Order: Variation), Re; *sub nom* X (Restraint Order: Payment Out), Re
  [2004] EWHC 861; [2005] Q.B. 133; [2004] 3 W.L.R. 906; [2004] 3 All E.R.
  1077; [2004] A.C.D. 51; *Times*, June 3, 2004, QBD (Admin) .... *Digested*, 04/**883**
X and Y (Children), Re see F *v.* Newsquest Ltd
X BV *v.* Head of Y Revenue Service 7 I.T.L. Rep. 689, Hof (Amsterdam)
X CC *v.* DW see A Local Authority *v.* DW
X Council *v.* B (Emergency Protection Orders) see A Local Authority *v.* B (Emergency
  Protection Orders)
X Ltd *v.* Y Ltd [2005] EWHC 769; [2005] B.L.R. 341; [2005] T.C.L.R. 5, QBD (TCC)
Xansa Barclaycard Partnership Ltd *v.* Customs and Excise Commissioners [2005] B.V.C.
  2085; [2004] V. & D.R. 457; [2004] S.T.I. 2574, V&DTr (London)
Xi Software Ltd *v.* Laing (Inspector of Taxes); Collins *v.* Laing (Inspector of Taxes)
  [2005] S.T.C. (S.C.D.) 249; [2005] S.T.I. 141, Sp Comm .... *Digested*, 05/**4063**
Xi Software Ltd *v.* Laing (Inspector of Taxes) (Costs); *sub nom* Collins *v.* Laing
  (Inspector of Taxes) (Costs) [2005] S.T.C. (S.C.D.) 453; [2005] S.T.I. 921, Sp
  Comm .... *Digested*, 05/**4140**
XL Communications Group Plc (In Liquidation), Re; *sub nom* Green *v.* BDO Stoy
  Hayward LLP [2005] EWHC 2413; *Times*, November 8, 2005, Ch D
XY Ex p. Haes, Re [1902] 1 K.B. 98, CA .... *Considered*, 05/**2288**

Y *v.* Norway (56568/00) (2005) 41 E.H.R.R. 7, ECHR .... *Digested*, 05/**2091**
Y (Leave to Remove from Jurisdiction), Re [2004] 2 F.L.R. 330; [2004] Fam. Law 650, Fam
  Div.. *Digested*, 05/**1635**
Y (Minors) (Adoption: Jurisdiction), Re; *sub nom* Adoption Application (AA 125/1983),
  Re [1985] Fam. 136; [1985] 3 W.L.R. 601; [1985] 3 All E.R. 33; [1986] 1
  F.L.R. 152; [1986] Fam. Law 26, Fam Div............................... *Digested*, 85/**2201**:
    Not followed, 05/1670
Yacoubou *v.* Secretary of State for the Home Department; G (Liberia) *v.* Secretary of
  State for the Home Department [2005] EWCA Civ 1051; [2005] Imm. A.R. 691,
  CA (Civ Div)
YAKAZI/Divisional (J40/03) [2005] E.P.O.R. 5, EPO (Legal Bd App) .... *Digested*, 05/**2458**
Yaman *v.* Turkey (32446/96) (2005) 40 E.H.R.R. 49, ECHR .... *Digested*, 05/**2130**
Yamanouchi Europe BV *v.* Almiral Prodesfarma SA; *sub nom* Yamanouchi Europe BV's
  Trade Mark Application [2005] E.T.M.R. 40, PO (Irl)
Yamanouchi Europe BV's Trade Mark Application see Yamanouchi Europe BV *v.* Almiral
  Prodesfarma SA
Yamanouchi Pharma UK Ltd *v.* Stop Huntingdon Animal Cruelty see Daiichi
  Pharmaceuticals UK Ltd *v.* Stop Huntingdon Animal Cruelty
Yankov *v.* Bulgaria (39084/97) (2005) 40 E.H.R.R. 36; 15 B.H.R.C. 592, ECHR ...... *Digested*, 04/**1974**
Yapici *v.* Secretary of State for the Home Department [2005] EWCA Civ 826; *Times*,
  July 28, 2005, CA (Civ Div) .... *Digested*, 05/**2184**
Yarburgh Childrens Trust *v.* Customs and Excise Commissioners; *sub nom* Customs and
  Excise Commissioners *v.* Yarburgh Children's Trust [2002] S.T.C. 207; [2001]
  B.T.C. 5651; [2002] B.V.C. 141; [2001] S.T.I. 1661; [2001] N.P.C. 173, Ch D;
  affirming [2001] B.V.C. 2307; [2001] V. & D.R. 342; [2001] S.T.I. 1170, V&DTr .. *Digested*, 02/**4811**:
    Followed, 05/4383
Yates *v.* Hawthorne (Unreported, November 16, 2004), CC (Birkenhead) [*Ex rel.*
  Michael J Pickavance, Barrister, 7 Harrington St, Liverpool] .... *Digested*, 05/**3095**
Yates *v.* Yates (1913) 33 N.Z.L.R. 281 .... *Distinguished*, 05/2692
Yates (A Bankrupt), Re; *sub nom* Carman *v.* Yates [2005] B.P.I.R. 476, Ch D .... *Digested*, 05/**2341**

Yaxley v. Gotts; *sub nom* Yaxley v. Gott [2000] Ch. 162; [1999] 3 W.L.R. 1217; [2000] 1 All E.R. 711; [1999] 2 F.L.R. 941; (2000) 32 H.L.R. 547; (2000) 79 P. & C.R. 91; [1999] 2 E.G.L.R. 181; [1999] Fam. Law 700; [1999] E.G.C.S. 92; (1999) 96(28) L.S.G. 25; (1999) 143 S.J.L.B. 198; [1999] N.P.C. 76; (1999) 78 P. & C.R. D33; *Times*, July 8, 1999 ; *Independent*, July 6, 1999, CA (Civ Div) . . . .   *Digested*, 99/**848**:
           Applied, 05/987: *Considered*, 02/2655: *Distinguished*, 00/4670:
                        Referred to, 02/4342

Yazhou Travel Investment Co Ltd v. Bateson Starr (A Firm) [2005] P.N.L.R. 31, CFI (HK)

Yearwood v. Commissioner of Police of the Metropolis; Commissioner of Police of the Metropolis v. Miller; Chief Constable of Merseyside v. Husain; Kochar v. Commissioner of Police of the Metropolis; Jeffrey v. Commissioner of Police of the Metropolis [2004] I.C.R. 1660, EAT . . . .   *Digested*, 05/**3333**

Yemen v. Aziz see Aziz v. Yemen

Yeshiva Properties No 1 Pty Ltd v. Marshall (2004-05) 7 I.T.E.L.R. 577, CA (NSW) . . . .   *Digested*, 05/**4294**

Yetkinsekerci v. United Kingdom (71841/01), *Times*, November 14, 2005, ECHR

YF v. Turkey (24209/94) (2004) 39 E.H.R.R. 34, ECHR . . . .   *Digested*, 05/**2119**

Yilmaz v. Secretary of State for the Home Department see R. (on the application of Yilmaz) v. Secretary of State for the Home Department

Yissum Research & Development Co of the Hebrew University of Jerusalem v. Comptroller-General of Patents [2004] EWHC 2880; (2005) 28(2) I.P.D. 28010, Ch D (Patents Ct)

Yonge v. Toynbee [1910] 1 K.B. 215, CA. . . . .   *Considered*, 05/489

Yoon v. R. 8 I.T.L. Rep. 129, Tax Ct (Can)

Yorkshire Building Society v. United Kingdom (21675/93) see National & Provincial Building Society v. United Kingdom (21319/93)

Yorkshire Water Services Ltd v. Coal Authority [2005] R.V.R. 99, Lands Tr

Yorkshire Water Services Ltd v. Taylor Woodrow Construction Northern Ltd (Application for Extension of Time) [2004] B.L.R. 409, QBD (TCC) . . . .   *Digested*, 05/**320**

Yorkshire Water Services Ltd v. Taylor Woodrow Construction Northern Ltd (No.3) [2005] EWCA Civ 894; [2005] B.L.R. 395; [2005] N.P.C. 96, CA (Civ Div); affirming [2004] EWHC 1660, QBD (TCC) . . . .   *Digested*, 05/**651**

Young v. Bemstone Ltd (t/a Bemstone Homes) [2004] EWHC 2651; 99 Con. L.R. 222, QBD (TCC) . . . .   *Digested*, 05/**967**

Young v. United Kingdom (A/44); James v. United Kingdom (A/44); Webster v. United Kingdom (A/44) [1982] E.C.C. 264; [1981] I.R.L.R. 408; (1982) 4 E.H.R.R. 38, ECHR; affirming [1980] E.C.C. 332; (1981) 3 E.H.R.R. 20, Eur Comm HR . . . . .   *Considered*, 05/2040:
                        Referred to, 01/3466

Young (Inspector of Taxes) v. Pearce; Young (Inspector of Taxes) v. Scrutton [1996] S.T.C. 743; 70 T.C. 331, Ch D; reversing (Unreported, May 25, 1995), Sp Comm .   *Digested*, 98/**4683**

Young (Inspector of Taxes) v. Scrutton see Young (Inspector of Taxes) v. Pearce

Younger Homes (Northern) Ltd v. First Secretary of State [2004] EWCA Civ 1060; [2005] Env. L.R. 12; [2005] 1 P. & C.R. 14; [2005] 3 P.L.R. 21; [2005] J.P.L. 354, CA (Civ Div); affirming [2003] EWHC 3058; [2004] J.P.L. 950, QBD (Admin) . . . .   *Digested*, 05/**3308**:
                        Distinguished, 05/3300

Younghusband v. Coutts & Co (No.1) see Pauling's Settlement Trusts (No.1), Re

Yukos Oil Co v. Dardana Ltd see Dardana Ltd v. Yukos Oil Co (No.1)

Yuksel v. Turkey (40154/98) (2005) 41 E.H.R.R. 19, ECHR

Yumsak v. Enfield LBC [2002] EWHC 280; [2003] H.L.R. 1, QBD (Admin). . . . .   *Digested*, 03/**2062**:
                        Considered, 05/1987

Yusuf v. Council of the European Union (T306/01) [2005] 3 C.M.L.R. 49, CFI (2nd Chamber)

Yusupova v. Russia (57948/00) see Isayeva v. Russia (57947/00)

Yvon v. France (44962/98) (2005) 40 E.H.R.R. 41, ECHR

Z v. Finland (1998) 25 E.H.R.R. 371; (1999) 45 B.M.L.R. 107, ECHR . . . .   *Digested*, 98/**3104**:
              Considered, 98/3105: *Referred to*, 05/1785

Z v. Secretary of State for the Home Department (No.2) [2004] EWCA Civ 1578; [2005] Imm. A.R. 75, CA (Civ Div) . . . .   *Digested*, 05/**2140**:
                        Considered, 05/2176

Z v. United Kingdom (29392/95) [2001] 2 F.L.R. 612; [2001] 2 F.C.R. 246; (2002) 34 E.H.R.R. 3; 10 B.H.R.C. 384; (2001) 3 L.G.L.R. 51; (2001) 4 C.C.L. Rep. 310; [2001] Fam. Law 583; *Times*, May 31, 2001, ECHR [2000] 2 F.C.R. 245; (2000) 2 L.G.L.R. 212, Eur Comm HR . . . .   *Digested*, 01/**3459**:
        Applied, 03/3004, 04/665, 05/1553: *Considered*, 02/763

Z v. Z (Abduction: Children's Views) [2005] EWCA Civ 1012; [2005] Fam. Law 763, CA (Civ Div) [2005] EWHC 1234; [2005] Fam. Law 691, Fam Div

Z (A Child) (Shared Parenting Plan: Publicity), Re [2005] Fam. Law 942, Fam Div

Z (An Adult: Capacity), Re see Z (Local Authority: Duty), Re

Z (Attorney General for Northern Ireland's Reference), Re see R. v. Z

Z (Local Authority: Duty), Re; *sub nom* A Local Authority *v.* Z; Z (An Adult: Capacity), Re [2004] EWHC 2817; [2005] 1 W.L.R. 959; [2005] 3 All E.R. 280; [2005] 1 F.L.R. 740; [2005] 2 F.C.R. 256; [2005] H.R.L.R. 2; [2005] U.K.H.R.R. 611; [2005] B.L.G.R. 709; (2005) 8 C.C.L. Rep. 146; (2005) 84 B.M.L.R. 160; [2005] Fam. Law 212; (2005) 102(2) L.S.G. 29; (2004) 154 N.L.J. 1894; *Times*, December 9, 2004; *Independent*, December 8, 2004, Fam Div . . . .   *Digested*, 05/**3946**

ZA *v.* Secretary of State for the Home Department; *sub nom* ZA (S58(9): Abandonment: Date of Grant: Ethiopia), Re [2004] UKIAT 241; [2004] Imm. A.R. 538, IAT . . . .   *Digested*, 05/**2189**

ZA (S58(9): Abandonment: Date of Grant: Ethiopia), Re see ZA *v.* Secretary of State for the Home Department

Zafar *v.* DPP [2004] EWHC 2468; (2005) 169 J.P. 208; [2005] R.T.R. 18; (2005) 169 J.P.N. 360; (2004) 148 S.J.L.B. 1315; *Times*, January 7, 2005, QBD (Admin) . . . .   *Digested*, 05/**779**

Zafaris *v.* Liu see Zafiris *v.* Liu

Zafiris *v.* Liu; *sub nom* Zafaris *v.* Liu [2005] EWCA Civ 1698; (2005) 149 S.J.L.B. 149; *Times*, March 3, 2005, CA (Civ Div)

Zawadka *v.* Poland (48542/99); *sub nom* Zawadkaw *v.* Poland (48542/99) [2005] 2 F.L.R. 897; [2005] Fam. Law 774, ECHR

Zdanoka *v.* Latvia (58278/00) (2005) 41 E.H.R.R. 31, ECHR

Zebra Industrial Projects Ltd (In Liquidation), Re; *sub nom* Zebra Products Ltd, Re [2004] EWHC 549; [2005] B.C.C.104; [2005] B.P.I.R.1022, Ch D

Zebra Products Ltd, Re see Zebra Industrial Projects Ltd (In Liquidation), Re

Zebrarise Ltd *v.* De Nieffe [2004] EWHC 1842; [2005] 2 All E.R. (Comm) 816; [2005] 1 Lloyd's Rep.154, QBD (Comm) . . . .   *Digested*, 05/**616**

Zelger *v.* Salinitri (129/83) [1984] E.C.R. 2397; [1985] 3 C.M.L.R. 366, ECJ (4th Chamber) . . . .   *Digested*, 85/**1380**: *Applied*, 92/3534, 93/3569, 01/5419, 04/579: *Considered*, 05/468

Zeqaj *v.* Secretary of State for the Home Department; *sub nom* Secretary of State for the Home Department *v.* Zeqaj [2002] EWCA Civ 1919; [2003] Imm. A.R. 298; [2003] I.N.L.R.109, CA (Civ Div) . . . .   *Digested*, 03/**2233**: *Followed*, 05/2148

Zermalt Holdings SA *v.* Nu-Life Upholstery Repairs Ltd [1985] 2 E.G.L.R. 14; (1985) 275 E.G.1134, QBD (Comm) . . . .   *Digested*, 85/**95**: *Applied*, 05/202: *Approved*, 89/3857: *Considered*, 93/169, 93/182, 94/208, 94/227, 96/3796, 97/3326, 05/2678: *Followed*, 04/2522

Zhu *v.* Secretary of State for the Home Department (C200/02) see Chen *v.* Secretary of State for the Home Department (C200/02)

Zino Davidoff SA *v.* A&G Imports Ltd; Levi Strauss & Co *v.* Costco Wholesale UK Ltd (C416/99); Levi Strauss & Co *v.* Tesco Stores Ltd (C415/99) [2002] Ch. 109; [2002] 2 W.L.R. 321; [2002] All E.R. (EC) 55; [2001] E.C.R. I-8691; [2002] 1 C.M.L.R. 1; [2002] C.E.C. 154; [2002] E.T.M.R. 9; [2002] R.P.C. 20; *Times*, November 23, 2001; *Daily Telegraph*, November 27, 2001, ECJ [2001] E.C.R. I-8691; [2001] E.T.M.R. 67; [2001] R.P.C. 44, AGO . . . .   *Digested*, 01/**4032**: *Applied*, 05/2572, 05/2573: *Considered*, 03/2621: *Subsequent proceedings*, 02/2905

Zita Modes Sarl *v.* Administration de l'Enregistrement et des Domaines (C497/01) [2005] S.T.C. 1059; [2003] E.C.R. I-14393; [2004] 2 C.M.L.R. 24; [2004] C.E.C.183; [2005] B.T.C. 5741; [2005] B.V.C. 772; [2003] S.T.I. 2225, ECJ (5th Chamber) (Unreported, September 26, 2002), AGO . . . .   *Digested*, 04/**1427**

ZM *v.* Slovakia (50232/99) [2005] 2 F.C.R. 415, ECHR

Znamenskaya *v.* Russia (77785/01) [2005] 2 F.C.R. 406, ECHR

Zockoll Group Ltd *v.* Mercury Communications Ltd (No.1) [1998] F.S.R. 354, CA (Civ Div); affirming 97 Z 1815, Ch D . . . .   *Digested*, 98/**525**

Zondi *v.* Member of the Executive Council for Traditional and Local Government Affairs 18 B.H.R.C. 436, Const Ct (SA)

Zoological Society of London *v.* Customs and Excise Commissioners (C267/00); *sub nom* Customs and Excise Commissioners *v.* Zoological Society of London (C267/00) [2002] Q.B. 1252; [2002] 3 W.L.R. 829; [2002] All E.R. (EC) 465; [2002] S.T.C. 521; [2002] E.C.R. I-3353; [2002] 2 C.M.L.R. 13; [2002] C.E.C. 316; [2002] B.T.C. 5224; [2002] B.V.C. 414; [2002] S.T.I. 356; *Times*, April 11, 2002, ECJ (5th Chamber) . . . .   *Digested*, 02/**4758**: *Applied*, 05/4356

Zoological Society of Wales *v.* Customs and Excise Commissioners [2005] B.V.C. 2157; [2004] S.T.I. 2578; (2004) 148 S.J.L.B.1313, V&DTr (London)

ZT *v.* Secretary of State for the Home Department [2005] EWCA Civ 1421; *Times*, December 23, 2005, CA (Civ Div)

Zurich Insurance Co *v.* Revenue and Customs Commissioners; *sub nom* Revenue and Customs Commissioners *v.* Zurich Insurance Co; CH/2005/APP/0592, Ch D; reversing [2005] S.T.I.1733, V&DTr (London)

PART II

SCOTTISH CASE CITATOR

This section contains:

(a) Details of cases decided or judicially considered in the Scottish courts during 2005.

(b) References to English Cases judicially considered in Scotland during 2005.

Scottish cases published in English Law Reports are included in both the English and Scottish sections.

Figures appearing in bold type indicate the main substantive paragraph.

A v. HM Advocate (No.1) 2005 S.C.C.R. 707; 2005 G.W.D. 30-566, HCJ
A v. HM Advocate (No.2) 2005 G.W.D. 30-569, HCJ
A v. Murray 2004 S.L.T.1273; 2004 Rep. L.R. 110; 2004 G.W.D. 29-610, OH . . . .   *Digested*, 05/**5610**
Abdulaziz v. Secretary of State for the Home Department 2005 G.W.D. 24-449, OH
Aberdeen City Council v. McCarthy 2004 Hous. L.R. 53; 2004 G.W.D. 14-309, Sh Ct
    (Grampian) . . . .   *Digested*, 05/**5474**
Aberdeen College Board of Management v. Youngson 2005 S.C. 335; 2005 S.L.T. 371;
    2005 G.W.D. 8-122, OH. . . . .   *Digested*, 05/**5612**
Aberdeenshire Council v. R; *sub nom* Aberdeenshire Council, Petitioners 2004 Fam.
    L.R. 93; 2004 G.W.D. 23-494, OH . . . .   *Digested*, 05/**5244**
Aberdeenshire Council, Petitioners see Aberdeenshire Council v. R
Accountant in Bankruptcy v. Butler 2005 G.W.D. 36-674, Sh Ct (North Strathclyde)
Accountant in Bankruptcy v. Orr 2005 S.L.T.1019; 2005 G.W.D. 28-528, OH . . . .   *Digested*, 05/**5445**
Adam (Daniel McNeil) v. HM Advocate 2005 S.C.C.R. 479, HCJ
Adams v. Thorntons WS (No.3) 2005 S.C. 30; 2005 S.L.T. 594; 2004 S.C.L.R. 1016;
    2005 G.W.D.13-234, IH (Ex Div) . . . .   *Digested*, 05/**5611**
Adamson v. HM Advocate (Sentencing) 2005 G.W.D.12-204, HCJ
Advocate General for Scotland v. Taylor 2004 S.C. 339; 2003 S.L.T. 1340; 2003 G.W.D.
    36-998, IH (Ex Div) . . . .   *Digested*, 04/**4956**:
        Followed, 05/4967
Affleck v. HM Advocate 2005 S.C.C.R. 503; 2005 G.W.D. 21-375, HCJ
Ahmed v. Ahmed; *sub nom* Syed v. Ahmed 2005 Fam. L.R. 71; 2005 G.W.D. 34-644,
    IH (Ex Div)
Aitken v. Aitken 2005 Fam. L.R. 59, OH
Aitken v. McMaster 2005 G.W.D. 20-369, Sh Ct (Grampian)
Aitken v. Poole 2005 G.W.D. 20-367, Sh Ct (Grampian)
Aitken v. Spencer 2005 S.C.C.R. 721, HCJ
Aitken v. Weatherford UK Ltd; *sub nom* Weatherford UK Ltd v. Aitken 2005 S.C. 360,
    IH (1 Div); affirming EATS/0049/03, EAT (SC)
Aitken (William) v. Wood 1921 J.C. 84; (1921) 2 S.L.T.124, HCJ. . . . .   *Applied*, 94/5621:
    Considered, 05/5153: *Referred to*, 94/5639
AJ v. FJ; *sub nom* J, Petitioner 2005 S.C. 428; 2005 Fam. L.R. 31; 2005 G.W.D. 15-
    251, IH (2 Div); reversing 2004 G.W.D. 27-568, OH
Alcan Aluminium UK Ltd v. Highland and Western Isles Valuation Joint Board Assessor
    [2005] R.A. 161, Lands Tr (Scot) . . . .   *Digested*, 05/**5621**
Alderdice (Francis Robert) v. HM Advocate (No.1) see Du Plooy (Devonne) v. HM
    Advocate (No.1)
Ali v. Secretary of State for the Home Department 2003 S.L.T. 674; 2003 G.W.D. 6-
    149, OH . . . .   *Digested*, 03/**5734**:
    Applied, 05/5443
Allan v. HM Advocate 2005 G.W.D. 23-427, HCJ
Allan Water Developments Ltd v. Revenue and Customs Commissioners [2005] S.T.I.
    661, V&DTr (Edinburgh)
Allan (Alexander Leonard) v. HM Advocate 2005 S.C.C.R. 613, HCJ
Allison v. Higson 2004 S.C.C.R. 720, HCJ. . . . .   *Digested*, 05/**5100**
AMT, Petitioners see T, Petitioner

Anchor International Ltd *v.* Inland Revenue Commissioners; *sub nom* Inland Revenue
Commissioners *v.* Anchor International Ltd [2005] S.T.C. 411; 2005 S.C. 76;
2005 S.L.T. 710; 2004 S.C.L.R. 1045; 77 T.C. 38; [2005] B.T.C. 97; [2004] S.T.I.
2298; 2004 G.W.D. 35-712, IH (Ex Div); affirming [2003] S.T.C. (S.C.D.) 115;
[2003] S.T.I. 246, Sp Comm . . . .   *Digested*, 05/**5691**
Anderson *v.* Griffiths 2005 G.W.D. 24-443, HCJ
Anderson *v.* HM Advocate 2005 G.W.D. 16-283, HCJ
Anderson (Keith Penfold) *v.* Griffiths 2005 J.C. 169; 2005 S.L.T. 86; 2005 S.C.C.R. 41;
2004 G.W.D. 38-778, HCJ. . . . .   *Digested*, 05/**5107**
Angus *v.* HM Advocate 2005 G.W.D. 40-749, HCJ
Angus Housing Association *v.* Fraser 2004 Hous. L.R. 83; 2004 G.W.D. 11-249, Sh Ct
(Tayside). . . . .   *Digested*, 05/**5477**
Anstruther Gough Calthorpe *v.* McOscar; *sub nom* Calthorpe *v.* Mcoscar [1924] 1 K.B.
716, CA; reversing [1923] 2 K.B. 573, KBD. . . . .   *Applied*, 47-51/**5413**,
57/1929, 64/2094, 05/5467: *Considered*, 63/1958
AR *v.* HM Advocate 2005 S.C.C.R. 677, HCJ
Archibald *v.* Fife Council [2004] UKHL 32; [2004] 4 All E.R. 303; 2004 S.C. (H.L.)
117; 2004 S.L.T. 942; 2004 S.C.L.R. 971; [2004] I.C.R. 954; [2004] I.R.L.R.
651; (2005) 82 B.M.L.R. 185; (2004) 101(31) L.S.G. 25; (2004) 148 S.J.L.B.
826; 2004 G.W.D. 23-505; *Times*, July 5, 2004, HL; reversing 2004 S.C. 495;
2004 S.L.T. 931; [2004] I.R.L.R. 197; 2004 G.W.D. 11-247; *Times*, January 23,
2004, IH (Ex Div); affirming EATS/0025/02, EAT . . . .   *Digested*, 04/**4707**:
Applied, 05/1229
Armia Ltd *v.* Daejan Developments Ltd 1979 S.C. (H.L.) 56; 1979 S.L.T. 147, HL;
reversing 1978 S.C. 152, IH (1 Div); affirming 1977 S.L.T. (Notes) 49, OH . . . . . .   *Digested*, 79/**3117**:
Applied, 89/3854, 96/6570, 00/6467, 05/5470: *Followed*, 91/5346,
93/5383
Armstrong *v.* HM Advocate 2005 G.W.D. 21-386, HCJ
Arthur *v.* Arthur 2005 S.C.L.R. 350, Sh Ct (Glasgow)
Aslam *v.* Secretary of State for the Home Department 2005 S.C. 10; 2004 G.W.D. 9-
210, OH
Attorney General's Reference (No.152 of 2002), Re; *sub nom* R. *v.* Crump (Richard
James); R. *v.* Cooksley (Robert Charles); R. *v.* Stride (Ian Paul); R. *v.* Cook (Neil
Terence) [2003] EWCA Crim 996; [2003] 3 All E.R. 40; [2003] 2 Cr. App. R.
18; [2004] 1 Cr. App. R. (S.) 1; [2003] R.T.R. 32; (2003) 100(23) L.S.G. 36;
Times, April 8, 2003; *Independent*, June 30, 2003 (C.S), CA (Crim Div) . . . . . .   *Digested*, 04/**3333**:
Applied, 04/3294, 04/3295, 04/3296, 04/3298, 05/3547, 05/3550,
05/3554: *Considered*, 04/3297, 05/3546, 05/3549, 05/3551, 05/3552,
05/3553, 05/3581, 05/3766, 05/5657: *Followed*, 04/3467, 04/4371,
05/3548
Aykol *v.* Secretary of State for the Home Department 2005 G.W.D. 7-101, OH

B, Applicant 2005 S.L.T. (Sh Ct) 95; 2005 G.W.D. 19-334, Sh Ct (Glasgow) . . . .   *Digested*, 05/**5028**
B, Petitioner see M *v.* Secretary of State for the Home Department
B *v.* B (Residence Order: Jurisdiction) see B (A Child) (Court's Jurisdiction), Re
B *v.* HM Advocate see RB *v.* HM Advocate
B *v.* Murray (No.2) 2005 S.L.T. 982, OH . . . .   *Digested*, 05/**5048**
B (A Child) (Court's Jurisdiction), Re; *sub nom* B *v.* B (Residence Order: Jurisdiction)
[2004] EWCA Civ 681; [2004] 2 F.L.R. 741; [2004] 2 F.C.R. 391; [2004] Fam.
Law 788, CA (Civ Div) . . . .   *Digested*, 05/**1645**
B&Q Plc *v.* Renfrewshire Valuation Joint Board Assessor [2004] R.A. 220, Lands Tr
(Scot). . . . .   *Digested*, 05/**5619**
Baird *v.* HM Advocate (Sentencing) 2005 G.W.D. 11-177, HCJ
Baitrum *v.* Dyer 2005 G.W.D. 24-438, HCJ
Baker Hughes Ltd *v.* CCG Contracting International Ltd 2005 S.C. 65; 2005 S.C.L.R.
1084, OH
Ballast Plc *v.* Laurieston Properties Ltd (In Liquidation) 2005 G.W.D. 9-133, OH
Bank of Credit and Commerce International (Overseas) Ltd (In Liquidation) *v.* Price
Waterhouse (No.2) [1998] Lloyd's Rep. Bank. 85; [1998] B.C.C. 617; [1998]
E.C.C. 410; [1998] P.N.L.R. 564; (1998) 95(15) L.S.G. 32; (1998) 142 S.J.L.B.
86; *Times*, March 4, 1998, CA (Civ Div); reversing [1997] B.C.C. 585; *Times*,
February 10, 1997, Ch D . . . .   *Digested*, 98/**3921**:
Applied, 01/4538, 05/5577: *Considered*, 00/4216
Bank of Scotland *v.* Kunkel-Griffin 2005 S.C.L.R. 538, OH
Bank of Scotland *v.* Kunkel-Griffin (Leave to Reclaim) 2005 G.W.D. 7-90, IH (1 Div)
Banks *v.* Banks 2005 Fam. L.R. 116, OH
Banks *v.* CGU Insurance Plc 2005 S.C.L.R. 556, OH
Barclay *v.* Dyer 2005 G.W.D. 23-425, HCJ
Barclay *v.* HM Advocate 2005 G.W.D. 30-586, HCJ
Barnfather *v.* Bell 2005 G.W.D. 16-292, HCJ
Baroness Goudie *v.* Oceanic Development Ltd 2005 S.C.L.R. 10, Sh Ct (Glasgow)
Barr (Anthony James) *v.* HM Advocate 2005 S.C.C.R. 680, HCJ
Barrett *v.* Thompsons 2005 G.W.D. 37-691, OH

Barrie v. Williams 2005 G.W.D. 11-191, HCJ
Beaton v. HM Advocate 2005 G.W.D. 35-658, HCJ
Beaton (Michael Anthony) v. HM Advocate 2004 S.C.C.R. 467; 2004 G.W.D. 24-517,
 HCJ . . . . *Digested,* 05/**5151**
Beattie v. HM Advocate 2005 G.W.D. 29-539, HCJ
Beattie (Jeffrey) v. Scott 1990 J.C. 320; 1991 S.L.T. 110; 1990 S.C.C.R. 296, HCJ . . . . . *Digested,* 91/**4568**:
 Considered, 05/5134
Beavon v. Fraser 2005 G.W.D. 16-275, HCJ
Beck v. Chief Constable of Strathclyde 2005 S.C. 149; 2005 S.L.T. 367; 2005 Rep.
 L.R. 6; 2005 G.W.D. 7-103, IH (2 Div) . . . . *Digested,* 05/**5607**
Beggs, Petitioner 2005 J.C. 174; 2005 S.L.T. 165; 2005 S.C.C.R. 47; 2005 G.W.D. 3-24,
 HCJ . . . . *Digested,* 05/**5124**
Beggs v. Scottish Ministers (Contempt of Court) 2005 S.C. 342; 2005 S.L.T. 305;
 2005 S.C.L.R. 640; 2005 G.W.D. 10-145, IH (1 Div) . . . . *Digested,* 05/**5026**
Beggs v. Scottish Ministers (Transfer of Prisoners) 2004 S.L.T. 755; 2004 G.W.D. 22-
 490, OH . . . . *Digested,* 04/**4958**:
 Considered, 05/4964
Beglan, Petitioner 2002 S.L.T. 1175; 2002 S.C.C.R. 923; 2002 G.W.D. 27-936, HCJ . . . *Digested,* 02/**5487**:
 Followed, 05/5160
Belhaven Brewery Co Ltd v. Bradbury 2005 G.W.D. 2-22, OH
Bell v. Inkersall Investments Ltd 2005 G.W.D. 18-314, OH
Bennett v. Criminal Injuries Compensation Appeal Panel 2005 G.W.D. 2-20, IH (Ex
 Div); affirming 2003 G.W.D. 40-1066, OH
Bennett v. HM Advocate 2005 G.W.D. 18-316, HCJ
Bennett v. Scottish Downs Syndrome Assocation 2005 G.W.D. 25-464, IH (Ex Div)
Benson v. Edinburgh City Council 2005 S.C. 24; 2004 S.L.T. 1227; 2004 G.W.D. 31-
 647, OH . . . . *Digested,* 05/**5040**
Berk v. Secretary of State for the Home Department 2005 G.W.D. 18-327, OH
Berktas v. Secretary of State for the Home Department 2005 G.W.D. 5-67, OH
Bermingham (John William) v. HM Advocate 2005 J.C. 17; 2004 S.L.T. 692; 2004
 S.C.C.R. 354; 2004 G.W.D. 18-359, HCJ . . . . *Digested,* 04/**4626**
Birt v. McQuaid 2005 G.W.D. 15-262, HCJ
Bishopsgate Investment Management Ltd (In Provisional Liquidation) v. Maxwell;
 Cooper (Provisional Liquidator of Bishopsgate Investment Management Ltd) v.
 Maxwell; Mirror Group Newspapers Plc v. Maxwell [1993] Ch. 1; [1992] 2
 W.L.R. 991; [1992] 2 All E.R. 856; [1992] B.C.C. 222; (1992) 136 S.J.L.B. 69;
 Times, January 30, 1992; *Independent,* January 30, 1992; *Financial Times,*
 February 4, 1992; *Guardian,* February 5, 1992, CA (Civ Div); affirming [1992]
 B.C.C. 214; [1992] B.C.L.C. 470; *Guardian,* January 22, 1992, Ch D . . . . *Digested,* 92/**2557**:
 Applied, 05/5449: *Approved,* 03/2400: *Considered,* 92/2559, 02/2687
Black v. Black 1995 G.W.D. 33-1713, Sh Pr . . . . *Considered,* 05/5251
Blackburn v. Cowie 2004 Hous. L.R. 135, Sh Ct (Glasgow) . . . . *Digested,* 05/**5447**
Blessing v. Watt 2005 G.W.D. 16-298, HCJ
Bluestone Estates Ltd v. Fitness First Clubs Ltd 2004 S.L.T. (Sh Ct) 140; 2003 G.W.D.
 27-768, Sh Ct (Tayside) . . . . *Digested,* 05/**5407**
Blyth (Kenneth John) v. HM Advocate 2005 S.C.C.R. 710, HCJ
Board v. HM Advocate 2005 G.W.D. 29-549, HCJ
Boath v. HM Advocate 2005 G.W.D. 35-659, HCJ
Bochell v. Urquhart see McAdam v. Urquhart
Bon Accord Granite Ltd v. Buchan 2005 G.W.D. 28-531, Sh Ct (Grampian)
Bone (Andrea Lorraine) v. HM Advocate 2005 S.C.C.R. 829; 2005 G.W.D. 37-687,
 HCJ
Booth v. West Highland Housing Association 2005 Hous. L.R. 32, Sh Ct (North
 Strathclyde)
Bott v. MacLean; *sub nom* MacLean v. Bott 2005 J.C. 83; 2003 S.C.C.R. 547, HCJ
Bott v. Morton 2005 S.C.C.R. 311, HCJ
Bovey v. Auditor of the Court of Session 2005 G.W.D. 38-715, OH
Bowie v. Falkirk Football & Athletic Club Ltd 2005 G.W.D. 40-756, Sh Ct (Tayside)
BP v. Williams see P v. Williams
BP Express Shopping Ltd v. Perth and Kinross Licensing Board 2005 S.L.T. 862; 2005
 G.W.D. 25-491, IH (1 Div) . . . . *Digested,* 05/**5507**
BP Oil Grangemouth Refinery Ltd v. Central Scotland Assessor [2005] R.A. 277, Lands
 Tr (Scot)
Bradford & Bingley Plc v. Semple 2005 Hous. L.R. 6, Sh Pr; reversing 2004 Hous. L.R.
 133, Sh Ct (Tayside) . . . . *Digested,* 05/**5052**
Brady v. Hutton & Philp 2005 G.W.D. 13-232, OH
Brand v. Aitken 2005 G.W.D. 19-340, HCJ
British Home Stores Ltd v. Burchell [1980] I.C.R. 303; [1978] I.R.L.R. 379; (1978) 13
 I.T.R. 560, EAT (SC) . . . . *Digested,* 80/**1004**:
 Applied, 80/1005, 80/1006, 82/113, 82/2856, 83/1348, 90/1929, 90/1975,
 97/2286, 97/6017, 99/2139, 03/1312, 03/1340: *Approved,* 00/2237:
 Considered, 84/1304, 84/1312, 86/1266, 87/1395, 91/1696, 97/2289,
 02/1387, 05/5218: *Referred to,* 89/1504, 96/2656
Broadley (Rose) v. HM Advocate 2005 S.C.C.R. 620; 2005 G.W.D. 28-520, HCJ

Brogan v. O'Rourke Ltd 2005 S.L.T. 29; 2005 S.C.L.R. 337; 2004 G.W.D. 39-788, IH
(Ex Div); affirming 2004 S.L.T. 774; 2004 G.W.D. 23-497, OH . . . .   *Digested,* 05/**5055**
Brown, Petitioner see Wright, Petitioner
Brown v. Frame 2005 J.C. 320; 2005 S.L.T. 744; 2005 S.C.C.R. 400; 2005 G.W.D.
25-499, HCJ . . . .   *Digested,* 05/**5109**
Brown v. Yorkhill NHS Trust 2004 S.C.L.R. 660; 2003 G.W.D. 29-815, OH . . . .   *Digested,* 05/**5588**
Bruce v. Dignity Funerals Ltd; *sub nom* Dignity Funerals Ltd v. Bruce 2005 S.C. 59;
2004 S.L.T. 1223; 2005 S.C.L.R. 951; [2005] I.R.L.R. 189; (2004) 148 S.J.L.B.
1313; 2004 G.W.D. 32-662, IH (2 Div); reversing EATS/0015/02, EAT (SC). . . .   *Digested,* 05/**5217**
Bruce v. Shetland Islands Council 2005 G.W.D. 1-18, OH
Bryden v. Miller 2005 G.W.D. 16-286, HCJ
Bryson v. Cameron see Bryson v. Currie
Bryson v. Currie; *sub nom* Bryson v. Cameron 2005 J.C. 119; 2005 S.L.T. 253; 2005
S.C.C.R. 4; 2004 G.W.D. 39-807, HCJ . . . .   *Digested,* 05/**5659**
Bulbul v. Secretary of State for the Home Department see Sepet v. Secretary of State
for the Home Department
Bunton v. HM Advocate 2005 G.W.D. 40-746, HCJ
Burgun v. HM Advocate 2005 G.W.D. 40-742, HCJ
Burke v. Glasgow City Council 2005 G.W.D. 37-689, OH
Burnett v. Menzies Dougal WS 2005 S.L.T. 929; 2005 S.C.L.R. 1061; 2005 G.W.D. 27-
534, IH (Ex Div); reversing 2005 S.C.L.R. 133; 2004 G.W.D. 15-344, OH . . . . . .   *Digested,* 05/**5051**
Butt v. Secretary of State for the Home Department 2005 S.L.T. 865; 2005 G.W.D.
26-512, OH . . . .   *Digested,* 05/**5434**
Bvunzai v. Glasgow City Council; Glasgow City Council v. Bvunzai 2005 G.W.D. 39-
725, IH (Ex Div); reversing EATS/0004/04, EATS/0015/04, EAT (SC)

C v. G 2005 G.W.D. 1-3, Sh Pr
Cadder Housing Association Ltd v. McVeigh 2005 Hous. L.R. 85, Sh Ct (Glasgow)
Cain v. HM Advocate 2005 G.W.D. 27-524, HCJ
Cairns v. Downie 2005 S.L.T. (Sh Ct) 14; 2005 S.C.L.R. 766; 2005 Rep. L.R. 30;
2005 G.W.D. 1-16, Sh Pr. . . . .   *Digested,* 05/**5046**
Cairns (William James) v. HM Advocate 2005 S.L.T. 541; 2005 S.C.C.R. 239; 2005
G.W.D. 14-240, HCJ
Calder, Petitioner 2005 G.W.D. 29-534, OH
Caledonia Subsea Ltd v. Micoperi Srl 2005 G.W.D. 9-131, OH
Calthorpe v. Mcoscar see Anstruther Gough Calthorpe v. McOscar
Cameron v. Fife Council 2005 S.L.T. (Sh Ct) 115; 2005 G.W.D. 29-558, Sh Ct
(Tayside). . . . .   *Digested,* 05/**5504**
Cameron v. Gibson see Cameron v. MacIntyre's Executor
Cameron v. MacIntyre's Executor; *sub nom* Cameron v. Gibson 2005 Fam. L.R. 108,
IH (1 Div); reversing 2004 S.L.T. 79; 2004 S.C.L.R. 219; 2003 Fam. L.R. 120;
2004 G.W.D. 1-5; *Times,* January 20, 2004, OH. . . . .   *Digested,* 04/**4736**
Campbell v. Dunoon & Cowal Housing Association Ltd (Leave to Appeal) 1992 S.L.T.
1136, IH (Ex Div). . . . .   *Digested,* 92/**5723**:
                                                     Considered, 05/5437
Campbell v. East Renfrewshire Council 2004 Rep. L.R. 89; 2004 G.W.D. 13-296, OH . .   *Digested,* 05/**5403**
Campbell v. Highland Council 2005 S.L.T. (Sh Ct) 141; 2005 G.W.D. 37-695, Sh Ct
(Grampian)
Campbell v. HM Advocate (Sentencing) 2005 G.W.D. 35-662, HCJ
Campbell v. Ramage 2005 G.W.D. 26-505, HCJ
Canmore Housing Association Ltd v. Bairnsfather (t/a BR Autos) 2004 S.L.T. 673;
2005 S.C.L.R. 185; 2004 G.W.D. 16-352, OH . . . .   *Digested,* 04/**4554**
Canon (UK) Ltd v. Craig 2005 G.W.D. 10-156, OH
Capello v. Secretary of State for Work and Pensions 2004 S.L.T. 1155; 2005 S.C.L.R.
28; 2004 G.W.D. 30-629, OH . . . .   *Digested,* 04/**5128**
Carmichael v. Murray 2005 G.W.D. 12-198, HCJ
Carnegie v. MJ Gleeson Group Ltd 2005 G.W.D. 40-753, Sh Ct (North Strathclyde)
Carroll v. Carroll 2005 Fam. L.R. 99, Sh Pr
Carter v. Carter 2005 G.W.D. 9-141, OH
Carter v. Ritchie see Carter v. Robertson
Carter v. Robertson; *sub nom* Carter v. Ritchie 2005 S.C.C.R. 181; 2005 G.W.D. 16-
271, HCJ
Castle View Services Ltd v. Howes; *sub nom* Howes v. Castle View Services Ltd 2000
S.C. 419; 2000 S.L.T. 696; 2000 G.W.D. 10-357, IH (1 Div) . . . .   *Digested,* 00/**6220**:
                                                     Considered, 05/5215
Caterleisure Ltd v. Glasgow Prestwick International Airport Ltd 2005 S.L.T. 1083;
2005 S.C.L.R. 943; 2005 G.W.D. 33-623, IH (Ex Div); reversing 2005 S.C.L.R.
306; 2004 G.W.D. 37-759, OH
Chakal v. Brown; *sub nom* Chakal v. Gallacher 2004 S.C.C.R. 541; 2004 G.W.D. 35-
713, HCJ. . . . .   *Digested,* 05/**5092**
Chakal v. Gallacher see Chakal v. Brown
Chalmers v. Griffiths; *sub nom* MacLeod v. Griffiths 2005 J.C. 158; 2005 S.L.T. 172;
2005 S.C.C.R. 30; 2005 G.W.D. 4-38, HCJ . . . .   *Digested,* 05/**5123**

Chapman *v.* Lord Advocate 2005 G.W.D. 37-696, OH
Charterhall Marketing Ltd *v.* Customs and Excise Commissioners [2005] B.V.C. 2566; [2005] S.T.I. 1027,V&DTr (Edinburgh)
Chas Stewart Plumbing & Heating Ltd *v.* Lowe 2005 S.C.L.R. 235, Sh Pr
Chatham (Nicola) *v.* HM Advocate 2005 S.C.C.R. 373; 2005 G.W.D. 14-242, HCJ
Chaudry *v.* Chaudry 2005 G.W.D. 5-65, Sh Ct (South Strathclyde)
Cheesman *v.* International Travel Service Ltd 2005 G.W.D. 40-732, OH
Chief Constable of Lothian and Borders *v.* Lothian and Borders Police Board 2005 S.L.T. 315; 2005 G.W.D. 8-104, OH . . . . *Digested,* 05/**4968**
Christensen (Peter Joseph) *v.* HM Advocate 2005 S.C.C.R. 825, HCJ
Christian *v.* Aberdeen City Council 2005 Hous. L.R. 71, Sh Ct (Grampian)
Christiani & Nielsen Ltd *v.* Birmingham City Council 52 Con. L.R. 56, QBD (OR). . . . . .   *Digested,* 97/**923**:
                                                     Considered, 05/**5069**
Christie (William) *v.* HM Advocate; Young (Sean James) *v.* HM Advocate; Scott (James Campbell) *v.* HM Advocate 2004 J.C. 13; 2003 S.L.T. 1352; 2003 S.C.C.R. 673; 2003 G.W.D. 35-984, HCJ. . . . . *Digested,* 04/**4658**:
                                                 Distinguished, 05/**5130**
City Leisure (Musselburgh) Ltd *v.* East Lothian Licensing Board 2004 S.L.T. 1210; 2004 G.W.D. 18-410, OH . . . . *Digested,* 05/**5505**
City Link Development Co Ltd *v.* Lanarkshire Housing Association Ltd 2005 S.C.L.R. 862, OH
City Wall Properties (Scotland) Ltd *v.* Pearl Assurance Plc (No.2) 2005 G.W.D. 35-666, OH
Clark *v.* BET Plc [1997] I.R.L.R. 348; [1997] O.P.L.R. 1, QBD . . . . *Digested,* 97/**2207**:
                           Considered, 05/1212: *Distinguished,* 05/**5220**
Clark *v.* Clark 2005 Fam. L.R. 28, Sh Pr
Clark *v.* HM Advocate (Sentencing) 2005 G.W.D. 11-180, HCJ
Clark *v.* Patrick 2005 G.W.D. 18-322, HCJ
Clark *v.* R&J Simpson Ltd 2005 G.W.D. 31-598, Sh Ct (Grampian)
Clark (Christopher John) *v.* Kelly [2003] UKPC D1; [2004] 1 A.C. 681; [2003] 2 W.L.R. 1586; [2003] 1 All E.R. 1106; 2003 S.C. (P.C.) 77; 2003 S.L.T. 308; 2003 S.C.C.R. 194; [2003] H.R.L.R. 17; [2003] U.K.H.R.R. 1167; 14 B.H.R.C. 369; (2003) 100(17) L.S.G. 27; (2003) 147 S.J.L.B. 234; 2003 G.W.D. 7-164; *Times,* February 12, 2003; *Independent,* March 17, 2003 (C.S), PC (Sc); affirming 2001 J.C. 16; 2000 S.L.T. 1038; 2000 S.C.C.R. 821; 2000 G.W.D. 27-1041, HCJ .   *Digested,* 03/**5167**:
                                                 Disapproved, 05/**5123**
Clarke *v.* Fennoscandia Ltd (No.3) 2005 S.L.T. 511; 2005 S.C.L.R. 322; 2005 G.W.D. 13-217, IH (2 Div); affirming 2004 S.C. 197; 2003 S.C.L.R. 894; 2003 G.W.D. 31-855, OH. . . . . *Digested,* 05/**5032**
Clarke *v.* Mackenzie 2005 S.C. 174; 2005 S.L.T. 389; 2005 G.W.D. 9-132, IH (Ex Div) . .   *Digested,* 05/**5056**
Claymore Dairies Ltd *v.* Director General of Fair Trading (Disclosure: Confidentiality Ring) [2003] CAT 12; [2004] Comp. A.R. 63, CAT. . . . . *Digested,* 04/**521**:
                                                 Followed, 05/**5061**
Claymore Dairies Ltd *v.* Office of Fair Trading (Disclosure: Further Information) [2004] CAT 16; [2005] Comp. A.R. 1, CAT. . . . . *Digested,* 05/**5061**
Clegg *v.* Rogerson 2005 G.W.D. 26-514, OH
Clydesdale Bank Plc *v.* Hyland 2004 Hous. L.R. 116; 2002 G.W.D. 37-1229, Sh Ct (Tayside) . . . . *Digested,* 05/**5053**
Clydesdale Bank Plc *v.* Lanarkshire Valuation Joint Board Assessor see Lanarkshire Valuation Joint Board Assessor *v.* Clydesdale Bank Plc
Cochrane *v.* Gaughan; *sub nom* Dall *v.* Gaughan 2004 S.C.L.R. 1073; 2004 Rep. L.R. 73 (Note); 2004 G.W.D. 9-215, OH . . . . *Digested,* 05/**5589**
Cochrane *v.* HM Advocate (Sentencing) 2005 G.W.D. 12-208, HCJ
Cole *v.* HM Advocate 2005 G.W.D. 21-380, HCJ
Colley *v.* Poland 2005 S.L.T. 436; 2005 G.W.D. 8-110, HCJ . . . . *Digested,* 05/**5285**
Collins *v.* Scottish Homes 2005 Hous. L.R. 120; 2005 G.W.D. 31-602, OH
Commissioner of Police *v.* Stunt see R. (on the application of Stunt) *v.* Mallett
Connelly *v.* GA Group Ltd (Expenses) 2005 S.L.T. (Sh Ct) 16, Sh Pr. . . . . *Digested,* 05/**5043**
Connolly *v.* Connolly 2005 Fam. L.R. 106, IH (1 Div)
Cooke *v.* Telford 2005 S.C.L.R. 367, Sh Ct (Glasgow)
Cooper *v.* HM Advocate 2005 G.W.D. 40-744, HCJ
Cooper (Provisional Liquidator of Bishopsgate Investment Management Ltd) *v.* Maxwell see Bishopsgate Investment Management Ltd (In Provisional Liquidation) *v.* Maxwell
Costain Ltd *v.* Strathclyde Builders Ltd 2004 S.L.T. 102; 2004 S.C.L.R. 707; 100 Con. L.R. 41; 2004 G.W.D. 1-9, OH . . . . *Digested,* 04/**4600**
Costigan *v.* Cook (t/a World of Heat, The Fireplace Shop) 2005 G.W.D. 34-637, Sh Ct (Tayside)
Council of the Law Society of Scotland *v.* Shepherd 2005 G.W.D. 37-694, IH (1 Div)
Cowan *v.* Ramsay 2005 S.L.T. (Sh Ct) 65; 2005 G.W.D. 7-97, Sh Ct (South Strathclyde) . . . . *Digested,* 05/**5038**
Coyle *v.* HM Advocate 2005 G.W.D. 23-420, HCJ

Coyle *v.* William Fairey Installations Ltd 1991 S.C. 16; 1991 S.L.T. 638; 1991 S.C.L.R. 248, IH (Ex Div); reversing 1990 S.C.L.R. 346, OH . . . .   *Digested,* 91/**5001**: *Considered,* 05/5041

Coyle *v.* Williams 2005 G.W.D. 15-263, HCJ

Craigie *v.* Lanarkshire Health Board 2005 G.W.D. 31-603, OH

Crawford (James Dair) *v.* HM Advocate 2005 S.L.T. 1056; 2005 S.C.C.R. 628; 2005 G.W.D. 25-474, HCJ . . . .   *Digested,* 05/**5130**

Creevy *v.* HM Advocate 2005 S.C.C.R. 272, HCJ

Crocket *v.* Tantallon Golf Club 2005 S.L.T. 663; 2005 S.C.L.R. 657; 2005 G.W.D. 16-265, OH . . . .   *Digested,* 05/**4966**

Crooks (William) *v.* HM Advocate (No.1) see Du Plooy (Devonne) *v.* HM Advocate (No.1)

Cruickshank *v.* Fairfield Rowan Ltd 2005 S.L.T. 462; 2005 Rep. L.R. 33, OH. . . . .   *Digested,* 05/**5166**

Cunningham *v.* Cunningham 2001 Fam. L.R. 12; 2000 G.W.D. 36-1362, OH . . . .   *Digested,* 01/**6519**: *Followed,* 05/5252

Cunningham *v.* HM Advocate (Sentencing) 2005 G.W.D. 38-710, HCJ

Cunningham *v.* M 2005 S.L.T. (Sh Ct) 73; 2005 Fam. L.R. 14; 2004 G.W.D. 40-811, Sh Pr . . . .   *Digested,* 05/**5253**

Cunningham *v.* Ralph 2004 S.C.C.R. 549; 2004 G.W.D. 29-603, HCJ . . . .   *Digested,* 05/**5128**

D *v.* D 2005 G.W.D. 9-128, Sh Ct (Tayside)

D *v.* H 2004 S.L.T. (Sh Ct) 73; 2004 Fam. L.R. 41; 2004 G.W.D. 8-164, Sh Pr . . . .   *Digested,* 04/**4744**: *Distinguished,* 05/5250

D *v.* Irvine 2005 S.L.T. (Sh Ct) 131; 2005 Fam. L.R. 94; 2005 G.W.D. 33-619, Sh Pr

D *v.* Secretary of State for the Home Department see DD *v.* Secretary of State for the Home Department

Dall *v.* Gaughan see Cochrane *v.* Gaughan

Darroch *v.* East Renfrewshire Council 2005 Hous. L.R. 26, Lands Tr (Scot)

Davidov *v.* Secretary of State for the Home Department 2005 S.C. 540; 2005 S.L.T. 953; 2005 G.W.D. 30-579, IH (1 Div) . . . .   *Digested,* 05/**5439**

Davidson, Petitioner (No.1) see Davidson *v.* Scottish Ministers (No.1)

Davidson, Petitioner (No.2) see Davidson *v.* Scottish Ministers (No.2)

Davidson, Petitioner (No.3) see Davidson *v.* Scottish Ministers (Incidental Petition: Dismissal of Appeal)

Davidson *v.* Scottish Ministers (Incidental Petition: Dismissal of Appeal); *sub nom* Davidson, Petitioner (No.3) 2005 S.C. (H.L.) 1, HL

Davidson *v.* Scottish Ministers (No.1); *sub nom* Scott *v.* Scottish Ministers; Scott, Petitioner; Davidson, Petitioner (No.1) [2005] UKHL 74; *Times,* December 19, 2005, HL; reversing 2002 S.C. 205; 2002 S.L.T. 420; 2002 G.W.D. 1-9, IH (Ex Div); affirming 2002 S.C.L.R. 166; 2001 G.W.D. 35-1341, OH. . . . .   *Digested,* 02/**5239**

Davidson *v.* Scottish Ministers (No.2); *sub nom* Davidson, Petitioner (No.2) [2004] UKHL 34; 2005 S.C. (H.L.) 7; 2004 S.L.T. 895; 2004 S.C.L.R. 991; [2004] H.R.L.R. 34; [2004] U.K.H.R.R. 1079; [2005] A.C.D. 19; 2004 G.W.D. 27-572; *Times,* July 16, 2004, HL; affirming in part 2003 S.C. 103; 2002 S.L.T. 1231; 2002 G.W.D. 28-959, IH (2 Div) . . . .   *Digested,* 04/**4467**: *Considered,* 05/2908: *Followed,* 03/5168

Davies *v.* Renfrewshire Council; *sub nom* Renfrewshire Council *v.* Davies 2005 S.C. 315; 2005 S.L.T. 445; 2005 G.W.D. 11-186, IH (Ex Div) . . . .   *Digested,* 05/**5503**

Davis *v.* Chief Constable for Central Scotland 2005 G.W.D. 30-575, Sh Ct (Tayside)

Davis *v.* United Kingdom (28901/95) see Rowe *v.* United Kingdom (28901/95)

Dawson *v.* Shaw 2005 G.W.D. 12-200, Sh Ct (Grampian)

DD *v.* Secretary of State for the Home Department; *sub nom* D *v.* Secretary of State for the Home Department 2005 S.C. 415; 2005 G.W.D. 24-448, IH (2 Div)

Dean (t/a Abbey Mill Business Centre) *v.* Freeman 2005 G.W.D. 9-137, OH

Deans *v.* Thus Plc 2005 S.C.L.R. 148; 2004 G.W.D. 9-220, OH

Deighan *v.* Edinburgh City Council 2004 Hous. L.R. 89, Sh Ct (Lothian). . . . .   *Digested,* 05/**5473**

Dempsey (Stephen) *v.* HM Advocate 2005 J.C. 252; 2005 S.L.T. 201; 2005 S.C.C.R. 169; 2005 G.W.D. 4-43, HCJ. . . . .   *Digested,* 05/**5154**

Dempster *v.* Spiers 2005 G.W.D. 21-389, HCJ

Dench *v.* HM Advocate 2005 G.W.D. 21-381, HCJ

Dhesi *v.* Glasgow City Council; *sub nom* Glasgow City Council *v.* Dhesi 2005 G.W.D. 39-726, IH (Ex Div); reversing EATS/0027/04, EAT (SC)

Di Rollo *v.* Di Rollo 1959 S.C. 75; 1959 S.L.T. 278, OH . . . .   *Digested,* 59/**3556**: *Considered,* 05/5270

Diamond Offshore Drilling (UK) Ltd *v.* Gulf Offshore NS Ltd 2005 S.L.T. 589; 2005 G.W.D. 17-301, IH (1 Div); affirming 2003 G.W.D. 29-804, OH . . . .   *Digested,* 05/**5078**

Dickson (Ryan Patrick) *v.* HM Advocate 2005 S.C.C.R. 344, HCJ

Dignity Funerals Ltd *v.* Bruce see Bruce *v.* Dignity Funerals Ltd

Dingwall (Anthony Paul) *v.* HM Advocate 2005 S.C.C.R. 700; 2005 G.W.D. 29-561, HCJ

Do *v.* Immigration Appeal Tribunal see R. (on the application of Ullah) *v.* Special Adjudicator

Do *v.* Secretary of State for the Home Department see R. (on the application of Ullah)
　　v. Special Adjudicator
Docherty *v.* HM Advocate 2005 G.W.D. 29-543, HCJ
Docherty *v.* HM Advocate (Sentencing) 2005 G.W.D. 12-205, HCJ
Dodds *v.* Walker [1981] 1 W.L.R. 1027; [1981] 2 All E.R. 609; (1981) 42 P. & C.R. 131;
　　125 S.J. 463, HL; affirming [1980] 1 W.L.R. 1061; [1980] 2 All E.R. 507; (1980)
　　40 P. & C.R. 487; (1980) 255 E.G. 53; 124 S.J. 575, CA (Civ Div) . . . . 　　　*Digested*, 81/**1518**:
　　　　　　　　　　　　Applied, 85/1847, 05/892: *Considered*, 04/4594: *Distinguished*, 05/5214:
　　　　　　　　　　　　　　　　　　　　　　　　　　　　　　　　　　Followed, 04/440
Dolphin Drilling Ltd *v.* Tor Drilling (UK) Ltd 2005 S.L.T. 1214; 2005 G.W.D. 31-599, IH
　　(1 Div); affirming EATS/0101/03, EAT (SC)
Donaldson *v.* Hays Distribution Services Ltd 2005 S.C. 523; 2005 S.L.T. 733; 2005
　　S.C.L.R. 717; 2005 Rep. L.R. 92; 2005 G.W.D. 22-410, IH (1 Div); affirming 2004
　　Rep. L.R. 57; 2004 G.W.D. 7-153, OH . . . . 　　　*Digested*, 05/**5168**
Donaldson *v.* Ord (1855) 17 D.1053 . . . . 　　*Considered*, 05/5030
Donaldson *v.* Reith 2005 G.W.D. 21-379, HCJ
Donnell (David Thomas) *v.* HM Advocate 2005 S.C.C.R. 728, HCJ
Donnelly *v.* FAS Products Ltd 2004 S.C.L.R. 678; 2004 Rep. L.R. 76 (Note); 2004
　　G.W.D. 12-266, OH . . . . 　　　*Digested*, 05/**5591**
Donohoe *v.* Queens Cross Housing Association 2004 Hous. L.R. 42, Lands Tr (Scot) . . 　　*Digested*, 05/**5424**
Dooner *v.* North Ayrshire Council 2005 G.W.D. 38-703, Sh Ct (North Strathclyde)
Dow *v.* Sweeney see Sweeney *v.* Sweeney (No.2)
Drinnan *v.* Bone Group Ltd 2005 S.L.T. (Sh Ct) 119; 2005 Rep. L.R. 75; 2005 G.W.D.
　　25-495, Sh Ct (South Strathclyde)
Drummond (Andrew Page) *v.* HM Advocate 2003 S.L.T. 295; 2003 S.C.C.R. 108;
　　2003 G.W.D. 1-16, HCJ . . . . 　　　*Digested*, 03/**5431**:
　　　　　　　　　　　　　　　　　　　　　　　　　　　　　　　Considered, 05/5149
Du Plooy (Devonne) *v.* HM Advocate (No.1); Alderdice (Francis Robert) *v.* HM
　　Advocate (No.1); Crooks (William) *v.* HM Advocate (No.1); O'Neil (David William)
　　v. HM Advocate (No.1) 2005 J.C. 1; 2003 S.L.T. 1237; 2003 S.C.C.R. 640;
　　2003 G.W.D. 31-865, HCJ. . . . . 　　　*Digested*, 03/**5404**:
　　　　　　　　　　　　　　　　　　　　　　　　　　　　　　　Considered, 05/5650
Duffy (John) *v.* HM Advocate 2005 S.C.C.R. 697; 2005 G.W.D. 30-570, HCJ
Duncan *v.* MacGillivray 1989 S.L.T. 48; 1988 S.C.C.R. 488, HCJ Appeal . . . . 　　　*Digested*, 88/**4845**:
　　　　　　　　　　　　　　　　　　　　　　　　　　　　　　　Considered, 05/5109
Dundee City Council *v.* McPhee 2005 Hous. L.R. 30, Sh Ct (Tayside)
Dundee Taxi Cab Co Ltd *v.* Dundee City Council 2005 S.C. 503; 2005 S.L.T. 401; 2005
　　G.W.D. 11-185, IH (Ex Div) . . . . 　　　*Digested*, 05/**5501**
Dyer *v.* Customs and Excise Commissioners [2005] S.T.C. 715; 2005 S.L.T. 255;
　　[2005] B.T.C. 5356; [2005] B.V.C. 387; [2005] S.T.I. 191; 2005 G.W.D. 3-32, IH
　　(Ex Div) . . . . 　　　*Digested*, 05/**5720**
Dysart *v.* Daldrup see Service *v.* Daldrup

E *v.* E 2004 Fam. L.R. 115; 2004 G.W.D. 26-548, Sh Ct (Tayside) . . . . 　　*Digested*, 05/**5250**
East Lothian Council *v.* Skeldon 2004 Hous. L.R. 123; 2004 G.W.D. 32-666, Sh Ct
　　(Lothian) . . . . 　　*Digested*, 05/**5478**
Edinburgh City Council *v.* 3Maxblack LLP 2005 S.L.T. (Sh Ct) 86; 2005 G.W.D. 25-
　　492, Sh Ct (Lothian) . . . . 　　*Digested*, 05/**5502**
Edinburgh City Council *v.* Johnston 2005 S.L.T. (Sh Ct) 100; 2005 Hous. L.R. 80;
　　2005 G.W.D. 26-513, Sh Ct (Lothian) . . . . 　　*Digested*, 05/**5479**
Edinburgh City Council *v.* Porter 2004 Hous. L.R. 46; 2004 G.W.D. 16-358, Sh Ct
　　(Lothian) . . . . 　　*Digested*, 05/**5476**
Edinburgh City Council *v.* Z 2005 S.L.T. (Sh Ct) 7; 2005 G.W.D. 5-68, Sh Pr. . . . . 　　*Digested*, 05/**5685**
Edinburgh Leisure *v.* Customs and Excise Commissioners [2005] B.V.C. 2146; [2004]
　　V. & D.R. 394; [2004] S.T.I. 2577, V&D Tr (Edinburgh)
Edinburgh Telford College *v.* Customs and Excise Commissioners; *sub nom* Edinburgh's
　　Telford College *v.* Revenue and Customs Commissioners; TNS, IH (1 Div);
　　reversing [2005] B.V.C. 2328; [2005] V. & D.R. 71, V&D Tr (Edinburgh)
Edinburgh's Telford College *v.* Revenue and Customs Commissioners see Edinburgh
　　Telford College *v.* Customs and Excise Commissioners
Edminson *v.* Murray 2005 G.W.D. 37-698, HCJ
Edwards *v.* United Kingdom (A/247B) (1993) 15 E.H.R.R. 417; *Times*, January 21,
　　1993, ECHR . . . . 　　　*Digested*, 93/**2125**:
　　　　　　　　　　　　　Applied, 01/1097: *Considered*, 05/5136: *Distinguished*, 00/3219
Emcor Drake & Scull Ltd *v.* Edinburgh Royal Joint Venture 2005 S.L.T. 1233; 2005
　　G.W.D. 35-656, OH
Empowerment Enterprises Ltd *v.* Customs and Excise Commissioners [2005] B.V.C.
　　2445; [2005] S.T.I. 876, V&D Tr (Edinburgh)
Esso Petroleum Co Ltd *v.* Hall Russell & Co Ltd (No.2) 1995 S.L.T. 127; 1995 S.C.L.R.
　　36, OH . . . . 　　　*Digested*, 94/**6118**:
　　　　　　　　　　　　　　　　　　　　　　　　　　　　　　　Considered, 05/2890
Europe and Jersey Estates Ltd *v.* Reid 2005 G.W.D. 40-759, Sh Ct (North Strathclyde)
Evans *v.* Motor Insurers Bureau see White (Brian) *v.* White (Shane)

Everest Ltd *v.* Dillon 2005 S.C. 560; 2005 G.W.D. 25-482, IH (1 Div); affirming EATS/
    0052/03, EAT (SC)
Ewos Ltd *v.* Mainland 2005 S.L.T. 1227; 2005 G.W.D. 38-713, OH

Fairley *v.* Thomson 2004 Rep. L.R. 142; 2004 G.W.D. 28-591, Sh Ct (Lothian) . . . .   *Digested*, 05/**5586**
Fairlie *v.* Perth and Kinross Healthcare NHS Trust 2004 S.L.T. 1200; 2004 G.W.D. 31-
    649, OH . . . .   *Digested*, 05/**5575**
Falconer *v.* Service 2005 G.W.D. 11-196, HCJ
Farquhar *v.* Ralph 2005 G.W.D. 22-397, HCJ
Farrell *v.* HM Advocate (Sentencing) 2005 G.W.D. 35-660, HCJ
Farrell (Anthony Thomas) *v.* HM Advocate 2005 S.C.C.R. 411, HCJ
Feeney *v.* Griffiths 2005 G.W.D. 22-402, HCJ
Fergus *v.* Eadie 2005 S.C.L.R. 176, Sh Pr
Ferguson *v.* City Refrigeration Holdings (UK) Ltd 2005 Rep. L.R. 117; 2005 G.W.D.
    24-446, Sh Ct (Grampian)
Ferguson *v.* HM Advocate 2005 S.C.C.R. 603, HCJ Appeal
FIM Holdings Ltd *v.* Assessor for Grampian Valuation Joint Board; *sub nom* FIM
    Holdings Ltd *v.* Grampian Valuation Joint Board Assessor 2005 S.C. 1; 2004
    S.L.T. 97; 2004 S.C.L.R. 725; [2004] R.A. 135; 2004 G.W.D. 1-21, LVAC . . . . . .   *Digested*, 04/**5098**
FIM Holdings Ltd *v.* Grampian Valuation Joint Board Assessor see FIM Holdings Ltd *v.*
    Assessor for Grampian Valuation Joint Board
Findlay *v.* Frame 2005 G.W.D. 10-165, HCJ
Fitzpatrick *v.* Advocate General 2005 S.C.L.R. 1089, Sh Ct (Lothian)
Fleming *v.* HM Advocate 2005 G.W.D. 22-395, HCJ
Flynn (Patrick Anthony) *v.* HM Advocate (No.2); Meek (Peter Mitchell) *v.* HM
    Advocate (No.2); Nicol (John Gary) *v.* HM Advocate (No.2); McMurray (Peter)
    v. HM Advocate (No.2) 2005 J.C. 271; 2004 S.L.T. 1195; 2004 S.C.C.R. 702;
    2004 G.W.D. 35-715, HCJ . . . .   *Digested*, 05/**5652**:
                                                                              Previous proceedings, 04/5109
Follen (Garry John) *v.* HM Advocate 2004 S.C.C.R. 647, HCJ . . . .   *Digested*, 05/**5661**
Forbes *v.* Forbes (1869) 8 M. 85. . . . .   *Applied*, 05/5033
Forbes *v.* Johnstone 1995 S.C. 220; 1995 S.L.T. 158; 1995 S.C.L.R. 154, IH (Ct of 5
    judges) . . . .   *Digested*, 95/**6384**:
                                                                              Applied, 05/5033
Forrester *v.* Chief Constable of Grampian Constabulary 2005 G.W.D. 28-524, Sh Ct
    (Grampian)
Foster Yeoman Ltd *v.* Highland and Western Isles Valuation Joint Board Assessor
    [2005] R.A. 189, Lands Tr (Scot) . . . .   *Digested*, 05/**5624**
Fowler *v.* Falkirk Council 2005 S.L.T. 404; 2005 S.C.L.R. 626; 2005 G.W.D. 11-187,
    OH . . . .   *Digested*, 05/**5521**
Frame *v.* Aberdeen Journals Ltd 2005 S.L.T. 949; 2005 S.C.C.R. 579; 2005 G.W.D.
    23-417, HCJ
Frankenberg *v.* Dundee City Council 2005 Hous. L.R. 55, Sh Ct (Tayside)
Fraser *v.* Adams 2005 S.C.C.R. 54; 2005 G.W.D. 1-8, Sh Ct (Lothian). . . . .   *Digested*, 05/**5104**
Fraser *v.* Irvine 2005 G.W.D. 20-371, Sh Ct (Lothian)
Fraser *v.* Professional Golfers Association Ltd; *sub nom* Fraser *v.* Professional Golf
    Association Ltd 2005 S.C.L.R. 769; 2005 G.W.D. 20-356, IH (Ex Div); reversing
    2005 S.C.L.R. 1; 2004 Rep. L.R. 69; 2004 G.W.D. 9-200, OH . . . .   *Digested*, 04/**658**
Free Church of Scotland *v.* General Assembly of the Free Church of Scotland 2005 S.C.
    396; 2005 S.L.T. 348; 2005 G.W.D. 11-181, OH . . . .   *Digested*, 05/**5170**
Friend *v.* Lord Advocate; *sub nom* Whaley *v.* Lord Advocate 2005 G.W.D. 30-577, IH
    (Ex Div); affirming 2004 S.C. 78; 2004 S.L.T. 425; 2003 G.W.D. 22-651, OH . . .   *Digested*, 04/**4480**
Friends Provident Life & Pensions Ltd *v.* McGuinness 2005 S.C.L.R. 1093; 2005 G.W.D.
    21-374, OH
Fulton (Stewart Farquharson) *v.* HM Advocate 2005 S.C.C.R. 159; 2005 G.W.D. 4-39,
    HCJ

Gafar *v.* Secretary of State for the Home Department 2005 G.W.D. 22-408, OH
Gallacher *v.* Bott 2005 G.W.D. 16-276, HCJ
Gallacher *v.* Reith 2005 G.W.D. 21-390, HCJ
Gallagher *v.* Jones (Inspector of Taxes) see Threlfall *v.* Jones (Inspector of Taxes)
Gallagher *v.* Parole Board for Scotland 2005 G.W.D. 30-585, OH
Gardiner *v.* HM Advocate (Sentencing) 2005 G.W.D. 19-343, HCJ
Gerrard *v.* Edinburgh NHS Trust Royal Infirmary 2005 S.C. 192; 2005 G.W.D. 3-30, IH
    (Ex Div); affirming 2002 G.W.D. 2-86, OH
Gholami *v.* Secretary of State for the Home Department 2005 G.W.D. 7-102, OH
Gibb *v.* Teale 2005 G.W.D. 36-671, HCJ
Gilchrist (Kenneth Alexander) *v.* HM Advocate; Quinn (Dennis James) *v.* HM Advocate
    2005 J.C. 34; 2004 S.L.T. 1167; 2004 S.C.C.R. 595; 2004 G.W.D. 34-689,
    HCJ . . . .   *Digested*, 05/**5086**
Gillanders *v.* Arthur Bell (Scotch Tweeds) Ltd 2005 Rep. L.R. 81, OH
Gillespie *v.* Toondale Ltd 2005 G.W.D. 31-590, OH

Gillies *v.* Lynch (No.1) 2002 S.L.T. 1420; 2003 S.C.L.R. 467; 2002 Rep. L.R. 133; 2002 G.W.D. 33-1114, OH . . . . *Digested*, 03/**5439**:
Not applied, 05/5163
Gillies *v.* Lynch (No.2) 2005 Rep. L.R. 9; 2004 G.W.D. 35-710, OH . . . . *Digested*, 05/**5164**
Gillon *v.* HM Advocate 2005 G.W.D. 33-627, HCJ
Glasgow City Council *v.* Bvunzai see Bvunzai *v.* Glasgow City Council
Glasgow City Council *v.* Dhesi see Dhesi *v.* Glasgow City Council
Glasgow Housing Association *v.* O'Donnell 2004 Hous. L.R. 78; 2004 G.W.D. 29-604, Sh Ct (Glasgow) . . . . *Digested*, 05/**5417**:
Considered, 05/5416
Glasgow Housing Association *v.* Sharkey 2005 S.L.T. (Sh Ct) 59; 2004 Hous. L.R. 130, Sh Pr . . . . *Digested*, 05/**5416**
Gloag *v.* Hamilton 2004 Hous. L.R. 91, Sh Ct (Grampian) . . . . *Digested*, 05/**5466**
Gonshaw *v.* Bamber (No.1) 2004 S.C.C.R. 482, HCJ . . . . *Digested*, 05/**5089**
Gonshaw *v.* Bamber (No.2) 2004 S.L.T. 1270; 2004 S.C.C.R. 696; 2004 G.W.D. 34-695, HCJ . . . . *Digested*, 05/**5155**
Gordon (Graham) *v.* HM Advocate 2004 S.C.C.R. 641; 2004 G.W.D. 34-692, HCJ . . . . *Digested*, 05/**5091**
Gorman *v.* Aberdeen Trades Council Social Club 2005 G.W.D. 34-636, Sh Ct (Grampian)
Gould *v.* Glasgow City Council see Wilson *v.* Glasgow City Council
Graham *v.* HM Advocate 2005 S.C.C.R. 544, HCJ Appeal
Grainger (Darren Michael) *v.* HM Advocate 2005 S.L.T. 364; 2005 S.C.C.R. 175; 2005 G.W.D. 7-92, HCJ . . . . *Digested*, 05/**5125**
Grampian Housing Association *v.* Pyper 2004 Hous. L.R. 22; 2004 G.W.D. 13-293, Sh Pr . . . . *Digested*, 05/**5425**
Grant *v.* Highland Council 2004 S.C.L.R. 1067, Sh Ct (Grampian) . . . . *Digested*, 05/**5594**
Grant *v.* McHale 2005 S.L.T. 1057; 2005 S.C.C.R. 559; 2005 G.W.D. 27-535, HCJ
Gray *v.* HM Advocate 2005 G.W.D. 31-594, HCJ
Gray (Inspector of Taxes) *v.* Seymours Garden Centre (Horticulture) [1995] S.T.C. 706; 67 T.C. 401; [1995] E.G.C.S. 99; *Times*, May 31, 1995; *Independent*, June 19, 1995 (C.S.), CA (Civ Div); affirming [1993] 2 All E.R. 809; [1993] S.T.C. 354; [1993] E.G.C.S. 72; *Times*, April 7, 1993, Ch D . . . . *Digested*, 96/**5563**:
Approved, 96/5564: *Considered*, 05/5691: *Followed*, 96/5566
Gray (William) *v.* HM Advocate; O'Rourke (James Bernard) *v.* HM Advocate 2005 J.C. 233; 2005 S.L.T. 159; 2005 S.C.C.R. 106; 2005 G.W.D. 5-62, HCJ . . . . *Digested*, 05/**5153**
Green Environmental Industries Ltd, Re see R. *v.* Hertfordshire CC Ex p. Green Environmental Industries Ltd
Green Environmental Industries Ltd *v.* Hertfordshire CC see R. *v.* Hertfordshire CC Ex p. Green Environmental Industries Ltd
Greenhill *v.* HM Advocate 2005 G.W.D. 3-22, HCJ
Griffiths *v.* Hart 2005 J.C. 313; 2005 S.L.T. 495; 2005 S.C.C.R. 392; 2005 G.W.D. 15-255, HCJ . . . . *Digested*, 05/**5095**
Griffiths *v.* Scottish Water 2005 G.W.D. 17-303, Sh Ct (Tayside)
Griffiths *v.* Simon Howie Butchers Ltd 2005 G.W.D. 37-690, Sh Ct (Tayside)
Gupta *v.* Ross 2005 S.L.T. 548; 2005 G.W.D. 4-44, IH (Ex Div) . . . . *Digested*, 05/**5042**

Haddow *v.* Glasgow City Council 2005 S.L.T. 1219; 2005 G.W.D. 38-714, OH
Haggarty *v.* Woodrow 2005 G.W.D. 35-654, Sh Ct (North Strathclyde)
Hallam *v.* Scottish Commission for the Regulation of Care; *sub nom* Hallam, Petitioner 2005 S.C.L.R. 982; 2005 G.W.D. 24-458, OH
Hallam Land Management Ltd *v.* Perratt 2005 S.C.L.R. 230; 2004 G.W.D. 35-720, IH (Ex Div)
Hamid *v.* HM Advocate (Sentencing) 2005 G.W.D. 12-209, HCJ
Hamilton *v.* Allied Domecq Plc 2005 S.L.T. 1151; 2005 G.W.D. 37-697, IH (2 Div); reversing 2004 S.L.T. 191; 2003 G.W.D. 31-877, OH . . . . *Digested*, 04/**5052**
Hamilton *v.* HM Advocate 2005 G.W.D. 29-556, HCJ
Hamilton *v.* Murray 2005 G.W.D. 19-351, HCJ
Hamilton *v.* Seamark Systems Ltd 2004 S.C. 543; 2004 G.W.D. 8-167, OH . . . . *Digested*, 05/**5031**
Hamilton (Martin Joseph) *v.* HM Advocate 2005 J.C. 285; 2005 S.C.C.R. 316; 2005 G.W.D. 29-541, HCJ
Hansen (Flemming Leif) *v.* HM Advocate 2005 S.C.C.R. 293, HCJ
Harper *v.* HM Advocate 2005 S.C.C.R. 245, HCJ
Harris *v.* Appeal Committee of the Institute of Chartered Accountants of Scotland 2005 S.L.T. 487; 2005 G.W.D. 15-248, OH . . . . *Digested*, 05/**4962**
Harris *v.* HM Advocate 2005 G.W.D. 35-670, HCJ
Harris *v.* Wyre Forest DC see Smith *v.* Eric S Bush (A Firm)
Harrison *v.* West of Scotland Kart Club 2004 S.C. 615; 2004 Rep. L.R. 126; 2004 G.W.D. 12-275, IH (1 Div); reversing in part 2001 S.C. 367; 2001 S.L.T. 1171; 2001 Rep. L.R. 2; 2000 G.W.D. 38-1422, OH . . . . *Digested*, 05/**5576**
Harvey (Devon Lloyd) *v.* HM Advocate see Sinclair (Kevin Andrew) *v.* HM Advocate
Hastie *v.* Scottish Commission for the Regulation of Care 2005 G.W.D. 12-215, Sh Pr; affirming 2004 S.L.T. (Sh Ct) 131; 2004 G.W.D. 34-704, Sh Ct (Tayside) . . . . . . *Digested*, 05/**5249**
Hay *v.* Bott 2005 G.W.D. 25-480, HCJ

Heath *v.* Darby Glass Ltd 2004 S.C.L.R. 1093, Sh Ct (North Strathclyde) . . . .   *Digested*, 05/**5590**
Henderson *v.* 3052775 Nova Scotia Ltd TNS, HL; reversing 2005 S.C. 325; 2005
   G.W.D. 17-300, IH (Ex Div); affirming 2004 G.W.D. 40-831, OH
Henderson *v.* HM Advocate 2005 G.W.D. 40-747, HCJ
Henderson *v.* HM Advocate 2005 G.W.D. 40-751, HCJ
Henderson *v.* Laing 2005 G.W.D. 11-192, HCJ
Henderson (Alexander) *v.* HM Advocate; Marnoch (Douglas John) *v.* HM Advocate
   2005 J.C. 301; 2005 S.L.T. 429; 2005 S.C.C.R. 354; 2005 G.W.D. 13-222,
   HCJ . . . .   *Digested*, 05/**5088**
Henderson (David Christopher) *v.* HM Advocate 2005 J.C. 184; 2005 G.W.D. 21-376;
   2005 G.W.D. 18-317, HCJ
Henvey (Steven) *v.* HM Advocate; Reid (George) *v.* HM Advocate 2005 S.L.T. 384;
   2005 S.C.C.R. 282; 2005 G.W.D. 8-108, HCJ . . . .   *Digested*, 05/**5111**
Hepburn *v.* Griffiths 2005 G.W.D. 7-93, HCJ
Herkes *v.* Bott 2005 G.W.D. 24-441, HCJ
Heyder *v.* Lochridge Ltd 2005 G.W.D. 18-328, Sh Ct (Lothian)
Hill (Brian David) *v.* HM Advocate 2005 J.C. 259; 2005 S.L.T. 634; 2005 S.C.C.R.
   208; 2005 G.W.D. 19-337, HCJ . . . .   *Digested*, 05/**5082**
HJ Banks & Co Ltd *v.* Shell Chemicals UK Ltd 2005 G.W.D. 29-557, OH   *Digested*, 05/**5081**
HM Advocate *v.* A 2005 S.L.T. 975; 2005 S.C.C.R. 593; 2005 G.W.D. 25-471, HCJ . . .   *Digested*, 05/**5081**
HM Advocate *v.* Airs (Gordon) 1975 J.C. 64; 1975 S.L.T. 177, HCJ . . . .   *Digested*, 75/**3687**:
   Considered, 05/5122
HM Advocate *v.* Alexander 2005 S.C.C.R. 537, HCJ Appeal
HM Advocate *v.* Booth (Raymond Glenn) 2005 S.L.T. 337; 2005 S.C.C.R. 6; 2004
   G.W.D. 40-826, HCJ . . . .   *Digested*, 05/**5648**
HM Advocate *v.* Brady (Finbar Matthew) see HM Advocate *v.* Fleming (Douglas Colin)
HM Advocate *v.* Campbell (Robert); HM Advocate *v.* Wallace (John) 2004 S.C.C.R.
   529, HCJ . . . .   *Digested*, 05/**5087**
HM Advocate *v.* Crawford (James Dair) 2005 S.C.C.R. 836; 2005 G.W.D. 39-724,
   HCJ
HM Advocate *v.* DS; *sub nom* HM Advocate *v.* S 2005 S.C.C.R. 655; 2005 G.W.D.
   26-504, HCJ
HM Advocate *v.* Edge 2005 G.W.D. 20-360, HCJ
HM Advocate *v.* Fleming (Douglas Colin); HM Advocate *v.* Brady (Finbar Matthew)
   2005 J.C. 291; 2005 S.C.C.R. 324, HCJ
HM Advocate *v.* Freeman (Anthony Russell) 2005 S.C.C.R. 571; 2005 G.W.D. 36-675,
   HCJ
HM Advocate *v.* Graham (Frederick) 1985 S.L.T. 498, HCJ Appeal . . . .   *Digested*, 85/**3912**:
   Applied, 95/5674: *Considered*, 05/5149
HM Advocate *v.* Greig (David Andrew) 2005 S.C.C.R. 465, Sh Ct (Tayside)
HM Advocate *v.* Headrick (Robert John) (No.1) 2005 S.C.C.R. 787, Sh Ct
HM Advocate *v.* Headrick (Robert John) (No.2) 2005 S.C.C.R. 787, Sh Ct
HM Advocate *v.* Holbein (John) 2005 J.C. 178; 2005 S.L.T. 242; 2005 S.C.C.R. 74;
   2005 G.W.D. 1-9, HCJ . . . .   *Digested*, 05/**5131**
HM Advocate *v.* JT see HM Advocate *v.* T
HM Advocate *v.* Lord Watson of Invergowrie 2005 G.W.D. 29-553, Sh Ct (Grampian)
HM Advocate *v.* M 2005 G.W.D. 31-592, OH
HM Advocate *v.* Macpherson (Thomas Donald) see HM Advocate *v.* Macpherson
   (Thomas Macdonald)
HM Advocate *v.* Macpherson (Thomas Macdonald); *sub nom* HM Advocate *v.*
   Macpherson (Thomas Donald) 2005 S.L.T. 397; 2004 S.C.C.R. 579; 2004
   G.W.D. 34-702, HCJ . . . .   *Digested*, 05/**5657**:
   Considered, 04/3298
HM Advocate *v.* Malley (Sentencing) 2005 G.W.D. 12-207, HCJ
HM Advocate *v.* McGale 2005 S.C.C.R. 473, Sh Ct
HM Advocate *v.* McMillan 2005 G.W.D. 36-678, HCJ
HM Advocate *v.* Murray (Paul Francis) 2004 S.L.T. 1230; 2004 S.C.C.R. 585; 2004
   G.W.D. 34-696, HCJ . . . .   *Digested*, 05/**5651**
HM Advocate *v.* Norris (David Ian) 2005 S.C.C.R. 482, HCJ
HM Advocate *v.* R; *sub nom* R *v.* HM Advocate [2002] UKPC D3; [2004] 1 A.C. 462;
   [2003] 2 W.L.R. 317; 2003 S.C. (P.C.) 21; 2003 S.L.T. 4; 2003 S.C.C.R. 19;
   [2003] U.K.H.R.R. 1; 2002 G.W.D. 39-1280; *Times*, December 6, 2002, PC (Sc);
   reversing 2002 S.L.T. 834; 2002 S.C.C.R. 697; 2002 G.W.D. 19-622, HCJ
   Appeal; affirming 2001 S.L.T. 1366; 2001 S.C.C.R. 915; 2001 G.W.D. 32-1275,
   HCJ . . . .   *Digested*, 03/**5410**:
   Considered, 05/5137: *Not followed*, 04/884
HM Advocate *v.* Roulston (Thomas Samuel) 2005 S.C.C.R. 193, HCJ
HM Advocate *v.* S see HM Advocate *v.* DS
HM Advocate *v.* Southwick 2005 G.W.D. 35-669, HCJ
HM Advocate *v.* T; *sub nom* HM Advocate *v.* JT 2005 J.C. 86; 2005 S.L.T. 43; 2004
   S.C.C.R. 619, HCJ . . . .   *Digested*, 05/**5655**
HM Advocate *v.* Transco Plc 2005 G.W.D. 32-617, HCJ
HM Advocate *v.* Wallace (John) see HM Advocate *v.* Campbell (Robert)
HM Advocate *v.* Weir (Robert) 2005 S.C.C.R. 821; 2005 G.W.D. 38-708, HCJ

HMV Fields Properties Ltd *v.* Bracken Self Selection Fabrics Ltd 1991 S.L.T. 31; 1990
S.C.L.R. 677, IH (1 Div) . . . . *Digested,* 91/**5174**:
Applied, 05/**5470**: *Followed,* 97/**6180**
Holland (James) *v.* HM Advocate [2005] UKPC D1; 2005 S.C. (P.C.) 3; 2005 S.L.T.
563; 2005 S.C.C.R. 417; [2005] H.R.L.R. 25; 18 B.H.R.C. 500; 2005 G.W.D. 17-
305; *Times,* June 1, 2005, PC (Sc) . . . . *Digested,* 05/**5134**:
Previous proceedings, 03/5338, 04/4672
Holland (James) *v.* HM Advocate (No.1) 2003 S.L.T. 1119; 2003 S.C.C.R. 616; 2003
G.W.D. 28-778, HCJ . . . . *Digested,* 03/**5338**:
Overruled in part, 05/5134
Holland (James) *v.* HM Advocate (No.2) 2004 S.L.T. 762; 2004 S.C.C.R. 452; 2004
G.W.D. 21-455, HCJ . . . . *Digested,* 04/**4672**:
Overruled in part, 05/5134
Hone *v.* Page [1980] F.S.R. 500, Ch D . . . . *Digested,* 81/**2791**:
Applied, 89/2923, 90/3580: *Considered,* 90/3584, 05/5026
Hood *v.* Carnegie 2005 G.W.D. 23-430, HCJ
Hope, Petitioner 2004 S.C.L.R. 943; 2004 G.W.D. 18-388, OH . . . . *Digested,* 05/**4940**
Hopkins (John) *v.* HM Advocate see Mills (Arthur) *v.* HM Advocate
Horne *v.* Ralph 2005 G.W.D. 16-280, HCJ
Horne *v.* Whyte 2005 G.W.D. 28-525, OH
Hoseini *v.* Secretary of State for the Home Department 2005 S.L.T. 550; 2005 G.W.D.
15-261, IH (1 Div) . . . . *Digested,* 05/**5437**
Howes *v.* Castle View Services Ltd see Castle View Services Ltd *v.* Howes
Howie *v.* CGU Insurance Plc 2005 S.C.L.R. 1122, OH
Huang *v.* Secretary of State for the Home Department 2005 G.W.D. 30-578, IH (1
Div)
Hughes *v.* Barratt Urban Construction (Scotland) Ltd (Expenses) 2004 S.C. 445;
2004 S.C.L.R. 338; 2004 G.W.D. 8-188, IH (Ex Div); reversing 2003 G.W.D. 40-
1078, OH . . . . *Digested,* 05/**5039**
Hume *v.* HM Advocate 2005 G.W.D. 22-411, HCJ
Humphrey *v.* Royal and Sun Alliance Plc 2005 S.L.T. (Sh Ct) 31, Sh Pr . . . . *Digested,* 05/**5034**
Hunt *v.* British Bakeries Ltd 2005 S.C.L.R. 178; 2004 G.W.D. 35-718, OH
Hussein *v.* Secretary of State for the Home Department 2005 S.C. 509, IH (Ex Div)
Hutchison *v.* Cameron 2005 S.C.L.R. 773, Sh Pr
Hutchison *v.* Poland 2005 S.C.C.R. 220, HCJ
Hynd *v.* Armstrong 2005 G.W.D. 11-182, IH (1 Div)

I&H Brown (Kirkton) Ltd *v.* Hutton 2005 S.L.T. 885; 2005 G.W.D. 27-518, IH (Ex Div) . *Digested,* 05/**5459**
ICL Plastics Ltd, Petitioner; *sub nom* ICL Plastics Ltd *v.* Scottish Ministers 2005 S.L.T.
675; 2005 S.C.L.R. 489; 2005 G.W.D. 21-373, OH . . . . *Digested,* 05/**4958**
Inland Revenue Commissioners *v.* Anchor International Ltd see Anchor International Ltd
v. Inland Revenue Commissioners
Inland Revenue Commissioners *v.* Scottish Provident Institution see Scottish Provident
Institution *v.* Inland Revenue Commissioners
Inland Revenue Commissioners *v.* William Grant & Sons Distillers Ltd see Revenue and
Customs Commissioners *v.* William Grant & Sons Distillers Ltd
Inland Revenue Commissioners, Petitioners see Revenue and Customs Commissioners,
Petitioners
Intranet Services Ltd *v.* Cooper 2005 G.W.D. 25-493, Sh Ct (Grampian)
Inverclyde Council *v.* Dunlop 2005 S.L.T. 967; 2005 G.W.D. 27-536, IH (2 Div) . . . . *Digested,* 05/**5702**
Iqbal *v.* Bott 2005 G.W.D. 24-450, HCJ
Irvine *v.* MacDonald 2005 S.C.C.R. 299; 2005 G.W.D. 20-361, HCJ
Irvine *v.* Royal Burgess Golfing Society of Edinburgh 2004 S.C.L.R. 386; 2004 G.W.D.
8-161, OH . . . . *Digested,* 05/**4967**
ITP SA *v.* Coflexip Stena Offshore Ltd 2005 S.C. 116; 2004 S.L.T. 1285; 2005 S.C.L.R.
254; (2005) 28(2) I.P.D. 28002; *Times,* November 29, 2004, IH (1 Div);
reversing 2003 S.L.T. 1197; 2003 G.W.D. 31-879, OH . . . . *Digested,* 05/**5452**

J, Petitioner see AJ *v.* FJ
J&H Ritchie Ltd *v.* Lloyd Ltd 2005 S.C. 155; 2005 S.L.T. 64; 2005 S.C.L.R. 447; 2005
G.W.D. 2-38, IH (Ex Div) . . . . *Digested,* 05/**5647**
Jackson *v.* Laurieston Homes (Howwood) Ltd 2005 G.W.D. 10-146, OH
Jackson *v.* McDougall 2004 S.L.T. 770; 2004 G.W.D. 21-450, OH . . . . *Digested,* 04/**4551**:
Followed, 05/5058
Jacques *v.* Jacques; *sub nom* Lightbody *v.* Jacques 1997 S.C. (H.L.) 20; 1997 S.L.T.
459; 1997 S.C.L.R. 108; [1997] 1 F.L.R. 748; [1997] Fam. Law 395; *Times,*
December 6, 1996, HL; affirming 1995 S.C. 327; 1995 S.L.T. 963; 1995 S.C.L.R.
585, IH (1 Div) . . . . *Digested,* 97/**6053**:
Considered, 05/5267
James Gibb Property Management *v.* Manders 2005 Hous. L.R. 97, Sh Ct (Lothian)

James Howden & Co Ltd *v.* Taylor Woodrow Property Co Ltd 1998 S.C. 853; 1999
S.L.T. 841; 1998 S.C.L.R. 903; 1998 G.W.D. 27-1386, IH (Ex Div); affirming 1997
G.W.D. 32-1637; *Times*, December 8, 1997, OH . . . .   *Digested*, 98/**5550**:
    Applied, 05/5470

Jarrold (Inspector of Taxes) *v.* John Good & Sons Ltd [1963] 1 W.L.R. 214; [1963] 1 All
E.R. 141; [1962] R.A. 681; [1963] R.V.R. 25; 9 R.R.C. 270; 40 T.C. 681; [1962]
41 A.T.C. 335; [1962] T.R. 371; 107 S.J. 153, CA; affirming [1962] 1 W.L.R. 1101;
[1962] 2 All E.R. 971; [1962] R.A. 273; [1962] R.V.R. 653; 9 R.R.C. 188;
(1962) 41 A.T.C. 170; [1962] T.R. 181; 106 S.J. 688, Ch D . . . .   *Digested*, 63/**1705**:
    Approved, 82/470, 85/2878, 91/3037, 96/5564: *Considered*, 74/1811,
    82/475, 87/3184, 05/5691

JD Wetherspoon Plc *v.* Assessor for Highland and Western Isles Valuation Joint Board
2005 S.L.T. (Lands Tr) 6; 2004 G.W.D. 33-683, Lands Tr (Scot) . . . .   *Digested*, 05/**5630**

Jeromson *v.* Gallacher 2005 G.W.D. 18-330, HCJ

John Doyle Construction Ltd *v.* Laing Management (Scotland) Ltd; *sub nom* Laing
Management (Scotland) Ltd *v.* John Doyle Construction Ltd 2004 S.C. 713;
2004 S.C.L.R. 872; [2004] B.L.R. 295; (2004) 20 Const. L.J. 477; [2004]
C.I.L.L. 2135; 2004 G.W.D. 20-434; *Times*, June 18, 2004, IH (Ex Div); affirming
2004 S.L.T. 678; [2002] B.L.R. 393; [2002] T.C.L.R. 24; 85 Con. L.R. 98;
(2003) 19 Const. L.J. 152; 2002 G.W.D. 14-461; *Times*, July 10, 2002, OH . . . . .   *Digested*, 05/**5071**

John Holland Construction & Engineering Pty Ltd *v.* Kvaerner RJ Brown Pty Ltd 82
B.L.R. 81, Sup Ct (Vic) . . . .   *Digested*, 97/**932**:
    Applied, 05/5071: *Considered*, 97/939, 02/5404

Johnson *v.* Secretary of State for the Home Department 2005 S.L.T. 393; 2004
G.W.D. 39-801, OH . . . .   *Digested*, 05/**5440**

Johnston *v.* Donaldson 2005 G.W.D. 25-478, HCJ

Johnstone *v.* Service 2005 G.W.D. 29-538, HCJ

Johnstone (Gordon) *v.* HM Advocate 2004 S.C.C.R. 727; 2004 G.W.D. 39-790, HCJ . .   *Digested*, 05/**5083**

Jonas *v.* Bamford (Inspector of Taxes) [1973] S.T.C. 519; 51 T.C. 1; [1973] T.R. 225 . . . .   *Digested*, 74/**1866**:
    Applied, 05/4090, 05/4098

Jones *v.* Feather Brooksbank Ltd 2005 G.W.D. 3-27, OH

Jones *v.* George Leslie Ltd 2005 S.L.T. (Sh Ct) 113; 2005 Rep. L.R. 125; 2005 G.W.D.
26-508, Sh Pr. . . . .   *Digested*, 05/**5059**

Jones *v.* MK Leslie Ltd 2004 Rep. L.R. 136; 2004 G.W.D. 16-354, OH . . . .   *Digested*, 05/**5050**

Jones *v.* Wood 2005 S.L.T. 655; 2005 G.W.D. 17-304, IH (Ex Div) . . . .   *Digested*, 05/**5408**

Kain *v.* Aberdeen City Council 2005 G.W.D. 31-587, Sh Ct (Grampian)

Kane *v.* Murray 2005 G.W.D. 18-320, HCJ

Karkhanehcehe *v.* Secretary of State for the Home Department 2005 G.W.D. 10-161,
OH

Karling *v.* Purdue 2004 S.L.T. 1067; 2005 S.C.L.R. 43; [2005] P.N.L.R. 13; 2004
G.W.D. 30-627; *Times*, October 15, 2004, OH . . . .   *Digested*, 04/**4466**

Kaur *v.* Singh see Singh *v.* Singh

Kay *v.* HM Advocate 2005 G.W.D. 14-243, HCJ

Keaney *v.* HM Advocate 2005 G.W.D. 26-506, HCJ

Kearney (Arthur) *v.* HM Advocate; *sub nom* Kearny *v.* HM Advocate; 1 of 2005, PC
(Sc); affirming 2005 S.L.T. 74; 2005 S.C.C.R. 79; 2005 G.W.D. 2-26, HCJ . . . . .   *Digested*, 05/**5135**

Kearny *v.* HM Advocate see Kearney (Arthur) *v.* HM Advocate

Keenan *v.* HM Advocate 2005 G.W.D. 16-278, HCJ

Kelly *v.* HM Advocate 2005 G.W.D. 29-544, HCJ

Kelly *v.* Stoddart Sekers International Plc 2005 Rep. L.R. 12; 2004 G.W.D. 38-783, OH .   *Digested*, 05/**5047**

Kelly (Colin Hugh) *v.* HM Advocate 2005 G.W.D. 40-736, HCJ

Kelman *v.* HM Advocate (Sentencing) 2005 G.W.D. 19-344, HCJ

Kelvin Homes Ltd *v.* Ritchie Brothers (PWC) Ltd 2004 S.C.L.R. 506, Sh Pr . . . .   *Digested*, 05/**5025**

Kelvin Homes Ltd *v.* Ritchie Brothers (PWC) Ltd (Proof before Answer) 2005 Rep. L.R.
128; 2005 G.W.D. 25-466, Sh Pr

Kennedy *v.* Aldington 2005 G.W.D. 14-245, OH

Kennedy *v.* Frame 2005 G.W.D. 8-125, HCJ

Kennedy *v.* Laing 2005 G.W.D. 1-10, HCJ

Kenward *v.* Adams, *Times*, November 29, 1975 . . . .   *Digested*, 75/**3591**:
    Considered, 05/3971: *Not followed*, 97/4733

Kernan *v.* HM Advocate 2005 G.W.D. 40-748, HCJ

Kerr *v.* East Ayrshire Council; *sub nom* Nimmo *v.* East Ayrshire Council 2005 S.L.T. (Sh
Ct) 67; 2005 Hous. L.R. 35; 2005 G.W.D. 18-329, Sh Ct (North Strathclyde) . . .   *Digested*, 05/**5169**

Khairandish *v.* Secretary of State for the Home Department 2003 S.L.T. 1358; 2003
G.W.D. 14-471, OH. . . . .   *Digested*, 04/**4963**:
    Applied, 05/5443: *Considered*, 04/4962

Khan *v.* Aberdeen City Council 2005 G.W.D. 9-138, Sh Ct (Grampian)

Kidd (Stewart Anderson) *v.* HM Advocate 2005 S.L.T. 375; 2005 S.C.C.R. 200, HCJ . .   *Digested*, 05/**5156**

Kilna *v.* De la Salle 2005 S.C.L.R. 154; 2004 G.W.D. 18-393, OH

Kim (Hyung Joon) *v.* HM Advocate 2005 S.L.T. 1119; 2005 G.W.D. 32-612, HCJ

Kimmins *v.* HM Advocate 2005 G.W.D. 23-426, HCJ

King *v.* Dyer 2005 G.W.D. 8-123, HCJ

King v. University Court of the University of St Andrews 2005 G.W.D. 20-363, IH (Ex Div); affirming 2003 G.W.D. 24-693, OH

Kingston Communications (Hull) Plc v. Stargas Nominees Ltd; *sub nom* Stargas Nominees Ltd v. Kingston Communications (Hull) Plc 2005 S.C. 139; 2005 S.L.T. 413; 2005 G.W.D. 10-162, IH (1 Div); affirming 2003 G.W.D. 33-946, OH . — *Digested*, 05/**5469**

Koca v. Secretary of State for the Home Department 2005 S.C. 487; 2005 S.L.T. 838; [2005] I.N.L.R. 506; 2005 G.W.D. 25-488, IH (1 Div); reversing 2002 G.W.D. 38-1263, OH. . . . . — *Digested*, 05/**5433**

Krishna v. Argyll and Bute Council 2005 S.C. 549; 2005 G.W.D. 22-404, IH (Ex Div)

Krotov v. Secretary of State for the Home Department [2004] EWCA Civ 69; [2004] 1 W.L.R. 1825; [2004] I.N.L.R. 304; *Times*, February 26, 2004, CA (Civ Div) . . . — *Digested*, 05/**2178**: *Applied*, 05/**5439**

Kundi v. East Coast Insurance Services Ltd 2005 G.W.D. 30-581, Sh Ct (Grampian)

L v. HM Advocate 2004 S.C.C.R. 713; 2004 G.W.D. 34-691, HCJ . . . . — *Digested*, 05/**746**

Laing Management (Scotland) Ltd v. John Doyle Construction Ltd see John Doyle Construction Ltd v. Laing Management (Scotland) Ltd

Lamarra v. Capital Bank Plc 2005 S.L.T. (Sh Ct) 21; 2004 G.W.D. 40-817, Sh Pr . . . . . . — *Digested*, 05/**5075**

Lanarkshire Valuation Joint Board Assessor v. Clydesdale Bank Plc; *sub nom* Clydesdale Bank Plc v. Lanarkshire Valuation Joint Board Assessor; Marks & Spencer Plc v. Lanarkshire Valuation Joint Board Assessor; Marks & Spencer Plc v. Renfrewshire Valuation Joint Board Assessor 2005 S.L.T. 167; 2005 S.C.L.R. 415; [2005] R.A. 1; 2004 G.W.D. 38-786, LVAC . . . . — *Digested*, 05/**5618**

Land Securities Group Plc v. North Lanarkshire Council 2005 S.L.T. 849; 2005 G.W.D. 26-516, OH . . . . — *Digested*, 05/**5598**

Laneres v. Marks & Spencer Plc; *sub nom* Marks & Spencer Plc v. Laneres 2005 G.W.D. 12-211, IH (Ex Div); reversing EATS/0033/03, EAT (SC)

Langstane Housing Association Ltd v. Morrow 2005 Hous. L.R. 103; 2005 G.W.D. 34-647, Sh Ct (Grampian)

Lappin v. Williams 2005 G.W.D. 16-285, HCJ

Larkin (Thomas Connell) v. HM Advocate 2005 S.L.T. 1087; 2005 S.C.C.R. 302; 2005 G.W.D. 30-565, HCJ

Lassence v. Tierney 41 E.R. 1379; (1849) 1 Mac. & G. 551 . . . . — *Applied*, 47-51/**1173**, 47-51/**9343**, 57/**3726**, 67/**3070**, 68/**3573**, 81/**1996**: *Considered*, 47-51/**10786**, 67/**410**, 67/**4081**, 05/**3972**: *Distinguished*, 60/**2896**, 67/**4097**: *Followed*, 84/**1801**, 85/**3134**

Latona v. Murray 2005 G.W.D. 19-352, HCJ

Lawrie (Jeanie) v. Muir 1950 J.C. 19; 1950 S.L.T. 37; 1949 S.L.T. (Notes) 58, HCJ Appeal . . . . — *Digested*, 47-51/**2075**: *Applied*, 47-51/**2076**, 47-51/**4013**, 01/**6303**, 05/**5088**: *Considered*, 94/**5508**: *Referred to*, 01/**6385**

Lawson v. Hutchison 2005 S.L.T. 872; 2005 G.W.D. 25-479, HCJ . . . . — *Digested*, 05/**5162**

Leggatt v. HM Advocate 2005 G.W.D. 16-273, HCJ

Leith v. HM Advocate 2005 G.W.D. 30-5873, HCJ

Lemon v. Aberdeen City Council 2005 G.W.D. 12-212, Sh Ct (Grampian)

Lennox v. Bishop 2005 S.C.L.R. 1107; 2005 Rep. L.R. 109; 2005 G.W.D. 32-613, OH

Lightbody v. Jacques see Jacques v. Jacques

Lin v. Secretary of State for the Home Department; *sub nom* Quin Shue Lin (also known as Chen Ri Lin), Petitioner 2005 S.L.T. 301; 2004 G.W.D. 39-800, IH (1 Div); reversing 2004 S.C.L.R. 608; 2003 G.W.D. 15-490, OH . . . . — *Digested*, 05/**5436**

Lindsay v. Lindsay 2005 S.L.T. (Sh Ct) 81; 2005 Fam. L.R. 53; 2005 G.W.D. 25-484, Sh Pr . . . . — *Digested*, 05/**5266**

Lindsay (Mark James) v. HM Advocate 2005 J.C. 332; 2005 S.C.C.R. 515, HCJ

Lingfield Park (1991) Ltd v. Shove (Inspector of Taxes) see Shove (Inspector of Taxes) v. Lingfield Park 1991 Ltd

Liquidator of Tay Square Properties Ltd, Noter; *sub nom* McLennan, Noter 2005 S.L.T. 468; 2005 S.C.L.R. 563; 2005 G.W.D. 13-231, OH . . . . — *Digested*, 05/**5449**

Lister v. Hesley Hall Ltd [2001] UKHL 22; [2002] 1 A.C. 215; [2001] 2 W.L.R. 1311; [2001] 2 All E.R. 769; [2001] I.C.R. 665; [2001] I.R.L.R. 472; [2001] Emp. L.R. 819; [2001] 2 F.L.R. 307; [2001] 2 F.C.R. 97; (2001) 3 L.G.L.R. 49; [2001] E.L.R. 422; [2001] Fam. Law 595; (2001) 98(24) L.S.G. 45; (2001) 151 N.L.J. 728; (2001) 145 S.J.L.B. 126; [2001] N.P.C. 89; *Times*, May 10, 2001; *Independent*, June 11, 2001 (C.S); *Daily Telegraph*, May 8, 2001, HL; reversing *Times*, October 13, 1999; *Independent*, November 22, 1999 (C.S.), CA (Civ Div). . — *Digested*, 01/**5359**: *Applied*, 02/**1531**, 03/**432**, 03/**3033**, 03/**3046**, 04/**655**, 05/**4199**, 05/**4200**: *Cited*, 02/**5360**, 02/**2975**: *Considered*, 05/**5573**

Lochridge v. Gilchrist see Lochridge v. Miller

Lochridge v. Miller; *sub nom* Lochridge v. Gilchrist 2002 S.L.T. 906; 2002 S.C.C.R. 628; 2002 G.W.D. 12-361, HCJ Appeal. . . . . — *Digested*, 02/**5493**: *Approved*, 05/**5137**

Lochrie v. HM Advocate (Sentencing) 2005 G.W.D. 11-176, HCJ

Logan v. Scottish Water 2005 S.L.T. 1183; 2005 G.W.D. 38-717, IH (Ex Div)

London & Edinburgh Inns Ltd v. North Ayrshire Licensing Board; *sub nom* London & Edinburgh Inns Ltd, Petitioners 2004 S.L.T. 848; 2005 S.C.L.R. 193; [2004] 29 S.L.L.P. 30; 2004 G.W.D. 15-345, OH .... *Digested,* 04/**5022**

London & Edinburgh Inns Ltd, Petitioners see London & Edinburgh Inns Ltd v. North Ayrshire Licensing Board

Lothian and Borders Police Board v. MacDonald 2004 S.L.T. 1295; 2005 S.C.L.R. 77; 2004 G.W.D. 33-682, OH .... *Digested,* 05/**5605**

Lousada & Co Ltd v. JE Lesser (Properties) Ltd 1990 S.C. 178; 1990 S.L.T. 823, IH (2 Div) .... *Digested,* 90/**5365**: *Applied,* 00/**6467**, 05/**5470**: *Followed,* 93/**5383**

Love v. Dyer 2005 G.W.D. 2-31, HCJ

Lyell v. Sun Microsystems Scotland BV 2005 S.C.L.R. 786; 2005 G.W.D. 11-189, OH

M, Petitioner 2005 S.L.T. 2; 2005 S.C.L.R. 396; 2004 Fam. L.R. 134, OH .... *Digested,* 05/**5248**

M v. Hendron 2005 S.L.T. 1122; 2005 G.W.D. 35-663, OH

M v. HM Advocate 2005 G.W.D. 16-272, HCJ

M v. HM Advocate 2005 G.W.D. 30-571, HCJ

M v. HM Advocate; *sub nom* NFM v. HM Advocate 2005 S.L.T. 1209; 2005 S.C.C.R. 747; 2005 G.W.D. 34-641, HCJ

M v. HM Advocate 2005 G.W.D. 40-750, HCJ

M v. Irvine 2005 Fam. L.R. 113, Sh Pr

M v. McQuaid 2005 G.W.D. 16-277, HCJ

M v. North Lanarkshire Council 2005 Fam. L.R. 22, Sh Ct (South Strathclyde)

M v. Secretary of State for the Home Department; *sub nom* B, Petitioner 2005 S.L.T. 721; 2005 G.W.D. 25-487, OH .... *Digested,* 05/**5441**

Macauley v. Houston 2005 S.L.T. 834; 2005 S.C.C.R. 589; 2005 G.W.D. 25-477, HCJ.   *Digested,* 05/**5656**

MacDonald (or Dalton) v. Turcan Connell (Trustees) Ltd 2005 S.C.L.R. 159; 2004 G.W.D. 20-439, OH

Mack v. Glasgow City Council 2005 Rep. L.R. 136; 2005 Hous. L.R. 66; 2005 G.W.D. 28-523, Sh Pr

Mackay v. MacLeod (Unreported, January 10, 1952), IH (1 Div) .... *Considered,* 05/**5170**

Mackay v. Teale 2005 G.W.D. 16-291, HCJ

Mackay (Alisdair John) v. HM Advocate 2005 J.C. 24; 2004 S.C.C.R. 478; 2004 G.W.D. 26-553, HCJ .... *Digested,* 05/**5085**

Mackenzie v. Teale 2005 G.W.D. 2-30, HCJ

Mackie v. Stott; *sub nom* Mackie v. Ward 2005 J.C. 41; 2004 S.L.T. 1319; 2004 S.C.C.R. 545; 2004 G.W.D. 37-762, HCJ .... *Digested,* 05/**5653**

Mackie v. Ward see Mackie v. Stott

Mackintosh (or Petrie) v. North Milk Cooperative Ltd 2005 S.C.L.R. 841, OH

MacLean v. Bott see Bott v. MacLean

MacLean v. HM Advocate 2005 S.C.C.R. 586, HCJ Appeal

MacLeod v. Griffiths see Chalmers v. Griffiths

Magell Ltd v. Dumfries and Galloway Regional Assessor (No.1) 2005 S.L.T. 453; [2004] R.A. 188; 2004 G.W.D. 27-581, LVAC...................... *Digested,* 04/**3186**

Magell Ltd v. Dumfries and Galloway Regional Assessor (No.2) 2005 S.L.T. 726; 2005 S.C.L.R. 1118; [2005] R.A. 306; 2005 G.W.D. 25-498, LVAC .... *Digested,* 05/**5620**

Mahechani v. Scottish Ambulance Service 2005 G.W.D. 11-168, IH (Ex Div)

Mahmood v. Secretary of State for the Home Department 2005 G.W.D. 19-348, OH

Malik v. Ali 2004 S.L.T. 1280; 2004 G.W.D. 26-551, IH (1 Div) .... *Digested,* 05/**5412**

Manners v. Strong's Judicial Factor (1902) 4 F. (Ct. of Sess.) 829................ *Applied,* 05/**4940**

MAR v. Dyer 2005 S.C.C.R. 818, HCJ

Marks & Spencer Plc v. Lanarkshire Valuation Joint Board Assessor see Lanarkshire Valuation Joint Board Assessor v. Clydesdale Bank Plc

Marks & Spencer Plc v. Laneres see Laneres v. Marks & Spencer Plc

Marks & Spencer Plc v. Renfrewshire Valuation Joint Board Assessor see Lanarkshire Valuation Joint Board Assessor v. Clydesdale Bank Plc

Marnoch (Douglas John) v. HM Advocate see Henderson (Alexander) v. HM Advocate

Marr v. Hutchison 2005 G.W.D. 10-166, HCJ

Mars UK Ltd v. Small (Inspector of Taxes); *sub nom* Small (Inspector of Taxes) v. Mars UK Ltd; William Grant & Sons Distillers Ltd v. Inland Revenue Commissioners [2005] EWHC 553; [2005] S.T.C. 958; [2005] B.T.C. 236; [2005] S.T.I. 833; *Times,* May 11, 2005, Ch D; reversing [2004] S.T.C. (S.C.D.) 253; [2004] S.T.I. 1282, Sp Comm .... *Digested,* 05/**4022**: *Overruled,* 05/**5692**

Marshall v. North Ayrshire Council 2005 G.W.D. 29-559, Sh Ct (North Strathclyde)

Martin v. Bott see Martin v. Howdle

Martin v. Had-Fab Ltd 2004 S.L.T. 1192; 2005 S.C.C.R. 129; 2004 G.W.D. 33-674, OH

Martin v. Howdle; *sub nom* Martin v. Bott 2005 S.L.T. 730; 2005 S.C.C.R. 554; 2005 G.W.D. 20-357, HCJ .... *Digested,* 05/**5108**

Martin v. McGuiness; *sub nom* Martin v. McInnes 2003 S.L.T. 1424; 2003 S.C.L.R. 548; 2003 Rep. L.R. 106; 2003 G.W.D. 13-385, OH .... *Digested,* 03/**5271**: *Applied,* 05/**5219**

Martin v. McInnes see Martin v. McGuiness

Martin v. Miller 2005 G.W.D. 16-295, HCJ
Marvin v. Spiers 2005 G.W.D. 18-331, HCJ
Matheson v. Mazars Solutions Ltd 2005 S.C. 420; 2005 S.L.T. 457; 2005 G.W.D. 14-
246, IH (Ex Div); affirming EATS/0048/03, EAT (SC) . . . . *Digested*, 05/**5216**
Mathieson v. HM Advocate 2005 G.W.D. 29-551, HCJ
Matthew v. Aitken; *sub nom* Matthew v. Procurator Fiscal, Wick 2004 S.C.C.R. 515;
[2005] Eu. L.R. 48, HCJ . . . . *Digested*, 05/**5284**
Matthew v. Procurator Fiscal, Wick see Matthew v. Aitken
Matthews v. Glasgow City Council 2004 Hous. L.R. 136; 2004 G.W.D. 30-618, Sh Ct
(Glasgow) . . . . *Digested*, 05/**5402**
Maxwell v. Fraser 2005 G.W.D. 7-95, HCJ
May v. Jeeves Parcels Ltd (t/a ANC (Aberdeen)) 2005 S.C.L.R. 1099; 2005 Rep. L.R.
131, OH
Mayer (John) v. HM Advocate; *sub nom* Mayer, Petitioner 2005 J.C. 121; 2004 S.L.T.
1251; 2004 S.C.C.R. 734; 2004 G.W.D. 37-761, HCJ . . . . *Digested*, 05/**5122**:
Previous proceedings, 03/5361
McAdam v. Boxpak Ltd TNS, IH (Ex Div); affirming 2005 S.L.T. (Sh Ct) 47; 2005
G.W.D. 9-127, Sh Pr . . . . *Digested*, 05/**4973**
McAdam v. Chick 2005 G.W.D. 29-560, OH
McAdam v. Urquhart; McAlpine v. Urquhart; Bochell v. Urquhart; McEwan v. Urquhart
2005 J.C. 28; 2004 S.L.T. 790; 2004 S.C.C.R. 506; 2004 G.W.D. 23-501, HCJ . *Digested*, 04/**4629**
McAlpine v. Urquhart see McAdam v. Urquhart
McArthur v. Lord Advocate 2005 G.W.D. 40-733, OH
McAuley v. Dyer 2005 G.W.D. 24-445, HCJ
McAuslane v. Highland Council 2004 Hous. L.R. 30; 2004 G.W.D. 12-270, Lands Tr
(Scot) . . . . *Digested*, 05/**5423**
McCall v. Dumfries and Galloway Rugby Football Club 1999 S.C.L.R. 977, Sh Ct . . . . . *Digested*, 00/**5896**:
Disapproved, 05/5576
McCall v. Scottish Ministers 2005 G.W.D. 39-720, OH
McCaskill v. McCaskill 2004 Fam. L.R. 123, Sh Pr . . . . *Digested*, 05/**5267**
McConway v. Dyer 2005 G.W.D. 30-567, HCJ
McCrae (David) v. HM Advocate 2005 J.C. 182; 2005 G.W.D. 23-416, HCJ
McCreaddie (Derek Alexander) v. HM Advocate (Appeal against Sentence) 2002 S.L.T.
1311; 2002 S.C.C.R. 912, HCJ Appeal. . . . . *Digested*, 02/**6079**:
Overruled, 05/5652
McCulloch v. Murray 2005 S.C.C.R. 775; 2005 G.W.D. 38-706, HCJ
McDonald v. Kwok 1999 S.L.T. 593; 1999 G.W.D. 3-125, OH . . . . *Digested*, 99/**5665**:
Considered, 04/4550, 04/4589: *Followed*, 05/5058: *Overruled*, 05/5055
McEwan v. Urquhart see McAdam v. Urquhart
McFarlane v. Scottish Borders Council 2005 S.L.T. 359; 2005 G.W.D. 8-120, IH (Ex
Div); reversing 2004 G.W.D. 1-20, OH. . . . . *Digested*, 05/**5405**
McFarlane v. Thain TNS, IH (2 Div); affirming 2005 S.L.T. 221; 2005 G.W.D. 7-89, OH . *Digested*, 05/**5054**
McGee v. South Lanarkshire Council [2005] R.V.R. 218; 2005 Hous. L.R. 41, Lands Tr
(Scot) . . . . *Digested*, 05/**5596**
McGiffen v. Williams 2005 G.W.D. 24-454, HCJ
McGilviray v. John Meiklem Drainage Contractors Ltd 2005 G.W.D. 2-33, OH
McGinty v. HM Advocate 2005 G.W.D. 11-171, HCJ
McGowan v. Scottish Water [2005] I.R.L.R. 167, EAT (SC) . . . . *Digested*, 05/**5219**
McGowan (Steven Henry) v. HM Advocate; O'Donnell (Kevin Barry) v. HM Advocate
2005 J.C. 327; 2005 S.C.C.R. 499, HCJ
McGradie v. Spiers 2005 G.W.D. 23-422, HCJ
McGraw (Steven Martin) v. HM Advocate 2004 S.C.C.R. 637, HCJ. . . . . *Digested*, 05/**5098**
McGruther, Noter see McGruther v. James Scott Ltd
McGruther v. Blin see McGruther v. James Scott Ltd
McGruther v. James Scott Ltd; *sub nom* McGruther v. Blin; McGruther, Noter 2004
S.C. 514; 2005 S.L.T. 264; 2004 S.C.L.R. 328, IH (Ex Div); affirming 2003 S.C.
495; 2004 S.L.T. 88; 2003 S.C.L.R. 144; 2002 G.W.D. 39-1309, OH . . . . *Digested*, 05/**5448**
McGruther v. Walton 2004 S.C.L.R. 319, Sh Pr . . . . *Digested*, 05/**5444**
McGuire v. Morris & Spottiswood (t/a Tarr (Roofing)) 2005 G.W.D. 23-415, OH
McGuire (Robert) v. HM Advocate see Mills (Arthur) v. HM Advocate
McIlravie v. Wallace; *sub nom* Superintendent of Fife Constabulary's Application, Re
2005 S.L.T. (Sh Ct) 2; 2005 G.W.D. 4-48, Sh Ct (Tayside) . . . . *Digested*, 05/**5415**
McIlvaney v. HM Advocate 2005 G.W.D. 29-552, HCJ
McInnes v. HM Advocate 2005 G.W.D. 37-686, HCJ
McInnes v. Onslow Fane [1978] 1 W.L.R. 1520; [1978] 3 All E.R. 211; 122 S.J. 844,
Ch D . . . . *Digested*, 78/**21**:
Applied, 82/1906, 83/3147, 05/4967: *Considered*, 86/9, 86/2054, 94/43
McIntosh v. British Railways Board (No.1) 1990 S.C. 338; 1990 S.L.T. 637, IH (1 Div) . . *Digested*, 90/**5624**:
Considered, 05/5041: *Referred to*, 91/5001
McIntyre (Colin McLean) v. HM Advocate 2005 S.L.T. 757; 2005 S.C.C.R. 380; 2005
G.W.D. 25-470, HCJ . . . . *Digested*, 05/**5080**
McKay v. Lloyds TSB Mortgages Ltd 2005 S.C.L.R. 547; 2004 G.W.D. 37-757, OH
McKellar v. Aberdeen City Council (No.2) see McKeller v. Aberdeen City Council
(No.2)

McKeller v. Aberdeen City Council (No.2); *sub nom* McKellar v. Aberdeen City Council
(No.2) 2005 S.C. 186; 2005 S.L.T. 95; 2005 G.W.D. 2-21, OH . . . .   *Digested*, 05/**4960**
McKenna v. HM Advocate 2005 G.W.D. 27-527, HCJ
McKenzie v. HM Advocate 2005 G.W.D. 30-576, HCJ
McKenzie v. Scottish Ministers 2004 S.L.T. 1236; 2004 G.W.D. 26-563, OH . . . .   *Digested*, 05/**4964**
McKidd v. Manson (1882) 9 R. 790, IH (1 Div) . . . .   *Applied*, 05/5055:
Considered, 90/5131: *Followed*, 96/7343
McLaren v. North Ayrshire Council 2005 Hous. L.R. 9, LandsTr (Scot)
McLaren Murdoch & Hamilton Ltd v. Abercromby Motor Group Ltd 2003 S.C.L.R. 323;
100 Con. L.R. 63; 2002 G.W.D. 38-1242, OH . . . .   *Digested*, 03/**5323**
McLarnon v. Griffiths see McLarnon v. McLeod
McLarnon v. McLeod; *sub nom* McLarnon v. Griffiths 2004 S.C.C.R. 397; 2004
G.W.D. 22-482, HCJ . . . .   *Digested*, 05/**5133**
McLaughlin v. McQuade see McLaughlin v. McQuaid
McLaughlin v. McQuaid; *sub nom* McLaughlin v. McQuade 2005 S.L.T. 972; 2005
S.C.C.R. 630; 2005 G.W.D. 25-476, HCJ . . . .   *Digested*, 05/**5654**
McLean v. Carnegie 2005 S.C.C.R. 549; 2005 G.W.D. 33-633, HCJ
McLean v. William Denny & Bros Ltd 2004 S.C. 656; 2004 S.L.T. 1099; 2004 Rep.
L.R. 82; 2004 G.W.D. 14-306, IH (1 Div); affirming 2004 S.L.T. 422; 2004
S.C.L.R. 675; 2004 Rep. L.R. 2; 2003 G.W.D. 39-1058, OH . . . .   *Digested*, 04/**5074**:
Applied, 04/5075: *Considered*, 05/5593
McLennan, Noter see Liquidator of Tay Square Properties Ltd, Noter
McLeod v. Millar; McLeod v. Tierney 2004 S.C.C.R. 419, HCJ . . . .   *Digested*, 05/**5148**
McLeod (Alistair), Petitioner see McLeod (Alistair) v. HM Advocate (No.2)
McLeod v. Tierney see McLeod v. Millar
McLeod (Alistair) v. HM Advocate (No.2); *sub nom* McLeod (Alistair), Petitioner 1998
J.C. 67; 1998 S.L.T. 233; 1998 S.C.C.R. 77; 1998 G.W.D. 4-161, HCJ . . . .   *Digested*, 98/**5607**:
Applied, 01/6347: *Considered*, 01/6314, 02/5518, 04/4671, 05/5136
McLeod (Peter) v. HM Advocate 2005 S.C.C.R. 736; 2005 G.W.D. 39-723, HCJ
McMillan v. Currie 2005 G.W.D. 2-27, HCJ
McMillan v. HM Advocate 2005 G.W.D. 29-546, HCJ
McMurray (Peter) v. HM Advocate (No.2) see Flynn (Patrick Anthony) v. HM
Advocate (No.2)
McNairn (George Douglas) v. HM Advocate 2005 S.L.T. 1071; 2005 S.C.C.R. 741; 2005
G.W.D. 33-628, HCJ
McNaughton v. HM Advocate 2005 G.W.D. 27-525, HCJ
McPherson v. HM Advocate 2005 G.W.D. 38-709, HCJ
McSorley (Timothy), Petitioner 2005 S.C.C.R. 508, HCJ Appeal
McTear v. Imperial Tobacco Ltd; *sub nom* McTear's Executrix v. Imperial Tobacco Ltd
2005 2 S.C. 1; 2005 G.W.D. 20-365; *Times*, June 14, 2005, OH
McTear's Executrix v. Imperial Tobacco Ltd see McTear v. Imperial Tobacco Ltd
Meek (Peter Mitchell) v. HM Advocate (No.2) see Flynn (Patrick Anthony) v. HM
Advocate (No.2)
Melville Dundas Ltd (In Receivership) v. George Wimpey UK Ltd TNS, IH (Ex Div);
reversing 2005 S.L.T. 24; 2005 S.C.L.R. 116, OH. . . . .   *Digested*, 05/**5070**
Meyl (Vadim Izrailevich) v. HM Advocate 2005 S.C.C.R. 338, HCJ
Middleton v. Chief Constable of Grampian 2005 G.W.D. 5-59, OH
Midlothian Council v. W 2005 S.L.T. (Sh Ct) 146; 2005 Fam. L.R. 104; 2005 G.W.D.
36-683, Sh Ct (Lothian)
Mighell v. Reading see White (Brian) v. White (Shane)
Millar v. Inland Revenue Commissioners; *sub nom* Millar v. Revenue and Customs
Commissioners 2005 S.L.T. 1074; 2005 G.W.D. 32-615, IH (Ex Div); reversing
EATS/0022/04, EAT (SC)
Millar v. Revenue and Customs Commissioners see Millar v. Inland Revenue
Commissioners
Millar v. Watt 2005 S.C.L.R. 143; 2004 G.W.D. 25-530, OH
Miller v. Bell 2004 S.C.C.R. 534; 2004 G.W.D. 26-564, HCJ . . . .   *Digested*, 05/**5102**
Miller v. Wood 2005 G.W.D. 15-259, HCJ
Mills (Arthur) v. HM Advocate; Hopkins (John) v. HM Advocate; McGuire (Robert) v.
HM Advocate 2005 S.C.C.R. 1, HCJ . . . .   *Digested*, 05/**5118**
Milne v. Normand 1994 S.L.T. 760; 1993 S.C.C.R. 1058, HCJ Appeal . . . .   *Digested*, 94/**5601**:
Distinguished, 05/5148
Mirror Group Newspapers Plc v. Maxwell see Bishopsgate Investment Management Ltd
(In Provisional Liquidation) v. Maxwell
Mitchell v. Edinburgh City Council 2004 Hous. L.R. 59; 2004 G.W.D. 26-557, Sh Ct
(Lothian) . . . .   *Digested*, 05/**5426**
Mitchell v. Glasgow City Council 2005 S.L.T. 1100; 2005 S.C.L.R. 920; 2005 Rep.
L.R. 101; 2005 G.W.D. 34-645, OH
Mitchell v. Reith 2004 S.C.C.R. 433, HCJ . . . .   *Digested*, 05/**5147**
Mitchells & Butlers Retail Ltd v. Aberdeen City Licensing Board 2005 S.L.T. 13; [2005]
30 S.L.L.P. 24, OH . . . .   *Digested*, 05/**4965**
MM v. HM Advocate see Moir (Mitchell John) v. HM Advocate
Moggach v. Milne 2005 G.W.D. 8-107, Sh Pr

Mohammadi v. Advocate General for Scotland; *sub nom* Mohammadi v. Secretary of
State for the Home Department 2004 S.C.L.R. 612; 2003 G.W.D. 15-491, OH . .   *Digested,* 05/**5438**
Mohammadi v. Secretary of State for the Home Department see Mohammadi v.
Advocate General for Scotland
Mohammed v. HM Advocate 2005 G.W.D. 21-384, HCJ
Moir (Mitchell John) v. HM Advocate; *sub nom* MM v. HM Advocate 2005 J.C. 102;
2004 S.C.C.R. 658, HCJ . . . .   *Digested,* 05/**5084**
Moir (Mitchell John) v. HM Advocate (Leave to Appeal) [2004] UKPC D2; 2005 S.C.
(P.C.) 1; 2005 S.L.T. 981, PC (Sc) . . . .   *Digested,* 05/**5127**
Moncrieff v. Jamieson 2005 S.C. 281; 2005 S.L.T. 225; 2005 S.C.L.R. 463; 2005
G.W.D. 5-66, IH (Ex Div); affirming 2004 S.C.L.R. 135, Sh Ct (Grampian) . . . . .   *Digested,* 05/**5409**
Montgomerie v. Glasgow Prestwick International Airport Ltd 2004 Rep. L.R. 117, OH . .   *Digested,* 05/**5634**
Moore v. Alexander Stephen & Sons Ltd 1954 S.C. 331; 1954 S.L.T. 289, IH (2 Div) . . .   *Digested,* 54/**4244**:
   Approved, 56/13000: *Considered,* 05/5031
Moore v. East Renfrewshire Council 2005 G.W.D. 30-584, OH
Moore (Anthony James) v. HM Advocate see Salmon (Donald) v. HM Advocate
Moorov v. Lord Advocate see Moorov (Samuel) v. HM Advocate
Moorov (Samuel) v. HM Advocate; *sub nom* Moorov v. Lord Advocate 1930 J.C. 68;
1930 S.L.T. 596, HCJ Appeal; reversing in part(Unreported, May 7, 1930), HCJ .   *Applied,* 52/3860,
   58/3658, 61/9728, 71/2781, 83/4097, 88/3892, 92/5375, 92/5376, 94/5523,
   04/4626: *Approved,* 73/524: *Cited,* 03/5346: *Considered,* 70/3068, 71/2781,
   79/469, 85/3852, 94/5524, 95/5616, 95/5617, 95/5618, 96/6813:
   Distinguished, 05/5151: *Followed,* 47-51/3808: *Not applied,* 63/3761,
   83/4096, 93/4895: *Referred to,* 03/5401
Morris v. Fife Council 2005 S.C. 72; 2004 S.L.T. 1139; 2005 S.C.L.R. 182; 2004
G.W.D. 33-672, IH (Ex Div); affirming 2003 S.L.T. 926; 2003 G.W.D. 24-684,
OH . . . .   *Digested,* 04/**4571**
Morris v. Morris 2005 Fam. L.R. 68, OH
Morris v. Williams 2005 G.W.D. 19-350, HCJ
Morrison v. Donaldson 2005 G.W.D. 23-423, HCJ
Morrison v. Gardiner 2005 G.W.D. 38-716, OH
Morrison v. Leckie 2005 G.W.D. 40-734, Sh Ct (North Strathclyde)
Morrison-Low v. Paterson's Executors 2005 S.L.T. (Land Ct) 2; 2005 G.W.D. 16-266,
Land Ct . . . .   *Digested,* 05/**5460**
Morrow v. HM Advocate 2005 G.W.D. 21-387, HCJ
Morton v. West Lothian Council 2005 G.W.D. 35-667, OH
Mowat v. HM Advocate 2005 G.W.D. 29-550, HCJ
Mowlem Plc (t/a Mowlem Marine) v. Scrabster Harbour Trust see Scrabster Harbour
Trust v. Mowlem Plc (t/a Mowlem Marine)
Mowlem Technical Services (Scotland) Ltd v. King 2005 S.C. 514, IH (Ex Div)
Moyarget Developments Ltd v. Mathis 2005 G.W.D. 33-621, OH
MRS Distribution Ltd v. DS Smith (UK) Ltd 2004 S.L.T. 631; 2005 S.C.L.R. 208; 2004
G.W.D. 18-391, OH . . . .   *Digested,* 04/**4615**
MT Hojgaard A/S v. Forth Estuary Transport Authority 2005 S.L.T. 187; 2005 S.C.L.R.
552, OH . . . .   *Digested,* 05/**5073**
Muir v. North Ayrshire Council 2005 S.L.T. 963; 2005 G.W.D. 30-582, OH . . . .   *Digested,* 05/**5574**
Muldoon, Applicant 2005 S.L.T. (Sh Ct) 52; 2005 S.C.L.R. 611; 2005 G.W.D. 5-57, Sh Ct
(Glasgow) . . . .   *Digested,* 05/**5676**
Mullan v. Murray 2005 G.W.D. 16-296, HCJ
Murdoch v. Moray Council 2005 Rep. L.R. 83, Sh Pr
Murphy v. Gallacher 2005 G.W.D. 15-257, HCJ
Murphy v. General Teaching Council for Scotland 1997 S.C. 172; 1997 S.L.T. 1152; 1997
S.C.L.R. 362, IH (2 Div) . . . .   *Digested,* 97/**6008**:
   Applied, 05/4967: *Considered,* 05/4962
Murphy v. HM Advocate 2005 G.W.D. 29-545, HCJ
Murray v. Ralph 2005 G.W.D. 24-457, HCJ
Murray's Executrix v. Greenock Dockyard Co Ltd 2004 S.L.T. 1104; 2004 Rep. L.R. 86;
2004 G.W.D. 14-305, IH (1 Div); reversing 2004 S.L.T. 346; 2004 S.C.L.R. 647;
2003 Rep. L.R. 115; 2003 G.W.D. 20-608, OH . . . .   *Digested,* 04/**5075**:
   Considered, 05/5166
Musaj v. Secretary of State for the Home Department 2004 S.L.T. 623; 2004 G.W.D.
18-406, OH . . . .   *Digested,* 04/**4962**:
   Applied, 05/5443
Musselburgh and Fisherrow Cooperative Society Ltd v. Mowlem Scotland Ltd 2004
S.C.L.R. 412; 2004 G.W.D. 9-219, OH. . . . .   *Digested,* 05/**5609**

Napier v. Scotsman Publications Ltd 2005 Rep. L.R. 2; 2004 G.W.D. 21-469, OH . . . . .   *Digested,* 05/**5404**
Napier v. Scottish Ministers 2005 S.C. 307; 2005 S.L.T. 379; [2005] U.K.H.R.R. 268;
2005 G.W.D. 9-136, IH (1 Div); affirming 2005 S.C. 229; 2004 S.L.T. 555; 2004
S.C.L.R. 558; [2004] U.K.H.R.R. 881; 2004 G.W.D. 14-316; *Times,* May 13,
2004, OH . . . .   *Digested,* 05/**5430**:
   Considered, 05/4964: *Previous proceedings,* 01/6834

Narden Services Ltd v. Inverness Retail & Business Park Ltd 2005 S.C.L.R. 704; 2005 G.W.D. 33-620, OH
Neil v. East Ayrshire Council 2005 Rep. L.R. 18; 2005 G.W.D. 4-53, OH
Neill v. Frame 2005 G.W.D. 3-25, HCJ
Nelson v. Donaldson 2005 G.W.D. 19-346, HCJ
Nelson v. Strathclyde Passenger Transport Executive 2005 G.W.D. 38-700, OH
New v. HM Advocate 2005 G.W.D. 40-740, HCJ
Newman Shopfitters Ltd v. MJ Gleeson Group Plc 2003 S.L.T. (Sh Ct) 83; 2003 S.C.L.R. 235; 2003 G.W.D. 10-271, Sh Pr . . . . *Digested*, 03/**5291**: *Applied*, 05/5036
Next Plc v. Assessor for Highland and Western Isles Valuation Joint Board 2005 S.L.T. (Lands Tr) 7; 2003 G.W.D. 29-827, Lands Tr (Scot) . . . . *Digested*, 05/**5623**
NFM v. HM Advocate see M v. HM Advocate
Nicol (John Gary) v. HM Advocate (No.2) see Flynn (Patrick Anthony) v. HM Advocate (No.2)
Nimmo v. Bank of Scotland 2005 S.L.T. (Sh Ct) 133; 2005 G.W.D. 28-518, Sh Ct (Tayside)
Nimmo v. East Ayrshire Council see Kerr v. East Ayrshire Council
Nolan (James) v. HM Advocate 2005 S.L.T. 474; 2005 S.C.C.R. 67; 2005 G.W.D. 5-61, HCJ . . . . *Digested*, 05/**5094**
North Ayrshire Council v. JM 2004 S.C.L.R. 956, Sh Ct (North Strathclyde) . . . . *Digested*, 05/**5530**
North British Trust Hotels Ltd v. Assessor for the Highland and Western Isles Area; *sub nom* North British Trust Hotels Ltd v. Highland and Western Isles Area Assessor 2005 S.L.T. 419; [2004] R.V.R. 300; 2004 G.W.D. 32-663, LVAC . . . . *Digested*, 05/**5613**
North British Trust Hotels Ltd v. Highland and Western Isles Area Assessor see North British Trust Hotels Ltd v. Assessor for the Highland and Western Isles Area
North Lanarkshire Council v. Kenmure 2004 Hous. L.R. 50; 2004 G.W.D. 20-433, Sh Pr . . . . *Digested*, 05/**5475**
North Lanarkshire Council v. Sexton [2004] R.V.R. 301; 2004 G.W.D. 27-571, Sh Pr . . . *Digested*, 05/**5030**
Northern Rock Plc v. Goodwin 2004 Hous. L.R. 88, Sh Ct (South Strathclyde) . . . . . . *Digested*, 05/**5035**: *Applied*, 05/5052
Numast v. P&O Scottish Ferries [2005] I.C.R. 1270, EAT (SC) . . . . *Digested*, 05/**5215**
NVC Constructional Services Ltd v. Teal 2005 G.W.D. 12-199, Sh Ct (Grampian)

O'Brien v. HM Advocate 2005 G.W.D. 40-743, HCJ
O'Brien v. Pacitti Jones (A Firm) see Pacitti Jones (A Firm) v. O'Brien
O'Connor v. Bullimore Underwriting Agency Ltd (t/a Leisure Consortium at Lloyd's) 2004 S.C.L.R. 346, OH . . . . *Digested*, 05/**5450**
O'Connor v. Bullimore Underwriting Agency Ltd (t/a Leisure Consortium at Lloyd's) (Expenses) 2005 S.C.L.R. 1111, OH
O'Dalaigh (aka Daly) v. Frame see Robertson v. Frame
O'Donnell (Kevin Barry) v. HM Advocate see McGowan (Steven Henry) v. HM Advocate
O'Neil v. HM Advocate 2005 G.W.D. 29-547, HCJ
O'Neil (David William) v. HM Advocate (No.1) see Du Plooy (Devonne) v. HM Advocate (No.1)
O'Rourke (James Bernard) v. HM Advocate see Gray (William) v. HM Advocate
Office of Fair Trading v. MB Designs (Scotland) Ltd 2005 S.L.T. 691; 2005 S.C.L.R. 894; 2005 G.W.D. 22-393; *Times*, August 11, 2005, OH . . . . *Digested*, 05/**5074**
Ogg v. Perth & Kinross Council 2005 Hous. L.R. 18, Lands Tr (Scot)
Ogg (Peter Allan) v. HM Advocate 1938 J.C. 152; 1938 S.L.T. 513, HCJ Appeal . . . . *Applied*, 03/5346: *Considered*, 92/5374, 96/6813, 05/5151
Ord v. HM Advocate 2005 G.W.D. 10-150, HCJ
Orr v. Metcalfe 1973 S.C. 57; 1973 S.L.T. 133; 1973 S.L.T. (Notes) 30, IH (1 Div) . . . . *Digested*, 78/**712**: *Considered*, 05/5039
Owens v. Donaldson 2005 G.W.D. 24-437, HCJ

P v. HM Advocate see Sneddon (Graham) v. HM Advocate
P v. HM Advocate; *sub nom* RWP v. HM Advocate 2005 S.C.C.R. 764, HCJ
P v. Williams; *sub nom* BP v. Williams 2005 S.L.T. 508; 2005 S.C.C.R. 234; 2005 G.W.D. 13-223, HCJ . . . . *Digested*, 05/**5090**
Pacitti v. Frame; *sub nom* Vettesse v. Frame 2005 S.C.C.R. 487, HCJ
Pacitti Jones (A Firm) v. O'Brien; *sub nom* O'Brien v. Pacitti Jones (A Firm) 2005 S.L.T. 793; [2005] I.R.L.R. 888; 2005 G.W.D. 25-483, IH (Ex Div); affirming EATS/ 0025/04, EAT (SC) . . . . *Digested*, 05/**5214**
Parkes v. McGregor 2005 G.W.D. 38-701, OH
Paterson v. HM Advocate 2005 G.W.D. 11-173, HCJ
Paterson v. Paterson 2005 S.L.T. (Sh Ct) 148; 2005 G.W.D. 36-673, Sh Pr
Paterson (Robert Kirk) v. Webster 2005 S.C.C.R. 492, HCJ
Patrick v. Williams 2005 G.W.D. 24-456, HCJ
Patterson v. HM Advocate 2005 G.W.D. 20-358, HCJ

Patterson v. Lanarkshire Acute Hospitals NHS Trust 2004 S.C.L.R. 1062; 2004 G.W.D.
2-35, OH .... *Digested*, 05/**5587**
Patterson v. Sommerville 2005 Rep. L.R. 32, OH
Peden (Marie) v. HM Advocate 2003 S.L.T. 1047; 2003 S.C.C.R. 605; 2003 G.W.D.
28-783, HCJ. .... *Digested*, 03/**5418**:
                                                 Considered, 05/5154
Percy v. Church of Scotland Board of National Mission [2005] UKHL 73; *Times*,
December 16, 2005; *Independent*, December 20, 2005, HL; reversing 2001 S.C.
757; 2001 S.L.T. 497; 2001 G.W.D. 12-434, IH (1 Div). .... *Digested*, 02/**5576**
Perth and Kinross Council v. Scott 2005 S.L.T. 89; 2005 S.C.L.R. 297; 2004 G.W.D.
37-766, OH .... *Digested*, 05/**5641**
Peterson's Crane Hire v. FE Beaumont Ltd 2005 G.W.D. 19-336, OH
Phillips v. Dumfries and Galloway Acute and Maternity Hospitals NHS Trust 2005
S.C.L.R. 1115, IH (Ex Div)
Phipps, Petitioner (No.2); *sub nom* Phipps v. Royal College of Surgeons of Edinburgh
(No.2) 2005 S.C.L.R. 886, OH
PIK Facilities Ltd v. Shell UK Ltd 2005 S.C.L.R. 958, OH
PIK Facilities Ltd v. Watson's Ayr Park Ltd 2005 S.L.T. 1041; 2005 G.W.D. 31-591, OH .. *Digested*, 05/**5045**
Pineview Housing Cooperative Ltd v. Smith 2005 Hous. L.R. 99, Sh Ct (Glasgow)
Pioneer Aggregates (UK) Ltd v. Secretary of State for the Environment [1985] A.C. 132;
[1984] 3 W.L.R. 32; [1984] 2 All E.R. 358; 82 L.G.R. 488; (1984) 48 P. &
C.R. 95; (1984) 272 E.G. 425; [1984] J.P.L. 651; (1984) 81 L.S.G. 2148; (1984)
128 S.J. 416, HL; affirming 82 L.G.R. 112; (1983) 46 P. & C.R. 313; (1983) 267
E.G. 941; [1983] J.P.L. 733, CA (Civ Div); affirming (1983) 46 P. & C.R. 113;
[1982] J.P.L. 371, QBD .... *Digested*, 84/**3465**:
                Applied, 85/3476, 86/3348, 92/4357, 00/4515, 05/3269:
         Approved, 99/4255: *Considered*, 89/3569, 90/3917, 90/4435, 91/3457,
         92/4272, 92/4373, 93/3956, 95/4770, 98/6136: *Distinguished*, 86/3337,
                           87/3710: *Followed*, 88/3517, 89/3553
Pirie v. Clydesdale Bank Plc 2005 G.W.D. 13-226, OH
Porter v. Oakbank School 2004 S.C. 603; 2004 G.W.D. 10-230, IH (Ex Div); reversing
EATS/0042/02, EAT (SC)... *Digested*, 05/**5218**
Porter (Thomas) v. HM Advocate 2005 J.C. 141; 2005 S.L.T. 271; 2005 S.C.C.R. 13;
2004 G.W.D. 40-822, HCJ .... *Digested*, 05/**5079**
Pratt v. Scottish Ministers 2005 G.W.D. 14-237, OH
Prescription Pricing Authority v. Ferguson 2005 S.C. 171; 2005 S.L.T. 63; 2005 G.W.D.
1-11, IH (1 Div); affirming EATS/0032/03, EAT (SC) .... *Digested*, 05/**5213**
Prior v. HM Advocate 2005 G.W.D. 21-383, HCJ
Procurator Fiscal, Dunoon v. Dominick see Webster v. Dominick
Profile Software Ltd v. Becogent Ltd [2005] E.C.D.R. 26, OH
Prole v. Allen [1950] 1 All E.R. 476, Assizes (Somerset) .... *Digested*, 47-51/**1199**:
         Applied, 97/3859: *Considered*, 92/1553, 05/5576: *Distinguished*, 90/3274
Purac Ltd v. Byzak Ltd 2005 S.L.T. 37; 2005 S.C.L.R. 244, OH .... *Digested*, 05/**5072**
PW v. AL (or W) see W v. W

Queen's Cross Housing Association Ltd v. Glasgow City Council 2004 Hous. L.R. 125,
SS Comm .... *Digested*, 05/**5669**
Quin Shue Lin (also known as Chen Ri Lin), Petitioner see Lin v. Secretary of State for the
Home Department
Quinan v. Carnegie; *sub nom* Quinan v. Donnelly 2005 J.C. 279; 2005 S.L.T. 707;
2005 S.C.C.R. 267; 2005 G.W.D. 22-394, HCJ .... *Digested*, 05/**5099**
Quinan v. Donnelly see Quinan v. Carnegie
Quinn (Dennis James) v. HM Advocate see Gilchrist (Kenneth Alexander) v. HM
Advocate

R v. HM Advocate see HM Advocate v. R
R v. HM Advocate 2005 G.W.D. 28-521, HCJ
R. v. Ali (Mudassir Mohammed) see R. v. Lambert (Steven)
R. v. Cook (Neil Terence) see Attorney General's Reference (No.152 of 2002), Re
R. v. Cooksley (Robert Charles) see Attorney General's Reference (No.152 of 2002),
Re
R. v. Crump (Richard James) see Attorney General's Reference (No.152 of 2002), Re

R. *v.* Hertfordshire CC Ex p. Green Environmental Industries Ltd; *sub nom* Green Environmental Industries Ltd, Re; Green Environmental Industries Ltd *v.* Hertfordshire CC [2000] 2 A.C. 412; [2000] 2 W.L.R. 373; [2000] 1 All E.R. 773; [2000] Eu. L.R. 414; [2000] Env. L.R. 426; [2000] E.H.L.R. 199; [2000] H.R.L.R. 359; [2000] U.K.H.R.R. 361; (2000) 2 L.G.L.R. 754; [2000] B.L.G.R. 215; [2000] 1 P.L.R. 108; [2000] C.O.D. 223; [2000] E.G.C.S. 27; (2000) 97(9) L.S.G. 42; (2000) 150 N.L.J. 277; [2000] N.P.C. 15; *Times*, February 22, 2000; *Independent*, February 22, 2000, HL; affirming [1998] Env. L.R. 153; [1998] J.P.L. 481; *Times*, October 9, 1997, CA (Civ Div); affirming [1997] Env. L.R. 114; [1996] N.P.C. 119, DC. . . . . *Digested*, 00/**2300**:
    Applied, 03/4720: *Considered*, 05/5449: *Followed*, 00/1057

R. *v.* Immigration Appeal Tribunal Ex p. Mehta (No.2) [1976] Imm. A.R. 174, QBD . . . . .   *Applied*, 05/5438

R. *v.* Jordan (Shirley) see R. *v.* Lambert (Steven)

R. *v.* Lambert (Steven); R. *v.* Ali (Mudassir Mohammed); R. *v.* Jordan (Shirley) [2001] UKHL 37; [2002] 2 A.C. 545; [2001] 3 W.L.R. 206; [2002] 1 All E.R. 2; [2001] 3 All E.R. 577; [2001] 2 Cr. App. R. 28; [2001] H.R.L.R. 55; [2001] U.K.H.R.R. 1074; [2001] Crim. L.R. 806; (2001) 98(33) L.S.G. 29; (2001) 145 S.J.L.B. 174; *Times*, July 6, 2001; *Independent*, July 19, 2001; *Daily Telegraph*, July 17, 2001, HL; affirming [2002] Q.B. 1112; [2001] 2 W.L.R. 211; [2001] 1 All E.R. 1014; [2001] 1 Cr. App. R. 14; [2001] H.R.L.R. 4; [2000] U.K.H.R.R. 864; (2000) 97(35) L.S.G. 36; *Times*, September 5, 2000, CA (Crim Div) . . . .   *Digested*, 01/**3504**:
    Applied, 01/2315, 03/780, 03/4064, 05/875: *Considered*, 02/785, 02/795, 03/761, 03/802, 04/707, 04/800, 04/4066, 05/5111: *Distinguished*, 02/813, 03/814: *Followed*, 01/1193, 01/5271, 02/844, 02/849, 02/1526, 02/2663

R. *v.* Land (Michael) [1999] Q.B. 65; [1998] 3 W.L.R. 322; [1998] 1 All E.R. 403; [1998] 1 Cr. App. R. 301; (1998) 162 J.P. 29; [1998] 1 F.L.R. 438; [1998] Crim. L.R. 70; [1998] Fam. Law 133; (1997) 161 J.P.N. 1173; (1997) 94(42) L.S.G. 32; *Times*, November 4, 1997; *Independent*, October 16, 1997, CA (Crim Div) . . .   *Digested*, 97/**1160**:
    Considered, 05/800: *Followed*, 05/5095

R. *v.* Mallett Ex p. Stunt see R. (on the application of Stunt) *v.* Mallett

R. *v.* Metropolitan Police Service Ex p. Stunt see R. (on the application of Stunt) *v.* Mallett

R. *v.* Secretary of State for the Home Department Ex p. Doody; R. *v.* Secretary of State for the Home Department Ex p. Pierson; R. *v.* Secretary of State for the Home Department Ex p. Smart; R. *v.* Secretary of State for the Home Department Ex p. Pegg [1994] 1 A.C. 531; [1993] 3 W.L.R. 154; [1993] 3 All E.R. 92; (1995) 7 Admin. L.R. 1; (1993) 143 N.L.J. 991; *Times*, June 29, 1993; *Independent*, June 25, 1993, HL; affirming [1993] Q.B. 157; [1992] 3 W.L.R. 956; [1993] 1 All E.R. 151; (1993) 5 Admin. L.R. 93; [1992] C.O.D. 458; *Times*, May 8, 1992; *Independent*, May 7, 1992; *Guardian*, May 13, 1992, CA (Civ Div) . . . . *Digested*, 93/**1213**:
    Applied, 94/768, 94/3848, 95/960, 97/1335, 97/3929, 99/5437, 03/2058, 04/2772, 05/1785, 05/4967: *Considered*, 93/1679, 94/44, 94/49, 94/3841, 95/42, 95/162, 95/2534, 96/1954, 96/4579, 96/6855, 97/1595, 97/2443, 98/4079, 00/3334, 00/4326, 02/3234, 04/1904: *Followed*, 95/81, 95/3228, 96/1953, 96/3981, 97/1626, 97/2672, 97/2678, 99/5212:
    Referred to, 95/1314

R. *v.* Secretary of State for the Home Department Ex p. Pegg see R. *v.* Secretary of State for the Home Department Ex p. Doody

R. *v.* Secretary of State for the Home Department Ex p. Pierson see R. *v.* Secretary of State for the Home Department Ex p. Doody

R. *v.* Secretary of State for the Home Department Ex p. Smart see R. *v.* Secretary of State for the Home Department Ex p. Doody

R. *v.* Stride (Ian Paul) see Attorney General's Reference (No.152 of 2002), Re

R. (on the application of Ahsak) *v.* Secretary of State for the Home Department [2002] EWHC 2182, QBD (Admin) . . . .   *Distinguished*, 05/5438

R. (on the application of Bulbul) *v.* Secretary of State for the Home Department see Sepet *v.* Secretary of State for the Home Department

R. (on the application of Inland Revenue Commissioners) *v.* Aberdeen General Commissioners of Income Tax see Revenue and Customs Commissioners, Petitioners

R. (on the application of Nadarajah) *v.* Secretary of State for the Home Department see R. (on the application of Razgar) *v.* Secretary of State for the Home Department (No.2)

R. (on the application of Razgar) *v.* Secretary of State for the Home Department (No.2); *sub nom* Secretary of State for the Home Department *v.* Razgar; R. (on the application of Soumahoro) *v.* Secretary of State for the Home Department; R. (on the application of Nadarajah) *v.* Secretary of State for the Home Department [2004] UKHL 27; [2004] 2 A.C. 368; [2004] 3 W.L.R. 58; [2004] 3 All E.R. 821; [2004] H.R.L.R. 32; [2004] Imm. A.R. 381; [2004] I.N.L.R. 349; [2004] A.C.D. 83; (2004) 101(28) L.S.G. 33; (2004) 154 N.L.J. 986; (2004) 148 S.J.L.B. 761; *Times,* June 21, 2004; *Independent,* June 23, 2004, HL; affirming [2003] EWCA Civ 840; [2003] Imm. A.R. 529; [2003] I.N.L.R. 543; [2003] A.C.D. 81, CA (Civ Div); affirming [2002] EWHC 2554; [2003] Imm. A.R. 269, QBD (Admin) . . . . *Digested, 04/***2029**:
Applied, 04/2032, 04/2041, 04/2052, 05/2159, 05/2181, 05/2192:
Considered, 04/839, 05/2179, 05/2213, 05/5431:
Previous proceedings, 03/2234

R. (on the application of Septet) *v.* Secretary of State for the Home Department see Sepet *v.* Secretary of State for the Home Department

R. (on the application of Soumahoro) *v.* Secretary of State for the Home Department see R. (on the application of Razgar) *v.* Secretary of State for the Home Department (No.2)

R. (on the application of Stunt) *v.* Mallett; *sub nom* Commissioner of Police *v.* Stunt; R. *v.* Metropolitan Police Service Ex p. Stunt; R. *v.* Mallett Ex p. Stunt [2001] EWCA Civ 265; [2001] I.C.R. 989; (2001) 98(16) L.S.G. 34; (2001) 145 S.J.L.B. 76; *Times,* March 20, 2001; *Independent,* March 6, 2001, CA (Civ Div); reversing *Independent,* June 12, 2000 (C.S), QBD . . . . *Digested, 01/***4778**:
Applied, 04/2822, 05/5605: *Distinguished,* 03/5843

R. (on the application of Ullah) *v.* Special Adjudicator; *sub nom* Ullah (Ahsan) *v.* Special Adjudicator; Do *v.* Secretary of State for the Home Department; R. (on the application of Ullah (Ahsan)) *v.* Secretary of State for the Home Department; Do *v.* Immigration Appeal Tribunal [2004] UKHL 26; [2004] 2 A.C. 323; [2004] 3 W.L.R. 23; [2004] 3 All E.R. 785; [2004] H.R.L.R. 33; [2004] U.K.H.R.R. 995; [2004] Imm. A.R. 419; [2004] I.N.L.R. 381; (2004) 101(28) L.S.G. 33; (2004) 154 N.L.J. 985; (2004) 148 S.J.L.B. 762; *Times,* June 18, 2004; *Independent,* June 22, 2004, HL; affirming [2002] EWCA Civ 1856; [2003] 1 W.L.R. 770; [2003] 3 All E.R. 1174; [2003] H.R.L.R. 12; [2003] U.K.H.R.R. 302; [2003] Imm. A.R. 304; [2003] I.N.L.R. 74; [2003] A.C.D. 30; (2003) 100(10) L.S.G. 28; (2003) 147 S.J.L.B. 28; *Times,* December 18, 2002; *Independent,* December 20, 2002, CA (Civ Div); affirming [2002] EWHC 1584; [2002] Imm. A.R. 601; *Times,* September 5, 2002; *Independent,* October 14, 2002 (C.S), QBD (Admin) . . . . *Digested, 04/***2009**:
Applied, 04/2052, 05/401, 05/2195: *Considered,* 04/839, 04/2038, 05/2140, 05/5431

R. (on the application of Ullah (Ahsan)) *v.* Secretary of State for the Home Department see R. (on the application of Ullah) *v.* Special Adjudicator

Ralston *v.* Scottish Ministers 2004 S.L.T. 1263; 2005 S.C.L.R. 385, OH . . . . *Digested, 05/***4963**

Rankin *v.* HM Advocate 2005 G.W.D. 29-548, HCJ

Rashid *v.* Secretary of State for the Home Department 2005 G.W.D. 20-364, IH (Ex Div)

RB *v.* HM Advocate; *sub nom* B *v.* HM Advocate 2004 S.C.C.R. 443; 2004 G.W.D. 21-453, HCJ. . . . . *Digested, 05/***5650**

RB *v.* MB 2005 Fam. L.R. 49, IH (Ex Div)

RBS Deutschland Holdings GmbH *v.* Customs and Excise Commissioners [2004] V. & D.R. 447; [2005] S.T.I. 123, V&DTr (Edinburgh)

Rebika *v.* Secretary of State for the Home Department 2005 G.W.D. 37-692, OH

Redpath *v.* HM Advocate 2005 G.W.D. 23-434, HCJ

Redpath *v.* HM Advocate 2005 G.W.D. 36-681, HCJ

Reedie (Graham John) *v.* HM Advocate 2005 S.L.T. 742; 2005 S.C.C.R. 407; 2005 G.W.D. 25-475, HCJ . . . . *Digested, 05/***5132**

Reid (George) *v.* HM Advocate see Henvey (Steven) *v.* HM Advocate

Reith *v.* Bates (Ross) 1998 J.C. 224; 1999 S.L.T. 380; 1998 S.C.C.R. 426; 1998 G.W.D. 20-1008, HCJ . . . . *Digested, 98/***5631**:
Applied, 05/5147

Renfrewshire Council *v.* Davies see Davies *v.* Renfrewshire Council

Rennie *v.* Frame 2005 S.C.C.R. 608, HCJ

Rennie *v.* Norquoy 2005 S.C.L.R. 171; 2004 G.W.D. 31-648, Sh Pr

Revenue and Customs Commissioners *v.* Robertson's Electrical Ltd see Robertson's Electrical Ltd *v.* Customs and Excise Commissioners

Revenue and Customs Commissioners *v.* William Grant & Sons Distillers Ltd; *sub nom* William Grant & Sons Distillers Ltd *v.* Inland Revenue Commissioners; Inland Revenue Commissioners *v.* William Grant & Sons Distillers Ltd 2005 S.L.T. 888; [2005] B.T.C. 483; [2005] S.T.I. 1647; 2005 G.W.D. 29-536, IH (Ex Div) . . . . . . *Digested, 05/***5692**:
Previous proceedings, 04/3712

Revenue and Customs Commissioners, Petitioners; *sub nom* R. (on the application of Inland Revenue Commissioners) *v.* Aberdeen General Commissioners of Income Tax; Inland Revenue Commissioners, Petitioners 2005 S.L.T. 1061; [2005] S.T.I. 1755; 2005 G.W.D. 33-634, OH

Reynard *v.* Exquisite Quisine Ltd (t/a Latours Cuisine) 2005 G.W.D. 36-682, OH

Riddell *v.* Riddell 2005 G.W.D. 18-324, Sh Pr

Ritchie *v.* HM Advocate 2005 G.W.D. 2-25, HCJ

Ritchie Brothers (PWC) Ltd *v.* David Philp (Commercials) Ltd 2005 S.C. 384; 2005 S.L.T. 341; 2005 S.C.L.R. 829; [2005] B.L.R. 384; 2005 G.W.D. 11-169; *Times*, May 24, 2005, IH (2 Div); reversing 2004 S.L.T. 471; [2004] B.L.R. 379; 2004 G.W.D. 13-282, OH . . . . *Digested*, 05/**5068**

Riva *v.* HM Advocate 2005 G.W.D. 23-419, HCJ

Robb *v.* Gillan 2004 Fam. L.R. 120; 2004 G.W.D. 32-651, Sh Pr . . . . *Digested*, 05/**5251**

Robb *v.* M&I Salamis Ltd 2005 S.L.T. 523; 2005 S.C.L.R. 676; 2005 Rep. L.R. 42; 2005 G.W.D. 16-290, IH (Ex Div); affirming 2004 S.C.L.R. 672; 2003 G.W.D. 33-949, Sh Ct (Grampian) . . . . *Digested*, 05/**5406**

Roberts *v.* Chisholm 2004 S.L.T. 1171; 2004 G.W.D. 31-633, OH . . . . *Digested*, 05/**5058**

Roberts *v.* Johnstone [1989] Q.B. 878; [1988] 3 W.L.R. 1247; (1989) 86(5) L.S.G. 44; (1989) 132 S.J. 1672; *Times*, April 15, 1988, CA (Civ Div); reversing in part (Unreported, July 25, 1986), HC . . . . *Digested*, 89/**1202**:

Applied, 94/1542, 99/1415, 00/1515, 01/1554: *Cited*, 05/5587:
Considered, 89/1185, 91/4896, 92/5639, 02/3412: *Not followed*, 87/1171:
Referred to, 90/1578

Roberts (Peter John) *v.* HM Advocate 2005 S.C.C.R. 717; 2005 G.W.D. 31-596, HCJ

Robertson *v.* Frame; *sub nom* Robertson *v.* Higson; Ruddy *v.* Procurator Fiscal, Perth; O'Dalaigh (aka Daly) *v.* Frame; Ruddy *v.* Griffiths; Nos. 2, 3 and 4 of 2005, PC (Sc); affirming 2005 J.C. 210; 2005 S.L.T. 131; 2005 S.C.C.R. 134; 2005 G.W.D. 3-23, HCJ . . . . *Digested*, 05/**5137**

Robertson *v.* Higson see Robertson *v.* Frame

Robertson *v.* HM Advocate 2005 G.W.D. 16-269, HCJ

Robertson Group (Construction) Ltd *v.* Amey-Miller (Edinburgh) Joint Venture 2005 S.C.L.R. 854; [2005] B.L.R. 491, OH

Robertson's Electrical Ltd *v.* Customs and Excise Commissioners; *sub nom* Revenue and Customs Commissioners *v.* Robertson's Electrical Ltd 2005 S.L.T. 1149; [2005] S.T.I. 1813; 2005 G.W.D. 37-699, IH (2 Div); reversing [2005] B.V.C. 2070; [2004] V. & D.R. 481; [2004] S.T.I. 2570, V&DTr (Edinburgh)

Robson *v.* Council of the Law Society of Scotland (No.2) 2005 S.C. 125; 2005 S.L.T. 244; 2005 S.C.L.R. 596; 2004 G.W.D. 40-833, IH (Ex Div) . . . . *Digested*, 05/**5496**

Rodger (Builders) Ltd *v.* Fawdry 1950 S.C. 483; 1950 S.L.T. 345, IH (2 Div); affirming (Unreported, March 8, 1949), OH . . . . *Digested*, 50/**4871**:

Applied, 83/4888, 83/4889: *Distinguished*, 05/5407: *Referred to*, 95/5982, 96/6577

Ross *v.* HM Advocate 2005 G.W.D. 23-424, HCJ

Ross *v.* Pryde 2004 Rep. L.R. 129; 2004 G.W.D. 25-529, OH . . . . *Digested*, 05/**5163**

Rotchford *v.* Carnegie 2005 G.W.D. 19-345, HCJ

Rowe *v.* United Kingdom (28901/95); Davis *v.* United Kingdom (28901/95) (2000) 30 E.H.R.R. 1; 8 B.H.R.C. 325; [2000] Crim. L.R. 584; *Times*, March 1, 2000, ECHR [1999] Crim. L.R. 410, Eur Comm HR . . . . *Digested*, 00/**3219**:

Applied, 01/988: *Considered*, 00/1059, 01/989, 01/1100, 05/5136

Roxburgh DC *v.* Collins 1991 S.L.T. (Sh. Ct.) 49; 1991 S.C.L.R. 575, Sh Pr . . . . *Digested*, 91/**5195**:

Considered, 05/5478: *Distinguished*, 00/6537

Royal Bank of Scotland Plc *v.* Bannerman Johnstone Maclay 2005 S.C. 437; 2005 S.L.T. 579; [2005] P.N.L.R. 43; 2005 Rep. L.R. 66; 2005 G.W.D. 17-309, IH (2 Div); reversing in part 2003 S.C. 125; 2003 S.L.T. 181; [2005] B.C.C. 235; [2003] P.N.L.R. 6; 2002 G.W.D. 26-917; *Times*, August 1, 2002, OH . . . . *Digested*, 05/**5572**

Royal Bank of Scotland Plc *v.* Kinnear 2005 Hous. L.R. 2; 2001 G.W.D. 3-124, Sh Pr

Royal Insurance (UK) Ltd *v.* Amec Construction Scotland Ltd 2005 G.W.D. 38-704, OH

Royal Scottish Assurance Plc *v.* Scottish Equitable Plc 2005 G.W.D. 13-221, OH

Ruddy *v.* Griffiths see Robertson *v.* Frame

Ruddy *v.* Procurator Fiscal, Perth see Robertson *v.* Frame

Russell *v.* Russell 2005 Fam. L.R. 96; 2005 G.W.D. 30-574, Sh Pr

Ruxton *v.* Starrs see Starrs *v.* Ruxton

RWP *v.* HM Advocate see P *v.* HM Advocate

Ryan *v.* Fairfield Rowan Ltd 2004 Rep. L.R. 138; 2004 G.W.D. 32-661, OH . . . . *Digested*, 05/**5593**

S *v.* Criminal Injuries Compensation Board 2004 S.L.T. 1173; 2004 G.W.D. 31-632, OH . *Digested*, 05/**4959**

S *v.* M 2005 G.W.D. 32-607, Sh Ct (Tayside)

S *v.* Q 2005 S.L.T. 53; 2004 Fam. L.R. 106, OH . . . . *Digested*, 05/**5252**

S *v.* S 2005 S.C.L.R. 587; 2004 Fam. L.R. 127; 2004 G.W.D. 35-705, OH . . . . *Digested*, 05/**5247**

S *v.* S 2005 G.W.D. 9-130, IH (Ex Div)

Sachdev *v.* Secretary of State for the Home Department 2005 G.W.D. 7-100, OH

Salisbury *v.* Dyer 2005 G.W.D. 19-347, HCJ

Salmon (Donald) v. HM Advocate; Moore (Anthony James) v. HM Advocate 1999 J.C.
67; 1999 S.L.T. 169; 1998 S.C.C.R. 740; 1998 G.W.D. 39-2002, HCJ . . . .   *Digested*, 99/**5832**:
Considered, 01/6387, 05/5111

Scott, Petitioner see Davidson v. Scottish Ministers (No.1)
Scott v. Fraser 2005 G.W.D. 30-564, HCJ
Scott v. Gilchrist 2005 G.W.D. 12-213, HCJ
Scott v. Scottish Ministers see Davidson v. Scottish Ministers (No.1)
Scott v. Service 2005 G.W.D. 22-403, HCJ
Scott v. Vieregge 2005 Rep. L.R. 59; 2005 G.W.D. 22-392, OH
Scott (James Campbell) v. HM Advocate see Christie (William) v. HM Advocate
Scottish Power Generation Ltd v. Scottish Environment Protection Agency (No.1) 2005
S.L.T. 98; [2005] Eu. L.R. 449; [2005] Env. L.R. 38; 2005 G.W.D. 1-1, OH . . . . .   *Digested*, 05/**4970**
Scottish Power Generation Ltd v. Scottish Environment Protection Agency (No.2) 2005
S.L.T. 641; 2005 G.W.D. 18-312, OH . . . .   *Digested*, 05/**4969**
Scottish Provident Institution v. Inland Revenue Commissioners; *sub nom* Inland
Revenue Commissioners v. Scottish Provident Institution [2004] UKHL 52;
[2004] 1 W.L.R. 3172; [2005] 1 All E.R. 325; [2005] S.T.C. 15; 2005 S.C. (H.L.)
33; 76 T.C. 538; [2004] B.T.C. 426; 7 I.T.L. Rep. 403; [2004] S.T.I. 2433;
(2004) 148 S.J.L.B. 1404; *Times*, November 26, 2004; *Independent*, December
1, 2004, HL; reversing [2003] S.T.C. 1035; 2004 S.C. 135; 2003 S.C.L.R. 867;
[2004] B.T.C. 105; [2003] S.T.I. 1416; 2003 G.W.D. 24-699, IH (1 Div); affirming
[2002] S.T.C. (S.C.D.) 252; [2002] S.T.I. 901, Sp Comm . . . .   *Digested*, 05/**4158**:
Considered, 05/4084
Scrabster Harbour Trust v. Mowlem Plc (t/a Mowlem Marine); Mowlem Plc (t/a
Mowlem Marine) v. Scrabster Harbour Trust; TNS, IH (1 Div); affirming 2005
S.L.T. 499; 2005 S.C.L.R. 795; 2005 G.W.D. 15-254, OH . . . .   *Digested*, 05/**5069**
Secretary of State for the Home Department v. Razgar see R. (on the application of
Razgar) v. Secretary of State for the Home Department (No.2)
Secretary of State for Trade and Industry v. Blackwood 2003 S.L.T. 120; [2005] B.C.C.
366; 2002 G.W.D. 27-930, IH (1 Div) . . . .   *Digested*, 03/**5303**
Secretary of State for Work and Pensions v. Cunningham 2005 S.C. 19; 2004 S.L.T. 1007;
2004 G.W.D. 25-546, IH (Ex Div) . . . .   *Digested*, 04/**5124**
Secretary of State for Work and Pensions v. Gault 2005 S.C.L.R. 973, Sh Ct (South
Strathclyde)
Secretary of State for Work and Pensions v. McNamara 2005 S.L.T. (Sh Ct) 125; 2005
G.W.D. 33-618, Sh Ct (North Strathclyde)
Selfridge v. Gallacher 2005 G.W.D. 10-151, HCJ
Senior v. Frame 2005 G.W.D. 24-451, HCJ
Sepet v. Secretary of State for the Home Department; *sub nom* R. (on the application
of Septet) v. Secretary of State for the Home Department; R. (on the application
of Bulbul) v. Secretary of State for the Home Department; Bulbul v. Secretary
of State for the Home Department [2003] UKHL 15; [2003] 1 W.L.R. 856;
[2003] 3 All E.R. 304; 14 B.H.R.C. 238; [2003] Imm. A.R. 428; [2003] I.N.L.R.
322; (2003) 100(18) L.S.G. 35; (2003) 147 S.J.L.B. 389; *Times*, March 21,
2003; *Independent*, March 25, 2003, HL; affirming [2001] EWCA Civ 681;
[2001] Imm. A.R. 452; [2001] I.N.L.R. 376; *Times*, July 12, 2001; *Independent*,
May 18, 2001, CA (Civ Div); affirming [2000] Imm. A.R. 445, IAT . . . .   *Digested*, 03/**2229**:
Applied, 05/5439: *Considered*, 03/5732, 04/1925, 05/2178
Service v. Daldrup; *sub nom* Dysart v. Daldrup 2005 S.C.C.R. 693; 2005 G.W.D. 23-
433, HCJ
SH v. KH 2005 S.L.T. 1025; 2005 Fam. L.R. 80; 2005 G.W.D. 32-616, IH (Ex Div);
reversing 2003 S.L.T. 515; 2003 G.W.D. 11-314, OH . . . .   *Digested*, 05/**5271**
Shambrook v. Fraser 2005 G.W.D. 16-297, HCJ
Sharp v. Highland and Islands Fire Board 2005 S.L.T. 855; 2005 S.C.L.R. 1049; 2005
Rep. L.R. 112; 2005 G.W.D. 26-515, OH . . . .   *Digested*, 05/**5573**
Sharp (or Chisholm) v. Wardrope 2005 S.C.L.R. 530; 2004 G.W.D. 34-688, OH
Sheikh v. Sheikh 2005 Fam. L.R. 7; 2005 G.W.D. 11-183, OH
Shetland Sea Farms Ltd v. Assuranceforeningen Skuld; *sub nom* Shetland Seafarms Ltd
v. Assuranceforeningen Skuld 2005 G.W.D. 12-214, IH (Ex Div); affirming 2004
S.L.T. 30; 2001 G.W.D. 24-915, OH . . . .   *Digested*, 04/**4539**
Shevill v. Presse Alliance SA [1996] A.C. 959; [1996] 3 W.L.R. 420; [1996] 3 All E.R.
929; [1996] I.L.Pr. 798; [1996] E.M.L.R. 533; (1996) 93(38) L.S.G. 42; (1996)
140 S.J.L.B. 208; *Times*, July 26, 1996, HL; affirming [1992] 2 W.L.R. 1; [1992]
1 All E.R. 409; [1991] I.L.Pr. 568; *Times*, March 13, 1991; *Independent*, March 13,
1991; *Financial Times*, March 20, 1991, CA (Civ Div) . . . .   *Digested*, 96/**1083**:
Applied, 05/974: *Considered*, 05/5046: *Distinguished*, 98/748:
Followed, 01/1835: *Previous proceedings*, 95/3127:
Subsequent proceedings, 95/3127
Shevill v. Presse Alliance SA (C68/93) [1995] 2 A.C. 18; [1995] 2 W.L.R. 499;
[1995] All E.R. (E.C.) 289; [1995] E.C.R. I-415; [1995] I.L.Pr. 267; [1995]
E.M.L.R. 543; *Times*, April 6, 1995; *Financial Times*, March 21, 1995, ECJ . . . . . .   *Digested*, 95/**3127**:
Considered, 99/715, 99/717, 05/5046: *Followed*, 04/562:
Previous proceedings, 92/2790: *Referred to*, 97/895:
Subsequent proceedings, 96/1083

Shove (Inspector of Taxes) v. Lingfield Park 1991 Ltd; *sub nom* Lingfield Park (1991) Ltd v. Shove (Inspector of Taxes) [2004] EWCA Civ 391; [2004] S.T.C. 805; 76 T.C. 363; [2005] B.T.C. 89; [2004] S.T.I. 987; (2004) 101(18) L.S.G. 35; (2004) 148 S.J.L.B. 537; *Times*, April 26, 2004; *Independent*, April 20, 2004, CA (Civ Div); affirming [2003] EWHC 1684; [2003] S.T.C. 1003; [2003] B.T.C. 422; [2003] S.T.I. 1146; (2003) 100(35) L.S.G. 38; *Times*, August 11, 2003, Ch D . . . . *Digested*, 04/**3691**:
Distinguished, 05/5691

Sinclair v. MacDougall Estates Ltd 1994 S.L.T. 76, OH . . . . *Digested*, 94/**6161**:
Applied, 05/5609: *Approved*, 01/6866

Sinclair v. Sinclair 2005 G.W.D. 8-105, Sh Pr

Sinclair (Alvin Lee) v. HM Advocate [2005] UKPC D2; 2005 S.C. (P.C.) 28; 2005 S.L.T. 553; 2005 S.L.T. 446; [2005] H.R.L.R. 26; 18 B.H.R.C. 527; 2005 G.W.D. 17-306; *Times*, June 1, 2005, PC (Sc); reversing 2004 S.L.T. 794; 2004 S.C.C.R. 499; 2004 G.W.D. 23-503, HCJ. . . . . *Digested*, 05/**5136**

Sinclair (Kevin Andrew) v. HM Advocate; Harvey (Devon Lloyd) v. HM Advocate 2005 S.L.T. 1177; 2005 S.C.C.R. 755; 2005 G.W.D. 33-624, HCJ

Singh v. Singh; *sub nom* Kaur v. Singh 2005 S.L.T. 749; 2005 S.C.L.R. 1000; 2005 Fam. L.R. 42; 2005 G.W.D. 25-485, OH. . . . . *Digested*, 05/**5270**

Singh (Daljit) v. Secretary of State for the Home Department 2000 S.C. 219; 2000 S.L.T. 243; 2000 G.W.D. 2-63, IH (1 Div) . . . . *Digested*, 00/**6491**:
Applied, 05/5439: *Distinguished*, 03/5730

Singh (Harpal) v. HM Advocate 2005 S.L.T. 478; 2004 S.C.C.R. 604, HCJ. . . . . *Digested*, 05/**5024**

Singh (Jasvir) v. Secretary of State for the Home Department (Continued Appeal) 2001 G.W.D. 26-1060, IH (1 Div)

Skinner v. Scottish Ambulance Service 2004 S.C. 790; 2004 S.L.T. 834; [2005] Eu. L.R. 54; 2004 Rep. L.R. 103; 2004 G.W.D. 23-498, IH (Ex Div); reversing 2004 G.W.D. 9-196, OH . . . . *Digested*, 04/**4903**

Slaven v. Spiers 2005 S.C.C.R. 308; 2005 G.W.D. 20-362, HCJ

Small (Inspector of Taxes) v. Mars UK Ltd see Mars UK Ltd v. Small (Inspector of Taxes)

Smiles v. Edinburgh City Council 2005 G.W.D. 34-643, Sh Ct (Lothian)

Smillie v. Lothian and Borders Police Board 2005 S.L.T. 1091; 2005 G.W.D. 34-650, OH

Smillie v. Olympic House Ltd 2004 S.L.T. 1244; 2004 S.C.L.R. 403; 2004 G.W.D. 24-525, OH . . . . *Digested*, 05/**5446**

Smith v. Buckett 2005 G.W.D. 2-23, Sh Ct (Grampian)

Smith v. Eric S Bush (A Firm); Harris v. Wyre Forest DC [1990] 1 A.C. 831; [1989] 2 W.L.R. 790; [1989] 2 All E.R. 514; (1989) 21 H.L.R. 424; 87 L.G.R. 685; [1955-95] P.N.L.R. 467; [1989] 18 E.G. 99; [1989] 17 E.G. 68; (1990) 9 Tr. L.R. 1; (1989) 153 L.G. Rev. 984; (1989) 139 N.L.J. 576; (1989) 133 S.J. 597, HL; affirming [1988] Q.B. 743; [1987] 3 All E.R. 179; (1987) 19 H.L.R. 287; [1987] 1 E.G.L.R. 157; (1987) 283 E.G. 56; (1987) 84 L.S.G. 3260; (1987) 137 N.L.J. 362; (1987) 131 S.J. 1423, CA (Civ Div) . . . . *Digested*, 89/**2566**:
Applied, 88/2457, 90/3258, 90/3266, 92/1547, 92/3207, 95/3718, 01/4540, 01/4541, 03/2993, 05/5577: *Considered*, 88/2433, 88/2456, 89/2565, 90/3306, 90/3307, 90/3315, 91/2657, 92/1553, 93/2997, 95/770, 95/2496, 96/2993, 98/3921, 99/477: *Distinguished*, 97/3851: *Followed*, 99/4058:
Referred to, 92/6078

Smith v. Gallacher 2005 G.W.D. 23-435, HCJ

Smith v. Houston 2005 G.W.D. 22-412, HCJ

Smith v. Jack 2005 G.W.D. 1-14, Sh Ct (Grampian)

Smith v. North Lanarkshire Licensing Board 2005 S.L.T. 544; 2005 G.W.D. 8-117, IH (Ex Div) . . . . *Digested*, 05/**5500**

Smith v. Patrick; *sub nom* Smith (James David) v. HM Advocate 2005 S.C.C.R. 704; 2005 G.W.D. 33-630, HCJ

Smith (Craig Charles) v. HM Advocate 2004 S.C.C.R. 521, HCJ. . . . . *Digested*, 05/**5649**

Smith (Gregory Alexander) v. Lees 1997 J.C. 73; 1997 S.L.T. 690; 1997 S.C.C.R. 139; 1997 G.W.D. 6-225, HCJ. . . . . *Digested*, 97/**5761**:
Applied, 04/4624: *Distinguished*, 05/5092

Smith (James David) v. HM Advocate see Smith v. Patrick

Smith (Pamela) v. Donnelly 2002 J.C. 65; 2001 S.L.T. 1007; 2001 S.C.C.R. 800; 2001 G.W.D. 26-1011, HCJ Appeal . . . . *Digested*, 01/**6702**:
Applied, 03/5359: *Considered*, 04/4632, 05/5098

Smith (Roy Dickson) v. HM Advocate 2005 J.C. 242; 2005 G.W.D. 4-36, HCJ

Smith (William Geddes) (Fatal Accident Inquiry) 2005 S.C.L.R. 355, Sh Ct (Grampian)

Sneddon (Graham) v. HM Advocate; P v. HM Advocate 2005 S.L.T. 651; 2005 S.C.C.R. 367; 2005 G.W.D. 19-339, HCJ . . . . *Digested*, 05/**5110**

Snelling v. Thomson Alarm & Communication System Ltd 2005 Rep. L.R. 127; 2003 G.W.D. 21-638, OH

Sohal v. Gallacher 2004 S.C.C.R. 577, HCJ . . . . *Digested*, 05/**5658**

South Lanarkshire Council v. Taylor 2005 S.C. 182; 2005 G.W.D. 1-17, IH (1 Div)

Spence v. Ayrshire and Arran Health Board see Urquhart v. Ayrshire and Arran Health Board

Spendiff (Robert James) v. HM Advocate 2005 J.C. 338; 2005 S.C.C.R. 522, HCJ

Spey District Fishery Board *v.* Scottish Ministers 2005 S.C.L.R. 810; 2005 G.W.D. 13-216, OH

Stafford *v.* HM Advocate 2005 S.L.T. 836; 2005 G.W.D. 27-530, HCJ . . . . *Digested*, 05/**5660**

Standard Commercial Property Securities Ltd *v.* Glasgow City Council 2005 S.L.T. 144; 2005 S.C.L.R. 423; 2005 G.W.D. 3-21, IH (1 Div); reversing 2004 S.L.T. 655; 2004 G.W.D.18-395, OH. . . . . *Digested*, 05/**5599**

Standard Life Assurance Co *v.* Scottish Ministers [2005] 15 E.G.C.S.123, IH (Ex Div)

Stanley *v.* HM Advocate 2005 G.W.D. 40-752, HCJ

Stargas Nominees Ltd *v.* Kingston Communications (Hull) Plc see Kingston Communications (Hull) Plc *v.* Stargas Nominees Ltd

Starrs *v.* Ruxton; *sub nom* Ruxton *v.* Starrs 2000 J.C. 208; 2000 S.L.T. 42; 1999 S.C.C.R. 1052; [2000] H.R.L.R. 191; [2000] U.K.H.R.R. 78; 8 B.H.R.C. 1; 1999 G.W.D. 37-1793; *Times*, November 17, 1999, HCJ. . . . . *Digested*, 99/**5884**:
Considered, 00/6091, 00/6095, 01/6372, 02/5493, 04/4588:
Distinguished, 01/92, 01/358: *Followed*, 00/478, 05/5137:
Referred to, 00/5841

Stephen *v.* Peters; *sub nom* Stephen *v.* Peter 2005 S.C.L.R. 513; 2005 Rep. L.R. 53, OH

Stevenson *v.* Donaldson 2005 G.W.D.12-210, HCJ

Stevenson *v.* Morrison Construction Ltd 2005 Rep. L.R. 120; 2005 G.W.D. 23-432, OH

Stewart *v.* Brown see Stewart *v.* Crowe

Stewart *v.* Crowe; *sub nom* Stewart *v.* Brown 1999 S.L.T. 899; 1999 S.C.C.R. 327; 1999 G.W.D.15-723, HCJ Appeal. . . . . *Digested*, 99/**5870**:
Followed, 05/5102

Stewart *v.* Donaldson 2005 G.W.D. 22-399, HCJ

Stewart *v.* Griffiths 2005 S.C.C.R. 291; 2005 G.W.D.11-172, HCJ

Stewart *v.* HM Advocate 2005 S.C.C.R. 565; 2005 G.W.D. 25-481, HCJ

Stewart *v.* Wylie 2005 G.W.D.16-284, HCJ

Stewart (Dean) *v.* HM Advocate 2005 S.C.C.R. 635; 2005 G.W.D. 27-523, HCJ

Stewart (William) *v.* HM Advocate (Sentencing) 2002 S.L.T. 1307; 2002 S.C.C.R. 915; 2002 G.W.D. 28-971, HCJ Appeal . . . . *Digested*, 02/**6080**:
Applied, 04/5108: *Considered*, 03/5888: *Followed*, 02/6079:
Overruled, 05/5652

Stirling *v.* McFadyen 2000 S.C.C.R. 239; 2000 G.W.D. 8-274, HCJ Appeal . . . . *Digested*, 00/**6005**:
Considered, 05/5092

Stirling Council *v.* Neil 2005 Hous. L.R.108, Sh Ct (Tayside)

Stork, Pursuer 2004 S.C.L.R. 513, Sh Ct (South Strathclyde). . . . . *Digested*, 05/**5529**

Stott *v.* Packer 2005 G.W.D. 20-359, Sh Ct (Lothian)

Strain *v.* Byers 2005 S.C.L.R.157; 2004 G.W.D.10-224, OH

Strang, Petitioner see Strang (Garry) *v.* HM Advocate

Strang *v.* Zulquernain 2005 G.W.D. 32-608, Sh Pr

Strang (Garry) *v.* HM Advocate; *sub nom* Strang, Petitioner 2005 S.L.T. 1114; 2005 S.C.C.R. 669; 2005 G.W.D. 26-502, HCJ

Strathclyde Joint Police Board *v.* McKinlay 2005 S.L.T. 764; 2005 G.W.D. 25-497, OH . *Digested*, 05/**5604**

Struk *v.* Secretary of State for the Home Department 2005 G.W.D. 7-99, OH

Stuart *v.* Telecom Services Ltd 2005 S.L.T. (Sh Ct) 39; 2005 G.W.D. 10-154, Sh Ct (Glasgow) . . . . *Digested*, 05/**5220**

Sturgeon *v.* Service 2005 G.W.D. 29-554, HCJ

Superdrug Stores Plc *v.* Network Rail Infrastructure Ltd TNS, IH (1 Div); reversing 2005 S.L.T. (Sh Ct) 105; 2005 G.W.D. 25-468, Sh Pr . . . . *Digested*, 05/**5057**

Superintendent of Fife Constabulary's Application, Re see McIlravie *v.* Wallace

Sutherland *v.* Foard 2005 G.W.D. 22-396, HCJ

Sweeney *v.* Sweeney (No.2); *sub nom* Dow *v.* Sweeney 2005 S.L.T. 1141; 2005 S.C.L.R. 1073; 2005 Fam. L.R. 62; 2005 G.W.D. 29-555, IH (Ex Div)

Sweets Service Ltd *v.* MacCallum 2005 S.C.L.R. 376, Sh Pr

Syed *v.* Ahmed see Ahmed *v.* Ahmed

Sykes *v.* Grant 2005 G.W.D.1-7, OH

Symanski *v.* Symanski 2005 Fam. L.R. 2, Sh Pr

Symanski *v.* Symanski (Further Evidence) 2005 Fam. L.R. 6, Sh Ct (Lothian)

T, Applicant 2005 S.L.T. (Sh Ct) 97; 2005 G.W.D. 26-501, Sh Ct (Glasgow). . . . . *Digested*, 05/**5027**

T, Petitioner; *sub nom* AMT, Petitioners 1997 S.L.T. 724; 1996 S.C.L.R. 897; [1997] Fam. Law 8; [1997] Fam. Law 225; *Times*, August 20, 1996, IH (1 Div) . . . . *Digested*, 96/**6596**:
Applied, 00/6485, 05/5250

Tant *v.* Gallacher 2005 G.W.D.11-170, HCJ

Taylor *v.* Griffiths 2005 G.W.D.11-197, HCJ

Taylor *v.* Russo 1977 S.L.T. (Sh. Ct.) 60, Sh Pr . . . . *Digested*, 77/**3218**:
Distinguished, 05/5444

Taylor *v.* Scottish Ministers 2005 S.C. 92; 2005 S.C.L.R. 577; 2004 G.W.D. 34-700, OH

Tayplan Ltd *v.* D&A Contracts 2005 S.L.T. 195; [2005] E.C.D.R. 20; 2005 G.W.D. 4-55, OH . . . . *Digested*, 05/**5451**

Telfer v. Kellock 2004 S.L.T. 1290, OH . . . . *Digested*, 05/**5165**
Temel v. Secretary of State for the Home Department 2005 S.L.T. 204, OH . . . . *Digested*, 05/**5443**
Thain v. Thain 2005 G.W.D. 9-135, Sh Pr
Thomas v. Council of the Law Society of Scotland 2005 G.W.D. 38-705, IH (2 Div)
Thomas v. HM Advocate 2005 G.W.D. 36-679, HCJ
Thompson v. Jardine 2004 S.C. 590; 2004 S.L.T. 1214; 2004 S.C.L.R. 806; 2004
    G.W.D. 35-711, IH (Ex Div) . . . . *Digested*, 05/**5033**
Thomson v. HM Advocate 2005 G.W.D. 14-239, HCJ
Thomson v. HM Advocate 2005 G.W.D. 14-241, HCJ
Thomson v. Newey & Eyre Ltd 2005 S.C. 373; 2005 S.L.T. 439; 2005 G.W.D. 8-118,
    IH (Ex Div); reversing 2004 G.W.D. 35-721, OH. . . . . *Digested*, 05/**5049**
Threlfall v. Jones (Inspector of Taxes); Gallagher v. Jones (Inspector of Taxes) [1994]
    Ch. 107; [1994] 2 W.L.R. 160; [1993] S.T.C. 537; 66 T.C. 77; (1993) 90(32)
    L.S.G. 40; (1993) 137 S.J.L.B. 174; *Times*, July 1, 1993; *Independent*, July 26,
    1993, CA (Civ Div); reversing [1993] S.T.C. 199; *Times*, February 10, 1993, Ch D
    . . . . *Digested*, 94/**2522**:
                  Approved, 99/4722: *Considered*, 94/639, 95/896, 96/3334, 05/5692
Tierney v. Biffa Waste Services Ltd 2005 G.W.D. 4-33, OH
Tonner v. Reiach & Hall 2005 S.L.T. 936; 2005 G.W.D. 25-463, OH . . . . *Digested*, 05/**5037**
Tony Beal Ltd v. Boyd (t/a Boyd Roofing) 2005 G.W.D. 15-252, Sh Pr
Towns v. Insurance Direct (Underwriting) Ltd 2005 G.W.D. 39-722, Sh Pr
Transco Plc v. Glasgow City Council 2005 S.L.T. 958; 2005 S.C.L.R. 733; 2005
    G.W.D. 29-562, OH. . . . . *Digested*, 05/**5704**
Transco Plc v. HM Advocate (No.1) 2004 J.C. 29; 2004 S.L.T. 41; 2004 S.C.C.R. 1;
    [2005] B.C.C. 296; 2003 G.W.D. 38-1039, HCJ. . . . . *Digested*, 04/**4634**
Transco Plc v. HM Advocate (No.2) 2005 J.C. 44; 2004 S.L.T. 995; 2004 S.C.C.R.
    553; 2004 G.W.D. 29-602, HCJ . . . . *Digested*, 04/**4655**
Transco Plc v. HM Advocate (No.3) 2005 J.C. 194; 2005 S.L.T. 211; 2005 S.C.C.R. 117;
    2005 G.W.D. 4-40, HCJ . . . . *Digested*, 05/**5152**
Trichem Scotland Ltd v. Stott 2005 G.W.D. 2-34, HCJ
Trico Shipping AS v. Frame 2005 G.W.D. 9-142, HCJ
Tudhope v. Finlay Park (t/a Park Hutchison Solicitors) 2004 S.L.T. 783; 2005 S.C.L.R.
    125; 2004 G.W.D. 3-46, OH. . . . . *Digested*, 04/**4590**
Turner v. Grovit (C159/02); *sub nom* Turner (C159/02), Re [2005] 1 A.C. 101; [2004] 3
    W.L.R. 1193; [2004] All E.R. (EC) 485; [2004] 2 All E.R. (Comm) 381; [2004]
    2 Lloyd's Rep. 169; [2004] E.C.R. I-3565; [2004] 1 C.L.C. 864; [2004] I.L.Pr.
    25; [2005] I.C.R. 23; [2004] I.R.L.R. 899; *Times*, April 29, 2004, ECJ [2004] 1
    Lloyd's Rep. 216; [2004] E.C.R. I-3565, AGO . . . . *Digested*, 04/**1393**:
                  Considered, 05/599, 05/2357, 05/5032: *Previous proceedings*, 02/641
Turner (C159/02), Re see Turner v. Grovit (C159/02)

Ullah (Ahsan) v. Special Adjudicator see R. (on the application of Ullah) v. Special
    Adjudicator
Unity Trust Bank Plc v. Frost (No.5) 2005 G.W.D. 19-335, OH
University Court of the University of Glasgow v. Customs and Excise Commissioners see
    University of Glasgow v. Customs and Excise Commissioners
University Court of the University of St Andrews v. Customs and Excise Commissioners
    [2005] B.V.C. 2621, V&DTr (Edinburgh)
University of Edinburgh v. Onifade 2005 S.L.T. (Sh Ct) 63; 2005 G.W.D. 5-60, Sh Pr . . *Digested*, 05/**5076**
University of Glasgow v. Customs and Excise Commissioners; *sub nom* University
    Court of the University of Glasgow v. Customs and Excise Commissioners
    [2005] B.V.C. 2583; [2005] V. & D.R. 198, V&DTr (Edinburgh)
UPS Supply Chain Solutions v. Glasgow Airport Ltd 2005 S.C.L.R. 67; 2004 G.W.D.
    39-802, OH
Urquhart v. Ayrshire and Arran Health Board; *sub nom* Spence v. Ayrshire and Arran
    Health Board 2000 S.L.T. 829; 2000 G.W.D. 20-812, OH . . . . *Digested*, 01/**6245**:
                                            Approved, 05/5042
Urquhart v. MacDonald 2005 G.W.D. 16-270, HCJ
Urquhart v. Sweeney 2005 S.L.T. 422; 2004 S.C.L.R. 796; 2004 G.W.D. 11-242, IH (2
    Div) . . . . *Digested*, 05/**4930**

Valentine v. HM Advocate 2005 G.W.D. 22-401, HCJ
Vannet v. Milligan 1998 S.L.T. 1018; 1998 S.C.C.R. 305; 1998 G.W.D. 13-644, HCJ
    Appeal . . . . *Digested*, 98/**5622**:
                                            Applied, 05/5147
Vaughan v. Griffiths 2004 S.C.C.R. 537, HCJ. . . . . *Digested*, 05/**5161**
Vettesse v. Frame see Pacitti v. Frame

W v. W; *sub nom* PW v. AL (or W) 2004 S.C. 63; 2003 S.L.T. 1253; 2003 S.C.L.R. 685; 2003 Fam. L.R. 85; 2003 G.W.D. 22-650, IH (1 Div); reversing 2003 S.C.L.R. 478; 2003 G.W.D. 11-298, OH . . . . *Digested*, 03/**5520**:
Considered, 05/5248

W's Guardian, Applicant 2005 G.W.D. 39-721, Sh Ct (Glasgow)
Walker v. Tidewater Cyprus Ltd 2004 S.C. 369; 2004 S.C.L.R. 505; 2003 G.W.D. 40-1070, IH (1 Div); affirming (Unreported, April 16, 2003), Sh Pr; reversing in part 2001 G.W.D. 39-1477, Sh Ct (Grampian) . . . . *Digested*, 05/**5029**
Wallis v. Wallis 1993 S.C. (H.L.) 49; 1993 S.L.T. 1348; 1993 S.C.L.R. 800; [1993] E.G.C.S. 148; *Times*, August 5, 1993, HL; affirming 1992 S.C. 455; 1992 S.L.T. 676; 1993 S.C.L.R. 7; Scotsman, June 10, 1992, IH (1 Div); reversing 1991 S.C.L.R. 192, Sh Ct (Tayside) . . . . *Digested*, 94/**2186**:
Considered, 01/6823, 05/5267: *Followed*, 94/5782, 04/4755, 04/4756:
Referred to, 95/5878
Wani v. Secretary of State for the Home Department 2005 S.L.T. 875; 2005 G.W.D. 27-533, OH . . . . *Digested*, 05/**5442**
Wanza v. Secretary of State for the Home Department 2005 G.W.D. 34-649, OH
Waqa v. Gallacher 2005 G.W.D. 10-164, HCJ
Wardrop (Alastair John) v. HM Advocate 2005 S.C.C.R. 226, HCJ
Watson v. Cheque Shop Ltd 2005 G.W.D. 31-589, OH
Watson v. Griffiths 2004 S.C.C.R. 723; 2004 G.W.D. 34-694, HCJ . . . . *Digested*, 05/**5149**
Watson v. HM Advocate (Sentencing) 2005 G.W.D. 3-26, HCJ
Watson v. Williams 2005 G.W.D. 19-353, HCJ
Watson's Executors v. Watson 2005 G.W.D. 29-535, Sh Ct (North Strathclyde)
Watt v. Bridges 2004 Rep. L.R. 96; 2004 G.W.D. 13-287, OH . . . . *Digested*, 05/**5592**
Waugh (Jean) v. HM Advocate; *sub nom* Waugh, Petitioner 2005 S.L.T. 451; 2005 S.C.C.R. 102; 2005 G.W.D. 10-149, HCJ . . . . *Digested*, 05/**5160**
Weatherford UK Ltd v. Aitken see Aitken v. Weatherford UK Ltd
Webster v. Dominick; *sub nom* Procurator Fiscal, Dunoon v. Dominick 2005 J.C. 65; 2003 S.L.T. 975; 2003 S.C.C.R. 525; 2003 G.W.D. 26-734, HCJ . . . . *Digested*, 03/**5371**:
Considered, 05/5110
Welding v. Wilson 2005 S.C.L.R. 570; 2005 G.W.D. 1-13, Sh Pr
West v. HM Advocate 2005 G.W.D. 40-738, HCJ
West Castle Properties Ltd v. Scottish Ministers 2004 S.C.L.R. 899; 2004 G.W.D. 20-444, OH . . . . *Digested*, 05/**5467**
West Dunbartonshire Council v. Barnes 2004 Hous. L.R. 64, Sh Ct (North Strathclyde) *Digested*, 05/**5410**
Westcrowns Contracting Services Ltd v. Daylight Insulation Ltd 2005 G.W.D. 23-429, OH
WH Smith Plc v. Glasgow Assessor [2004] R.A. 197, Lands Tr (Scot) . . . . *Digested*, 05/**5625**
Whaley v. Lord Advocate see Friend v. Lord Advocate
Whitbread Group Plc v. Goldapple Ltd (No.2) 2005 S.L.T. 281; 2005 S.C.L.R. 263; 2005 G.W.D. 8-114, OH . . . . *Digested*, 05/**5468**
White v. White 2001 S.C. 689; 2001 S.L.T. 485; 2001 S.C.L.R. 607; 2001 Fam. L.R. 21; 2001 G.W.D. 10-327, IH (1 Div); reversing 1999 S.L.T. (Sh Ct) 106; 1999 G.W.D. 28-1308, Sh Pr . . . . *Digested*, 01/**6510**:
Considered, 05/5250: *Not followed*, 00/6267
White (Brian) v. White (Shane); Mighell v. Reading; Evans v. Motor Insurers Bureau [2001] UKHL 9; [2001] 1 W.L.R. 481; [2001] 2 All E.R. 43; [2001] 1 All E.R. (Comm) 1105; [2001] 1 Lloyd's Rep. 679; [2001] R.T.R. 25; [2001] 2 C.M.L.R. 1; [2001] Lloyd's Rep. I.R. 493; [2001] P.I.Q.R. P20; (2001) 98(15) L.S.G. 33; (2001) 151 N.L.J. 350; (2001) 145 S.J.L.B. 67; *Times*, March 6, 2001; *Independent*, April 30, 2001 (C.S), HL; reversing [1999] 1 C.M.L.R. 1251; [1999] Eu. L.R. 389; [1999] Lloyd's Rep. I.R. 30; [1999] P.I.Q.R. P101; *Times*, October 12, 1998, CA (Civ Div); affirming [1997] 3 C.M.L.R. 1218; *Times*, November 10, 1997, QBD (Comm) . . . . *Digested*, 01/**3828**:
Applied, 05/5054: *Considered*, 04/2231: *Followed*, 03/2472
Whitehead v. Johnson; *sub nom* Whitehead v. Johnston 2005 G.W.D. 38-711, Sh Pr; reversing in part 2005 G.W.D. 38-712, Sh Ct (South Strathclyde)
Wiles v. Bothwell Castle Golf Club 2005 S.L.T. 785; 2005 G.W.D. 25-460, OH . . . . *Digested*, 05/**4961**
Wilkie v. HM Advocate 2005 G.W.D. 27-528, HCJ
William Grant & Sons Distillers Ltd v. Inland Revenue Commissioners see Mars UK Ltd v. Small (Inspector of Taxes)
William Grant & Sons Distillers Ltd v. Inland Revenue Commissioners see Revenue and Customs Commissioners v. William Grant & Sons Distillers Ltd
William Hill Organisation Ltd v. Glasgow City Licensing Board 2005 S.C. 102; 2005 S.L.T. 178; 2004 G.W.D. 40-810, IH (Ex Div) . . . . *Digested*, 05/**5499**
William Tracey Ltd v. Scottish Ministers 2005 S.L.T. 191; 2005 G.W.D. 4-56, IH (2 Div). . *Digested*, 05/**5597**
Wilson v. DM Hall & Sons [2005] P.N.L.R. 22, OH . . . . *Digested*, 05/**5577**
Wilson v. Dyer; *sub nom* Wilson v. Higson 2005 S.C.C.R. 686; 2005 G.W.D. 32-609, HCJ
Wilson v. Glasgow City Council; Gould v. Glasgow City Council 2004 S.L.T. 1189; 2004 S.C.L.R. 638; 2004 G.W.D. 14-307, OH . . . . *Digested*, 05/**5041**
Wilson v. Higson see Wilson v. Dyer
Wilson v. HM Advocate 2005 G.W.D. 31-595, HCJ

Wilson v. Shiels; *sub nom* Wilson v. Stott 2004 J.C. 169; 2004 S.C.C.R. 436; 2004
    G.W.D. 20-435, HCJ . . . . *Digested*, 05/**5150**
Wilson v. Stott see Wilson v. Shiels
Wilson (t/a TW Contractors) v. Drake & Scull Scotland Ltd; *sub nom* Wilson (t/a TW
    Contractors) v. Drake & Skull Ltd 2005 S.L.T. (Sh Ct) 35; 2005 G.W.D. 10-143,
    Sh Ct (Glasgow) . . . . *Digested*, 05/**5036**
Wolanski & Co Trustees Ltd v. First Quench Retailing Ltd 2004 Hous. L.R. 110; 2004
    G.W.D. 33-678, Sh Ct (Glasgow) . . . . *Digested*, 05/**5470**
Woodhouse v. Wright Johnston & Mackenzie 2004 S.L.T. 911; 2005 S.C.L.R. 222;
    2004 G.W.D. 25-541, OH . . . . *Digested*, 04/**5055**
Woodland v. Advocate General 2005 S.C.L.R. 163; 2004 Rep. L.R. 63; 2004 G.W.D.
    12-257, OH . . . . *Digested*, 04/**4902**
Wordie Property Co Ltd v. Secretary of State for Scotland 1984 S.L.T. 345, IH (1 Div) . .   *Digested*, 84/**4735**:
                     Applied, 89/5083, 92/5890, 93/5939, 96/7151, 97/6113, 04/5080:
                  Considered, 00/6491, 00/6500, 04/5024, 05/5438: *Followed*, 97/6144,
                                 99/6411: *Referred to*, 93/5937
Wright, Petitioner; *sub nom* Wright (Robert Bruce) v. HM Advocate; Brown, Petitioner
    2005 J.C. 11; 2004 S.L.T. 491; 2004 S.C.C.R. 324; 2004 G.W.D. 13-289, HCJ . .   *Digested*, 04/**4734**
Wright v. Scottish Ministers (No.2) 2005 S.C. 453; 2005 S.L.T. 613; 2005 G.W.D. 17-
    307, IH (Ex Div); affirming 2004 S.L.T. 823; 2004 G.W.D. 24-523, OH . . . . *Digested*, 05/**5431**
Wright (James David) v. HM Advocate 2005 S.C.C.R. 780; 2005 G.W.D. 34-639, HCJ
Wright (Robert Bruce) v. HM Advocate see Wright, Petitioner
WS Karoulias SA v. Drambuie Liqueur Co Ltd (No.2) 2005 S.L.T. 813; 2005 S.C.L.R.
    1014; 2005 G.W.D. 27-520, OH . . . . *Digested*, 05/**5077**
Wu v. Secretary of State for the Home Department 2005 G.W.D. 10-160, OH
Wylie v. Wood see Wyllie v. Wood
Wylie (James Williamson) v. HM Advocate 1966 S.L.T. 149; [1967] Crim. L.R. 422,
    HCJ Appeal . . . . *Digested*, 67/**715**:
                              Considered, 96/6855, 05/5122
Wyllie v. Wood; *sub nom* Wylie v. Wood 2005 S.L.T. 521; 2005 S.C.C.R. 277; 2005
    G.W.D. 13-225, HCJ

X v. BBC 2005 S.L.T. 796; 2005 S.C.L.R. 740; 2005 G.W.D. 26-500, OH . . . .   *Digested*, 05/**5044**

Yashi Care Ltd v. Scottish Commission for the Regulation of Care 2004 S.L.T. (Sh Ct)
    134; 2004 G.W.D. 34-703, Sh Pr . . . . *Digested*, 05/**5683**
Young (Andrew) v. Guild 1985 J.C. 27; 1985 S.L.T. 358, HCJ Appeal . . . .   *Digested*, 85/**3853**:
                                   Followed, 05/5123
Young (Sean James) v. HM Advocate see Christie (William) v. HM Advocate

Zaery v. Secretary of State for the Home Department 2005 G.W.D. 2-37, OH
Zubrytska v. Secretary of State for the Home Department 2005 G.W.D. 35-665, OH

Aegeon,The (No.1) [2002] EWCA Civ 247; [2003] Q.B. 556; [2002] 3 W.L.R. 616; [2002]
1 All E.R. (Comm) 714; [2002] 2 Lloyd's Rep. 42; [2002] C.L.C. 886; [2002] Lloyd's
Rep. I.R. 573; (2002) 99(16) L.S.G. 38; (2002) 146 S.J.L.B. 66, CA (Civ Div);
affirming [2002] Lloyd's Rep. I.R. 191, QBD (Comm) . . . . *Digested,* 02/**2732**:
Considered, 05/2359: *Referred to,* 05/2387
Afrapearl,The [2004] EWCA Civ 864; [2004] 1 W.L.R. 3111; [2004] 2 All E.R. (Comm) 578;
[2004] 2 Lloyd's Rep. 305; [2004] 2 C.L.C. 199; (2004) 101 (33) L.S.G. 37; *Times,*
August 24, 2004, CA (Civ Div); reversing [2003] EWHC 1904; [2004] 1 All
E.R. (Comm) 269; [2003] 2 Lloyd's Rep. 671, QBD (Comm) . . . . *Digested,* 05/**3784**
Agios Dimitrios,The [2004] EWHC 2232; [2005] 1 Lloyd's Rep. 23, QBD (Comm) . . . *Digested,* 05/**3795**
Al Tawwab, The [1991] 1 Lloyd's Rep. 201; *Times,* November 21, 1990; *Independent,*
December 3, 1990 (C.S.); *Financial Times,* November 13, 1990, CA (Civ Div) . . . *Digested,* 91/**3204**:
Applied, 99/494, 05/89: *Followed,* 96/890: *Not followed,* 05/315
Albaforth,The [1984] 2 Lloyd's Rep. 91; (1984) 81 L.S.G. 1360, CA (Civ Div) . . . . *Digested,* 84/**2671**:
Applied, 05/978: *Considered,* 00/769
Aliza Glacial,The [2002] EWCA Civ 577; [2002] 2 All E.R. (Comm) 39; [2002] 2 Lloyd's
Rep. 421; [2002] C.L.C. 1227; [2003] Lloyd's Rep. I.R. 10, CA (Civ Div) . . . . . . *Digested,* 02/**4107**:
Applied, 05/2352
Allobrogia,The [1978] 3 All E.R. 423; [1979] 1 Lloyd's Rep. 190, Ch D (Companies Ct) . *Digested,* 78/**262**:
Considered, 05/2366
Angelic Grace,The [1995] 1 Lloyd's Rep. 87, CA (Civ Div); affirming [1994] 1 Lloyd's Rep.
168, QBD (Comm) . . . . *Digested,* 94/**4066**:
Applied, 98/239, 05/599, 05/2357: *Considered,* 97/880, 99/733, 99/745,
99/4441, 01/950, 05/625
Antaios,The [1985] A.C. 191; [1984] 3 W.L.R. 592; [1984] 3 All E.R. 229; [1984] 2 Lloyd's
Rep. 235; (1984) 81 L.S.G. 2776; (1984) 128 S.J. 564, HL; affirming [1983] 1 W.L.R.
1362; [1983] 3 All E.R. 777; [1983] 2 Lloyd's Rep. 473; [1983] Com. L.R. 262;
(1983) 127 S.J. 730, CA (Civ Div) . . . . *Digested,* 84/**96**:
Applied, 85/113, 86/1909, 90/193, 90/2850, 92/2745, 98/807, 00/874,
01/332: *Considered,* 85/2602, 86/91, 86/92, 86/1907, 86/2711, 87/146,
89/104, 90/180, 91/201, 91/203, 91/2269, 92/2721, 94/2760, 02/208,
03/204, 05/475: *Referred to,* 87/2216
Atlantic Crusader,The [2005] EWHC 380; [2005] 2 All E.R. (Comm) 389; [2005] 1 Lloyd's
Rep. 699; [2005] 1 C.L.C. 413; (2005) 155 N.L.J. 594, QBD (Admlty) . . . . *Digested,* 05/**3794**
Atlantic Emperor,The [1992] 1 Lloyd's Rep. 342; [1991] E.C.R. I-3855; [1991] I.L.Pr. 524;
Times, September 20, 1991; *Financial Times,* October 16, 1991, ECJ . . . . *Digested,* 91/**3930**:
Applied, 97/883, 02/642: *Considered,* 97/4484, 05/599, 05/604:
Followed, 97/4584
Atlas Pride,The [2004] EWCA Civ 48; [2004] 2 All E.R. (Comm) 221; [2004] 1 Lloyd's Rep.
445; [2004] 1 C.L.C. 423; [2004] I.L.Pr. 29, CA (Civ Div); reversing [2003] EWHC
550; [2004] I.L.Pr. 3, QBD (Comm). . . . . *Digested,* 05/**468**
Azuero,The [1967] 1 Lloyd's Rep. 464; 117 N.L.J. 680, QBD (Comm). . . . . *Digested,* 67/**3622**:
Applied, 05/3813
Azur Gaz,The [2005] EWHC 2528; [2005] 2 C.L.C. 815, QBD (Comm)

Baltic Flame,The [2001] EWCA Civ 418; [2001] 1 All E.R. (Comm) 993; [2001] 2 Lloyd's
Rep. 203; [2001] C.L.C. 1151; *Times,* April 5, 2001, CA (Civ Div) . . . . *Digested,* 01/**610**:
Applied, 05/2396
Bow Spring, The [2004] EWCA Civ 1007; [2005] 1 W.L.R. 144; [2004] 4 All E.R. 899;
[2005] 1 All E.R. (Comm) 53; [2005] 1 Lloyd's Rep. 1; [2005] 1 C.L.C. 394; *Times,*
August 19, 2004; *Independent,* October 8, 2004, CA (Civ Div); affirming
[2003] EWHC 1802; [2004] 1 Lloyd's Rep. 647, QBD (Admlty) . . . . *Digested,* 04/**3495**:
Considered, 05/3794
Bunga Saga Lima,The [2005] EWHC 244; [2005] 2 Lloyd's Rep. 1, QBD (Comm)
Byzantio,The [2004] EWHC 3067; [2005] 1 Lloyd's Rep. 531, QBD (Comm). . . . . *Digested,* 05/**341**

Cape Equinox,The [2005] EWHC 8; [2005] 1 All E.R. (Comm) 528; [2005] 1 Lloyd's Rep.
390; [2005] 1 C.L.C. 1, QBD (Comm) . . . . *Digested,* 05/**3817**
Cape Providence, The [2002] EWCA Civ 1407; [2003] Q.B. 679; [2002] 3 W.L.R. 1617;
[2002] 4 All E.R. 689; [2002] 2 All E.R. (Comm) 999; [2002] 2 Lloyd's Rep. 653;
[2003] 2 C.L.C. 16; (2002) 99(43) L.S.G. 34; (2002) 152 N.L.J. 1616; [2002]
N.P.C. 127; *Times,* October 17, 2002; *Independent,* October 22, 2002, CA (Civ
Div); affirming (2001) 151 N.L.J. 1696, QBD (Comm) . . . . *Digested,* 02/**720**:
Applied, 04/383, 04/472: *Considered,* 05/516

Captain Panagos DP, The [1985] 1 Lloyd's Rep. 625; [1985] Fin. L.R. 224, QBD (Comm)   *Digested*, 85/**3205**:
                                                                                        Applied, 05/2386
Casco, The [2005] EWHC 273; [2005] 1 Lloyd's Rep. 565; [2005] 1 C.L.C. 232, QBD
    (Comm) . . . .   *Digested*, 05/**3816**
Caspiana, The [1957] A.C. 149; [1957] 2 W.L.R. 45; [1956] 3 All E.R. 957; [1956] 2 Lloyd's
    Rep. 379, HL; affirming [1956] 1 Q.B. 462; [1956] 2 W.L.R. 238; [1956] 1 All E.R.
    209; [1955] 2 Lloyd's Rep. 722; 101 S.J. 43, CA; reversing [1955] 3 W.L.R. 535;
    [1955] 3 All E.R. 251; [1955] 2 Lloyd's Rep. 301; 99 S.J. 762, QBD . . . .   *Digested*, 57/**3300**:
                                Considered, 57/3297, 57/3299, 57/3306, 58/565, 58/3141, 69/3293:
                                                    Followed, 59/3033, 03/3887, 05/3787

Demetra K, The [2002] EWCA Civ 1070; [2002] 2 Lloyd's Rep. 581; [2003] 1 C.L.C. 579;
    [2002] Lloyd's Rep. I.R. 795, CA (Civ Div); affirming 1197, QBD (Comm). . . . . . .   *Digested*, 05/**2385**
Denise, The [2004] EWHC 3305; [2005] 2 All E.R. (Comm) 47, QBD (Admlty) . . . . . .   *Approved*, 05/3801
Diana Prosperity, The [1976] 1 W.L.R. 989; [1976] 3 All E.R. 570; [1976] 2 Lloyd's Rep. 621;
    120 S.J. 719, HL; affirming [1976] 2 Lloyd's Rep. 60; 120 S.J. 329, CA (Civ Div)   *Digested*, 77/**2816**:
                        Applied, 78/338, 83/2127, 91/311, 01/2287, 01/4950, 02/671, 05/288:
                        Approved, 97/2189: *Considered*, 76/1204, 80/2458, 81/16, 86/1513, 93/2519,
                        94/332, 94/3430, 95/1974, 98/2300: *Followed*, 76/333, 77/2668, 79/813
Duke of Yare, The [1992] Q.B. 502; [1992] 2 W.L.R. 319; [1992] 2 All E.R. 450; [1991] 2
    Lloyd's Rep. 557; [1992] I.L.Pr. 164; (1991) 135 S.J.L.B. 126; *Times*, August 8, 1991;
    Financial Times, August 2, 1991, CA (Civ Div) . . . .   *Digested*, 92/**3534**:
                        Applied, 94/482, 94/487, 01/830: *Considered*, 96/920, 03/595, 05/468:
                                                    Distinguished, 92/3401, 93/3127

Eastern Venture, The [1985] 1 All E.R. 923; (1983) 80 L.S.G. 2683; (1983) 127 S.J. 682, CA
    (Civ Div) . . . .   *Digested*, 85/**2628**:
                                                                                        Distinguished, 05/345
El Amria, The [1981] 2 Lloyd's Rep. 119; [1981] Com. L.R. 136, CA (Civ Div); affirming [1980]
    1 Lloyd's Rep. 390, QBD (Admlty) . . . .   *Digested*, 81/**2198**:
                        Applied, 83/387, 93/454, 00/760, 02/4688, 05/2406: *Considered*, 85/1291,
                                                    97/872, 97/881: *Followed*, 98/771
Eleftheria, The [1970] P. 94; [1969] 2 W.L.R. 1073; [1969] 2 All E.R. 641; [1969] 1 Lloyd's
    Rep. 237; 113 S.J. 407, PDAD. . . . .   *Digested*, 69/**3293**:
                        Applied, 81/2198, 01/4902: *Considered*, 79/308, 79/311, 80/317, 00/4685,
                                                                                        05/625
Endeavour, The [2004] S.T.C. (S.C.D.) 207; [2004] S.T.I. 992, Sp Comm . . . .   *Digested*, 05/**4003**
Epaphus, The [1987] 2 Lloyd's Rep. 215; [1987] 2 F.T.L.R. 213; *Times*, May 18, 1987, CA
    (Civ Div); affirming [1986] 2 Lloyd's Rep. 387, QBD (Comm) . . . .   *Digested*, 88/**3165**:
                                                                                        Considered, 05/267
Esso Bernicia, The [1989] A.C. 643; [1988] 3 W.L.R. 730; [1989] 1 All E.R. 37; [1989] 1
    Lloyd's Rep. 8; 1988 S.L.T. 874; (1988) 85(42) L.S.G. 48; (1988) 132 S.J. 1459;
    Times, October 7, 1988, HL; affirming in part 1988 S.L.T. 33, IH (1 Div) . . . .   *Digested*, 89/**3392**:
                                                    Considered, 05/2890: *Distinguished*, 03/3613

Fanti, The [1991] 2 A.C. 1; [1990] 3 W.L.R. 78; [1990] 2 All E.R. 705; [1990] 2 Lloyd's Rep.
    191; [1990] B.C.L.C. 625; (1990) 134 S.J. 833, HL; reversing [1989] 1 Lloyd's Rep.
    239; *Times*, December 27, 1988, CA (Civ Div); reversing in part [1987] 2
    Lloyd's Rep. 299, QBD (Comm) . . . .   *Digested*, 90/**4098**:
                        Applied, 92/3972, 93/3619, 97/4597, 00/3514, 03/2468:
                        Considered, 95/2926, 96/1136, 05/2366: *Distinguished*, 98/3354:
                        Followed, 97/3139, 99/3227, 00/4693: *Previous proceedings*, 88/3239
Flintermar, The [2005] EWCA Civ 17; [2005] 1 All E.R. (Comm) 497; [2005] 1 Lloyd's Rep.
    409; [2005] 1 C.L.C. 40, CA (Civ Div) . . . .   *Digested*, 05/**3813**
Front Comor, The [2005] EWHC 454; [2005] 2 All E.R. (Comm) 240; [2005] 2 Lloyd's
    Rep. 257; [2005] 1 C.L.C. 347, QBD (Comm) . . . .   *Digested*, 05/**2357**

Game Boy, The [2004] EWHC 15; [2004] 1 All E.R. (Comm) 560; [2004] 1 Lloyd's Rep.
    238; [2004] Lloyd's Rep. I.R. 867, QBD (Comm) . . . .   *Digested*, 04/**2211**:
                                                                                        Referred to, 05/2387
Global Mariner, The [2005] EWHC 380; [2005] 2 All E.R. (Comm) 389; [2005] 1 Lloyd's
    Rep. 699; [2005] 1 C.L.C. 413; (2005) 155 N.L.J. 594, QBD (Admlty) . . . .   *Digested*, 05/**3794**
Golden Victory, The [2005] EWCA Civ 1190; [2005] 2 Lloyd's Rep. 747; [2005] 2 C.L.C.
    576; (2005) 102(43) L.S.G. 31; *Times*, October 21, 2005, CA (Civ Div); affirming
    [2005] EWHC 161; [2005] 1 All E.R. (Comm) 467; [2005] 1 Lloyd's Rep. 443;
    [2005] 1 C.L.C. 138; *Times*, March 4, 2005, QBD (Comm)

Great Peace,The [2002] EWCA Civ 1407; [2003] Q.B. 679; [2002] 3 W.L.R. 1617; [2002] 4
  All E.R. 689; [2002] 2 All E.R. (Comm) 999; [2002] 2 Lloyd's Rep. 653; [2003] 2
  C.L.C. 16; (2002) 99(43) L.S.G. 34; (2002) 152 N.L.J. 1616; [2002] N.P.C. 127;
  Times, October 17, 2002; *Independent*, October 22, 2002, CA (Civ Div);
  affirming (2001) 151 N.L.J. 1696, QBD (Comm) . . . . *Digested*, 02/**720**:
                                                                     Applied, 04/383, 04/472: *Considered*, 05/516

Halki,The [1998] 1 W.L.R. 726; [1998] 2 All E.R. 23; [1998] 1 Lloyd's Rep. 465; [1998]
  C.L.C. 583; (1998) 142 S.J.L.B. 44; [1998] N.P.C. 4; *Times*, January 19, 1998;
  Independent, January 12, 1998 (C.S.), CA (Civ Div); affirming [1997] 1 W.L.R.
  1268; [1997] 3 All E.R. 833; [1998] 1 Lloyd's Rep. 49; (1997) 94(28) L.S.G. 26;
  (1997) 141 S.J.L.B. 172; *Times*, October 13, 1997, QBD (Admlty) . . . . *Digested*, 98/**246**:
                                    Applied, 03/648, 04/588, 04/593, 05/642: *Considered*, 04/652, 05/198:
                                                                                       Followed, 00/227
Hari Bhum,The (No.1) [2004] EWCA Civ 1598; [2005] 1 All E.R. (Comm) 715; [2005] 1
  Lloyd's Rep. 67; [2004] 2 C.L.C. 1189; [2005] I.L.Pr. 30; (2004) 148 S.J.L.B. 1435,
  CA (Civ Div); reversing in part [2003] EWHC 3158; [2004] 1 Lloyd's Rep. 206;
  [2004] 1 C.L.C. 794, QBD (Comm) . . . . *Digested*, 05/**599**:
                                                                                       Applied, 05/2357
Hari Bhum,The (No.2) [2005] EWHC 455; [2005] 2 Lloyd's Rep. 378; [2005] 1 C.L.C. 376,
  QBD (Comm) . . . . *Digested*, 05/**200**
Hoegh Anapa,The [1983] 2 A.C. 570; [1983] 2 W.L.R. 778; [1983] 2 All E.R. 189; [1983] 2
  Lloyd's Rep. 1; [1983] I.C.R. 490; [1983] I.R.L.R. 218; (1983) 133 N.L.J. 577; (1983)
  127 S.J. 306, HL; affirming [1983] 2 W.L.R. 45; [1982] 1 All E.R. 334; [1983] 1
  Lloyd's Rep. 154; [1983] I.C.R. 178; [1982] I.R.L.R. 26; (1983) 80 L.S.G. 213; (1983)
  133 N.L.J. 186; 126 S.J. 745; *Times*, November 5, 1982, CA (Civ Div) . . . . *Digested*, 83/**3794**:
                                                   Applied, 84/3553, 85/3384, 86/3443, 87/3769: *Considered*, 87/3759,
                                                                                   88/3417, 89/3519, 05/4189

Ibaraki Maru,The [1986] A.C. 1; [1985] 3 W.L.R. 381; [1985] 2 All E.R. 935; [1985] 2 Lloyd's
  Rep. 303; (1985) 82 L.S.G. 2912; (1985) 135 N.L.J. 677; (1985) 129 S.J. 506, PC
  (Aus) . . . . *Digested*, 85/**2310**:
                                               Applied, 05/3239: *Considered*, 85/2311, 86/2252, 86/2270:
                                                    Distinguished, 90/1535: *Referred to*, 87/3582, 88/3408
Irbenskiy Proliv,The [2004] EWHC 2924; [2005] 1 All E.R. (Comm) 328; [2005] 1 Lloyd's
  Rep. 383, QBD (Comm) . . . . *Digested*, 05/**3788**
Island Archon,The [1995] 1 All E.R. 595; [1994] 2 Lloyd's Rep. 227; *Times*, July 8, 1994;
  Independent, July 20, 1994, CA (Civ Div); affirming [1993] 2 Lloyd's Rep. 388,
  QBD (Comm) . . . . *Digested*, 94/**4059**:
                                                                                       Applied, 05/3814
Italia Express, The (No.3) [1992] 2 Lloyd's Rep. 281; *Financial Times*, February 12, 1992,
  QBD (Comm) . . . . *Digested*, 93/**3619**:
                                                 Followed, 97/3139, 05/2358: *Referred to*, 97/3121
Ivan Zagubanski,The [2002] 1 Lloyd's Rep. 106, QBD (Comm) . . . . *Digested*, 02/**642**:
                                                                     Approved, 05/599: *Followed*, 04/560

Jalagouri,The [2000] 1 All E.R. (Comm) 700; [2000] 1 Lloyd's Rep. 515; [2000] C.L.C.
  1051; *Independent*, April 7, 2000, CA (Civ Div); affirming [1999] 1 Lloyd's Rep.
  903; [1998] C.L.C. 1054, QBD (Comm) . . . . *Digested*, 00/**4703**:
                                                                                       Applied, 05/3812
Jordan II,The [2004] UKHL 49; [2005] 1 W.L.R. 1363; [2005] 1 All E.R. 175; [2005] 1 All
  E.R. (Comm) 1; [2005] 1 Lloyd's Rep. 57; [2004] 2 C.L.C. 1172; 2005 A.M.C. 1;
  (2004) 148 S.J.L.B. 1405; *Times*, November 26, 2004, HL; affirming [2003]
  EWCA Civ 144; [2003] 1 All E.R. (Comm) 747; [2003] 2 Lloyd's Rep. 87;
  [2003] 1 C.L.C. 885, CA (Civ Div); reversing in part [2002] EWHC 1268;
  [2002] 2 All E.R. (Comm) 364, QBD (Comm) . . . . *Digested*, 05/**3787**:
Jotunheim,The [2004] EWHC 671; [2005] 1 Lloyd's Rep. 181, QBD (Comm) . . . . *Digested*, 05/**3793**

KastorToo,The [2004] EWCA Civ 277; [2005] 2 All E.R. (Comm) 720; [2004] 2 Lloyd's
  Rep. 119; [2004] 2 C.L.C. 68; [2004] 4 Costs L.R. 569; [2004] Lloyd's Rep. I.R. 481;
  Times, April 29, 2004, CA (Civ Div); reversing in part [2002] EWHC 2601;
  [2003] 1 All E.R. (Comm) 277; [2003] 1 Lloyd's Rep. 296; [2003] 2 C.L.C.
  489; [2003] Lloyd's Rep. I.R. 262, QBD (Comm) . . . . *Digested*, 04/**2225**
Key Singapore,The [2004] EWHC 2227; [2005] 1 All E.R. (Comm) 99; [2005] 1 Lloyd's
  Rep. 91, QBD (Comm) . . . . *Digested*, 05/**3810**:
Kitsa,The [2005] EWHC 177; [2005] 1 Lloyd's Rep. 432; [2005] 1 C.L.C. 153, QBD (Comm) *Digested*, 05/**3814**
Komninos S, The [1991] 1 Lloyd's Rep. 370; *Financial Times*, January 16, 1991, CA (Civ
  Div); reversing [1990] 1 Lloyd's Rep. 541; *Financial Times*, January 16, 1990, QBD
  (Comm) . . . . *Digested*, 92/**3925**:
                                                                                       Applied, 05/616

La Pintada,The (No.1) [1985] A.C.104; [1984] 3 W.L.R.10; [1984] 2 All E.R. 773; [1984] 2
   Lloyd's Rep. 9; [1984] C.I.L.L.110; (1984) 81 L.S.G.1999; (1984) 128 S.J. 414, HL;
   reversing [1983] 1 Lloyd's Rep. 37; [1982] Com. L.R. 250; *Times*, November 1,
   1982, QBD (Comm) . . . . *Digested*, 84/**123**:
         Applied, 84/120, 85/3160: *Cited*, 00/1453: *Considered*, 84/2346, 86/2760,
         87/2429, 97/3839, 98/1433, 05/3984: *Followed*, 98/231
Laemthong Glory,The (No.1) [2004] EWHC 2226; [2004] 2 All E.R. (Comm) 797; [2005]
   1 Lloyd's Rep. 100; [2005] 2 C.L.C. 644, QBD (Comm) . . . . *Digested*, 05/**413**
Laemthong Glory, The (No.2) [2005] EWCA Civ 519; [2005] 2 All E.R. (Comm) 167;
   [2005] 1 Lloyd's Rep. 688; [2005] 1 C.L.C. 739, CA (Civ Div); affirming [2004]
   EWHC 2738; [2005] 1 Lloyd's Rep. 632, QBD (Comm) . . . . *Digested*, 05/**3791**
Leon,The [1985] 2 Lloyd's Rep. 470, QBD (Comm) . . . . *Digested*, 86/**3107**:
                                                    Considered, 05/388
Lips,The [1988] A.C. 395; [1987] 3 W.L.R. 572; [1987] 3 All E.R.110; [1987] 2 Lloyd's Rep.
   311; [1987] 2 F.T.L.R. 477; [1987] Fin. L.R. 313; (1987) 84 L.S.G. 2765; (1987) 137
   N.L.J. 734; (1987) 131 S.J.1085, HL; reversing [1987] 2 W.L.R. 906; [1987] 1 All
   E.R. 957; [1987] 1 Lloyd's Rep.131; [1987] 1 F.T.L.R. 50; [1987] Fin. L.R. 91; (1987)
   84 L.S.G.1333; (1987) 131 S.J. 422; *Financial Times*, November 4, 1986, CA (Civ
   Div); reversing [1985] 2 Lloyd's Rep. 180; (1984) 134 N.L.J. 969, QBD
   (Comm) . . . . *Digested*, 87/**3399**:
                          Applied, 92/3972, 93/3619: *Followed*, 05/2358
Lorico,The [1997] 4 All E.R. 514; [1997] 2 Lloyd's Rep. 386; [1997] C.L.C.1274, CA (Civ
   Div); reversing [1997] 1 Lloyd's Rep. 578, QBD (Comm) . . . . *Digested*, 97/**4534**:
                                       Applied, 05/697

Maciej Rataj,The (C406/92) [1999] Q.B. 515; [1999] 2 W.L.R.181; [1995] All E.R. (E.C.)
   229; [1995] 1 Lloyd's Rep. 302; [1994] E.C.R. I-5439; [1995] I.L.Pr. 81; *Times*,
   December 28, 1994; *Financial Times*, December 13, 1994, ECJ. . . . . *Digested*, 95/**704**:
         Applied, 96/7098, 99/732, 00/738, 00/776, 05/624: *Considered*, 97/900,
         99/715, 00/5442, 05/604: *Followed*, 96/1089, 02/5366, 05/622
Maersk Colombo,The [2001] EWCA Civ 717; [2001] 2 Lloyd's Rep. 275; (2001) 98(24)
   L.S.G. 43; (2001) 145 S.J.L.B.149; *Times*, June 13, 2001, CA (Civ Div); affirming
   [1999] 2 Lloyd's Rep. 491; [1999] C.L.C.1814, QBD (Admlty). . . . . *Digested*, 01/**4501**:
                           Considered, 05/374: *Followed*, 03/939
Manzanillo II,The [2004] EWCA Civ 1007; [2005] 1 W.L.R. 144; [2004] 4 All E.R. 899;
   [2005] 1 All E.R. (Comm) 53; [2005] 1 Lloyd's Rep.1; [2005] 1 C.L.C. 394; *Times*,
   August 19, 2004; *Independent*, October 8, 2004, CA (Civ Div); affirming
   [2003] EWHC 1802; [2004] 1 Lloyd's Rep. 647, QBD (Admlty) . . . . *Digested*, 04/**3495**:
                                          Considered, 05/3794
Maridive VII,The [2004] EWHC 2227; [2005] 1 All E.R. (Comm) 99; [2005] 1 Lloyd's Rep.
   91, QBD (Comm) . . . . *Digested*, 05/**3810**
Marinor,The [1996] 1 Lloyd's Rep. 301; [1996] C.L.C. 337, QBD (Comm) . . . . *Applied*, 97/**4514**:
                                           Distinguished, 05/3816
Martin P,The [2003] EWHC 3470; [2004] 1 Lloyd's Rep. 389; [2005] Lloyd's Rep. I.R.174,
   QBD (Comm) . . . . *Digested*, 05/**2384**:
                                          Considered, 05/2390
Mediana,The [1900] A.C. 113, HL; affirming [1899] P. 127, CA. . . . . *Applied*, 47-51/2554,
                   47/2554, 03/943, 05/4193: *Considered*, 52/893, 78/44.u
Mineral Transporter,The [1986] A.C.1; [1985] 3 W.L.R. 381; [1985] 2 All E.R. 935; [1985] 2
   Lloyd's Rep. 303; (1985) 82 L.S.G. 2912; (1985) 135 N.L.J. 677; (1985) 129 S.J.
   506, PC (Aus). . . . . *Digested*, 85/**2310**:
         Applied, 05/3239: *Considered*, 85/2311, 86/2252, 86/2270:
         Distinguished, 90/1535: *Referred to*, 87/3582, 88/3408
Moorcock,The (1889) L.R.14 P.D. 64; [1886-90] All E.R. Rep. 530, CA; affirming (1888)
   L.R. 13 P.D.157, PDAD. . . . . *Applied*, 83/2064,
         93/2407: *Considered*, 76/1532, 86/421, 98/2492, 05/697:
      Distinguished, 80/1643: *Doubted*, 47-51/1756: *Referred to*, 84/1935, 85/1929

Nai Genova,The [1984] 1 Lloyd's Rep. 353, CA (Civ Div); affirming [1983] 2 Lloyd's Rep.
   333; [1983] Com. L.R.170; (1983) 133 N.L.J. 621, QBD (Comm) . . . . *Digested*, 84/**378**:
          Applied, 95/3063, 96/3756, 96/3815, 05/2386: *Considered*, 05/717:
                                    Followed, 94/558
Nai Superba,The [1984] 1 Lloyd's Rep. 353, CA (Civ Div); affirming [1983] 2 Lloyd's Rep.
   333; [1983] Com. L.R.170; (1983) 133 N.L.J. 621, QBD (Comm) . . . . *Digested*, 84/**378**:
          Applied, 95/3063, 96/3756, 96/3815, 05/2386: *Considered*, 05/717:
                                      Followed, 94/558

New Vanguard,The [1994] 1 W.L.R.1634; [1995] 1 All E.R. 641; [1995] 1 Lloyd's Rep.191;
   Times, August 15, 1994; *Independent*, August 22, 1994 (C.S.), CA (Civ Div) . . . . *Digested*, 95/**4213**:
                                             Considered, 05/206

Noel Bay, The [1989] 1 Lloyd's Rep. 361, CA (Civ Div) . . . . *Digested*, 90/**4121**:
Distinguished, 05/3790
Nore Challenger, The [2005] EWHC 421; [2005] 2 Lloyd's Rep. 534, QBD (Comm)

Ocean Frost, The [1986] A.C. 717; [1986] 2 W.L.R. 1063; [1986] 2 All E.R. 385; [1986] 2
Lloyd's Rep.109; (1986) 83 L.S.G. 2002; (1986) 130 S.J. 430, HL; affirming [1985]
3 W.L.R. 640; [1985] 3 All E.R. 795; [1985] 1 Lloyd's Rep. 1; (1984) 81 L.S.G. 2169;
(1984) 129 S.J. 362, CA (Civ Div) . . . . *Digested*, 86/**37**:
Applied, 89/55, 94/537, 95/763, 99/456, 05/2959: *Considered*, 93/64,
94/106

Pacifica, The [1994] 1 W.L.R. 1634; [1995] 1 All E.R. 641; [1995] 1 Lloyd's Rep. 191; *Times*,
August 15, 1994; *Independent*, August 22, 1994 (C.S.), CA (Civ Div) . . . . *Digested*, 95/**4213**:
Considered, 05/206
Pamphilos, The [2002] EWHC 2292; [2002] 2 Lloyd's Rep. 681, QBD (Comm) . . . . . . *Digested*, 03/**3894**:
Applied, 05/205
Popi M, The [1985] 1 W.L.R. 948; [1985] 2 All E.R. 712; [1985] 2 Lloyd's Rep. 1; (1985) 82
L.S.G. 2995; (1985) 129 S.J. 503, HL; reversing [1984] 2 Lloyd's Rep. 555, CA (Civ
Div); reversing in part [1983] 2 Lloyd's Rep. 235, QBD (Comm) . . . . *Digested*, 85/**3207**:
Applied, 90/3232, 90/3252, 92/3975, 95/4534, 02/349:
Considered, 05/292: *Distinguished*, 00/2984: *Followed*, 02/4123

Rafaela S, The [2005] UKHL 11; [2005] 2 A.C. 423; [2005] 2 W.L.R. 554; [2005] 2 All E.R.
86; [2005] 1 All E.R. (Comm) 393; [2005] 1 Lloyd's Rep. 347; [2005] 1 C.L.C. 172;
2005 A.M.C. 913; *Times*, February 21, 2005, HL; affirming [2003] EWCA Civ
556; [2004] Q.B. 702; [2004] 2 W.L.R. 283; [2003] 3 All E.R. 369; [2003] 2
All E.R. (Comm) 219; [2003] 2 Lloyd's Rep. 113; [2003] 2 C.L.C. 94; 2003
A.M.C. 2035; (2003) 100(26) L.S.G. 38; *Times*, May 5, 2003, CA (Civ Div);
reversing [2002] EWHC 593; [2002] 2 Lloyd's Rep. 403; [2002] C.L.C. 1043,
QBD (Comm) . . . . *Digested*, 05/**3785**
Rays, The [2005] EWHC 1694; [2005] 2 Lloyd's Rep. 479, QBD (Comm) . . . . *Digested*, 05/**3811**
River Gurara, The [1998] Q.B. 610; [1997] 3 W.L.R. 1128; [1997] 4 All E.R. 498; [1998] 1
Lloyd's Rep. 225; [1997] C.L.C. 1322; (1997) 94(33) L.S.G. 27; (1997) 141 S.J.L.B.
175; *Times*, July 29, 1997, CA (Civ Div); affirming [1996] 2 Lloyd's Rep. 53;
[1996] C.L.C. 927; *Times*, March 6, 1996, QBD (Admlty). . . . . *Digested*, 98/**4405**:
Followed, 05/3786

Sardinia Sulcis, The [1991] 1 Lloyd's Rep. 201; *Times*, November 21, 1990; *Independent*,
December 3, 1990 (C.S.); *Financial Times*, November 13, 1990, CA (Civ Div) . . . *Digested*, 91/**3204**:
Applied, 99/494, 05/89: *Followed*, 96/890: *Not followed*, 05/315
Scaptrade, The [1983] 2 A.C. 694; [1983] 3 W.L.R. 203; [1983] 2 All E.R. 763; [1983] 2
Lloyd's Rep. 253, HL; affirming [1983] Q.B. 529; [1983] 2 W.L.R. 248; [1983] 1 All
E.R. 301; [1983] 1 Lloyd's Rep. 146; (1983) 133 N.L.J. 133; 126 S.J. 853; *Times*,
November 30, 1982, CA (Civ Div); affirming [1981] 2 Lloyd's Rep. 425; [1981]
Com. L.R. 214, QBD (Comm) . . . . *Digested*, 83/**3405**:
Considered, 83/421, 84/1326, 93/2495, 05/3793: *Distinguished*, 85/2604,
05/422
Selby Paradigm, The [2004] EWHC 1804; [2004] 2 Lloyd's Rep. 714; (2004) 154 N.L.J.
1362, QBD (Admlty) . . . . *Digested*, 05/**310**
Spiliada, The [1987] A.C. 460; [1986] 3 W.L.R. 972; [1986] 3 All E.R. 843; [1987] 1 Lloyd's
Rep. 1; [1987] E.C.C. 168; [1987] 1 F.T.L.R. 103; (1987) 84 L.S.G. 113; (1986) 136
N.L.J. 1137; (1986) 130 S.J. 925; *Financial Times*, November 25, 1986, HL;
reversing [1985] 2 Lloyd's Rep. 116; (1985) 82 L.S.G. 1416, CA (Civ Div) . . . . . . *Digested*, 87/**3135**:
Applied, 85/2597, 86/2705, 89/1722, 89/3095, 89/3394, 90/3768, 91/475,
91/476, 92/475, 93/3571, 93/5876, 94/483, 94/4040, 95/696, 96/846,
97/908, 98/4398, 99/717, 99/719, 99/750, 99/2405, 00/775, 01/815,
03/599, 04/1493, 05/622: *Considered*, 87/3095, 88/2911, 89/2725,
89/3042, 92/3072, 94/3252, 94/3256, 95/3484, 96/1089, 96/1091,
98/764, 02/477, 02/2756, 05/611: *Distinguished*, 87/3024, 03/2215:
Explained, 00/769: *Followed*, 91/5142, 95/690, 95/6052, 97/2453, 98/748,
98/749, 05/978
Star Sea, The [2001] UKHL 1; [2003] 1 A.C. 469; [2001] 2 W.L.R. 170; [2001] 1 All E.R. 743;
[2001] 1 All E.R. (Comm) 193; [2001] 1 Lloyd's Rep. 389; [2001] C.L.C. 608;
[2001] Lloyd's Rep. I.R. 247; *Times*, January 23, 2001, HL; affirming [1997] 1
Lloyd's Rep. 360; [1997] C.L.C. 481; [1997] 6 Re. L.R. 175; *Times*, January 23,
1997, CA (Civ Div); affirming [1995] 1 Lloyd's Rep. 651, QBD (Comm) . . . . *Digested*, 01/**3825**:
Applied, 00/4696, 00/4744, 02/2732, 02/2739, 04/471:
Considered, 01/3827, 05/2359
Stena Pacifica, The [1990] 2 Lloyd's Rep. 234, QBD (Comm). . . . . *Digested*, 91/**182**:
Followed, 05/3816